THE ONE SHOW

THE ONE SHOW

THE
54TH
ANNUAL
OF
ADVERTISING,
EDITORIAL,
AND
TELEVISION
ART
AND
DESIGN
WITH
THE
15TH
ANNUAL
COPY
AWARDS

Art Director/Designer	**Kiyoshi Kanai**
Editors	**Jo Yanow, Jennifer Place**
Editorial Assistants	**Jody Uttal, Wendy Addiss**
	Barbara Egan, Glenda Spencer
	Claire Hardiman, Joan Fisher
Writer, Hall of Fame	**Naomi Andrews**
Cover Art	**Charles White III**
Production Coordinator	**Frank DeLuca**
Design, Show Section	**Jim Craig, Bob Fillie**
Mechanicals	**Jay Anning, Peter Siepmann**
Typographers	**Gerard Associates/Graphic Arts, Inc.**
	TypoGraphics Communications
Printing and Binding	**Halliday Lithograph Corp.**
Color Separations	**Color Tech/CA Magazine, Toppan Graphic Arts**
Paper	**Avery Super Smooth**
Endpapers	**Multicolor Antique**
Cover	**Tyveck, printed by Largene Press**
Photos	**Tom Yahashi, Harold Zipkowitz**

The 54th Annual of Advertising, Editorial &
Television Art & Design with the 15th Annual Copy Awards

Published by Watson Guptill Publications
a Division of Billboard Publications, Inc.
One Astor Plaza, New York, New York 10036
Library of Congress Catalog Number 22-5058
ISBN 0-8230-1907-1

Cities are listed in the credits only where work is by
agency branch offices or by International entrants.

THE ONE SHOW

THE 54TH ANNUAL OF ADVERTISING, EDITORIAL, AND TELEVISION ART AND DESIGN WITH THE 15TH ANNUAL COPY AWARDS

CONTENTS

THE GOLD AWARDS

ADVERTISING

Print Advertising 1–263
Photography & Art 264–304
Radio Commercials 305–360A
Television Commercials & Films 361–505
International Advertising 506–553

EDITORIAL AND GRAPHIC DESIGN

Consumer and Trade Publications 554–679
Graphic Design 680–989
Photography & Art 990–1133
International Editorial & Graphic Design 1134–1182

THE HALL OF FAME

CLUB NEWS

INDEX

THE GOLD AWARDS

Can Elizabeth keep Richard dry?
People
The new way to reach people.

39 years later, Betty Bloomer moved into the White House.
People
The new way to reach people.

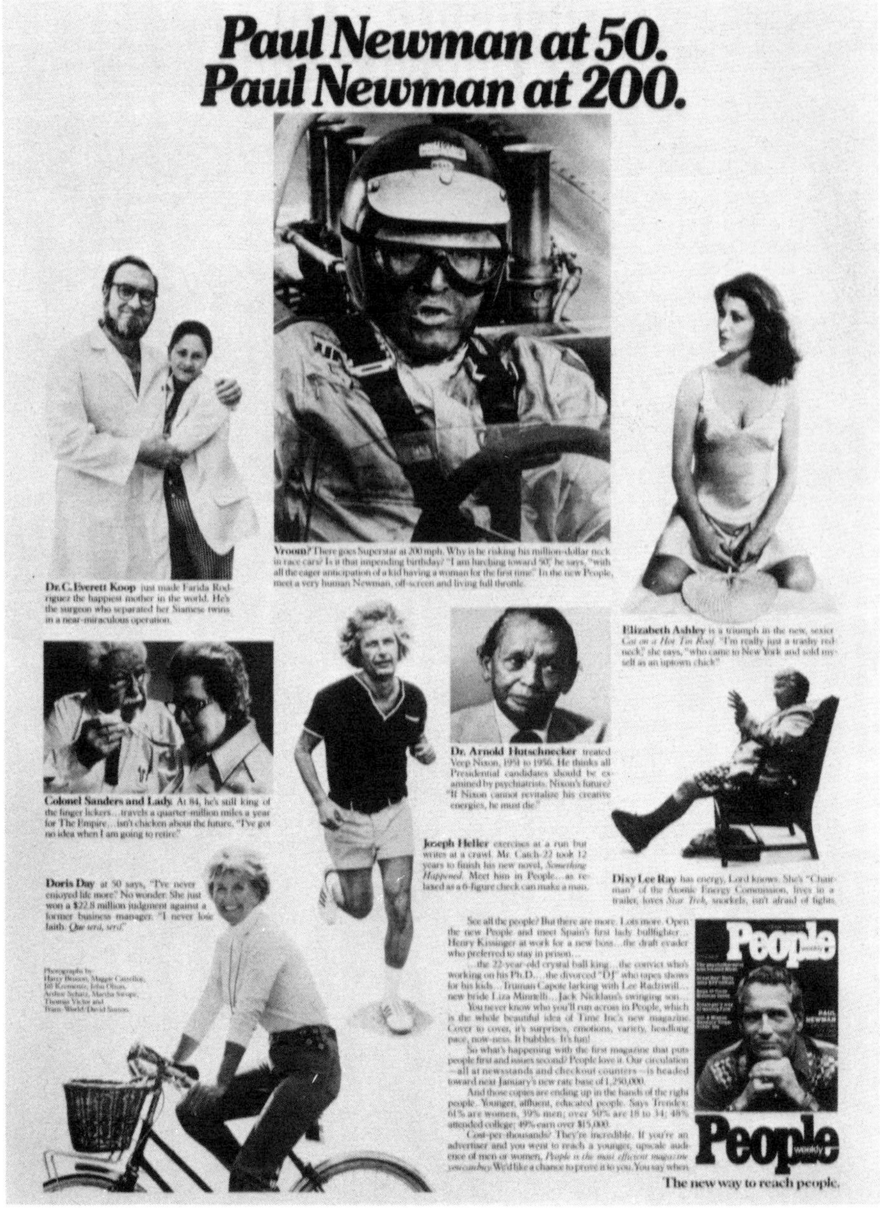

Paul Newman at 50. Paul Newman at 200.
Vroom? There goes Superstar at 200 mph. Why is he risking his million-dollar neck in race cars? Is it that impending birthday? "I am lurching toward 50," he says, "with all the eager anticipation of a kid having a woman for the first time." In the new People, meet a very human Newman, off-screen and living full throttle.
Dr. C. Everett Koop just made Farida Rodriguez the happiest mother in the world. He's the surgeon who separated her Siamese twins in a near-miraculous operation.
Elizabeth Ashley is a triumph in the new, sexier Cat on a Hot Tin Roof. "I'm really just a trashy redneck," she says, "who came to New York and sold myself as an uptown chick."
Colonel Sanders and Lady. At 84, he's still king of the finger lickers...travels a quarter-million miles a year for The Empire...isn't chicken about the future. "I've got no idea when I am going to retire."
Dr. Arnold Hutschnecker treated Veep Nixon, 1951 to 1956. He thinks all Presidential candidates should be examined by psychiatrists. Nixon's future? "If Nixon cannot revitalize his creative energies, he must die."
Joseph Heller exercises at a run but writes at a crawl. Mr. Catch-22 took 12 years to finish his new novel, Something Happened. Meet him in People...as relaxed as a 6-figure check can make a man.
Dixy Lee Ray has energy, Lord knows. She's "Chairman" of the Atomic Energy Commission, lives in a trailer, loves Star Trek, snorkels, isn't afraid of fights.
Doris Day at 50 says, "I've never enjoyed life more." No wonder. She just won a $22.8 million judgment against a former business manager. "I never lost faith. Que sera, sera."
See all the people? But there are more. Lots more. Open the new People and meet Spain's first lady bullfighter...Henry Kissinger at work for a new boss...the draft evader who preferred to stay in prison...
...the 22-year-old crystal ball king...the convict who's working on his Ph.D....the divorced "DJ" who tapes shows for his kids...Truman Capote larking with Lee Radziwill...new bride Liza Minnelli...Jack Nicklaus's swinging son...
You never know who you'll run across in People, which is the whole beautiful idea of Time Inc's new magazine. Cover to cover, it's surprises, emotions, variety, headlong pace, now-ness. It bubbles. It's fun!
So what's happening with the first magazine that puts people first and issues second? People love it. Our circulation—all at newsstands and checkout counters—is headed toward next January's new rate base of 1,250,000.
And those copies are ending up in the hands of the right people. Younger, affluent, educated people. Says Trendex: 61% are women, 39% men; over 50% are 18 to 34; 48% attended college; 49% earn over $15,000.
Cost-per-thousands? They're incredible. If you're an advertiser and you want to reach a younger, upscale audience of men or women, People is the most efficient magazine you can buy. We'd like a chance to prove it to you. You say when.
People weekly
The new way to reach people.

35

Art Director Bob Czernysz
Writer Richard Olmsted
Photographer Editorial
Agency Young & Rubicam International
Client People Magazine

WE SELL MORE CARS THAN FORD, CHRYSLER,
CHEVROLET AND BUICK COMBINED.
MATCHBOX.

T
t
T
is for
Twins,
who look
just the same.
U
u
U
is for
Umbrella
to get
out of the
rain.

74
171
195
Art Directors Allan Beaver
Ken Sausville
Writers Larry Plapler
Frank Anton
Designers Allan Beaver
Ken Sausville
Photographer Cailor/Resnick
Agency Levine, Huntley, Schmidt
Client Lesney Products Corp.

1150
Art Director David Pocknell
Designer David Pocknell
Photographer Harri Peccinotti
Agency David Pocknell
Client Absorba, Ltd.

At 204 pounds, I had pudgy cheeks, big thighs and a bottom that was out of sight.

Now that I see these photographs of me side by side, I realize what a tremendous difference coming down to 138 pounds has made in my appearance. And my outlook on life, ma

The thought of wearing a bathing suit made me lose 66 pounds.

By Mavis Molina — as told to Ruth L. McCarthy

From my own personal experience, I know there's nothing quite like being lonely, homesick and snowbound to turn a person's appetite on. In my case, I ate everything in sight and wound up weighing 204 pounds.

You see, I'm English by birth, married to an American Air Force man. Happily for me, our first years together were spent "at home" near my parents. But soon after our third child was born, we were transferred to the States. We had hoped to be sent to Florida, because I love the sun and swimming so much. But instead, we ended up in North Dakota.

I don't think I've ever felt so lonely in my life. Not that the people were unfriendly. But drifts of snow separated the 18 houses on the base and instead of ploughing out to visit neighbors, I stayed indoors, eating and fussing over the children from December until almost June.

I didn't have a scale or a full length mirror at the time. And although my jeans were getting tighter, I had no idea how big I really was until the summer thaw came. My parents had arrived for a visit about then, and one day we drove 35 miles into the nearest town for a look around.

That's when I saw a reflection of myself in a store window. I was so huge, I nearly died. Why, the very thought of my getting into a bathing suit made me shudder.

Right then I knew that I had to take some action. So I walked into a drug store and bought a bathroom scale and a box of Ayds®, the chocolate mint kind. You see, while I was snowbound, I'd read those stories of people who'd lost weight on the Ayds plan. And since I'd learned that Ayds Reducing Plan Candy contains vitamins and minerals, but no drugs, I wasn't afraid to start on the plan the next day.

I took one or two Ayds before each meal with a hot drink, and they really helped me cut down on what I ate. For breakfast, I'd have an egg and sometimes bacon. At noon, I'd have Ayds and coffee and maybe a chef's salad. For dinner, I'd have my Ayds and coffee again, then eat what the rest of the family did, but much smaller portions. And in the evening, instead of a piece of cake, I'd have a couple more Ayds. Soon the weight started coming off. The first two weeks on the Ayds plan, I lost nearly eight pounds. Then I tapered off to two pounds a week and later one pound, until at the end of the year I'd lost 66 pounds.

I think I ought to mention that during the time I was losing weight, we moved from North Dakota to Panama City, Florida, which gave me even more incentive to reduce.

You see, I couldn't stand the idea of being a fat blob on a beach of bikini-slim women. But that Ayds plan worked beautifully for me and it brought a lot of sunshine into my life.

One last thing. And I say this for the benefit of people like me who overeat when they get upset. Ayds are marvelous for controlling your appetite, whether you want to lose a little weight or a lot. I know, because several months ago my husband went off on a special tour of duty and loneliness moved right in on me. I immediately began to overeat and put on pounds again. But this time, thank goodness, I knew what the Ayds plan could do. In very short order, it made my bathing suit look great on me again.

BEFORE AND AFTER MEASUREMENTS

	Before	After
Height	5' 9"	5' 9"
Weight	204 lbs.	138 lbs.
Bust	42"	36½"
Waist	34"	28½"
Hips	44"	36½"
Dress	20½	12-14

When I saw this photo, I [illegible] to cut off some of my 178 pounds.

Now I'm 118 pounds, my husband loves to be first on the dance floor with me.

I cheated on weekends and lost 60 pounds.

By Diane Gabriele — as told to Ruth L. McCarthy

It was always on Sundays for me. Saturdays, too. I'm talking about the cheating I used to do when I finally decided to reduce. You see, no matter how strict I was with my diet Monday through Friday, I'd weaken on weekends. On Saturdays, visiting my folks, I'd eat Pennsylvania Dutch goodies. And on Sundays with my husband's family, I'd eat Italian-style. Yet, believe it or not, I still went from 178 to 118 pounds. But I never could have done it just on my own. I had to have a plan for losing the weight.

I didn't have a weight problem until I began having children. My first three were born in just three years, so the pounds accumulated fast. And when I carried my fourth, my husband Jim was out of work five months, so I ate out of worry. Then when he went back to the job, I was so happy, I stuffed myself.

The only person who thought I looked great was Jim's godfather. When we'd go over to his house, he'd say: "Eat. Eat. God bless you. You eat." Then he'd pat me and say: "You get nice and fat."

But there were others who sent darts right through me with their remarks. Yet each time I looked in a full length mirror, I would just turn to my best side and refuse to see my bulges and my heavy thighs.

Well, that's the way I kidded myself, until one day I borrowed one of Mom's dresses and couldn't fit into it. What a shock, since I always thought of her as bigger than I. But it was just the shaking up I needed to make me do something about losing.

Fortunately, I'd been reading the ads about people who had lost weight on the Ayds® plan, so I decided to try it. I bought a box of the chewy vanilla caramel Ayds candies at the drug store. And since they contain vitamins and minerals, but no drugs, I wasn't afraid to eat them.

It was June and two things made me want to take off weight by August. First, Jim's vacation. And second, a pair of hip huggers he'd bought for me in size 16, too small to fit. But I didn't want Jim to know, so each time he'd ask me to try them on, I would say "Later . . . later," until he didn't ask me any more.

Well, once on the plan, I took one Ayds with a hot drink (tea for me) before each meal, and it actually helped my stomach stop growling. That doesn't sound nice, I know, but I had the kind of stomach that was always talking to me. But on the Ayds plan, I was able to cut down on what I ate and still feel satisfied.

For instance, at breakfast, I'd have one Ayds and tea, then a boiled egg and juice. At lunch, one Ayds, tea and maybe a tuna fish salad and fruit. Then at dinner, Ayds and tea followed by meat, a green vegetable, sometimes a potato and a salad. And in the evening, Ayds and tea, and perhaps a pretzel. There was no starving myself at all, and the weight began to come off — and off.

By August, when it was time for vacation, I'd lost 26 pounds on the Ayds plan and said to Jim: "See, my hip huggers fit!" When we got back home (to Norwood, Pa.) though, I learned the best thing of all. Thanks to the Ayds plan, I hadn't gained a pound. I'd controlled my weight even away from home.

That's when I decided to change the Ayds plan to suit my life. I stayed strict with myself on weekdays, but cheated a little on weekends. And it worked, believe me.

In the end, I lost 60 pounds on the Ayds plan and I'm the talk of every wedding and wake I go to. Not that I'm the one who brings up the subject. It's that everybody who sees me slim asks how I lost the weight and I have to tell them — the Ayds plan. And I'll tell you this, it's wonderful knowing that people notice just as much when you lose as when you gain.

BEFORE AND AFTER MEASUREMENTS

	Before	After
Height	5'6½"	5'5½"
Weight	178 lbs.	118 lbs.
Bust	38"	33½"
Waist	35"	25"
Hips	42-44	34"
Dress	18	8-10

Watch me lose 125 pounds —a picture at a time.

By Betty O'Neal—as told to Ruth L. McCarthy

270 pounds Here I am at my top weight. And it began years ago with Mom saying: "If you're a good girl, you'll get an extra cookie." I was so good, my thighs wound up as big as most girls' waists.

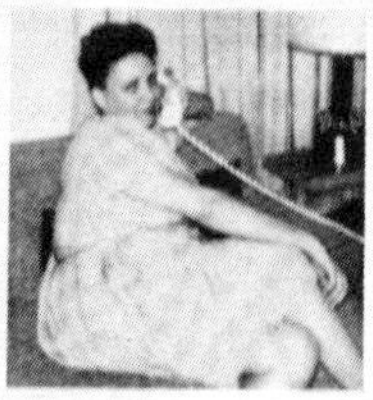

255 pounds I'd lost 15 pounds, yet I still preferred sofas to chairs. I once sat in an arm chair and when I stood up, it wouldn't let go. But what really got me losing was those ads about a reducing plan candy that helps curb your appetite.

232 pounds Down 38 pounds! Quite a record for someone who loved to eat. But I'd never have done it on will-power alone. I needed help and those Ayds® candies gave it to me. I'd take a couple with a hot drink before a meal and I'd actually eat less.

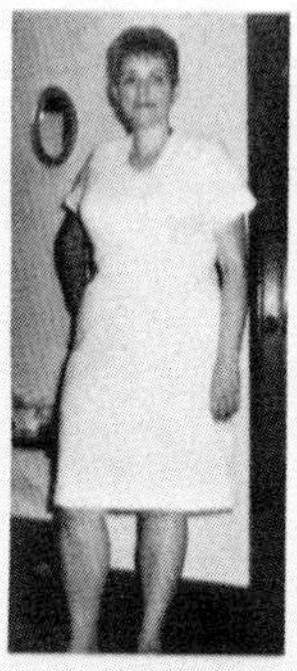

215 pounds No question the Ayds plan was really working for me now. Why, when I saw those scales down 55 pounds, I knew nothing could stop me until I got to my goal — below 150. Another thing. I found I could pass up pies, donuts and cakes more easily because those Ayds also satisfied my sweet tooth.

195 pounds A big turning point! I'd broken the 200-pound barrier. To reward myself I decided to have a huge meal and gooey dessert one day a week. Something to look forward to. And it worked. I still lost.

The new me!
Betty O'Neal

145 pounds Success! I was down to my goal. And just look at that beautiful waist! I don't know who is more proud — my husband or I. But we're both very happy, thanks to the Ayds plan.

Note: *Photos are from the personal album of Betty O'Neal, Chicago, Illinois. The picture at right was for laughs: Betty in a dress she wore before losing 125 pounds on the Ayds plan. Incidentally, Ayds contain vitamins and minerals, no drugs, and are available at drug counters.*

BEFORE AND AFTER MEASUREMENTS

	Before	After
Height	5'6"	5'6"
Weight	270 lbs.	145 lbs.
Bust	53"	38½"
Waist	46"	28"
Hips	55"	36"
Dress	26½	12

133

Art Director Charley Aromando
Writer Ruth L. McCarthy
Photographers Irwin Cohn
Jerry Cohen
Agency Wilson Haight & Welch
Client Campana Corp.

AT CLUB MEDITERRANEE GUADELOUPE, YOU DO ABSOLUTELY EVERYTHING FOR ABSOLUTELY NOTHING.

A week on Guadeloupe costs no more than a week at an ordinary resort. Except all the extras don't cost extra.

Included in the initial price are comfortable, air-conditioned rooms, three meals a day (unlimited food at every meal) and all the free wine you can drink at lunch and supper.

All you have to pay for are drinks at the bar.

The activities are free too. There's free tennis. Free sailing. Free water skiing and scuba diving. Free picnic excursion boat rides. Free yoga and calisthenics. What's more, there's free group lessons and equipment in all sports.

And, free live entertainment every night.

Not only that but you have your choice of Club Mediterranee's two villages on the island. Fort Royal, a smaller, more personal village with a mini club for kids. And the larger more luxurious Caravelle, with its famous Antilles beach.

If you'd like to know more, come in and see us or call.

A vacation at Club Mediterranee on Guadeloupe is a place where you can do a lot more without having to pay a lot more.

TRAVEL AGENT

CLUB MEDITERRANEE/MEXICO. GO SOMEPLACE WHERE MONEY ISN'T THE ONLY LANGUAGE PEOPLE SPEAK.

At Club Mediterranee/Playa Blanca near Manzanillo, nobody talks money. That's because after you pay for your room and board, nobody asks you to pay for anything else.

For that initial cost, which is no more than what you'd pay at an ordinary resort, you get air-conditioned bungalows, three meals a day (unlimited food at every meal) and all the free wine you can drink at lunch and supper. As a matter of fact, all you have to pay for are drinks at the bar.

And all the activities you could possibly want are free.

There's free tennis. Free snorkeling. Free sailing. Free scuba diving. Free yoga and calisthenics. Free picnic excursion boat rides. What's more, there's free group lessons and equipment in all sports. And, free live entertainment every night.

If you'd like to hear more, come in and see us or call.

At Club Mediterranee in Mexico, you can not only leave your troubles behind, you can leave your money behind.

TRAVEL AGENT

CLUB MEDITERRANEE/HAWAII. IN ADDITION TO LEAVING YOUR TROUBLES BEHIND, LEAVE YOUR MONEY BEHIND.

These days, nobody wants to have to go through money like water on their vacation. That's why you should know about Club Mediterranee.

A week at Club Mediterranee in Hawaii costs about the same as a week at an ordinary resort. Except all the extras don't cost extra.

Luxurious, comfortable, air-conditioned rooms, three meals a day (unlimited food at every meal) and all the free wine you can drink at lunch and supper are included in the initial cost. All you have to pay for are drinks at the bar.

Besides that, there's free tennis. Free water skiing. Free sailing. Free snorkeling. Free golf lessons. Free deep sea fishing. Free yoga and calisthenics.

Not to mention the big sport, surfing. And that's free too. There's also free picnic excursion boat rides. What's more, there's free group lessons and equipment in all sports. And free live entertainment every night.

If you'd like to hear more, come in and see us or give us a call.

All in all, you'll not only come back with a beautiful tan, your wallet will come back a healthy shade of green.

TRAVEL AGENT

222

Art Director Bill Kamp
Writers John Russo
Larry Plapler
Designer Bill Kamp
Artist Whistlin Dixie
Agency Levine, Huntley, Schmidt
Client Club Mediterranee

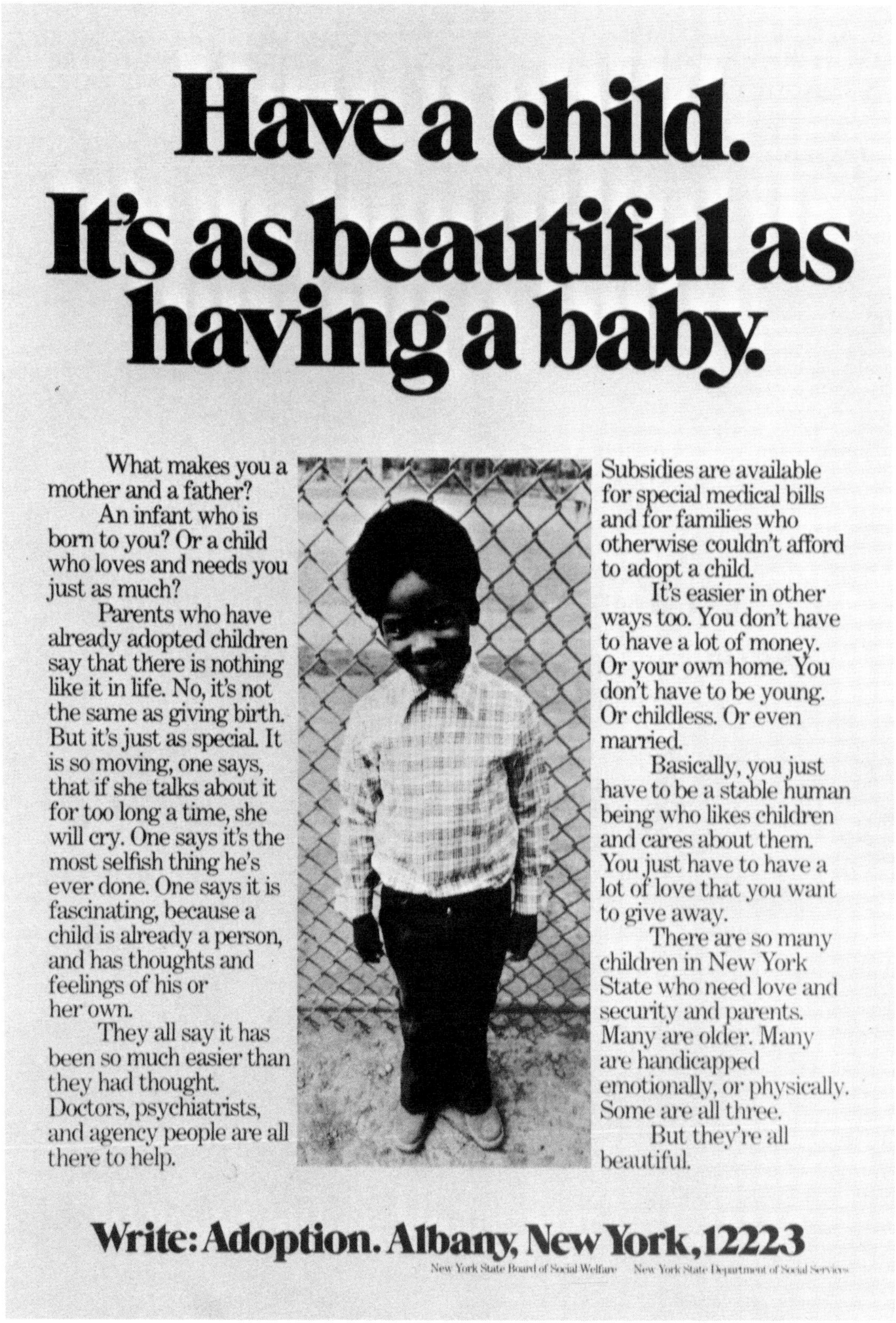
Have a child.
It's as beautiful as having a baby.
What makes you a mother and a father?
An infant who is born to you? Or a child who loves and needs you just as much?
Parents who have already adopted children say that there is nothing like it in life. No, it's not the same as giving birth. But it's just as special. It is so moving, one says, that if she talks about it for too long a time, she will cry. One says it's the most selfish thing he's ever done. One says it is fascinating, because a child is already a person, and has thoughts and feelings of his or her own.
They all say it has been so much easier than they had thought. Doctors, psychiatrists, and agency people are all there to help.
Subsidies are available for special medical bills and for families who otherwise couldn't afford to adopt a child.
It's easier in other ways too. You don't have to have a lot of money. Or your own home. You don't have to be young. Or childless. Or even married.
Basically, you just have to be a stable human being who likes children and cares about them. You just have to have a lot of love that you want to give away.
There are so many children in New York State who need love and security and parents. Many are older. Many are handicapped emotionally, or physically. Some are all three.
But they're all beautiful.
Write: Adoption. Albany, New York, 12223
New York State Board of Social Welfare
New York State Department of Social Services

254
Art Director Alan Kupchick
Writer Enid Futterman
Designer Alan Kupchick
Photographer Joe Toto
Agency Grey Advertising
Client New York State Board of Adoption

If you can't decide between a Shepherd, a Setter or a Poodle, get them all.
Adopt a mutt at the MSPCA and get everything you're looking for, all in one dog. The intelligence of a poodle and the loyalty of a lassie. The bark of a shepherd and the heart of a Saint Bernard. The spots of a Dalmatian, the size of a schnauzer, and the speed of a greyhound. A genuine, all-American mutt has it all.
And the MSPCA has lots of all-American mutts waiting for you. There are genuine, all-American alley kittens, too. Just come to the MSPCA Adoption Ward, 180 Longwood Avenue, Boston. We're open 10:30 to 3:30, Monday through Saturday.
Massachusetts Society for the Prevention of Cruelty to Animals.
Get the best of everything. Adopt a mutt.

Now you can prove your dog is a genuine, All-American Mutt.
M.S.P.C.A.
ALL-AMERICAN MUTT
REGISTRATION CERTIFICATE
When you adopt a pup from the MSPCA, you get a certificate just like this one to prove he's a genuine, All-American Mutt.
Our All-American Alley Kittens have papers, too!
They're all waiting for you at the MSPCA Adoption Ward, 180 Longwood Avenue, Boston. Come in 10:30 to 3:30, Monday through Saturday. We guarantee you'll leave with the best of everything.
Massachusetts Society for the Prevention of Cruelty to Animals.
Get the best of everything. Adopt a mutt.

262

Art Directors June Corley
Mary Moore
Writers Katina Mills
Veronica Nash
Artist Joe Patti
Photographer David Doss
Agency Humphrey Browning MacDougall
Client Massachusetts Society
for the Prevention of
Cruelty to Animals

All the king's horses and all the king's men can't put King Richard together again.

On May 12, 1973, the National Council of the National Emergency Civil Liberties Committee resolved to conduct a campaign for the impeachment of Richard Milhous Nixon, by petition, advertising and public meetings.

Nearly a year later, the impeachment issue has become the most important issue before the nation.

Now, with Congress only moments away from the critical decision it must face, we are publishing this advertisement to ask for your participation by notifying your Congress-person of your position on this issue.

Please fill in the coupons below, and send them immediately to us, together with whatever you can afford, to permit us to place this ad in other publications. We will forward your ballot to Washington.

We have come so far, and we are now so near, and you can help to make the vital difference.

After all, do you know anyone who is proud to have that man as President?

Nadel

National Impeachment Poll

Name of Representative: ______
House Office Building, Washington, D.C.
☐ I believe that the Congress should impeach Richard M. Nixon immediately.
☐ I think he should resign.
Name ______
Address ______
City ______ State ______ Zip ______

Enclosed is my contribution of $100, $50, $25, $15, $10, $5, $ ______
Name ______
Address ______
City ______ State ______ Zip ______

National Emergency Civil Liberties Committee
25 East 26 Street, New York, NY 10010

Edith Tiger, Director
Corliss Lamont, Chairman
Leonard Boudin, General Counsel

263
Art Director Barbara Schubeck
Writer Dick Calderhead
Artist Marc Nadel
Agency Calderhead, Jackson
Client National Emergency Civil Liberties Committee

ON POURRAIT SE PASSER DE CINZANO.
ON POURRAIT AUSSI SE PASSER DE NOËL.
CINZANO
CINZANO BITTER®. NOUS NE CHANGERONS JAMAIS.
PREPARE SELON LA RECETTE DE FRANCESCO CINZANO.
CINZANO

507
Art Directors Martin Reavley
Rosette Holzer
Writer Pierre Berville
Photographer David Thorpe
Agency Tragos Bonnage
Wiesendanger Ajroldi
Paris
Client Cinzano

Gensler and Associates Architects
Gensler and Associates Architects
Tenant Development
Clients

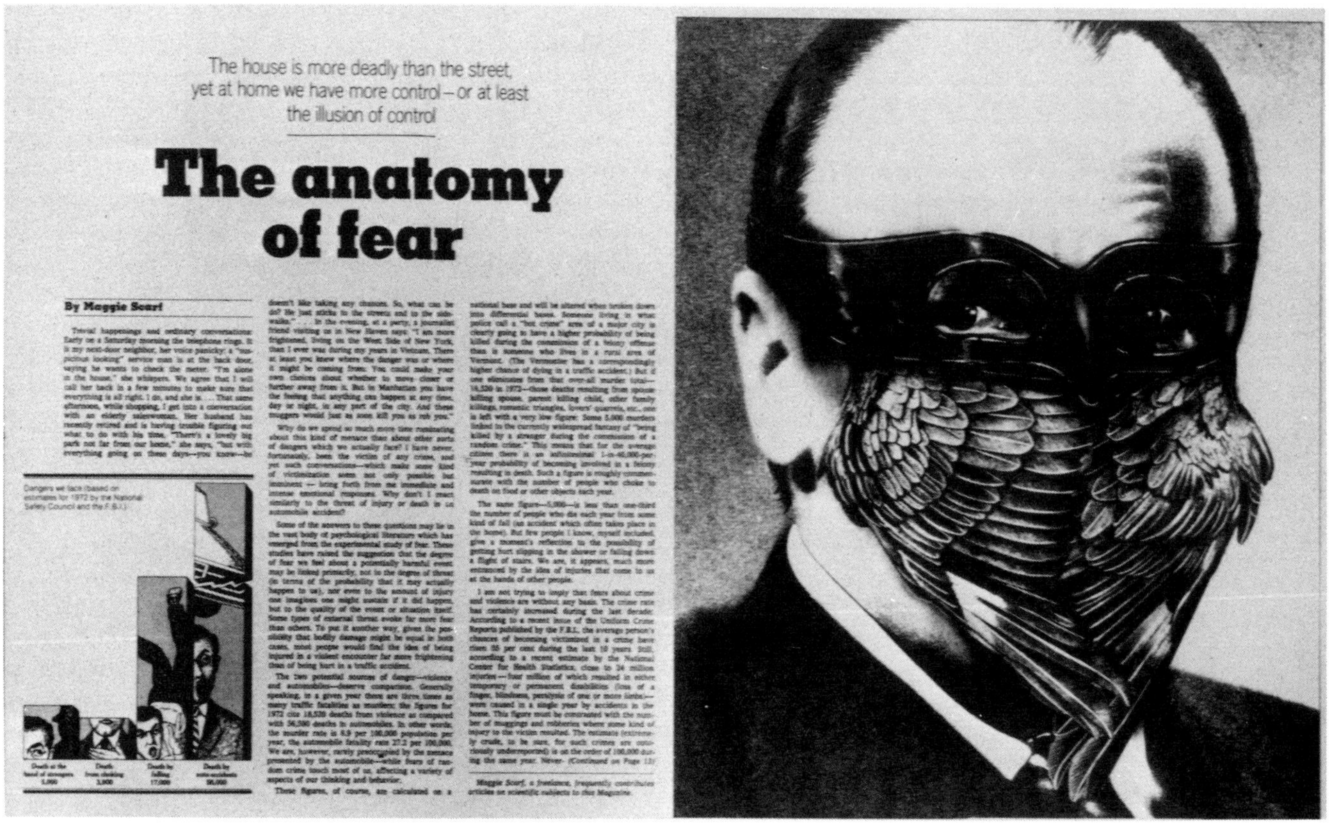
The house is more deadly than the street, yet at home we have more control—or at least the illusion of control
The anatomy of fear
By Maggie Scarf

736
Art Director Harry Murphy
Designer Harry Murphy
Artist Kate Keating
Writer Art Odel
Agency Harry Murphy & Friends
Client Gensler & Assoc. Architects

1074
Art Director Ruth Ansel
Designer Ruth Ansel
Artist Christian Piper
Editors Lewis Bergman
Jack Rosenthal
Publisher The New York Times Magazine

Hot Shots
• Photographs by Norman Seeff •

1051
Art Director Herbert Wise
Designer Norman Seeff
Photographer Norman Seeff
Publisher Flash Books

A VOLVO DISCOVERY: RAIN FALLS ON REAR WINDOWS, TOO.

Volvo is the only wagon maker with the foresight to provide its rear window with a wiper and washer as standard equipment.

Volvo has also discovered that everyone doesn't buy a wagon to be fashionable. Many people buy wagons to carry things.

So we didn't design Volvo's cargo area low and sleek to accommodate a styling trend. We designed it high and practical, to accommodate things like a six-foot sofa and two chairs (with the rear seat down). Or three six-foot people and 12 two-suiters (with the rear seat up).

Volvo's rear area not only holds a lot, it comes with a lot. It has its own heating and ventilation vents, its own three-point seat belts, electric rear window defogger, carpeting, tinted glass and childproof door locks.

And Volvo's back door swings up out of your way, instead of out into your stomach. Or down into your knee caps.

It doesn't take a college degree to appreciate the thinking behind our wagon. So we leave you to consider this. If the rear end of your car isn't as well thought-out as Volvo's, what other part might not be?

VOLVO
The wagon for people who think.

RR-7902
VOLVO
245 DL

Art Director Robert Reitzfeld
Writer Thomas J. Nathan
Photographer Henry Sandbank
Agency Scali, McCabe, Sloves
Client Volvo of America Corp.

IT TAKES A LOT OF DUMMIES TO DESIGN A CAR FOR PEOPLE WHO THINK.

By smashing Volvos into barriers with dummies inside, we've made them safer for people. These tests helped develop a front end which absorbs highway-speed impacts to protect the passenger compartment. And a three-point seat belt which can restrain 3½ tons of force.

By bouncing a dummy bottom on a seat for hours, we designed one to stay comfortable for years. But all our improvements aren't suggested by dummies. Some come from common sense.

All cars have head restraints. Volvo's have openings, so you can see behind you.

All cars have windshield wipers. But instead of shiny ones that glare, Volvo has dull black ones.

Volvo provides four wheel power-assisted disc brakes, steel-belted radial tires, fuel injection, new suspension that makes the car corner flatter and smoother. And a heating-circulation system that can freshen the air, warm your feet and defog the front windows all at once.

At Volvo, the smallest details get careful consideration. Which is why, all things considered, Volvo may well be the world's most carefully thought-out car.

It's not surprising then, that Volvo has a special appeal for people who think. 87% of the people who buy Volvos are college educated.

The other 13% must be just plain smart.

VOLVO
The car for people who think.

800-TJN

A CAR SEAT HAS TO BE MORE THAN A PLACE TO SIT. OURS MAKES YOU A BETTER DRIVER.

The average car seat is designed to fit a person who doesn't exist ...the average size driver.

So Volvo developed a seat that accommodates *every* size driver.

The Volvo seat is built to help you drive. It's adjustable to your dimensions, to afford you complete control over the controls.

If your calves are shorter than average, you can lower the seat height to get closer to the pedals.

If your arms are longer than average, you can lean back without moving back. (The seat angle is adjustable.)

If your back gets tired, a lumbar adjustment will support you in the style you prefer: from soft to firm. And if your legs get tired, you can tilt back the seat cushion to brace your thighs. Or push back the seat to stretch them.

The Volvo seat even improves your visibility. Our head restraints have openings, so you can see in back of you.

If this seems like a lot of thought to put into the place where you sit, you'll be even more impressed by something else. The thinking that went into the place where we put our seat.

Our car.

VOLVO
The car for people who think.

DID IT EVER OCCUR TO YOU THAT YOUR CAR MIGHT PANIC IN A CRISIS?

The 1975 Volvo 240 series was planned with the unexpected in mind.

Because, while it's human to err, driving errors can be fatal. Volvos are designed to compensate.

Jamming on the brakes may make them work too well.

When a car stops fast, its weight shifts forward. The rear wheels tend to lock before the front ones. This can cause a skid.

Volvo's 4-wheel power disc brake system has a pressure-proportioning valve on each rear brake line. It minimizes premature rear wheel lock-up, and helps keep you on the straight and narrow.

Road debris could damage a brake line. So Volvo has two independent braking systems. Each works on *three* wheels—two front, one rear. (According to Volvo's math, you could lose 50% of your braking system, and have about 80% of its effectiveness left.)

If you can't stop, you've got to go around. Volvo's rack and pinion steering is similar to a racing car's. It's extremely quick. And even in high speed dodging, Volvo's new suspension holds you steady, smooth and flat.

No matter how good your reflexes are, you have to rely on your car's reactions. And when it comes to avoiding accidents, Volvo thinks you can't go too far.

VOLVO
The car for people who think.

Art Director Robert Reitzfeld
Writers Thomas J. Nathan
Edward A. McCabe
Photographers Henry Sandbank
Steve Horn
Agency Scali, McCabe, Sloves
Client Volvo of America Corp.

1971
BLUE NUN®
WHITE WINE
H. SICHEL SÖHNE, MAINZ ESTD. 1857
LIEBFRAUMILCH QUALITATSWEIN
Schieffelin & Co.—New York
SINCE 1794
SOLE U.S.
The nun who turned wine into profits.
Her name is Blue Nun.
And she's on the label of the largest selling imported premium white wine on the market today.
It's Blue Nun wine. The delicious white wine that's correct with any dish. The wine that's delicate enough for fish, yet hearty enough for meat. The wine more and more people are asking for everyday.
And the wine more and more people are going to be hearing about everyday, too. That's because Blue Nun commercials are the most popular wine advertising ever done on radio. And now they'll reach more people in your market than ever before.
So if you'd like to turn wine into profits, stock and display the German white wine that sells more, and makes more than any other. Blue Nun wine.
We think you'll find the results are miraculous.
Blue Nun. The delicious white wine more people are converting to every year.

The nun's story.
The best part of this story is the fact that it never ends.
It just goes on and on. And gets better and better.
It's the success story of Blue Nun wine. The delicious white wine that's correct with any dish. The wine that's delicate enough for fish, yet hearty enough for meat. The wine more and more people are asking for everyday.
In fact, so many people are asking for Blue Nun that it's become the largest selling imported premium white wine.
Blue Nun has also become the most listened to imported premium white wine. That's because Blue Nun commercials are the most popular wine advertising ever done on radio. And now they'll reach more people in your market than ever before.
So if you want to be part of one of the greatest success stories ever told, stock and display Blue Nun wine in your store.
Blue Nun wine. It's one for the books.
Blue Nun. The delicious white wine more people are converting to every year.

Behind every success story stands a great woman.
The woman behind our success story is a Blue Nun.
And she's on the label of the largest selling imported premium white wine on the market today.
It's Blue Nun wine.
The delicious white wine that's correct with any dish. The wine that's delicate enough for fish, yet hearty enough for meat. The wine more and more people are asking for everyday.
And the wine more and more people are going to be hearing about everyday, too. That's because Blue Nun commercials are the most popular wine advertising ever done on radio. And now they'll reach more people in your market than ever before.
So if you want the Blue Nun success story to be part of your success story, stock and display Blue Nun wine in your store.
What you'll have is a great woman behind you. And a great future in front of you.
Blue Nun. The delicious white wine more people are converting to every year.
IMPORTED BY SCHIEFFELIN & CO., NEW YORK.

206

Art Director Mark Yustein
Writer Kay Kavanagh
Artists Cal Sachs
David Wilcox
Photographer Charlie Gold
Agency Della Femina, Travisano & Partners
Client Schieffelin & Co.

Does this Jewish couple dare to marry and have children?

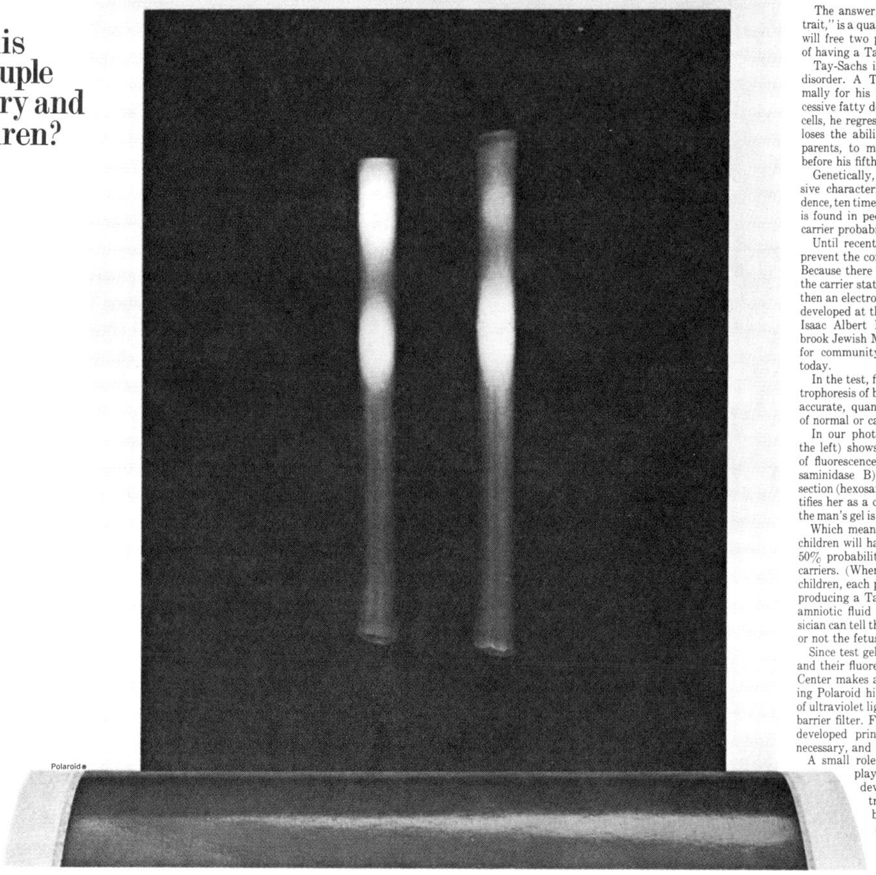
Polaroid

The answer, shown in our Polaroid "portrait," is a qualified "yes." It's an answer that will free two people from the haunting fear of having a Tay-Sachs child.

Tay-Sachs is a fatal, inherited, metabolic disorder. A Tay-Sachs child develops normally for his first six months. Then, as excessive fatty deposits accumulate in his brain cells, he regresses. Slowly and inexorably, he loses the ability to sit up, to recognize his parents, to manage a smile. Then, usually before his fifth birthday, he dies.

Genetically, Tay-Sachs is a simple recessive characteristic. Its highest carrier incidence, ten times that of the general population, is found in people of Jewish ancestry where carrier probability is 1 in 30.

Until recently, there was no sure way to prevent the conception of a Tay-Sachs baby. Because there was no sure way to determine the carrier status of prospective parents. And then an electrophoretic testing technique was developed at the Birth Defects Center of the Isaac Albert Research Institute at Kingsbrook Jewish Medical Center. It's being used for community screening in many centers today.

In the test, fluorescent acrylamide gel electrophoresis of blood samples provides a rapid, accurate, quantitative, visual determination of normal or carrier status.

In our photograph, the woman's gel (on the left) shows a relatively higher intensity of fluorescence in the upper section (hexosaminidase B) as compared to the lower section (hexosaminidase A). This pattern identifies her as a carrier. The reverse pattern in the man's gel is typical of a normal individual.

Which means there's *no* chance that their children will have the disease. But there *is* a 50% probability that their children will be carriers. (When two carriers decide to have children, each pregnancy holds a 25% risk of producing a Tay-Sachs child. By testing the amniotic fluid early in pregnancy, the physician can tell the prospective parents whether or not the fetus has the disease.)

Since test gels deteriorate within 12 hours, and their fluorescence dissipates rapidly, the Center makes a permanent record by exposing Polaroid high contrast film to 5 seconds of ultraviolet light through a Wratten No. 2A barrier filter. Fifteen seconds later, the fully developed print can be studied, reshot if necessary, and filed for future reference.

A small role for one of our products to play? Maybe. But when anybody develops a procedure that helps troubled people, we're proud to be involved.

Just for the record.

Polaroid Corporation

184

Art Director Lee Epstein
Writer Hal Silverman
Designer Lee Epstein
Photographer Henry Sandbank
Agency Doyle Dane Bernbach
Client Polaroid Corp.

12
CHIVAS REGAL
1801
SCOTCH
WHISKY
To your wealth.

232
Art Director Ed Flanagan
Writer Jim Copacino
Designer Ed Flanagan
Photographer John Conboy
Agency Promotion Plus
Doyle Dane Bernbach Div.
Client General Wine & Spirits

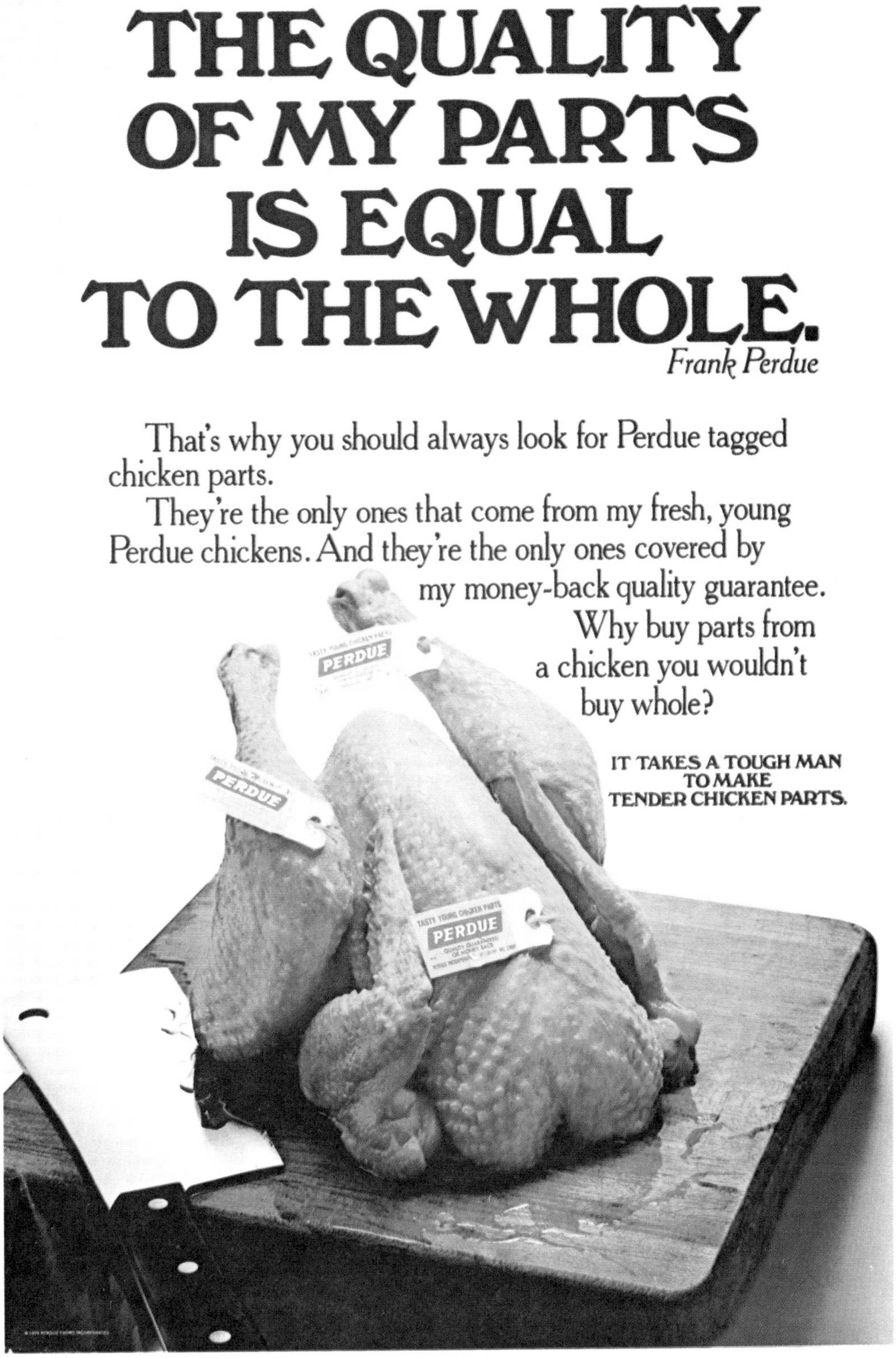
THE QUALITY OF MY PARTS IS EQUAL TO THE WHOLE.
Frank Perdue
That's why you should always look for Perdue tagged chicken parts.
They're the only ones that come from my fresh, young Perdue chickens. And they're the only ones covered by my money-back quality guarantee.
Why buy parts from a chicken you wouldn't buy whole?
IT TAKES A TOUGH MAN TO MAKE TENDER CHICKEN PARTS.
PERDUE
PERDUE
PERDUE

244
Art Director Sam Scali
Writer Edward A. McCabe
Photographer Phil Mazzurco
Agency Scali, McCabe, Sloves
Client Perdue Farms

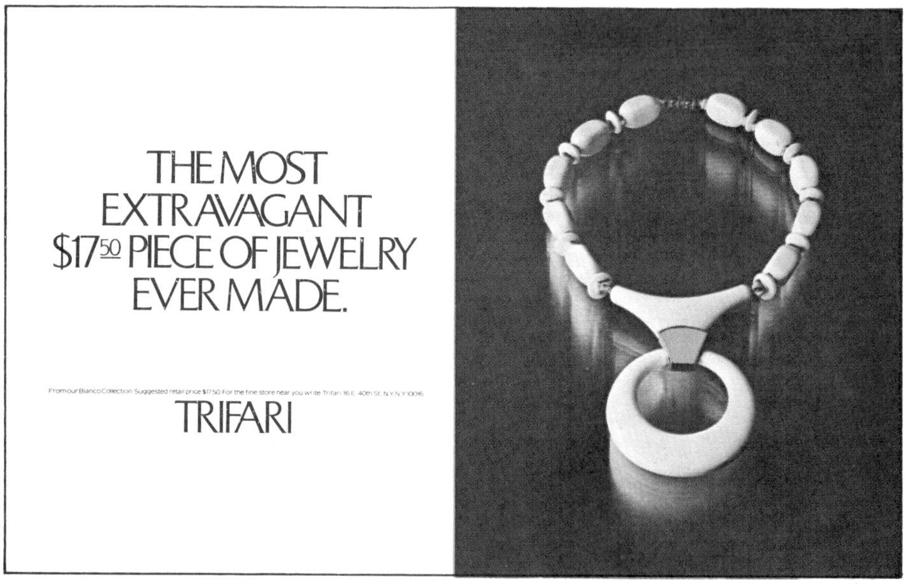
THE MOST
EXTRAVAGANT
$17.50 PIECE OF JEWELRY
EVER MADE.
From our Bianco Collection. Suggested retail price $17.50. For the fine store near you write Trifari, 16 E. 40th St., N.Y., N.Y. 10016.
TRIFARI

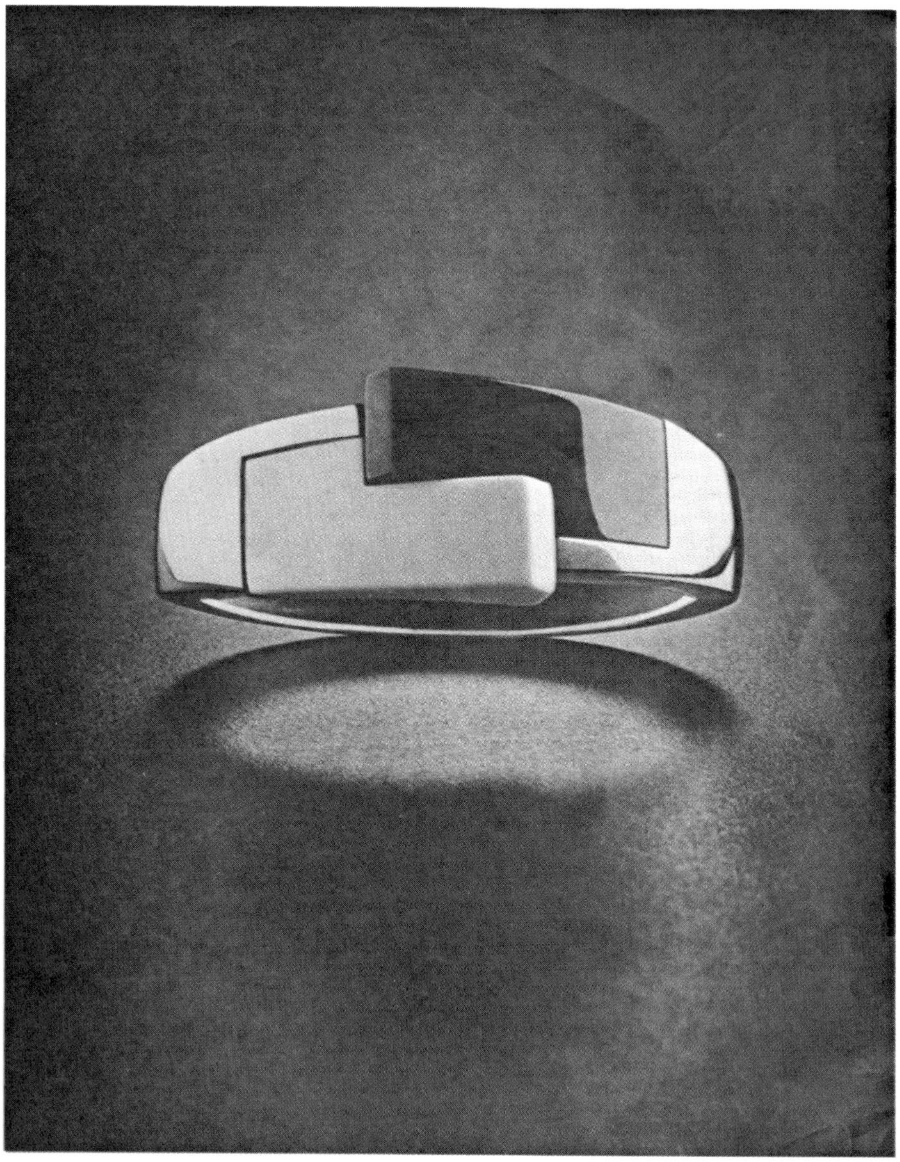

288

Art Director Dennis D'Amico
Photographer Michael O'Neill
Writer Dick Tarlow
Agency Sacks, Tarlow & Rosen
Client Trifari, Krussman & Fishel

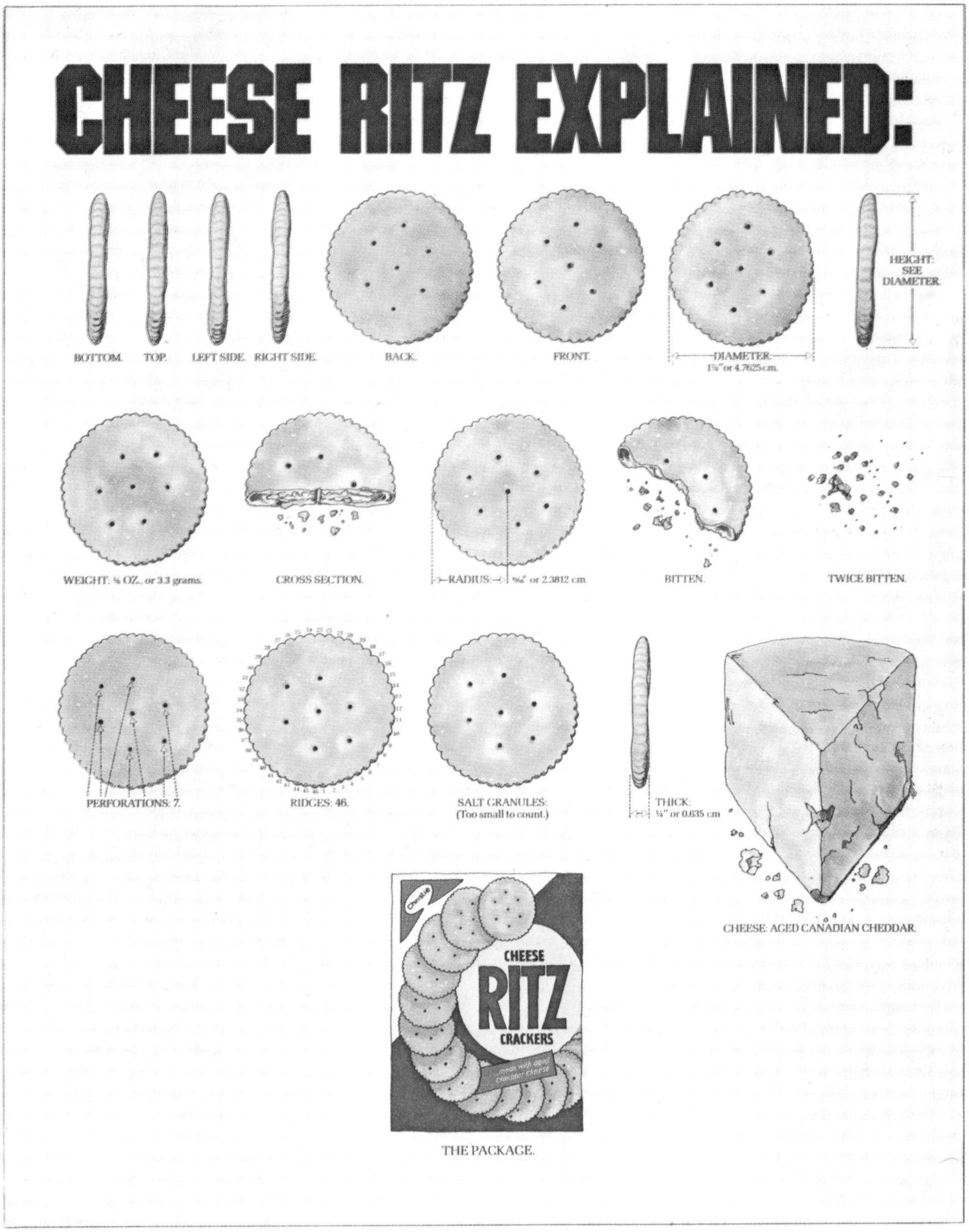
CHEESE RITZ EXPLAINED:
BOTTOM.
TOP.
LEFT SIDE.
RIGHT SIDE.
BACK.
FRONT.
DIAMETER:
1⅞" or 4.7625 cm.
HEIGHT: SEE DIAMETER.
WEIGHT: ⅛ OZ., or 3.3 grams.
CROSS SECTION.
RADIUS: 15/16" or 2.3812 cm.
BITTEN.
TWICE BITTEN.
PERFORATIONS: 7.
RIDGES: 46.
SALT GRANULES:
(Too small to count.)
THICK:
¼" or 0.635 cm
CHEESE: AGED CANADIAN CHEDDAR.
Christie
CHEESE
RITZ
CRACKERS
THE PACKAGE.

522

Art Director Brian Harrod
Writer Allan Kazmer
Designer Brian Harrod
Artist Tony Kew
Agency McCann-Erickson
Toronto
Client Christies Brown

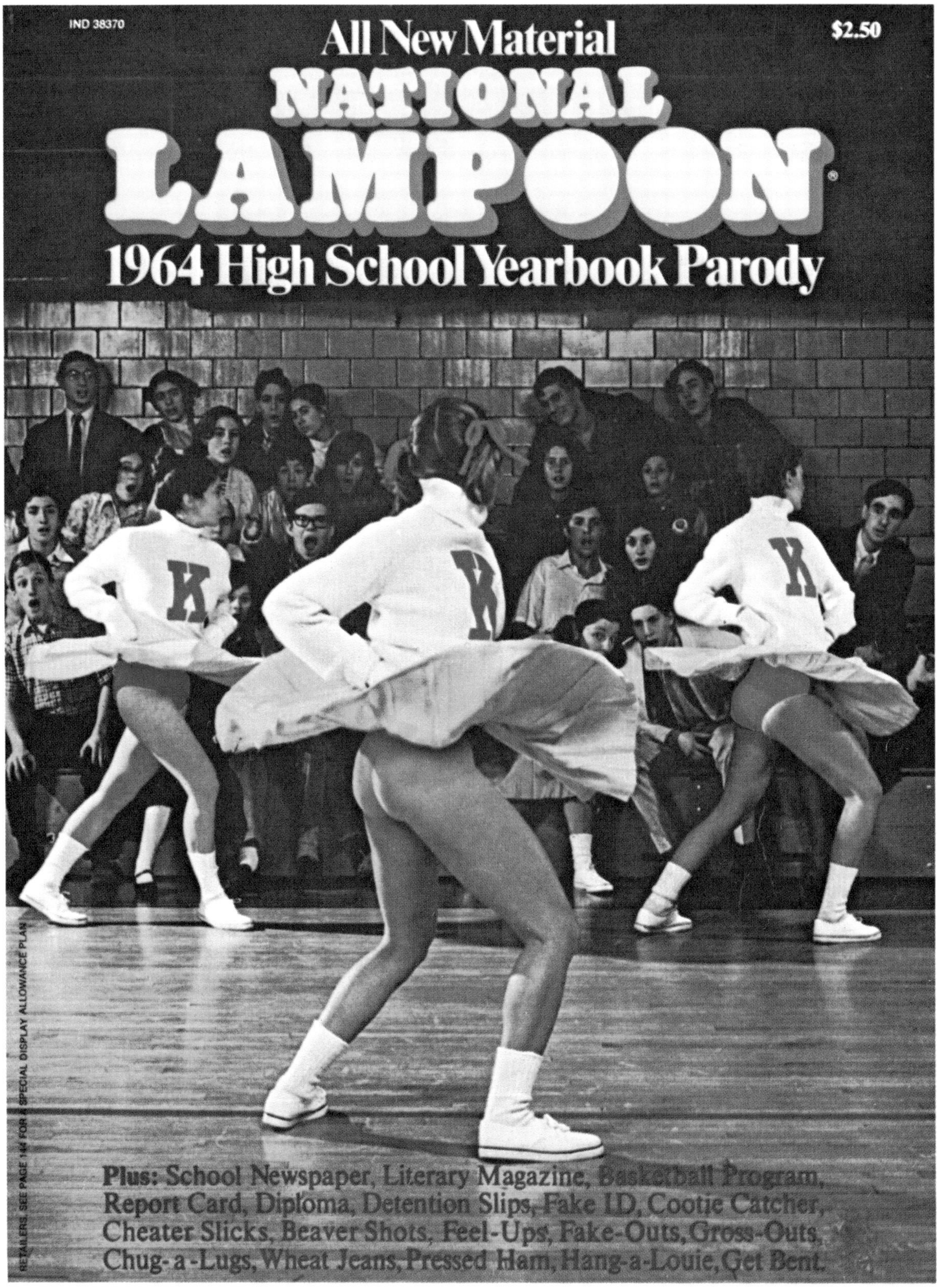
IND 38370
All New Material
$2.50
NATIONAL
LAMPOON®
1964 High School Yearbook Parody
Plus: School Newspaper, Literary Magazine, Basketball Program, Report Card, Diploma, Detention Slips, Fake I.D., Cootie Catcher, Cheater Slicks, Beaver Shots, Feel-Ups, Fake-Outs, Gross-Outs, Chug-a-Lugs, Wheat Jeans, Pressed Ham, Hang-a-Louie, Get Bent.
RETAILERS, SEE PAGE 144 FOR A SPECIAL DISPLAY ALLOWANCE PLAN

618

Art Director David Kaestle
Designer David Kaestle
Artists Alan Rose
Marc Arceneaux
Mara McAffee
Photographers David Kaestle
Vince Aiosa
Writers Doug Kenny
P. J. O'Rourke
Publisher National Lampoon

The Living World of
AUDUBON
by Roland C. Clement
The best of Audubon with the best of today's photography

PLATE
306
Common Loon
Gavia immer

How do Audubon's birds fare today?
A few have increased in number and even extended their ranges, but many others—like the loon—have decreased both in numbers and distribution. The "great northern diver" is still a common bird in appropriate places. In Audubon's day it nested as far south as the Wabash and Susquehanna; today only some of the northern-tier United States and parts of Canada know it as a nesting bird. With the coming of winter, it leaves the northern lakes and heads for the large bays and the coastal seas, where—singly or in small groups—it fishes and awaits the coming of another spring. "Whether it be fishing in deep water amid rolling billows," Audubon wrote, "or engaged in eluding its foes, it disappears beneath the surface so suddenly, remains so long in the water, and rises at so extraordinary a distance, often in a direction quite the reverse of that supposed to be followed by it, that your eyes become wearied in searching for it."

14

650
Art Director Albert Squillace
Designer Albert Squillace
Artist John James Audubon
Writer Roland Clement
Publishers Ridge Press
Grosset & Dunlap

CHARLES IVES
THE 100TH ANNIVERSARY
1874 - 1974

828
Art Directors John Berg
Henrietta Condak
Designer Henrietta Condak
Artist Richard Hess
Client Columbia Records

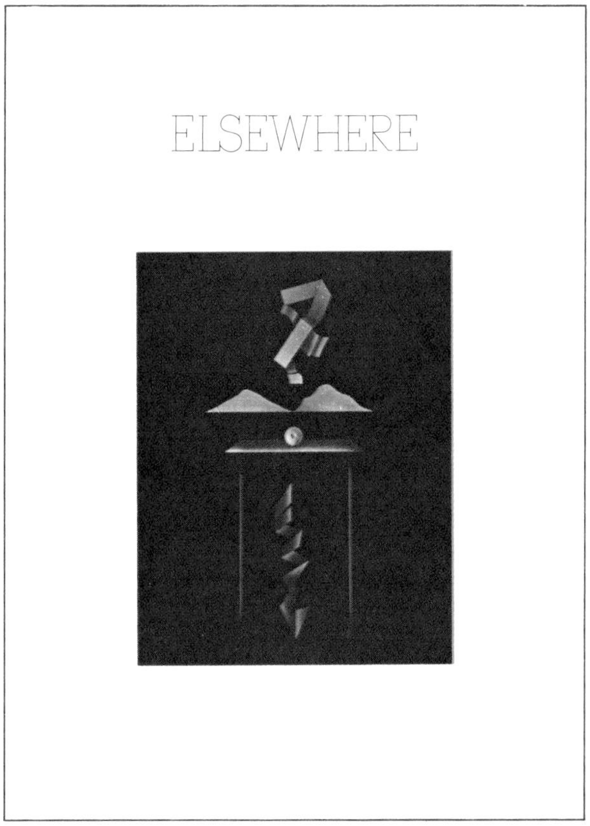
ELSEWHERE

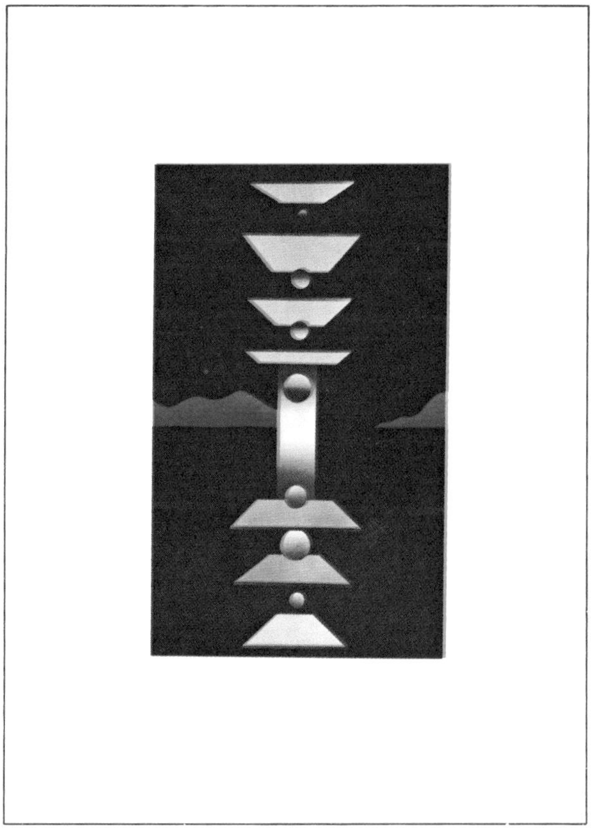

1126

Art Director Uli Boege
Designer Uli Boege
Artist Uli Boege
Photographer Jean-Marie Guyaux
Writers Franz Kafka
translated by Uli Boege
Publisher Links Books

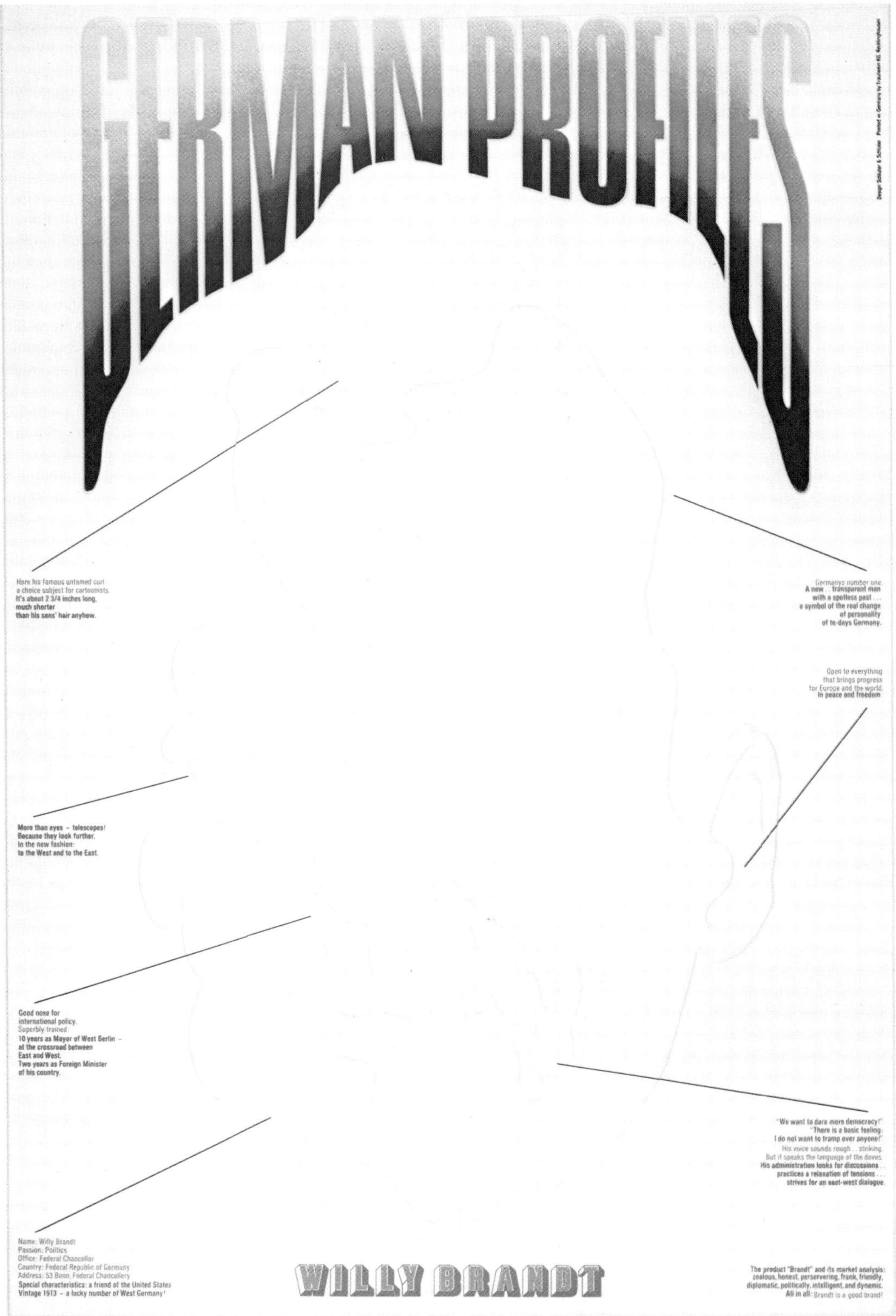

GERMAN PROFILES
Here his famous untamed curl
a choice subject for cartoonists.
It's about 2 3/4 inches long,
much shorter
than his sons' hair anyhow.
Germanys number one.
A new . . transparent man
with a spotless past . . .
a symbol of the real change
of personality
of to-days Germany.
Open to everything
that brings progress
for Europe and the world.
In peace and freedom
More than eyes – telescopes!
Because they look further.
In the new fashion:
to the West and to the East.
Good nose for
international policy.
Superbly trained:
10 years as Mayor of West Berlin –
at the crossroad between
East and West.
Two years as Foreign Minister
of his country.
"We want to dare more democracy!"
"There is a basic feeling:
I do not want to tramp over anyone!"
His voice sounds rough . . striking.
But it speaks the language of the doves.
His administration looks for discussions . .
practices a relaxation of tensions . . .
strives for an east-west dialogue.
Name: Willy Brandt
Passion: Politics
Office: Federal Chancellor
Country: Federal Republic of Germany
Address: 53 Bonn, Federal Chancellery
Special characteristics: a friend of the United States
Vintage 1913 – a lucky number of West Germany!
WILLY BRANDT
The product "Brandt" and its market analysis:
zealous, honest, perservering, frank, friendly,
diplomatic, politically, intelligent, and dynamic.
All in all: Brandt is a good brand!

1164

Art Directors Doris Schluter
Harald Schluter
Designers Doris Schluter
Harald Schluter
Artists Doris Schluter
Harald Schluter
Writer Jurgen Mehl
Agency Schluter, Schluter,
Mehl Ideealismus GmbH
West Germany
Client Inter Nationes

R Fox Limited 2 North Road, London N7 9HL.Telephone 01-607 7371 (10 lines)
Statement

1174
Art Directors Marcello Minale
Brian Tattersfield
Designers Marcello Minale
Brian Tattersfield
Alex Maranzano
Agency Minale, Tattersfield,
Provinciali Ltd.
London
Client Fox Ltd.

CLUB ATLANTIQUE
60-second

ANNCR: Stiller and Meara.

MEARA: Say, is this your first vacation at Club Atlantique?

STILLER: Yeah, last year I tried Le Club Dead Sea, but there wasn't much action. Ha ha ha ha . . .

MEARA: You're very humorous. Hey, that's a lovely sarong you're wearing.

STILLER: Thank you, it's a Pucci.

MEARA: Oh . . .

STILLER: Yours is kind of interesting too.

MEARA: Thank you. It's a towel I got at a singles weekend at Grossinger's.

STILLER: Very becoming, this is really an exotic spread. What are you having?

MEARA: Oh, I think I'll try the cracked crab Martinique.

STILLER: And I think I'll have the meatloaf Fantastique. And perhaps we could share a bottle of wine.

MEARA: That would be magnifique! Except that you're having meat and I'm having seafood. I mean what wine goes with both.

STILLER: Well, I noticed a little Blue Nun over there.

MEARA: Oh, is she the one in the black pedal pushers.

STILLER: No, Blue Nun is a wine. A delicious white wine that's correct with any dish. It goes as well with meat as it does with fish.

MEARA: That sounds like some wine. Is it expensive?

STILLER: It's not cheap. It's about four conch shells and a couple of red beads. Ha ha ha ha . . .

MEARA: Very witty . . .

STILLER: Say did you hear the one about the . . .

MEARA: Yes!

ANNCR: Blue Nun. The delicious white wine that's correct with any dish. Another Sichel Wine imported by Schieffelin & Co., New York.

315
Writers Kay Kavanagh
Mark Yustein
Producer Lewis Kuperman
Production Co. National Recording
Agency Della Femina, Travisano & Partners
Client Schieffelin & Co.

STANLEY
55-second

NARRATOR: Once upon a time there was a cab driver who had no opinion. Stanley knew every street in Detroit . . .

STANLEY: I can getcha to Sterling Heights in 11 minutes.

NARRATOR: . . . But he knew very little about the world. When the passengers in his cab would strike up a conversation . . .

PASSENGER: Boy, that's some bill they just passed in Lansing.

NARRATOR: Stanley didn't have much to say.

STANLEY: Uh . . . hot enough for ya?

NARRATOR: Then one day, the president of a well-known corporation said to him . . .

PRESIDENT: Stanley, if you read The Detroit News you know.

NARRATOR: Stanley began reading The Detroit News every day. He discovered he had a real gift for analyzing current events.

STANLEY: That's right, Mac, Greenland will be the next superpower.

NARRATOR: Soon leaders from all over the world were coming to Stanley for advice.

BRITISH DIPLOMAT: I say, Stanley, what should we do about this banana embargo?

NARRATOR: Stanley became famous and respected. Which proves beyond a shadow of a doubt what a good thing it is to Read The News and Know.

DIPLOMAT: I'm honored to meet you, Messieur Stanley. Hot enough for you?

YOUNG COUPLE
55-second

SINGLE LADY
55-second

348
Writer Lawrence Kasdan
Directors Lawrence Kasdan
Jim Dale
Producers Lawrence Kasdan
Jim Dale
Production Co. Bell Sound
Agency W. B. Doner & Co. Advertising
Client The Detroit News

AN ELEPHANT STEPPED ON IT
30-second

SPOKESMAN: Last year the Tonka Toy Co. ran a commercial to parents about broken toys.

In it children told their parents how their toys got broken.

One said, "An elephant stepped on it."

We wondered. What would happen if an elephant stepped on a Tonka Toy?

MUSIC

ANNCR: A toy shouldn't break just because a child plays with it.

376
Art Director Mike Tesch
Writer Patrick Kelly
Director Steve Horn
Producer Vera Samama
Production Co. Horn/Griner Productions
Agency Carl Ally
Client Tonka Corp.

Del Monte
TOMATO
CATSUP

CATSUP
30-second

VO: I see that your mother has gotten you Del Monte Catsup.

KID: Yup.

VO: And I'd say, makin' just a wild guess, that you like the deliciousness of it and the thickness, and you like what Del Monte's special blend of those seven herbs and spices is doin' to that hamburger.

KID: Yup.

VO: Trade ya my size 14 varsity baseball shoes for it.

KID: Nope.

VO: I'll send you to the moon.

KID: Nope.

VO: How 'bout if I sent your sister to the moon?

KID: I got two sisters.

VO: They'll both go.

ANNCR: When it comes to picking catsup, Mother really does know best.

FRENCH STYLE GREEN BEANS
30-second

425
Art Director Jerry Collamer
Writer Valerie Wagner
Director Denny Harris
Producer Harry Wypich
Production Co. Denny Harris Inc.
Agency McCann-Erickson
San Francisco
Client Del Monte

Southern

ORGY
60-second

STEWARDESS: Second cabin, please.

ANNCR: You know what the stewardess really means when she orders you to go back to the second cabin, don't you?

She means, get back there with the peasants. That's what she means.

Southern Airways believes that no man should be subjected to the indignity of being labeled or treated like a second class citizen.

Which is why, when you get on a Southern jet, you'll find no curtain separates the peasants from the nobility.

STEWARDESS: Hi, Mr. Gill, sit anywhere you like.

ANNCR: No one takes the legroom from you and gives it to someone else.

On Southern there's only one class of service and it isn't second.

SUPER: *Nobody's Second Class On Southern*

448
Art Director Jonis Gold
Writer Tom Little
Director Joe Sedelmaier
Producer Suzanne Carroll
Production Co. Sedelmaier Films
Agency McDonald & Little
Client Southern Airways

COMMUTER
60-second

ANNCR: This winter you need all the summer you can get.

SONG: Chasing the sunshine, looking to warm my soul and body, feeling so fine. Life is all mine in the sunshine. Chasing the rainbow, looking to cleanse my soul. wooo. . .

ANNCR: Did you know this island was discovered by Christopher Columbus in 1493? Florida, Mexico and the Vacation Islands of the Caribbean are filled with summer.
And you can do more than just dream about it.
With Eastern Airlines' new Personalized Vacation Planning you can have a vacation as unique as you are.
Talk to your Travel agent or call the airline that's working harder for your dollar.

CONDUCTOR: Irvington, Irvington.

ANNCR: Get the most summer this winter from Eastern . . . The Wings of Man.

JOGGER
60-second

HOUSEWIFE
60-second

468
Art Director Jim Swan
Writer Phil Peppis
Director Ed Bianchi
Producer Jim Swan
Production Co. Milan Films
Agency Young & Rubicam International
Client Eastern Airlines

Have a child.
It's as beautiful as
having a baby.

DADDY
30-second

OLDER CHILD: Daddy's coming home soon.

YOUNGER CHILD: He's not my Daddy. I'm adopted.

OLDER CHILD: Yes he is.

YOUNGER CHILD: How do you know?

OLDER CHILD: 'Cause I'm your sister. Daddy's home!

YOUNGER CHILD: Hi, Daddy.

ANNCR: There are so many children in New York who need parents. Have a child. It's as beautiful as having a baby. Write Adoption, Albany, New York.

474
Art Director Alan Kupchick
Writer Enid Futterman
Director Norman Griner
Producer Steve Novick
Production Co. Horn/Griner Productions
Agency Grey Advertising
Client New York State Board of Adoption

CELEBRITIES
60-second

ANNCR: Masterpiece Theatre has a strange effect on intelligent people.
It holds them spellbound.

It lures them to their television sets, and it doesn't let them go.

It warms the heart and it captures the mind. It may startle you . . . or amuse you . . . But it will never never bore you.

SUPER: Masterpiece Theatre.
Sunday evenings on P.B.S.
Brought to you by Mobil

497
Art Director Gordon Bowan
Writer Charlie Miesmer
Cameraman David Hoffman
Director David Hoffman
Producer Harry Wiland
Production Co. Varied Directions
Client Mobil Oil Corp.

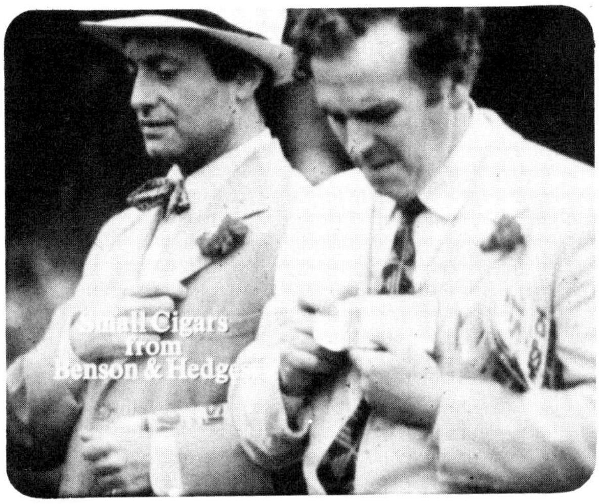
Small Cigars
from
Benson & Hedges

CARNATION

MUSIC UNDER

530
Art Director Geoff Krikland
Director Bob Brooks
Producer John Cigarini
Production Co. Brooks Fulford Cramer
Agency Collett Dickenson Pearce & Partners Ltd. London
Client Benson & Hedges Ltd.

PRINT ADS

ADVERTISING

Newspaper Ads	1–34
Newspaper Campaigns	35–47
Consumer Magazine Ads, b/w	48–76
Consumer Magazine Ads, color	77–125
Consumer Magazine Campaigns, b/w	126–139
Consumer Magazine Campaigns, color	140–158
Trade Magazine Ads, b/w	159–173
Trade Magazine Ads, color	174–191
Trade Magazine Campaigns, b/w	193–200
Trade Magazine Campaigns, color	201–206
Small Space Ads	207–221
Small Space Campaigns	222–226
Outdoor/Billboards	227–234
Outdoor Billboard Campaigns	235–237
Posters	238–245
Public Service	246–262
Political	263

At Club Mediterranee, you know how much your vacation costs before you go. Instead of after.
On an ordinary vacation, you pay for your room and meals and then every move you make is extra.
On a Club Mediterranee vacation, you pay just about the same price for your room and meals and virtually nothing else is extra.
Included at no extra cost is all the French and native cuisine you can eat at three meals a day. Plus all the free wine you can drink at lunch and dinner. You pay only for drinks at the bar.
And to work off all you've taken in, we give you free tennis. Free snorkeling. Free sailing. Free yoga. Free calisthenics. Free picnic excursions. A free private beach. Free scuba diving. Free water-skiing. And free deep sea fishing in Tahiti and Hawaii. What's more, with every sport, there's free equipment and a free group education from expert instructors.
The cost of Club Mediterranee doesn't go up when the sun goes down, either. There's after dinner dancing to a live band, native dancing, nightly cabaret and game shows, recorded classical music concerts along the beach and discotheques that stay open as long as you can stand up. All of which you can enjoy without ever having to dip into your wallet.
At Club Mediterranee, not only do we save you money in big chunks, we also save you money in small ones. At all Club Mediterranee vacation villages, tipping is prohibited. And transportation to and from local airports is free on Club Mediterranee group flights.
Flights leave regularly for Club Mediterranee vacation villages on Guadeloupe (Ft. Royal and Caravelle), Martinique, Mexico, Tahiti, Hawaii and Cape Skiring, Senegal in West Africa and our sixty other clubs around the world.
To find out more, contact your travel agent or fill out our coupon. We'll tell you everything else you won't have to pay for while you're on a Club Mediterranee vacation. Or after it's over.
CLUB MEDITERRANEE

1

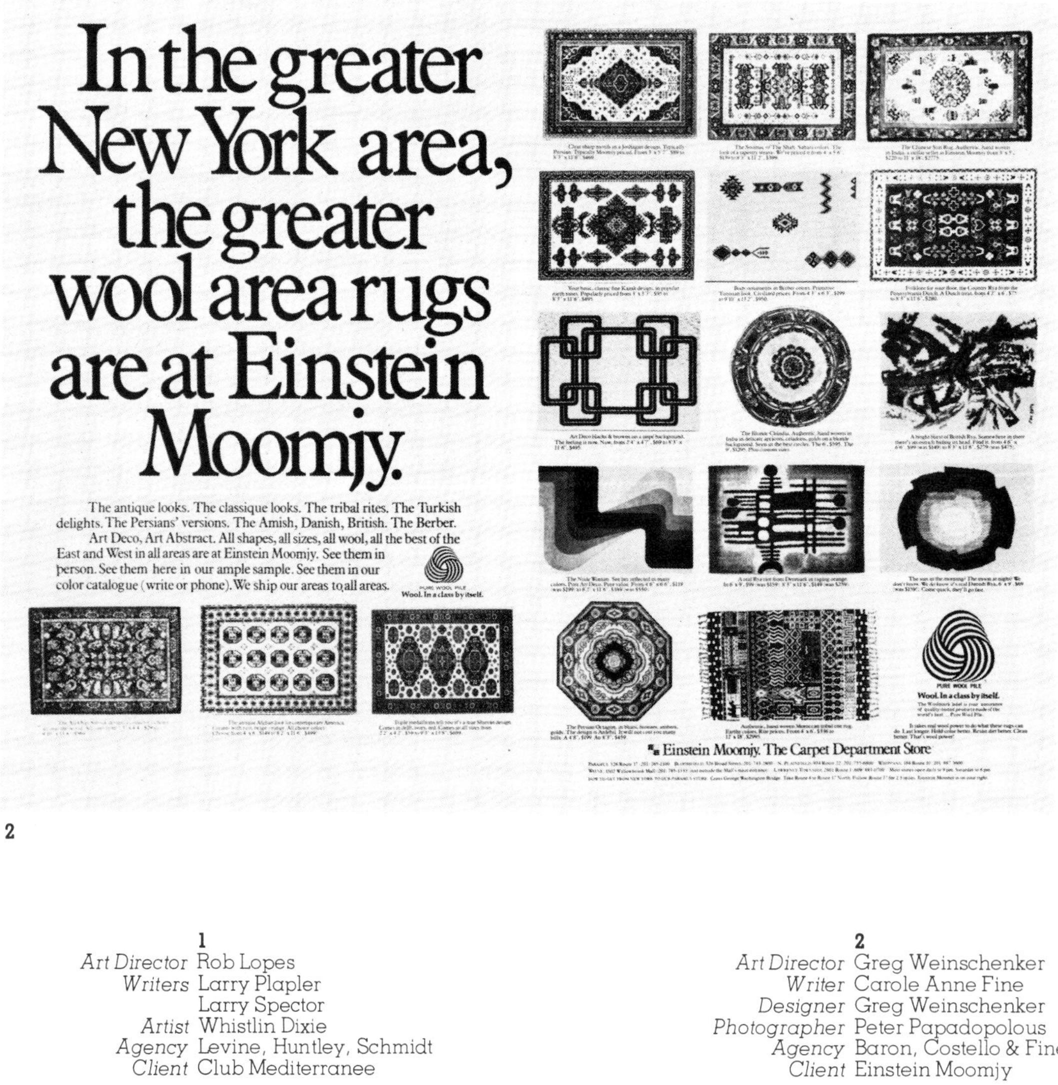
In the greater New York area, the greater wool area rugs are at Einstein Moomjy.
The antique looks. The classique looks. The tribal rites. The Turkish delights. The Persians' versions. The Amish, Danish, British. The Berber.
Art Deco, Art Abstract. All shapes, all sizes, all wool, all the best of the East and West in all areas are at Einstein Moomjy. See them in person. See them here in our ample sample. See them in our color catalogue (write or phone). We ship our areas to all areas.
PURE WOOL PILE
Wool. In a class by itself.
Einstein Moomjy. The Carpet Department Store

2

1
Art Director Rob Lopes
Writers Larry Plapler
Larry Spector
Artist Whistlin Dixie
Agency Levine, Huntley, Schmidt
Client Club Mediterranee

2
Art Director Greg Weinschenker
Writer Carole Anne Fine
Designer Greg Weinschenker
Photographer Peter Papadopolous
Agency Baron, Costello & Fine
Client Einstein Moomjy

Translating "Travelese" into English.

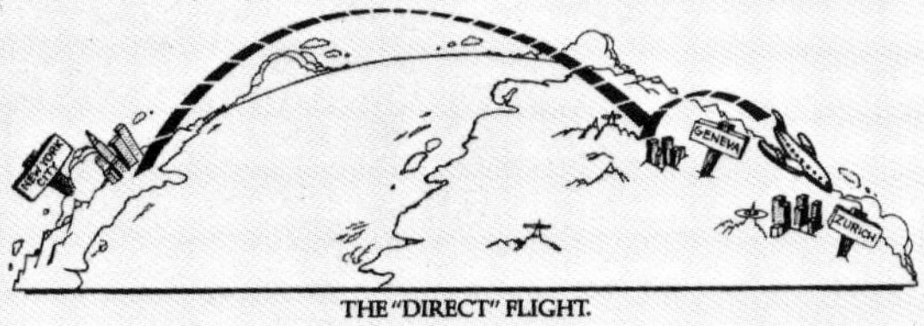
NEW YORK CITY
GENEVA
ZURICH

THE "DIRECT" FLIGHT.

NEW YORK CITY
GENEVA
ZURICH

THE "NON-STOP" FLIGHT.

Travel literature has a language all its own. But once you understand it, planning your trip becomes a lot easier. It becomes fun, instead of work.

Of course first you have to get the literature. Which is easy enough. The travel section of your newspaper, and various magazines, have countless ads describing European vacations and airfares. And these ads have coupons and addresses where you can write for travel brochures describing these trips in detail. You can also, if it's convenient, pick up this literature at the offices of various international airlines, and at your travel agent.

Travel literature is easy to get. And free.

One more tip. The local tourist offices of the countries you want to visit can provide you with an enormous amount of information.

Reading It All

Now that you've got all the ads, brochures, and booklets spread out in front of you on the coffee table (and if you're really serious it's probably spilling over onto the floor) you'll need some help deciphering it. Let's start with some basics, like airfares.

Airfares

There are many different airfares that can take you from the United States to Europe. You can, of course, buy a first class or economy class ticket. But to save money on a special promotional airfare, you must abide by certain restrictions. Restrictions that apply to the length of your stay, the time of year you travel, how far in advance you buy your ticket, and whether you're willing to buy land arrangements in Europe. These land arrangements are usually part of a "tour package" which includes things like hotels, meals, sightseeing, and air travel. Swissair has already published an ad explaining the transatlantic airfare system. If you missed it, you can get a copy by writing to Swissair at 608 Fifth Ave., New York, N.Y. 10020.

A Tour Package.

Legalisms, Fine Print And Asterisks

Travel advertising is subject to certain legal restrictions. Restrictions that are written into the ad or brochure. They're there to help you. To tell you what you're getting. And not getting. But they can also be confusing. For example:

Fares subject to government approval—An organization called IATA (International Air Transport Association) composed of most scheduled international airlines agrees on standardized fares for all their members. But final approval for flights to, and from, the United States must come from both the Civil Aeronautics Board, and the government of the other country. So while you can buy a fare that is still "subject to government approval," there is a very slight possibility that you may have to pay more, or less, before you leave.

G.I.T.—This stands for Group Inclusive Tour. And you'll usually see it in conjunction with special promotional airfares. But to take advantage of these lower airfares, you'll have to: 1.) Fly in a group that the airline or the travel agent makes up, of at least 10 people. 2.) Make your reservations and purchase your ticket at least 15 days before you go. 3.) Purchase a certain amount of land arrangements, i.e., hotels, cars and meals.

Per person/double occupancy—Even though the price of the package is for one, the condition here is that hotel accommodations and cars are based on two people sharing. If you're going with a relative or friend, this is obviously no problem. However, when you're going alone, you may want a room, or a car, by yourself. In that case there will be an additional charge (this is called a single supplement.)

Continental Breakfast (CB)—Europeans aren't accustomed to large meals in the morning. So when you find a package that gives you a Continental Breakfast every day don't expect eggs and bacon. What you get are rolls (probably brioches or croissants) jams, jellies and coffee.

Hotel Categories—These can vary from country to country. The best accommodations are called Deluxe or First Class. After that it ranges from Standard to Guesthouse (or Pension). In the first two categories you'll usually get a private bath. In the latter two you may be sharing a bath.

Transfers—Most tour packages include "transfers." It refers to the fact that your transportation from the airport to your hotel, and back, is taken care of.

TRANSFER
AIRPORT
HOTEL

Direct flights—Even though you stay on one plane to your destination, there will be one or more stops along the way.

Non-Stop flights—You fly to, or from your destination with no stops in between.

Services included—A service charge simply means tipping. If it's not included in the package price, then most European hotels and restaurants automatically add it on to the bill. It's usually anywhere from 10 to 15 per cent. If you're not certain if a service charge has been added on, ask your concierge or waiter.

AMERICAN PLAN
MODIFIED AMERICAN PLAN
EUROPEAN PLAN

American Plan—This is also called full board or full pension. It means three meals a day are included.

Modified American Plan—This is sometimes called demi-pension and means you'll get two meals a day. Breakfast plus lunch or dinner.

European Plan—No meals are included.

Departure Tax—There is a tax of 3 dollars for anyone leaving the United States. Other countries may have a departure tax too.

What You Get And What You Don't Get

Make sure you know what's included in the price of a package.

Notice what the rates are for the different times of the year. Because they do change.

Check to see if the package includes airfare and land arrangements. Or just land arrangements.

If you're travelling with your family, find out if there are extra charges for extra beds in your room.

If you're planning to rent a car in Europe, can you save a significant amount of money by renting your car in a country where there are lower taxes on rental cars?

Is sightseeing included? And if so, is your trip fully escorted or semi-escorted? Or are you on your own?

ITALY
ZURICH

An "escorted" tour is best for some people.

Pay attention to cancellation clauses. How far in advance can you cancel without losing all or part of your money? And if you can't cancel, see what kind of insurance is available to protect you against loss.

Remember too that the brochure you're reading was printed weeks, even months, before. So make sure the prices are current. Finally, don't ignore packages that include certain things you may not be interested in. Even with those unwanted extras it may be cheaper in the long run. Add it all up before you decide.

Some Gentle Warnings And Tips

Don't make irrevocable decisions right away. Get your information and study it. If at all possible try to be flexible about how long you can get away for, and when you can go. If you can get away for three weeks in March it may be cheaper than going for two weeks in April. Also, don't plan to do too much. Take your time. Europe is still going to be there next year when you've become an old hand at travelling. Finally, as we said earlier, enjoy it. Planning a European vacation can be, and should be, fun. So relax.

Now What Do You Do?

You've gotten all the information you can get your hands on. Maybe you've even read a couple of books and talked to friends who went through the same thing last year. You've decided, in general, which countries you want to see. And how much you have to spend. Now you need a professional to put it together. A travel agent.

Meanwhile, if you have any questions please call us at (212) 995-4400. Outside the New York Metropolitan area Swissair has set up toll free numbers for your convenience. In New York State and Suffolk County call (800) 522-6906. In New Jersey, Connecticut, and Massachusetts call (800) 221-4480. Or drop into your local Swissair office. Like many major airlines, we have a tour department that has years of experience in making travelling easier than you think.

SWISSAIR

3

3
Art Director Howard Title
Writer Chuck Cohen
Designer Howard Title
Artist Robert Dale
Agency Waring & LaRosa
Client Swissair

Welcome to our Back Yd.

A whole new way to carpet your front rm. for, for example, $139.

If remnants have put you on your guard, relax, buy remnants at our Back Yd.

No dogs, no losers, no mill seconds, no cast-offs, no rejects, no colors gone kaput, no imperfects. (We have laws against flaws.)

And no back numbers in The Back Yd.

6000 gorgeous sq. ft. of the same sq. yds. of carpets de-luxe that sell for a lot more bucks Up Front at Einstein Moomjy.

We have wall-to-wall. We install. We have room-size pieces. We'll fringe, we'll bind them. We have custom pieces. Ask, we'll find them. We have area rugs and runners. All stunners.

What if you can't find the carpet you want in a big enough size?

Peace! We can piece pieces of the same carpet and keep you in stitches (under your sofa, for instance, where they'll never be seen) and there you are, with a wall-to-wall windfall!

What if you find the carpet you want in a too-big size? Don't worry. We'll cut to measure. It's our pleasure.

Hark, hark, where to park?

To park is a lark at The Back Yd. Just pull your car around to our Back Yd. loading dock and we'll carry on from there. (Our sturdy take-out carpet bags are free.) Delivery? No task. Just ask.

Ouch, the backbreak of remnant departments! Ah, but not at The Back Yd. Benches to sit on while you ponder. 6000 ft. of room to wander. We'll unroll rolls so you can feel for real and treat your feet.

Where besides The Back Yd. can you have such a picnic before you pick?

Pick an unseedy tweedy, 12′ x 12′, $79. A bronze in velvet, 15′ x 11′, $49. A sunny shag, supersize, $185.

A Saxony silver fern, $79. A Sundance orange, $69. A popcorn plush, $99. Plus 700 other picks. The pickins' grow on trees in The Back Yd.

In case you can't come to Paramus (home of The Back Yd.), our other Carpet Department Stores will show you Back Yd. samples and steer you right.

Problem: You come to Einstein Moomjy. You fall in love with a carpet. But you have a budget and you can't budge it. Moan, groan. What do you do?

Solution: You may very well find the very same carpet in just the right size at just the right price back in our own Back Yd.

As The Einsteins, The Moomjys and Back YdMaster Steve Finston always say: "It's not what's Up Front that always counts. Welcome to The Back Yd. at Einstein Moomjy."

The Back Yd. at
Einstein Moomjy. The Carpet Department Store®

Paramus, 526 Route 17 (201) 265-1100 Bloomfield, 326 Broad Street (201) 743-2800 N. Plainfield, 934 Route 22 (201) 755-6800 Whippany, 184 Route 10 (201) 887-3600
Wayne, 1502 Willowbrook Mall (201) 785-1333 (just outside the Mall's main entrance) Lawrence Township, 2801 Route 1 (609) 883-0700 Most stores open daily to 9 pm, Saturday to 6 pm.
How to get from New York to our Paramus store. Cross George Washington Bridge. Take Route 4 to Route 17 North. Follow Route 17 for 2.5 miles. Einstein Moomjy is on your right.

4

BIG FAT CARPETS! NOW ON 8 DAY REDUCING PLAN AT EINSTEIN MOOMJY!

Dear A. Moomjy:

"Your big fat carpets are gorgeous. We've been waiting and watching for you to reduce them. Fat chance."

The Wait Watchers.

Dear Wait Watchers:

"I'm not dense. From now through May 10th, my big fat carpets are taking off dollars. Now's your big fat chance."

A. Moomjy.

Get my beefy shag for $5.99. My maxi-saxy (a thick Saxony) for $8.99. My triple shag (like 3 shags rolled into 1) for $8.99.

My posh plush with a glimmer of shimmer for a price that is slimmer. $8.99. My marbled for $8.99.

My popular earthy look. Why on earth am I selling it for $11.99? I'll hand you my handcrafted look for $13.99. My California shag (the toast of the coast) coasted to $13.99. My ample Antron® nylon is $14.99. My highest and mightiest shag has come down to $15.99.

My heavyweight Berber wool, it's a knockout, is chomped to $15.99. My pounds and pounds of wool velvet, $18.99. How thick is my wall-to-wall Moroccan? Only the toes knows. $45.99.

Right foot: "I'm in over my toes."
Left foot: "No you're not. This carpet's only $15.99."

What more could I take more off?

I've got rugs from Persia for less. I've got rugs from India for least. I've got Ryas as big as a room. Down to $119. Couristans as big as a room. Down to $199.

I've got odds at half-price, I've got ends that begin at just $29. You'll eat it all up. Don't wait. Take off for the big reductions at

Einstein Moomjy
The Carpet Department Store®

Paramus, 526 Route 17 (201) 265-1100 Bloomfield, 326 Broad Street (201) 743-2800 N. Plainfield, 934 Route 22 (201) 755-6800 Whippany, 184 Route 10 (201) 887-3600
Wayne, 1502 Willowbrook Mall (201) 785-1333 (just outside the Mall's main entrance) Lawrence Township, 2801 Route 1 (609) 883-0700 Most stores open daily to 9 pm. Saturday to 6 pm
How to get from New York to our Paramus store. Cross George Washington Bridge. Take Route 4 to Route 17 North. Follow Route 17 for 2.5 miles. Einstein Moomjy is on your right.

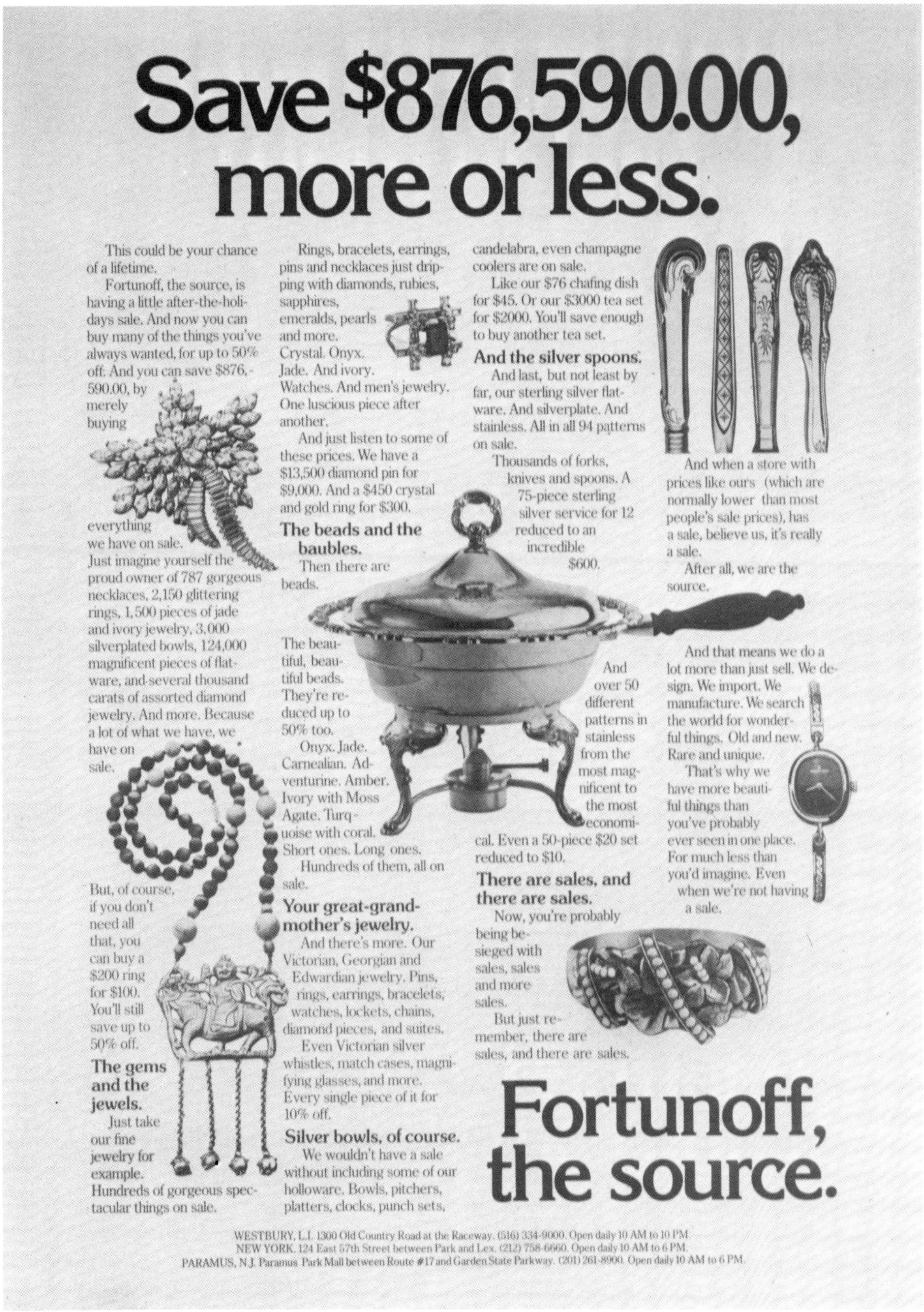
Save $876,590.00, more or less.
This could be your chance of a lifetime.
Fortunoff, the source, is having a little after-the-holidays sale. And now you can buy many of the things you've always wanted, for up to 50% off. And you can save $876,590.00, by merely buying everything we have on sale.
Just imagine yourself the proud owner of 787 gorgeous necklaces, 2,150 glittering rings, 1,500 pieces of jade and ivory jewelry, 3,000 silverplated bowls, 124,000 magnificent pieces of flatware, and several thousand carats of assorted diamond jewelry. And more. Because a lot of what we have, we have on sale.
But, of course, if you don't need all that, you can buy a $200 ring for $100. You'll still save up to 50% off.
The gems and the jewels.
Just take our fine jewelry for example. Hundreds of gorgeous spectacular things on sale.
Rings, bracelets, earrings, pins and necklaces just dripping with diamonds, rubies, sapphires, emeralds, pearls and more. Crystal. Onyx. Jade. And ivory. Watches. And men's jewelry. One luscious piece after another.
And just listen to some of these prices. We have a $13,500 diamond pin for $9,000. And a $450 crystal and gold ring for $300.
The beads and the baubles.
Then there are beads.
The beautiful, beautiful beads. They're reduced up to 50% too.
Onyx. Jade. Carnealian. Adventurine. Amber. Ivory with Moss Agate. Turquoise with coral. Short ones. Long ones.
Hundreds of them, all on sale.
Your great-grandmother's jewelry.
And there's more. Our Victorian, Georgian and Edwardian jewelry. Pins, rings, earrings, bracelets, watches, lockets, chains, diamond pieces, and suites.
Even Victorian silver whistles, match cases, magnifying glasses, and more. Every single piece of it for 10% off.
Silver bowls, of course.
We wouldn't have a sale without including some of our holloware. Bowls, pitchers, platters, clocks, punch sets, candelabra, even champagne coolers are on sale.
Like our $76 chafing dish for $45. Or our $3000 tea set for $2000. You'll save enough to buy another tea set.
And the silver spoons.
And last, but not least by far, our sterling silver flatware. And silverplate. And stainless. All in all 94 patterns on sale.
Thousands of forks, knives and spoons. A 75-piece sterling silver service for 12 reduced to an incredible $600.
And over 50 different patterns in stainless from the most magnificent to the most economical. Even a 50-piece $20 set reduced to $10.
There are sales, and there are sales.
Now, you're probably being besieged with sales, sales and more sales.
But just remember, there are sales, and there are sales.
And when a store with prices like ours (which are normally lower than most people's sale prices), has a sale, believe us, it's really a sale.
After all, we are the source.
And that means we do a lot more than just sell. We design. We import. We manufacture. We search the world for wonderful things. Old and new. Rare and unique.
That's why we have more beautiful things than you've probably ever seen in one place. For much less than you'd imagine. Even when we're not having a sale.
Fortunoff, the source.
WESTBURY, L.I. 1300 Old Country Road at the Raceway. (516) 334-9000. Open daily 10 AM to 10 PM.
NEW YORK. 124 East 57th Street between Park and Lex. (212) 758-6660. Open daily 10 AM to 6 PM.
PARAMUS, N.J. Paramus Park Mall between Route #17 and Garden State Parkway. (201) 261-8900. Open daily 10 AM to 6 PM.

6

4
Art Director Harvey Baron
Writer Carole Anne Fine
Designer Harvey Baron
Photographer Peter Papadopolous
Agency Baron, Costello & Fine
Client Einstein Moomjy

5
Art Director Greg Weinschenker
Writer Carole Anne Fine
Designer Greg Weinschenker
Photographer Peter Papadopolous
Agency Baron, Costello & Fine
Client Einstein Moomjy

6
Art Director Arnie Arlow
Writer Jennifer Berne
Designer James Clarke
Photographer Michael Harris
Agency Martin Landey, Arlow Advertising
Client Fortunoff

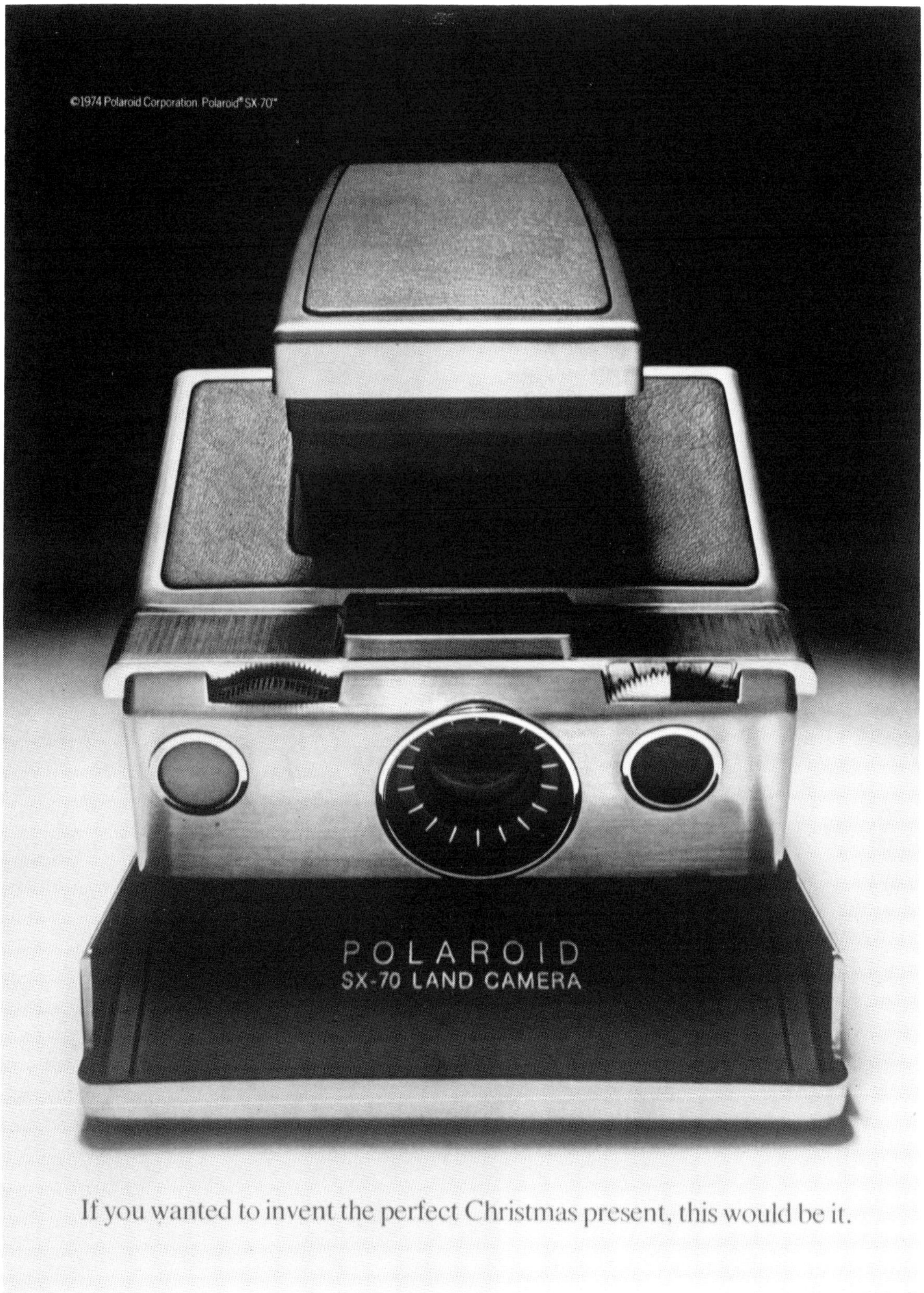
©1974 Polaroid Corporation. Polaroid® SX-70™
POLAROID
SX-70 LAND CAMERA
If you wanted to invent the perfect Christmas present, this would be it.

7

7
Art Director Robert Gage
Writer Phyllis Robinson
Photographer Bill Stettner
Agency Doyle Dane Bernbach
Client Polaroid Corp.

8
Art Director Harvey Baron
Writer Carole Anne Fine
Designer Harvey Baron
Photographer Nick Samardge
Agency Baron, Costello & Fine
Client Einstein Moomjy

9
Art Director Howard Title
Writer Chuck Cohen
Designer Howard Title
Artist Push Pin Studios
Agency Waring & LaRosa
Client Swissair

Einstein's theory of relativity: Give strangers the same price you give your relatives.

$4.99 to $8.99

Starting now through Sat. April 12th, blood won't be thicker than water at The Carpet Department Stores.

We're giving you family prices. The prices we give our own family.

Example: Our short shag. The beefy new shag recommended by our Aunt Fanny's fanny.

She paid $4.99 a sq. yd. She saved plenty.

You'll pay $4.99 a sq. yd. You'll save plenty.

We can give you our velvety plush in Acrilan® acrylic for $5.99. Our trim office tweed for $5.99.

Mr. Moomjy charged his mama only $5.99 for this gorgeous carpet. And that's all he's charging you.

We can give you our soft Saxony for $6.99. We can give you our triple toned twist for $6.99.

Would you want to spend $7.99? We can give you our sculptured shag for $7.99. We can give you our sky (high) shag for $7.99.

Would you want to go to $8.99? Our tailored plush has been tailored to $8.99. Our antique marble has been chiseled to $8.99.

Even our $14.99 shag (its furry depth is the height of luxury) has come all the way down to only $8.99.

You may say to Einstein Moomjy: "You're giving me the same prices you give your relatives.

Okay, terrific.

But how do I know I'll love your carpets? How do I know I'll find what I want?

Your papa's posh plush could be my poison. It's all relative."

Ladies, you're right.

Maybe you'll think our wet look (it's only $8.99) is all wet. Maybe our warm bedroom carpet (it's only $8.49) will leave you cold.

Think nothing of it.

We've got hundreds more carpets in hundreds more colors to show you.

We've got hundreds more styles and piles and prices to show you.

We're The Carpet Department Store. We've got more of more for your floor.

Please drive us crazy until you find the carpet you want at Einstein Moomjy.

After all, our relatives have been driving us crazy for years at

Einstein Moomjy
The Carpet Department Store

PARAMUS, 526 Route 17 (201) 265-1100 BLOOMFIELD, 326 Broad Street (201) 743-2800 N. PLAINFIELD, 934 Route 22 (201) 755-6800 WHIPPANY, 184 Route 10 (201) 887-3600
WAYNE, 1502 Willowbrook Mall (201) 785-1333 (just outside the Mall's main entrance) LAWRENCE TOWNSHIP, 2801 Route 1 (609) 883-0700 Most stores open daily to 9 pm, Saturday to 6 pm.
HOW TO GET FROM NEW YORK TO OUR PARAMUS STORE: Cross George Washington Bridge. Take Route 4 to Route 17 North. Follow Route 17 for 2.5 miles. Einstein Moomjy is on your right.

Monsanto

8

Our 27,000 shareholders and 14,000 employees believe that the more you know about Swissair the better it is for you. And us.

A few words from Swissair in a language all businesspeople understand.

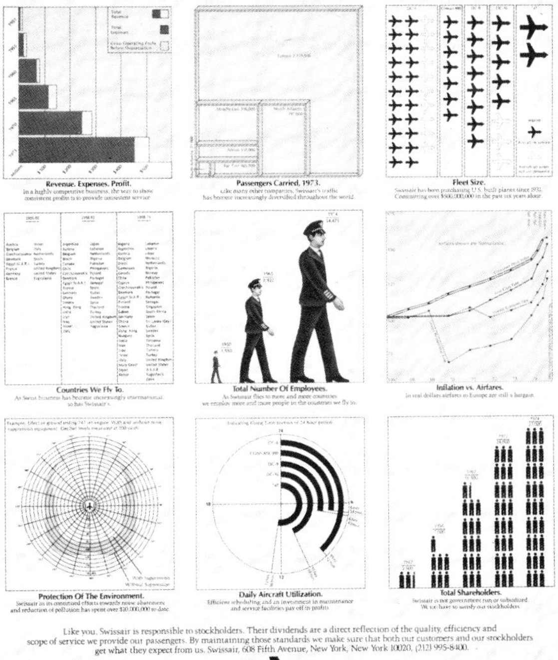

Revenue. Expenses. Profit.
In a highly competitive business, the way to show consistent profits is to provide consistent service.
Passengers Carried, 1973.
Like many other companies, Swissair's traffic has become increasingly diversified throughout the world.
Fleet Size.
Swissair has been purchasing U.S. built planes since 1931. Committing over $560,000,000 in the past six years alone.
Countries We Fly To.
As Swiss business has become increasingly international so has Swissair's.
Total Number Of Employees.
As Swissair flies to more and more countries we employ more and more people in the countries we fly to.
Inflation vs. Airfares.
In real dollars airfares to Europe are still a bargain.
Protection Of The Environment.
Swissair in its continued efforts towards noise abatement and reduction of pollution has spent over $10,000,000 to date.
Daily Aircraft Utilization.
Efficient scheduling and an investment in maintenance and service facilities pay off in profits.
Total Shareholders.
Swissair is not government run or subsidized. We too have to satisfy our stockholders.

Like you, Swissair is responsible to stockholders. Their dividends are a direct reflection of the quality, efficiency and scope of service we provide our passengers. By maintaining those standards we make sure that both our customers and our stockholders get what they expect from us. Swissair, 608 Fifth Avenue, New York, New York 10020, (212) 995-8400.

SWISSAIR

9

"I ASKED THE GUY AT ATLANTIS SOUND WHAT HI-FI I SHOULD GET, AND HERE'S WHAT HE SAID IN A NUTSHELL."

"This is probably the first major leisure purchase of your life—be thorough, be careful, and don't be ripped-off. Hi-fi components are like any other equipment that has to perform: it's no damn good if it doesn't work reliably or if, when it breaks, it can't be fixed quickly at a reasonable cost, if not free under warranty. (Atlantis Sound has the strongest warranty in the industry. In fact, it is far stronger than many manufacturers' own warranties).

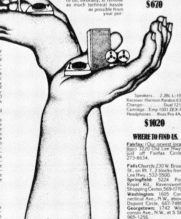

Buying a system consists of figuring out where to buy, what to buy, what price to pay and when to buy. Let's take them in that order.

WHERE TO BUY.

Buy from an audio component specialist near where you live. Then, it's not a hassle to get satisfaction if you've got a problem. Remember, not all products work perfectly out of the box: in fact some don't work at all. This holds true for even the best manufacturer's equipment. If you buy from a distant dealer or one that offers only the manufacturer's warranty, the smallest problem becomes a nightmare. Even though mass merchandisers in the appliance business may be able to sell you hi-fi equipment and maybe even service it, they're not equipped to advise you on your purchase. The worst use of the money you had budgeted for hi-fi is to end up with a mismatched system. It can only sound as good as the least effective component.

Remember: before you select a hi-fi system, select what type of dealer you are going to buy from—an audio components specialist, a mass merchandiser, an appliance chain or someone selling out of his apartment. Only a component specialist can give you proper assistance, good brand selection, and super service after the sale.

WHAT TO BUY.

A component system generally consists of a pair of speakers, a receiver (tuner-amplifier), and a record changer or manual turntable with a stereo cartridge. The item that makes the biggest difference in the sound is the loudspeaker. It is the speakers that make the system sound good, bad, mediocre, clean, honky, objectionable or maybe even just plain rotten.

HOT TO EVALUATE LOUDSPEAKERS.

The quality of sound from a loudspeaker is not as subjective a judgment as many people claim. Be very careful when auditioning speakers and make sure you follow the cardinal rules for speaker evaluation.

Speakers must be compared:

—at the same volume level since it is a law of psyco-acoustics that if one speaker is playing louder (no matter how slightly) it will sound "better".

—only two at a time (A-B comparison) since "hearing has no memory" and, consequently, comparison of three or more speakers at one time is meaningless.

—in a properly engineered sound room with adequate wiring to assure the speakers are receiving all the power the amplifier is delivering.

—in a roughly the same physical location, at least on the same wall, otherwise the room acoustics alter the sound of the speaker being compared.

Note: Only the very best in high fidelity dealers will have properly engineered sound rooms with speaker switching facilities that can automatically equalize the sound pressure level (volume) of the speakers being compared. Facilities of this type are extremely expensive and show the audio component specialists' dedication to the component sound equipment business.

WHAT TO LISTEN FOR.

The novice will often listen for obvious defects (many of which are not the speakers' fault), rather than the more subtle (but recognizable) attributes that distinguish a really fine speaker from the many available. Below is a list of the fine frequency or spectral characteristics to listen for, and how these characteristics relate to speaker quality and ultimate listening satisfaction. A qualified audio specialist at Atlantis Sound will point out these features for you.

1. Bass response. When you listen for bass, which is traditionally what people listen for first, make sure the record or tape really has deep bass on it, not just medium bass as found in most rock recordings. Use music like a pipe organ, a closed-miked bass guitar or bass drums recorded in a large hall. Bass drums are particularly good since these notes are clean and distinct and easily discernable even to the novice. Come in and listen on an Advent or Bose speaker with the right program material and our audio specialist will point out what deep bass really is!

2. High frequency dispersion. Most speakers will reproduce high frequencies, but many concentrate the high frequency output in a narrow path directly in front of the speaker. This generally isn't

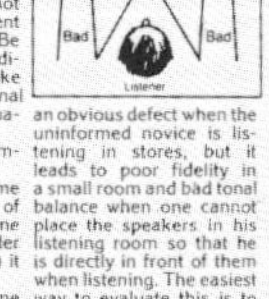

Dispersion
Left Speaker
Right Speaker
Good
Bad
Bad
Listener

an obvious defect when the uninformed novice is listening in stores, but it leads to poor fidelity in a small room and bad tonal balance when one cannot place the speakers in his listening room so that he is directly in front of them when listening. The easiest way to evaluate this is to tune an FM receiver between the stations where you hear only hiss (white noise—a random mixture of high frequencies). Then walk by the front of the speaker and notice if the hiss becomes lower in pitch as you walk off-center. If the speaker is good in this regard, this effect should hardly be noticeable.

3. Transient response. This is the hardest criterion for the novice to evaluate. A speaker with good transient response will reproduce sharp sounds (like a clicking noise or percussive sounds) with an open lifelike clarity. This is true because transient response means that ability of a speaker to follow the wave form of the music. A speaker with poor transient response will make drums sound muddy. A solo trumpeter is often a good test. It should have considerable "razz" on an accurate speaker, and will sound too smooth on a poor speaker.

What makes transient response so difficult to judge is that good transient response will expose defects in the rest of the sound system—and a novice listener may blame what he hears on the speakers. Dirty or defective records, mistracking of the cartridge stylus, or amplifier distortion will be completely exposed by a speaker with good transient response. So when you audition speakers, make sure you use a clean recording and listen through an amplifier with plenty of power and low distortion.

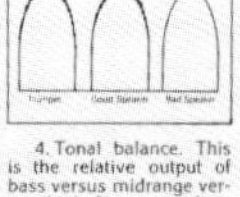

Transient Response
Good Speaker
Bad Speaker

4. Tonal balance. This is the relative output of bass versus midrange versus high frequency. It is also especially difficult for the novice listener to judge. Fortunately, most name brands have fairly good balance. Advent and EPI are the standards of

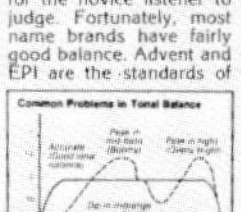

Common Problems in Tonal Balance

the industry in this regard. A speaker that has a disproportionate amount of treble or bass response has poor tonal balance.

5. Efficiency. This is the relative ability of a speaker to produce a certain sound pressure level (volume) with a certain amount of power input; or, the relationship between the power input versus the volume output. An efficient speaker will play to a louder volume with the same power (wattage) than an inefficient speaker. This is certainly a desirable characteristic, but generally deep bass is sacrificed in order to achieve an efficient speaker.

A special word about spatial and temporal response: The ideal speaker would be a sphere with sound emmanating in all directions (360°). This is desirable because live music is not projected directly at the listener, but is dispersed to him in a combination of direct and reflected sound. This can best be simulated by a loudspeaker that projects the sound to a listener from more than one plane. Most loudspeakers on the market over $200 have good frequency characteristics, but for this kind of money, the consumer should get much more—a speaker that provides the realism of the original rock concert, the symphony hall, or the tiny night club. Bose and EPI are the pioneers of spatial response as an important speaker criterion. Styling and efficiency are the only two reasons, other than spatial relations, to spend more than $200.

ELECTRONICS. WHAT DO SPECIFICATIONS MEAN?

As far as the electronics are concerned, their performance specifications can be quantitatively measured and the actual test results for A-rated and other receivers are available in our stores. Fortunately, the small differences between all good-quality amplifiers will make very little difference, if any, in how the total system sounds. The important criteria for receiver selection is that it have adequate power to drive the speakers taking into account desired listening level, and the amplifier must put out this power at less than one percent total distortion. Then, the important criteria for brand selection are reliability, warranty (both the manufacturer's and the dealer's), features, and even styling.

A few words about receivers in general.

A receiver is actually three components in one: the tuner, which converts radio waves in the air to an electrical musical signal; the preamp, which is the control center that selects the desired input (tuner, phono or tape) that controls the volume, tone and channel balance, and boosts the signal slightly before it goes to the third component — the power amp, which amplifies the signal to a sufficient power level to travel through the speaker wires and drive the loudspeakers. Receivers account for 80 percent of the consumer hi-fi electronic business. A receiver also takes up roughly one-third the space of individual components. With these advantages in mind, we rate receivers as the best buy in electronics.

Now, about the differences in the performance of various price range receivers.

Under $200—economy. To achieve reliability, a reputable manufacturer compromises features and some performance. In this price category are a myriad of non hi-fi products that may look fine, but be careful, don't get ripped off!

$200—good. In this price range are receivers that deliver adequate power and with all the essential features, but no frills.

$200 to $300—better. Receivers in this price range may have:

- more power at less distortion
- more sensitive tuner
- more convenience features
- better styling
- and greater reliability

$300 to $400—better yet. Again, an improvement in the areas outlined above.

$400—best. This is the price range that gives you a really superb receiver, high power, super FM reception, lifetime reliability and excellent convenience and styling.

$500—superior. There is no better. This buys the ultimate stereo receiver, high power at inaudible distortion, an FM tuner that can receive better than most stations can transmit, maximum features, convenience and great styling. Then ask yourself, which brand?

There's a small cadre of electronic manufacturers who are the leaders. They're competent and sincere, and realize that they must (1) design and produce components of high quality, performance and reliability at reasonable prices (value) and (2) distribute them through the leading audio component specialists who provide consumer education and protection (service). Only a few manufacturers have the ability and desire to achieve these goals. In our opinion, Pioneer, Harmon Kardon, JVC, and Onkyo are in this category.

The price of a good stereo system is a significant amount of money and an investment in the art of music that should last a very long time. Don't take any chances with your hard-earned money. Stick with A-rated components. Hi-fi should be an enjoyable experience, not a nightmare of C-rated products and F-rated service.

Now for some technical details.

The power output of an amplifier is measured in watts. Although there is only one meaningful way of measuring watts, many of today's manufacturers use other methods to achieve higher figures. Methods such as IPP, EIA, and IHF ("Music Power") are examples that tend to give higher power ratings. They measure the instantaneous power capacity of the amplifiers under controlled test conditions (not normal use), sometimes using laboratory power source! These figures can be further inflated by using a less common speaker impedence such as four ohms. This generally results in a higher power rating than the more common impedence of eight ohms. Other methods of deception are rating the amp at mid-frequency (1,000 Hz) and rating it with only one channel driven.

We rate our amplifiers under normal conditions using the average, continuous (RMS) wattage with both channels driving into 8 ohms, over a full audible spectrum (20 Hz-20,000 Hz) and not exceeding the stated distortion level. The other methods are great for advertising but misleading for you.

Equally important to power output is distortion, i.e., the amount of extraneous noise added by the electronics. It is rated in percent, and, obviously, the less the better.

Five years ago, 1 percent distortion was considered acceptable for high fidelity music reproduction. Today, the better receivers boast not more than 0.2 percent. Therefore, you hear the music and not the electronics producing it. But be careful—most of the receiver manufacturers have gotten themselves into a power race where each new model has higher and higher power, often at the expense of other important performance characteristics such as inter-modulation distortion. The crucial IM distortion is at the lower power levels. This means the amplifier or receiver might deliver seldom, if ever used, maximum power at 0.2% distortion, but may be a poor performer (1-2% IM) when playing at the important normal levels where you do 99% of your listening.

The frequency response of an amp is the highest and lowest audio frequencies that it will reproduce faithfully. It is measured in Hz (an abbreviation for Hertz) which stands numerically for the pitch of a tone. A normal human ear can detect tones as low as about 20 Hz and as high as 20,000 Hz, and the closer an amp comes to these parameters the better. To make the specification mean anything, it must be coupled with a ±dB factor which reveals how far off the response is from being perfectly flat, i.e., the extent to which the amp is unfaithful in perfectly reproducing the tone. The smaller the dB rating, the better.

The power bandwidth is a specification most manufacturers would rather not discuss.

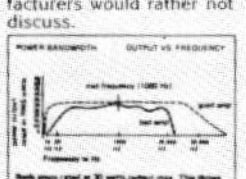

POWER BANDWIDTH
OUTPUT VS. FREQUENCY

The reason is that where any amplifier will deliver its rated power at mid-frequency (1,000 Hz), most won't be able to do so at the extremes (20 Hz and 20,000 Hz) of the audible spectrum. The reduced power results in poorly defined or even badly distorted bass and a loss of high frequency overtones. Some manufacturers specify RMS power but only at 1,000 Hz; our Electronic Evaluation Program only considers the amount of power at the full power bandwidth of 20-20,000 cycles (the ten octaves that make up music).

Finally, you should know about selectivity.

It refers to the tuner's ability to select only the desired station from the multitude of frequencies available, and to receive a weak station that's close to a strong one in frequency. This assures accurate tuning of the station as well as rejection of unwanted distant stations which are operating at the same frequencies. The higher this figure (rated in dB), the better.

TURNTABLES AND CARTRIDGES.

The turntable is the device that rotates the record and whose tonearm holds the cartridge as it picks the sound off the record groove. A changer does all this, plus automatically changes the records. For a given amount of money, you can get more performance from a turntable, and it is more reliable. In all Atlantis Sound Systems, a turntable can be substituted for a changer if desired.

The important criteria for turntables or changers are reliability, ease of operation, and its gentleness to your records.

Last but not least is the cartridge, a very important item, almost as important as the loudspeakers. Most of the name brands on the market use different design concepts to achieve roughly the same level of performance for the same selling price. However, their sound output levels vary widely as does the delicateness of their stylii and susceptability to damage.

WHAT PRICE TO PAY.

Up until a couple of years ago systems costing less than $800 weren't perfect in regard to the musical parameters. There were compromises.

Today, good systems are available from $370 to $450. There are significant improvements in the better systems between $550 and $840, such as increased power handling capacity and spatial relations. Systems costing say, $1000 or more offer further improvements in spatial relations or efficiency and volume output. But a good system is a necessity of life today; better systems are a luxury. Below $350, the economy systems, some compromises are necessary. There is less degradation in this price range than ever before, but still some exists. Remember though, the "how much" at Atlantis Sound is less than anywhere else.

WHEN TO BUY.

Because of increased cost and inflation both here and overseas, prices will be going up later in the fall. If you want a system and can afford to purchase now, do so.

What about waiting for a sale? If you wait for one of our competitors' sales, their price may become as low as ours. We sell our systems at the lowest prices possible. It's a lot easier that way—for us, for you, and for the friends that you will refer to us later.

A LITTLE ABOUT ATLANTIS SOUND.

The common notion that all hi-fi dealers are the same is a fallacy. The dealer you buy from is very important. Even among the various audio component specialists, you'll find important difference. They're generally broken down into four distinct areas: price, selection, warranty, and service.

At this point, it's impossible for us to stay modest. We excel over our competition in all four areas above. That's a pretty broad statement, but we can back it up as follows.

Price. If, within 30 days of purchase, you discover any authorized dealer selling the same equipment with comparable guarantee for a lower price, bring in the proof and Atlantis Sound will gladly refund the difference. Likewise, of course, we'll beat this quote if you haven't purchased yet.

Selection. We carry all major brands and only brand name products (no private label). If you don't see a particular item or brand, ask; we have many products in stock for immediate delivery that may not be on display in the particular store where you're shopping.

Warranty. We're one of the miniscule number of hi-fi dealers whose warranty is actually better and longer than most of the manufacturers themselves:

We guarantee the speaker system (parts **and** labor) five years. So the Advent, or Pioneer speaker you buy from us is different than the Advent or Pioneer you could buy from the dealer down the street.

We guarantee the electronic component (parts **and** labor) three years. The turntable or changer, or tape recorder, one year. (Repair parts subject to wear, such as styli, tape heads, belts, etc., are guaranteed for 90 days only).

We also have a money-back guarantee in case you change your mind within 7 days. And a 100% equipment exchange program if you prefer something else within 90 days (we'll credit you full price toward the purchase of any other component or combination of components at the normal list price).

We have a one year speaker exchange, as follows. Atlantis will allow your full purchase price towards any more expensive speaker we carry, with one year. (Reductions will be made for cabinet damage, and the policy doesn't apply to speakers that are the same except for cabinet style).

Now for the fine print. The guarantees extend from original date of purchase and are limited to the original purchaser only and are not transferable. They're in lieu of all other warranties or guarantees, express or implied; they're automatically voided by the misuse or abuse of any component; they're applicable only to those components or sound systems specifically recommended by Atlantis Sound in its print advertising; and lastly, they require that all equipment returned under any of the provisions of the warranty be in original condition with all packing material, accessories, and instruction books intact and not defaced.

Which is only fair.

Okay, now the fourth area. Service. What we try to do, basically, is remove as much technical hassle as possible from your purchase. We have a reasonable payment plan; we take BankAmericard, Master Charge, and Central Charge; we deliver, set-up and install free; and we have a loaner program to take the misery out of being without your music if something's on the blink.

Last but not least, should you ever encounter any problems, with your system or with us, or have any comments, please feel free to call The Wizard of Atlantis, Ken Kanzler, who is really concerned about your satisfaction. Call him at his office, 532-5500, or his home, 620-9559.

WHAT IS AN ATLANTIS SOUND SYSTEM?

First the Wizard uses an elaborate Electronic Evaluation Program and selects the A-rated products in each price range—receivers, speakers, turntables, etc. Then he puts it all together, carefully matching each component to the others.

However, it goes farther than just a genius matching up the world's best components. It's the absolute best value in its price range, and each system is backed by the Atlantis Sound Consumer Protection Plan— a combination of the strongest warranty and the most generous services in the industry.

So not only do you get the best possible equipment for your money, you also get the best protection. It sounds trite, but you simply can't make a mistake buying from us.

BRING THIS AD AND HEADPHONES ARE INCLUDED FREE.

This week's special Atlantis Sound Systems have everything going for them: brands, warranties, service, the Wizard's personal blessing, and a price so low we dare anyone to beat it. Each represents the best buy in its particular price range—if there were any better value, we'd recommend it. But there isn't.

To make them completely irresistible, we're including the headphones, this week only, **at no additional charge,** when you bring this ad with you.

Speakers .... 2 EPI 100v's
Receiver .... Harmon Kardon 330B
Changer BSR-510X
Headphones ..... Koss K6 L-C

$400

Speakers .... 2 large Advents
Receiver .... Pioneer 525
Changer .... PE 3012
Cartridge .. Emp 999 AEX-11
Headphones ...... Koss HV-1

$570

Speakers .... 2 Bose 501
Receiver .... Onkyo 440
Changer .... PE 3012
Cartridge .. Emp 999 AEX-11
Headphones Pioneer SEL-240

$670

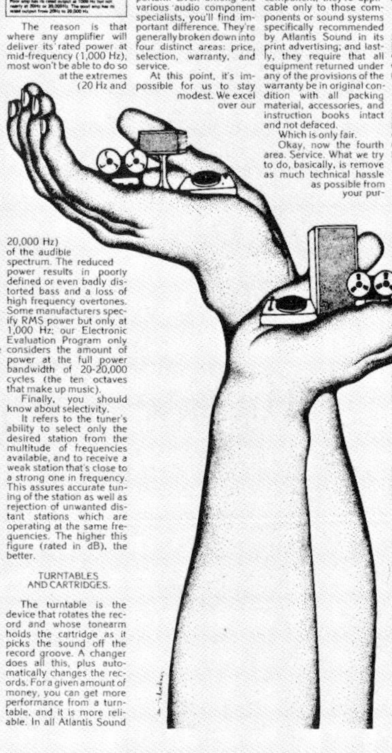

Speakers ... 2 JBL L-100
Receiver Harmon Kardon 630
Changer .... Dual 1218
Cartridge .. Emp 1001 ZEX-III
Headphones ... Koss Pro 4AA

$1020

WHERE TO FIND US.

Fairfax: (Our newest location) 3220 Old Lee Hwy., just off Fairfax Circle, 273-8634.

Falls Church: 230 W. Broad St., on Rt. 7, 2 blocks from Lee Hwy., 532-5500.
Springfield: 5224 Port Royal Rd., Ravensworth Shopping Center, 569-1770.
Washington: 1605 Connecticut Ave., N.W., above Dupont Circle, 667-7480.
Georgetown: 1742 Wisconsin Ave., N.W., at S St., 965-1256.
Bethesda: 7811 Old Georgetown Rd., at Arlington Rd., 652-6462.
Coming soon — **Rockville.**"

ATLANTIS SOUND

© 1974 Atlantis Sound

10

10
Art Director Dan Rosenthal
Writer Dan Rosenthal
Designer Dan Rosenthal
Artists Ginny Rinaldo
Jan Schockner
Agency Weitzman & Assoc.
Client Atlantis Sound

11
Art Director Howard Title
Writer Chuck Cohen
Designer Howard Title
Artists John Collier
Arton Assoc.
Agency Waring & LaRosa
Client Swissair

12
Art Director Alan Wolsky
Writers Bill Quirk
Alan Wolsky
Designer Hy Didia
Photographer Klaus Lucka
Agency Alan Wolsky & Friends
Client The Franklin Society
Federal Savings & Loan Assoc.

We know you want to fly to Europe
for as little as possible.
So you decide how little is possible.
SWISSAIR

11

SOCIAL SECURITY
LEE THOMAS
IF THIS IS YOUR RETIREMENT FUND, YOU'D BETTER READ THIS AD.
by the Answer Man
Pretend you're 65.
And you're living on $266 a month. (Make it $399 if there are two of you.)
That's the most you can get from Social Security. And you could get a lot less.
So you pay your rent. You buy a little food. You count your pennies. And you wait for your next check.
Of course, the payments will go up over the years. But then so will everything else.
Maybe you're counting on a pension. So were a lot of other people. The welfare offices are full of them.
Senator Javits estimates that, for one reason or another, pension benefits go to as few as one out of twelve covered employees.
You may not qualify for a pension if you change jobs, change unions (or locals), you don't work continuously, you leave before you're 65, your company calls it quits before you do, or any one of a lot of little regulations hidden in the fine print.
Shouldn't you have something to fall back on? Or look ahead to? And somebody to help you plan for the future?
You should. And you do.
There's an Answer Man in every one of our branches to answer your questions about retirement planning. (And he's got a free book on planning your retirement that you'll find invaluable.)
He'll help you figure out how much you'll need to retire. And how you should save to get it.
He'll even show you lots of ways to spend less now so you can put more away for later.
Maybe you'll never be rich. But you'll never be poor either. It's something to think about. And talk about. Come in and ask the Answer Man.
Downtown at 217 Broadway, the Answer Man is Rudy Stoya.
On Lexington Avenue at 44th St., ask for George Bambrick.
In Forest Hills, at Queens Blvd. and Continental Avenue, George Ruschmeyer is the Answer Man.
In our Bronx office at Fordham Rd. on Jerome Avenue, he's John Berardi.
And John Davis is the Answer Man in our office on East Central Avenue in Pearl River, New York.
Call (212) 267-4000 for an appointment. Or just stop by.
In Pearl River, call (914) PE 5-4023.
The Franklin Society Federal Savings & Loan Association
Our interest doesn't stop with your money

12

Great beer comes from places where there's not much to do but make great beer.
Take Utica, New York, for example. It's not exactly New York, New York. You might say the life here is a bit slower.
That may be bad, but it's also good.
For, it means that when we have a job to do we can take our time and do it good, instead of merely fast.
Our beer, Utica Club, is a prime example of that.
While many beers in the United States today are made with commercial syrups or extracts, it would go against our grain to use anything but whole grains in our beer. That's not very commercial of us.
The malt we use in Utica Club is "choice grade" malt. That's the choicest grade malt money can buy.
The water we use comes from the pure Adirondack streams nearby. It's so delicious we could probably bottle it and sell it by itself.
We use choice hops, pure corn and, as if all that weren't enough, we even use brewer's rice for extra lightness. A step only a handful of brewers in the United States see the need for.
Then, after introducing all these great ingredients to each other, we do something else that's rare in beer making these days. We let them sit around and get acquainted. Naturally. So that they lose their edge, but not their individuality.
You see, we just couldn't accept the idea of forcing carbonation down the throat of our beer, a very accepted practice today. So Utica Club is aged for months, instead of weeks. Natural aging gives you a more mellow better blended beer with a natural life that lasts right down to the bottom of the glass or the keg. So it's not a race till the finish between you and your beer. But it gives us heartaches.
For it requires a lot of extra equipment. And it ties up thousands of barrels of beer.
However, we feel artificial carbonation would be even more expensive. It would cost us a great beer.
See for yourself if all that extra time and effort pays off. Go out and get some Utica Club.
Or, better yet, hop into your car and pay us a visit in person. We'd love to show you around our brewery. And buy you a beer.
In fact, we'll ask you to do something we wouldn't do. Hurry.
Utica Club
Utica Club
Pilsener Lager Beer
Utica Club

13

13
Art Director Ken Berris
Writer Neil Drossman
Designer Ken Berris
Artist Ken Lombardo
Photographer George Cochran
Agency Della Femina, Travisano & Partners
Client West End Brewing Co.

The city where every 43rd person is a millionaire.
Welcome to Boca Raton
The city is Boca Raton, Florida. Population, 40,000. Millionaires, 907.
Only six other cities of any size, anywhere in the country, can claim to have attracted a greater number of millionaires.
But no other city of any size, anywhere, can claim a more remarkable reason for attracting such wealth.
And that reason is the city itself. A city tenaciously maintaining an idea conceived 50-odd years ago by an eccentric entrepreneur named Addison Mizner: to create a resort town that would make the millionaires paradise of Palm Beach "look like servants' quarters."
Today it is difficult to drive through Boca Raton without getting the distinct feeling that only millionaires live here.
Because the 40,000 people in Boca Raton display an almost fanatical concern for their city.
Because they have seen to it that no building will ever be erected until a special committee is satisfied with its shape, size and color. Not to mention its appearance from the nearby road. Or from passing trains. Or even from the ridge at the end of town.
Because in Boca Raton, billboards are banned and signs of all kinds are subject to careful scrutiny as careful as approving the entrance and exit signs on apartment house parking lots.
Because in Boca Raton, if a company's national image clashes with the city's image, it is not the city's image that gives way. (The bright, yellow arches of a hamburger chain may be acceptable to most of America, but not to Boca Raton.)
And probably the most important "because" of all: it is against the law for Boca Raton to grow beyond 40,000 dwellings.
We, at Porta Bella, invite you to Boca Raton to see 660 of those dwellings.
We invite you to live on the Intracoastal Waterway in the heart of this millionaires city. With a millionaires view from your balcony.
We invite you to enjoy our yachting facilities. And to join our Racquet Club.
We invite you, knowing that you may not yourself be a millionaire. And that you might even require a little help from us with your financing.
To come to Porta Bella, take Exit 28 on Florida's Turnpike, drive East to Highway 1, North to East Jeffery Street, then turn right.
Or call or write for our brochure, Porta Bella, 700 East Jeffery Street, Boca Raton, Florida 33432. Dade: (305) 944-5615; Broward: (305) 421-7090.
Porta Bella. The place in Boca.
One, two and three-bedroom apartments from $46,000 to $113,000.

14

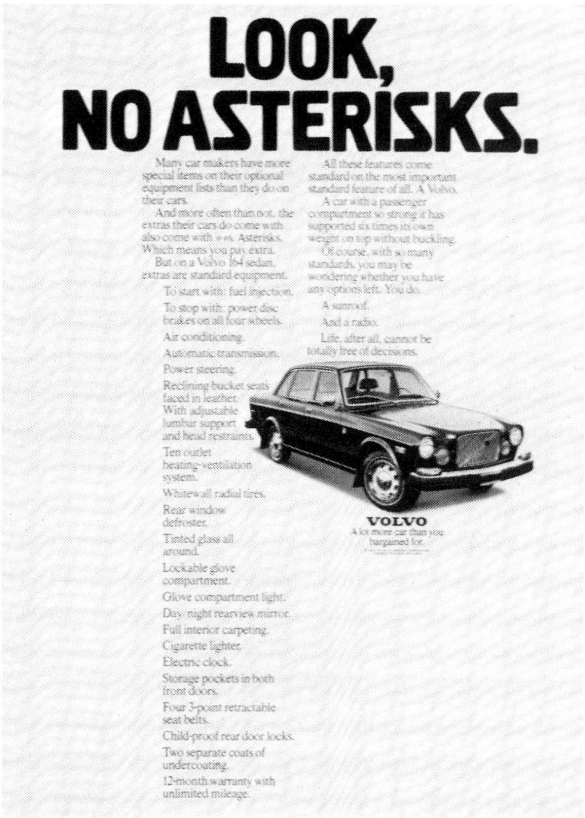
LOOK, NO ASTERISKS.
Many car makers have more special items on their optional equipment lists than they do on their cars.
And more often than not, the extras their cars do come with also come with ***. Asterisks. Which means you pay extra.
But on a Volvo 164 sedan, extras are standard equipment.
To start with: fuel injection.
To stop with: power disc brakes on all four wheels.
Air conditioning.
Automatic transmission.
Power steering.
Reclining bucket seats faced in leather. With adjustable lumbar support and head restraints.
Ten outlet heating-ventilation system.
Whitewall radial tires.
Rear window defroster.
Tinted glass all around.
Lockable glove compartment.
Glove compartment light.
Day/night rearview mirror.
Full interior carpeting.
Cigarette lighter.
Electric clock.
Storage pockets in both front doors.
Four 3-point retractable seat belts.
Child-proof rear door locks.
Two separate coats of undercoating.
12-month warranty with unlimited mileage.
All these features come standard on the most important standard feature of all. A Volvo.
A car with a passenger compartment so strong it has supported six times its own weight on top without buckling.
Of course, with so many standards, you may be wondering whether you have any options left. You do.
A sunroof.
And a radio.
Life, after all, cannot be totally free of decisions.
VOLVO
A lot more car than you bargained for.

15

"The same price I charge my mother, I charge you."
Shore's Discount Drugs

16

14
Art Director Cary Howard
Writer Burt Klein
Designer Cary Howard
Photographer Jeff Turnau
Agency Michael Schack Advertising
Client Porta Bella

15
Art Director Robert Reitzfeld
Writers Edward A. McCabe
Larry Cadman
Agency Scali, McCabe, Sloves
Client Volvo of America Corp.

16
Art Director Marty Malone
Writer Burt Klein
Designer Marty Malone
Photographer Bob Gelberg
Agency Michael Schack Advertising
Client Shore's Discount Drugs

*DIN 70030 ©Volkswagen of America, Inc.
Presenting the 84 mpg Volkswagen.
Since all the car manufacturers are conducting their own mileage tests these days, we at Volkswagen thought we'd conduct one too.
So we modified our body—and our engine. And, of course, we got someone who didn't weigh much to drive.
Lo and behold, we got 84 miles per gallon!
Ridiculous? Nobody normally drives like this? Of course. That's precisely our point.
Nobody normally drives like most of those tests you're seeing.
Volkswagen: An honest 25* miles per gallon.

17

17
Art Director Charles Piccirillo
Writer Mike Mangano
Photographer Frank Cowan
Agency Doyle Dane Bernbach
Client Volkswagen of America Corp.

The Renaissance of the Curious Reader
Smithsonian
Smithsonian Magazine
The curious truth

18

CHARGING LUNCH VS. FINANCING IT.
Carte Blanche
Carte Blanche

19

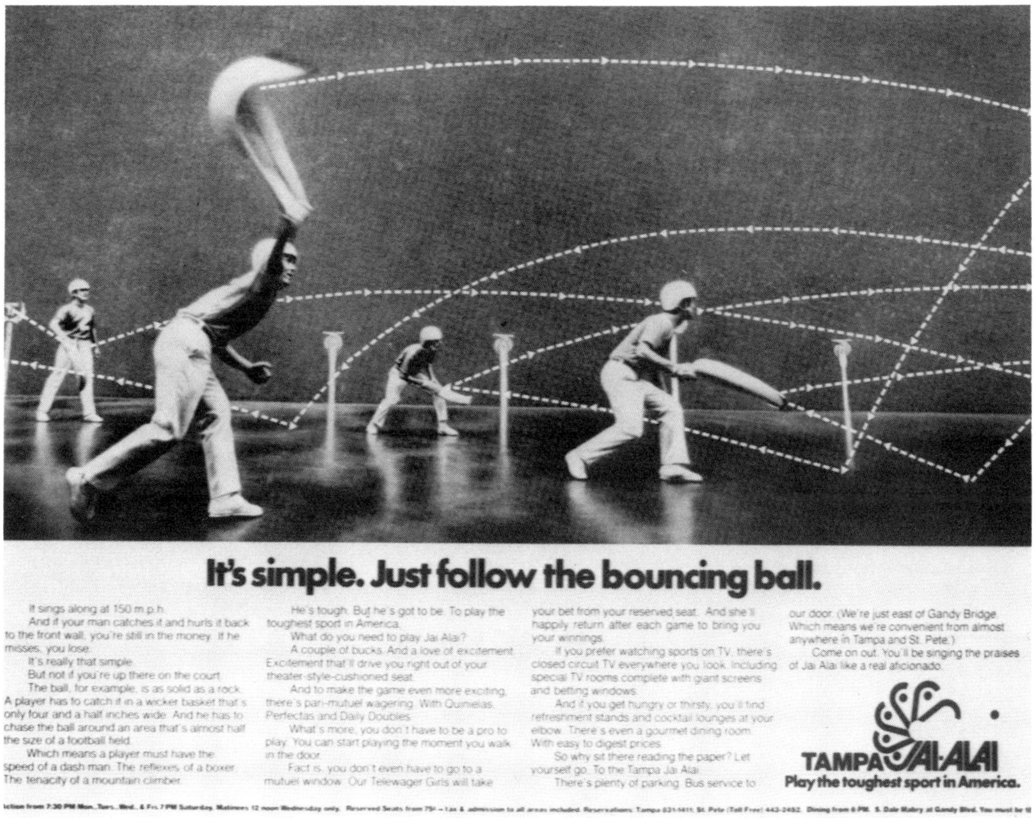
It's simple. Just follow the bouncing ball.
It sings along at 150 m.p.h.
And if your man catches it and hurls it back to the front wall, you're still in the money. If he misses, you lose.
It's really that simple.
But not if you're up there on the court.
The ball, for example, is as solid as a rock. A player has to catch it in a wicker basket that's only four and a half inches wide. And he has to chase the ball around an area that's almost half the size of a football field.
Which means a player must have the speed of a dash man. The reflexes of a boxer. The tenacity of a mountain climber.
He's tough. But he's got to be. To play the toughest sport in America.
What do you need to play Jai Alai?
A couple of bucks. And a love of excitement. Excitement that'll drive you right out of your theater-style-cushioned seat.
And to make the game even more exciting, there's pari-mutuel wagering. With Quinielas, Perfectas and Daily Doubles.
What's more, you don't have to be a pro to play. You can start playing the moment you walk in the door.
Fact is, you don't even have to go to a mutuel window. Our Telewager Girls will take your bet from your reserved seat. And she'll happily return after each game to bring you your winnings.
If you prefer watching sports on TV, there's closed circuit TV everywhere you look. Including special TV rooms complete with giant screens and betting windows.
And if you get hungry or thirsty, you'll find refreshment stands and cocktail lounges at your elbow. There's even a gourmet dining room. With easy to digest prices.
So why sit there reading the paper? Let yourself go. To the Tampa Jai Alai.
There's plenty of parking. Bus service to our door. (We're just east of Gandy Bridge. Which means we're convenient from almost anywhere in Tampa and St. Pete.)
Come on out. You'll be singing the praises of Jai Alai like a real aficionado.
TAMPA JAI-ALAI
Play the toughest sport in America.

20

18
Art Director Hy Varon
Writer Charles Gowl
Designer Hy Varon
Artist Gene Calogero
Agency Warwick, Welsh & Miller
Client Smithsonian Magazine

19
Art Director Mark Yustein
Writer Kay Kavanagh
Designer Mark Yustein
Photographer Allen Vogel
Agency Della Femina, Travisano & Partners
Client Carte Blanche

20
Art Director Dave Romano
Writer William Drier
Photographer Dan Forer
Agency Hume, Smith, Mickelberry
Client World Jai-Alai

TODAY AN Rh POSITIVE CAN FALL IN LOVE WITH AN Rh NEGATIVE.
Now they can look forward to a blessed event without fear.
Because today a doctor can protect an unborn child from Rh disease, if he knows in advance the Rh factors of both the mother and father.
This was just one of the fears we were able to put to rest in a recent editorial about birth defects.*
We pointed out some of the startling advances medicine has made in recent years.
Today these advances promise a relatively normal life to children born with clubfoot, open spine, cleft lip and palate, or even water on the brain.
And we let parents know what they can do to protect their children from diseases like PKU, rubella and sickle-cell.
It's editorials like this that keep 23 million people reading Better Homes and Gardens.
Our readers not only want to know about everyday things like home furnishings, cooking, sewing and the best way to repave a driveway, but they also want to know about all the things that affect the lives and future of their entire family.
And our readers hate to part with us. They refer back to us for information, help and advice. In fact, an average issue is kept around the house for 22 months.
And they don't think of Better Homes and Gardens as just an ordinary magazine, they think of us as more of a professional journal for husbands and wives who are making a home and raising a family.
Because we give them more ideas and information on food, home furnishings, home improvement and even travel than magazines like Family Circle, Good Housekeeping, Ladies' Home Journal, McCall's, Redbook or Woman's Day.
We even have more husbands and wives who buy new cars, own their own homes and buy major appliances than they do.**
Because we do more for our readers than they do. But then we have more readers than they do.
Everything we talk about is close to home.
That's why Better Homes and Gardens is the third most widely read magazine in America.
Better Homes and Gardens
BETTER HOMES
and Gardens®
*March 1974 issue of BH&G
**Source: W.R. Simmons 1975

21

SILVER

21

Art Director Nick Scordato
Writer Ken Charof
Designer Nick Scordato
Photographer Cailor-Resnick
Agency Doherty, Mann & Olshan
Client Better Homes & Gardens

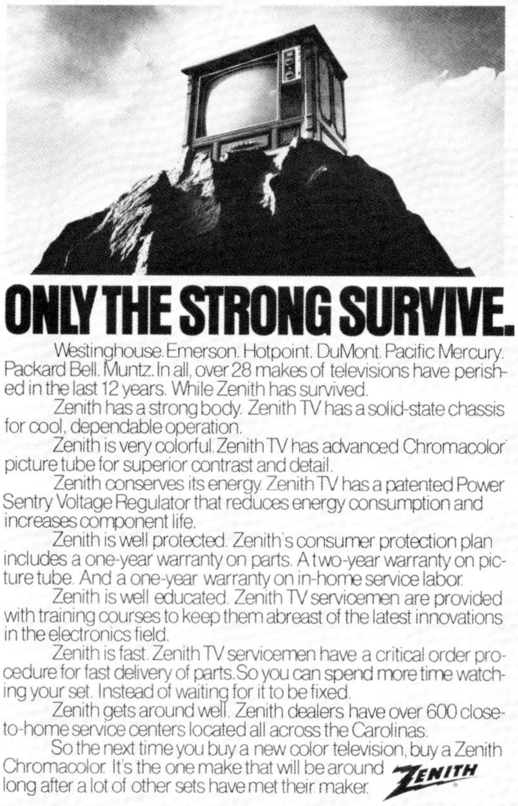
ONLY THE STRONG SURVIVE.
Westinghouse. Emerson. Hotpoint. DuMont. Pacific Mercury. Packard Bell. Muntz. In all, over 28 makes of televisions have perished in the last 12 years. While Zenith has survived.
Zenith has a strong body. Zenith TV has a solid-state chassis for cool, dependable operation.
Zenith is very colorful. Zenith TV has advanced Chromacolor picture tube for superior contrast and detail.
Zenith conserves its energy. Zenith TV has a patented Power Sentry Voltage Regulator that reduces energy consumption and increases component life.
Zenith is well protected. Zenith's consumer protection plan includes a one-year warranty on parts. A two-year warranty on picture tube. And a one-year warranty on in-home service labor.
Zenith is well educated. Zenith TV servicemen are provided with training courses to keep them abreast of the latest innovations in the electronics field.
Zenith is fast. Zenith TV servicemen have a critical order procedure for fast delivery of parts. So you can spend more time watching your set. Instead of waiting for it to be fixed.
Zenith gets around well. Zenith dealers have over 600 close-to-home service centers located all across the Carolinas.
So the next time you buy a new color television, buy a Zenith Chromacolor. It's the one make that will be around long after a lot of other sets have met their maker.
ZENITH

22

For 144 years, the hands that were good enough to sew our country's flags were not considered worthy to cast a ballot.
From 1776 to 1920, women had no say in government.
Betsy Ross was not allowed to vote. Neither was Dolly Madison. Or Martha Washington.
Or even Barbara Frietchie ("Shoot, if you must, this old gray head, but spare your country's flag," she said).
But voting wasn't the half of it.
Women were expected to keep their political opinions to themselves.
In one state, a man could legally beat his wife whenever he thought she needed it, provided the stick he used was no thicker than the local judge's thumb.
Women didn't win the right to vote until 1920. And things have been changing ever since.
Struggles like this still grip our attention.
So, as we approach our Bicentennial, we look behind us…to see how we got to where we are today.
CBS is doing just that.
In an exciting series of broadcasts entitled, appropriately enough, "The American Parade." And sponsored by Eaton Corporation.
The parade will be led by "We the Women," which will trace America's continuing – and sometimes bitter – struggle for women's equal rights.
"We the Women" will be followed by a dozen other Bicentennial perspectives on the Presidency, the Industrial Revolution, Slavery, the Armed Forces, the Winning of the West, Congress, Labor, and other aspects of our common heritage.
Next will be "Mr. President," which takes us from George Washington to Teddy Roosevelt, the first President of the 20th Century.
It will be followed by "The 34th Star." It will tell the story of Kansas, the 34th star in the Union flag – how it grew from buffalo prairie through the coming of the railroad, the Indian and Civil Wars, the coming of the locusts, and the growth of cities.
In producing this series, CBS News thus takes a thematic, rather than a chronological approach to history, and allows it to be seen from a variety of new and different perspectives.
It is safe to say you and your family will learn a lot about America that you never knew before.
The American Parade
"We the Women"
The first in the series premieres Sunday, March 17, 8-9PM.
CBS 2

23

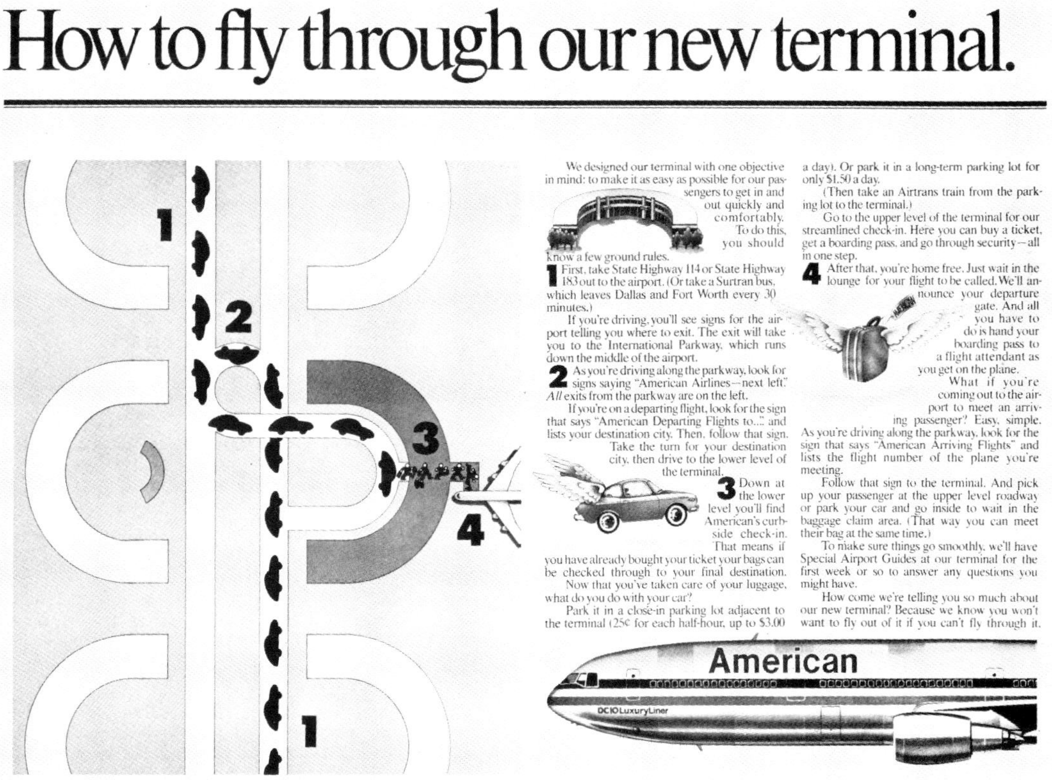
How to fly through our new terminal.
1
2
3
4
1
We designed our terminal with one objective in mind: to make it as easy as possible for our passengers to get in and out quickly and comfortably. To do this, you should know a few ground rules.
1 First, take State Highway 114 or State Highway 183 out to the airport. (Or take a Surtran bus, which leaves Dallas and Fort Worth every 30 minutes.)
If you're driving, you'll see signs for the airport telling you where to exit. The exit will take you to the International Parkway, which runs down the middle of the airport.
2 As you're driving along the parkway, look for signs saying "American Airlines—next left." All exits from the parkway are on the left.
If you're on a departing flight, look for the sign that says "American Departing Flights to…" and lists your destination city. Then, follow that sign. Take the turn for your destination city, then drive to the lower level of the terminal.
3 Down at the lower level you'll find American's curbside check-in. That means if you have already bought your ticket your bags can be checked through to your final destination.
Now that you've taken care of your luggage, what do you do with your car?
Park it in a close-in parking lot adjacent to the terminal (25¢ for each half-hour, up to $3.00 a day). Or park it in a long-term parking lot for only $1.50 a day.
(Then take an Airtrans train from the parking lot to the terminal.)
Go to the upper level of the terminal for our streamlined check-in. Here you can buy a ticket, get a boarding pass, and go through security—all in one step.
4 After that, you're home free. Just wait in the lounge for your flight to be called. We'll announce your departure gate. And all you have to do is hand your boarding pass to a flight attendant as you get on the plane.
What if you're coming out to the airport to meet an arriving passenger? Easy, simple. As you're driving along the parkway, look for the sign that says "American Arriving Flights" and lists the flight number of the plane you're meeting.
Follow that sign to the terminal. And pick up your passenger at the upper level roadway or park your car and go inside to wait in the baggage claim area. (That way you can meet their bag at the same time.)
To make sure things go smoothly, we'll have Special Airport Guides at our terminal for the first week or so to answer any questions you might have.
How come we're telling you so much about our new terminal? Because we know you won't want to fly out of it if you can't fly through it.
American
DC10 LuxuryLiner

24

22
Art Director Preuit Holland
Writer Roger Feuerman
Designer Preuit Holland
Photographer Tom Walters
Agency Cargill, Wilson & Acree
Client Allison-Erwin Co.

23
Art Director Lou Dorfsman
Writer Dick Jackson
Designers Lou Dorfsman
Ted Andresakes
Artist Nick Fasciano
Photographer David Spindell
Agency CBS/Broadcast Group
Client CBS Television Network

24
Art Director Stu Weisselberg
Writer Stevie Pierson
Designer Stu Weisselberg
Artist Kim Whitesides
Agency Doyle Dane Bernbach
Client American Airlines

We write
War and Peace
once a week.
And again this week. As drama unfolded in Washington and London, and as the bargaining continued in the Middle East, TIME correspondents filed a volume of words bigger than Tolstoy's "War and Peace." And from the 600,000 words that poured into TIME's editors, this week's issue was distilled.
No other newsmagazine starts with so much information. Because, for one thing, no other has anything approaching TIME's reporting staff: 450 correspondents and stringers working out of 30 editorial offices around the world.
The result? There's simply more substance in TIME. More color. More stories you won't find anyplace else. More of the small, human details that bring the news to life. More of the subtle lights and shadings of the real world.
More solidity, too. Because what you read is just the tip of the iceberg. Underneath is that vast substructure of fact, analysis, personal insight—and experience—that sets TIME apart from every other newsmagazine.
Real wars and real peacemaking are only part of the story TIME tells. In books or art or business or politics or medicine, ideas meet and clash and TIME is there on the battle lines, digging deeper and reporting more fully. Out of this massive flow of ideas, this river of words, comes finally a sharper understanding. So that a busy person really can keep up with every important trend of thought in two hours of reading a week.
TIME starts with more so TIME readers can get more. It's a good reason why more people get their news from TIME every week than from any other single news source. Over 26 million readers around the world.
TIME
CHARGING NIXON'S MEN
TIME makes everything more interesting. Including you.

25

My daddy can lick your daddy.
People
The new way to reach people.

26

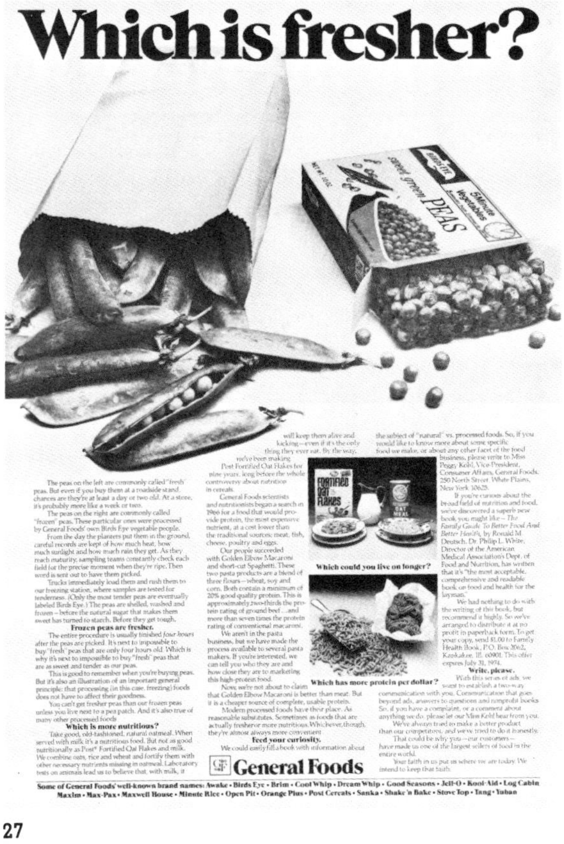
Which is fresher?
PEAS
Which could you live on longer?
Which has more protein per dollar?
General Foods

27

25
Art Director Bob Czernysz
Writer Richard Olmsted
Photographer Editorial
Agency Young & Rubicam International
Client Time Magazine

26
Art Director Bob Czernysz
Writer Richard Olmsted
Photographer Editorial
Agency Young & Rubicam International
Client People Magazine

27
Art Director Gary Carlisle
Writers Art Naiman
Forrest Long
Photographer Ron De Milt
Agency Young & Rubicam International
Client General Foods

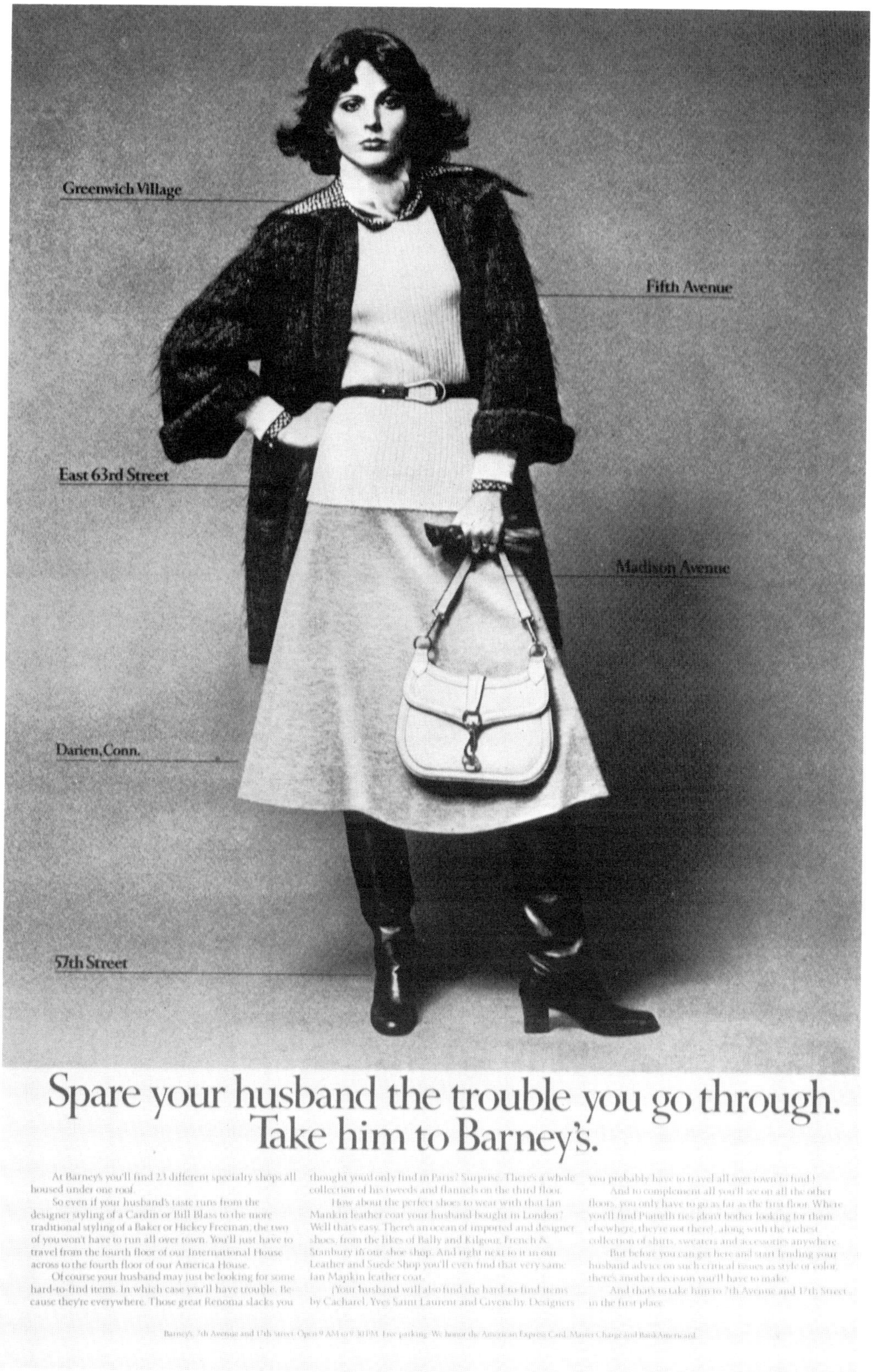
Greenwich Village
Fifth Avenue
East 63rd Street
Madison Avenue
Darien, Conn.
57th Street
Spare your husband the trouble you go through.
Take him to Barney's.

28

28
Art Director Louis Colletti
Writer Michael Lichtman
Photographer Hal Davis
Agency Scali, McCabe, Sloves
Client Barney's

EDITION
WEATHER: Sunny, Breezy, Cooler.
BIG THREE GO UP!
G.M., Ford, Chrysler Hike Prices.
Little One Stays Down!
Still $2625

29

A VOLVO DISCOVERY: RAIN FALLS ON REAR WINDOWS, TOO.
Volvo is the only wagon maker with the foresight to provide its rear window with a wiper and washer as standard equipment.
Volvo has also discovered that everyone doesn't buy a wagon to be fashionable. Many people buy wagons to carry things.
So we didn't design Volvo's cargo area low and sleek to accommodate a styling trend. We designed it high and practical, to accommodate things like a six-foot sofa and two chairs (with the rear seat down). Or three six-foot people and 12 two-suiters (with the rear seat up).
Volvo's rear area not only holds a lot, it comes with a lot. It has its own heating and ventilation vents, its own three-point seat belts, electric rear window defogger, carpeting, tinted glass and childproof door locks.
And Volvo's back door swings up out of your way, instead of out into your stomach. Or down into your knee caps.
It doesn't take a college degree to appreciate the thinking behind our wagon. So we leave you to consider this. If the rear end of your car isn't as well thought-out as Volvo's, what other part might not be?
VOLVO
The wagon for people who think.
VOLVO
RP-7902
245 DL

30

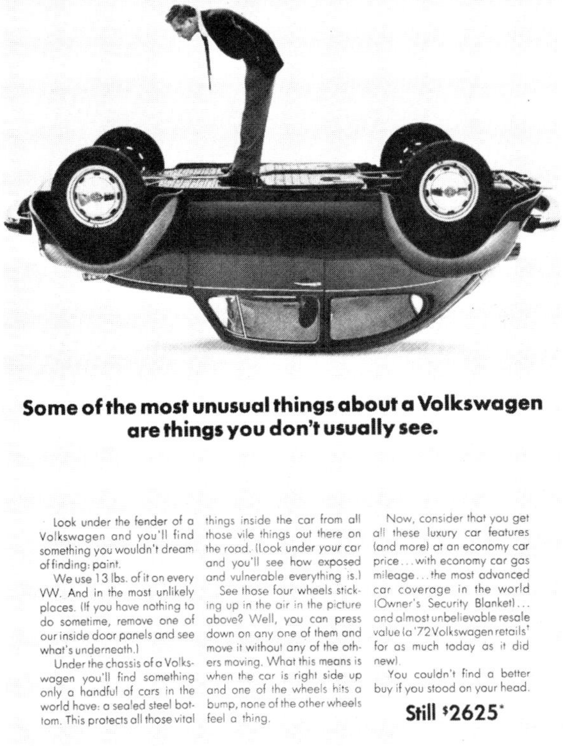
Some of the most unusual things about a Volkswagen are things you don't usually see.
Look under the fender of a Volkswagen and you'll find something you wouldn't dream of finding: paint.
We use 13 lbs. of it on every VW. And in the most unlikely places. (If you have nothing to do sometime, remove one of our inside door panels and see what's underneath.)
Under the chassis of a Volkswagen you'll find something only a handful of cars in the world have: a sealed steel bottom. This protects all those vital things inside the car from all those vile things out there on the road. (Look under your car and you'll see how exposed and vulnerable everything is.)
See those four wheels sticking up in the air in the picture above? Well, you can press down on any one of them and move it without any of the others moving. What this means is when the car is right side up and one of the wheels hits a bump, none of the other wheels feel a thing.
Now, consider that you get all these luxury car features (and more) at an economy car price...with economy car gas mileage...the most advanced car coverage in the world (Owner's Security Blanket)...and almost unbelievable resale value (a '72 Volkswagen retails[†] for as much today as it did new).
You couldn't find a better buy if you stood on your head.
Still $2625*

31

SILVER

29
Art Director Charles Piccirillo
Writer Mike Mangano
Photographer Larry Sillen
Agency Doyle Dane Bernbach
Client Volkswagen of America Corp.

30
Art Director Robert Reitzfeld
Writer Thomas J. Nathan
Photographer Henry Sandbank
Agency Scali, McCabe, Sloves
Client Volvo of America Corp.

31
Art Director Charles Piccirillo
Writer Mike Mangano
Photographer David Langley
Agency Doyle Dane Bernbach
Client Volkswagen of America Corp.

IT TAKES A LOT OF DUMMIES TO MAKE A CAR FOR PEOPLE WHO THINK.

By smashing Volvos into barriers with dummies inside, we've made them safer for people. These tests helped develop a front end which absorbs highway-speed impacts to protect the passenger compartment. And a three-point seat belt which can restrain 3½ tons of force.

By bouncing a dummy bottom on a seat for hours, we designed one to stay comfortable for years. But all our improvements aren't suggested by dummies. Some come from common sense.

All cars have head restraints. Volvo's have openings, so you can see behind you.

All cars have windshield wipers. But instead of shiny ones that glare, Volvo has dull black ones.

Volvo provides four wheel power-assisted disc brakes, steel-belted radial tires, fuel injection, new suspension that makes the car corner flatter and smoother. And a heating-circulation system that can freshen the air, warm your feet and defog the front windows all at once.

At Volvo, the smallest details get careful consideration. Which is why, all things considered, Volvo may well be the world's most carefully thought-out car.

It's not surprising then, that Volvo has a special appeal for people who think. 87% of the people who buy Volvos are college educated.

The other 13% must be just plain smart.

VOLVO
The car for people who think.

800·IJN

32

Movie fans, we hear you!

Ok, for the first time anywhere, here's an almost complete list of WCCO-TV's movie library.

The idea is for us to get to know our movie fans better.

So sit down with a pencil and check off the films you want us to show in the next couple months. We hope you'll answer the questions, too.

When you're all done, send this whole ad to: The Movie Man, WCCO-TV, 52 So. 9th St., Minneapolis, 55402.

1. WCCO-TV regularly shows movies at 3:30 pm, 10:30—and on Friday night, a second Classic Film about midnight. Which time do you like best?______

2. Are we giving you enough movies? Or too many?______

3. Would you like more movies scheduled late at night?______ Which nights?______

4. To give us a better idea of what our movie audience is like, would you tell us your age?____ Occupation?____ Male____ Female____ City____

5. Are there other movies not on the list you'd like us to try to get for you?______

Old Silents, But Goodies

Gems from the 30's & 40's

Singing & Dancing Extravaganzas

Chilling Tales, Horror & Sci-Fi

The Best of the West

Comedies, Dramas and More

Juicy New Titles Just Added!

POP CORN
4 WCCO TV

The most popular moviehouse in town.

34

32
Art Director Robert Reitzfeld
Writer Thomas J. Nathan
Photographer Henry Sandbank
Agency Scali, McCabe, Sloves
Client Volvo of America Corp.

34
Art Director Sue Crolick
Writer Sandra Bucholtz
Designer Sue Crolick
Artist Thomas D. Drackert
Photographer Kent Severson
Agency Martin Williams Advertising
Client WCCO Television

Can Elizabeth keep Richard dry?
People
People
The new way to reach people.

39 years later, Betty Bloomer moved into the White House.
People
People
The new way to reach people.

Paul Newman at 50. Paul Newman at 200.
Vroom? There goes Superstar at 200 mph. Why is he risking his million-dollar neck in race cars? Is it that impending birthday? "I am lurching toward 50," he says, "with all the eager anticipation of a kid having a woman for the first time." In the new People, meet a very human Newman, off-screen and living full throttle.
Dr. C. Everett Koop just made Farida Rodriguez the happiest mother in the world. He's the surgeon who separated her Siamese twins in a near-miraculous operation.
Elizabeth Ashley is a triumph in the new, sexier Cat on a Hot Tin Roof. "I'm really just a trashy red-neck," she says, "who came to New York and sold my-self as an uptown chick."
Colonel Sanders and Lady. At 84, he's still king of the finger lickers…travels a quarter-million miles a year for The Empire…isn't chicken about the future. "I've got no idea when I am going to retire."
Dr. Arnold Hutschnecker treated Veep Nixon, 1951 to 1956. He thinks all Presidential candidates should be examined by psychiatrists. Nixon's future? "If Nixon cannot revitalize his creative energies, he must die."
Joseph Heller exercises at a run but writes at a crawl. Mr. Catch-22 took 12 years to finish his new novel, Something Happened. Meet him in People…as relaxed as a 6-figure check can make a man.
Dixy Lee Ray has energy, Lord knows. She's "Chairman" of the Atomic Energy Commission, lives in a trailer, loves Star Trek, snorkels, isn't afraid of fights.
Doris Day at 50 says, "I've never enjoyed life more." No wonder. She just won a $22.8 million judgment against a former business manager. "I never lose faith. Que sera, sera."
See all the people? But there are more. Lots more. Open the new People and meet Spain's first lady bullfighter… Henry Kissinger at work for a new boss…the draft evader who preferred to stay in prison…
…the 22-year-old crystal ball king…the convict who's working on his Ph.D.…the divorced "DJ" who tapes shows for his kids…Truman Capote larking with Lee Radziwill…new bride Liza Minnelli…Jack Nicklaus's swinging son…
You never know who you'll run across in People, which is the whole beautiful idea of Time Inc's new magazine. Cover to cover, it's surprises, emotions, variety, headlong pace, now-ness. It bubbles. It's fun!
So what's happening with the first magazine that puts people first and issues second? People love it. Our circulation—all at newsstands and checkout counters—is headed toward next January's new rate base of 1,250,000.
And those copies are ending up in the hands of the right people. Younger, affluent, educated people. Says Trendex: 61% are women, 39% men; over 50% are 18 to 34; 48% attended college; 49% earn over $15,000.
Cost-per-thousands? They're incredible. If you're an advertiser and you want to reach a younger, upscale audience of men or women, People is the most efficient magazine you can buy. We'd like a chance to prove it to you. You say when.
People
PAUL NEWMAN
People weekly
The new way to reach people.

35

GOLD

35
Art Director Bob Czernysz
Writer Richard Olmsted
Photographer Editorial
Agency Young & Rubicam International
Client People Magazine

Di-hydrogen oxide.
What's it doing in your food?
A pinch of sodium chloride
General Foods

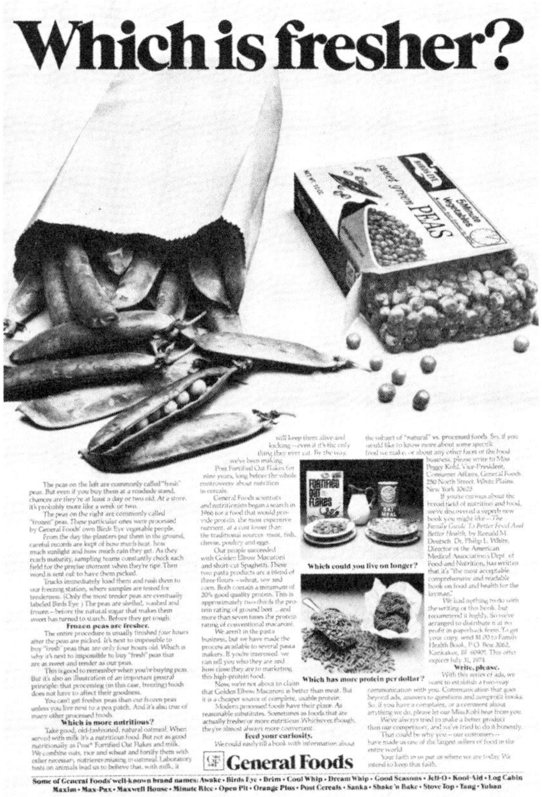
Which is fresher?
Which could you live on longer?
Which has more protein per dollar?
General Foods

Is the Small Family Size bigger than the
Giant Economy Carton
or cheaper than the Jumbo Value Pack?
Small Family Size
Giant Economy Carton
Jumbo Valu-Pak
The shell game isn't our game.
Where does it tell how to make instant by the pot?
General Foods

36

36
Art Director Gary Carlisle
Writers Art Naiman
Forrest Long
Artist Chris Corey
Photographer Ron De Milt
Agency Young & Rubicam International
Client General Foods

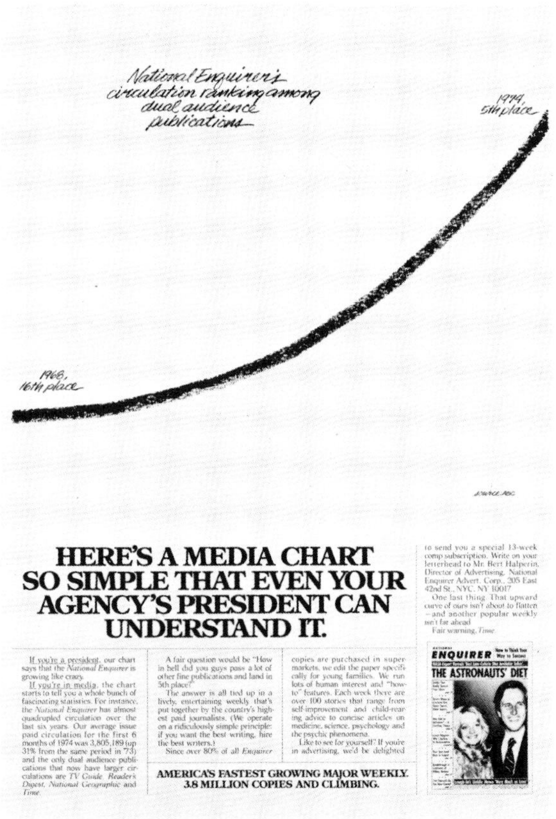
National Enquirer's circulation ranking among dual audience publications
1974, 5th place
1968, 16th place
HERE'S A MEDIA CHART SO SIMPLE THAT EVEN YOUR AGENCY'S PRESIDENT CAN UNDERSTAND IT.
AMERICA'S FASTEST GROWING MAJOR WEEKLY.
3.8 MILLION COPIES AND CLIMBING.

OUR READERS CHALLENGE YOU TO A GORILLA-NAMING CONTEST.
AMERICA'S FASTEST GROWING MAJOR WEEKLY.
3.8 MILLION COPIES AND CLIMBING.

WE TOLD OUR READERS ABOUT SOME OF GEORGE'S ...AHEM...WHOPPERS.
AMERICA'S FASTEST GROWING MAJOR WEEKLY.
3.8 MILLION COPIES AND CLIMBING.

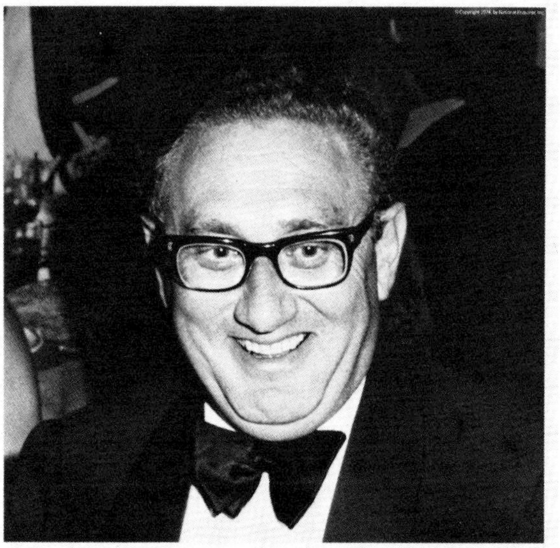
OUR READERS KNEW HENRY WAS GETTING MARRIED BEFORE HENRY KNEW.
AMERICA'S FASTEST GROWING MAJOR WEEKLY.
3.8 MILLION COPIES AND CLIMBING.

37

37

Art Director Gerry Severson
Writer John Emmerling
Photographers Various
Agency Richard K. Manoff
Client National Enquirer

AT CLUB MEDITERRANEE GUADELOUPE, IF YOU DO EVERYTHING THAT'S FREE YOU'LL NEED A VACATION.
After you pay as little as $217* for a week at Club Mediterranee Caravelle or Ft. Royal on Guadeloupe, virtually everything you'd pay extra for at most resorts is free.
You can over-indulge yourself with all the French and native cuisine you can eat at three meals a day. And wash it down with all the free wine you can drink at lunch and dinner. You pay only for drinks at the bar.
In between meals, there's free tennis. A free private beach. Free scuba diving. Free sailing. Free water-skiing. Free snorkeling. Free sailing picnics. Free French lessons. Free yoga and calisthenics. Equipment and group instruction are just as reasonably priced. They're also free.
Our free prices don't go up at night, either. There's a free live band, free cabaret or game shows, free recorded classical music concerts and a free discotheque that stays open as long as your eyes do.
You also have freedom to choose between two different clubs on Guadeloupe. Our new Caravelle Club is for people who want to be surrounded by luxury but not with crowds. It has superb accommodations and a beach that's nearly a mile long. And our smaller, more intimate club, Ft. Royal, offers special family rates, hotel rooms or secluded bungalows and a supervised children's mini-club where your kids don't always have to keep an eye on you.
Direct flights leave weekly from New York to Guadeloupe.
To find out more, contact your travel agent or fill out our coupon.
CLUB MEDITERRANEE
GUADELOUPE

At Club Mediterranee/Mexico, you can do everything or nothing for the same price.
At Club Mediterranee/Mexico, we believe having fun on a vacation shouldn't cost you extra.
So after you pay $293* for a week at our new vacation village, Playa Blanca, near Manzanillo, on the Pacific coast of Mexico, you'll find virtually all your money can stay at home.
At most resorts, your vacation package includes two ordinary meals. At Club Mediterranee/Playa Blanca we give you three meals a day of all the French, Mexican and Continental cuisine you can eat. And instead of one complimentary rum cocktail, we give you, free, all the red and rosé wine you can drink at lunch and dinner. You pay only for drinks at the bar. And even there, tipping is absolutely not allowed.
At Club Mediterranee/Playa Blanca, along with a beautiful beach, we have: Free tennis. Free sailing picnics. Free sailing. Free scuba diving. Free spear fishing. Free snorkeling. Free calisthenics. Free judo. Free yoga. And a huge swimming pool. And since you can't enjoy many of these activities unless you know how to do them, we also include equipment and expert group instruction. Also at no extra cost.
You include evening entertainment in your vacation. So we include it in the price of ours. Every evening, there are recorded classical music concerts alongside the beach, a live dance band, cabaret or game shows and a discoteque that stays open as long as your eyes do. All free.
And when your eyes can't stay open, you can rest them in an air-conditioned, secluded hacienda-style bungalow facing the ocean.
Flights to Club Mediterranee/Playa Blanca leave regularly from New York, Los Angeles, Houston, Montreal and Toronto. To find out more, call your travel agent or fill out this coupon.
CLUB MEDITERRANEE
MEXICO

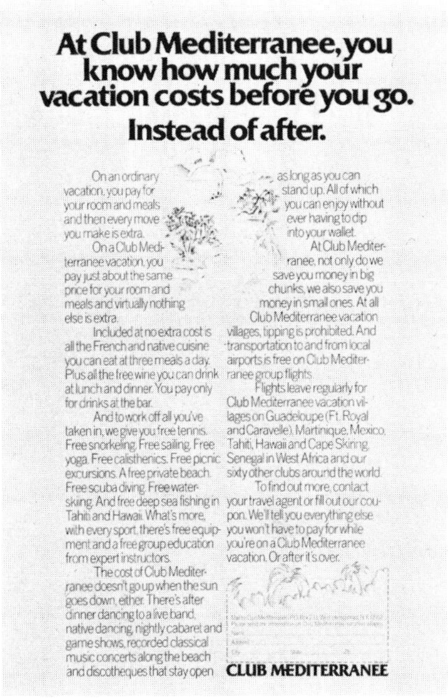
At Club Mediterranee, you know how much your vacation costs before you go. Instead of after.
On an ordinary vacation, you pay for your room and meals and then every move you make is extra.
On a Club Mediterranee vacation, you pay just about the same price for your room and meals and virtually nothing else is extra.
Included at no extra cost is all the French and native cuisine you can eat at three meals a day. Plus all the free wine you can drink at lunch and dinner. You pay only for drinks at the bar.
And to work off all you've taken in, we give you free tennis. Free snorkeling. Free sailing. Free yoga. Free calisthenics. Free picnic excursions. A free private beach. Free scuba diving. Free water-skiing. And free deep sea fishing in Tahiti and Hawaii. What's more, with every sport, there's free equipment and a free group education from expert instructors.
The cost of Club Mediterranee doesn't go up when the sun goes down, either. There's after dinner dancing to a live band, native dancing, nightly cabaret and game shows, recorded classical music concerts along the beach and discotheques that stay open as long as you can stand up. All of which you can enjoy without ever having to dip into your wallet.
At Club Mediterranee, not only do we save you money in big chunks, we also save you money in small ones. At all Club Mediterranee vacation villages, tipping is prohibited. And transportation to and from local airports is free on Club Mediterranee group flights.
Flights leave regularly for Club Mediterranee vacation villages on Guadeloupe (Ft. Royal and Caravelle), Martinique, Mexico, Tahiti, Hawaii and Cape Skirring, Senegal in West Africa and our sixty other clubs around the world.
To find out more, contact your travel agent or fill out our coupon. We'll tell you everything else you won't have to pay for while you're on a Club Mediterranee vacation. Or after it's over.
CLUB MEDITERRANEE

38

38
Art Director Rob Lopes
Writer Larry Spector
Designer Rob Lopes
Artist Whistlin Dixie
Agency Levine, Huntley, Schmidt
Client Club Mediterranee

If I'm going to smoke,
I'm going to do it right.
Some people smoke a brand for its image.
I don't. You can't taste image.
I smoke for taste. I smoke Winston.
All Winston will ever give you is real taste.
And real pleasure. For some of us,
that's enough. Winston is for real.

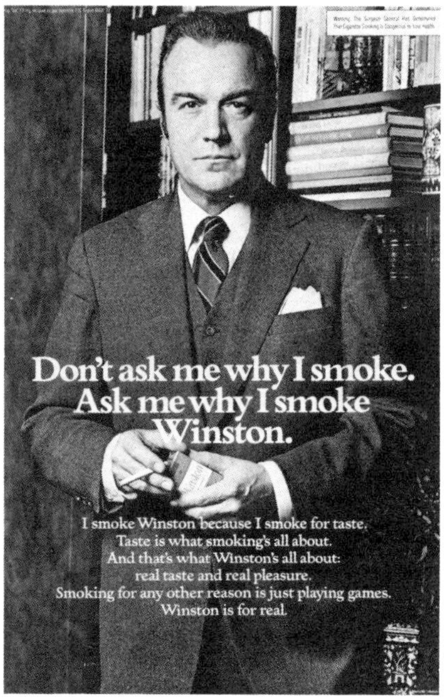
Don't ask me why I smoke.
Ask me why I smoke
Winston.
I smoke Winston because I smoke for taste.
Taste is what smoking's all about.
And that's what Winston's all about:
real taste and real pleasure.
Smoking for any other reason is just playing games.
Winston is for real.

19 mg. "tar," 1.2 mg. nicotine av. per cigarette, FTC Report MAR. '74.
Warning: The Surgeon General Has Determined
That Cigarette Smoking Is Dangerous to Your Health
If it wasn't for Winston,
I wouldn't smoke.
Winston
Taste isn't everything. It's the only thing.
I smoke for pleasure. That's spelled T-A-S-T-E.
That means Winston. Winston won't give you a new image.
All Winston will ever give me is taste.
A taste that's very real. If a cigarette isn't real,
it isn't anything. Winston is for real.

39

39
Art Director Jeffery Hill
Writers William Giles
Dana Blackmar III
Agency Dancer-Fitzgerald-Sample
Client R. J. Reynolds Tobacco Co.

Smart Parisiennes adore the creations of Christian Dior, like this beguiling black silk chiffon tea gown brilliantly patterned with gold metallic flowers, $398. Exclusively S.F.A., of course, Designer Collections.
SAKS FIFTH AVENUE
CELEBRATING FIFTY YEARS OF FASHION
30
VOGUE, September, 1974

SAKS FIFTH AVENUE
CELEBRATING FIFTY YEARS OF FASHION

SAKS FIFTH AVENUE
CELEBRATING FIFTY YEARS OF FASHION

40

40
Art Director Richard Martino
Writer Jerry Bennet
Designer Max Jordan
Artists Pedro Barrious
Jim Howard
Photographers Deborah Turbeville
Maureen Lambray
Arthur Elgort
Richard Blinkoff
Agency Saks Advertising Department
Client Saks Fifth Avenue

Live today. Tomorrow will cost more.
PAN AM.
The world's most experienced airline.

How can you think of a vacation abroad at a time like this?
PAN AM.

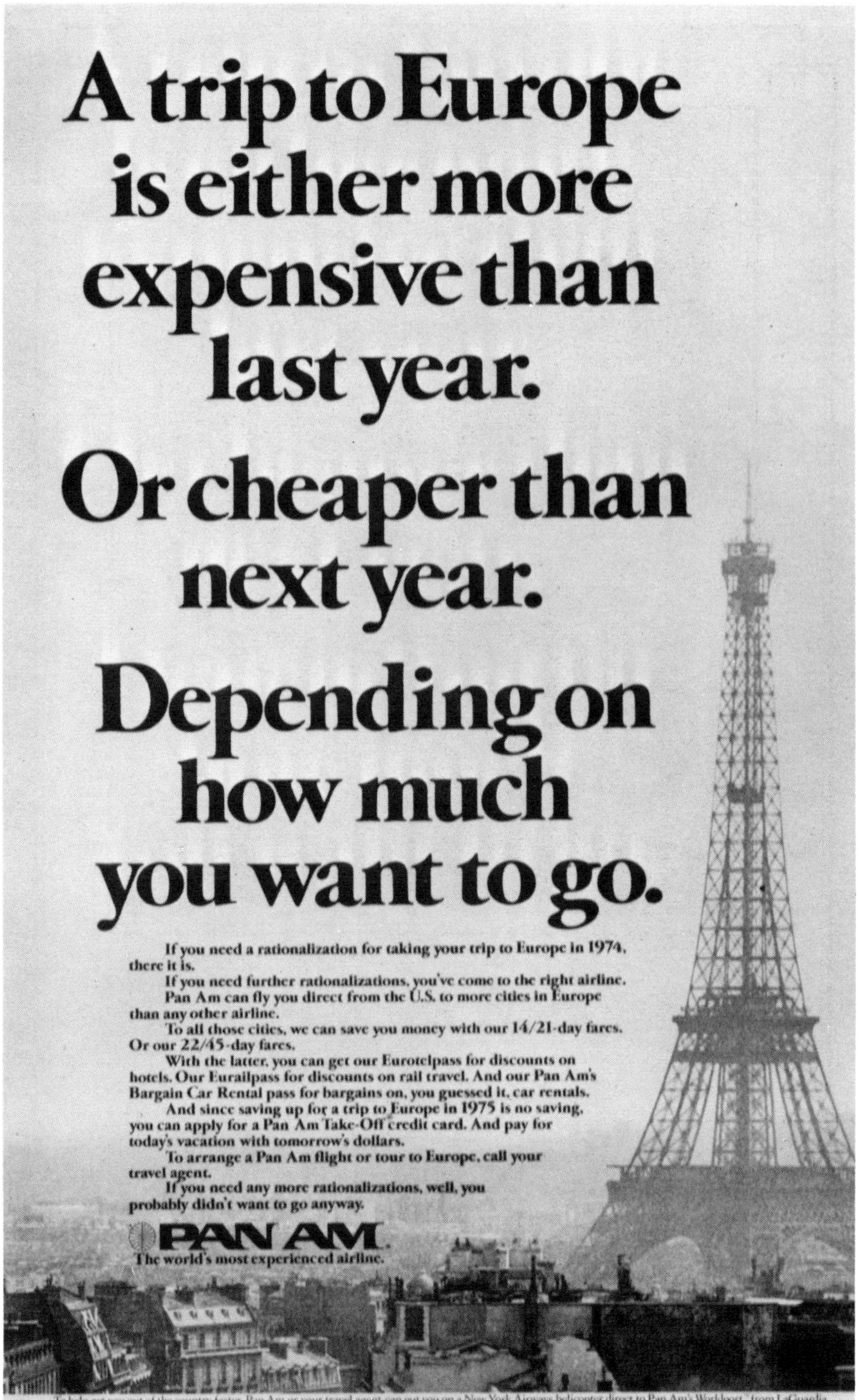
A trip to Europe is either more expensive than last year.
Or cheaper than next year.
Depending on how much you want to go.
If you need a rationalization for taking your trip to Europe in 1974, there it is.
If you need further rationalizations, you've come to the right airline.
Pan Am can fly you direct from the U.S. to more cities in Europe than any other airline.
To all those cities, we can save you money with our 14/21-day fares. Or our 22/45-day fares.
With the latter, you can get our Eurotelpass for discounts on hotels. Our Eurailpass for discounts on rail travel. And our Pan Am's Bargain Car Rental pass for bargains on, you guessed it, car rentals.
And since saving up for a trip to Europe in 1975 is no saving, you can apply for a Pan Am Take-Off credit card. And pay for today's vacation with tomorrow's dollars.
To arrange a Pan Am flight or tour to Europe, call your travel agent.
If you need any more rationalizations, well, you probably didn't want to go anyway.
PAN AM.
The world's most experienced airline.
To help get you out of the country faster, Pan Am or your travel agent can put you on a New York Airways helicopter direct to Pan Am's Worldport from LaGuardia, Newark, and Teterboro Airports, Wall Street and Morristown. See your travel agent or call Pan Am at 973-4000. Or visit one of our 10 convenient ticket offices. In New Jersey, MI 3 In Westchester, 472-6404. In Conn.: Bridgeport, 366-3843; Greenwich, 661-2154; Hartford, 249-9651; New Haven, 777-4716; Stamford, 348-2678.

41

41
Art Director John Danza
Writers Tom Messner
Jim Durfee
Agency Carl Ally
Client Pan American World Airways

Save $876,590.00, more or less.
The beads and the baubles.
Your great-grand-mother's jewelry.
Silver bowls, of course.
The gems and the jewels.
And the silver spoons.
There are sales, and there are sales.
Fortunoff, the source.

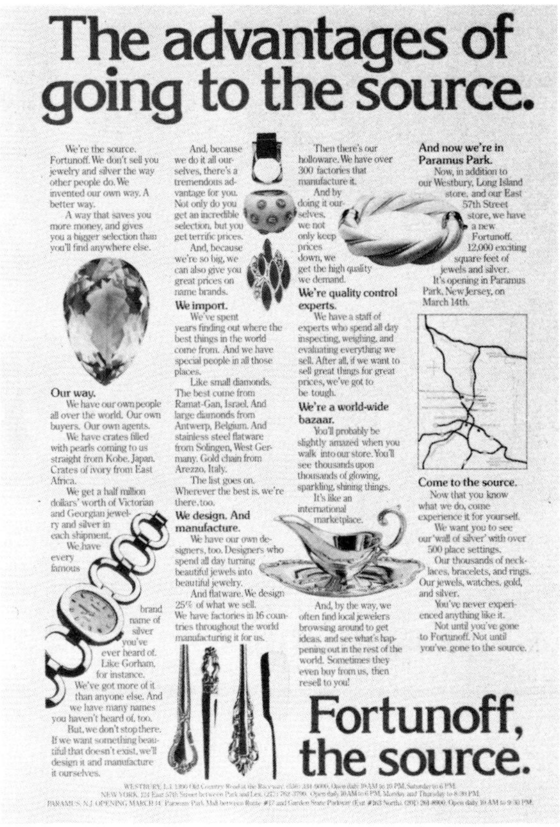
The advantages of going to the source.
Our way.
We import.
We design. And manufacture.
We're quality control experts.
We're a world-wide bazaar.
And now we're in Paramus Park.
Come to the source.
Fortunoff, the source.

Twenty-five gifts from the slightly unusual to the absolutely unheard of.
Fortunoff, the source.

42

42

Art Director Arnie Arlow
Writer Jennifer Berne
Designer James Clarke
Photographer Michael Harris
Agency Martin Landey, Arlow Advertising
Client Fortunoff

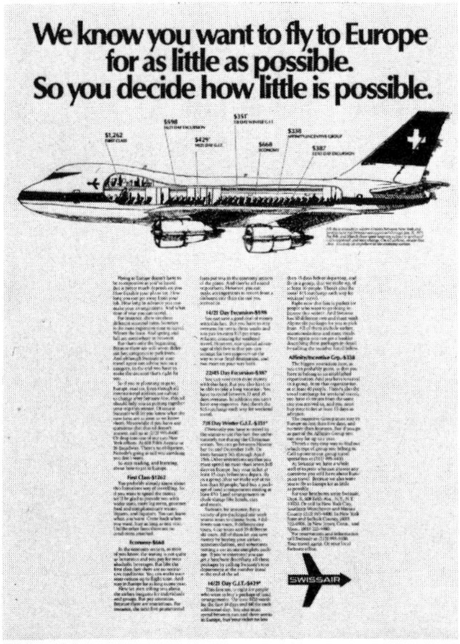
We know you want to fly to Europe for as little as possible.
So you decide how little is possible.
SWISSAIR

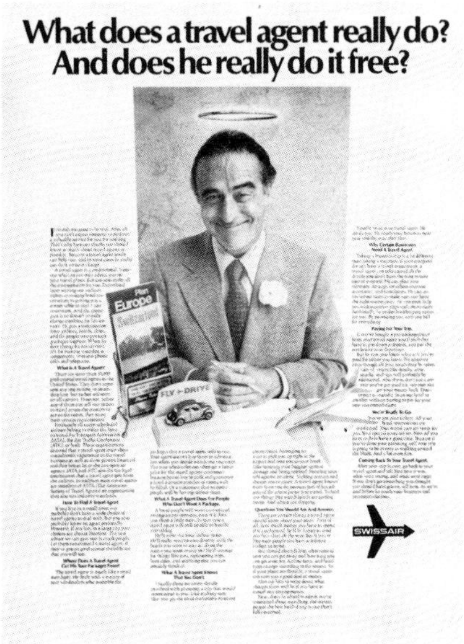
What does a travel agent really do?
And does he really do it free?
Europe
SWISSAIR

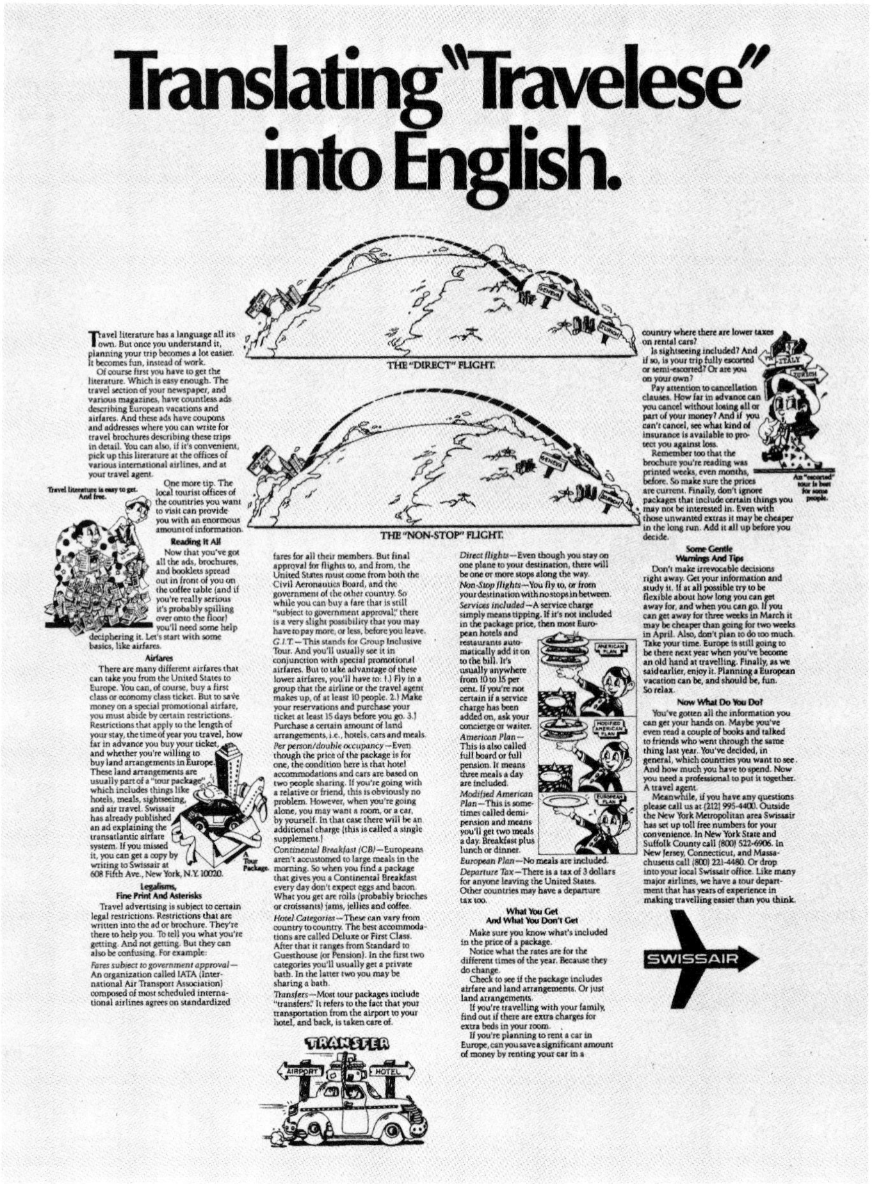
Translating "Travelese" into English.
THE "DIRECT" FLIGHT.
THE "NON-STOP" FLIGHT.
Travel literature has a language all its own. But once you understand it, planning your trip becomes a lot easier. It becomes fun, instead of work.
Of course first you have to get the literature. Which is easy enough. The travel section of your newspaper, and various magazines, have countless ads describing European vacations and airfares. And these ads have coupons and addresses where you can write for travel brochures describing these trips in detail. You can also, if it's convenient, pick up this literature at the offices of various international airlines, and at your travel agent.
One more tip. The local tourist offices of the countries you want to visit can provide you with an enormous amount of information.
Travel literature is easy to get. And free.
Reading It All
Now that you've got all the ads, brochures, and booklets spread out in front of you on the coffee table (and if you're really serious it's probably spilling over onto the floor) you'll need some help deciphering it. Let's start with some basics, like airfares.
Airfares
There are many different airfares that can take you from the United States to Europe. You can, of course, buy a first class or economy class ticket. But to save money on a special promotional airfare, you must abide by certain restrictions. Restrictions that apply to the length of your stay, the time of year you travel, how far in advance you buy your ticket, and whether you're willing to buy land arrangements in Europe. These land arrangements are usually part of a "tour package" which includes things like hotels, meals, sightseeing, and air travel. Swissair has already published an ad explaining the transatlantic airfare system. If you missed it, you can get a copy by writing to Swissair at 608 Fifth Ave., New York, N.Y. 10020.
A Tour Package.
Legalisms, Fine Print And Asterisks
Travel advertising is subject to certain legal restrictions. Restrictions that are written into the ad or brochure. They're there to help you. To tell you what you're getting. And not getting. But they can also be confusing. For example:
Fares subject to government approval—An organization called IATA (International Air Transport Association) composed of most scheduled international airlines agrees on standardized fares for all their members. But final approval for flights to, and from, the United States must come from both the Civil Aeronautics Board, and the government of the other country. So while you can buy a fare that is still "subject to government approval," there is a very slight possibility that you may have to pay more, or less, before you leave.
G.I.T.—This stands for Group Inclusive Tour. And you'll usually see it in conjunction with special promotional airfares. But to take advantage of these lower airfares, you'll have to: 1.) Fly in a group that the airline or the travel agent makes up, of at least 10 people. 2.) Make your reservations and purchase your ticket at least 15 days before you go. 3.) Purchase a certain amount of land arrangements, i.e., hotels, cars and meals.
Per person/double occupancy—Even though the price of the package is for one, the condition here is that hotel accommodations and cars are based on two people sharing. If you're going with a relative or friend, this is obviously no problem. However, when you're going alone, you may want a room, or a car, by yourself. In that case there will be an additional charge (this is called a single supplement.)
Continental Breakfast (CB)—Europeans aren't accustomed to large meals in the morning. So when you find a package that gives you a Continental Breakfast every day don't expect eggs and bacon. What you get are rolls (probably brioches or croissants) jams, jellies and coffee.
Hotel Categories—These can vary from country to country. The best accommodations are called Deluxe or First Class. After that it ranges from Standard to Guesthouse (or Pension). In the first two categories you'll usually get a private bath. In the latter two you may be sharing a bath.
Transfers—Most tour packages include "transfers." It refers to the fact that your transportation from the airport to your hotel, and back, is taken care of.
TRANSFER
AIRPORT
HOTEL
Direct flights—Even though you stay on one plane to your destination, there will be one or more stops along the way.
Non-Stop flights—You fly to, or from your destination with no stops in between.
Services included—A service charge simply means tipping. If it's not included in the package price, then most European hotels and restaurants automatically add it on to the bill. It's usually anywhere from 10 to 15 per cent. If you're not certain if a service charge has been added on, ask your concierge or waiter.
American Plan—This is also called full board or full pension. It means three meals a day are included.
Modified American Plan—This is sometimes called demi-pension and means you'll get two meals a day. Breakfast plus lunch or dinner.
AMERICAN PLAN
MODIFIED AMERICAN PLAN
EUROPEAN PLAN
European Plan—No meals are included.
Departure Tax—There is a tax of 3 dollars for anyone leaving the United States. Other countries may have a departure tax too.
What You Get And What You Don't Get
Make sure you know what's included in the price of a package.
Notice what the rates are for the different times of the year. Because they do change.
Check to see if the package includes airfare and land arrangements. Or just land arrangements.
If you're travelling with your family, find out if there are extra charges for extra beds in your room.
If you're planning to rent a car in Europe, can you save a significant amount of money by renting your car in a country where there are lower taxes on rental cars?
Is sightseeing included? And if so, is your trip fully escorted or semi-escorted? Or are you on your own?
Pay attention to cancellation clauses. How far in advance can you cancel without losing all or part of your money? And if you can't cancel, see what kind of insurance is available to protect you against loss.
Remember too that the brochure you're reading was printed weeks, even months, before. So make sure the prices are current. Finally, don't ignore packages that include certain things you may not be interested in. Even with those unwanted extras it may be cheaper in the long run. Add it all up before you decide.
ITALY
ZURICH
An "escorted" tour is best for some people.
Some Gentle Warnings And Tips
Don't make irrevocable decisions right away. Get your information and study it. If at all possible try to be flexible about how long you can get away for, and when you can go. If you can get away for three weeks in March it may be cheaper than going for two weeks in April. Also, don't plan to do too much. Take your time. Europe is still going to be there next year when you've become an old hand at travelling. Finally, as we said earlier, enjoy it. Planning a European vacation can be, and should be, fun. So relax.
Now What Do You Do?
You've gotten all the information you can get your hands on. Maybe you've even read a couple of books and talked to friends who went through the same thing last year. You've decided, in general, which countries you want to see. And how much you have to spend. Now you need a professional to put it together. A travel agent.
Meanwhile, if you have any questions please call us at (212) 995-4400. Outside the New York Metropolitan area Swissair has set up toll free numbers for your convenience. In New York State and Suffolk County call (800) 522-6906. In New Jersey, Connecticut, and Massachusetts call (800) 221-4480. Or drop into your local Swissair office. Like many major airlines, we have a tour department that has years of experience in making travelling easier than you think.
SWISSAIR

43

43
Art Director Howard Title
Writer Chuck Cohen
Designer Howard Title
Artists Push Pin Studios
Robert Dale
John Collier
Arton Assoc.
Photographer Carl Fischer
Agency Waring & LaRosa
Client Swissair

Smile, you tightwad.
Liquor in half gallons (and what a selection) has arrived at Surdyk's.
Surdyk's LIQUOR STORE
201 East Hennepin (One block off University Avenue) Minneapolis

They're the same until you open your wallet.
Theirs.
Ours.
Surdyk's LIQUOR STORE

Surdyk's presents 18 gift ideas you couldn't have done better on in 1959.
Surdyk's LIQUOR STORE

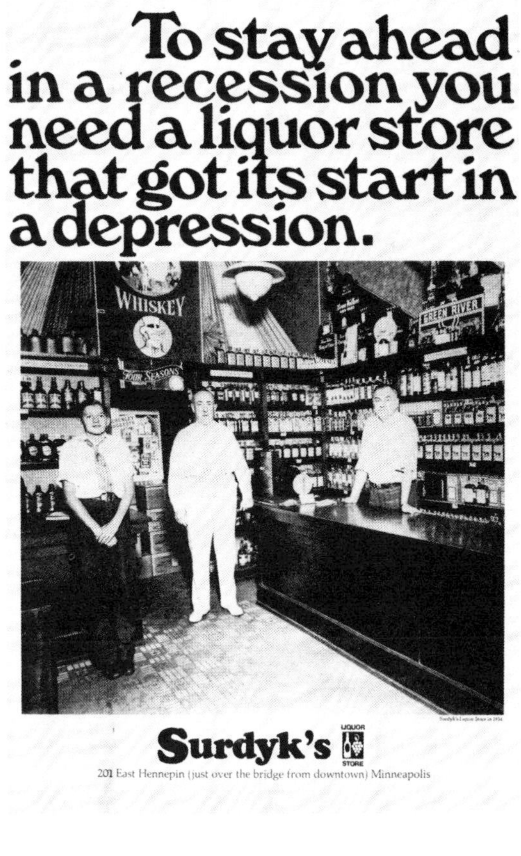
To stay ahead in a recession you need a liquor store that got its start in a depression.
Surdyk's LIQUOR STORE
201 East Hennepin (just over the bridge from downtown) Minneapolis

44

44
Art Directors Nancy Rice
Ron Anderson
Writer Tom McElligott
Designers Nancy Rice
Ron Anderson
Photographers Don Thoen
Bob Blanch
Don Getsug
Rick Dublin
Agency Knox Reeves Advertising
Client Surdyk's Liquor Store

Einstein's theory of relativity: Give strangers the same price you give your relatives.
$4.99 to $8.99
Starting now through Sat. April 12th, blood won't be thicker than water at The Carpet Department Stores.
We're giving you family prices. The prices we give our own family.
Example: Our short shag. The beefy new shag recommended by our Aunt Fanny's fanny.
She paid $4.99 a sq. yd. She saved plenty.
You'll pay $4.99 a sq. yd. You'll save plenty.
We can give you our velvety plush in Acrilan® acrylic for $5.99. Our trim office tweed for $5.99.
We can give you our soft Saxony for $6.99. We can give you our triple toned twist for $6.99.
Would you want to spend $7.99? We can give you our sculptured shag for $7.99. We can give you our sky (high) shag for $7.99.
Would you want to go to $8.99? Our tailored plush has been tailored to $8.99. Our antique marble has been chiseled to $8.99.
Even our $14.99 shag (its furry depth is the height of luxury) has come all the way down to only $8.99.
You may say to Einstein Moomjy: "You're giving me the same prices you give your relatives.
Okay, terrific.
But how do I know I'll love your carpets? How do I know I'll find what I want?
Your papa's posh plush could be my poison. It's all relative."
Ladies, you're right.
Maybe you'll think our wet look (it's only $8.99) is all wet. Maybe our warm bedroom carpet (it's only $8.49) will leave you cold.
Think nothing of it.
We've got hundreds more carpets in hundreds more colors to show you.
We've got hundreds more styles and piles and prices to show you.
We're The Carpet Department Store. We've got more of more for your floor.
Please drive us crazy until you find the carpet you want at Einstein Moomjy.
After all, our relatives have been driving us crazy for years at
Einstein Moomjy
The Carpet Department Store

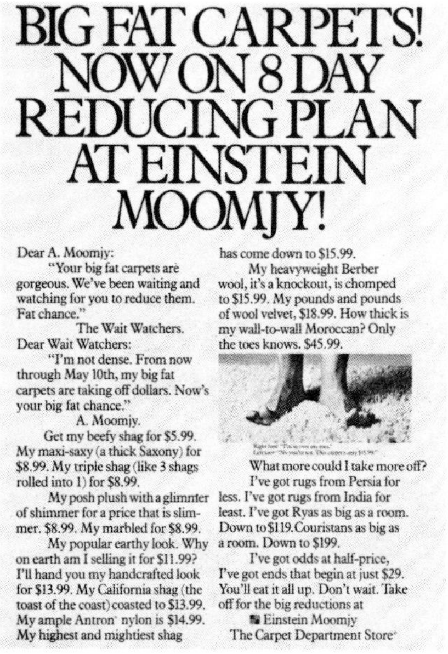
BIG FAT CARPETS! NOW ON 8 DAY REDUCING PLAN AT EINSTEIN MOOMJY!
Dear A. Moomjy:
"Your big fat carpets are gorgeous. We've been waiting and watching for you to reduce them. Fat chance."
The Wait Watchers.
Dear Wait Watchers:
"I'm not dense. From now through May 10th, my big fat carpets are taking off dollars. Now's your big fat chance."
A. Moomjy.
Get my beefy shag for $5.99. My maxi-saxy (a thick Saxony) for $8.99. My triple shag (like 3 shags rolled into 1) for $8.99.
My posh plush with a glimmer of shimmer for a price that is slimmer. $8.99. My marbled for $8.99.
My popular earthy look. Why on earth am I selling it for $11.99? I'll hand you my handcrafted look for $13.99. My California shag (the toast of the coast) coasted to $13.99. My ample Antron® nylon is $14.99. My highest and mightiest shag has come down to $15.99.
My heavyweight Berber wool, it's a knockout, is chomped to $15.99. My pounds and pounds of wool velvet, $18.99. How thick is my wall-to-wall Moroccan? Only the toes knows. $45.99.
What more could I take more off?
I've got rugs from Persia for less. I've got rugs from India for least. I've got Ryas as big as a room. Down to $119. Couristans as big as a room. Down to $199.
I've got odds at half-price, I've got ends that begin at just $29. You'll eat it all up. Don't wait. Take off for the big reductions at
Einstein Moomjy
The Carpet Department Store

45

Victory over de feet.
It's de Major General Moomjy carpet sale of de year. All soft on de feet, all soft on de finances, some as low as $5.99! De softest shags, shimmers, Saxonys, twists, velvets, Acrilan® acrylic plushes, marbles, earth tones, plaids, geometrics, Ryas, Couristans, customs, Orientals, odds, ends, all on sale now through Veterans Day. Fall in at
Einstein Moomjy
The Carpet Department Store

45
Art Directors Harvey Baron
Greg Weinschenker
Writer Carole Anne Fine
Designers Harvey Baron
Greg Weinschenker
Photographers Peter Papadopolous
Nick Samardge
Agency Baron, Costello & Fine
Client Einstein Moomjy

IT TAKES A LOT OF DUMMIES TO MAKE A CAR FOR PEOPLE WHO THINK.

By smashing Volvos into barriers with dummies inside, we've made them safer for people. These tests helped develop a front end which absorbs highway-speed impacts to protect the passenger compartment. And a three-point seat belt which can restrain 3½ tons of force.

By bouncing a dummy bottom on a seat for hours, we designed one to stay comfortable for years. But all our improvements aren't suggested by dummies. Some come from common sense.

All cars have head restraints. Volvo's have openings, so you can see behind you.

All cars have windshield wipers. But instead of shiny ones that glare, Volvo has dull black ones.

Volvo provides four wheel power-assisted disc brakes, steel-belted radial tires, fuel injection, new suspension that makes the car corner flatter and smoother. And a heating-circulation system that can freshen the air, warm your feet and defog the front windows all at once.

At Volvo, the smallest details get careful consideration. Which is why, all things considered, Volvo may well be the world's most carefully thought-out car.

It's not surprising then, that Volvo has a special appeal for people who think.

87% of the people who buy Volvos are college educated.

The other 13% must be just plain smart.

VOLVO
The car for people who think.

3
2
800-IJN

WHAT DO YOU DO WHEN YOU CAN'T AFFORD A VOLVO 164 OR A MERCEDES-BENZ?

The Volvo 164 and Mercedes are both lavishly endowed with the comforts and refinements people of means expect in a luxury car.

Unfortunately for some people, however, both cars are also endowed with stiff price tags.

Many of these people will find a consoling alternative in the Volvo 240. A car which shares many features with one, or both, of the higher priced cars.

For example, inside the Volvo 240, you sit on infinitely adjustable bucket seats. And while they may not be upholstered in leather like those in the Volvo 164, they do have adjustable lumbar supports for the small of your back.

The air around you is circulated by Volvo's 12-outlet heating and ventilation system. The glass around you is tinted. And kept clear by front, rear and front side window defoggers.

For performance and handling, there's fuel injection, 4-wheel power disc brakes, steel-belted radials and rack and pinion steering.

It's all standard on the Volvo 240. And if you want to exceed the standard, you can always add air conditioning, or power-assisted steering with automatic transmission.

If you think about it, all this luxury is enough to make you forget that in buying a Volvo 240, you're actually doing something very practical and down to earth.

Saving money.

VOLVO
The car for people who think.

177-EMO

A VOLVO DISCOVERY: RAIN FALLS ON REAR WINDOWS, TOO.

Volvo was the first wagon maker with the foresight to provide its rear window with a wiper and washer as standard equipment.

Volvo has also discovered that everyone doesn't buy a wagon to be fashionable. Many people buy wagons to carry things.

So we didn't design Volvo's cargo area low and sleek to accommodate a styling trend. We designed it high and practical, to accommodate things like a six-foot sofa and two chairs (with the rear seat down). Or three six-foot people and 12 two-suiters (with the rear seat up).

Volvo's rear area not only holds a lot, it comes with a lot. It has its own heating and ventilation vents, its own three-point seat belts, electric rear window defogger, carpeting, tinted glass and childproof door locks.

And Volvo's back door swings up out of your way, instead of out into your stomach. Or down into your knee caps.

It doesn't take a college degree to appreciate the thinking behind our wagon. So we leave you to consider this. If the rear end of your car isn't as well thought-out as Volvo's, what other part might not be?

VOLVO
The wagon for people who think.

RP-7902
VOLVO

46

46
Art Directors Robert Reitzfeld
Earl Cavanah
Writers Thomas J. Nathan
Edward A. McCabe
Larry Cadman
Photographer Henry Sandbank
Agency Scali, McCabe, Sloves
Client Volvo of America Corp.

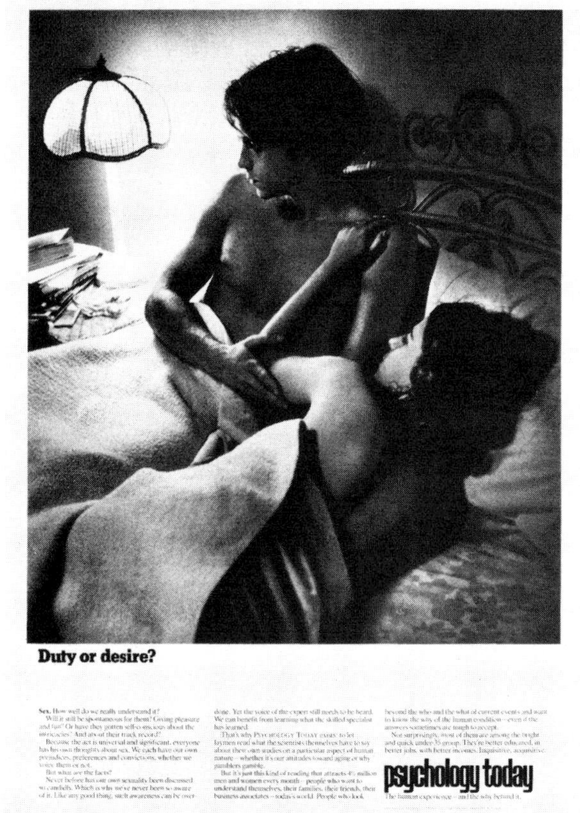
Duty or desire?
psychology today

Facade or feeling?
psychology today

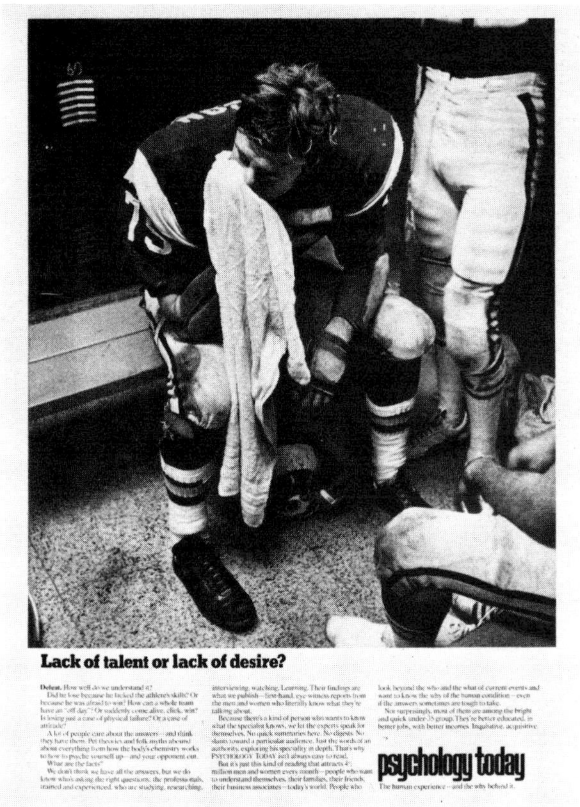
Lack of talent or lack of desire?
psychology today

Vent it or prevent it?
psychology today

47

47
Art Director Herb Stern
Writer Robin Jones
Designer Herb Stern
Photographers Mike Levins
Michael Rougier
Agency Ziff-Davis Publishing
Client Psychology Today

This is our most expensive number. The HP-810. Describing what it has that makes it sound so good requires technical talk. If you know the jargon, read on. Or you can simply listen to it, and hear what we mean.
The HP-810 has components like the acclaimed Dual 1211 changer which operates either automatically or manually. There's a magnetic stereo cartridge with a diamond stylus. And an anti-skating device, which lifts the arm automatically before it can leave a scratch.
And there's an amplifier powerful enough, so if you really want to, you can let all your neighbors know you have Sony's finest compact. Without even inviting them over.
The HP-810's FM tuner has a Field Effect Transistor (FET), which picks up weak signals, yet minimizes interference on strong ones.
Finally, with Sony's acoustic-suspension speakers, your ears hear what they're meant to hear. Low lows, high highs and everything in between.
The Sony HP-810. Our very best compact stereo. We don't know how to make it look better. Or sound better.
BEAUTY IS IN THE EAR OF THE BEHOLDER.
HP-810
SONY
Model HP-810 Compact Stereo System ©1975 Sony Corp. of America. SONY is a trademark of Sony Corp.
"IT'S A SONY."

48

48
Art Director Dom Marino
Writer Diane Till
Designer Dom Marino
Photographer Cosimo
Agency Doyle Dane Bernbach
Client Sony Corporation of America

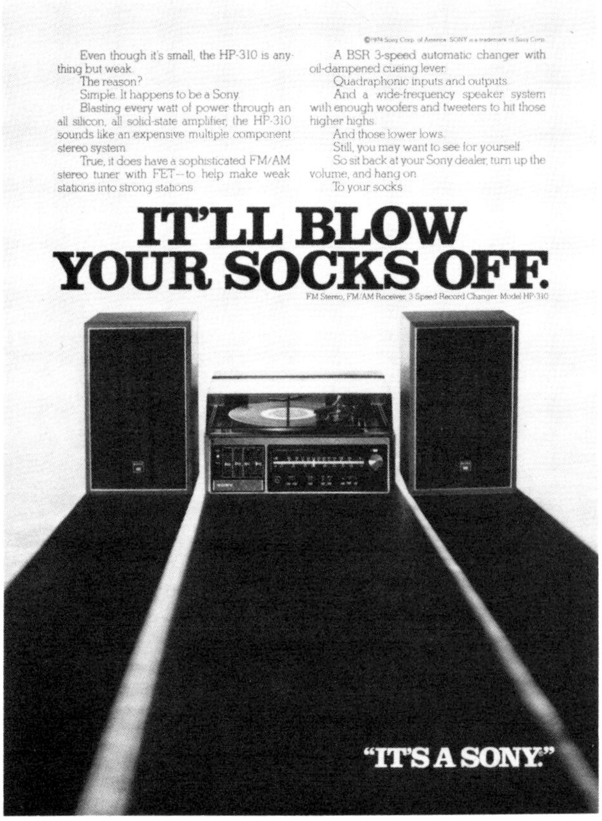
©1974 Sony Corp. of America. SONY is a trademark of Sony Corp.
Even though it's small, the HP-310 is anything but weak.
The reason?
Simple. It happens to be a Sony.
Blasting every watt of power through an all silicon, all solid-state amplifier, the HP-310 sounds like an expensive multiple component stereo system.
True, it does have a sophisticated FM/AM stereo tuner with FET—to help make weak stations into strong stations.
A BSR 3-speed automatic changer with oil-dampened cueing lever.
Quadraphonic inputs and outputs.
And a wide-frequency speaker system with enough woofers and tweeters to hit those higher highs.
And those lower lows.
Still, you may want to see for yourself.
So sit back at your Sony dealer, turn up the volume, and hang on.
To your socks.
IT'LL BLOW YOUR SOCKS OFF.
FM Stereo, FM/AM Receiver, 3-Speed Record Changer. Model HP-310
"IT'S A SONY."

49

Why the skin on certain parts of your body looks years younger than the skin on your face.
The most beautiful skin on your body hardly ever goes out in public.
Compare, for example, the skin on your face with the skin on the insides of your thighs.
Your face loses.
Yet when you were an infant, that skin looked and felt nearly the same. Years of exposure to harsh sunlight, drying wind, even grit and chemicals in the air, have left their mark.
Unfortunately, you can't undo the effects of time and nature. But you can compensate for them. By starting a program of 'Ultima' II Skim Milk Natural Skincare now.
Skim Milk Natural Skincare was created for the woman who wants to save her skin, but doesn't want to spend half her life doing it.
So we made it quick and easy. 'Skim Milk' is formulated with 100% fat-free milk protein. Nothing could be lighter. It goes to work instantly, conditioning, helping smooth out dry skin wrinkles.
There is no complicated ritual either. In just a few minutes a day, three little bottles can work wonders:
Skim Milk Lotion Cleanser cleans the skin without stripping away precious oils the way soap can. And it doesn't leave a film.
Skim Milk Toners purify and firm the skin by deep cleaning and tightening the pores. And make your skin feel more alive.
Skim Milk Moisturizer helps prevent moisture loss and provides a barrier of protective moisture between your skin and the elements.
To get the best results, use all three. Of course, you don't have to. Begin with just one or two. But do something. Soon.
Because nothing does less for your skin than nothing.
Skim Milk Natural Skincare
'ULTIMA' II / CHARLES REVSON

50

49
Art Director Reinhold Schwenk
Writer Robert Saxon
Designer Reinhold Schwenk
Photographer Henry Sandbank
Agency Doyle Dane Bernbach
Client Sony Corporation of America

50
Art Director Vincent Figliola
Writer Edward A. McCabe
Photographer Richard Avedon
Agency Scali, McCabe, Sloves
Client Revlon

Advertisement

DOLLARS AND SENSE

By Mike & Pat Cetta

	STEAK	POTATO	SALAD	TOTAL
PETER LUGER	10.50	1.65	1.75	13.90
GALLAGHERS	9.75	1.25	1.60	12.60
BROADWAY JOE	11.50			11.50
CHRIST CELLA	12.50		2.00	14.50
PALM	10.50	2.00	2.00	14.50
PEN & PENCIL	11.50	.95	1.95	14.40
SPARK'S	8.95			8.95

RAW FACTS

Wholesale Cost	What It Costs You
A raw baking potato costs 10¢	You pay up to $1.50
Yesterday's baked potatoes as today's hashbrowns	You pay up to $2.00
A whole case of lettuce costs $8.00 (24 heads make a hell of a lot of salads)	You pay $1.50 to $2.50
Quality shrimp cost about 25¢ each	You pay $3.75 to $4.00 for a shrimp cocktail
Scotch (1½ oz. Cutty or Dewars) 38¢	You pay $1.75 to $2.25
One portion of great real cream cheesecake costs 45¢	You pay up to $2.00
Great coffee costs 10¢ per person (if you use extra cream & sugar)	You pay 75¢ & up per person

Why do you pay $50 to $60 for two steaks before it's over?

Surely there is no mystery to tomatoes, potatoes, scotch, coffee or cheesecake; IT'S THE STEAK ISN'T IT?

Let's forget the dollars, maybe you're rich or maybe the company's paying for it. Let's talk about the sense.

Pat & Mike Cetta who are writing this ad or message, are professional meat men who are in the meat market themselves every day. We are owners and operators of a successful steak house (SPARKS STEAK HOUSE) for many years now.

We are going to make two simple statements.

ONE—The number of places that call themselves steak houses, that serve USDA PRIME, aged shell steaks exclusively could be counted on your right hand; and the number of fingers left over would horrify you. THAT'S RIGHT! You can count SPARKS STEAK HOUSE as #1 and the amount of fingers left over, (using just your right hand) is a disgrace.

TWO--Aging? Forget it. We know of no one who ages meat as long as we do. High prices are just high prices! They guarantee you *nothing!*

For those who refuse to believe that someone would sell the very best for half the price, while others are getting more and giving less quality for your dollars: DON'T COME TO SPARKS.

We are only interested in the real steak eater who knows or remembers what a great steak tastes like; not the person who is looking for just another restaurant to go to. Sparks is not an ordinary restaurant. SPARKS STEAK HOUSE is a legitimate steak house. We serve USDA PRIME, aged shell steaks exclusively—or filet mignon. We do not serve "other" things. Salad and potato is served with each steak.

We are always busy but come early before 7pm—or after 9pm there are tables—or come in between and have a drink at the bar. Relax and we will serve you the best steak you have ever eaten. Do make the effort because only then will you have something to judge all steak houses by, as to whether or not you have gotten USDA PRIME, aged shell steak or not. We are also open for lunch.

In today's unsettled meat market it is even more important than ever to be a professional with integrity who has been buying USDA PRIME exclusively.

This was proven recently in both the meat boycott and the meat shortage of August 1973. SPARKS STEAK HOUSE was the *only* steak house that served continuously and exclusively USDA PRIME, aged shell steaks and went into the New York Times stating it.

Pat and Mike Cetta whose family has been shopping in the New York wholesale meat markets for over half a century, will have no problem getting USDA PRIME for their customers now.

All the meat that we purchase at the market is brought directly to SPARKS STEAK HOUSE where it is aged, butchered and trimmed on the premises. The quality is maintained by us. We are not dependent on outside butchers, brokers etc.

We are equally proud of our staff—our waiters and waitresses who you will find a pleasant treat; our chefs who know how to cook rare, medium rare etc; our porters who know how to keep a place clean. Our bartenders are John and Ted.

The steak is USDA PRIME and aged. The owners are Pat & Mike Cetta who attest to the honesty and integrity of the above statement.

WE DON'T MIND BEING UNIQUE

Sparks Steak House
123 East 18 St.
(Between Park Ave. & Irving Place)
N.Y.C.—Gr 5-9696
No Reservation. No Credit Card.
Closed Sunday.

51

BY THE TIME VOLVO GETS OUT INTO THE WORLD, THE WORST IS OVER.

Before a Volvo ever so much as bumps bumpers with another car, we slammed dozens of Volvos into a concrete wall. These crash tests helped us develop a front end that's designed to absorb a fifty mile per hour barrier collision.

Before a Volvo will ever have to stop short on the highway, we disconnected a complete set of brakes on a fully-loaded Volvo and accelerated it to sixty miles per hour. It still stopped quickly, because every Volvo has *two* independent sets of three-wheel disc brakes. (If one should ever fail, the other still gives you about 80% of your braking power.)

Before you'll ever give'er the gas, we gave the Volvo engine the gas for the equivalent of 10,000 miles at continuous full throttle. It didn't quit.

Before you'll ever swerve to avoid a big bump, the Volvo had to complete 60,000 miles on our "life expectancy course": a special test track that combines more wrenching turns and suspension-numbing bumps than you'll probably ever face in a lifetime of driving.

And before you'll ever find yourself out in the middle of nowhere, almost every Volvo component that's subject to wear had to take at least three lifetimes of pounding, bumping and shaking on its own test rig.

So if you're looking for a car that can take the worst life has to offer, we can offer you something even better.

A car that can take the worst Volvo has to offer.

VOLVO

52

If President Nixon is kicked out of office, will he be eligible to collect unemployment insurance?

The answer, according to a gentleman in the Washington, D.C. Unemployment Bureau who prefers to remain nameless, is that Mr. Nixon would be disqualified for 10 weeks but then, for 24 weeks, he could collect $110 a week. (The highest in the nation, our friend points out.)

But the real question is, who would have the audacity to ask that question in the first place.

NEW TIMES Magazine, that's who. A brand new news magazine that's going to be, we can assure you, like nothing you've ever read.

First of all, there's our editorial policy. It's a two-word policy: Nothing's sacred. No individual. No institution. We told our prospective writers not to worry about who they might offend, just to go ahead and turn out the kind of magazine they've always said they'd love to write for.

With an offer like that, there weren't many writers who could refuse. As a result, in NEW TIMES you'll be reading the best group of writers ever gathered in one magazine at one time.

Jimmy Breslin, Joe McGinniss, Mike Royko, Sara Davidson, Larry L. King, Studs Terkel, Nicholas von Hoffman, Murray Kempton, Pete Hamill, Dick Schaap, J. Anthony Lukas, Jack Newfield, Joan Barthel, F. Reid Buckley, Marshall Frady, Brock Brower, Nora Sayre, Thomas Thompson.

Those are the names, the brightest stars in American journalism. They've written the bestsellers, they've won the Pulitzer Prizes, they're the best reporters and writers around.

There are also more than 100 other writers from all around the country on the NEW TIMES staff. They're young. You haven't heard of them. Yet. But we expect many of them will be among the next group of "best reporters and writers around."

NEW TIMES will be published every other week. Which means we won't cover the news in the traditional way, we won't summarize it or review it. Our writers will make sure that every time you read NEW TIMES you learn something you didn't know. They'll go out and dig up new news. And present it to you in words that jump off the page at you, words that are unexpected, revealing, full of insight. And irreverent.

For example, our look at the President as a potential candidate for unemployment. Or Texan Larry L. King's inside look at Texan John Connally: "Connally didn't smoke but he carried a cigarette lighter. He'd offer a light only to somebody who was very, very rich."

In short, NEW TIMES won't bore you. We'll avoid the obvious and focus instead on the stories and viewpoints you don't expect, the ones conventional journalists and conventional magazines never think of.

We'll cover whatever we know will interest you—politics, sports, consumerism, business, crime and the mob, labor, personalities, show business, art, architecture, science, medicine, daily living. There will be special newsletters that, in themselves, will be worth the price of admission. There will be articles dealing with issues of epic significance and pieces that stay light, because we're going to inform *and* entertain you.

It all starts October 19, with Volume 1, Number 1. We'd like to enroll you as a Charter Subscriber right now, with an offer that will do three things for you.

First, a Charter Subscription to NEW TIMES right now will save you money right now. NEW TIMES on the newsstand will cost 60¢ an issue, $15.60 a year (26 issues). The regular subscription price will be $12 a year. With this offer you get it for half the regular subscription price—just $6 a year.

Second, a Charter Subscription now will save you money later. You'll always get the lowest possible rate for yourself and on gift subscriptions you order.

And third, your Charter Subscription guarantees you Volume 1, Number 1—an issue we guarantee will quickly become a collector's item.

So fill in the coupon and mail it to us right away. Then you'll be eligible to collect the first news magazine to come along in 40 years. Right away.

NEW TIMES

The news magazine that's going to make news.

SPECIAL INTRODUCTORY CHARTER OFFER. SAVE $6.

Yes, I want to be a Charter Subscriber to NEW TIMES. Send me Volume 1, Number 1, plus 25 subsequent issues for only $6—half the regular subscription price of $12. I understand that, as a Charter Subscriber, I will receive the lowest possible prices on renewals and gift subscriptions and that I may cancel at any time, for any reason, and receive a full refund on any unmailed issues.

☐ PAYMENT ENCLOSED ☐ BILL ME LATER

6041

Name

Address

City State Zip

Mail to: New Times
P.O. Box 2948
Boulder, Colorado 80302

53

SILVER

51
Art Director Horace Minnar
Writers Mike Cetta
Pat Cetta
Designer Horace Minnar
Agency Minnar Advertising
Client Sparks Steak House

52
Art Director Earl Cavanah
Writer Scott Wadler
Agency Scali, McCabe, Sloves
Client Volvo of America Corp.

53
Art Director Bob Kuperman
Writer Dick Raboy
Designer Bob Kuperman
Agency Epstein, Raboy Advertising
Client New Times Communication Corp.

Why Only One Restaurant In The United States Is Named After A Subterranean European Fungus.

A truffle is a small, black, lumpy fungus. It looks like a walnut.

Because it grows underground around tree roots, it takes an experienced hunter, a shovel, and a trained pig or dog to find a truffle.

Because it grows underground around tree roots in France and Italy, a truffle also costs about $12 an ounce to buy.

None of which makes a truffle the most appealing thing you could put on a plate. That is, until you marinate it in champagne. Blanket it in pâte. Bake it in a puff-pastry shell. And serve it in a sauce périgourdine.

Ultimately turning the truffle into a totally unique, indescribably delicious food, a dish ranking as the epitome of fine gourmet fare.

It's the one delicacy no luxury restaurant would dare omit from its menu.

It's also the one standard only a very confident restaurant would dare name itself after.

Even The Best Truffles In The World Don't, By Themselves, Make The Best Dinner Menu In Chicago.

We serve the finest truffles obtainable. The ones from the Périgord region in France. And we serve them a variety of ways.

But a look at our menu will show you more. And it begins with the motto on the bottom.

"Prepare a few things perfectly."

Because that's exactly what we try to do.

The number of entrées is, therefore, limited. But the choice isn't.

There's Pheasant Souvarov.

A breast of pheasant prepared with a rich, hearty game stock, demi-glacé, and simmered vegetables. And then served with goose liver and sliced truffle garnish.

Or Tournedos Beaugency.

A prime filet en croûton, garnished and served with a delicate sauce Choron.

Or Fresh Trout Genèvoise.

A whole, deboned trout. Poached and served with a fine red wine and anchovy sauce.

Or Rack of Lamb Réforme. Scampi Provençale. Veal Sweetbreads aux Morilles. Médaillon of Veal. Roast Duckling.

All ready to be accompanied by Hors d'Oeuvres that include Truffle en Croûte Périgourdine, Imported Smoked Scottish Salmon, and a fluffy dumpling prepared with fresh pike and lobster called Quenelle of Pike. Soups that include Crab Bisque and Cream of Minted Peas. And desserts like Truffle Surprise, and three very exquisite soufflés.

Not a long menu.

But, a few things, prepared perfectly.

If You Can't Wait Until Dinner, You Don't Have To.

You can start right in with lunch. Because we do.

And choose from entrées that include exclusives like Filet of Striped Bass. And deliciously prepared things like Coq au Vin, Wiener Schnitzel, and Roast Rack of Lamb.

With salads like you've never seen before.

Like the Calcutta, prepared with fresh tossed greens, breast of chicken, and a delicate curry and chutney dressing.

Or the San Francisco, made with tiny bay shrimps and fresh tossed greens.

To give you a lunch you'll remember long after lunchtime.

A Sommelier Who Might Send You Home With The Label.

A prerequisite for any good wine steward seems to be a profound knowledge of fine wines and an equally profound sneer.

Our sommelier, Oswaldo Darnier, breaks that tradition.

He has a profound knowledge of fine domestic and European wines. He also has a profound knowledge of human nature.

He doesn't expect you to know as much about wines as he does. That's his job. Not yours.

So whether it's explaining what wine to accompany a Turbot Sautéed Naturale, explaining why a bottle or glass is shaped the way it is, or soaking the label from a bottle for your own future reference, Oswaldo is more help than he is "hauteur."

Some Of The People You'll Never See Are The Ones You'll Appreciate Most.

They include people like Chef Jacques Gassnier.

His assistant, Alain Trouboul.

And the Food and Beverage Director, Horst Schulze.

All people who have been in the business a long time.

People who are here because we know that, if we don't deliver what you expect the very first time, we won't see you a second.

You see, as a subterranean European fungus, truffles established a tradition among gourmets.

As a restaurant, we're committed to keeping that tradition.

Truffles

At the Hyatt Regency Chicago.
151 E. Wacker Drive. Telephone 565-1000.

54

5 M.P.H. BUMPERS ARE DESIGNED TO PROTECT CARS. 50 M.P.H. FRONT ENDS ARE DESIGNED TO PROTECT PEOPLE.

Before the Volvo you buy so much as taps bumpers with another car in a parking lot, we'll have slammed dozens of Volvos into reinforced concrete barriers.

We're sorry to report that this wasn't one of them.

But we're happy to report that the driver of this Volvo was able to go out and buy another one.

Note that behind the windshield, this Volvo has not been deformed.

That's because the front end is designed to absorb a 50 mph impact without passing it on to the passenger compartment.

And to protect the passengers even further, Volvo surrounds them with a steel cage. Six box-section steel pillars, strong enough to support six Volvos piled on top, are an integral part of every Volvo body.

A Volvo doesn't *have* to be built this strong.

It also didn't *have* to have a padded dashboard, three-point seat belts or dual independent braking systems back when we introduced them.

But it's the things a Volvo doesn't *have* to have, that make a Volvo worth having.

VOLVO

55

Why you should consider a Saab if you're looking at an Audi.

If you're thinking about buying an Audi 100 LS, you're making a reasonably good choice among automobiles. Because the Audi is reasonably well made, reasonably attractive, and offers a reasonable variety of features and gas economy for the money.

Which is precisely why you should also consider Saab. We're similar to Audi in many ways. Similar enough to be in the same class, but different enough to offer you things you can't find in the Audi.

It's these differences that you should know about

SAAB

before you spend your thousands of dollars on a car. Any car.

1. Our shape.

At Saab, we've always felt that form should follow function. So we developed the shape of the Saab 99 with the help of numerous wind tunnel tests. We know that aerodynamic testing and styling can do three important things for a car:

a. Improve gas mileage, since the engine doesn't have to work as hard.
b. Lower wind noise.
c. Give excellent stability in crosswinds.

Now, styling is a very subjective judgment, but we feel that the way our car looks, helps the way it works. And that in itself is very beautiful, indeed.

2. Smaller outside.
Just about as big (if not bigger) inside.

The table below compares the general dimensions of the Saab and Audi. As you can see, Saab is considerably smaller on the outside than the Audi. But on the inside, there are some surprises.

SAAB 99		AUDI 100	
Overall length	174.0″	Overall length	185.0″
Wheelbase	97.4″	Wheelbase	105.3″
Headroom, front	39.5″	Headroom, front	40.0″
Headroom, rear	38.5″	Headroom, rear	36.0″
Trunk space (by volume)	23.3 cu. ft.	Trunk space (by volume)	20.0 cu. ft.

a. The Saab has just about as much headroom in front as Audi. But more headroom in the rear.
b. The Saab has more trunk space than the Audi. (And that's even before you fold down the rear seat on Saab and find a little station wagon in back. A feature that Audi doesn't have.)

We think that once you sit in both a Saab and an Audi you'll find that in the other critical measurements Saab is just about the same as Audi.

3. Roll-cage construction.

Every Saab sedan is built with unitized steel body construction. The door sills are made of extra thick steel, the doors themselves are reinforced for extra strength and safety, and six steel pillars support the roof and protect you.

It's this kind of strong construction, with over 4,000 welds, that is engineered into every Saab to help make it strong, safe and dependable.

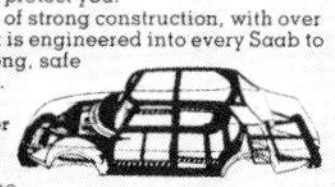

4. 4-wheel disc brakes (and other things you won't find in Audi).

Of course, the Audi has a lot of the same features that our Saab has. They both have front-wheel drive, for example, for excellent traction, control and handling on any kind of road surface.

They both have rack and pinion steering, for precise control on the curviest roads.

And they both have flow-thru ventilation and radial tires (standard).

But Audi doesn't give you power-assisted disc brakes on all four wheels. Saab does. Instead, Audi has disc brakes only on the front wheels, like many other cars.

We also give you tinted windows, fuel-injection, large 15 inch wheels, a heated driver's seat, and a fold-down rear seat, all standard.

5. More dealers than Audi.

There's no question about who has sold more cars in the U.S. up until now. Audi is ahead. And that tends to make a lot of people think that Saab just doesn't have the sales and service facilities necessary to handle a large volume of cars.

But Saab has more than 450 dealers nationwide. Which is more than Audi. More than Volvo. And more than any other car in our class.

To find the dealer nearest you, check the yellow pages.

6. Price.

Often the first—and final—decision on a new car is based on price. Saab and Audi are competitively priced. The P.O.E. price of the Saab 99LE two door with manual transmission, radial ply tires, and all other standard equipment is $4,698. The comparable model for Audi is the 100LS at $4,975.

7. The test drive is the test.

The real difference between two cars cannot be adequately judged until you have driven both cars. That's why we think everyone looking at an Audi is not being fair to themselves until they also test drive a Saab. We think that the fun of driving that you experience in a Saab will convince you that comfortable, safe, dependable, practical, economical transportation doesn't have to be dull.

We also think that no matter what other cars you may be considering, you'll be convinced to buy a Saab.

SAAB
It's what a car should be.

Price does not include dealer prep., taxes and optional equipment, if any.

56

54
Art Directors Hackenberg, Norman & Assoc. Creative Staff
Writers Hackenberg, Norman & Assoc. Creative Staff
Photographer Charles Smith
Agency Hackenberg, Norman & Assoc.
Client Hyatt Regency of Chicago

55
Art Director Robert Reitzfeld
Writer Thomas J. Nathan
Agency Scali, McCabe, Sloves
Client Volvo of America Corp.

56
Art Director Alan Torreano
Writer Michael Cox
Agency Cox & Co. Advertising
Client Saab-Scania of America

A child is someone who passes through your life, and then disappears into an adult.

Of all the people and things in your life, children are perhaps the best indicators of how quickly time passes.

All the clichés are true. They *do* grow up before your very eyes. They *are* little girls one moment, and college students the next.

And one day before you know it, your child becomes someone different, a full-fledged person with a life and a future all her own.

Nobody can slow the process down for you. But we can help make sure her future will be a secure one.

At Metropolitan Life, we've spent over a century helping people prepare for the future. Helping them prepare for college and a career and anything else that might arise. And we can do the same for your child as well.

Of course, nobody can say exactly what *will* happen in the future. But whatever does, it's nice to know your child will be ready for it.

Metropolitan Life
Where the future is now

57

57
Art Director Bob Engel
Writer Tom Thomas
Photographer Bert Stern
Agency Young & Rubicam International
Client Metropolitan Life Insurance Co.

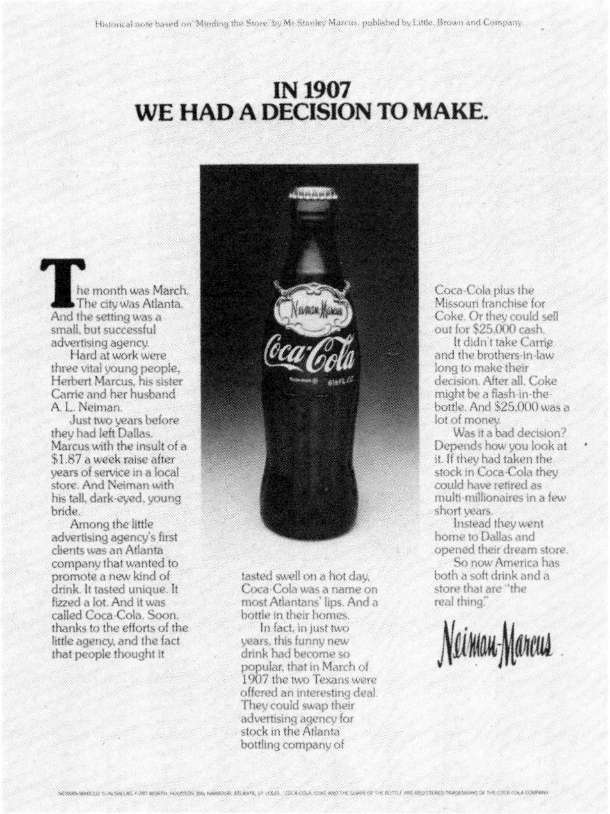
Historical note based on "Minding the Store" by Mr. Stanley Marcus, published by Little, Brown and Company.
IN 1907
WE HAD A DECISION TO MAKE.
The month was March. The city was Atlanta. And the setting was a small, but successful advertising agency.
Hard at work were three vital young people, Herbert Marcus, his sister Carrie and her husband A. L. Neiman.
Just two years before they had left Dallas. Marcus with the insult of a $1.87 a week raise after years of service in a local store. And Neiman with his tall, dark-eyed, young bride.
Among the little advertising agency's first clients was an Atlanta company that wanted to promote a new kind of drink. It tasted unique. It fizzed a lot. And it was called Coca-Cola. Soon, thanks to the efforts of the little agency, and the fact that people thought it
tasted swell on a hot day, Coca-Cola was a name on most Atlantans' lips. And a bottle in their homes.
In fact, in just two years, this funny new drink had become so popular, that in March of 1907 the two Texans were offered an interesting deal. They could swap their advertising agency for stock in the Atlanta bottling company of
Coca-Cola plus the Missouri franchise for Coke. Or they could sell out for $25,000 cash.
It didn't take Carrie and the brothers-in-law long to make their decision. After all, Coke might be a flash-in-the-bottle. And $25,000 was a lot of money.
Was it a bad decision? Depends how you look at it. If they had taken the stock in Coca-Cola they could have retired as multi-millionaires in a few short years.
Instead they went home to Dallas and opened their dream store.
So now America has both a soft drink and a store that are "the real thing."
Neiman-Marcus
Neiman-Marcus
Coca-Cola

58

I lost half of myself without taking diet pills.
By Donna Walker — as told to Ruth L. McCarthy
When I was 66 inches around, and 65 inches tall, even my favorite fat lady's store had a problem. I know, because at 278 pounds I wore the largest bloomers they had. And that's the only word for them — bloomers — even though I'm of the generation that usually refers to ladies' panties as briefs.
Fact is, the thought of having nothing to wear made me so panicky, I said to myself: "This is it! You've got to lose weight, Donna." Not that I was unaware of my size before. There were too many embarrassing reminders in my life for me to ignore my weight. For instance, at my fullest figure, I fit so snugly into a tub that the water was dammed up behind me when I pulled the plug out in front of me. And when I stood up in a shower stall, I couldn't even bend over to pick up a bar of soap. I was trapped by my appetite.
As for dresses, I had one — to go to work in. I washed it every night and every day for one whole year because it was the only dress that fit.
I think I ought to mention that chocolate and sweets were my undoing. But ironically, candy is what really helped me lose weight. Ayds* Reducing Plan Candy. I'd read ads about it in magazines and when I learned that Ayds contains vitamins and minerals, but no drugs, I thought maybe, at last, I'd found what I needed. I knew from past experience that diet pills, weekly reducing sessions and even a psychiatrist were not the answer for me. I needed something to help curb my appetite and my eternal craving for sweets.
So, I bought a box of chocolate fudge Ayds at the drug store and started on the plan in the fall. I took one or two Ayds about 15 minutes before each meal with a hot drink and it really helped me cut down on what I ate. And I ate regular meals, nothing special.
Right from the start, I had such a positive feeling about the Ayds plan, I took on a $50 bet from my friend's husband. He'd heard me talk about
When I weighed 278 pounds, my friends called me a Floating Island. See why?
Now I'm 136 pounds, my friends in West Hartford, Conn., hardly recognize me.
losing weight for 10 years, but never saw me do anything about it. So he figured it was going to be an easy win. Was he wrong! In the end, he had to pay up, because the weight came off.
Nobody really noticed it until I'd lost more than 50 pounds. You see, I hadn't bought any new clothes, so I was hidden under a lot of baggy pants and sacky tops. Then at Easter, when I'd taken off 78 pounds on the Ayds plan, I turned out in a new lavender pantsuit and everybody was amazed. I was thrilled, and more determined than ever to stick to the Ayds plan.
I guess, though, we never see ourselves as others do. Let me tell you about a remark my nephew made while I was still losing weight. He'd seen me at his sister's wedding, wearing a size 52 beige tent. Months after I'd been on the Ayds plan, I appeared at his wedding in a size 18 dress. He was so shocked, he said: "What were you wearing the last time I saw you — your beige Volkswagen?" Funny. I knew I was fat, but not that fat.
How long did it take me to lose 142 pounds on the Ayds plan? Just about a year, and now I can do things I never could before. For the first time, believe it or not, I can cross my legs — like a lady. I can also see all of me in a mirror. And I can even climb up a pool ladder without fear of breaking it.
On the serious side, my teenage nieces and nephews are now proud to introduce me as their aunt. In fact, everybody is a lot happier with me, now that I'm only 37½ inches around. Which makes me forever grateful for the Ayds plan.
BEFORE AND AFTER MEASUREMENTS
Before After
Height 5'5" 5'5"
Weight 278 lbs. 136 lbs.
Bust 49" 35¾"
Waist 45" 27"
Hips 66" 37½"
Dress 52 12

59

Xerox introduces nothing.
You'll find that nothing on the back of most every copy.
And most every Xerox copier and duplicator can copy something on that nothing.
Just turn over your copies and run them through again.
That nothing can save you paper.
That nothing can save you filing space.
That nothing can save you mailing costs.
Who ever thought nothing would be so valuable?
XEROX

60

58
Art Directors Alan Goodman
David Sillen
Writer Joyce Fabian
Designer Alan Goodman
Artist Alan Goodman
Photographer Charles Gold
Agency Leber Katz Partners
Client Neiman Marcus

59
Art Director Charley Aromando
Writer Ruth L. McCarthy
Designer Charley Aromando
Photographer Irwin Cohn
Agency Wilson Haight & Welch
Client Campana Corp.

60
Art Director Jeff Cohen
Writers Allen Kay
Roger Levinsohn
Photographer Stephen Steigman
Agency Needham, Harper & Steers
Client Xerox Corp.

Some of the most unusual things about a Volkswagen are things you don't usually see.
Look under the fender of a Volkswagen and you'll find something you wouldn't dream of finding: paint.
We use 13 lbs. of it on every VW. And in the most unlikely places. (If you have nothing to do sometime, remove one of our inside door panels and see what's underneath.)
Under the chassis of a Volkswagen you'll find something only a handful of cars in the world have: a sealed steel bottom. This protects all those vital things inside the car from all those vile things out there on the road. (Look under your car and you'll see how exposed and vulnerable everything is.)
See those four wheels sticking up in the air in the picture below? Well, you can press down on any one of them and move it without any of the others moving. What this means is when the car is right side up and one wheel hits a bump, none of the other wheels feel a thing.
Now, consider that you get all these luxury car features (and more) at an economy car price . . . with economy car gas mileage . . . the most advanced car coverage in the world (Owner's Security Blanket) . . . and almost unbelievable resale value (a '72 VW retails' for as much today as it did new).
You couldn't find a better buy if you stood on your head.
Still $2625*

61

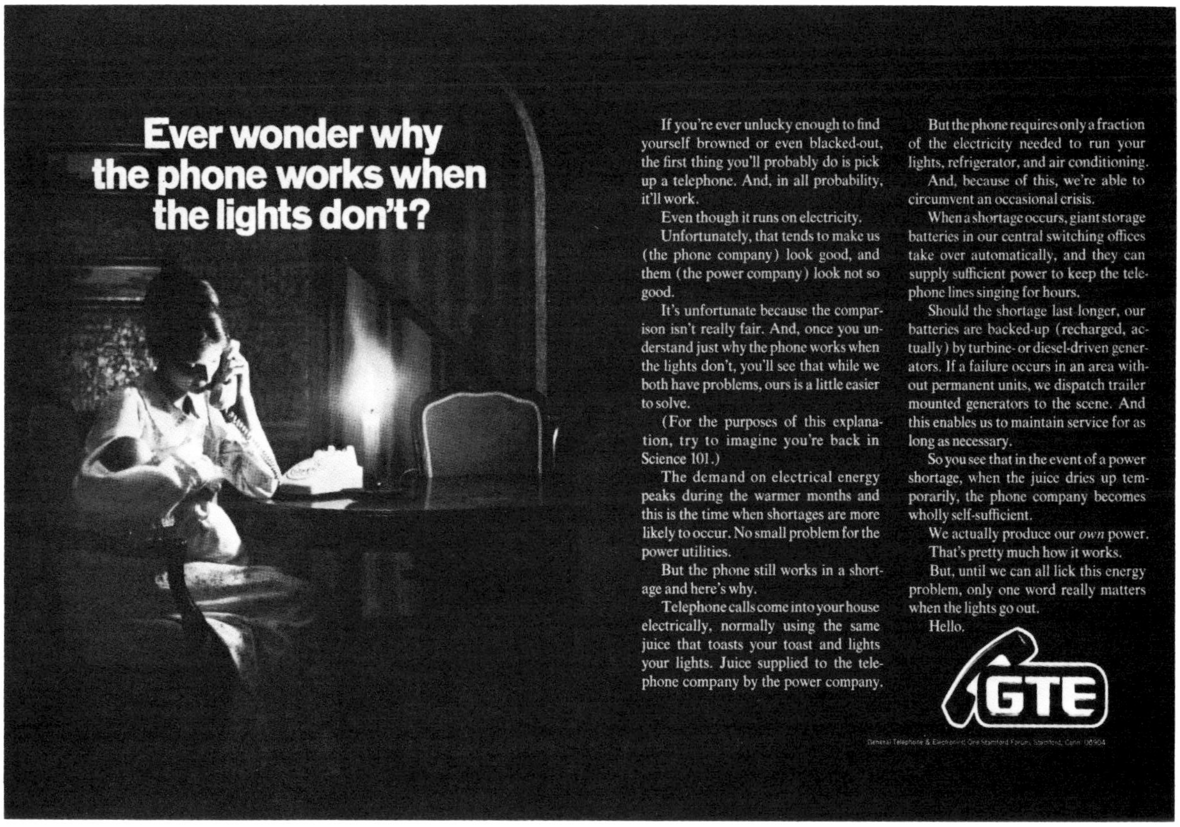
Ever wonder why the phone works when the lights don't?
If you're ever unlucky enough to find yourself browned or even blacked-out, the first thing you'll probably do is pick up a telephone. And, in all probability, it'll work.
Even though it runs on electricity.
Unfortunately, that tends to make us (the phone company) look good, and them (the power company) look not so good.
It's unfortunate because the comparison isn't really fair. And, once you understand just why the phone works when the lights don't, you'll see that while we both have problems, ours is a little easier to solve.
(For the purposes of this explanation, try to imagine you're back in Science 101.)
The demand on electrical energy peaks during the warmer months and this is the time when shortages are more likely to occur. No small problem for the power utilities.
But the phone still works in a shortage and here's why.
Telephone calls come into your house electrically, normally using the same juice that toasts your toast and lights your lights. Juice supplied to the telephone company by the power company.
But the phone requires only a fraction of the electricity needed to run your lights, refrigerator, and air conditioning.
And, because of this, we're able to circumvent an occasional crisis.
When a shortage occurs, giant storage batteries in our central switching offices take over automatically, and they can supply sufficient power to keep the telephone lines singing for hours.
Should the shortage last longer, our batteries are backed-up (recharged, actually) by turbine- or diesel-driven generators. If a failure occurs in an area without permanent units, we dispatch trailer mounted generators to the scene. And this enables us to maintain service for as long as necessary.
So you see that in the event of a power shortage, when the juice dries up temporarily, the phone company becomes wholly self-sufficient.
We actually produce our *own* power.
That's pretty much how it works.
But, until we can all lick this energy problem, only one word really matters when the lights go out.
Hello.
GTE

62

61
Art Director Charles Piccirillo
Writer Mike Mangano
Photographer David Langley
Agency Doyle Dane Bernbach
Client Volkswagen of America Corp.

62
Art Director Paul Jones
Writer Ted Bell
Designer Paul Jones
Photographer Tony Petrucelli
Agency Doyle Dane Bernbach
Client GTE

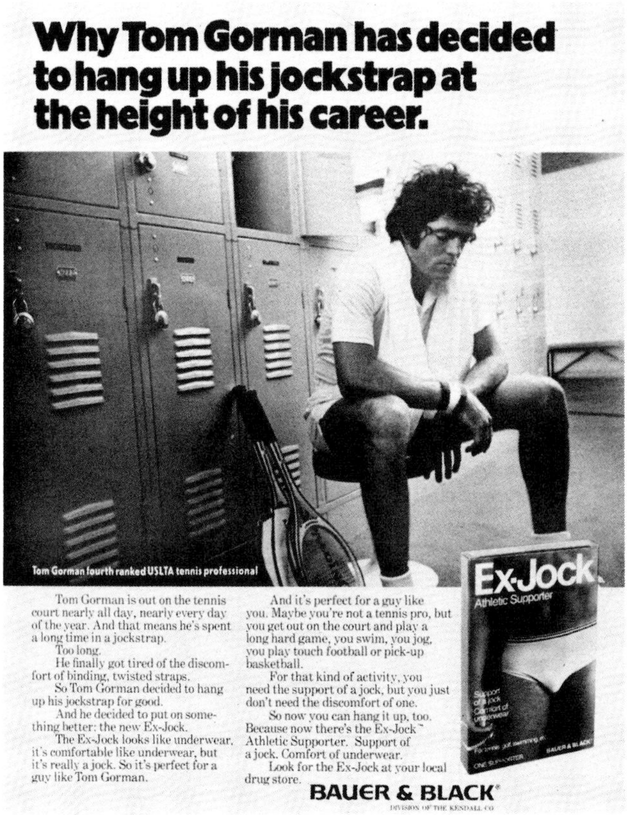
Why Tom Gorman has decided to hang up his jockstrap at the height of his career.
Tom Gorman fourth ranked USLTA tennis professional
Tom Gorman is out on the tennis court nearly all day, nearly every day of the year. And that means he's spent a long time in a jockstrap.
Too long.
He finally got tired of the discomfort of binding, twisted straps.
So Tom Gorman decided to hang up his jockstrap for good.
And he decided to put on something better: the new Ex-Jock.
The Ex-Jock looks like underwear, it's comfortable like underwear, but it's really a jock. So it's perfect for a guy like Tom Gorman.
And it's perfect for a guy like you. Maybe you're not a tennis pro, but you get out on the court and play a long hard game, you swim, you jog, you play touch football or pick-up basketball.
For that kind of activity, you need the support of a jock, but you just don't need the discomfort of one.
So now you can hang it up, too. Because now there's the Ex-Jock™ Athletic Supporter. Support of a jock. Comfort of underwear.
Look for the Ex-Jock at your local drug store.
Ex-Jock
Athletic Supporter
BAUER & BLACK®
DIVISION OF THE KENDALL CO

63

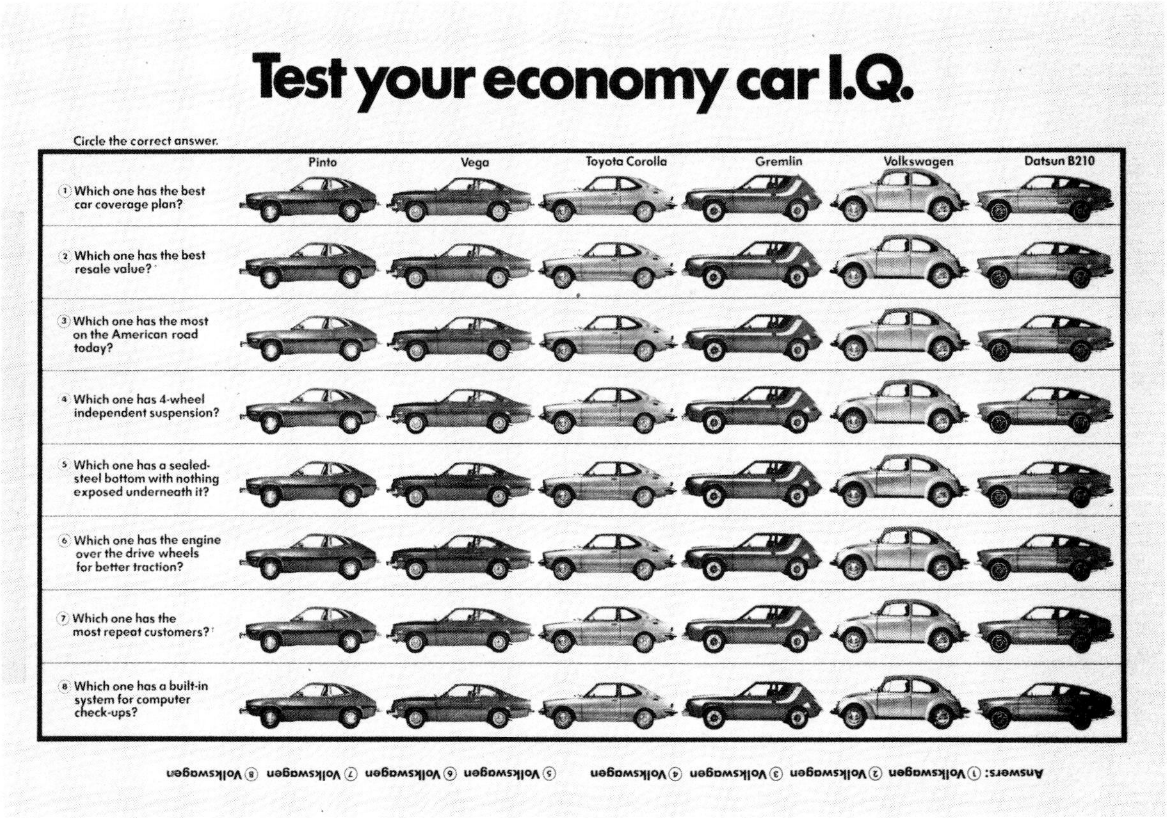
Test your economy car I.Q.
Circle the correct answer.
Pinto
Vega
Toyota Corolla
Gremlin
Volkswagen
Datsun B210
1 Which one has the best car coverage plan?
2 Which one has the best resale value?
3 Which one has the most on the American road today?
4 Which one has 4-wheel independent suspension?
5 Which one has a sealed-steel bottom with nothing exposed underneath it?
6 Which one has the engine over the drive wheels for better traction?
7 Which one has the most repeat customers?
8 Which one has a built-in system for computer check-ups?
Answers: 1 Volkswagen 2 Volkswagen 3 Volkswagen 4 Volkswagen 5 Volkswagen 6 Volkswagen 7 Volkswagen 8 Volkswagen

64

63
Art Director Ralph Moxcey
Writers Scott Miller
Tom Turner
Designer Ralph Moxcey
Agency Humphrey Browning MacDougall
Client Bauer & Black

64
Art Director Steve Graff
Writer Deanna Cohen
Designer Steve Graff
Photographer Ken Duskin
Agency Doyle Dane Bernbach
Client Volkswagen of America Corp.

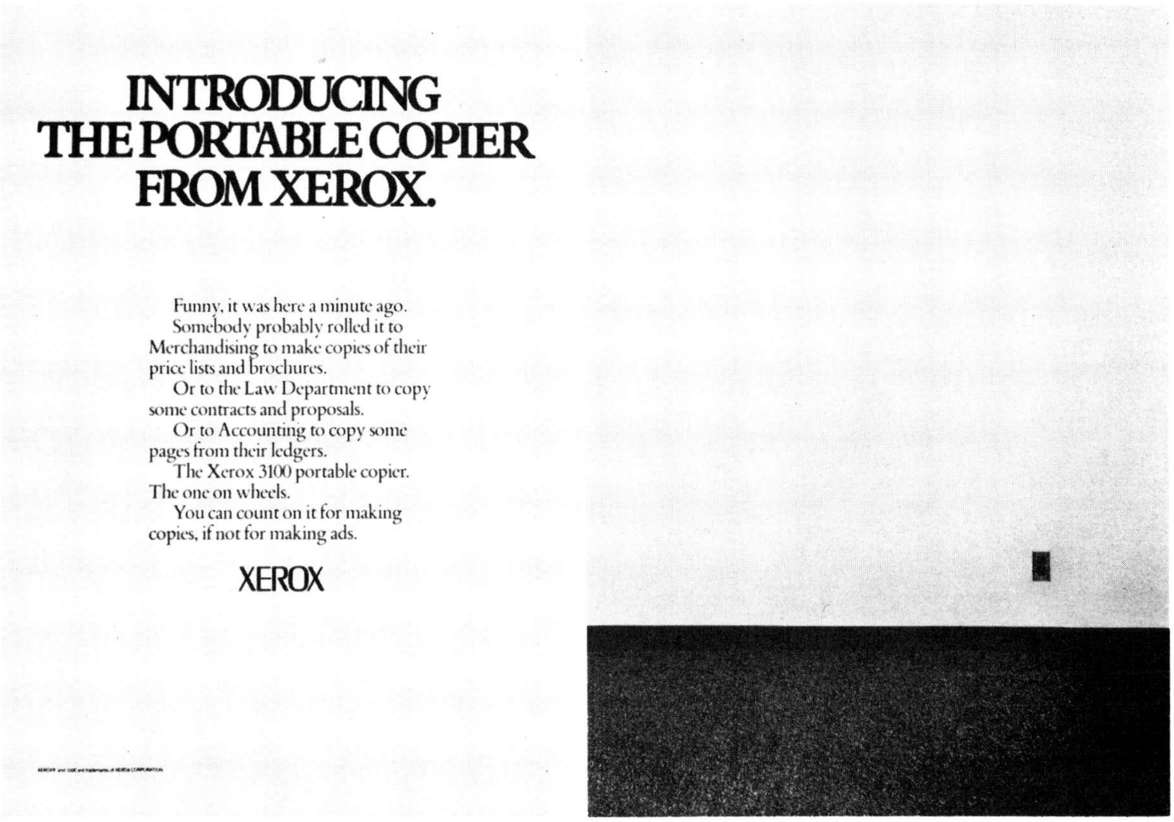
INTRODUCING
THE PORTABLE COPIER
FROM XEROX.
Funny, it was here a minute ago.
Somebody probably rolled it to Merchandising to make copies of their price lists and brochures.
Or to the Law Department to copy some contracts and proposals.
Or to Accounting to copy some pages from their ledgers.
The Xerox 3100 portable copier. The one on wheels.
You can count on it for making copies, if not for making ads.
XEROX

65

This is an ad about funerals.
The fact you don't want to read it
is exactly why you should.
Start talking about funerals and you usually find that most people don't want to talk about it.
Which is quite natural, because most people don't want to think about their dying.
It's also a mistake, because the facts are that you'll probably take part in the planning of funerals a number of times in your lifetime. For a loved one. A relative. A close friend. Or a business associate.
And knowing more about funerals now—ahead of time—can only help when the time of need comes.
Help before you need it
Helping people is what our business is all about. And anytime you find it convenient, we'd be pleased to discuss with you all that a funeral director can, and will, do for you.
Or if you prefer, we'd be happy to send you our 24-page booklet: "Knowledge About Funerals." It covers the facts, figures, and features of funerals. Things like the detail work involved, how to select a casket, considerations about vaults, church or funeral establishment facilities, cemetery arrangements, and a wide array of other information.
We think it will answer a lot of your questions. Help you plan any funeral exactly as you want it. At the price you want to pay for it. And the booklet is yours for the asking. Simply call, or stop by.
Help when you really need it
For nearly four decades, we at Darling & Fischer have been helping people through the troubled time of funerals.
With compassion, understanding, and professionalism.
We offer you a choice of four chapels: The Garden Chapel in San Jose, Memorial Chapel in Campbell, Chapel of the Hills in Los Gatos, and Los Gatos Memorial Park. A choice of services, with numerous features for your consideration. And you can make both cemetery and mortuary arrangements with us, too. (Few other funeral directors offer all this convenience.)
And we itemize the cost of all of our services. So you'll know what you're paying for. Before you pay for it.
A final note
Arranging for a funeral will always be one of the most difficult and painful experiences of your life. We can only try to make it a little less so.
That has been our dedication here in Santa Clara County, since 1935.
And it always will be.
Darling-Fischer Mortuaries.
Los Gatos Memorial Park. Phone 998-2226.
Darling-Fischer

66

65
Art Director Allen Kay
Writer Lois Korey
Photographer George Ehrlich
Agency Needham, Harper & Steers
Client Xerox Corp.

66
Art Director Charles Fillhardt
Writer Curtis Wright
Designer Charles Fillhardt
Photographer Charles Fillhardt
Agency Bergthold, Fillhardt, & Wright
Client Darling-Fischer Mortuaries

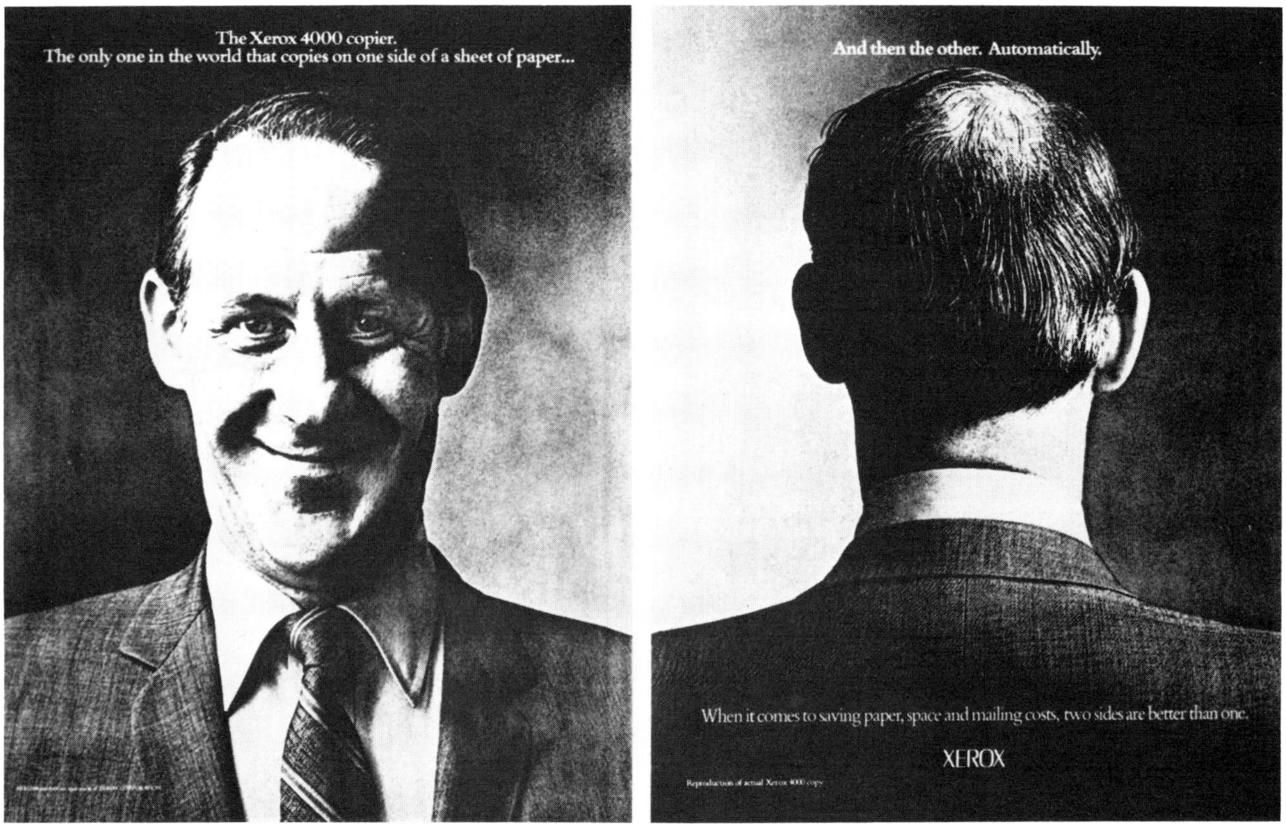
The Xerox 4000 copier.
The only one in the world that copies on one side of a sheet of paper...
And then the other. Automatically.
When it comes to saving paper, space and mailing costs, two sides are better than one.
XEROX
Reproduction of actual Xerox 4000 copy

67

THE BIG CAR EXPERTS.
SMALL
It's not that easy.
The people who've been bringing millions of big cars into the world for years and years aren't doing too much bragging about their big cars these days.
They've taken up another cry. Today they're "the small car experts."
For us at Fiat, small car expertise came not as painlessly or as suddenly. We've been making small cars for 70 years.
The difference between our slow evolution and their instant knowledge is obvious in the cars we make.
The Fiat 124 has almost a foot more legroom than a Maverick, a Nova, a Mustang II, and a Capri.
A small car shouldn't be a big car made smaller.
It even has more legroom than an Eldorado, an Imperial, and a Continental.*
The 124 isn't low and sleek like some of Detroit's small cars. Instead it gives you more headroom than a Rolls Royce.*
This height, plus exceptionally large windows, keeps you from the claustrophobia those sleek small cars are becoming famous for.
The backseat of the 124 isn't the typical small car backseat. There's enough room in the back for two people 6'6" without their knees being up around their chins. And the trunk will hold 7 pieces of luggage for those full-sized people.
Unlike many small cars, the 124 isn't underpowered. It'll cruise faster than you'd normally care to go.
It corners flat and steers precisely. (Which is unique even in Detroit's big cars.) Of course, we did learn a few things from the big car boys. Our 124 comes with automatic transmission and air conditioning.
Now it's their turn to learn a few things from us.
Most people who make small cars really want to sell you something else.
FIAT
The biggest selling car in Europe.
Overseas delivery arranged through your dealer.

68

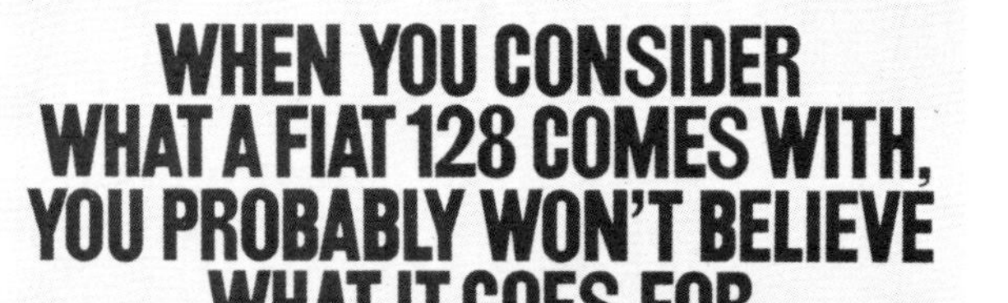
WHEN YOU CONSIDER WHAT A FIAT 128 COMES WITH, YOU PROBABLY WON'T BELIEVE WHAT IT GOES FOR.
This year, more Americans than ever will be going out and buying small cars. Many will be disappointed.
Mainly because most people, while accepting the idea of a small car, still don't want to give up the comfort and performance of a big car.
We suggest these people take a look at a Fiat 128.
The Fiat 128 has more legroom inside than an Eldorado, yet it's smaller outside than a Volkswagen Super Beetle.
And you'll not only feel more comfortable sitting in it, but you'll feel more comfortable driving it, as well.
It has a longer wheel base than Toyota and Datsun and the Fiat's radial tires are standard (they usually run about $100 extra).
The 128 has all-independent suspension. And the same rack-and-pinion steering found in cars like Ferraris and Porsches.
The 128 has an overhead cam engine for quick acceleration, yet it still gets you about 34 miles to a gallon, according to an August, 1973 Motor Trend test. And it has self-adjusting, power-assisted front-disc brakes for quick, sure stops.
And if you live in a place where the winters are bad, you won't believe how the Fiat's front-wheel drive gets you through ice and snow.
The Fiat 128 comes in 2-door, 4-door, station wagon, and sport coupe models.
What exactly does each of these Fiats go for?
Why not see for yourself when you test drive a 128 at your local Fiat showroom.
After all, if we tell you everything now, we won't have anything left to tell you when you get there.
FIAT
The biggest selling car in Europe.
Overseas delivery arranged through your dealer.

69

67
Art Director Jeff Cohen
Writer Allen Kay
Photographer Stephen Steigman
Agency Needham, Harper & Steers
Client Xerox Corp.

68
Art Director Roy Grace
Writer David Altschiller
Artist Lou Myers
Agency Carl Ally
Client Fiat-Roosevelt Motors

69
Art Director Nate Fiarman
Writer Ron Berger
Agency Carl Ally
Client Fiat-Roosevelt Motors

2½ min.
And the Farberware Electric Coffeemaker will give you two great cups of coffee.
FARBERWARE superfast
FARBERWARE AN LCA DIVISION
4 cups in 4 minutes. 8 cups in 7 minutes. 12 cups in 10 minutes. The Farberware® Stainless Steel Electric Coffeemaker, available in 4, 8, 12 cup sizes.

70

The 4-minute 3,000 mile.
When you have to get information somewhere fast—the Xerox Telecopier transceiver is a record breaker.
By simply dialing an ordinary telephone you can send copies of documents, diagrams, drawings, even photographs from anywhere in the country to anywhere else in the country.
Even from coast to coast in just four minutes or less.
And just think, with the Xerox Telecopier, if you're sending something from New York to California it gets there 2 hours and 56 minutes before you sent it.
For more information just call our toll free number, (800) 255-4180, and a Xerox representative will run right over.
XEROX
XEROX

71

70
Art Directors Stuart Pittman
Faith Popcorn
Writers Faith Popcorn
Stuart Pittman
Photographer Michael O'Neill
Agency Smith/Greenland Co.
Client Farberware

71
Art Director Allen Kay
Writer Lester Colodny
Photographer Dave Langley
Agency Needham, Harper & Steers
Client Xerox Corp.

THE BEST STYLER DRYER YOU CAN BUY ISN'T A STYLER DRYER.
CONAIR
CONAIR PRO STYLE
TWO HANDS ARE BETTER THAN ONE
THE PROFESSIONAL HAIRDRYER

72

WOULD YOU TAKE A FREE CANDY BAR FROM A TOTAL STRANGER?
STORE COUPON
10¢
GOOD FOR ONE FREE U-NO BAR.
U-NO

73

WE SELL MORE CARS THAN FORD, CHRYSLER, CHEVROLET AND BUICK COMBINED.
MATCHBOX.

74

GOLD

72
Art Director Nick Gisonde
Writer Mark Shenfield
Designer Nick Gisonde
Photographer Cailor-Resnick
Agency Della Femina, Travisano & Partners
Client Continental Hair Products

73
Art Director Mark Yustein
Writer Neil Drossman
Designer Mark Yustein
Photographer Arnold Beckerman
Agency Della Femina, Travisano & Partners
Client Ralston Purina

74
Art Director Allan Beaver
Writer Larry Plapler
Designer Allan Beaver
Photographer Cailor-Resnick
Agency Levine, Huntley, Schmidt
Client Lesney Products Corp.

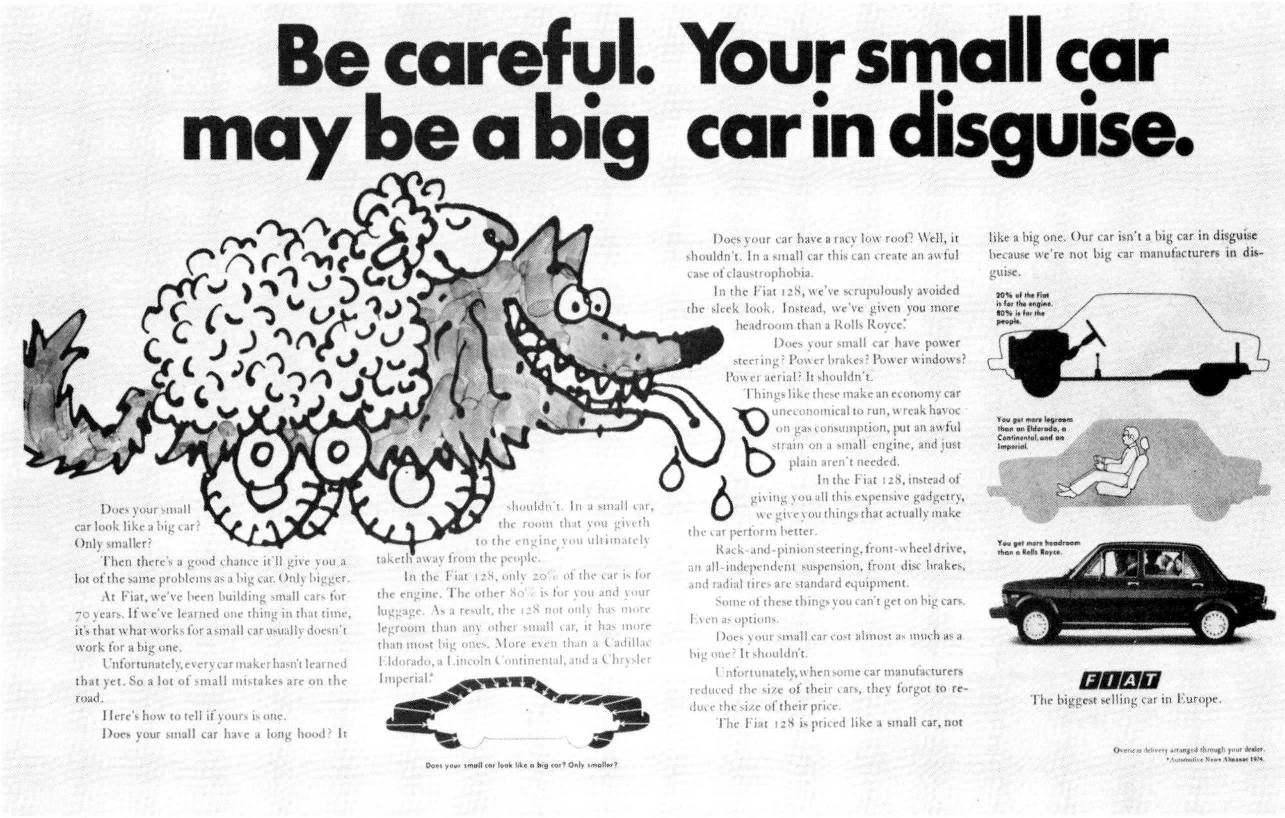
Be careful. Your small car may be a big car in disguise.
Does your small car look like a big car? Only smaller?
Then there's a good chance it'll give you a lot of the same problems as a big car. Only bigger.
At Fiat, we've been building small cars for 70 years. If we've learned one thing in that time, it's that what works for a small car usually doesn't work for a big one.
Unfortunately, every car maker hasn't learned that yet. So a lot of small mistakes are on the road.
Here's how to tell if yours is one.
Does your small car have a long hood? It shouldn't. In a small car, the room that you giveth to the engine you ultimately taketh away from the people.
In the Fiat 128, only 20% of the car is for the engine. The other 80% is for you and your luggage. As a result, the 128 not only has more legroom than any other small car, it has more than most big ones. More even than a Cadillac Eldorado, a Lincoln Continental, and a Chrysler Imperial.*
Does your small car look like a big car? Only smaller?
Does your car have a racy low roof? Well, it shouldn't. In a small car this can create an awful case of claustrophobia.
In the Fiat 128, we've scrupulously avoided the sleek look. Instead, we've given you more headroom than a Rolls Royce.*
Does your small car have power steering? Power brakes? Power windows? Power aerial? It shouldn't.
Things like these make an economy car uneconomical to run, wreak havoc on gas consumption, put an awful strain on a small engine, and just plain aren't needed.
In the Fiat 128, instead of giving you all this expensive gadgetry, we give you things that actually make the car perform better.
Rack-and-pinion steering, front-wheel drive, an all-independent suspension, front disc brakes, and radial tires are standard equipment.
Some of these things you can't get on big cars. Even as options.
Does your small car cost almost as much as a big one? It shouldn't.
Unfortunately, when some car manufacturers reduced the size of their cars, they forgot to reduce the size of their price.
The Fiat 128 is priced like a small car, not like a big one. Our car isn't a big car in disguise because we're not big car manufacturers in disguise.
20% of the Fiat is for the engine. 80% is for the people.
You get more legroom than an Eldorado, a Continental, and an Imperial.
You get more headroom than a Rolls Royce.
FIAT
The biggest selling car in Europe.
Overseas delivery arranged through your dealer.
*Automotive News Almanac 1974.

75

What's it like to be the mother of three kids when you're already the father?
There's no one way to describe it because it's different for every man who loses his wife.
But no matter what kind of an emotional adjustment he has to make, he still has to deal with the economic realities. Somebody's got to take care of the kids and the house. Which may mean hiring a full-time housekeeper.
If his wife had a job, as four out of ten mothers* do these days, that extra money is gone. Money that could have helped later on with the mortgage or the kids' education.
Maybe that's why the traditional idea of insuring the wife with only a token amount doesn't make as much sense anymore.
The Travelers life insurance people have developed a number of plans to meet the needs of today's family.
Since each plan is a little different, you really ought to look up your local Travelers agent in the Yellow Pages to find out which one's right for you.
But do it soon. And do it together.
*U.S. Department of Labor Statistics
THE TRAVELERS
Maybe we can help.
The Travelers Insurance Company, Hartford, Conn. 06115

76

SILVER

75
Art Director Roy Grace
Writer David Altschiller
Artist Lou Myers
Agency Carl Ally
Client Fiat-Roosevelt Motors

76
Art Director Mike Tesch
Writer Ed Butler
Photographer Peter Papadopolous
Agency Carl Ally
Client The Travelers Insurance Cos.

WHY A $33,500* MOTOR CAR MAKES SENSE DURING THESE TRYING TIMES.
If you wanted a motor car which could last you the rest of your life your options would be rather limited: the Rolls-Royce Silver Shadow or Corniche.
NEVER A USED CAR. SIMPLY A CLASSIC.
Each of these extraordinary road machines is designed, engineered and crafted for the ages. In fact, more than one-half of the Rolls-Royces produced since 1904 are still on the road, running as good as new. And, after six years, long after most luxury cars have been traded in, the Rolls-Royce is just entering adolescence.
It can be said, without fear of contradiction, that the Silver Shadow holds its resale value better than any ordinary luxury car.
TRUST. A HARD-EARNED VIRTUE.
The Rolls-Royce has earned it a thousandfold. For example, the Silver Shadow carries not one but *three* totally independent braking systems, including two sets of massive disc brakes.
The independent front *and* rear suspension systems offer uncanny lateral support even during rapid cornering.
The body is made of welded steel while the doors are an aluminum alloy braced internally like an airplane wing for maximum impact protection.
Before a Rolls-Royce engine is ever mounted into the chassis, it is run for over two hours to absolutely ensure that all running clearances are correct. At random, certain engines are tested under load for 24 hours and then completely torn down and inspected.
REGULAR GASOLINE.
There is a curious misconception that the Rolls-Royce aluminum V-8 engine demands the highest octane fuel.
This is a falsehood. In point of fact, the Silver Shadow and all 1974 Rolls-Royce motor cars are adjusted and tuned for regular gasoline. Such a happy economy.
Moreover, it is interesting and revealing to note that the Rolls-Royce Silver Shadow and the Rolls-Royce Corniche both offer better gasoline mileage than some domestic automobiles.
A WORD ABOUT MANNERS AND GRACE IN AN ALL TOO RUDE WORLD.
As always the Rolls-Royce maintains an almost religious devotion to silence. The interiors are of rare woods, fine English leathers and all-wool carpeting, not vinyls and other such synthetics. The seats are unusually accommodating, like those in an established men's club. The body paint is 14 coats deep—white like porcelain, black like polished marble, plus a choice of colors in between.
However, the real joy comes from the driving. Motoring in a Rolls-Royce is both sensuous and euphoric. Women appreciate its even temper and security. Gentlemen relish its responsiveness.
At your earliest opportunity visit your Rolls-Royce dealer and experiment for yourself. Or for a handsome leather-bound copy of The Rolls-Royce Owner's Manual send twenty-five dollars to Mr. Lynn Perkins, Public Relations and Advertising Manager, Rolls-Royce Motors Inc., Dept. S055A, Box 564, Paramus, N.J. 07652.

77

People either ask for Beefeater, or they ask for gin.
Beefeater. Distilled and bottled in London by James Burrough Ltd., the independent family firm since 1820.

78

This mascara cost $5.00
It's by Christian Dior.*
It gives you rich, lush lashes in your favorite rich, lush shades. Can you see any difference between it and the Yardley Slicker? Neither could 7 out of 10 girls we asked.*
This mascara cost $2.50
It's Yardley's Slicker.*
It gives you rich, lush lashes in your favorite rich, lush shades. Can you see any difference between it and the Dior mascara? Neither could 7 out of 10 girls we asked.*
Big plus: Slicker is waterproof! It's that exclusive Yardley "raincoat" formula.
*Test conducted by Nationwide Consumer Testing Institute, Inc.
There's no prettier face for love or money.

79

77
Art Director Lou Carvell
Writer Ted Pettus
Photographer Pete Turner
Agency McCaffrey & McCall
Client Rolls Royce

78
Art Director George Euringer
Writer David Altschiller
Photographer Arthur Beck
Agency Carl Ally
Client Kobrand Corp.

79
Art Director Marvin Goldman
Writer Carol Oelbaum
Designer Marvin Goldman
Photographers Bob Stone
Chuck LaMonica
Agency Ted Bates Advertising
Client Yardley of London

1925, A FRAGRANCE CAPTURES THE WORLD LIKE LE JAZZ HOT.
A transmuted sadness pours forth from jazz trumpets. The rhythms are compelling. It is The Jazz Age, and Guerlain creates a perfume of real power.
Shalimar. Heady, exciting, as intoxicating as Prohibition itself.
SHALIMAR
by Guerlain

80

1921, A FRAGRANCE WILL NOT LET HIM FORGET.
For one crazy moment he feels he will stay. Then he turns towards the gangplank and walks very slowly into the mist.
Each one of their moments—the shy beginnings, the electric touching of fingertips, the transporting passion—will disappear in the universal solvent of time plus distance.
Years later, an unknown woman in a silk dress will pass by wearing Mitsouko.
And 1921 will flash through him like a shock. He will not be able to forget the long black hair, the incredibly soft skin, the infinite tenderness…
MITSOUKO
by Guerlain

81

WHEN SHOULD YOU TRADE IN YOUR 1974 ROLLS-ROYCE?
When most people purchase a new automobile, they already know how long the relationship will last. They recognize, from the outset, that the car they drive out of the showroom today will rapidly lose both its value and its appeal.
Fortunately, there is an exception to this rule. The Rolls-Royce Silver Shadow or the Rolls-Royce Corniche. Traditionally, these cars have been designed, engineered and built not for the moment—but for the ages. Of all the Rolls-Royce motor cars built since 1904, more than half are still on the road. Perhaps this is why the Rolls-Royce holds its resale value better than any ordinary luxury car.
1977 After just 3 years, most luxury cars have been separated from their original owners in the classic syndrome of trade-in or trade-up.
Meanwhile, you and your Rolls-Royce are still enjoying the honeymoon. Practically every day you're still discovering new Rolls-Royce features: A sympathetic green light that comes on when your fuel supply is down to three gallons, an automatic speed control system, eight different adjustments for leg room, seat height and angle. Your Rolls still smells like a new car with its English-leather bucket seats, all-wool carpets and rare wood work.
1984 Maintenance is important with any car. Your Rolls-Royce owner's manual reminds you that after every 96,000 miles you should fit new flexible hoses into the braking systems. It is interesting to note that every Rolls carries not one, but three, independent braking systems, including two sets of massive disc brakes.
1992 An automobile with 180,000 miles under its belt can usually be expected to develop some rather disturbing noises and mannerisms.
Your Rolls-Royce will surprise you. The front and rear suspension systems will continue to support you with unflappable dignity, regardless of speed. The aluminum V-8 engine will purr in muffled silence, still decades away from replacement.
2009 Any 35-year-old car, which is still on the road, is certain to make heads turn. But it won't be dated styling which people will admire in your Rolls. It won't even be the miracle of mechanical endurance, for this has come to be expected from these fine motor cars. Rather, your Rolls will represent a worthy and almost timeless investment in the highest art of 4-wheeled transportation.
At your earliest convenience visit your Rolls-Royce Dealer (check listing on opposite page). And at the same time send for the 188-page, leather-bound Owner's Manual—a virtual encyclopedia of fascinating information on the specifics, maintenance and operation of this legendary motor car. Mail $25 to Mr. Lynn Perkins, Public Relations and Advertising Manager, Rolls-Royce Motors Inc., Department 8034M, Box 564, Paramus, N.J. 07652.
ROLLS RR ROYCE

82

80
Art Director Gennaro Andreozzi
Writer Paul Margulies
Designer Gennaro Andreozzi
Photographer Steve Horn
Agency Primaute Advertising
Client Guerlain

81
Art Director Gennaro Andreozzi
Writer Paul Margulies
Designer Gennaro Andreozzi
Photographer Steve Horn
Agency Primaute Advertising
Client Guerlain

82
Art Director Lou Carvell
Writer Ted Pettus
Photographer Pete Turner
Agency McCaffrey & McCall
Client Rolls Royce

Bye. Bye.
Grossingers.
Hello Grossingers. You should only live and be well!
As far as going to the country goes, you're about the biggest and the best your country has to offer.
But if anybody who goes to Grossingers would like once in a while a little something different, have we got a country for you!
Holland. It isn't the biggest country in Europe. But every square inch of us is like one giant resort.
We Dutch are so tuned in to welcoming people, we'll really make you feel at home.
Not just in our large cities like Amsterdam, Rotterdam and The Hague. With their museums, night clubs and excitements.
But in the countryside as well. A countryside made familiar by artists for centuries.
You'll find that every village and hamlet in Holland has facilities designed to take good care of people. Family people. With kids, grandkids, and in-laws and uncles and aunts.
In fact, you'll find a whole nation of Dutch uncles just waiting to entertain yours.
In times like these it's also good to remind you that Holland is a country that really likes Americans. (We liked America so much we bought Manhattan. Remember?)
And we'll never forget what you Americans did for us during World War II. (Who could forget that?)
So for a change come to Holland. To our dikes and windmills and tulips and seasides and countrysides and citysides.
And so it shouldn't be a total loss, remember. When you go back to Grossingers, you'll have a lot to talk about.
Holland.
Don't visit us. Live with us.
HOLLAND

83

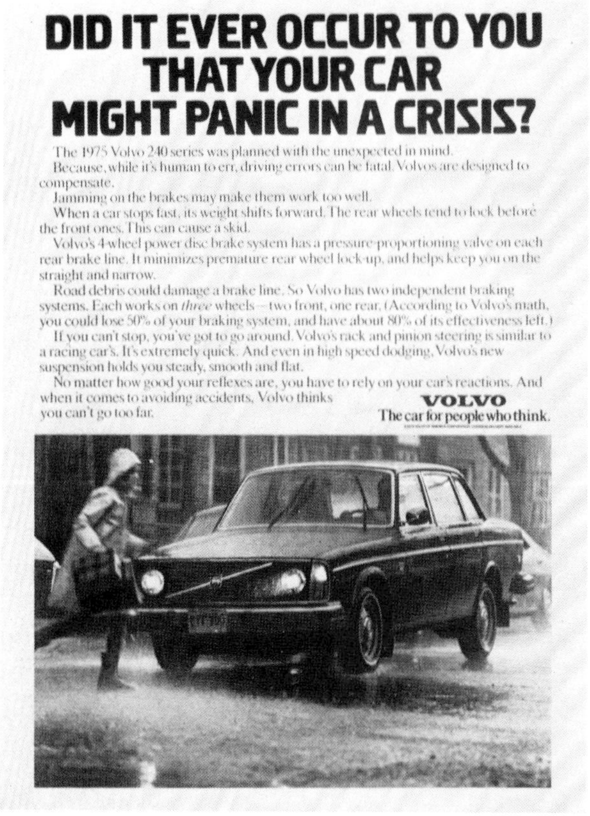
DID IT EVER OCCUR TO YOU THAT YOUR CAR MIGHT PANIC IN A CRISIS?
The 1975 Volvo 240 series was planned with the unexpected in mind.
Because, while it's human to err, driving errors can be fatal. Volvos are designed to compensate.
Jamming on the brakes may make them work too well.
When a car stops fast, its weight shifts forward. The rear wheels tend to lock before the front ones. This can cause a skid.
Volvo's 4-wheel power disc brake system has a pressure-proportioning valve on each rear brake line. It minimizes premature rear wheel lock-up, and helps keep you on the straight and narrow.
Road debris could damage a brake line. So Volvo has two independent braking systems. Each works on three wheels—two front, one rear. (According to Volvo's math, you could lose 50% of your braking system, and have about 80% of its effectiveness left.)
If you can't stop, you've got to go around. Volvo's rack and pinion steering is similar to a racing car's. It's extremely quick. And even in high speed dodging, Volvo's new suspension holds you steady, smooth and flat.
No matter how good your reflexes are, you have to rely on your car's reactions. And when it comes to avoiding accidents, Volvo thinks you can't go too far.
VOLVO
The car for people who think.

84

83
Art Director Norman Tanen
Writer Jack Silverman
Designer Norman Tanen
Artist Norman Tanen
Photographer Robert Freson
Agency Leber Katz Partners
Client Netherlands National Tourist Office

84
Art Director Robert Reitzfeld
Writers Edward A. McCabe
Thomas J. Nathan
Photographer Steve Horn
Agency Scali, McCabe, Sloves
Client Volvo of America Corp.

This scotch ad won't be interrupted by a commercial.

BY DICK CAVETT

I WISH PEOPLE would stop insisting that I reveal secret information that I do not possess.

I also wish they would stop insisting that I reveal secret information that I do possess.

Before I finish here, I hope you (and I) will know what I mean.

Almost weekly I am asked a question that, as we say in Nebraska, gets my goat. Ordinary people on the street grab me, spin me around and demand, "What is the secret of being a good conversationalist?" Others send a self-addressed airmail envelope, hoping for a snappy response by air.

More than once—twice in fact—editors of reputable magazines have asked me to write articles entitled, Dick Cavett Reveals the 10 Rules of Good Conversation.

When I ask how they know there are ten if they don't know what they are, they grin foolishly.

Truth is, I have never given any more thought to how to converse than I have to how those statues got on Easter Island.

(Actually, I have a theory on that, but no one cares. I think the statues were always there, and what appears to be an island was slid under them.)

Unhappily, people want to know more than just my alleged Secret of Talk. I am accused of hiding everything, of living a Garbo-like existence, beating a hasty retreat when spotted in public, and never speaking to strangers.

Horsefeathers! Or worse.

I am as gregarious as the next man.

And twice as gregarious as the next woman.

I mingle openly with the populace. Often I have struck up conversation with the lowliest fishmonger or honeydipper, accompanying him to the nearest pub and eventually to his Hogarthian abode where, in the company of his bawdy wife and callous friends, we roister til dawn. And without a thought as to what magic formula is keeping the talk lubricated.

Ask any lowly fishmonger or honeydipper.

In hopes of finally quelling the glut of letters that stuff my mailbox and clog my incinerator, all panting after the secret of gab (and any others I can spare) I sat down and wrote a book about myself. With a friend. We each wrote parts of it (they are clearly labeled).

I was surprised at how much I knew about myself, and floored at how much he knew.

The search for a clever title ended when in a moment of inspiration one of us came up with CAVETT. I forget which one of us thought of it, but I have a sickening feeling it was not him. He? Who(m)ever.

I only hope you can resist the temptation to judge my book by its title.

I also only hope no one has set too great a store by learning the most intimate details of my life.

Knowing them hasn't made me deliriously happy. Why should it you?

Cavett emptor, you might say.

As a bonus, I reveal in the book—at last—the 10 rules of good conversation.

How can I thank Teacher's Scotch for allowing me this space—uninterrupted by commercials—to put this matter to rest?

Perhaps by revealing the first rule here:—Try and have at least one language in common with the person to whom you are speaking.

There are, of course, more...

TEACHER'S
HIGHLAND CREAM
SCOTCH WHISKY

No scotch improves the flavour of water like Teacher's.

86 Proof Scotch Whisky Blended and Bottled in Scotland by Wm. Teacher & Sons, Ltd. © Schieffelin & Co., N.Y., Importers

85

85
Art Director Nick Gisonde
Writer Neil Drossman
Designer Nick Gisonde
Photographer Carl Fischer
Agency Della Femina, Travisano, & Partners
Client Schieffelin & Co.

This is
all we want to do.
But perfectly.
The engineering of high-fidelity turntables is a technical and controversial subject.
But the concept of a perfect turntable is perfectly simple.
Since a perfect turntable is what we at Garrard have been striving to make, we'd like to communicate this concept to you as unequivocally as possible. Then all the claims and counterclaims you hear will fall into place.
Think of it this way:
A phonograph record doesn't know and doesn't care what kind of mechanism is spinning it,
as long as it's spinning properly. If your hand could turn it at exactly 33⅓ RPM, without the slightest fluctuations in speed, and keep it moving in the horizontal plane only, without the slightest jiggling or vibrations up-and-down or sideways, you could expect perfect reproduction.
Similarly, a phono cartridge has no idea what's holding it in the groove, as long as it's properly held. If your other hand were holding it, correctly aligned, with the right amount of downward force and without resisting its movement across the record, it would perform faultlessly.
That's really all there is to it.
The basic point is that the turntable and tonearm have exceedingly simple and purely mechanical functions, just like a chemist's analytical balance or a gyroscope. That's why turntable manufacturing is, above all, a matter of precision and integrity, with the emphasis on perfect operation rather than hi-fi pizzazz or features for features' sake.
Of course, theoretical perfection in an actual mechanical device is an unrealizable ideal. But even though 100% is impossible, there's a big difference between 99.9% and 98%.
It's in this most fundamental sense, we feel, that Garrard turntables are in a class by themselves.
For example, in the case of the Zero 100c changer and the Zero 100SB single-play automatic, tracking error has been reduced to a virtually unmeasurable quantity (in effect, zero) by the geometry of the tonearm design. Rumble, wow and flutter figures are also coming ever closer to theoretical perfection in these and other top Garrard models. (The Zero 100c and the Zero 100SB are both priced at $209.95.)
To a less spectacular degree, the lower-priced models, from $49.95 up, also come quite close to the theoretical ideal because of this emphasis on fundamentals.
Remember: all we want is to make your record revolve perfectly and to position your phono cartridge perfectly.
And we're almost there.
For your free copy of The Garrard Guide, a 16-page full-color reference booklet, write to Garrard, Dept. 10, 100 Commercial Street, Plainview, N.Y. 11803.
Garrard
Division of Plessey Consumer Products

86

Please be patient.
We're making our shoes as fast as we can.
Who ever heard of standing in line for a pair of shoes?
We're amazed. Really amazed. At first people called our EARTH* brand negative heel shoes strange and ugly. And now they're standing in line to get them.
And while the ends of the lines are waiting to get into our stores, the beginnings of the lines are buying up all of our shoes.
Of course we always knew Earth* shoes were a great invention. And we knew people would love them. But we had no idea the word would spread so fast.
It all started with Anne Kalsø.
It started in Denmark 17 years ago, when Anne Kalsø had the idea for the negative heel shoe. A shoe with the heel lower than the toe.
The concept was that these shoes would allow you to walk naturally. Like when you walk barefoot in sand and your heel sinks down lower than your toes. Anne was convinced that this is the natural way the body is designed to walk. And that this shoe would work in harmony with your entire body.
So she worked for 10 years refining every delicate adjustment. Until finally they were perfected.
The shoe that works with your body.
And the result was the Earth shoe. The shoe that's not just for your feet.
Not only is the heel lower than the toe, but the entire sole is molded in a very special way. This allows you to walk in a gentle rolling motion. And to walk easily and comfortably on the hard, jarring cement of our cities.
Even the arch of the Earth shoe is different, and the toes are wide to keep your toes from being cramped or squashed.
Now everybody wants them.
So you started buying them. You told your friends about them. And they told their friends.
Until finally it's happened. Now you want them faster than we can make them.
It takes time to make a good shoe.
Earth negative heel shoes take time to make. Of course we could knock them out fast, by leaving out a lot of important features. Or by not paying attention to quality. But then it wouldn't be the Earth brand shoe.
To get an idea of how the EARTH shoe works, stand barefoot with your toes up on a book. Feel what begins to happen.
Lowering the heel isn't enough.
We knew we had a good idea. And we knew others would try to imitate us by making negative heel shoes too.
But just because a shoe looks like ours doesn't mean it works like ours.
The 10 years that went into perfecting the Earth shoe are very important. We have many, many features built into our shoes to make them work. And that is why they are patented.
So to be sure you're getting the Earth negative heel shoe, look on the sole for our Earth trademark and U.S. patent number 3305947.
They're worth waiting for.
Please be patient. We're sending out more and more shoes to our stores every month. And if they've run out of your size or style, they'll have it soon.
And when you do try them, you'll see, perhaps for the first time in your life, what it's like to walk more gracefully, naturally and comfortably.
And, believe us, that's worth waiting for.
The EARTH* shoe comes in styles for men and women, from open sandals to high boots. From $25.50 to $42.50. Prices slightly higher in the west.
KALSØ earth shoe
*EARTH is the registered trademark of Kalsø Systemet, Inc. for its negative heel shoes and other products.
Anne Kalsø.
Inventor of the EARTH negative heel shoe.
Our shoes are sold at stores that sell only the EARTH shoe. For a list of these stores please see the facing page.

87

4 Swiss Virgins
Discover what Europeans have known about for years. The Alps of Switzerland's Lake of Geneva region. Where the skiing is wide open. The lift lines are almost non-existent. And the prices will remind you of less inflationary days. Eight days of skiing costs from just $183 to $220.* And for that you get double occupancy accommodations for 7 nights, 2 meals a day, and a lift pass good for unlimited use at all four resorts. And when you land in Geneva you're just a few hours away from any one of them.
Les Diablerets is located at the foot of the famed Diablerets glacier, where you can ski all year around. Below the glacier you have skiing as varied as the nine mile Martinsberg run or the relatively simple Meilleret system. But no matter where you start you'll probably end your run in the charming village. A casual easy-going place that's perfect for families, or people who just want to get away from it all.
Villars faces the French Alps and gives skiers open slopes reached by a cog railway, two gondolas and more than a dozen drag lifts. There are over 30 miles of marked runs. Plus at the base, there's the kind of relaxed country village the Swiss themselves have been coming to for years.
In Leysin you can take a gondola up to the Berneuse and take it easy down to the Lac d'Ai level. Or go over to the Chaux de Mont for some slightly more adventurous runs. Back down, you'll find Leysin offers both the younger, and the slightly older sets, the kinds of night life they expect. (Separately, of course.)
Château-D'Oex, located near Gstaad, shares the quiet chicness of that famed resort. Whether you're on one of the 40 lifts, or celebrating at night, you're likely to meet someone you usually only see on a movie screen. Château-D'Oex offers an enormous variety of winter sports. But, best of all, its famed White Highlands gives skiers the opportunity to practice and improve.
So if you're looking for an Alp, try one in the Lake of Geneva region. They're everything you expect from a European vacation. But the nicest part is that you can be the first one in your neighborhood to find it out.
LES DIABLERETS
VILLARS
LEYSIN
CHÂTEAU-D'OEX
For reservations, or our free "Alps of Lake Geneva" folder, see your local travel agent, Swissair office, or write: Swissair, 608 Fifth Avenue, New York, N.Y. 10020.
*Based on $1=2.80 Swiss Francs. Subject to currency change.
The Lake of Geneva Region

88

86
Art Director Dick Calderhead
Writer Peter Aczel
Designer Barbara Schubeck
Artist Don Ivan Punchatz
Agency Calderhead, Jackson
Client Garrard

87
Art Director Mel Platt
Writer Jennifer Berne
Artist Norman Green
Agency Martin Landey, Arlow Advertising
Client Kalsø

88
Art Director Howard Title
Writer Chuck Cohen
Designer Howard Title
Artists John Collier
Arton Assoc.
Agency Waring & LaRosa
Client Swissair

"I was wondering if I could possibly borrow a cup
of Johnnie Walker Black Label."
12 YEAR OLD BLENDED SCOTCH WHISKY, 86.8 PROOF. BOTTLED IN SCOTLAND. IMPORTED BY SOMERSET IMPORTERS, LTD., N.Y., N.Y.

89

SILVER

89

Art Directors Stuart Pittman
Faith Popcorn
Writer Murray L. Klein
Photographer Michael O'Neill
Agency Smith/Greenland Co.
Client Somerset Importers

Love thyself.
Johnnie Walker
Black Label Scotch
YEARS 12 OLD
JOHNNIE WALKER® BLACK LABEL 12 YEAR OLD BLENDED SCOTCH WHISKY, 86.8 PROOF. BOTTLED IN SCOTLAND. IMPORTED BY SOMERSET IMPORTERS, LTD., N.Y.

90

©Volkswagen of America. *Sedan 110 P.O.E., Suggested Retail Price, Local Taxes and Other Dealer Delivery Charges Additional.
Now.
Fuel
Injection
for the
frugal.
PORSCHE
66
AUDI
You'll find fuel injection on some of the fastest cars in the world.
On some of the most expensive cars in the world.
And now, through a miracle of modern technology, you'll find it on one of the most inexpensive cars in the world.
The new, advanced '75 Beetle. '75 $2895*

91

90
Art Directors Stuart Pittman
Faith Popcorn
Alan Friedlander
Writers Faith Popcorn
Stuart Pittman
Artist Gervasio Gallardo
Agency Smith/Greenland Co.
Client Somerset Importers

91
Art Director Charles Piccirillo
Writer Mike Mangano
Photographer David Langley
Agency Doyle Dane Bernbach
Client Volkswagen of America Corp.

You can probably name the best known automatic typewriter. Guess who makes one that's twice as fast?

We've hidden a clue in the picture on the right.
Surprised?
Well, you're looking at the new Xerox 800 electronic typing system.
An automatic typewriter with a memory, that can type by itself at the incredible rate of up to 350 error-free words per minute.
And our typewriter has a combination of features that the other automatic typewriter doesn't.
Features like automatic carriage return. Reverse printout. Right margin justification. And pica, elite, and proportional spacing. All on one machine.
All of which means that typing gets done faster, and looks better than it ever did before.
The new Xerox 800 electronic typing system.
Years ahead of its time. And about 175 words per minute ahead of the best known automatic typewriter.

XEROX

92

These are the things that litter our beaches. Not beer cans, paper cups and candy wrappers.

Spend a few days on the beaches of South Carolina, and you'll go home with a lot more than sandy sneakers and a suntan.
Because this just may be the most diverse collection of places to go, and things to do, ever strung together along one coastline.
Island beaches so untouched, you can only reach them by boat. Where you don't even have to look for shells to find them.
Myrtle Beach, hub of the famous Grand Strand, where there's generally more nightlife than wildlife. But where the beaches, like all the beaches here, are wide and sandy and unpolluted.
Places where you can golf, play tennis, camp, fish, sail, or just wander a while and get back in touch with yourself.
Nearby you'll find historic homes, world-famous gardens, and old cities like Charleston.
So you can soak up some history, if you get tired of soaking up sun.
And, since so much of what you can do costs so little, you won't have to cut corners to cut the cost of your vacation.
Just write for our free Trip Kit, to help you plan. Then come enjoy the good things South Carolina has to give you.
There's only one thing we'd like to ask you to do for us, in return.
When you leave our beaches, please make sure you haven't left anything more permanent than your footprints behind you.

South Carolina

93

SILVER

92
Art Director Allen Kay
Writer Lloyd Fink
Photographer Carl Fischer
Agency Needham, Harper & Steers
Client Xerox Corp.

93
Art Director Michael Winslow
Writer Harriet Frye
Designer Michael Winslow
Artist Michael Winslow
Photographers Phil Marco
Ralph Holland
Agency McKinney & Silver
Client State of South Carolina
Division of Tourism

"If you think Tennessee music is one long hoe~down, bite your tongue."
"Dick walked in after an interview at Vanderbilt University and said, 'Honey, think a couple of New Yorkers can find true happiness in Nashville? Seriously, it's a great offer. The department is terrific. We've got to make the move.'
"Gulp! Is that going to put a crimp in my music career? Country music is fine, but I'm no banjo player.
"But, I put on a brave smile and tagged along. Good husbands are hard to find.
"I was in for quite a surprise. Nashville really is Music City. And not just country music. It's chamber music. Recitals. Symphonies. To say nothing of good rock and jazz.
"Things happened fast. I started teaching. Gave a few concerts. Got my Master's from George Peabody College. Joined the faculty at Peabody and at Blair Academy a great pre-college music school. As you can see, I haven't been sitting still. That's me on the opposite page rehearsing for an appearance with the Nashville Symphony under Thor Johnson.
"We're doing what we want to do with our lives. And it's happening in Tennessee.
"Naturally, we're into a lot of other activities, too. Camping, for example. That's a switch for a couple of city kids. Did you know that the Tennessee countryside has been likened to the green, hilly countryside of England? And by English travellers, yet.
"That's my story. Dick's is just as good. He's now Chairman of the Psychology Department at Vanderbilt. And he's into everything he loves to do. Writing. Research. Consulting for the National Institute of Mental Health. I'm getting prouder of him every day.
"Best of all, we're enjoying our life — Tennessee Style."
Thank you, Enid. We're proud of both of you. You're absolutely right about Tennessee's cultural environment. Nashville has 14 colleges and the State has 54. Maybe that's the reason for our growing art colony. Painters and sculptors and crafts people from all over the country are settling here. Not having a State Property Tax or Personal Income Tax doesn't hurt either, does it?
You folks thinking about plant relocation or industrial expansion owe it to yourselves to come down and look us over. Or write to me, Dr. Pat Choate, Commissioner of Economic and Community Development, Andrew Jackson Building, Nashville, Tennessee 37219. As Enid so beautifully points out, we've got a lot more going than our waterways, TVA power, coal and natural gas. You'll like doing business Tennessee style.
We like doing business
TENNESSEE STYLE

94

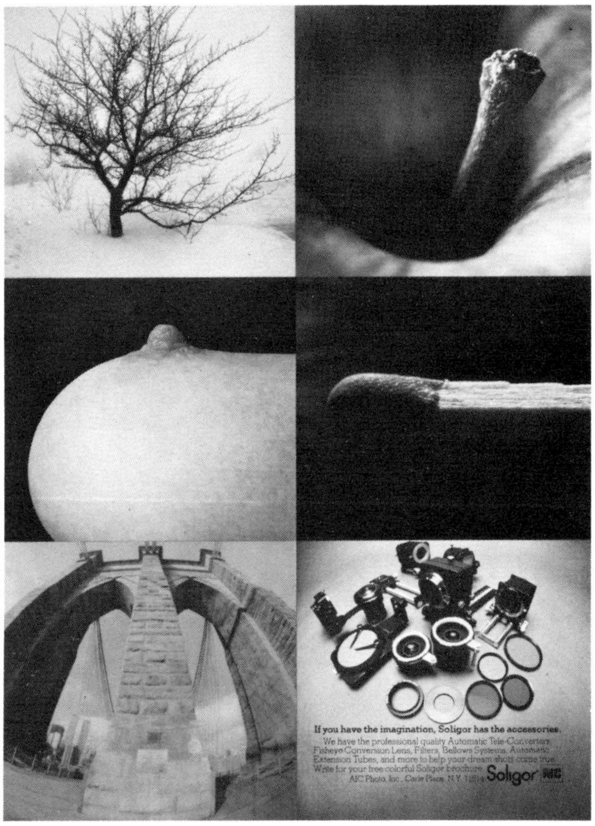
If you have the imagination, Soligor has the accessories.
We have the professional quality Automatic Tele-Converters, Fisheye Conversion Lens, Filters, Bellows Systems, Automatic Extension Tubes, and more to help your dream shots come true. Write for your free colorful Soligor brochure.
Soligor

95

94
Art Director Chet Sailor
Writer George Mitchell
Designer Chet Sailor
Photographer Tabor Chadwick
Agency Noble-Dury & Assoc.
Client State of Tennessee, Industrial Development Div.

95
Art Directors Lew-Dave-Marv
Writers Lew-Dave-Marv
Designers Lew-Dave-Marv
Photographer Dick Frank
Agency KSS&G
Client Soligor

9 OUT OF EVERY 10,000 AMERICANS PREFER CAMPARI & SODA.
Campari & Soda is a favorite cocktail refresher all over Europe. In America, it's practically unheard of.
There are certain Viennese bars, in fact, that serve more Campari & Soda on a single day than all of Boston.
Yet we, the makers of Campari, are not discouraged. For our figures indicate that a few more Americans each day discover the unique taste of the Campari & Soda cocktail (light, tongue-tingling).
We are also happy to note isolated pockets of Campari & Tonic activity in American restaurants. This too contributes to the inexorable rise of Campari consumption in the United States.
Campari comes from Italy where we have a saying: Rome wasn't built in a day; nor is the love of Campari & Soda.
ITALY
CAMPARI
CLUB SODA

96

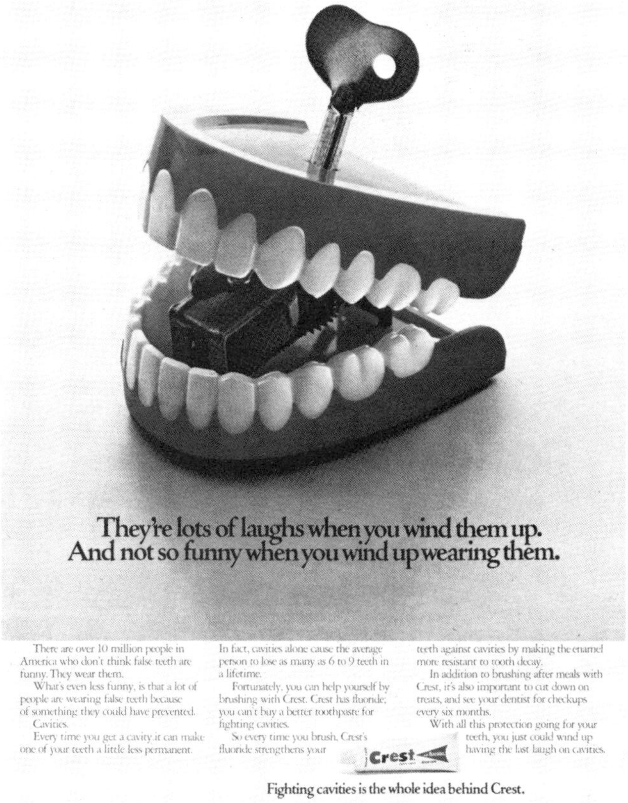
They're lots of laughs when you wind them up.
And not so funny when you wind up wearing them.
There are over 10 million people in America who don't think false teeth are funny. They wear them.
What's even less funny, is that a lot of people are wearing false teeth because of something they could have prevented.
Cavities.
Every time you get a cavity it can make one of your teeth a little less permanent.
In fact, cavities alone cause the average person to lose as many as 6 to 9 teeth in a lifetime.
Fortunately, you can help yourself by brushing with Crest. Crest has fluoride; you can't buy a better toothpaste for fighting cavities.
So every time you brush, Crest's fluoride strengthens your teeth against cavities by making the enamel more resistant to tooth decay.
In addition to brushing after meals with Crest, it's also important to cut down on treats, and see your dentist for checkups every six months.
With all this protection going for your teeth, you just could wind up having the last laugh on cavities.
Crest
Fighting cavities is the whole idea behind Crest.

97

A VOLVO DISCOVERY: RAIN FALLS ON REAR WINDOWS, TOO.
Volvo is the only wagon maker with the foresight to provide its rear window with a wiper and washer as standard equipment.
Volvo has also discovered that everyone doesn't buy a wagon to be fashionable. Many people buy wagons to carry things.
So we didn't design Volvo's cargo area low and sleek to accommodate a styling trend. We designed it high and practical, to accommodate things like a six-foot sofa and two chairs (with the rear seat down). Or three six-foot people and 12 two-suiters (with the rear seat up).
Volvo's rear area not only holds a lot, it comes with a lot. It has its own heating and ventilation vents, its own three-point seat belts, electric rear window defogger, carpeting, tinted glass and childproof door locks.
And Volvo's back door swings up out of your way, instead of out into your stomach. Or down into your knee caps.
It doesn't take a college degree to appreciate the thinking behind our wagon. So we leave you to consider this. If the rear end of your car isn't as well thought-out as Volvo's, what other part might not be?
VOLVO
The wagon for people who think.
RP-7902
VOLVO
245 DL

98

GOLD

96
Art Director Irwin Goldberg
Writer Bob Larimer
Designer Irwin Goldberg
Photographer Buddy Endress
Agency Nadler & Larimer
Client Austin, Nichols & Co.

97
Art Director Joe Gregorace
Writer Marv Jacobson
Photographer Phil Marco
Agency Benton & Bowles
Client Procter & Gamble

98
Art Director Robert Reitzfeld
Writer Thomas J. Nathan
Photographer Henry Sandbank
Agency Scali, McCabe, Sloves
Client Volvo of America Corp.

Guess what Scotch is about to be served.
CHIVAS REGAL • 12 YEARS OLD WORLDWIDE • BLENDED SCOTCH WHISKY • 86 PROOF • GENERAL WINE & SPIRITS CO., NEW YORK, N.Y.
99

99
Art Director Mike Lawlor
Writer Mike Mangano
Designer Mike Lawlor
Photographer Rudy Legname
Agency Doyle Dane Bernbach
Client Chivas Regal

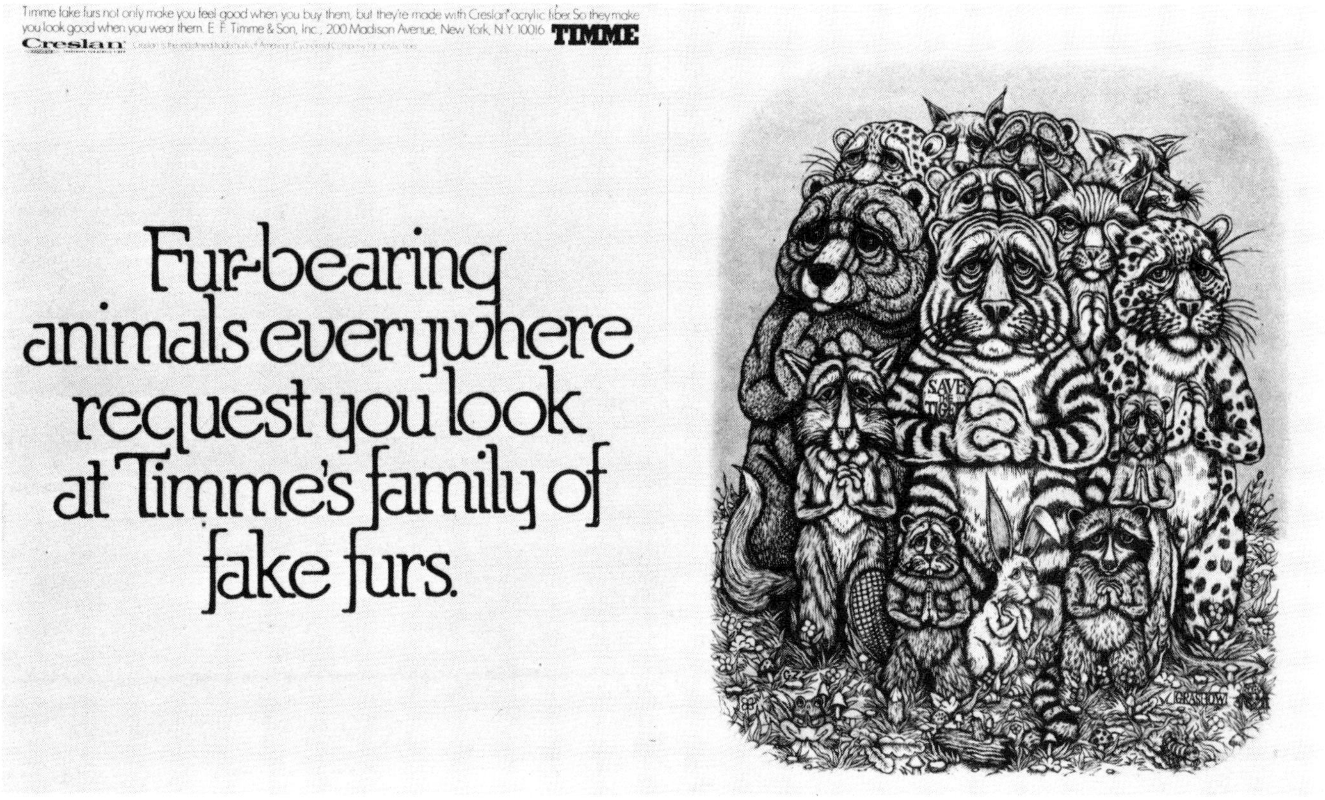
Timme fake furs not only make you feel good when you buy them, but they're made with Creslan® acrylic fiber. So they make you look good when you wear them. E. F. Timme & Son, Inc., 200 Madison Avenue, New York, N.Y. 10016
TIMME
Creslan
Fur-bearing animals everywhere request you look at Timme's family of fake furs.
SAVE THE TIGER
GRASHOW

100

GOOD DAYS START WITH GOOD NIGHTS.
How you feel during the day depends a lot on how you sleep during the night. And that depends a lot on your mattress.
Get your marriage off to a good start every day. Get your Beautyrest,® by Simmons. America's great firm mattress.
Beautyrest's unique pocketed coil construction provides firmness where you need it. Under your back. Yet it gives you all the comfort you want for a deep, restful and refreshing night's sleep.
Vist your Simmons dealer and try a Beautyrest. All sizes are available, but a lot of today's brides pick the Queen because it offers 20% more room than a standard double bed.
And there are a variety of Beautyrest firmnesses to choose from. From firm to extra-firm. One of them was just made for the two of you.
GET YOUR BEAUTYREST AND HAVE A GOOD DAY.
BEAUTYREST BY SIMMONS

101

100
Art Director Rob Lopes
Writers Mike Lichtman
Larry Plapler
Artist James Grashow
Agency Levine, Huntley, Schmidt
Client E. F. Timme & Son

101
Art Director Janet Monte
Writer Jim Johnston
Photographer Steve Horn
Agency Young & Rubicam International
Client Simmons Co.

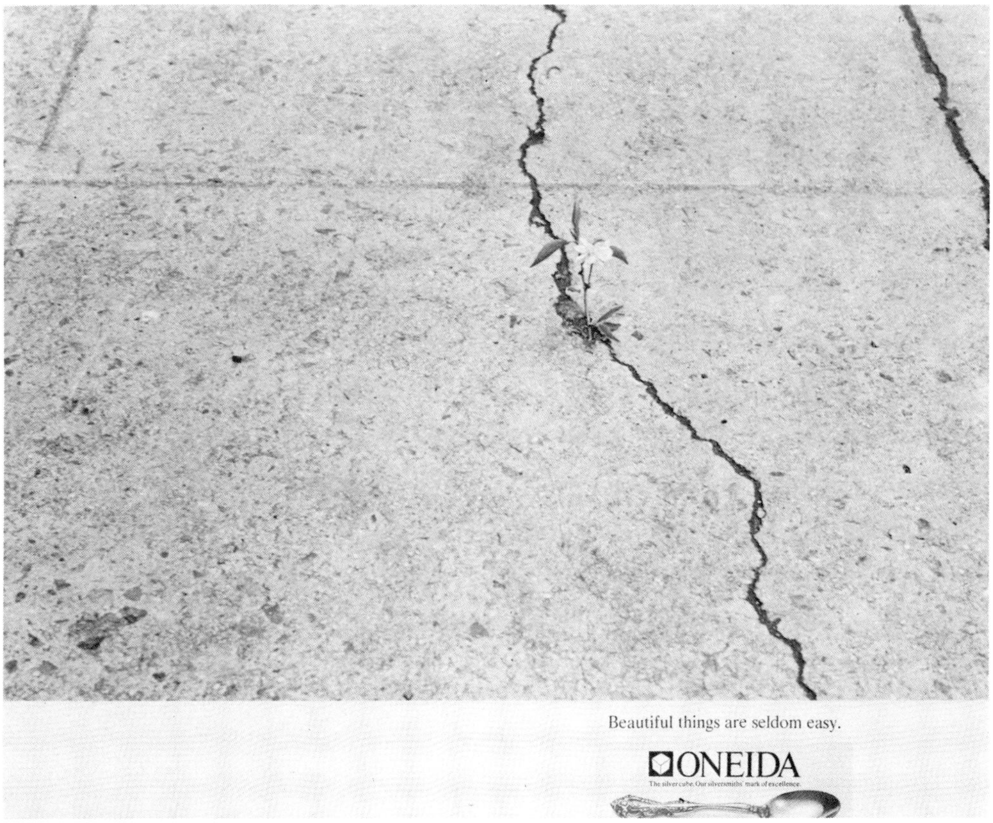
Beautiful things are seldom easy.
ONEIDA
The silvercube. Our silversmiths' mark of excellence.

102

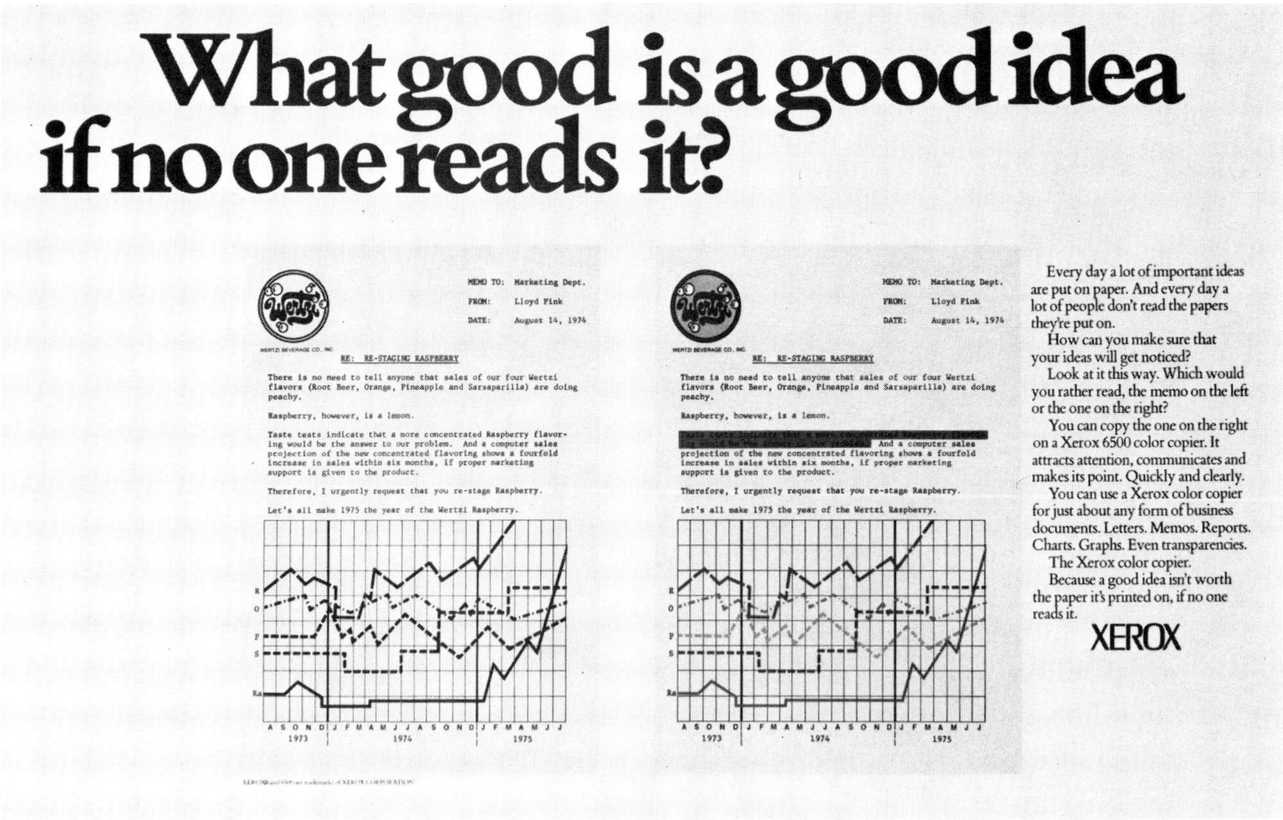
What good is a good idea if no one reads it?
MEMO TO: Marketing Dept.
FROM: Lloyd Fink
DATE: August 14, 1974
WERTZI BEVERAGE CO. INC.
RE: RE-STAGING RASPBERRY
There is no need to tell anyone that sales of our four Wertzi flavors (Root Beer, Orange, Pineapple and Sarsaparilla) are doing peachy.
Raspberry, however, is a lemon.
Taste tests indicate that a more concentrated Raspberry flavoring would be the answer to our problem. And a computer sales projection of the new concentrated flavoring shows a fourfold increase in sales within six months, if proper marketing support is given to the product.
Therefore, I urgently request that you re-stage Raspberry.
Let's all make 1975 the year of the Wertzi Raspberry.
1973
1974
1975
Every day a lot of important ideas are put on paper. And every day a lot of people don't read the papers they're put on.
How can you make sure that your ideas will get noticed?
Look at it this way. Which would you rather read, the memo on the left or the one on the right?
You can copy the one on the right on a Xerox 6500 color copier. It attracts attention, communicates and makes its point. Quickly and clearly.
You can use a Xerox color copier for just about any form of business documents. Letters. Memos. Reports. Charts. Graphs. Even transparencies.
The Xerox color copier.
Because a good idea isn't worth the paper it's printed on, if no one reads it.
XEROX

103

102
Art Directors David Deutsch
Rocco E. Campanelli
Writer Robert G. Kilzer
Designers David Deutsch
Rocco E. Campanelli
Photographer Ben Somoroff
Agency David Deutsch Assoc.
Client Oneida Silversmiths

103
Art Director Jeff Cohen
Writer Lloyd Fink
Agency Needham, Harper & Steers
Client Xerox Corp.

Ignore them.
Maybe they'll go away.
It's a simple fact of life, the less attention you pay to your children's teeth, the more cavities they'll have.
And cavities can lead to tooth loss.
In fact, we found out that the average person loses 6 to 9 teeth in a lifetime due to cavities.
And the biggest cause of cavities is neglect. But you can do something about cavities by having your children brush with Crest. The fluoride in Crest combines with tooth enamel to make teeth more resistant to decay.
In addition, be careful with treats and snacks.
And have your children see the dentist regularly.
Since teeth are sensitive, living things, if you don't pay attention to them, one day they'll probably leave. And never come back.
So take care of your teeth with Crest.
Crest
You can't beat Crest for fighting cavities.

104

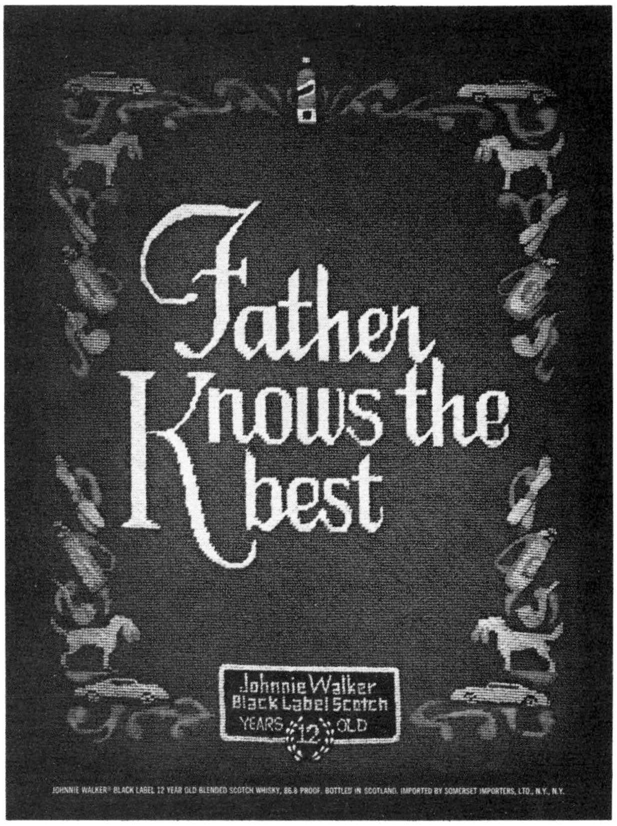
Father Knows the best
Johnnie Walker
Black Label Scotch
YEARS 12 OLD
JOHNNIE WALKER® BLACK LABEL 12 YEAR OLD BLENDED SCOTCH WHISKY, 86.8 PROOF. BOTTLED IN SCOTLAND. IMPORTED BY SOMERSET IMPORTERS, LTD., N.Y., N.Y.

105

We asked her if she'd like a female cigarette. She said, "Let's keep sex out of smoking."
O.K. We got your message. So we changed Eve. And we changed it good. Cut the flowers. Put in the flavor. A fresh, full-bodied, satisfying flavor. Eve. In regular or menthol. The new filter cigarette for women. A lot less flowers. A lot more flavor.
EVE
PREMIUM LENGTH
Re-Introducing Eve.
Because you've got a right to a real cigarette.
Warning: The Surgeon General Has Determined That Cigarette Smoking Is Dangerous to Your Health.

106

104
Art Director Jim Burton
Writer Marv Jacobson
Photographer Alen MacWeeney
Agency Benton & Bowles
Client Procter & Gamble

105
Art Directors Stuart Pittman
Faith Popcorn
Writer Adam Hanft
Designer Stuart Pittman
Artist David Smiton
Photographer Michael O'Neill
Agency Smith/Greenland Co.
Client Somerset Importers

106
Art Director Mel Rustom
Writers Peggy Flynn
Joy Golden
Photographer William Connors
Agency Norman, Craig & Kummel
Client Liggett & Myers

Johnnie Walker
Black Label Scotch
YEARS 12 OLD
Now there are two kinds of gold
you can buy in bars.
JOHNNIE WALKER® BLACK LABEL 12 YEAR OLD BLENDED SCOTCH WHISKY, 86.8 PROOF. BOTTLED IN SCOTLAND. IMPORTED BY SOMERSET IMPORTERS, LTD., N.Y.

107

107
Art Director Ivan Sherman
Writer Murray L. Klein
Photographer Henry Sandbank
Agency Smith/Greenland Co.
Client Somerset Importers

This is what we give you in return for getting up each time the record is over.
A typical evening for the Manual Turntable Owner: Up and down, up and down, up and down, up and down.
A typical evening for the Automatic Turntable Owner: Up and down.
If this is true, and it is, then why do manual turntables, trip-producers that they are, account for an overwhelming majority of all turntable models over $200?
Because in relinquishing convenience, something far more progressive is recaptured: perfection. But before we go into the glory details, let's first get our terminology sorted out.
Separating the turntables from the turntables from the turntables.
Four categories of turntables exist. You can buy a single-play manual, which is just what it sounds like. You can buy a single-play semi-automatic, which means it has a manual cueing device, but an automatic shut off. You can buy a single-play automatic, which has both automatic cueing and shut off. Or you can buy a multiple-play automatic turntable—a changer. This is the only kind of turntable that lets you play a stack of records.
What makes semi's run (And single-play and automatics, too.)
There are three ways that turntables turn. Way #1: rim or idler drive. A wheel is attached to the turntable's motor. This wheel presses against the edge of the turntable and spins it around.
Way #2: belt drive. A belt that is attached to the shaft of the motor is wrapped around the edge of the turntable.
Way #3: direct drive. The newest. The best. The simplest. Basically, the shaft of the motor is the spindle of the turntable. The motor is controlled electronically to turn at the speed you want the turntable to turn. No belts. No idlers. (Doesn't that sound like a girdle ad?)
You can only get direct drive on manual and semi-automatic turntables. Direct drive gives you lower rumble and less wow and flutter than any other method of platter spinning. That's one thing you get in return for getting up each time the record is over.
Other things that justify inconvenience.
If you've ever noticed a record changer changing, you've seen a funny thing happen: one record falls on top of another. Now new records are designed so the fall won't scratch them. But old records weren't designed that way.
Old records also cannot be replaced. So if you have some, think twice about a changer.
Another interesting thing happens when records pile up. The angle of the needle to the groove changes as the stack gets higher. The higher the stack, the more the difference in the angle, the greater the distortion.
Some changers are equipped with a complicated gizmo that compensates for this error by automatically changing the angle of the needle. That's what they do. What they don't do is work very well. They are delicate and temperamental. They demand a lot of attention. (But wait a second, aren't changers supposed to be convenient.)
And getting up each time the record is over is certainly preferable to getting up and bringing your changer to the repair shop.
SONY

108

IT TAKES A LOT OF DUMMIES TO MAKE A CAR FOR PEOPLE WHO THINK.
800-TJN
For years, we've employed dummies to help us plan our Volvos.
By smashing our cars into concrete barriers with dummies strapped inside, we've learned how to make them safer for people.
From these tests, we developed a front end which absorbs highway-speed impacts to protect the passenger compartment.
Dummies helped us perfect a three-point seat belt capable of restraining 3½ tons of force.
And after bouncing a dummy bottom on our seats for hours on end, we devised a body support system that will cradle you comfortably for years on end.
But not all the things we do depend on a lot of dummies. Some simply require a little common sense.
All cars have head restraints. Volvo's have openings, so you can see behind you.
All cars have windshield wipers. But instead of shiny ones that glare in your eyes, Volvo had a brighter idea.
Dull black ones.
Volvo provides four-wheel power disc brakes, steel-belted radial tires, fuel injection, new suspension that makes the car corner flatter and smoother. And a heating-circulation system so versatile it can freshen the air, warm your feet and defog the front windows at the same time.
Volvo even improved on the lowly gas cap. To make it hard to leave behind, we installed a holder behind its door.
At Volvo, the smallest details are worthy of careful consideration. Which is why, all things considered, Volvo may well be the world's most carefully thought-out car.
It's not surprising then, that Volvo has a special appeal for people who think.
87% of the people who buy Volvos are college-educated.
The other 13% must be just plain smart.
VOLVO
The car for people who think.

109

108
Art Director Don Slater
Writer Adam Hanft
Designer Don Slater
Photographer Pete Turner
Agency Rosenfeld, Sirowitz & Lawson
Client Sony Corporation of America

109
Art Director Robert Reitzfeld
Writer Thomas J. Nathan
Photographer Henry Sandbank
Agency Scali, McCabe, Sloves
Client Volvo of America Corp.

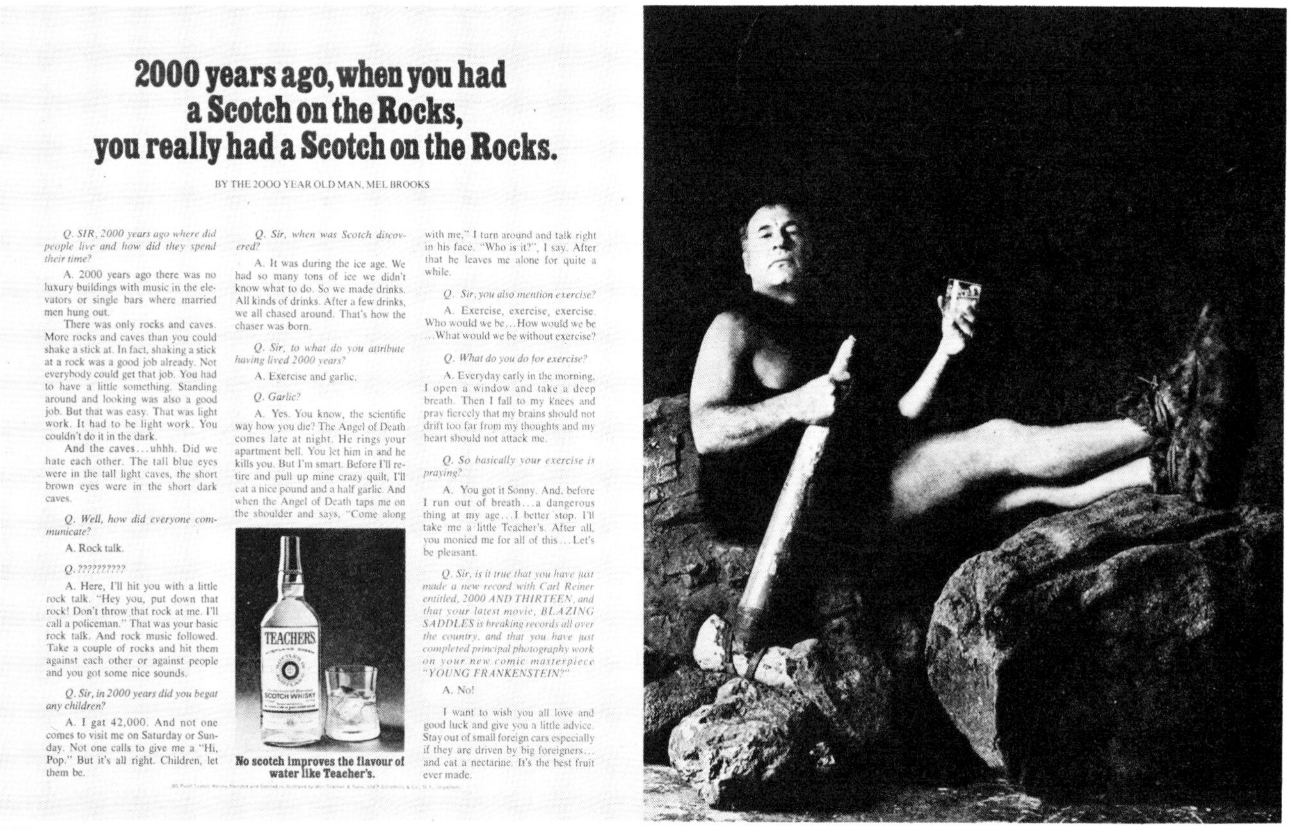
2000 years ago, when you had a Scotch on the Rocks, you really had a Scotch on the Rocks.
BY THE 2000 YEAR OLD MAN, MEL BROOKS
Q. SIR, 2000 years ago where did people live and how did they spend their time?
A. 2000 years ago there was no luxury buildings with music in the elevators or single bars where married men hung out.
There was only rocks and caves. More rocks and caves than you could shake a stick at. In fact, shaking a stick at a rock was a good job already. Not everybody could get that job. You had to have a little something. Standing around and looking was also a good job. But that was easy. That was light work. It had to be light work. You couldn't do it in the dark.
And the caves...uhhh. Did we hate each other. The tall blue eyes were in the tall light caves, the short brown eyes were in the short dark caves.
Q. Well, how did everyone communicate?
A. Rock talk.
Q. ??????????
A. Here, I'll hit you with a little rock talk. "Hey you, put down that rock! Don't throw that rock at me. I'll call a policeman." That was your basic rock talk. And rock music followed. Take a couple of rocks and hit them against each other or against people and you got some nice sounds.
Q. Sir, in 2000 years did you begat any children?
A. I gat 42,000. And not one comes to visit me on Saturday or Sunday. Not one calls to give me a "Hi, Pop." But it's all right. Children, let them be.
Q. Sir, when was Scotch discovered?
A. It was during the ice age. We had so many tons of ice we didn't know what to do. So we made drinks. All kinds of drinks. After a few drinks, we all chased around. That's how the chaser was born.
Q. Sir, to what do you attribute having lived 2000 years?
A. Exercise and garlic.
Q. Garlic?
A. Yes. You know, the scientific way how you die? The Angel of Death comes late at night. He rings your apartment bell. You let him in and he kills you. But I'm smart. Before I'll retire and pull up mine crazy quilt, I'll eat a nice pound and a half garlic. And when the Angel of Death taps me on the shoulder and says, "Come along with me," I turn around and talk right in his face. "Who is it?", I say. After that he leaves me alone for quite a while.
Q. Sir, you also mention exercise?
A. Exercise, exercise, exercise. Who would we be...How would we be ...What would we be without exercise?
Q. What do you do for exercise?
A. Everyday early in the morning, I open a window and take a deep breath. Then I fall to my knees and pray fiercely that my brains should not drift too far from my thoughts and my heart should not attack me.
Q. So basically your exercise is praying?
A. You got it Sonny. And, before I run out of breath...a dangerous thing at my age...I better stop. I'll take me a little Teacher's. After all, you monied me for all of this...Let's be pleasant.
Q. Sir, is it true that you have just made a new record with Carl Reiner entitled, 2000 AND THIRTEEN, and that your latest movie, BLAZING SADDLES is breaking records all over the country, and that you have just completed principal photography work on your new comic masterpiece "YOUNG FRANKENSTEIN?"
A. No!
I want to wish you all love and good luck and give you a little advice. Stay out of small foreign cars especially if they are driven by big foreigners... and eat a nectarine. It's the best fruit ever made.
TEACHER'S
SCOTCH WHISKY
No scotch improves the flavour of water like Teacher's.

110

Konica takes the worry out of being close.
Macrophotography. Another way to be creative with Konica.
Now tiny spiders and slithering snakes don't have to frighten grown-ups with cameras.
Because thanks to Konica's Autoreflex T3, the problems of macrophotography have become no problem at all.
How do you shoot a smiling spider, or a snake having his lunch?
Automatically!
With the ingenious Konica Autoreflex T3, and the unbelievable new Konica Auto Macro 55mm f/3.5 lens with automatic exposure control and open aperture metering. So the whole exciting world of macrophotography is just a click away.
The Konica Auto Macro 55mm lens can also be used as a standard lens, focusing from as close as 8½" to infinity. And the magnification ratio is 1:2 (half life-size), or 1:1 (life-size) with an adapter.
When using flash, its automatic effective aperture compensation eliminates exposure calculations.
Macro made easy is just one of Konica's many accomplishments. To see them all, visit your local Konica dealer and actually hold the T3 in your hands. You'll know why we say the T3 "outperforms any other automatic SLR in existence. At any price!"
Or write for our detailed Fact File: Konica Camera Co., Woodside, N.Y. 11377. In Canada: Garlick Films, Ltd., Ontario.
KONICA Berkey
World's most experienced automatic SLR system.

111

110
Art Director Mark Yustein
Writer Neil Drossman
Designer Mark Yustein
Photographer Arnold Beckerman
Agency Della Femina, Travisano & Partners
Client Schieffelin & Co.

111
Art Director Lew-Dave-Marv
Writer Lew-Dave-Marv
Designer Lew-Dave-Marv
Photographer Dick Frank
Agency KSS&G
Client Konica Camera Co.

Little girls don't grow up too fast. Fathers are just too slow to notice.

Hidden somewhere in every father's mind is the belief that, all evidence to the contrary, his little girl will remain little forever.

That's why we'd like to remind you that she won't.

Little girls become college freshmen, brides and career women with such astonishing quickness that it could catch you unprepared. So if you'd like to secure your daughter's future, it's never too early to start.

At Metropolitan Life we're helping over 40 million people secure their financial future. And what we're doing for them, we can do for you.

Of course, we can't tell you exactly what will happen in the future. But whatever does, it's nice to know it won't take your little girl by surprise.

Metropolitan Life
Where the future is now

112

112
Art Director Bob Engel
Writer Tom Thomas
Photographer Art Kane
Agency Young & Rubicam International
Client Metropolitan Life Insurance Co.

113

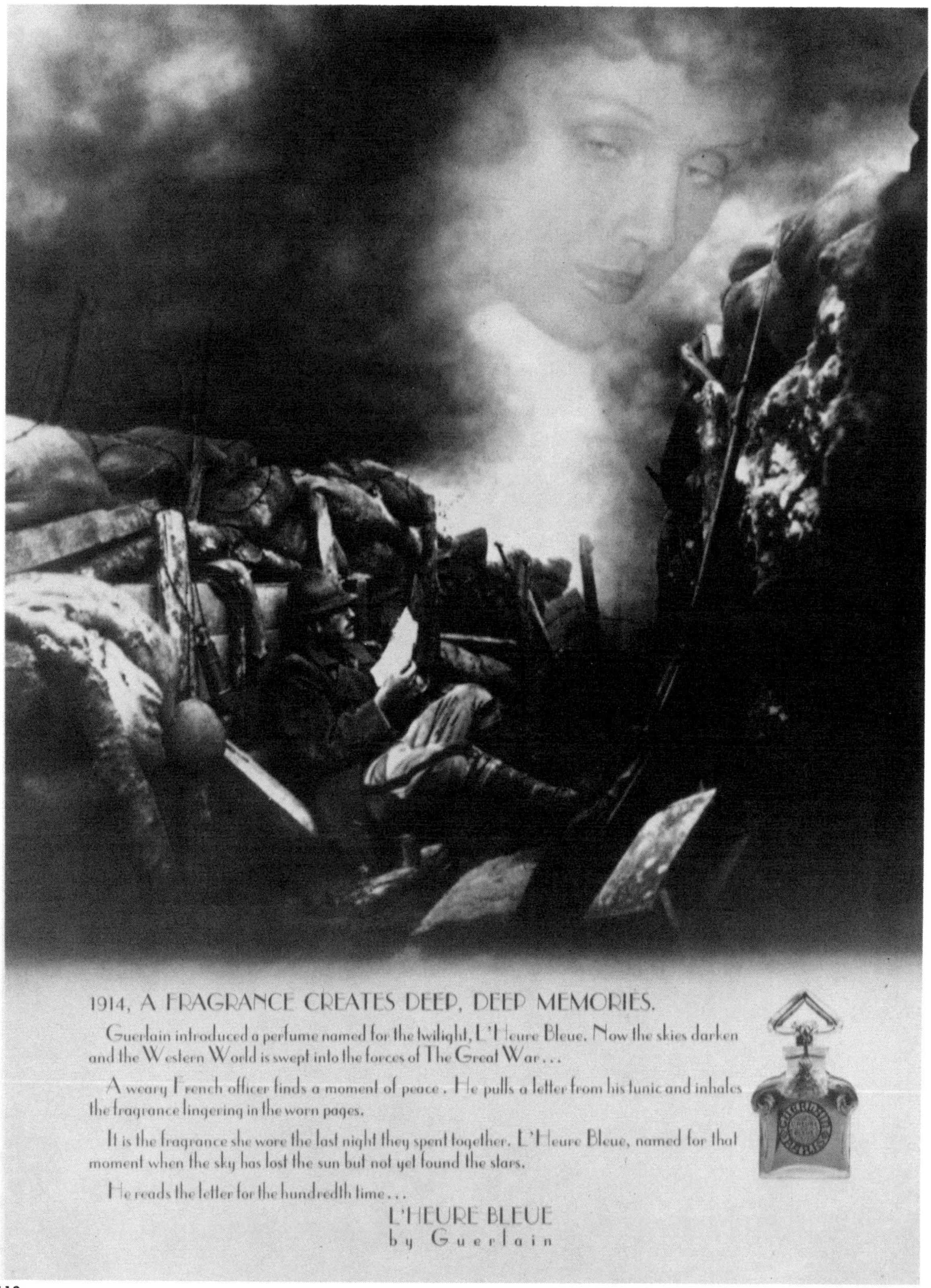
1914, A FRAGRANCE CREATES DEEP, DEEP MEMORIES.
Guerlain introduced a perfume named for the twilight, L'Heure Bleue. Now the skies darken and the Western World is swept into the forces of The Great War...
A weary French officer finds a moment of peace. He pulls a letter from his tunic and inhales the fragrance lingering in the worn pages.
It is the fragrance she wore the last night they spent together. L'Heure Bleue, named for that moment when the sky has lost the sun but not yet found the stars.
He reads the letter for the hundredth time...
L'HEURE BLEUE
by Guerlain

113
Art Director Gennaro Andreozzi
Writer Paul Margulies
Designer Gennaro Andreozzi
Photographer Steve Horn
Agency Primaute Advertising
Client Guerlain

The Volvo 164
A CIVILIZED CAR BUILT FOR AN UNCIVILIZED WORLD.
After thousands of years of progress, man continues to spend a great deal of his time standing still.
Trapped in endless traffic jams that can wear him out before his day even begins.
So when we designed the Volvo 164, we did all we could to make entrapment as painless as possible.
The 164's seats, for example, can keep you from crawling out of your skin no matter how long you've been crawling in traffic. Because instead of having them designed by a stylist, we called upon an engineer with the perfect background for the job. A bad back. What he developed were massive bucket seats (faced in genuine leather instead of genuine vinyl) that not only conform to the contours of the back, but can be adjusted to give the small of your back the exact support it requires.
This same precise thinking was also applied to the 164's interior. Which explains why it doesn't simply have ten-outlet air conditioning and heating, but a heated driver's seat as well. And why it doesn't simply have ample legroom for five adults, but enough for even a 6'6" driver.
Of course, the 164 is just as impressive going somewhere as it is going nowhere. With an aggressive, three liter fuel-injected engine and a thoughtful combination of safety features. Including disc brakes on all four wheels. Front and rear ends designed to help absorb the impact of a collision rather than passing it on to the passenger compartment. And a single-unit body so strong, any one of its thousands of spot welds is capable of supporting the weight of the entire body.
Yet with all this strength and comfort, the 164 is surprisingly nimble. Its turning circle is actually smaller than the Volkswagen Beetle's. A virtue you'll be particularly grateful for when tucking into tight parking spaces more ungainly luxury cars are forced to pass by.
Another 164 virtue—one that seems to grow more virtuous all the time—is its relatively meager need for gasoline. Latest government figures show the 164 gets about fifty percent more gas mileage than the most popular domestic cars in its price range.
So when you're not waiting on lines at gas stations, you can conserve your frustrations for the jammed-up roads ahead.
VOLVO

114

THE
FAMOUS GROUSE
90° PROOF SCOTCH WHISKY
100% SCOTCH WHISKIES BLENDED
Matthew Gloag & S
Perth, Scotlan
ESTABLISHED IN 180
4/5 QUART
PRODUCT OF SCOTLAND
BLENDED
AUSTIN, NICHOLS & CO
BOTTLED IN SCO
Bottled in Scotland
200
150
100
50
The Effects of Ice on Scotch
How fast a drink of Scotch whisky over rocks loses its flavor depends on the proof of the Scotch and the richness of its blend. These two factors are optimized for "on the rocks" Scotch drinkers in 90-Proof Famous Grouse, a venerable old brand from Scotland only recently introduced to America.
Pursuing a Perfect Proof
The Masters of Perth

115

114
Art Director Robert Reitzfeld
Writer Michael Drazen
Photographer Hal Davis
Agency Scali, McCabe, Sloves
Client Volvo of America Corp.

115
Art Director Irwin Goldberg
Writer Bob Larimer
Designers Irwin Goldberg
Arthur Zimmerman
Photographer Tom Seaton
Agency Nadler & Larimer
Client Austin Nichols & Co.

Nature also makes holes in teeth.
The Grand Canyon is a work of nature. So is a cavity.
The Canyon was formed over millions of years by wind and water tearing away at rock. A cavity is formed by the forces of nature at work in your mouth.
The bacteria in your mouth change the sugar in some food particles to acids that, day after day, eat away at tooth enamel – the hardest substance in your body.
Eventually the result is a cavity.
A tiny "canyon" in one of your teeth.
But you're not helpless, so cavities don't have to be an inevitability of nature.
Some of the things you can do may sound pretty basic. Getting yourself to do them can be the hardest part.
First, be sure you brush regularly with Crest. Especially after meals. That way, while you clean your teeth, the fluoride in Crest makes your tooth enamel more resistant to decay.
Next, see your dentist every six months. Give him a chance to catch little problems before they become big ones.
Third, use dental floss as your dentist recommends it.
And finally, you have to cut down on between-meal treats.
If you do all these things, you can help yourself have fewer cavities.
In a sense, you'll be taming one of the forces of nature.
Crest
Fighting cavities is the whole idea behind Crest.

116

Chase the chill with a few ounces of light Scotch. Eagle's Clydella sportshirt.
It's light-bodied. It makes you feel warm all over. It's blended in Scotland of 80% cotton and 20% lamb's wool. Eagle's great Clydella sportshirt comes in tartans, checks, tattersalls and solids. This one is the authentic Dress Douglas tartan. All of them mix well with water (just drop into a washing machine and shake).
Clydella, the other cheerful product of Scotland. Tailored by Eagle, the shirtmaker's shirtmaker.
EAGLE

117

116
Art Director Joe Gregorace
Writer Marv Jacobson
Photographer Four by Five Inc.
Agency Benton & Bowles
Client Procter & Gamble

117
Art Director Joseph Nissen
Writer Ed Hanft
Photographer Carl Fischer
Agency Chalk, Nissen, Hanft
Client Eagle Shirtmakers

Eagle proudly presents a brand new shirt with holes in it.
The business Aertex®

Why use the most comfortable fabrics only for sportshirts? It's during business and dress-up hours

that you really need a shirt that lets the cool air in and body heat out. Which is why Eagle designed a new collection of dress shirts out of what was originally only a sportshirt fabric. Aertex® the hole-iest fabric in the world. It's woven of polyester and cotton in stripes, checks and windowpane plaids, as shown here with Eagle's textured solid bowtie. For sports wear, we still make our Aertex® knit with the same open-air construction. Now Aertex® is all work and all play.

Eagle. The shirtmakers' shirtmaker.

118

When the old Saratoga trunks were packed, this is the kind of shirt that went along.

When Saratoga was in its original heyday and men flocked there to take the plunge (in the waters or at the races), there was no such thing as a sportshirt. Fabrics like this—brighter and more informal—served both purposes. It's time, Eagle feels, for the restoration of Saratoga Square. And for your convenience, we've done it now in durable press Dacron® polyester and cotton. (Illustrated here with Eagle's corded tambour tie).

Saratoga Square. Think of it as a vestige of our past that wears well.

From Eagle, the shirtmakers' shirtmaker.

119

118
Art Director Joseph Nissen
Writer Ed Hanft
Photographer Carl Fischer
Agency Chalk, Nissen, Hanft
Client Eagle Shirtmakers

119
Art Director Joseph Nissen
Writer Ed Hanft
Photographer Carl Fischer
Agency Chalk, Nissen, Hanft
Client Eagle Shirtmakers

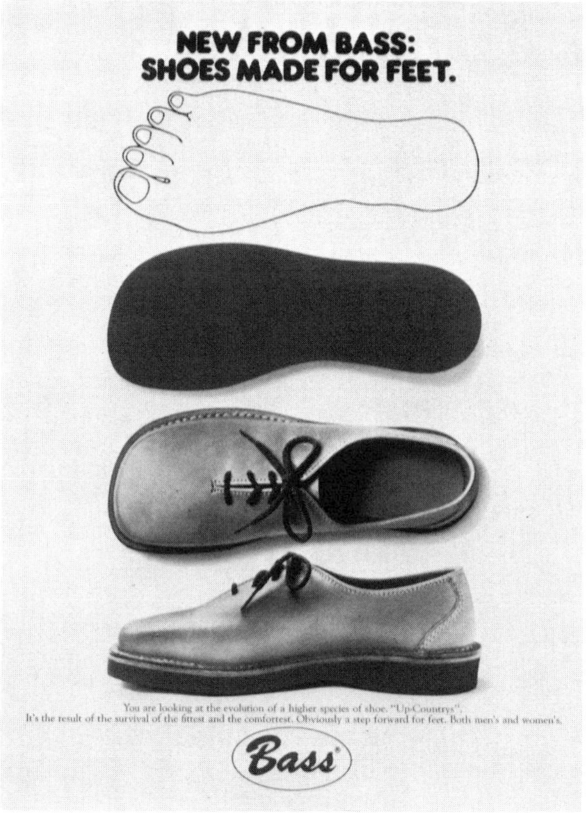
NEW FROM BASS:
SHOES MADE FOR FEET.
You are looking at the evolution of a higher species of shoe. "Up-Countrys".
It's the result of the survival of the fittest and the comfortest. Obviously a step forward for feet. Both men's and women's.
Bass

119A

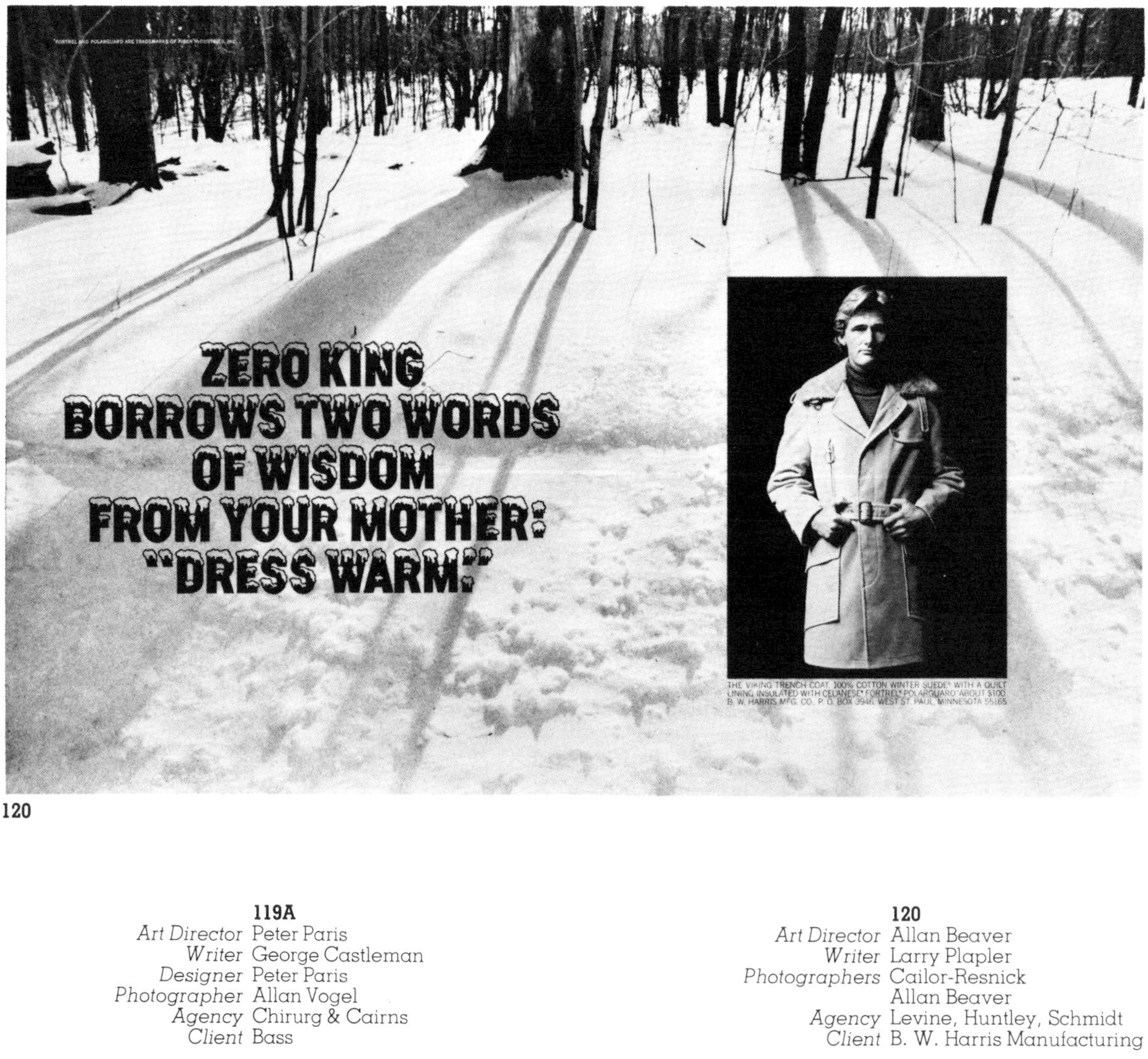
ZERO KING
BORROWS TWO WORDS
OF WISDOM
FROM YOUR MOTHER:
"DRESS WARM."
THE VIKING TRENCH COAT. 100% COTTON WINTER SUEDE* WITH A QUILT
LINING INSULATED WITH CELANESE* FORTREL* POLARGUARD* ABOUT $100
B. W. HARRIS MFG. CO., P. O. BOX 3946, WEST ST. PAUL, MINNESOTA 55165

120

119A
Art Director Peter Paris
Writer George Castleman
Designer Peter Paris
Photographer Allan Vogel
Agency Chirurg & Cairns
Client Bass

120
Art Director Allan Beaver
Writer Larry Plapler
Photographers Cailor-Resnick
Allan Beaver
Agency Levine, Huntley, Schmidt
Client B. W. Harris Manufacturing

AT LAST, A SONY. FOR MAHONEY.
Our new 19-inch-diagonal screen should be large enough even for large families. Well anyway—large, close families.
It's a Sony for Patrick Mahoney. Or his neighbor, Renaldo Carboni.
It has, of course, our famous one-gun, one-lens Trinitron system to give the Mahoneys our famous bright, sharp picture. And to make that picture even brighter and sharper, we've put in the world's widest-angle picture tube.
The wide, flat 114° angle shortens the distance the color beams must travel to the front of the tube. Which means color's more intense, and less subject to distortion.
It also means the set's thinner from back to front. And in crowded quarters, that's an advantage that isn't phony.
Right, Mrs. Mahoney? THE 19-INCH-DIAGONAL TRINITRON.
12

121

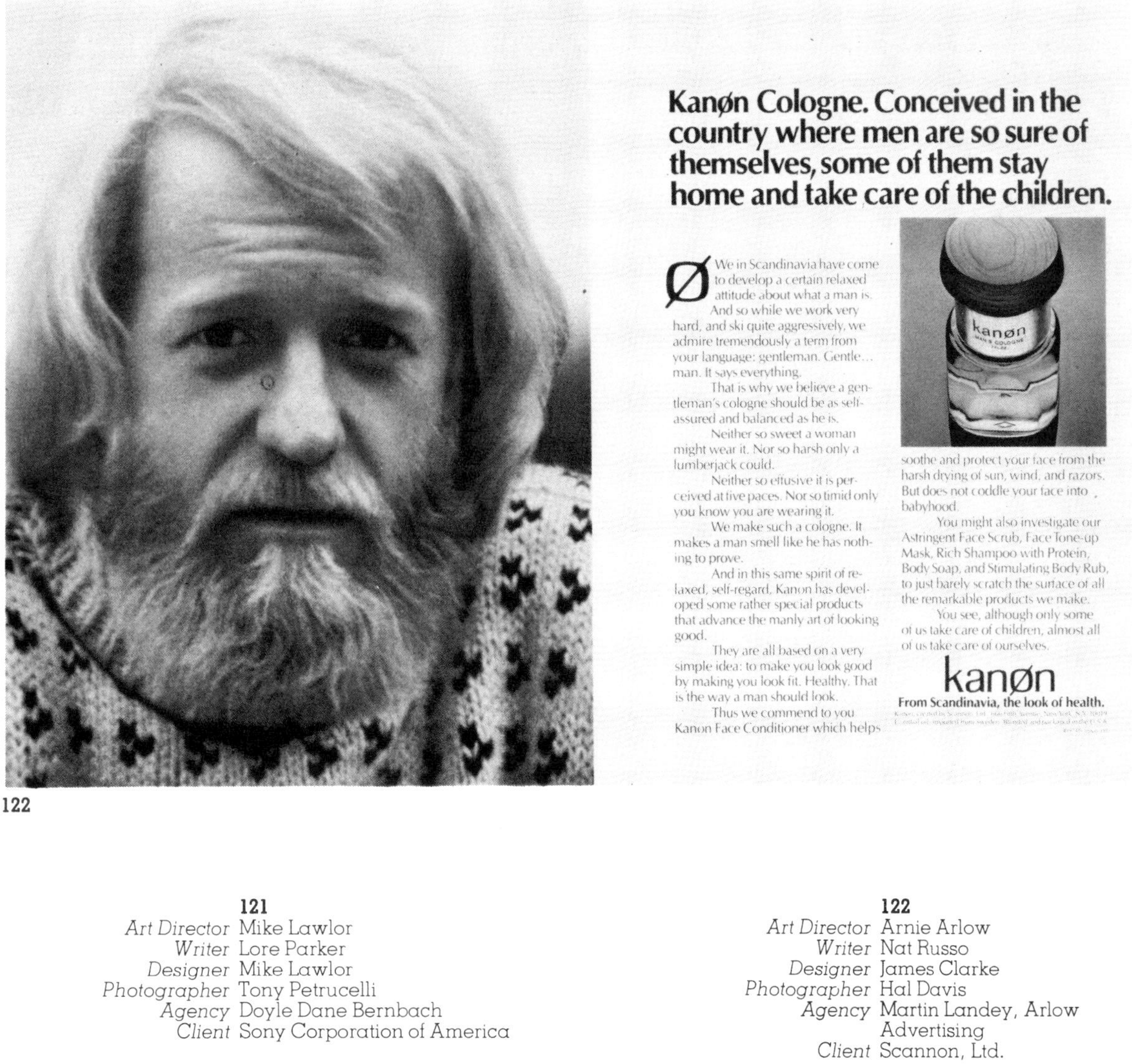
Kanøn Cologne. Conceived in the country where men are so sure of themselves, some of them stay home and take care of the children.
Ø We in Scandinavia have come to develop a certain relaxed attitude about what a man is.
And so while we work very hard, and ski quite aggressively, we admire tremendously a term from your language: gentleman. Gentle... man. It says everything.
That is why we believe a gentleman's cologne should be as self-assured and balanced as he is.
Neither so sweet a woman might wear it. Nor so harsh only a lumberjack could.
Neither so effusive it is perceived at five paces. Nor so timid only you know you are wearing it.
We make such a cologne. It makes a man smell like he has nothing to prove.
And in this same spirit of relaxed, self-regard, Kanon has developed some rather special products that advance the manly art of looking good.
They are all based on a very simple idea: to make you look good by making you look fit. Healthy. That is the way a man should look.
Thus we commend to you Kanon Face Conditioner which helps soothe and protect your face from the harsh drying of sun, wind, and razors. But does not coddle your face into babyhood.
You might also investigate our Astringent Face Scrub, Face Tone-up Mask, Rich Shampoo with Protein, Body Soap, and Stimulating Body Rub, to just barely scratch the surface of all the remarkable products we make.
You see, although only some of us take care of children, almost all of us take care of ourselves.
kanøn
From Scandinavia, the look of health.

122

121
Art Director Mike Lawlor
Writer Lore Parker
Designer Mike Lawlor
Photographer Tony Petrucelli
Agency Doyle Dane Bernbach
Client Sony Corporation of America

122
Art Director Arnie Arlow
Writer Nat Russo
Designer James Clarke
Photographer Hal Davis
Agency Martin Landey, Arlow Advertising
Client Scannon, Ltd.

The Beech-Nut Baby Research Report.
DO FAT BABIES BECOME FAT ADULTS?
A lot of mothers think fat babies are cute babies and fat babies are healthy babies. But actually, overfeeding a baby could be the beginning of a life-long problem. It's one of the most common causes of adult overweight.
Many fat adults are fat because they were fat babies.
Why do mothers overfeed babies?
It's very, very easy to confuse food and love. When you feed your baby you feel like he's accepting love from you. It's very satisfying when he takes food from you.
You might feel the more he eats, the healthier he's getting. And when he rejects food, very often it can feel like he's rejecting you and 'your' nourishment.
But, that's not true. And feeling like this could make you overfeed your baby.
Your baby knows more about how much he should eat than you do.
It's alright to let your baby tell you when he's finished. He knows. In your baby's body is a natural mechanism that regulates his food intake. This tells him how much he should eat, automatically. It's nature's way of taking care of your baby.
If you force your baby to eat more than he wants, you could be interfering with that mechanism and causing him to overeat.
And, if your baby seems to have any special eating problems, consult your pediatrician.
What happens when your baby is fed too much?
Your baby uses food to do more than give him energy. He uses food to grow. And he will eat a great deal of food in his first year, because in that time he'll triple in weight.
But, if he gets more than he wants, more than he needs, this extra food could grow into extra fat cells. Fat cells he will carry around with him for the rest of his life. And those extra fat cells will demand extra food, and make him fat.
Fat cells just sit there sending out their little messages, 'feed me, feed me.' And they usually get fed.
Eat. Eat.
Somewhere toward the end of the first year, your baby's growing appetite will begin slowing down. Don't worry. This is normal.
Your baby is reducing his rate of growing, and he is regulating his food intake. This is often the time when mothers think something has gone wrong with their baby's appetite, and force him to eat more than he needs.
But, if your baby kept gaining at his original rate, he'd end up weighing hundreds of pounds.
He'll decide how much. You decide what.
So, you see, the quantity of food is really up to your baby. Your job is making sure he gets the right quality. The kind of foods that satisfy his nutritional needs.
And that's where we can help. By offering you a complete line of wholesome, nourishing foods, full of the nutrients your baby needs.
All of our ingredients are scientifically measured to assure consistent, uniform nutrition. Then they are cooked with careful and continuous quality control.
We add no artificial colors, no artificial flavors, and no monosodium glutamate. And many of our foods are fortified with vitamins and minerals for extra nutrition.
For instance, when your baby is ready for cereal, that is the time when many babies need extra iron in their diets. So we fortify our cereal with extra iron to meet this need.
And, no matter which of our foods you choose, you can feel sure you are getting a nutritious, quality product for your baby.
The more you know, the more you can relax.
So, since you know that nature is taking care of your baby's appetite and Beech-Nut is taking care of his food, you can relax. Chances are, if you don't show any anxiety about food and eating, neither will your baby.
And feeding will become a happy, calm, close relationship that you can share with your baby.
This report is one of a series. If you are interested in reading the others, write to Baker/Beech-Nut Corporation, Consumer Service, Dept 101, Canajoharie, N.Y. 13317, and we'll be glad to send them to you.
This report is brought to you by Beech-Nut Baby Food. Wholesome, nutritious food for your baby.
Beech-Nut
cereal
Fortified with Vitamins & Minerals plus Iron
Baby Food

123

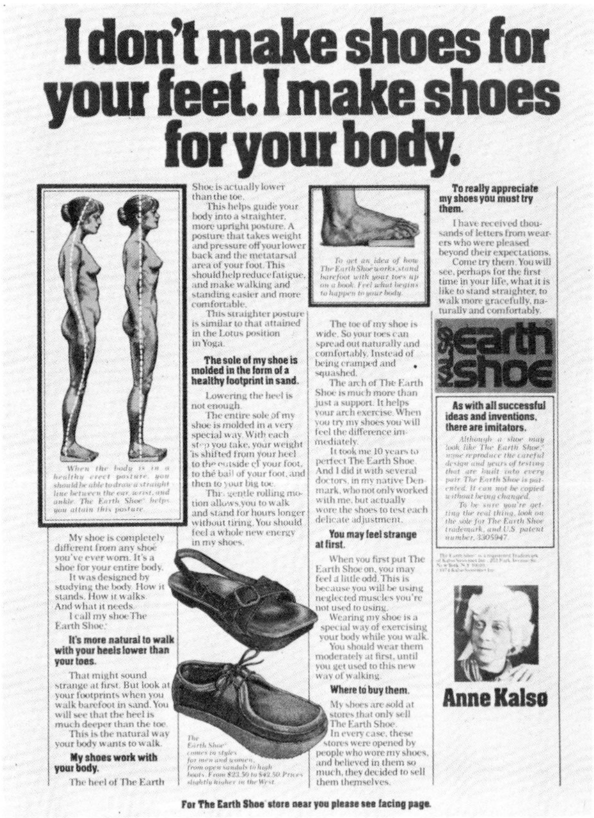
I don't make shoes for your feet. I make shoes for your body.
When the body is in a healthy erect posture, you should be able to draw a straight line between the ear, wrist, and ankle. The Earth Shoe helps you attain this posture.
My shoe is completely different from any shoe you've ever worn. It's a shoe for your entire body.
It was designed by studying the body. How it stands. How it walks. And what it needs.
I call my shoe The Earth Shoe.
It's more natural to walk with your heels lower than your toes.
That might sound strange at first. But look at your footprints when you walk barefoot in sand. You will see that the heel is much deeper than the toe.
This is the natural way your body wants to walk.
My shoes work with your body.
The heel of The Earth Shoe is actually lower than the toe.
This helps guide your body into a straighter, more upright posture. A posture that takes weight and pressure off your lower back and the metatarsal area of your foot. This should help reduce fatigue, and make walking and standing easier and more comfortable.
This straighter posture is similar to that attained in the Lotus position in Yoga.
The sole of my shoe is molded in the form of a healthy footprint in sand.
Lowering the heel is not enough.
The entire sole of my shoe is molded in a very special way. With each step you take, your weight is shifted from your heel to the outside of your foot, to the ball of your foot, and then to your big toe.
This gentle rolling motion allows you to walk and stand for hours longer without tiring. You should feel a whole new energy in my shoes.
The Earth Shoe comes in styles for men and women, from open sandals to high boots. From $23.50 to $42.50. Prices slightly higher in the West.
To get an idea of how The Earth Shoe works, stand barefoot with your toes up on a book. Feel what begins to happen to your body.
The toe of my shoe is wide. So your toes can spread out naturally and comfortably. Instead of being cramped and squashed.
The arch of The Earth Shoe is much more than just a support. It helps your arch exercise. When you try my shoes you will feel the difference immediately.
It took me 10 years to perfect The Earth Shoe. And I did it with several doctors, in my native Denmark, who not only worked with me, but actually wore the shoes to test each delicate adjustment.
You may feel strange at first.
When you first put The Earth Shoe on, you may feel a little odd. This is because you will be using neglected muscles you're not used to using.
Wearing my shoe is a special way of exercising your body while you walk.
You should wear them moderately at first, until you get used to this new way of walking.
Where to buy them.
My shoes are sold at stores that only sell The Earth Shoe.
In every case, these stores were opened by people who wore my shoes, and believed in them so much, they decided to sell them themselves.
To really appreciate my shoes you must try them.
I have received thousands of letters from wearers who were pleased beyond their expectations.
Come try them. You will see, perhaps for the first time in your life, what it is like to stand straighter, to walk more gracefully, naturally and comfortably.
Kalsø earth shoe
As with all successful ideas and inventions, there are imitators.
Although a shoe may look like The Earth Shoe, none reproduce the careful design and years of testing that are built into every pair. The Earth Shoe is patented. It can not be copied without being changed.
To be sure you're getting the real thing, look on the sole for The Earth Shoe trademark, and U.S. patent number, 3305947.
Anne Kalsø
For The Earth Shoe store near you please see facing page.

124

Why everybody's pretending they're us.
These are not Earth shoes. Just because they look like Earth shoes doesn't mean they are Earth brand shoes.
There was a time when the EARTH* negative heel shoe was the only shoe in the world with the heel lower than the toe.
In those days the other people who made shoes just laughed at us.
But things have changed.
And now that you love our Earth brand shoes, now that you're standing in line to get them, the shoe companies have stopped laughing and started copying.
The shoes that look like, seem like, but don't work like the Earth shoe.
Today, a lot of people are trying to imitate our shoe. Some even use names that sound like ours, and have ads that look like ours!
It seems like everybody's trying to be us.
But what they don't understand is this. Merely lowering the heel of a shoe isn't enough. And imitating the outside of our shoe isn't enough. Just because a shoe looks like the Earth shoe doesn't mean it works like the Earth shoe.
It took many years to perfect the Earth brand shoe. And those years are crucial. They make our shoe different from all its imitators.
How the Earth Shoe was invented.
It started years ago when Anne Kalsø had the original idea for the negative heel shoe.
She saw footprints in the sand, and realized that with every footprint the body was designing a shoe.
A natural shoe. A shoe with the heel lower than the toe. A shoe that would work in harmony with your entire body.
But that was just the beginning. Then came the years of research and hard work to get every detail just right. To perfect the arch. To make the toes wide, comfortable and functional. To balance the shoe. To mold the sole in a special way so that it would allow you to walk in a natural rolling motion. Gently and easily even on the hard jarring cement of our cities.
To get an idea of how the Earth shoe works, stand barefoot with your toes up on a book. Feel what begins to happen.
The Earth brand shoe comes in styles for men and women, from open sandals to high boots. From $23.50 to $42.50. Prices slightly higher in the west.
Patent 3305947. Why the Earth shoe is unique.
The Earth shoe is patented. That means it can't be copied without being changed.
And if it's changed it just isn't the Earth shoe.
So to be sure you're getting the real thing, look on the sole for our patent number and our trademark, Earth. If they're not there, it's not the Earth brand shoe.
Sold only at Earth shoe stores.
And there's one more thing that makes our shoes so special. Our stores.
Earth shoes are sold only at Earth shoe stores. Stores that sell no other shoe but ours, and are devoted entirely to the Earth shoe concept.
How our shoes fit you is very important to us. There's a special technique to fitting them. Our people are trained to fit you properly and we wouldn't trust anyone else to do it.
Find out for yourself.
To really appreciate Earth shoes you must try them.
When you do you'll see, perhaps for the first time in your life, what it's like to walk more gracefully, naturally and comfortably.
Kalsø earth shoe
*EARTH is the registered trademark of Kalsø Systemet, Inc. for its negative heel shoes and other products.
Anne Kalsø.
Inventor of the EARTH negative heel shoe.
You can only buy Earth shoes at Earth Shoe Stores in the cities listed on the facing page.

125

123
Art Director Mel Platt
Writer Jennifer Berne
Designer Mel Platt
Photographer Michael O'Neill
Agency Martin Landey, Arlow Advertising
Client Beech-Nut Baby Food

124
Art Director Mel Platt
Writer Jennifer Berne
Designer Mel Platt
Artist Norman Green
Agency Martin Landey, Arlow Advertising
Client Kalsø

125
Art Director Mel Platt
Writer Jennifer Berne
Designer Mel Platt
Artist Norman Green
Photographer Lee Batlin
Agency Martin Landey, Arlow Advertising
Client Kalsø

The 4-minute 3,000 mile.
When you have to get information somewhere fast—the Xerox Telecopier transceiver is a record breaker.
By simply dialing an ordinary telephone you can send copies of documents, diagrams, drawings, even photographs from anywhere in the country to anywhere else in the country.
Even from coast to coast in just four minutes or less.
And just think, with the Xerox Telecopier, if you're sending something from New York to California it gets there 2 hours and 56 minutes before you sent it.
For more information just call our toll free number, (800) 255-4180, and a Xerox representative will run right over.
XEROX
XEROX® and TELECOPIER® are trademarks of XEROX CORPORATION
XEROX

INTRODUCING THE PORTABLE COPIER FROM XEROX.
Funny, it was here a minute ago.
Somebody probably rolled it to Merchandising to make copies of their price lists and brochures.
Or to the Law Department to copy some contracts and proposals.
Or to Accounting to copy some pages from their ledgers.
The Xerox 3100 portable copier. The one on wheels.
You can count on it for making copies, if not for making ads.
XEROX

The new Xerox 4500 copier. Scrooge would have loved it.
Of course he would have. Scrooge was no fool. Especially when it came to saving. And that's exactly what the new Xerox 4500 copier does. It saves. With two features you just can't find in any other copier.
First, the 4500 copier isn't just one of your ordinary everyday copiers. This one also copies on both sides of the same piece of paper, automatically. So naturally it saves paper. And that saves mailing costs. Not to mention saving filing space.
Second, there's the built-in sorter. This little penny pincher collects all the copies and puts them together in order, in just seconds. Which is a real convenience when it comes to saving time. And energy. And aggravation.
The Xerox 4500 copier. For the little bit of Scrooge in all of us.
XEROX

126

SILVER

126
Art Directors Allen Kay
Jeff Cohen
Writers Lester Colodny
Lois Korey
Photographers Dave Langley
Howard Menken
George Ehrlich
Agency Needham, Harper & Steers
Client Xerox Corp.

Salvatore Ferragamo knows the art of strewing men at your feet. The pump, meant for appreciation, for adoration. Gilded with an ornament. Taupe, brown or black calf, from Italy and ours alone. $64. Shoe Salon.
SAKS FIFTH AVENUE
CELEBRATING FIFTY YEARS OF FASHION

SAKS FIFTH AVENUE
CELEBRATING FIFTY YEARS OF FASHION

Our Dancing Daughters know youth must have its fling. And all the rage is the chic T-strap slipper created by our own Beth in camel, grey or black kid, $58. An absolute "must" for the lady about town. Beth's Bootery.
SAKS FIFTH AVENUE
CELEBRATING FIFTY YEARS OF FASHION

127

127
Art Director Richard Martino
Writer Jerry Bennett
Designer Max Jordan
Artists Redro Barrious
Jim Howard
Photographers Deborah Turbeville
Maureen Lambray
Arthur Elgort
Richard Blinkoff
Agency Saks Advertising Department
Client Saks Fifth Avenue

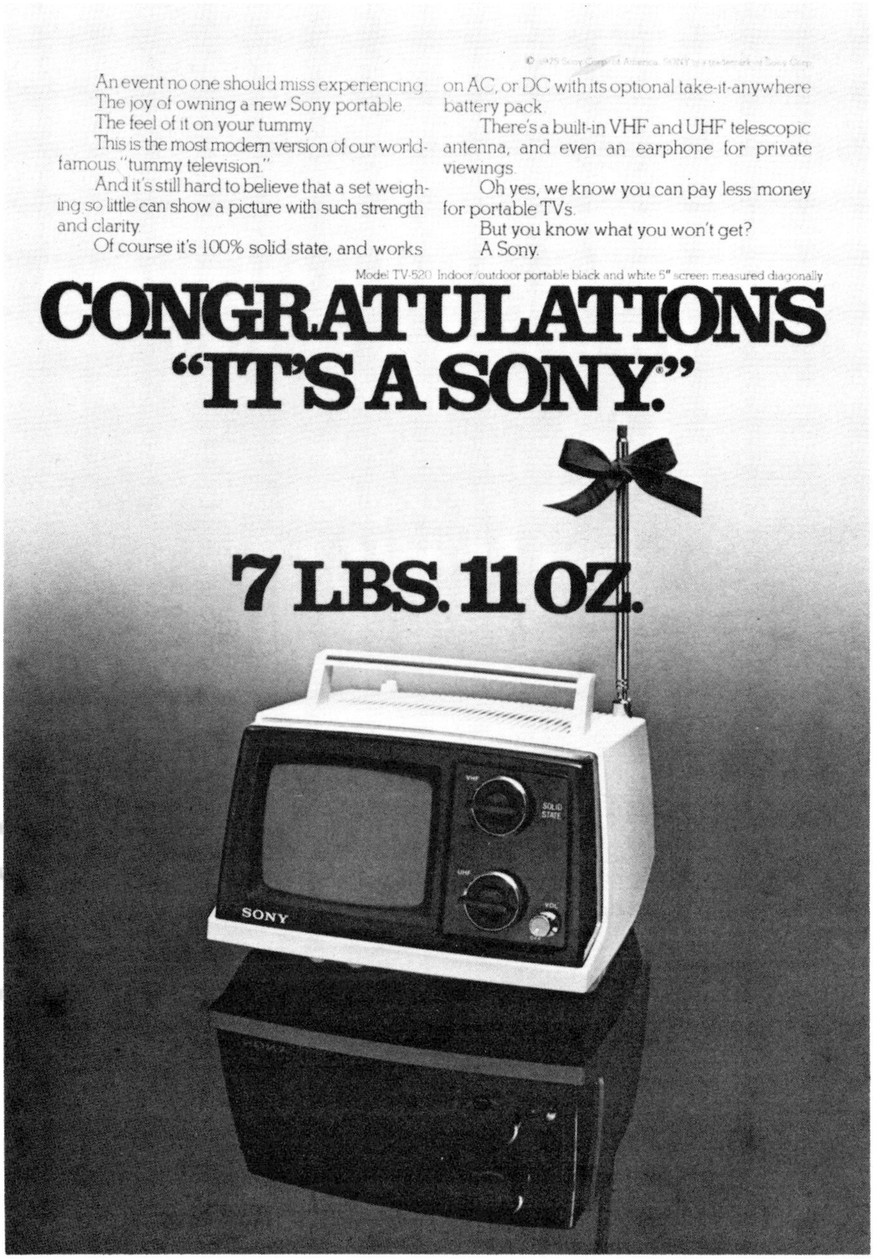
An event no one should miss experiencing.
The joy of owning a new Sony portable.
The feel of it on your tummy.
This is the most modern version of our world-famous "tummy television."
And it's still hard to believe that a set weighing so little can show a picture with such strength and clarity.
Of course it's 100% solid state, and works on AC, or DC with its optional take-it-anywhere battery pack.
There's a built-in VHF and UHF telescopic antenna, and even an earphone for private viewings.
Oh yes, we know you can pay less money for portable TVs.
But you know what you won't get?
A Sony.
Model TV-520. Indoor/outdoor portable black and white 5" screen measured diagonally
CONGRATULATIONS
"IT'S A SONY."
7 LBS. 11 OZ.
SONY

You have to wake up at least once every day. So why not make the best of it?
And this Sony Digimatic Clock Radio is the best of it.
It not only tells you the hour, minute and second, it lets you know the day and the date.
You can choose FM or AM, music alarm or buzzer alarm.
Or you can hit the "Snooze Bar" and make it all go away for another 8 minutes. And then automatically come back.
What you perhaps wouldn't know is how such a rich, beautiful sound can come out of a radio less than 5" high.
Because the same technology and precision the world admires in Sony television sets, can be admired in Sony radios.
So shop around. There are a lot of radios that do a lot of the things our radios do.
But a radio by any other name is not a Sony.
EVERYTHING
YOU'VE ALWAYS WANTED
TO KNOW IN YOUR BEDROOM.
"IT'S A SONY."

There's not a wasted inch of space. Top, sides and front. Switches, toggle switches and dials.
Sony technology has mastered the portable radio.
Here's a list of things this radio can do.
First, and most important, it makes a tremendous sound. Only 8" high, the speaker is an over-sized 4¾".
That's backed up by a powerful 2.8-watt (max.) output.
And that's backed up by a "Squelch Switch" to suppress interfering noise.*
So what you end up with are the rich velvety tones that normally come out of radios too big to carry around.
There are three bands, FM, AM, and Public Service. (Police car transmissions, for instance.)
A "moving film" style tuning dial.
And a 60-minute timer that turns the radio on and off.
Why not stop in at a Sony dealer and get checked out.
Then find a lonely stretch of road, and open her up.
THE COCKPIT.
SONY
"IT'S A SONY."

PRINT ADVERTISING

128
Art Director John Caggiano
Writer Marvin Honig
Designer John Caggiano
Photographer George Hausman
Agency Doyle Dane Bernbach
Client Sony Corporation of America

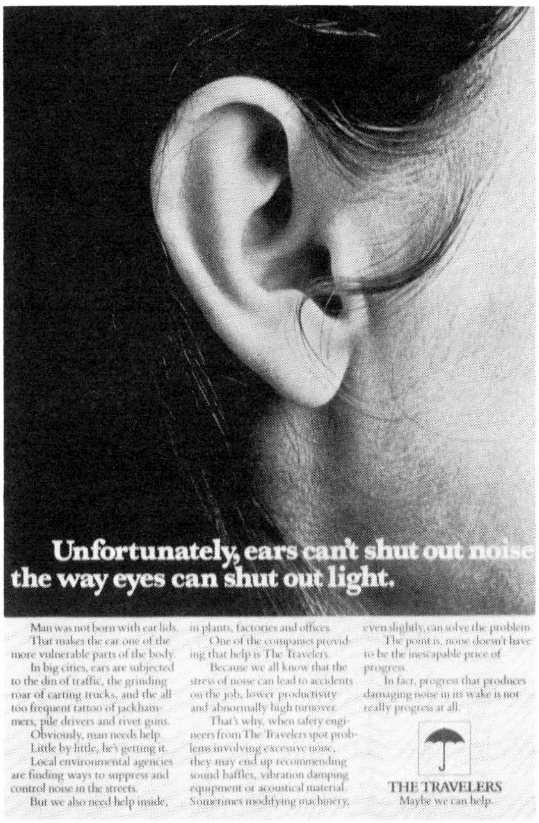
Unfortunately, ears can't shut out noise the way eyes can shut out light.
Man was not born with ear lids. That makes the ear one of the more vulnerable parts of the body.
In big cities, ears are subjected to the din of traffic, the grinding roar of carting trucks, and the all too frequent tattoo of jackhammers, pile drivers and rivet guns.
Obviously, man needs help.
Little by little, he's getting it.
Local environmental agencies are finding ways to suppress and control noise in the streets.
But we also need help inside, in plants, factories and offices.
One of the companies providing that help is The Travelers.
Because we all know that the stress of noise can lead to accidents on the job, lower productivity and abnormally high turnover.
That's why, when safety engineers from The Travelers spot problems involving excessive noise, they may end up recommending sound baffles, vibration damping equipment or acoustical material. Sometimes modifying machinery, even slightly, can solve the problem.
The point is, noise doesn't have to be the inescapable price of progress.
In fact, progress that produces damaging noise in its wake is not really progress at all.
THE TRAVELERS
Maybe we can help.

What's it like to be the mother of three kids when you're already the father?
There's no one way to describe it because it's different for every man who loses his wife.
But no matter what kind of an emotional adjustment he has to make, he still has to deal with the economic realities. Somebody's got to take care of the kids and the house. Which may mean hiring a full-time housekeeper.
If his wife had a job, as four out of ten mothers* do these days, that extra money is gone. Money that could have helped later on with the mortgage or the kids' education.
Maybe that's why the traditional idea of insuring the wife with only a token amount doesn't make as much sense anymore.
The Travelers life insurance people have developed a number of plans to meet the needs of today's family.
Since each plan is a little different, you really ought to look up your local Travelers agent in the Yellow Pages to find out which one's right for you.
But do it soon. And do it together.
THE TRAVELERS
Maybe we can help.
*U.S. Department of Labor Statistics

LANGLEY & BUTLER
466-8721
MOVING
Local-Long Distance
The neighbors didn't know the Forans were moving. Neither did the Forans.
You're looking at a burglary in progress.
While the Forans were away on vacation, three bogus moving men pulled up in a van, let themselves in through the back door, and emptied the house. In broad daylight.
This little story is true. Only the names have been changed.
Granted, it's not the kind of problem the average homeowner has to deal with on a day-to-day basis.
More typical are those once-in-a-lifetime things that seem to happen two or three times a year. Like the day someone gets hurt tripping over your welcome mat. Or the night that old maple blows over on your garage.
Obviously, you're going to need insurance. The question is, how much and what kind of protection is enough?
The Travelers knows how confusing that can be. That's why our Homeowners policy not only covers the big things, it also covers more of the little unsuspected things, the ones that can seem very big if you have to pay for them out of your own pocket.
If you'd like to know just how comprehensive a comprehensive Homeowners policy can be, talk to your local Travelers agent. See the Yellow Pages.
THE TRAVELERS
Maybe we can help.

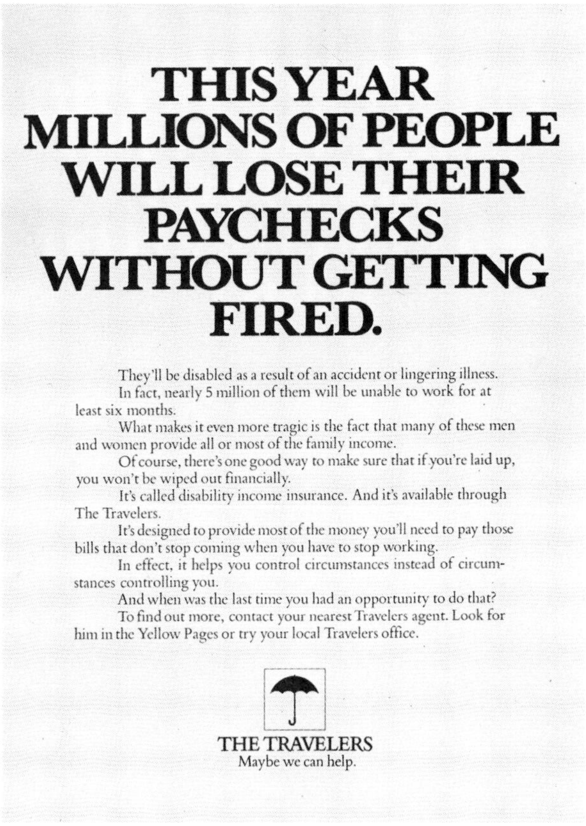
THIS YEAR MILLIONS OF PEOPLE WILL LOSE THEIR PAYCHECKS WITHOUT GETTING FIRED.
They'll be disabled as a result of an accident or lingering illness.
In fact, nearly 5 million of them will be unable to work for at least six months.
What makes it even more tragic is the fact that many of these men and women provide all or most of the family income.
Of course, there's one good way to make sure that if you're laid up, you won't be wiped out financially.
It's called disability income insurance. And it's available through The Travelers.
It's designed to provide most of the money you'll need to pay those bills that don't stop coming when you have to stop working.
In effect, it helps you control circumstances instead of circumstances controlling you.
And when was the last time you had an opportunity to do that?
To find out more, contact your nearest Travelers agent. Look for him in the Yellow Pages or try your local Travelers office.
THE TRAVELERS
Maybe we can help.

129

129
Art Director Mike Tesch
Writer Ed Butler
Photographers Alen MacWeeney
Peter Papadopolous
David Langley
Agency Carl Ally
Client The Travelers Insurance Cos.

Historic note based on "Minding the Store" by Mr. Stanley Marcus published by Little Brown & Company.
OUR CHIEF RESOURCE.
When a former Texan and good customer of ours, was appointed ambassador to New Zealand, he teased his wife by saying they were finally moving to a place where no one ever heard of Neiman-Marcus.
After they had been at their new post for a while, the Australian Minister of External Territories invited the Ambassador and his wife to New Guinea. To the wildest and most unsettled parts. Where the natives had never seen an American before.
On the appointed morning the Ambassador's party flew to remote Papua and were taken up river by boat. Past little villages they travelled. Amidst overgrown jungle. The sound of drums told them they were approaching the village of the native Chief. They disembarked and, in torrents of rain, hacked their way through the undergrowth until they got to the Chieftain's hut.
The excited natives and New Guinea officials assured the Ambassador and his wife that they would see marvelous native handcrafts. Rare and exotic objects never before available to tourists.
Soon the Chieftain arrived. Through an interpreter he was told that his visitor was an important ambassador. From the great state of Texas. Where cattle with enormous horns roamed the land. The Chieftain broke into a great smile. "Texas," he said. "Ah, Neiman-Marcus."
You see, just a little while earlier one of our buyers had chartered a bush plane to take her to this same tiny village, in hopes of finding rare native crafts. She had just placed a large order with the Chief. And had made him a friend of Neiman-Marcus for life.
Proving once again that in their quest for the unusual, our buyers are hunters who use their heads.
Neiman-Marcus

IN 1907
WE HAD A DECISION TO MAKE.
The month was March. The city was Atlanta. And the setting was a small, but successful advertising agency.
Hard at work were three vital young people. Herbert Marcus, his sister Carrie and her husband A.L. Neiman.
Just two years before they had left Dallas. Marcus with the insult of a $1.87 a week raise after years of service in a local store. And Neiman with his tall, dark-eyed, young bride.
Among the little advertising agency's first clients was an Atlanta company that wanted to promote a new kind of drink. It tasted unique. It fizzed a lot. And it was called Coca Cola. Soon, thanks to the efforts of the little agency, and the fact that people thought it tasted swell on a hot day Coca-Cola was a name on most Atlantans' lips. And a bottle in their homes.
In fact, in just two years, this funny new drink had become so popular, that in March of 1907 the two Texans were offered an interesting deal. They could swap their advertising agency for stock in the Atlanta bottling company of Coca-Cola plus the Missouri franchise for Coke. Or they could sell out for $25,000 cash.
It didn't take Carrie and the brothers-in-law long to make their decision. After all, Coke might be a flash in the bottle. And $25,000 was a lot of money.
Was it a bad decision? Depends how you look at it. If they had taken the stock in Coca-Cola they could have retired as multi-millionaires in a few short years.
Instead they went home to Dallas and opened their dream store.
So now America has both a soft drink and a store that are "the real thing."
Neiman-Marcus

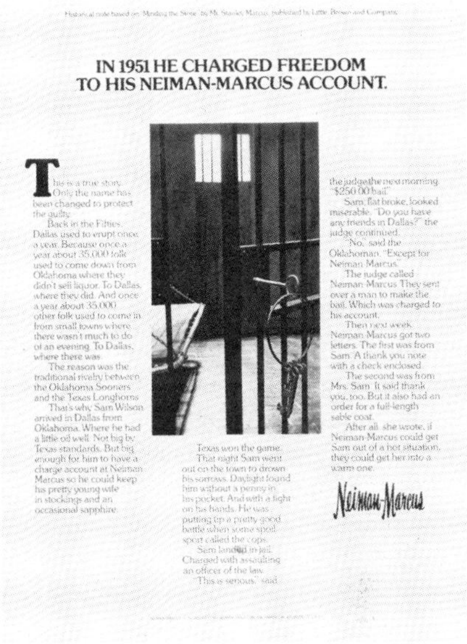
IN 1951 HE CHARGED FREEDOM
TO HIS NEIMAN-MARCUS ACCOUNT.
This is a true story. Only the name has been changed to protect the guilty.
Back in the Fifties, Dallas used to erupt once a year. Because once a year about 35,000 folk used to come down from Oklahoma where they didn't sell liquor. To Dallas, where they did. And once a year about 35,000 other folk used to come in from small towns where there wasn't much to do of an evening. To Dallas, where there was.
The reason was the traditional rivalry between the Oklahoma Sooners and the Texas Longhorns.
That's why Sam Wilson arrived in Dallas from Oklahoma. Where he had a little oil well. Not big by Texas standards. But big enough for him to have a charge account at Neiman Marcus so he could keep his pretty young wife in stockings and an occasional sapphire.
Texas won the game.
That night Sam went out on the town to drown his sorrows. Daylight found him without a penny in his pocket. And with a fight on his hands. He was putting up a pretty good battle when some spoil sport called the cops.
Sam landed in jail. Charged with assaulting an officer of the law.
"This is serious," said the judge the next morning. "$250.00 bail."
Sam, flat broke, looked miserable. "Do you have any friends in Dallas?" the judge continued.
"No," said the Oklahoman. "Except for Neiman Marcus."
The judge called Neiman Marcus. They sent over a man to make the bail. Which was charged to his account.
Then next week, Neiman Marcus got two letters. The first was from Sam. A thank you note with a check enclosed.
The second was from Mrs. Sam. It said thank you, too. But it also had an order for a full-length sable coat.
After all, she wrote, if Neiman-Marcus could get Sam out of a hot situation, they could get her into a warm one.
Neiman-Marcus

130

Art Director Alan Goodman
Writers Joyce Fabian
Susan Fraser
Designer Alan Goodman
Artist Alan Goodman
Photographers Charles Gold
Richard Noble
Klaus Lucka
Steve Dolce
Agency Leber Katz Partners
Client Neiman Marcus

STEINWAY IS A STEINWAY IS A STEINWAY.
There are different sizes. And different prices.
But large or small, when a piano bears the Steinway name you may be certain that it was built to the standard set by Henry E. Steinway 435,000 pianos ago: "Build the finest piano possible and sell it at the lowest price consistent with quality."
From smallest vertical to concert grand, all Steinway pianos are built by the same hands. Regardless of size, they share patented and exclusive features (like Steinway's Diaphragmatic® Sound Board). Features which endow the instrument with the Steinway sound.
We make no "cheaper" piano. We make no second-line piano sold under another name. We make only the Steinway.®
And no one else has ever managed to build anything quite like it.
For more information please write to Mr. John H. Steinway, 109 West 57th Street, New York, New York 10019.
STEINWAY & SONS

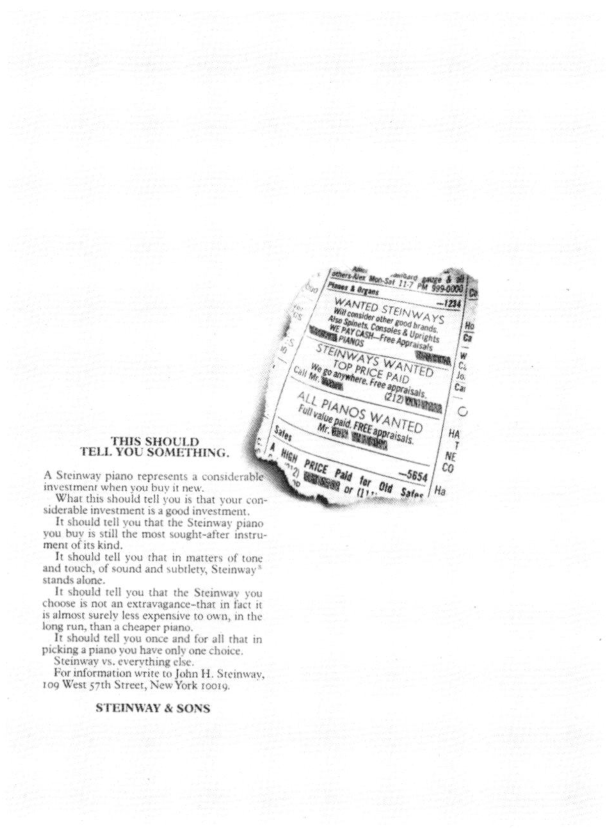
WANTED STEINWAYS
STEINWAYS WANTED TOP PRICE PAID
ALL PIANOS WANTED
THIS SHOULD TELL YOU SOMETHING.
A Steinway piano represents a considerable investment when you buy it new.
What this should tell you is that your considerable investment is a good investment.
It should tell you that the Steinway piano you buy is still the most sought-after instrument of its kind.
It should tell you that in matters of tone and touch, of sound and subtlety, Steinway® stands alone.
It should tell you that the Steinway you choose is not an extravagance–that in fact it is almost surely less expensive to own, in the long run, than a cheaper piano.
It should tell you once and for all that in picking a piano you have only one choice.
Steinway vs. everything else.
For information write to John H. Steinway, 109 West 57th Street, New York 10019.
STEINWAY & SONS

HOW WE PERSUADE SO MANY ARTISTS TO PLAY THE STEINWAY PIANO.
Something ineffable exists between an artist and an instrument.
The relationship is intensely personal, and most pianists pick instruments with greater care and deliberation than one might use in choosing a mate.
So it's significant that all over the world most of the important pianists, the immortals if you will, own one or more Steinway pianos.
We do not lend them, or any other artists, instruments for their homes.
Nor do we pay them for their kind words of endorsement.
We convince them to buy and play the Steinway® with the same unanswerable sales argument we have used since 1853...by building the finest piano we know how to build. Which is a special kind of artistry all its own.
For more about it write to Mr. John H. Steinway, 109 West 57th Street, New York, New York 10019.
STEINWAY & SONS

THE WIZARD OF WALKER STREET.
The pianos of the day had a thin, nasal sound when Henry E. Steinway set up shop in Walker Street in New York City.
Starting in 1853, he and his descendants quietly began to "re-invent" the instrument.
They redesigned scales, repositioned bridges, reworked actions. They literally changed the shape of the piano for all time and produced an instrument of unprecedented sensitivity, and power – the most technically advanced piano of its time.
Today under the guidance of Henry E. Steinway's heirs, the company he founded is still the unchallenged technical leader.
Today only a Steinway® has the touch, the tone, the sensitivity, and the power of a Steinway. Because it continues to be the most advanced and modern piano being built.
The Wizard lives!
For more information please write to Henry E. Steinway's great-great grandson, William T. Steinway, 109 West 57th Street, New York 10019.
STEINWAY & SONS

131

131
Art Director Cathie Campbell
Writer Arthur Einstein
Designer Cathie Campbell
Photographers David Langley
John Paul Endress
Carl Fischer
(Mathew Brady)
Agency Lord, Geller, Federico
Client Steinway & Sons

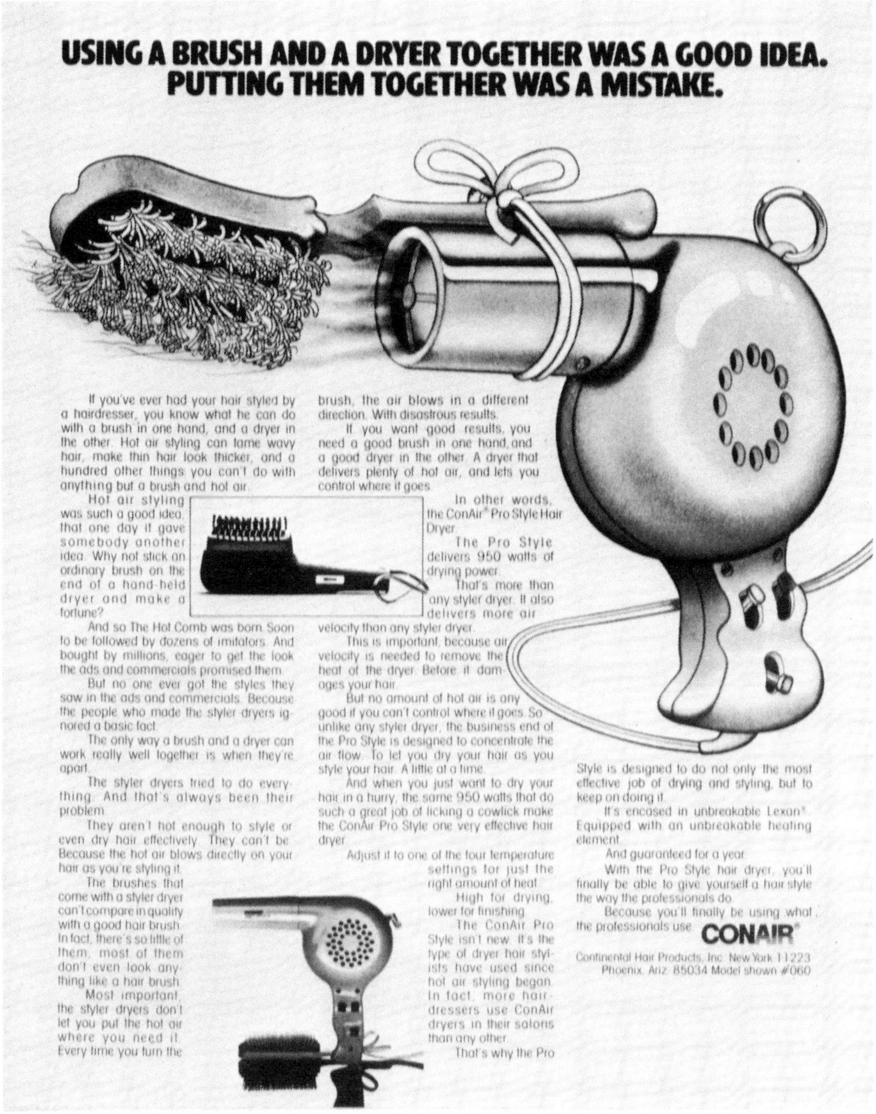
USING A BRUSH AND A DRYER TOGETHER WAS A GOOD IDEA.
PUTTING THEM TOGETHER WAS A MISTAKE.
If you've ever had your hair styled by a hairdresser, you know what he can do with a brush in one hand, and a dryer in the other. Hot air styling can tame wavy hair, make thin hair look thicker, and a hundred other things you can't do with anything but a brush and hot air.
Hot air styling was such a good idea, that one day it gave somebody another idea. Why not stick an ordinary brush on the end of a hand-held dryer and make a fortune?
And so The Hot Comb was born. Soon to be followed by dozens of imitators. And bought by millions, eager to get the look the ads and commercials promised them.
But no one ever got the styles they saw in the ads and commercials. Because the people who made the styler dryers ignored a basic fact.
The only way a brush and a dryer can work really well together is when they're apart.
The styler dryers tried to do everything. And that's always been their problem.
They aren't hot enough to style or even dry hair effectively. They can't be. Because the hot air blows directly on your hair as you're styling it.
The brushes that come with a styler dryer can't compare in quality with a good hair brush. In fact, there's so little of them, most of them don't even look anything like a hair brush.
Most important, the styler dryers don't let you put the hot air where you need it. Every time you turn the brush, the air blows in a different direction. With disastrous results.
If you want good results, you need a good brush in one hand, and a good dryer in the other. A dryer that delivers plenty of hot air, and lets you control where it goes.
In other words, the ConAir® Pro Style Hair Dryer.
The Pro Style delivers 950 watts of drying power.
That's more than any styler dryer. It also delivers more air velocity than any styler dryer.
This is important, because air velocity is needed to remove the heat of the dryer. Before it damages your hair.
But no amount of hot air is any good if you can't control where it goes. So unlike any styler dryer, the business end of the Pro Style is designed to concentrate the air flow. To let you dry your hair as you style your hair. A little at a time.
And when you just want to dry your hair in a hurry, the same 950 watts that do such a great job of licking a cowlick make the ConAir Pro Style one very effective hair dryer.
Adjust it to one of the four temperature settings for just the right amount of heat.
High for drying, lower for finishing.
The ConAir Pro Style isn't new. It's the type of dryer hair stylists have used since hot air styling began. In fact, more hairdressers use ConAir dryers in their salons than any other.
That's why the Pro Style is designed to do not only the most effective job of drying and styling, but to keep on doing it.
It's encased in unbreakable Lexan®. Equipped with an unbreakable heating element.
And guaranteed for a year.
With the Pro Style hair dryer, you'll finally be able to give yourself a hair style the way the professionals do.
Because you'll finally be using what the professionals use.
CONAIR®
Continental Hair Products, Inc. New York 11223
Phoenix, Ariz. 85034 Model shown #060

WHAT MAKES IT TWICE THE DRYER
IS THAT IT WORKS IN HALF THE TIME.
CONAIR®

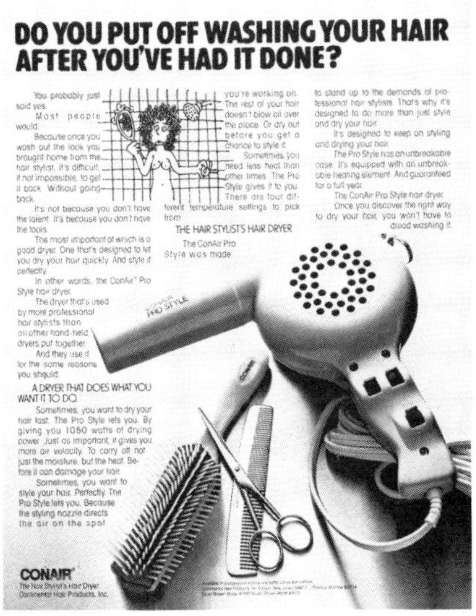
DO YOU PUT OFF WASHING YOUR HAIR
AFTER YOU'VE HAD IT DONE?
THE HAIR STYLIST'S HAIR DRYER
A DRYER THAT DOES WHAT YOU WANT IT TO DO.
CONAIR®

132
Art Director Nick Gisonde
Writer Mark Shenfield
Designer Nick Gisonde
Artist Whistlin Dixie
Photographer Cailor-Resnick
Agency Della Femina, Travisano & Partners
Client Continental Hair Products

The thought of wearing a bathing suit made me lose 66 pounds.

By Mavis Molina — as told to Ruth L. McCarthy

I cheated on weekends and lost 60 pounds.

By Diane Gabriele — as told to Ruth L. McCarthy

Watch me lose 125 pounds —a picture at a time.

By Betty O'Neal—as told to Ruth L. McCarthy

270 pounds Here I am at my top weight. And it began years ago with Mom saying: "If you're a good girl, you'll get an extra cookie." I was so good, my thighs wound up as big as most girls' waists.

255 pounds I'd lost 15 pounds, yet I still preferred sofas to chairs. I once sat in an arm chair and when I stood up, it wouldn't let go. But what really got me losing was those ads about a reducing plan candy that helps curb your appetite.

232 pounds Down 38 pounds! Quite a record for someone who loved to eat. But I'd never have done it on will-power alone. I needed help and those Ayds® candies gave it to me. I'd take a couple with a hot drink before a meal and I'd actually eat less.

215 pounds No question the Ayds plan was really working for me now. Why, when I saw those scales down 55 pounds, I knew nothing could stop me until I got to my goal — below 150. Another thing. I found I could pass up pies, donuts and cakes more easily because those Ayds also satisfied my sweet tooth.

195 pounds A big turning point! I'd broken the 200-pound barrier. To reward myself I decided to have a huge meal and gooey dessert one day a week. Something to look forward to. And it worked. I still lost.

145 pounds Success! I was down to my goal. And just look at that beautiful waist! I don't know who is more proud — my husband or I. But we're both very happy, thanks to the Ayds plan.

The new me! Betty O'Neal

Note: *Photos are from the personal album of Betty O'Neal, Chicago, Illinois. The picture at right was for laughs: Betty in a dress she wore before losing 125 pounds on the Ayds plan. Incidentally, Ayds contain vitamins and minerals, no drugs, and are available at drug counters.*

BEFORE AND AFTER MEASUREMENTS

	Before	After
Height	5'6"	5'6"
Weight	270 lbs.	145 lbs.
Bust	53"	38½"
Waist	46"	28"
Hips	55"	36"
Dress	26½	12

133

GOLD

133

Art Director Charley Aromando
Writer Ruth L. McCarthy
Designer Charley Aromando
Photographers Irwin Cohn
Jerry Cohen
Agency Wilson Haight & Welch
Client Campana Corp.

Presenting the 84 mpg Volkswagen.
Since all the car manufacturers are conducting their own mileage tests these days, we at Volkswagen thought we'd conduct one too.
So we modified our body—and our engine. And, of course, we got someone who didn't weigh much to drive.
Lo and behold, we got 84 miles per gallon!
Ridiculous? Nobody normally drives like this? Of course. That's precisely our point.
Nobody normally drives like most of those tests you're seeing.
Volkswagen. An honest 25* miles per gallon.

LATE CITY ★★★★ EDITION
WEATHER: Sunny, Breezy, Cooler.
BIG THREE GO UP!
G.M., Ford, Chrysler Hike Prices.
Little One Stays Down!
Still $2625*

Some of the most unusual things about a Volkswagen are things you don't usually see.
Look under the fender of a Volkswagen and you'll find something you wouldn't dream of finding: paint.
We use 13 lbs. of it on every VW. And in the most unlikely places. (If you have nothing to do sometime, remove one of our inside door panels and see what's underneath.)
Under the chassis of a Volkswagen you'll find something only a handful of cars in the world have: a sealed steel bottom. This protects all those vital things inside the car from all those vile things out there on the road. (Look under your car and you'll see how exposed and vulnerable everything is.)
See those four wheels sticking up in the air in the picture below? Well, you can press down on any one of them and move it without any of the others moving. What this means is when the car is right side up and one wheel hits a bump, none of the other wheels feel a thing.
Now, consider that you get all these luxury car features (and more) at an economy car price . . . with economy car gas mileage . . . the most advanced car coverage in the world (Owner's Security Blanket) . . . and almost unbelievable resale value (a '72 VW retails† for as much today as it did new).
You couldn't find a better buy if you stood on your head.
Still $2625*

134

134
Art Director Charles Piccirillo
Writer Mike Mangano
Photographers Larry Sillen
David Langley
Frank Cowan
Agency Doyle Dane Bernbach
Client Volkswagen of America Corp.

THE MIGHTY AND CUNNING SEA IS NO PLACE FOR A BARGAIN BOAT.
Dozens of boats lie scattered along the bottom of the Florida Keys.
Coral-encrusted galleons. Seeping tankers.
Clouds of fry spook and shimmer in the blue, filtered sunlight of the warm waters as they dart amongst rusting hulks and fiberglass hulls.
Yes, fiberglass hulls.
The Caribbean is the spawning ground of sudden squalls and blackening cloud fronts that can catch a small open boat like a cornered fox.
At a time like this, a 'salesman's special' can make your heart pound faster than a bonefish skiff in a chop.
A boat the experts trust.
Check with Florida fishing clubs and you'll find out which boat the experts put their trust in.
SeaCraft. It's chosen by more fishing club members in South Florida than any other boat.
You could ride out seas in a SeaCraft where other boats would crack. SeaCrafts are braced with fiberglass beams laminated to the hull. For incredible rigidity and strength.
You could sit out a wave-frothing storm in a SeaCraft while other boats scurried for port. SeaCrafts have self-bailing cockpits that flush out water like a downspout. Even when the boat is not moving. And actually suck it out when it is.
Or you could beat them home to port. SeaCraft holds the Miami/Nassau twin-outboard world speed record.
There isn't a boat anywhere, that has SeaCraft's ride, performance, or speed in its matching class. Because no other boat has SeaCraft's hull, the VDH.
The patented VDH hull.
The VDH or Variable Deadrise Hull, is a vee hull consisting of a series of different-angle planes. It is the only hull that combines the deep vee's soft ride with the shallow-draft's great stability at rest.
The VDH lays down a film of air between the hull and the water. This air gives our hull two astonishing properties. It acts like a lubricant, greasing a SeaCraft's speed up to 10% faster than a comparable deep vee. And it acts like a cushion. To give the SeaCraft a ride as soft as a goosedown pillow.
Cost where it counts.
It costs money to build boats of great strength and water-riding efficiency.
Neither show in a showroom.
But when you're far from port and angry black clouds are moving low across the sea toward you, you'll find out where you spent your money.
For an illustrated brochure on the complete SeaCraft line, write: SeaCraft, Dept. 2B 24400 S.W. 137th Avenue, Princeton, Florida 33030.
SEACRAFT

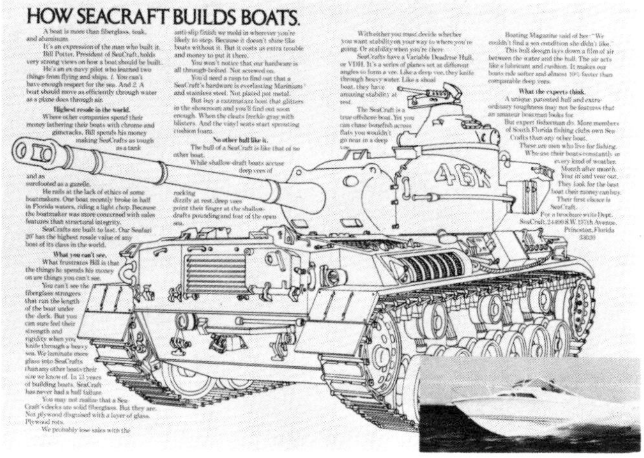
HOW SEACRAFT BUILDS BOATS.
46K

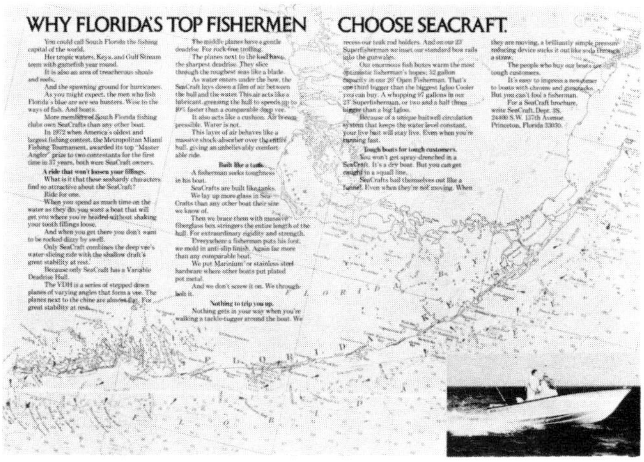
WHY FLORIDA'S TOP FISHERMEN CHOOSE SEACRAFT.

135

135
Art Director Joe Ciccarone
Writer Peter Evans
Designer Joe Ciccarone
Artist Peter Evans
Agency Peter Evans Advertising
Client Seacraft

CLASS OF '58
If this seems like only yesterday, imagine how soon tomorrow will be here.
If you're wondering where the years went since the '58 Prom, we can't help you. But if you're wondering where they're likely to go from here, we can.
Sometime very soon—probably while you're busy trying to cope with the present—your children will grow up. They won't give notice; you'll simply wake up and find yourself the parent of undergraduates, instead of grade schoolers.
Which is why we'd like to remind you that the future is no time to plan for the future. You have to do it while you're young. And that's the best reason for seeing a Metropolitan Life representative now.
At Metropolitan, we're helping over 40 million people secure their financial future. And what we do for them, we can do for you.
Of course, nobody can tell you exactly what will happen in the future. But whatever does, it's nice to know you and your family will be ready for it.
Metropolitan Life
Where the future is now

A child is someone who passes through your life, and then disappears into an adult.
Of all the people and things in your life, children are perhaps the best indicators of how quickly time passes.
All the cliches are true. They do grow up before your very eyes. They are little girls one moment, and college students the next.
And one day before you know it, your child becomes someone different, a full-fledged person with a life and a future all her own.
Nobody can slow the process down for you. But we can help make sure her future will be a secure one.
At Metropolitan Life, we've spent over a century helping people prepare for the future. Helping them prepare for college and a career and anything else that might arise. And we can do the same for your child as well.
Of course, nobody can say exactly what will happen in the future. But whatever does, it's nice to know your child will be ready for it.
Metropolitan Life
Where the future is now

Someone you love has had a heart attack. You can panic. Or you can save his life.
It happens with terrifying suddenness. What do you do? Try and comfort him? Call for help? Call a doctor and hope he arrives in time?
There's no adequate preparation for a moment like this. But you can do something besides standing by helplessly.
You don't have to be a doctor to save someone's life. If a heart attack victim is attended to within the first two minutes, his chances of survival are still good. And to help him, all you need is a little training.
We'd like to urge you to get that training. Before you need it.
There's a life-saving technique currently being used with great success by hospitals and by rescue squads. It's called Cardio-Pulmonary Resuscitation (CPR), but don't be scared off by the name. It can be learned in as little as 3 hours.
We can't teach CPR, but there are many qualified organizations who can—your local Heart Association and Red Cross among them. Contact one of these. And if you write us, we'll send along a wallet-sized card describing the elementary steps of the CPR procedure. Write: "CPR," Metropolitan Life, One Madison Avenue, New York, N.Y. 10010.
Our interest in this is simple. At Metropolitan Life, everything we do is connected with people's futures. And making sure those futures are not only secure, but long.
Metropolitan Life
Where the future is now

136
Art Director Bob Engel
Writer Tom Thomas
Photographers Bert Stern
Joe Toto
Tony Petrucelli
Agency Young & Rubicam International
Client Metropolitan Life Insurance Co.

THE BIG CAR EXPERTS.
SMALL
It's not that easy.
The people who've been bringing millions of big cars into the world for years and years aren't doing too much bragging about their big cars these days.
They've taken up another cry. Today they're "the small car experts."
For us at Fiat, small car expertise came not as painlessly or as suddenly. We've been making small cars for 70 years.
The difference between our slow evolution and their instant knowledge is obvious in the cars we make.
The Fiat 124 has almost a foot more legroom than a Maverick, a Nova, a Mustang II, and a Capri.
A small car shouldn't be a big car made smaller.
It even has more legroom than an Eldorado, an Imperial, and a Continental.*
The 124 isn't low and sleek like some of Detroit's small cars. Instead it gives you more headroom than a Rolls Royce.*
This height, plus exceptionally large windows, keeps you from the claustrophobia those sleek small cars are becoming famous for.
The backseat of the 124 isn't the typical small car backseat. There's enough room in the back for two people 6'6" without their knees being up around their chins. And the trunk will hold 7 pieces of luggage for those full-sized people.
Unlike many small cars, the 124 isn't underpowered. It'll cruise faster than you'd normally care to go.
Most people who make small cars really want to sell you something else.
It corners flat and steers precisely. (Which is unique even in Detroit's big cars.) Of course, we did learn a few things from the big car boys. Our 124 comes with automatic transmission and air conditioning.
Now it's their turn to learn a few things from us.
FIAT
The biggest selling car in Europe.
*Automotive News Almanac 1974
Overseas delivery arranged through your dealer.

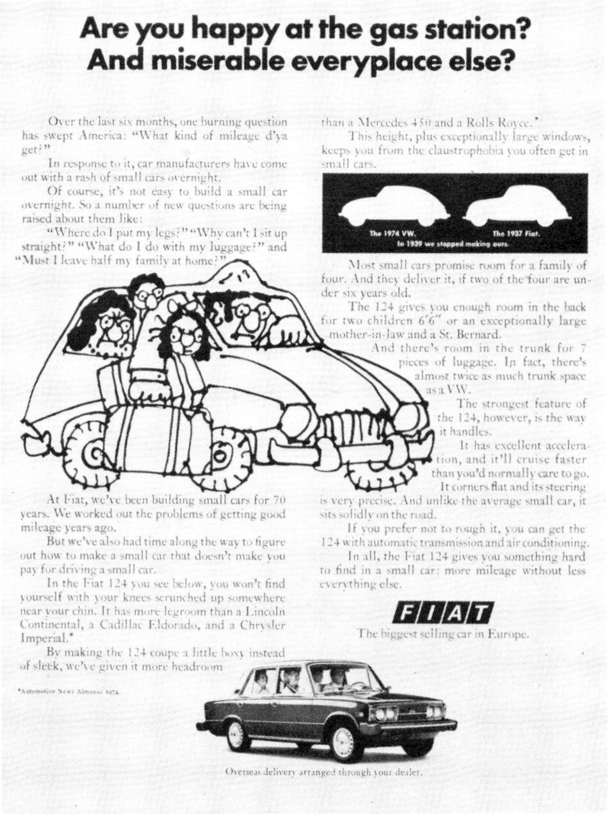
Are you happy at the gas station?
And miserable everyplace else?
Over the last six months, one burning question has swept America: "What kind of mileage d'ya get?"
In response to it, car manufacturers have come out with a rash of small cars overnight.
Of course, it's not easy to build a small car overnight. So a number of new questions are being raised about them like:
"Where do I put my legs?" "Why can't I sit up straight?" "What do I do with my luggage?" and "Must I leave half my family at home?"
At Fiat, we've been building small cars for 70 years. We worked out the problems of getting good mileage years ago.
But we've also had time along the way to figure out how to make a small car that doesn't make you pay for driving a small car.
In the Fiat 124 you see below, you won't find yourself with your knees scrunched up somewhere near your chin. It has more legroom than a Lincoln Continental, a Cadillac Eldorado, and a Chrysler Imperial.*
By making the 124 coupe a little boxy instead of sleek, we've given it more headroom than a Mercedes 450 and a Rolls Royce.*
This height, plus exceptionally large windows, keeps you from the claustrophobia you often get in small cars.
The 1974 VW.
The 1937 Fiat.
In 1939 we stopped making ours.
Most small cars promise room for a family of four. And they deliver it, if two of the four are under six years old.
The 124 gives you enough room in the back for two children 6'6" or an exceptionally large mother-in-law and a St. Bernard.
And there's room in the trunk for 7 pieces of luggage. In fact, there's almost twice as much trunk space as a VW.
The strongest feature of the 124, however, is the way it handles.
It has excellent acceleration, and it'll cruise faster than you'd normally care to go.
It corners flat and its steering is very precise. And unlike the average small car, it sits solidly on the road.
If you prefer not to rough it, you can get the 124 with automatic transmission and air conditioning.
In all, the Fiat 124 gives you something hard to find in a small car: more mileage without less everything else.
FIAT
The biggest selling car in Europe.
*Automotive News Almanac 1974.
Overseas delivery arranged through your dealer.

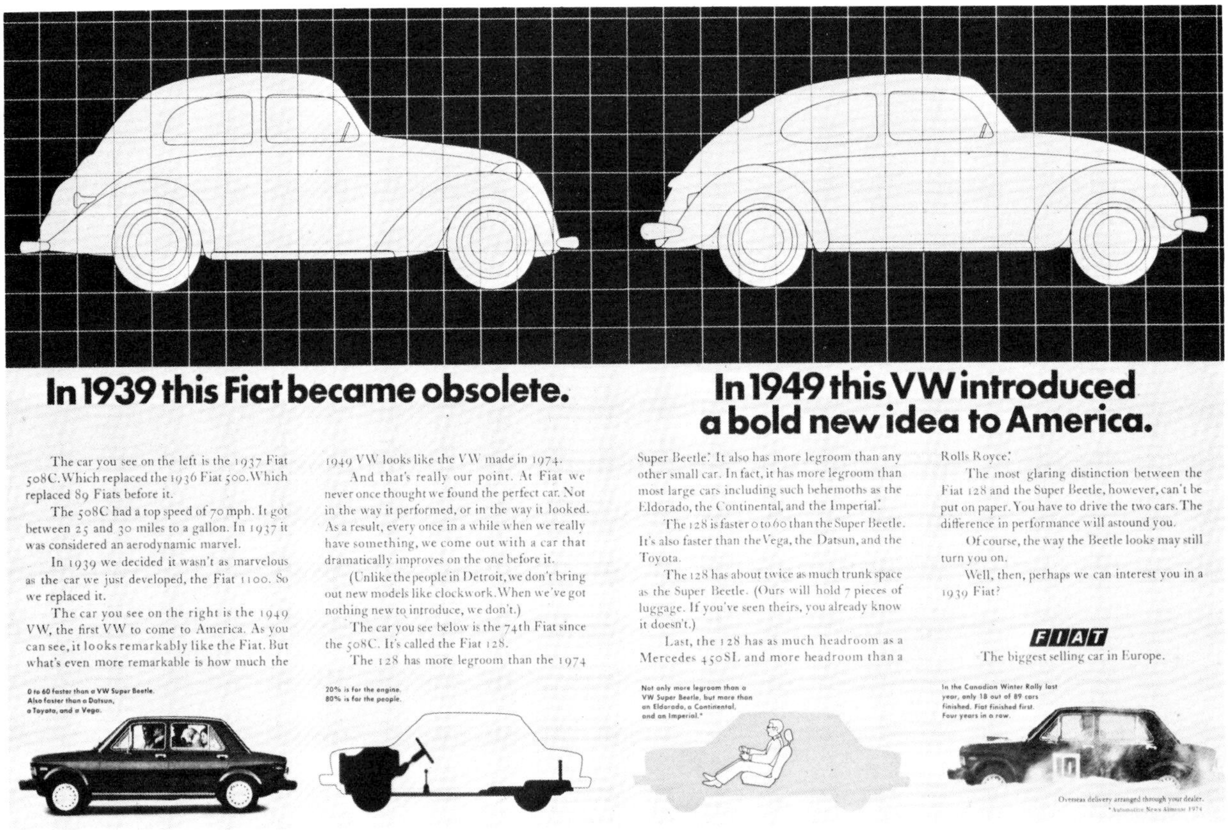
In 1939 this Fiat became obsolete.
In 1949 this VW introduced a bold new idea to America.
The car you see on the left is the 1937 Fiat 508C. Which replaced the 1936 Fiat 500. Which replaced 89 Fiats before it.
The 508C had a top speed of 70 mph. It got between 25 and 30 miles to a gallon. In 1937 it was considered an aerodynamic marvel.
In 1939 we decided it wasn't as marvelous as the car we just developed, the Fiat 1100. So we replaced it.
The car you see on the right is the 1949 VW, the first VW to come to America. As you can see, it looks remarkably like the Fiat. But what's even more remarkable is how much the 1949 VW looks like the VW made in 1974.
And that's really our point. At Fiat we never once thought we found the perfect car. Not in the way it performed, or in the way it looked. As a result, every once in a while when we really have something, we come out with a car that dramatically improves on the one before it.
(Unlike the people in Detroit, we don't bring out new models like clockwork. When we've got nothing new to introduce, we don't.)
The car you see below is the 74th Fiat since the 508C. It's called the Fiat 128.
The 128 has more legroom than the 1974 Super Beetle.* It also has more legroom than any other small car. In fact, it has more legroom than most large cars including such behemoths as the Eldorado, the Continental, and the Imperial.*
The 128 is faster 0 to 60 than the Super Beetle. It's also faster than the Vega, the Datsun, and the Toyota.
The 128 has about twice as much trunk space as the Super Beetle. (Ours will hold 7 pieces of luggage. If you've seen theirs, you already know it doesn't.)
Last, the 128 has as much headroom as a Mercedes 450SL and more headroom than a Rolls Royce.*
The most glaring distinction between the Fiat 128 and the Super Beetle, however, can't be put on paper. You have to drive the two cars. The difference in performance will astound you.
Of course, the way the Beetle looks may still turn you on.
Well, then, perhaps we can interest you in a 1939 Fiat?
FIAT
The biggest selling car in Europe.
0 to 60 faster than a VW Super Beetle. Also faster than a Datsun, a Toyota, and a Vega.
20% is for the engine. 80% is for the people.
Not only more legroom than a VW Super Beetle, but more than an Eldorado, a Continental, and an Imperial.*
In the Canadian Winter Rally last year, only 18 out of 89 cars finished. Fiat finished first. Four years in a row.
Overseas delivery arranged through your dealer.
*Automotive News Almanac 1974

137

137
Art Director Roy Grace
Writer David Altschiller
Artist Lou Meyers
Photographers Tony Petrucelli
Mick Pateman
Agency Carl Ally
Client Fiat-Roosevelt Motors

What becomes a Legend most?
Blackglama
BLACKGLAMA® IS THE WORLD'S FINEST NATURAL DARK RANCH MINK BRED ONLY IN AMERICA BY THE GREAT LAKES MINK MEN.

138

What becomes a Legend most?
Blackglama
BLACKGLAMA® IS THE WORLD'S FINEST NATURAL DARK RANCH MINK BRED ONLY IN AMERICA BY THE GREAT LAKES MINK MEN.

What becomes a Legend most?
Blackglama
BLACKGLAMA® IS THE WORLD'S FINEST NATURAL DARK RANCH MINK BRED ONLY IN AMERICA BY THE GREAT LAKES MINK MEN.

138
Art Director Peter Rogers
Writer Jane Trahey
Photographer Bill King
Agency Trahey/Rogers
Client Great Lakes Mink Assoc.

A copier should solve problems, not create them.
In the late '50s, the copier became the wonder of the American office.
A thing of beauty, serving a vital role despite the waste and bottlenecks it sometimes caused.
Since then, copying has grown into a major office function. And now that the copier has lost its novelty, we at IBM have developed a way to make sure it solves problems, rather than creates them.
It goes beyond just selling you a copier. It involves our total office experience to match the copier to your office requirements. To your people. Your procedures. Your flow of work.
In other words, we're prepared to help you better manage your entire copying system.
Further, we have something else rather unique.
A pricing plan that lets you know *beforehand* what the limits of your copier costs will be. No matter how many copies you make.
Call our Office Products Division. One of our Representatives will be happy to go to work on your problems. Even those that may not be problems yet.
IBM
Word Processing

A copier either works for your office, or against it.
IBM
Word Processing

The last thing you need is a copier you don't need.
IBM
Word Processing

139

139
Art Director Jerry Whitley
Writer Jim Durfee
Photographer Bill Tiadecki
Agency Carl Ally
Client IBM-Office Products

In whiskey,
you're not good because you're famous
...you're famous because you're good.
AMERICAN LIGHT WHISKEY • A BLEND • 100% AMERICAN WHISKEY • 86 PROOF • ©1974 FOUR ROSES DIST. CO., N.Y.C.

In whiskey,
this picture is worth a thousand words...

How to ask for a choice whiskey
in two choice words.

140

Art Directors Wally Littman
Tony Zamora
Writers Gordon Bushell
Robert Feinberg
Designers Wally Littman
Tony Zamora
Artist Osborn Charles
Agency William Esty
Client Four Roses Distillers

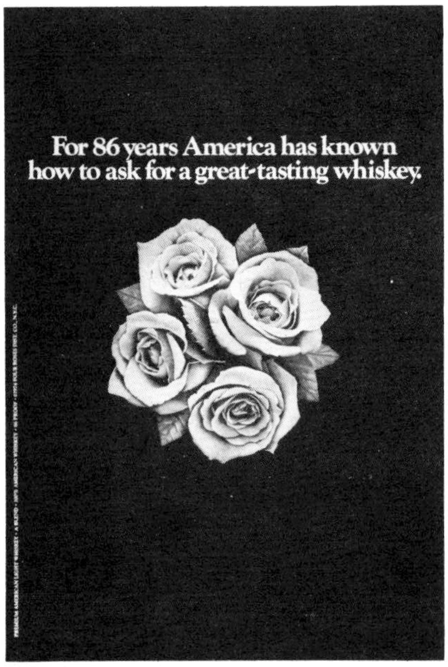
For 86 years America has known
how to ask for a great-tasting whiskey.

Quick,
think of a great whiskey
...to give*
*Elegantly gift packaged, with the famous eggnog recipe included.

Quick...think of a great whiskey.
PREMIUM AMERICAN LIGHT WHISKEY · A BLEND · 100% AMERICAN WHISKEY · 86 PROOF · ©1974 FOUR ROSES DIST. CO., N.Y.C.

141

141
Art Directors Wally Littman
Tony Zamora
Writers Gordon Bushell
Robert Feinberg
Designers Wally Littman
Tony Zamora
Artist Osborn Charles
Agency William Esty
Client Four Roses Distillers

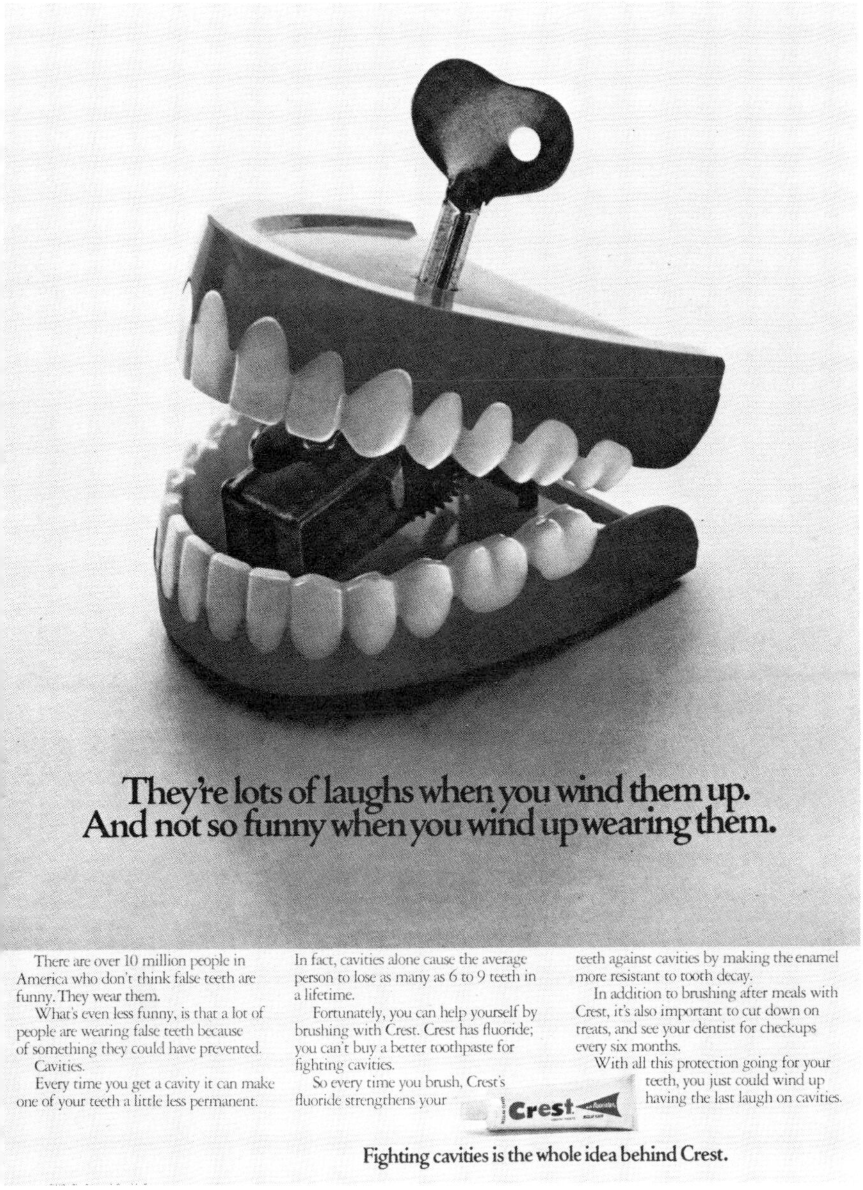
They're lots of laughs when you wind them up.
And not so funny when you wind up wearing them.
There are over 10 million people in America who don't think false teeth are funny. They wear them.
What's even less funny, is that a lot of people are wearing false teeth because of something they could have prevented.
Cavities.
Every time you get a cavity it can make one of your teeth a little less permanent.
In fact, cavities alone cause the average person to lose as many as 6 to 9 teeth in a lifetime.
Fortunately, you can help yourself by brushing with Crest. Crest has fluoride; you can't buy a better toothpaste for fighting cavities.
So every time you brush, Crest's fluoride strengthens your teeth against cavities by making the enamel more resistant to tooth decay.
In addition to brushing after meals with Crest, it's also important to cut down on treats, and see your dentist for checkups every six months.
With all this protection going for your teeth, you just could wind up having the last laugh on cavities.
Crest
Fighting cavities is the whole idea behind Crest.

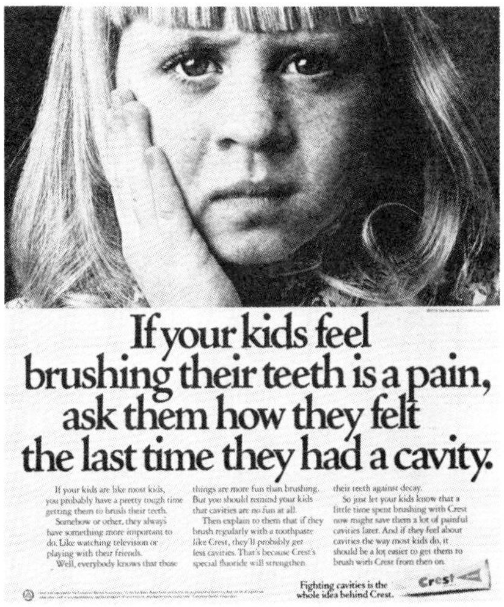
If your kids feel brushing their teeth is a pain, ask them how they felt the last time they had a cavity.
If your kids are like most kids, you probably have a pretty tough time getting them to brush their teeth.
Somehow or other, they always have something more important to do. Like watching television or playing with their friends.
Well, everybody knows that those things are more fun than brushing. But you should remind your kids that cavities are no fun at all.
Then explain to them that if they brush regularly with a toothpaste like Crest, they'll probably get less cavities. That's because Crest's special fluoride will strengthen their teeth against decay.
So just let your kids know that a little time spent brushing with Crest now might save them a lot of painful cavities later. And if they feel about cavities the way most kids do, it should be a lot easier to get them to brush with Crest from then on.
Fighting cavities is the whole idea behind Crest.
Crest

Nature also makes holes in teeth.
Crest
Fighting cavities is the whole idea behind Crest.

SILVER

142

Art Directors Joe Gregorace
Harvey Cohen
Dick Wolf
Writers Marv Jacobson
Charlie Kornberger
Michael Norica
Photographers Joe Toto
Four by Five, Inc.
Phil Marco
Agency Benton & Bowles
Client Procter & Gamble

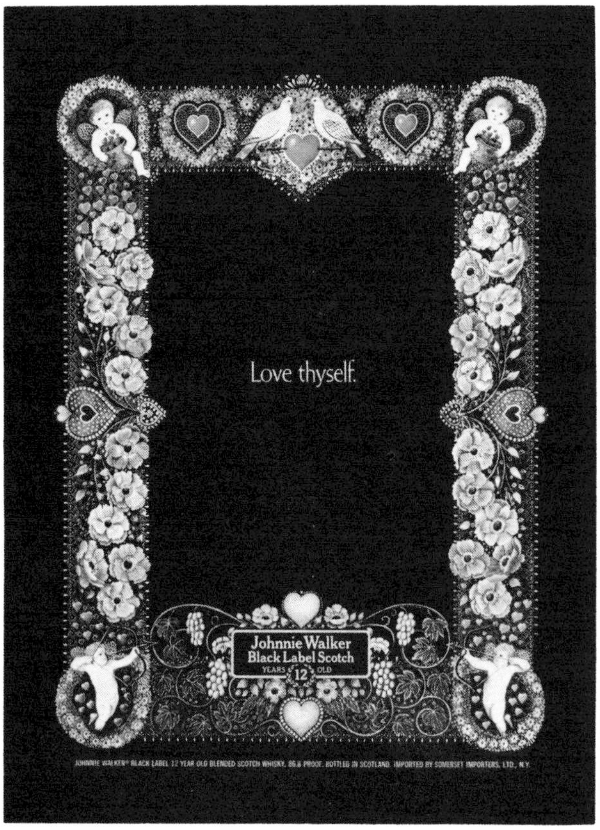
Love thyself.
Johnnie Walker
Black Label Scotch
YEARS 12 OLD
JOHNNIE WALKER® BLACK LABEL 12 YEAR OLD BLENDED SCOTCH WHISKY, 86.8 PROOF. BOTTLED IN SCOTLAND. IMPORTED BY SOMERSET IMPORTERS, LTD., N.Y.

Father Knows the best
Johnnie Walker
Black Label Scotch
YEARS 12 OLD
JOHNNIE WALKER® BLACK LABEL 12 YEAR OLD BLENDED SCOTCH WHISKY, 86.8 PROOF. BOTTLED IN SCOTLAND. IMPORTED BY SOMERSET IMPORTERS, LTD., N.Y., N.Y.

"I was wondering if I could possibly borrow a cup of Johnnie Walker Black Label."
12 YEAR OLD BLENDED SCOTCH WHISKY. 86.8 PROOF. BOTTLED IN SCOTLAND. IMPORTED BY SOMERSET IMPORTERS, LTD., N.Y., N.Y.

Johnnie Walker
Black Label Scotch
YEARS 12 OLD
Now there are two kinds of gold you can buy in bars.
JOHNNIE WALKER® BLACK LABEL 12 YEAR OLD BLENDED SCOTCH WHISKY, 86.8 PROOF. BOTTLED IN SCOTLAND. IMPORTED BY SOMERSET IMPORTERS, LTD., N.Y.

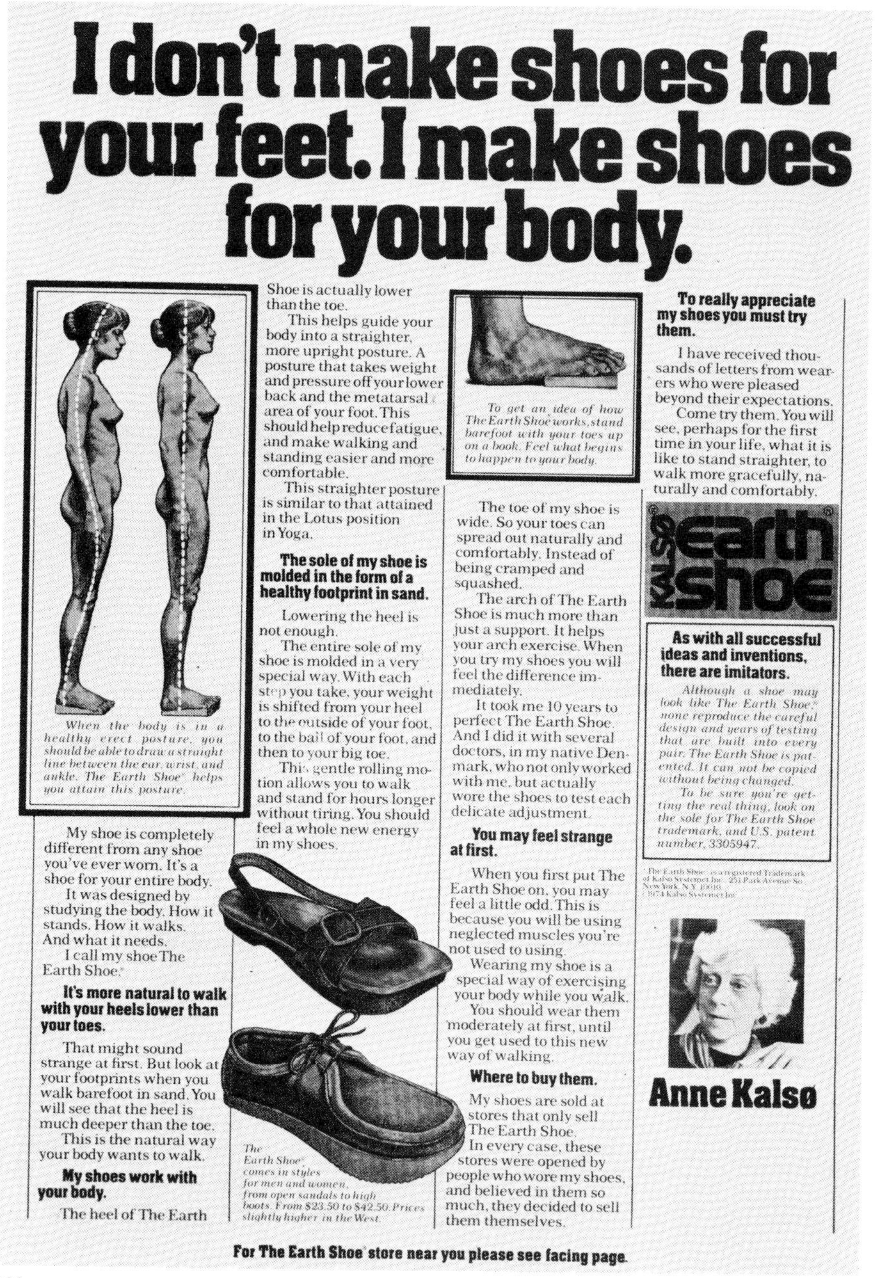
I don't make shoes for your feet. I make shoes for your body.
When the body is in a healthy erect posture, you should be able to draw a straight line between the ear, wrist, and ankle. The Earth Shoe® helps you attain this posture.
My shoe is completely different from any shoe you've ever worn. It's a shoe for your entire body.
It was designed by studying the body. How it stands. How it walks. And what it needs.
I call my shoe The Earth Shoe®.
It's more natural to walk with your heels lower than your toes.
That might sound strange at first. But look at your footprints when you walk barefoot in sand. You will see that the heel is much deeper than the toe.
This is the natural way your body wants to walk.
My shoes work with your body.
The heel of The Earth Shoe is actually lower than the toe.
This helps guide your body into a straighter, more upright posture. A posture that takes weight and pressure off your lower back and the metatarsal area of your foot. This should help reduce fatigue, and make walking and standing easier and more comfortable.
This straighter posture is similar to that attained in the Lotus position in Yoga.
The sole of my shoe is molded in the form of a healthy footprint in sand.
Lowering the heel is not enough.
The entire sole of my shoe is molded in a very special way. With each step you take, your weight is shifted from your heel to the outside of your foot, to the ball of your foot, and then to your big toe.
This gentle rolling motion allows you to walk and stand for hours longer without tiring. You should feel a whole new energy in my shoes.
The Earth Shoe® comes in styles for men and women, from open sandals to high boots. From $23.50 to $42.50. Prices slightly higher in the West.
To get an idea of how The Earth Shoe works, stand barefoot with your toes up on a book. Feel what begins to happen to your body.
The toe of my shoe is wide. So your toes can spread out naturally and comfortably. Instead of being cramped and squashed.
The arch of The Earth Shoe is much more than just a support. It helps your arch exercise. When you try my shoes you will feel the difference immediately.
It took me 10 years to perfect The Earth Shoe. And I did it with several doctors, in my native Denmark, who not only worked with me, but actually wore the shoes to test each delicate adjustment.
You may feel strange at first.
When you first put The Earth Shoe on, you may feel a little odd. This is because you will be using neglected muscles you're not used to using.
Wearing my shoe is a special way of exercising your body while you walk.
You should wear them moderately at first, until you get used to this new way of walking.
Where to buy them.
My shoes are sold at stores that only sell The Earth Shoe.
In every case, these stores were opened by people who wore my shoes, and believed in them so much, they decided to sell them themselves.
To really appreciate my shoes you must try them.
I have received thousands of letters from wearers who were pleased beyond their expectations.
Come try them. You will see, perhaps for the first time in your life, what it is like to stand straighter, to walk more gracefully, naturally and comfortably.
KALSØ earth shoe
As with all successful ideas and inventions, there are imitators.
Although a shoe may look like The Earth Shoe®, none reproduce the careful design and years of testing that are built into every pair. The Earth Shoe is patented. It can not be copied without being changed.
To be sure you're getting the real thing, look on the sole for The Earth Shoe trademark, and U.S. patent number, 3305947.
Anne Kalsø
For The Earth Shoe® store near you please see facing page.

144

Why everybody's pretending they're us.
The shoes that look like, seem like, but don't work like the Earth shoe.
How the Earth Shoe was invented.
Patent 3305947. Why the Earth shoe is unique.
Sold only at Earth shoe stores.
Find out for yourself.
Anne Kalsø.
You can only buy Earth shoes at Earth Shoe Stores in the cities listed on the facing page.

143
Art Directors Stuart Pittman
Faith Popcorn
Ivan Sherman
Writers Murray L. Klein
Faith Popcorn
Adam Hanft
Stuart Pittman
Artists Gervasio Gallardo
David Smiton
Photographers Michael O'Neill
Henry Sandbank
Agency Smith/Greenland Co.
Client Somerset Importers

144
Art Director Mel Platt
Writer Jennifer Berne
Designer Mel Platt
Artist Norman Green
Photographer Lee Batlin
Agency Martin Landey, Arlow Advertising
Client Kalsø

Guess what Scotch is about to be served.
CHIVAS REGAL · 12 YEARS OLD WORLDWIDE · BLENDED SCOTCH WHISKY · 86 PROOF · GENERAL WINE & SPIRITS CO., NEW YORK, N.Y.

12
CHIVAS REGAL
No other scotch makes you wonder what you did to deserve it.
12 YEARS OLD WORLDWIDE · BLENDED SCOTCH WHISKY · 86 PROOF · GENERAL WINE & SPIRITS CO., NEW YORK, N.Y.

Just a reminder that the most impressive thing about Chivas Regal is what's in the bottle, not what's on it.
12 YEARS OLD WORLDWIDE · BLENDED SCOTCH WHISKY · 86 PROOF · GENERAL WINE & SPIRITS CO., NEW YORK, N.Y.

BY APPOINTMENT TO
HER MAJESTY THE QUEEN
PURVEYORS OF PROVISIONS
FOUNDED
1801
If this is all our label says to you, you obviously haven't tasted our Scotch.
12 YEARS OLD WORLDWIDE · BLENDED SCOTCH WHISKY · 86 PROOF · GENERAL WINE & SPIRITS CO., NEW YORK, N.Y.

145

145

Art Directors	Mike Lawlor
	Bill Harris
Writers	Mike Mangano
	Larry Levenson
Designers	Mike Lawlor
	Bill Harris
Photographers	Rudy Legname
	Henry Sandbank
	Chuck Lamonica
	Charles Gold
Agency	Doyle Dane Bernbach
Client	Chivas Regal

Iced Water by Lenox
Crystal, hand-blown and hand-cut, with the same breed of artistry that gives Lenox China its stature the world over.
LENOX CRYSTAL
TRENTON, N.J. 08605

Lemon Ice by Lenox
Hand-blown, hand-finished lead crystal created with the same breed of artistry that gives Lenox China its stature the world over.
LENOX CRYSTAL

Vin ordinaire by Lenox.
Hand blown, hand finished lead crystal created with the same breed of artistry that gives Lenox China its stature the world over.
LENOX CRYSTAL

146

146
Art Director Alexander Mohtares
Writer Alexander Mohtares
Designer Alexander Mohtares
Photographer Jim Vicari
Agency Chirurg & Cairns
Client Lenox

A CAR SEAT HAS TO BE MORE THAN A PLACE TO SIT. OURS MAKES YOU A BETTER DRIVER.
The average car seat is designed to fit a person who doesn't exist ...the average size driver.
So Volvo developed a seat that accommodates every size driver.
The Volvo seat is built to help you drive. It's adjustable to your dimensions, to afford you complete control over the controls.
If your calves are shorter than average, you can lower the seat height to get closer to the pedals.
If your arms are longer than average, you can lean back without moving back. (The seat angle is adjustable.)
If your back gets tired, a lumbar adjustment will support you in the style you prefer: from soft to firm. And if your legs get tired, you can tilt back the seat cushion to brace your thighs. Or push back the seat to stretch them.
The Volvo seat even improves your visibility. Our head restraints have openings, so you can see in back of you.
If this seems like a lot of thought to put into the place where you sit, you'll be even more impressed by something else. The thinking that went into the place where we put our seat.
Our car.
VOLVO
The car for people who think.

A VOLVO DISCOVERY: RAIN FALLS ON REAR WINDOWS, TOO.
Volvo is the only wagon maker with the foresight to provide its rear window with a wiper and washer as standard equipment.
Volvo has also discovered that everyone doesn't buy a wagon to be fashionable. Many people buy wagons to carry things.
So we didn't design Volvo's cargo area low and sleek to accommodate a styling trend. We designed it high and practical, to accommodate things like a six-foot sofa and two chairs (with the rear seat down). Or three six-foot people and 12 two-suiters (with the rear seat up).
Volvo's rear area not only holds a lot, it comes with a lot. It has its own heating and ventilation vents, its own three-point seat belts, electric rear window defogger, carpeting, tinted glass and childproof door locks.
And Volvo's back door swings up out of your way, instead of out into your stomach. Or down into your knee caps.
It doesn't take a college degree to appreciate the thinking behind our wagon. So we leave you to consider this. If the rear end of your car isn't as well thought out as Volvo's, what other part might not be?
VOLVO
The wagon for people who think.
RP 7902
VOLVO
245 DL

DID IT EVER OCCUR TO YOU THAT YOUR CAR MIGHT PANIC IN A CRISIS?
The 1975 Volvo 240 series was planned with the unexpected in mind.
Because, while it's human to err, driving errors can be fatal. Volvos are designed to compensate.
Jamming on the brakes may make them work too well.
When a car stops fast, its weight shifts forward. The rear wheels tend to lock before the front ones. This can cause a skid.
Volvo's 4-wheel power disc brake system has a pressure-proportioning valve on each rear brake line. It minimizes premature rear wheel lock-up, and helps keep you on the straight and narrow.
Road debris could damage a brake line. So Volvo has two independent braking systems. Each works on *three* wheels—two front, one rear. (According to Volvo's math, you could lose 50% of your braking system, and have about 80% of its effectiveness left.)
If you can't stop, you've got to go around. Volvo's rack and pinion steering is similar to a racing car's. It's extremely quick. And even in high speed dodging, Volvo's new suspension holds you steady, smooth and flat.
No matter how good your reflexes are, you have to rely on your car's reactions. And when it comes to avoiding accidents, Volvo thinks you can't go too far.
VOLVO
The car for people who think.

147

GOLD

147

Art Director Robert Reitzfeld
Writers Thomas J. Nathan, Edward A. McCabe
Photographers Henry Sandbank, Steve Horn
Agency Scali, McCabe, Sloves
Client Volvo of America Corp.

GF
GENERAL FOODS KITCHENS
Your husband always eats his peas.
With pearl onions, he might even notice them.
Regular vegetables are fine. But you can get tired of anything after twenty or thirty years.
That's why Birds Eye® came up with Combination Vegetables. Like our Peas with Pearl Onions, for example. They're better than just peas. And better than just onions.
Your husband might even mention them. And for vegetables, that's saying quite a lot.
BIRDS EYE
COMBINATIONS
Green Peas and Pearl Onions
Birds Eye Combinations
The first vegetables your husband might even notice.
(Above photograph is 3 times actual size.)

Once he notices the Hollandaise Sauce he can't ignore the broccoli.
Your husband probably likes broccoli. But chances are, he's never paid much attention to it. After all, broccoli is broccoli.
That's why we put Birds Eye® broccoli in combination with broccoli's best friend, Hollandaise Sauce. The thick, golden sauce will catch your husband's eye and before he knows it, he'll be sinking his teeth into our tender broccoli spears and actually noticing them.
Hollandaise Sauce may not make broccoli the main topic of dinner conversation. But at least it'll deserve a mention.
Broccoli Spears
Birds Eye® Combinations
The first vegetables your husband might even notice.

Without almonds your husband would think this is just a hill of beans.
All by themselves, you can't expect green beans to grab your husband's attention. They're good alright. But not too interesting.
That's why we make Birds Eye* Combinations. Like our French Beans with Toasted Almonds, for example.
They have the look and flavor to catch a husband's eye. The same goes for our French Beans and Mushrooms.
Like all our Combinations, they amount to a lot more than just plain vegetables.
French Green Beans Toasted Almonds
Birds Eye® Combinations
The first vegetables your husband might even notice.

148

148
Art Director Tom Balchunas
Writer Peter Cornish
Photographer Henry Sandbank
Agency Young & Rubicam International
Client General Foods

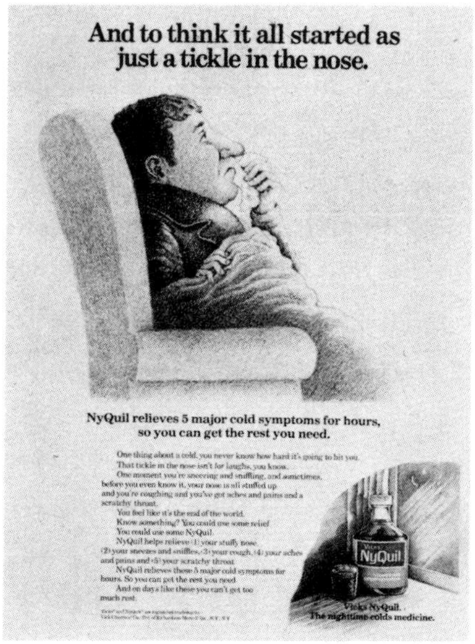

And to think it all started as just a tickle in the nose.
NyQuil relieves 5 major cold symptoms for hours,
so you can get the rest you need.
Vicks NyQuil.
The nighttime colds medicine.

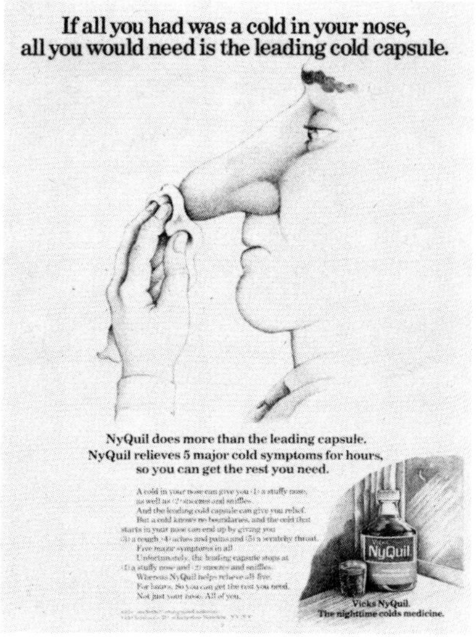

If all you had was a cold in your nose,
all you would need is the leading cold capsule.
NyQuil does more than the leading capsule.
NyQuil relieves 5 major cold symptoms for hours,
so you can get the rest you need.
Vicks NyQuil.
The nighttime colds medicine.

Today's forecast:
Cold followed by gradual clearing
and brighter days ahead.
NyQuil relieves 5 major cold symptoms for hours,
so you can get the rest you need.
When you get a cold, let's face it. You're not just under the weather. You feel rotten.
It always seems like everything hits you at once.
You're sneezing and sniffling something awful.
Your nose is all stuffed up.
You're coughing and coughing. You ache all over.
And your throat feels like you've been swallowing sand.
Just as there's a calm after a storm, there can be rest after your turmoil.
Take NyQuil.
NyQuil helps relieve (1) your stuffed-up nose, (2) your sneezing and sniffling, (3) your coughing, (4) your aches and pains and (5) your scratchy throat.
NyQuil relieves these 5 major cold symptoms for hours. So you can get the rest you need.
And that's as important as remembering to wear your rubbers when it rains.
Vicks® and NyQuil® are registered trademarks—
Vick Chemical Co., Div. of Richardson-Merrell Inc., N.Y., N.Y.
Vicks
NyQuil
Vicks NyQuil.
The nighttime colds medicine.

149

149
Art Director Sam Cooperstein
Writer Rupert Johnson
Artist Sam Cooperstein
Agency Benton & Bowles
Client Vick Chemical Co.

Standing close together is hard enough to learn.
And then they ask you to move your feet.
Kodak film. For the times of your life.
Kodak Film

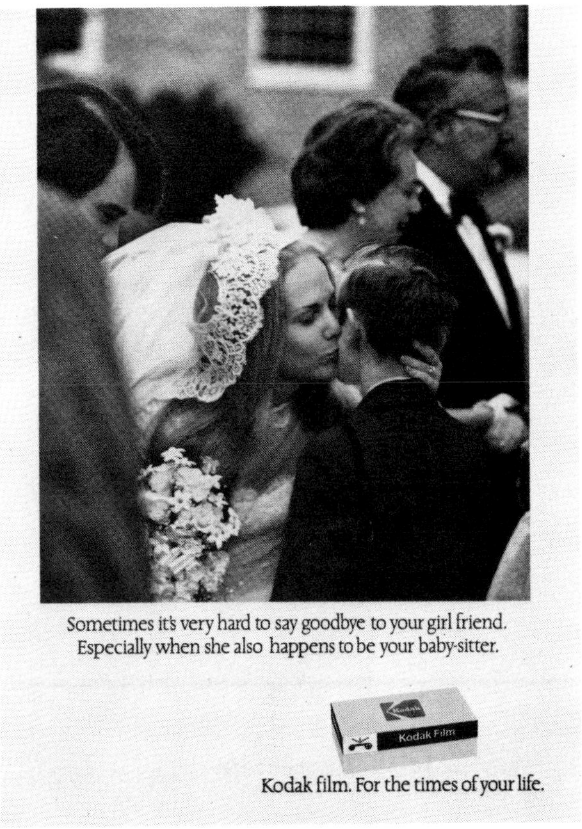
Sometimes it's very hard to say goodbye to your girl friend.
Especially when she also happens to be your baby-sitter.
Kodak Film
Kodak film. For the times of your life.

DORSEY
Who'll ever forget the day you took the kickoff on your own two and ran 98 glorious yards for dear old Dorsey Service Station.
Kodak Film
Kodak film. For the times of your life.

150

150
Art Director Fred Kittel
Writer Bill Lane
Designer Fred Kittel
Photographer Tom McCarthy
Agency J. Walter Thompson
Client Eastman Kodak Co.

1970, A FRAGRANCE IS CREATED FOR A WOMAN WHO IS SURE OF HERSELF.
Guerlain introduces Chamade. It is purely female. Deep, rich and sensuous.
It is a fragrance for a woman who doesn't care about pleasing anyone but herself. And if you think that this is somewhat narcissistic, perhaps it is. But all real love starts here. You can't really love another unless you yourself feel worthy of love.
CHAMADE
by Guerlain

1921, A FRAGRANCE WILL NOT LET HIM FORGET.
For one crazy moment he feels he will stay. Then he turns towards the gangplank and walks very slowly into the mist.
Each one of their moments—the shy beginnings, the electric touching of fingertips, the transporting passion—will disappear in the universal solvent of time plus distance.
Years later, an unknown woman in a silk dress will pass by wearing Mitsouko.
And 1921 will flash through him like a shock. He will not be able to forget the long black hair, the incredibly soft skin, the infinite tenderness...
MITSOUKO
by Guerlain

1914, A FRAGRANCE CREATES DEEP, DEEP MEMORIES.
Guerlain introduced a perfume named for the twilight, L'Heure Bleue. Now the skies darken and the Western World is swept into the forces of The Great War...
A weary French officer finds a moment of peace. He pulls a letter from his tunic and inhales the fragrance lingering in the worn pages.
It is the fragrance she wore the last night they spent together. L'Heure Bleue, named for that moment when the sky has lost the sun but not yet found the stars.
He reads the letter for the hundredth time...
L'HEURE BLEUE
by Guerlain

1925, A FRAGRANCE CAPTURES THE WORLD LIKE LE JAZZ HOT.
A transmuted sadness pours forth from jazz trumpets. The rhythms are compelling. It is The Jazz Age, and Guerlain creates a perfume of real power.
Shalimar. Heady, exciting, as intoxicating as Prohibition itself.
SHALIMAR
by Guerlain

151

151
Art Director Gennaro Andreozzi
Writer Paul Margulies
Designer Gennaro Andreozzi
Photographer Steve Horn
Agency Primaute Advertising
Client Guerlain

The Beech-Nut Baby Research Report.
DO FAT BABIES BECOME FAT ADULTS?
A lot of mothers think fat babies are cute babies and fat babies are healthy babies. But actually, overfeeding a baby could be the beginning of a life-long problem. It's one of the most common causes of adult overweight.
Many fat adults are fat because they were fat babies.
Why do mothers overfeed babies?
It's very, very easy to confuse food and love. When you feed your baby you feel like he's accepting love from you. It's very satisfying when he takes food from you.
You might feel the more he eats, the healthier he's getting. And when he rejects food, very often it can feel like he's rejecting you and 'your' nourishment.
But, that's not true. And feeling like this could make you overfeed your baby.
Your baby knows more about how much he should eat than you do.
It's alright to let your baby tell you when he's finished. He knows. In your baby's body is a natural mechanism that regulates his food intake. This tells him how much he should eat, automatically. It's nature's way of taking care of your baby.
If you force your baby to eat more than he wants, you could be interfering with that mechanism and causing him to overeat.
And, if your baby seems to have any special eating problems, consult your pediatrician.
What happens when your baby is fed too much?
Your baby uses food to do more than give him energy. He uses food to grow. And he will eat a great deal of food in his first year, because in that time he'll triple in weight.
But, if he gets more than he wants, more than he needs, this extra food could grow into extra fat cells. Fat cells he will carry around with him for the rest of his life. And those extra fat cells will demand extra food, and make him fat.
Fat cells just sit there sending out their little messages, 'feed me, feed me.' And they usually get fed.
Eat. Eat.
Somewhere toward the end of the first year, your baby's growing appetite will begin slowing down. Don't worry. This is normal.
Your baby is reducing his rate of growing, and he is regulating his food intake. This is often the time when mothers think something has gone wrong with their baby's appetite, and force him to eat more than he needs.
But, if your baby kept gaining at his original rate, he'd end up weighing hundreds of pounds.
He'll decide how much. You decide what.
So, you see, the quantity of food is really up to your baby. Your job is making sure he gets the right quality. The kind of foods that satisfy his nutritional needs.
And that's where we can help. By offering you a complete line of wholesome, nourishing foods, full of the nutrients your baby needs.
All of our ingredients are scientifically measured to assure consistent, uniform nutrition. Then they are cooked with careful and continuous quality control.
We add no artificial colors, no artificial flavors, and no monosodium glutamate. And many of our foods are fortified with vitamins and minerals for extra nutrition.
For instance, when your baby is ready for cereal, that is the time when many babies need extra iron in their diets. So we fortify our cereal with extra iron to meet this need.
And, no matter which of our foods you choose, you can feel sure you are getting a nutritious, quality product for your baby.
The more you know, the more you can relax.
So, since you know that nature is taking care of your baby's appetite and Beech-Nut is taking care of his food, you can relax. Chances are, if you don't show any anxiety about food and eating, neither will your baby.
And feeding will become a happy, calm, close relationship that you can share with your baby.
This report is one of a series. If you are interested in reading the others, write to Baker-Beech-Nut Corporation, Consumer Services, Dept. 101, Canajoharie, N.Y. 13317, and we'll be glad to send them to you.
This report is brought to you by Beech-Nut Baby Food. Wholesome, nutritious food for your baby.
Beech-Nut
cereal
Fortified with Vitamins & Minerals plus Iron
Baby Food

The Beech-Nut Baby Research Report.
SHOULD FATHERS FEED BABIES?
This report is brought to you by Beech-Nut Baby Food. Wholesome, nutritious food for your baby.
Beech-Nut
cereal

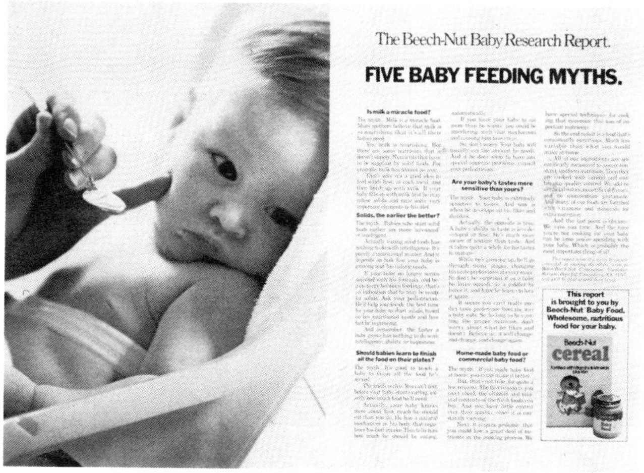
The Beech-Nut Baby Research Report.
FIVE BABY FEEDING MYTHS.
This report is brought to you by Beech-Nut Baby Food. Wholesome, nutritious food for your baby.
Beech-Nut
cereal

152

152
Art Director Mel Platt
Writer Jennifer Berne
Designer Mel Platt
Photographer Michael O'Neill
Agency Martin Landey, Arlow Advertising
Client Beech-Nut Baby Food

Eagle proudly presents a brand new shirt with holes in it.
The business Aertex®.
Why use the most comfortable fabrics only for sportshirts? It's during business and dress-up hours that you really need a shirt that lets the cool air in and body heat out. Which is why Eagle designed a new collection of dress shirts out of what was originally only a sportshirt fabric. Aertex®, the hole-iest fabric in the world. It's woven of polyester and cotton in stripes, checks and windowpane plaids, as shown here with Eagle's textured solid bowtie. For sports wear, we still make our Aertex® knit with the same open-air construction. Now Aertex® is all work and all play.
Eagle. The shirtmakers' shirtmaker.

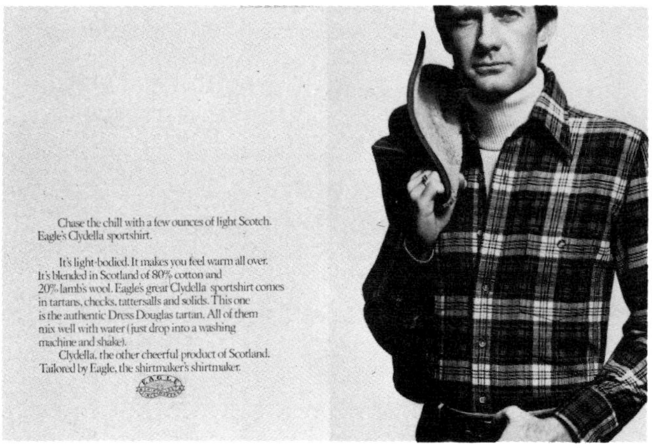
Chase the chill with a few ounces of light Scotch. Eagle's Clydella sportshirt.
It's light-bodied. It makes you feel warm all over. It's blended in Scotland of 80% cotton and 20% lamb's wool. Eagle's great Clydella sportshirt comes in tartans, checks, tattersalls and solids. This one is the authentic Dress Douglas tartan. All of them mix well with water (just drop into a washing machine and shake).
Clydella, the other cheerful product of Scotland. Tailored by Eagle, the shirtmaker's shirtmaker.

When the old Saratoga trunks were packed, this is the kind of shirt that went along.
When Saratoga was in its original heyday and men flocked there to take the plunge (in the waters or at the races), there was no such thing as a sportshirt. Fabrics like this—brighter and more informal—served both purposes. It's time, Eagle feels, for the restoration of Saratoga Square. And for your convenience, we've done it now in durable press Dacron® polyester and cotton. (Illustrated here with Eagle's corded tambour tie).
Saratoga Square. Think of it as a vestige of our past that wears well.
From Eagle, the shirtmakers' shirtmaker.

153

153
Art Director Joseph Nissen
Writer Ed Hanft
Photographer Carl Fischer
Agency Chalk, Nissen, Hanft
Client Eagle Shirtmakers

How to buy a set of sheets and still have nothing to put on your bed.
If you've never used Martex® sheets on anything except your bed, there's probably only one reason.
You never thought of it.
Decorators have. In fact, they've been using Martex sheets instead of fabric or wallpaper all through the home.
And for three very good reasons.
First, they're easy to use. That's because Martex sheets come in widths that start at 72 inches (twin-size flat) and go up to 108 inches (king-size flat). So there are fewer seams when you're covering a wall. And no seams when you're covering a table or making a shower curtain.
Second, they save you money.
For example, if you used Martex sheets to cushion a chair, dress up a window, give new life to an old table and lamp, and covered the walls of a 9 x 14 room, (all the things we did here), it would cost less than $125.
The third reason, and probably the most important, is the way we design them.
We call it the Martex Master Plan. It means that each design is created to work with the others.
Take, for example, these prints from our Paris-Out-of-Town collection. They play against each other perfectly. The flowers seem to have been plucked from the same garden in Provence. And the colors from the same sun-drenched landscape.
Now that you know how Martex sheets can change the look of your house, isn't it about time you stopped buying them just to change the look of your bed.
Martex
We change more than just your bed.

The Martex Master Plan.
It lets you mix color with color. Pattern with pattern. Country with country.

The Martex Master Plan. It can start with a pillow. And end with a room.

154

154
Art Directors Martin Lipsitt
Mike Withers
Writers Neil Calet
Sandy Berger
Designer Martin Lipsitt
Photographer Jerry Abromowitz
Agency DKG
Client West Point Pepperell

THE MOST
EXTRAVAGANT
$30 PIECE OF JEWELRY
EVER MADE.
From our Winter Ice Collection. In jet and rhinestone.
Suggested retail price $30.00. For the fine store near you write: Trifari, 16 East 40th Street, New York, New York, 10016.
TRIFARI

THE
MOST EXTRAVAGANT
$65 WATCH EVER
MADE.
TRIFARI

THE MOST
EXTRAVAGANT
$12.50 PIECE OF JEWELRY
EVER MADE.
TRIFARI

155

155
Art Director Dennis D'Amico
Writer Dick Tarlow
Designer Dennis D'Amico
Photographer Michael O'Neill
Agency Sacks, Tarlow and Rosen
Client Trifari, Krussman and Fishel

©1974 R. J. Reynolds Tobacco Co.
If it wasn't for Winston, I wouldn't smoke.
Winston
Taste isn't everything. It's the only thing.
I smoke for pleasure. That's spelled T-A-S-T-E.
That means Winston. Winston won't give you a new image.
All Winston will ever give me is taste.
A taste that's very real. If a cigarette isn't real,
it isn't anything. Winston is for real.
Warning: The Surgeon General Has Determined
That Cigarette Smoking Is Dangerous to Your Health.
19 mg. "tar," 1.3 mg. nicotine av.
per cigarette, FTC Report
MAR. '74.

If I'm going to smoke, I'm going to do it right.
Some people smoke a brand for its image.
I don't. You can't taste image. I smoke for taste.
I smoke Winston. All Winston will ever give you
is real taste. And real pleasure. For some of us,
that's enough. Winston is for real.

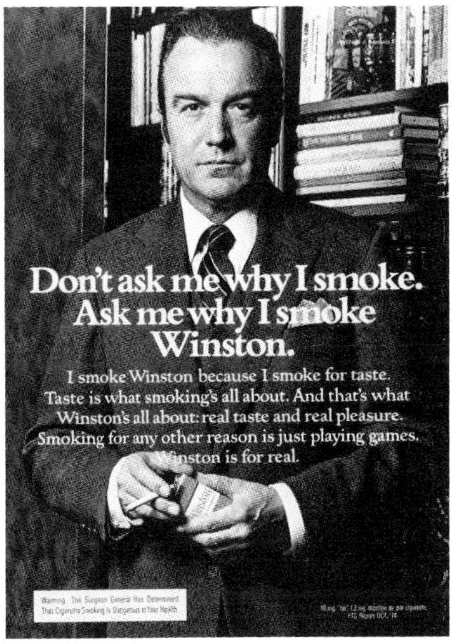
Don't ask me why I smoke.
Ask me why I smoke
Winston.
I smoke Winston because I smoke for taste.
Taste is what smoking's all about. And that's what
Winston's all about: real taste and real pleasure.
Smoking for any other reason is just playing games.
Winston is for real.

156

156
Art Director Jeffery Hill
Writers William Giles
Dana Blackmar III
Agency Dancer-Fitzgerald-Sample
Client R. J. Reynolds Tobacco Co.

2000 years ago, when you had a Scotch on the Rocks, you really had a Scotch on the Rocks.
BY THE 2000 YEAR OLD MAN, MEL BROOKS
Q. SIR, 2000 years ago where did people live and how did they spend their time?
A. 2000 years ago there was no luxury buildings with music in the elevators or single bars where married men hung out.
There was only rocks and caves. More rocks and caves than you could shake a stick at. In fact, shaking a stick at a rock was a good job already. Not everybody could get that job. You had to have a little something. Standing around and looking was also a good job. But that was easy. That was light work. It had to be light work. You couldn't do it in the dark.
And the caves...uhhh. Did we hate each other. The tall blue eyes were in the tall light caves, the short brown eyes were in the short dark caves.
Q. Well, how did everyone communicate?
A. Rock talk.
Q. ??????????
A. Here, I'll hit you with a little rock talk. "Hey you, put down that rock! Don't throw that rock at me. I'll call a policeman." That was your basic rock talk. And rock music followed. Take a couple of rocks and hit them against each other or against people and you got some nice sounds.
Q. Sir, in 2000 years did you begat any children?
A. I gat 42,000. And not one comes to visit me on Saturday or Sunday. Not one calls to give me a "Hi, Pop." But it's all right. Children, let them be.
Q. Sir, when was Scotch discovered?
A. It was during the ice age. We had so many tons of ice we didn't know what to do. So we made drinks. All kinds of drinks. After a few drinks, we all chased around. That's how the chaser was born.
Q. Sir, to what do you attribute having lived 2000 years?
A. Exercise and garlic.
Q. Garlic?
A. Yes. You know, the scientific way how you die? The Angel of Death comes late at night. He rings your apartment bell. You let him in and he kills you. But I'm smart. Before I'll retire and pull up mine crazy quilt, I'll eat a nice pound and a half garlic. And when the Angel of Death taps me on the shoulder and says, "Come along with me," I turn around and talk right in his face. "Who is it?", I say. After that he leaves me alone for quite a while.
Q. Sir, you also mention exercise?
A. Exercise, exercise, exercise. Who would we be...How would we be ...What would we be without exercise?
Q. What do you do for exercise?
A. Everyday early in the morning, I open a window and take a deep breath. Then I fall to my knees and pray fiercely that my brains should not drift too far from my thoughts and my heart should not attack me.
Q. So basically your exercise is praying?
A. You got it Sonny. And, before I run out of breath...a dangerous thing at my age...I better stop. I'll take me a little Teacher's. After all, you monied me for all of this...Let's be pleasant.
Q. Sir, is it true that you have just made a new record with Carl Reiner entitled, 2000 AND THIRTEEN, and that your latest movie, BLAZING SADDLES is breaking records all over the country, and that you have just completed principal photography work on your new comic masterpiece "YOUNG FRANKENSTEIN?"
A. No!
I want to wish you all love and good luck and give you a little advice. Stay out of small foreign cars especially if they are driven by big foreigners... and eat a nectarine. It's the best fruit ever made.
TEACHER'S
SCOTCH WHISKY
No scotch improves the flavour of water like Teacher's.

Half the fun of writing this critique was becoming totally immersed in the subject matter.
BY REX REED
THE ASSIGNMENT was the same as hundreds of others I've had in the past. I was to write a critical evaluation on a given subject.
As always, I would have to first get to know my subject by soaking up as much information as possible about it. I knew this wouldn't be too difficult because this time my subject was Teacher's Scotch.
I've reviewed hundreds of movies and interviewed hundreds of stars in the last few years. Recently, I went through three galaxies of them for my new book, People Are Crazy Here.
I usually like to get to know my subject over a few drinks. It helps break the ice. And loosen the tongue.
So, that's what I decided to do. Is there a better way to get to know a scotch than over a few drinks?
I was at an advantage this time. Teacher's wasn't a total stranger.
Our first meeting took place at an opening night party in Beverly Hills. Beverly Hills, by the way, is the only place in the world where the police have an unlisted phone number.
I forget the name of the movie that opened that night. A lot of people must have. Because that night we also celebrated its closing.
I do remember someone coming up to me, giving me a scotch and leaving.
There I was, drinking alone. Critics do that a lot you know.
I wondered what kind of budget the movie had if they were serving scotch instead of champagne.
I consoled myself with the fact that the scotch they were serving was Teacher's Scotch. That showed very good taste in my opinion. As a matter of fact, it was the only thing I saw all night that did.
Most opening night parties are a bore. I go because people say things at parties that you don't normally see in the papers. And if you do see them in the papers, it's because I go to the parties.
I spent most of the night observing people. You can tell a lot from the way a person holds a scotch glass.
Most people at Hollywood parties use the classic four finger hold and nurse their scotch. I think this is fitting. I've always considered Hollywood an artificial nursery.
Anyway, back to the subject at hand. What I think of Teacher's Scotch.
When the Teacher's people gave me the assignment of writing this critique, they also gave me a bottle of their scotch for research.
We were to have our own little opening night party.
Once again, I was drinking alone. I poured the first drink. I liked it.
I then proceeded to drink it straight, on the rocks, I even tried it with a twist. I tried it with water, soda. I even tried one in an oversized wine glass...veddy British.
I don't generally like the idea of awards but if they ever give one for best performance as a scotch, Teacher's should get it. It also produces great technical effects. And even Technicolor couldn't improve on the way it looks.
I've always said, I write what I see, sense, smell and taste. And that's exactly what I did here.
You might say that while writing this critique, there wasn't a moment when I wasn't completely absorbed in my work.
TEACHER'S
SCOTCH WHISKY
No scotch improves the flavour of water like Teacher's.
86 Proof Scotch Whisky Blended and Bottled in Scotland by Wm. Teacher & Sons, Ltd. © Schieffelin & Co., N.Y., Importers

You can always tell a lot about a man by how he holds his liquor.
BY ZERO MOSTEL
A QUICK LOOK at the way I hold my liquor can tell you that I should have my head examined. A reasonable conclusion.
For, you see, I happen to have a hole in my head. When I first discovered this, I took advantage of the situation, quickly drilling a hole in my drinking glass and placing it over the hole in my head.
The scotch sifted deliciously through my body. Which sometimes has been referred to as a beached whale. As it passed my eyes, I chased it with a little eye wash. At my knees it ran into a large body of water. Scotch and water on the knee can be very painful. In fact, it's not commonly known but the drainage on my knee was the model for the Hoover Dam.
Drinking scotch my way does have its advantages. It allows me to chew gum and drink at the same time. Besides, it's because I drink that way that I drink Teacher's. I've tried a lot of other brands, but nothing sits better on me or goes down softer.
As a matter of fact, in the hope that the Teacher's people would ask me to endorse their scotch, I set down on tape some observations about my life. The following then are the transcripts from the scotch tapes of Zero Mostel.
"My Mother (bless her) carried me a long time. I was born at the immature old age of 2. Father (inaudible.)
"In (inaudible) school, I majored in hooky. I was even going for my masters, but I couldn't find their rooms. Later I fought with the Foreign Legion.
"And lost.
"In the theater, I've worked with Burbage, Kean, Rudolph Schildkraut and the divine Sarah Schwartz, learning nothing on my way to star failure. But I've also done a lot outside the theater. Under a pseudonym I wrote War and Peace, Beowulf, Godey's Lady's Book, Timon of Athens and Bei Mir Bis Du Schoen. I was turned down for the Knighthood only because I had one bad knee. I have affixed the names of Carivaggio, Le Nain, Menzel, Rembrandt, Turner, and Rosa Bonheur to the canvasses I've painted which hang by a rope in many (expletive) museums all over the world. In addition, I served and laundered for years as Gandhi's fashion consultant.
"I've often contemplated suicide, but I was out of town too much. Besides, as an actor, what do you do for an encore?
"(Gap)
"My (expletive deleted) secretary just kicked the tape recorder. (Expletive deleted, expletive deleted.)
"Altogether my life has been a happy one filled with sadness. And vice versa. When I was Lincoln Steffens, I saw the future and it didn't work. So, in the twilight of my life, I look behind me. Which can be a shattering experience when you're walking around with a glass on your head.
"As this ad draws to a close, if you didn't buy the hole in the head story, at least by now you must believe that I have rocks in my head. (Expletive, inaudible, gap, hic, haec, hoc, hup, nolo contendre, etcetera, ad infinitum, ad nauseum.)"
TEACHER'S
SCOTCH WHISKY
No scotch improves the flavour of water like Teacher's.
86 Proof Scotch Whisky Blended and Bottled in Scotland by Wm. Teacher & Sons, Ltd. © Schieffelin & Co., N.Y., Importers

157

157

Art Directors Nick Gisonde
Mark Yustein
Jim Perretti
Writers Neil Drossman
John Russo
Designer Nick Gisonde
Photographers Joe Toto
Carl Fischer
Carl Furuta
Arnold Beckerman
Agency Della Femina, Travisano & Partners
Client Schieffelin & Co.

Purina
NEW!
TASTES SO GOOD CATS ASK FOR IT BY NAME
MEOW MIX
A Completely Nutritious Meal For Cats
A Tasty Combination of 3 Separate Flavors
INTRODUCING MEOW MIX.
The cat food cats ask for by name.
"Meow"
While man may love his cat, man and cat do not speak the same language. The same can be said for woman and cat.
A situation which has given rise to all sorts of communications problems.
For example, over the years cats have been accused of being finicky eaters.
Well, maybe we've never really understood what they've been asking for. (After all, you'd be finicky too, if you had to put up with just one taste at every meal.)
So we at Purina have come out with a whole new way to feed your cat. Not just a new variety of cat food, but a cat food with real variety in it.
We call it Meow Mix.™
For the first time, a cat can get his three favorite flavors, tuna, liver, and chicken, in one package. They're in separate bite-size morsels.
The tuna is red the liver is brown and the chicken is yellow. So they look as different as they taste.
Now, your cat doesn't have to wait till his next meal for a change of taste, he can get it in the next bite.
Which should keep him biting. All day long.
It should also help keep him healthy. Because Meow Mix contains all the proteins, vitamins and minerals cats are known to need.
And Meow Mix even has something for you, convenience. There's nothing to mix. Just pour some Meow Mix into a bowl and the fresh, tasty morsels will stay fresh and tasty all day long.
From now on, when your cat meows, you'll know what he's asking for.
15¢ Something for you to meow about. 15¢
STORE COUPON
15¢ 15¢

FINALLY, CATS HAVE A CHANCE TO EAT THEIR WORDS.
Everyday, millions of people eat their words. (For example, hamburger is a word people eat. Not to mention chopped liver or bacon, lettuce and tomato.)
But things aren't that easy for cats.
After all, how many times have you seen a cat eating a meow.
It is this unfair situation that has given rise to a new cat food.
Meow Mix™. The cat food cats ask for by name.
Now, thanks to Meow Mix, a cat can have his meow and eat it too.
What's more, there's more to Meow Mix than just a meow.
For one thing, there's tuna. For another, there's liver. And for another, there's chicken. Your cat's three favorite flavors.
And now, he can get them all at once. So he gets a change of taste in every mouthful, instead of at every other meal.
Each flavor is a separate bite size morsel. With a color all its own. (The tuna is red, the liver is brown, the chicken is yellow.)
But Meow Mix brings more to a cat's diet than variety, it brings nutrition. For it contains all the protein, vitamins and minerals cats are known to need.
So the next time you're trying to decide what to feed your cat, take his word for it.
TASTES SO GOOD CATS ASK FOR IT BY NAME
Purina
TASTES SO GOOD CATS ASK FOR IT BY NAME
MEOW MIX
A Completely Nutritious Meal For Cats
A Tasty Combination of 3 Separate Flavors
Tuna Liver Chicken
NET WT. 18 OZ. (1 LB. 2 OZ.)

"Meow"
SPOT— PITTSBURGH, PA
"Meow"
S. KATZ—BROOKLYN, N.Y.
"Meow"
GEORGE— WASHINGTON, D.C.
"Meow"
LARUE— HOLLYWOOD, CALIF.
"Meow"
PERCY III—BOSTON, MASS.
"Meow"
LULUBELLE— SAVANNAH, GA.
THE BEST ADVERTISING FOR NEW MEOW MIX IS WORD OF MOUTH.
An ad can't tell you what a cat can.
And cats who've tasted Meow Mix™ have had one word for it. "Meow". (See above.)
You see, Meow Mix is a whole new way to feed a cat. More than just a new variety of cat food, it's a cat food with real variety.
For the first time, a cat can get his three favorite flavors, tuna, liver and chicken, in one package. They're in separate bite-size morsels. The tuna is red the liver is brown the chicken is yellow. So they look as different as they taste.
And not only does a cat get the variety he craves, he also gets the nourishment he needs. Because Meow Mix contains all the protein, vitamins and minerals cats are known to need.
So now your cat doesn't have to wait till his next meal for change of taste, he can get it in his next bite. Which should keep him biting all day long.
But don't take our word for it, we'd rather you get it right from the cat's mouth.
NEW!
MEOW MIX

158

158
Art Directors Steve Ohman
Bob Kuperman
Writer Neil Drossman
Photographers Dave Langley
Jerry Friedman
Agency Della Femina, Travisano & Partners
Client Ralston Purina

This is a get rich quick ad.
Money swore an oath that nobody that did not love her should ever have her. —Irish Proverb
Results! Action! Sales! Profits!
Magic words to the advertiser.
The acronym is RASP.
Something hard and sharp, that cuts through matter quickly and efficiently.
Which is how we see ourselves, and how we describe our advertising campaigns.
Our "style" is, as one of our clients has described it, Aggressive Creativity.
Which is another way of saying that we go right for the jugular.
Nicely.
If you consider the ads shown in this ad, you will notice that they are directed straight at the reader, to challenge him, confront him, and get him involved.
The results of this approach are spectacularly productive.
The abominable myth of rock speakers vs. classical speakers.
RECTILINEAR
Examples:
Subscription advertising for magazines has tended away from print, because print hasn't been working very well.
Calderhead, Jackson ads have recently been pulling like this:
Cost of ad: $3,000.
Return on ad: $12,000.
Suddenly our efforts, for a variety of publications, are showing remarkably profitable returns, in print.
We are seriously asking ourselves, "Have we ever had a bomb?" and so far, we haven't been able to think of even one.
Well, we have produced some less successful efforts than others.
How do you make small talk with a Chairman of the Board?
FORTUNE
More success stories.
For instance, we ran a four-color ad for a client, selling very expensive merchandise, and the ad turned a nice profit.
We ran the same ad in black and white, and it turned a much higher profit! (The difference in this case was that color was unnecessary, and didn't justify its expense in added returns.)
Then we ran an ad with a large coupon in the lower right hand corner. It did just fine.
But an alternate ad with a coupon ⅔ the size of the page absolutely broke the bank with coupons. That ad was paid for in the first day's returns.
Another time, we didn't put a coupon in the ad, because the offer was so good, and get this: ad space cost about $30,000, and the client wrote over $1,500,000 in sales. Within 4 days!
One of our clients wanted to try a new direct mail approach, so we prepared a package for him, one that shows his product off to best advantage, is clear, easy to read, and simple to order from.
His orders are rolling in, and at this point one thing is obvious to him: when he came to us, he struck gold.
He will pay us about $5,000 for our services, but he is looking at before-tax-income of $200,000.
(Which is why we scratch our heads in wonder when we hear that agencies are making a lot of money.)
The Corporate Ad.
We were approached by a large company with a very low price currently on their stock, and asked if we could do anything about it, through advertising.
We said, "Yes."
You may remember an earlier ad of ours, where we showed an example of a NYSE stock that went from $4 to $8, after an ad we prepared had run in the Wall Street Journal.
We explained this case history to our client. Who asked a lot of questions. Questions like "What was the trend of that stock?" "What was the volume that week?" "What was the market doing?" "What other factors contributed to the action?"
Our answers:
The stock was going nowhere.
The Dow was off again, and had been for several days, and remained off for several more.
The volume was moderate to low.
1000
We are the first to admit that a single ad has very little to do with changing the world.
But advertising that is properly conceived and executed can make whole businesses prosper.
In the case above, we are discussing a company that had a good story to tell, and had been telling it badly, until we came in.
Our ad was strong enough to cause a number of houses to switch their attitudes, and signal "BUY" to their customers.
Which brings us to another old saw about financial advertising: "The Street isn't influenced by advertising."
But how much will they bring at auction?
Hogwash.
They aren't influenced by silly puffery.
Neither are you.
But just as you are aware of countless products because of advertising, they, too, read and study advertising, and they are influenced by it. At least to the point of looking into companies that may have been overlooked, discounted, or ignored until then.
A word about us.
With success stories like these, you might wonder what kind of people we are.
Has success gone to our heads, are we creatively arrogant, or what?
Let's talk about us for a while.
First of all, we really believe in advertising.
We do enough of it for ourselves to demonstrate the truth in that statement.
This is the 12th ad we've run for ourselves, to the tune of over $75,000. (Some investment spending, right?)
We are an extremely easy agency to work with.
The reason for this is our confidence in the product we produce.
We don't panic.
We don't flail around.
We listen carefully to a client, and we learn from him what his company believes about the marketplace.
We don't go charging off in all directions until we've heard this kind of detail.
One of our new clients asked us, "What if I tell you that I don't like your ad?" Our answer to that was: "What don't you like about the ad?" You see, we can't begin to find a mutually acceptable answer to that question, until we get that answer.
(A surprising number of agencies never bother to find out what the client didn't like, they just deliver 10 more ads fast. That, in our opinion, is a waste of everybody's time.)
Our creative people always seem to be able to find an effective compromise, when it's required.
Our confidence comes from a solid feel for selling, and what it takes to sell a buyer.
And not just through advertising.
Some of the businesses we're in.
On the theory that there is no experience like experience, we have involved ourselves in several businesses other than advertising.
For one of our clients, we act as the Import Agent, the Sales Agent, and the Advertising Agent. Have you ever gone down to the docks to see about a tangled customs problem? We have. Or made the sales call at Macy's—yourself? We have.
Keeping the pipelines filled, in anticipation of new orders, and keeping out of back-order situations, is the kind of experience that makes us ten times more valuable to a client when we prepare a marketing plan, or write an ad.
We know our ads will work.
And when they do, we want our product on the shelf.
New products?
This is the trickiest part of the business, as we see it.
(Come up with a great idea, and chances are the client will take it to Grey.)
We have come up with dozens of sensational ideas.
An idea (which is for sale, as are all of the ideas described here) that will revolutionize the cosmetics industry.
It's been a long time since we were simply a can company.
An idea that will create a run on the cookie section of the A&P.
An idea that will smash a hole in the men's toiletries market.
An idea that all the women in the office want, just as soon as it can be made.
A cat food idea that Ralston doesn't want, but which could make you rich.
(Incidentally, some of the pros in our business know about these ideas, since they consult with us, and they give these concepts ★★★★.)
We are also heavily involved in launching new products for our clients.
Like a new Investment Advisory Service that is absolutely state of the art, and unsurpassed for effectiveness.
A new magazine devoted to women's sports.
A new magazine devoted to book lovers.
And a new Life Insurance policy.
In other words, we've got hot, creative ideas coming out of here in profusion.
And they're all for sale.
How to get rich quicker.
Get on the phone today.
You could have new copy in print or on the air in weeks. Or a new product in test by January.
And then you could see the difference, in sales. (As one of our clients always says, "Why guess when you can know.")
Or send for our agency presentation book.
Sorry, we don't sell yo-yo's.
If you are an advertiser we have to establish the ground rules.
Full-service advertising is impossible on commissionable billings of less than $1,000,000. (Talented advertising people are unbelievably expensive.)
There are really only a few exceptions to this, and they all have to do with fees:
One is direct response advertising.
Our direct response unit can operate profitably on small budgets, or test projects.
And our collateral department handles a number of small budget assignments.
Then comes the other major exception: If you are a smaller company with big growth plans, we can talk. Xerox was a tiny company with big plans, so was Polaroid. Or, if you are a blue-chip company with a brand that spends less than our minimum, we can talk. For obvious reasons.
Otherwise, fellas, it's no dice. We can't get involved with marginal enterprises.
In our business, the rich get richer quicker, and we aim to do the same.
If that's your goal, give us a call.
You'll learn all about us. But quick.
Calderhead, Jackson Inc.

159

A LITTLE FREE ADVICE FOR THE MEDIA DIRECTOR OF J. WALTER THOMPSON FROM THE MEDIA DIRECTOR OF D. ZACHARIA'S LIQUOR STORE.
Mr. D. Zacharia, Proprietor, Zachy's Wine & Liquor Store:
"How to reach the rich and the affluent is a problem that perplexes us all.
"Even in Westchester County where there is no shortage of wealthy people, there is also no shortage of liquor stores.
"Competition is fierce.
"For years, I tried all the usual local media, newspapers, radio, direct mail, even outdoor.
"And then, two years ago I discovered MNI. Which, as you no doubt know, is a way to buy groups of upscale national magazines at local, affordable prices.
"Since then, ads for Zachy's Liquor Store have appeared regularly in such publications as Time, Newsweek, U.S. News, Sports Illustrated and New York Magazine.
"How effective has it been, you ask?
"Sitting in my store is perhaps the most sophisticated device for measuring the effectiveness of media yet devised by man.
"It is called a cash register."
It began as a big idea for small spenders.
Before MNI's Magazine Networks, the only people who could afford to advertise in the big magazines were the big advertisers.
Unfair, we said.
So in 1968, we proceeded to remedy that unfortunate circumstance.
We put together groups of magazines and an ingenious idea of buying, selling and printing whole sections of advertising that not only made buying ads in national magazines feasible for advertisers smaller than General Motors, but also made it possible to buy them in markets smaller than Greater Metropolitan New York.
The how, the why, and the economics of what we did are all very interesting. But also very lengthy.
Suffice it to say that today, in 1974, MNI offers advertisers four compatible groups of magazines in 100 top metro and suburban markets. And two in the overseas military market.
It's threatening to become a big idea for big advertisers.
In accomplishing all this for the small, local advertiser, it seems we created a whole new and rather exciting opportunity for the big advertiser as well.
For the national and regional advertiser, MNI offers the selective characteristics of national magazines, but makes it possible to buy and use them the same way you buy and use spot TV.
It's a way to heavy up in special market areas.
It's a good test market vehicle.
It's even a beautiful way to boost—or get—co-op money from dealers and distributors.
All in all, in a business where new ideas are few and rare, MNI is a good new idea that might well bear some looking into.
If we've piqued your curiosity at all, we'd like to suggest you call Dick Timpone at (212) 661-4800.
Not only will he answer any questions you may have, he'll answer some you may not have thought of.
MAGAZINE NETWORKS
A Medium of Media Networks, Inc.
MN

160

159
Art Director Dick Calderhead
Writer Dick Calderhead
Designer Barbara Schubeck
Artists Marc Nadel
Bettman Archive
Agency Calderhead, Jackson
Client Calderhead, Jackson

160
Art Director Ralph Ammirati
Writer Martin Puris
Designer Ralph Ammirati
Artist Ralph Ammirati
Photographer Leon Kuzmanoff
Agency Ammirati Puris AvRutick
Client Media Networks

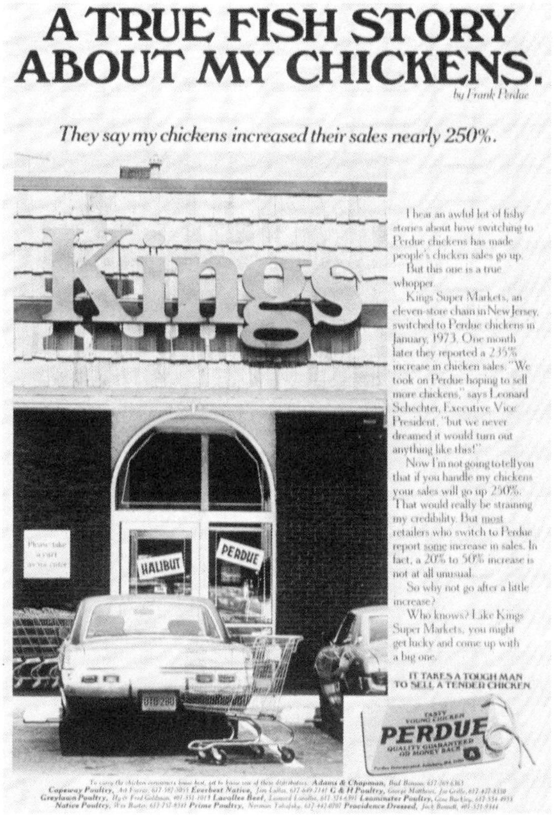
A TRUE FISH STORY
ABOUT MY CHICKENS.
by Frank Perdue
They say my chickens increased their sales nearly 250%.
Kings
HALIBUT
PERDUE
I hear an awful lot of fishy stories about how switching to Perdue chickens has made people's chicken sales go up.
But this one is a true whopper.
Kings Super Markets, an eleven-store chain in New Jersey, switched to Perdue chickens in January, 1973. One month later they reported a 235% increase in chicken sales. "We took on Perdue hoping to sell more chickens," says Leonard Schechter, Executive Vice President, "but we never dreamed it would turn out anything like this!"
Now I'm not going to tell you that if you handle my chickens your sales will go up 250%. That would really be straining my credibility. But most retailers who switch to Perdue report some increase in sales. In fact, a 20% to 50% increase is not at all unusual.
So why not go after a little increase?
Who knows? Like Kings Super Markets, you might get lucky and come up with a big one.
IT TAKES A TOUGH MAN
TO SELL A TENDER CHICKEN.
TASTY YOUNG CHICKEN
PERDUE
QUALITY GUARANTEED OR MONEY BACK

161

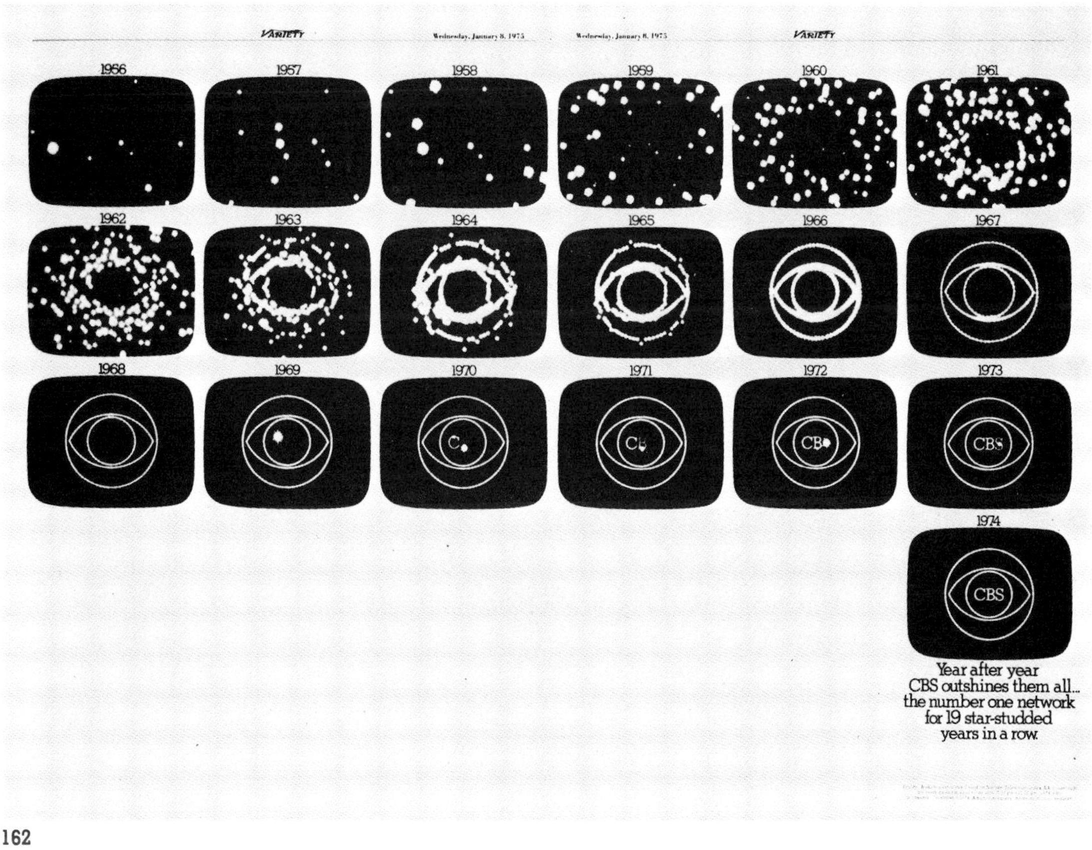
VARIETY
VARIETY
1956
1957
1958
1959
1960
1961
1962
1963
1964
1965
1966
1967
1968
1969
1970
1971
1972
1973
1974
CBS
Year after year
CBS outshines them all...
the number one network
for 19 star-studded
years in a row.

162

161
Art Director Sam Scali
Writer Edward A. McCabe
Photographer Alan Dolgins
Agency Scali, McCabe, Sloves
Client Perdue Farms

162
Art Director Lou Dorfsman
Writers Lou Dorfsman
Jacques Sammes
Designers Lou Dorfsman
Ted Andresakes
Artists George McGinnis
Stan Beck
Agency CBS/Broadcast Group
Client CBS Television Network

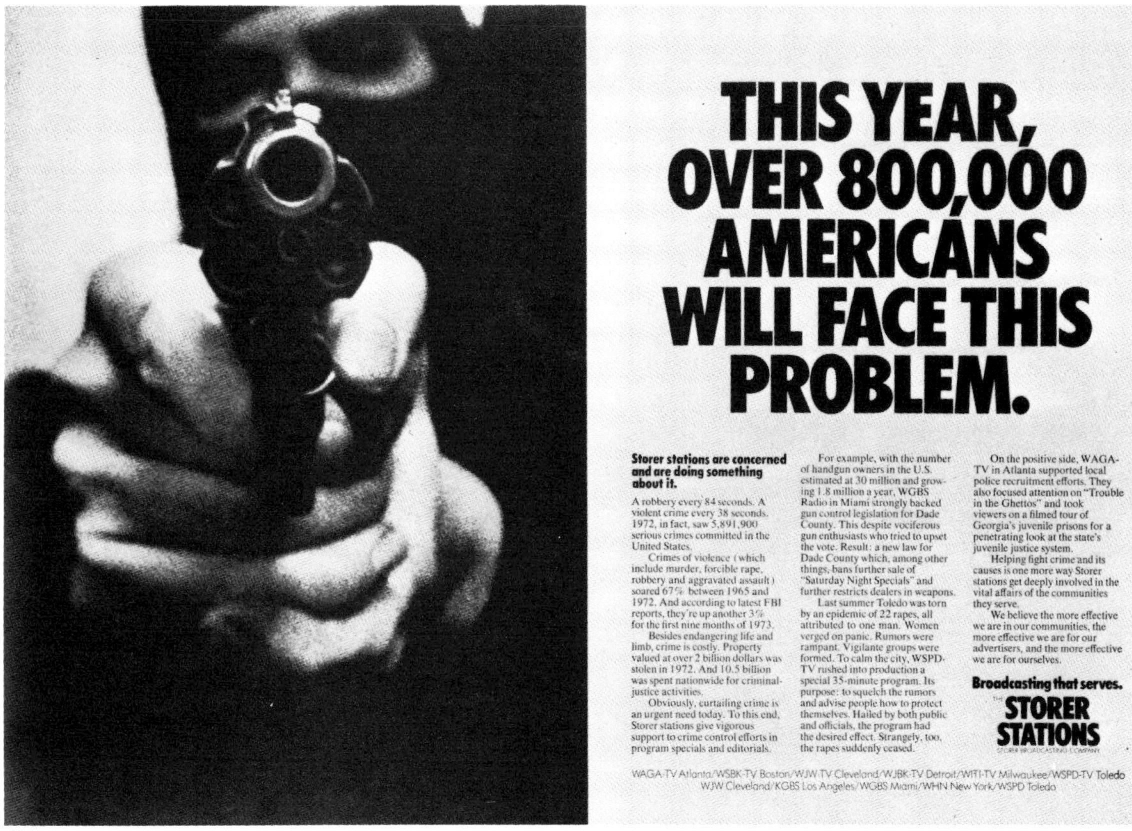
THIS YEAR, OVER 800,000 AMERICANS WILL FACE THIS PROBLEM.
Storer stations are concerned and are doing something about it.
A robbery every 84 seconds. A violent crime every 38 seconds. 1972, in fact, saw 5,891,900 serious crimes committed in the United States.
Crimes of violence (which include murder, forcible rape, robbery and aggravated assault) soared 67% between 1965 and 1972. And according to latest FBI reports, they're up another 3% for the first nine months of 1973.
Besides endangering life and limb, crime is costly. Property valued at over 2 billion dollars was stolen in 1972. And 10.5 billion was spent nationwide for criminal-justice activities.
Obviously, curtailing crime is an urgent need today. To this end, Storer stations give vigorous support to crime control efforts in program specials and editorials.
For example, with the number of handgun owners in the U.S. estimated at 30 million and growing 1.8 million a year, WGBS Radio in Miami strongly backed gun control legislation for Dade County. This despite vociferous gun enthusiasts who tried to upset the vote. Result: a new law for Dade County which, among other things, bans further sale of "Saturday Night Specials" and further restricts dealers in weapons.
Last summer Toledo was torn by an epidemic of 22 rapes, all attributed to one man. Women verged on panic. Rumors were rampant. Vigilante groups were formed. To calm the city, WSPD-TV rushed into production a special 35-minute program. Its purpose: to squelch the rumors and advise people how to protect themselves. Hailed by both public and officials, the program had the desired effect. Strangely, too, the rapes suddenly ceased.
On the positive side, WAGA-TV in Atlanta supported local police recruitment efforts. They also focused attention on "Trouble in the Ghettos" and took viewers on a filmed tour of Georgia's juvenile prisons for a penetrating look at the state's juvenile justice system.
Helping fight crime and its causes is one more way Storer stations get deeply involved in the vital affairs of the communities they serve.
We believe the more effective we are in our communities, the more effective we are for our advertisers, and the more effective we are for ourselves.
Broadcasting that serves.
STORER STATIONS
WAGA-TV Atlanta/WSBK-TV Boston/WJW-TV Cleveland/WJBK-TV Detroit/WITI-TV Milwaukee/WSPD-TV Toledo
WJW Cleveland/KGBS Los Angeles/WGBS Miami/WHN New York/WSPD Toledo

163

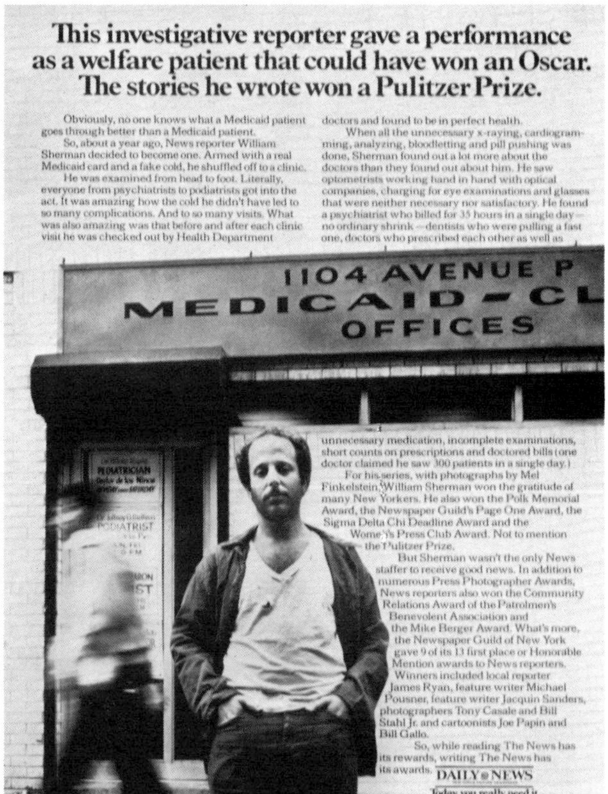
This investigative reporter gave a performance as a welfare patient that could have won an Oscar. The stories he wrote won a Pulitzer Prize.
Obviously, no one knows what a Medicaid patient goes through better than a Medicaid patient.
So, about a year ago, News reporter William Sherman decided to become one. Armed with a real Medicaid card and a fake cold, he shuffled off to a clinic.
He was examined from head to foot. Literally, everyone from psychiatrists to podiatrists got into the act. It was amazing how the cold he didn't have led to so many complications. And to so many visits. What was also amazing was that before and after each clinic visit he was checked out by Health Department doctors and found to be in perfect health.
When all the unnecessary x-raying, cardiogramming, analyzing, bloodletting and pill pushing was done, Sherman found out a lot more about the doctors than they found out about him. He saw optometrists working hand in hand with optical companies, charging for eye examinations and glasses that were neither necessary nor satisfactory. He found a psychiatrist who billed for 35 hours in a single day—no ordinary shrink—dentists who were pulling a fast one, doctors who prescribed each other as well as unnecessary medication, incomplete examinations, short counts on prescriptions and doctored bills (one doctor claimed he saw 300 patients in a single day.)
1104 AVENUE P
MEDICAID - CL
OFFICES
For his series, with photographs by Mel Finkelstein, William Sherman won the gratitude of many New Yorkers. He also won the Polk Memorial Award, the Newspaper Guild's Page One Award, the Sigma Delta Chi Deadline Award and the Women's Press Club Award. Not to mention the Pulitzer Prize.
But Sherman wasn't the only News staffer to receive good news. In addition to numerous Press Photographer Awards, News reporters also won the Community Relations Award of the Patrolmen's Benevolent Association and the Mike Berger Award. What's more, the Newspaper Guild of New York gave 9 of its 13 first place or Honorable Mention awards to News reporters. Winners included local reporter James Ryan, feature writer Michael Pousner, feature writer Jacquin Sanders, photographers Tony Casale and Bill Stahl Jr. and cartoonists Joe Papin and Bill Gallo.
So, while reading The News has its rewards, writing The News has its awards.
DAILY NEWS
Today, you really need it.

164

163
Art Director John Cenatiempo
Writer Andrew Issacson
Photographer Cailor-Resnick
Agency Gaynor & Ducas
Client Storer Broadcasting Co.

164
Art Director Ed Rotondi
Writer Neil Drossman
Designer Ed Rotondi
Photographer David Vine
Agency Della Femina, Travisano & Partners
Client The Daily News

WITH MY CHICKENS YOU CAN COUNT YOUR PROFITS BEFORE THEY HATCH.
Frank Perdue
Past experience on the part of retailers who have taken on my chickens has proven it time and again.
Virtually every store that switched to Perdue has sold more chickens than ever.
In some instances, the increase is staggering. There's an 11-store chain in New Jersey that put all their eggs in one basket by selling strictly Perdue and chicken sales nearly tripled.
The reason for this phenomenon is simple. People are more aware of Perdue chickens than all the other brands combined. And not only are they willing to go out of their way to find my chickens, they're also willing to pay more for them.
If you'd like to take advantage of this highly predictable situation, call 301-742-7161, collect.
PERDUE

165

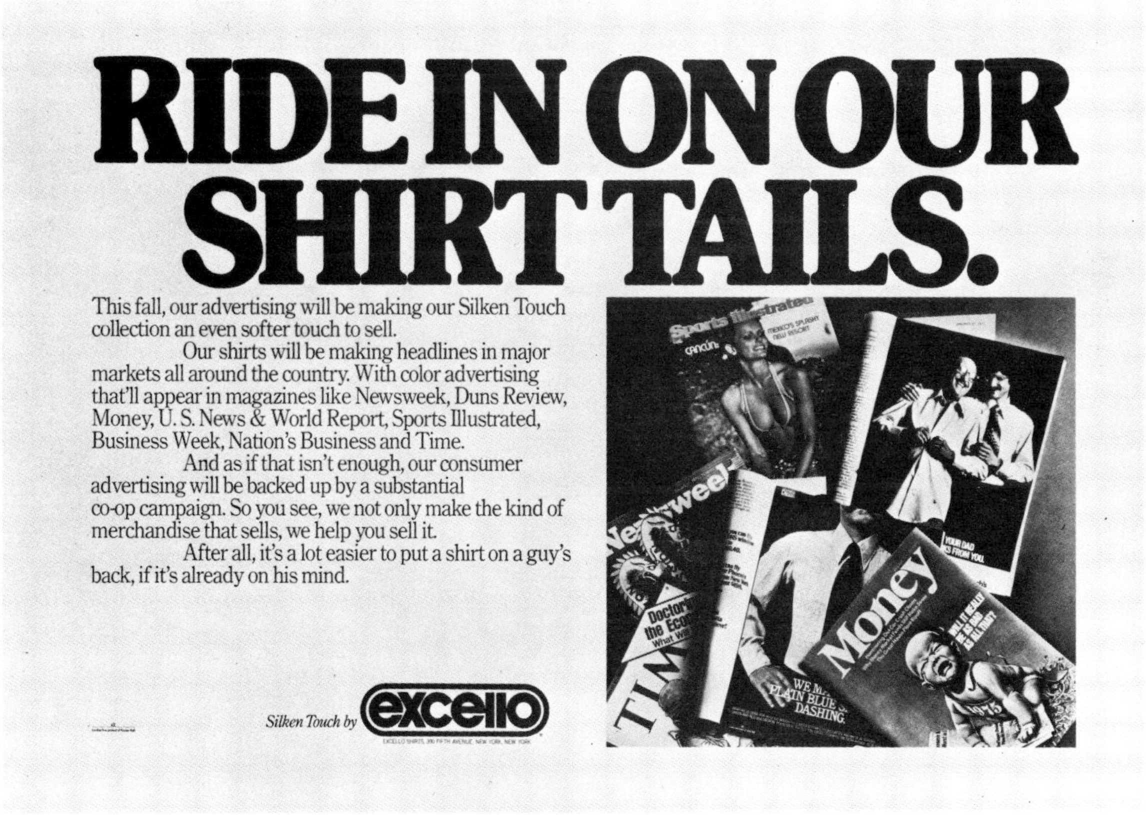
RIDE IN ON OUR SHIRT TAILS.
This fall, our advertising will be making our Silken Touch collection an even softer touch to sell.
Our shirts will be making headlines in major markets all around the country. With color advertising that'll appear in magazines like Newsweek, Duns Review, Money, U. S. News & World Report, Sports Illustrated, Business Week, Nation's Business and Time.
And as if that isn't enough, our consumer advertising will be backed up by a substantial co-op campaign. So you see, we not only make the kind of merchandise that sells, we help you sell it.
After all, it's a lot easier to put a shirt on a guy's back, if it's already on his mind.
Silken Touch by excello
Money

166

165
Art Director Sam Scali
Writer Edward A. McCabe
Photographer Alan Dolgins
Agency Scali, McCabe, Sloves
Client Perdue Farms

166
Art Director Bill Kamp
Writer John Russo
Designer Bill Kamp
Photographer Andrew Unangst
Agency Levine, Huntley, Schmidt
Client Excello Shirts

MORE MEN READ PLAYBOY
THAN WATCH
MONDAY NIGHT FOOTBALL ON TV
Monday Night Football traditionally draws the largest male audience of any regularly televised sports show.
But when it comes to attracting men, not even pro football can match the editorial appeal of PLAYBOY.
The facts: PLAYBOY gathers 14,800,000 men to its pages each month, while Monday Night Football reaches 11,780,000. And if your game plan concentrates on men 18-34, the point spread is even greater: 9,480,000 for PLAYBOY vs. 4,250,000 for pro football.
While PLAYBOY provides a far greater male audience than television sports, it also offers another extremely important advantage. And that's involvement with your advertising message.
PLAYBOY commands the highest attention to advertising of any major medium—print or broadcast. Nearly 80% of our audience pays attention to the advertising in PLAYBOY vs. 54% for Monday Night Football.*
Enormous coverage of the male market combined with maximum attention to advertising: an unbeatable combination. And only PLAYBOY provides it. That's why PLAYBOY is in a class by itself when it comes to influencing men.
PLAYBOY
IN A CLASS BY ITSELF

167

167
Art Director Richard Manzo
Writer Robert Carr
Designer Richard Manzo
Photographer Don Azuma
Agency Playboy Promotion Department
Client Playboy Magazine

Another fine product of Kayser-Roth
THE FIRST THING TO LOOK BAD IN OTHER SHIRTS IS NOW THE LAST THING TO LOOK BAD IN OURS.
INTRODUCING THE XLO-100 COLLAR.
excello
Permanent Press
Wrinkled collars are a pain in the neck. So at Excello we've developed a new kind of collar. One that doesn't wrinkle or pucker. Even after 100 launderings.
We call it the XLO-100 Collar. Its lining is fused to the top-ply of the collar, giving it more body.
So it can resist wrinkling and puckering. And always look good, while staying soft and comfortable. Because of its unique construction, the XLO-100 Collar runs rings around other collars.
excello
Excello Shirts, 390 Fifth Avenue, New York, New York 10018

168

How to tighten your belt without cutting off your circulation.

Spending your advertising money like it's going out of style is now out of style.

And as you well know, you can't spend fewer dollars in the same ways and places as you can spend lots of dollars.

So, how do you get as much out of your advertising budget without putting as much into it?

We at the Daily News think we have the answer.

The Daily News.

The News has nearly twice the circulation of any major daily in the nation, with over 5 million readers.

In fact, according to a recent survey conducted by Markets In Focus, the Daily News has more readers in the nation's number one market than the Times and Post combined.

What's more, The News has 875,000 more adults in families owning homes than the Times, 400,000 more working women, and 55% more adults in families earning between $15,000 and $25,000.

Besides, the strength of The News knows no city limits. For just as we're number one in the city, we're also number one in the suburbs.

Now let's take a look at TV.

At a time when you're tightening your belt, you really should stay away from things that are too rich for your blood.

Yet despite this fact there are still a lot of advertisers who only have eyes for TV.

Well, if the Daily News were a TV show, its audience would be greater in GRP's than any of the top TV shows of this season. And you can buy the Daily News for a lot less.

Furthermore in the New York ADI, nothing on the tube can give you more penetration than The News.

If you'd like to get an even better grasp of our reach, call Lou Francis, the Daily News Research Manager, (212) 682-1234.

After all, if today's business headlines have you looking at newspapers again, there's no newspaper you should take a closer look at than the New York Daily News.

DAILY NEWS
BAR PANEL RIPS
5 STATE JUDGES

DAILY NEWS
Today...you really need it!

169

SILVER

168
Art Director Rob Lopes
Writer Larry Spector
Designer Rob Lopes
Photographer Elbert Budin
Agency Levine, Huntley, Schmidt
Client Excello Shirts

169
Art Director Ed Rotondi
Writer Neil Drossman
Designer Ed Rotondi
Photographer David Vine
Agency Della Femina, Travisano & Partners
Client The Daily News

Mac Porter makes $23,000. Do you still think management starts at $15,000?
If you've had your house painted lately, you know what kind of wages painters command these days.
Why not? Wages and prices all across the board have been going nowhere but up. So isn't it strange that some advertising people still paint themselves into a corner when it comes to defining the management market?
Too many of them still consider $15,000 the starting point for management. Obviously, it just isn't true anymore—with salaries being what they are now. Today, you've got to raise your sights at least to $25,000 if real corporate decision-makers are your target.
The most efficient way to reach these middle and top managers is Fortune. For Managers and Officials over $25,000, Fortune has the lowest cost per thousand of any major publication.*
But CPMs are just one way your advertising dollar buys more leverage in Fortune. Other ways? Take frequency. A lot fewer ads are a lot heavier schedule. Six Fortune insertions is one in every two issues. In the newsweeklies, it's less than one in eight.
This is no trivial distinction. You get more continuity for less money. Every advertisement in Fortune keeps working. Through the whole month. People read it at home. They pick it up again and again. They have to, because there's solid meat here. For anybody who's concerned with business decisions, it's essential reading from front cover to back. There's no telling how many times they'll see your messages or how long your advertising will keep pulling.
The lowest cost per thousand to decision-makers. And the most efficient continuity for your advertising. In today's economic climate, they're pretty convincing reasons to schedule Fortune.
FORTUNE
Real management starts at $25,000.

170

WE SELL MORE CARS THAN FORD, CHRYSLER, CHEVROLET AND BUICK COMBINED.
MATCHBOX.

171

GOLD

170
Art Director Bob Czernysz
Writer Richard Olmsted
Photographer Richard Noble
Agency Young & Rubicam International
Client Fortune Magazine

171
Art Director Allan Beaver
Writer Larry Plapler
Designer Allan Beaver
Photographer Cailor-Resnick
Agency Levine, Huntley, Schmidt
Client Lesney Products Corp.

It's only natural that a person would rather hear what they won't have to pay for on their vacation.
That's the reason you should know about Club Mediterranee.
When you sell a Club Mediterranee vacation, there's a lot to talk about on the subject of saving money.
At Club Mediterranee, the price ends with the initial cost. A week in Mexico, Hawaii, Tahiti, one of our three villages in the Caribbean or any of our other sixty villages around the world costs no more than a week at an ordinary resort.
But that price includes comfortable rooms, three meals a day (unlimited food), all the free wine you can drink at lunch and dinner, and all the exercise you can stand.
With activities like free tennis. Free sailing. Free scuba diving. Free water skiing. Free yoga and calisthenics. Free picnic excursions and boat rides. And a lot more that's free too. We even give free lessons and equipment in all these sports. And at night, there's free live entertainment. Every night.
What's more, because everything is included, you, as a travel agent are included in everything. You receive a commission on the whole package.
And for a travel agent who sells a Club Mediterranee vacation, one commission leads to another.
A recent survey has shown that, on the average, every client you send to Club Mediterranee brings at least five new customers to Club Mediterranee. That proves that good news travels fast. And that's good news for us. And for you. All in all, a Club Mediterranee vacation pays not only because of what your clients won't have to pay. But because of what it'll pay you.
For more information about Club Mediterranee vacations, call (212) 977-2121 or write: Club Mediterranee 40 West 57th Street, New York, New York 10019.
Free Scuba Diving
Free Sailing
Free Food & Wine
Free Tennis
Free Water Skiing
Free Entertainment
TELL YOUR CLIENTS WHAT THEIR VACATION WON'T COST FOR A CHANGE.
CLUB MEDITERRANEE
CARIBBEAN/SOUTH PACIFIC/MEXICO
and 60 other locations around the world

172

"People laughed.
"When I directed 'Where's Poppa?', a serious film about the problems of old age, people laughed. Another picture I did, 'The Comic', with Dick Van Dyke, people laughed.
"Now, I'm not so immodest as to think that what I wrote or directed and put in front of them made them laugh, because I was serious. Those were serious pieces as far as I was concerned. And 'The New Dick Van Dyke Show' is a serious work. But people laugh.
"So I have to assume that it's because Kodak makes funny film.
"When people say they're laughing at my film, it's really Kodak's film. But then again it's mine because I bought it from them. I think they sell the same film to some of my friends because their films make people laugh, too.
"I understand that they also have a serious film that they sell to Swedish and Russian directors. And that film is almost certain not to make people laugh.
"I'm negotiating for the film rights to 'Dante's Inferno', and if I do secure them, I'll order Kodak's serious film."
Carl Reiner. Writer, director, actor, interviewer of a 2013-year-old man and a personal friend of Mel Brooks. Currently producing "The New Dick Van Dyke Show."
EASTMAN KODAK COMPANY

173

172
Art Director Bill Kamp
Writer John Russo
Designer Bill Kamp
Artist Whistlin Dixie
Agency Levine, Huntley, Schmidt
Client Club Mediterranee

173
Art Director Ben Kuwata
Writer Carl Reiner
Designer Ben Kuwata
Photographer Carl Furuta
Agency J. Walter Thompson
Client Eastman Kodak Co.

INDUSTRY MANAGERS SHOULD HAVE MISTRESSES INSTEAD OF WIVES.

The best solution to the problem of the corporate wife is to eliminate her.

Or substitute a mistress.

To compete in the executive rat race, some psychiatrists believe that the executive should become a bit of a rat.

Why? Because the system denies the corporate wife independence and self expression. She becomes ripe for tippling and tranquilizing. And a pain in his ascent up the corporate ladder.

She becomes identified in his mind with inferior hamburgers. And competes with temptations of sexy secretaries, scintillating stewardesses and unlimited expense accounts.

Where will industry managers find answers to this serious problem?

One of their best idea sources is Industry Week.

It informs them. Leads them. Motivates them.

It helps them become better managers. Gives them new answers to old problems. Old answers to new ones.

That's why when TGI reported recently that Industry Week reaches 1.8 million readers, we were only mildly surprised.

That's also why IW's up 25% in advertising dollars in the first quarter of 1974.

Because Industry Week helps managers understand their wives, it has made a beautiful marriage with advertisers.

INDUSTRY WEEK

The magazine managers read.

174

IT'S GOING TO BE ANOTHER OF THOSE 3-BENNIE, 2-DEXY DAYS.

Many industrial companies are being managed by junkies. Men and women addicted to nicotine, alcohol and pills.

When they can't sleep, they take pills.

When they have hangovers, they take pills.

When they face a particularly tough day, they take pills.

And then there's tea. And coffee. And three martini lunches.

Between 90 million and 110 million Americans swallow the most abused drug—alcohol.

About 80 to 90 million use mind altering drugs.

About 20 million have tried marijuana.

Where will industry managers find answers to the drug problem in their companies?

One of their best idea sources is Industry Week.

It informs them. Leads them. Motivates them.

It helps them become better managers. Gives them new answers to old problems. Old answers to new ones.

That's why when TGI reported recently that Industry Week reaches 1.8 million readers, we were only mildly surprised.

That's also why IW's up 25% in advertising dollars in the first quarter of 1974.

Because Industry Week has become a habit with its readers, it has become a habit with advertisers.

INDUSTRY WEEK

The magazine managers read.

175

174
Art Director Bob Kwait
Writer Mike Marino
Photographer Bob Bender
Agency Griswold-Eshleman
Client Industry Week

175
Art Director Bob Kwait
Writer Mike Marino
Photographer Bob Bender
Agency Griswold-Eshleman
Client Industry Week

BALLERO
WAR
*Say [BY · 'YAIR · O]
UA-XW432-W
A new single from "War Live" on United Artists Records & Tapes.
Produced by Jerry Goldstein in association with Lonnie Jordan & Howard Scott for Far Out Productions, Inc.
© MCMLXXIV United Artists Records, Inc.

175A

175A
Art Director Bob Cato
Writer John Kehe
Designer John Kehe
Artist John Kehe
Photographer David Alexander
Agency United Artists Artists
Client United Artists Records

THERE'S A FORTUNE TO BE MADE IN MEADOW MUFFINS.

You don't bake them.

You just find them lying there, ready to be made into energy. The kind that lights lights, heats houses, and drives drills.

Plain, ordinary cow manure may become one of the most practical solutions to the energy crisis.

Because a gadget called an "anerobic digester" converts meadow muffins, road apples and buffalo chips into usable methane fuel. And methane produces energy.

Industry managers first read about this novel raw material in Industry Week. That's where they get a lot of their new ideas.

And that's why they like it.

Industry Week informs them. Leads them. Motivates them.

It helps them become better managers. Gives them new answers to old problems. Old answers to new ones.

That's why when TGI reported recently that Industry Week reaches 1.8 million readers, we were only mildly surprised.

That's also why IW's up 25% in advertising dollars in the first quarter of 1974.

And that's no meadow muffin.

INDUSTRY WEEK

The magazine managers read.

176

ALMOST AS MUCH STEALING GOES ON IN INDUSTRY TODAY AS IN GOVERNMENT.

With all the hooting and hollering about payoffs, under-table deals and kickbacks, one would think that all the stealing and cheating is going on in political circles.

Not so.

Pilfering is costing American industry over $2 billion each year. And it's getting worse. A lot worse.

Who pays for it?

The consumer. In higher prices. In higher insurance rates. In shoddy products.

Where will industry managers find answers to stopping industrial pilferage?

One of their best idea sources is Industry Week.

It informs them. Leads them. Motivates them.

It helps them become better managers. Gives them new answers to old problems. Old answers to new ones.

That's why when TGI reported recently that Industry Week reaches 1.8 million readers, we were only mildly surprised.

That's also why IW's up 25% in advertising dollars in the first quarter of 1974.

Because Industry Week is helping managers put a stop to in-plant stealing, it has become a real steal for advertisers.

INDUSTRY WEEK

The magazine managers read.

177

SILVER

176
Art Directors Bob Kwait
Tom Gilday
Writer Mike Marino
Designer Bob Kwait
Photographer Jan Czyrba
Agency Griswold-Eshleman
Client Industry Week

177
Art Director Bob Kwait
Writer Mike Marino
Photographer Bob Bender
Agency Griswold-Eshleman
Client Industry Week

A LOT OF MANAGERS WITH TOP-DRAWER POTENTIAL END UP HERE.

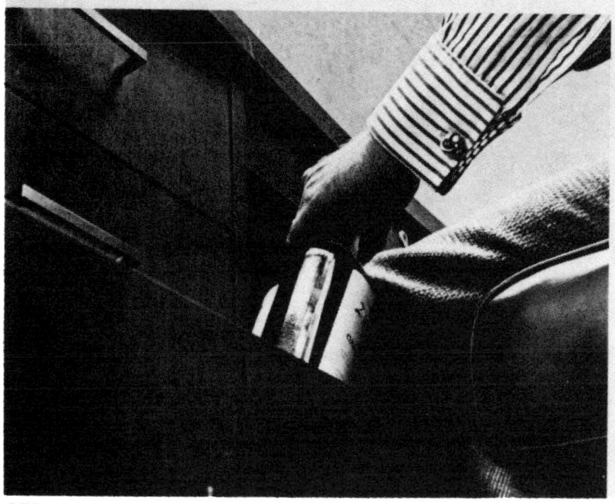

Many managers try to find the answers to their problems in the bottom drawer. In a bottle.

One in ten will become an alcoholic.

The cost to industry? Staggering. $40 billion in lost time and fuzzy on-the-job performance.

An undetected alcoholic authorized to sign contracts or make investments can lose his company millions in minutes.

But there are other, more serious costs.

Alcoholics are more susceptible to liver disorders. Colds. Ulcers. And their life expectancy is twelve years shorter than non-drinkers.

Where will industry managers find answers to alcoholism?

One of their best idea sources is Industry Week.

It informs them. Leads them. Motivates them.

It helps them become better managers. Gives them new answers to old problems. Old answers to new ones.

That's why when TGI reported recently that Industry Week reaches 1.8 million readers, we were only mildly surprised.

That's also why IW's up 25% in advertising dollars in the first quarter of 1974.

Because Industry Week helps keep top-drawer talent out of the bottom drawer, it has become a top-drawer advertising buy.

INDUSTRY WEEK
The magazine managers read.

178

THAT BELLY WILL KILL HIM BEFORE HE'S 54.

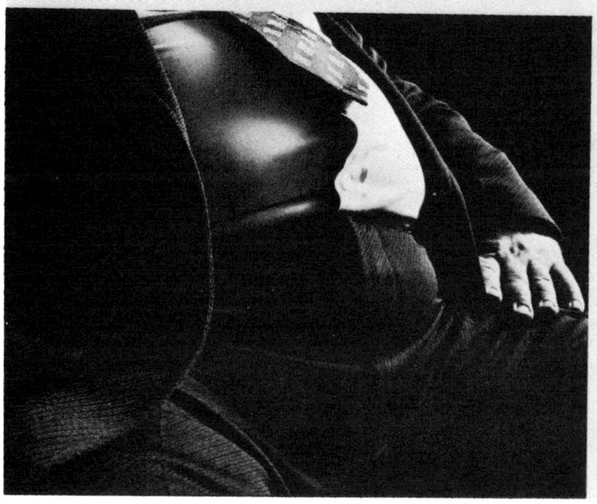

Joe's an average middle manager.

In his forties. Always on the job, usually early. Often works late.

He's bucking for the plant manager's job—has to beat out two other guys.

Joe has a 50-50 chance of dying from some type of heart ailment by the time he's fifty-four.

There's one chance in four that he'll get cancer.

And there's about a 10% chance he's already suffering from some mental or emotional disorder.

He's a $15 billion-a-year industrial problem.

Where will industry managers find answers to this health problem?

One of their best idea sources is Industry Week.

It informs them. Leads them. Motivates them.

It helps them become better managers. Gives them new answers to old problems. Old answers to new ones.

That's why when TGI reported recently that Industry Week reaches 1.8 million readers, we were only mildly surprised.

That's also why IW's up 25% in advertising dollars in the first quarter of 1974.

Helping Joe solve his health problems is what is helping Industry Week become more and more healthy.

INDUSTRY WEEK
The magazine managers read.

179

178
Art Director Bob Kwait
Writer Mike Marino
Photographer Bob Bender
Agency Griswold-Eshleman
Client Industry Week

179
Art Director Bob Kwait
Writer Mike Marino
Photographer Bob Bender
Agency Griswold-Eshleman
Client Industry Week

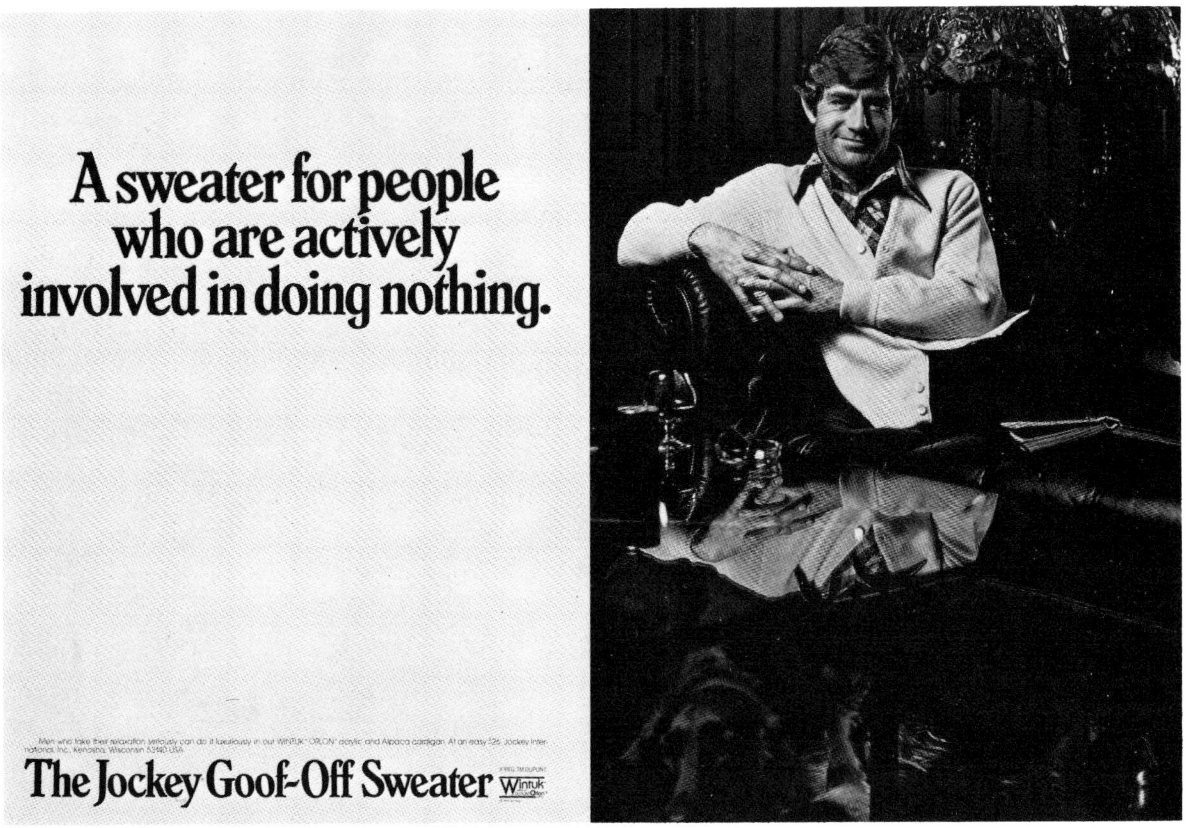
A sweater for people who are actively involved in doing nothing.
Men who take their relaxation seriously can do it luxuriously in our WINTUK* ORLON* acrylic and Alpaca cardigan. At an easy $26. Jockey International, Inc., Kenosha, Wisconsin 53140 USA.
The Jockey Goof-Off Sweater
*REG. TM DUPONT
Wintuk
Orlon

180

"Even more terrifying than the stunts we filmed for the Fiat 'Stunt Driver' commercial was the fact that we had no more than one chance to get each one on film.
"In fact, deciding what to do was easy. All we had to do was let our imaginations run amok. Roof jumps, ferryboat leaps, running down three flights of steps. Since the idea was to demonstrate how extraordinarily durable these cars are made, no stunt could be too wild.
"But working out a thoroughly efficient, totally foolproof way of shooting the stunts—and doing it within a very strict budget—was another matter.
"We put together a multinational crew. Our director was Giacomo Battiato, a brilliant young man from Milan. Our cinematographer was Pasquolino DeSantis, who did the feature film, 'Romeo and Juliet.'
"Then, after months of planning how each stunt would proceed second by second, plotting exactly how each would be filmed, where each camera would be placed, which lens to use for what, we started shooting in Italy.
"We used four cameras to film each stunt. Two going at regular speed and two at 120 frames per second. The idea here was to allow ourselves every possibility in the editing room and to provide for a backup in case one camera failed.
"The Eastman film we used was the kind they use for most feature films. And, at the risk of sounding like a commercial for Kodak, deciding what film to use was the easiest decision we made on the whole project."
Ralph Ammirati, Partner in Ammirati Puris AvRutick Advertising Agency, New York.
Kodak
EASTMAN KODAK COMPANY

181

180
Art Director Louis Colletti
Writer Larry Spector
Designer Louis Colletti
Photographer Richard Noble
Agency Levine, Huntley, Schmidt
Client Jockey International

181
Art Director Ben Kuwata
Writer Robert Bishopric
Designer Ben Kuwata
Photographer Leon Kuzmanoff
Agency J. Walter Thompson
Client Eastman Kodak Co.

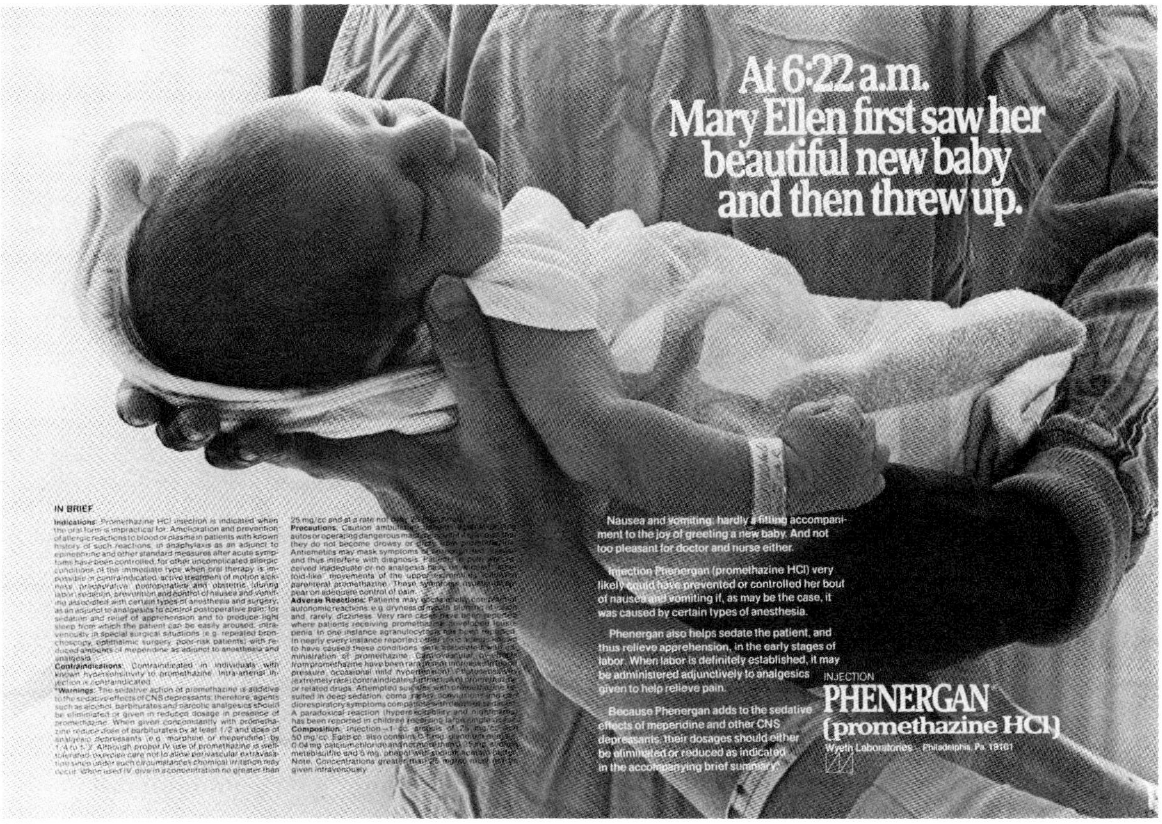
At 6:22 a.m.
Mary Ellen first saw her beautiful new baby and then threw up.
IN BRIEF
Nausea and vomiting: hardly a fitting accompaniment to the joy of greeting a new baby. And not too pleasant for doctor and nurse either.
Injection Phenergan (promethazine HCl) very likely could have prevented or controlled her bout of nausea and vomiting if, as may be the case, it was caused by certain types of anesthesia.
Phenergan also helps sedate the patient, and thus relieve apprehension, in the early stages of labor. When labor is definitely established, it may be administered adjunctively to analgesics given to help relieve pain.
Because Phenergan adds to the sedative effects of meperidine and other CNS depressants, their dosages should either be eliminated or reduced as indicated in the accompanying brief summary.
INJECTION
PHENERGAN
(promethazine HCl)
Wyeth Laboratories Philadelphia, Pa. 19101

182

Since we helped so many retailers get where they are, we'd like to show you where they've been.
In 1921, a department store on 34th Street ran its first ad in the Daily News.
Its name was Macy's.
Today, millions and millions of advertising dollars later, Macy's, the world's largest store, spends the largest part of its advertising budget with the Daily News.
And Macy's may not have told Gimbels, but Gimbels found out about us too. In 1921.
In 1920, despite the fact that we were wet behind the ears, Sears decided to try us. With over a million lines. You don't have to read between the lines to realize they liked us. Because today they're still running over a million lines.
A&P checked us out in 1921. And once they saw how we delivered, they didn't stop.
Ohrbach's has been with us since the Gatsby look came and went. The first time.
Martin's and Mays joined the fold in the 20's. So did A&S. (Fifty years later A&S runs more lines in The News than any other advertiser.)
In the 30's it was Alexander's and Gertz.
Castro has been with us since Bernadette was bouncing around in her crib.
Why have so many retailers grown up with us?
Retailers buy what sells. And the fact is that even before many of today's leading retailers were who they are, we were what we are. The number one retail medium in the nation's number one market. For the past 43 years.
And number one in circulation for 50 years.
As you can tell from the ads pictured, retail ads may not look the same today as they did way back when, but there's one thing about retail advertising that's remained the same. Us.
DAILY NEWS
NEW YORK'S PICTURE NEWSPAPER
Today...you really need it!
Macy's Rubber Soled
SANDALS
Are All-'Round Sandals
79c
MACY'S
See Mays 2-Page Adv.
Mays
510 FULTON ST
Smartest
WHITE
HATS
55c
Just at the Right Time
BEAUTIFUL WHITE SHOES
Richly Furred
Winter Coats
$48
ABRAHAM & STRAUS
Sun Suits
50c
$10 DOWN PUTS A GARAGE
EASY PAYMENTS
SEARS, ROEBUCK AND CO.
THIRD FLOOR
The New GIMBELS

183

182
Art Director Alan Kline
Writer Bernard Ostrof
Designer Alan Kline
Photographer Leonard Cohen
Agency Lewis & Gilman
Client Wyeth Laboratories

183
Art Director Ron Travisano
Writer Neil Drossman
Designer Ron Travisano
Agency Della Femina, Travisano & Partners
Client The Daily News

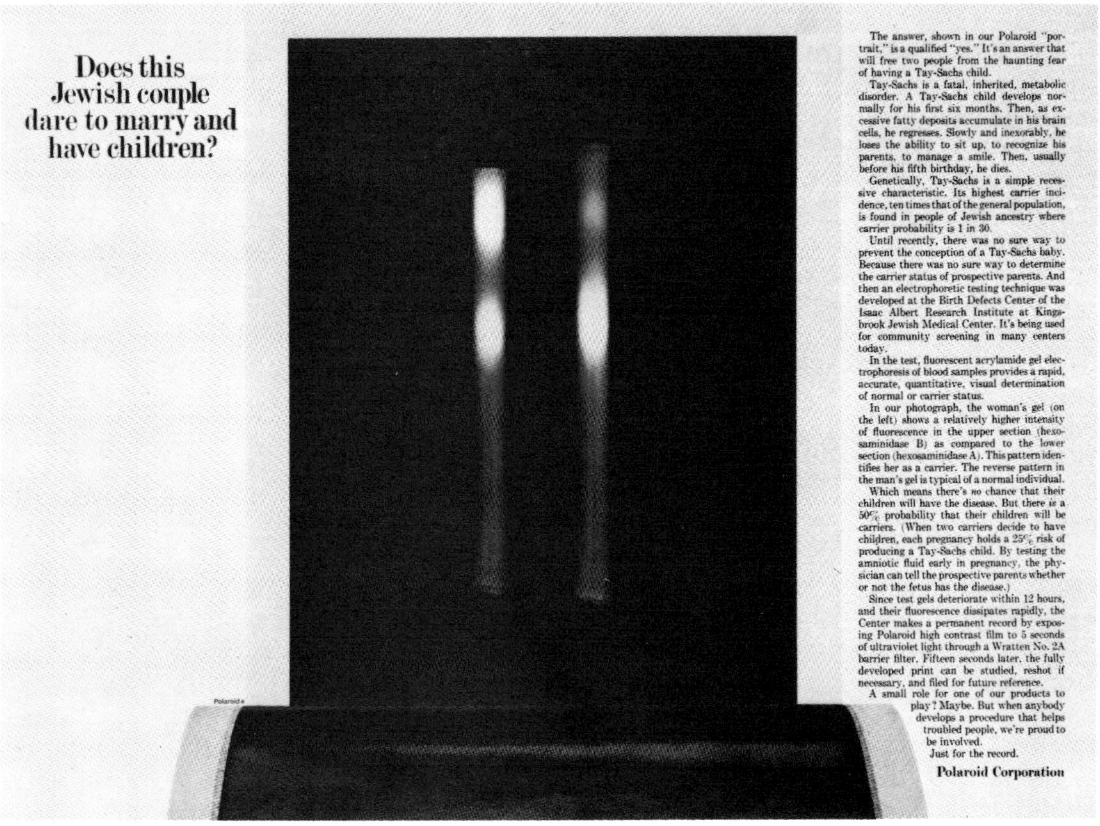
Does this Jewish couple dare to marry and have children?
The answer, shown in our Polaroid "portrait," is a qualified "yes." It's an answer that will free two people from the haunting fear of having a Tay-Sachs child.
Tay-Sachs is a fatal, inherited, metabolic disorder. A Tay-Sachs child develops normally for his first six months. Then, as excessive fatty deposits accumulate in his brain cells, he regresses. Slowly and inexorably, he loses the ability to sit up, to recognize his parents, to manage a smile. Then, usually before his fifth birthday, he dies.
Genetically, Tay-Sachs is a simple recessive characteristic. Its highest carrier incidence, ten times that of the general population, is found in people of Jewish ancestry where carrier probability is 1 in 30.
Until recently, there was no sure way to prevent the conception of a Tay-Sachs baby. Because there was no sure way to determine the carrier status of prospective parents. And then an electrophoretic testing technique was developed at the Birth Defects Center of the Isaac Albert Research Institute at Kingsbrook Jewish Medical Center. It's being used for community screening in many centers today.
In the test, fluorescent acrylamide gel electrophoresis of blood samples provides a rapid, accurate, quantitative, visual determination of normal or carrier status.
In our photograph, the woman's gel (on the left) shows a relatively higher intensity of fluorescence in the upper section (hexosaminidase B) as compared to the lower section (hexosaminidase A). This pattern identifies her as a carrier. The reverse pattern in the man's gel is typical of a normal individual.
Which means there's *no* chance that their children will have the disease. But there *is* a 50% probability that their children will be carriers. (When two carriers decide to have children, each pregnancy holds a 25% risk of producing a Tay-Sachs child. By testing the amniotic fluid early in pregnancy, the physician can tell the prospective parents whether or not the fetus has the disease.)
Since test gels deteriorate within 12 hours, and their fluorescence dissipates rapidly, the Center makes a permanent record by exposing Polaroid high contrast film to 5 seconds of ultraviolet light through a Wratten No. 2A barrier filter. Fifteen seconds later, the fully developed print can be studied, reshot if necessary, and filed for future reference.
A small role for one of our products to play? Maybe. But when anybody develops a procedure that helps troubled people, we're proud to be involved.
Just for the record.
Polaroid Corporation

184

DIFFERENT SOCKS FOR DIFFERENT JOCKS.
Presenting a complete line of socks for the active as well as not so active sportsman. They're made for cycling, basketball, jogging, tennis, whatever, in 17 different styles. And come in a variety of colors for men and boys. So stock up now. From the one man with all the socks, your Hanes distributor.
PRO'S CHOICE
Hanes

185

GOLD

184
Art Director Lee Epstein
Writer Hal Silverman
Designer Lee Epstein
Photographer Henry Sandbank
Agency Doyle Dane Bernbach
Client Polaroid Corp.

185
Art Director Frank Rogers
Writer Roger Feuerman
Designer Frank Rogers
Photographer Gary Ludwick
Agency Cargill, Wilson & Acree
Client Hanes-Millis Sales Corp.

Your problems magnified in seconds.
The Polaroid MP-4 Camera. Instant photomacrography is only one of the things it does.
Maybe you're measuring the growth rate of cracks in metals under stress. Or maybe you're studying the growth of a certain strain of bacteria under no stress.
If you're using Polaroid's MP-4 you can make your problems up to 32 times bigger than they actually are and get finished pictures in seconds. In full color, or in black and white (with or without an instant negative).
Polaroid's instant pictures tell you right away if you've got the shot you want and, in some cases, how your test is going. Whichever way it goes you'll have time to do something about it without starting all over again.
You won't have to reshoot difficult sequences or restage complex experiments. And you've got a permanent record to study—one minute or one year after the metal has cracked and the bacteria has grown up.
In addition to instant delivery, Polaroid's multi-purpose camera has a number of features you'd expect to find only in specialized macrophotographic systems. A reflex viewer for precise focusing (with aerial image focusing screens for extremely critical focusing at high magnifications). And a system of interchangeable lenses for a wide range of magnifications and greater flexibility. (The MP-4 can do photomicrography and photocopying as well as photomacrography.)
If you have small problems, write us and we'll tell you more about how to enlarge them.
Polaroid Corporation, Dept. 28-286, 549 Technology Square, Cambridge, Mass. 02139. If you're in a hurry, call collect (617) 547-5176.
Polaroid
Ion exchange resin beads X34
Type 58 Polacolor film
Insect eye X30
Type 46-L transparency film
Watch balance wheel assembly X30
Type 107 high speed film
Bullet striations X32
Type 105
positive/negative film
"Polaroid" and "Polacolor"®

186

This is all we want to do. But perfectly.
The engineering of high-fidelity turntables is a technical and controversial subject.
But the concept of a perfect turntable is perfectly simple.
Since a perfect turntable is what we at Garrard have been striving to make, we'd like to communicate this concept to you as unequivocally as possible. Then all the claims and counterclaims you hear will fall into place.
Think of it this way:
A phonograph record doesn't know and doesn't care what kind of mechanism is spinning it,
as long as it's spinning properly. If your hand could turn it at exactly 33⅓ RPM, without the slightest fluctuations in speed, and keep it moving in the horizontal plane only, without the slightest jiggling or vibrations up-and-down or sideways, you could expect perfect reproduction.
Similarly, a phono cartridge has no idea what's holding it in the groove, as long as it's properly held. If your other hand were holding it, correctly aligned, with the right amount of downward force and without resisting its movement across the record, it would perform faultlessly.
That's really all there is to it.
The basic point is that the turntable and tonearm have exceedingly simple and purely mechanical functions, just like a chemist's analytical balance or a gyroscope. That's why turntable manufacturing is, above all, a matter of precision and integrity, with the emphasis on perfect operation rather than hi-fi pizzazz or features for features' sake.
Of course, theoretical perfection in an actual mechanical device is an unrealizable ideal. But even though 100% is impossible, there's a big difference between 99.9% and 98%.
It's in this most fundamental sense, we feel, that Garrard turntables are in a class by themselves.
For example, in the case of the Zero 100c changer and the Zero 100SB single-play automatic, tracking error has been reduced to a virtually unmeasurable quantity (in effect, zero) by the geometry of the tonearm design. Rumble, wow and flutter figures are also coming ever closer to theoretical perfection in these and other top Garrard models. (The Zero 100c and the Zero 100SB are both priced at $209.95.)
To a less spectacular degree, the lower-priced models, from $49.95 up, also come quite close to the theoretical ideal because of this emphasis on fundamentals.
Remember: all we want is to make your record revolve perfectly and to position your phono cartridge perfectly.
And we're almost there.
For your free copy of The Garrard Guide, a 16-page full-color reference booklet, write to Garrard, Dept. 10, 100 Commercial Street, Plainview, N.Y. 11803.
Garrard

187

Remember when they laughed at yellow tennis balls?
Today, bright colored tennis balls are taking over the market. And bright colored tennis clothes are taking over the market. And it only stands to reason that, before long, bright colored tennis shoes will be taking over the market.
Which is where we come in.
INTRODUCING VOLARE TENNIS SHOES. A RAINBOW FOR YOUR FEET.
Initially, Volares are available in six colors. Powder blue. Royal blue. Forest green. Sunshine yellow. Ruby red. And good old white. Eventually, Volares will be available in about fifty different colors. Everything from hot pink to sandy beige to black. For very formal games.
But don't get us wrong, we're more than just a pretty face.
WE'RE COLORFUL. BUT WE'RE DEAD SERIOUS ABOUT OUR TENNIS.
Volares are built to compete with the finest men's and women's professional tennis shoes on the market. With features like fully padded rims and raised tendon protectors. With soft burnished suede uppers. With fine, orthopedically designed arch supports. With unique multi-directional skid resistant soles.
And with one more very important feature.
VOLARES ARE PROBABLY THE LIGHTEST PROFESSIONAL TENNIS SHOES IN THE WORLD.
Light shoes are better than heavy shoes. They make your feet go faster. And they make your legs less tired. That's why we've designed and built Volares to be the lightest top quality tennis shoe you can buy.
Without sacrificing comfort. Without sacrificing durability.
FOR THE WHOLE BEAUTIFUL STORY GIVE US A CALL.
Volares will be sold through pro shops and better stores only. If that's you, call Sandy Magnes, collect, at (305) 573-6700. He'll answer any questions, he'll send our catalog, or if you like, he'll send a salesman by with our samples.
Or write: Volare Sport, Division of Volare Shoe Company, 3415 N.E. 2nd Ave., Miami, Florida 33137.
Volare

188

186
Art Director John Eding
Writer Dodds Musser
Designer John Eding
Artist R & V Studio
Photographer Henri Janson
Agency Doyle Dane Bernbach
Client Polaroid Corp.

187
Art Director Dick Calderhead
Writer Peter Aczel
Designer Barbara Schubeck
Artist Don Ivan Punchatz
Agency Calderhead, Jackson
Client Garrard

188
Art Director Burt Klein
Writer Breen & Porter
Designer Burt Klein
Photographer Bob Panuska
Agency Saunders Bell Hicks
Client Volare Shoe Co.

Believe in Blue Nun and you shall be rewarded.
Rewarded with profits.
The profits you earn carrying the largest selling imported premium white wine on the market.
Blue Nun wine.
Blue Nun is the delicious white wine that's correct with any dish. Delicious enough for fish, yet hearty enough for meat. It's the wine more and more people are asking for every day.
It's also the wine more and more people are hearing about every day. That's because Blue Nun commercials are the most popular wine advertising ever done on radio. And now they'll be reaching more people in your market than ever before.
So if you want profits to rain down like pennies from heaven, stock and display Blue Nun wine.
We think it'll be blue skies from then on.
Blue Nun. The delicious white wine more people are converting to every year.

189

1971
BLUE NUN®
WHITE WINE
H. SICHEL SÖHNE, MAINZ ESTD. 1857
A. P. Nr. 4907189/006/73
LIEBFRAUMILCH QUALITÄTSWEIN
Schieffelin & Co.—New York
IMPORTERS SINCE 1794
SOLE U.S. DISTRIBUTORS
The nun who turned wine into profits.
Her name is Blue Nun.
And she's on the label of the largest selling imported premium white wine on the market today.
It's Blue Nun wine. The delicious white wine that's correct with any dish. The wine that's delicate enough for fish, yet hearty enough for meat. The wine more and more people are asking for everyday.
And the wine more and more people are going to be hearing about everyday, too. That's because Blue Nun commercials are the most popular wine advertising ever done on radio. And now they'll reach more people in your market than ever before.
So if you'd like to turn wine into profits, stock and display the German white wine that sells more, and makes more than any other. Blue Nun wine.
We think you'll find the results are miraculous.
Blue Nun. The delicious white wine more people are converting to every year.

190

189
Art Director Mark Yustein
Writer Kay Kavanagh
Designer Mark Yustein
Artist David Wilcox
Photographer Charles Gold
Agency Della Femina, Travisano & Partners
Client Schieffelin & Co.

190
Art Director Mark Yustein
Writer Kay Kavanagh
Designer Mark Yustein
Photographer Charles Gold
Agency Della Femina, Travisano & Partners
Client Schieffelin & Co.

The story of Blue Nun as told by the profits.
When it came to wine there used to be an unbreakable commandment. Red wine for meat, white wine for fish.
Then along came Blue Nun to change all that. Blue Nun is the delicious white wine that's correct with any dish. It's delicate enough for fish, yet hearty enough for meat.
In fact, so many people have converted to Blue Nun that today it's the largest selling imported premium white wine on the market. The one more and more people are asking for every day.
And when Blue Nun's followers aren't asking for her, they're hearing about her. That's because Blue Nun commercials are the most popular wine advertising on radio. And now they're reaching more people in your market than ever before.
If you want to hear your own story as told by the profits, stock and display Blue Nun wine.
Pretty soon we think you'll have a flock of new customers. And that's the gospel truth.
Blue Nun. The delicious white wine more people are converting to every year.
IMPORTED BY SCHIEFFELIN & CO., NEW YORK, N.Y.

191

191
Art Director Mark Yustein
Writer Kay Kavanagh
Designer Mark Yustein
Artist Cal Sacks
Agency Della Femina, Travisano & Partners
Client Schieffelin & Co.

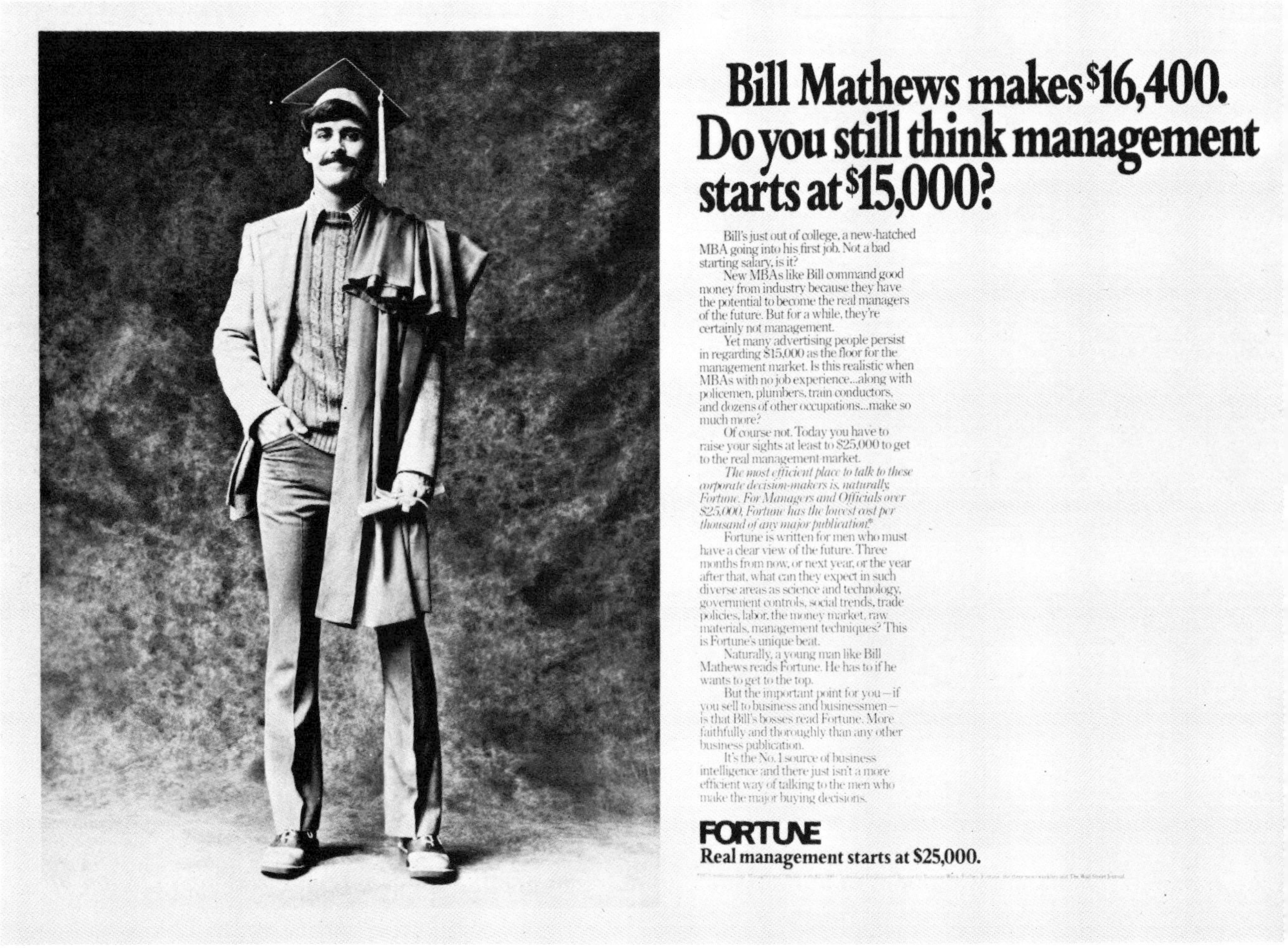
Bill Mathews makes $16,400.
Do you still think management starts at $15,000?
Bill's just out of college, a new-hatched MBA going into his first job. Not a bad starting salary, is it?
New MBAs like Bill command good money from industry because they have the potential to become the real managers of the future. But for a while, they're certainly not management.
Yet many advertising people persist in regarding $15,000 as the floor for the management market. Is this realistic when MBAs with no job experience...along with policemen, plumbers, train conductors, and dozens of other occupations...make so much more?
Of course not. Today you have to raise your sights at least to $25,000 to get to the real management market.
The most efficient place to talk to these corporate decision-makers is, naturally, Fortune. For Managers and Officials over $25,000, Fortune has the lowest cost per thousand of any major publication.*
Fortune is written for men who must have a clear view of the future. Three months from now, or next year, or the year after that, what can they expect in such diverse areas as science and technology, government controls, social trends, trade policies, labor, the money market, raw materials, management techniques? This is Fortune's unique beat.
Naturally, a young man like Bill Mathews reads Fortune. He has to if he wants to get to the top.
But the important point for you—if you sell to business and businessmen—is that Bill's bosses read Fortune. More faithfully and thoroughly than any other business publication.
It's the No. 1 source of business intelligence and there just isn't a more efficient way of talking to the men who make the major buying decisions.
FORTUNE
Real management starts at $25,000.

Harry Stengle makes $19,900.
Do you still think management starts at $15,000?
FORTUNE
Real management starts at $25,000.

Sal Petrone makes $22,500.
Do you still think management starts at $15,000?
FORTUNE
Real management starts at $25,000.

193

193
Art Director Bob Czernysz
Writer Richard Olmsted
Photographer Richard Noble
Agency Young & Rubicam International
Client Fortune Magazine

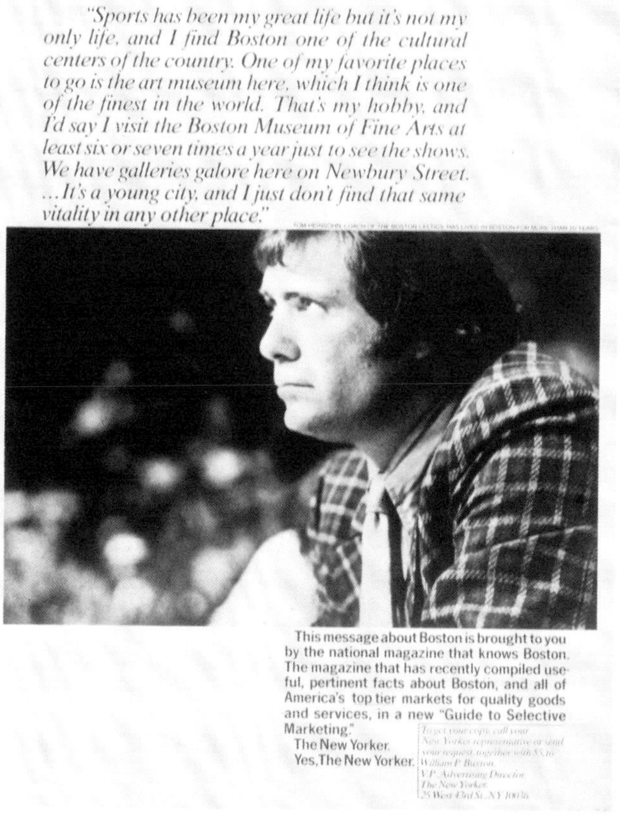
"Sports has been my great life but it's not my only life, and I find Boston one of the cultural centers of the country. One of my favorite places to go is the art museum here, which I think is one of the finest in the world. That's my hobby, and I'd say I visit the Boston Museum of Fine Arts at least six or seven times a year just to see the shows. We have galleries galore here on Newbury Street. ...It's a young city, and I just don't find that same vitality in any other place."
This message about Boston is brought to you by the national magazine that knows Boston. The magazine that has recently compiled useful, pertinent facts about Boston, and all of America's top tier markets for quality goods and services, in a new "Guide to Selective Marketing."
The New Yorker.
Yes, The New Yorker.

"The people of Dallas are very warm. They welcome and greet newcomers without making them go through a probationary period. They have a tendency to accept people rather than waiting for them to prove themselves right. Many people have come here from other parts of the country. They are always astounded by the warmth and hospitality they encounter in Dallas."
This message about Dallas is brought to you by the national magazine that knows Dallas. The magazine that has recently compiled useful, pertinent facts about Dallas, and all of America's top tier markets for quality goods and services, in a new "Guide to Selective Marketing."
The New Yorker.
Yes, The New Yorker.

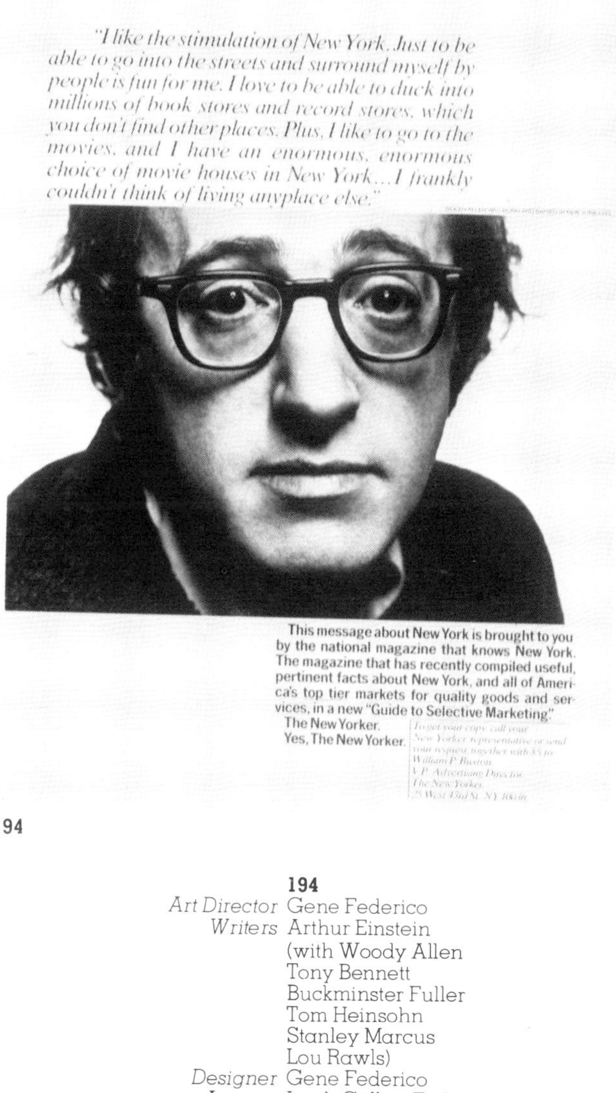
"I like the stimulation of New York. Just to be able to go into the streets and surround myself by people is fun for me. I love to be able to duck into millions of book stores and record stores, which you don't find other places. Plus, I like to go to the movies, and I have an enormous, enormous choice of movie houses in New York... I frankly couldn't think of living anyplace else."
This message about New York is brought to you by the national magazine that knows New York. The magazine that has recently compiled useful, pertinent facts about New York, and all of America's top tier markets for quality goods and services, in a new "Guide to Selective Marketing."
The New Yorker.
Yes, The New Yorker.
To get your copy, call your
New Yorker representative or send
your request, together with $5, to
William P. Buxton,
V.P. Advertising Director,
The New Yorker,
25 West 43rd St., NY 10036.

194

194

Art Director Gene Federico
Writers Arthur Einstein
(with Woody Allen
Tony Bennett
Buckminster Fuller
Tom Heinsohn
Stanley Marcus
Lou Rawls)
Designer Gene Federico
Agency Lord, Geller, Federico
Client The New Yorker

WE SELL MORE CARS THAN FORD, CHRYSLER,
CHEVROLET AND BUICK COMBINED.
MATCHBOX.

195

GOLD

195

Art Directors Allan Beaver
Ken Sausville
Writers Larry Plapler
Frank Anton
Designers Allan Beaver
Ken Sausville
Photographer Cailor-Resnick
Agency Levine, Huntley, Schmidt
Client Lesney Products Corp.

HOW TO BUY PORK THAT SELLS ITSELF.
WILSON'S Cert-i Select
PORK
Corn King
PORK
Look to Wilson. We've been in business for over 120 years. We're one of America's leading meat processors, and the world's largest processor of pork. And we program our pork from the very beginning to be the best well-trimmed, no-waste fresh pork in the business.
Wilson's distinguished brands. Wilson's Cert-I-Select and Wilson's Corn King—our two great pork brands—retain their profit potential, turn over fast and taste as good on the table as they look in your counter. Both brands are available at case cost to you, so you can buy and sell the best for less. And these special lines offer complete flexibility in satisfying your individual marketing needs.
HAM
Wilson's special pork. Cert-I-Select is available in a complete variety and range of bone-in loins from 12 through 16 pounds, plus boneless loins, center cut loins, butts, ribs and boneless ham roasts. Corn King offers a complete variety and range of bone-in loins from 16 to 20 pounds, plus center cut loins, butts and ribs.
RIB
Wilson's special quality. Wilson has more pork to choose from than anyone else in the world. Cert-I-Select and Corn King come only from the finest lean-meat-type hogs available, processed under the strictest quality standards in the industry.
BUTT
Each cut is hand-trimmed and block-ready. Wilson trimming specialists perform with exacting uniformity cut-after-cut-after-cut, giving you the type of consistency that's almost impossible to master while handling dozens of assignments behind the market counter. This uniformity pays off in greater efficiency and more salable pork in your counter instead of your scrap barrel.
Wilson's Sno-cap process delivers this special pork to you with a beautifully preserved appearance. Because our CO_2 "snow" evaporates instead of melting, your pork arrives fresh and without a trace of moisture. The Sno-cap process also retards bacteria growth, and that means longer case life.
Proven representation. When it comes to pork—or any meat at all—Wilson serves you better. Even in this time of turmoil in the meat industry, our reputation for service remains. If you're thinking about improving your pork department, let us prove our advanced capabilities to you.
LOIN
See your Wilson representative or write Manager, Fresh Pork Department, Wilson & Co., Inc., 4545 Lincoln Blvd., Oklahoma City, 73105. You'll learn more about Wilson . . . the company with pork that practically sells itself.
PICNIC
WILSON.
WILSON'S TOTAL MEAT PROGRAM
WILSON'S CERTIFIED
Corn King
TOTAL SERVICE
THE TOTAL MEAT COMPANY WITH THE TOTAL MEAT PROGRAM.
LOIN
HAM
BUTT
RIB
PICNIC
Wilson & Co., Inc., Gen. Off., 4545 N. Lincoln Blvd., Oklahoma City 73105

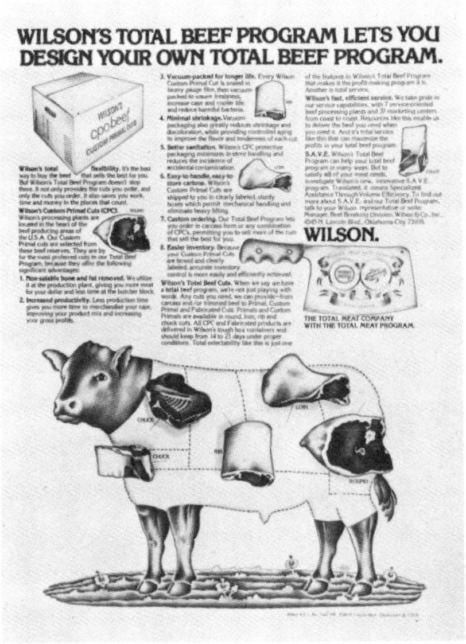
WILSON'S TOTAL BEEF PROGRAM LETS YOU DESIGN YOUR OWN TOTAL BEEF PROGRAM.
WILSON.
THE TOTAL MEAT COMPANY WITH THE TOTAL MEAT PROGRAM.

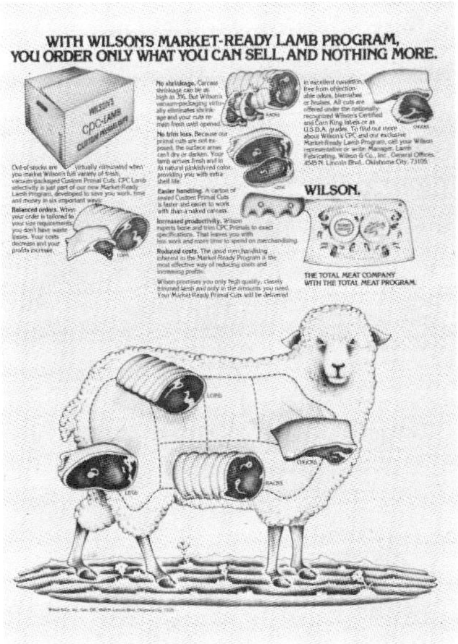
WITH WILSON'S MARKET-READY LAMB PROGRAM, YOU ORDER ONLY WHAT YOU CAN SELL, AND NOTHING MORE.
WILSON.
THE TOTAL MEAT COMPANY WITH THE TOTAL MEAT PROGRAM.

196

Art Directors Vin Scheihagen
Lois Tischler
Writer Ray Baron
Artist Woody Pirtle
Agency Tracy-Locke Advertising
Client Wilson & Co.

If she can run a $3,500 cash register, she can run a $200,000 deli.

69¢

Running a checkout counter requires a good deal of concentration, a fair amount of expertise, and an ability to meet customers and keep them happy.

So does running a deli.

The only real difference is in the training.

And we have a way to help.

It's called "The Armour Deli Personnel Merchandising Workshop." A long name for an intensive course.

It includes a slide presentation. A lecture. And a participating workshop program. All aimed at the people out there on the front line.

So they'll learn about simple things, like organizing the case. Display. How to help eliminate shrinkage and waste.

And more difficult things. Like salesmanship. And functioning as a vital part of your store's public relations program. So you'll sell more. And sell more often.

Another program we offer takes place at a different level.

The management level.

Officially, it's known as "The Armour Deli Marketing Presentation."

Practically, it's designed to hand you everything we know about a deli operation. Marketing and product data. Space and equipment requirements. Personnel selection and training. And merchandising directions.

Backing up this program is product. A lot of it.

There are over 75 items in the Armour Deli line. Including thirteen different loaves, sixteen sausages, nine specialty meats, three kinds of poultry, seventeen Wisconsin cheeses, and a dozen prepared entrees in the Armour Deli Fare™ line. Plus plans for sandwiches, salads, and party trays.

All of which get an added boost from our no-cost merchandising programs.

If you'd like it all spelled out for you, write Dick Cray, Director, Deli Marketing, Armour Food Company, Greyhound Tower, Phoenix, Arizona 85077. Or, contact your local Armour representative.

We'll give you an honest look at the market. How a sensible, organized approach to it can do a lot for you.

And how we can give that deli employee a much bigger cash register to run.

The Armour Deli Service Group.
Not a new idea. Just a new way of making it work.

Selling public relations by the pound.

Years ago, a lot of grocery products went home wrapped in paper just because there wasn't anything better.

Then, the age of plastics came around. And wraps became air-tight, waterproof, crushproof and transparent.

Everyone recognized it as a big improvement. Some even called it a revolution.

And it was. For everyone except a segment of the market that had $3 billion a year to spend.

Some careful research had shown that, as far as this part of the market was concerned, we'd all left something behind with that old paper wrap.

Something called personalized service.

It's the kind of service that says hello when you place your order. Maybe even remembers your name.

The kind that lets you spend a little time making up your mind. Getting something cut just the way you like it.

e Deli The Deli The

And the kind that hands you a cool, weighty package that somehow tastes better than the plastic-wrapped, pre-sliced variety when it's unwrapped at home.

And, while we were finding all this out, we came across another fact; even the shoppers who would rarely, if ever, buy their deli items this way, were looking for this kind of service in their store.

It made them feel good that it was available. That their store still sold to people in a personal way.

And it added another dimension to that $3 billion market. Selling deli products in that old paper wrap made more than profits. For everyone, it made good public relations.

Now it takes a considerable amount of skill to integrate an old-fashioned idea like a deli into a modern operation like a supermarket.

And that's just where we come in. The Armour Deli Service Group.

We've spent a long time organizing the deli service concept. Take products, for instance. Over 75 items.

That includes thirteen different loaves. Ham and Cheese. Ham and Bacon. Liver Cheese. Olive. Pickle. Old-Fashioned. Peppered. B.B.Q. Macaroni and Cheese. Pizza. Kulbassy. Star. Ham-Ett. All of them made with our "Bake and Browned" process. Then vacuum-packed in Cryovac and individually boxed for added protection.

There are many different sausages. Ranging from standards like bologna and summer, to specialties like genoa salami and calabrese.

Ten varieties of ham. Eleven of poultry. Plus corned beef, roast beef, peppered beef, chopped ham, chopped pork and spiced luncheon meat.

We can also give you a choice of more than 25 Wisconsin and imported cheeses. From a mellow-aged cheddar. To a smoked provolone aged salami.

And something we call Deli Fare.™ A long line of prepared entrees. Including beef stew, lasagna, stuffed green peppers, beef stroganoff and salisbury steak.

O.K. But you need more than products. And we've got that, too.

You get all the help you need from our Armour Deli staff. From original planning to determining equipment.

There's also a complete training program for deli personnel available.

And other things like no-cost merchandising packages. Plus plans to minimize shrinkage waste through additional sales of salads and sandwiches.

For a detailed look at this market, how it can work, and what it can mean to you, write Dick Cray, Director, Deli Marketing, Armour Food Company, Greyhound Tower, Phoenix, Arizona 85077. Or contact your local Armour representative.

We'll show you that a little wrapping paper and the right approach can sell a product, and your store, all at the same time.

The Armour Deli Service Group.
Not a new idea. Just a new way of making it work.

For the next few hours, this room will be filled with people learning how to take business away from you.

The people who'll be in this room are supermarket employees.

And, over a period of several hours, they'll receive intensive instruction on a subject that's unique in the business.

They'll learn how to sell their store.

Because they're all enrolled in the Armour Deli Personnel Training Workshop.

A special program developed by the Armour Deli Service Group, this seminar is designed to give deli employees virtually every basic, practical piece of knowledge necessary to run an efficient and profitable in-store deli.

The entire course is organized around a slide presentation that begins with instruction on a deli fundamental: sanitation. It's strongly stressed because deli purchases are usually highly impulsive, and are initially dependent on a clean case and work area.

Tied tightly into how clean a deli is, is how attractive a deli looks. And that's covered too. Case organization, display and garnishing make up the second course section.

From there, instruction goes on to include administrative functions like product selection and ordering, pricing, and proper equipment and supply usage. Everything an employee needs to run a successful deli behind the case.

To make sure this success continues on the other side of the case the second half of the seminar deals with the aspects of public relations and promotion. Things like proper usage of point-of-sale materials are covered. Development of seasonal promotions. Effective tie-ins with in-store specials. Plus the importance of a smile, a warm welcome, and a free sample.

Pulling everything together at the seminar's conclusion is a special section titled, "What's In It For Me And My Company?"

And the answer to that is the same as it is for you: the pride and profitability of a well-run deli operation.

The Armour Deli Personnel Training Workshop is a unique approach to ensuring an in-store deli's success. But it's only one of several we have.

There's product. And lots of it. Over 100 items, ranging from a long line of sausages, over a dozen different loaves, over two dozen imported and Wisconsin cheeses, to Deli Fare, a long line of prepared entrees.

There's highly-qualified help, in the form of an experienced Armour Deli staff. To assist you in all phases of deli operations, from original planning to customer relations.

There are other things like no-cost merchandising packages and techniques that minimize shrinkage waste through additional sales of salads and sandwiches.

For more information on all of it, write Dick Cray, Director, Deli Marketing, Armour Food Company, Greyhound Tower, Phoenix, Arizona 85077. Or contact your local Armour Salesman.

And then maybe the next time a group of employees sits down to learn a business, they won't be learning how to take away from yours.

But how to add to it.

The Armour Deli Service Group.
Not a new idea. Just a new way of making it work.

198

198
Art Director HN&A Creative Staff
Writer HN&A Creative Staff
Photographers Joel Snyder
Rich Tomlinson
Agency Hackenberg, Norman and Assoc.
Client Armour Food Co.

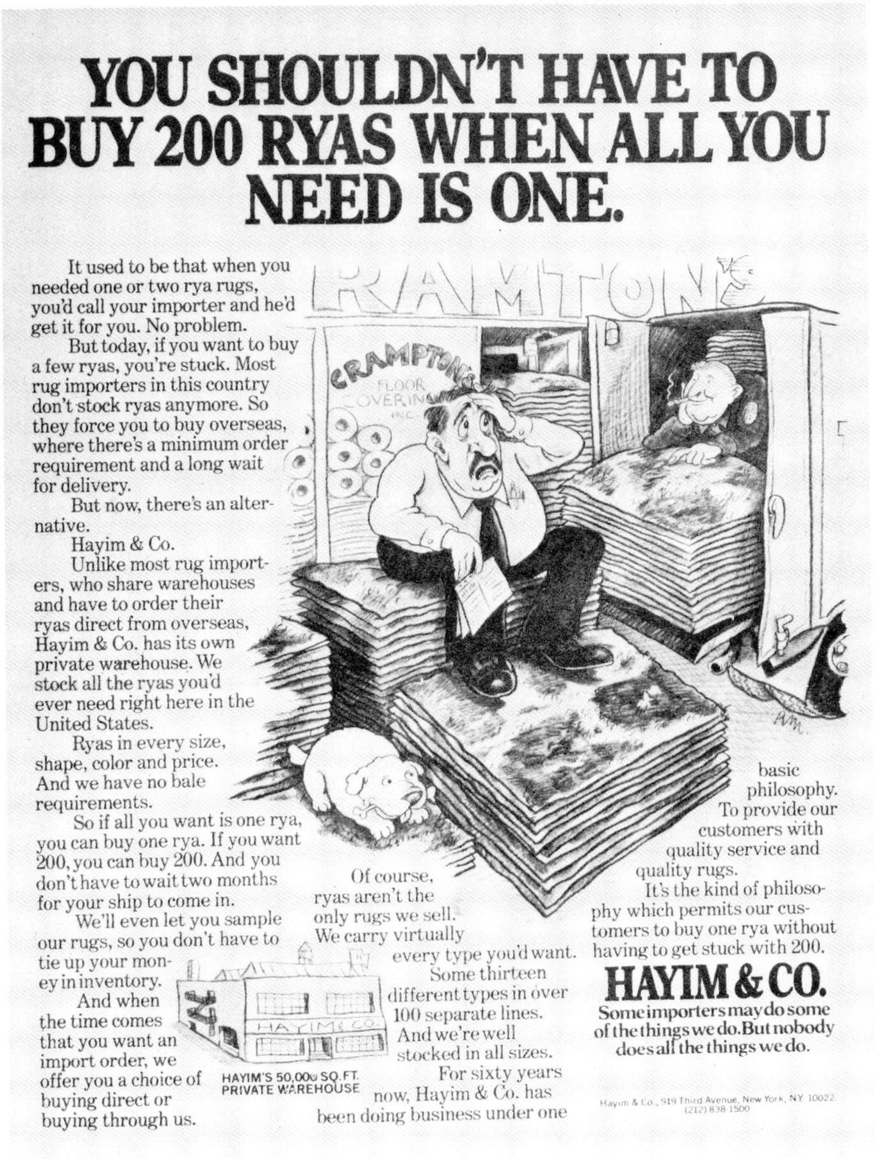
YOU SHOULDN'T HAVE TO BUY 200 RYAS WHEN ALL YOU NEED IS ONE.
It used to be that when you needed one or two rya rugs, you'd call your importer and he'd get it for you. No problem.
But today, if you want to buy a few ryas, you're stuck. Most rug importers in this country don't stock ryas anymore. So they force you to buy overseas, where there's a minimum order requirement and a long wait for delivery.
But now, there's an alternative.
Hayim & Co.
Unlike most rug importers, who share warehouses and have to order their ryas direct from overseas, Hayim & Co. has its own private warehouse. We stock all the ryas you'd ever need right here in the United States.
Ryas in every size, shape, color and price. And we have no bale requirements.
So if all you want is one rya, you can buy one rya. If you want 200, you can buy 200. And you don't have to wait two months for your ship to come in.
We'll even let you sample our rugs, so you don't have to tie up your money in inventory.
And when the time comes that you want an import order, we offer you a choice of buying direct or buying through us.
Of course, ryas aren't the only rugs we sell. We carry virtually every type you'd want. Some thirteen different types in over 100 separate lines. And we're well stocked in all sizes.
For sixty years now, Hayim & Co. has been doing business under one basic philosophy. To provide our customers with quality service and quality rugs.
It's the kind of philosophy which permits our customers to buy one rya without having to get stuck with 200.
CRAMPTON'S
CRAMPTON'S FLOOR COVERING INC.
HAYIM & CO.
HAYIM'S 50,000 SQ.FT. PRIVATE WAREHOUSE
HAYIM & CO.
Some importers may do some of the things we do. But nobody does all the things we do.
Hayim & Co., 919 Third Avenue, New York, NY 10022 (212) 838-1500

RUGS CAN MAKE YOU RICHER THAN CARPETS.
The trend in floor covering is becoming abundantly clear. More and more people are turning away from conventional carpeting and buying beautiful imported area rugs.
There are several good reasons for this.
To begin with, rugs are much less expensive than carpets.
Secondly, more and more homes and apartments are being built with finished parquet floors. Consequently, people are complementing their floors with rugs, not covering them with carpet.
Thirdly, we live in a transient society and people want the mobility area rugs have to offer.
And lastly, unlike carpet which is basically bland floor covering, area rugs, by their very design, add another dimension to a room.
Rugs not only offer many advantages to your customers, they offer many advantages to you.
For instance, rugs offer a quick and clean sale that requires a minimum amount of a salesman's time.
Further, unlike carpeting which requires premeasuring, rugs can be delivered on the spot. Obviously, there are no labor costs.
And most important of all, rugs simply are more profitable than carpeting. While carpeting is usually marked up 50-60%, Hayim area rugs are designed to be marked up a minimum of 100%.
Now that we've shown you how rugs can make you richer than carpet, we'd like to show you some examples.
Our all wool Kashmir rugs are an example of Hayim innovation in design: an innovation that's designed to offer you more profit potential.
Instead of the traditional styled orientals with their typical floral patterns and bright hues, Kashmir is styled with straight line geometric patterns and muted antique colors.
As an example of how successful this rug can be, Bloomingdale's had over $300,000 in retail sales after running just two ads.
Another example of Hayim ingenuity is what we do with our American Flokati rugs. Unlike other importers, we buy these rugs by the roll and cut it ourselves. The result is a savings on labor, not quality. And because of this the markup passed on to the retailer is extraordinarily high. Over 100%.
For over sixty years Hayim and Co. has been selling rugs to stores like Sloane's, The Broadway, Lazarus, Carsons, and others.
Sure, these stores do a good business in carpet. But they're getting rich on rugs.
American Flokati
Kashmir
Kashmir
HAYIM & CO.
Some importers may do some of the things we do. But nobody does all the things we do.

JUST BECAUSE WE DO BUSINESS WITH BLOOMINGDALE'S, DOESN'T MEAN WE DON'T BREAK OUR BACK FOR BENSON'S.
Benson's is a small retail store in Bayonne, New Jersey. Total purchase last year: five rugs.
Bloomingdale's is a large retail store in New York. Total purchases last year: 2,000 rugs.
Yet as different as these stores are, they have two things in common.
Both buy area rugs from Hayim & Co. and both receive the same care and attention.
That's because, for over 60 years, Hayim & Co. has prided itself in providing all our customers, large and small, with the same courteous, reliable service.
BENSON'S FLOOR COVERINGS
Oran
Oran
For information and catalog, write or call: Hayim & Co., 919 Third Ave., New York, N.Y. (212) 838-1500.
HAYIM & CO.
Some importers may do some of the things we do. But nobody does all the things we do.

199

199
Art Director Stan Schofield
Writer Steve Penchina
Agency Stan Schofield
Client Hayim & Co.

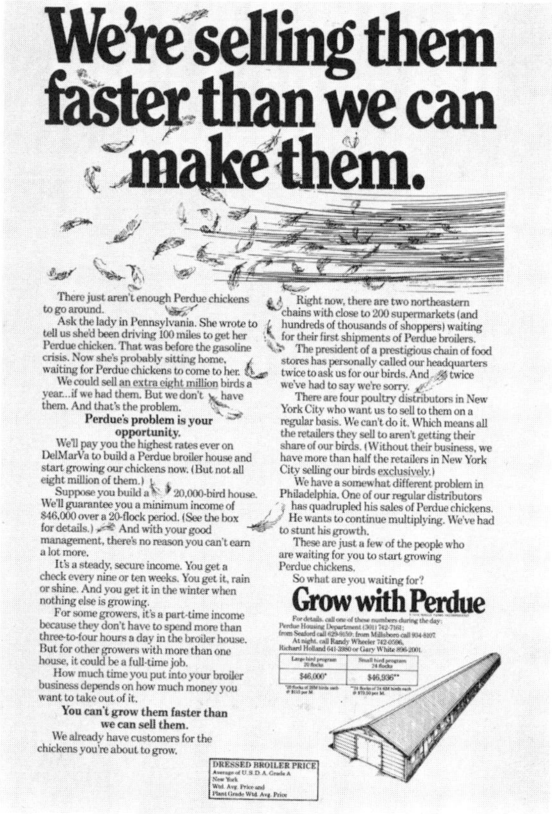
We're selling them faster than we can make them.
There just aren't enough Perdue chickens to go around.
Ask the lady in Pennsylvania. She wrote to tell us she'd been driving 100 miles to get her Perdue chicken. That was before the gasoline crisis. Now she's probably sitting home, waiting for Perdue chickens to come to her.
We could sell an extra eight million birds a year...if we had them. But we don't have them. And that's the problem.
Perdue's problem is your opportunity.
We'll pay you the highest rates ever on DelMarVa to build a Perdue broiler house and start growing our chickens now. (But not all eight million of them.)
Suppose you build a 20,000-bird house. We'll guarantee you a minimum income of $46,000 over a 20-flock period. (See the box for details.) And with your good management, there's no reason you can't earn a lot more.
It's a steady, secure income. You get a check every nine or ten weeks. You get it, rain or shine. And you get it in the winter when nothing else is growing.
For some growers, it's a part-time income because they don't have to spend more than three-to-four hours a day in the broiler house. But for other growers with more than one house, it could be a full-time job.
How much time you put into your broiler business depends on how much money you want to take out of it.
You can't grow them faster than we can sell them.
We already have customers for the chickens you're about to grow.
Right now, there are two northeastern chains with close to 200 supermarkets (and hundreds of thousands of shoppers) waiting for their first shipments of Perdue broilers.
The president of a prestigious chain of food stores has personally called our headquarters twice to ask us for our birds. And twice we've had to say we're sorry.
There are four poultry distributors in New York City who want us to sell to them on a regular basis. We can't do it. Which means all the retailers they sell to aren't getting their share of our birds. (Without their business, we have more than half the retailers in New York City selling our birds exclusively.)
We have a somewhat different problem in Philadelphia. One of our regular distributors has quadrupled his sales of Perdue chickens. He wants to continue multiplying. We've had to stunt his growth.
These are just a few of the people who are waiting for you to start growing Perdue chickens.
So what are you waiting for?
Grow with Perdue
For details, call one of these numbers during the day: Perdue Housing Department (301) 742-7161; from Seaford call 629-9159; from Millsboro call 934-8107.
At night, call Randy Wheeler 742-0596, Richard Holland 641-3980 or Gary White 896-2001.
Large-bird program 20 flocks
$46,000*
Small-bird program 24 flocks
$46,936**
DRESSED BROILER PRICE
Average of U.S.D.A. Grade A
New York
Wtd. Avg. Price and
Plant Grade Wtd. Avg. Price

Perdue's money-back guarantees:
TASTY YOUNG CHICKEN
PERDUE
QUALITY GUARANTEED OR MONEY BACK
KEEP REFRIGERATED
For the housewife
For the grower
Every Perdue chicken and chicken part we sell carries our money-back quality guarantee. Yet the number of housewives who don't take advantage of it is amazing.
For every 39,000 chickens we ship out, our Salisbury postman delivers just one request for a refund. JUST ONE! Which means that about 99.999974% of our customers are satisfied customers. And when we hear from one who isn't, we investigate. Often as not, we find that what was wrong was the cook. Not the chicken.
What's sauce for the goose...
We want our new growers to be as satisfied as our customers. So when you build a broiler house and qualify for Perdue's new-house guarantee, we put that guarantee in writing. While you do a good job growing our chickens, it commits us to supply you with 20 or 24 flocks. And so far, all our new growers have done a good job. We're satisfied with them. And vice versa.
Our Perdue guarantee is a kind of crop insurance that every good broiler grower should be carrying. And any farmer who wants to reduce his risks should, too.
So look into building a Perdue broiler house. We guarantee to keep the fox away from the door.
For details, call one of these numbers during the day: Perdue Housing Department (301) 742-7161; from Seaford call 629-9159; from Millsboro call 934-8107.
At night, call Charles Carpenter 742-6986, Richard Holland 641-3980 or Gary White 896-2001.
Grow with Perdue
DRESSED BROILER PRICE
Average of U.S.D.A. Grade A
New York
Wtd. Avg. Price and
Plant Grade Wtd. Avg. Price

We'll pay you $25,875 to raise our broilers' grandmothers.
Breeder Pullet
Replacement Pullet
Broiler
In the chicken business, there's no question about which comes first, the primary breeder pullet or the broiler. The pullet does...by two generations. So to meet the demand for at least eight million more Perdue broilers a year, we need more high-quality breeder pullets right now.
If you want extra income but don't want to work hard...
Build a primary pullet house to Perdue specifications. We'll put in flocks of about 5,000 birds for seven months each. You put in one to three hours a day—no more—checking the birds and hand-feeding them. What you get out of it is $5,175 a year—no less—for five years.
That's a guaranteed $25,875. If your pullets were broilers, it's the equivalent of earning $180 per thousand birds over a 28-flock period.
and if your farm isn't large...
All primary pullet houses are the same size. Small. Just 5100 square feet. So it doesn't take much land to build one. But for the pullets' health, we require a lot of land between houses. No more than one to a farm and no closer than one mile to the nearest chicken house.
we need you.
We can't afford a lost generation of Perdue broilers. And you probably can't afford the cost of living these days. So let's get together. You grow our breeder pullets. We pay you a second income.
For details, call us today.
Grow with Perdue
DRESSED BROILER PRICE
Average of U.S.D.A. Grade A
New York
Wtd. Avg. Price and
Plant Grade Wtd. Avg. Price
For details, call one of these numbers during the day: Perdue Housing Department (301) 742-7161; from Seaford call 629-9159; from Millsboro call 934-8107; from Vienna call 376-3144.
At night call Charles Carpenter 742-6986; Stanley F. Baker 896-2945; Roger Covey 749-7984.

Dairy farmer Harold Hostetler found greener pastures. Chickens.
When you own 45 Holsteins and your farm isn't big enough to keep them all in clover, hay, alfalfa and corn, you have to go outside to buy feed. Expensive feed.
Then watch your cows chew up part of your profits.
That's what finally drove Harold Hostetler and partner Leon Overholt of Westover, Maryland to build a Perdue replacement pullet house. (For the birds that produce our broilers.)
On a half-acre that can't support one cow, they'll be growing 11,300 birds. Three flocks a year. Perdue supplies all the feed. (Good news for these dairymen.) And a second income that should make any farmer happy.
Earn $58,374 in 5 years. Guaranteed.
Once you build a replacement pullet house and start to grow, you collect a Perdue check every month. They add up to $11,675 a year. And they keep coming for five years. Guaranteed.
The guarantee more than covers the building costs. It exceeds them by about $5,000. And you may not have to touch your savings to put a house up. Many Perdue growers have received complete financing.
Come see a model house.
The Hostetler/Overholt house will be open for inspection this Friday. (Details below.) Outside, it looks like a broiler house. Inside, it's different. A Perdue supervisor will show you around and explain the program in detail. (One detail: for an average three-hour day, 46 weeks a year, it pays you about $12 an hour.)
Take some time and go. It'll be worth every hour of it.
Grow Replacement Pullets with Perdue
For details, call one of these numbers during the day: Perdue Housing Department (301) 742-7161; from Seaford call 629-9519; from Millsboro call 934-8107; from Vienna call 376-3144.
At night call
Charles Carpenter 742-6986;
Stanley F. Baker 896-2945;
Roger Covey 749-7984.
Perdue Open House
Friday, Dec. 13th, 3-7 pm at the Hostetler/Overholt farm.
Come see this new Perdue replacement pullet house in Westover, Maryland.
DRESSED BROILER PRICE
Average of U.S.D.A. Grade A
New York
Wtd. Avg. Price and
Plant Grade Wtd. Avg. Price

200

200
Art Director Joe Schindelman
Writer Ray Myers
Artist Sandy Huffaker
Agency Scali, McCabe, Sloves
Client Perdue Farms

IT'S GOING TO BE ANOTHER OF THOSE 3-BENNIE, 2-DEXY DAYS.

Many industrial companies are being managed by junkies. Men and women addicted to nicotine, alcohol and pills.

When they can't sleep, they take pills.

When they have hangovers, they take pills.

When they face a particularly tough day, they take pills.

And then there's tea. And coffee. And three martini lunches.

Between 90 million and 110 million Americans swallow the most abused drug—alcohol.

About 80 to 90 million use mind altering drugs.

About 20 million have tried marijuana.

Where will industry managers find answers to the drug problem in their companies?

One of their best idea sources is Industry Week.

It informs them. Leads them. Motivates them.

It helps them become better managers. Gives them new answers to old problems. Old answers to new ones.

That's why when TGI reported recently that Industry Week reaches 1.8 million readers, we were only mildly surprised.

That's also why IW's up 25% in advertising dollars in the first quarter of 1974.

Because Industry Week has become a habit with its readers, it has become a habit with advertisers.

INDUSTRY WEEK

The magazine managers read.

ALMOST AS MUCH STEALING GOES ON IN INDUSTRY TODAY AS IN GOVERNMENT.

With all the hooting and hollering about payoffs, under-table deals and kickbacks, one would think that all the stealing and cheating is going on in political circles.

Not so.

Pilfering is costing American industry over $2 billion each year. And it's getting worse. A lot worse.

Who pays for it?

The consumer. In higher prices. In higher insurance rates. In shoddy products.

Where will industry managers find answers to stopping industrial pilferage?

One of their best idea sources is Industry Week.

It informs them. Leads them. Motivates them.

It helps them become better managers. Gives them new answers to old problems. Old answers to new ones.

That's why when TGI reported recently that Industry Week reaches 1.8 million readers, we were only midly surprised.

That's also why IW's up 25% in advertising dollars in the first quarter of 1974.

Because Industry Week is helping managers put a stop to in-plant stealing, it has become a real steal for advertisers.

INDUSTRY WEEK

The magazine managers read

INDUSTRY MANAGERS SHOULD HAVE MISTRESSES INSTEAD OF WIVES.

The best solution to the problem of the corporate wife is to eliminate her.

Or substitute a mistress.

To compete in the executive rat race, some psychiatrists believe that the executive should become a bit of a rat.

Why? Because the system denies the corporate wife independence and self expression. She becomes ripe for tippling and tranquilizing. And a pain in his ascent up the corporate ladder.

She becomes identified in his mind with inferior hamburgers. And competes with temptations of sexy secretaries, scintillating stewardesses and unlimited expense accounts.

Where will industry managers find answers to this serious problem?

One of their best idea sources is Industry Week.

It informs them. Leads them. Motivates them.

It helps them become better managers. Gives them new answers to old problems. Old answers to new ones.

That's why when TGI reported recently that Industry Week reaches 1.8 million readers, we were only mildly surprised.

That's also why IW's up 25% in advertising dollars in the first quarter of 1974.

Because Industry Week helps managers understand their wives, it has made a beautiful marriage with advertisers.

INDUSTRY WEEK

The magazine managers read

201

SILVER

201
Art Director Bob Kwait
Writer Mike Marino
Photographer Bob Bender
Agency Griswold-Eshleman
Client Industry Week

This 300-year-old portrait looks well restored.

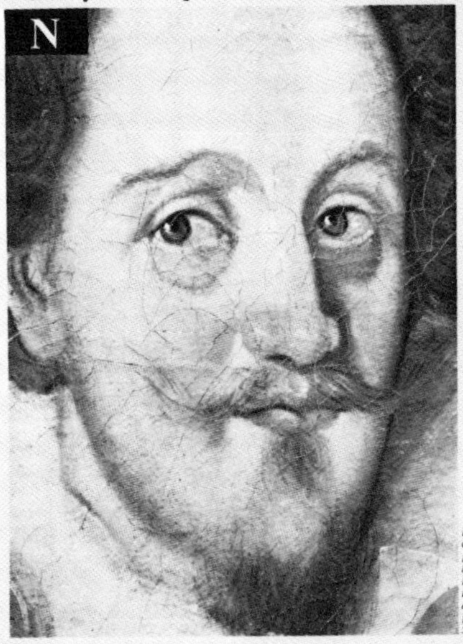
N

Portrait of Colonel Nels Assersen, painted in 1623 by Georg Günther Kräil de Bemeberg. Both photographs are enlarged from Polaroid Type 55 negatives.

Until you look beneath the surface.

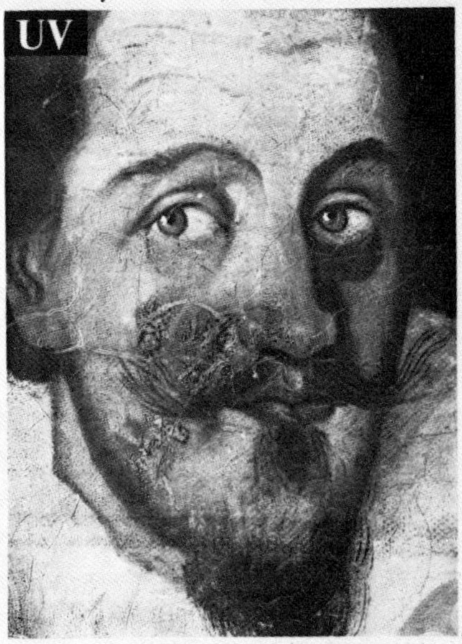
UV
Polaroid

These two prints from Polaroid instant negatives reveal a problem which must be solved in our lifetime. The price of failure will be the loss of many of our noblest paintings from the past.

That is the opinion of Dr. Björn Hallström, director of the Institute of Technology of Artistic Materials and head of the Art Conservation School of the Royal Swedish Academy of Fine Arts in Stockholm.

Dr. Hallström is specifically concerned about the long-term effects of certain early relining techniques on paintings. In these commonly employed restoration procedures, a painting threatened by flaking pigment or decomposing canvas has a new fabric pasted to its back. The painting may then appear quite revitalized. But beneath the "restored" surface, deterioration may actually accelerate.

Our Polaroid prints, for example, show a detail from a portrait painted in 1623. The painting was relined around 1930 and photographed some 40 years later. Under normal light (left) it looks fine. But the ultraviolet reflectogram (right) shows dark areas of decomposition in the relining paste. In time, such deterioration irreversibly alters a painting's color and characteristic craquelure.

Dr. Hallström suggests that the Polaroid instant photographs which reveal this problem can also help to solve it. Essentially, he proposes a standardized system of photoanalysis for all public collections. Each painting would be photographed using different kinds of radiation.

White light, flatly illuminating the canvas, gives a normal picture. *Raked white light* reveals surface damage, undulations in the canvas, etc. *Ultraviolet light with UV absorbing filters* on the camera shows fluorescence in the painting and indicates previous retouching. *Ultraviolet light plus a lens filter which absorbs visible fluorescent light* gives a UV reflectogram which can reveal decomposition invisible to the naked eye.

Polaroid Type 105 (3¼ x 4¼ pack format) and Type 55 (4 x 5 sheet format) positive/negative films are basic to Dr. Hallström's system for several reasons:

First, of course, they are *instant* films. This is particularly helpful in terms of UV reflectograms because some filters separate fluorescent areas better than others. If the Polaroid print shows poor separation, the filter can be changed, and the picture retaken on the spot.

Second, Type 105 and Type 55 provide an instant high resolution negative with the positive print. So enlargements can be made for closer scrutiny.

Finally, the superb tonal qualities of these films are especially useful in recording the low-brightness range of UV reflectograms.

Because of these advantages, and because Hallström's Polaroid technique is quick, economical and effective, it could be used to analyze all of our great paintings. And deterioration could often be detected and stopped before it went too far. Furthermore, periodic examination of newly relined paintings would indicate the restoration techniques most likely to truly conserve the art which we hold in trust for future generations.

The conservation of art treasures: A new use for Polaroid Instant Positive/Negative Films.

Does this Jewish couple dare to marry and have children?

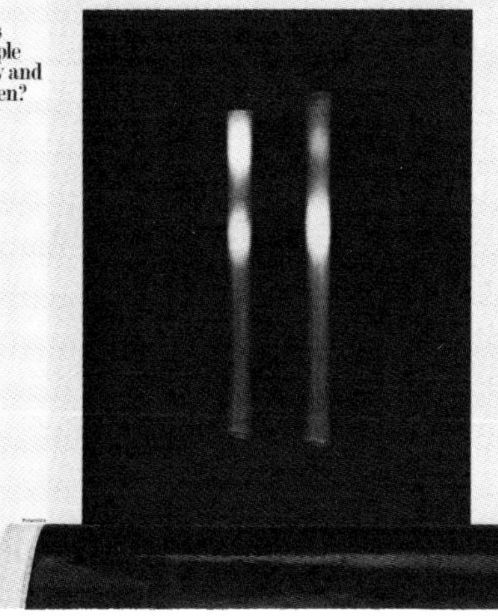

The answer, shown in our Polaroid "portrait," is a qualified "yes." It's an answer that will free two people from the haunting fear of having a Tay-Sachs child.

Tay-Sachs is a fatal, inherited, metabolic disorder. A Tay-Sachs child develops normally for his first six months. Then, as extensive fatty deposits accumulate in his brain cells, he regresses. Slowly and inexorably, he loses the ability to sit up, to recognize his parents, to manage a smile. Then, usually before his fifth birthday, he dies.

Genetically, Tay-Sachs is a simple recessive characteristic. Its highest carrier incidence, ten times that of the general population, is found in people of Jewish ancestry where carrier probability is 1 in 30.

Until recently, there was no sure way to prevent the conception of a Tay-Sachs baby. Because there was no sure way to determine the carrier status of prospective parents. And then an electrophoretic testing technique was developed at the Birth Defects Center of the Isaac Albert Research Institute at Kingsbrook Jewish Medical Center. It's being used for community screening in many centers today.

In the test, fluorescent acrylamide gel electrophoresis of blood samples provides a rapid, accurate, quantitative, visual determination of normal or carrier status.

In our photograph, the woman's gel (on the left) shows a relatively higher intensity of fluorescence in the upper section (hexosaminidase B) as compared to the lower section (hexosaminidase A). This pattern identifies her as a carrier. The reverse pattern in the man's gel is typical of a normal individual.

Which means there's no chance that their children will have the disease. But there is a 50% probability that their children will be carriers. (When two carriers decide to have children, each pregnancy holds a 25% risk of producing a Tay-Sachs child. By testing the amniotic fluid early in pregnancy, the physician can tell the prospective parents whether or not the fetus has the disease.)

Since test gels deteriorate within 12 hours, and their fluorescence dissipates rapidly, the Center makes a permanent record by exposing Polaroid high contrast film to 5 seconds of ultraviolet light through a Wratten No. 2A barrier filter. Fifteen seconds later, the fully developed print can be studied, reshot if necessary, and filed for future reference.

A small role for one of our products to play? Maybe. But when anybody develops a procedure that helps troubled people, we're proud to be involved.

Just for the record.

Polaroid Corporation

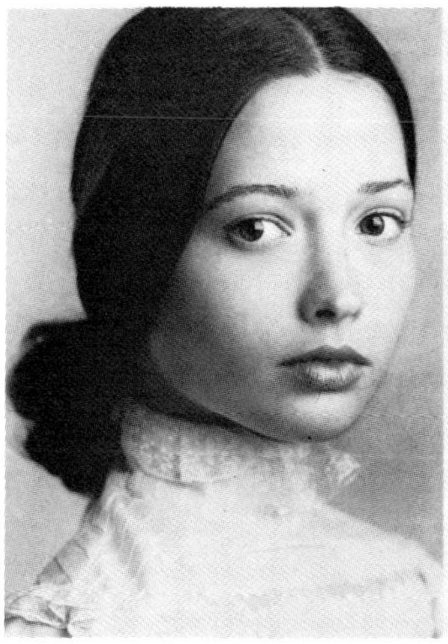

We never thought a Polaroid product could have so many negative qualities.

Until we invented instant Positive/Negative Pack Film.

Polaroid's new
3¼x4¼ Pack Film.

202

202
Art Director Lee Epstein
Writer Hal Silverman
Designer Lee Epstein
Photographers Melvin Sokolsky
Henry Sandbank
Dr. Bjorn Hallström
Agency Doyle Dane Bernbach
Client Polaroid Corp.

ROLLING STONE
Rolling Stone East: the new team.
Just off Park Avenue on 56th Street (New York) is Rolling Stone Sales headquarters. Everything new. New faces . . . new furnishings . . . something new in the air: an exciting mixture of enthusiasm and experience that you will like.
78 E 56
Joe.
Manager of the team is Joe Armstrong, a Texan, who came to Rolling Stone via Family Weekly (Asst. Publisher), law and Wall Street. Is he Over 30? No. On the other hand, he isn't Under 30 either. Joe's right on. Y'all are going to like Joe.
Les & Ann & Carol & Earl & Valerie
It's a strong team; look 'em over. Les Kent, 12 years at Playboy . . . Ann Pilkington, A.E., at Della Femina . . . Carol Davis, NBC Sales . . . Earl Butler from Harper's Bazaar Marketing and Research. Valerie Kosorek, 3½ years at Rolling Stone in San Francisco.
Rolling Stone: a general interest magazine covering contemporary American culture, politics and arts, with a special interest in music.
Meanwhile, in S.F. L.A. and London.
New York City is sales headquarters; we also have sales teams in our offices in San Francisco, Los Angeles and London. Gary Walters (Western Sales Director) is in L.A. We're also at conventions and shows, as many as we can cover. We've got a great story to tell. We're ready to go wherever there's a good audience to hear it. How about you?
Fast Facts:
Net paid circulation: 400,000
Total Audience: 2,000,000
Average Age: 22
Between 18 and 35: 83%
Male 78%
In college or have gone to college: 69%
Invitation.
If you are an advertiser or an agency with a quality product or service that belongs in Rolling Stone, we have two questions: (1) Are you on our mailing list? (2) Would you like to come for lunch (just off Park Avenue) and get better acquainted? Lunch is informal, Japanese, delicious, it makes talking business a pleasure. Either way, (1) or (2), get in touch with Joe. Let's go.
(212) 486-9560
New York: (212) 486-9560
San Francisco: (415) 362-4730
Los Angeles: (213) 461-3571
London: (01) 637-4038

ROLLING STONE
Our readers like nice things.
Think of the Rolling Stone reader this way:
Anyone who buys a highly sophisticated component music system—and buys 57 LP records and 10 unrecorded tapes a year to go with it—has to be a helluva good prospect for a lot of other things as well.
Travel, for instance. (64% of Rolling Stone buyers traveled to a foreign country on vacation or as a student in the 3 years prior to our Roper/Seasonwein Study.)
He's a very good prospect for cars, motorcycles, campers. There is at least one camera in 85% of households of Rolling Stone readers. In 30% of Rolling Stone homes, the camera cost over $100.
JAGUAR
CIRCULATION (Net paid): 400,000
Total audience: 2 million
Average age: 22 69% 18-25
78% male 83% 18-35
76% single 47% working
69% in college or went to college
Once you understand his life style, you realize that his basic living costs are low, which leaves a surprisingly large number of discretionary dollars for beer, wine, apparel, books, movies, radios, TV sets, anything to do with music.
He's an acquisitive guy, and the ONE magazine he reads and believes is Rolling Stone. You really ought to get to know him (and us) better.
Rolling Stone and The Generation Gap
A funny thing happens at a few of the big advertising agencies. We'll be talking with a big Media Decision Maker and he'll say, "I really don't know much about Rolling Stone . . . except that my kids read it . . ."
He's right; they do. This is the Rolling Stone audience: bright, middle-class young people who are either in or just out of college. Early twenties. More sophisticated, better read, broader in their interests than their parents were at the same age. For them, Rolling Stone has evolved into a general interest magazine, covering the whole contemporary scene.
Rolling Stone: Who needs it? You do.
The man on your right is Our Man in National Affairs: Hunter S. Thompson.
"This country's greatest political reporter," says the San Francisco Chronicle. TIME, in describing Rolling Stone's "editorial maturity," calls Hunter "the hottest staff member at the moment." Newsweek describes him as a "refreshing phenomenon." Which he is.
So is Rolling Stone. A refreshing phenomenon. A whole new way to communicate: reporting that is non-objective, deeply involved. Our readers love it: they get as deeply involved as we do. Call it The New Journalism . . . call it exciting, honest, fearless reporting . . . whatever you call it, it's very successful. It is winning raves from the critics . . . and more and more readers with every issue. From a handful to 2 million in less than 7 years is quite a success story.
Rolling Stone offers you a unique selling opportunity. The responsive young audience that swears by it is an audience that you really can't reach any other way.
ROOM
They're an audience you must reach: They're the future.
Rolling Stone: who needs it? You do. Want to get better acquainted and get down to business? We do.
New York: (212) 486-9560
San Francisco: (415) 362-4730
Los Angeles: (213) 461-3571
London: (01) 637-4038

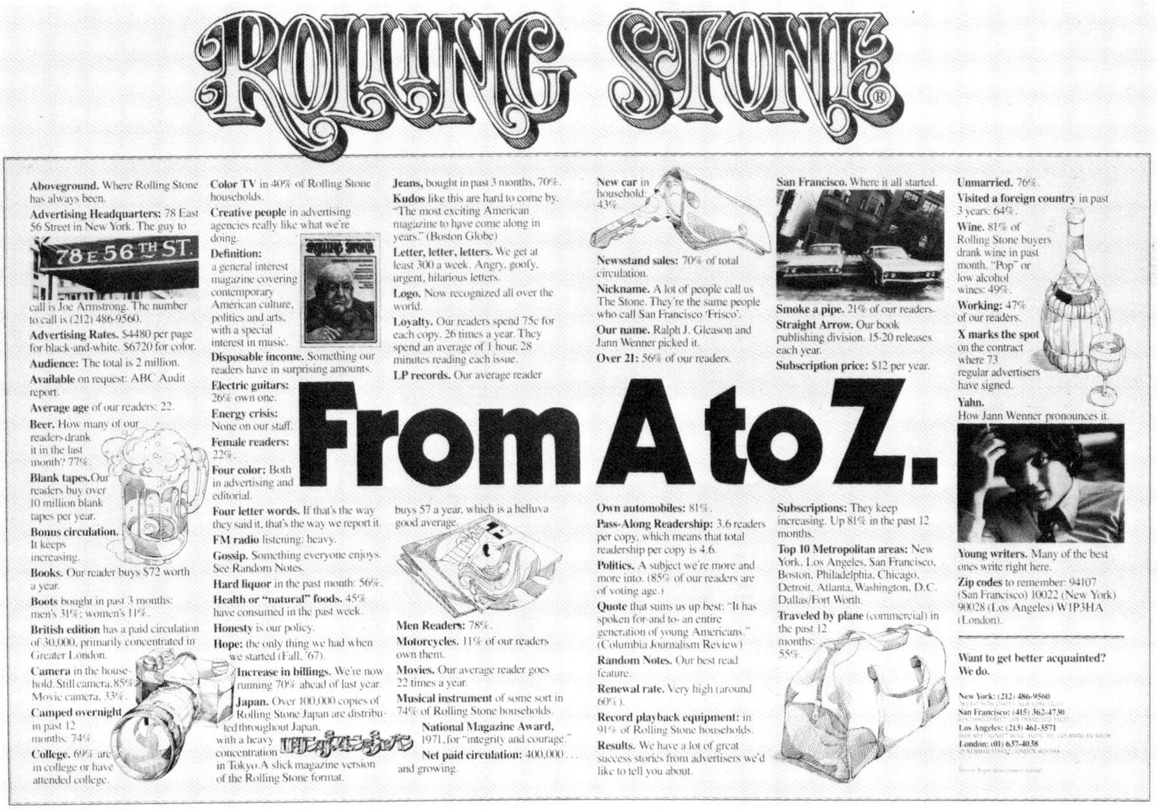
ROLLING STONE
From A to Z.
Aboveground. Where Rolling Stone has always been.
Advertising Headquarters: 78 East 56 Street in New York. The guy to call is Joe Armstrong. The number to call is (212) 486-9560.
78 E 56 TH ST.
Advertising Rates. $4480 per page for black-and-white. $6720 for color.
Audience: The total is 2 million.
Available on request: ABC Audit report.
Average age of our readers: 22.
Beer. How many of our readers drank it in the last month? 77%.
Blank tapes. Our readers buy over 10 million blank tapes per year.
Bonus circulation. It keeps increasing.
Books. Our reader buys $72 worth a year.
Boots bought in past 3 months: men's 31%; women's 11%.
British edition has a paid circulation of 30,000, primarily concentrated in Greater London.
Camera in the household. Still camera, 85%. Movie camera, 33%.
Camped overnight in past 12 months: 74%.
College. 69% are in college or have attended college.
Color TV in 40% of Rolling Stone households.
Creative people in advertising agencies really like what we're doing.
Definition: a general interest magazine covering contemporary American culture, politics and arts, with a special interest in music.
Disposable income. Something our readers have in surprising amounts.
Electric guitars: 26% own one.
Energy crisis: None on our staff.
Female readers: 22%.
Four color: Both in advertising and editorial.
Four letter words. If that's the way they said it, that's the way we report it.
FM radio listening: heavy.
Gossip. Something everyone enjoys. See Random Notes.
Hard liquor in the past month: 56%.
Health or "natural" foods. 45% have consumed in the past week.
Honesty is our policy.
Hope: the only thing we had when we started (Fall, '67).
Increase in billings. We're now running 70% ahead of last year.
Japan. Over 100,000 copies of Rolling Stone Japan are distributed throughout Japan, with a heavy concentration in Tokyo. A slick magazine version of the Rolling Stone format.
Jeans, bought in past 3 months, 70%.
Kudos like this are hard to come by. "The most exciting American magazine to have come along in years." (Boston Globe)
Letter, letter, letters. We get at least 300 a week. Angry, goofy, urgent, hilarious letters.
Logo. Now recognized all over the world.
Loyalty. Our readers spend 75c for each copy. 26 times a year. They spend an average of 1 hour, 28 minutes reading each issue.
LP records. Our average reader buys 57 a year, which is a helluva good average.
Men Readers: 78%.
Motorcycles. 11% of our readers own them.
Movies. Our average reader goes 22 times a year.
Musical instrument of some sort in 74% of Rolling Stone households.
National Magazine Award, 1971, for "integrity and courage."
Net paid circulation: 400,000 . . . and growing.
New car in household: 43%.
Newsstand sales: 70% of total circulation.
Nickname. A lot of people call us The Stone. They're the same people who call San Francisco 'Frisco'.
Our name. Ralph J. Gleason and Jann Wenner picked it.
Over 21: 56% of our readers.
Own automobiles: 81%.
Pass-Along Readership: 3.6 readers per copy, which means that total readership per copy is 4.6.
Politics. A subject we're more and more into. (85% of our readers are of voting age.)
Quote that sums us up best: "It has spoken for-and to- an entire generation of young Americans." (Columbia Journalism Review)
Random Notes. Our best read feature.
Renewal rate. Very high (around 60%).
Record playback equipment: in 91% of Rolling Stone households.
Results. We have a lot of great success stories from advertisers we'd like to tell you about.
San Francisco. Where it all started.
Smoke a pipe. 21% of our readers.
Straight Arrow. Our book publishing division. 15-20 releases each year.
Subscription price: $12 per year.
Subscriptions: They keep increasing. Up 81% in the past 12 months.
Top 10 Metropolitan areas: New York, Los Angeles, San Francisco, Boston, Philadelphia, Chicago, Detroit, Atlanta, Washington, D.C. Dallas/Fort Worth.
Traveled by plane (commercial) in the past 12 months: 55%.
Unmarried. 76%.
Visited a foreign country in past 3 years: 64%.
Wine. 81% of Rolling Stone buyers drank wine in past month. "Pop" or low alcohol wines: 49%.
Working: 47% of our readers.
X marks the spot on the contract where 73 regular advertisers have signed.
Yahn. How Jann Wenner pronounces it.
Young writers. Many of the best ones write right here.
Zip codes to remember: 94107 (San Francisco) 10022 (New York) 90028 (Los Angeles) W1P3HA (London).
Want to get better acquainted? We do.
New York: (212) 486-9560
San Francisco: (415) 362-4730
Los Angeles: (213) 461-3571
London: (01) 637-4038

203

203
Art Director Dick Thomas
Writer Whit Hobbs
Designer Dick Thomas
Artist Bob Deschamps
Photographer Editorial
Agency Blue Green, Inc.
Client Rolling Stone

Pictures of inner space in no time.
The Polaroid MP-4 Camera. Instant photomicrography is only one of the things it does.
Explore canyons on the edge of a razor blade. Shrink into worlds of giant bacteria. Track continents in a fossil. And bring back sharp, clear pictures in a matter of seconds. With Polaroid's MP-4, a multi-purpose camera that anyone can use. With a modular design that lets you do gross specimen and photomacrography as well as photomicrography.
The MP-4 has interchangeable backs, so you can use Polaroid roll, pack, or 4x5 sheet film. And get prints in color; transparencies, prints, and negatives in black and white.
It has special aerial image focusing screens for critical focusing at high magnifications.
A system which uses the optics of the microscope to form the image directly on the film. So there's no distortion of the final result because of intermediate lenses in the camera.
And, most important of all, there's instant delivery, to give you a finished picture in a matter of seconds. So you're always sure you've got exactly the result you want.
You don't have to waste the time and money involved in setting up your subject for a retake. Or, possibly not having it at all.
If your business is involved with inner space, write us and we'll tell you how to conquer it. Instantly.
Polaroid Corporation, Dept. 27-287, 549 Technology Square, Cambridge, Mass. 02139.
If you're in a hurry, call collect (617) 547-5176.
Polaroid

Your problems magnified in seconds.
The Polaroid MP-4 Camera. Instant photomacrography is only one of the things it does.
Maybe you're measuring the growth rate of cracks in metals under stress. Or maybe you're studying the growth of a certain strain of bacteria under no stress.
If you're using Polaroid's MP-4 you can make your problems up to 32 times bigger than they actually are and get finished pictures in seconds. In full color, or in black and white (with or without an instant negative).
Polaroid's instant pictures tell you right away if you've got the shot you want and, in some cases, how your test is going. Whichever way it goes you'll have time to do something about it without starting all over again.
You won't have to reshoot difficult sequences or restage complex experiments. And you've got a permanent record to study—one minute or one year after the metal has cracked and the bacteria has grown up.
In addition to instant delivery, Polaroid's multipurpose camera has a number of features you'd expect to find only in specialized macrophotographic systems. A reflex viewer for precise focusing (with aerial image focusing screens for extremely critical focusing at high magnifications). And a system of interchangeable lenses for a wide range of magnifications and greater flexibility. (The MP-4 can do photomicrography and photocopying as well as photomacrography.)
If you have small problems, write us and we'll tell you more about how to enlarge them.
Polaroid Corporation, Dept. 28-286, 549 Technology Square, Cambridge, Mass. 02139. If you're in a hurry, call collect (617) 547-5176.
Polaroid

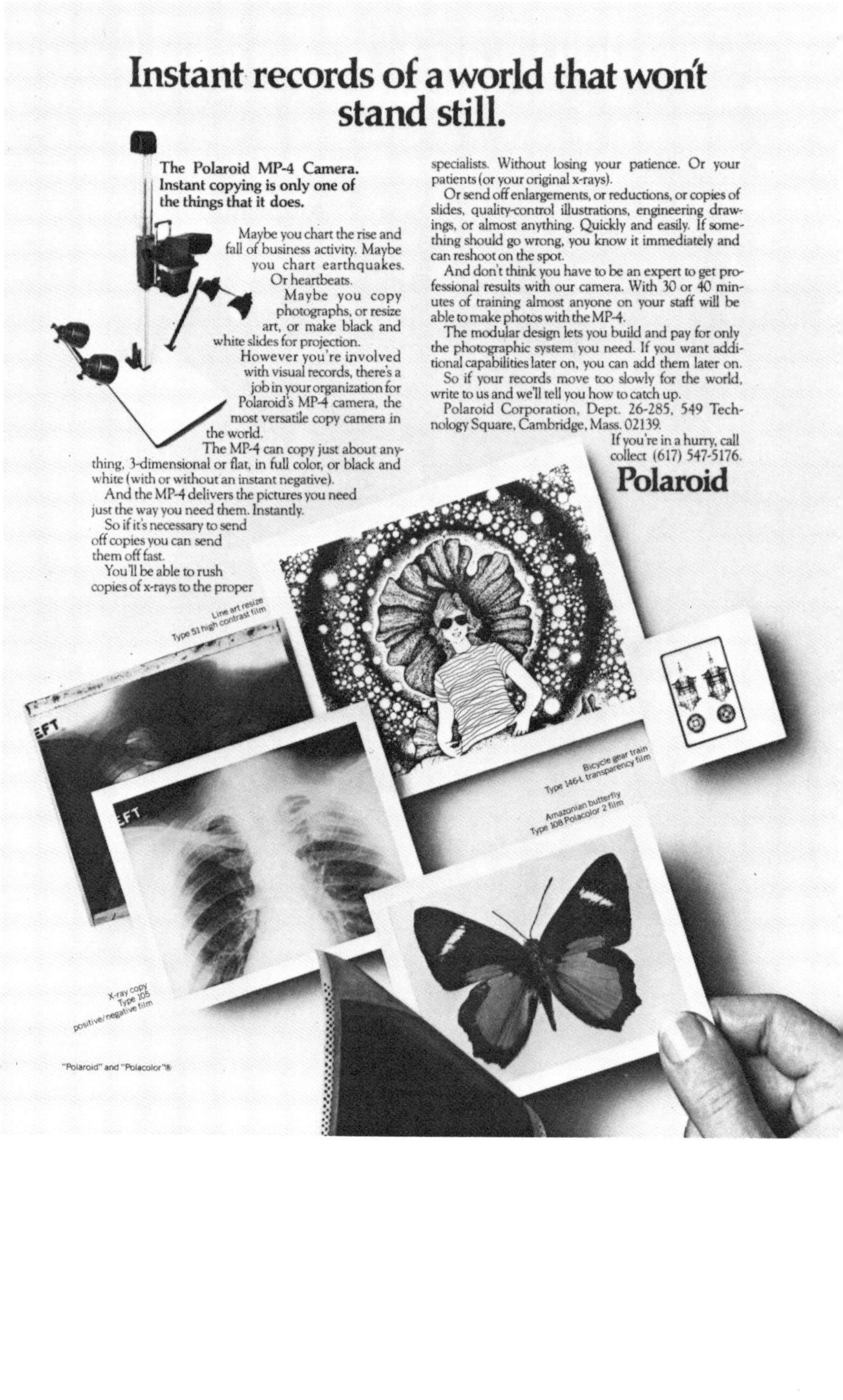
Instant records of a world that won't stand still.
The Polaroid MP-4 Camera. Instant copying is only one of the things that it does.
Maybe you chart the rise and fall of business activity. Maybe you chart earthquakes. Or heartbeats.
Maybe you copy photographs, or resize art, or make black and white slides for projection.
However you're involved with visual records, there's a job in your organization for Polaroid's MP-4 camera, the most versatile copy camera in the world.
The MP-4 can copy just about anything, 3-dimensional or flat, in full color, or black and white (with or without an instant negative).
And the MP-4 delivers the pictures you need just the way you need them. Instantly.
So if it's necessary to send off copies you can send them off fast.
You'll be able to rush copies of x-rays to the proper specialists. Without losing your patience. Or your patients (or your original x-rays).
Or send off enlargements, or reductions, or copies of slides, quality-control illustrations, engineering drawings, or almost anything. Quickly and easily. If something should go wrong, you know it immediately and can reshoot on the spot.
And don't think you have to be an expert to get professional results with our camera. With 30 or 40 minutes of training almost anyone on your staff will be able to make photos with the MP-4.
The modular design lets you build and pay for only the photographic system you need. If you want additional capabilities later on, you can add them later on.
So if your records move too slowly for the world, write to us and we'll tell you how to catch up.
Polaroid Corporation, Dept. 26-285, 549 Technology Square, Cambridge, Mass. 02139.
If you're in a hurry, call collect (617) 547-5176.
Polaroid
Line art resize
Type 51 high contrast film
Bicycle gear train
Type 146-L transparency film
Amazonian butterfly
Type 108 Polacolor 2 film
X-ray copy
Type 105
positive/negative film
"Polaroid" and "Polacolor"®

204

204
Art Director John Eding
Writer Dodds Musser
Designer John Eding
Artist R & V Studio
Photographer Henri Janson
Agency Doyle Dane Bernbach
Client Polaroid Corp.

COCO CHANEL.
SHE REALLY HAD OUR NUMBER.
She changed the shape of women. And, incidentally, of the future.
In the 1920's Coco Chanel realized the Victorian Era of frills and lace was not going to work for the modern woman. So she put them in the sleek, effortless clothes that are still in style today. And she went on to invent the short hairdo. Costume jewelry. The sling-back pump.
She even made the suntan fashionable.
Quite a lot for anyone. And in a very real way Chanel's instinct for what was going to be needed in the future symbolizes our thinking at Union Carbide. That's why we'd like to start talking with you now about your future.
Together we might be able to figure out exactly what you'll need in the years ahead. What sort of raw materials you'll be depending upon. And how we can plan to get them to you.
You see, we can admire an innovator like Coco Chanel because innovation has been part of our philosophy for over 50 years.
And, who knows, if your company and our company start planning now, we just might change the shape of a few things ourselves.
PEOPLE PLANNING THE FUTURE.
UNION CARBIDE
Chemicals and Plastics

LEO HENDRIK BAEKELAND.
HE DID HIS BEST WORK UNDER PRESSURE.
He molded theory into hard reality. He learned how to control the action of formaldehyde and phenol under pressure to create something totally new and different. Phenolic plastic.
But it wasn't easy. The basic idea he was working with—the reaction of aldehydes with phenols—had been discovered some twenty years before. However, in and of itself this condensation doesn't produce anything of value.
Only under very special conditions is it possible to produce the unique, amberlike, highly resistant properties of Bakelite phenolic resins. It took Dr. Baekeland five years of failure, disappointment and incredible work to establish these necessary conditions.
But in 1908 he succeeded. And opened up the frontiers of modern plastics to the world's ever increasing appetites.
At Union Carbide we inherited Dr. Baekeland's dedication to systematic research and his faith in the future. That's why we'd like to start discussing your future plans and needs as soon as possible.
Together we can pinpoint what some of your requirements will be in the years ahead. Gauge where your research is taking you. And evaluate the kind of technological assistance you'll need.
PEOPLE PLANNING THE FUTURE.

WILHELM KONRAD ROENTGEN.
HE SAW THINGS IN PEOPLE NO ONE ELSE EVER SAW.
On November 8, 1895 Wilhelm Roentgen startled his wife and made a place for himself in history by producing the world's first X-ray of the human body. It was such an incredible breakthrough he called the phenomenon "X," unknown, rather than give it his name.
Roentgen's discovery grew out of his work with vacuum tubes. But so quick was his understanding of its possibilities that within two weeks he had completed the foundations of modern X-ray practice. And, incidentally, helped to usher in the era of Modern Physics.
At Union Carbide we admire a man like Wilhelm Roentgen because we too are planning for the future. Looking for better ways to apply our knowledge. Experimenting with new possibilities.
That's why we want to start planning the future now. To discuss long-range plans. To try to predict your changing needs.
Innovation has been our philosophy for more than fifty years. And we know that if we get together soon enough, we just might make some history ourselves.
PEOPLE PLANNING THE FUTURE.
UNION CARBIDE

205

205
Art Director Ray Groff
Writer Alan Fraser
Agency Needham, Harper & Steers
Client Union Carbide Corp.

1971
BLUE NUN
WHITE WINE
H. SICHEL SÖHNE, MAINZ ESTD. 1857
LIEBFRAUMILCH QUALITATSWEIN
Schieffelin & Co.—New York
IMPORTERS SINCE 1794 SOLE U.S. DISTRIBUTORS
The nun who turned wine into profits.
Her name is Blue Nun.
And she's on the label of the largest selling imported premium white wine on the market today.
It's Blue Nun wine. The delicious white wine that's correct with any dish. The wine that's delicate enough for fish, yet hearty enough for meat. The wine more and more people are asking for everyday.
And the wine more and more people are going to be hearing about everyday, too. That's because Blue Nun commercials are the most popular wine advertising ever done on radio. And now they'll reach more people in your market than ever before.
So if you'd like to turn wine into profits, stock and display the German white wine that sells more, and makes more than any other. Blue Nun wine.
We think you'll find the results are miraculous.
Blue Nun. The delicious white wine more people are converting to every year.

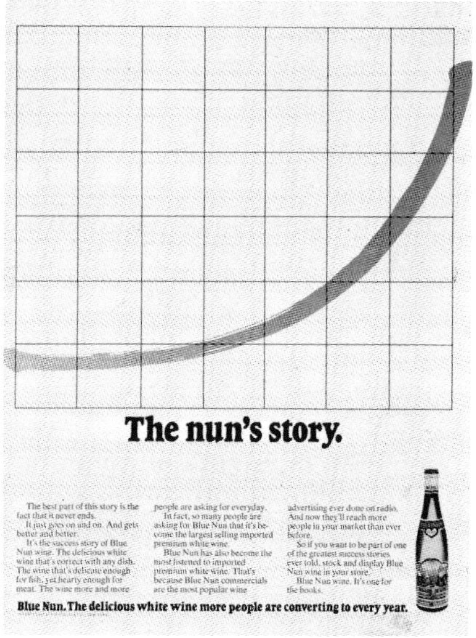
The nun's story.
The best part of this story is the fact that it never ends.
It just goes on and on. And gets better and better.
It's the success story of Blue Nun wine. The delicious white wine that's correct with any dish. The wine that's delicate enough for fish, yet hearty enough for meat. The wine more and more people are asking for everyday.
In fact, so many people are asking for Blue Nun that it's become the largest selling imported premium white wine.
Blue Nun has also become the most listened to imported premium white wine. That's because Blue Nun commercials are the most popular wine advertising ever done on radio. And now they'll reach more people in your market than ever before.
So if you want to be part of one of the greatest success stories ever told, stock and display Blue Nun wine in your store.
Blue Nun wine. It's one for the books.
Blue Nun. The delicious white wine more people are converting to every year.

Believe in Blue Nun and you shall be rewarded.
Rewarded with profits.
The profits you earn carrying the largest selling imported premium white wine on the market.
Blue Nun wine.
Blue Nun is the delicious white wine that's correct with any dish. Delicious enough for fish, yet hearty enough for meat. It's the wine more and more people are asking for every day.
It's also the wine more and more people are hearing about every day. That's because Blue Nun commercials are the most popular wine advertising ever done on radio. And now they'll be reaching more people in your market than ever before.
So if you want profits to rain down like pennies from heaven, stock and display Blue Nun wine.
We think it'll be blue skies from then on.
Blue Nun. The delicious white wine more people are converting to every year.
IMPORTED BY SCHIEFFELIN & CO., NEW YORK, N.Y.

206

GOLD

206
Art Director Mark Yustein
Writer Kay Kavanagh
Artists Cal Sachs
David Wilcox
Photographer Charlie Gold
Agency Della Femina, Travisano & Partners
Client Schieffelin & Co.

AT CLUB MEDITERRANEE GUADELOUPE, YOU DO ABSOLUTELY EVERYTHING FOR ABSOLUTELY NOTHING.
A week on Guadeloupe costs no more than a week at an ordinary resort. Except all the extras don't cost extra.
Included in the initial price are comfortable, air-conditioned rooms, three meals a day (unlimited food at every meal) and all the free wine you can drink at lunch and supper.
All you have to pay for are drinks at the bar.
The activities are free too. There's free tennis. Free sailing. Free water skiing and scuba diving. Free picnic excursion boat rides. Free yoga and calisthenics. What's more, there's free group lessons and equipment in all sports.
And, free live entertainment every night.
Not only that but you have your choice of Club Mediterranee's two villages on the island. Fort Royal, a smaller, more personal village with a mini club for kids. And the larger more luxurious Caravelle, with its famous Antilles beach.
If you'd like to know more, come in and see us or call.
A vacation at Club Mediterranee on Guadeloupe is a place where you can do a lot more without having to pay a lot more.
TRAVEL AGENT

207

Here comes the bribe.
Free wedding gift. 41-piece glassware set.
gingiss formalwear

208

207
Art Director Bill Kamp
Writers Larry Plapler
John Russo
Designer Bill Kamp
Artist Whistlin Dixie
Agency Levine, Huntley, Schmidt
Client Club Mediterranee

208
Art Director Barry Vetere
Writer Jan Zechman
Designer Ray Nyquist
Photographer Kazu
Agency Zechman Lyke Vetere
Client Gingiss International

BEFORE INFLATION, YOU COULD GET A 12 COURSE MEAL IN ITALY FOR $5. NOW, IT'S ALL THE WAY UP TO $6.

Even with inflation, it's amazing what a dollar can still buy in Italy.

Take the restaurant Ambasciata D'Abruzzo in Rome.

Feasting on their 12-course meal of ham, sausages, antipasto, pasta, roasts, salad, cheese, fruit, coffee, cake, wine and Sambuca used to cost $5. Today it's $6.

Or, if you prefer, something a little more expensive. You can eat in a restaurant where Hemingway ate. Piccolo Padre in Milan.

Before inflation its 22-course meal was $8. Today it's $10. Including all the wine you can drink.

Alitalia has more non-stop flights from the U.S. to Italy than any other airline.

And we have almost 50 different tours of Italy, leaving from New York, Boston and Philadelphia.

What's more, there isn't a scheduled airline in the world that can beat our new low fares to Italy.

For more information, call an expert, your travel agent. He can help plan your trip and make all arrangements for you completely free of charge. Or call Alitalia.

Alitalia's Italy
All you ever dreamed of.
And more.

209

FAILING BUSINESS FOR SALE. $50,000.

It's not failing because it doesn't work. It's failing because we don't have the time to make it work.

But we know it *can* work because our president went on the road himself and proved it. What he was selling were some of the most effective and innovative syndicated advertising packages that the automotive industry has ever seen. Packages that have already helped car dealers all over the country make remarkable increases in their sales and profits.

But we're a major advertising agency and running that subsidiary company just took up too much of our time and energy.

But maybe you have the time and energy it takes to get our neglected business moving.

If you do, it could make you very rich. Write Box No. 8165, c/o Automotive News, 965 East Jefferson, Detroit, MI 48207.

210

209
Art Director Paul Singer
Writer Joe Tantillo
Designer Paul Singer
Photographer Rudy Legname
Agency DKG
Client Alitalia Airlines

210
Art Director Jerry Esposito
Writers Don Dickison
Jay Stevens
Designer Jerry Esposito
Agency Van Leeuwen Advertising
Client Van Leeuwen Productions

Instead of coming home from Europe with a car rental receipt, come home with a car.
Buy a Fiat here and pick it up in Europe. For more information write to: Overseas Delivery Dept., Fiat Distributors, Inc., 532 Sylvan Ave., Englewood Cliffs, N.J. 07632.
Name
Address
City State Zip
FIAT
That's where the automobile is going.

211

YOU HAVEN'T TASTED SPAGHETTI UNTIL YOU'VE HAD IT COOKED IN A PAPER BAG.
Unless you've been to the Trattoria di Ciccio in Amalfi, you don't know how spaghetti should taste.
First, Ciccio makes a sauce with clams and olives. Next, he boils some spaghetti. Then he puts both things into a paper bag, folds it shut and heats it in an oven.
What comes out of that paper bag isn't just spaghetti with sauce on it. But spaghetti with sauce in it.
The food is so good in Ciccio's, you almost forget to look out the window at one of the most incredible coastlines in the world. Amalfi.
Alitalia has more non-stop flights from the U.S. to Italy than any other airline.
And, we have almost 50 different tours of Italy leaving from New York, Boston and Philadelphia. Some of which include Amalfi.
What's more, there isn't a scheduled airline in the world that can beat our new low fares to Italy.
For more information, call an expert, your travel agent. He can help plan your trip and make all arrangements for you completely free of charge. Or call Alitalia.
Alitalia's Italy
All you ever dreamed of.
And more.

212

211
Art Director Joe Cappadona
Writer Ron Berger
Photographer Peter Papadopolous
Agency Carl Ally
Client Fiat-Roosevelt Motors

212
Art Director Paul Singer
Writer Joe Tantillo
Designer Paul Singer
Photographer Rudy Legname
Agency DKG
Client Alitalia Airlines

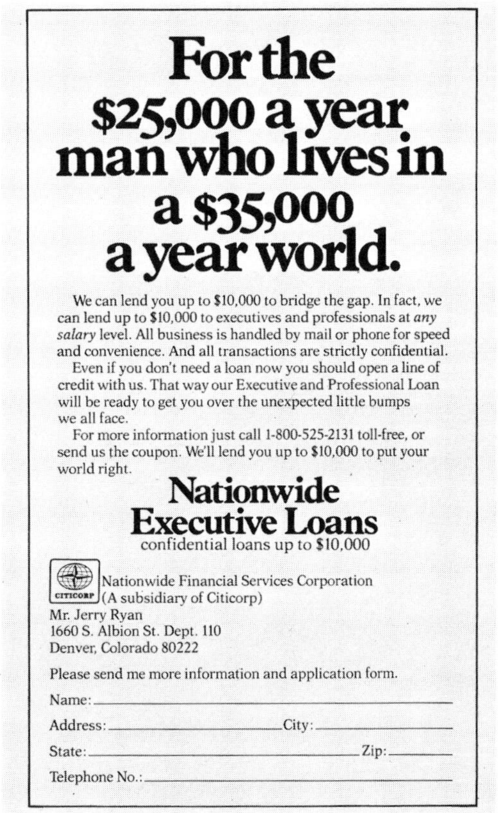
For the $25,000 a year man who lives in a $35,000 a year world.
We can lend you up to $10,000 to bridge the gap. In fact, we can lend up to $10,000 to executives and professionals at *any salary* level. All business is handled by mail or phone for speed and convenience. And all transactions are strictly confidential.
Even if you don't need a loan now you should open a line of credit with us. That way our Executive and Professional Loan will be ready to get you over the unexpected little bumps we all face.
For more information just call 1-800-525-2131 toll-free, or send us the coupon. We'll lend you up to $10,000 to put your world right.
Nationwide Executive Loans
confidential loans up to $10,000
CITICORP
Nationwide Financial Services Corporation
(A subsidiary of Citicorp)
Mr. Jerry Ryan
1660 S. Albion St. Dept. 110
Denver, Colorado 80222
Please send me more information and application form.
Name:
Address: City:
State: Zip:
Telephone No.:

213

WE HEAR YOU NEED A NEW MUFFLER.
And so do your neighbors. And if you want to put a hush to those not-so-nice things they may be saying about your exhaust system . . .
Come to Korman. We started right here in Cleveland. And we're the oldest muffler specialists in the business.
We've got five convenient locations to serve you. So when the man sings "Come to Korman," he's not asking you to go very far.
At Korman, we'll practically guarantee to save you money over anyone else in the business. Not by cutting quality. But by trimming unnecessary overhead.
And maybe best of all, when you come to Korman you can leave Korman pretty fast. We've developed a system of operation that completely fixes most car's systems within a half hour. So you won't be stuck standing around humming our jingle all day.
Come to Korman.
Both of us will be glad.
KORMAN MUFFLER

214

We neexd two sharp secretaries, a classxxy reception-est, and xxxxxtwo xxxxxxxx accxuratxe clexrk typists.
Call Mr.Ivey foxr an appointment at xxMetzdorf Adv., 526-5361.

215

SILVER

213
Art Director Nick Nickerson
Writers Ronald M. Rosenfeld
Dick Meylan
Agency Rosenfeld, Sirowitz & Lawson
Client Nationwide Financial Services

214
Art Director Tom Smith
Writers Walt Woodward
Tom Smith
Designer Tom Smith
Artist Curilla & Assoc.
Agency Griswold-Eshleman
Client Korman Muffler

215
Art Director Lyle Metzdorf
Client Lyle Metzdorf
Designer Lyle Metzdorf
Agency Metzdorf Advertising
Client Metzdorf Advertising

CLUB MEDITERRANEE/HAWAII.
IN ADDITION TO LEAVING
YOUR TROUBLES BEHIND, LEAVE YOUR
MONEY BEHIND.
These days, nobody wants to have to go through money like water on their vacation. That's why you should know about Club Mediterranee.
A week at Club Mediterranee in Hawaii costs about the same as a week at an ordinary resort. Except all the extras don't cost extra.
Luxurious, comfortable, air-conditioned rooms, three meals a day (unlimited food at every meal) and all the free wine you can drink at lunch and supper are included in the initial cost. All you have to pay for are drinks at the bar.
Besides that, there's free tennis. Free water skiing. Free sailing. Free snorkeling. Free golf lessons. Free deep sea fishing. Free yoga and calisthenics.
Not to mention the big sport, surfing. And that's free too.
There's also free picnic excursion boat rides. What's more, there's free group lessons and equipment in all sports. And free live entertainment every night.
If you'd like to hear more, come in and see us or give us a call.
All in all, you'll not only come back with a beautiful tan, your wallet will come back a healthy shade of green.
TRAVEL AGENT

216

"Dear
American Tourister:
The stuff is so easy
to carry, my wife
carries it."
James Spero, Los Angeles
American Tourister
The Verylite
In 8 soft-sided sizes and 3 colors. From $32.50 to $57.50

217

216
Art Director Bill Kamp
Writer John Russo
Designer Bill Kamp
Artist Whistlin Dixie
Agency Levine, Huntley, Schmidt
Client Club Mediterranee

217
Art Director Jack Mariucci
Writer Marcia Bell Grace
Designer Jack Mariucci
Photographer Cosimo
Agency Doyle Dane Bernbach
Client American Tourister

Spend a week in the sun without getting burned.
Waikiki One-Weeker. 8 days-Waikiki, $298
Island Combination. 8 days-Waikiki and Maui, $337
Most Hawaii vacations promise you everything under the sun but what you actually get is sometimes a little cloudy.
On Pan Am's World Hawaii Tours, we make everything you get very clear.
You get your round trip GIT economy air fare. Air-conditioned hotel accommodations based on double occupancy. Transportation between the airports and hotels. Sightseeing. And all hotel taxes and service charges.
You also get our "Hawaii Fancy Free," a booklet of coupons good for two-for-the-price-of-one lunches and dinners, free drinks and free greens fees for a round of golf.
Call your travel agent and ask him to put you on one of 12 Pan Am's World Hawaii One- and Two-Weeker vacations.
That way, the only thing you'll have to worry about getting for your money is a good tan.
PAN AM.
The world's most experienced airline.
See your travel agent.

218

"Dear American Tourister:
After going 20,000 miles in three weeks, I only wish I looked as good."
Janet Smerling, New York
American Tourister
The Verylite
In 8 soft-sided sizes and 3 colors. From $32.50 to $57.50.

219

8 days in solitary. $259.
Jamaica is the kind of place you wouldn't mind being sentenced to for life.
But at this price, the best we can do is give you 8 days and 7 nights at the air-conditioned Jamaica Hilton (double occupancy) with private balcony in Ocho Rios.
And we'll throw in your round trip GIT midweek economy air fare (for groups of 15 or more booked 7 days in advance), transportation between the airport and hotel, shows every night, a free tennis lesson and 2 cocktail parties.
Call your travel agent now for reservations on our "Jamaica Hilton Pleasure Chest" vacation.
So then, all you'll have to do is plan your escape.
Welcome to our world.
PAN AM.
The world's most experienced airline.
See your travel agent.

220

218
Art Director Peter Kingman
Writer Ron Berger
Agency Carl Ally
Client Pan American World Airways

219
Art Director Jack Mariucci
Writer Marcia Bell Grace
Designer Jack Mariucci
Photographer Cosimo
Agency Doyle Dane Bernbach
Client American Tourister

220
Art Director Peter Kingman
Writer Ron Berger
Agency Carl Ally
Client Pan American World Airways

HOW TO CATCH THE 5:25 FERRY AT 5:26.

The Fiat 124 is an ideal car if you have a tendency to miss the boat.

It has a high-performance overhead cam engine that lets you take off quickly.

It has 4-wheel disc brakes and radial tires for surer stops on wet surfaces.

And it has front-wheel independent suspension, so it takes bumps well.

Of course, if you're not in a big hurry to catch the 5:25, the Fiat 124 offers a convenient accessory.

An AM-FM radio.

So you can hear how backed up traffic is on the bridge.

FIAT

The biggest selling car in Europe.

Overseas delivery arranged through your dealer.

(Dealer Name)

221

221
Art Director Nate Fiarman
Writer Ron Berger
Agency Carl Ally
Client Fiat-Roosevelt Motors

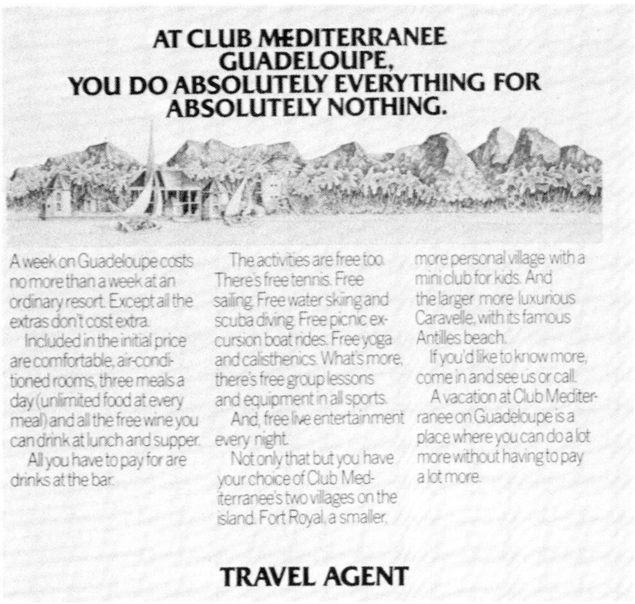
AT CLUB MEDITERRANEE GUADELOUPE, YOU DO ABSOLUTELY EVERYTHING FOR ABSOLUTELY NOTHING.
A week on Guadeloupe costs no more than a week at an ordinary resort. Except all the extras don't cost extra.
Included in the initial price are comfortable, air-conditioned rooms, three meals a day (unlimited food at every meal) and all the free wine you can drink at lunch and supper.
All you have to pay for are drinks at the bar.
The activities are free too. There's free tennis. Free sailing. Free water skiing and scuba diving. Free picnic excursion boat rides. Free yoga and calisthenics. What's more, there's free group lessons and equipment in all sports.
And, free live entertainment every night.
Not only that but you have your choice of Club Mediterranee's two villages on the island. Fort Royal, a smaller, more personal village with a mini club for kids. And the larger more luxurious Caravelle, with its famous Antilles beach.
If you'd like to know more, come in and see us or call.
A vacation at Club Mediterranee on Guadeloupe is a place where you can do a lot more without having to pay a lot more.
TRAVEL AGENT

CLUB MEDITERRANEE/MEXICO. GO SOMEPLACE WHERE MONEY ISN'T THE ONLY LANGUAGE PEOPLE SPEAK.
At Club Mediterranee/Playa Blanca near Manzanillo, nobody talks money. That's because after you pay for your room and board, nobody asks you to pay for anything else.
For that initial cost, which is no more than what you'd pay at an ordinary resort, you get air-conditioned bungalows, three meals a day (unlimited food at every meal) and all the free wine you can drink at lunch and supper. As a matter of fact, all you have to pay for are drinks at the bar.
And all the activities you could possibly want are free.
There's free tennis. Free snorkeling. Free sailing. Free scuba diving. Free yoga and calisthenics. Free picnic excursion boat rides. What's more, there's free group lessons and equipment in all sports. And, free live entertainment every night.
If you'd like to hear more, come in and see us or call.
At Club Mediterranee in Mexico, you can not only leave your troubles behind, you can leave your money behind.
TRAVEL AGENT

CLUB MEDITERRANEE/HAWAII. IN ADDITION TO LEAVING YOUR TROUBLES BEHIND, LEAVE YOUR MONEY BEHIND.
These days, nobody wants to have to go through money like water on their vacation. That's why you should know about Club Mediterranee.
A week at Club Mediterranee in Hawaii costs about the same as a week at an ordinary resort. Except all the extras don't cost extra.
Luxurious, comfortable, air-conditioned rooms, three meals a day (unlimited food at every meal) and all the free wine you can drink at lunch and supper are included in the initial cost. All you have to pay for are drinks at the bar.
Besides that, there's free tennis. Free water skiing. Free sailing. Free snorkeling. Free golf lessons. Free deep sea fishing. Free yoga and calisthenics.
Not to mention the big sport, surfing. And that's free too. There's also free picnic excursion boat rides. What's more, there's free group lessons and equipment in all sports. And free live entertainment every night.
If you'd like to hear more, come in and see us or give us a call.
All in all, you'll not only come back with a beautiful tan, your wallet will come back a healthy shade of green.
TRAVEL AGENT

222

GOLD

222
Art Director Bill Kamp
Writers John Russo
Larry Plapler
Designer Bill Kamp
Artist Whistlin Dixie
Agency Levine, Huntley, Schmidt
Client Club Mediterranee

223
Art Director Paul Singer
Writer Joe Tantillo
Designer Paul Singer
Photographer Rudy Legname
Agency DKG
Client Alitalia Airlines

YOU HAVEN'T TASTED SPAGHETTI UNTIL YOU'VE HAD IT COOKED IN A PAPER BAG.

Unless you've been to the Trattoria di Ciccio in Amalfi, you don't know how spaghetti should taste.

First, Ciccio makes a sauce with clams and olives. Next, he boils some spaghetti. Then he puts both things into a paper bag, folds it shut and heats it in an oven.

What comes out of that paper bag isn't just spaghetti with sauce on it. But spaghetti with sauce in it.

The food is so good in Ciccio's, you almost forget to look out the window at one of the most incredible coastlines in the world. Amalfi.

Alitalia has more non-stop flights from the U.S. to Italy than any other airline.

And, we have almost 50 different tours of Italy leaving from New York, Boston and Philadelphia. Some of which include Amalfi.

What's more, there isn't a scheduled airline in the world that can beat our new low fares to Italy.

For more information, call an expert, your travel agent. He can help plan your trip and make all arrangements for you completely free of charge. Or call Alitalia.

Alitalia's Italy
All you ever dreamed of.
And more.

COME TO SICILY AND BE EMBARRASSED BY A FOUNTAIN.

Rome has Bernini's Fountain of the Triton, 3 fountains in the Piazza Navona and of course, the Fountain of Trevi.

But only Palermo has the Fountain of Shame.

The nakedness of the statues is lifelike and sensual. But even more obvious is the affection some of the statues have for each other.

The Fountain of Shame, like everything else in Sicily, is a little bit different than what you'll find in the rest of Italy.

Alitalia has more non-stop flights from the U.S. to Italy than any other airline.

And we have almost 50 different tours of Italy leaving from New York, Boston and Philadelphia. All of which can be combined with a stay in Sicily.

What's more, there isn't a scheduled airline in the world that can beat our new low fares to Italy.

For more information, call your travel agent. He can help plan your trip and make all arrangements for you completely free of charge. Or call Alitalia.

Alitalia's Italy
All you ever dreamed of.
And more.

BEFORE INFLATION, YOU COULD GET A 12 COURSE MEAL IN ITALY FOR $5. NOW, IT'S ALL THE WAY UP TO $6.

Even with inflation, it's amazing what a dollar can still buy in Italy.

Take the restaurant Ambasciata D'Abruzzo in Rome.

Feasting on their 12-course meal of ham, sausages, antipasto, pasta, roasts, salad, cheese, fruit, coffee, cake, wine and Sambuca used to cost $5. Today it's $6.

Or, if you prefer, something a little more expensive. You can eat in a restaurant where Hemingway ate. Piccolo Padre in Milan.

Before inflation its 22-course meal was $8. Today it's $10. Including all the wine you can drink.

Alitalia has more non-stop flights from the U.S. to Italy than any other airline.

And we have almost 50 different tours of Italy, leaving from New York, Boston and Philadelphia.

What's more, there isn't a scheduled airline in the world that can beat our new low fares to Italy.

For more information, call an expert, your travel agent. He can help plan your trip and make all arrangements for you completely free of charge. Or call Alitalia.

Alitalia's Italy
All you ever dreamed of.
And more.

CHASING YOUR TAIL WON'T HELP YOU MAKE BOTH ENDS MEET.

Relax. Slow down. Unpanic.
Chasing your tail will only make you dizzy.
This is a time for cool cogitation and efficiency.

For example, why not use the current business slowdown as an opportunity to improve the efficiency of your media buying?

Stop paying for readers you don't need. Or buyers who don't buy what you sell.

Try Industry Week. It's the most efficient way to reach managers who buy products for use in industry. Over 1.8 million readers, says TGI. Only pennies per contact.

We're just as uncertain about the economy as you are. But we're not chasing our tails. We're chasing business prospects instead. Efficiently!

That's what we can help you do, too.

INDUSTRY WEEK
The magazine managers read.

WHAT MOST AMERICANS NEED THESE DAYS IS A SLIGHT IMPEDIMENT IN THEIR REACH.

The days of "the more the better" are gone now. Efficiency is in. Extravagance is out.

And inefficiency is as outmoded in media buying as it is in any other activity today.

Wasting big money on big numbers isn't the answer anymore. Now advertisers want selective control. Every advertising dollar has to work harder.

Industry Week has been preaching efficiency to its readers for some time. In their living, working, eating and spending.

It has been preaching efficiency to its advertisers, too. We've been saying: if industry managers buy your products, we can prove Industry Week is your most efficient and effective media buy to reach them. Over 1.8 million readers, says TGI. Only pennies per contact.

Be efficient! Ask us to prove that extravagant claim.

INDUSTRY WEEK
The magazine managers read.

HOW MANY ADVERTISING MEN JUMPED OUT OF WINDOWS ON BLACK TUESDAY?

Our guess? Not many.

Because advertising people are optimists. If they weren't, they wouldn't be advertising people.

We're optimists, too, and we have some sage advice. To make 1975 a better business year than the pessimists are predicting, keep advertising.

Companies that advertise in slowdowns protect their share of market. And when times get better, their business gets better faster than competitors' who don't advertise.

Instead of thinking about jumping out of windows on Black Tuesdays, jump into Industry Week every Monday. That's where over 1.8 million readers (TGI, 1974) will see your message first.

It will keep you optimistic.

INDUSTRY WEEK
The magazine managers read.

THINGS ARE SO UNCERTAIN THESE DAYS EVEN THE YES MEN ARE MERELY NODDING.

Times are tough for yes men. Their bosses can't make up their minds.

Ask any of your clients how he sees his business prospects for 1975 and he'll give you a positive "I don't know!"

We have a suggestion for any of you who want to guard against slowdowns or recessions in your businesses. Keep advertising. Companies that keep advertising during business slowdowns protect and even increase their share of market.

Keep advertising! But buy your media wisely. Put your advertising dollars to work in the most powerful voice talking to powerful men in industry today: Industry Week. Over 1.8 million readers, says TGI. Only pennies per contact.

Even your yes men will look good agreeing with you on this decision.

INDUSTRY WEEK
The magazine managers read.

224

224
Art Director Bob Kwait
Writer Mike Marino
Agency Griswold-Eshleman
Client Industry Week

We can show you the best places to sleep in Puerto Rico.
With the kind of nightlife you find at the hotels in Puerto Rico, the thing you need is a good beach to sleep on the next day.
One of these hotels is the Caribe Hilton, where for only $244, we can give you an air-conditioned room (based on double occupancy) with private balcony for 8 days and 7 nights.
The price also includes your round trip air fare, a welcome cocktail, an escorted tour of San Geronimo and a free scuba lesson.
Call your travel agent for reservations. And ask for the Pan Am/Hilton Pleasure Chest.
For $244, you can go to sleep every day counting the money you save.
PAN AM
The world's most experienced airline.
See your travel agent.

Take the wife out dancing. $298.
The price includes your round trip GIT economy air fare with convenient Saturday departures, 8 days and 7 nights at an air-conditioned hotel (based on double occupancy), transportation between the airport and hotel, and a Pearl Harbor cruise.
And, of course, a traditional lei greeting to welcome you to Hawaii.
To welcome you to Pan Am we not only have this Waikiki One-Weeker but 13 other Hawaii vacations as well.
Call your travel agent now for more information.
For $298, even if you can't dance, you can afford to take lessons.
PAN AM
The world's most experienced airline.
See your travel agent.

8 days in solitary. $259.
Jamaica is the kind of place you wouldn't mind being sentenced to for life.
But at this price, the best we can do is give you 8 days and 7 nights at the air-conditioned Jamaica Hilton (double occupancy) with private balcony in Ocho Rios.
And we'll throw in your round trip GIT midweek economy air fare (for groups of 15 or more booked 7 days in advance), transportation between the airport and hotel, shows every night, a free tennis lesson and 2 cocktail parties.
Call your travel agent now for reservations on our "Jamaica Hilton Pleasure Chest" vacation.
So then, all you'll have to do is plan your escape.
Welcome to our world.
PAN AM
The world's most experienced airline.
See your travel agent.

225

225
Art Director Peter Kingman
Writer Ron Berger
Designer Peter Kingman
Agency Carl Ally
Client Pan American World Airways

"Dear
American Tourister:
You don't have to
be a superwoman
to carry it."
Mrs. Elsie Green, Cleveland
American Tourister
The Verylite
In 8 soft-sided sizes and 3 colors. From $32.50 to $57.50.

"Dear
American Tourister:
After going 20,000
miles in three weeks,
I only wish I looked
as good."
Janet Smerling, New York
American Tourister
The Verylite
In 8 soft-sided sizes and 3 colors. From $32.50 to $57.50.

"Dear
American Tourister:
The stuff is so easy
to carry, my wife
carries it."
James Spero, Los Angeles
American Tourister
The Verylite
In 8 soft-sided sizes and 3 colors. From $32.50 to $57.50.

226

226
Art Director Jack Mariucci
Writer Marcia Bell Grace
Designer Jack Mariucci
Photographer Cosimo
Agency Doyle Dane Bernbach
Client American Tourister Luggage

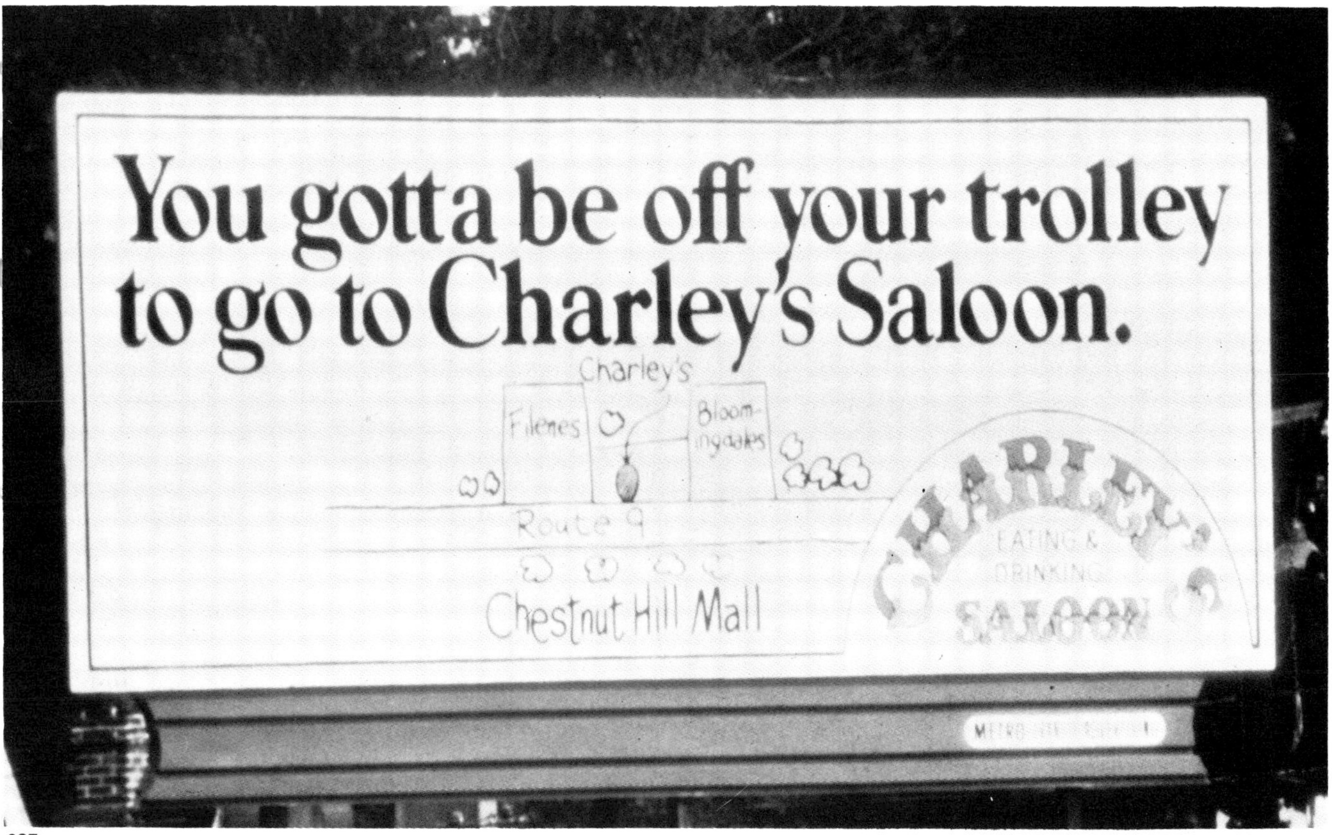
You gotta be off your trolley
to go to Charley's Saloon.
Charley's
Filenes
Bloom-
ingdales
Route 9
Chestnut Hill Mall
CHARLEY'S
EATING &
DRINKING
SALOON

227

When long ago
is far away –
call Long Distance.

228

SILVER

227
Art Director Tony Viola
Writers Seumas McGuire
Tony Winch
Designer Dick Pantano
Artist Tony Viola
Agency Hill, Holliday, Connors
Cosmopulos
Client Charley's Eating &
Drinking Saloon

228
Art Director Mitch Leichner
Writer Andy Certner
Designer Mitch Leichner
Photographer Cosimo
Agency Doyle Dane Bernbach
Client GTE

SCE&G
3236
Save gas. Ride to work with a friend.

229

Take your herd west.
CALICO SALOON
AMERICAN AIRLINES TO CALIFORNIA

230

229
Art Director Jerry Torchia
Writer Michael Gaffney
Designer Jerry Torchia
Photographer Jim Collins
Agency Cargill, Wilson & Acree
Client South Carolina Electric & Gas

230
Art Director Stan Jones
Writer David Butler
Photographer Carl Furuta
Agency Doyle Dane Bernbach
Los Angeles
Client American Airlines

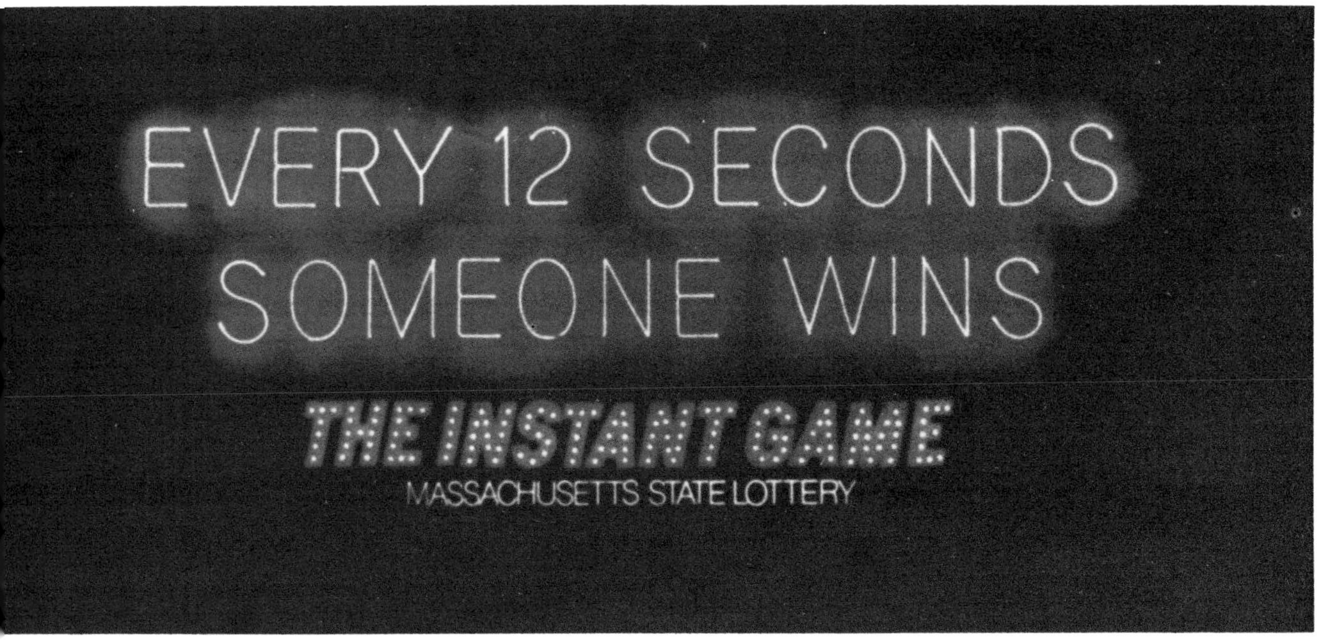
EVERY 12 SECONDS
SOMEONE WINS
THE INSTANT GAME
MASSACHUSETTS STATE LOTTERY

231

To your wealth.
CHIVAS REGAL
1801
SCOTCH
WHISKY

232

231
Art Director Tom McCarthy
Writer Tom McCarthy
Designer Mike Solazzo
Photographer Frank Foster
Agency Humphrey Browning MacDougall
Client Massachusetts State Lottery Commission

GOLD

232
Art Director Ed Flanagan
Writer Jim Copacino
Designer Ed Flanagan
Photographer John Conboy
Agency Promotion Plus Doyle Dane Bernbach Div.
Client General Wine & Spirits

We pick up and deliver.
SCE&G

233

Dallas to Houston: $2.59
HONDA

234

233
Art Director Jerry Torchia
Writer Barbara Ford
Designer Jerry Torchia
Photographer Bill Barley
Agency Cargill, Wilson & Acree
Client South Carolina Electric & Gas

234
Art Directors Norm Friant
Leland Miyawaki
Writer J. R. Navarro
Designers Norm Friant
Leland Miyawaki
Photographer Sam Kwong
Agency Grey Advertising
Los Angeles
Client American Honda Motor Co.

Boston to filly.
Tunnel to Rt.1. Suffolk Downs.
Post-time 12:30
Donnelly

235

235
Art Director Bill Murphy
Writer Joan McArthur
Designer Bill Murphy
Agency Ingalls Assoc.
Client Ogden Recreation

My Mom Really Knows her Catsup
Del Monte
Catsup

My Mom Really Knows her Tomato Sauce
Del Monte
Tomato Sauce

My Mom Really Knows her Green Beans
Del Monte
Green Beans

236

SILVER

236
Art Director Jerry Collamer
Writer Valerie Wagner
Designer Jerry Collamer
Artist Lowell Herrero
Agency McCann-Erickson San Francisco
Client Del Monte

237
Writer Garth DeCew
Designer Marty Neumeier
Artist Marty Neumeier
Agency Garth De Cew Group
Client Dos Pesos Restaurants

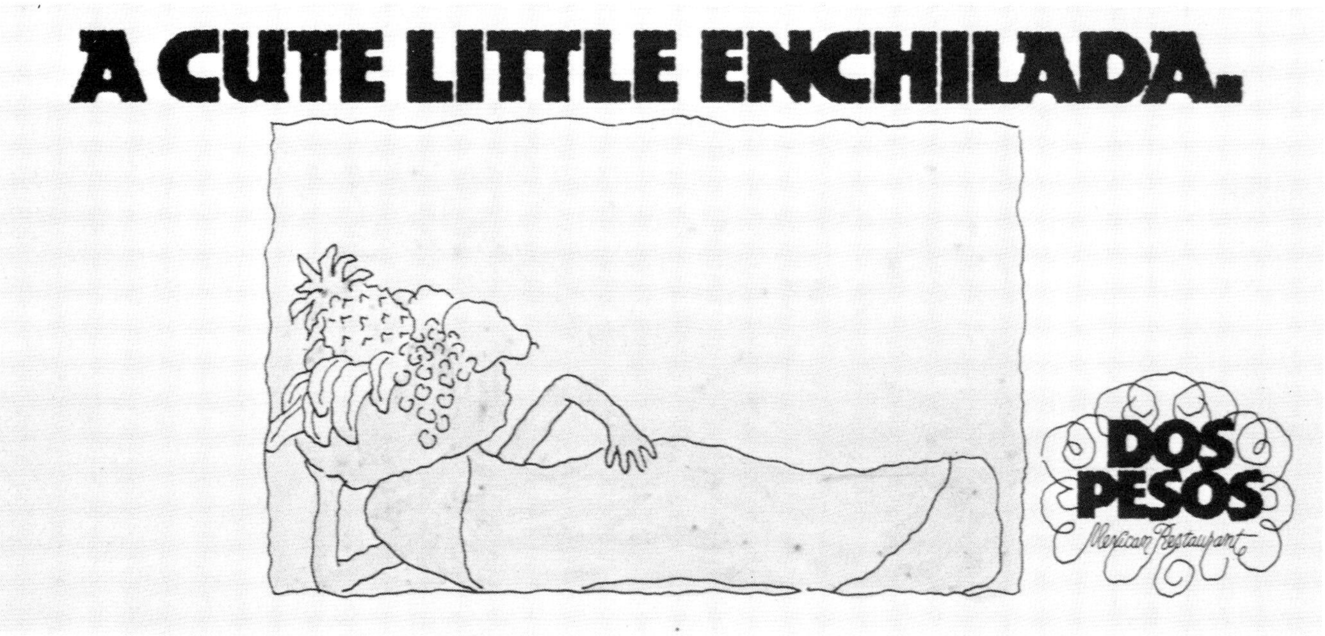
A CUTE LITTLE ENCHILADA.
DOS PESOS
Mexican Restaurant

HERE TODAY, GONE TAMALE.
DOS PESOS
Mexican Restaurant

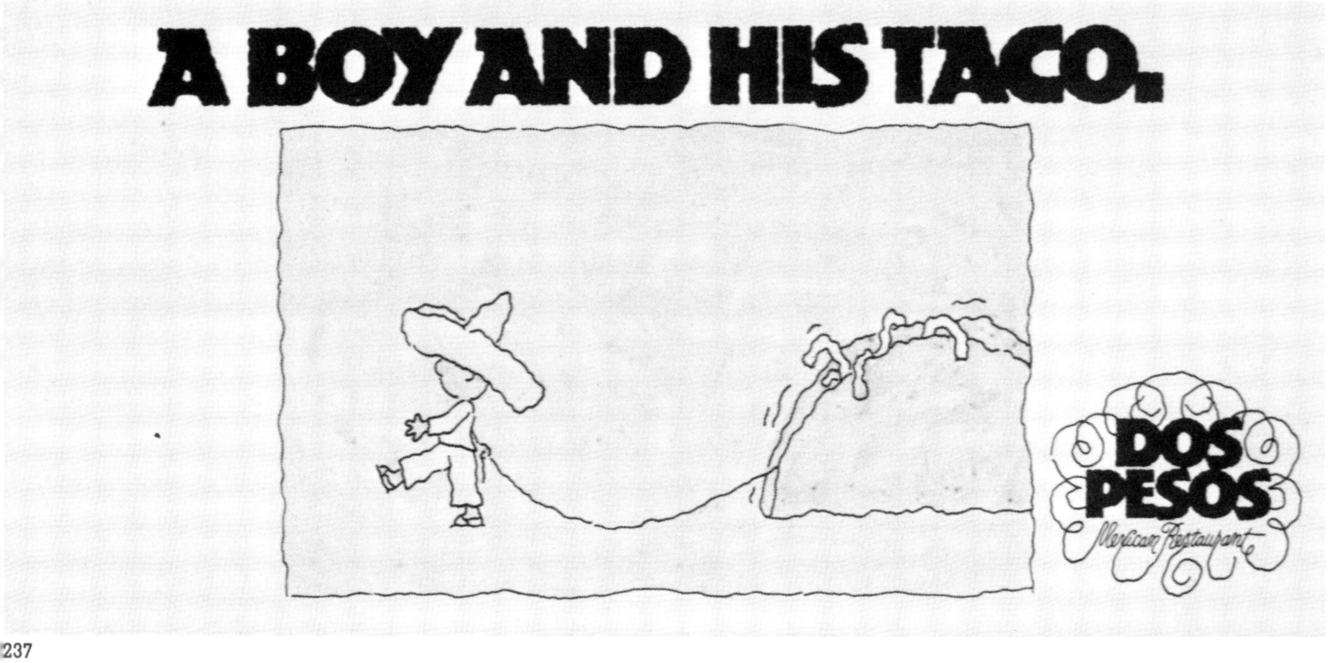
A BOY AND HIS TACO.
DOS PESOS
Mexican Restaurant

If you think she's beautiful now wait till you see her move.
Aqueduct.
The fastest animals in the world. Thoroughbred racing October 14 through January 4.

238

You don't have to leave the city to get away from it all.
Aqueduct.
The fastest animals in the world. Thoroughbred racing through July 27.
First race 1:30.

239

238
Art Director Richard Brown
Writer Rick Johnson
Designer Richard Brown
Photographer Steve Steigmann
Agency McCann-Erickson
Client New York Racing Assoc.

239
Art Director Richard Brown
Writer Rich Johnson
Designer Richard Brown
Photographer Gus Boyd
Agency McCann-Erickson
Client New York Racing Assoc.

Now
you can
save your bread
where you buy
your butter.
Announcing Citibank at Pathmark.
A full service bank in a supermarket.
Member FDIC

240

Eat,
eat, eat.
Doesn't anybody drink anymore?
CHARLEY'S
EATING &
DRINKING
SALOON
LADIES INVITED/344 NEWBURY ST./267-8645 · CHESTNUT HILL MALL/244-1200

241

240
Art Director Nick Scordato
Writer Mike Bookman
Designer Nick Scordato
Agency Doherty, Mann & Olshan
Client First National City Corp.

241
Art Director Tony Viola
Writers Tony Winch
Seumas McGuire
Designer Dick Pantano
Artist Tony Viola
Agency Hill, Holliday,
Connors, Cosmopulos
Client Charley's Eating &
Drinking Saloon

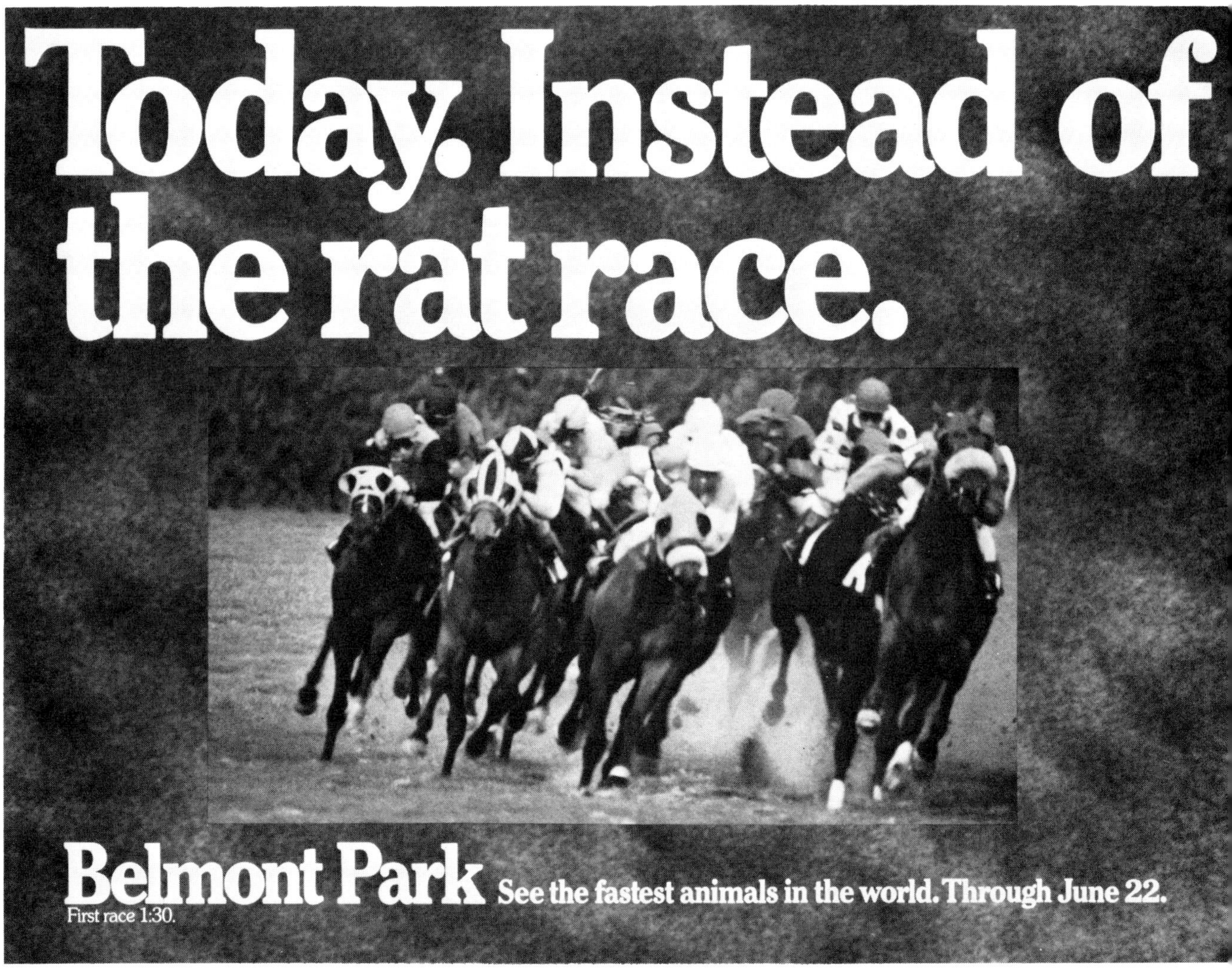
Today. Instead of the rat race.
Belmont Park
See the fastest animals in the world. Through June 22.
First race 1:30.

242

242
Art Director Harvey Gabor
Writer Rick Johnston
Designer Harvey Gabor
Photographer Gus Boyd
Agency McCann-Erickson
Client New York Racing Assoc.

"The Pursuit of Youth"
A Xerox Season Presentation. Thursday, May 30.
10 P.M. EDT on NBC-TV Network.
Americans spend an incredible amount of time and billions of dollars trying to make themselves look young.
On May 30, Xerox will sponsor a 60-minute special exploring our obsession with youth, and why we are afraid to grow old.
Tune in. It won't make you any younger but it may make you a little wiser.
XEROX

243

THE QUALITY OF MY PARTS IS EQUAL TO THE WHOLE.
Frank Perdue
That's why you should always look for Perdue tagged chicken parts.
They're the only ones that come from my fresh, young Perdue chickens. And they're the only ones covered by my money-back quality guarantee.
Why buy parts from a chicken you wouldn't buy whole?
IT TAKES A TOUGH MAN TO MAKE TENDER CHICKEN PARTS.

244

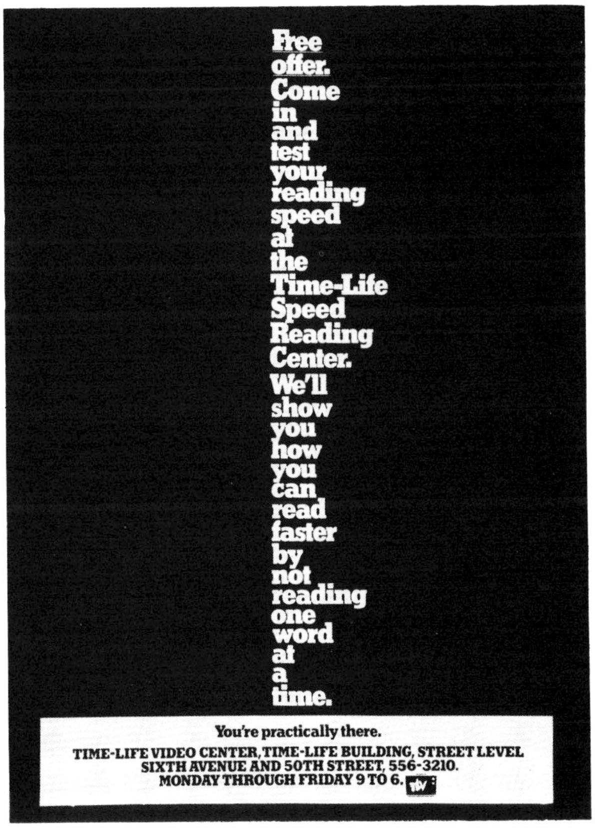
Free offer. Come in and test your reading speed at the Time-Life Speed Reading Center. We'll show you how you can read faster by not reading one word at a time.
You're practically there.
TIME-LIFE VIDEO CENTER, TIME-LIFE BUILDING, STREET LEVEL
SIXTH AVENUE AND 50TH STREET, 556-3210.
MONDAY THROUGH FRIDAY 9 TO 6.

245

GOLD

SILVER

243
Art Director Allen Kay
Writer Lloyd Fink
Photographer Carl Fischer
Agency Needham, Harper & Steers
Client Xerox Corp.

244
Art Director Sam Scali
Writer Edward A. McCabe
Photographer Phil Mazzurco
Agency Scali, McCabe, Sloves
Client Perdue Farms

245
Art Director Bill Weinstein
Writer Lawrence Brown
Designer Bill Weinstein
Agency Scali, McCabe, Sloves
Client Time-Life Video

Get the best of everything. Adopt a mutt.
The smarts of a Lassie.
The spots of a Dalmatian.
The friendliness of a Beagle.
The bark of a Shepherd.
The heart of a St. Bernard.
The paw of a Great Dane.
Bring home a genuine All-American Mutt from the MSPCA and get everything you're looking for, all in one dog.
There are lots of genuine All-American Alley Kittens waiting for you too. Just come to the MSPCA Adoption Ward, 180 Longwood Ave., Boston. We're open 10:30 to 3:30, Monday through Saturday.
Massachusetts Society for the Prevention of Cruelty to Animals.

246

Now you can prove your dog is a genuine, All-American Mutt.
M.S.P.C.A.
ALL-AMERICAN MUTT
REGISTRATION CERTIFICATE
When you adopt a pup from the MSPCA, you get a certificate just like this one to prove he's a genuine, All-American Mutt.
Our All-American Alley Kittens have papers, too!
They're all waiting for you at the MSPCA Adoption Ward, 180 Longwood Avenue, Boston. Come in 10:30 to 3:30, Monday through Saturday. We guarantee you'll leave with the best of everything.
Massachusetts Society for the Prevention of Cruelty to Animals.
Get the best of everything. Adopt a mutt.

247

If you can't decide between a Shepherd, a Setter or a Poodle, get them all.
Adopt a mutt at the MSPCA and get everything you're looking for, all in one dog. The intelligence of a poodle and the loyalty of a lassie. The bark of a shepherd and the heart of a Saint Bernard. The spots of a Dalmatian, the size of a schnauzer, and the speed of a greyhound. A genuine, all-American mutt has it all.
And the MSPCA has lots of all-American mutts waiting for you. There are genuine, all-American alley kittens, too. Just come to the MSPCA Adoption Ward, 180 Longwood Avenue, Boston. We're open 10:30 to 3:30, Monday through Saturday.
Massachusetts Society for the Prevention of Cruelty to Animals.
Get the best of everything. Adopt a mutt.

248

246
Art Directors June Corley, Mary Moore
Writers Katina Mills, Veronica Nash
Photographer David Doss
Agency Humphrey Browning MacDougall
Client Massachusetts Society for the Prevention of Cruelty to Animals

247
Art Directors June Corley, Mary Moore
Writers Katina Mills, Veronica Nash
Artist Joe Patti
Photographer David Doss
Agency Humphrey Browning MacDougall
Client Massachusetts Society for the Prevention of Cruelty to Animals

248
Art Directors June Corley, Mary Moore
Writers Katina Mills, Veronica Nash
Photographer David Doss
Agency Humphrey Browning MacDougall
Client Massachusetts Society for the Prevention of Cruelty to Animals

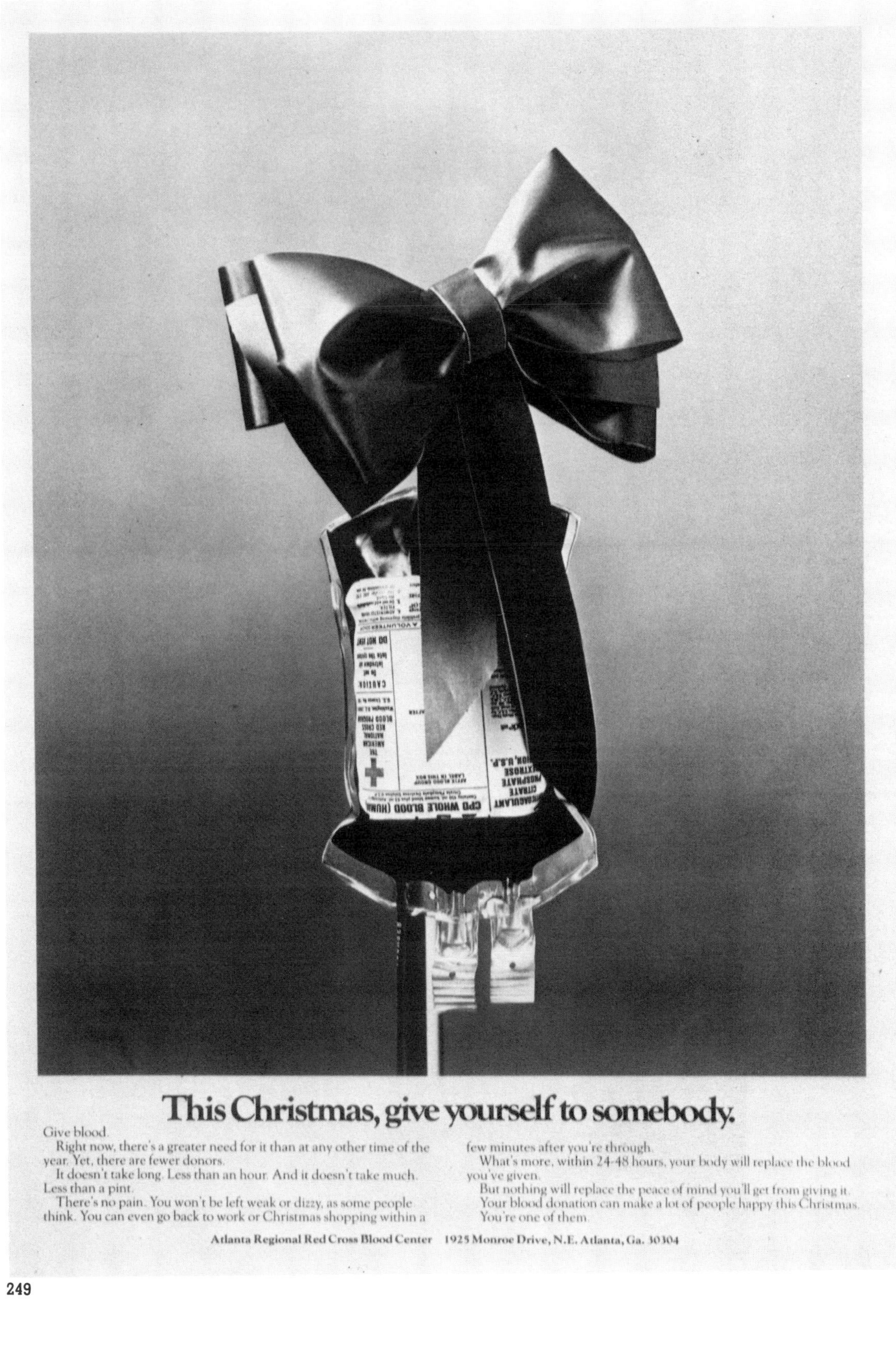
This Christmas, give yourself to somebody.
Give blood.
Right now, there's a greater need for it than at any other time of the year. Yet, there are fewer donors.
It doesn't take long. Less than an hour. And it doesn't take much. Less than a pint.
There's no pain. You won't be left weak or dizzy, as some people think. You can even go back to work or Christmas shopping within a few minutes after you're through.
What's more, within 24-48 hours, your body will replace the blood you've given.
But nothing will replace the peace of mind you'll get from giving it.
Your blood donation can make a lot of people happy this Christmas.
You're one of them.
Atlanta Regional Red Cross Blood Center 1925 Monroe Drive, N.E. Atlanta, Ga. 30304

249

249

Art Director Bill Sweney
Writer Russ Dymond
Designer Bill Sweney
Photographer Arthur Tilley
Agency Lawler Ballard Little
Client Red Cross, Metropolitan Atlanta Chapter

You're afraid to drive through a neighborhood like this.
Imagine what it's like to live there.
There are muggers in there. And rapists. And addicts. Not to mention fires, and filth, and rats.
Yet people still live there.
In fact, there isn't even a problem filling those tenements. Because for many members of Cleveland minorities, it's the only housing they can get.
Prejudice built these slums. And it's keeping people in them.
The answer, the only answer, to neighborhoods like this is open housing in all communities.
To an extent, that will be reached through fair housing laws and complete enforcement of those laws.
But more importantly, open housing depends on individual action. It depends on you.
If you're a renter, or a landlord, or if you're buying or selling real estate, find out how you can help assure fair housing to every Clevelander.
Call Operation Equality at 295-1600.
You may be able to avoid that neighborhood.
But the person behind you may have to go in there. And stop.
Operation Equality, 4102 Lee Road; Joseph H. Battle, Director. An affiliate of the Urban League of Cleveland.

250

From oil, she knows nothing.
She knows fear and sorrow and loneliness.
One woman. Alone.
One of thousands of new immigrants in Israel, familiar with the frustrations of waiting. For a visa, a train, a place to sleep, a plate of food.
One of thousands of aged in New York, familiar with the frustrations of waiting. For a safe place to live, someone to care, a reason for living.
She needs all the help we can give. For it is up to us, the Jewish community, to care for all of our aged here at home and overseas. To house, clothe, heal, sustain them. To maintain the social welfare and health services vital to their lives.
The issue is survival. Survival of the Jewish community, the Jewish spirit, the Jewish future. The price runs higher today than ever before. But, working together, we will meet it.
Help her to know that, as Jews:
We are one.
The Israel Emergency Fund
United Jewish Appeal of Greater New York
Federation of Jewish Philanthropies
of Greater New York

251

Some people call him a pusher.
But he's really a magician.
In six weeks he can turn you into an animal.
It takes more to stop crime than police alone. It takes a community dedicated to stopping the kind of vermin that commit crimes.
Because as long as you allow the pushers, thieves, rapists, murderers and other criminals to hide beneath the surface of the city, they'll go right on committing their ugly crimes.
Until someday they affect you, or somebody close to you. If they haven't already.
So if you have good reason to suspect someone of committing a crime, call the Minneapolis Police Department. Anonymously.
Trap the rat, before he traps you.
Rat on a Rat. Call 348-2179

252

250
Art Director Tom Gilday
Writer Mike Faems
Photographer Jan Czyrba
Agency Griswold-Eshleman
Client Urban League of Cleveland

251
Art Director Dick Thomas
Writer Dick Lord
Designer Irena Steckiv
Agency Lord, Geller, Federico
Client United Jewish Appeal Federation of Jewish Philanthropies

252
Art Director Ron Anderson
Writer Tom McElligott
Designer Ron Anderson
Photographer Gregory Edwards
Agency Knox Reeves Advertising
Client Minneapolis Police Department

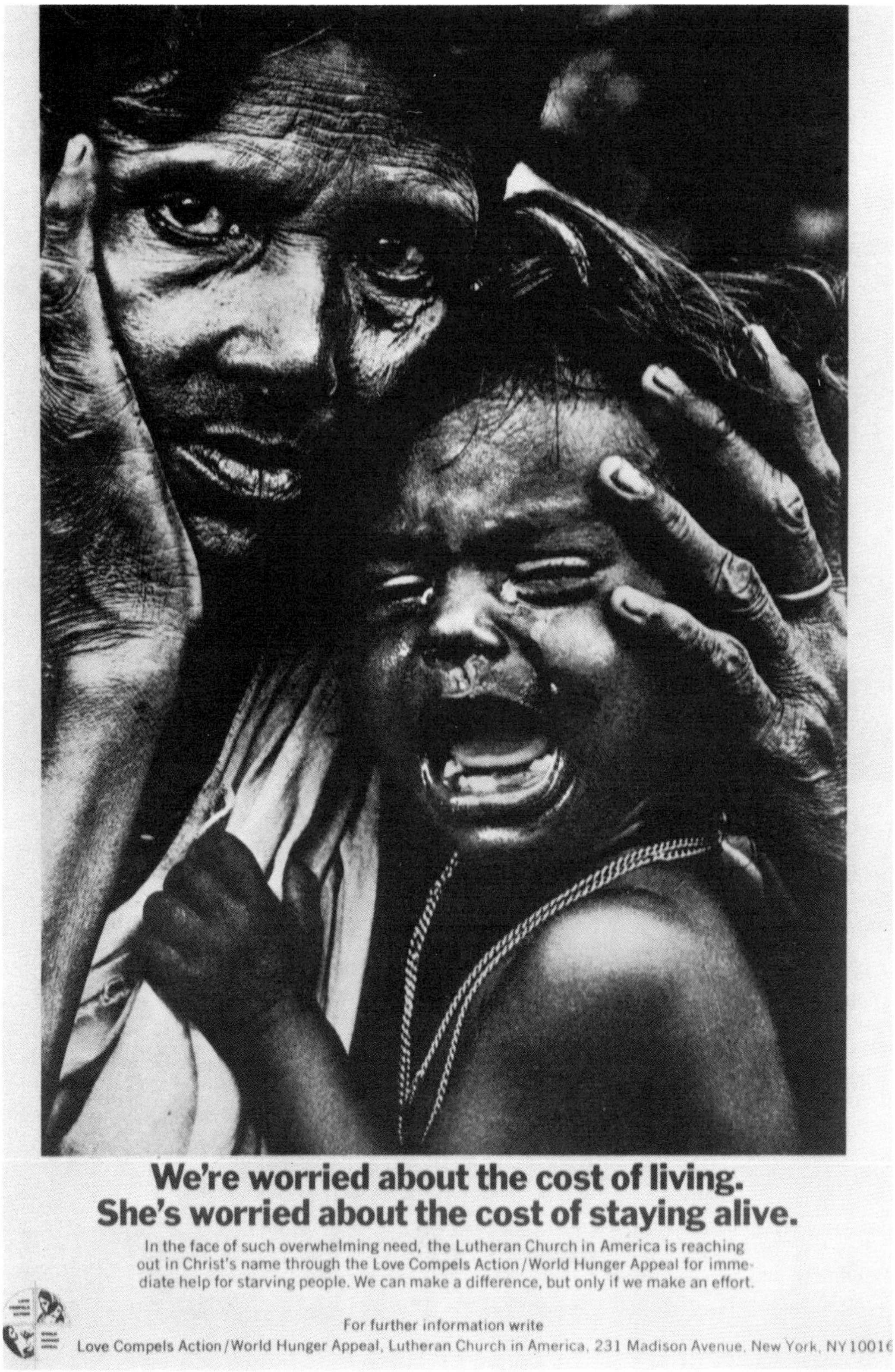
We're worried about the cost of living.
She's worried about the cost of staying alive.
In the face of such overwhelming need, the Lutheran Church in America is reaching out in Christ's name through the Love Compels Action/World Hunger Appeal for immediate help for starving people. We can make a difference, but only if we make an effort.
For further information write
Love Compels Action/World Hunger Appeal, Lutheran Church in America, 231 Madison Avenue, New York, NY 10016

253

GOLD

253
Art Director Brian O'Neill
Writers Jon Bittmann
Brian O'Neill
Designer Brian O'Neill
Photographer Donald McCullin
Agency Brian O'Neill Design
Client Lutheran Church in America

254
Art Director Alan Kupchick
Writer Enid Futterman
Designer Alan Kupchick
Photographer Joe Toto
Agency Grey Advertising
Client New York State Board of Adoption

255
Art Director Alan Kupchick
Writer Enid Futterman
Designer Alan Kupchick
Photographer Joe Toto
Agency Grey Advertising
Client New York State Board of Adoption

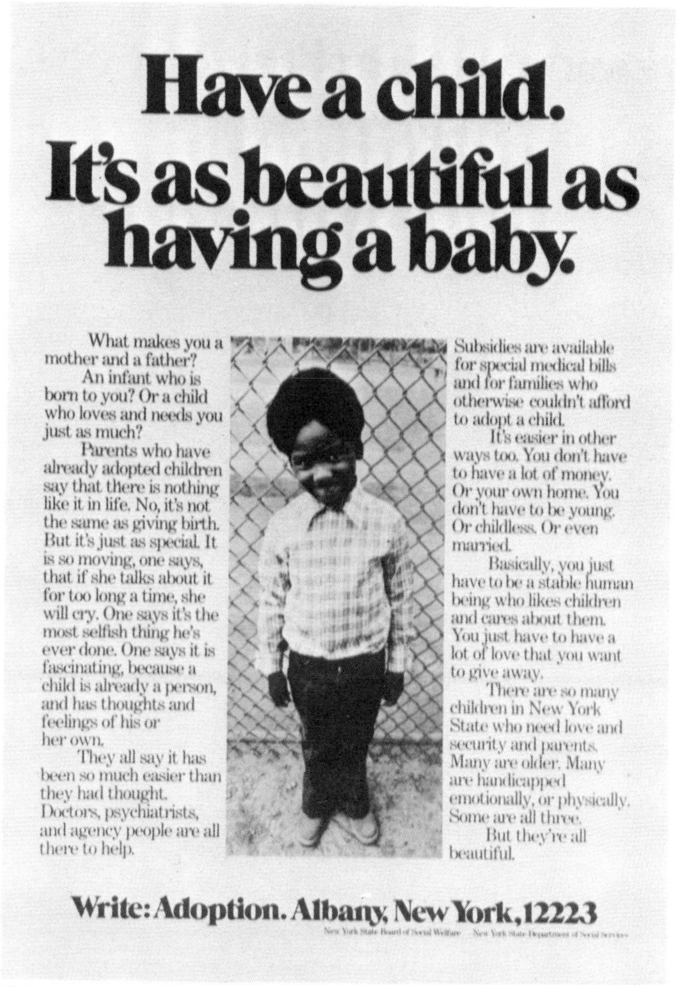
Have a child.
It's as beautiful as having a baby.
What makes you a mother and a father?
An infant who is born to you? Or a child who loves and needs you just as much?
Parents who have already adopted children say that there is nothing like it in life. No, it's not the same as giving birth. But it's just as special. It is so moving, one says, that if she talks about it for too long a time, she will cry. One says it's the most selfish thing he's ever done. One says it is fascinating, because a child is already a person, and has thoughts and feelings of his or her own.
They all say it has been so much easier than they had thought. Doctors, psychiatrists, and agency people are all there to help.
Subsidies are available for special medical bills and for families who otherwise couldn't afford to adopt a child.
It's easier in other ways too. You don't have to have a lot of money. Or your own home. You don't have to be young. Or childless. Or even married.
Basically, you just have to be a stable human being who likes children and cares about them. You just have to have a lot of love that you want to give away.
There are so many children in New York State who need love and security and parents. Many are older. Many are handicapped emotionally, or physically. Some are all three.
But they're all beautiful.
Write: Adoption. Albany, New York, 12223

254

How to have a child:
First, want a child. Even if that child is older or handicapped. If you really want to be a parent, you will probably be a good one.
Second, contact an adoption agency. There aren't many rules anymore. You just have to be stable, at least 21, and have a steady income. You don't have to be young, childless, married or rich. You don't have to own your home.
Third, get to know your caseworker so he or she can help you choose the right child. Look at pictures together, and talk about the children and what they're like. Until you think you've found your child.
Fourth, meet your child and bring him, or her, home for six months.
Last and best, go to court and adopt your child. Forever.
Except for a few small details, that's about it. Write to the address below, if you would like to receive a brochure with more information. Adopting a child is much simpler than you thought. And more beautiful than you could imagine.
Have a child. It's as beautiful as having a baby.
Write: Adoption. Albany, New York, 12223
New York State Board of Social Welfare
New York State Department of Social Services

255

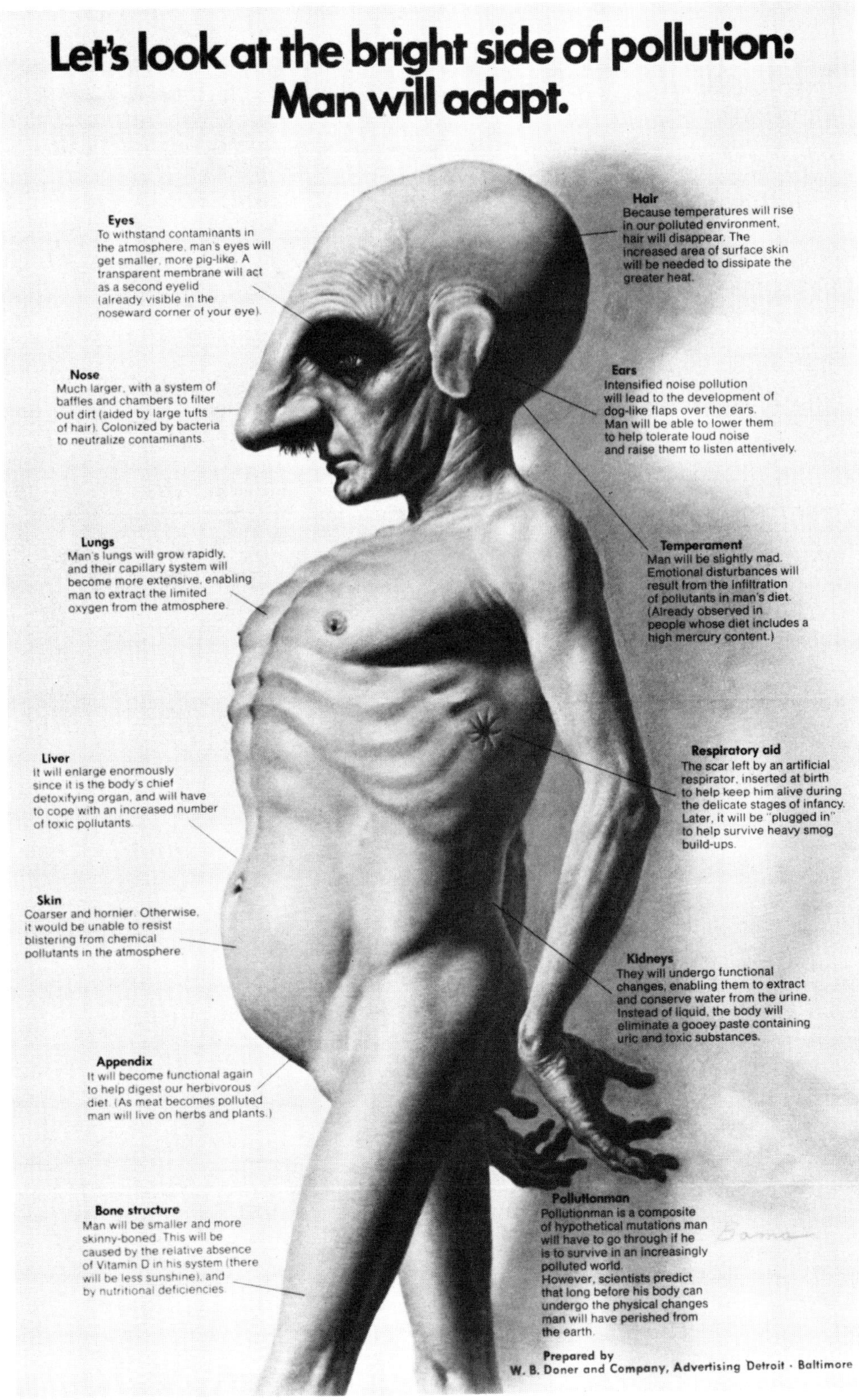
Let's look at the bright side of pollution: Man will adapt.
Eyes
To withstand contaminants in the atmosphere, man's eyes will get smaller, more pig-like. A transparent membrane will act as a second eyelid (already visible in the noseward corner of your eye).
Hair
Because temperatures will rise in our polluted environment, hair will disappear. The increased area of surface skin will be needed to dissipate the greater heat.
Nose
Much larger, with a system of baffles and chambers to filter out dirt (aided by large tufts of hair). Colonized by bacteria to neutralize contaminants.
Ears
Intensified noise pollution will lead to the development of dog-like flaps over the ears. Man will be able to lower them to help tolerate loud noise and raise them to listen attentively.
Lungs
Man's lungs will grow rapidly, and their capillary system will become more extensive, enabling man to extract the limited oxygen from the atmosphere.
Temperament
Man will be slightly mad. Emotional disturbances will result from the infiltration of pollutants in man's diet. (Already observed in people whose diet includes a high mercury content.)
Liver
It will enlarge enormously since it is the body's chief detoxifying organ, and will have to cope with an increased number of toxic pollutants.
Respiratory aid
The scar left by an artificial respirator, inserted at birth to help keep him alive during the delicate stages of infancy. Later, it will be "plugged in" to help survive heavy smog build-ups.
Skin
Coarser and hornier. Otherwise, it would be unable to resist blistering from chemical pollutants in the atmosphere.
Kidneys
They will undergo functional changes, enabling them to extract and conserve water from the urine. Instead of liquid, the body will eliminate a gooey paste containing uric and toxic substances.
Appendix
It will become functional again to help digest our herbivorous diet. (As meat becomes polluted man will live on herbs and plants.)
Bone structure
Man will be smaller and more skinny-boned. This will be caused by the relative absence of Vitamin D in his system (there will be less sunshine), and by nutritional deficiencies.
Pollutionman
Pollutionman is a composite of hypothetical mutations man will have to go through if he is to survive in an increasingly polluted world. However, scientists predict that long before his body can undergo the physical changes man will have perished from the earth.
Bama
Prepared by
W. B. Doner and Company, Advertising Detroit · Baltimore

256

256
Art Director Steve LaGattuta
Writer Jim Herbert
Designer Steve LaGattuta
Artist James Bama
Agency W. B. Doner & Co.
Client W. B. Doner & Co.

"When I grow up I wanna be a pimp like the guy next door."
Kids take their heroes where they find them.
When a boy growing up in the ghetto sees a pimp, he sees a big, beautiful, block-long car. A girl sees that hookers have fancy clothes. Numbers runners have money, pushers have cool.
If they've never seen any better, how can they know any better?
That's why we've got to be there too. In the same neighborhood. On the same streets.
At a Neighborhood Center, a kid can find everything from a cub scout pack to drug counseling. From a part-time job to a free breakfast.
While we're getting families into new apartments, we're getting rats out of old ones.
While we're teaching one kid how to read a newspaper, we're teaching his older brother how to print one.
We figure the more a kid learns about himself and the rest of the world, the more heroes he'll have to choose from.
And the better his choice will be.
232 Madison Avenue, New York, N.Y. 10016
National Federation of Settlements
The other heroes on the block.

257

257
Art Director Merrick Gagliano
Writers Ritch Kassof
SRA Copy Group
Photographer Mike Raab
Agency Shaller Rubin Assoc.
Client National Federation of Settlements

"We just had a ten year old boy."
"Adopting Steven has been like giving birth in a lot of ways. After all, even though he has already lived for ten years, he's brand new to us.
I don't think I can explain to you what I felt the night Steven came home to us. After so many years of so many homes he wanted to believe he was really home at last. But he was afraid to.
When I told him that this would be his room until he grew up, I could almost see the fear going away. No one had ever said that before, and Steven knew it. He just looked at me for a long time until he was sure I wasn't lying. He looked at his father the same way. And he smiled. It was the first time we had ever seen him smile.
I think we were all born that night."
There are so many children in New York who need parents. And just about all you need to have, is love to give.
Many of the children are older. Many are handicapped emotionally, or physically. Some are all three.
But they're all beautiful.
Have a child. It's as beautiful as having a baby.
Write: Adoption. Albany, New York, 12223

258

"Someday I'm gonna be a rich hooker and wear all those beautiful clothes."
A prostitute's wardrobe has to look good to a girl whose new clothes are her sister's old ones.
And how can a kid whose family's never owned a car help envying a pimp with a flashy one? Who has more money than a numbers runner? More cool than a pusher?
Every kid needs a hero. The trouble is, the ghetto doesn't give you all that much of a choice.
That's why Neighborhood Centers have to be there.
At a Center, kids discover people who want to do something for them, instead of to them.
They can learn how to read from Sesame Street or learn about drugs from someone who's been on the street.
They can get into scouting. Spend the summer on a job instead of on the corner. See a doctor when they have to, make a friend when they want to.
At a Neighborhood Center, kids find more than their heroes. They find themselves.
232 Madison Avenue, New York, N.Y. 10016
National Federation of Settlements
The other heroes on the block.

259

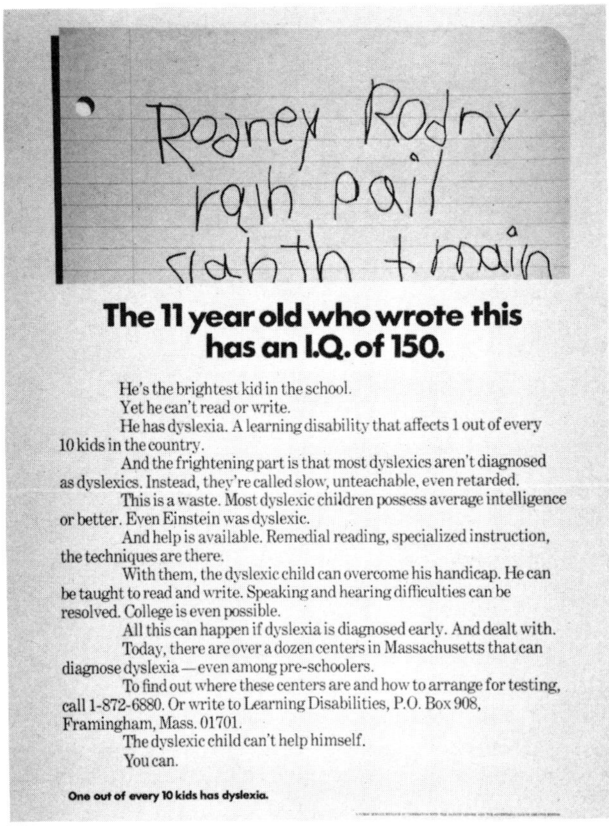
Roaney Rodny
raih pail
The 11 year old who wrote this has an I.Q. of 150.
He's the brightest kid in the school.
Yet he can't read or write.
He has dyslexia. A learning disability that affects 1 out of every 10 kids in the country.
And the frightening part is that most dyslexics aren't diagnosed as dyslexics. Instead, they're called slow, unteachable, even retarded.
This is a waste. Most dyslexic children possess average intelligence or better. Even Einstein was dyslexic.
And help is available. Remedial reading, specialized instruction, the techniques are there.
With them, the dyslexic child can overcome his handicap. He can be taught to read and write. Speaking and hearing difficulties can be resolved. College is even possible.
All this can happen if dyslexia is diagnosed early. And dealt with.
Today, there are over a dozen centers in Massachusetts that can diagnose dyslexia—even among pre-schoolers.
To find out where these centers are and how to arrange for testing, call 1-872-6880. Or write to Learning Disabilities, P.O. Box 908, Framingham, Mass. 01701.
The dyslexic child can't help himself.
You can.
One out of every 10 kids has dyslexia.

260

SILVER

258
Art Director Alan Kupchick
Writer Enid Futterman
Designer Alan Kupchick
Photographer Joe Toto
Agency Grey Advertising
Client New York State Board of Adoption

259
Art Director Merrick Gagliano
Writers Ritch Kassof
SRA Copy Group
Photographer Mike Raab
Agency Shaller Rubin Assoc.
Client National Federation of Settlements

260
Art Director Milt Wuilleumier
Writer Ken Henderson
Designer Milt Wuilleumier
Artist Barbara Dubé
Photographer Edward Bishop
Agency Ingalls Assoc.
Client Learning Disabilities

"We just had a ten year old boy."
"Adopting Steven has been like giving birth in a lot of ways. After all, even though he has already lived for ten years, he's brand new to us.
I don't think I can explain to you what I felt the night Steven came home to us. After so many years of so many homes he wanted to believe he was really home at last. But he was afraid to.
When I told him that this would be his room until he grew up, I could almost see the fear going away. No one had ever said that before, and Steven knew it. He just looked at me for a long time until he was sure I wasn't lying. He looked at his father the same way. And he smiled. It was the first time we had ever seen him smile.
I think we were all born that night."
There are so many children in New York who need parents. And just about all you need to have, is love to give.
Many of the children are older. Many are handicapped emotionally, or physically. Some are all three.
But they're all beautiful.
Have a child. It's as beautiful as having a baby.
Write: Adoption. Albany, New York, 12223
New York State Board of Social Welfare New York State Department of Social Services

How to have a child:
First, want a child. Even if that child is older or handicapped. If you really want to be a parent, you will probably be a good one.
Second, contact an adoption agency. There aren't many rules anymore. You just have to be stable, at least 21, and have a steady income. You don't have to be young, childless, married or rich. You don't have to own your home.
Third, get to know your caseworker so he or she can help you choose the right child. Look at pictures together, and talk about the children and what they're like. Until you think you've found your child.
Fourth, meet your child and bring him, or her, home for six months.
Last and best, go to court and adopt your child. Forever.
Except for a few small details, that's about it. Write to the address below, if you would like to receive a brochure with more information. Adopting a child is much simpler than you thought. And more beautiful than you could imagine.
Have a child. It's as beautiful as having a baby.
Write: Adoption. Albany, New York, 12223

Have a child. It's as beautiful as having a baby.
What makes you a mother and a father?
An infant who is born to you? Or a child who loves and needs you just as much?
Parents who have already adopted children say that there is nothing like it in life. No, it's not the same as giving birth. But it's just as special. It is so moving, one says, that if she talks about it for too long a time, she will cry. One says it's the most selfish thing he's ever done. One says it is fascinating, because a child is already a person, and has thoughts and feelings of his or her own.
They all say it has been so much easier than they had thought. Doctors, psychiatrists, and agency people are all there to help.
Subsidies are available for special medical bills and for families who otherwise couldn't afford to adopt a child.
It's easier in other ways too. You don't have to have a lot of money. Or your own home. You don't have to be young. Or childless. Or even married.
Basically, you just have to be a stable human being who likes children and cares about them. You just have to have a lot of love that you want to give away.
There are so many children in New York State who need love and security and parents. Many are older. Many are handicapped emotionally, or physically. Some are all three.
But they're all beautiful.
Write: Adoption. Albany, New York, 12223

261

261
Art Director Alan Kupchick
Writer Enid Futterman
Designer Alan Kupchick
Photographer Joe Toto
Agency Grey Advertising
Client New York State Board of Adoption

If you can't decide between a Shepherd, a Setter or a Poodle, get them all.
Adopt a mutt at the MSPCA and get everything you're looking for, all in one dog. The intelligence of a poodle and the loyalty of a lassie. The bark of a shepherd and the heart of a Saint Bernard. The spots of a Dalmatian, the size of a schnauzer, and the speed of a greyhound.
A genuine, all-American mutt has it all.
And the MSPCA has lots of all-American mutts waiting for you. There are genuine, all-American alley kittens, too. Just come to the MSPCA Adoption Ward, 180 Longwood Avenue, Boston. We're open 10:30 to 3:30, Monday through Saturday.
Massachusetts Society for the Prevention of Cruelty to Animals.
Get the best of everything. Adopt a mutt.

Now you can prove your dog is a genuine, All-American Mutt.
M.S.P.C.A.
ALL-AMERICAN MUTT
REGISTRATION CERTIFICATE
When you adopt a pup from the MSPCA, you get a certificate just like this one to prove he's a genuine, All-American Mutt.
Our All-American Alley Kittens have papers, too!
They're all waiting for you at the MSPCA Adoption Ward, 180 Longwood Avenue, Boston. Come in 10:30 to 3:30, Monday through Saturday. We guarantee you'll leave with the best of everything.
Massachusetts Society for the Prevention of Cruelty to Animals.
Get the best of everything. Adopt a mutt.

262

GOLD

262

Art Directors June Corley
Mary Moore
Writers Katina Mills
Veronica Nash
Artist Joe Patti
Photographer David Doss
Agency Humphrey Browning MacDougall
Client Massachusetts Society for the Prevention of Cruelty to Animals

All the king's horses and all the king's men can't put King Richard together again.

On May 12, 1973, the National Council of the National Emergency Civil Liberties Committee resolved to conduct a campaign for the impeachment of Richard Milhous Nixon, by petition, advertising and public meetings.

Nearly a year later, the impeachment issue has become the most important issue before the nation.

Now, with Congress only moments away from the critical decision it must face, we are publishing this advertisement to ask for your participation by notifying your Congress-person of your position on this issue.

Please fill in the coupons below, and send them immediately to us, together with whatever you can afford, to permit us to place this ad in other publications. We will forward your ballot to Washington.

We have come so far, and we are now so near, and you can help to make the vital difference.

After all, do you know anyone who is proud to have that man as President?

National Impeachment Poll

Name of Representative: ____________
House Office Building, Washington, D.C.

☐ I believe that the Congress should impeach Richard M. Nixon immediately.
☐ I think he should resign.

Name
Address
City State Zip

Enclosed is my contribution of $100, $50, $25, $15, $10, $5, $ ____________

Name
Address
City State Zip

National Emergency Civil Liberties Committee
25 East 26 Street, New York, NY 10010

Edith Tiger, Director
Corliss Lamont, Chairman
Leonard Boudin, General Counsel

263

GOLD

263
Art Director Barbara Schubeck
Writer Dick Calderhead
Artist Marc Nadel
Agency Calderhead, Jackson
Client National Emergency Civil Liberties Committee

ADVERTISING PHOTOGRAPHY & ART

Advertising Photography, b/w	264–266
Advertising Photography, color	267–288
Advertising Art, b/w	289–294
Advertising Art, color	296–304

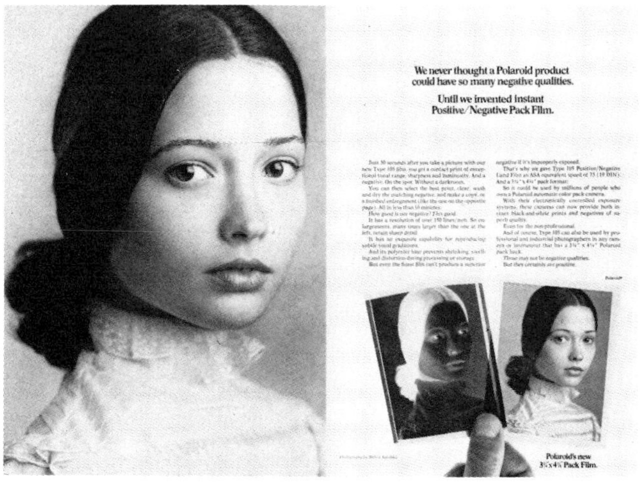

We never thought a Polaroid product could have so many negative qualities.
Until we invented instant Positive/Negative Pack Film.
Polaroid's new 3¼x4¼ Pack Film.

264

"The Pursuit of Youth"
A Xerox Season Presentation. Thursday, May 30.
10 P.M. EDT on NBC-TV Network.
XEROX

265

SILVER

264
Art Director Lee Epstein
Designer Lee Epstein
Photographer Melvin Sokolsky
Writer Hal Silverman
Agency Doyle Dane Bernbach
Client Polaroid Corp.

265
Art Director Allen Kay
Photographer Carl Fischer
Writer Roy Fink
Agency Needham, Harper & Steers
Client Xerox Corp.

The more our neighborhoods grow,
the harder it is to grow up.
GTE

266

Have it made! Quote Newsweek
the world's most quoted newsweekly
COACH
19
12
22
18
31
37
© Newsweek Inc., 1974

267

266
Art Director Bob Starr
Photographer Carl Fischer
Writer Bob Matheo
Agency Doyle, Dane Bernbach
Client GTE

267
Art Director Ed Di Benedetto
Photographer Carl Fischer
Writer Jerry Pfiffner
Agency N. W. Ayer Abh International
Client Newsweek Magazine

149
The city's full of kids who could use a job.
If you run a business, big or small,
give a high school or college kid better things to do
than hang around this summer. Give a kid a job.
And help a kid learn to contribute to life.
We'll make it easy. Write us or call 741-5940.
Give a kid a job this summer.

268

You'll never have a better excuse to buy a Suzuki.
SUZUKI

269

268
Art Director Tony Oliveto
Photographer Carl Fischer
Writer Dorothy Linder
Agency Young & Rubicam International
Client National Alliance of Businessmen

269
Art Director Hal Silverman
Writer Hal Silverman
Designer Hal Silverman
Photographer Marv Lyons
Agency Foote, Cone, Belding
Client Suzuki Motors

THE NIKON IMAGE
A magazine within a magazine devoted to today's great photographs and photographers...and the camera they have in common.
WOLF
"We'd worked for two days, I thought I had the shot, but she said 'I love Mangos, can I eat one?' That's how it happened."

270

270
Art Director Roy Tuck
Designer Roy Tuck
Photographer Henry Wolf
Agency Henry Wolf Productions
Client Nikon Camera

We're expecting a few extra people for dinner tonight.
Today, something we do will touch your life.

271

If you think she's beautiful now wait till you see her move.
4
Aqueduct.
The fastest animals in the world. Thoroughbred racing October 14 through January 4.

272

271
Art Directors Tony Oliveto
Art Harris
Photographers Carl Fischer
Steve Horn
Writers Helio Gonzalez-Adame
Dorothy Linder
Agency Young & Rubicam International
Client Union Carbide

272
Art Director Richard Brown
Designer Richard Brown
Photographer Steve Steigman
Writer Rick Johnson
Agency McCann-Erickson
Client New York Racing Assoc.

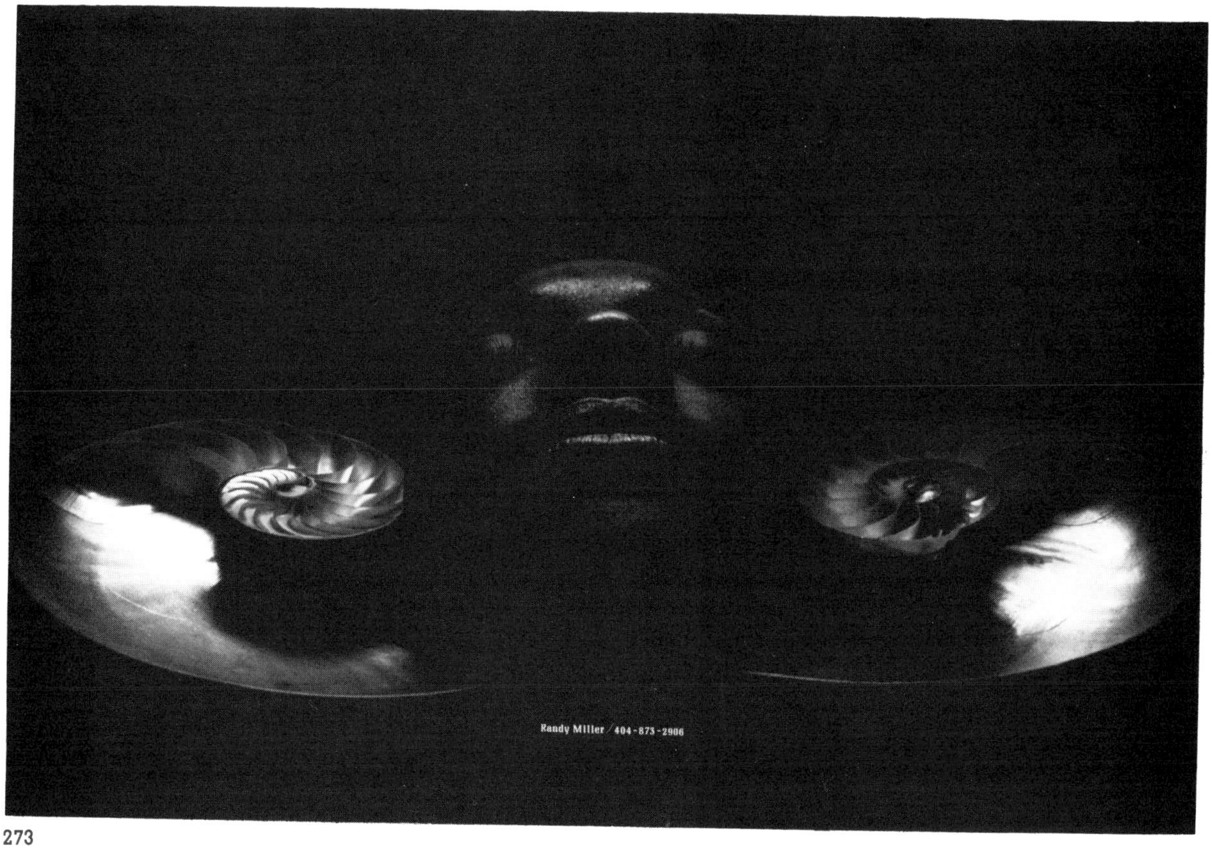
Randy Miller / 404-873-2906

273

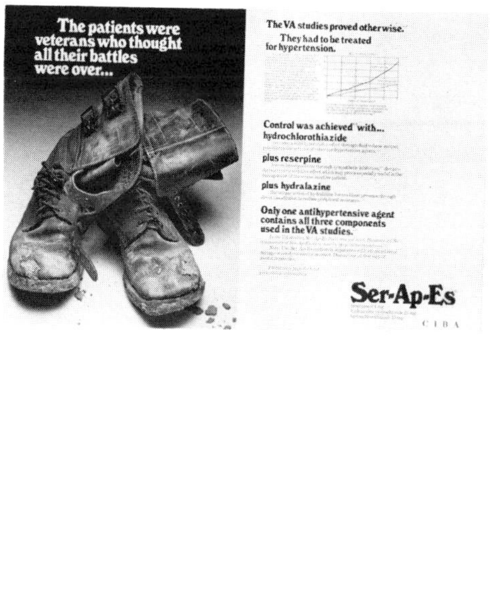
The patients were veterans who thought all their battles were over...
The VA studies proved otherwise.
They had to be treated for hypertension.
Control was achieved with...
hydrochlorothiazide
plus reserpine
plus hydralazine
Only one antihypertensive agent contains all three components used in the VA studies.
Ser-Ap-Es
CIBA

274

273
Art Director Randy Miller
Designer Randy Miller
Photographer Randy Miller
Writer Randy Miller
Agency Randy Miller, Inc.
Client Randy Miller, Inc.

274
Art Director Peter Belliveau
Designer Neil Ferrara
Photographer Al Francekevich
Writer Alan Theodore
Agency William Douglas McAdams
Client Ciba-Geigy Corp.

OBREMSKI
"I'm a perfectionist, and I'll shoot
until I get exactly what I want
...or what's wanted."

275

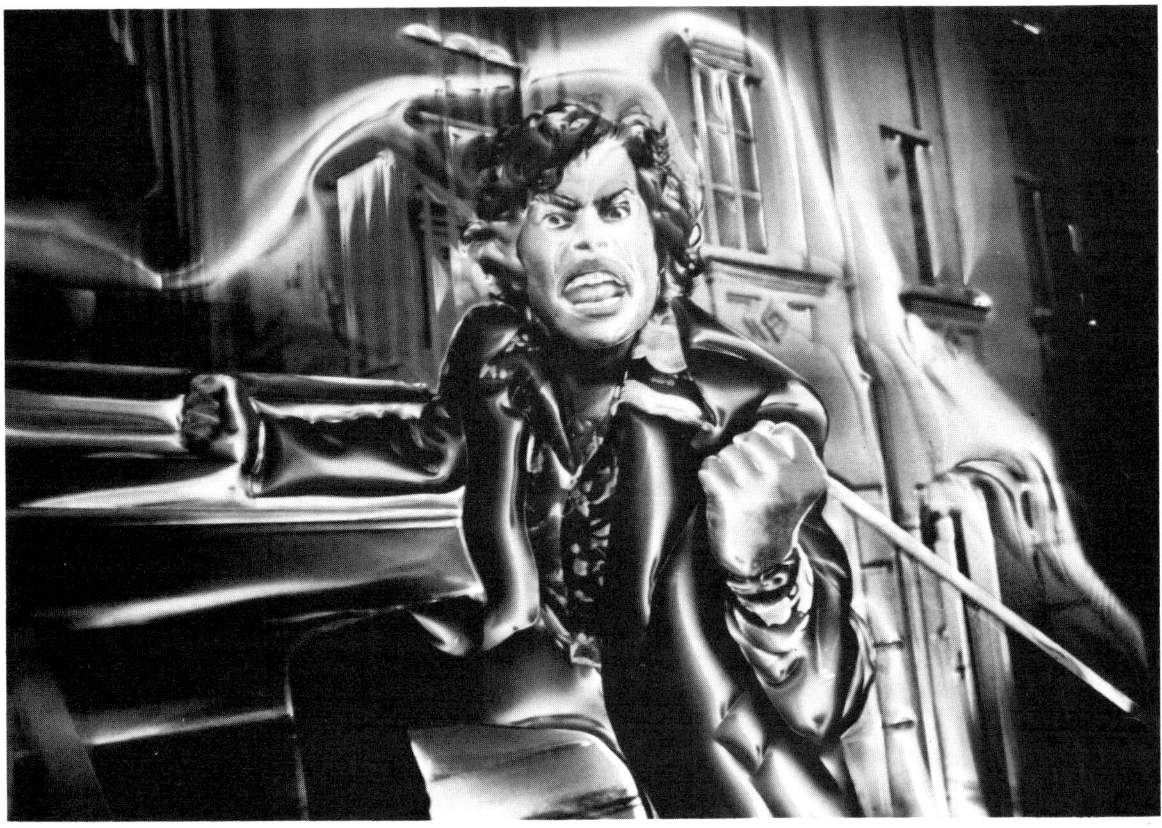

276

275
Art Director Roy Tuck
Designer Roy Tuck
Photographer George Obremski
Writer Bill Irvine
Agency Gilbert, Felix & Sharf
Client Nikon Camera

276
Art Director Marty Minch
Designer Marty Minch
Photographer Robert Monroe
Agency Kallir, Philips, Ross
Client McNeil Laboratories

Think of the computer as energy. As mental energy. Power to get things done. IBM.

277

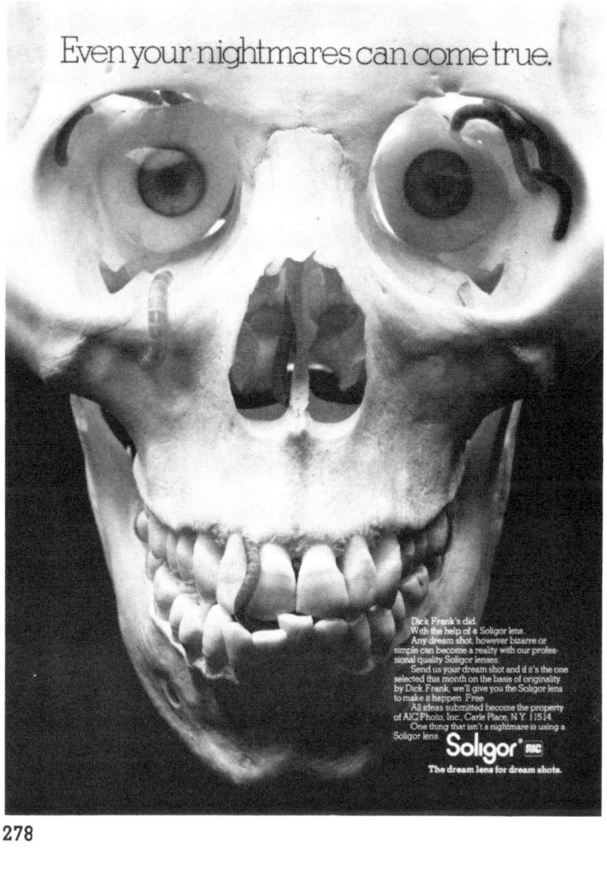
Even your nightmares can come true.
Dick Frank's did.
With the help of a Soligor lens.
Any dream shot, however bizarre or simple can become a reality with our professional quality Soligor lenses.
Send us your dream shot and if it's the one selected this month on the basis of originality by Dick Frank, we'll give you the Soligor lens to make it happen. Free.
All ideas submitted become the property of AIC Photo, Inc., Carle Place, N.Y. 11514.
One thing that isn't a nightmare is using a Soligor lens.
Soligor®
The dream lens for dream shots.

278

277
Art Director Ray Brown
Photographer Jay Maisel
Writer John Jackson
Agency Geer, Du Bois
Client IBM

278
Art Director Lew-Dave-Marv
Designer Lew-Dave-Marv
Photographer Dick Frank
Writer Lew-Dave-Marv
Agency KSS&G
Client Soligor

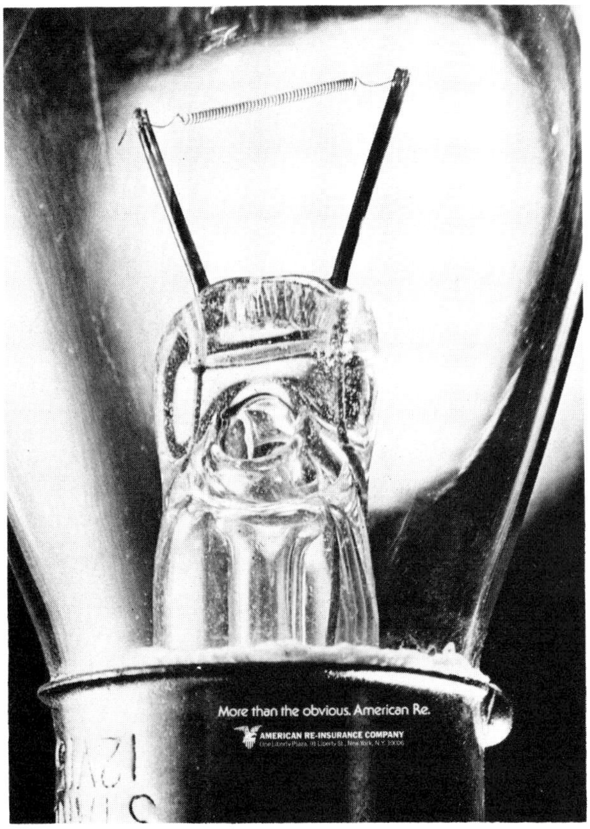
More than the obvious. American Re.
AMERICAN RE-INSURANCE COMPANY

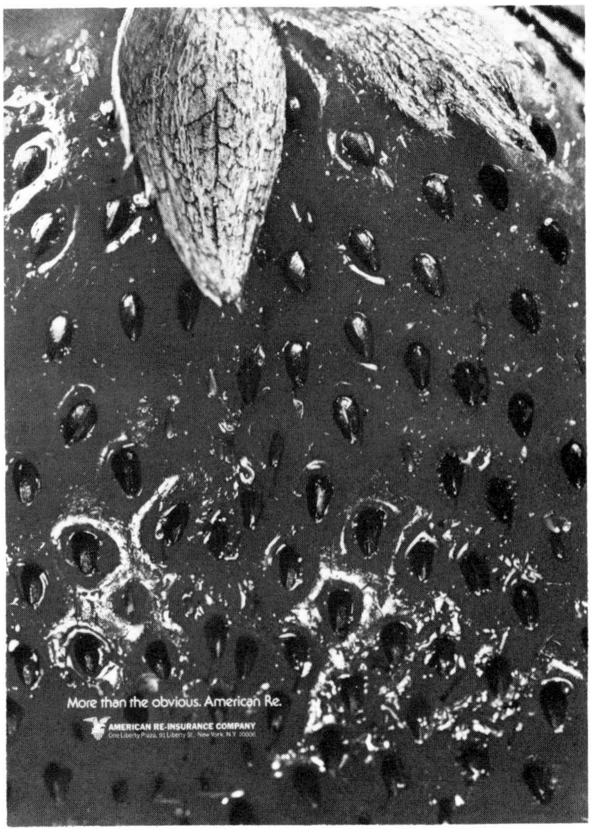
More than the obvious. American Re.
AMERICAN RE-INSURANCE COMPANY

More than the obvious. American Re.
AMERICAN RE-INSURANCE COMPANY

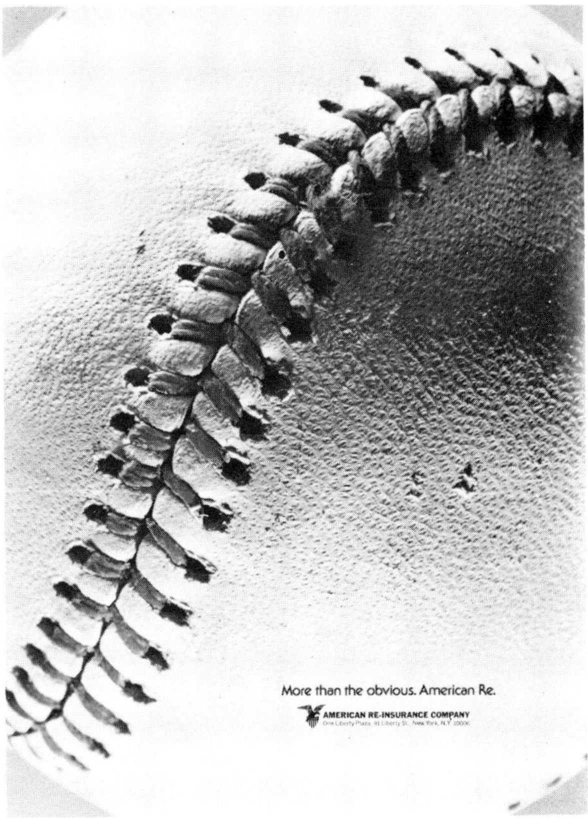
More than the obvious. American Re.
AMERICAN RE-INSURANCE COMPANY

278A

278A

Art Director Richard Murnak
Photographer Michael Geiger
Writer Tom Atkinson
Agency Doremus Uptown
Client American Re-Insurance Co.

ROCK SPRINGS
STORE
CAFE
HOTEL
COCKTAILS
If the people of Rock Springs, Arizona wanted to move their town to Massachusetts, they could.
American's 747 Freighter can do it in one trip.
Yes, we mean the whole town. In one plane. One of American's new 747 Freighters.
Freighter
The whole town includes the service station (with repair shop, tools and gas pumps). The homes with all their furnishings. The Rock Springs restaurant (where you can get a great green chili and Mexican sausage omelet). The hotel. The cafe with bar, tables and chairs, jukebox and pool table. And the general store with all its merchandise.
A total of 200,000 pounds of town.
Just imagine how much of your cargo our 747 Freighter can move with its 20,000 cubic feet of space, about the capacity of five railroad boxcars. Like maybe a six-ton generator, fully assembled. Or a small forest of trees, each eight feet high. Or an entire order of digital display devices. All easily shippable in American's new Ten Footer (96" x 96" x 125") air cargo container. Why, American's 747 Freighter can even take a yacht mast 35 feet long.
We can handle almost anything you want to ship. So contact American Freight. We'll do it safely, efficiently, economically—and fast.
Maybe it won't be a whole town. But then again, you never know.
American Airlines
Freight System

279

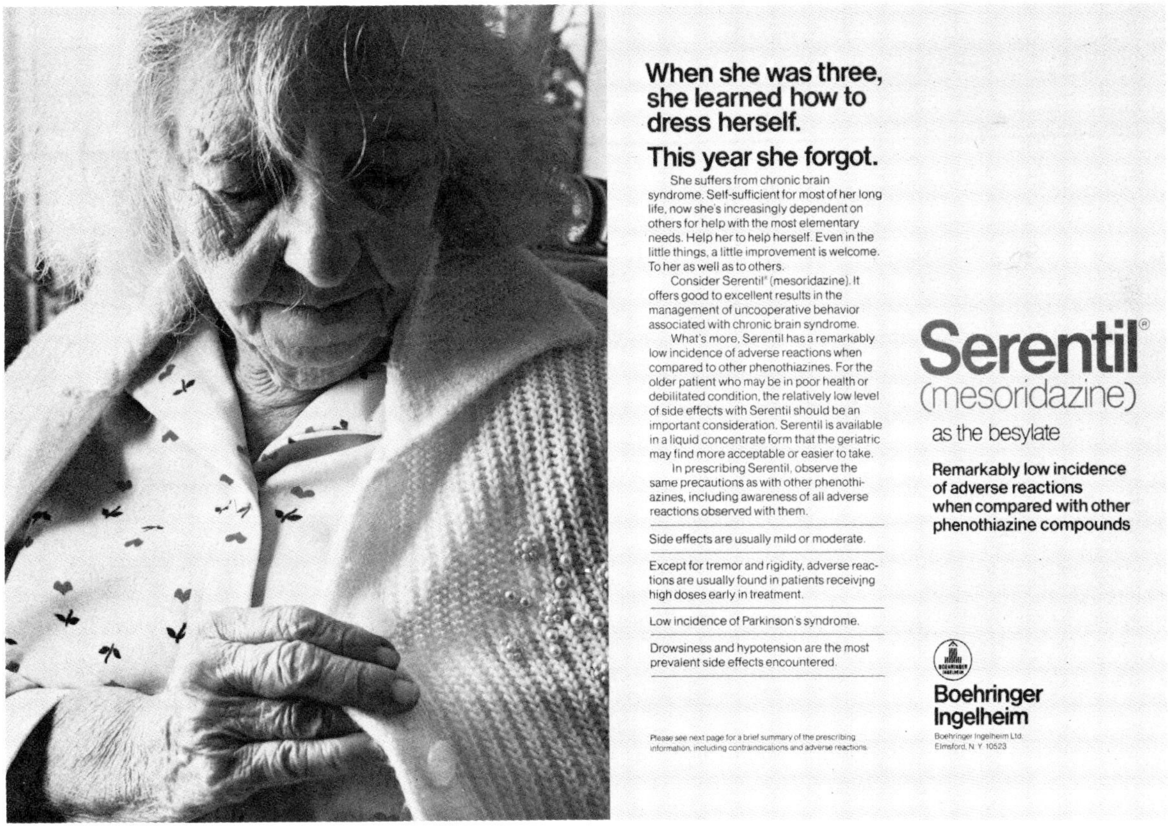
When she was three, she learned how to dress herself.
This year she forgot.
She suffers from chronic brain syndrome. Self-sufficient for most of her long life, now she's increasingly dependent on others for help with the most elementary needs. Help her to help herself. Even in the little things, a little improvement is welcome. To her as well as to others.
Consider Serentil® (mesoridazine). It offers good to excellent results in the management of uncooperative behavior associated with chronic brain syndrome.
What's more, Serentil has a remarkably low incidence of adverse reactions when compared to other phenothiazines. For the older patient who may be in poor health or debilitated condition, the relatively low level of side effects with Serentil should be an important consideration. Serentil is available in a liquid concentrate form that the geriatric may find more acceptable or easier to take.
In prescribing Serentil, observe the same precautions as with other phenothiazines, including awareness of all adverse reactions observed with them.
Side effects are usually mild or moderate.
Except for tremor and rigidity, adverse reactions are usually found in patients receiving high doses early in treatment.
Low incidence of Parkinson's syndrome.
Drowsiness and hypotension are the most prevalent side effects encountered.
Please see next page for a brief summary of the prescribing information, including contraindications and adverse reactions.
Serentil®
(mesoridazine)
as the besylate
Remarkably low incidence of adverse reactions when compared with other phenothiazine compounds
Boehringer Ingelheim
Boehringer Ingelheim Ltd.
Elmsford, N.Y. 10523

280

279
Art Director Lee Gardner
Designer Lee Gardner
Photographer Leon Kuzmanoff
Writer Martin Cohen
Agency Fuller & Smith & Ross
Client American Airlines Freight System

280
Art Director Lew Di Paolo
Designer Lew Di Paolo
Photographer Jack Wallach
Writer Bill Brown
Agency J. Walter Thompson
Client Boehringer-Ingelheim Ltd.

Confused and irrational?
Orientation often begins with
HALDOL
(haloperidol)
a first choice for starting therapy
Helps to correct confused thinking and behavior
Usually leaves patients relatively alert and responsive
Reduces risk of serious adverse reactions

281

Konica takes the worry out of being close.
Macrophotography. Another way to be creative with Konica.
KONICA

283

281
Art Director Marty Minch
Designer Marty Minch
Photographer Robert Monroe
Agency Kallir, Philips, Ross
Client McNeil Laboratories

283
Art Director Lew-Dave-Marv
Designer Lew-Dave-Marv
Photographer Dick Frank
Writer Lew-Dave-Marv
Agency KSS & G
Client Konica Camera Co.

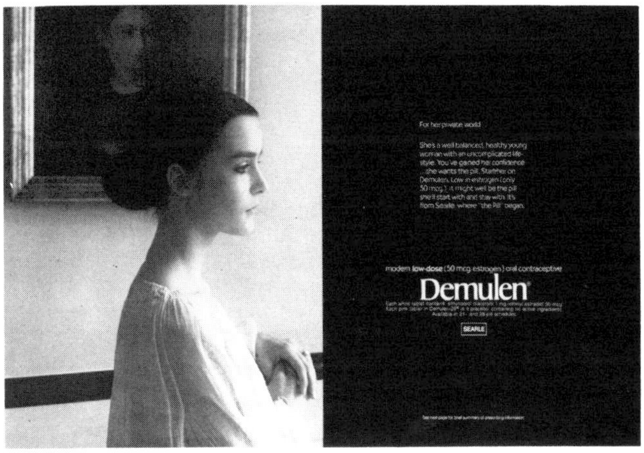
For her private world
modern low-dose (50 mcg estrogen) oral contraceptive
Demulen
SEARLE

284

284
Art Director Bill Alderisio
Designer Bill Alderisio
Photographer David Hamilton
Writer Gemma Just
Agency J. Walter Thompson
Client G. D. Searle & Co.

Slip into JOHNSON'S Baby Powder. It's pure and fresh and natural.
And slipping into JOHNSON'S after you bathe will keep your skin feeling baby soft and smooth and silky.
Before you slip into anything, slip into JOHNSON'S Baby Powder.
It's soft on you.
Johnson & Johnson
Johnson's baby powder
Slip into something soft.
Johnson's baby powder
© J&J 1974

285

285
Art Director Rick Urban
Photographer Gosta Peterson
Writer Morag McEwan
Agency Young & Rubicam International
Client Johnson & Johnson

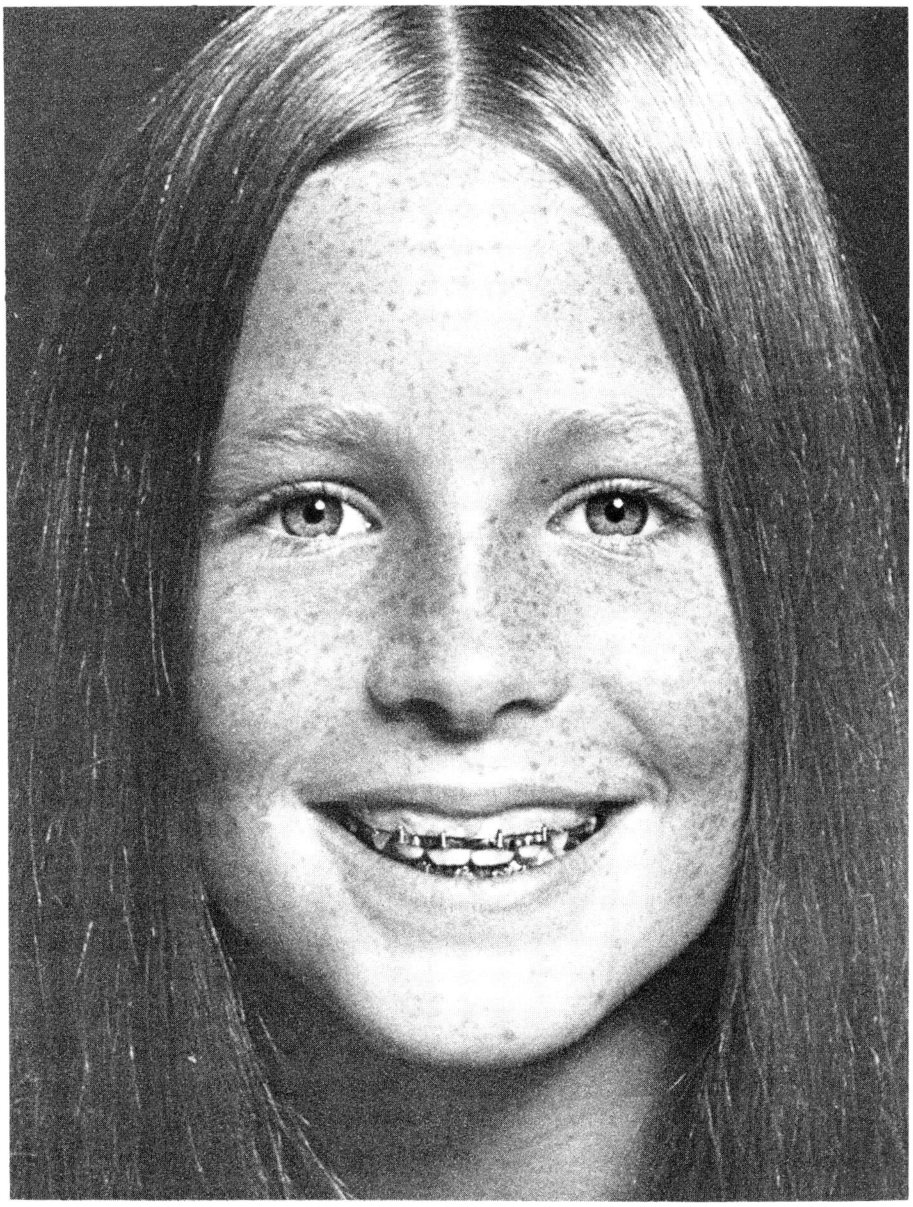

Some of the metals we mine
are more precious than gold.
UNION CARBIDE
Today, something we do
will touch your life.

286

286
Art Director Tony Oliveto
Photographer Carl Fischer
Writer Helio Gonzalez-Adame
Agency Young & Rubicam International
Client Union Carbide

Beautiful things are seldom easy.
ONEIDA
The silver cube. Our silversmiths' mark of excellence.

287

287
Art Directors David Deutsch
Rocco E. Campanelli
Designers David Deutsch
Rocco E. Campanelli
Photographer Ben Somoroff
Writer Robert G. Kilzer
Agency David Deutsch
Client Oneida Ltd. Silversmiths

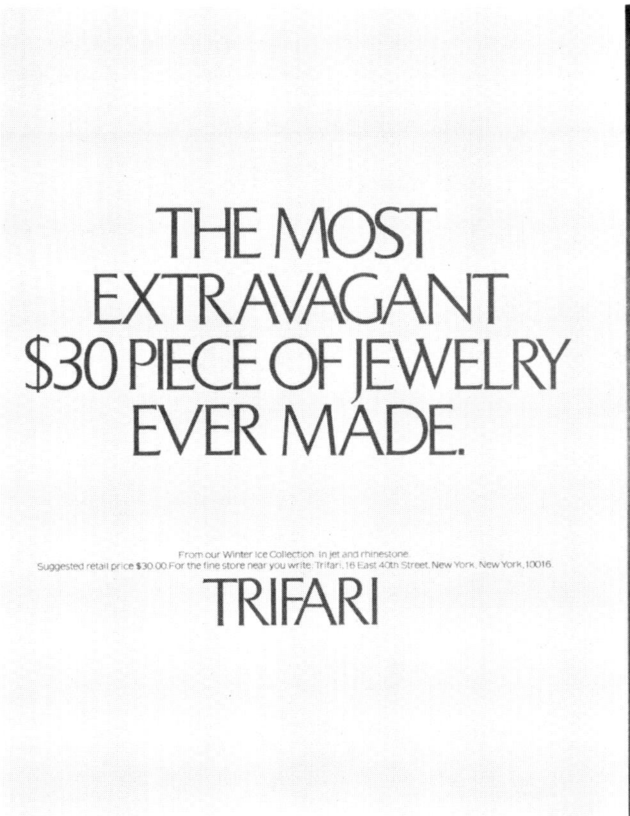
THE MOST EXTRAVAGANT $30 PIECE OF JEWELRY EVER MADE.
From our Winter Ice Collection. In jet and rhinestone.
Suggested retail price $30.00. For the fine store near you write: Trifari, 16 East 40th Street, New York, New York, 10016.
TRIFARI

288

GOLD

288
Art Director Dennis D'Amico
Photographer Michael O'Neill
Writer Dick Tarlow
Agency Sacks, Tarlow & Rosen
Client Trifari, Krussman & Fishel

Soup
SHRIMP BISQUE
There's one thing you often miss in shrimp bisque.
Shrimp.
Searching for shrimp in some shrimp bisques won't do any good.
They just aren't there.
What are there, are some strange little lumps. Pieces of shrimp.
Because some brands of shrimp bisque chop up the shrimp beyond recognition.
But not Hilton's.
Hilton's Shrimp Bisque has tender little shrimp, and lots of them. Plus other good things. Like fresh whole milk, cream, sauterne, onions and savory spices.
The result is a flavorful gourmet bisque with shrimp in nearly every spoonful. Or a superb sauce for fish and seafoods. And an excellent dip, as well.
Next time you decide on soup, decide on Hilton's Shrimp Bisque.
One of Hilton's delicious seafood soups. For people who like seafood as much as they like soup.
Hilton's
SHRIMP BISQUE
You don't have to search for the seafood in Hilton's seafood soups.

With the amount of oysters you find in some oyster stew, you'd think half of them escaped.
No matter how hard you hunt, you won't find many oysters in some brands of oyster stew.
And it isn't because they got away.
It's because they were never there in the first place.
Hilton's believes the main reason you buy oyster stew is for the oysters. So we put plenty of oyster meat in each can of Hilton's Oyster Stew.
We also give you fresh whole milk and pure creamery butter. So what you get is a canned oyster stew as good as homemade.
Hilton's Oyster Stew.
One of Hilton's delicious seafood soups. All with seafood you don't have to search for to find.
Hilton's
OYSTER STEW
You don't have to search for the seafood in Hilton's seafood soups.

289

289
Art Director Marilyn Katz
Designer Marilyn Katz
Artist Dave Willardson
Writer Roger Myers
Agency Van Brunt & Co.
Client New England Fish Co.

290
Art Director Dolores Gudzin
Designer Dolores Gudzin
Artist Wilson McLean
Agency NBC Advertising Dept.
Client National Broadcasting Co.

291
Art Director Dolores Gudzin
Designer Dolores Gudzin
Artist Bill Greer
Agency NBC Advertising Dept.
Client National Broadcasting Co.

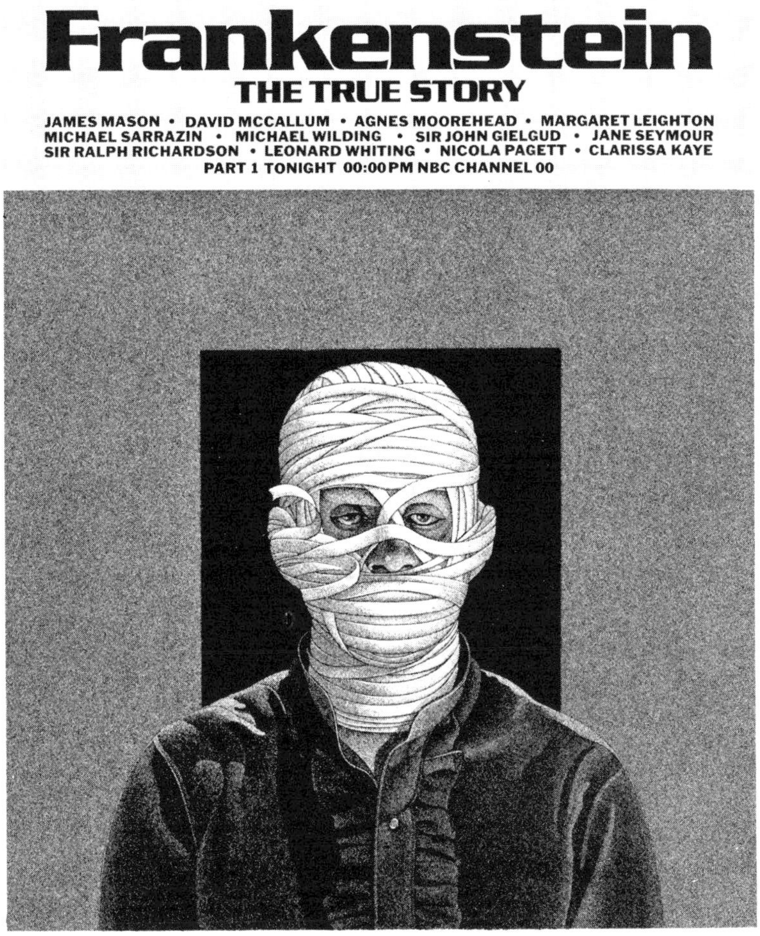
Frankenstein
THE TRUE STORY
JAMES MASON • DAVID McCALLUM • AGNES MOOREHEAD • MARGARET LEIGHTON
MICHAEL SARRAZIN • MICHAEL WILDING • SIR JOHN GIELGUD • JANE SEYMOUR
SIR RALPH RICHARDSON • LEONARD WHITING • NICOLA PAGETT • CLARISSA KAYE
PART 1 TONIGHT 00:00 PM NBC CHANNEL 00

290

world series
0:00PM NBC 00

291

The problem for most agencies isn't getting good advertising out of their people. It's getting good advertising out of their agency.
Anybody who's been around knows that bright creative ideas aren't the prerogative of any one advertising agency.
This business has more than its share of talented people. Tissues and boards of good ads and commercials float around the hallways of most shops.
Then why doesn't the good stuff get out?
Why do so many advertising agencies produce so many ads and commercials that are blah? That are striking only in their dull uniformity. That assault and insult the intelligence of consumers. That are unbelievably unbelievable.
How does it happen? We think the fault lies in the system.
Before the client ever gets to see an ad or commercial, it's usually been taken apart and put back together again by: the copy and art supervisor, group head, associate creative director, creative director, plans review board, the junior, middle and senior account execs, the research people, etc.
With everybody taking their whack out here and adding their piece in there, is it any wonder whatever's left has lost any clarity of design and purpose?
And looks and sounds like every other ad and commercial that's been whacked apart and taped back together again over at some other advertising agency?
We have a simple philosophy at our agency. Hire the best people and then leave them alone to do the work we hired them to do.
It's no surprise that this appeals to the best creative people. We've hired a lot of them. A lot more would like to work here.
What they do at our agency is make ads and commercials.
That's all they do. They don't supervise or administrate.
They get all the information and marketing strategies they need from our account people but they alone create the ads and commercials.
They work unencumbered by outside directives and a plans review board.
As a result, the client gets a chance to see some clear thinking on his products or services.
Ads and commercials that communicate effectively and that consumers find believable and involving.
Advertising that probably wouldn't have gotten past a plans review board.
In many agencies, the cleaning lady shovels more great advertising into her trashwagon than the client ever sees.
Not at ours.
Lee King & Partners, Inc.
360 N. Michigan Ave., Chicago, Illinois 60601

292

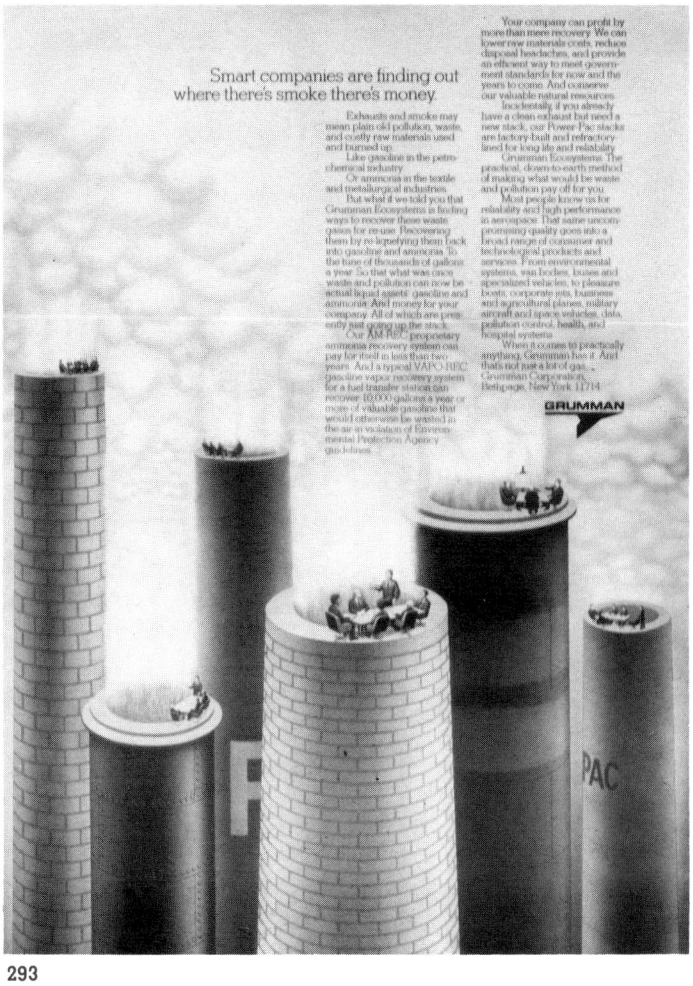
Smart companies are finding out where there's smoke there's money.
Exhausts and smoke may mean plain old pollution, waste, and costly raw materials used and burned up.
Like gasoline in the petrochemical industry.
Or ammonia in the textile and metallurgical industries.
But what if we told you that Grumman Ecosystems is finding ways to recover these waste gases for re-use. Recovering them by re-liquefying them back into gasoline and ammonia. To the tune of thousands of gallons a year. So that what was once waste and pollution can now be actual liquid assets: gasoline and ammonia. And money for your company. All of which are presently just going up the stack.
Our AM-REC proprietary ammonia recovery system can pay for itself in less than two years. And a typical VAPO-REC gasoline vapor recovery system for a fuel transfer station can recover 10,000 gallons a year or more of valuable gasoline that would otherwise be wasted in the air in violation of Environmental Protection Agency guidelines.
Your company can profit by more than mere recovery. We can lower raw materials costs, reduce disposal headaches, and provide an efficient way to meet government standards for now and the years to come. And conserve our valuable natural resources.
Incidentally, if you already have a clean exhaust but need a new stack, our Power-Pac stacks are factory-built and refractory-lined for long life and reliability.
Grumman Ecosystems. The practical, down-to-earth method of making what would be waste and pollution pay off for you.
Most people know us for reliability and high performance in aerospace. That same uncompromising quality goes into a broad range of consumer and technological products and services. From environmental systems, van bodies, buses and specialized vehicles, to pleasure boats, corporate jets, business and agricultural planes, military aircraft and space vehicles, data, pollution control, health, and hospital systems.
When it comes to practically anything, Grumman has it. And that's not just a lot of gas.
Grumman Corporation, Bethpage, New York 11714
GRUMMAN
PAC

293

R. Heindel
Henry Fonda
IN CLARENCE DARROW
0:00PM
On NBC 00

294

292
Art Director Hank Hechtman
Designer Hank Hechtman
Artist Edward Sorel
Writer Norman Kantor
Agency Lee King & Partners
Client Lee King & Partners

293
Art Directors Frank Perry
Art Christy
Designers Art Christy
Frank Perry
Artist Don Ivan Punchatz
Writers Art Christy
Martin Cohen
Agency Fuller & Smith & Ross
Client Grumman Corp.

294
Art Director Dolores Gudzin
Designer Dolores Gudzin
Artist Robert Heindel
Agency NBC Advertising Dept.
Client National Broadcasting Co.

Salt City Playhouse Performing Arts Center
CEREMONIES IN DARK OLD MEN
By Lonne Elder, III
Director: Anderson McCullough
November 14,15,16,17
November 21,22,23,24
Thursdays, Fridays & Saturdays 8:15PM
Sundays at 7:30PM
Reservations: 474-0124 474-1122
601 South Crouse Ave. Syracuse

296

DART EXTRAVAGANZA
NUMBER THREE 74
This year the Cleveland Darter Club will hold its tournament on April 6th and 7th at the Slovenian Auditorium (6409 St. Clair Avenue, Cleveland, Ohio). There's over $6,000 in prizes and trophies and Miss Dart Extravaganza will, in her own way, personally congratulate the winners. If you don't think you have a chance to win turn this poster 180° for additional information.

297

296
Art Director Ivan Powell
Designer Ivan Powell
Artist Ivan Powell
Agency Mastropaul Design
Client Salt City Playhouse Performing Arts Center

297
Art Director Tom Yurcich
Designer Tom Yurcich
Artist Tom Yurcich
Writer Tom Yurcich
Agency TY Graphics
Client The Cleveland Darter Club

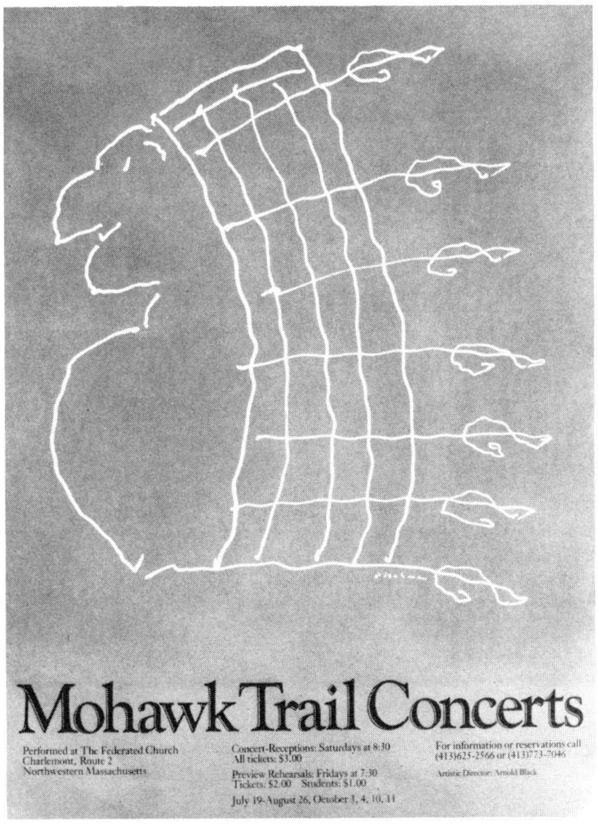
Mohawk Trail Concerts
Performed at The Federated Church
Charlemont, Route 2
Northwestern Massachusetts
Concert-Receptions: Saturdays at 8:30
All tickets: $3.00
Preview Rehearsals: Fridays at 7:30
Tickets: $2.00 Students: $1.00
July 19-August 26, October 3, 4, 10, 11
For information or reservations call
(413)625-2566 or (413)773-7046
Artistic Director: Arnold Black

298

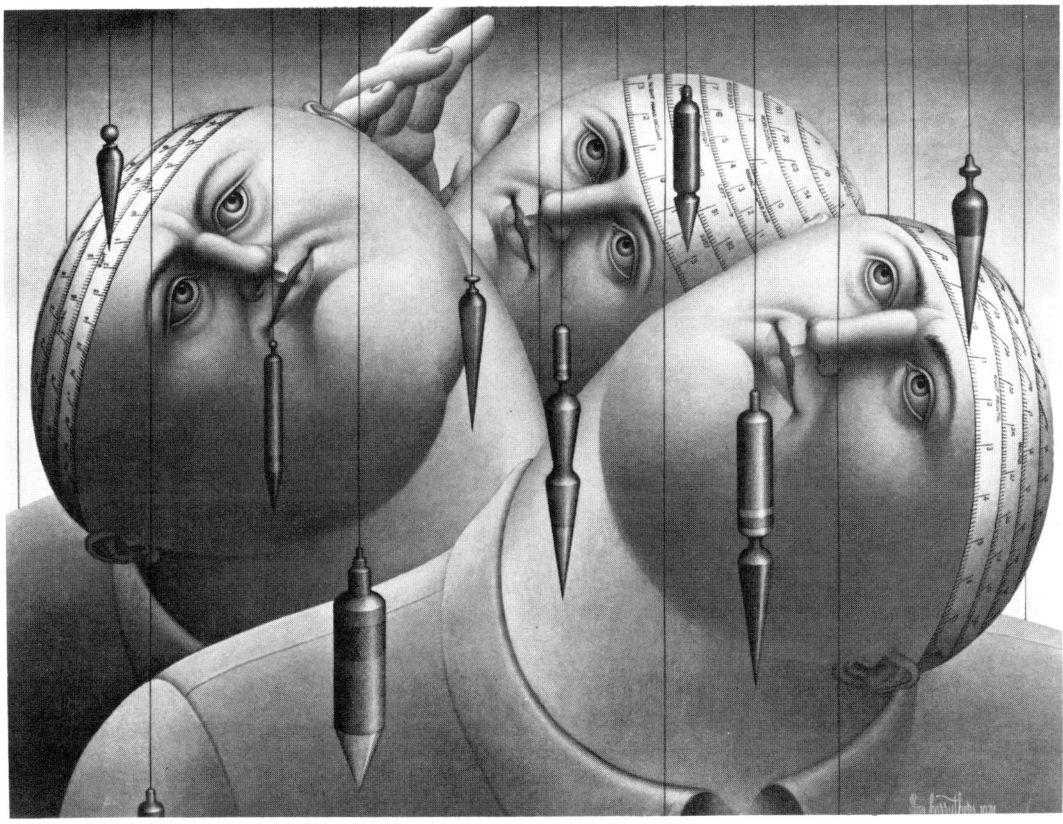

299

SILVER

298
Art Director Peter Rauch
Designer Peter Rauch
Artist R. O. Blechman
Agency R. O. Blechman
Client Mohawk Trail Concerts

299
Art Director Anthony V. Leone
Designer Anthony V. Leone
Artist Roy Carruthers
Writer Bernard Ostrof
Agency Lewis & Gilman
Client Roerig
Div. Pfizer Pharmaceuticals

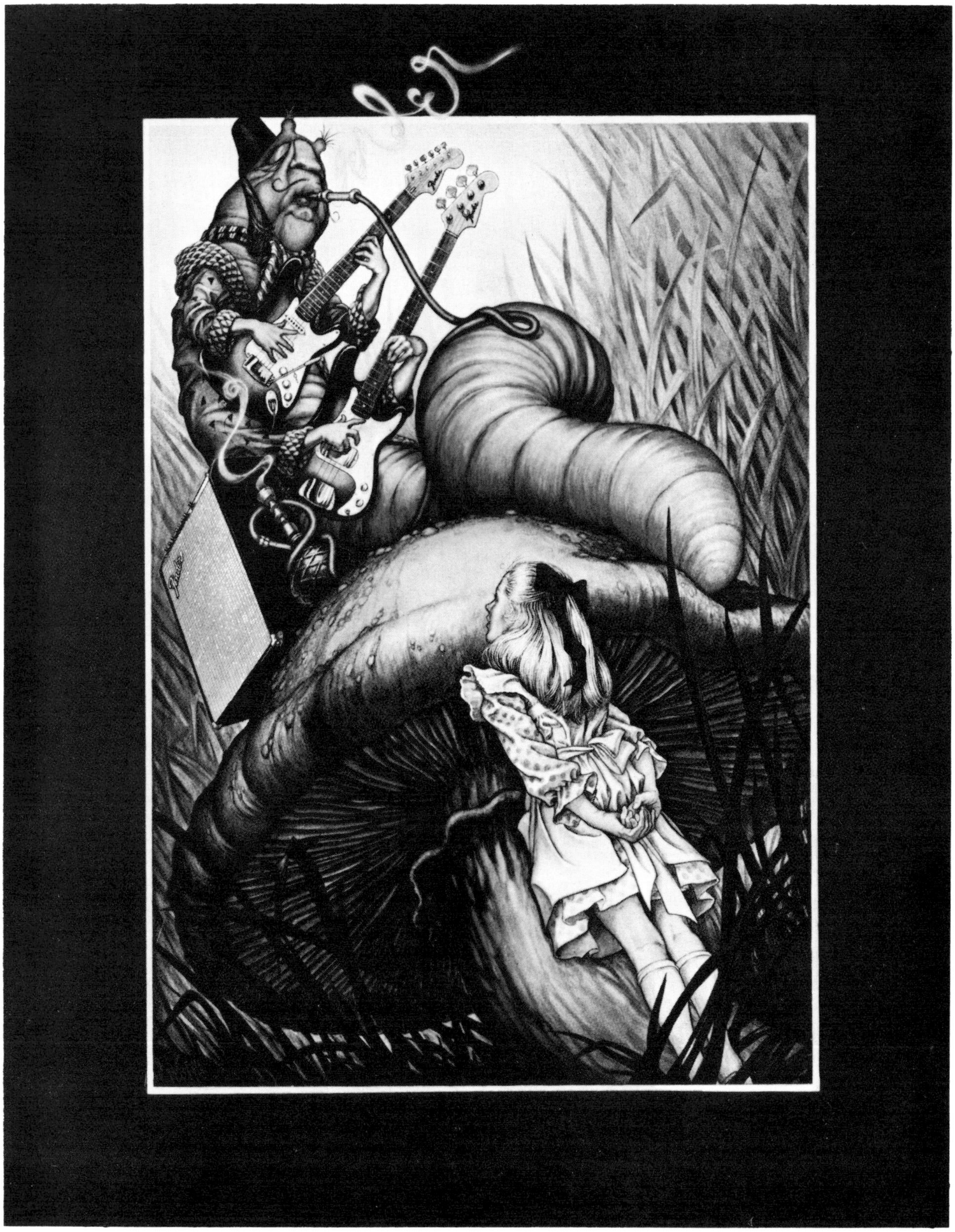

300

300
Art Director Ben Wong
Designers Bruce Wolfe
Ben Wong
Artist Bruce Wolfe
Writer David Perlstein
Agency Wenger-Michael
Client CBS Musical Instruments

SACO-LOWELL
CORPORATION
Service.
Twenty-four hours a day.
Seven days a week.
Around the clock.
Around the world.
Your future is our future.

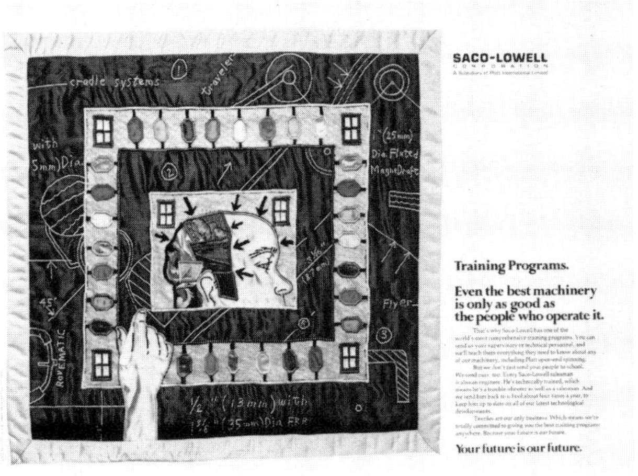
SACO-LOWELL
CORPORATION
Training Programs.
Even the best machinery
is only as good as
the people who operate it.
Your future is our future.

301

301
Art Director John Gregory
Designer Anne Raymo
Artist Anne Raymo
Photographer H. Neil Gillespie
Writers Walter Neubau
Francee Levin
Agency Henderson Advertising
Client Platt Saco Lowell

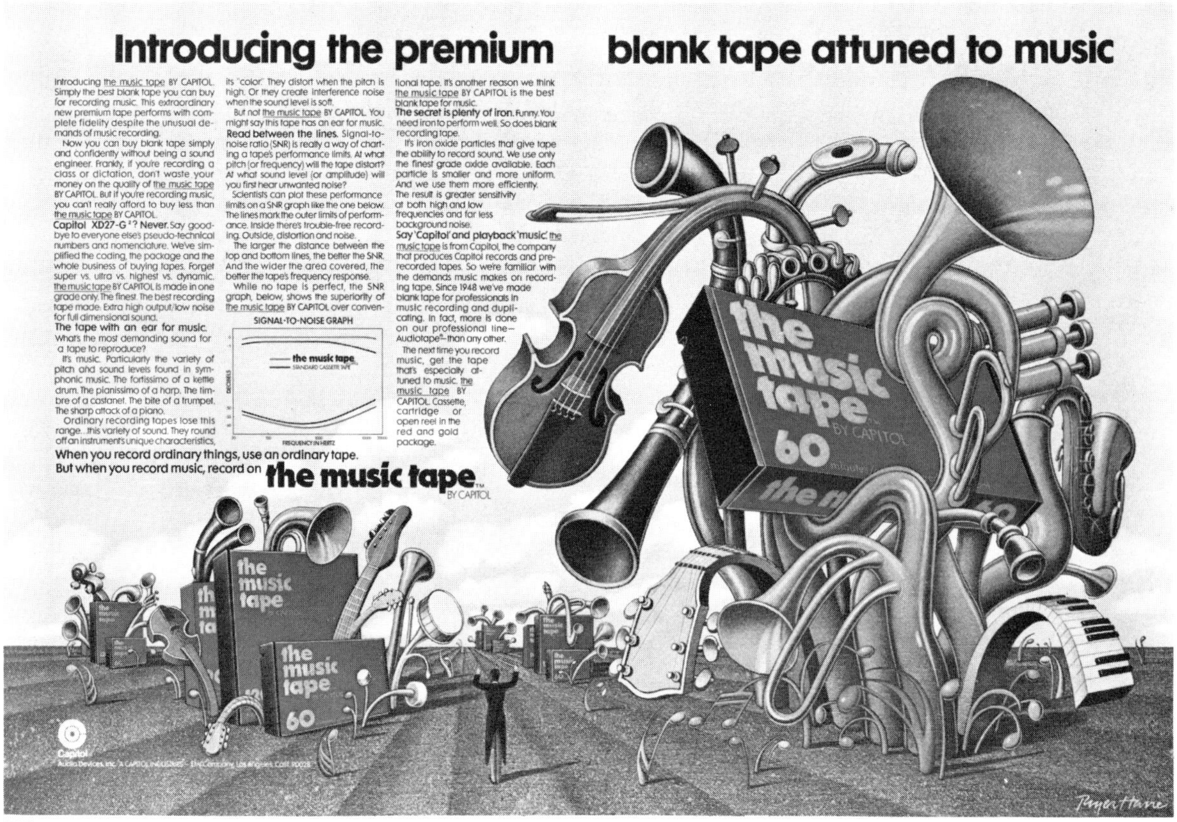

Introducing the premium blank tape attuned to music
Introducing the music tape BY CAPITOL. Simply the best blank tape you can buy for recording music. This extraordinary new premium tape performs with complete fidelity despite the unusual demands of music recording.
Now you can buy blank tape simply and confidently without being a sound engineer. Frankly, if you're recording a class or dictation, don't waste your money on the quality of the music tape BY CAPITOL. But if you're recording music, you can't really afford to buy less than the music tape BY CAPITOL.
Capitol XD27-G²? Never. Say good-bye to everyone else's pseudo-technical numbers and nomenclature. We've simplified the coding, the package and the whole business of buying tapes. Forget super vs. ultra vs. highest vs. dynamic. the music tape BY CAPITOL is made in one grade only. The finest. The best recording tape made. Extra high output/low noise for full dimensional sound.
The tape with an ear for music. What's the most demanding sound for a tape to reproduce?
It's music. Particularly the variety of pitch and sound levels found in symphonic music. The fortissimo of a kettle drum. The pianissimo of a harp. The timbre of a castanet. The bite of a trumpet. The sharp attack of a piano.
Ordinary recording tapes lose this range...this variety of sound. They round off an instrument's unique characteristics, its "color." They distort when the pitch is high. Or they create interference noise when the sound level is soft.
But not the music tape BY CAPITOL. You might say this tape has an ear for music.
Read between the lines. Signal-to-noise ratio (SNR) is really a way of charting a tape's performance limits. At what pitch (or frequency) will the tape distort? At what sound level (or amplitude) will you first hear unwanted noise?
Scientists can plot these performance limits on a SNR graph like the one below. The lines mark the outer limits of performance. Inside there's trouble-free recording. Outside, distortion and noise.
The larger the distance between the top and bottom lines, the better the SNR. And the wider the area covered, the better the tape's frequency response.
While no tape is perfect, the SNR graph, below, shows the superiority of the music tape BY CAPITOL over conventional tape. It's another reason we think the music tape BY CAPITOL is the best blank tape for music.
SIGNAL-TO-NOISE GRAPH
the music tape
STANDARD CASSETTE TAPE
DECIBELS
FREQUENCY IN HERTZ
The secret is plenty of iron. Funny. You need iron to perform well. So does blank recording tape.
It's iron oxide particles that give tape the ability to record sound. We use only the finest grade oxide available. Each particle is smaller and more uniform. And we use them more efficiently. The result is greater sensitivity at both high and low frequencies and far less background noise.
Say 'Capitol' and playback 'music.' the music tape is from Capitol, the company that produces Capitol records and pre-recorded tapes. So we're familiar with the demands music makes on recording tape. Since 1948 we've made blank tape for professionals in music recording and duplicating. In fact, more is done on our professional line—Audiotape®—than any other.
The next time you record music, get the tape that's especially attuned to music. the music tape BY CAPITOL. Cassette, cartridge or open reel in the red and gold package.
When you record ordinary things, use an ordinary tape.
But when you record music, record on the music tape™ BY CAPITOL
the music tape BY CAPITOL 60
the music tape 60
Capitol

302

Halston Dress
HALSTON
33 EAST 68TH STREET. NEW YORK. N.Y. 10021 U.S.A.

303

302
Art Director Alvin Ako
Writer Trisha Ingersoll
Agency J. Walter Thompson
Los Angeles
Client Capitol Magnetic Products

303
Art Director William McCaffery
Designer William McCaffery
Artist Larry Rivers
Agency Norton Simon Communications
Client Halston

304

304
Art Director Anthony V. Leone
Designer Anthony V. Leone
Artist Mark English
Writer Bernard Ostrof
Agency Lewis & Gilman
Client Roerig
Div. Pfizer Pharmaceuticals

RADIO & TELEVISION

ADVERTISING

Radio Commercials	305–345
Radio Commercial Campaigns	346–356
Public Service Radio Commercials	357–359
Public Service Radio Campaigns	360–360A
TV Commercials, 30 sec.	361–424
TV Commercial Campaigns, 30 sec.	425–432
TV Commercials, 60 sec.	433–463
TV Commercial Campaigns, 60 sec.	465–472
Public Service TV Commercials	473–482
Public Service TV Commercial Campaign	483
Animated TV Commercials	486–490
Animated Station & Network Promotion	492
Program Promotions	494–497
Station & Network Promotions	498–504
Industrial/Sales Film	505

THE APARTMENT
30-second

ANNCR: Here's a book that everybody in your apartment building could use. For instance, if the lady in 4A wants to indulge in a little self expression . . .

SFX: La, la, la, la, la, la (scale) . . .

ANNCR: She'll find voice lessons in the Yellow Pages. As for the young man in 3D who's into self defense . . .

SFX: Hai, Yaaah. (Lady doing scales continues)

ANNCR: He'll find karate instruction in the Yellow Pages. And here's a listing you might be interested in.

SFX: Door slams . . . then quiet.

ANNCR: For another apartment, check the Yellow Pages. Let your fingers do the walking.

305
Writer Blake Hunter
Producer Pam Den Hartog
Agency Chiat/Day
Client Pacific Northwest Bell Telephone Co.

RANCHER
30-second

RANCHER: Well, I was standing right here. I was looking for a lost heifer. Then I saw this thing. It was going up that ridge right over there.

At first, I thought that it was a motorcycle. But it was real quiet. It didn't make a sound like a motorcycle. And it didn't never stop, see. It just sorta snaked its way up that gully. And I just don't believe that there's any way in the world that a motorcycle could do that. None I ever seen. It might 'a been a motorcycle. But I think it was something else.

I don't have to tell you there's thousands of planets like ours in this universe. And it's only natural those people would try to contact us.

ANNCR: It's like no other motorcycle you have ever seen. The Cat, from Yamaha.

306
Writer Don Hadley
Director Sandra Marshall
Producers Don Hadley
Sandra Marshall
Production Co. Bell Sound
Agency Botsford Ketchum
San Francisco
Client Yamaha International Corp.

LOGGER
30-second

LOGGER: I'll tell you the honest truth, I'm real sorry I ever saw that thing. See my partner and I were just fixin' to come down off the hill when we see this thing going up over the other ridge.

Well now, there's nothin' but rocks and fallen logs over there. But here is this vehicle. Now it wasn't an animal—glidin' right up that ridge. Right over the rocks, right over the logs. And I have ridden a motorcycle. And there's nobody in the world goin' tell me that it's humanly possible for a motorcycle to do what I saw this thing do.

V.O.: What was it then?

LOGGER: Well, I'll tell you. If I was to go around telling people what I think it was, they'd haul me off to the county hospital.

ANNCR: It is like no other motorcycle you have ever seen. The Cat, from Yamaha.

IRV AND AL
30-second

AL: Go on Irv, I think you ought to tell us, you're the one that saw it first.

IRV: No, Al, you go ahead.

AL: Well, all right. We're comin' down this trail right about here and ol' Irv spots this thing working its way up that creek bed right over there.

IRV: Ya see those boulders over there? That thing just glided up over those boulders.

AL: Ya, but here's what knocked us for a loop. This thing paused for just about a second and then just choosh, it just went right straight up that cliff.

IRV: I never saw anything like it.

AL: I mean I'd like to think it was a motorcycle, but you got some problems there 'cause it was quiet. And you tell me, you walk over there and look at that cliff and then you tell me what motorcycle in the world is going to git up that cliff.

IRV: It wasn't a motorcycle . . . and it wasn't anything human.

It's like no other motorcycle you have ever seen.

The Cat from Yamaha.

RADIO

307
Writer Don Hadley
Directors Don Hadley
Sandra Marshall
Producer Sandra Marshall
Production Co. Bell Sound
Agency Botsford Ketchum
San Francisco
Client Yamaha International Corp.

308
Writer Don Hadley
Directors Don Hadley
Sandra Marshall
Producer Sandra Marshall
Production Co. Bell Sound
Agency Botsford Ketchum
San Francisco
Client Yamaha International Corp.

BETTE MIDLER
60-second

BETTE MIDLER: Hi, I'm Bette Midler, and I've been taking ballet dancing for years. It's very difficult. And the music. Please. It always sounds like this.

MUSIC

MIDLER: But the Joffrey Ballet is divine. Because the Joffrey sounds like this.

MUSIC

MIDLER: So come to the Joffrey. You'll be surprised. And you won't be bored. And it will cost you less than the price of a Broadway show.

Listen, if you like the ballet, you're gonna love the Joffrey. And if you hate the ballet, you're still going to love the Joffrey.

309
Writers Enid Futterman
Alan Kupchick
Producer Steve Novick
Production Cos. Aura Recording
Crescendo Productions
Agency Grey Advertising
Client Joffrey Ballet

SOUNDS OF HOHNER
60-second

Multi-musical accompaniments. Harmonica opens. Chorus follows lyrical classical guitar solo followed by switch to pianet then clavinet to banjo duet. Tempo also alternates from lyrical to fast, crisp full band to theme.

ANNCR: When you hear great harmonica sound, you know it's Hohner. But did you know that Hohner makes other great-sounding instruments? Like our guitars? Or our keyboards . . . There's the Hohner international piano, the pianet, and our funky clavinet. And our banjos . . . or our fretless bass, and Hohner mikes and amps.

Try all the great sounds from Hohner at your music store. Hohner. We also make harmonicas.

310
Writers Richard Murdock
Gregory Bruce
Producer Gil Matthies
Music Mega Music Corp.
David Briggs
Production Co. Quadrophonic Productions
Agency Rumrill-Hoyt
Client M. Hohner

MOTHER
30-second

MUSIC UNDER

ANNCR: Statistics show that there are 51,483,637 moms in the United States. And a somewhat larger number of devoted sons and daughters.

That means that on Mother's Day a lot of sons and daughters will make long distance calls to a lot of moms. General Telephone doesn't want your mother to be disappointed because of overloaded phone lines, so this year why not call her a day or two ahead of time, she'll understand.

Mother always understands.

311
Writer David Butler
Producer Mel Kane
Music Bennie Golson
Agency Doyle Dane Bernbach
Los Angeles
Client General Telephone

BILL RALPH USED CARS
50-second

SFX

BILL RALPH: Bill Ralph here. For Bill Ralph's Used Cars Flushing. "Prices so low, everybody gets to go."

Here I have a '72 Lincoln. Original sticker price $7,300. Now only $4,175. Or maybe you want a smaller car. Like a '72 Chevy Impala originally $3,700. Now only $2,350.

Or how about the famous Volkswagen Beetle. This '72 sold for $1,999. I can let you have it now for only $2,100. Er . . . wait a minute . . . these figures must be reversed.

ANNCR: No, those figures aren't reversed. According to the July '74 NADA Eastern Used Car Guide, a '72 Beetle actually retails for more today than it did new.

BILL RALPH: I didn't know that.

ANNCR: (Live dealer tag.)

312
Writer Michael Mangano
Producer Rosemary Barre
Agency Doyle Dane Bernbach
Client Volkswagen of America Corp.

SURGERY
60-second

DOCTOR: OK, nurse, I think we're ready to begin the operation. Gloves.

NURSE: Gloves.

DOCTOR: Ether.

NURSE: Ether.

DOCTOR: Sponge.

NURSE: Sponge.

DOCTOR: Scalpel.

NURSE: We're all out of scalpels, doctor. They were supposed to get here this morning, but they haven't arrived yet.

DOCTOR: No scalpels. Well, I suppose you expect me to open this patient with a corkscrew?

NURSE: I don't think we have a corkscrew, doctor.

ANNCR: If you've got a small package to ship, and someone is depending on it, it's important to have an air freight company you can depend on. At Emery, we reserve space on every key flight that carries freight around the world. And we speed things up on the ground, too. With personal pick up and delivery. And a computerized tracking system that lets you know where your shipment is—if it isn't where it's supposed to be. That's why so many people in so many businesses do business with Emery.

DOCTOR: Nurse, do you think you could get me a very sharp knife from the commissary?

NURSE: Can't promise.

ANNCR: Emery Air Freight. The shortest distance between two points.

313
Writers John Russo
Ken Berris
Producer Suzanne DePlautt
Agency Della Femina, Travisano & Partners
Client Emery Air Freight

DRIVE A COOL BARGAIN
50-second

SONG: It's so hot
Oh man am I beat.
It's so hot
I'm stickin' to my seat.
Oh Baby!
It's so hot.

ANNCR: Have we been playing your song?

Well here's some news that'll really cool you off. For a limited time you can get a new Volkswagen Beetle fully equipped with air conditioning for only $199 extra.

Maybe the heat has gotten to us, but for only $199 extra you can drive a real cool bargain.

After riding in an air-conditioned Volkswagen Beetle, it won't take you long to change your tune.

SONG: It's so cool
I can feel the breeze
So cool
Think I'm gonna sneeze
So cool
Thanks for makin' me
Makin' me
So cool.

MUSIC

ANNCR: Drive a cool bargain at (Dealer name—tag) . . . Distribution suggested retail price on selected Beetles at participating dealers. Offer expires July 31st.

314
Writer Patty Volk Blitzer
Producer Paul Conti
Music Anacrusis Music
Production Co. SDC
Agency Doyle Dane Bernbach
Client Volkswagen of America Corp.

CLUB ATLANTIQUE
60-second

ANNCR: Stiller and Meara.

MEARA: Say, is this your first vacation at Club Atlantique?

STILLER: Yeah, last year I tried Le Club Dead Sea, but there wasn't much action. Ha ha ha ha . . .

MEARA: You're very humorous. Hey, that's a lovely sarong you're wearing.

STILLER: Thank you, it's a Pucci.

MEARA: Oh . . .

STILLER: Yours is kind of interesting too.

MEARA: Thank you. It's a towel I got at a singles weekend at Grossinger's.

STILLER: Very becoming, this is really an exotic spread. What are you having?

MEARA: Oh, I think I'll try the cracked crab Martinique.

STILLER: And I think I'll have the meatloaf Fantastique. And perhaps we could share a bottle of wine.

MEARA: That would be magnifique! Except that you're having meat and I'm having seafood. I mean what wine goes with both.

STILLER: Well, I noticed a little Blue Nun over there.

MEARA: Oh, is she the one in the black pedal pushers.

STILLER: No, Blue Nun is a wine. A delicious white wine that's correct with any dish. It goes as well with meat as it does with fish.

MEARA: That sounds like some wine. Is it expensive?

STILLER: It's not cheap. It's about four conch shells and a couple of red beads. Ha ha ha ha . . .

MEARA: Very witty . . .

STILLER: Say did you hear the one about the . . .

MEARA: Yes!

ANNCR: Blue Nun. The delicious white wine that's correct with any dish. Another Sichel Wine imported by Schieffelin & Co., New York.

GOLD

315
Writers Kay Kavanagh
Mark Yustein
Producer Lewis Kuperman
Production Co. National Recording
Agency Della Femina, Travisano & Partners
Client Schieffelin & Co.

JAPANESE MEAL
60-second

ANNCR: Stiller & Meara:

STILLER: Hi Gert. Hubby's home.

MEARA: Come in happy wanderer. Take off your shoes.

STILLER: Why, did you shampoo the rugs today?

MEARA: No, I cooked Japanese food.

STILLER: (Sniff) Smells funny.

MEARA: That's incense burning.

STILLER: Quick, take it off the stove. Maybe we can save it.

MEARA: Incense is a Japanese scent, one of those mysteries of the Orient.

STILLER: I'm more interested in mysteries of the oven. Let's eat.

MEARA: Can my big samuri handle chopsticks?

STILLER: Easy. You oughta hear me play Malaguena.

MEARA: Oh, Fletcher. Here, have some Sashimi.

STILLER: Uhg—looks like raw fish!

MEARA: It is raw fish. A Japanese delicacy. Then we're having Beef Teryaki.

STILLER: Lucky, I brought home a little Blue Nun.

MEARA: Fletcher, a Buddhist Monk would add more atmosphere.

STILLER: Gert, Blue Nun is a wine. A delicious white wine.

MEARA: I didn't slave over a hot Hibachi to see my beef served with white wine.

STILLER: Blue Nun is the white wine that's correct with any dish. It goes as well with meat as it does with fish.

MEARA: Sounds expensive.

STILLER: Oh, Lotus blossom money's no object when you've got a yen for something.

SFX: Gong

ANNCR: Blue Nun, the delicious white wine that's correct with any dish. Another Sichel Wine imported by Schieffelin & Co., New York.

316
Writers Mark Yustein
Kay Kavanagh
Producer Lewis Kuperman
Production Co. National Recording
Agency Della Femina, Travisano & Partners
Client Schieffelin & Co.

CAROL
60-second

MUSIC

WOMAN: Hi, there. My name is Carol. You know, until recently two things terrified me. Mice. And Volkswagen Busses. You know, the ones that look like Brontosauruses. But then last week I drove the new 1975 Volkswagen Bus. It is tremendously big inside—almost twice as big as an ordinary station wagon—but it parks and handles just like an ordinary medium-sized car, even without the optional automatic transmission. (It gets great mileage too!)

So now that a great big bus can drive me all over town . . . why does a little, tiny mouse still drive me up a wall?

ANNCR: (Tag) See the 1975 Volkswagen Station Wagon at . . .

317
Writer Dodds Musser
Director Rosemary Barre
Producer Rosemary Barre
Music Joe Brooks
Agency Doyle Dane Bernbach
Client Volkswagen of America Corp.

PROPOSAL
60-second

ANNCR: A pushbutton phone, from General Telephone, has an esthetic side that old-style phones don't have. As you push the buttons, each one plays a different musical note. When you think about it, that could open up a whole new level of communication.

SFX: Phone ringing.

SHE: Hello?

HE: Hi . . . . . . Louise?

SHE: Richard?

HE: Yeah . . . Uh . . . Louise . . .

SHE: Yes. . .

HE: There's something I've been wanting to ask you. I could never find the right words. But I think I found the right buttons . . .

SFX: First eight notes of "Here Comes the Bride."

SHE: Ohhh . . . Richard . . .

HE: Yea . . .

ANNCR: And the pushbutton phone has advantages besides the musical interludes. For example, it's easier to use than the dial phone, so you make fewer mistakes. And it's faster. A lot faster.

Pushbutton phones are now available to all our customers in many colors and styles. Why not order one from your General Telephone business office? And make your own kind of music.

318
Writer David Butler
Producer Mel Kane
Agency Doyle Dane Bernbach
Los Angeles
Client General Telephone

FROZEN POKED
60-second

ANNCR: Ladies and Gentlemen, the President of Perdue Farms, Mr. Frank Perdue.

FRANK PERDUE: Mrs. Robert Gertner of Brooklyn, wrote to ask me if my chicken and chicken parts are frozen. Frozen? My chickens aren't frozen. I pack my tender, young Perdue chicken, and my Pedigreed parts, in ice. So they'll arrive at your store completely fresh—and *unfrozen*. Now, at one time it was easy to recognize a frozen chicken. You poked it. And if it was hard, it was frozen. Nowadays, it's not as easy as that. There's a new thing called chill-packing. This process freezes the chicken just a little bit. So it's hard for you to tell.

The only way I know to be absolutely sure of getting an honest-to-goodness fresh chicken, is to look for one with my name tag on it. That tag not only guarantees my chicken is tender, juicy and delicious. It guarantees it's not frozen, or you get your money back.

ANNCR: When it comes to chicken, Frank Perdue is even tougher than you are. He *has* to be. Because everyone of his chickens comes with a money-back quality guarantee. It takes a tough man to make a tender chicken. Perdue.

319
Writers Edward A. McCabe
Jon Goward
Production Co. The Mix Place
Agency Scali, McCabe, Sloves
Client Perdue Farms

FROZEN PACKAGES
60-second

ANNCR: Ladies and Gentlemen, the President of Perdue Farms, Mr. Frank Perdue:

FRANK PERDUE: Mrs. Ruth Block of Yonkers, New York wrote to ask me why I don't put my Perdue chicken in frozen packages. I don't believe in freezing my packages. Or my chickens. Not even a little bit. Why, I had a guy come by trying to sell me on chilling my chicken. But do you know what he wanted to do? Take my tender, young chicken and put it on a conveyor belt; run it into a room and blast it with air that was 20° to 30° below zero! I said he might call that "chilling", but it sounded suspiciously like freezing to me. So I sent him packing.

And I continue to pack my Perdue chickens in ice. And ship them in my own refrigerated trucks. That way, I know they'll arrive at your store completely fresh. If there's one thing that makes me hot under the collar, it's a chicken with frostbite.

ANNCR: When it comes to chicken, Frank Perdue is even tougher than you are. He *has* to be. Because every one of his chickens comes with a money-back quality guarantee. It takes a tough man to make a tender chicken. Perdue.

320
Writers Edward A. McCabe
Jon Goward
Production Co. The Mix Place
Agency Scali, McCabe, Sloves
Client Perdue Farms

164—ANGRY COMMUTERS
55-second

SFX: Traffic noises.

ANNCR: Recently two traffic policemen went on strike by blockading a major highway with their own cars, trapping thousands of hapless commuters for more than eight hours.

SFX: (Woman driver: Hurry up!)

ANNCR: So it seems that in addition to the approximately 17 million accidents a year, the 23 thousand miles of road construction and the 112 million other vehicles, now you can get stuck behind the people who are supposed to keep you moving.

SFX: (Man driver: Get em off the road.)

ANNCR: The Volvo 164 was designed with such madness in mind. Knowing you're destined to spend a great deal of your driving life standing still, we've provided the 164 with massive seats that actually adjust to the needs of your spine. With air conditioning for when you are hot. A heated driver's seat for when you are cold. And enough legroom to keep a six-foot six-inch commuter from crawling out of his skin.

SFX: (Man: Why doesn't somebody call a cop?)

ANNCR: The Volvo 164. A civilized car built for an uncivilized world.

321
Writer Michael Drazen
Production Co. National Recording
Agency Scali, McCabe, Sloves
Client Volvo of America Corp.

FROZEN ICE
60-second

ANNCR: Ladies and Gentlemen, the President of Perdue Farms, Mr. Frank Perdue:

FRANK PERDUE: Mrs. Clare Stevens of Wayne, Pennsylvania wrote me a letter that says, "Please advise if freezing a chicken makes it tough. My butcher says it doesn't hurt." Well, freezing a chicken isn't the problem. It's thawing it out that messes it up. You see, when you freeze a chicken, all the natural juices turn to ice. So when you thaw it out, a lot of the juices can run out of the chicken, leaving you with a bird that isn't nearly what it could be.

That's the reason why my Perdue chicken arrives at your store ice-packed and completely fresh. Because when you cook a fresh, unfrozen chicken like mine, you seal in the natural juices so they can't escape. And the chicken can't help but come out tender, juicy, and delicious. I suppose there may be a chicken that freezing won't hurt. But it won't be one of mine.

ANNCR: When it comes to chicken, Frank Perdue is even tougher than you are. He has to be. Because every one of his chickens comes with a money-back quality guarantee. It takes a tough man to make a tender chicken. Perdue.

322
Writers Edward McCabe
Jon Goward
Production Co. The Mix Place
Agency Scali, McCabe, Sloves
Client Perdue Farms

BASKETBALL
60-second

SFX: Whistle, basketball dribbling, jump

ANNCR: When a basketball player makes a jump shot, it looks like a simple graceful motion.

SFX: Swish.

ANNCR: But it demands the coordination of over 400 muscles. Come inside your body and see.

SFX: Pounding basketball to pounding muscles.

ANNCR: Over 140 in your back and upper body, 68 in your neck and shoulders, 64 in your arms, 20 in each hand. Almost all the muscles in your body to make a simple jump shot. But if you only play ball on Saturday, you may exert certain muscles that get little exercise during the week. You can strain them, and wake up Sunday feeling pain. The pain of muscle ache.

Take Excedrin. Excedrin provides fast effective relief for many kinds of simple pain. In two medical research studies on two different kinds of pain, Excedrin was significantly more effective than the common asprin tablet. When you need pain relief, take Excedrin. Take it as directed on the label. Excedrin. The extra-strength pain reliever.

323
Writer Peter Berkhard
Producer Jim Coyne
Production Co. Radio Band of America
Agency Young & Rubicam International
Client Bristol-Myers Co.

KINNEY SHOES—$13.88
60-second

ANNCR: (In rhythm) This is the week that you've got to consider your feet . . .

SFX: (Voice echo: Hello feet!)

ANNCR: 'Cause if your feet could only talk, they'd take the rest of you for a walk and they'd wail about a Kinney Shoe Sale . . .

MUSIC CHANGE TO UP TEMPO

SONG: Ooh! Hey! Everytime we're out wanna boogie! Wanna boogie! Wanna shake and shout about a flipped out casual Kinney Shooo---
One . . . three . . . eight . . . eight

MUSIC CHANGE TO CASUAL SOUNDS

ANNCR: And that's great. $13.88. For each of the five popular casual comfortable easy go'in suede and leather men's styles in the store.

SFX: (Voice echo: In the store . . .)

ANNCR: Yeah, this is the week alright . . .
The only week . . .

SFX: (Voice echo: That's right)

ANNCR: Cause if your feet could only talk they'd take the rest of you for a walk and they'd wail about a Kinney Shoe Sale . . .

SONG REPEAT CHORUS

ANNCR: $13.88 and that's great leather and suede The Kinney Shoe Sale.

SONG: For guys . . .

ANNCR: Hello feet . . .

324
Writers George Miller
Harley Flaum
Paul Messing
Director Harley Flaum
Producer George Miller
Production Co. Radio Band of America
Agency Sawdon & Bess
Client Kinney Shoe Corp.

HOT APPLE CIDER
60-second

SONG: (Chorus): Apple Cider, Apple Cider, Apple Cider, Apple Cider, Hot Apple Cider.

Apple Cider, Apple Cider, Apple Cider, Apple Cider, Hot Apple Cider.

Now there's a new way to warm up. At Carrols, at Carrols, Apple Cider. At Carrols.

Now when you come to us there's something new. Apple Cider. Apple Cider. At Carrols. Apple Cider.

ANNCR: Try Carrols new Hot Apple Cider with a pinch of cinnamon.

SONG: At Carrols . . . at Carrols. Hot Apple Cider.

325
Writers Eric Mower
Warren Margulies
Directors Eric Mower
Warren Margulies
Producers Eric Mower
Warren Margulies
Music George F. Handel
Production Co. Dick Lavsky's Music House
Agency Silverman & Mower Advertising
Client Carrols Restaurants

WOLFMAN
60-second

WOLFMAN: Hey, hey this is Wolfman Jack comin' at ya, baby. Got to whisper some importance in your ear gonna save your posterior come prom night. Why you can't go to the prom lookin' like you do. Unless you gonna drag a big, ole tree with you to hide behind. You got to drip elegance, sweetheart. You got to get down with your bad self at any one of the 27 Chicago-land Gingiss Formalwear Centers. Else, you ain't even gonna get close to that wicked witch's third ugly sister. Gingiss is gonna dress you in one of them After Six tuxedos, you know, hide the fact you been out heardin' sheep. And Gingiss has 25 different styles to climb into. And colors.

SFX: Snort, growl.

WOLFMAN: Let me tell ya. Pinks, yellows, blues, browns, apricots, even blacks and whites. So get down to Gingiss. And bring a student ID with ya, won't ya please, so's you can get that 20% off. And remember, baby, after you hung up them ballet slippers prom night . . . when the moon's shinin' on you in that Gingiss tuxedo . . . and you hear some heavy breathin' somewhere

. . . remember, baby, it was the Wolfman told you so.

SILVER

326
Writer Jeff Gorman
Producer Jeff Gorman
Production Co. Radio & Records
Agency Zechman Lyke Vetere
Client Gingiss International

BOGIE
55-second

SFX: Doorbell rings inside house. Dog barking.

GIRL: Daddy! Herbie's here! Will you get the door?

FATHER: Save me from another prom night.

SFX: Doorbell

FATHER: Okay, kid. Quit leaning on it. I'm here. I'm here.

MUSIC: Gushy, 1930's piano music, to end.

HERBIE: (Dead-ringer for Humphrey Bogart) Evening, Mr. Biggins.

FATHER: Herbie??

HERBIE: Great night for a prom, ain't it?

FATHER: Herbie? Is this you? You look different.

HERBIE: Must be the tuxedo, sweetheart.

FATHER: It's beautiful.

HERBIE: Uh huh. You wanna quit fondling the merchandise? It's reserved for another member of the family.

ANNCR: A strange thing happens when you slip into a tuxedo on prom night. Your entire image changes. And Gingiss has so many tuxedo styles in so many colors, that come prom night, you can be whoever you want to be.

HERBIE: Whaddya mean have her home by 10:30, Mr. Biggins?

327
Writer Jeff Gorman
Producer Janet Collins
Production Co. Studio One
Agency Zechman Lyke Vetere
Client Gingiss International

HOTDOGS
60-second

ANNCR: America, what's your favorite sport?

AMERICA: Baseball!

ANNCR: Sandwich?

AMERICA: Hotdogs!

ANNCR: Pie?

AMERICA: Apple!

ANNCR: And what's your favorite car, America?

AMERICA: Chevrolet!

ANNCR: Let's see—that's baseball, hotdogs, apple pie and Chevrolet, huh? Well, you sure sound like America to me.

AMERICA: We are.

ANNCR: Well then you better tell me again, cause I just might forget.

SONG: We love baseball, hotdogs, apple pie and Chevrolet . . . baseball, hotdogs, apple pie and Chevrolet.

ANNCR: That's baseball, hotdogs, apple pie and Chevrolet.

AMERICA: Baseball, hotdogs, apple pie and Chevrolet.

ANNCR: I think you better tell me again.

AMERICA: We love baseball, hotdogs, apple pie and Chevrolet. Baseball, hotdogs, apple pie and Chevrolet.

ANNCR: In case you're wondering, this message is brought to you by . . . baseball, hotdogs, apple pie. And America's favorite car.

SONG: They go together in the good old USA, baseball, hotdogs, apple pie and Chevrolet.

ANNCR: Makes sense to me.

AMERICA: Baseball, hotdogs, apple pie and Chevrolet.

ANNCR: That's right.

AMERICA: Baseball, hotdogs, apple pie and Chevrolet.

328
Writer James W. Hartzell
Producer Molly A. Hudson
Composer Ed Labunski
Production Co. Labunski Productions
Agency Campbell-Ewald Co.
Client General Motors

7 DAYS A WEEK
50-second

ANNCR: The continuing story of the Volkswagen Campmobile.

SFX: VW engine, music under

ANNCR: It gets you and your family up to the mountains on Friday . . .
sleeps you there on Saturday . . .
feeds you there on Sunday.

It takes 6 commuters to work on Monday . . .
passes up your favorite gas station on Tuesday . . .
fits into a tiny VW-size parking space on Wednesday . . .
and carries home a Spinnet piano on Thursday . . .

It gets you and your family up to the mountains on Friday . . .
sleeps you there on Saturday . . .
feeds you there on Sunday.

The Volkswagen Campmobile
It keeps you going 7 days a week.

ANNCR: See the incredibly versatile Volkswagen Campmobile at (Live dealer tag.)

PEDIGREED PARTS - CUT UP
60-second

ANNCR: Ladies and Gentlemen, the President of Perdue Farms, Mr. Frank Perdue.

FRANK PERDUE: A Mr. Kabren of Wantagh, Long Island wants to know how to cut up a whole chicken. Now listen carefully. The way you cut up the body into breast and back sections is to place the chicken on the neck end and cut from the tail along each side of the back bone, through the rib joints to the neck. Then cut through the skin that attaches the neck and back strip to the breast. Place the neck and back strip skin side up on the cutting board and cut the chicken into two pieces.

But I wouldn't bother to go through all that. I'd forget about cutting up chickens and buy my Perdue pedigreed chicken parts instead. They're always cut up right. I know because my Perdue pedigreed parts go through three more inspections than even my whole chickens. And my whole chickens go through more inspections than anybody else's I know of.

ANNCR: When it comes to chicken, Frank Perdue is even tougher than you are. He *has* to be. Because every one of his chicken parts comes with a money-back quality guarantee. It takes a tough man to make a tender chicken. Perdue.

329
Writer John Noble
Producer Rosemary Barre
Music Grant & Murtaugh
Agency Doyle Dane Bernbach
Client Volkswagen of America Corp.

330
Writers Edward McCabe
Jon Goward
Production Co. The Mix Place
Agency Scali, McCabe, Sloves
Client Perdue Farms

CHICKEN FAT
60-second

ANNCR: Ladies and Gentlemen, the President of Perdue Farms, Mr. Frank Perdue.

FRANK PERDUE: Mrs. Viola Borsos of Doyltown, Pennsylvania wrote me a letter that says: "Your chickens are fat! Why don't you make some for all of us who have to cut down on fat?" My chickens are fat because they're well-fed. Fat's a sign of good health and something you want to look for in any chicken. It means the chicken's tender, juicy and delicious.

A skinny chicken is going to be a tough bird. Besides, even a fat chicken isn't fat by other meat standards. The fat's *on* the meat, not in it. So you don't have to eat it. But you shouldn't throw it away, either. My chicken fat makes a great vegetable seasoning, a great ingredient in chicken soup and goes great in chopped liver. But it's not bad for anything. So you shouldn't worry about getting too much fat in my chicken. What you should worry about is getting a chicken with too little fat.

ANNCR: When it comes to chicken, Frank Perdue is even tougher than you are. He *has* to be. Because every one of his chickens comes with a money-back quality guarantee. It takes a tough man to make a tender chicken. Perdue.

331
Writers Edward McCabe
Jon Goward
Production Co. The Mix Place
Agency Scali, McCabe, Sloves
Client Perdue Farms

18 DAYS
60-second

DICK: Norm, I'll give you ten dollars if you make a move right now.

BERT: Let's see, if I move here then you'll move there and connect four in a row and you'll beat me.

DICK: Norman?

BERT: If I move—what? Hm.

DICK: See, eighteen days is too long between moves, Norm. Ha, Ha.

BERT: I could move here, no I couldn't, you'll block me. I'm sorry.

DICK: Connect Four is only a game, Norm.

BERT: On the other hand, if I move here, then you'll have to . . . no you won't, no you won't . . .

DICK: I know my lovely wife is probably wondering what happened to me.

BERT: Boy, this Connect Four is more than a vertical checkers game.

DICK: I know my boss. He's going to be mad.

BERT: It's vertical and horizontal and diagonal strategy.

DICK: Know, I think I was supposed to be in Pittsburgh last Tuesday.

BERT: It's a challenge! That's what I like.

DICK: I really do miss my wife Shirley though.

BERT: Isn't it Sheila?

DICK: Yes, Sheila, Right, Sheila.

BERT: It's like two minds locked in battle.

DICK: Not for eighteen days, Norman. Make a move!

BERT: But you've snuck up on me, I can't move anywhere! I give up.

DICK: I win Connect Four?

BERT: You win Connect Four!

DICK: Ha, Ha, I win, thank goodness!

BERT: Harry . . . it's two out of three, remember.

SFX: Thud!

ANNCR: Connect Four, the new strategy game of vertical checkers from Milton Bradley.

332
Writer Dick Orkin Creative Services
Producer Dick Orkin Creative Services
Production Co. Dick Orkin Creative Services
Agency Young & Rubicam International
Client Milton Bradley Co.

GOOD DAY
60-second

SONG: Yes, it's a good day
A Beautyrest day

ANNCR: Get your Beautyrest America and have a good day
Have a Beautyrest day

SONG: Yes, it's a good day
A Beautyrest day
Yes, it's a good day
A Beautyrest day . . .
When you have a good night
Your day is okay
So get your Beautyrest
and have a good day!

ANNCR: (Live dealer tag under.)

SONG: Go get your Beautyrest and have a good day . . .
Go get your Beautyrest
and have a good day.
go get your Beautyrest
and have a good day.

DEAR AUNT ROSE

SFX: Nursery music

CINDY: Dear Aunt Rose and Uncle Jack,

The last few weeks have opened up a whole new world for Mark and me. Michelle is one month old today. And as I write this, I can hear her in the nursery.

We were really surprised when we opened your gift. With stuffed animals, pink blankets and all, we never expected a Kodak X-15 Color Outfit. It's lovely, and we thank you.

Mark loaded the color film into the Instamatic camera and took this picture of me and my daughter. My daughter. I never thought those words could mean so much to me . . . She waved her little fists . . .

ANNCR: The Kodak Instamatic X-15 color outfit. An X-15 camera for flash without batteries—magicube and color film—all for less than nineteen dollars. It's a way to remember they'll never forget.

CINDY: And I know if Michelle could talk, she'd thank you for your thoughtfulness. I hope you enjoy the snapshots as much as we enjoy the camera.

Love from the three of us, Cindy.

SFX: Baby gurgles.

333
Writer Jim Johnston
Producer Buck Warnick
Music HEA Assoc.
Production Co. A&R Recording Studio
Agency Young & Rubicam International
Client Simmons Co.

334
Writer Steve Klausner
Producer Nick Ullett
Production Co. J. Walter Thompson
Agency J. Walter Thompson Co.
Client Eastman Kodak Co.

KISSINGER
30-second

HENRY: I'm so tired, Nancy, Egypt to Israel. Israel to Egypt. I don't even have time to balance my checkbook.

NANCY: I know, Henry. But thank goodness we have Fultime Checking.

HENRY: Attacking? Who's attacking?

NANCY: No, "checking," Henry. Fultime Checking, with Consec-U-Check. It makes balancing our checkbook so easy.

HENRY: (Relieved) Oh.

NANCY: Plus it gives us five other checking services—all free if we keep a balance of $250.

HENRY: The most concessions I ever got. And I didn't even have to negotiate for them.

ANNCR: Fultime Checking from Fulton National Bank. It's a checking service. Not just a checking account. Member F.D.I.C.

335
Writer Russ Dymond
Director Russ Dymond
Producer Russ Dymond
Production Co. National Recording Studios
Agency Lawler Ballard Little
Client Fulton National Bank

MORE OF THE UNEXPECTED-UNDERGROUND
60-second

ANNCR: You never know what to expect at Barney's Underground. One day you might come in to buy a sweater and suddenly find yourself walking out in a shirt called Post Time with horses and jockeys galloping all over the place. Or a pair of appliqued jeans sewn from denim patches. Or one of our luxurious gabardine vested suits by Yves St. Laurent that could well be the best-fitting suit you've ever worn.

Of course, we don't expect you to come down to the Underground just for the unexpected. So we also keep on hand a heady selection of blue serge blazers, Sisley and Mustang jeans, Shetland sweaters and western shirts. Some other places carry some of these things. The Underground carries them all. So if you're running low on jeans or could use a new blazer, come down to the Underground. And if on the way out you spot an incredibly supple, short leather jacket with three front zippers and eight sash pockets, pass it right on by. Because if you don't, you don't stand a chance.

Barney's Underground. More of the expected. And more of the unexpected. At 7th Avenue and 17th Street. Free parking. Open 9 to 9:30.

336
Writer Michael Drazen
Production Co. National Recording Studios
Agency Scali, McCabe, Sloves
Client Barney's Clothes

FIRST CLASS
60-second

MUSIC UNDER

ANNCR: First class on Japan Air Lines is like first class used to be. From the moment your kimono hostess greets you with a shy smile, you'll be struck by the careful attention that is placed on little things.

Your wine is not just French—it's a grand cru from the great vineyards of Burgundy and Bordeaux. Your caviar is not just any caviar—it's caviar from Iran.

You're living in a perfect world. Where you're never rushed, never overlooked, never forgotten . . . all the way to JAL's Orient.

337
Writer Terry Coveny
Producer Merl Bloom Assoc.
Music HEA Productions
Production Co. HEA Productions
Agency Ketchum, MacLeod & Grove
Client Japan Air Lines

NIGHTMARES AND OTHER TALES FROM THE VINYL JUNGLE
60-second

SFX: Howling wind; church bell tolling in the distance. Establish then under

ANNCR: (Very sinister) Midnight. And all over town people are safe in their beds. Suddenly —

SFX: Floor creak.

ANNCR: A sound.

SFX: Tension music under.

ANNCR: Is it real or is it a nightmare?

SFX: Footsteps.

ANNCR: It's coming nearer

SFX: Door creak . . .

ANNCR: And nearer. Is it real or is it a nightmare?

SFX: Door opening slowly . . .

ANNCR: This creature with twelve legs and six heads . . .

SFX: Woman screams . . .

ANNCR: It's opening its mouth to speak. What does it want to say?

SFX: Chord of anticipation, then band music.

SONG: I musta got lost
I musta got lost
I musta got lost
Somewhere down the line . . . and under

ANNCR: Nightmares and Other Tales from the Vinyl Jungle. The shocking new album from the J. Geils Band. On Atlantic Records and Tapes.

SONG: Nightmares. . . .

338
Writer Elin Guskind
Producer Elin Guskind
Music J. Geils Band
Agency Atlantic Records
Client Atlantic Records

GLADYS
60-second

SFX: Milk squirting into pail.

ANNCR: You're listening to Gladys . . . a big, beautiful 1400 pound dairy cow. At the business end, Tracy Andreg . . . believed by many to have the fastest pair of hands in the West.

TRACY: I'm just coastin' milkin' this cow. Just takin' my time.

ANNCR: Tracy's in training for the big hand milking contest at the P.I. this year . . . with 2000 bucks in prize money.

TRACY: . . . if she didn't have a good grip and a good strong arm, you wouldn't have much luck milkin' cows.

ANNCR: The P.I. "Milk-Offs." 60 seconds of gripping excitement held every day, along with all the livestock displays, the home and craft show and the championship rodeo/horse show.

TRACY: Ah . . . if you want to milk fast this is about the way it'd go . . .

ANNCR: The Pacific International Livestock Exposition. At the Expo Center, November 9 through 16.

SFX: Squirting stops.

TRACY: You get a free bath every once in awhile.

ANNCR: It's a lot of good clean fun.

SFX: Final squirts.

339
Writer Bill Borders
Director Bill Borders
Producer Bill Borders
Production Co. Spectrum Studios
Agency Cole & Weber
Client Pacific International Livestock Expo

JOAN RIVERS
60-seconds

JOAN RIVERS: Hello. I'm Joan Rivers. When I was a kid I took ballet lessons. And I was the worst. When we did Swan Lake, they made me wear water wings. And the music. Eccch. It always sounded like this.

MUSIC

RIVERS: But I adore the Joffrey Ballet. The Joffrey sounds like this.

MUSIC

RIVERS: And that's only the half of it. Come and see the other half. You're gonna love it. Take my word. If you like the ballet you'll love the Joffrey. And if you hate the ballet, you'll love the Joffrey.

340
Writers Enid Futterman
Alan Kupchick
Producer Steve Novick
Production Co. Aura Recording
Agency Grey Advertising
Client Joffrey Ballet

DINING ALONE
60-second

ANNCR: Stiller and Meara.

STILLER: Good evening, Miss. Will you be dining alone?

MEARA: Sob, yes!

STILLER: What can I get you?

MEARA: Manacotti.

STILLER: Oh, I'm sorry, Miss. We're all out.

MEARA: No, I mean Carmine Manacotti. He just broke our engagement. He had his mother call and tell me.

STILLER: Oh, the swine.

MEARA: No, she was very sweet about it.

STILLER: No, I meant Carmine. Anyway, may I suggest the Surf 'N Turf tonight.

MEARA: Is that some new singles bar?

STILLER: No, the Surf 'N Turf is our delicious combination of Lobster Tail and Filet Mignon. Perhaps to raise your spirits a very special wine to go with it.

MEARA: Can I get a wine that goes with seafood and meat?

STILLER: Certainly. May I bring a little Blue Nun to your table?

MEARA: Oh, I'm sure she would be very sympathetic. But I'd much rather be alone.

STILLER: No, no, Miss. Blue Nun is a wine. A delicious white wine that's correct with any dish. It goes as well with meat as it does with fish. And perhaps after dinner, cantelope?

MEARA: I don't see cantelope on the menu.

STILLER: No, that's me. Stanley Cantelope. I get off at 11:00. Maybe we could go out on the town.

ANNCR: Blue Nun. The delicious white wine that's correct with any dish. Another Sichel Wine imported by Schieffelin and Co., New York.

341
Writers Kay Kavanagh
Mark Yustein
Producer Lewis Kupperman
Production Co. National Recording
Agency Della Femina, Travisano & Partners
Client Schieffelin & Co.

BEETHOVEN
60-second

ANNCR: If Beethoven were alive today, he'd be recording music something like this.

MUSIC: (Modern rock version of the "Fifth" complete with dissonances and distortion.)

ANNCR: And he'd be recording it on Scotch Magnetic Tape. Because nearly eighty percent of all master recording studios use Scotch Magnetic Tape.

MUSIC: (More of the rock "Fifth".)

ANNCR: So, next time you record something, take a hint from the master.
Use Scotch . . . the Master Tape.

344
Writer Bob Mallin
Producer Kathi Golden
Music Dave Mathews
Production Co. Grant & Murtough
Agency BBDO
Client 3M Company

BRAITHWAITE
60-second

BRAITHWAITE: Mumbles, chuckles unintelligibly in agreement throughout.

BIG BANKER: Oh, I say, Braithwaite—I suppose you've heard this new bank in Decatur called Fidelity National. It claims it's going to take on the big banks. It's pure poppycock. Why, Fidelity National doesn't even have any branches. They're simply a bank. They do such unbanklike things, like keeping their drive-in teller open from 8 to 6, having hot coffee available all day long inside the bank, no service charge for personal checking, and staying open on Saturday from 9 to noon. It's absurd.

And who do they send against our hundreds of assistant Vice Presidents? One man who will make a decision for you.

Now really, the public's simply not ready for a bank without red tape. Our computer says so.

Now let me put it to you plainly, Braithwaite. Fidelity National. No red tape. No branches. A helping hand. A living, breathing person you can talk to. A bank you can call your own. Braithwaite, it's ridiculous.

ANNCR: Fidelity National. We're a bank. Not a branch.

345
Art Director Norman Grey
Writers Mel Stein
A. Goldsmith
Producers Mel Stein
Norman Grey
Production Co. Master Sound
Agency Doran Stein Grey
Client Fidelity National

MAINTAINING
50-second

MUSIC: Instrumental throughout

KAREN: It would be awful if you didn't like people, it would be a terrible job.

ANNCR: Karen Iozzo works for American Airlines in reservations. She's one of 30,000 men and women at American who are going out of their way in 1974. So you won't have to go out of yours.

KAREN: We establish a rapport, with the passengers by assuring them that we do understand what they need and, letting them know it.

ANNCR: Everybody at American is working to get you where you're going, when you want to go.

American is maintaining convenient schedules, so there should be seats available, even to the most popular destinations. And with people like Karen working for American you'll not only get there, you'll get there with a smile.

SONG: American Airlines, American Airlines . . .

MUSIC OUT

346
Writer Stevie Pierson
Producer Paul Conti
Music Labunski Productions
Agency Doyle Dane Bernbach
Client American Airlines

HEADACHE
60-second

ANNCR: It's been estimated that it would take a computer the size of a football stadium to do what your brain does. Come inside your body and see.

SFX: Transition music.

ANNCR: Thousands of messages bombard your brain. It receives them, sorts, files, orders reactions.

To perform its massive task, your brain needs oxygen. Hundreds of tiny vessels crisscross your brain to supply it.

But sometimes, some of the vessels expand and you feel the pressure as pain—the pain of headache.

You can effectively relieve headache and many other kinds of pain with Excedrin.

Two different research projects, on two different kinds of pain, studied the effectiveness of Excedrin. In both tests, Excedrin was significantly more effective than the common aspirin tablet. Significantly more effective.

When you need effective pain relief, take Excedrin as directed on the label. Excedrin, the extra-strength pain reliever.

MUSCLE ACHE
60-second

TEETH
60-second

352
Writer Peter Burkhard
Producer Jim Coyne
Production Co. Radio Band of America
Agency Young & Rubicam International
Client Bristol-Myers

TOMATO CATSUP
60-seconds

COSBY: Tomato Catsup. There's probably not a kid in the world who doesn't like tomato catsup.

'Cept for Lamont, who used to live a couple miles down the road. Now at Lamont's house, they didn't have the good tasting Del Monte Catsup, they always had some kinda weird stuff that did nothin' for a hamburger. So whenever Lamont ate over at our house we'd say, "Have a little catsup, Lamont", Lamont'd say, "No thanks. I don't want to mess up the taste of my french fries." So one day I said to Lamont, "My Mom buys Del Monte Catsup. It's got seven terrific herbs and spices and you're gonna love it." So Lamont said, "Is that a fact?" and he tried some on his french fries. "Mmmm, that's pretty good," he says. "Your Mom really knows her catsup." Then he tries some on my french fries. "Mmmm, that's even better," he says. Then he tries some on the magnolia bush outside the front door.

Right about then we decided it was time for Lamont to leave. So we gave him the catsup and a ride home in my father's new car. But before we even made it out the driveway, ol' Lamont had catsup on the dashboard and was eatin' that too.

ANNCR: Del Monte Catsup. When it comes to picking catsup, Mother really does know best.

PEARS
60-second

CORN
60-second

SILVER

353
Writer Valerie Wagner
Producer Harry Wypich
Production Co. Coast Recorders
Agency McCann-Erickson San Francisco
Client Del Monte

HAVE A GOOD TIME FROM HOUSTON
60-second

SFX: Jet roar, cocktail chatter, tinkling piano.

GIRL: You know you can always have a good time on Southwest Airlines. Three times a day to San Antonio . . .
Every hour from 7:30 A.M. to Love.

DIRECTOR: Every hour . . .

SINGERS: Every hour . . .

DIRECTOR: From Houston's Hobby . . .

SINGERS: From Houston's Hobby . . .

DIRECTOR: Southwest has a good time to Love.

SINGERS: We have a good time to Love.

DIRECTOR: And the same is true . . .

SINGERS: And the same is true . . .

DIRECTOR: Coming back to Hou . . .

SINGERS: Coming back to Hou . . .

DIRECTOR: Ston!

SINGERS: Stonnnnn!

DIRECTOR: Everybody!

SINGERS: And Southwest go-oes . . . to San Antonio . . . three good times a day.

ANNCR: Now Southwest has even more good times to Dallas and San Antonio. And our Pleasure Class Flights are still just fifteen dollars.

SINGERS: You have a good time . . . on Southwest Airlines.

HAVE A GOOD TIME FROM SAN ANTONIO
60-second

HAVE A GOOD TIME FROM DALLAS
60-second

TOWER
60-second

ANNCR: Throughout the civilized world, the St. Francis has always been known as a fine hotel.

Perhaps the only problem was that not everyone who wanted to stay at the St. Francis could stay at the St. Francis.

No more. That's all been changed. We've added the Tower. Now, instead of having 600 rooms fill up too fast, we have 1200 guest rooms that fill up comfortably. Plus grand ballrooms and assorted meeting rooms. The Tower is taller than the original. 32 stories. The view is grander. And glass elevators travel up the outside.

But there are important similarities. The stonework outside. The wide hallways and carpeting inside. And, of course, the mood, the feel—and the service—are exactly the same. Because we want you to feel at home in the St. Francis, wherever you go. Or stay.

St. Francis, California. The city within The City.

LEGEND
60-second

COINS
60-second

RADIO

354
Writer Richard Schiera
Director Richard Schiera
Harvey Greenberg
Producer Harvey Greenberg
Agency The Bloom Agency
Client Southwest Airlines

355
Writers Nadine Pasnick
Hal Dixon
Director Larry Field
Producer Larry Field
Production Co. Cole & Weber
Agency Cole & Weber
Client St. Francis Hotel

STANLEY
55-second

NARRATOR: Once upon a time there was a cab driver who had no opinion. Stanley knew every street in Detroit . . .

STANLEY: I can getcha to Sterling Heights in 11 minutes.

NARRATOR: . . . But he knew very little about the world. When the passengers in his cab would strike up a conversation . . .

PASSENGER: Boy, that's some bill they just passed in Lansing.

NARRATOR: Stanley didn't have much to say.

STANLEY: Uh . . . hot enough for ya?

NARRATOR: Then one day, the president of a well-known corporation said to him . . .

PRESIDENT: Stanley, if you read The Detroit News you know.

NARRATOR: Stanley began reading The Detroit News every day. He discovered he had a real gift for analyzing current events.

STANLEY: That's right, Mac, Greenland will be the next superpower.

NARRATOR: Soon leaders from all over the world were coming to Stanley for advice.

BRITISH DIPLOMAT: I say, Stanley, what should we do about this banana embargo?

NARRATOR: Stanley became famous and respected. Which proves beyond a shadow of a doubt what a good thing it is to Read The News and Know.

DIPLOMAT: I'm honored to meet you, Messieur Stanley. Hot enough for you?

YOUNG COUPLE
55-second

SINGLE LADY
55-second

GOLD

348
Writer Lawrence Kasdan
Directors Lawrence Kasdan
Jim Dale
Producers Lawrence Kasdan
Jim Dale
Production Co. Bell Sound
Agency W. B. Doner & Co.
Client The Detroit News

JAPANESE MEAL
60-second

ANNCR: Stiller & Meara:

STILLER: Hi Gert. Hubby's home.

MEARA: Come in happy wanderer. Take off your shoes.

STILLER: Why, did you shampoo the rugs today?

MEARA: No, I cooked Japanese food.

STILLER: Sniff—smells funny.

MEARA: That's incense burning.

STILLER: Quick, take it off the stove. Maybe we can save it.

MEARA: Incense is a Japanese scent, one of those mysteries of the Orient.

STILLER: I'm more interested in mysteries of the oven. Let's eat.

MEARA: Can my big samurai handle chopsticks?

STILLER: Easy. You oughta hear me play Malaguena.

MEARA: Oh, Fletcher. Here, have some Sashimi.

STILLER: Uhg—looks like raw fish!

MEARA: It is raw fish. A Japanese delicacy. Then we're having Beef Teryaki.

STILLER: Lucky, I brought home a little Blue Nun.

MEARA: Fletcher, a Buddhist Monk would add more atmosphere.

STILLER: Gert, Blue Nun is a wine. A delicious white wine.

MEARA: I didn't slave over a hot Hibachi to see my beef served with white wine.

STILLER: Blue Nun is the white wine that's correct with any dish. It goes as well with meat as it does with fish.

MEARA: Sounds expensive.

STILLER: Oh, Lotus blossom money's no object when you've got a yen for something.

SFX: Gong

ANNCR: Blue Nun, the delicious white wine that's correct with any dish. Another Sichel Wine imported by Schieffelin & Co., New York.

CLUB ATLANTIQUE
60-second

DINING ALONE
60-second

349
Writers Mark Yustein
Kay Kavanagh
Producer Lewis Kuperman
Production Co. National Recording
Agency Della Femina, Travisano & Partners
Client Schieffelin & Co.

HELLO SUNSHINE
60-second

SONG: Hello Sunshine . . .
Hello Mountain Dew.
With the lemony look of sunshine . . .
And the different taste that's right for you . . .

It's fresh as sunrise, Mountain Dew.
It pours like sunshine, Mountain Dew.
Refreshing as morning the whole day through . . .
The lemony taste of Mountain Dew

Hello Sunshine . . .

Hello Sunshine . . .
Hello Mountain Dew.
Hello Sunshine . . .
Hello Mountain Dew.

DIXIE
60-second

STANDARD
60-second

350
Writer Spencer Michlin
Producers Spencer Michlin
John Hill
Composers Spencer Michlin
John Hill
Production Co. Michlin & Hill
Agency BBD&O
Client PepsiCo

STANDARD
30-second

SONG: You can do it (zip!) we can help.
One calorie, one calorie Diet Pepsi can help.
You can do it (zip!) we can help.
You can do it if you wanna . . .
You can do it if you wanna . . .
And Diet Pepsi can help.

Yes you can if you try . . .
One calorie Diet Pepsi's one good reason why.
(zip! zip!)
You can do it if you wanna . . .
You can do it if you wanna . . .
And Diet Pepsi can help.
(zip!)
Great tasting one calorie Diet Pepsi can help.
(zip! zip!)

DIXIE
30-second

351
Writer Spencer Michlin
Producers John Hill
Spencer Michlin
Composers Spencer Michlin
John Hill
Production Co. Michlin & Hill
Agencie BBDO
Michlin & Hill
Client PepsiCo

RED LIPS
55-second

SONGWRITER: I'm Lionel Cirken, the songwriter. The Cheap Jeans people are turning one of my best songs, "Red Lips," into a commercial. But everybody knows about Cheap Jeans. So, so when they sing Cheap Jeans, just substitute "Red Lips" and you'll get an idea what I'm trying to say.

SONG: There is long hair, but no one has long hair like yours. There are blue eyes, but no one has blue eyes like yours. There are Cheap Jeans, Cheap Jeans, but no one has Cheap Jeans like yours.

SONGWRITER: Did ya do it? Did ya substitute "Red Lips"? So forget Cheap Jeans just forget they say it . . .

SONG: No one has Cheap (songwriter overlaps with "Red Lips") Jeans (songwriter again with "Like Yours") like yours . . .
There are Cheap Jeans, Cheap Jeans, no one has Cheap Jeans like yours . . .

SONGWRITER: Oh, that's beautiful, I wrote that, I wrote it.

FADE: Cheap Jeans, Cheap Jeans . . .

ROCK GROUP
55-second

SINGER
55-second

TRASHBALL
60-second

SONG: Trashball . . . a neat game . . . everybody wins, let me show you how to play. Well, you pick up some trash . . . pretend it's a ball . . . and then you throw it in the bucket, you're playing trashball. Jump shot, hook, you got to put it away . . . we're gonna' play that trashball everyday.

Jump shot, hook, ya' gotta put it away . . .
we're gonna' play that trashball everyday . . .
We're gonna' play that trashball everyday . . .
We're gonna' play that trashball everyday . . .
We're Gonna' play that trashball everyday.

356
Writer Jennifer Berne
Directors Arnie Arlow
Jennifer Berne
Producer Barbara Gans
Music Mega Music
Production Co. Mega Music
Agency Martin Landley
Arlow Advertising
Client Cheap Jeans

357
Writer Susan Russell
Producer Dennis Gray
Music Lucas/McFaul Productions
Agency VanSant Dugdale
Client City of Baltimore

LULLABY
60-second

SINGER: (Speaking) Lullaby for my brand new child.
His name is Michael. His eyes are brown. His hair is black.
He only just arrived today. He is ten years old.

SONG: Sleep Michael sleep
You got nothing to be scared of
Dream Michael dream
You got nothing but love
I am your mama
That's all you got to know
And daddy's your papa
And you never have to go.

ANNCR: There are so many children in New York who need mamas and papas. And just about all you need to have, is love to give. Write to Adoption, Albany, N.Y. for information. Have a child. It's as beautiful as having a baby.

SONG: I am your mama
That's all you got to know
And daddy's your papa
And you never have to go

ANNCR: A message from the New York State Board of Social Welfare and the State Department of Social Services.

358
Writer Enid Futterman
Producer Steve Novick
Composer Michael Cohen
Production Cos. Generation Sound
Crescendo Productions
Agency Grey Advertising
Client New York State
Board of Adoption

PIED PIPER
55-second

SONG (BOY): When you're a Scout,
You're a Scout all the way,
From your first Tenderfoot,
To your Eagle Scout days.

CHORUS: When you're a Scout,
Black or White, Red or Tan,
You've got Brothers around,
You're a family man.

You're never alone,
You're never disconnected.

When you're a Scout,
You're the top cat in town,
You're the Gold Medal kid,
With the Heavyweight crown.

When you're a scout,
You're the swinginest thing,
Little boy you're a man,
Little man you're a King.

Here come the Scouts, yeah,
And we're gonna sign every last boy in town,
In the whole lovin' town,
In this big, movin', ever-lovin' town!

ANNCR: Go to your school on Thursday, November 14th and join our gang, the New York Scouts, 'cause in this town you'd better be prepared.

SILVER

359
Writer Jim Johnston
Producer Ken Yagoda
Music HEA Assoc.
Production Co. A&R Recording
Agency Young & Rubicam International
Client Boy Scouts of New York

DOUBLE UP, AMERICA
30-second

MUSIC: Double up, America . . .

ANNCR: If you drive to work alone, it's costing you twice as much to commute as it should. And that's too much. Cut it in half. Take a friend. Double up, America. Two can ride cheaper than one.

MUSIC: Double up, America . . .

ANNCR: A public service—U.S. Department of Transportation, this station and The Ad Council.

DOUBLE UP
60-second

360
Writer Ed Flamma
Director Ron Watts
Music Tom Dawes Productions
Production Co. Tom Dawes Productions
Agency APCL&K
Client United States Department of Transportation

BROTHERS & SISTERS
60-second

SONG: I knew a 19 year old lady
who passed away today
She died in a car with her 20 year old man
He was drinking wine
He was feeling fine
He was driving with one hand
And now nobody knows just what to say.

REFRAIN: It's not just the mothers and the fathers
It's the brothers and the sisters too
And now's the time to talk before it's you.

SONG: Thousands of us are killed or hurt badly in drunk driving crashes every year. Please don't let your friends drive if they're drunk. Say something, refuse to ride with them. Offer to drive, something—before there's nothing to say. Be a friend, don't loose one.

REFRAIN: It's not just the mothers and the fathers
It's the brothers and the sisters too
And now's the time to talk before it's you.

FRIENDS
60-second

TOM
60-second

SILVER

360A
Writers Enid Futterman
John Simpson
Producer Patty Wineapple
Music Richard Berg
John Simpson
Agency Grey Advertising
Client National Highway Traffic Safety Administration

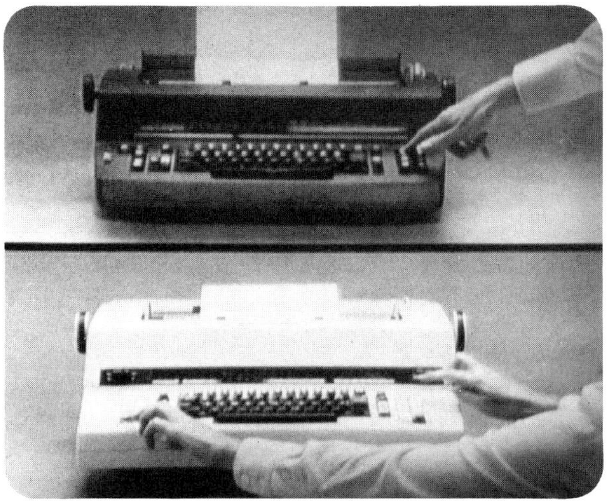

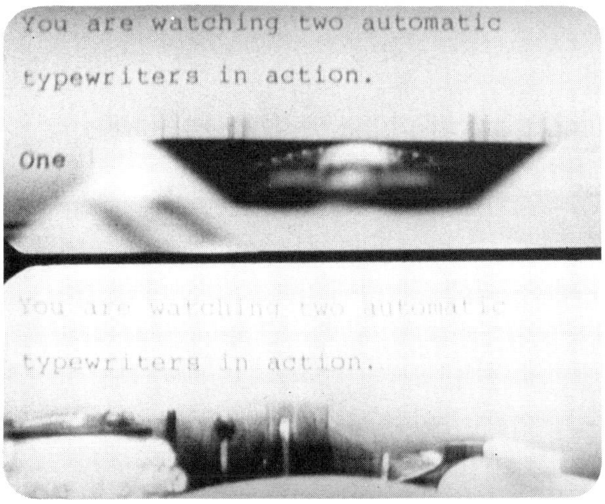

You are watching two automatic
typewriters in action.
One
You are watching two automatic
typewriters in action.

XEROX

EXODUS
30-second

ANNCR: You are watching two automatic typewriters in action.

One is the best known.

The other has just been introduced.

The new one can automatically type in both directions at the rate of up to 350 words per minute.

The automatic typewriter that's twice as fast is made by Xerox.

That's right. Xerox.

SUPER: *Xerox*

SILVER

361
Art Director Allen Kay
Writers Lois Korey
Lloyd Fink
Director Mickey Trenner
Producer Syd Rangell
Production Co. EUE/Screen Gems
Agency Needham, Harper & Steers
Client Xerox Corp.

Brigitte Bardot

AIR FRANCE
French Government
Tourist Office

BARDOT
30-second

BRIGITTE: When I go away on vacation, I stay home.

I walk along the Seine. Swim on the Riviera.

See great art. And eat some of the best food in the world.

When you go away on vacation, come to France.

You too will feel at home.

MUSIC

ANNCR: Call The French Government Tourist Office or Air France.

SUPER: *French Government Tourist Office*

362
Art Director Allen Kay
Writers Lois Korey
Alan Fraser
Director Laurent Vergess
Producers Syd Rangell
Allen Kay
Production Co. Hamster Films
Agency Needham, Harper & Steers
Client French Government
Tourist Office

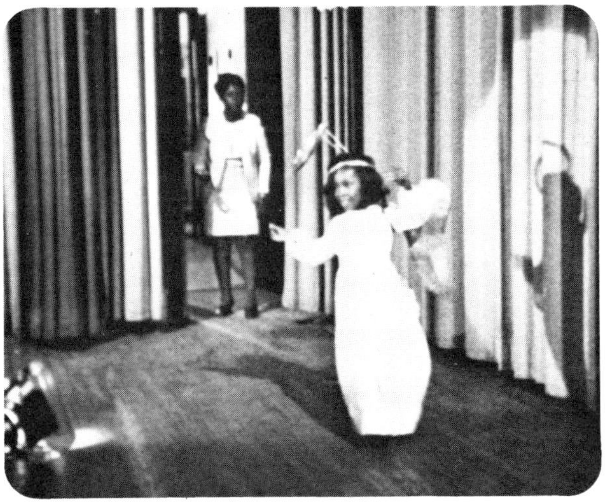

DO YOUR OWN SING
30-second

EMCEE: (Singing) "Killing Me Softly" . . .

SFX: Crowd boos.

SFX: Record needle drops.

SINGERS: (Singing) "Let Your Love Shine Through"

CHILD: (Singing) "A Million to One"

SFX: Applause and cheering.

EMCEE: Great show! Now let's bring out the band . . .

That's right . . .

This album was our band tonight. The music for all our wonderful singers was right here . . . All the latest hits without the vocals

You do the vocals . . . That's why they call it "Do your Own Sing." . . . Begins to sing "Me and Mrs. Jones."

363
Cameraman Julian Townsand
Writer Thomas McNamee
Director Arnold Levine
Agency Gotham Advertising
Client Epic Records

EXCELLO MAGIC OVAL
30-second

ANNCR: Shirt collars come in standard sizes. But unfortunately people's necks don't.

SFX

ANNCR: So Excello offers . . .

The Magic Oval Comfort Collar.

It works without a button.

Like other collars it comes in standard sizes, but unlike others it adjusts to fit any neck perfectly.

The Magic Oval Collar by Excello. It always fits perfectly.

SUPER: *The Magic Oval by Excello*

364
Art Director Rob Lopes
Writer Mike Lichtman
Director Elbert Budin
Production Co. Ampersand Productions
Agency Levine, Huntley, Schmidt
Client Excello Shirts

Gelatin–Pudding
Section
Little Lunch
strawberry

Section

In the gelatin-pudding section.
Little Lunch
strawberry

SUPERMARKET
30-second

HE: Louise? This is new? The Little Lunch from Del Monte? (To himself) Little Lunch. I'll put it with the small salami.

SHE: It's made from yogurt.

HE: I'll put it with the yogurt.

SHE: It's made from yogurt.

HE: I'll put it with the yogurt.

SHE: But don't put it with the yogurt. *Yogurt never tasted like this.* Comes in raspberry, strawberry, blueberry, pineapple, and peach.

SON: Put it with the bananas.

HE: I'll put it with the bananas.

SHE: *It's nutritious.* You eat it at lunchtime.

HE: (To his son) We eat it at lunchtime.

VO: You don't have to have a big lunch to have a good lunch. With *new Little Lunch products from Del Monte.*

SHE: Sam, are you putting it away?

HE: I'm putting it away.

365
Art Director Jerry Collamer
Writer Valerie Wagner
Director Joe Sedelmaier
Producer Harry Wypich
Production Co. Sedelmaier Films
Agency McCann-Erickson San Francisco
Client Del Monte

The Poulan CounterVibe.

TWO-GUYS
30-second

SFX: Rattling.

ANNCR: Both of these guys spent all morning cutting with chain saws. One used an ordinary chain saw. The other used . . .

the Poulan CounterVibe, a powerful new lightweight with automatic chain oiling, a super quiet muffler, and a shock absorbing system that reduces vibration up to 78%.

So . . . which guy used the new Poulan CounterVibe . . . and which one didn't?

SFX: Ice cubes jingling under beauty shot.

SUPER: *The Super XXV Countervibe Yellow Page Info*

366
Art Director Vin Scheihagen
Writer Harold Schwartz
Director Joe Sedelmaier
Producer Billy Ray Smith
Production Co. Sedelmaier Films
Agency Tracy-Locke Advertising
Client Beaird-Poulan

FREE

FREE

CLUB MEDITERRANEE
TAHITI
See your travel agent.

CLUB MEDITERRANEE
30-second

SFX: Exciting Caribbean music.

ANNCR: After you pay for your room and board at Club Med, virtually everything else is free.

At Club Med/Tahiti, you can not only leave your troubles home, you can leave your money home.

SUPER: *Club Mediterranee/Tahiti*

367
Art Director Bill Kamp
Writer John Russo
Producer Sandy Sinclair
Production Co. Duffix Productions
Agency Levine, Huntley Schmidt
Client Club Mediterranee

Hefty

Hefty
TRASH
BAGS

ROMEO AND JULIET
30-second

JULIET: Romeo, oh Romeo, wherefore art thou, Romeo?

WINTERS: Here, sweet Juliet!

JULIET: My garbage is ready!
Oh! Twas thirty pounds of garbage!

ROMEO: My, how strong these are! What are they? . . . . . gasp. . . . . Hefty! I can read!

JULIET: Quickly, take these as token of my love!

ROMEO: This is a token of her love. Strange child.

SUPER: *From Mobil*

368
Art Director Ken Kimura
Writer Ethan Revsin
Designers Ethan Revsin
Ken Kimura
Director Victor Haboush
Producer Ethan Revsin
Production Co. Haboush Co.
Agency Lee King and Partners
Client Mobil Chemical Co.

HOLLOW SUITCASE
30-second

KARL MALDEN: You are about to witness a crime.

An unsuspecting traveler, her wallet buried safely in a canvas bag . . .

Watch closely . . .

Don't carry cash. Carry American Express Travelers Checks.

Now, there are other brands of travelers checks, but they're not the same. Only American Express can give you emergency refunds 365 days a year. So insist on American Express Travelers Checks.

369
Art Director Mark Ross
Writer Brendan Kelley
Director Bob Giraldi
Producer Phil Suarez
Agency Ogilvy & Mather
Client American Express Travelers Checks

BRIAN
30-second

BRIAN: I was ten when my father started saving for my college education. "Brian," he said, "you're gonna have it better than me. You just do the studying. I'll do the saving."

He had it all planned. There was only one thing he didn't plan. He didn't plan on dying.

MUSIC

ANNCR: When a man dies, his dreams don't have to die with him. Talk to us about your life insurance needs.

ANIMATED LOGO: *Mutual of New York MONY. For the future*

370
Art Director Andrew Langer
Writer Marshall Karp
Director Steve Horn
Producer Diane Jeremias
Production Co. Steve Horn, Inc.
Agency The Marschalk Co.
Client Mutual of New York

Chester Gould
Gillette
the dry look

HEROES
30-second

ANNCR: Dick Tracy, Wethead.
Dick Tracy, The Dry Look.
Clark Kent, Wethead.
Clark Kent, The Dry Look.

SFX: Shazam! (Thunder, lightning)

ANNCR: . . . Wethead.

SFX: Shazam! (Thunder, lightning)

ANNCR: . . . The Dry Look.

The Dry Look makes a good guy look even better.

And only Gillette has the adjustable valve to spray as light and dry as you like.

So c'mon, hero—get rid of that wet look. Get with The Dry Look.

The Dry Look aerosol hair control. From Gillette.

371
Art Director Frank Vero
Writer Brian Dillon
Designer Hal Silvermintz
Artists Chester Gould
National Periodical Publications
Director Steve Elliot
Producer Bert Mangel
Production Cos. Perpetual Motion
EUE Video
Agency BBDO
Boston
Client Gillette

The Freeman
Free-Flex.

FREEMAN SHOES
30-second

ANNCR: This fresh egg is going to help us sell . . .

this brand new Free-Flex shoe from Freeman.

Watch.

You can press harder.

SUPER: *Think that was a fluke?*

ANNCR: You can do it with any new Freeman Free-Flex.

Let's use the same egg.

SUPER: *The Freeman Free-Flex*

372
Art Director Norman Tanen
Writer Laurel Cutler
Director David Vine
Producer Susan Kirchmeier
Production Co. Grapevine Productions
Agency Leber Katz Partners
Client United States Shoe Corp.

10
9
Belmont Park
First Race 1:30

THOROUGHBRED TRAINING
30-second

ANNCR: The Thoroughbred. He's born fast.

But up until the day he runs his first race, he has to be carefully, patiently trained . . .

Because the same instincts that make him wary enough to survive in the wild . . . would only hold him back on a race track.

And then one day, his natural fears of noise and crowds and the touch of man are gone . . .

Replaced by a single purpose: to win. He's ready to take his place among the fastest animals in the world.

SUPER: *Belmont Park*
1st Race 1:30

373
Art Director Harvey Gabor
Writer Rick Johnston
Director Peter Israelson
Producer Phil Messina
Production Co. EUE/Screen Gems
Agency McCann-Erickson
Client The New York Racing Assoc.

Probe

PROBE-TAXI
30-second

MAVEN: Does your word have an *X*, Petrucci?

PETRUCCI: Yeah, 15 points for you.

MAVEN: You don't need to know big words to win at Probe. Probe's a different kind of word game. How about an *A*?

PETRUCCI: 10 points.

MAVEN: What you gotta remember is which letters have been guessed . . . A - X - I. . . What kinda word can you make from A - X - I?

LADY: Taxi! Taxi!

ANNCR: Probe from Parker Brothers. It's a different kind of word game. You don't have to be a genius to win.

MAVEN: Does your word have a *P*?

374
Art Directors Ken Amaral
Dick Gage
Writers Peter Caroline
Stan Schulman
Director Joe Pytka
Producer Jerry Kreeger
Production Co. Wylde and Assoc.
Agency Humphrey Browning MacDougall
Client Parker Brothers

converse
an Eltra company

ALL STARS - SLAM DUNK
30-second

KID: A poem to my Converse All Star basketball shoes:

You are the greatest and that's no jive.
You're standard equipment on the B Street five.
As I fly through the air doing my famous slam dunk
I'm flying first class and that's no bunk.
My shoes will be wearing the Converse name.
Till they bronze my feet for the Hall of Fame.
Converse All Stars . . . Limousines for the feet.

ANNCR: Converse All Stars. An Eltra Company.

SILVER

375
Art Director Ralph Moxcey
Writer Scott Miller
Director Joe Hanwright
Producer Thomas Anabel
Production Co. Wakeford/Orloff
Agency Humphrey Browning MacDougall
Client Converse Rubber Corp.

AN ELEPHANT STEPPED ON IT
30-second

SPOKESMAN: Last year the Tonka Toy Co. ran a commercial to parents about broken toys.

In it children told their parents how their toys got broken.

One said, "An elephant stepped on it."

We wondered. What would happen if an elephant stepped on a Tonka Toy?

MUSIC

ANNCR: A toy shouldn't break just because a child plays with it.

GOLD

376
Art Director Mike Tesch
Writer Patrick Kelly
Director Steve Horn
Producer Vera Samama
Production Co. Horn/Griner Productions
Agency Carl Ally
Client Tonka Corp.

Vacation in Rio

STAY HOME/GO AWAY
30-second

MAN 1: Gas problems, political problems, economic problems. How can you think of a vacation at a time like this?

MAN 2: With all those problems, how can you stay home?

MAN 3: If I take my two weeks at home, I could paint the house.

MAN 4: If I'd stayed home I would have spent two weeks painting the house.

MAN 5: I'll probably get away next year.

MAN 6: Who knows, maybe next year I won't be able to get away.

376A
Art Director John Danza
Writer David Altschiller
Director Jeff Lovinger
Producer Maureen Kearns
Agency Carl Ally
Client Pan American World Airways

THE BIG CAR EXPERTS.

SMAL

THE SMALL CAR EXPERTS.

SMALL CAR EXPERTS
30-second

ANNCR: One night, while America was sleeping, the people who've been making all those big cars—underwent a magical change.

They became "The Small Car Experts."

At Fiat we said to ourselves, "Isn't that wonderful?"

That they could do overnight what it took Fiat 70 years to achieve.

Fiat . . . The biggest selling car in Europe.

377
Art Director Roy Grace
Writer David Altschiller
Director Dick Loew
Producer Maureen Kearns
Production Co. Gomes-Loew
Agency Carl Ally
Client Fiat-Roosevelt Motors

DRIVING CONDITIONS
30-second

ANNCR: In Europe, the driving conditions are among . . . The most difficult in the world.

And the price of gas is possibly the highest in the world. As much as $1.80 a gallon.

To deal with these conditions, Europeans have over fifty different kinds of cars to choose from.

And for the last twelve straight years, the car they chose . . . Fiat.

FIAT
The biggest selling car in Europe.

378
Art Director Ted Shaine
Writers David Altschiller
Ed Butler
Director Massimo Magri
Producer Bob Schenkel
Production Co. Politecne Cinematografica
Agency Carl Ally
Client Fiat-Roosevelt Motors

Traveling Banker
262-5252
MEMBER FDIC

COUPLE
30-second

BANKER: And what is your full name please?

MAN: Alvin John Manelis.

BANKER: And how much would you like to borrow, Mr. Manelis?

WIFE: (Interrupting) Only nine hundred . . .

MAN: A thousand and nine hundred if you don't mind.

ANNCR: The Citibank Traveling Banker. From now on whenever you need a loan, instead of going to the bank, he'll come to you any time, any day of the week.

SUPER: *The Citibank Traveling Banker. The banker that makes house calls. Call: 262-5252*

379
Art Director Jay Wolf
Writer Mike Bookman
Director Bob Giraldi
Producer Joe Scibetta
Production Co. Ampersand Productions
Agency Doherty, Mann & Olshan
Client First National City Corp.

FLUFF-OUT FACIAL TISSUES
30-second

SNEEZE

JOEY: Hi. I'm Joey Faye. I've been sneezing for a living since I started in vaudeville, age 14.

SNEEZE UNDER

I'm going to sneeze into Kleenex. 2-ply tissue. 200 to the box.

SNEEZE

Very soft. Now I'm going to sneeze into Marcal. 2-ply tissue. 200 to the box.

SNEEZE

Also very soft. But if you sneezed as much as I sneeze . . .

SNEEZE

you'd sneeze into Marcal. Because Marcal costs about 10 cents less than Kleenex. And 10 cents a box is nothing to . . .

SNEEZE

sneeze at.

380
Art Director Frank Nicolo
Writer Robert Hildt
Director Don Tortoriello
Producer Frank Nicolo
Production Co. EUE/Screen Gems
Agency Chalek & Dreyer
Client Marcal Paper Mills

Suggested

$5.00 LESS
30-second

ANNCR: Here's the MX-25 Bowmar Brain.

Here's the 2510 Texas Instrument's calculator.

Now, they're both called full-featured calculators. But Bowmar gives you a percent key. They don't.

Bowmar has an automatic constant. They have a manual one.

And the Bowmar fits in your pocket, easily. Texas Instrument's doesn't.

Now, you know what these extras cost you with Bowmar—about $5 less.

The Bowmar Brain $34.95.

381
Art Director Stan Block
Writer Frank DiGiacomo
Designer Stan Block
Director Jeff Lovinger
Production Co. Lovinger, Tardio, Melsky
Agency Rosenfeld, Sirowitz & Lawson
Client Bowmar Instrument Corp.

ATTIC
30-second

MUSIC

SINGER: "The best minute of the day.
The best minute of the day.
From Polaroid."

ANNCR: The Square Shooter 2 Land Camera.

The lowest priced color camera from Polaroid.

MUSIC

SINGER: "Is there any other way?"

ANNCR: Only $24.95.

382
Art Director Robert Gage
Writer Jack Dillon
Cameraman Richard Dubbleman
Director Robert Gage
Producer Cliff Fagin
Production Co. Directors Studio
Agency Doyle Dane Bernbach
Client Polaroid Corp.

MINER
30-second

IRV: I saw it first. It was kinda glidin' up through that arroyo. At first I thought it was a motorcycle, but it was real quiet. You'd have a heck of a time gettin' a mule up through there let alone a motorcycle. I don't think you could get a mule up through there. What do you think, Al?

AL: I think it should be reported to the Air Force.

ANNCR: It's like no other motorcycle you've ever seen. The Cat. From Yamaha.

384
Art Director Gerald Andelin
Writer Don Hadley
Artist William Littlejohn
Director Dick Snider
Producer Gerald Andelin
Production Co. N. Lee Lacy
Agency Botsford Ketchum
San Francisco
Client Yamaha International Corp.

ARTHUR ASHE
30-second

ARTHUR: Hi, I'm Arthur Ashe.

You can't have a good backhand in tennis if you ignore your backbone.

So I don't.

See this curve?

Look what happens to it on a Simmons Beautyrest Mattress. The coils are free to push up and fill in under the curve. But, at equal pressure, these ordinary coils don't fill in as readily.

So I sleep on a firm Beautyrest. Have for years. 'Cause I like the way it supports my backbone, which supports my backhand, which supports me.

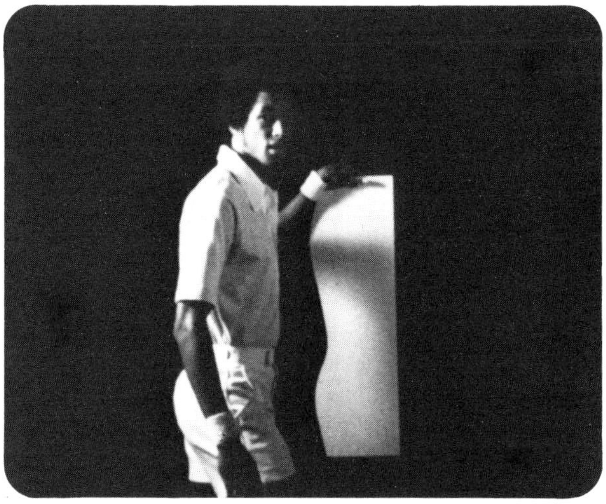

BEAUTYREST
THE OVERNIGHT VACATION

385
Art Director Matt Basile
Writer Gretta Basile
Director Marty Goldman
Producer Nancy Bacal
Production Co. EUE/Screen Gems
Agency Young & Rubicam International
Client Simmons Corp.

CAR
30-second

ANNCR: Robert Ammon . . . Michigan

Mrs. James Simonds . . . New Hampshire.

Mrs. Frank O'Brien . . . Alabama.

Mrs. Travis Wiginton . . . California.

Robert Geroy . . . North Carolina.

James Edelstein . . . Wisconsin.

Mrs. D. M. Olson . . . Minnesota.

Ask them whether an American Tourister is a great suitcase to have . . . when you hit the road.

SUPER: *American Tourister*

388
Art Director Jack Mariucci
Writer Marcia Bell Grace
Designer Jack Mariucci
Director Steve Horn
Producer Susan Calhoun
Production Co. Horn/Griner Productions
Agency Doyle Dane Bernbach
Client American Tourister

Frank Perdue

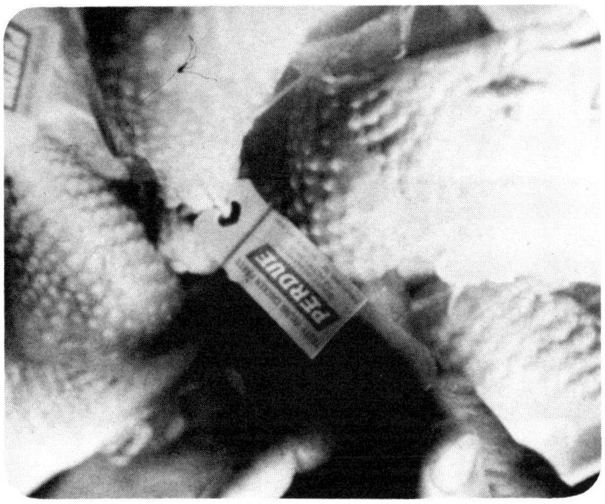
PERDUE

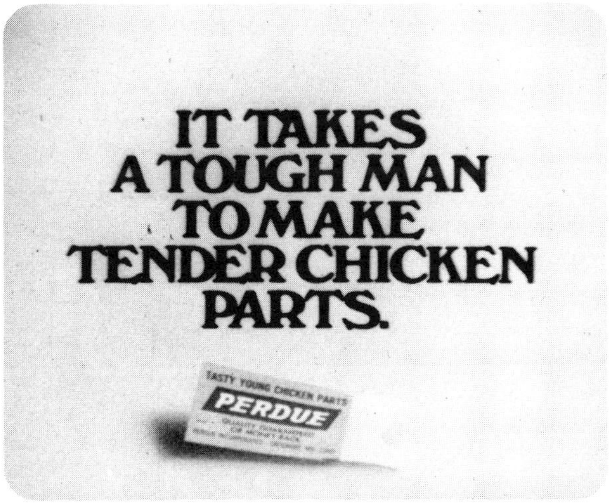
IT TAKES
A TOUGH MAN
TO MAKE
TENDER CHICKEN
PARTS.
TASTY YOUNG CHICKEN PARTS
PERDUE

UNKNOWN ANCESTRY
30-second

FRANK PERDUE: Most chicken parts are of unknown ancestry. Where do you suppose these came from? The fact is when you buy most chicken parts you have no way of knowing.

Unless they're my chicken parts.

Perdue Pedigreed Parts. They're the only ones that come from tender young Perdue chickens.

And the only ones identified with a name tag and my money-back guarantee.

I don't know about you, but when I was a little boy my father told me never to take chicken from a stranger.

SUPER: *It takes a tough man to make tender chicken parts*

389
Art Director Sam Scali
Writer Edward A. McCabe
Director Frank Herman
Production Co. Televideo Productions
Agency Scali, McCabe, Sloves
Client Perdue Farms

WALL STREET
30-second

ANNCR: The man who just walked out that door is Wall Street financial expert Allan D. Sutton, who's about to give you some advice on how to get through those uncertain times.

Something you can buy low, yields great dividends while you have it . . .

and, if you ever decide to unload it, chances are it'll sell high.

SFX

SUTTON: Buy a Volkswagen.

SFX: Car noises.

391
Art Director Charles Piccirillo
Writer Mike Mangano
Cameraman Ernie Caparros
Directors Mike Mangano
Charles Piccirillo
Producer Rosemary Barre
Production Co. Directors Studio
Agency Doyle Dane Bernbach
Client Volkswagen of America Corp.

30 m.p.h. barrier test.

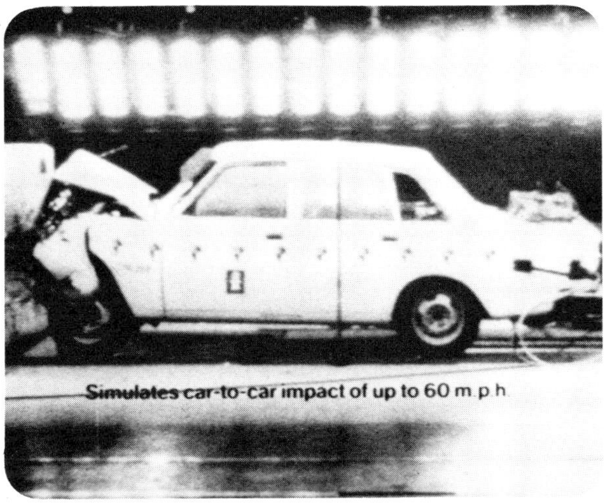
Simulates car-to-car impact of up to 60 m.p.h.

VOLVO
The car for people
who think.

CORPORATE CRASH TEST/75
30-second

MUSIC UNDER

ANNCR: The government says car makers must provide five-mile-per-hour bumpers to protect their cars.

But Volvo doesn't stop there.

Volvo's front end is designed to absorb highway-speed impacts to protect the passenger compartment.

Bumpers are designed to protect cars.

Volvo's front end is designed to protect people.

SUPER: *Volvo. The car for people who think*

392
Art Director Robert Reitzfeld
Writer Thomas J. Nathan
Directors Robert Reitzfeld
Thomas J. Nathan
Producers Robert Reitzfeld
Thomas J. Nathan
Production Co. Scali, McCabe, Sloves
Agency Scali, McCabe, Sloves
Client Volvo of America Corp.

Today, you

VARIETY
30-second

ANNCR: The Daily News has so many grocery coupons that some people can't get together on what's more important:

Good reading on one side of the page or a good bargain on the other.

But anytime a ten cent newspaper can inform, entertain, and help save a few dollars on food, it's got to be the best deal in town.

The Daily News. Today you really need it.

SUPER: *The Daily News. Today you really need it*

392A
Art Director Ed Rotondi
Writer Joe O'Neill
Directors Ed Rotondi
Ralph Weissinger
Producer Lewis Kuperman
Production Co. Avon Productions
Agency Della Femina, Travisano & Partners
Client The Daily News

Jack-in-the-Box

RODNEY VARIETY
30-second

RODNEY: Hi, I'm Rodney Allen Rippy . . .

There's a lot of things you can eat at Jack-in-the-Box.

This is a . . . Jack steak sandwich . . . and these are pretty delicious too.

And this is a taco . . .

this is an onion ring.

There must be ten thousand things at Jack-in-the-Box.

RODNEY (singing): Pack up the kids, crank up the car to Jack-in-the-Box. Come as you like, come as you are to Jack-in-the-Box.

SUPER: *Jack-in-the-Box*

393
Art Director Mas Yamashita
Writer John Annarino
Director Jack DeSort
Producer Jim Grumish
Production Co. DeSort/Sam
Agency Doyle Dane Bernbach
Los Angeles
Client Jack-in-the-Box

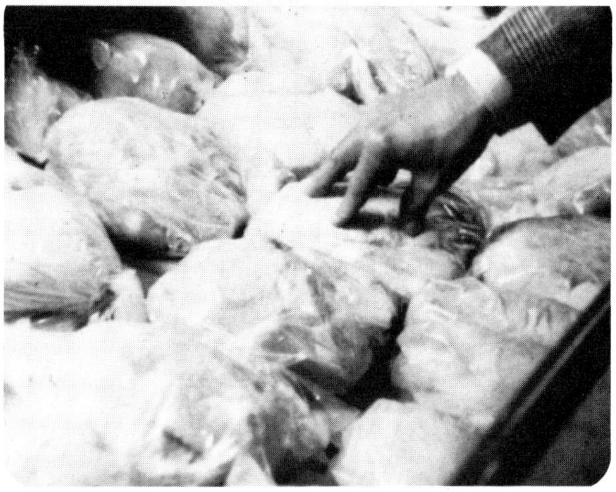

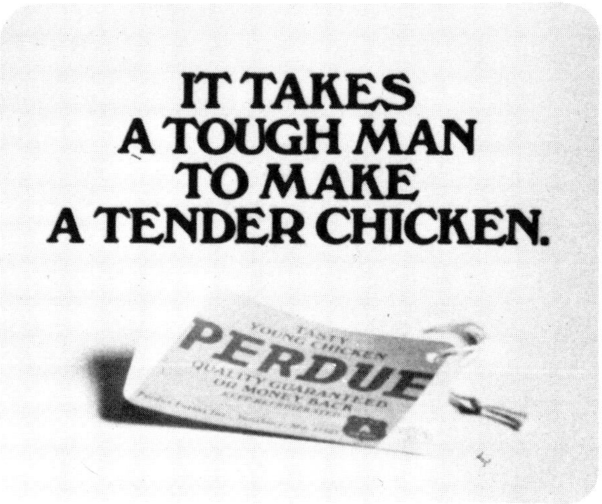
IT TAKES
A TOUGH MAN
TO MAKE
A TENDER CHICKEN.
PERDUE

HARD NOSED
30-second

FRANK PERDUE: You just can't take a chicken at face value.

These chickens put up a good front. But they've got drawbacks in their backs.

They're hard because somewhere along the line they've been partially frozen. And just cannot be the same as my fresh, tender Perdue chickens.

That's why you should always insist on a chicken that has my name on it. If there's one thing I'm hardnosed about, it's a hard-backed chicken.

SUPER: *It takes a tough man to make a tender chicken*

394
Art Director Sam Scali
Writer Edward A. McCabe
Director Frank Herman
Production Co. Televideo Productions
Agency Scali, McCabe, Sloves
Client Perdue Farms

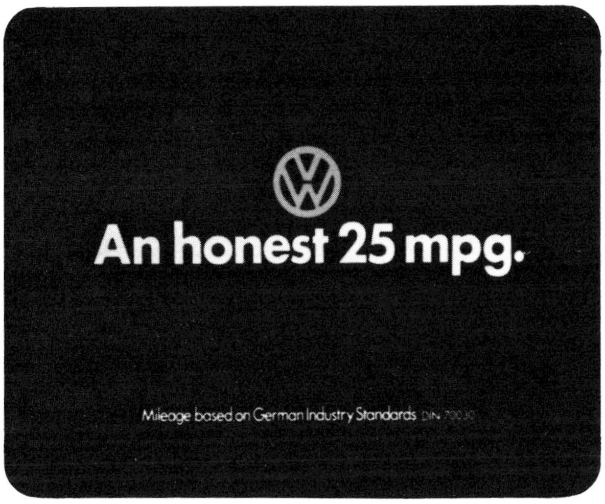
An honest 25 mpg.
Mileage based on German Industry Standards

84 MPG

84 MPG
30-second

MUSIC UNDER

ANNCR: Since everyone's conducting a mileage test, we at Volkswagen thought we'd conduct one.

So, we modified our body and our engine, and used someone who didn't weigh too much to drive.

And we got 84 miles per gallon.

Ridiculous? Nobody normally drives like this?

That's precisely our point.

Nobody normally drives like most of those tests.

SUPER: *An honest 25 mpg.*

395
Art Director Charles Piccirillo
Writer Mike Mangano
Cameraman Ernie Capparros
Directors Charles Piccirillo
Mike Mangano
Producer Jim DeBarros
Production Co. Directors Studio
Agency Doyle Dane Bernbach
Client Volkswagen of America Corp.

30

fresh'n
fresh'n
The cleaner you are,
the better you feel.

CHAUFFEUR II
30-second

CHAUFFEUR: They don't use toilet paper.

BOY: My Daddy doesn't use toilet paper. And neither do I.

ANNCR: Now you don't need toilet paper either. Introducing Fresh'n.

The new pre-moistened toilet tissue that gets you cleaner than ordinary toilet tissue can.

Fresh'n isn't dry. It's lightly moistened to get you cleaner.

SUPER: Fresh'n. The cleaner you are, the better you feel.

TENNIS PLAYER: I've never played better since I stopped using toilet paper.

396
Art Director Sam Scali
Writer Edward A. McCabe
Director Barry Brown
Production Co. Brillig Productions
Agency Scali, McCabe, Sloves
Client American Can Co.

SAVING TIME
30-second

MAN: I get about a half-hour at the most to read the newspaper every day.

So I had to make a choice:

I could read a newspaper that handles a story like this. Or I could read a newspaper that covers the same story like this.

The Daily News.

It gets to the point a lot faster. So I can read 10 or 15 stories in the same time it takes me to read 3 or 4 in the other paper.

And after I read all the things I need to know, I don't feel so guilty reading the things I really want to know. Like how my favorite team made out.

ANNCR: The Daily News today. You really need it.

SUPER: *The Daily News today*
You really need it

396A
Art Director Ed Rotondi
Writer Joe O'Neill
Directors Ed Rotondi
Ralph Weissinger
Producer Lewis Kuperman
Production Co. Avon Productions
Agency Della Femina, Travisano & Partners
Client The Daily News

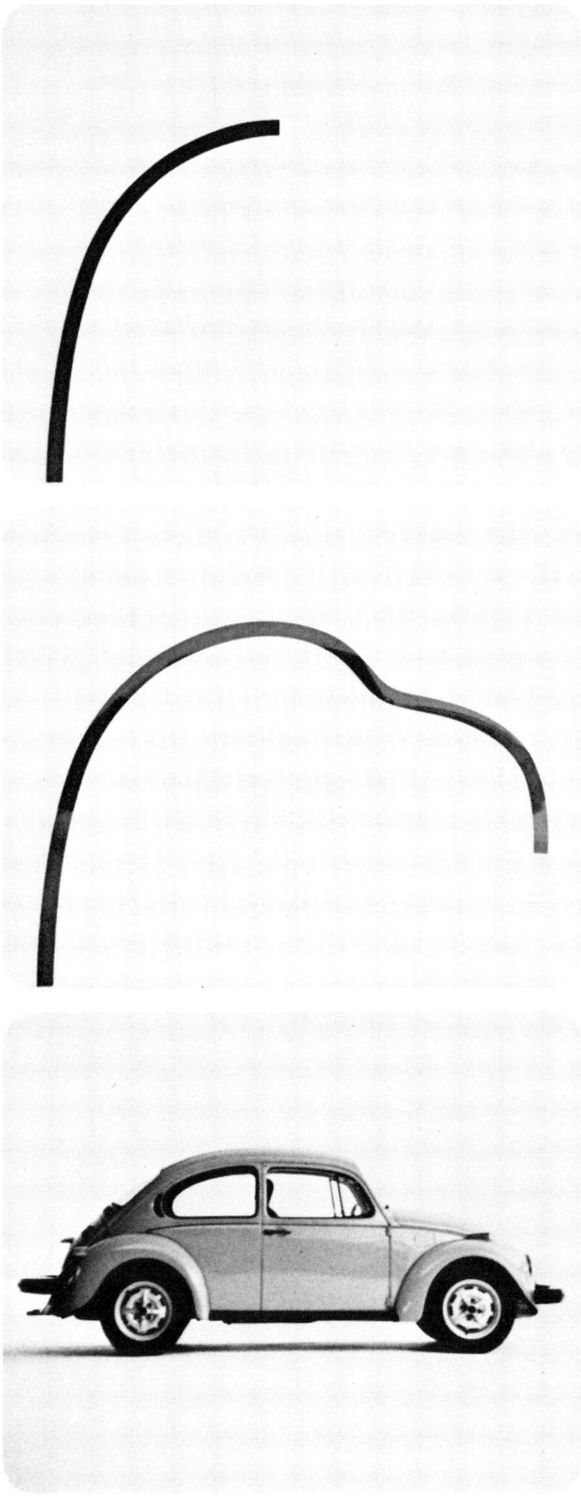

RISING COSTS
30-second

ANNCR: Seventh GM increase hikes cars an average of $550.00 this year.

Ford up sixth time, raising their cars an average of $584.00 over the year.

Today, as cars go up, up, up . . . believe it or not, there's one that's gone down.

Volkswagen introduces the specially equipped $2499.00 Love Bug.

You'd better hurry, though.

There's a limit to our love.

SUPER: *The $2499 Love Bug Limited Edition*

397
Art Director Charles Piccirillo
Writer Mike Mangano
Designer Charles Piccirillo
Artist A/D Associaties
Directors Charles Piccirillo
Mike Mangano
Producer Jim DeBarros
Production Co. Directors Studio
Agency Doyle Dane Bernbach
Client Volkswagen of America Corp.

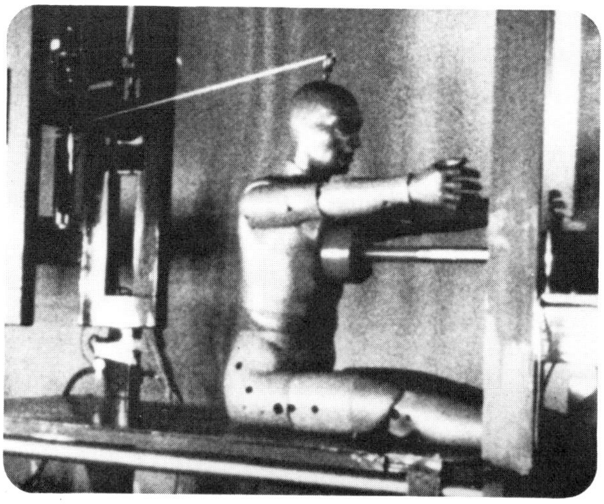

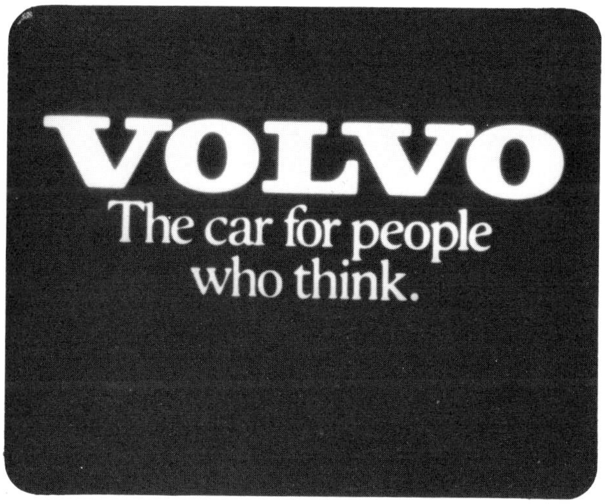
VOLVO
The car for people
who think.

GENERIC-DUMMIES
30-second

MUSIC THROUGHOUT

ANNCR: At Volvo, we employ a lot of dummies to help us plan our cars.

They've shown us how to make Volvo bodies protect your body better.

They gave us ideas for a more comfortable interior and suggested ways to keep you safer.

We think Volvo is the world's most intelligently thought-out car.

It's because we've learned a lot from dummies.

SUPER: *Volvo. The car for people who think*

SILVER

398
Art Director Robert Reitzfeld
Writer Thomas J. Nathan
Director Henry Sandbank
Production Co. Henry Sandbank Films
Agency Scali, McCabe, Sloves
Client Volvo of America Corp.

SCENE
1
TAKE
2
SOUND
17
PRODUCT
PINTO
DIRECTOR
J. DE BARROS
B. EVANS

SCENE
3
TAKE
9
SOUND
32
PRODUCT
CAPRI
C. PICCIRILLO
R. BARR

TAKE ONE
30-second

1ST MAN: Pinto, take two.

ANNCR: Lately, Volkswagen has been starring in a lot of other car commercials.

2ND MAN: Mercury, take five.

ANNCR: It seems they're all comparing themselves to us.

3RD MAN: Capri, take nine.

ANNCR: Now . . . we always knew how good we were.

4TH MAN: Volkswagen, take one.

ANNCR: But we never thought we'd see them admit it. Thank you, gentlemen.

399
Art Director Charles Piccirillo
Writer Mike Mangano
Directors Mike Mangano
Charles Piccirillo
Producer Jim DeBarros
Production Co. Directors Studio
Agency Doyle Dane Bernbach
Client Volkswagen of America Corp.

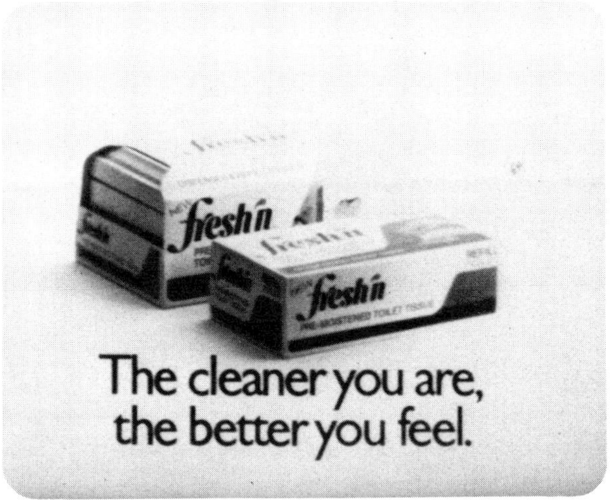
fresh'n
fresh'n
The cleaner you are,
the better you feel.

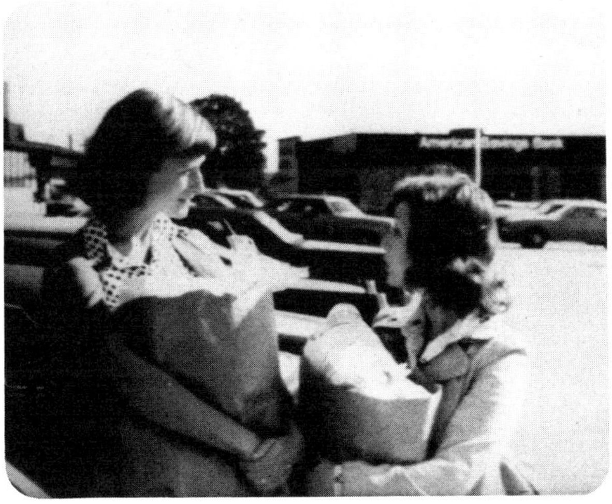

FOOTBALL II
30-second

FOOTBALL PLAYER: I don't use toilet paper.

WIFE: We've never felt better since we stopped using toilet paper.

ANNCR: Now you don't need toilet paper either. Introducing Fresh'n.

The new pre-moistened toilet tissue that gets you cleaner than ordinary toilet tissue can.

Fresh'n isn't dry. It's lightly moistened to get you cleaner.

And the cleaner you are, the better you feel.

FIRST GIRL: Oh, hi Janie! How are you?

SECOND GIRL: Fine . . . never felt better since I stopped using toilet paper.

400
Art Director Sam Scali
Writer Edward A. McCabe
Director Barry Brown
Production Co. Brillig Productions
Agency Scali, McCabe, Sloves
Client American Can Co.

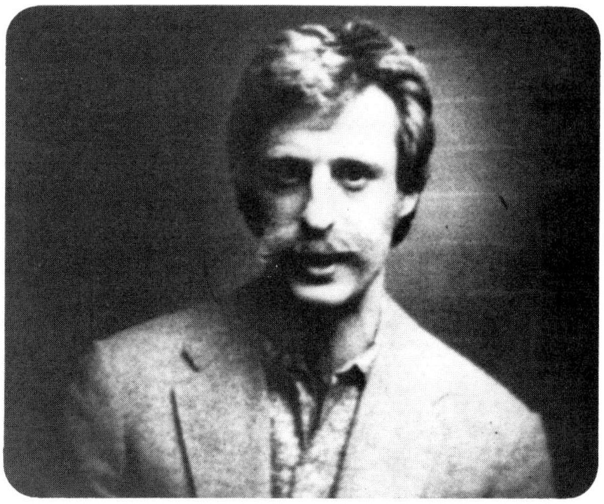

DAILY

REPORTER
30-second

MAN: If a Daily News reporter always looked like a reporter, some of the people he has to talk to wouldn't be very talkative.

One reporter posed as a Spanish speaking customer in order to expose druggists who were overcharging on prescriptions.

Another reporter became an old man with a bad cold to nail doctors who were cheating on Medicaid.

Daily News reporters have posed as hardhats, business executives, even as junkies.

Sometimes the best way to cover a story these days, is to go undercover.

ANNCR: The Daily News. Today, you really need it.

SUPER: *The Daily News. Today, you really need it*

401A
Art Director Ed Rotondi
Writer Joe O'Neill
Directors Ed Rotondi
Ralph Weissinger
Producer Lewis Kuperman
Production Co. Avon Productions
Agency Della Femina, Travisano & Partners
Client The Daily News

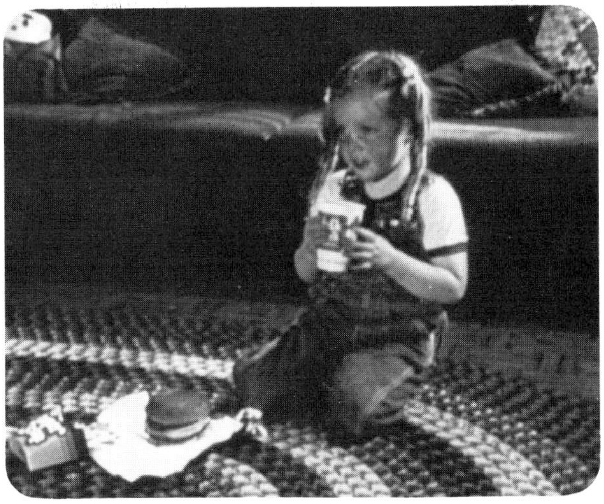

Jack-in-the-Box

SING ALONG WITH RODNEY
30-second

RODNEY: (Singing) Take life a little easier. Make life . . .

LITTLE GIRL: (Singing along with Rodney) life . . .

RODNEY: . . . a little easier.

LITTLE GIRL: (Singing along with Rodney) . . . easier.

RODNEY: Pack up the kids, crank up the car . . .

LITTLE GIRL: . . . car . . .

RODNEY: Come as you like, come as you are . . . to Jack-in-the-Box.

LITTLE GIRL: (Loud bursts of giggling).

SUPER: *Jack-in-the-Box*

402
Art Director Mas Yamashita
Writer John Annarino
Director Harry Hamburg
Producer Jim Grumish
Production Co. McGraw-Hill Pacific Productions
Agency Doyle Dane Bernbach
Los Angeles
Client Jack-in-the-Box

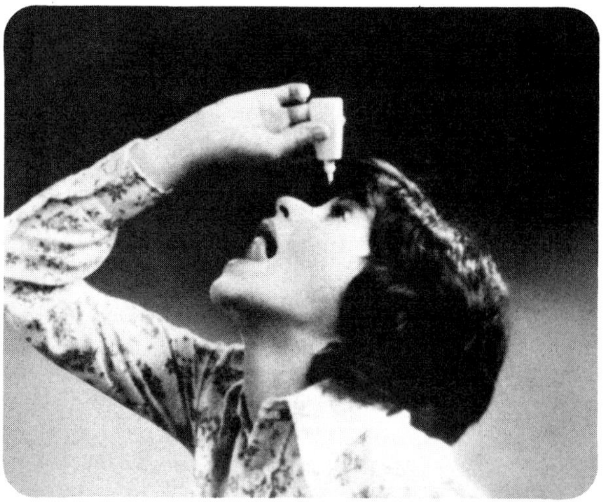

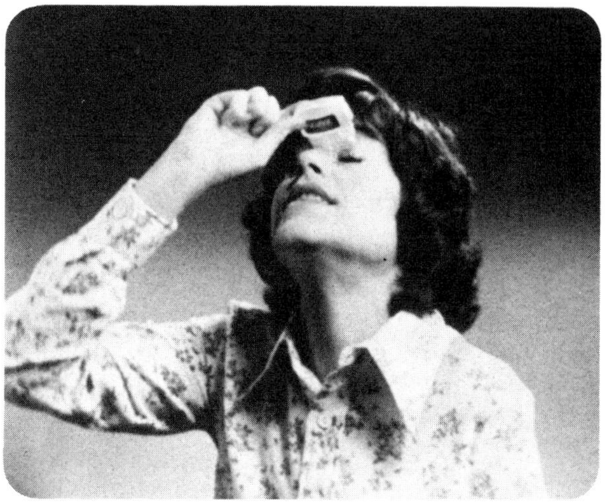

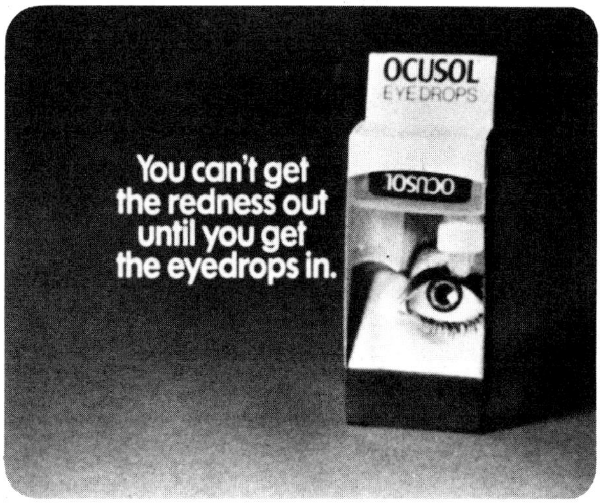
OCUSOL
EYE DROPS
OCUSOL
You can't get the redness out until you get the eyedrops in.

KLEENEX
30-second

MUSIC UNDER

WOMAN: You know how it is. You're trying to get up the courage to put the eyedrops in . . .

your hand wavers just a little bit . . .

and the drop (ping) drops down your face.

Well, that can't happen . . .
with Ocusol.

Because Ocusol has a little nose bridge . . . that helps hold it steady until you're ready to open your eye.

ANNCR: You can't get the redness out, until you get the eyedrops in.

403
Art Director Al Silver
Writer Edward Caffrey
Producer Glenn DeBona
Production Co. Flickers
Agency Benton & Bowles
Client Norwich Pharmacal Co.

SCOTTI
MUFFLER
CENTER
COAST TO COAST
We give you a 100% guarantee
on 100% of our work.
Check the Yellow Pages

SCOTTI VS. MIDAS
30-second

ANNCR: When Midas installs an exhaust system, their lifetime guarantee covers the muffler. If anything else fails, Midas can charge you about 15 bucks for a tailpipe, $35 for an exhaust pipe or $5 for clamps and hangers.

When Scotti installs an exhaust system, should any part go we'll replace it free for as long as you own the car. So you can go to Midas and get the Midas touch. Or you can come to Scotti and get off Scott-free from then on.

VO: We give you a 100% guarantee on 100% of our work.

404
Art Director Ray Alban
Writer Steve Smith
Director Joe DeVoto
Production Co. Ramsey Enterprises
Agency Scali, McCabe, Sloves
Client Scotti Muffler Centers

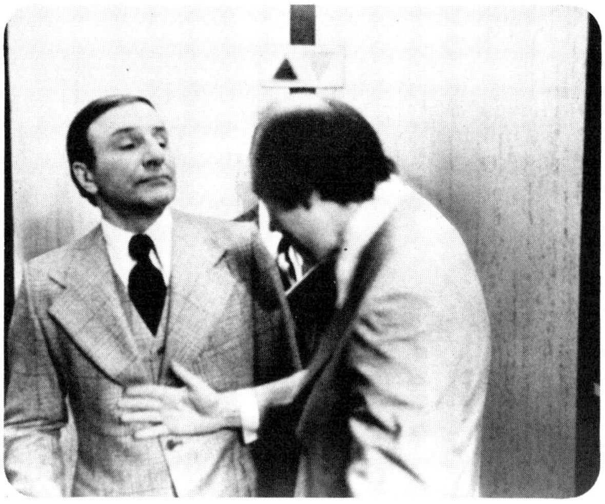

LAST LAUGH
30-second

1ST MAN: Frank, you ol sonofagun, how ya doin?

2ND MAN: Fine, fine.

1ST MAN: Gee, you look great . . . that suit is dynamite. Where ja get that?

2ND MAN: Robert Hall.

1ST MAN: Robert Hall! Ha Ha Ha . . . Yer never serious.

What 'ya pay for it, forty dollars?

2ND MAN: No . . . I think it was seventy.

1ST MAN: Ha Ha Ha Ha Ha Ha.

2ND MAN: What'ya pay for yours?

1ST MAN: Hunnerd an' sixty-five.

2ND MAN: Hundred sixty-five? A hundred sixty-five.

Ha Ha Ha Ha Ha Ha Ha Ha Ha Ha.

ANNCR: Robert Hall. Good clothes that don't cost the shirt off your back.

SUPER: *Robert Hall . . . Good clothes that don't cost the shirt off your back*

406
Art Director Al Bensusan
Writer Chet Lane
Producer Joanne Ruesing
Production Co. Wylde and Assoc.
Agency Benton & Bowles
Client Robert Hall Clothes

Midas

RICHEST MAN
30-second

ATTORNEY TYPE: Mr. Overcash would like to know the terms of your Midas guarantee.

MIDAS MAN: He's the world's richest man?

MIDAS MAN: Hi . . . well . . . our guarantee is good on any Midas muffler we install on any American car. And it says that if anything goes wrong, we'll replace the muffler free of charge . . . and now that includes the installation.

SECRETARY: Sorry, he's in conference now.

MIDAS MAN: And a Midas guarantee is good for as long as you own your car.

ATTORNEY TYPE: Will other Midas shops around the country honor it?

MIDAS MAN: Of course!

OVERCASH: Excellent.

MIDAS MAN: Mind if I ask you a personal question H. J.? Why does a man like you even bother with a guarantee?

OVERCASH: My boy, how do you think a man like me got to be a man like me?

SUPER: *Midas. We're Specialists.*
We have to do a Better Job

407
Art Director Michael Ulick
Writer Jeff Frey
Cameraman Ed Rosson
Director Michael Ulick
Producers Sue Becton
John Gramaglia
Production Co. Kaleidoscope Films
Agency Wells, Rich, Greene
Client Midas Mufflers

Barney's
7th Avenue and 17th Street

YOU'RE BIG ENOUGH TO DRESS YOURSELF
30-second

ANNCR: From the very beginning, people have been dressing you.
Your mother . . .

your schoolmates . . .

your country . . .

even the clothing stores you shopped in.

Well at Barney's, we think you're big enough to dress yourself. So when you come to Barney's, you'll be able to choose from the widest range of American and International fashions in the world.

MAN: What do you think?

SALESMAN: What do *you* think?

MAN: Terrific.

ANNCR: Barney's. We let you be you.

408
Art Director Louis Coletti
Writer Michael Drazen
Director Steve Horn
Production Co. Steve Horn, Inc.
Agency Scali, McCabe, Sloves
Client Barney's Clothes

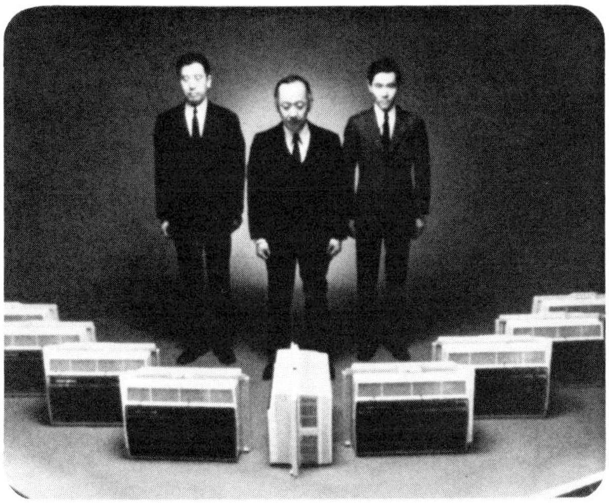

PICK UP
30-second

MAN (Japanese accent): We have been most successful in making things small.

Radios small, TV's small . . .

But now an American company, Fedders, makes a rotary-powered air conditioner. Very powerful, but small.

Fedders call them "Pick-Ups."

Pick it up, take it home, put it in the window, plug it in.

In the bedroom, den.

One small "Pick-Up" does a big job.

Fedders, we salute you.

409
Art Director Dan Schwartz
Writers Howard Stabin
Mel Stein
Director George Gomes
Producer Tom McGrath
Production Co. Gomes/Loew
Agency Kenyon & Eckhardt
Client Fedders Corp.

Frank Perdue

TASTY
YOUNG CHICKEN
PERDUE
QUALITY GUARANTEED
OR MONEY BACK

IT TAKES
A TOUGH MAN
TO MAKE
A TENDER CHICKEN.
PERDUE

CONSUMER PROTECTION
30-second

FRANK PERDUE: I make sure my chickens are well bred. I make sure my chickens are well fed.

I make sure they're well cared for. I make sure that the only place my chickens *could* get fouled up is in your kitchen.

So I'm doing something to make sure you can't. From now on, every Perdue chicken wing-tag . . . has a great recipe on the back. It tells you exactly what to do with my chicken.

Look for a different recipe every time you shop.

I'm not taking any chances. I'm bringing my quality standards right into your home.

SUPER: *It takes a tough man to make a tender chicken*

410
Art Director Sam Scali
Writer Edward A. McCabe
Director Frank Herman
Production Co. Televideo Productions
Agency Scali, McCabe, Sloves
Client Perdue Farms

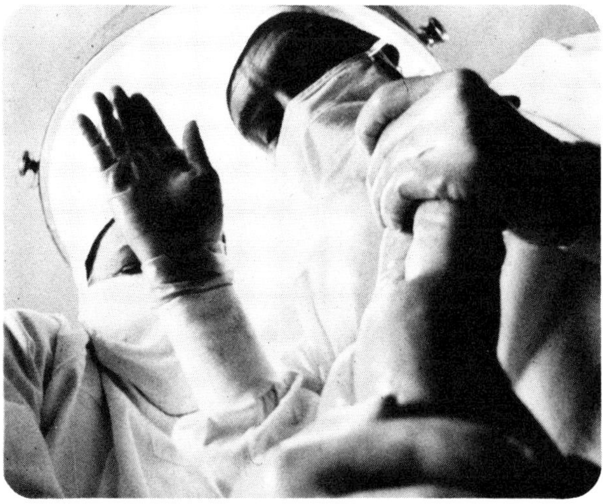

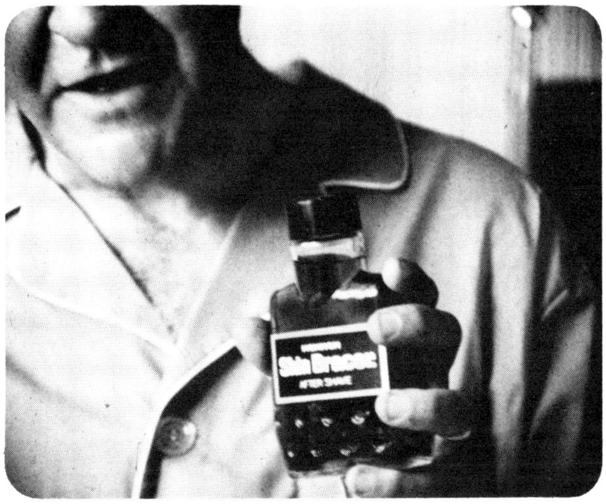
Skin Bracer

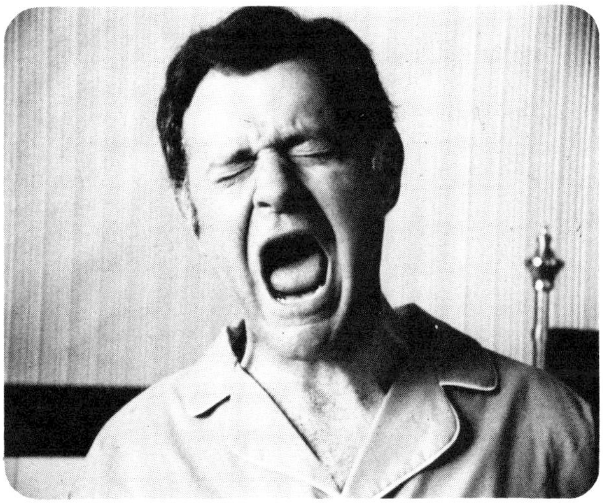

BIRTH
30-second

MAN: I'll never forget my first cold slap.

MUSIC UNDER

It was the day I was born. I was scared. Where was I? It was the doctor who brought me to my senses.

MUSIC OUT

SFX: Slap! Slap!

SFX: Waaaaaaaaaa!

I couldn't say "Thanks, I needed that" then.

MAN: But I *needed* that then, and I need it now. And I get it, every morning, from Skin Bracer. Its skin tightener and chin chillers wake me up like a cold slap in the face.

SFX: Slap! Slap!

Waaaaaa!

411
Art Director John Triolo
Writer Mike Leonard
Director Barry Brown
Producer Kimberly Hoeck
Production Co. Brillig Productions
Agency Case & McGrath
Client The Mennen Co.

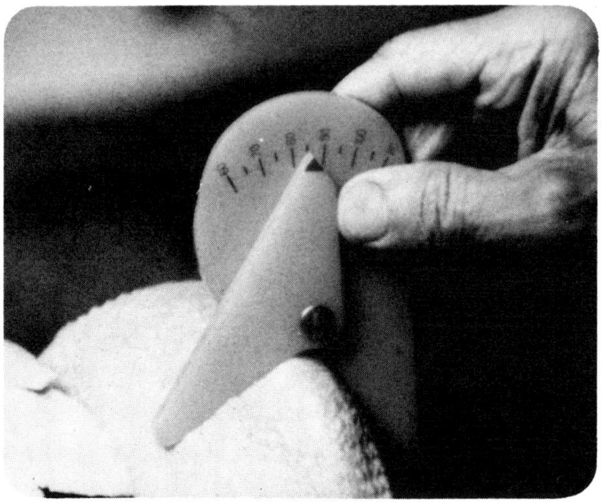

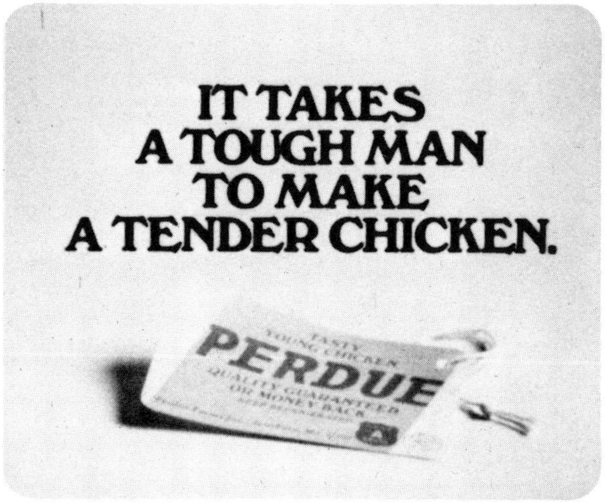
IT TAKES
A TOUGH MAN
TO MAKE
A TENDER CHICKEN.
PERDUE

BREAST GAUGE
30-second

FRANK PERDUE: One way you can tell a great chicken from an ordinary one is by the size of the breast.

Perdue chicken is bred to have the broadest, plumpest breast of any chicken you can buy.

And measures at least 84 on the breast gauge. You don't have a breast gauge? Don't let that stand between you and a better chicken.

Send me two Perdue wing-tags and a dollar, and I'll send you a Perdue breast gauge along with instructions for use.

See for yourself how the chicken you buy stacks up against mine.

SUPER: *It takes a tough man to make a tender chicken*

412
Art Director Sam Scali
Writer Edward A. McCabe
Director Frank Herman
Production Co. Televideo Productions
Agency Scali, McCabe, Sloves
Client Perdue Farms

SOUVENIRS

SOUVENIRS

SOUVENIRS

HOME OR AWAY
30-second

JIM: Could you just keep one thing in mind about diarrhea? Pepto Bismol relieves it.

Whether you get common diarrhea right there in your own home or away on vacation, Pepto Bismol will help get you back to normal. Pepto Bismol coats and soothes, helps relieve the misery, the nausea . . .

So next time you get common diarrhea, whether you're at home or away, you're in luck! Cause Pepto Bismol really works!

SFX: Applause

SUPER: *Use only as directed*

413
Art Director Al Silver
Writer Edward Caffrey
Producer Patrick Boyriven
Production Co. EUE/Screen Gems
Agency Benton & Bowles
Client Norwich Pharmacal Co.

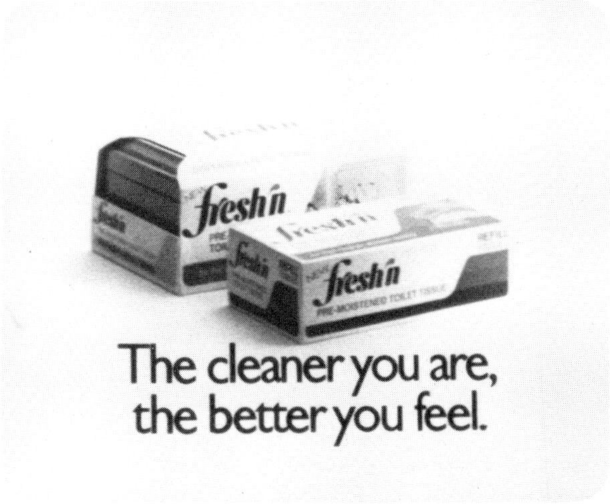
fresh'n
fresh'n
PRE-MOISTENED TOILET TISSUE
The cleaner you are,
the better you feel.

LADIES II
30-second

FIRST LADY: Fred just bought me a mink coat.

SECOND LADY: Our new car is coming next week.

THIRD LADY: You know what? I don't use toilet paper.

ANNCR: Now you don't need toilet paper either. Introducing Fresh'n.

The new pre-moistened toilet tissue that gets you cleaner than ordinary toilet tissue can.

Fresh'n isn't dry. It's lightly moistened to get you cleaner.

And the cleaner you are, the better you feel.

FIRST PILOT: Great flight, Chet.

CAPTAIN: I've never flown better since I stopped using toilet paper.

414
Art Director Sam Scali
Writer Edward A. McCabe
Director Barry Brown
Production Co. Brillig Productions
Agency Scali, McCabe, Sloves
Client American Can Co.

Frank

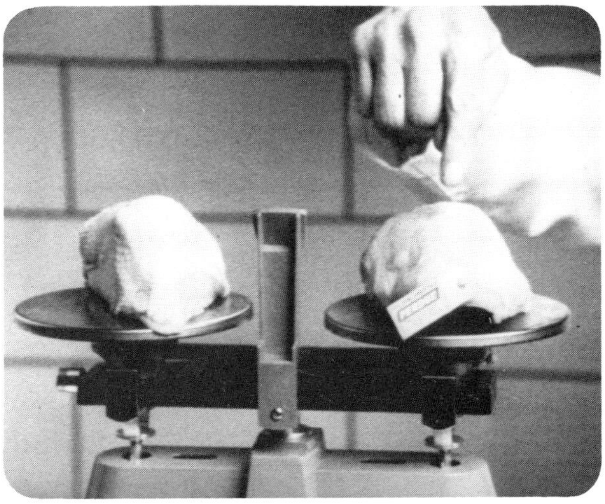

IT TAKES
A TOUGH MAN
TO MAKE
TENDER CHICKEN
PARTS.
TASTY YOUNG CHICKEN PARTS
PERDUE

EXTRA BITE
30-second

FRANK PERDUE: Never go into a store and just ask for a pound of chicken breasts. Because you could be cheating yourself out of some meat.

Here's an ordinary one-pound breast, and here's a one pound breast of mine.

They weigh the same. But as you can see, mine has more meat. And theirs has more bone.

I breed the broadest breasted, meatiest chicken you can buy.

So don't buy chicken by the pound. Buy them by the tag, and get an extra bite in every breast.

SUPER: *It takes a tough man to make tender chicken parts*

415
Art Director Sam Scali
Writer Edward A. McCabe
Director Frank Herman
Production Co. Televideo Productions
Agency Scali, McCabe, Sloves
Client Perdue Farms

FRUIT OF THE LOOM
We keep making it better...
not expensive.

WATER SKIS—TERRY THOMAS
30-second

TERRY: Terry Thomas for Fruit of the Loom underwear. Today I'll demonstrate its strength and quality by attaching it to my ski rope. Thank you. This all cotton brief is comfy, but is it strong? You bet!

ASSISTANT: He says he's all set!!

TERRY: No, no, I said bet, not set! Whooaa!

SFX

TERRY: I say what super strength.

Fruit of the Loom. Only a dollar. They keep making it better, not expensive.

LOGO: *Fruit of the Loom*

SUPER: *Mens and boys underwear*

416
Art Director Tom Krumwiede
Writer Tony Alfano
Director Sid Myers
Producer Ira Lassman
Production Co. Myers & Eisenstat
Agency Grey Advertising
Client Union Underwear Co.

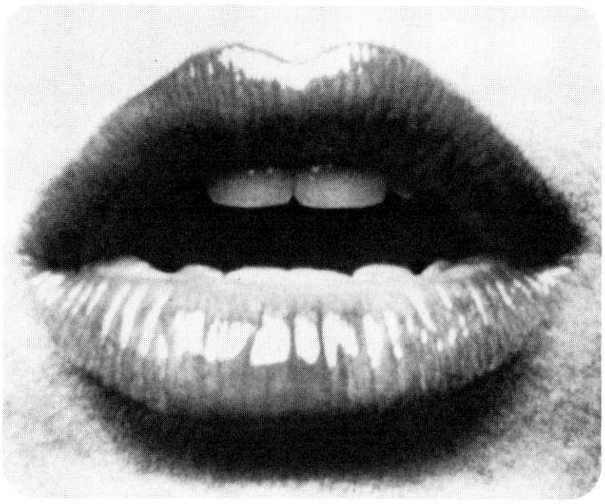

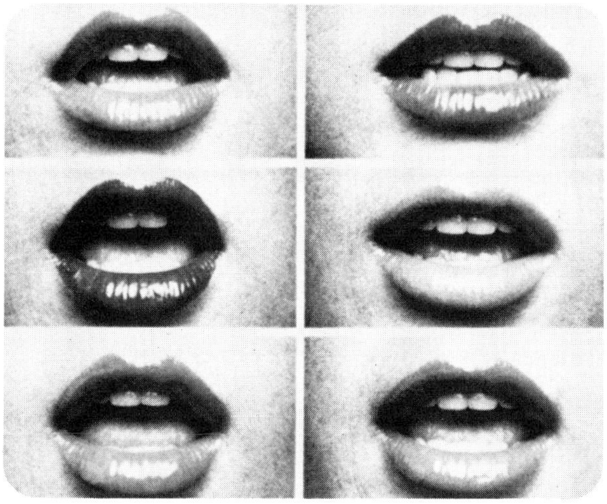

Pure Magic
Great Shine Lipstick
MAX FACTOR

GREAT SHINE
30-second

LIPS: (Singing) There's a brand new lipstick on my lips.

Do Do Do Do Do
Pure Magic Great Shine
on my lips. Pure Magic.

It has the color of lipstick. The shine of gloss.
Color, color, shine, shine.

Color of lipstick, shine of gloss. Color of lipstick, shine of gloss.

Pure Magic Great Shine Lipstick from Max Factor.

SUPER: *Pure Magic Great Shine Lipstick. Max Factor*

417
Art Director Frank Kirk
Writer Judith Brolin Fitzgerald
Designer Frank Kirk
Director Harold Becker
Producer Paul Chesloff
Production Co. N. Lee Lacy
Agency Rosenfeld, Sirowitz & Lawson/West Beverly Hills
Client Max Factor

SAAB 99

BLOWOUT
30-second

SFX: Natural sounds.

ANNCR: You are about to see a demonstration you may find hard to believe.

The driver of this Saab sedan will have a blowout at sixty miles per hour, yet he'll stop straight. Even in a panic stop there's virtually no swerving . . . no pulling, because Saab has front-wheel drive.

Saab. It's what a car should be.

418
Art Directors Alan Torreano
John Armistead
Writers Michael Cox
Bob Wright
Director Larry Williams
Producer Lou Puopolo
Production Co. Lou Puopolo, Inc.
Agency Cox & Co. Advertising
Client Saab-Scania of America

SYBIL

SYBIL
30-second

SYBIL: I'm not a freak. I'm Sybil. I am Sybil.

MAN: I'm so glad I'm not a woman.

SYBIL: Oh, Sybil, you make me sick. You should be ashamed, Sybil, dancing and lipstick.

Oh, why are you doing this to me?

ANNCR: Everything you've heard about her is true. She's sixteen personalities. There's never been a woman like her. Now, she's in paperback.

419
Art Director Steve Frankfurt
Writers Lou Du Charme
Gail Silver
Designer Steve Frankfurt
Cameraman Dick Stone
Director Dick Stone
Producers Lou Puopolo
Bertille Selig
Production Co. Lou Puopolo, Inc.
Agency Frankfurt Communications
Client Warner Publishing

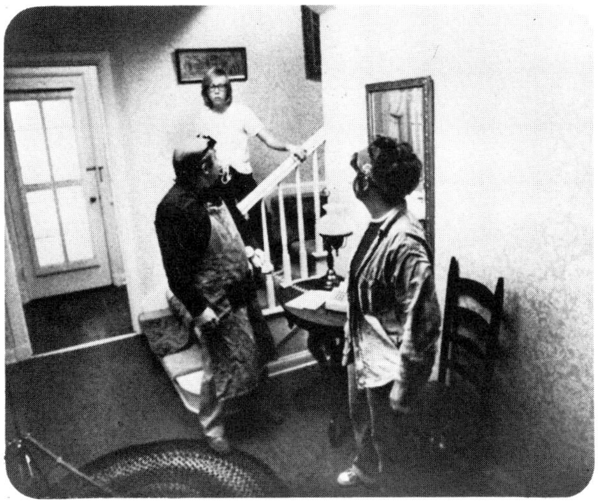

FAMILY
30-second

SFX: Ring, Ring

MOM: Honey, can you get the phone?

Andrew, get the phone, honey. Mother is very busy.

DAD: Can't anyone answer the phone up there, Sweetie?

ANNCR: For some reason, the telephone never seems to ring unless you're way at the other end of the house. That's why it's nice to have more than one. You can add an extension for only about 3c a day, you know.

And if you can use *three* phones, ask about our Pushbutton Package Deal . . .

that's three Touch-Tone phones—any style, any color—at a special bargain price.

Call your Illinois Bell Service Representative for details . . .

DAD: Hello?

ANNCR: before you miss any more calls.

SON: Hey Dad, was that for me?

SUPER: *Illinois Bell*

420
Art Director Bill Smith
Writer Ray Thiem
Director Hil Covington
Producer Michael Paradise
Production Co. Hil Covington
Agency NW Ayer ABH International Chicago
Client Illinois Bell

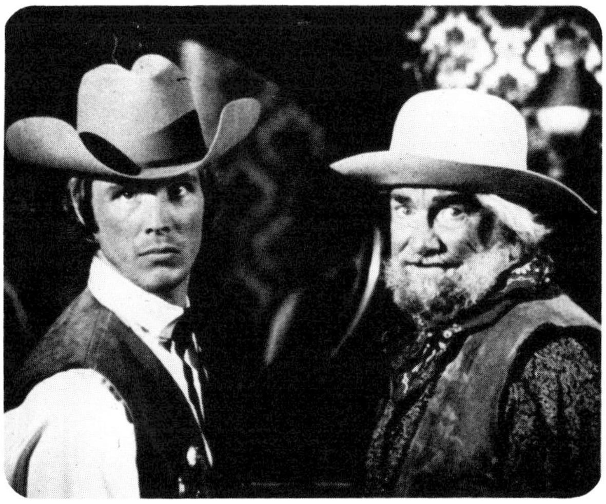

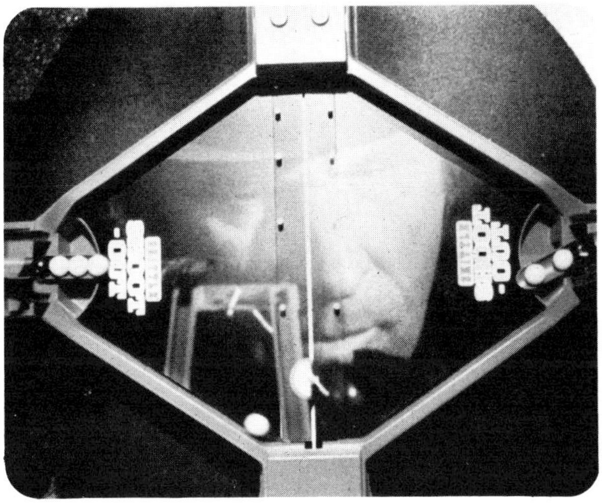

MOONDANCE KID SHOOTOUT
30-second

SFX: Music and shots.

FOSTER: Who's that?
The Moondance Kid? eh?
The Moondance Kid!!

MOONDANCE: Howdy Marshall.

MARSHALL: Howdy Moondance.

MOONDANCE: We've got a score to settle.

FOSTER: It's a Skittle Shoot Out.

SFX: Screams

MOONDANCE KID: OK. Shoot. The last one to hit the moving target before it disappears, scores.

MOONDANCE KID: I win.

FOSTER: But the good guys always win in the movies.

MOONDANCE KID: This is television.

FOSTER: I'd like to say hello to all my friends out there in television land.

ANNCR: Skittle Shootout from Aurora.

421
Art Director Wally Pfeiffer
Writer Buddy Radish
Director Don Adams
Producers Manning Rubin
Vinnie Infantino
Production Co. Entertainment Concepts
Agency Grey Advertising
Client Aurora Products Corp.

RYDER
RYDER
Ryder. We keep 'em rolling.

VAROOM
30-second

MAN: Ryder. We lease and rent trucks.

New GMC and Chevy trucks.

SFX: Varoom!

And we've kept 'em rolling through hurricanes . . .

SFX: Sh-h-h!

floods, panics . . .

SFX: Varoom!

we've even kept them rolling through fuel shortages.

SFX: Varoom!

Because Ryder just does smart things with trucks.

Like, uh, not using fuel to do this commercial.

SFX: Varoom!

SUPER: *Ryder. We keep 'em rolling*

422
Art Director Frank Siebke
Writer Mel Richman
Director Judd Maze
Producer Bertelle Selig
Production Co. Flickers
Agency Mike Sloan
Client Ryder Truck Rental

PURINA DOG CHOW

PURINA DOG CHOW

CHOWHOUNDS
30-second

MUSIC THROUGHOUT

DISC JOCKEY: All right . . . it's Little Charles and the Chowhounds.

LITTLE CHARLES: Purina Dog Chow.

CHOWHOUNDS: Chow wow wow wow. Purina Dog Chow. Dog Food.

LITTLE CHARLES: Chow wow wow wow wow . . . Oh, oh, oh, oh, oh, oh, oh, oh.

GROUP: Purina Dog Chow.

WALDO: Darlin' . . . I'd be lost without delicious, nutritious Purina Dog Chow.

GROUP: Purina Dog Chow.

423
Art Director Harvey Gabor
Writer Bert Neufeld
Director Michael Ulick
Producers Diane Flynn
John Gramaglia
Production Co. Uncle Film Co.
Agency Wells, Rich, Greene
Client Ralston Purina

FIAT
The biggest selling car in Europe.

CHOICE
30-second

MAN: Deciding on which small car to buy is becoming a difficult decision for many people.

Because there are now over a dozen makes to choose from.

But in Europe, where there are over fifty makes to choose from, there's no difficulty at all.

Because Europeans have had over sixty years experience with small cars.

And the car they buy most is Fiat.

Fiat. The biggest selling car in Europe.

424
Art Director Ted Shaine
Writers David Altschiller
Ed Butler
Jim Durfee
Director Massimo Magri
Producer Bob Schenkel
Production Co. Politecne Cinematografica
Agency Carl Ally
Client Fiat-Roosevelt Motors

Del Monte
TOMATO
CATSUP

CATSUP
30-second

VO: I see that your mother has gotten you Del Monte Catsup.

KID: Yup.

VO: And I'd say, makin' just a wild guess, that you like the deliciousness of it and the thickness, and you like what Del Monte's special blend of those seven herbs and spices is doin' to that hamburger.

KID: Yup.

VO: Trade ya my size 14 varsity baseball shoes for it.

KID: Nope.

VO: I'll send you to the moon.

KID: Nope.

VO: How 'bout if I sent your sister to the moon?

KID: I got two sisters.

VO: They'll both go.

ANNCR: When it comes to picking catsup, Mother really does know best.

FRENCH STYLE GREEN BEANS
30-second

GOLD

425
Art Director Jerry Collamer
Writer Valerie Wagner
Director Denny Harris
Producer Harry Wypich
Production Co. Denny Harris Inc.
Agency McCann-Erickson San Francisco
Client Del Monte

Today, you really need it.

VARIETY
30-second

ANNCR: The Daily News has so many grocery coupons that some people can't get together on what's more important:

Good reading on one side of the page or a good bargain on the other.

But anytime a ten cent newspaper can inform, entertain, and help save a few dollars on food, it's got to be the best deal in town.

The Daily News. Today you really need it.

SUPER: *The Daily News. Today you really need it*

SAVING TIME
30-second

REPORTER
30-second

425A
Art Director Ed Rotondi
Writer Joe O'Neill
Directors Ed Rotondi
Ralph Weissinger
Producer Lewis Kuperman
Production Co. Avon Productions
Agency Della Femina, Travisano & Partners
Client The Daily News

SALOON

SALOON

DOLLAR SAVINGS BANK
The better way.
Sixth largest savings bank in the nation.
Member FDIC.

PARLAY
30-second

SFX: Traffic sounds.

MAN: Wilma, we still have 150 dollars and four nights to parlay that into thousands.

WOMAN: Mickey, it only took you two nights to parlay thousands into 150 dollars.

MAN: Well, sometimes you gotta lose a little to win a lot.

WOMAN: I'd settle for losing a little. Seven years you've been coming here to win a bundle. Even if you win this year, we're still down six bundles. There's gotta be a better way.

ANNCR: Dollar Savings Bank. Maybe we're the better way.

SUPER: *Dollar Savings Bank the better way.*
The 6th largest savings bank in the nation
Member FDIC

SHIRT
30-second

426
Art Director Mike Withers
Writer Barry Greenspon
Directors Norman Toback
Dave de Vries
Producers Joanne Michels
Dave de Vries
Production Co. Toback & Assoc.
Petersen Co.
Agency DKG
Client Dollar Savings Bank

AMERICAN EXPRESS
JOHN McGIVER

SILVER

427
Art Director Mark Ross
Writer Bill Taylor
Director Dick Miller
Producers Judith Stevens
Mark Ross
Production Co. Wylde and Assoc.
Agency Ogilvy & Mather
Client American Express

DO YOU KNOW ME?
30-second

JOHN McGIVER: Do you know me?

People often look at me and say, "You're somebody." But they haven't the foggiest notion who.

That's why I carry an American Express Card.

I use it in stores, restaurants, airlines, hotels, worldwide. Even in places where they've never seen my pretty face.

True it's a bit more difficult to get, but it means much more when you get it.

SFX

ANNCR: To apply for a card, call 800-528-8000.

JOHN McGIVER: American Express Card. Don't leave home without it.

NORMAN FELL
30-second

WILLIAM MILLER
30-second

DIET PEPSI

ZIPPER BOUTIQUE
30-second

SONG: You can do it . . .

We can help. Zip!

One calorie, one calorie . . .
Diet Pepsi can help.

You can do it . . .
We can help.

You can do it if you wanna.

One calorie Diet Pepsi can help.

Yes you can . . .
If you try.

One calorie Diet Pepsi's . . .
One good reason why.

You can do it if you wanna . . .
One calorie . . .

Diet Pepsi can help.

Great tasting one calorie . . .
Diet Pepsi can help.

ZIP!!

SUPER: *You can do it. We can help*

COSTUME PARTY
30-second

427A
Art Directors Stan Richards
Merl Bloom
Kong Wu
Spencer Michlin
Writer Spencer Michlin
Directors Mel Sokolsky
Richard Heimann
Producer George Bragg
Production Cos. Michlin & Hill
Sunlight Pictures
Wakeford/Orloff
Agencies BBDO
Michlin & Hill, Inc.
Client PepsiCo

HAREM
30-second

TURKISH MUSIC THROUGHOUT.

PAUL POE: Last week I'm touring Istanbul, looking like a million in my Splendor double knit shirt from Van Heusen. Suddenly, two guys grab me and say, "Prince Taruna, come with us." Well I told 'em . . . I'm Paul Poe. Next thing I know, I'm face to face with the Sultan of Shagur. I told 'em, I'm Paul Poe. He tells me he's making me a gift of 15 harem girls. I told 'em, 8 would have been plenty.

ANNCR: Splendor double knit dress and sport shirts only from Van Heusen.

SUPER: *Van Heusen Splendor Double Knit*

RESTAURANT
30-second

PLANTATION
30-second

VAN HEUSEN
SPLENDOR
DOUBLE KNIT

428
Art Director Bob Schlesinger
Writer Jeff Wolff
Directors Dominic Rossetti, Norm Griner
Producer Vinnie Infantino
Production Cos. Rossetti Films, Griner/Cuesta
Agency Grey Advertising
Client Van Heusen Co.

FRUIT OF THE LOOM

QUICKSAND
30-second

TERRY: Terry Thomas for Fruit of the Loom underwear. Hello. Today I'll demonstrate its strength and quality while rapidly sinking in this dreadful ooze. This all cotton brief is comfy, but is it strong enough to rescue me?

Rodney pull me out.

Rodney . . .

Rodney . . .
I shant ask you again.
Run . . .

I say . . .

What super strength! Fruit of the Loom. Only a dollar. They keep making it better, not expensive.

LOGO: *Fruit of the Loom*

SUPER: *Mens and Boys Underwear*

RAILROAD TRACKS
30-second

WATERSKIS
30-second

429
Art Director Tom Krumwiede
Writer Tony Alfano
Director Sid Myers
Producer Ira Lassman
Production Co. Myers & Eisenstat
Agency Grey Advertising
Client Union Underwear Co.

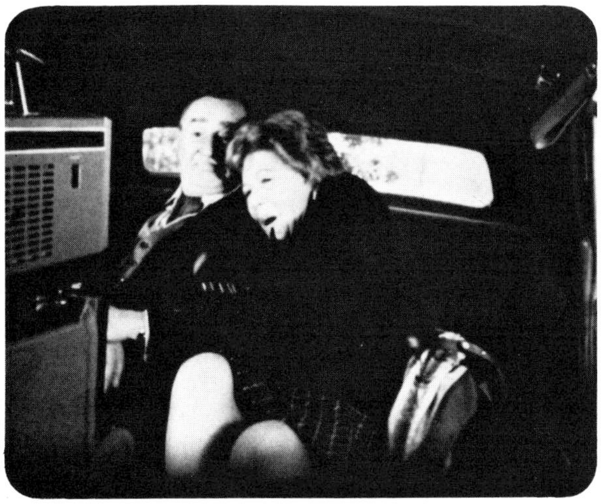

"IT'S A SONY"

WEALTHY COUPLE
30-second

MAN: I have a birthday present for you my love.

LADY: Oh goody.

MAN: It's outside.

LADY: Another car. How nice, now we have a set.

MAN: No, this is our same car. Your present's in the back.

LADY: Oh?

Oh, thank you, bumpkins!

It's a Sony.

ANNCR: All the money in the world couldn't buy a better set. That's why when there's a TV in the back seat, usually it's a Sony.

LADY: Let's watch the billionaire.

AUNT TESS
30-second

430
Art Director John Caggiano
Writer Marvin Honig
Designer John Caggiano
Directors John Caggiano
Bob Giraldi
Producers Phil Worcester
Frank Disalvo
Production Cos. D.S.I.
Giraldi Productions
Agency Doyle Dane Bernbach
Client Sony Corp.

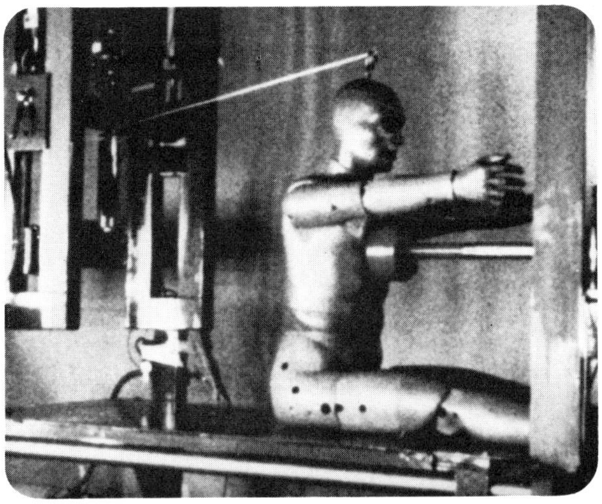

VOLVO
The car for people
who think.

GENERIC-DUMMIES
30-second

MUSIC THROUGHOUT

ANNCR: At Volvo, we employ a lot of dummies to help us plan our cars.

They've shown us how to make Volvo bodies protect your body better.

They gave us ideas for a more comfortable interior and suggested ways to keep you safer.

We think Volvo is the world's most intelligently thought-out car.

It's because we've learned a lot from dummies.

SUPER: *Volvo. The car for people who think*

164—STANDARDS OF LUXURY
30-second

CORPORATE CRASH TEST
30-second

431
Art Director Robert Reitzfeld
Writer Thomas J. Nathan
Directors Robert Reitzfeld
Henry Sandbank
Production Co. Sandbank Films
Agency Scali, McCabe, Sloves
Client Volvo of America Corp.

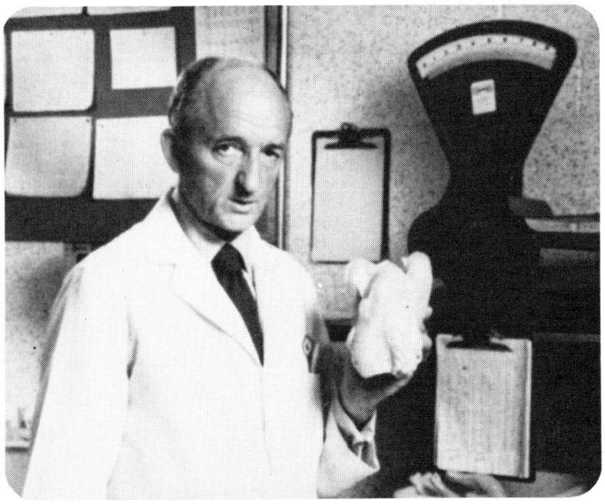

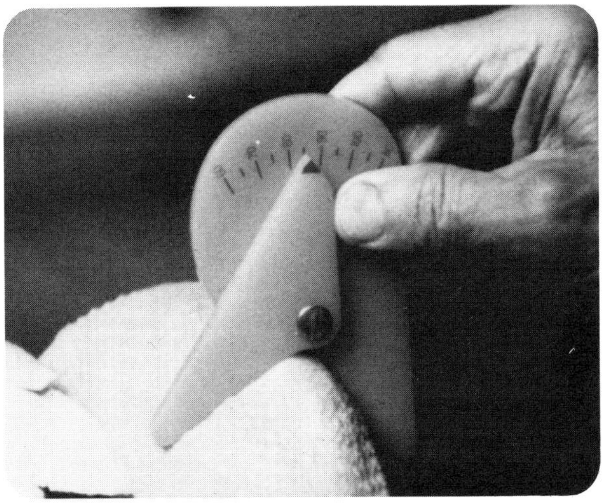

IT TAKES
A TOUGH MAN
TO MAKE
A TENDER CHICKEN.
PERDUE
QUALITY GUARANTEED
OR MONEY BACK

BREAST GAUGE
30-second

FRANK PERDUE: One way you can tell a great chicken from an ordinary one is by the size of the breast.

Perdue chicken is bred to have the broadest, plumpest breast of any chicken you can buy.

And measures at least 84 on the breast gauge. You don't have a breast gauge? Don't let that stand between you and a better chicken.

Send me two Perdue wing-tags and a dollar, and I'll send you a Perdue breast gauge along with instructions for use.

See for yourself how the chicken you buy stacks up against mine.

SUPER: *It takes a tough man to make a tender chicken*

FEED SAMPLES
30-second

HARD NOSED
30-second

432
Art Director Sam Scali
Writer Edward A. McCabe
Director Frank Herman
Production Co. Televideo Productions
Agency Scali, McCabe, Sloves
Client Perdue Farms

BABY ANIMALS
60-second

MUSIC THROUGHOUT

ANNCR: Have you ever seen something that was so . . .

Soft . . . you just had to touch it.

Something that was also colorful . . .

And stayed soft even after being washed.

That's out new comforter made of one of the softest fibers in the world, Arnel from Celanese.

Arnel is soft . . . and cuddley . . . and *very* lush.

Comforters of Arnel come in 5 rich colors . . .

And they come in a jungle pattern called Afrique. And comforters of Arnel are *very . . . very . . .* comfortable.

Comforters by Countess York

433
Art Director Jim Scalfone
Writer Robin Needleman
Director Neil Tardio
Producer Fletcher Coleman
Production Co. Lovinger, Tardio, Melsky
Agency Doyle, Dane, Bernbach
Client Celanese

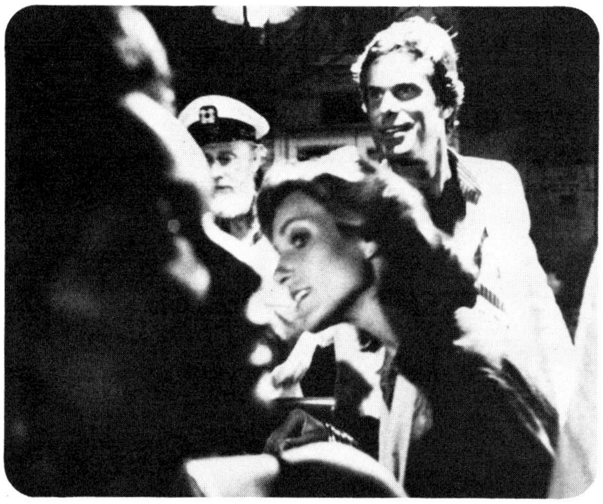

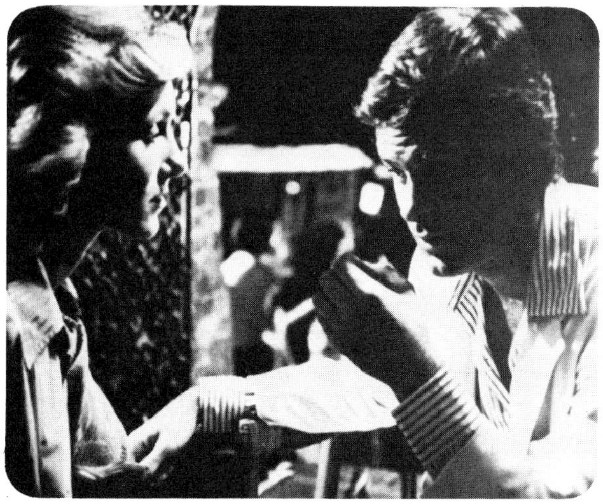

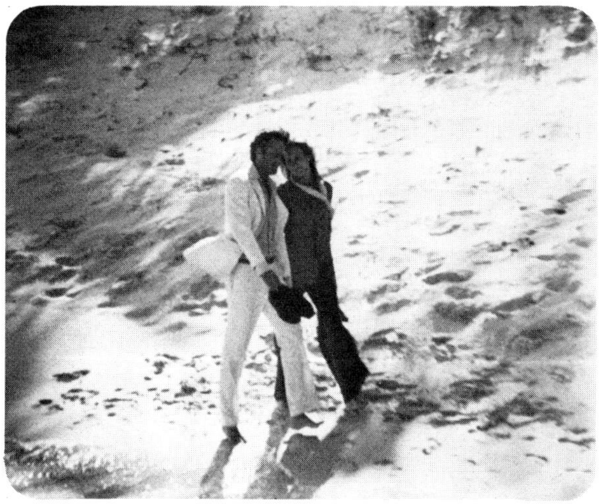

VIRGIN ISLANDS
60-second

MUSIC UNDER: "What a life" theme.

ANNCR: Down in the Caribbean . . . in the United States Virgin Islands . . . the sun appears daily.

Some people wait up for it.

The United States Virgin Islands. What a life.

SUPER: *United States Virgin Islands. What a life*

434
Art Director Reggie Troncone
Cameraman Nicolas Roeg
Writers Richard Gaetano Ferrelli
Gad Romann
Director Nicolas Roeg
Producer Reggie Troncone
Production Co. James Garrett and Partners
Agency Greengage Assoc.
Client United States Virgin Islands

60% less
calories
EX BIER

EX BIER
60-second

ANNCR: Not far from the Rhine, in Switzerland's leading brewery, they've come up with something remarkable.

Ex Bier. It looks and tastes like great imported beer, but has 60% less calories.

The Swiss have been drinking Ex Bier for some time—but there's never been anything like it in America.

Ex Bier is brewed with the richest malt, hops, and pure Swiss mountain water—and a yeast so good it's exported to breweries all over the world.

Then something unique happens to Ex Bier. After it's aged, the alcohol is removed by a special process no other beer has ever used.

So you get all the taste, aroma, and creamy head you want. With 60% less calories.

We'd like to show you how they do it. But only the brewmaster knows.

(And maybe his wife.)

Ex Bier: New from Switzerland. Tastes like the great imports, but 60% less calories.

435
Art Director Dan Weiss
Writer Liz Buttke
Designer Dan Weiss
Director Lear Levin
Producer Dan Weiss
Production Co. Lear Levin Productions
Agency Firestone & Assoc.
Client Ex Bier

TEENAGERS
60-second

MIKE: Hello, Debbie? Hi, this is Mike.

DEBBIE: Hi Mike.

MUSIC UNDER

MIKE: Remember the other day when we were in the cafeteria and I kinda spilled my soup?

DEBBIE: Yeah!

MIKE: Hey, well listen, I was about to tell you something, and didn't get around to it.

Uh, I wanted to tell you that . . . I think I love you.

DEBBIE: What?

MIKE: Surprised huh?

DEBBIE: I . . . I

MIKE: What is it Debbie?

DEBBIE: I can't talk because my parents are sitting right beside me.

MIKE: Speak up!

DEBBIE: I can't.

ANNCR: There are times when a family really needs the privacy an extension phone can give it. And you can have one for only about 3 cents a day.

In fact, if you can use *three* phones, ask about our Pushbutton Package at a special bargain rate. Call your Illinois Bell Service Representative for details.

MIKE: Really, if you don't like me it's fine.

ANNCR: And make life a lot simpler for everyone.

DEBBIE: I couldn't talk before because my parents were sitting right here.

436
Art Director Bill Smith
Writer Ray Thiem
Director Hil Covington
Producer Michael Paradise
Production Co. Hil Covington
Agency NW Ayer ABH International Chicago
Client Illinois Bell

NO DIME
60-second

ANNCR: Pick up the receiver and you get a dial tone right away, so you know the phone is working.

If you have no change, just dial the Operator, who'll place your call for you—for an extra charge on local calls.

MAN #2: Operator? Will you charge this call to my home phone?

MAN #1: Only got pennies, huh?

OLD LADY: Well, let's see . . . one, two.

MAN #1: Yeah, one, two unbelievable.

ANNCR: Dial Tone First. It could save you a lot of trouble sometime.

MAN #1: (Singing) I'll pay you back if you loan me a dime in time.

MAN #1: Do you have a dime on ya by any chance?

STRANGER: I'm sorry. What?

MAN #1: I, uh happen to have no change.

STRANGER: I never lend money to strangers.

MAN: Listen, could I borrow a dime? I gotta make a call.

ANNCR: We don't think a dime should ever stand between you and an important phone call.

So we're installing the new Dial Tone First coin phones that work with or without a dime. They're identified by the instruction card.

437
Art Director Bill Smith
Writer Hugh Wells
Director Hil Covington
Producer Michael Paradise
Production Co. Hil Covington
Agency NW Ayer ABH International Chicago
Client Illinois Bell

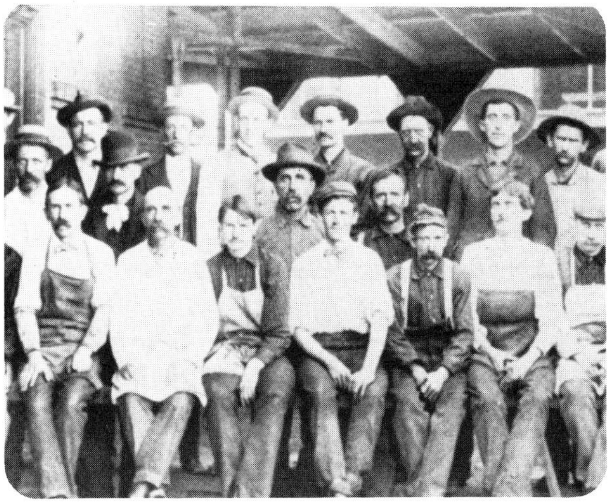

CALIFORNIA HERE I COME
90-second

Scenes of southern California from 1900 to the present run throughout.

MUSIC: "California Here I Come"

ANNCR: Over the years, clean natural gas has helped make life better in Southern California.

It has been and will continue to be the most efficient energy source for heating, cooking and hot water. And that saves natural resources. So if you're thinking about the future, think about gas.

It's been a fuel of the future for a long, long time.

438
Art Director Bob Matsumoto
Writer David Balkan
Producer Mel Kane
Production Co. Waterbarrel
Agency Doyle Dane Bernbach
Los Angeles
Client Southern California Gas Co.

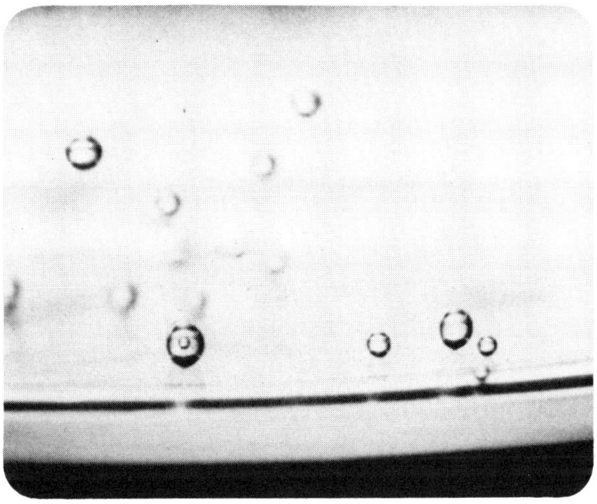

THE BUBBLE
60-second

ANNCR: You could be wasting valuable energy without even knowing it.

SFX: Natural sounds.

You could be leaving your pots and pans uncovered when you cook.

Or you might not be using the most efficient energy source.

Using gas for cooking consumes about one-third less energy than using electricity. So if you need a new range choosing gas will actually help save energy.

But no matter what the energy source . . .

you should always try to cover your pots and pans when cooking.

Let's say 20% of the homes in Southern California are doing that now.

If everyone did, we'd save enough energy in a year . . .

so that every household in a city the size of Pasadena could cook all their meals for over two years.

Energy is our business. Conserving it is everyone's business.

SUPER: *Energy is our business . . . conserving it is everyone's business*

439
Art Director Bob Matsumoto
Writer Terry Taketa
Producer Reed Springer
Production Co. Ampersand Productions
Agency Doyle Dane Bernbach
Los Angeles
Client Southern California Gas Co.

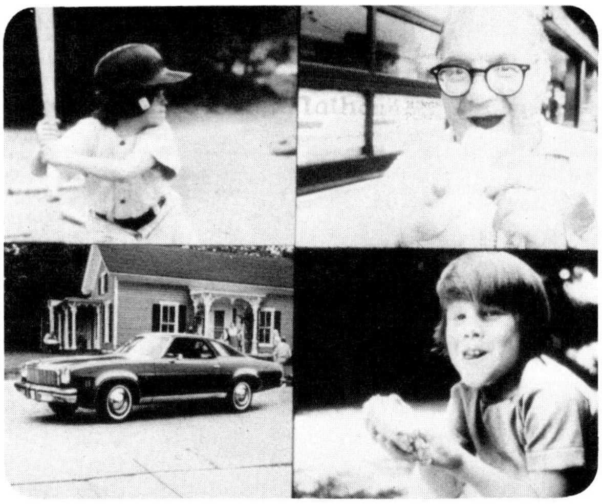

HOTDOGS
60-second

ANNCR: America, what's your favorite sport?

AMERICA: Baseball!

ANNCR: Sandwich?

AMERICA: Hotdogs!

ANNCR: Pie?

AMERICA: Apple!

ANNCR: And what's your favorite car, America?

AMERICA: Chevrolet!

ANNCR: Let's see—that's baseball, hotdogs, apple pie, and Chevrolet, Well you sure sound like America to me.

AMERICA: We are!

ANNCR: Well then you better tell me again . . . 'cause I just might forget.

AMERICA: (Singing) We love baseball, hot-dogs, apple pie, and Chevrolet . . . baseball, hotdogs, apple pie, and Chevrolet.

ANNCR: That's Baseball, hotdogs, apple pie, and Chevrolet.

AMERICA: Baseball and hotdogs, apple pie and Chevrolet.

ANNCR: In case you're wondering, this commercial is brought to you by . . . baseball, hotdogs, apple pie, and your favorite car.

AMERICA: (Singing) They go together in the good old U.S.A., baseball . . .

ANNCR: Makes sense to me.

AMERICA: (Singing) Baseball, hotdogs, apple pie, and Chevrolet.

440
Art Director Audrey Clugston
Writer James W. Hartzell
Producers David E. Davis, Jr.
Virginia Heyl
Production Cos. Braverman Productions
Brillig Productions
Agency Campbell-Ewald Co.
Client General Motors

PORTRAIT OF ROBBIE
60-second

ANNCR: This is Robbie.

MUSIC UNDER

ANNCR: This is a portrait of Robbie taken with Polaroid's SX-70 Land Camera, and developing in minutes into a print so real it wants to speak to you.

ANNCR: But the camera won't let you stop there. Robbie is a lot of things . . . and the camera seems to search them out . . . effortlessly . . . leading you to new discoveries about Robbie . . . and about yourself.

ANNCR: A portrait of Robbie . . . you could have taken it. You . . . and Polaroid's SX-70.

441
Art Director Robert Gage
Writer Phyllis Robinson
Cameraman Richard Dubbleman
Director Robert Gage
Producer Cliff Fagin
Production Co. Directors Studio
Agency Doyle Dane Bernbach
Client Polaroid Corp.

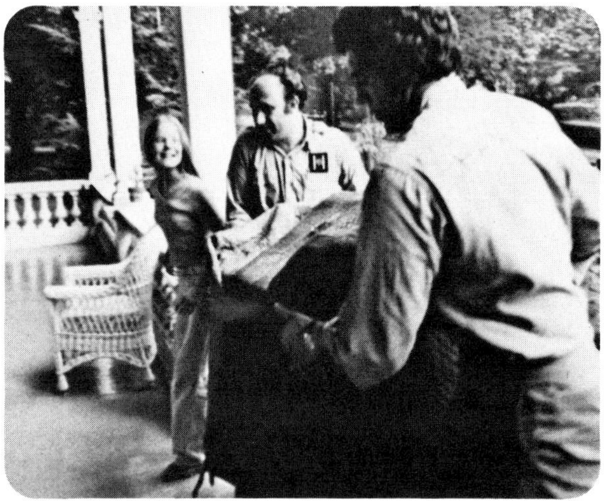

Hammond
$439.95 to $7,500.

DELIVERY
60-second

ANNCR: At Hammond, we realize it's very easy to put off buying an organ.

There's always a bedroom to carpet . . . or a television set on its last legs.

But no child ever grew up with happy memories of everybody singing . . . around the new aluminum siding.

And nobody ever learned to play music on a trash compactor. So even though you can always find perfectly sensible reasons . . . for waiting buy an organ . . . maybe you should think of all the reasons for not waiting.

After all, while this family is having an experience they'll keep forever . . . all your family is doing . . . is watching a television commercial.

442
Art Director Jack Piccolo
Writer Diane Rothschild
Director Jack Piccolo
Producer Barbara Cowan
Production Co. Director's Studio
Agency Doyle Dane Bernbach
Client Hammond Organ

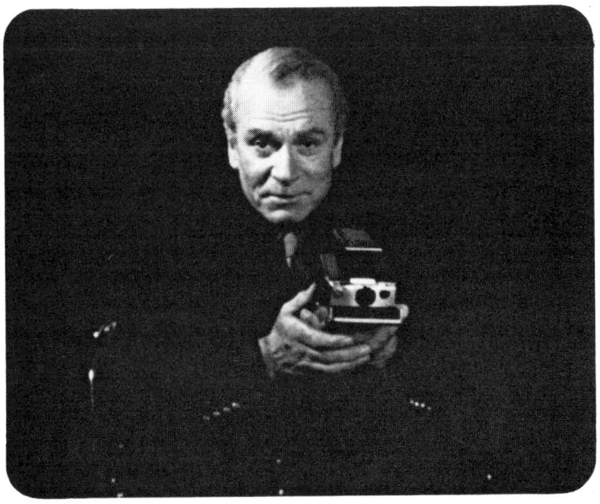

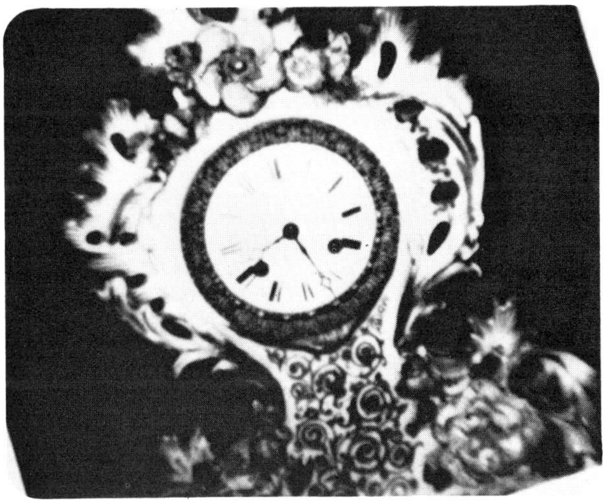

HARDWARE
60-second

OLIVIER: The age of miracles. A pocket-sized folding . . . electronically controlled motor driven single lens reflex camera, that, quite simply, does the impossible. Come a bit closer.

MUSIC

OLIVIER: The Polaroid SX-70 Land camera. The 10-picture film pack . . . inside this there is a waferthin battery providing fresh power to the camera every time you load. A protective cover. For indoors, the Flashbar . . . Now focus, frame, touch the electric button and the impossible happens.

MUSIC

OLIVIER: In minutes, you have a finished photograph of dazzling beauty. That . . . is the Polaroid SX-70 Experience.

443
Art Director Robert Gage
Writer Roy Grace
Cameraman Richard Dubbleman
Director Robert Gage
Producer Cliff Fagin
Production Co. Directors Studio
Agency Doyle Dane Bernbach
Client Polaroid Corp.

VOLVO

164—GO HOME
60-second

MAITRE D': Ah, Mr. and Mrs. Baxter.

WOMAN: Charles, very nice to see you again.

MAITRE D': How nice to see you again. You look delightful.

MAN: Everything looks good.

MAITRE D': Would you like to order now?

MAN: No, Charles, why don't you order for us?

ANNCR: The Volvo 164 has disc brakes on all four wheels . . .

SFX: Road noises

MAITRE D': Carré d'agneau . . . the rack of lamb.

WOMAN: Ah, Charles, it's magnificent!

ANNCR: . . . radial tires . . .

WOMAN: Mmm, so tender.

ANNCR: . . . an enormously strong all-welded body . . .

WOMAN: I'm going to have some of everything.

MAN: Sure you don't want a crepe?

ANNCR: . . . and precise handling.

MAN: Let's go home.

WOMAN: What a lovely idea.

ANNCR: The Volvo 164. Because no matter how far you've come in life . . .

DOORMAN: Have a pleasant trip home, Mr. and Mrs. Baxter.

ANNCR: . . . sooner or later, you have to go home.

444
Art Director Robert Reitzfeld
Writer Michael Drazen
Director Steve Horn
Cameraman Steve Horn
Production Co. Steve Horn, Inc.
Agency Scali, McCabe, Sloves
Client Volvo of America Corp.

VAC-730

VOLVO
The car for people who think.

240 DETAILS
60-second

ANNCR: Volvo thinks the design of a car should be as intelligent as the person who drives it.

Consider the thinking that went into Volvo's gas filler cap. Volvo provides a receptacle, so it shouldn't be mislaid. So it shouldn't be missed, Volvo colors it red.

The seat provides more than a place to sit. It can make you a better driver.

You can see through it. And it's infinitely adjustable, to afford you better control over the controls. A lumbar support may be firmed or softened to your liking.

And if an important light burns out, this lights up.

It's no surprise that a car this carefully thought-out should appeal to people who think. 87% of all Volvo buyers are college-educated.

The other 13% are just plain smart.

SUPER: *Volvo. The car for people who think*

445
Art Director Robert Reitzfeld
Writer Thomas J. Nathan
Director Henry Sandbank
Agency Scali, McCabe, Sloves
Client Volvo of America Corp.

LEE TREVINO SONG AND DANCE
60-second

GIRLS: Lee Trevino sings his favorite pop tune.

LEE: (Singing) You think I'm a golfer . . . maybe so . . . Could be a dancer . . . you never really know.

Now this looks like a cola, but it's not. You ought try the special taste its got.

Don't you believe nobody else . . . Take it from me . . . find out for yourself.

CHORUS: Dr. Pepper so misunderstood. It tastes different, and millions of people love . . . the difference of . . . Dr. Pepper . . .

so misunderstood. It tastes different . . .

446
Art Director Ed Bianchi
Writer Rich DePascal
Director Ed Bianchi
Producer Nancy Bacal
Production Co. Wakeford/Orloff
Agency Young & Rubicam International
Client Dr. Pepper

USLIFE SAVINGS
and Loan Association

ARTHUR DANEMAN
60-second

ARTHUR DANEMAN: I'm not an actor, I'm a 75-year-old retired book distributor. I used to earn a minimum of $25,000 a year.

And that was a lot of money back then. Today in retirement my wife and I have an income of about $5,000 plus Social Security.

I do have some savings, but my gosh . . . in my working years I could have saved a couple hundred thousand dollars. Take a tip from me. Save ten percent of your salary, at a place like the company that asked me to do this commercial, USLIFE Savings.

Stop by any USLIFE Savings office for a free book about retirement planning . . . I used to think nothing of spending a hundred dollars for an evening out. I used to think tomorrow never comes.

Tomorrow does come.

447
Art Director Ross Van Dusen
Writer Bob Sundland
Cameraman Jordan Cronewith
Director Bob Gyrs
Producer Pam Den Hartog
Production Co. Filmfair
Agency Chiat/Day
Client USLIFE Savings & Loan Assoc.

Southern

ORGY
60-second

STEWARDESS: Second cabin, please.

ANNCR: You know what the stewardess really means when she orders you to go back to the second cabin, don't you?

She means, get back there with the peasants. That's what she means.

Southern Airways believes that no man should be subjected to the indignity of being labeled or treated like a second class citizen.

Which is why, when you get on a Southern jet, you'll find no curtain separates the peasants from the nobility.

STEWARDESS: Hi, Mr. Gill, sit anywhere you like.

ANNCR: No one takes the legroom from you and gives it to someone else.

On Southern there's only one class of service and it isn't second.

SUPER: *Nobody's Second Class On Southern*

GOLD

448

Art Director Jonis Gold
Writer Tom Little
Director Joe Sedelmaier
Producer Suzanne Carroll
Production Co. Sedelmaier Films
Agency McDonald & Little
Client Southern Airways

PROJECT CABLE

SAN FRANCISCO POLICE DEPARTMENT
60-second

SFX: Police department and car noises.

CAPTAIN FEDER: I'm Captain Lou Feder of the San . . . Francisco Police Department . . .

and this system, built with the help of . . . GTE Information System . . .

is called . . . Project . . . Cable Computer Assisted . . . Bay Area Law Enforcement.

SFX: Siren and car chase

CAPTAIN FEDER: Jerome Summers . . . was just another speeder . . . when we started . . . chasing him . . .

SFX: Car hits ground.

CAPTAIN FEDER: but in less than a minute we learned a lot . . . more about Jerome Summers.

POLICE OFFICER: Turning right on Montgomery . . . Do you have any results?

CAPTAIN FEDER: We learned that he was armed, dangerous, and wanted for . . . murder in Wisconsin.

With Project Cable, Jerome Summers was apprehended . . . and held on the murder charge.

Without it he might . . . still be riding around.

POLICE OFFICER: All right out of the car with your hands . . .

ANNCR: GTE Information System.

448A
Art Director Charles Gennarelli
Writer Larry Levenson
Director William Fraker
Producer Paul Schulman
Production Co. Independent Artists
Agency Doyle Dane Bernbach
Client General Telephone & Electronics

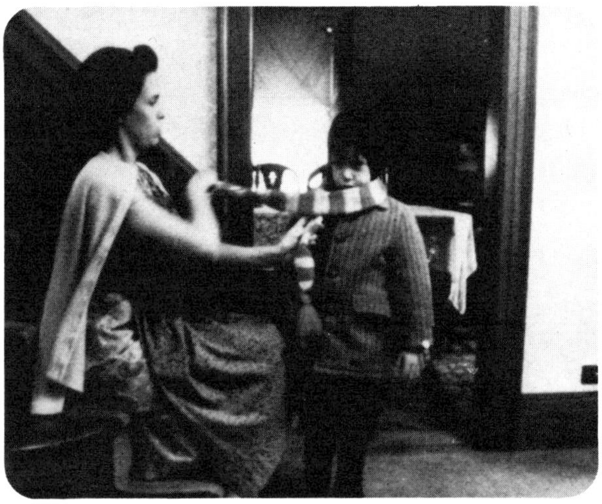

Barney's
7th Avenue and 17th Street

YOU'RE BIG ENOUGH TO DRESS YOURSELF
60-second

ANNCR: From the very beginning people have been dressing you. Your mother . . . your schoolmates . . . your country . . .

SERGEANT: You're out of uniform, Soldier!

ANNCR: Even the clothing stores you shopped in.

YOUNG MAN: Don't you have something with just a little different look?

SALESMAN: Sir, that is *the* look.

ANNCR: Well at Barney's, we think you're big enough to dress yourself.

So when you come to Barney's, you'll be able to choose from the widest range of American and international fashions in the world.

MAN: What do you think?

SALESMAN: What do *you* think?

MAN: Terrific!

ANNCR: Barney's. We let you be you.

SILVER

449
Art Director Louis Colletti
Writer Michael Drazen
Director Steve Horn
Production Co. Steve Horn
Agency Scali, McCabe, Sloves
Client Barney's Clothes

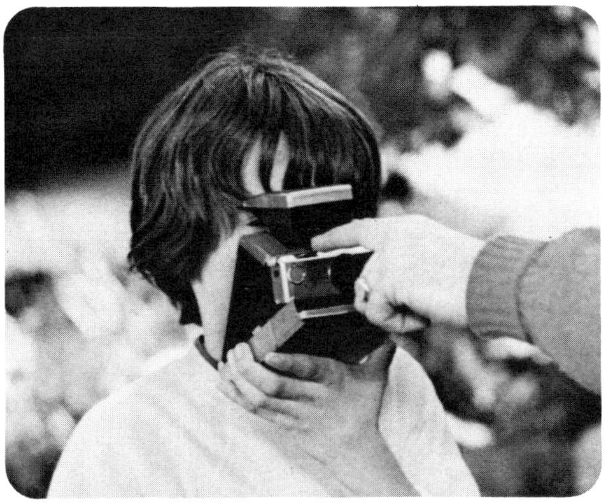

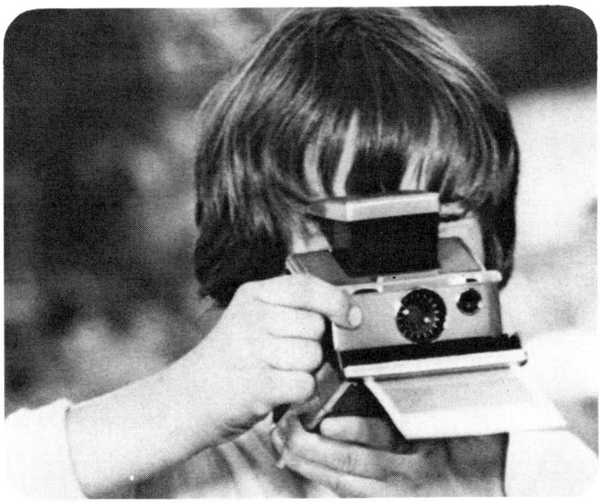

FATHER & SON
60-second

MUSIC UNDER

FATHER: Now hold it in your left hand, rest it against your chin, and look through the viewer.
Now all you use is one finger.
You turn this focusing wheel to make everything sharp.

ANNCR: Now there is a new way to open up the world for someone.

FATHER: Press the electric button . . .

ANNCR: The SX-70 . . .
Almost effortlessly, it slips through life—

MUSIC

ANNCR: searching out—recording—

MUSIC

ANNCR: You watch your creation come to life, growing more vivid, more detailed.
Until minutes later, you're looking at a print; almost as real as life itself.
Polaroid's SX-70 Land Camera.
It can open up the world.

450
Art Director Robert Gage
Writer Phyllis Robinson
Cameraman Richard Dubbleman
Director Robert Gage
Producer Cliff Fagin
Production Co. Directors Studio
Agency Doyle Dane Bernbach
Client Polaroid Corp.

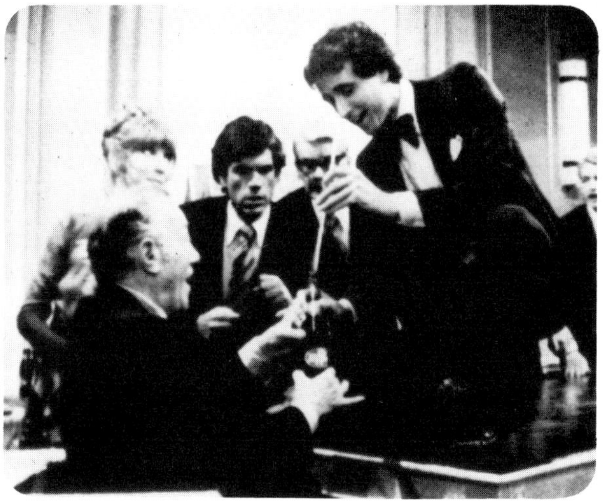

EXECUTIVE LUNCH
60-second

BOSS: (Singing) I'll have my usual, Nellie Sue.

SECRETARY: (Singing) Lettuce on toast, and a cola too.

2ND MAN: (Singing) I'll have the same, Boss, the same as you.

3RD MAN: (Singing) Me too!

4TH MAN: (Singing) Me too!

5TH MAN: (Singing) Me too!

6TH MAN: (Singing) Me too!

HERO: (Singing) Oh no, not for me, Sir!
I need originality Sir.
Give me innovation, variation, Dr. Pepper . . .
Dr. Pepper!
It's not a cola.
It's something much, much more
It's not a root beer, there are root beers by the score.

ALL: (Singing) Dr. Pepper . . .
The joy of every boy and girl,
It's the most original soft drink
ever in the whole wide world.
Dr. Pepper . . .,

BOSS: Fine speech, my boy!

HERO: Thanks, Dad.

ALL: (Singing) Dr. Pepper . . .

451
Art Director Jim Swan
Writer Curvin O'Rielly
Director Ed Bianchi
Producer Dennis Powers
Production Co. Dick Levine Productions
Agency Young & Rubicam International
Client Dr. Pepper

USLIFE SAVINGS
and Loan Association

I'M NOT AN ACTOR
60-second

WARREN MORGAN: I'm not an actor. I'm a 74-year-old man in some financial difficulty. I was a top executive with 40 years of service for three of America's largest corporations. I retired 10 years ago with what I thought was plenty to see me through my retirement in comfort.

But it just wasn't enough. Inflation . . . medical expenses . . . stock market losses . . . I've got one piece of advice for young people. The time to start saving for retirement is when you first start working.

The company that asked me to do this commercial, USLIFE Savings, is a good place to do it. And if you stop in at one of their offices they'll give you a free copy of the book "The Complete Guide To Retirement."

I'm glad I had the chance to do this commercial for USLIFE Savings.

I needed the money.

452

Art Director Ross Van Dusen
Cameraman Fred Peterman
Writer Bob Sundland
Director Fred Peterman
Producer Pam Den Hartog
Production Co. Harvest Films
Agency Chiat/Day
Client USLIFE Savings & Loan Assoc.

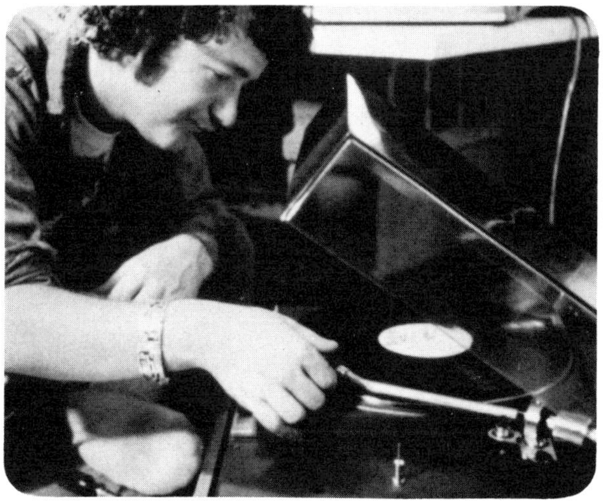

OUR SONG
60-second

MOTHER: Harry, Harry what's going on in there? Why is it so dark, let's get some light in here.

FATHER: So this is it? This is it?

MOTHER: Harry, you spend a whole summer making pizzas and buy a record player that doesn't even fit together?

SON: Mom, this is Sony equipment . . . you can't get any better.

MOTHER: When does the cabinet arrive?

SON: It's got sixty watts RMS per channel over the entire band width. Listen to the bass guitar on that speaker.

FATHER: You call that music!? Here . . . play this.

MOTHER: What's that?

FATHER: It's our song.

MOTHER: Hey, not bad.

FATHER: I never heard those french horns before.

ANNCR: You can talk about Sony equipment endlessly—you can praise it lavishly . . . but there's nothing that can take the place of listening to it.

MOTHER: Does it come in French Provincial?

FATHER: You don't know how to talk to the kid.

ANNCR: Let a Sony sell you a Sony.

453
Art Director Don Slater
Writer Adam Hanft
Director Jeff Lovinger
Producer Tom Fenton
Production Co. Lovinger, Tardio, Melsky
Agency Rosenfeld, Sirowitz & Lawson
Client Sony Corporation of America

TOM & BOB'S
OLD FASHIONED
HOME MADE
CIDER
by
GALLON

TOM&BOB'S

PARTNERSHIP
60-second

ANNCR: Sometimes your future may be captured in a single moment in the present.

CHORUS: Sun is shining.
Things are growing.
Things are going well with you and me.
A future planned together.
A rich, full life together
and things look bright as they can be.

We're helping 40 million people,
more than 40 million people,
who know the future is now.

At Metropolitan Life, we help to plan your future.

ANNCR: The future will be here in a moment. Don't let it take you by surprise.

At Metropolitan Life we've spent over a century helping people prepare for the future.

And Metropolitan can do the same for you.

Metropolitan Life, where the future is now.

454
Art Director Robert Engle
Writer Tom Thomas
Director Art Kane
Producer Robert Engle
Production Co. Wylde and Assoc.
Agency Young & Rubicam International
Client Metropolitan Life

Mass., 1920

FROSTED

CLARENCE BIRDSEYE
30-second

MUSIC UNDER

ANNCR: Yes, there really was a Clarence Birdseye, and this is his story.

While ice fishing in 50° below . . . the young scientist discovered the secret of quick freezing foods. Clarence Birdseye couldn't get the idea out of his mind . . . so in 1920 in his own kitchen sink he invented the first process for quick freezing foods. Cooked months later, it still tasted fresh.

CLARENCE: With this invention, I can freeze fresh vegetables at the peak of perfection. People will eat my good tasting vegetables even in the winter. Housewives won't have to waste time shelling peas, washing green beans . . . These vegetables are picked garden fresh. Ladies, I will only freeze the best . . . because my name is on the box. I can't settle for anything less than the best you can grow.

ANNCR: So if you're as fussy as Clarence Birdseye, don't serve your family just anybody's vegetables . . . Serve the vegetables that bear the name of the father of frozen foods.

455
Art Director Stew Birbrower
Writer Mike Becker
Director Steve Horn
Producer Phylis Landi
Production Co. Horn/Griner Productions
Agency Young & Rubicam International
Client General Foods

SUGAR

MUSICAL
60-second

GIRL: (Singing) I asked the man for a diet
soft drink.
He brought me a glass right away.
Took one sip and suddenly knew it most
likely wasn't his day.
I looked at this drink in front of me.
Took another sip.

MUSIC

It just can't be . . .
this just can't be a diet soft drink.
It tastes too good to be true.

CHORUS: It's Sugar Free Dr. Pepper. It tastes
too good to be true.

GIRL: (Singing) It really is a diet soft drink.

CHORUS: It tastes too good to be true.

GIRL: (Singing) Bye!

CHORUS: It's Sugar Free Dr. Pepper.
It tastes too good to be true.
It tastes too good to be . . .
it tastes too good to be true.

456
Art Director Jim Swan
Writer Mara Connolly
Director Rick Levine
Producer Linda Mevorach
Production Co. Rick Levine Productions
Agency Young & Rubicam International
Client Dr. Pepper

BRIAN COE
60-second

MUSIC UNDER

ANNCR: Maybe you remember this boy. His name is Brian Coe. We introduced you to him over six years ago . . . in a General Electric commercial.

Brian lived and played in Stoneham, Massachusetts. And his heart ran on batteries. Every beat of Brian's heart . . . was triggered by a General Electric Pacemaker. A small electronic device implanted under his skin.

Today, Brian Coe still lives and plays in Stoneham . . . his heart still runs on batteries.

Brian's GE Pacemaker keeps his heart beating at about 71 beats per minute. Enough for him to grow like any boy. Enough for him to grow into a man.

Progress for people from General Electric.

SUPER: *Progress for People*
General Electric

457
Art Director Len McCarron
Writer Bob McLoughlin
Director Lear Levin
Producer Tom Anderson
Production Co. Lear Levin Productions
Agency BBDO
Client GE Corporate

CABIN
60-second

WOMAN: George and I fell in love with this place on a day just like this one. The cabin was run down and the roof leaked, but that didn't matter.

Even though we couldn't put much money into it we put in a lot of hard work. George fixed the roof and I snooped around the auctions looking for furniture to refinish.

We only came up on weekends, but to us it was home.

I never thought we'd give it up. But then I never thought George would die.

MUSIC

ANNCR: When a man dies, one of the saddest things his family has to face is what they'll lose after they've lost him.

We at MONY, Mutual Of New York, know how reluctant some people can be to discuss life insurance.

But we also know how much it can mean when it's needed.

Call us. Because your family can't live on memories alone.

ANIMATED LOGO: *Mutual Of New York. MONY. For the future*

458
Art Director Andrew Langer
Writer Marshall Karp
Director Steve Horn
Producer Diane Jeremias
Production Co. Steve Horn Inc.
Agency The Marschalk Co.
Client Mutual of New York

OPEN

BRIAN
60-second

BRIAN: I remember the day my father started saving for my college education. It was my 10th birthday, and he opened a savings account for ten dollars.

"Brian," he said, "you're gonna have it better than me. You're not gonna have to stand on your feet all day just to make a buck. You do the studying. I'll do the saving."

He had it all planned. There was only one thing he didn't plan. He didn't plan on dying.

MUSIC

ANNCR: Sometimes the saddest thing about a man's death is to watch his dreams die with him.

We at MONY, Mutual Of New York, understand how reluctant some people can be to discuss life insurance.

But if you have children, you should talk to a MONY representative about insuring their future. Because as painful as it might be for your family to go on without you, it would be even more painful for them to go on without anything.

ANIMATED LOGO: *Mutual Of New York MONY. For the future*

459
Art Director Andrew Langer
Writer Marshall Karp
Director Steve Horn
Producer Diane Jeremias
Production Co. Steve Horn, Inc.
Agency The Marschalk Co.
Client Mutual of New York

POLICE

POLICE CALLS
60-second

MUSIC UNDER

SON: Hey, Mom, where's Dad?

MOM: I don't know. He's half an hour late already.

DISPATCHER: All Units. I have a 1053 in Sector 5.

COP: Charlie 3 responding.

SFX: Siren

DISPATCHER: Charlie 3. Proceed to Route 6 overpass. Probable injuries.

MOM: Nancy, come set the table before your Daddy gets home.

ANNCR: What would your family do if one night you didn't come home?

COP: I have an injured and a possible fatal. Request two ambulances and a couple of wreckers.

DISPATCHER: They're on their way.

ANNCR: What would they do if you became the other guy in a car accident?

COP: I'm 1098 here.

DISPATCHER: Make notifications to the families involved.

ANNCR: We at MONY, Mutual Of New York, know how reluctant some people are to discuss life insurance. But if you'll call a MONY representative, we'll help plan your family's future. Just in case, one night, you're the one who doesn't come home.

COP: Mrs. Hayden? Your husband's been in an accident. He'll be all right. He was the lucky one.

ANNCR: Mutual Of New York. MONY. For the future.

460
Art Director Andrew Langer
Writer Marshall Karp
Director Steve Horn
Producer Diane Jeremias
Production Co. Steve Horn, Inc.
Agency The Marschalk Co.
Client Mutual of New York

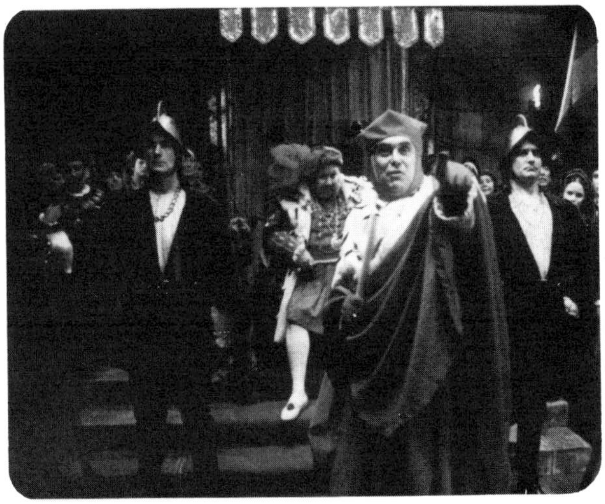

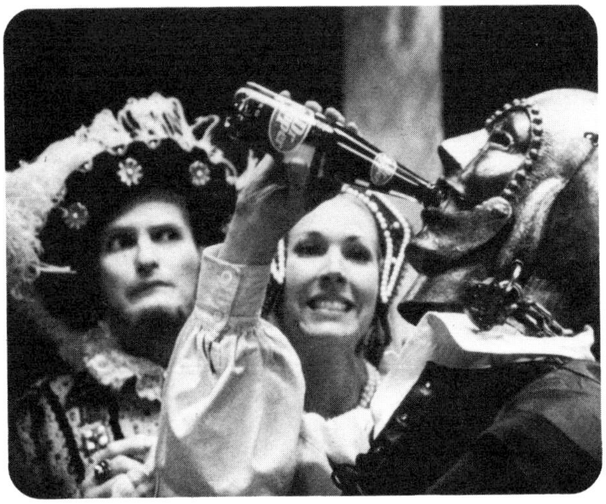

MAN IN IRON MASK
60-second

GUARD: Let the prisoner approach the throne.

CARDINAL: The Crown decrees Prince Richard be freed of the iron mask . . .

KING: Providing he meets my condition.

RICHARD: Then the mask remains!

LADY ANNE: (Aside) Ten years since last that handsome face I saw! (to Richard) Consent my love!

RICHARD: I cannot!

LADY ANNE: I shall wed Sir Chauncey!

RICHARD: What see you in him?

LADY ANNE: Firstly . . . I see his face!

RICHARD: I submit!

ANNCR: Dr. Pepper. It looks like a cola, but it tastes different and millions of people love that difference.

RICHARD: Gadzooks! Magnificent!

LADY ANNE: Oooh!

461
Art Director Lou DiJoseph
Writer Tom Attea
Designer Howard Barker
Cameraman Gerald Cotts
Director Rick Levine
Producer Geoff Mayo
Production Co. Rick Levine Productions
Agency Young & Rubicam International
Client Dr. Pepper

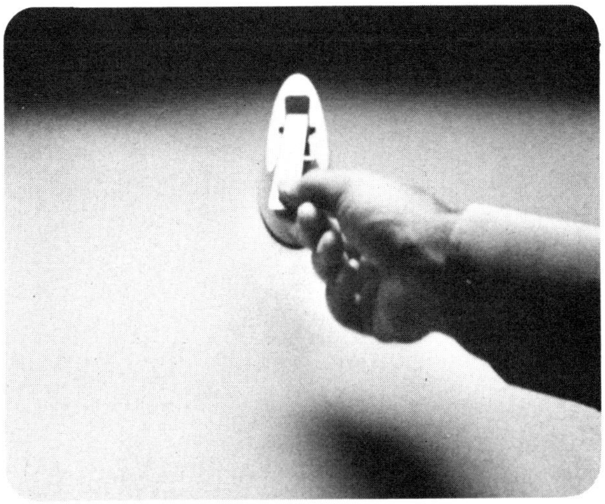

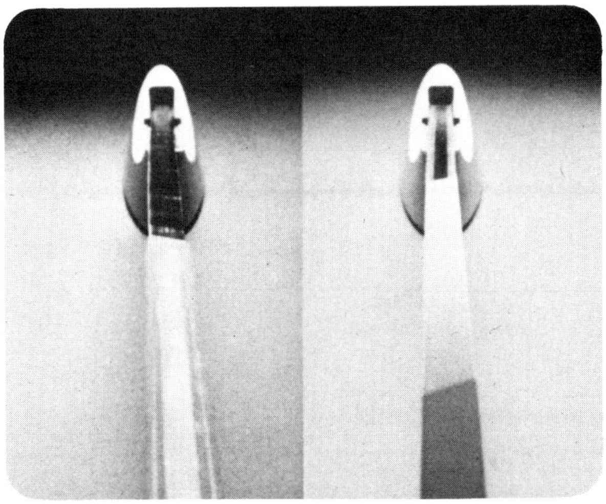

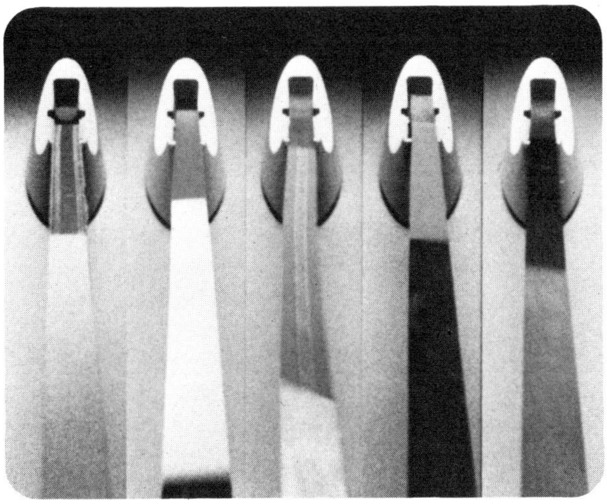

TAPE
60-second

ANNCR: In 1925, a young man working for the 3M Company had a novel idea. He called it masking tape.

MUSIC: Pomp and Circumstance

From that humble beginning came the now famous Scotch brand transparent tape. And from that idea sprang electrical tape. Followed closely by bookbinding tape and fireproofing tape. Pretty soon 3M was into so many different tapes, it was hard even for 3M to handle it all. So to keep things running smoothly, they started putting different kinds of tape into their own small groups.

Like the magnetic audio-video people.

And the medical products people. As the groups grew, they split up into even more businesses.

And today, 3M has a lot of separate groups making over 600 different kinds of tape for nearly every customer need.

All because we *haven't* created a lot of red tape.

The 3M Company.

LOGO: *3M Company*
The Kind of Climate That
Grows Good Products

462
Art Director Brian Stewart
Writer Gibson Carothers
Director Gene McGarr
Producer Brian Stewart
Production Co. Phoenix Films Corp.
Agency BBDO
Client 3M Co.

BOEING
Getting people together

FAMILY OF PLANES
60-second

MUSIC: Harp gliss.

ANNCR: Boeing has been getting people together almost since man learned to fly.

SONG: Man left the ground with a whirling sound. He took to the sky cause he wanted to fly in big beautiful flying ships taking historic trips
making new friends that you've known through the years.
Now and forever, getting people together.
Wherever we go
together we go . . .

ANNCR: Can you imagine what air travel would be like if there hadn't been a Boeing?

SONG: Almost every hour of every day
There's a 747 flying your way.
Take off . . .

ANNCR: Boeing.
We've been getting people together for almost 60 years.

463
Writer Hal Newsom
Directors Mike Olds
Larry Field
Producer Cole & Weber
Production Co. N. Lee Lacy
Agency Cole & Weber
Client Boeing Airplane Co.

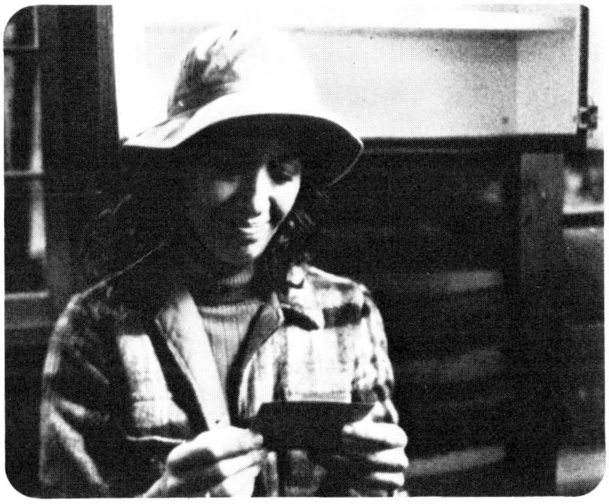

CABIN
60-second

WOMAN: George and I fell in love with this place on a day just like this one. The cabin was run down and the roof leaked, but that didn't matter.

Even though we couldn't put much money into it we put in a lot of hard work. George fixed the roof and I snooped around the auctions looking for furniture to refinish.

We only came up on weekends, but to us it was home.

I never thought we'd give it up. But then I never thought George would die.

MUSIC UNDER

ANNCR: When a man dies, one of the saddest things his family has to face is what they'll lose after they've lost him.

We at MONY, Mutual Of New York, know how reluctant some people can be to discuss life insurance.

But we also know how much it can mean when it's needed.

Call us. Because your family can't live on memories alone.

ANIMATED LOGO: *Mutual Of New York MONY. For the future*

POLICE CALLS
60-second

BRIAN
60-second

465
Art Director Andrew Langer
Writer Marshall Karp
Director Steve Horn
Producer Diane Jeremias
Production Co. Steve Horn, Inc.
Agency The Marschalk Co.
Client Mutual Of New York

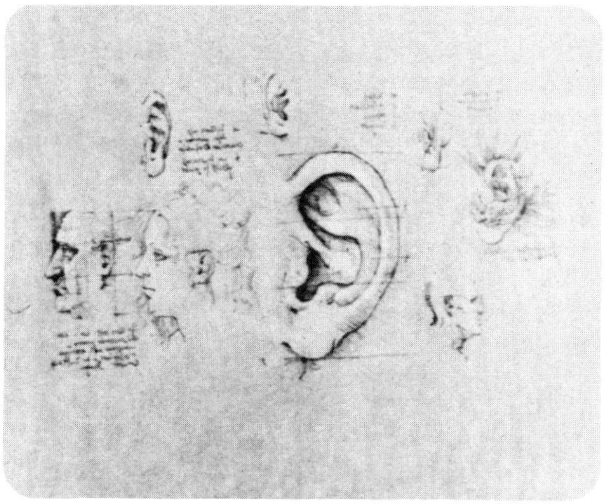

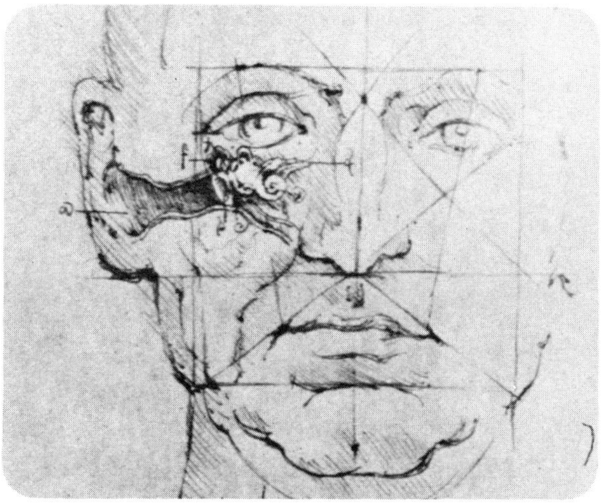

SONY
COMPONENTS

EAR
60-second

ANNCR: The human ear is a stunningly engineered instrument.

The eardrum is sensitive to within a billionth of a centimeter.

A tiny bone called the incus can vibrate 20,000 times a second.

Yes, the ear is a remarkable piece of equipment. And when choosing stereo components, we at Sony say trust it.

Put aside the spec sheets and the multitude of contradictory opinions.

And let your equipment sell you our equipment.

OUR SONG
60-second

CHIP MONCK
60-second

466
Art Director Don Slater
Writer Adam Hanft
Artist Gary Cooley
Directors Jeff Lovinger
Jack Zander
Producer Tom Fenton
Production Cos. Lovinger, Tardio, Melsky
Zander's Animation Parlour
Agency Rosenfeld, Sirowitz & Lawson
Client Sony Corporation of America

EXHAUSTO

COMPETITIVE
60-second

MIDAS MAN: Help you?

TALL MAN: Is it true that Midas usually takes 30 minutes to install a muffler?

MIDAS MAN: Yeah . . . or less.

SHORT MAN: Or less, ha, ha.

TALL MAN: This is your inventory? Mufflers for over 1700 different car models, I believe.

MIDAS MAN: Yeah . . .

TALL MAN: And is it true that you have a guarantee good on every Midas Muffler you install?

MIDAS MAN: Yeah.

TALL MAN: Otto, the guarantee.

SHORT MAN: If anything goes wrong, we'll replace the muffler free of charge.

MIDAS MAN: Right . . . but . . .

SHORT MAN: It's good on any American car for as long as you own it.

MIDAS MAN: Say, are you guys customers . . . or . . .

TALL MAN: And *that* is why your prices are high.

MIDAS MAN: But they're not.

TALL MAN: They're not?

MIDAS MAN: No.

VOICE OVER: At Midas are prices make our customers happy and our competition a little sad.

SHORT MAN: What do we do, Jerry? How do we compete with those guys?

TALL MAN: Shh—I need time to think.

ANNCR: At Midas we're specialists. We have to do a better job.

SUPER: *Midas.*
We're Specialists.
We Have to Do a Better Job.

TOO FAST
60-second

RICHEST MAN
60-second

467
Art Director Michael Ulick
Writer Jeff Frey
Cameraman Ed Rosson
Director Michael Ulick
Producers Sue Becton
John Gramaglia
Production Co. Kaliedoscope Films
Agency Wells, Rich, Greene
Client Midas Mufflers

COMMUTER
60-second

ANNCR: This winter you need all the summer you can get.

SONG: Chasing the sunshine, looking to warm my soul and body, feeling so fine. Life is all mine in the sunshine. Chasing the rainbow, looking to cleanse my soul. wooo. . .

ANNCR: Did you know this island was discovered by Christopher Columbus in 1493? Florida, Mexico and the Vacation Islands of the Caribbean are filled with summer.
And you can do more than just dream about it.
With Eastern Airlines' new Personalized Vacation Planning you can have a vacation as unique as you are.
Talk to your Travel agent or call the airline that's working harder for your dollar.

CONDUCTOR: Irvington, Irvington.

ANNCR: Get the most summer this winter from Eastern . . . The Wings of Man.

JOGGER
60-second

HOUSEWIFE
60-second

GOLD

468
Art Director Jim Swan
Writer Phil Peppis
Director Ed Bianchi
Producer Jim Swan
Production Co. Milan Films
Agency Young & Rubicam International
Client Eastern Airlines

POTTED PALM
60-second

ANNCR: At her annual gala, the Countess of Ruritania is a vision in a gown she made herself from a fabulous Ultressa print by Burlington/Klopman. Adventuress Cindy Starr is really turning heads with her naughty little number daringly cut from an Alluressa Knit by the Klopman Division of Burlington.

COUNTESS: "My jewels!"

EVERYBODY: Ahhhhhhhhhh........

ANNCR: Why, just everyone's wearing a tuxedo in a Burlington Worsted fabric. Notice the tasty tidbits of furniture created by Burlington House? The Countess has crammed her posh villa with them.

As a really stylish finishing touch, the potted palm is sporting comfy canary yellow Burlington socks.

That yummy, red carpet is by Burlington House, the big, big name in home fashions.

DUNGEON ESCAPE
60-second

GANGSTER APARTMENT
60-second

469
Art Director Mike Lawlor
Writer Denis Schmidt
Director Steve Horn
Producer Nancy Campbell
Production Co. Horn/Griner Productions
Agency Doyle Dane Bernbach
Client Burlington

QUIET PLEASE

Dr Pepper.
The most original
soft drink

LIBRARIAN
60-second

STUDENT 1: (Singing) Why don't you get out of those books for a while?

STUDENT 2: (Singing) Have some excitement, Emma Lou.

EMMA LOU: (Singing) I've all the thrills that anybody ever needs. Why just today, there're two books overdue.

STUDENT 3: (Singing) You're gonna let life pass you by.

STUDENT 4: (Singing) You're making a mistake.

EMMA LOU: I won't discuss it anymore. I'm going to take my cola break.

STUDENT 5: (Singing) A cola break . . . the perfect time to live adventurously.

SEVERAL STUDENTS: (Singing) Have a Dr. Pepper.

ALL: (Singing) Taste some originality.

EMMA LOU: Dr. Pepper? Elucidate, please.

ALL: (Singing) It's not a cola.

EMMA LOU: Am I the type?

ALL: (Singing) It's something much much more.

EMMA LOU: Yes . . . yes, maybe I am!

ALL: (Singing) It's not a root beer. There are root beers by the score.

EMMA LOU: Oh, I am . . . I am!

ALL: (Singing) Drink Dr. Pepper! The joy of every boy and girl. It's the most original soft drink in the whole wide world. Dr. Pepper! Dr. Pepper! Dr. Pepper! . . .

PROM
60-second

TEXAS
60-second

EXECUTIVE LUNCH
60-second

MEALS ON WHEELS
60-second

SILVER

470
Art Director Jim Swan
Writers Curvin O'Rielly
Lou Di Joseph
Director Ed Bianchi
Producer Dennis Powers
Production Co. Dick Levine Productions
Agency Young & Rubicam International
Client Dr. Pepper

BALLERINA
60-second

MUSIC UNDER

OLIVIER: The Polaroid SX-70 Land Camera. Lights . . . Action . . . Now these pictures, developing themselves, outside the camera, are hard and dry.

MUSIC

OLIVIER: There's nothing to peel, nothing even to throw away, nothing to time.

MUSIC

OLIVIER: In minutes, you have finished photographs of dazzling beauty.

MUSIC

OLIVIER: That . . . is the Polaroid SX-70 Experience.

HARDWARE
60-second

471
Art Director Robert Gage
Writers Phyllis Robinson
Roy Grace
Cameraman Richard Dubbleman
Director Robert Gage
Producer Cliff Fagin
Production Co. Directors Studio
Agency Doyle Dane Bernbach
Client Polaroid Corp.

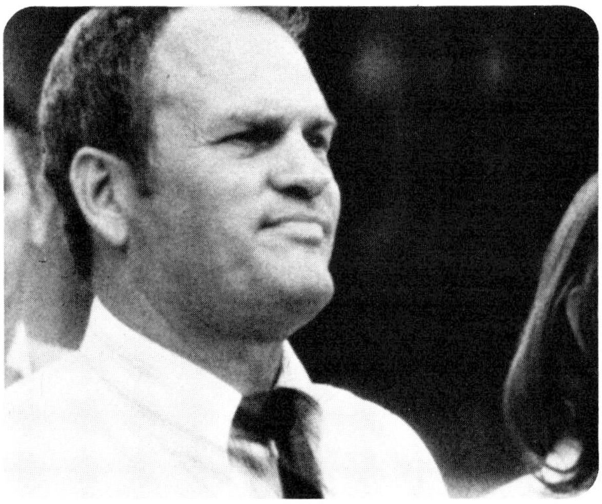

F.D.I.C.

DOCTOR
60-second

ANNCR: Charlie Hudson.

For all the world you'd think he has everything going for him.

Three year letterman in college. Still plays handball, tennis and jogs a couple of miles a week.

Charlie, his wife and three kids just moved into a big new house. In a nice neighborhood.

Maybe he did extend himself a little. But it's something Mary wanted. And something he never dreamed he'd have before the age of 40.

NURSE: "Mr. Hudson, the doctor will see you now."

DOCTOR: "Oh, hi Charlie. Charlie, I'm going to put you in the hospital for a few days."

CHARLIE: "Hospital?"

ANNCR: The Hudsons' ready cash: a grand total of $263.00.

Even with a good medical program, you still need ready cash.

Please. Start a regular savings program for your family. At National Bank of Commerce. Or any bank for that matter. Someday your life may depend on it.

HUDSON: "What do you think it is, Doc?"

RETIREMENT
60-second

472
Writer Hal Newsom
Cameraman Terry Clairmont
Director Dick Snyder
Producer Cole & Weber
Production Co. N. Lee Lacy
Agency Cole & Weber
Client Rainier National Bank

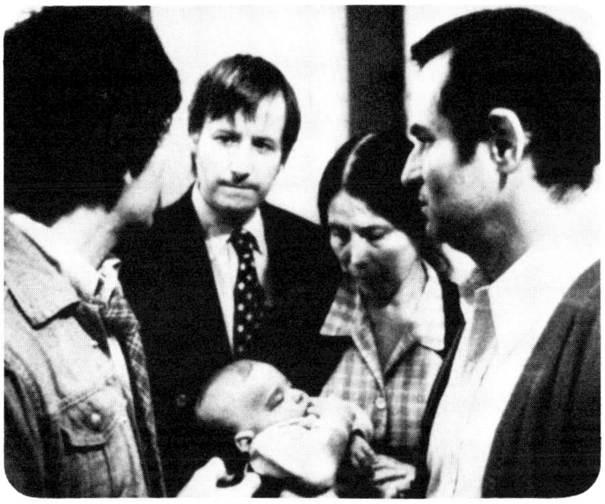

SLUMLORD
120-seconds

ANNCR: This is a slumlord, the worst of his kind. He's been getting away with murder.

LEGAL AID: Make a note of it. (In Spanish) Oh, Mr. Lopes, we're here, Legal Aid.

INTERPRETER: He says it's no use, the landlord won't fix the building.

LEGAL AID: Cover the floors, the ceilings, the walls . . . and I want everything that you see covered on film.

TENANT: The water is so dirty, it comes up from the sewer.

LEGAL AID: This place stinks . . . you know nobody's been around here for quite awhile.

LEGAL AID: Tell me what happened.

WOMAN: My baby died of pneumonia from the cold in this place. I took him to the hospital . . . but . . . the doctor said there was no hope, he was so bad off.

ANNCR: When it's the poor against the powerful, it's good to have Legal Aid around to make the fight a little fairer. But with a quarter of a million people to fight for, we need money.

LEGAL AID: Let's take him to court.

ANNCR: Give money.

473
Art Director Georgia Shankel
Writer Dorothy Linder
Producer Manny Perez
Production Co. Stan Lang Productions
Agency Young & Rubicam International
Client Legal Aid Society

Have a child.
It's as beautiful as
having a baby.

DADDY
30-second

OLDER CHILD: Daddy's coming home soon.

YOUNGER CHILD: He's not my Daddy. I'm adopted.

OLDER CHILD: Yes he is.

YOUNGER CHILD: How do you know?

OLDER CHILD: 'Cause I'm your sister. Daddy's home!

YOUNGER CHILD: Hi, Daddy.

ANNCR: There are so many children in New York who need parents. Have a child. It's as beautiful as having a baby. Write Adoption, Albany, New York.

GOLD

474
Art Director Alan Kupchick
Writer Enid Futterman
Director Norman Griner
Producer Steve Novick
Production Co. Horn/Griner Productions
Agency Grey Advertising
Client New York State Board of Adoption

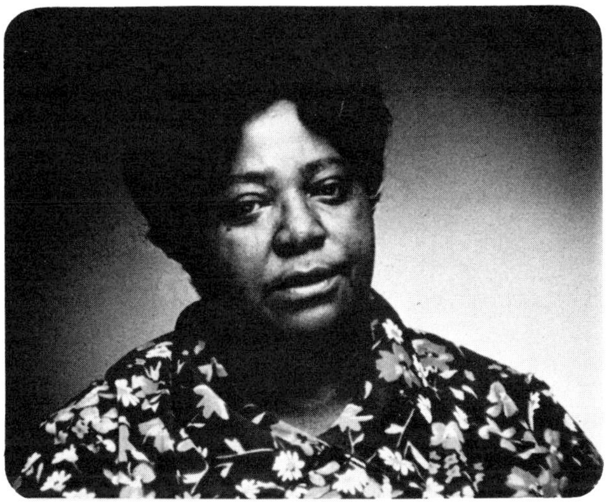

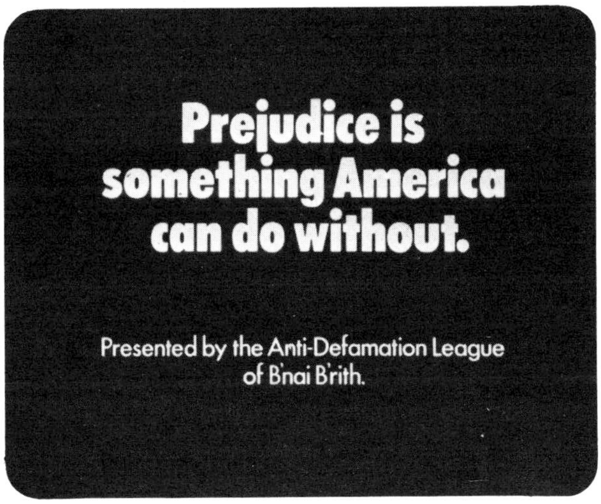
Prejudice is
something America
can do without.
Presented by the Anti-Defamation League
of B'nai B'rith.

DIFFERENT VOICES—FACES
30-second

IRISH: You know it wouldn't really matter if a Chinese-American talked like this.

SWEDISH: Or if an American-Indian looked like this . . .

JAPANESE: Because if you're a real American you wouldn't even care.

SCOTTISH: But some people here believe that everyone should look and talk and think the same way they do, or they should not be living in the same place.

EUROPEAN: A man called Adolf Hitler felt the same way.

ANNCR: Prejudice is something America can do without.

SUPER: *Prejudice is something America can do without*

SILVER

475
Art Director Stu Rosenwasser
Writer Bob Veder
Designer Seymour Chwast
Director Norm Griner
Producer Vinnie Infantino
Production Cos. Griner/Cuesta
Push Pin Studio
Agency Grey Advertising
Client Anti Defamation League

RP Foundation
Post Office Box 5773
Baltimore, Maryland 21208

MARY TYLER MOORE
30-second

M.T.M.: There are thousands of children faced with the terror of going blind from a disease called Retinitis Pigmentosa. RP.

It begins with loss of side vision and slowly narrows—until there is nothing left.

And the most tragic part is there is no known cure. Doctors are now working to fight RP. But diseases are fought with money.

Please send a contribution to the RP Foundation.

Children have so much to see. Give them a chance to see it.

SUPER: *Send your contribution to: RP Foundation, Box XXX, Baltimore, Maryland*

477
Art Director Ann-Marie Light
Writer Joline LaMond
Producer Tom Fenton
Production Cos. Mary Tyler Moore Productions
Agency Rosenfeld, Sirowitz & Lawson
Client National Retinitis Pigmentosa Foundation

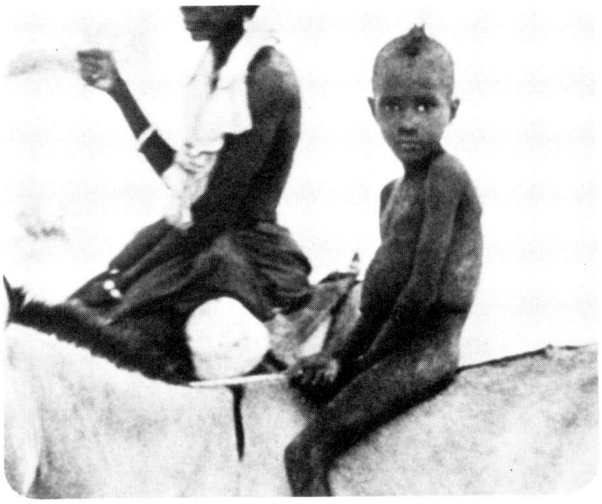

Church World Service
P.O. Box 19455
Kansas City, Mo. 64141

LADY BUG
60-second

ANNCR: When disaster strikes, Church World Service and CROP, its community hunger appeal, sends in food, blankets, and medicine to save people's lives.

But when this little creature caused a disaster in West Africa by destroying thousands of food producing trees, we had to be more creative with the kind of help we sent in.

So we helped develop a new kind of lady bug. Specially bred to devour 400 insects a day.

Right now the lady bug is helping to save thousands of food producing trees. And thousands of people from starvation.

But without your money to go on, we can't send in the food, clothing and medicine that save lives, and we certainly can't send in the bugs.

SUPER: *Church World Service, P.O. Box 19455, Kansas City, Mo. 64141*

ANNCR: Please give directly to Church World Service or through your local church or through BankAmericard or Master Charge. For 27 years we've been feeding people, educating people . . . saving their lives.

478
Art Director Jim Handloser
Writer Ken Charof
Director Elbert Budin
Producer Joe Scibetta
Production Co. Ampersand Productions
Agency Doherty, Mann & Olshan
Client Church World Service

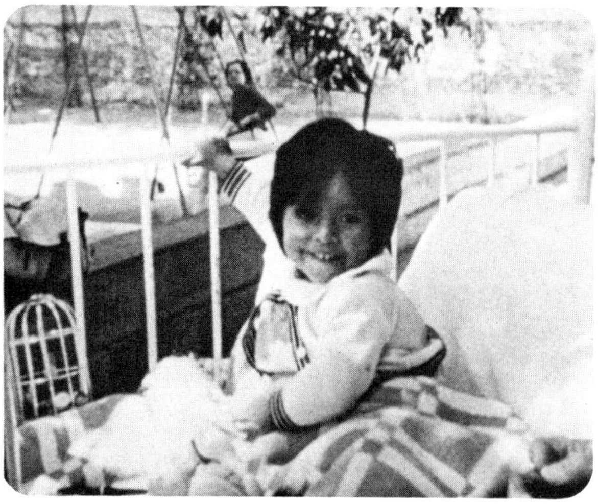

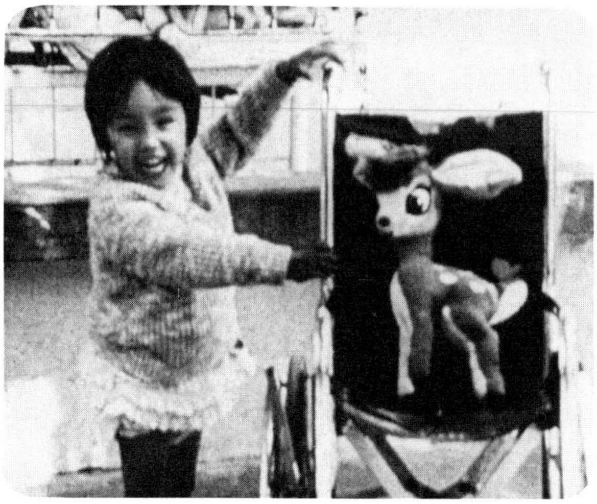

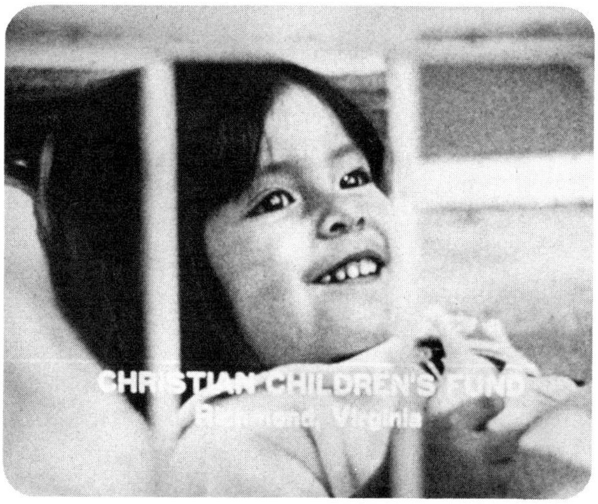
CHRISTIAN CHILDREN'S FUND
Richmond, Virginia

ROSITA
60-second

MUSIC UNDER

ANNCR: Rosita Sanchez is a pretty little girl who lives in Mexico . . . She is an orphan who has been crippled from birth. And she lost both her parents when she was only two years old.

But now Rosita is happy and well cared for at a home for crippled children. The home is affiliated with the Christian Children's Fund and Rosita has a kind sponsor in America who is helping to support her. After several operations, she'll be able to get around in a wheel chair, and before long, she may even walk. She's a cheerful, happy little girl, but none of this would have been possible without the love of her sponsor here in the United States.

To find out how you can help a child like Rosita, write the Christian Children's Fund, Richmond, Virginia.

479
Designer Peter J. Coughter, Jr.
Writer Peter J. Coughter, Jr.
Cinematographer Medford Taylor
Director Medford Taylor
Producer Peter J. Coughter, Jr.
Production Co. Cabell Eanes Advertising
Agency Cabell Eanes Advertising
Client Christian Children's Fund

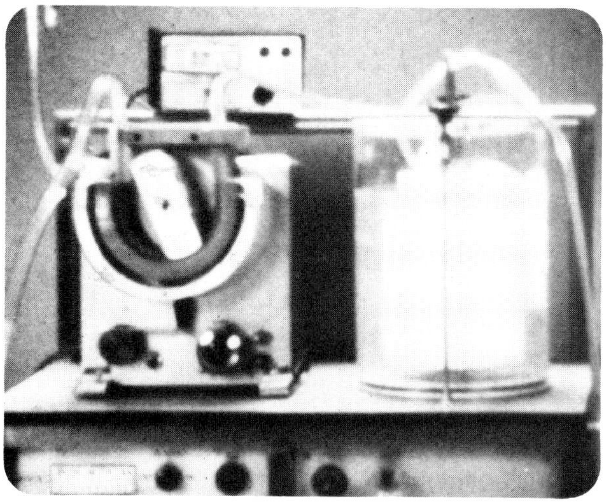

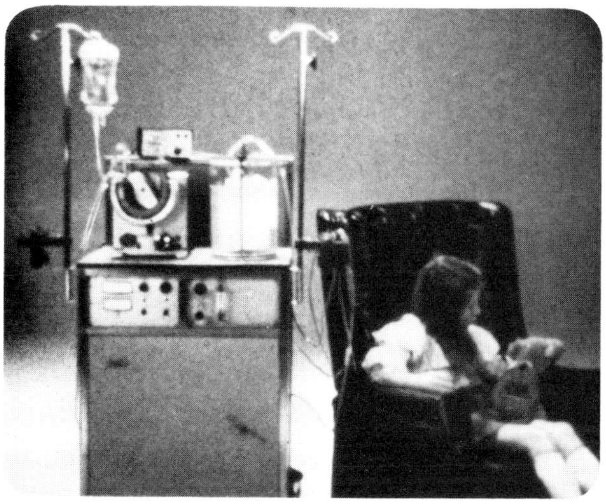

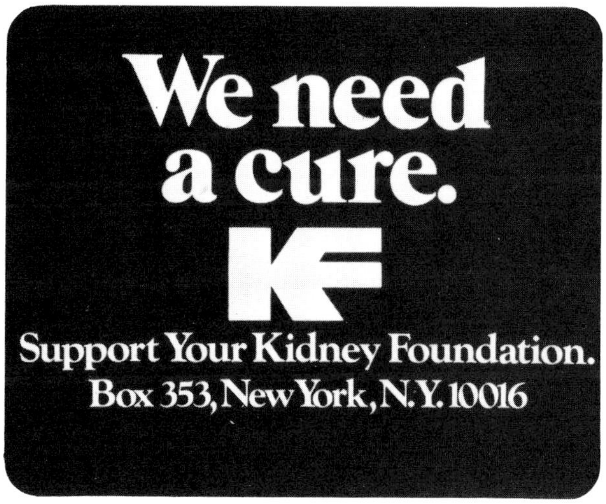
We need
a cure.
KF
Support Your Kidney Foundation.
Box 353, New York, N.Y. 10016

CHILD
20-second

SFX: Kidney Machine

ANNCR: This is a Kidney Machine. If your kidneys fail, you can stay alive by spending 6 hours a day, 3 days a week connected to it. It's no way to spend a childhood. We need a cure.

SFX

ANNCR: Support your Kidney Foundation

480
Art Director Ron De Vito
Writer Herb Fried
Designers Sy Davis
Ted Amber
Cinematographer John Knoop
Director Ralph De Vito
Producer Ralph De Vito
Production Co. Taliesen Productions
Agency DFK Sales Promotions
Client National Kidney Foundation

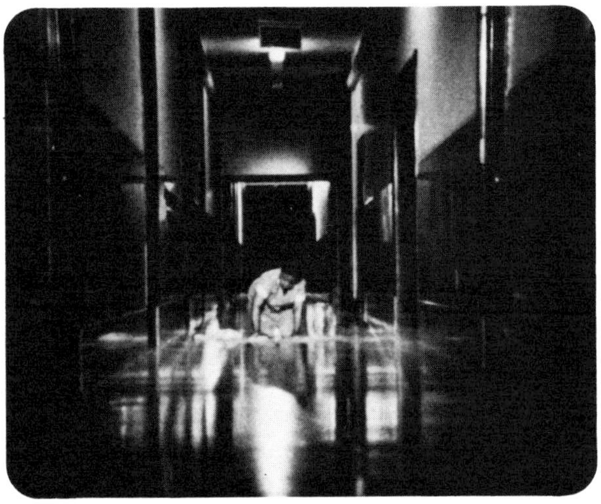

MOTHER
30-second

SON (Off camera): My mother works nights scrubbing floors, Mr. Campbell . . . just to get the extra money to send me to college.

Now, the school needs money? . . . and you're telling me, my chemistry class may be discontinued. I'll never be a doctor . . . and that's Mama's dream.

She's always praying, I'll be able to get my degree . . . now . . . How am I gonna tell her what's happening to the school?

ANNCR: Give, now, to the United Negro College Fund. A mind is a terrible thing to waste.

481
Art Director Harry Webber
Writer Joan Blache
Director Steve Horn
Producers John Scott
Percy Hall
Production Co. Horn/Griner Productions
Agency Young & Rubicam International
Client United Negro College Fund

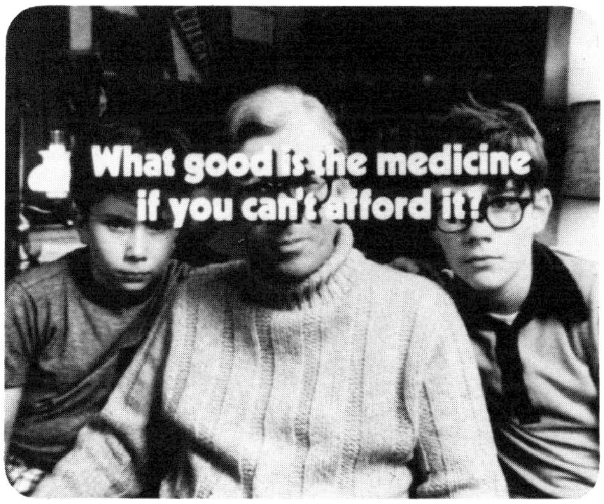
What good is the medicine
if you can't afford it?

FATHER & SONS
60-second

JOE: I'm Joe Dowd. I'm not an actor, I'm a father. So forgive me if I'm not good at this, but there's something I'd like to ask you. If you can understand what it's like for a kid to hear he has hemophilia . . . the bleeders disease . . . and there's no cure for it. Well then think what it's like to hear there's a medicine that can stop your bleeding but you can't afford it.

It must be like torture. The medicine is called a clotting factor, but it costs about $26,000 every year. So most hemophilia kids can't afford the medicine they need.

That's the problem my son Tim has. And my son Joey too. Hemophilia needs your help.

A few dollars to do research that will bring down the cost of the medicine so kids like mine can afford the help their fathers can't give them. Please.

Help Hemophilia. Because what good is the medicine if you can't afford it?

482
Art Director Bob Petrocelli
Writer Hal Friedman
Director Bob Giraldi
Producer Phil Suarez
Production Co. Bob Giraldi Productions
Agency Warren Muller Dolobowsky
Client National Hemophilia Foundation

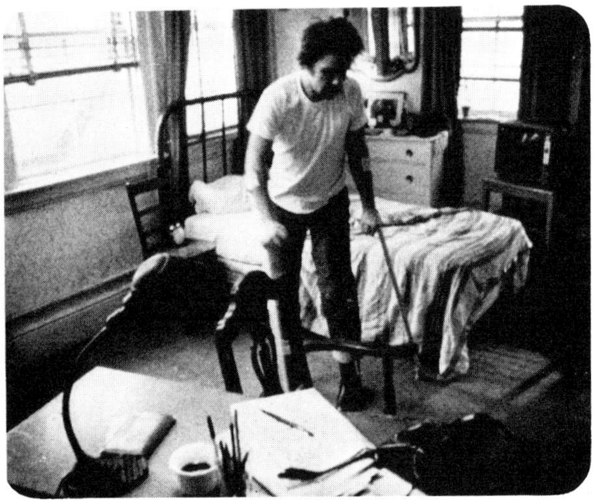

DREAM
60-second

SFX: Battle field.

ANNCR: Isn't it incredible to think that while most people were going into work, guys like this were going into battle.

But what's even more incredible is that when these able, mature and experienced men finally came home they had to start fighting all over again.

For a job.

And those that couldn't get work, got welfare.

That's why the National Alliance of Businessmen wants you to give disabled vets jobs.

Because a man who should be on the payroll, shouldn't end up on the welfare roll.

The way to get this country working, is to get people working.

So if you have a job to give, call the National Alliance of Businessmen.

Help America work.

SLUM
60-second

TOY SOLDIERS
60-second

483

Art Directors Ed Nussbaum
Stu Rosenwasser
Writers Joan LaMell
Bob Veder
Directors Elbert Budin
Steve Horn
Producers Barbara Barrow
Vinnie Infantino
Production Cos. Ampersand Productions
Steve Horn, Inc.
Agency Grey Advertising
Client National Alliance of Businessmen

TREE
30-second

ANNCR: If Levi's made a tree instead of shirts and slacks and jeans, now that'd be a tree, with mighty limbs that never break.

If Levi's made a tree, it'd be the kind of tree you'd wanna be in. It'd be the best dressed, naturally.

If Levi's made a tree, tremendous. But only nature makes a tree. Yeah. Commercials are made by fools like me.

486
Art Director Chris Blum
Writer Mike Koelker
Designer Roger Chouinard
Artists Roger Chouinard
Mel Sommer
Animator Vince Davis
Director Roger Chouinard
Production Co. Duck Soup Productions
Agency Foote, Cone & Belding/Honig
San Francisco
Client Levi Strauss

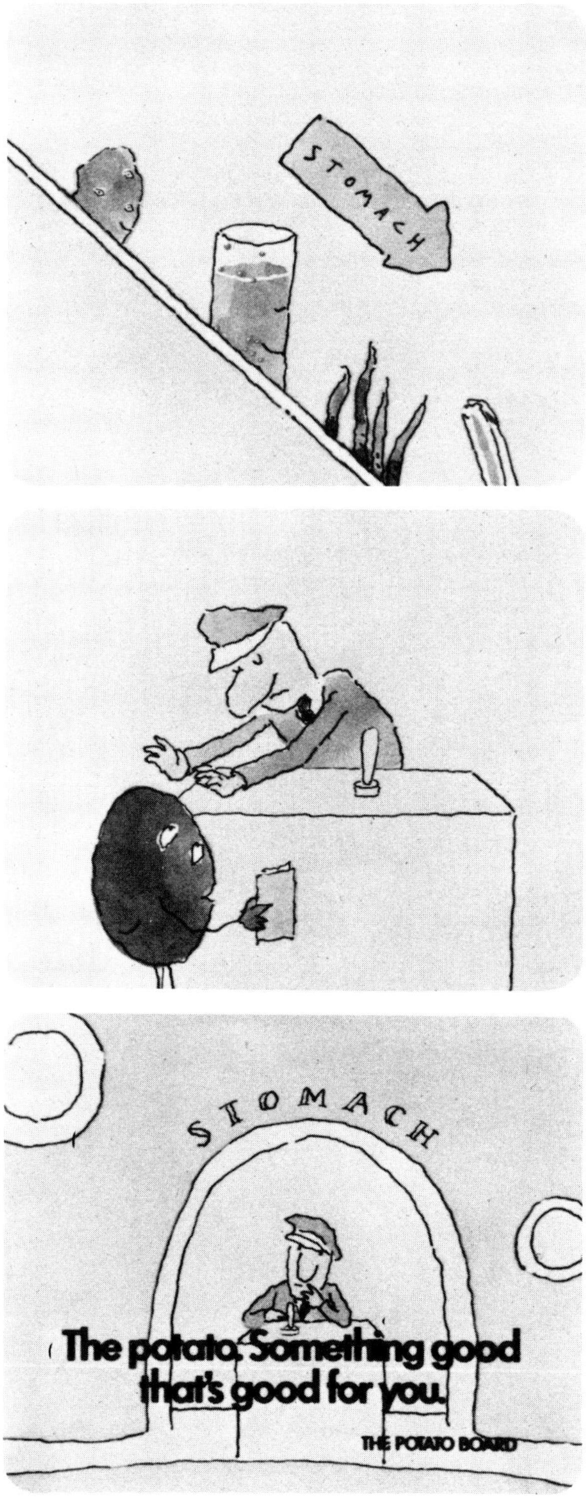
STOMACH
STOMACH
The potato. Something good that's good for you.
THE POTATO BOARD

FRED
30-second

GUARD: Hold it, fella . . . . We're watching our calories down here . . .

FRED: Here's my papers, sir. I think you'll find everything in order.

GUARD: Let's see. Potato, Fred. Medium. Baked. *90* calories? Yessir.

FRED: And I'm sure you'll find my vitamins and minerals are all there, too.

GUARD: Okay. Potato, proceed.

FRED: Thank you, sir.

GUARD: 90 calories, huh? Why just yesterday I had a cup o' cottage cheese that came in at 170 . . .

The potato. Something good that's good for you.

486A
Art Director Jim Lacey
Writer Jill Murray
Artist R. O. Blechman
Animator Ed Smith
Director R. O. Blechman
Producers Jim Lacey
Jill Murray
Production Co. R. O. Blechman, Inc.
Agency Botsford Ketchum
San Francisco
Client The Potato Board

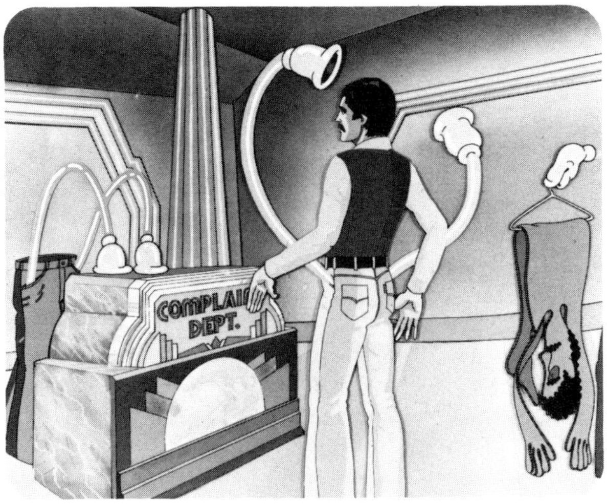
COMPLAINT DEPT.

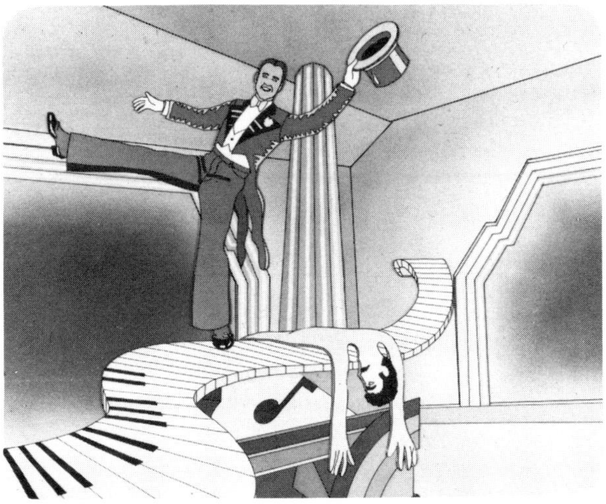

CHAMELEON
60-second

COMPLAINT DEPT: May I help you?

JEANS: Yeah—I want to return this person.

COMPLAINT DEPT: Squeaky elbows?

JEANS: Naw, us Levi's jeans want color, style, variety, not your person's dull, drab, rubby dudds. Look at us, lemon cords, khaki denims, coral bells—Levi's jeans have variety!

COMPLAINT DEPT: Well . . . there's our chameleon model.

JEANS: Ah, that I like, like . . . Levi's, Levi's . . . Uh—oh—oh—it was only a dream. Sure, a dream, go back to sleep.

487
Art Director Chris Blum
Writer Mike Koelker
Designer Roger Chouinard
Artists Roger Chouinard
Mel Sommer
Animator Duane Crowther
Directors Roger Chouinard
Duane Crowther
Producer Mark Levy
Production Co. Duck Soup Productions
Agency Foote, Cone & Belding/Honig
Client Levi Strauss

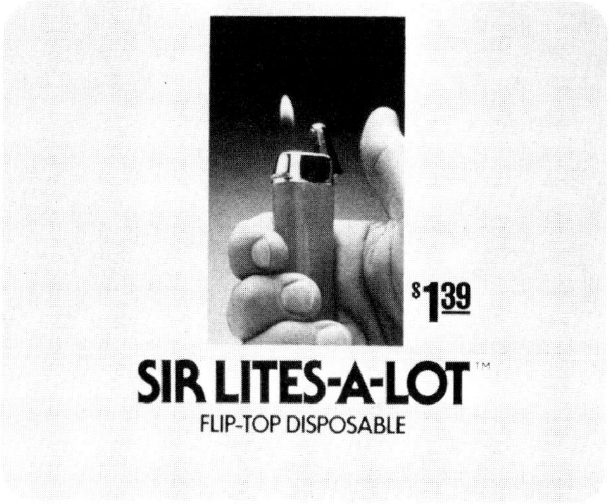
$1.39
SIR LITES-A-LOT™
FLIP-TOP DISPOSABLE

ROUND TABLE
30-second

ART: One of you knights got a light?

LAL: Sir Lites-A-Lot, your majesty. And you don't have to fight me to light me.

ART: A knight that don't fight?

LAL: I'm a lighter. Not a fighter.

GWEN: And a good looker, too.

ART: Mmm. Lights with no fight.

LAL: For thousands of lights.

GWEN: Without spinning wheels . . . a snap of his cap turns him on.

ALL: Sir Lites-A-Lot!

ANNCR: Sir Lites-A-Lot flip top disposable. You don't have to fight him to light him.

SUPER: *Sir Lites-A-Lot, flip-top disposable, $1.39*

488
Art Director Marvin Mitchneck
Writers Dick Bernstein
Jack Keane
Designer Mordy Gerstein
Artist Mordy Gerstein
Cameraman George Davis
Director Mordy Gerstein
Producers Jack Keane
Dick Bernstein
Marvin Mitchneck
Production Co. Phil Kimmelman & Assoc.
Agency David, Oksner & Mitchneck
Client Consolidated Cigar Corp.

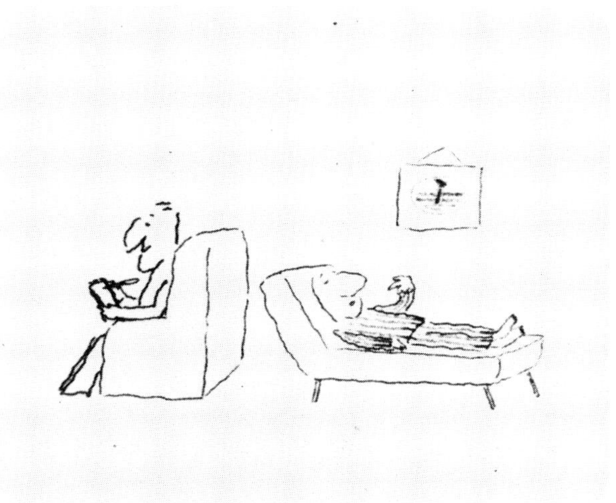

THE OLD PHILOSOPHER/CAR
30-second

ANNCR: You say you dreamed your brand new car rolled downhill and crashed into a pizza parlor?

And you ran for help and somebody stole your tires and sprained his ankle and now he's suing you. . . and you're not fully covered?

Is that what's troubling you, Bunky?

Well stand up and take a walk in the sun—straight to your independent insurance agent.

He's an expert on trouble. Independent of any one company, he works to find the best policies for you.

Look him up in the yellow pages. If he can't help you . . . nobody can.

SUPER: *Your Independent Insurance Agent serves you first. If he can't help you, nobody can*

489
Art Director Rod Capawana
Writer Dee Maskaleris
Designer R. O. Blechman
Artist R. O. Blechman
Director Rod Capawana
Producer Paula Del Nunzio
Production Co. R. O. Blechman Studio
Agency Doremus
Client National Assoc. of Insurance Agents

UNITED STATES AIR FORCE
GOOD
JOBS
HERE

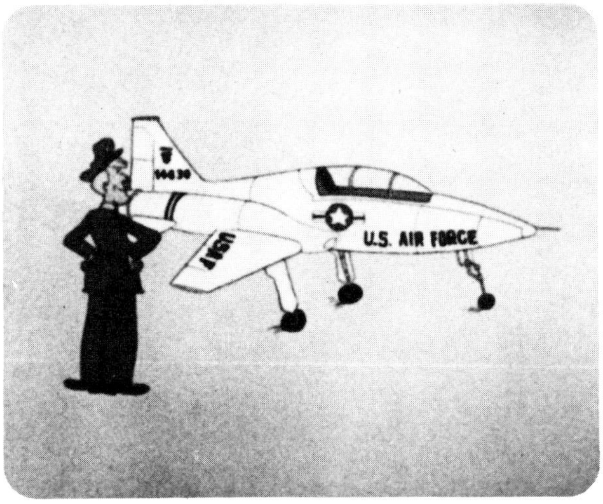
U.S. AIR FORCE
USAF

CORNER OF THE SKY
60-second

MUSIC THROUGHOUT

490
Art Director Gil Rosoff
Writer Gil Rosoff
Designer Bob Mitchel
Artist Bob Mitchel
Director Bob Mitchel
Producer Gil Rosoff
Production Co. EUE/Screen Gems
Agency D'Arcy MacManus & Masius
Client United States Air Force Recruiting Service

AMERICA
60-second

MUSIC THROUGHOUT

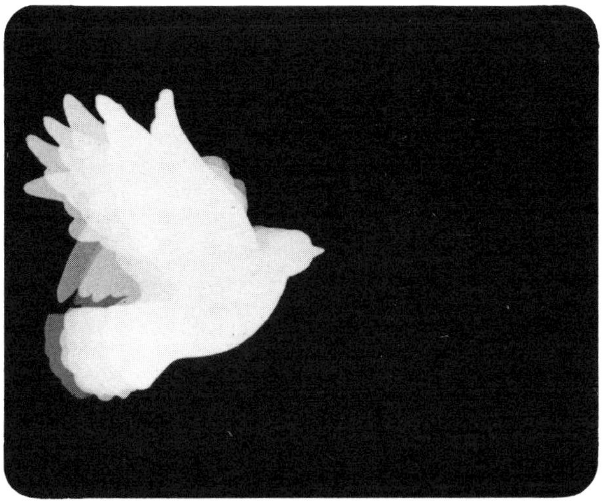

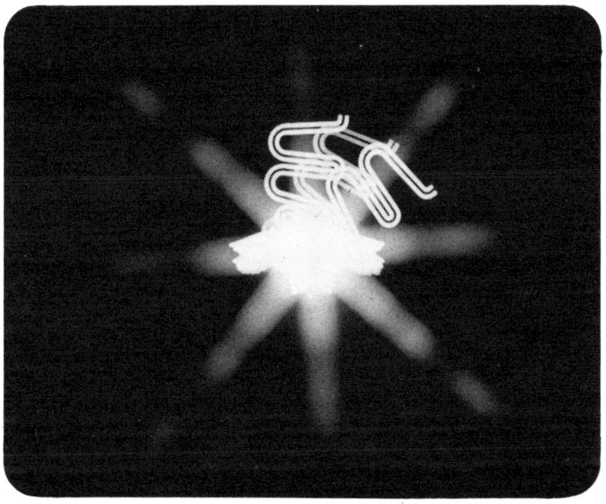

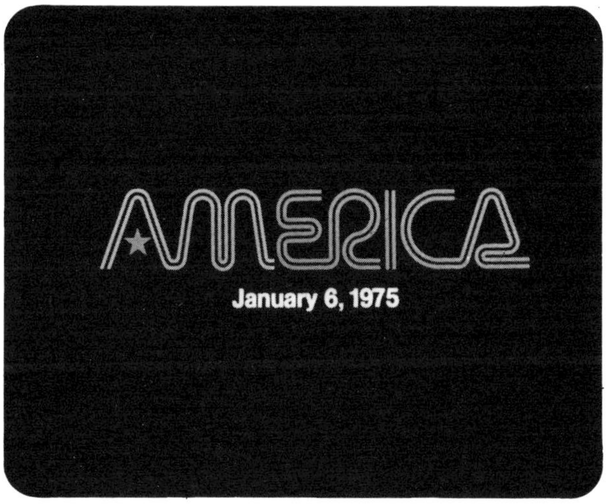
AMERICA
January 6, 1975

492

Art Directors	George McGinnis Mark Howard
Designers	George McGinnis Mark Howard
Artists	George McGinnis Mark Howard
Animators	Michael Sporn Mark Howard
Cinematographers	George McGinnis Mark Howard
Directors	George McGinnis Mark Howard
Producers	George McGinnis Mark Howard
Production Co.	Image Factory
Agency	Visualscope
Client	ABC Network

FRIDAY NIGHT MOVIES
60-second

MUSIC THROUGHOUT

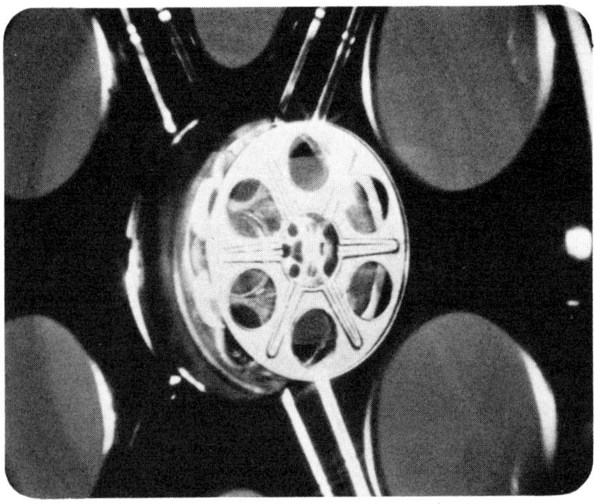

CBS

THE CBS
FRIDAY NIGHT
MOVIES
CBS

494
Art Director Lou Dorfsman
Designer Lou Dorfsman
Artist Lou Dorfsman
Director Lou Dorfsman
Producer Lou Dorfsman
Agency CBS/Broadcast Group
Client CBS Television Network

CLIO AWARDS
60-second

MUSIC THROUGHOUT

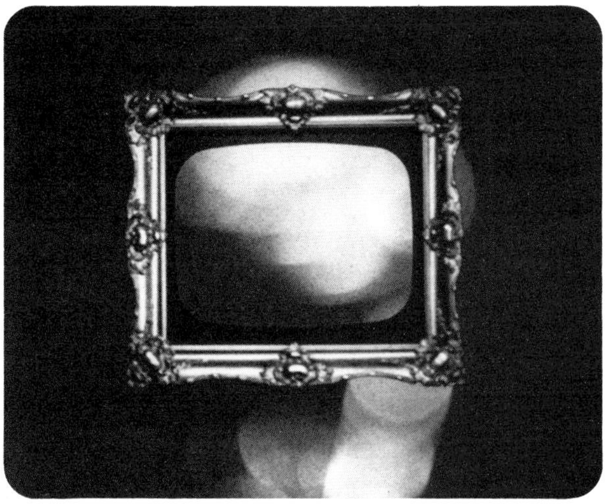

1974 CLIO AWARDS

495
Designer Arthur Eckstein
Cinematographer Jerry E. Kalogeratos
Director Arthur Eckstein
Producer Miles Harmon
Production Co. Arthur Eckstein & Assoc.
Client CLIO

NEWSROOM
30-second

ANNCR: In the beginning, the Eyewitness News Team wasn't all that big.

BILL: Oh, french fries.

ANNCR: But as they caught on, more warm and friendly newscasters joined up.

ALL: Oh, french fries.

ANNCR: So today, The Eyewitness News Team is bigger and better than ever.

ALL: Oh, french fries.

ANNCR: But as successful as they are Eyewitness News will always be Eyewitness News.

SUPER: *Eyewitness News, 6 & 11 P.M.*

496
Art Director Stan Block
Writer Adam Hanft
Designer Stan Block
Director Robert Giraldi
Producer Magi Durham
Production Co. Ampersand Productions
Agency Rosenfeld, Sirowitz & Lawson
Client WABC-TV
New York

CELEBRITIES
60-second

ANNCR: Masterpiece Theatre has a strange effect on intelligent people.
It holds them spellbound.

It lures them to their television sets, and it doesn't let them go.

It warms the heart and it captures the mind. It may startle you . . . or amuse you . . . But it will never never bore you.

SUPER: Masterpiece Theatre.
Sunday evenings on P.B.S.
Brought to you by Mobil

GOLD

497
Art Director Gordon Bowan
Writer Charlie Miesmer
Cameraman David Hoffman
Director David Hoffman
Producer Harry Wiland
Production Co. Varied Directions
Client Mobil Oil Corp.

Field Stream

NEWSSTAND
60-second

SILVER

498
Art Director Lou Dorfsman
Writer Lou Dorfsman
Designer Lou Dorfsman
Director Dick Loew
Producer Lou Dorfsman
Production Co. Gomes Loew
Agency CBS/Broadcast Group
Client WCBS Newsradio 88

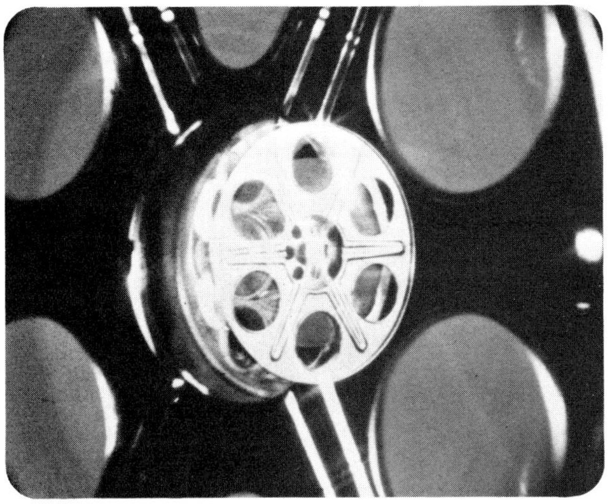

CBS

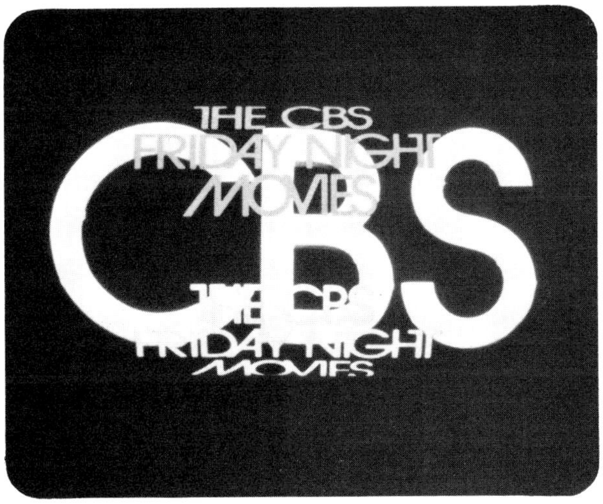
THE CBS
FRIDAY NIGHT
MOVIES
CBS

FRIDAY NIGHT MOVIES
60-second

MUSIC THROUGHOUT

498A
Art Director Lou Dorfsman
Designer Lou Dorfsman
Artist Lou Dorfsman
Director Lou Dorfsman
Producer Lou Dorfsman
Production Cos. Petersen Co.
Director's Circle
Edstan Studio
Agency CBS/Broadcast Group
Client CBS Television Network

QUARTET
30-second

MUSIC (Badly played)

ANNCR: No matter how hard they practice, Chuck Moore, Jim Axel, Guy Sharpe, and Thom Boyd will never make it to Symphony Hall.

But at the serious business of bringing you the news, you'll never find a better quartet.

SUPER: *WAGA-TV5 News Scene*

499
Art Director Norman Grey
Writer Melvin Stein
Director Alan Brooks
Producers Norman Grey
Mel Stein
Production Co. Alan Brooks
Agency Doran Stein Grey
Client WAGA TV-5
Atlanta

CBS AMERICA'S BEST
FOR 18 YEARS IN A ROW

CALIFORNIA
60-second

SONG: I came to California to thank the folks
out West,
For watching again and staying our
friends,
And help make us the best.

They like you to know,
18 years in a row,
America's best is CBS.

Wo, wo, wo, wo, Wow!
Wait till you see what's coming,
Wait till you see what's new.
We got something going this fall,
For you and you and you.

We're the best, we're the best,
CBS!
Who's the best, who's the best?
CBS!
America's best,
CBS!
We're the best, we're the best,
CBS!
See the best, see the best,
CBS!
Wo, wo, wo, wo, Wow!"

KANSAS
60-second

MAINE
60-second

RODEO
60-second

504
Art Director Lou Dorfsman
Writers Lou Dorfsman
Ken Chandler
Designer Lou Dorfsman
Director Rick Levine
Producer Richard Goldberg
Production Co. Rick Levine Productions
Agency CBS/Broadcast Group
Client CBS Television Network

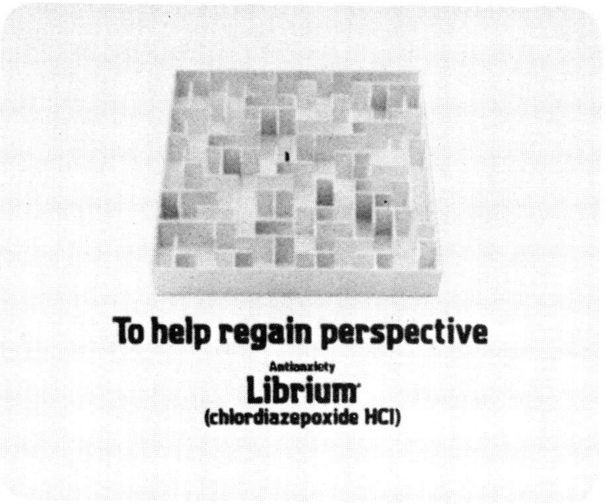
To help regain perspective
Antianxiety
Librium
(chlordiazepoxide HCl)

LIBRIUM MAZE
60-second

MUSIC THROUGHOUT

ANNCR: Sometimes anxiety . . . can overwhelm a man. Mental processes are disrupted . . . and . . . physical sensations are bewildering.

When this happens to one of your patients . . . he loses his perspective . . . and sense of direction. Every attempt . . . to orient himself . . . only produces new obstacles.

And every turn creates more problems. He's confused . . . apprehensive . . . alone. That's why he needs your reassurance and expertise. Often just talking things over is enough.

But when it isn't, and . . . relief is needed, Librium (chlordiazepoxide hydrochloride) can be a valuable adjunct to your counseling. Librium generally reduces excessive anxiety promptly . . . without impairment of mental activity.

For the patient who needs an antianxiety agent . . . consider Librium.

SUPER: *To help regain emotional perspective antianxiety Librium (chlordiazepoxide HC1)*

505
Art Director Stan Dornfest
Writers Maurice Peizer
Nancy Smith
Designer Stan Dornfest
Photographer David Nagata
Director David Nagata
Producer Michael Wolf
Production Co. David Nagata Productions
Agency William Douglas McAdams
Client Roche Laboratories

INTERNATIONAL ADVERTISING

International Magazine Ads & Campaigns, b/w & color	506–517
International Newspaper Ads & Campaigns, b/w & color	518–522
International TV Commercials	529–540
International Radio Commercials	541–542
International Posters & Billboards	544–549
International Advertising Art	550
International Advertising Photography	552–553

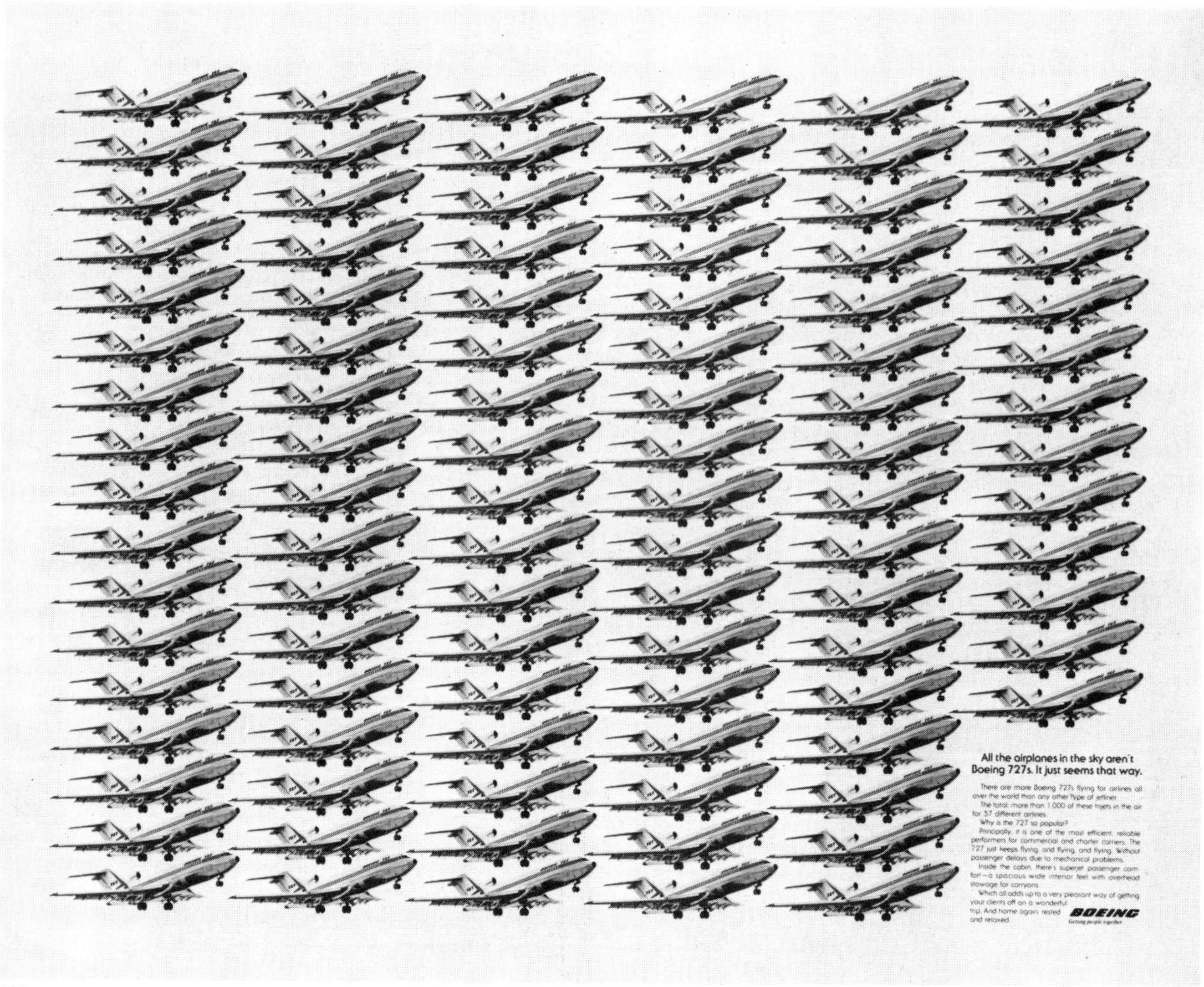
All the airplanes in the sky aren't Boeing 727s. It just seems that way.
There are more Boeing 727s flying for airlines all over the world than any other type of jetliner.
The total: more than 1,000 of these trijets in the air for 57 different airlines.
Why is the 727 so popular?
Principally, it is one of the most efficient, reliable performers for commercial and charter carriers. The 727 just keeps flying, and flying, and flying. Without passenger delays due to mechanical problems.
Inside the cabin, there's superjet passenger comfort—a spacious wide interior feel with overhead stowage for carryons.
Which all adds up to a very pleasant way of getting your clients off on a wonderful trip. And home again, rested and relaxed.
BOEING

506

506
Art Director Dan Snope
Writer Hal Newsom
Designer Dan Snope
Artists Chris Reilly
Win Brown
Agency Cole & Weber
Client Boeing Airplane Co.

Vini ou*
Nos amis seront vos amis.
Venez*. Venez nous rejoindre aux Antilles, ou au Sénégal, à la Réunion, à Hawaï, à l'île Maurice, en Egypte, Tahiti, en Côte d'Ivoire, au Maroc, au Mexique, en Tunisie, en Espagne, ou en Israël.
Au Club, l'eau est chaude, la nature généreuse. La découverte vous attend. Celle que vous saisissez au passage.
Le sourire d'un pêcheur, un vol de pélican au couchant, une conque déposée pour vous par la vague. Au Club, tout est compris : le voyage, le séjour, les repas, les sports, les distractions.
Pas de surprises. Sauf celle d'une ambiance chaleureuse, d'une architecture conçue pour le pays et d'un émerveillement constant, solitaire ou partagé, comme il vous plaira.
Demandez-nous la brochure. Club Méditerranée place de la Bourse Paris 2e.
Avec le Club Méditerranée, cet hiver.
Place de la Bourse Paris 2e / 86 avenue des Champs-Elysées Paris 8e / Tél. 266 52 52. Agences Havas-Voyages de votre ville.

506A

ON POURRAIT SE PASSER DE CINZANO.
ON POURRAIT AUSSI SE PASSER DE NOËL.
CINZANO
CINZANO BITTER. NOUS NE CHANGERONS JAMAIS.

507

GOLD

506A
Art Director Rolland Della Monta
Writers Marie Petit
Michel Clairon
Photographer Philippe Quidor
Agency Synergie/K&E
Paris
Client Club Mediterranee

507
Art Director Martin Reavley
Writer Pierre Berville
Cameraman David Thorpe
Agency Tragos Bonnage
Wiesendanger Ajroldi
Paris
Client Cinzano

Dans les magasins il y a plusieurs marques de pése-personne.
Au Musée d'Art Moderne de New York, il n'y en a qu'une.
Terraillon.
Un pèse-personne doit être précis. Un pèse-personne peut être beau.

509

quand on n'a plus vingt ans, et que cela commence à se voir...
Révolutionnaire !
Tous les produits anti-rides disent qu'ils le sont. Mais leurs résultats ne sont pas toujours à la hauteur de leurs ambitions.
Révolutionnaire ! Le mot n'est pas trop fort pour qualifier le nouveau Specific Vitalizer de Lancaster.
C'est une crème anti-rides, un véritable traitement de choc dont les résultats sont proprement extraordinaires : 3 ans de tests en laboratoire ont démontré l'efficacité parfaite de Specific Vitalizer sur toutes les peaux même les plus abimées.
Essayez Specific Vitalizer : en quelques jours vous verrez déjà un changement. Votre peau sera plus souple, vos rides moins marquées. Cette efficacité est dûe à sa conception vraiment originale : composée d'éléments biologiques homologues à ceux de l'épiderme, ce traitement permet à celui-çi de se régénérer rapidement et complètement.
Specific Vitalizer s'applique tous les soirs en cure de 30 jours. Présenté en pot scellé, ce produit est léger, agréable à mettre, il hydrate et détend la peau, pénètre profondément, ne tache pas.
Specific Vitalizer fait partie de la gamme des Specifics Lancaster dont les résultats dans le traitement des rides sont bien connus.
Demandez-le à votre parfumeur conseil agréé Lancaster. Après tout vous pouvez être bien dans votre peau à n'importe quel âge... mais ne pas avoir envie de paraître cet âge.
SPECIFIC VITALIZER
LANCASTER

510

509
Art Director Robert Dubarle
Writers Uli Wiesendanger
Isabelle Brun
Photographer Del Bocca
Agency Tragos Bonnange
Wiesendanger
Ajroldi
Paris
Client Terraillon

510
Art Director Mafia Staff
Writer France Brécard
Photographer Guy Bourdin
Agency Maïmé Arnodin, Fayolle,
International, Assoc.
Paris
Client Lancaster

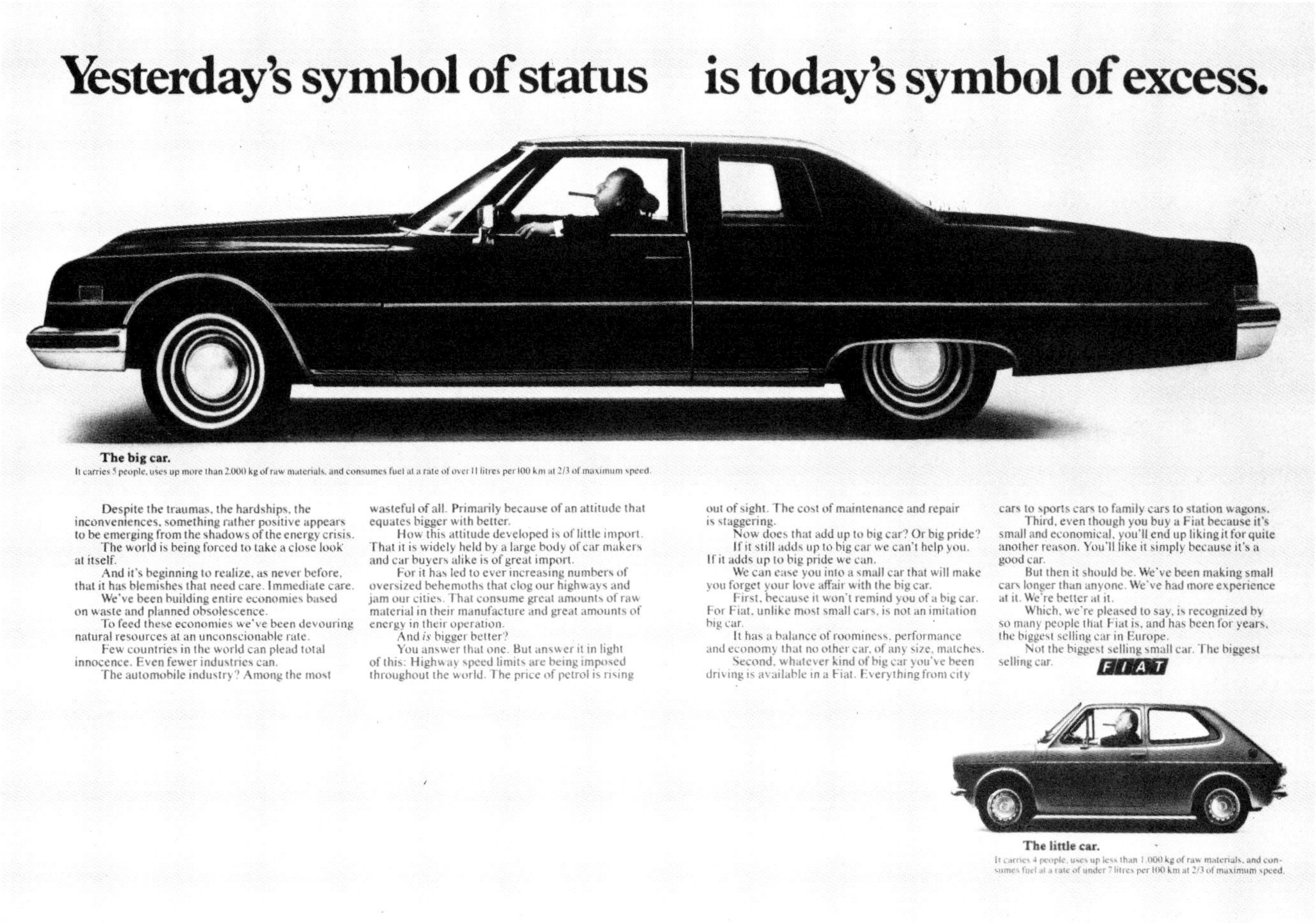
Yesterday's symbol of status is today's symbol of excess.
The big car.
It carries 5 people, uses up more than 2.000 kg of raw materials, and consumes fuel at a rate of over 11 litres per 100 km at 2/3 of maximum speed.
Despite the traumas, the hardships, the inconveniences, something rather positive appears to be emerging from the shadows of the energy crisis.
The world is being forced to take a close look at itself.
And it's beginning to realize, as never before, that it has blemishes that need care. Immediate care.
We've been building entire economies based on waste and planned obsolescence.
To feed these economies we've been devouring natural resources at an unconscionable rate.
Few countries in the world can plead total innocence. Even fewer industries can.
The automobile industry? Among the most wasteful of all. Primarily because of an attitude that equates bigger with better.
How this attitude developed is of little import. That it is widely held by a large body of car makers and car buyers alike is of great import.
For it has led to ever increasing numbers of oversized behemoths that clog our highways and jam our cities. That consume great amounts of raw material in their manufacture and great amounts of energy in their operation.
And *is* bigger better?
You answer that one. But answer it in light of this: Highway speed limits are being imposed throughout the world. The price of petrol is rising out of sight. The cost of maintenance and repair is staggering.
Now does that add up to big car? Or big pride?
If it still adds up to big car we can't help you. If it adds up to big pride we can.
We can ease you into a small car that will make you forget your love affair with the big car.
First, because it won't remind you of a big car. For Fiat, unlike most small cars, is not an imitation big car.
It has a balance of roominess, performance and economy that no other car, of any size, matches.
Second, whatever kind of big car you've been driving is available in a Fiat. Everything from city cars to sports cars to family cars to station wagons.
Third, even though you buy a Fiat because it's small and economical, you'll end up liking it for quite another reason. You'll like it simply because it's a good car.
But then it should be. We've been making small cars longer than anyone. We've had more experience at it. We're better at it.
Which, we're pleased to say, is recognized by so many people that Fiat is, and has been for years, the biggest selling car in Europe.
Not the biggest selling small car. The biggest selling car.
FIAT
The little car.
It carries 4 people, uses up less than 1.000 kg of raw materials, and consumes fuel at a rate of under 7 litres per 100 km at 2/3 of maximum speed.

511

511
Art Director Amil Gargano
Writer Jim Durfee
Designer Amil Gargano
Photographer Peter Papadopolous
Agency Carl Ally
Client Fiat S.P.A.

"Every girl has a favourite colour. I have 26," says Mary Quant.
Quick, think of a colour.
Pale or bright, shiny or muted. Jezebel or Plum Rock, Ivory or Forever Amber. You name it, Mary has it.
Not only in her lipsticks, but matching in her nail polishes.
Whatever the colour is going to be tomorrow, today, Mary will have it.
26 in her lipsticks and 26 in her nail polishes. 52 in all.
How many favourites have you?
Mary Quant Lip and Nail Colours.
No-one else has them,
because no-one else has Mary.

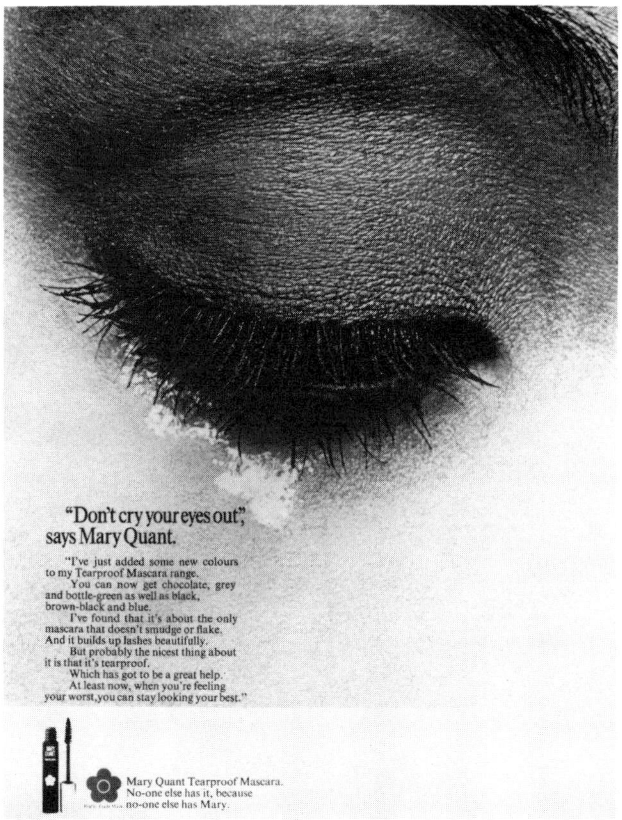
"Don't cry your eyes out," says Mary Quant.
"I've just added some new colours to my Tearproof Mascara range.
You can now get chocolate, grey and bottle-green as well as black, brown-black and blue.
I've found that it's about the only mascara that doesn't smudge or flake.
And it builds up lashes beautifully.
But probably the nicest thing about it is that it's tearproof.
Which has got to be a great help.
At least now, when you're feeling your worst, you can stay looking your best."
Mary Quant Tearproof Mascara.
No-one else has it, because
no-one else has Mary.

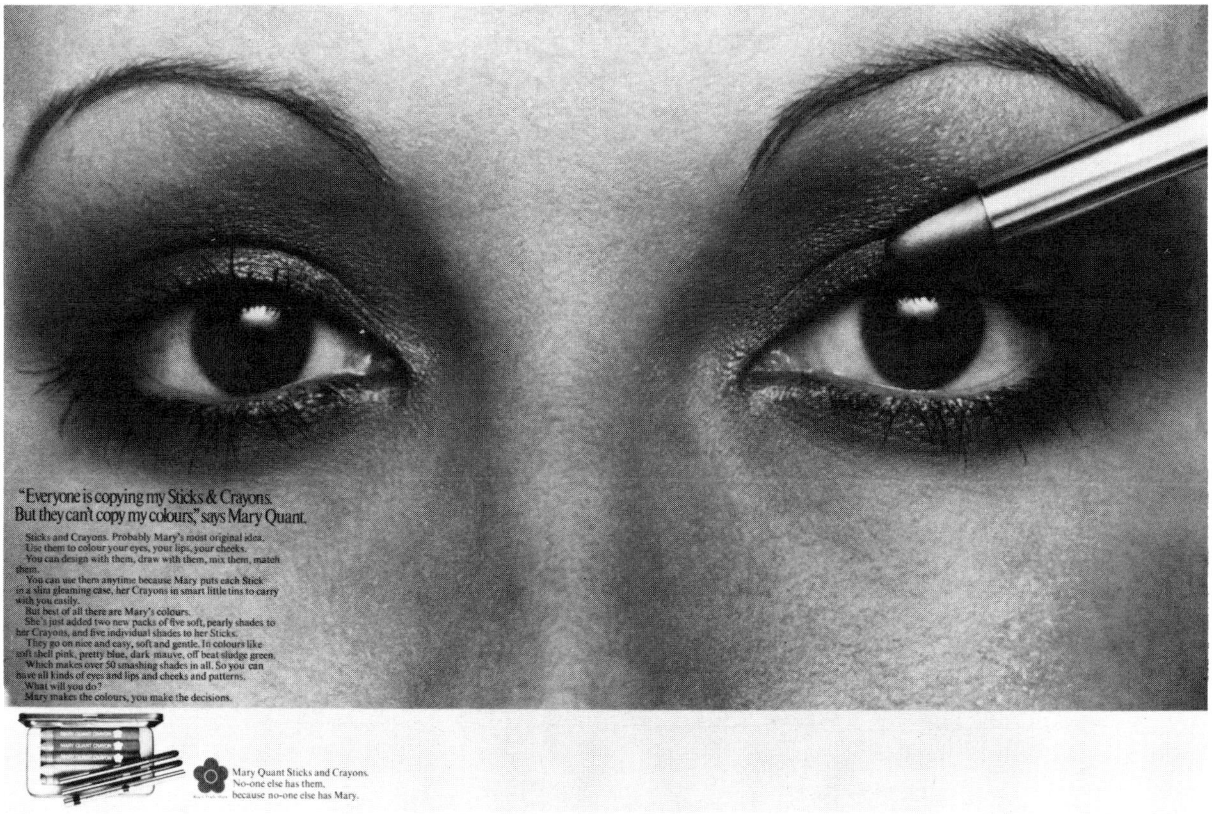
"Everyone is copying my Sticks & Crayons. But they can't copy my colours," says Mary Quant.
Sticks and Crayons. Probably Mary's most original idea.
Use them to colour your eyes, your lips, your cheeks.
You can design with them, draw with them, mix them, match them.
You can use them anytime because Mary puts each Stick in a slim gleaming case, her Crayons in smart little tins to carry with you easily.
But best of all there are Mary's colours.
She's just added two new packs of five soft, pearly shades to her Crayons, and five individual shades to her Sticks.
They go on nice and easy, soft and gentle. In colours like soft shell pink, pretty blue, dark mauve, off beat sludge green.
Which makes over 50 smashing shades in all. So you can have all kinds of eyes and lips and cheeks and patterns.
What will you do?
Mary makes the colours, you make the decisions.
Mary Quant Sticks and Crayons.
No-one else has them,
because no-one else has Mary.

512

SILVER

512
Art Director Bob Marchant
Writers Wayne Garland
Lindsey Dale
Designer Bob Marchant
Photographers Brian Duffy
Richard Dunkley
Agency Aalders & Marchant
London
Client Mary Quant Cosmetics

One, two, buckle my shoe. Three, four, fall on the floor.
Some of the shoes you see these days are a positive health hazard. It is a wonder those girls can stand up in some of the ridiculous styles they are wearing these days. Let alone walk in them. Or run down the stairs. Or drive a car.
At Clarks Joyflex we have long held the belief that a shoe doesn't have to be painful to be stylish. And to prove the point we have designed a whole new range of shoes, each of which has two things in common. It looks good. And it feels good.
Just like the shoe illustrated. It's called Bravo and it comes in a range of three different fittings in Maple/Tartan Rub off. Suggested retail price $17.99.
All our shoes are smart, stylish and comfortable. At Clarks Joyflex we will never make a shoe that hurts. Either your feet. Or your pocket.
Clarks Joyflex. Painless fashion.

514

If you need to take them off, you need to take them back.
How many times have you kicked them off under the table? Or under your seat at the movies?
Maybe you think that uncomfortable shoes are part of being a woman.
Not any more. At Clarks Joyflex we reckon that if you need to take your shoes off because they hurt you, you need to take them back and ask for another brand.
So we've made Australia's first range of painless fashion shoes. They are elegantly styled, but also incorporate all our know-how in comfort and fit. The know-how we have gained from 60 years of working on famous Clarks Children's Shoes.
The shoe illustrated is called Cindy and is available in three different fittings in White, Bone, Jute, Campari and Navy. Suggested retail price $20.99.
These new Joyflex shoes are not available from every shoe store. But they are available from the following select group of retailers, who care just as much about your feet as we do.
In New South Wales: Brooks, Bruce Jones, Francis Dale, Gays, Goldsmith, David Jones, Murray Bros., and Sparks.
In Victoria: Colliers, Farmers, Simons, and Vogue.
In Queensland: Myers, McDonald and East, and Beresfords.
In Western Australia: Cecil Bros., and Myers.
In South Australia: Miller Anderson, McKenzies, and Pitter Patter.
Clarks Joyflex. Painless fashion.

515

514
Art Director Gordon Trembath
Writer Lionel Hunt
Designer Gordon Trembath
Photographers John Beale
Bob Bourne
Agency Pritchard Wood-Quadrant
Melbourne
Client Clarks Shoes Ltd.

515
Art Director Gordon Trembath
Writer Lionel Hunt
Designer Gordon Trembath
Photographer John Beale
Agency Pritchard Wood-Quadrant
Melbourne
Client Clarks Shoes Ltd.

GUINNES
GUINNESS EXTRA STOUT
REGISTERED TRADE MARK
ST JAMES'S GATE DUBLIN
L/G 122276
CONTENTS 12 FL.OZS.
LABATT'S ONTARIO BREWERIES LTD.
LONDON ONTARIO
GUINNESS
IS GOOD
If you think it looks different, wait till you taste it.
Remember how surprised you were at your very first taste of beer? And how much you got to like it once you got used to it? Well, you might be surprised at your first taste of our dark beer as well. But we think you'll find it's also worth getting used to. For Guinness has a unique, deep dark taste you might discover is a welcome change from the ordinary. Of course, it won't be easy . . . your first beer wasn't easy . . . but remember: all good things in life are worth working for.
Guinness. Unlike any other beer.

516

516
Art Director Mike Fromowitz
Writers Mike Gill
Mike Fromowitz
Designer Mike Fromowitz
Photographer Gillean Proctor
Agency J. Walter Thompson Co. Ltd.
Toronto
Client Guinness Canada

517
Art Director Mike Fromowitz
Writers Mike Gill
Mike Fromowitz
Designer Mike Fromowitz
Photographer Gillean Proctor
Agency J. Walter Thompson Co. Ltd.
Toronto
Client Guinness Canada

GUINNESS
In a country that loves blondes, it's a brunette.
Let's be honest: Guinness is not one of your ordinary blonde Canadian beers. And we don't expect everyone to give up their blonde beers over-night. After all, Guinness can't promise untold happiness. Guinness doesn't star in beautiful TV commercials. Guinness doesn't even have a song. In fact Guinness is just not your normal Canadian beer. It just isn't like any other beer. For Guinness has a deep, dark taste that's all its own. But if you're the kind of person who seeks out new adventures…who isn't afraid of a bit of sultry mystery…try a Guinness. You might find the difference of Guinness a welcome change.
Guinness. Unlike any other beer.

NNESS
Guinness. Unlike
r beer.
In these days of an abundance of
it's
refreshing
an authentic original
s been
nothing to
deep dark taste of
since Arthur
first brought it to
Dublin in
1759. And today
inness is brewed in
da
the
same sec
formula. Which means that
satiated
your ordinary beers, you
have
unique d
taste of Guinness to turn
We th
you'll find the difference
Guin
refreshing
erience…rather unlike
you

"If I can't wear my old Wrangler shirt I'm not going."

518

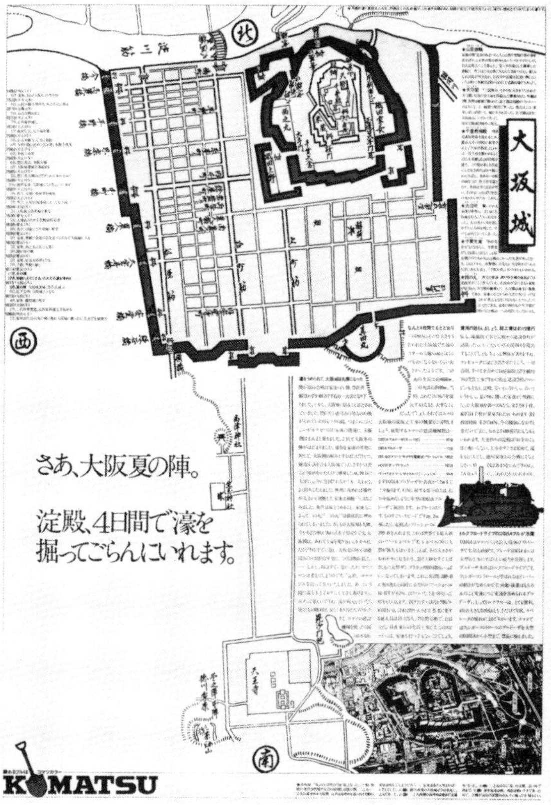
大坂城
さあ、大阪夏の陣。
淀殿、4日間で濠を掘ってごらんにいれます。
KOMATSU

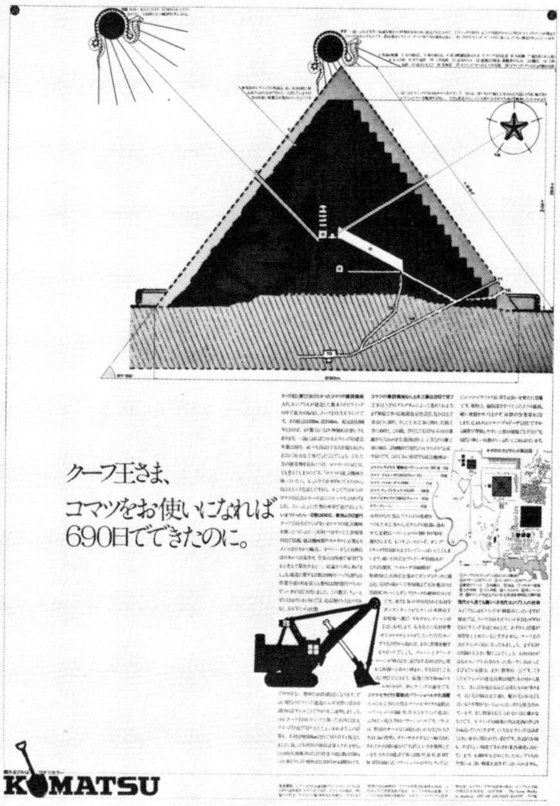
クーフ王さま、
コマツをお使いになれば
690日でできたのに。
KOMATSU

519

518
Art Directors Gordon Trembath
Lindsay Crethar
Writer Lionel Hunt
Designer Gordon Trembath
Photographer Brian Morris
Agency The Campaign Palace
South Melbourne
Client Wrangler

519
Art Directors Hiroaki Koga
Tadashi Ishiura
Writer Kazuo Kikuchi
Designers Tadashi Ishiura
Yasunobu Aso
Photographer Kazuo Aoki
Agency Hakuhodo Inc.
Tokyo
Client Komatsu, Ltd.

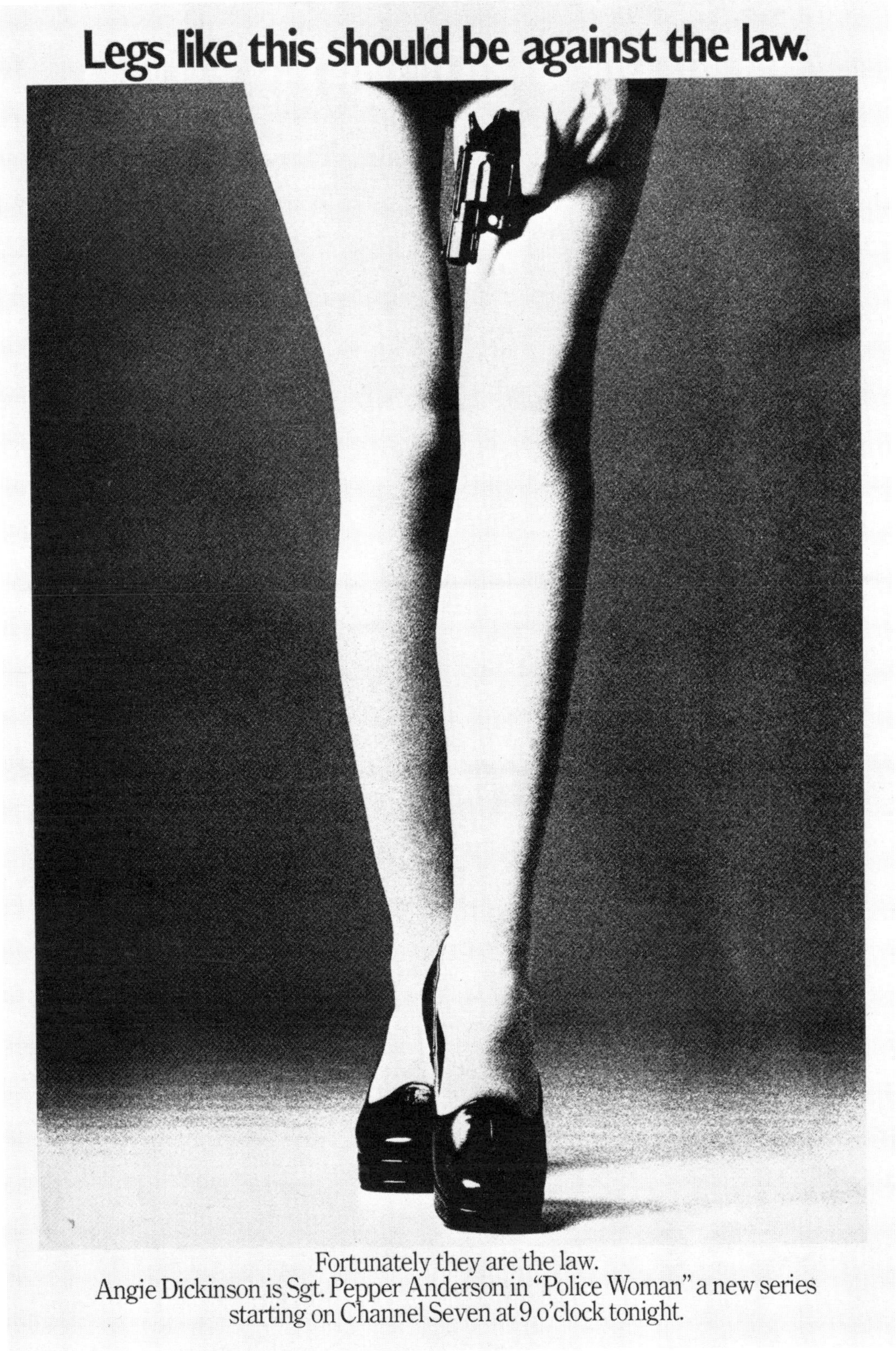
Legs like this should be against the law.
Fortunately they are the law.
Angie Dickinson is Sgt. Pepper Anderson in "Police Woman" a new series
starting on Channel Seven at 9 o'clock tonight.

520

520
Art Director Gordon Trembath
Writers Lionel Hunt
Garrie Hutchinson
Designer Gordon Trembath
Artist Steve Warren
Photographer Bob Bourne
Agency The Campaign Palace
South Melbourne
Client Seven Color Television

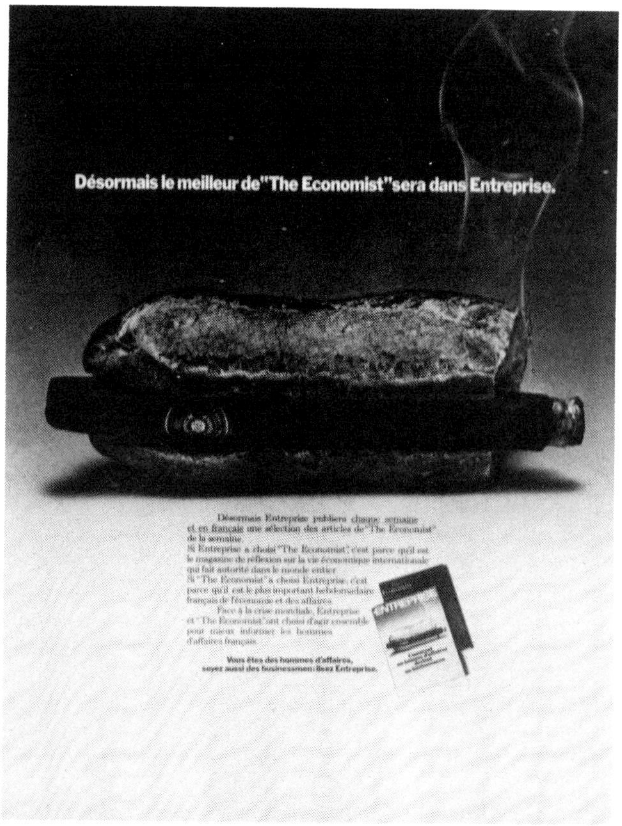
Désormais le meilleur de "The Economist" sera dans Entreprise.
Désormais Entreprise publiera chaque semaine et en français une sélection des articles de "The Economist" de la semaine.
Si Entreprise a choisi "The Economist", c'est parce qu'il est le magazine de réflexion sur la vie économique internationale qui fait autorité dans le monde entier.
Si "The Economist" a choisi Entreprise, c'est parce qu'il est le plus important hebdomadaire français de l'économie et des affaires.
Face à la crise mondiale, Entreprise et "The Economist" ont choisi d'agir ensemble pour mieux informer les hommes d'affaires français.
Vous êtes des hommes d'affaires, soyez aussi des businessmen: lisez Entreprise.

521

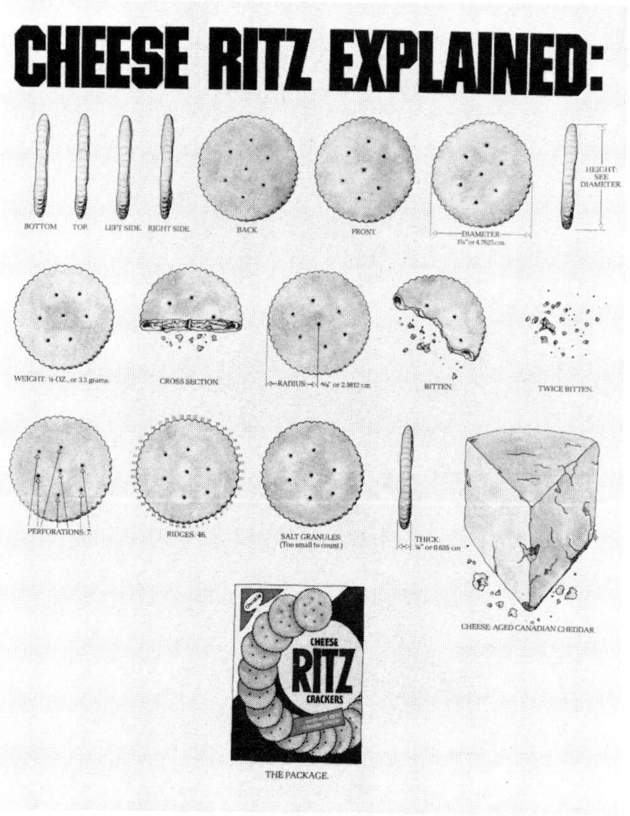
CHEESE RITZ EXPLAINED:
BOTTOM
TOP
LEFT SIDE
RIGHT SIDE
BACK
FRONT
HEIGHT: SEE DIAMETER.
WEIGHT
CROSS SECTION
RADIUS
BITTEN
TWICE BITTEN
PERFORATIONS: 7.
RIDGES: 46.
SALT GRANULES (Too small to count.)
THICK
CHEESE: AGED CANADIAN CHEDDAR
CHEESE
RITZ
CRACKERS
THE PACKAGE.

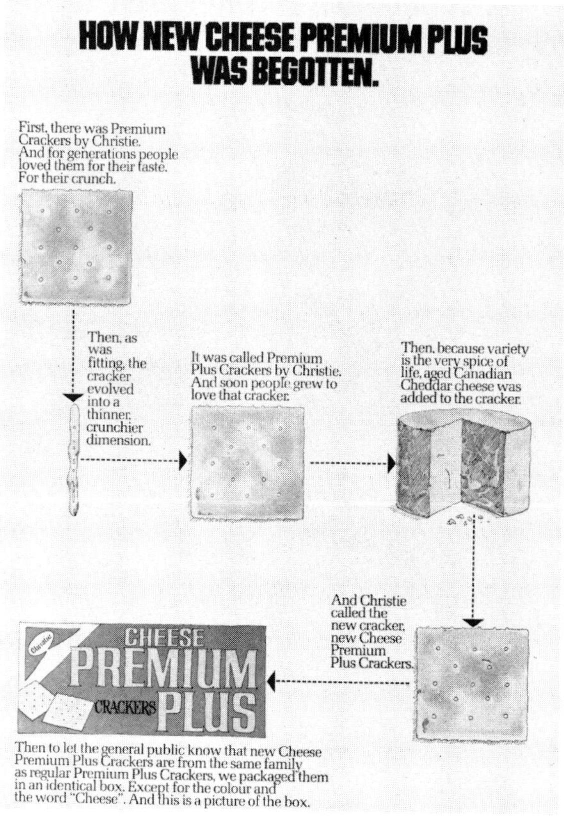
HOW NEW CHEESE PREMIUM PLUS WAS BEGOTTEN.
First, there was Premium Crackers by Christie. And for generations people loved them for their taste. For their crunch.
Then, as was fitting, the cracker evolved into a thinner, crunchier dimension.
It was called Premium Plus Crackers by Christie. And soon people grew to love that cracker.
Then, because variety is the very spice of life, aged Canadian Cheddar cheese was added to the cracker.
And Christie called the new cracker, new Cheese Premium Plus Crackers.
CHEESE
PREMIUM
CRACKERS
PLUS
Then to let the general public know that new Cheese Premium Plus Crackers are from the same family as regular Premium Plus Crackers, we packaged them in an identical box. Except for the colour and the word "Cheese". And this is a picture of the box.

522

GOLD

521
Art Director Robert Dubarle
Photographer Daniel Fauchon
Writer Thierry Ardisson
Agency Tragos Bonnange Wiesendanger Ajroldi Paris
Client R.E.C.

522
Art Director Brian Harrod
Writer Allan Kazmer
Designer Brian Harrod
Artist Tony Kew
Agency McCann-Erickson Toronto
Client Christie Brown

One of life's
sweet mysteries.
CARAMILK

MONA LISA
30-second

LEONARDO: (Imploringly) Mona, smile . . .

ANNCR: Maestro Da Vinci, have you finally figured out how Cadbury gets the soft flowing caramel inside the Caramilk bar?

LEONARDO: Ah yes, Caramilk . . . a fascinating problem. Mona, take a break.

I thought this might work, and then this machine . . . but that's not it . . .

(Off camera) And then this ancient Roman technique . . . but I need more time . . . more thought

(Joyous) Mona, hold it . . .

Magnifico!

SUPER: *One of life's sweet mysteries*

529
Art Director A. Morkel
Writer G. Prouk
Director E. Beck
Producer L. Jensen
Production Co.: Rabko Television Productions Ltd.
Agency Doyle Dane Bernbach
Toronto
Client Cadbury, Schweppes, Powell Ltd.

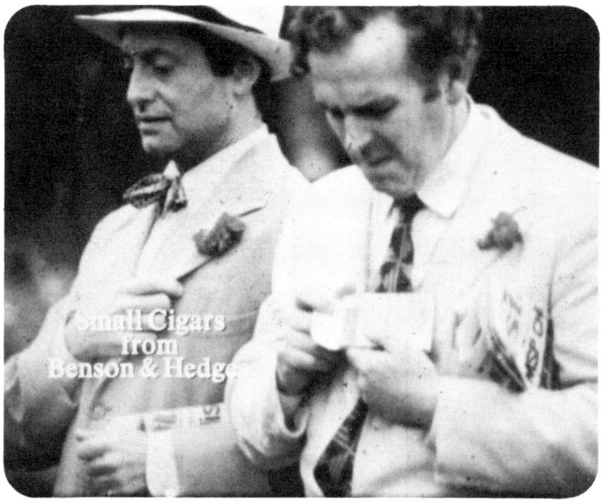
Small Cigars
from
Benson & Hedges

CARNATION

MUSIC UNDER

GOLD

530

Art Director Geoff Krikland
Director Bob Brooks
Producer John Cigarini
Production Co. Brooks Fulford Cramer
Agency Collett Dickenson
Pearce & Partners Ltd.
London
Client Benson & Hedges Ltd.

SUITCASE

MUSIC UNDER

531
Director Bob Brooks
Producer John Cigarini
Production Co. Brooks Fulford Cramer Ltd.
Agency Collett Dickenson
Pearce & Partners Ltd.
London
Client Benson and Hedges Ltd.

HUNTER
30-second

SFX: Natural Sounds

ANNCR: Where does your Candidate stand on the killing of baby seals?

SUPER: *Where does your candidate stand on the killing of baby seals?*

Demand an answer

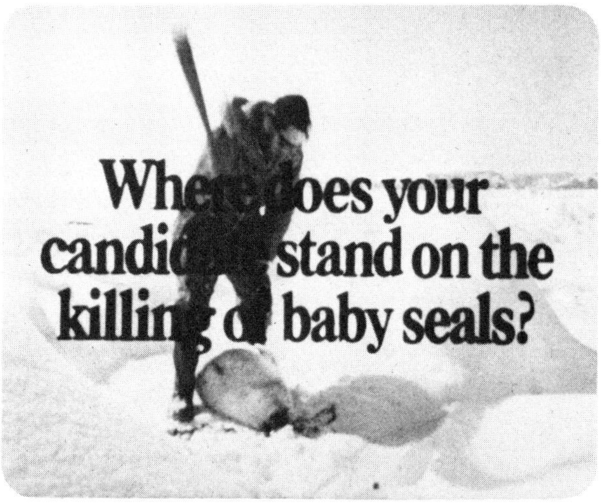
your
stand on the
baby seals?

Demand an answer.

532
Art Director Brian Harrod
Writer Allan Kazmer
Cameraman Steve Best
Director Steve Best
Producer William Fahnestock
Production Co. Mobius Productions Ltd.
Agency McCann-Erickson
Toronto
Client International Fund for Animal Welfare

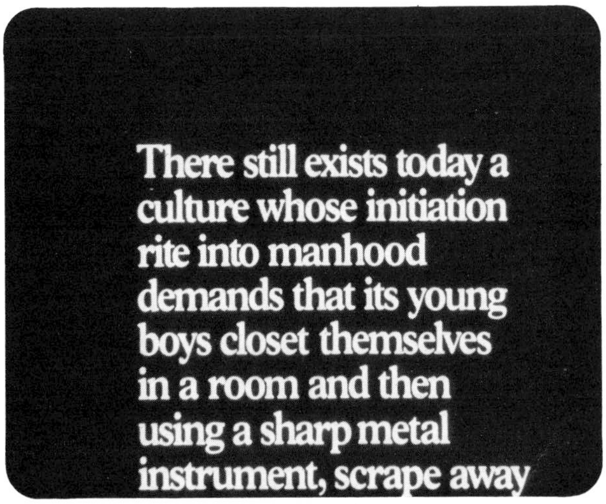
There still exists today a culture whose initiation rite into manhood demands that its young boys closet themselves in a room and then using a sharp metal instrument, scrape away

their facial hair without grimacing or physically marring their face.

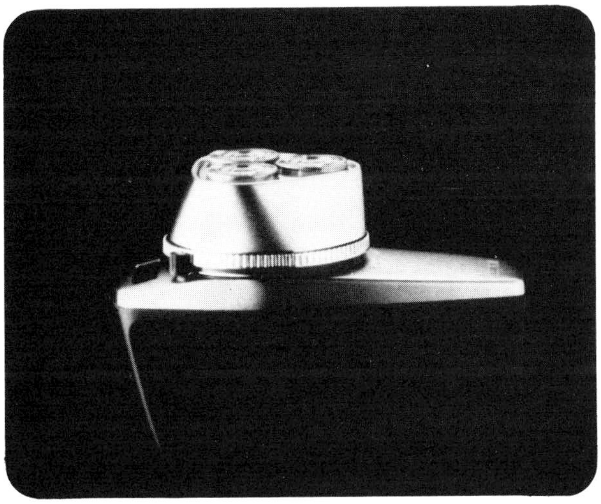

INITIATION RITES
30-second

ANNCR: There still exists today a culture whose initiation rite into manhood demands its young boys closet themselves in a room and then using a sharp metal instrument scrape away their facial hair without grimacing or physically marring their face.

Fortunately, the custom seems to be changing and many enlightened elders are presenting their sons with a Philishave.

They've discovered the removal of facial hair is complete and the failure rate into manhood is nil.

Philishave by Philips.

533
Art Director Brian Harrod
Writer Allan Kazmer
Cameraman Ray Kellgran
Director Paul Herriott
Producer Karen Hays
Production Co. Paul Herriott
Agency McCann-Erickson Toronto
Client Cos Capone

HOLLAND

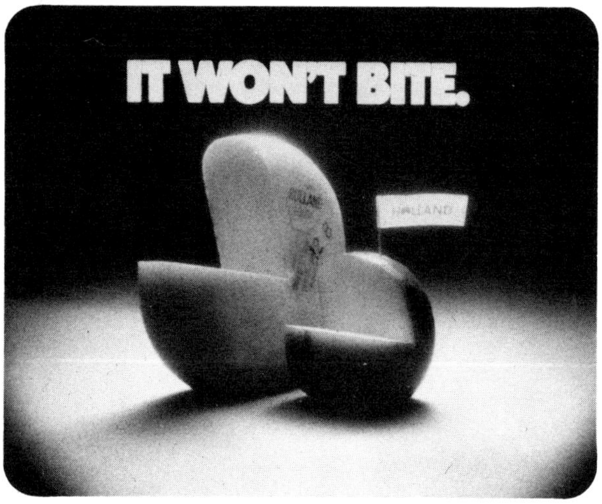
IT WON'T BITE.

EDAM AND GOUDA
30-second

WOMAN: Come on. You're a big grown up person now. You're not afraid of a little ball of imported cheese, are you?

Just because it says it's imported doesn't mean it's going to taste strong. Edam and Gouda cheese from Holland, wouldn't want . . .

to scare you for the world. Both Edam and Gouda are very easy on the taste buds. And easy on the . . . food budget. Come on. Try Edam and Gouda . . .

from . . . Holland.

It won't bite.

534
Art Director Brian Harrod
Writer Allan Kazmer
Cameraman Stephen Goldblatt
Director Stephen Goldblatt
Producer Willie Fahnestock
Agency McCann-Erickson Toronto
Client Holland Cheese Exporters Assoc.

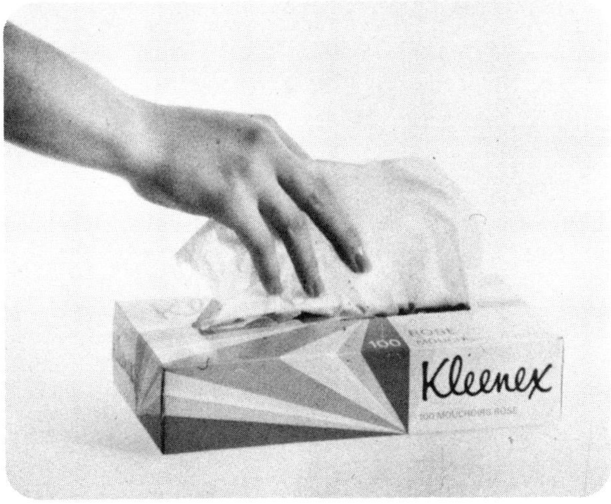
100
Kleenex

COCKTAIL
10-second

ANNCR: Kleenex, and everything disappears with a caress.

535
Art Director Philippe Pouzol
Writer Marie Quennessen
Cameraman Colin Mounier
Director Pascal Thomas
Production Co. Telema
Agency Intermarco Elvinger Paris
Client Sopalin

DUAL RADIO
60-second

ANNCR: This is a record . . . I've only been around for a little while, but have I been abused . . . scratched . . .

SFX

ANNCR: Nicked . . .

SFX

ANNCR: . . . hurt to the point where I can't even be understood,

SFX

ANNCR: . . . understood . . . understood. Listen to me, stammering at my age. Not too long ago I sounded like this . . .

MUSIC

ANNCR: . . . Beautiful, wasn't I? . . . Then bad turntables go to me . . . they cut my highs . . . slashed my lows . . . you see I've been getting the point now for a long, long time. Now I think it's time you get the point. Clear, accurate sound is good for your ears and what's good for your ears is good for your head. You know a record can't really talk, but it can be a spokesman.

I'd like to recommend a company that makes gentle turntables. Dual. Dual turntables are engineered with precision and have features that take care of sensitive records. And that's good for me, and if it's good for me, I'll be good for you.

After all, one good turn deserves another.

541
Writer Syd Kessler
Producers Syd Kessler
Raymond Lee
Production Co. WAMO
Agency Raymond Lee & Assoc. Ltd.
Toronto
Client Noresco Ltd.

WEDDING DAY
30-second

MINISTER: Welcome to my church, is this the tall handsome groom?

FATHER: I'm the fat bald father.

MINISTER: Ha ha, of course you are. A little levity helps to relax the bridal party. Where is the groom?

BRIDE: Where's Harold?

MOTHER: Where's Harold?

MINISTER: Best man, where's Harold.

BEST MAN: He's not coming.

FATHER: Not coming.

BRIDE: Not coming.

MOTHER: Not coming.

BEST MAN: Nup, he's not coming.

BRIDE: Why not?

FATHER: Why not?

BEST MAN: He said if I can't wear my old Wrangler shirt I'm not going.

BRIDE: He's really not coming?

FATHER: I told you he was immature.

BRIDE: Oh.

MOTHER: My daughter's life ruined by a smelly old Wrangler shirt.

BRIDE: Oh.

542
Writers Street Remley
Lionel Hunt
Director Street Remley
Producer Street Remley
Production Co. Pepper Studios
Agency The Campaign Palace
South Melbourne
Client Wrangler

Join the debating society.

Separate fact from faction.

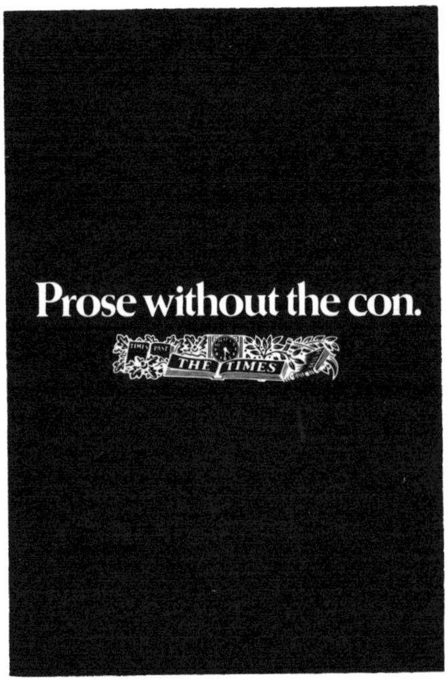
Prose without the con.

Sit down
with a paper of standing.

You supply the mind.
We'll provide the matter.

No pomp.
Just the circumstances.

544

544
Art Director Bob Byrne
Writer Ken Mullen
Designer Bob Byrne
Agency Leo Burnett Ltd.
London
Client The Times

THE ONE BANK
THAT MUST NEVER
RUN DRY.
GIVE BLOOD.
Contact your local Blood Transfusion Centre.
(Or call 01-628 4590 day or night.)

PUT A LITTLE
IN THE BANK.
GIVE BLOOD.
Contact your local Blood Transfusion Centre.
(Or call 01-628 4590 day or night.)

OPEN A
LIFE SAVINGS
ACCOUNT WITH
OUR BANK.
GIVE BLOOD.
Contact your local Blood Transfusion Centre.
(Or call 01-628 4590 day or night.)

546

546
Art Director Derrick Hass
Writer Stuart Blake
Designer Derrick Hass
Artist Doyle Dane Bernbach Studio
Agency Doyle Dane Bernbach Ltd.
London
Client Central Office of Information

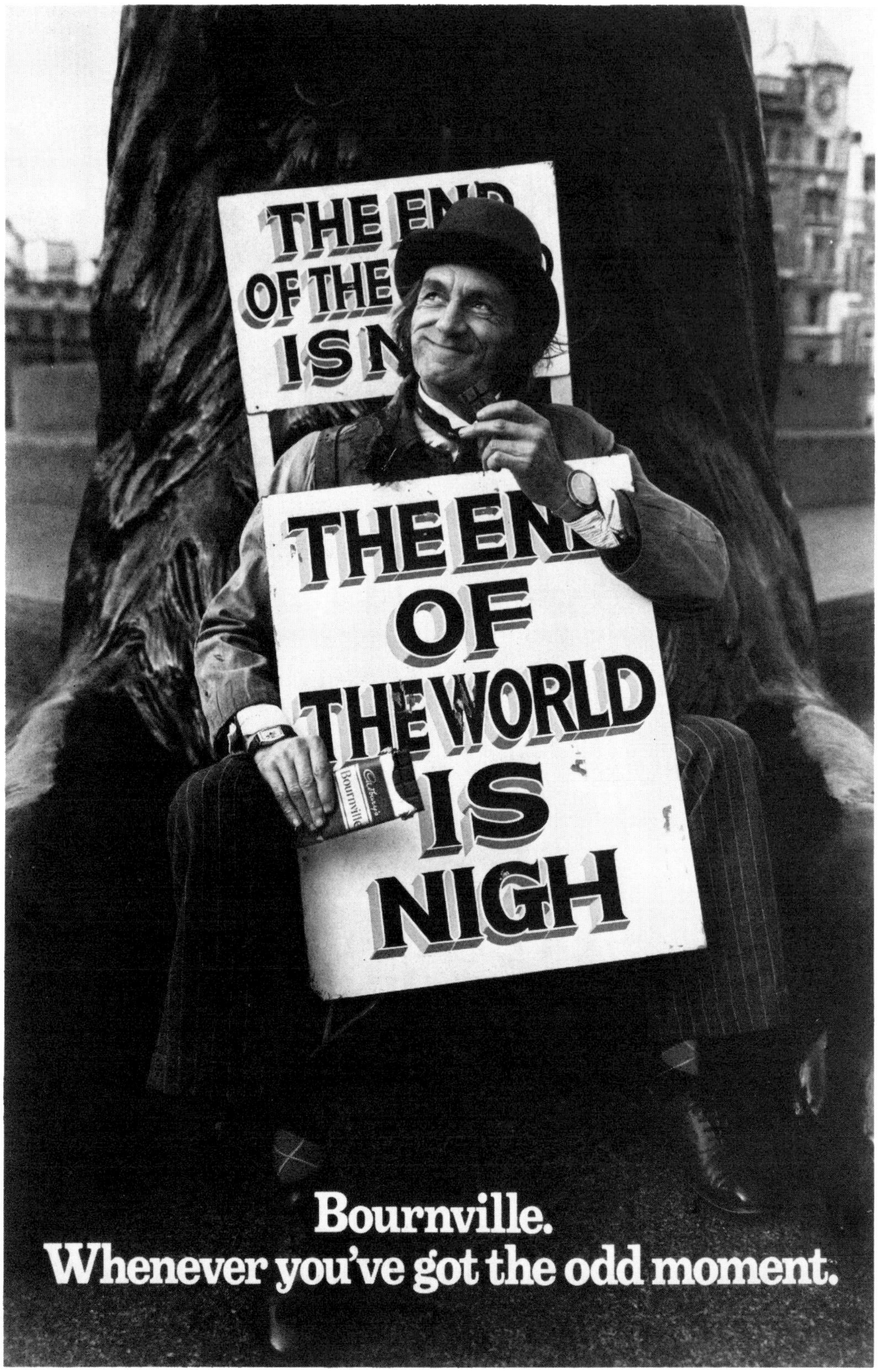
THE END OF THE WORLD IS NIGH
Bournville
Bournville.
Whenever you've got the odd moment.

547

547
Art Director Bob Byrne
Writer Ken Mullen
Designer Bob Byrne
Photographer Lester Bookbinder
Agency Leo Burnett Ltd.
London
Client Cadbury Ltd.

548
Art Director Derrick Hass
Writer Derrick Hass
Designer Derrick Hass
Agency Doyle Dane Bernbach Ltd.
London
Client Women's Recognition

549
Art Director Brian Harrod
Writer Allan Kazmer
Designer Brian Harrod
Photographer Bert Bell
Agency McCann-Erickson
Toronto
Client Holland Cheese
Exporters Assoc.

Male
supremacy
is all cock.
WOMEN'S RECOGNITION.

548

IT WON'T BITE.
HOLLAND
GOUDA
Contrary to a popular myth,
the cheese of Holland is neither
expensive, nor strong tasting.

549

ON POURRAIT SE PASSER DE CINZANO.
ON POURRAIT AUSSI SE PASSER DE NOËL.
CINZANO
CINZANO BITTER. NOUS NE CHANGERONS JAMAIS.
PREPARE SELON LA RECETTE DE FRANCESCO CINZANO.
CINZANO
4EME GROUPE

550

550
Art Directors Martin Reavley
Rosette Holzer
Writer Pierre Derville
Artist Stag
Photographer David Thorpe
Agency Tragos Bonnange
Wiesendanger
Ajroldi
Paris
Client Cinzano

quand on n'a plus vingt ans,
et que cela commence à se voir...
Révolutionnaire !
Tous les produits anti-rides disent qu'ils le sont. Mais leurs résultats ne sont pas toujours à la hauteur de leurs ambitions.
Révolutionnaire ! Le mot n'est pas trop fort pour qualifier le nouveau Specific Vitalizer de Lancaster.
C'est une crème anti-rides, un véritable traitement de choc dont les résultats sont proprement extraordinaires : 3 ans de tests en laboratoire ont démontré l'efficacité parfaite de Specific Vitalizer sur toutes les peaux même les plus abimées.
Essayez Specific Vitalizer : en quelques jours vous verrez déjà un changement. Votre peau sera plus souple, vos rides moins marquées. Cette efficacité est dûe à sa conception vraiment originale : composée d'éléments biologiques homologues à ceux de l'épiderme, ce traitement permet à celui-ci de se régénérer rapidement et complètement.
Specific Vitalizer s'applique tous les soirs en cure de 30 jours. Présenté en pot scellé, ce produit est léger, agréable à mettre, il hydrate et détend la peau, pénètre profondément, ne tache pas.
Specific Vitalizer fait partie de la gamme des Specifics Lancaster dont les résultats dans le traitement des rides sont bien connus.
Demandez-le à votre parfumeur conseil agréé Lancaster. Après tout vous pouvez être bien dans votre peau à n'importe quel âge... mais ne pas avoir envie de paraître cet âge.
SPECIFIC VITALIZER
LANCASTER

552

Déroutez-vous
Venez bavarder avec nos voisins.
Laissez-vous vivre. A votre rythme. Venez nous rejoindre au Maroc, en Tunisie, au Sénégal, aux Antilles, à l'Ile Maurice ou à Tahiti.
La découverte vous attend. Celle que vous saisissez au passage. Une rose des sables sous vos pas, la savoureuse brûlure du thé à la menthe, le rire d'un petit berger.
Au Club, tout est compris : le voyage, le séjour, les repas, les sports, les distractions. Pas de surprises. Sauf celle d'une ambiance chaleureuse, d'une architecture conçue pour le pays et d'un émerveillement constant solitaire ou partagé, comme il vous plaira.
Demandez-nous la brochure. Club Méditerranée place de la Bourse 75083 Paris - Cédex 02.
Avec le Club Méditerranée, cet hiver.
Place de la Bourse Paris 2e / 86 avenue des Champs-Elysées Paris 8e / Tél. 266 52 52. Agence Havas-Voyages de votre ville.

553

552
Art Director Mafia Staff
Writer France Brécard
Photographer Guy Bourdin
Agency Maïmé Arnodin, Fayolle International, Assoc. Paris
Client Lancaster

553
Art Director Rolland Della Monta
Writers Marie Petit
Michel Clairon
Photographer Philippe Quidor
Agency Synergie/K&E
Paris
Client Club Mediterranee

EDITORIAL DESIGN

Consumer Publication Pages 554–555
Consumer Publication Spreads 556–593
Consumer Publication Sections 595–614
Complete Issues 615–619
Consumer Publication Covers 620–627
Trade Publication Pages 628–629
Trade Publication Spreads 630–632
Trade Publication Sections 633–634
Trade Issues 635–637
Trade Publication Covers 638–643
Design of Complete Books 646–671
Individual Spread from a Book 672
Book Jackets 673–679

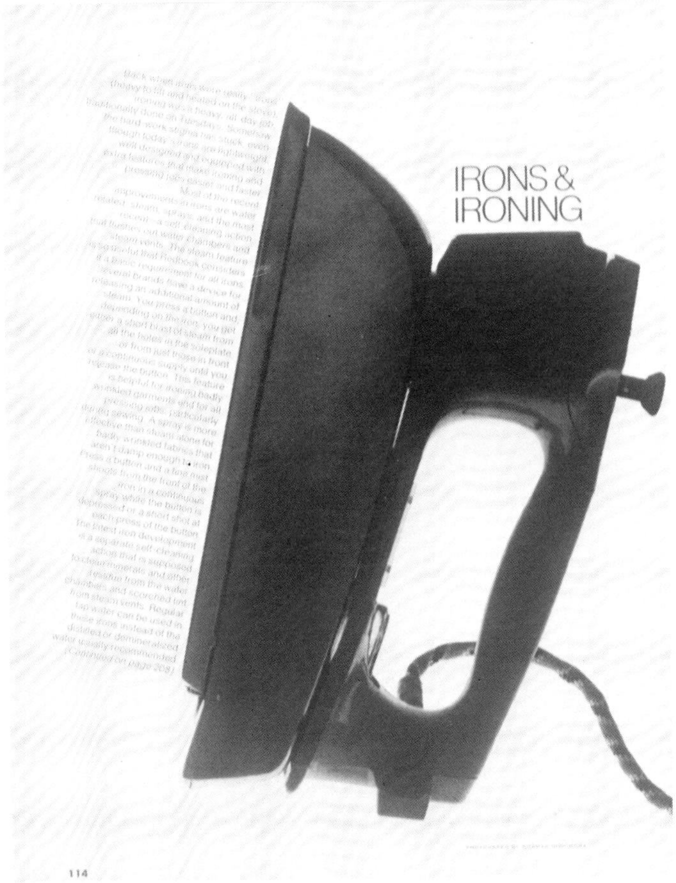
IRONS & IRONING
114

554

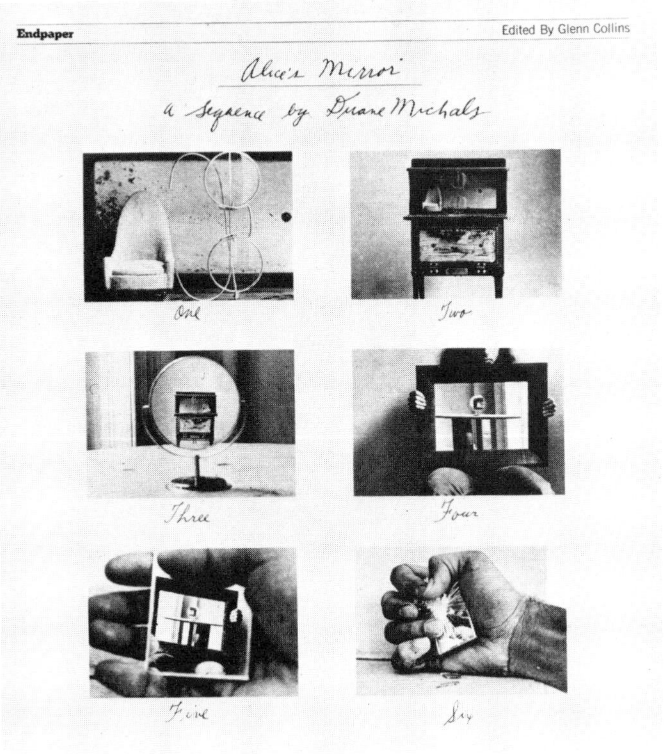
Endpaper
Edited By Glenn Collins
Alice's Mirror
a Sequence by Duane Michals
One
Two
Three
Four
Five
Six

555

554
Art Directors William Cadge
Verdun Cook
Designer Verdun Cook
Photographer Norman Nishimura
Editor Ann Arnott
Publisher Redbook

555
Art Director Ruth Ansel
Designer Ruth Ansel
Photographer Duane Michals
Editor Glenn Collins
Publisher The New York Times Magazine

Finding capital for U.S. industry
PRODUCTION
The massive task of expanding capacity

556

Government intervention
REGULATION
The surprisingly high cost of a safer environment

557

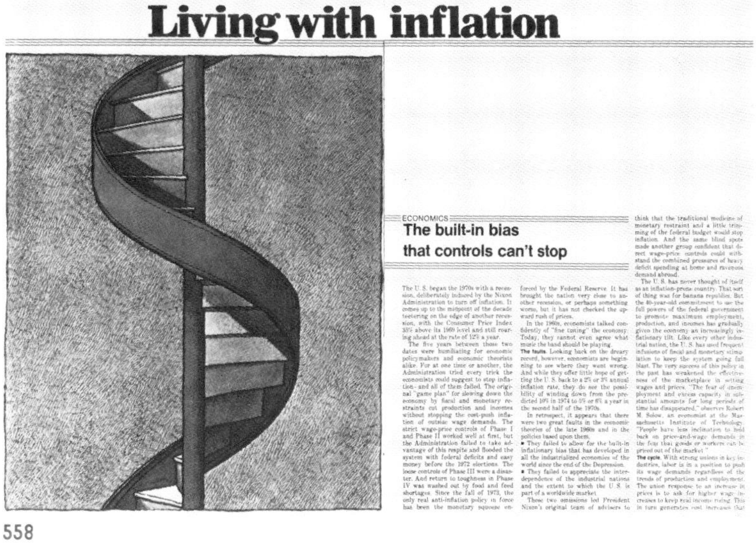
Living with inflation
ECONOMICS
The built-in bias that controls can't stop

558

SILVER

556
Art Director Robert N. Essman
Designers Robert N. Essman
Berni Schoenfield
Artist Pierre Le-Tan
Publisher Business Week

557
Art Director Robert N. Essman
Designers Robert N. Essman
Berni Schoenfield
Artist Pierre Le-Tan
Publisher Business Week

558
Art Director Robert N. Essman
Designers Robert N. Essman
Berni Schoenfield
Artist Pierre Le-Tan
Publisher Business Week

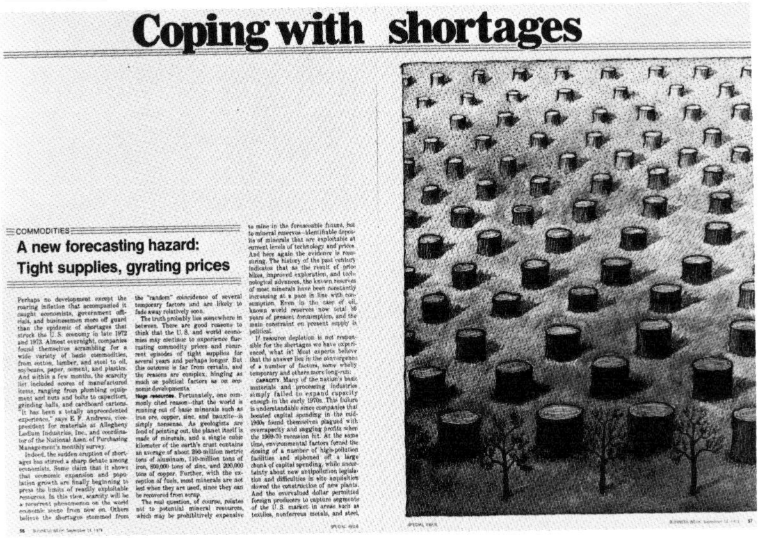
Coping with shortages
COMMODITIES
A new forecasting hazard:
Tight supplies, gyrating prices

559

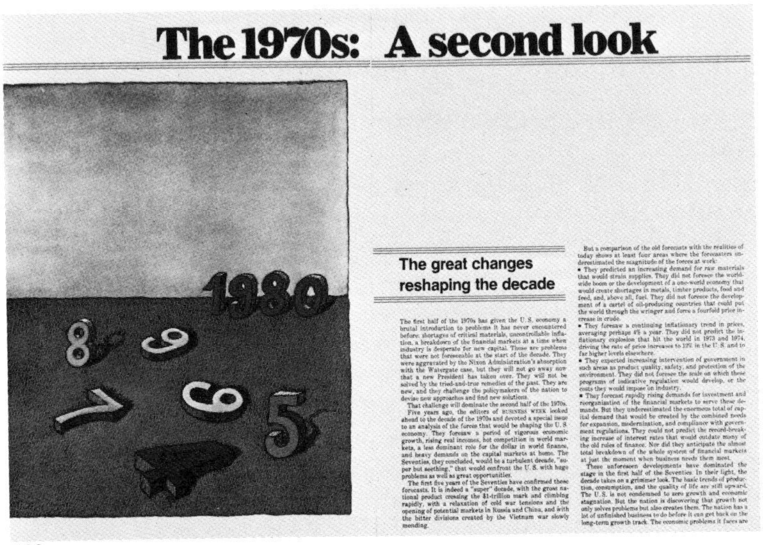
The 1970s: A second look
1980
The great changes
reshaping the decade

560

Answers from technology
RESEARCH & DEVELOPMENT
Even the smallest machine
will have its own 'brain'

561

559
Art Director Robert N. Essman
Designers Robert N. Essman
Berni Schoenfield
Artist Pierre Le-Tan
Publisher Business Week

560
Art Director Robert N. Essman
Designers Robert N. Essman
Berni Schoenfield
Artist Pierre Le-Tan
Publisher Business Week

561
Art Director Robert N. Essman
Designers Robert N. Essman
Berni Schoenfield
Artist Pierre Le-Tan
Publisher Business Week

Intermission: A few words for future daddies

You are looking at one good reason for having kids: To bring into the world a boy or girl who, at age twelve or thirteen, gets to experience life's first—and best—passionate moment. Think back: Was anything as great as the first kiss on the lips, the first bare skin? Can anything ever come close?

Painting by Jean-Paul Goude

562

THE LAST GOODBYE

IN THE birthplace of jazz—New Orleans, Louisiana—the funeral of a musician is a very special ceremony. It may begin with the bitter-sweet wail of a clarinet floating a tune like "Do You Know What It Means to Miss New Orleans" across a procession of mourners. It may run the gamut of emotions from solemn sorrow to dancing joy. And it always seems to say to participant and spectator alike that, in the fearsome presence of death, the only really appropriate response is the joyful, uninhibited reaffirmation of life.

The jazz funeral is a procession on foot through the streets, spurred on by the melodies of marching jazz bands, generally made up of colleagues and friends of the departed musician. A relic of days gone by, it never fails to attract a crowd. The mere idea of a funeral procession on foot is a novelty to Americans because most modern funerals feature a caravan of automobiles, their headlights turned on to warn other vehicles to yield the right-of-way.

Not so in the jazz world of New Orleans. There the mourners divide themselves into three groups or phases, as the accompanying pictures, made at several jazz funerals in the last few years, show. There are the spectators who line the streets. There are those who march in the procession. And (Continued)

Pall bearers (left) carry a coffin with solemn dignity while jazz band (immediately below) plays accompaniment. Tuxedos and full dress are common.

563

562
Art Director Richard Weigand
Designer Richard Weigand
Artist Jean Paul Goude
Publisher Esquire

563
Art Director Thaddeus A. Miksinski, Jr.
Designer Thaddeus A. Miksinski, Jr.
Photographer Leo Touchet
Writer Lucien Agniel
Publisher Topic Magazine

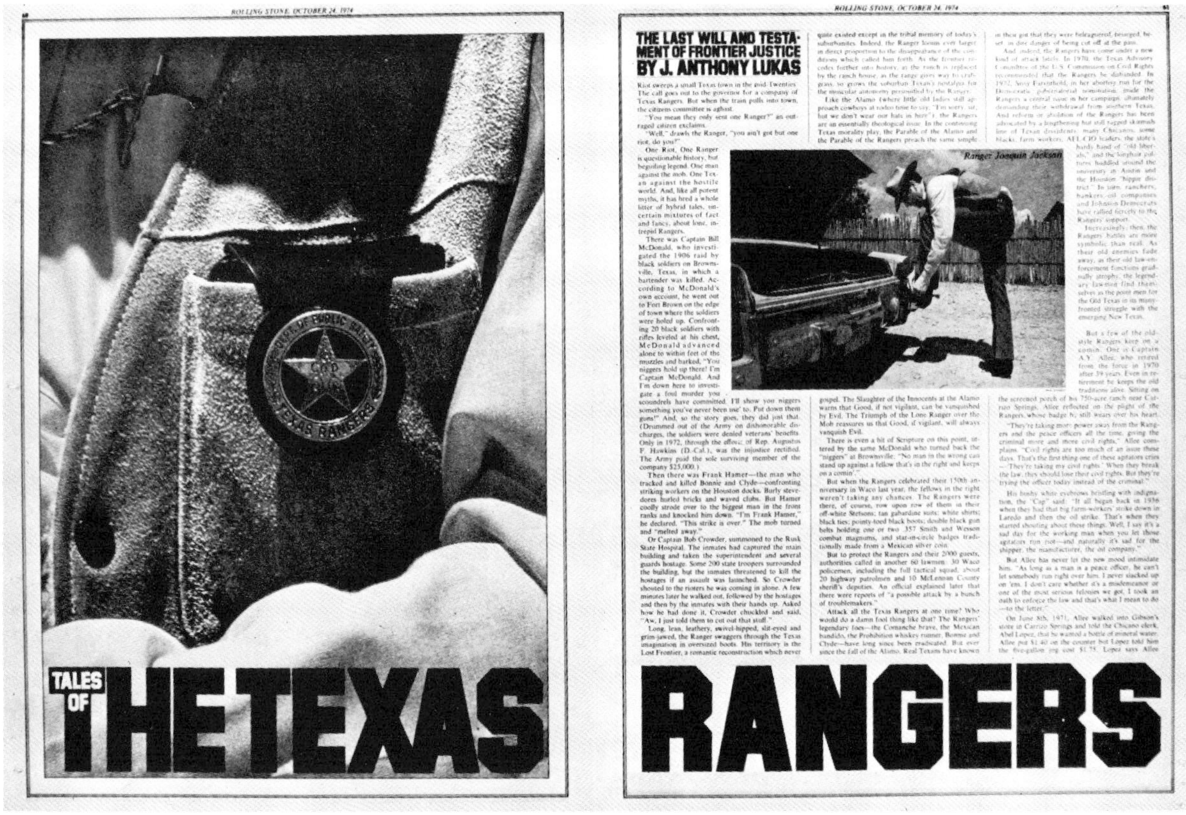

ROLLING STONE, OCTOBER 24, 1974

TALES OF THE TEXAS RANGERS

THE LAST WILL AND TESTAMENT OF FRONTIER JUSTICE
BY J. ANTHONY LUKAS

Riot sweeps a small Texas town in the mid-Twenties. The call goes out to the governor for a company of Texas Rangers. But when the train pulls into town, the citizens committee is aghast.

"You mean they only sent one Ranger?" an outraged citizen exclaims.

"Well," drawls the Ranger, "you ain't got but one riot, do you?"

One Riot, One Ranger is questionable history, but beguiling legend. One man against the mob. One Texan against the hostile world. And, like all potent myths, it has bred a whole litter of hybrid tales, uncertain mixtures of fact and fancy, about lone, intrepid Rangers.

There was Captain Bill McDonald, who investigated the 1906 raid by black soldiers on Brownsville, Texas, in which a bartender was killed. According to McDonald's own account, he went out to Fort Brown on the edge of town where the soldiers were holed up. Confronting 20 black soldiers with rifles leveled at his chest, McDonald advanced alone to within feet of the muzzles and barked, "You niggers hold up there! I'm Captain McDonald. And I'm down here to investigate a foul murder you scoundrels have committed. I'll show you niggers something you've never been use' to. Put down them guns!" And, so the story goes, they did just that. (Drummed out of the Army on dishonorable discharges, the soldiers were denied veterans' benefits. Only in 1972, through the efforts of Rep. Augustus F. Hawkins (D-Cal.), was the injustice rectified. The Army paid the sole surviving member of the company $25,000.)

Then there was Frank Hamer—the man who tracked and killed Bonnie and Clyde—confronting striking workers on the Houston docks. Burly stevedores hurled bricks and waved clubs. But Hamer coolly strode over to the biggest man in the front ranks and knocked him down. "I'm Frank Hamer," he declared. "This strike is over." The mob turned and "melted away."

Or Captain Bob Crowder, summoned to the Rusk State Hospital. The inmates had captured the main building and taken the superintendent and several guards hostage. Some 200 state troopers surrounded the building, but the inmates threatened to kill the hostages if an assault was launched. So Crowder shouted to the rioters he was coming in alone. A few minutes later he walked out, followed by the hostages and then by the inmates with their hands up. Asked how he had done it, Crowder chuckled and said, "Aw, I just told them to cut out that stuff."

Long, lean, leathery, swivel-hipped, slit-eyed and grim-jawed, the Ranger swaggers through the Texas imagination in oversized boots. His territory is the Lost Frontier, a romantic reconstruction which never quite existed except in the tribal memory of today's suburbanites. Indeed, the Ranger looms ever larger in direct proportion to the disappearance of the conditions which called him forth. As the frontier recedes further into history, as the ranch is replaced by the ranch house, as the range gives way to crabgrass, so grows the suburban Texan's nostalgia for the muscular autonomy personified by the Ranger.

Like the Alamo (where little old ladies still approach cowboys at rodeo time to say, "I'm sorry, sir, but we don't wear our hats in here"), the Rangers are an essentially theological issue. In the continuing Texas morality play, the Parable of the Alamo and the Parable of the Rangers preach the same simple gospel. The Slaughter of the Innocents at the Alamo warns that Good, if not vigilant, can be vanquished by Evil. The Triumph of the Lone Ranger over the Mob reassures us that Good, if vigilant, will always vanquish Evil.

There is even a bit of Scripture on this point, uttered by the same McDonald who turned back the "niggers" at Brownsville: "No man in the wrong can stand up against a fellow that's in the right and keeps on a comin'."

But when the Rangers celebrated their 150th anniversary in Waco last year, the fellows in the right weren't taking any chances. The Rangers were there, of course, row upon row of them in their off-white Stetsons; tan gabardine suits; white shirts; black ties; pointy-toed black boots; double black gun belts holding one or two .357 Smith and Wesson combat magnums, and star-in-circle badges traditionally made from a Mexican silver coin.

But to protect the Rangers and their 2000 guests, authorities called in another 60 lawmen: 30 Waco policemen, including the full tactical squad, about 20 highway patrolmen and 10 McLennan County sheriff's deputies. An official explained later that there were reports of "a possible attack by a bunch of troublemakers."

Attack all the Texas Rangers at one time? Who would do a damn fool thing like that? The Rangers' legendary foes—the Comanche brave, the Mexican bandido, the Prohibition whiskey runner, Bonnie and Clyde—have long since been eradicated. But ever since the fall of the Alamo, Real Texans have known in their gut that they were beleaguered, besieged, beset, in dire danger of being cut off at the pass.

And indeed, the Rangers have come under a new kind of attack lately. In 1970, the Texas Advisory Committee of the U.S. Commission on Civil Rights recommended that the Rangers be disbanded. In 1972, Sissy Farenthold, in her abortive run for the Democratic gubernatorial nomination, made the Rangers a central issue in her campaign, ultimately demanding their withdrawal from southern Texas. And reform or abolition of the Rangers has been advocated by a lengthening but still ragged skirmish line of Texan dissidents: many Chicanos, some blacks, farm workers, AFL-CIO leaders, the state's hardy band of "old liberals," and the longhair vultures huddled around the university in Austin and the Houston "hippie district." In turn, ranchers, bankers, oil companies and Johnson Democrats have rallied fiercely to the Rangers' support.

Increasingly, then, the Rangers' battles are more symbolic than real. As their old enemies fade away, as their old law-enforcement functions gradually atrophy, the legendary lawmen find themselves as the point men for the Old Texas in its many-fronted struggle with the emerging New Texas.

Ranger Joaquin Jackson

But a few of the old-style Rangers keep on a comin'. One is Captain A.Y. Allee, who retired from the force in 1970 after 39 years. Even in retirement he keeps the old traditions alive. Sitting on the screened porch of his 750-acre ranch near Carrizo Springs, Allee reflected on the plight of the Rangers, whose badge he still wears over his heart.

"They're taking more power away from the Rangers and the peace officers all the time, giving the criminal more and more civil rights," Allee complains. "Civil rights are too much of an issue these days. That's the first thing one of these agitators cries —'They're taking my civil rights.' When they break the law, they should lose their civil rights. But they're trying the officer today instead of the criminal."

His bushy white eyebrows bristling with indignation, the "Cap" said: "It all began back in 1936 when they had that big farm-workers' strike down in Laredo and then the oil strike. That's when they started shouting about these things. Well, I say it's a sad day for the working man when you let these agitators run riot—and naturally it's sad for the shipper, the manufacturer, the oil company."

But Allee has never let the new mood intimidate him. "As long as a man is a peace officer, he can't let somebody run right over him. I never slacked up on 'em. I don't care whether it's a misdemeanor or one of the most serious felonies we got, I took an oath to enforce the law and that's what I mean to do —to the letter."

On June 8th, 1971, Allee walked into Gibson's store in Carrizo Springs and told the Chicano clerk, Abel Lopez, that he wanted a bottle of mineral water. Allee put $1.40 on the counter but Lopez told him the five-gallon jug cost $1.75. Lopez says Allee

564

Mural, mural, on the wall,
You make this the loveliest block of all,
And so by now, it's become our rule,
To pass this way, as we walk to school;
And yet we wonder, each time we do,
Why our city has no other walls like you?
Shirts and skirts march back to school from left to right.
cotton knit goes with a black circular skirt banded with color. Girltown, 7-14. Shirt, $8; skirt, $9.50. 2d floor, Altman's. Jumping Jacks shoes. Bosic bag, Accessories Unlimited.
Continued on Page 53

565

564
Art Director Tony Lane
Designer Tony Lane
Photographer Nicki Simpson
Publisher Rolling Stone

565
Art Director Ruth Ansel
Designer Ruth Ansel
Photographer Bill Binzen
Editor Mary Simons
Publisher The New York Times Magazine

Hail, Mary

a revival of devoted interest in the only religious symbol asserting the femininity of the Ultimate

By Andrew M. Greeley

When my generation was starting out in the parochial schools of the nineteen-thirties, the older nuns used to tell a story of the Boss complaining to St. Peter about certain very disreputable characters he had seen walking the streets of the heavenly city. "Why did you let those fellows get in?" the Boss demanded of his gatekeeper.

"Can't help it," replied the hapless Peter. "I turn them away from the main gate and your mother lets them in through the kitchen door."

One could hardly grow up Catholic in those days without a reverence for Mary. She was a central figure in such staples of religious life as processions, May crownings and "living rosaries" (in which children formed a rosary in the schoolyard, with one or more of them representing each "bead." Each bead then recited in turn the "Hail Mary," the prayer that echoes the greetings to Mary in the gospel from her cousin, Elizabeth, and the angel Gabriel—"Hail Mary, full of grace/The Lord is with thee . . .") The Mary myth was for the most part benign and tender when I was a youngster, a soft, gentle, reassuring aspect of religion. In a Counter Reformation Catholicism which was notably devoid of sentiment and emotion, Mary appealed to something more than defense of the faith and stern moral obligation. The medieval poet sang of the same gentle lady that humanized our religious life:

I sing of a maiden that
Matchless is,
King of Kings is her son
I wis.

He came all so still
Where his mother was
As dew in April
That falleth on grass.

He came all so still
To his mother's bower
As dew in April
That falleth on shower.

He came all so still
Where his mother lay
As dew in April
That falleth on spray.

Mother and maiden
Was ne'er none but she
Well may such a lady
God's mother be.

We have lost the symbol in the last two decades. The church's intellectuals told us that Mary was irrelevant (even today in some élite circles mention of her is likely to occasion snide laughter). In my adolescence, our teachers converted the gentle lady into a stern, negative sex goddess who banned "dirty thoughts" and presided over the depth of necklines and the length of hemlines. Like most other young men who aspired to the priesthood, I said the rosary every day and would have claimed a "strong devotion" to Mary. But in my seminary years she became identified with the sweet, sickly, sentimental piety preached by the spiritual directors—long, flowery, elaborate prayers which said nothing. She was used to reinforce a religious viewpoint in which obedience had become more important than charity, chastity more important than dedication, and prudence more important than commitment. The people who claimed to be her devoted followers were creeps lugging statues about, preaching secret revelations rather than the gospel, and substituting ethereal pieties for both social concern and personal involvement. I turned the whole thing off.

In our enthusiastic discovery of the value of the "secular," we assumed that anything smacking of the sacred was probably steeped in superstition. Mary was part of a "maladroit fable," as one writer put it, a product of the superstitious medieval world view and quite out of place in a scientific, secular age. There was (Continued on Page 98)

The Rev. Andrew M. Greeley is a columnist and director of the Center for the Study of American Pluralism in Chicago. He has written a book called "The Mary Myth," to be published next year.

The Virgin of San Felipe, Oaxaca.

566

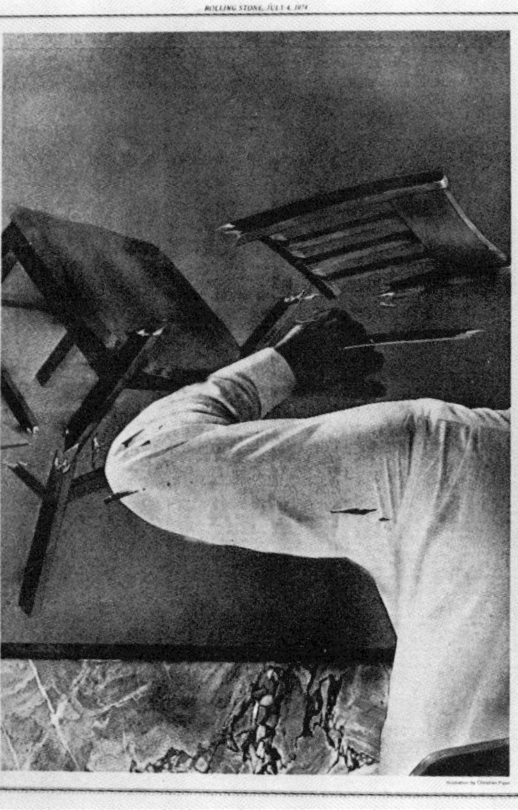

Illustration by Christian Piper

THE DEATH OF A HIGH SCHOOL

By JACK SLATER

By most estimates, it was a normal school year for Chicago. The 14-year-old son of a policeman fired a .38 caliber revolver and a .45 caliber pistol into the brain, chest and arms of the principal at Clara W. Barton Elementary School. At Hirsh High School, a 16-year-old sophomore, arguing over 25 cents, shot and killed another student in the school's crowded assembly hall. And at Metro High School, a 16-year-old girl, enraged by a poor grade she felt she did not deserve, quarreled bitterly with the teacher before pushing her down a flight of stairs. Elsewhere in the nation, in suburbs and cities alike, the school year followed a similar pattern.

Generally suburban high schools experience fewer incidents of violence, although recent events suggest some suburban schools, particularly in the East, are being sucked into the same defeat experienced by their urban counterparts. During this spring in New Jersey, for instance, fighting between black and white high-school students erupted in Morristown, New Brunswick, Pleasantville, Bridgeton and Montclair. And in Ardmore, an affluent suburb of Philadelphia, racial disorders between black and white students disrupted classes at Lower Merion High School for nearly a week.

Racial scrimmages everywhere so resemble one another that one doesn't need to know too many details surrounding the incident to know that a racial epithet triggered it. Indeed, "nigger" (or "honky") may have been the immediate cause of several other battles Lower Merion High experienced earlier last fall and winter. According to students, black and white girls sometimes squared off in the school washrooms and groups of boys battled occasionally after school.

"At first, it just seemed to be personal conflicts, not racial fighting, even though blacks and whites were involved," said a 16-year-old white girl who asked not to be identified.

"I don't think anyone wanted to recognize what it was: that black and white kids were actually fighting at Lower Merion," said another white girl, 17.

Finally, however, everyone had to recognize it. On March 27th, a group of angry black male students marched through the corridors of the school toward a chemistry laboratory. They opened the door to the classroom and immediately went after a white youth, 18-year-old John Sargent Jr., who had earlier, so it was alleged, shouted, "Niggers, nothing but niggers," at the black group. A few heated words were exchanged in the classroom, and a brawl involving more white students ensued. Squads of policemen arrived, and soon the entire school became implicated.

Two days later, 948 of Lower Merion High's 1500 students, including most of its 150 black students, boycotted classes and refused to return to school until the administration agreed to remove policemen from the halls and enforced a "no double standard" ruling which would give equal punishment to the white as well as the black students involved in the incident. As it turned out, however, two black students were expelled, and seven whites and blacks, including Sargent, were suspended.

If the same incident had taken place in a large city, it would have been viewed as a minor, almost routine, episode in the life of an urban high school. Yet at Lower Merion High, imbedded in a suburb whose residents earn an average of $30,000 annually, such an incident assumed "major" dimensions, partly because it was one of those episodes which "can never happen here" and partly because it pointed to the futility of suburban escape. For the incident not only publicly exposed the undercurrent of racial hostilities even among upper-income blacks and whites, but uncovered other "urban" problems plaguing the school.

"When I first came here," said Frank Peluso, a guidance counselor at Lower Merion High, "there was very little vandalism in the school. It was a shock to see graffiti, to see fixtures torn off in the bathrooms. It was a shock to see a fight. Today these are common occurrences." Or: "Drugs play a big role in a lot of the tension at the school," said Frank Kelly, a black senior at Lower Merion High. "And so many fights start because of drug rip-offs. You just can't deny that."

It was a normal year, then, for the usual loss of lives, the same financial cost of violence and the same predictable educational waste. Yet few school authorities, students or congressional leaders seem to understand the calamity of what violence in high schools portends, or what it says about life in the United States of America.

High-school violence, which largely affects black youths both as perpetrators and victims, began in the mid-Sixties at the height of the civil-rights movement, and rose dramatically after the collapse of that movement, after drug abuse became more widespread and after white affluent America, fleeing to private schools or to the suburbs with their tax-support dollars, left the remains of the urban school system to the poor. Expressed mostly as assaults against teachers, administrators and students, as well as against school property, violence was exacerbated by a complex of factors which included parental impotence, ghetto despair and an inflexible, unimaginative school system. These phenomena seemed to react with the advent of the civil-rights movement and released a new kind of energy.

"The civil-rights movement," said Dr. James P. Comer, a noted black psychiatrist at Yale University Medical School, "mobilized an aggression in many black youths by forcing them to challenge old notions about themselves. Perhaps for the first time in American history, young black people, collectively, began to feel good about themselves, since the new aggression became channeled and released as an urge toward achievement. And during that period, there was certainly a great amount of achievement by thousands of black students. Test scores shot up and grades generally improved. However, the civil-rights movement also mobilized in other youngsters an aggression which could not be channeled. The aggression became released as energy, but it couldn't be harnessed into curiosity or learning or an effort at mastery. The aggression simply remained exposed: Free. Unchanneled. And finally it turned itself into impulsive violent acts. Violence was a way — in a way, I think — for some

—Continued

Jack Slater, formerly an associate editor at 'Ebony' magazine, has joined 'The New York Times Magazine' staff as a manuscript editor.

568

566
Art Director Ruth Ansel
Designer Ruth Ansel
Photographer Paul Strand
"The Mexican Portfolio"
Editors Lewis Bergman
Jack Rosenthal
Publisher The New York Times Magazine

568
Art Director Mike Salisbury
Designers Mike Salisbury
Lloyd Ziff
Artist Christian Piper
Publisher Rolling Stone

"If you can read this, you're too damn close"

BY LUCIEN AGNIEL

The new Volkswagen, a sparkling yellow in the winter sunshine, was parked on one of the streets near Howard University in Washington, D.C. Behind the wheel sat a handsome student, intent on what the young woman beside him was saying. From time to time, a passing motorist sounded his car's horn—and each time the student raised an arm in acknowledgement without once losing interest in or turning away from the conversation.

Those horn blasts were elicited by a sticker which dominated the VW's rear bumper with this appealing message: HONK IF YOU LOVE JESUS. On this day, at least, motoring Christians were in a responsive mood.

The bumper sticker, a curiously American phenomenon, has had its ups and downs over the years, and at the moment it is up again. The messages are not confined to any single subject. They range from the trivial—BE ALERT: THIS COUNTRY NEEDS MORE LERTS—to the sociological—HAVING TROUBLE PARKING? SUPPORT PLANNED PARENTHOOD. There is even a bristling warning aimed at those who approach too rapidly or too close in traffic: IF YOU CAN READ THIS, YOU'RE TOO DAMN CLOSE.

Why do Americans advertise their peeves and preferences, their political favorites and their dogmas? No one is quite sure, but some social scientists think it's a combination of flamboyance and loneliness, a groping effort in a mechanized age to achieve a sense of community. It is often said of Americans that they treasure the freedom of movement and the privacy afforded them by the automobile. Yet somehow, when the car door slams shut, the windows close and the driver fastens his safety belt, he is overcome with a feeling of isolation. That's when the desire to reach out to strangers wells up—and that's when the motorist goes out and buys himself a bumper sticker.

Many of the stickers contain a deeply felt message. Thus, a political activist exhibits this slogan: AMERICA—CHANGE IT OR LOSE IT. A person resentful of permissiveness toward the young displays: IF YOU HATE POLICEMEN, NEXT TIME YOU NEED HELP CALL A HIPPIE. And one who feels that the American Indian was exploited and persecuted blares from his bumper: CUSTER HAD IT COMING, an allusion to the slaying by Indians of the famed Indian fighter, George Custer, in 1876.

Aldine Printing Company of Los Angeles, perhaps the nation's largest maker of bumper stickers, turned out 18 million of the little adhesive strips of luminescent writing in the presidential election year of 1972, most of which exhorted voters to favor candidates of the drivers' choice. The stickers usually sell for about 35 cents. Overall, it's estimated that the annual sale of bumper stickers runs around 50 million; that makes it a $17-million business.

The origin of the bumper sticker craze is obscure. It goes back at least to the ill-fated presidential campaign of Alfred Landon in 1936, when those who supported the Kansas Republican bolted metal sunflowers—the Kansas state flower—to the rear bumpers of their automobiles. One theory holds that the bumper sticker evolved from advertising placards in buses and streetcars around the turn of the century.

In today's era of mass communication, word of clever bumper stickers gets around fast. Some current ones: STAMP OUT OLD AGE—SMOKE CIGARETTES; MY GOD'S NOT DEAD—SORRY ABOUT YOURS; KEEP YOUR CITY CLEAN—EAT A PIGEON; FIGHT INFLATION—HIBERNATE. The Texas Memorial Museum in Austin, Texas, has a collection of some 10,000 stickers. Mrs. Willena Adams, editor of museum publications, says: "We feel that bumper stickers are a vital part of the 20th century's legacy. There has been as much creativity shown by Americans in making bumper stickers as in some of the best-selling novels." □

LOVE
THINK TENNIS
BE A FRIEND
SAVE WATER
BATHE WITH A FRIEND
STAMP OUT OLD AGE
SMOKE CIGARETTES
KEEP AMERICA BEAUTIFUL
SWALLOW YOUR BEER CANS
PRESERVE WILD LIFE
THROW A PARTY
Re-elect U.S. Senator
CASE
Leave Your Brain to Science NOW
ESCHEW OBFUSCATION
SOYEZ A LA MODE
PARLEZ FRANCAIS
Green Survival
...it depends on you.
THINK SNOW
PEACE
TOMORROW IS CANCELED DUE TO LACK OF INTEREST
1378
Virginia is for lovers.
BUMPER STICKER
pollution STINKS
LIVE BETTER
WORK UNION
913·OVN
NEW YORK
THINK MORE TALK LESS
GREED KILLS

569

A CHRISTMAS PRESENCE

570

569
Art Director Thaddeus A. Miksinski, Jr.
Designer Thaddeus A. Miksinski, Jr.
Photographer Barry Blackman
Writer Lucien Agniel
Publisher Topic Magazine

570
Art Director Nancy Kent
Designer Nancy Kent
Photographer Joel Baldwin
Editor Anne Kampmann
Writer Mary Louise Ransdell
Publisher Town & Country

MARIA
BY DAVID SHAW

571

"Nothing Matters But the Fever"
Gregg Allman and Dicky Betts
by Tim Cahill

572

ROLLING STONE, JUNE 20, 1974

573

571
Art Director Mike Salisbury
Designer Lloyd Ziff
Photographer Annie Leibovitz
Publisher Rolling Stone

572
Art Director Tony Lane
Designer Tony Lane
Photographer Pete Turner
Publisher Rolling Stone

573
Art Director Mike Salisbury
Designer Lloyd Ziff
Photographer Warner Bros. Pictures
Publisher Rolling Stone

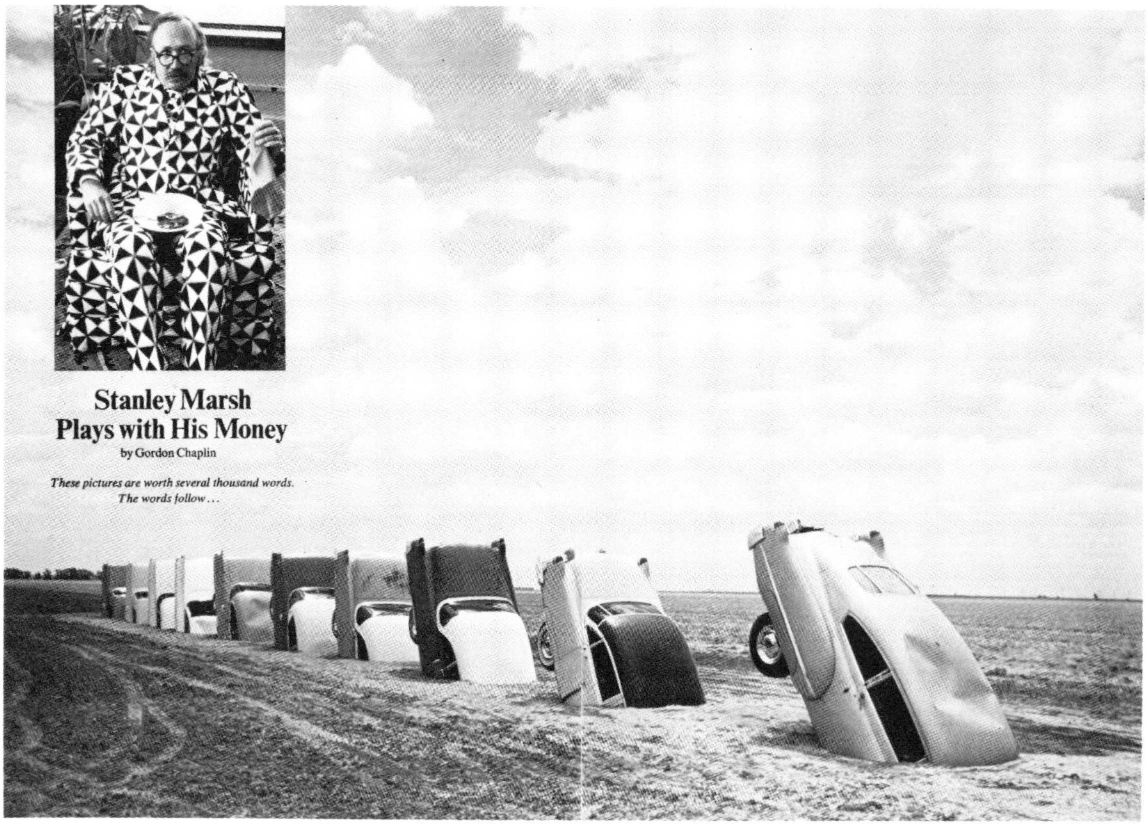
Stanley Marsh
Plays with His Money
by Gordon Chaplin
These pictures are worth several thousand words.
The words follow...

574

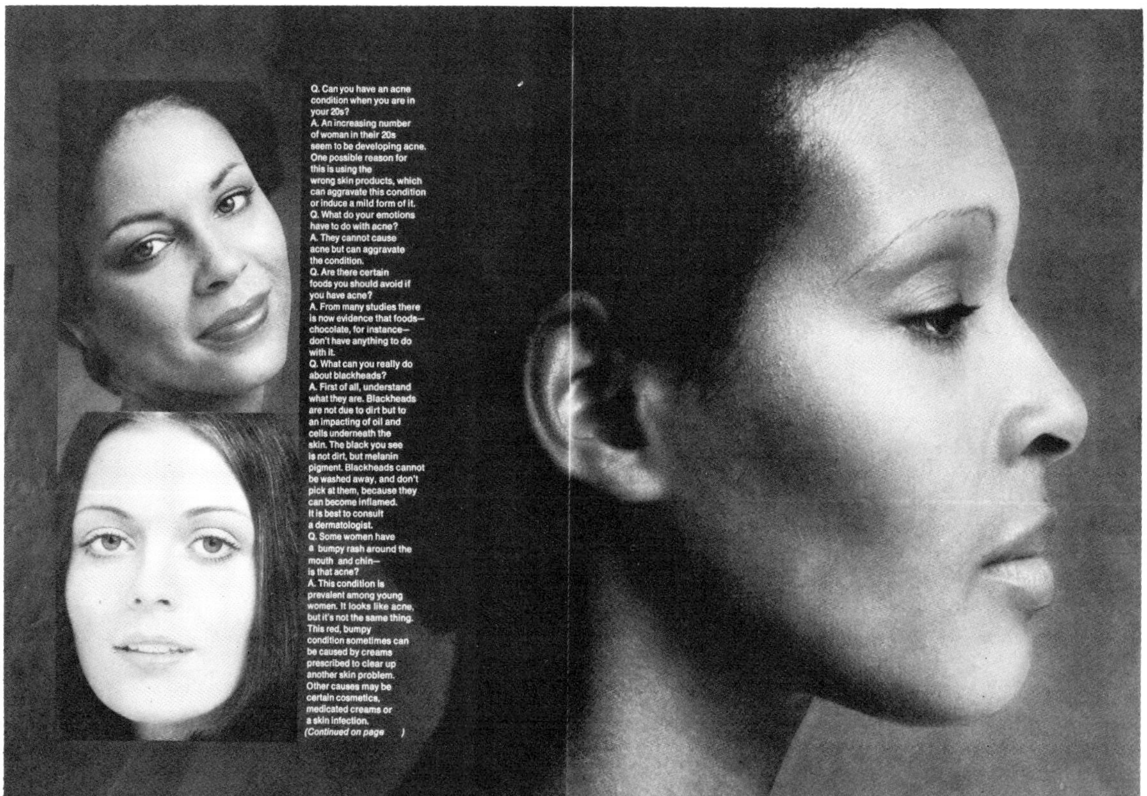
Q. Can you have an acne condition when you are in your 20s?
A. An increasing number of woman in their 20s seem to be developing acne. One possible reason for this is using the wrong skin products, which can aggravate this condition or induce a mild form of it.
Q. What do your emotions have to do with acne?
A. They cannot cause acne but can aggravate the condition.
Q. Are there certain foods you should avoid if you have acne?
A. From many studies there is now evidence that foods—chocolate, for instance—don't have anything to do with it.
Q. What can you really do about blackheads?
A. First of all, understand what they are. Blackheads are not due to dirt but to an impacting of oil and cells underneath the skin. The black you see is not dirt, but melanin pigment. Blackheads cannot be washed away, and don't pick at them, because they can become inflamed. It is best to consult a dermatologist.
Q. Some women have a bumpy rash around the mouth and chin—is that acne?
A. This condition is prevalent among young women. It looks like acne, but it's not the same thing. This red, bumpy condition sometimes can be caused by creams prescribed to clear up another skin problem. Other causes may be certain cosmetics, medicated creams or a skin infection.
(Continued on page)

575

574
Art Director Richard Weigand
Designer Richard Weigand
Photographer Bud Lee
Writer Gordon Chaplin
Publisher Esquire

575
Art Director William Cadge
Designer Ed Sobel
Photographer Ken Mori
Editor Jean Adams
Publisher Redbook

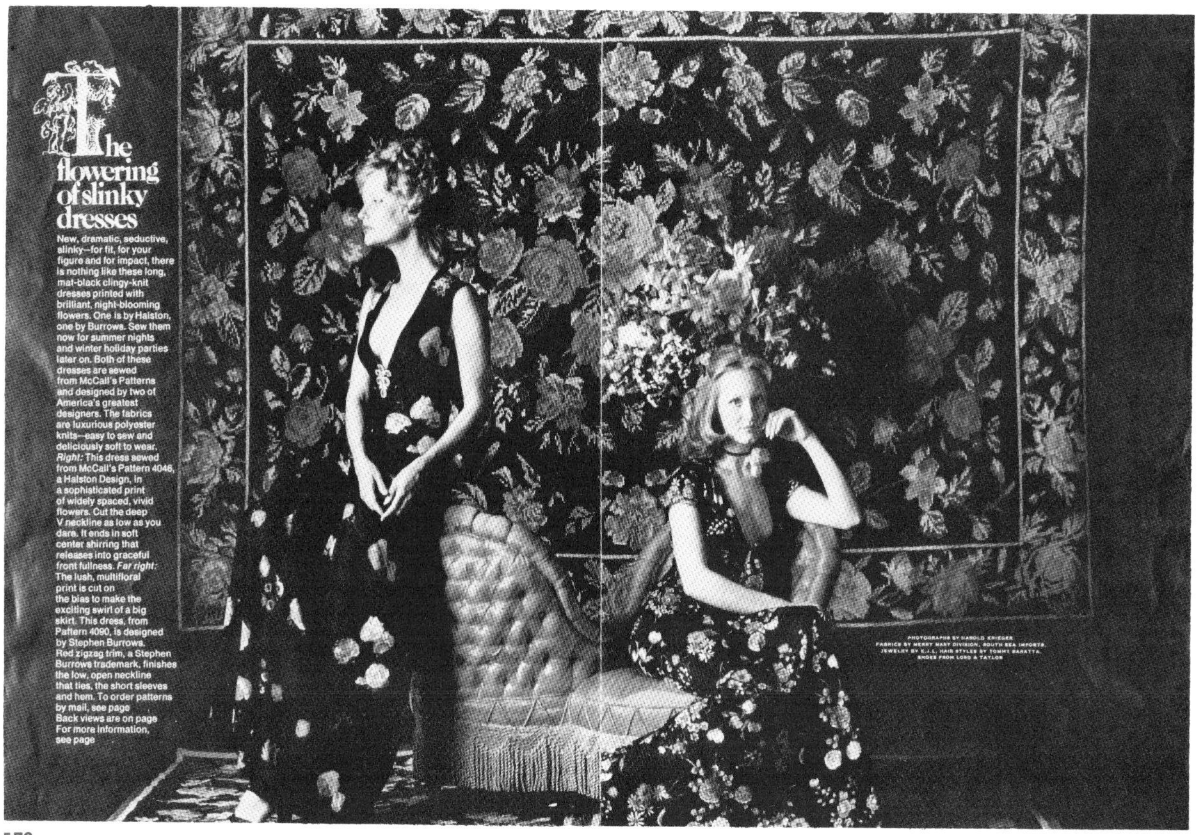
The flowering of slinky dresses
New, dramatic, seductive, slinky—for fit, for your figure and for impact, there is nothing like these long, mat-black clingy-knit dresses printed with brilliant, night-blooming flowers. One is by Halston, one by Burrows. Sew them now for summer nights and winter holiday parties later on. Both of these dresses are sewed from McCall's Patterns and designed by two of America's greatest designers. The fabrics are luxurious polyester knits—easy to sew and deliciously soft to wear. *Right:* This dress sewed from McCall's Pattern 4046, a Halston Design, in a sophisticated print of widely spaced, vivid flowers. Cut the deep V neckline as low as you dare. It ends in soft center shirring that releases into graceful front fullness. *Far right:* The lush, multifloral print is cut on the bias to make the exciting swirl of a big skirt. This dress, from Pattern 4090, is designed by Stephen Burrows. Red zigzag trim, a Stephen Burrows trademark, finishes the low, open neckline that ties, the short sleeves and hem. To order patterns by mail, see page
Back views are on page
For more information, see page
PHOTOGRAPHS BY HAROLD KRIEGER
FABRICS BY MERRY MART DIVISION, SOUTH SEA IMPORTS.
JEWELRY BY K.J.L. HAIR STYLES BY TOMMY SARATTA.
SHOES FROM LORD & TAYLOR

576

32
ROLLING STONE, MARCH 14, 1974

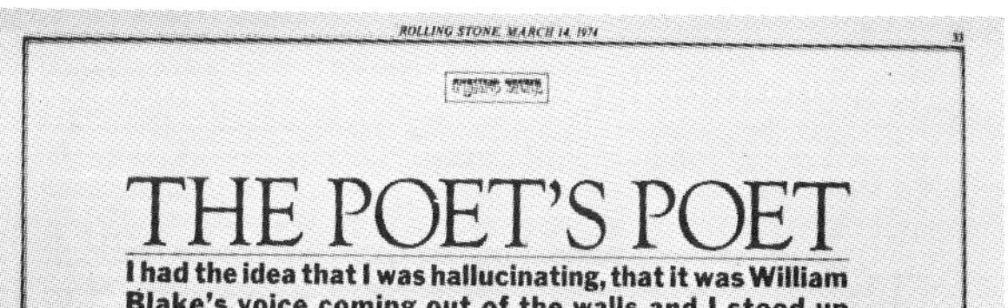

ROLLING STONE, MARCH 14, 1974 33

THE POET'S POET

I had the idea that I was hallucinating, that it was William Blake's voice coming out of the walls and I stood up and put my hands on the walls and they were vibrating.

By MICHAEL McCLURE

Memory is a beautiful thing—as I get older I learn to cherish it. It seems so beautiful or ugly that it is often more than real. Sometimes the vision is lit up with imagination; sometimes the imaginings have the shapes of real acts and gestures we call experience.

Experience is physical matter—and there is no sense in hanging onto it. It is a pleasure to let memory pour through the consciousness like nuggets of gold and moss agates and crystals of quartz clicking through the fingers at a rock shop. One never plans to keep those stones but the pleasure of feeling them is lovely.

The autoharp Bob Dylan gave me early in 1966 sat on the mantelpiece for six weeks before I picked it up and strummed it. A black and magical autoharp. Afraid of music, I had always felt totally unmusical—except in appreciation. Bob had asked me what instrument I'd like to play (I was writing song lyrics). I said autoharp out of the clear blue though I had no picture of what an autoharp looked like. There must have been people playing them on farms in my Kansas childhood.

San Francisco poets were poor in 1965 and it was an impressive present and it committed me to music. There was the interest in writing lyrics and perhaps a new way to use rhyme.

Rock had mutual attraction for all; a common tribal dancing ground whether we were poets, or printers, or sculptors, it was a form we all shared. I spent a year and a half learning to play autoharp in an eccentric way and wrote songs like "The Blue Lyon Laughs," "The Allen Ginsberg for President Waltz" and "Come on God, and Buy Me a Mercedes Benz."

I bought an old amplifier and stood in front of the mirror whanging on the autoharp. Obsessed with John Keats' question: What weapon has the lion but himself. I tried to make it a song and sang it so many times so loudly that I wonder what the neighbors thought in those old days when acid rock was a baby.

In December, 1965, when we had been bombing Vietnam for eight months, Dylan read "Poisoned Wheat," a long anti-war poem of mine. One day as we were eating chicken, I handed him another copy. He left huge greasy fingerprints and he did it with complete aplomb. It seemed very non-materialistic and natural not to notice the blotches. It seemed right to treat works of art as part of the transformations of life. Later I gave the copy to a girl who wanted Bob's fingerprints.

The first person to play a Dylan album for me was poet David Meltzer. It was Dylan's first album, and I heard it shortly after it came out in March or April of 1962. I could not understand what David heard in the album. In high school I knew people at the University of Chicago and in New York City who were singing like that—just some hillbilly-intellectual music that I'd gotten bored with earlier. In retrospect, Dylan must have shown a direct creative thrust without the "Art" self-consciousness of other singers.

Mr. McClure is a poet and a playwright. His latest play, "Gorf," debuted in San Francisco recently.

Early in 1965 a friend of my wife Joanna came to visit and brought the Dylan album with "She Belongs to Me." The album had changed her life-image from a tragic loser to a proud artist. Joanna heard and understood Dylan at once and completely, I think.

In 1965 everyone had been after me to listen to Dylan carefully—to sit down and listen to the words *and* the music. I absolutely did *not* want to hear Dylan. I imagined, without admitting it to myself, that Dylan was a threat to poetry—or to my poetry. I sensed that a new mode of poetry, or rebirth of an old one, might replace my mode. In the long run, rock lyrics have sensitized many people to words and brought them to discover poetry.

At last I could not resist Joanna's demand that I hear the album. We had a banged-up record player in the hallway at the top of the stairs. Late at night, in the pale-gray hallway-light, Joanna sat me down in front of the speaker and told me to listen to the words. I began to hear what the words were saying, not just the jangling of the guitar and the harmonica and the whining nasal voice. The next thing I knew I was crying. It was "Gates Of Eden": "At dawn my lover comes to me/ And tells me of her dreams/ With no attempts to shovel the glimpse/ Into the ditch of what each one means . . ."

I had the idea that I was hallucinating, that it was William Blake's voice coming out of the walls and I stood up and put my hands on the walls and they were vibrating.

Then I went back to those people who had tried to get me to listen and I told them that I thought the revolution had begun. "Gates Of Eden" and those other songs seemed to open up the post-Freudian and post-existentialist era. Everyone didn't have to use the old explanations and the mildewed rationalities any longer.

By the time I met Bob, his poetry was important to me in the way that Kerouac's writing was. It was not something to imitate or be influenced by; it was the expression of a unique individual and his feelings and perceptions.

There is no way to second-guess poetry or to predict poetry or to convince a poet that the very best songs in the world are poetry if they are not. Bob Dylan is a poet, whether he has cherubs in his hair and fairy wings, or feet of clay, he is a poet. Those other people called "rock poets," "song poets," "folk poets," or whatever the rock critic is calling them this week, will be better off if they are appreciated as songwriters.

At a party after his concert at the Berkeley Community Theater in December, 1965, Dylan told me that he had not read Blake and did not know the poetry. That seemed hard to believe so I recited a few stanzas. One was the motto to "The Songs of Innocence and Experience" which begins: "The Good are attracted by Men's perceptions/ And think not for themselves/ Till Experience teaches them to catch/ And to cage the Fairies & Elves . . ."

Bob was sitting on the floor and everyone crowded around him. Joanna, who has a tendency to go to sleep when she's pleased and in a crowd, started to sleep with her head in my lap. Someone told her in an ugly way that she ought to wake up—that if she didn't want to hear what was being said, there were plenty of others who would like her place close to Dylan. One wonders if those were honors being paid to a popular poet, or a worshipful voice in the crowd that the poet argues against.

In 1965 that first Dylan concert in the Bay Area was at the Masonic Auditorium. In those days the Masonic seemed huge and rather plush. It was the first time I'd heard Bob Dylan in person. The records were beautiful but this was better—an immaculate performance with inflections or nuances different from the albums. Dylan was purest poet. Like an elf being, so perfect was he and so ferocious in his persistence for perfection. There was a verge of anger in him waiting for any obstacle to the event.

After the Masonic Auditorium concert we went to the Villa Romano Motel, where Bob and the Hawks were staying, and met Al Grossman. He, Joan Baez, Allen Ginsberg, and I spoke for a while. Joan said that Allen and I should be Bob's conscience. It seemed a beautiful thing to say, though not clear at the time. Later Joan wrote that we should hold Bob in our consciousness.

A night or two later, after another concert, there was a party for Bob in San Francisco. Ken Kesey bounced through the door with a few of his Merry Pranksters. Ruddy with the vigor of good health, Los Gatos sunshine and acid, Kesey immediately hit Dylan with something like, "Hey, man, you should try playing while you're high on acid." Without a pause Dylan said, "I did and it threw off my timing." There was no way to one-up Bob or to get ahead of him at any level or any time. You knew that pop stars like Dylan or Lennon drove around in black cars and they were careful and they were very fast and they were staying where they were and they were not kidding.

Nine years later, on the plane going to Dylan's Philadelphia concert, I reread Robert Duncan's small book, *Seventeenth Century Suite*. Duncan has vowed not to commercially publish any of his new poetry for 15 years, so that no pressure would direct him to write anything other than what he wishes most deeply. By canceling formal publication he was essentially vowing to please only himself. Robert made an edition of 300 copies of *Seventeenth Century Suite* and gave them to friends for Christmas gifts.

How incredibly far it is from Duncan's private edition of *Seventeenth Century Suite* to Dylan's millions of albums. Both are fine poetry and though they seem poles apart, they almost touch in their subtle images and

Continued

577

576
Art Director William Cadge
Designer Ed Sobel
Photographer Harold Krieger
Editor Lee Miles
Publisher Redbook

577
Art Director Mike Salisbury
Designer Lloyd Ziff
Artist David Levine
Publisher Rolling Stone

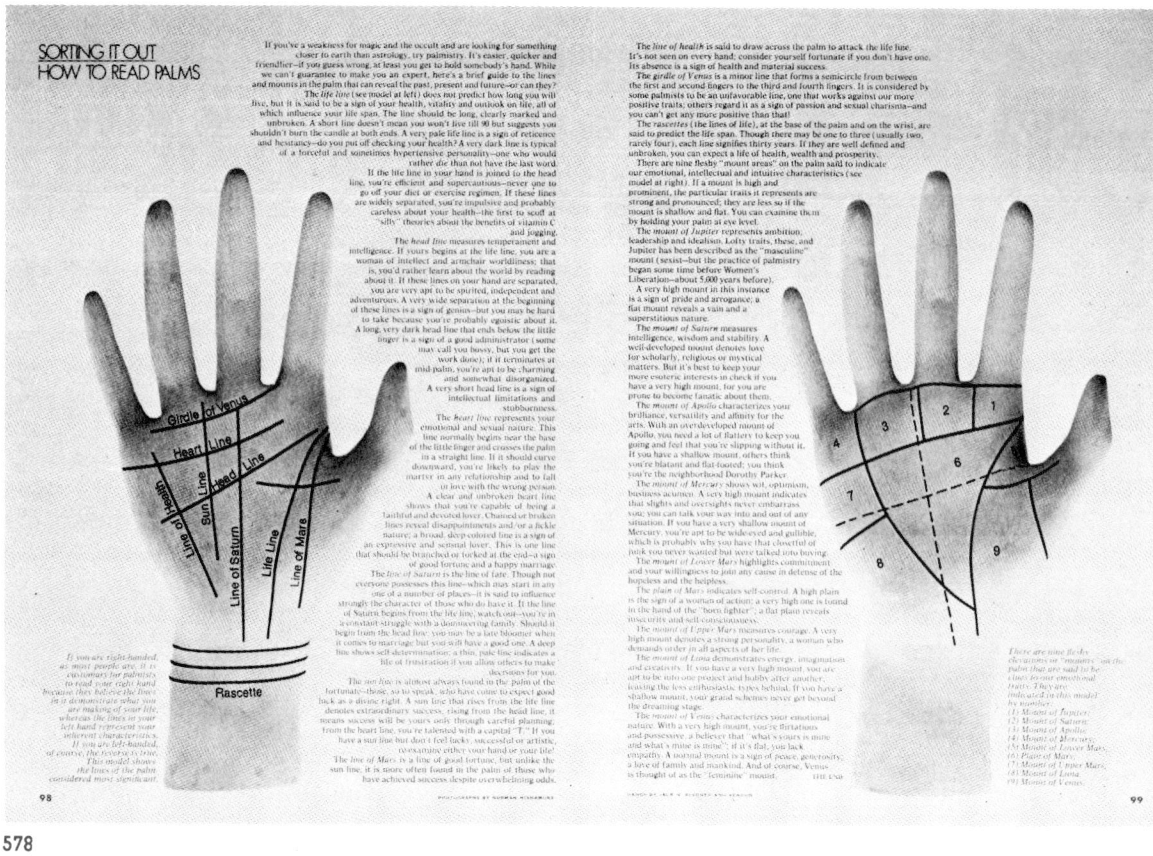

Girdle of Venus
Heart Line
Head Line
Line of Health
Sun Line
Line of Saturn
Life Line
Line of Mars
Rascette
1
2
3
4
6
7
8
9

SORTING IT OUT
HOW TO READ PALMS

If you've a weakness for magic and the occult and are looking for something closer to earth than astrology, try palmistry. It's easier, quicker and friendlier—if you guess wrong, at least you get to hold somebody's hand. While we can't guarantee to make you an expert, here's a brief guide to the lines and mounts in the palm that can reveal the past, present and future—or can they?

The *life line* (see model at left) does not predict how long you will live, but it is said to be a sign of your health, vitality and outlook on life, all of which influence your life span. The line should be long, clearly marked and unbroken. A short line doesn't mean you won't live till 90 but suggests you shouldn't burn the candle at both ends. A very pale life line is a sign of reticence and hesitancy—do you put off checking your health? A very dark line is typical of a forceful and sometimes hypertensive personality—one who would rather *die* than not have the last word.

If the life line in your hand is joined to the head line, you're efficient and supercautious—never one to go off your diet or exercise regimen. If these lines are widely separated, you're impulsive and probably careless about your health—the first to scoff at "silly" theories about the benefits of vitamin C and jogging.

The *head line* measures temperament and intelligence. If yours begins at the life line, you are a woman of intellect and armchair worldliness; that is, you'd rather learn about the world by reading about it. If these lines on your hand are separated, you are very apt to be spirited, independent and adventurous. A very wide separation at the beginning of these lines is a sign of genius—but you may be hard to take because you're probably egoistic about it. A long, very dark head line that ends below the little finger is a sign of a good administrator (some may call you bossy, but you get the work done); if it terminates at mid-palm, you're apt to be charming and somewhat disorganized. A very short head line is a sign of intellectual limitations and stubbornness.

The *heart line* represents your emotional and sexual nature. This line normally begins near the base of the little finger and crosses the palm in a straight line. If it should curve downward, you're likely to play the martyr in any relationship and to fall in love with the wrong person. A clear and unbroken heart line shows that you're capable of being a faithful and devoted lover. Chained or broken lines reveal disappointments and/or a fickle nature; a broad, deep-colored line is a sign of an expressive and sensual lover. This is one line that should be branched or forked at the end—a sign of good fortune and a happy marriage.

The *line of Saturn* is the line of fate. Though not everyone possesses this line—which may start in any one of a number of places—it is said to influence strongly the character of those who do have it. If the line of Saturn begins from the life line, watch out—you're in a constant struggle with a domineering family. Should it begin from the head line, you may be a late bloomer when it comes to marriage but you will have a good one. A deep line shows self-determination; a thin, pale line indicates a life of frustration if you allow others to make decisions for you.

The *sun line* is almost always found in the palm of the fortunate—those, so to speak, who have come to expect good luck as a divine right. A sun line that rises from the life line denotes extraordinary success; rising from the head line, it means success will be yours only through careful planning; from the heart line, you're talented with a capital "T." If you have a sun line but *don't* feel lucky, successful or artistic, re-examine either your hand or your life!

The *line of Mars* is a line of good fortune, but unlike the sun line, it is more often found in the palm of those who have achieved success despite overwhelming odds.

If you are right-handed, as most people are, it is customary for palmists to read your right hand because they believe the lines in it demonstrate what you are making of your life, whereas the lines in your left hand represent your inherent characteristics. If you are left-handed, of course, the reverse is true. This model shows the lines of the palm considered most significant.

PHOTOGRAPHS BY NORMAN NISHIMURA

98

The *line of health* is said to draw across the palm to attack the life line. It's not seen on every hand; consider yourself fortunate if you don't have one. Its absence is a sign of health and material success.

The *girdle of Venus* is a minor line that forms a semicircle from between the first and second fingers to the third and fourth fingers. It is considered by some palmists to be an unfavorable line, one that works against our more positive traits; others regard it as a sign of passion and sexual charisma—and you can't get any more positive than that!

The *rascettes* (the lines of life), at the base of the palm and on the wrist, are said to predict the life span. Though there may be one to three (usually two, rarely four), each line signifies thirty years. If they are well defined and unbroken, you can expect a life of health, wealth and prosperity.

There are nine fleshy "mount areas" on the palm said to indicate our emotional, intellectual and intuitive characteristics (see model at right). If a mount is high and prominent, the particular traits it represents are strong and pronounced; they are less so if the mount is shallow and flat. You can examine them by holding your palm at eye level.

The *mount of Jupiter* represents ambition, leadership and idealism. Lofty traits, these, and Jupiter has been described as the "masculine" mount (sexist—but the practice of palmistry began some time before Women's Liberation—about 5,000 years before).

A very high mount in this instance is a sign of pride and arrogance; a flat mount reveals a vain and a superstitious nature.

The *mount of Saturn* measures intelligence, wisdom and stability. A well-developed mount denotes love for scholarly, religious or mystical matters. But it's best to keep your more esoteric interests in check if you have a very high mount, for you are prone to become fanatic about them.

The *mount of Apollo* characterizes your brilliance, versatility and affinity for the arts. With an overdeveloped mount of Apollo, you need a lot of flattery to keep you going and feel that you're slipping without it. If you have a shallow mount, others think you're blatant and flat-footed; you think you're the neighborhood Dorothy Parker.

The *mount of Mercury* shows wit, optimism, business acumen. A very high mount indicates that slights and oversights never embarrass you; you can talk your way into and out of any situation. If you have a very shallow mount of Mercury, you're apt to be wide-eyed and gullible, which is probably why you have that closetful of junk you never wanted but were talked into buying.

The *mount of Lower Mars* highlights commitment and your willingness to join any cause in defense of the hopeless and the helpless.

The *plain of Mars* indicates self-control. A high plain is the sign of a woman of action; a very high one is found in the hand of the "born fighter"; a flat plain reveals insecurity and self-consciousness.

The *mount of Upper Mars* measures courage. A very high mount denotes a strong personality, a woman who demands order in all aspects of her life.

The *mount of Luna* demonstrates energy, imagination and creativity. If you have a very high mount, you are apt to be into one project and hobby after another, leaving the less enthusiastic types behind. If you have a shallow mount, your grand schemes never get beyond the dreaming stage.

The *mount of Venus* characterizes your emotional nature. With a very high mount, you're flirtatious and possessive, a believer that "what's yours is mine and what's mine is mine"; if it's flat, you lack empathy. A normal mount is a sign of peace, generosity, a love of family and mankind. And of course, Venus is thought of as the "feminine" mount. THE END

There are nine fleshy elevations or "mounts" on the palm that are said to be clues to our emotional traits. They are indicated in this model by number: (1) Mount of Jupiter; (2) Mount of Saturn; (3) Mount of Apollo; (4) Mount of Mercury; (5) Mount of Lower Mars; (6) Plain of Mars; (7) Mount of Upper Mars; (8) Mount of Luna; (9) Mount of Venus.

99

578

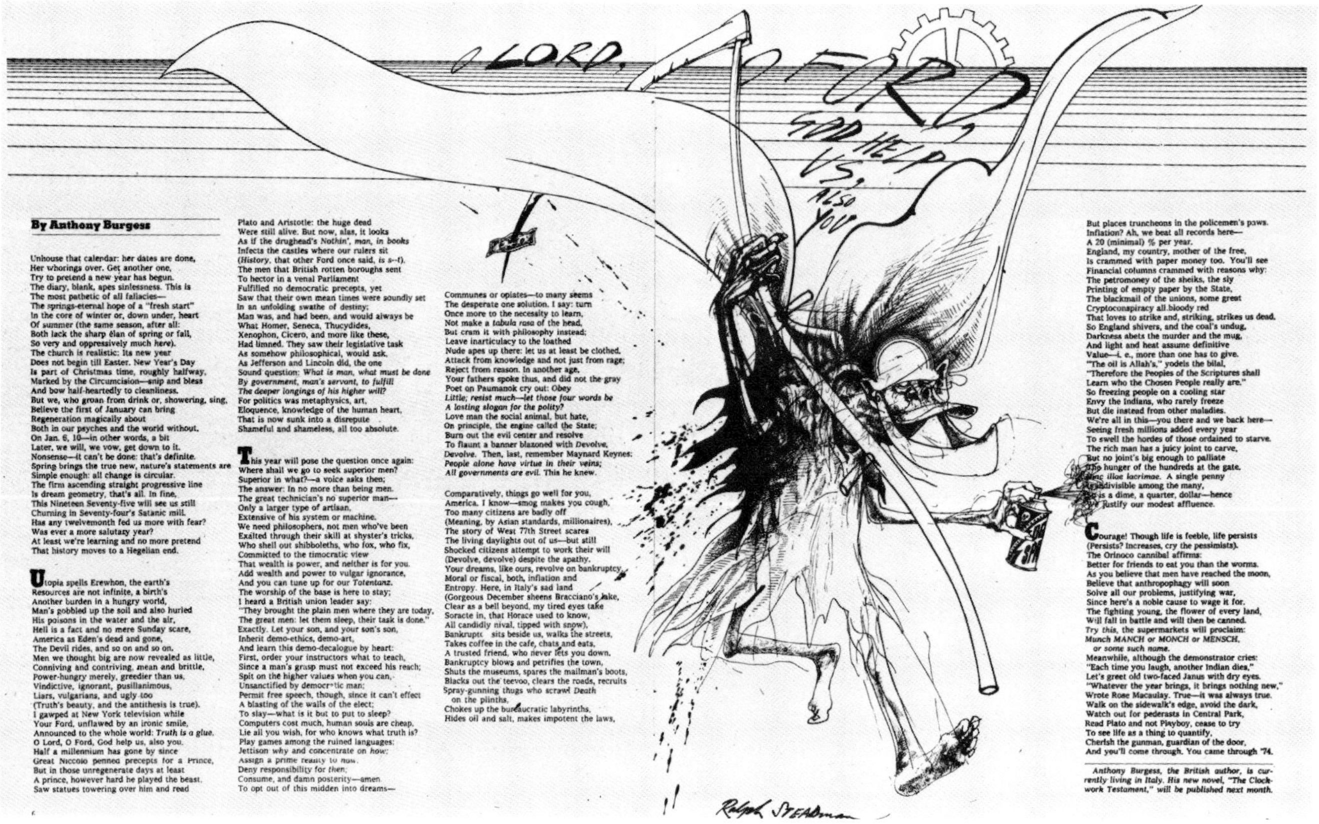

O LORD, O FORD,
GOD HELP US,
ALSO YOU
Ralph STEADMAN

By Anthony Burgess

Unhouse that calendar: her dates are done,
Her whorings over. Get another one,
Try to pretend a new year has begun.
The diary, blank, apes sinlessness. This is
The most pathetic of all fallacies—
The springs-eternal hope of a "fresh start"
In the core of winter or, down under, heart
Of summer (the same season, after all:
Both lack the sharp élan of spring or fall,
So very and oppressively much *here*).
The church is realistic: its new year
Does not begin till Easter. New Year's Day
Is part of Christmas time, roughly halfway,
Marked by the Circumcision—snip and bless
And bow half-heartedly to cleanliness.
But we, who groan from drink or, showering, sing,
Believe the first of January can bring
Regeneration magically about
Both in our psyches and the world without.
On Jan. 6, 10—in other words, a bit
Later, we will, we vow, get down to it.
Nonsense—it can't be done: that's definite.
Spring brings the true new, nature's statements are
Simple enough: all change is circular.
The firm ascending straight progressive line
Is dream geometry, that's all. In fine,
This Nineteen Seventy-five will see us still
Churning in Seventy-four's Satanic mill.
Has any twelvemonth fed us more with fear?
Was ever a more salutary year?
At least we're learning and no more pretend
That history moves to a Hegelian end.

Utopia spells Erewhon, the earth's
Resources are not infinite, a birth's
Another burden in a hungry world,
Man's gobbled up the soil and also hurled
His poisons in the water and the air,
Hell is a fact and no mere Sunday scare,
America as Eden's dead and gone,
The Devil rides, and so on and so on.
Men we thought big are now revealed as little,
Conniving and contriving, mean and brittle,
Power-hungry merely, greedier than us,
Vindictive, ignorant, pusillanimous,
Liars, vulgarians, and ugly too
(Truth's beauty, and the antithesis is true).
I gawped at New York television while
Your Ford, unflawed by an ironic smile,
Announced to the whole world: *Truth is a glue.*
O Lord, O Ford, God help us, also you.
Half a millennium has gone by since
Great Niccolo penned precepts for a Prince,
But in those unregenerate days at least
A prince, however hard he played the beast,
Saw statues towering over him and read
Plato and Aristotle: the huge dead
Were still alive. But now, alas, it looks
As if the drughead's *Nothin', man, in books*
Infects the castles where our rulers sit
(*History*, that other Ford once said, *is s--t*).
The men that British rotten boroughs sent
To hector in a venal Parliament
Fulfilled no democratic precepts, yet
Saw that their own mean times were soundly set
In an unfolding swathe of destiny;
Man was, and had been, and would always be
What Homer, Seneca, Thucydides,
Xenophon, Cicero, and more like these,
Had limned. They saw their legislative task
As somehow philosophical, would ask,
As Jefferson and Lincoln did, the one
Sound question: *What is man, what must be done*
By government, man's servant, to fulfill
The deeper longings of his higher will?
For politics was metaphysics, art,
Eloquence, knowledge of the human heart,
That is now sunk into a disrepute
Shameful and shameless, all too absolute.

This year will pose the question once again:
Where shall we go to seek superior men?
Superior in what?—a voice asks then;
The answer: In no more than being men.
The great technician's no superior man—
Only a larger type of artisan,
Extensive of his system or machine.
We need philosophers, not men who've been
Exalted through their skill at shyster's tricks,
Who shell out shibboleths, who fox, who fix,
Committed to the timocratic view
That wealth is power, and neither is for you.
Add wealth and power to vulgar ignorance,
And you can tune up for our *Totentanz*.
The worship of the base is here to stay;
I heard a British union leader say:
"They brought the plain men where they are today,
The great men: let them sleep, their task is done."
Exactly. Let your son, and your son's son,
Inherit demo-ethics, demo-art,
And learn this demo-decalogue by heart:
First, order your instructors what to teach,
Since a man's grasp must not exceed his reach;
Spit on the higher values when you can,
Unsanctified by democr*tic man;
Permit free speech, though, since it can't effect
A blasting of the walls of the elect;
To slay—what is it but to put to sleep?
Computers cost much, human souls are cheap.
Lie all you wish, for who knows what truth is?
Play games among the ruined languages;
Jettison *why* and concentrate on *how*;
Assign a prime reality to *now*.
Deny responsibility for *then*;
Consume, and damn posterity—amen.
To opt out of this midden into dreams—
Communes or opiates—to many seems
The desperate one solution. I say: turn
Once more to the necessity to learn,
Not make a *tabula rasa* of the head,
But cram it with philosophy instead;
Leave inarticulacy to the loathed
Nude apes up there: let us at least be clothed.
Attack from knowledge and not just from rage;
Reject from reason. In another age,
Your fathers spoke thus, and did not the gray
Poet on Paumanok cry out: *Obey*
Little; resist much—let those four words be
A lasting slogan for the polity?
Love man the social animal, but hate,
On principle, the engine called the State;
Burn out the evil center and resolve
To flaunt a banner blazoned with *Devolve,*
Devolve. Then, last, remember Maynard Keynes:
People alone have virtue in their veins;
All governments are evil. This he knew.

Comparatively, things go well for you,
America. I know—smog makes you cough,
Too many citizens are badly off
(Meaning, by Asian standards, millionaires).
The story of West 77th Street scares
The living daylights out of us—but still
Shocked citizens attempt to work their will
(Devolve, devolve) despite the apathy.
Your dreams, like ours, revolve on bankruptcy,
Moral or fiscal, both, inflation and
Entropy. Here, in Italy's sad land
(Gorgeous December sheens Bracciano's lake,
Clear as a bell beyond, my tired eyes take
Soracte in, that Horace used to know,
All candidly nival, tipped with snow),
Bankrupt[illegible] sits beside us, walks the streets,
Takes coffee in the cafe, chats and eats,
A trusted friend, who never lets you down.
Bankruptcy blows and petrifies the town,
Shuts the museums, spares the mailman's boots,
Blacks out the teevoo, clears the roads, recruits
Spray-gunning thugs who scrawl *Death*
on the plinths,
Chokes up the bureaucratic labyrinths,
Hides oil and salt, makes impotent the laws,
But places truncheons in the policemen's paws.
Inflation? Ah, we beat all records here—
A 20 (minimal) % per year.
England, my country, mother of the free,
Is crammed with paper money too. You'll see
Financial columns crammed with reasons why:
The petromoney of the sheiks, the sly
Printing of empty paper by the State,
The blackmail of the unions, some great
Cryptoconspiracy all bloody red
That loves to strike and, striking, strikes us dead.
So England shivers, and the coal's undug,
Darkness abets the murder and the mug,
And light and heat assume definitive
Value—i. e., more than one has to give.
"The oil is Allah's," yodels the bilal,
"Therefore the Peoples of the Scriptures shall
Learn who the Chosen People really are."
So freezing people on a cooling star
Envy the Indians, who rarely freeze
But die instead from other maladies.
We're all in this—you there and we back here—
Seeing fresh millions added every year
To swell the hordes of those ordained to starve.
The rich man has a juicy joint to carve,
But no joint's big enough to palliate
[illegible] hunger of the hundreds at the gate.
[illegible] *illae lacrimae.* A single penny
[illegible]divisible among the many,
[illegible] is a dime, a quarter, dollar—hence
[illegible] justify our modest affluence.

Courage! Though life is feeble, life persists
(Persists? Increases, cry the pessimists).
The Orinoco cannibal affirms:
Better for friends to eat you than the worms.
As you believe that men have reached the moon,
Believe that anthropophagy will soon
Solve all our problems, justifying war,
Since here's a noble cause to wage it for.
The fighting young, the flower of every land,
Will fall in battle and will then be canned.
Try this, the supermarkets will proclaim:
Munch MANCH or MONCH or MENSCH,
or some such name.
Meanwhile, although the demonstrator cries:
"Each time you laugh, another Indian dies,"
Let's greet old two-faced Janus with dry eyes.
"Whatever the year brings, it brings nothing new,"
Wrote Rose Macaulay. True—it was always true.
Walk on the sidewalk's edge, avoid the dark,
Watch out for pederasts in Central Park,
Read Plato and not Playboy, cease to try
To see life as a thing to quantify,
Cherish the gunman, guardian of the door,
And you'll come through. You came through '74.

Anthony Burgess, the British author, is currently living in Italy. His new novel, "The Clockwork Testament," will be published next month.

579

578
Art Directors William Cadge
Verdun Cook
Designer Ed Sobel
Artists Jack Rindner
Verdun Cook
Photographer Norman Nishimura
Editor Fran Ruffin
Publisher Redbook

579
Art Director Ruth Ansel
Designer Ruth Ansel
Artist Ralph Steadman
Editors Lewis Bergman
Jack Rosenthal
Publisher The New York Times
Magazine

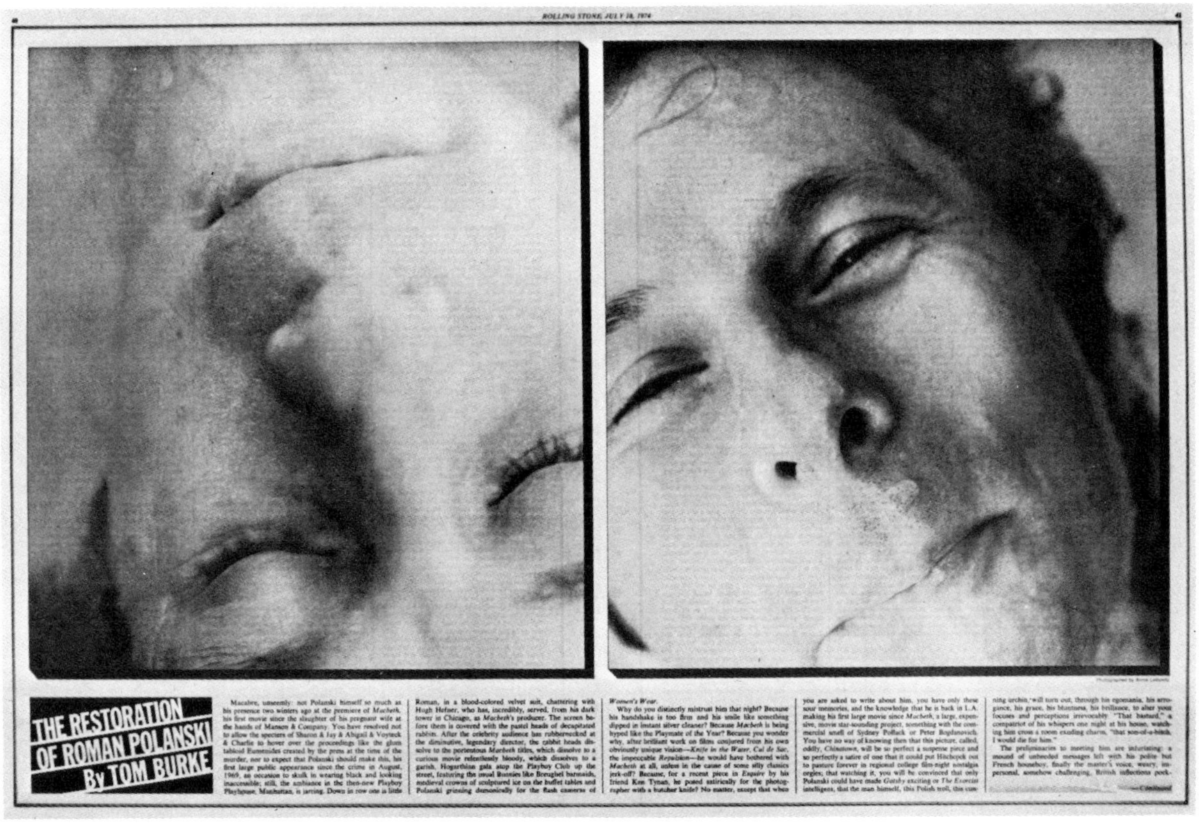

ROLLING STONE, JULY 18, 1974

THE RESTORATION OF ROMAN POLANSKI

By TOM BURKE

Macabre, unseemly: not Polanski himself so much as his presence two winters ago at the premiere of *Macbeth*, his first movie since the slaughter of his pregnant wife at the hands of Manson & Company. You have resolved not to allow the specters of Sharon & Jay & Abigail & Voytek & Charlie to hover over the proceedings like the glum tabloid Eumenides created by the press at the time of the murder, nor to expect that Polanski should make this, his first large public appearance since the crime in August, 1969, an occasion to skulk in wearing black and looking inaccessible; still, the ambiance in the then-new Playboy Playhouse, Manhattan, is jarring. Down in row one is little Roman, in a blood-colored velvet suit, chattering with Hugh Hefner, who has, incredibly, served, from his dark tower in Chicago, as *Macbeth's* producer. The screen before them is covered with the pastel heads of decapitated rabbits. After the celebrity audience has rubbernecked at the diminutive, legendary director, the rabbit heads dissolve to the portentous *Macbeth* titles, which dissolve to a curious movie relentlessly bloody, which dissolves to a garish, Hogarthian gala atop the Playboy Club up the street, featuring the usual Bunnies like Breughel barmaids, medieval crowns of sculptured ice on the buffet tables and Polanski grinning demonically for the flash cameras of *Women's Wear*.

Why do you distinctly mistrust him that night? Because his handshake is too firm and his smile like something dipped in instant silver cleaner? Because *Macbeth* is being hyped like the Playmate of the Year? Because you wonder why, after brilliant work on films conjured from his own obviously unique vision—*Knife in the Water*, *Cul de Sac*, the impeccable *Repulsion*—he would have bothered with *Macbeth* at all, unless in the cause of some silly classics jerk-off? Because, for a recent piece in *Esquire* by his friend Ken Tynan, he posed satirically for the photographer with a butcher knife? No matter, except that when you are asked to write about him, you have only these sour memories, and the knowledge that he is back in L.A. making his first large movie since *Macbeth*, a large, expensive, movie star-sounding project, something with the commercial smell of Sydney Pollack or Peter Bogdanovich. You have no way of knowing then that this picture, called, oddly, *Chinatown*, will be so perfect a suspense piece and so perfectly a satire of one that it could put Hitchcock out to pasture forever in regional college film-night nostalgia orgies; that watching it, you will be convinced that only Polanski could have made *Gatsby* exciting or *The Exorcist* intelligent; that the man himself, this Polish troll, this cunning urchin, will turn out, through his egomania, his arrogance, his grace, his bluntness, his brilliance, to alter your focuses and perceptions irrevocably. "That bastard," a compatriot of his whispers one night at his house, watching him cross a room exuding charm, "that son-of-a-bitch, I would die for him."

The preliminaries to meeting him are infuriating: a mound of unheeded messages left with his polite but French houseboy, finally the master's voice, weary, impersonal, somehow challenging, British inflections pock-

—Continued

580

ROLLING STONE, JANUARY 30, 1975

JOURNEY TO THE CENTER OF THE STAGE

BY CAMERON CROWE

"Have you heard the gag about the ten-year-old twin brothers, Peter and Paul?" A Howard Johnson's coffee shop full of ditchers from a nearby Pittsburgh high school casually eavesdrops on Rick Wakeman's lunch-time tale. "Well, they're the filthiest pair of kids you'd ever want to meet. I mean, it wasn't, 'Tuck me into bed, please mum?' It was, 'Fix the goddamn covers, bitch.'" Rick bends to take a loud slurp from a soup spoon, his blond waterfall of hair drawing a curtain across his face. "So anyway, one night their parents decide the only way to clean up Peter and Paul's language is to beat the crap out of the next one that swears.

"Sure enough, the next morning at breakfast, the mother asks Peter what he'd like to eat. 'I'll have some fucking corn flakes,' Peter growls. So the father immediately jumps up and begins to sock, stab, maim and ax the kid until he's just a pulpy mess lying in a pool of blood. Really gross. Dad sits back down and asks Paul what *he'd* like to eat. Paul just shrugs and says, 'Well, I'd be a cunt if I asked for corn flakes.'" The entire coffee shop explodes in guffaws. Wakeman, always the class clown, leans back in his seat, basking in the laughter. He loves it.

The lunch is a quick take of Wakeman, who at 25 seems to be at the front edge of a cresting wave of interest in a classically informed, jazz-inclined, rock-based hybrid music that encompasses John McLaughlin, Herbie Hancock, Yes, Pink Floyd, Emerson, Lake & Palmer and European groups like Magma, Tasavallan Presidentti and Tangerine Dream. Wakeman skates the classical perimeter like a caricature surfer, tall, lean and blond, loose and witty enough to cover the high-mindedness of it all in a mask of infectious humor.

It's been six months since he bailed out of Yes, surely one of the world's most prosperous bands, on the eve of a multimillion-dollar summer tour. There's been no time for regrets. With a two-album catalog of solo works to peddle, he promptly took off on a 20-stop tour of North America's largest halls and arenas. Despite sizable crowds, the month-long journey lost a substantial amount of money. Credit that to a payroll listing a 118-person entourage, a rented Lockheed Electra and the expensive David Measham and his National Philharmonic Orchestra and Choir of America. "It's not really a bloodbath," insists Yes/Wakeman manager Brian Lane, "just a light shower." One rock manager computes that it must have been a six-figure shower, but for Wakeman that's light. He invested $50,000 in the album production of *Journey to the Centre of the Earth* with the attitude, "It wasn't wasted, it was invested." *Journey* is approaching platinum status, its predecessor, *The Six Wives of Henry VIII*, is near gold, and the skyrocketing record sales are expected to more than recoup the tour expenses. More [illegible], one senses, the roadwork provided [illegible] with an inval-

581

580
Art Director Mike Salisbury
Designers Mike Salisbury
Lloyd Ziff
Photographer Annie Leibovitz
Publisher Rolling Stone

581
Art Director Tony Lane
Designer Tony Lane
Photographer Neal Preston
Publisher Rolling Stone

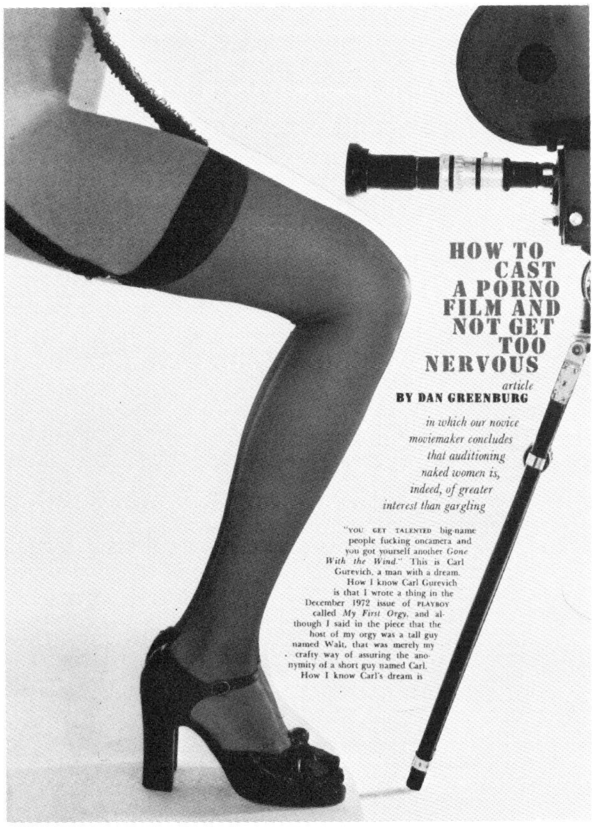

HOW TO CAST A PORNO FILM AND NOT GET TOO NERVOUS

article
BY DAN GREENBURG

in which our novice moviemaker concludes that auditioning naked women is, indeed, of greater interest than gargling

"YOU GET TALENTED big-name people fucking oncamera and you got yourself another *Gone With the Wind*." This is Carl Gurevich, a man with a dream.

How I know Carl Gurevich is that I wrote a thing in the December 1972 issue of PLAYBOY called *My First Orgy*, and although I said in the piece that the host of my orgy was a tall guy named Walt, that was merely my crafty way of assuring the anonymity of a short guy named Carl.

How I know Carl's dream is

HOW TO CAST A PORNO FILM AND NOT GET TOO NERVOUS
article
BY DAN GREENBURG
in which our novice moviemaker concludes that auditioning naked women is, indeed, of greater interest than gargling
"YOU GET TALENTED big-name people fucking oncamera and you got yourself another Gone With the Wind." This is Carl Gurevich, a man with a dream.
How I know Carl Gurevich is that I wrote a thing in the December 1972 issue of PLAYBOY called My First Orgy, and although I said in the piece that the host of my orgy was a tall guy named Walt, that was merely my crafty way of assuring the anonymity of a short guy named Carl.
How I know Carl's dream is

582

Fashion — By Patricia Peterson

As black as magic

Opposite page: Wild mysterious black keynotes winter fashion. A big black cape of soft mohair (big sketch and at right in inset) ties at the neck and swoops on over everything. $150. Hitch, Ltd. Bendel's. Shirt and pants of ebony satin, polyester for practicality (at left in inset), add to an evening's drama. By Calvin Klein. Shirt, $60; pants, $56. Saks Fifth Avenue.

This page: A billowing smock over a full skirt (at left in inset at top), both in a jersey blend, are by Liz Claiborne for Youth Guild. $90. Bloomingdale's. A Chanel-like suit (at right in inset) with longer jacket is hand-crocheted of deepest black bouclé. Designed by Joan Vass. The jacket is $115; the skirt, $110. On the third floor at Bloomingdale's.

68

The New York Times Magazine/November 24, 1974

583

582
Art Director Arthur Paul
Designer Tom Staebler
Photographer Pompeo Pozar
Writer Dan Greenburg
Publisher Playboy

583
Art Director Ruth Ansel
Designer Ruth Ansel
Artist Antonio
Editor Mary Simons
Publisher The New York Times Magazine

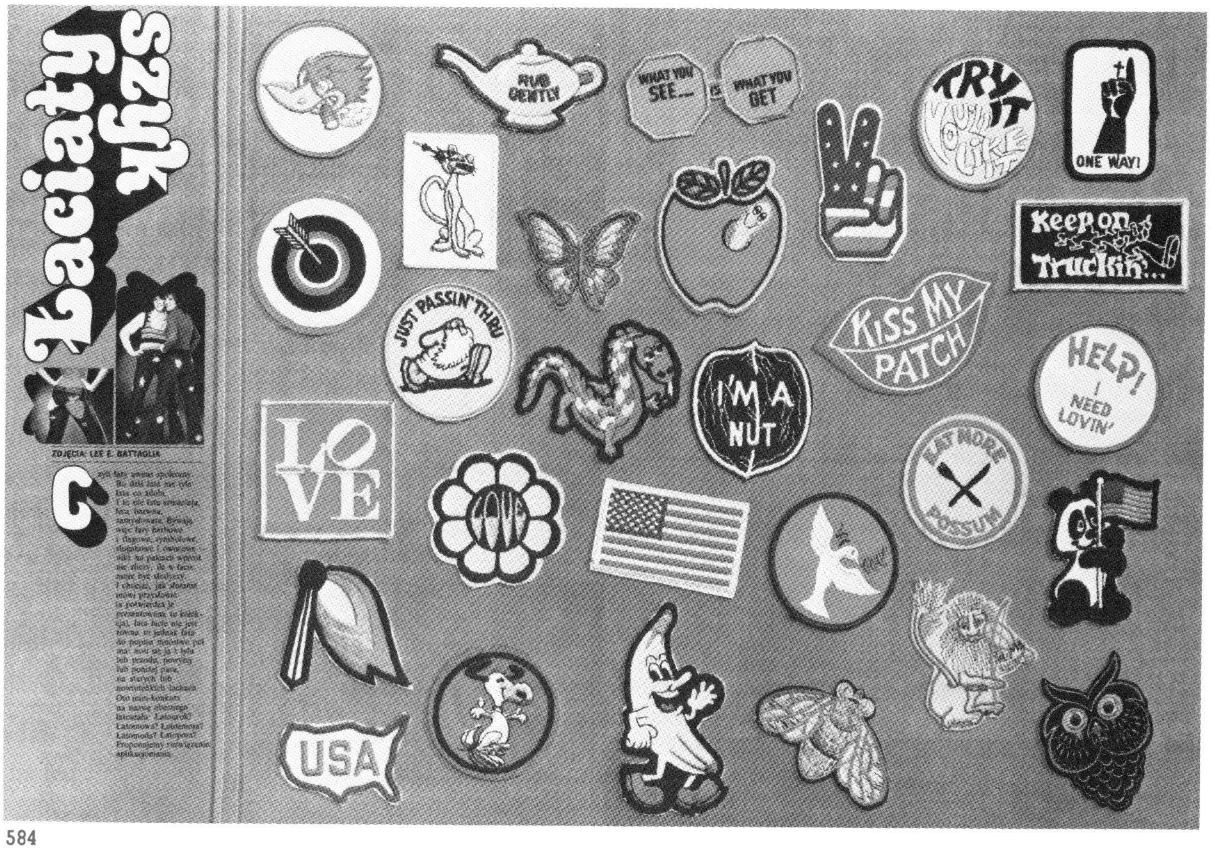
Łaciaty szyk
ZDJĘCIA: LEE E. BATTAGLIA
RUB GENTLY
WHAT YOU SEE... IS WHAT YOU GET
TRY IT YOU'LL LIKE IT
ONE WAY!
Keep on Truckin'...
JUST PASSIN' THRU
KISS MY PATCH
HELP! I NEED LOVIN'
I'M A NUT
LOVE
EAT MORE POSSUM
USA

584

PASTA
1 PASTA GOES GREAT WITH FISH! Think of spaghetti with clam sauce (red or white). Then try Redbook's Spaghetti with Mediterranean Tuna Sauce (above) and small-shell Pasta with Codfish Provençal (right, above). Both can be made in the time it takes to cook the pasta. Both will be favorites with adults and children alike. Pasta takes to many flavors.
2 PASTA GOES GREAT WITH MEAT! Spaghetti and meat balls is about as American as Christopher Columbus (or Leif Ericsson?), but try this delicious Chinese Noodle Meat Ball Soup for a real transcultural experience. Noodles, after all, are highly popular in China and Japan. Legend has it that noodles were brought to Italy by Marco Polo. Now turn the page for more PASTA.

585

584
Art Director David Moore
Designer Joseph Morgan
Artist Joseph Morgan
Photographer Lee Battaglia
Writer Sharon Ofenstein
Publisher America Illustrated

585
Art Director William Cadge
Designer Ed Sobel
Artist Verdun Cook
Photographer Leonard Nones
Editor Elizabeth Alston
Publisher Redbook

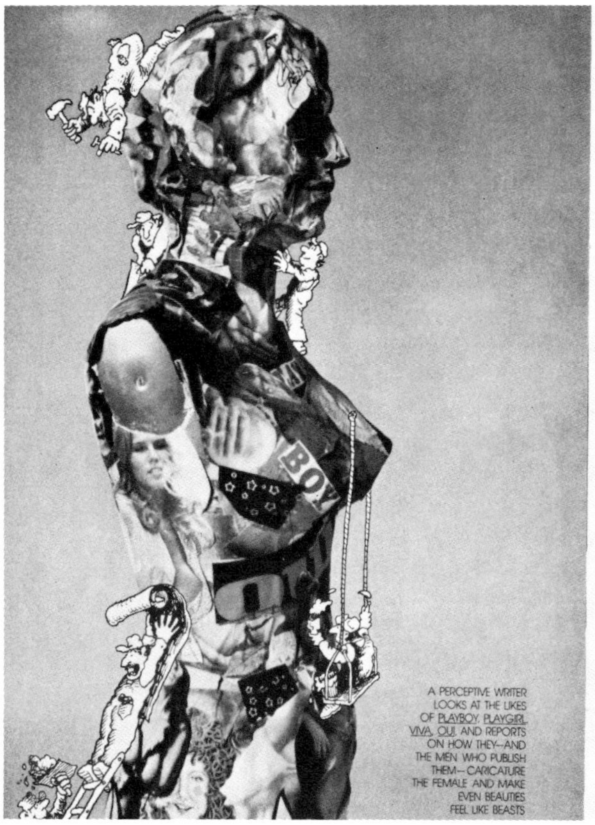
A PERCEPTIVE WRITER LOOKS AT THE LIKES OF PLAYBOY, PLAYGIRL, VIVA, OUI, AND REPORTS ON HOW THEY—AND THE MEN WHO PUBLISH THEM—CARICATURE THE FEMALE AND MAKE EVEN BEAUTIES FEEL LIKE BEASTS

A WOMAN SOUNDS OFF ON THOSE SEXY MAGAZINES

by Colette Dowling

It is a quiet afternoon in early spring. I am sitting in the room I both work and sleep in, surrounded by piles of girlie magazines, and I sit thumbing rather lazily through a copy of *Playboy*. Every month there are 14 million people who read *Playboy* and magazines like it (the latest comers in the field are *Playgirl* and *Viva*), and the editors of Redbook have asked me to have a look at them to see what they are saying to men and women about ourselves and our sexuality.

I had thought it was an interesting assignment, but now, flipping from one boring article to the next, I begin to wonder. First, an interminable *Playboy* interview with Himself (*yawn*), Hugh M. Hefner. Then an article—helpfully labeled "humor"—called, "Is It Nice to Have Sex With a Brussels Sprout?" I am beginning to contemplate a nice long nap when I hit page 101 and suddenly remember why it was I wanted to do this piece. There, in hideous four-color, is one of those vulgar cartoons whose humiliating messages haunted my adolescence.

Imagine a tiny roadside hamburger stand wedged between the fat thighs of an outsized figure of a kneeling woman pointing down toward the stand. A little man is sitting at the lunch counter between her kneeling thighs, and the counterman is telling him, "All I sell is cheeseburgers, but I sell a *lot* of cheeseburgers."

The grotesqueness of that female figure is riveting. She wears only boots, a cowboy hat and ranchers' gloves on her otherwise naked, neon pink body. Her hair is circus-blond and her nipples are drawn like nose cones on a pair of missiles. She is so freakish, I find it painful to look at her. Then my nine-year-old son comes into the room and glances at the cartoon, and he too is riveted. "Gross out!" he exclaims. It is his generation's idiom for that which is quintessentially disgusting.

I am embarrassed. My son's reaction to this caricature is embarrassing me, and I realize that the feeling has a long history. I want to get a firmer grip on my thoughts and feelings about the influence such publications have on me, my friends and potentially my children. Will my son's and daughters' lives be marked in the same way mine was marked long ago by *Playboy*?

To begin, I need to go back a bit in time. There is a feeling—or, rather, a state of being—I would like to recapture. It has to do with that tenuous but powerfully formative time when you are neither child nor adult.

The year *Playboy* was born I was 15 years old, a gawky girl who'd only lately arrived at puberty. If you can remember gray flannel suits and white buck shoes, Elvis ("The Pelvis") Presley singing "Heartbreak Hotel" and Marlon Brando in *On the Waterfront*, you've got the general time slot. Sex was just beginning to emerge as a million-dollar commodity. In the summer of 1953 a skinny young man named Hugh Hefner was sitting in his apartment in Chicago, putting together the first issue of a sexy magazine that eventually would make him a multimillionaire.

They say it cost him $600 to produce, that first issue. They say that $500 of it went to the Baumgarth Calendar Company for the rights to publish the famous picture of Marilyn Monroe in the pearly buff. Prescient, that move of Hefner's. As *Time* magazine put it: "He was the first publisher to see that the sky would not fall and mothers would not march if he published bare bosoms." Hefner's baby was a preview of the sexual sensationalism that was to preoccupy the entire country in the 1960s.

Of course, we didn't see it that way then. For me it was simply a time of confusion, a time of being terribly aware of my own body and trying desperately to ignore it. Five feet eight and a half inches tall and weighing about 110 pounds, I hunched my shoulders forward and sometimes walked with my knees buckled under my circle skirt to make myself seem shorter.

For a year or so I'd been hitching dutifully into a size 32-A bra with as much *savoir-faire* as anyone who is totally flat-chested can manage. For special occasions I padded the bra with nylon stockings—one stocking per cup—but there was always the problem of slipping. I took consolation from the fact that at least I was even. I knew a girl who was bigger on one side (*Continued on page 153*)

586

STEEL

The great strength of steel is being utilized in new design concepts that enable a steel building to bear greater loads as a whole than the strength of its individual parts would permit. In effect, through design, one steel part picks up strength from another. Standard steel bears as much as 248 megapascals; special steels are now proving to be three times as strong.

The steel skeleton of the Superdome, a mammoth sports and activities center being built in downtown New Orleans, Louisiana, has a span of 204 meters and will support a roof nearly four hectares in area.

588

586
Art Director William Cadge
Designer Ed Sobel
Artist Rick Meyerowitz
Photographer Mike Gold
Editor Bob Levin
Publisher Redbook

588
Art Director Joseph Morgan
Designer James Keaton
Photographer Robert Phillips
Picture Editor Lee Battaglia
Publisher Horizons USA

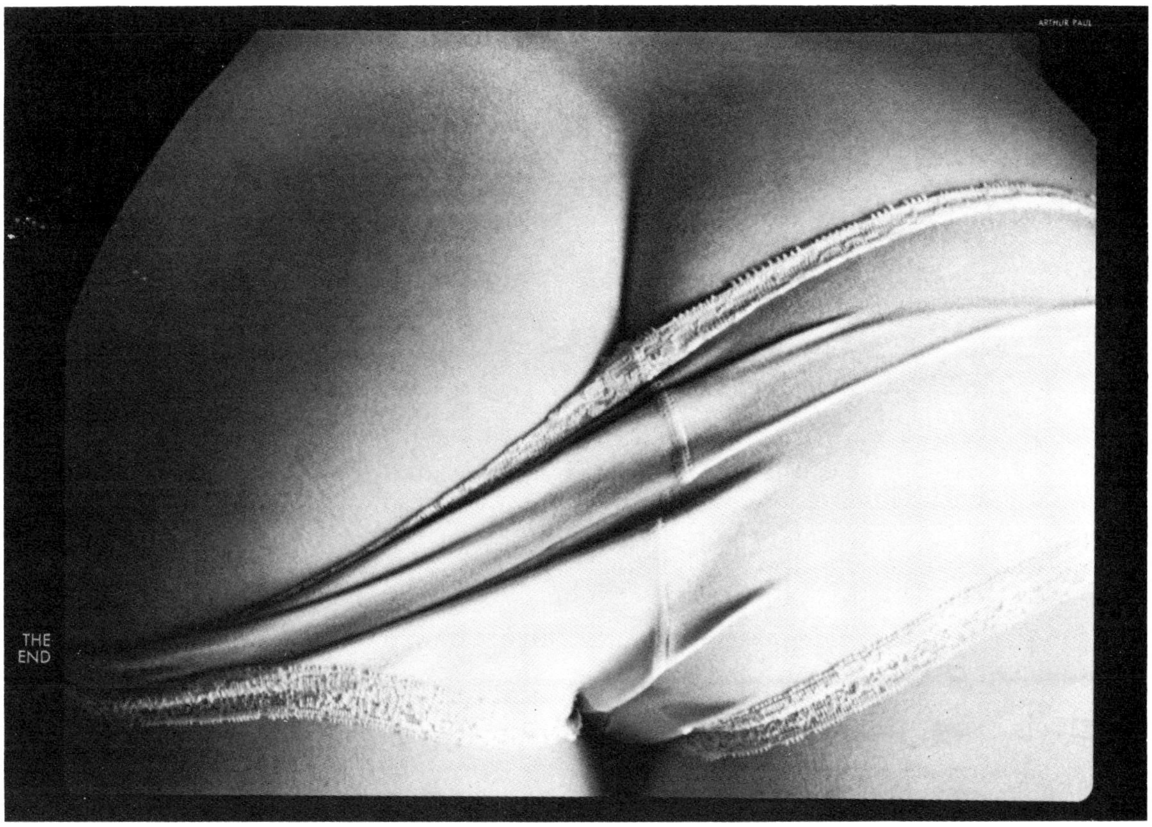
ARTHUR PAUL
THE END

589

Fresh

Clean, bouncy, healthy hair is always the prettiest hair, and keeping it that way is simply a matter of kind attention and good nutrition. "Hair is very much like a beautiful fabric," says top hair stylist Kenneth, "a remarkable material that will continue to look great in spite of the perils of everyday living *if* you treat it with respect." Being kind to your hair means protecting it from sea, sun, and wind. It means keeping it pristinely clean with frequent shampooing. And it means a simple haircut from time to time to get rid of split ends. Remember, once hair leaves your scalp the strand itself is no longer alive. It is a complex system of intricately put together protein but it has no capacity to heal itself; a split hair cannot grow back together again. That's why your own good health is likely to be your best asset when it comes to beautiful hair. And that means a vitamin-rich diet (red meat; green, leafy vegetables; cheese) and lots of protein (hair is protein, remember?).

H

Vidal Sassoon is another advocate of the body beautiful. The London-born hair stylist (whose client list, with Anne Bancroft, Julie Christie, Mia Farrow, Candice Bergen, reads like a show business *Who's Who*) believes that "physical exercise is absolutely essential to your hair's well-being." Still, it's nice to know that neglected hair may shine again with the proper restorative treatment. And there are many products that do promise help. Sassoon himself is bringing out his own private-label treatment products; look for them soon at favored salons across the country.

A

You can't baby your hair too much. Start with a good shampoo like Revlon's Milk Plus 6 Shampoo/Conditioner, Mennen's Protein 21, or Pantene's Ultra Control Shampoo; these are excellent and have the right pH level. Hair is slightly acidic and to best preserve its structure, shampoo should more or less match it chemically. To test shampoo you're not sure about, use Squibb & Sons' Nitrazine Paper—a yellowish tint will indicate correct acid-alkalinity balance for hair (4.5 to 5.5); if paper turns blue-green, the balance is not correct.

I

Try not to tangle your hair during shampooing; handle it carefully. Rinse hair thoroughly in shower with water on full—the force of the water will help detangle it. Because hair is weaker when it's wet, a brisk approach with a comb or brush may cause extensive breakage. Take your time. Start from the ends and work up to scalp. PURR is a fantastic little device by Clairol that distinguishes itself by vibrating out tangles in the most stubborn hair... Louis of Louis Guy D salon in New York finds it indispensable. A conditioning rinse or even a simple creme rinse will help make hair silky again. Try Revlon's Flex Balsam and Protein Instant Conditioner, or Pantene's Multi-Condition. For a really deep-penetrating conditioner, give yourself a longer treatment with Wella's Kolestral. This takes about fifteen minutes.

R

And if your hair has reached the point of no return, there's still no better solution than a short short haircut—leave all the problem hair on the salon floor and start fresh! Hair grows six inches or more a year so it doesn't take long to get going on a new mane—the kind that is lovely to look at... and to touch. ◻ Comb: Rahz. Sunglasses: Riviera. Photograph: Steve Hiett

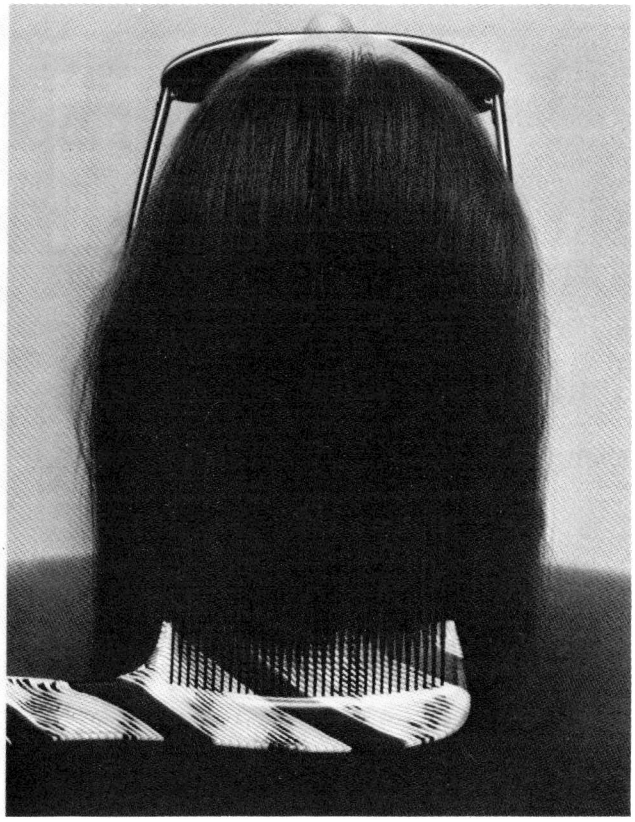

590

589
Art Director Arthur Paul
Designer Tom Staebler
Photographer Arthur Paul
Writer Carl Philip Snyder
Publisher Playboy

590
Art Directors Art Kane
Roy Carruthers
Designer Carl Barile
Photographer Steve Hiett
Editor Maureen Harris
Publisher Viva

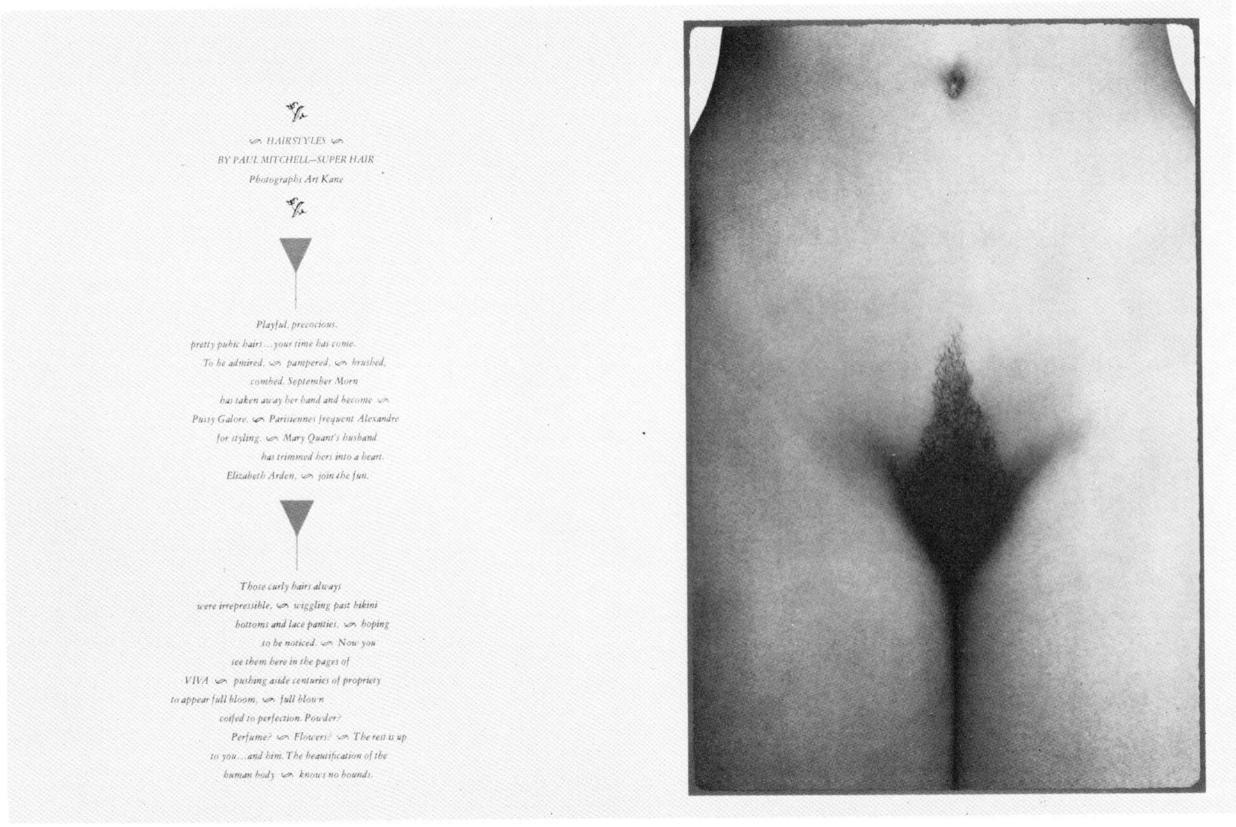
HAIRSTYLES
BY PAUL MITCHELL—SUPER HAIR
Photographs Art Kane
Playful, precocious,
pretty pubic hairs…your time has come.
To be admired, pampered, brushed,
combed. September Morn
has taken away her hand and become
Pussy Galore. Parisiennes frequent Alexandre
for styling. Mary Quant's husband
has trimmed hers into a heart.
Elizabeth Arden, join the fun.
Those curly hairs always
were irrepressible, wiggling past bikini
bottoms and lace panties, hoping
to be noticed. Now you
see them here in the pages of
VIVA pushing aside centuries of propriety
to appear full bloom, full blown
coifed to perfection. Powder?
Perfume? Flowers? The rest is up
to you…and him. The beautification of the
human body knows no bounds.

591

THE ULTIMATE CHOCOLATE CAKE
What makes a great recipe? Why is one cook's concoction better than another's? Given the right recipe, can anyone turn out great results? If we told you that the recipe for this chocolate cake is just about the world's best, would you believe us? Turn to page 000 and try it. Great, eh?

592

SILVER

591
Art Directors Art Kane
Carl Barile
Designers Claire Victor
Hector Marrero
Photographer Art Kane
Publisher Viva

592
Art Director William Cadge
Designer Ed Sobel
Photographer Gordon E. Smith
Editor Elizabeth Alston
Publisher Redbook

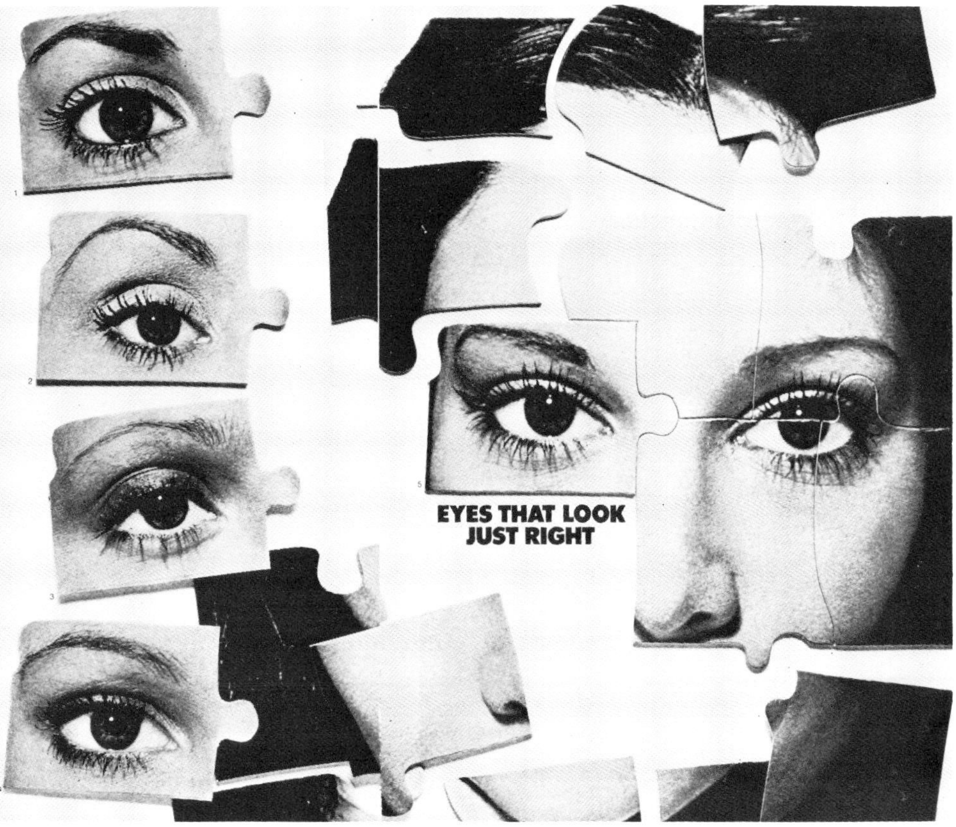

Your eyes give you away. More than any other feature they reflect your mood. That is why deft eye makeup is so important—to give your eyes added color and life. Stan Place gazed deep into the eyes of our five women and found certain assets to build up, certain faults to play down. Carol's eyes (1), for example, were somewhat small for the rest of her face and needed to be "opened up," made more important. Louise's deep-set eyes (2) benefited from being "pulled out," made larger. Maria had round, faintly bulging eyes (3), which needed to be narrowed and elongated so that they receded into the contours of her face. With just a few touches he was able to make Marcie's long, narrow eyes (4) appear deeper and rounder. And to Jane's wide-set eyes (5) he gave a softer, more subtle look.

To enlarge Carol's eyes, Stan pulled out the blue shadow in an elliptical shape, rounding the outer corners and ribboning the color under the lower lashes. Her brows are well tweezed for maximum space between lashes and brow. Long lashes add to the extending effect.

To make Louise's deep-set eyes look fuller and more alive, Stan used a pale, frosted-lavender shadow from lash line to brow, keeping the shadow soft, light and contained within the bone structure of the eye socket. The brow is a thin, rounded arch (a too-heavy brow makes deep-set eyes look even more so).

He played down Maria's round, too-prominent eyes by using a dark, smoky-brown shadow and winging it out beyond the eye to pull the eyes sideways (thus narrowing them). Lashes elongated with black mascara, and a long, light thin brow make the eyes look less heavy.

Marcie's long, narrow eyes were given a rounder look by Stan's use of a color eyeliner, domed in the middle to the ferny-green eyeshadow color. The shadow itself is rounded up over the eyeball and blended toward the arch of the brow.

Jane's eyes appeared "flat" as opposed to deep set. Stan created the illusion of depth by shadowing under the brow bone and contouring the hollow of the eye. He used a light, frosted silver-gray over the whole lid, a deeper shadow just in the middle of the eye and then rouge (or pearlized highlighter) at the brow bone. The eyebrows are precisely drawn in a winged arch.

EYES THAT LOOK JUST RIGHT

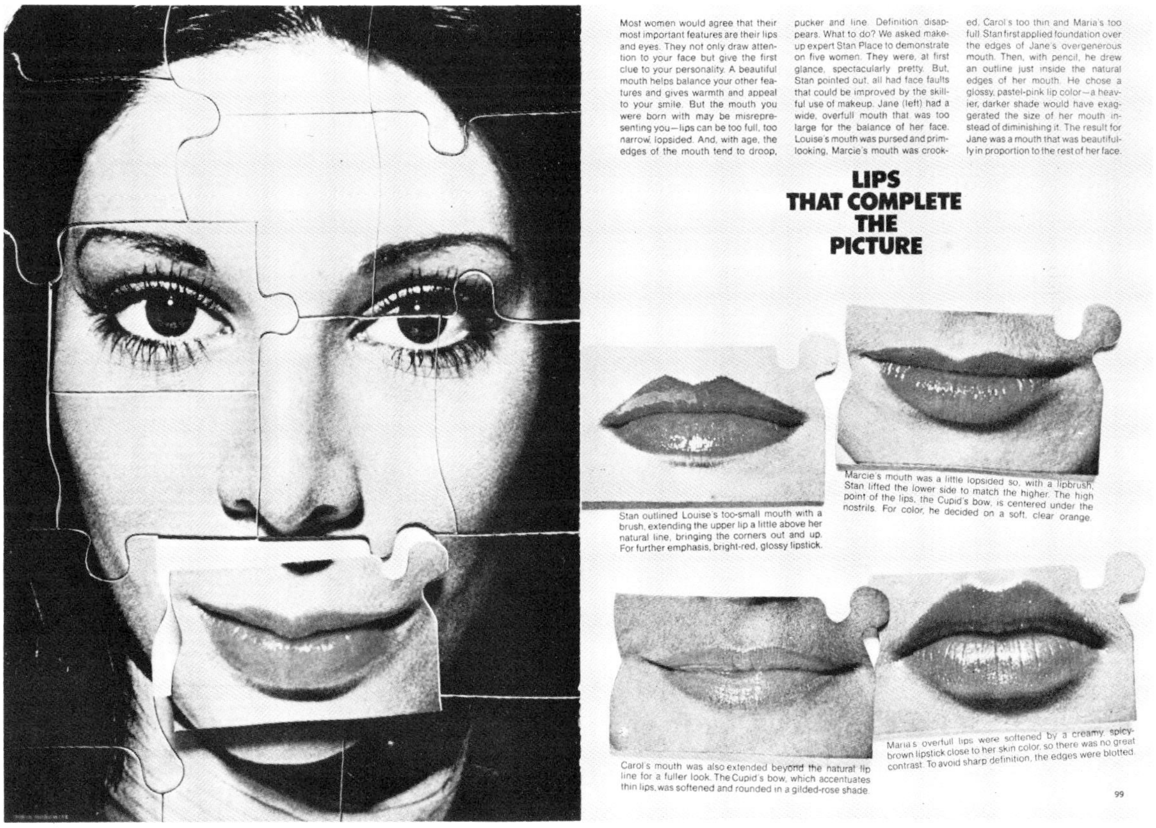

Most women would agree that their most important features are their lips and eyes. They not only draw attention to your face but give the first clue to your personality. A beautiful mouth helps balance your other features and gives warmth and appeal to your smile. But the mouth you were born with may be misrepresenting you—lips can be too full, too narrow, lopsided. And, with age, the edges of the mouth tend to droop, pucker and line. Definition disappears. What to do? We asked makeup expert Stan Place to demonstrate on five women. They were, at first glance, spectacularly pretty. But, Stan pointed out, all had face faults that could be improved by the skillful use of makeup. Jane (left) had a wide, overfull mouth that was too large for the balance of her face. Louise's mouth was pursed and prim-looking, Marcie's mouth was crooked, Carol's too thin and Maria's too full. Stan first applied foundation over the edges of Jane's overgenerous mouth. Then, with pencil, he drew an outline just inside the natural edges of her mouth. He chose a glossy, pastel-pink lip color—a heavier, darker shade would have exaggerated the size of her mouth instead of diminishing it. The result for Jane was a mouth that was beautifully in proportion to the rest of her face.

LIPS THAT COMPLETE THE PICTURE

Stan outlined Louise's too-small mouth with a brush, extending the upper lip a little above her natural line, bringing the corners out and up. For further emphasis, bright-red, glossy lipstick.

Marcie's mouth was a little lopsided so, with a lipbrush, Stan lifted the lower side to match the higher. The high point of the lips, the Cupid's bow, is centered under the nostrils. For color, he decided on a soft, clear orange.

Carol's mouth was also extended beyond the natural lip line for a fuller look. The Cupid's bow, which accentuates thin lips, was softened and rounded in a gilded-rose shade.

Maria's overfull lips were softened by a creamy, spicy-brown lipstick close to her skin color, so there was no great contrast. To avoid sharp definition, the edges were blotted.

99

593

593
Art Director Alvin Grossman
Designer Alvin Grossman
Photographer Irwin Horowitz
Editor Maureen Marwick
Publisher McCall's

The New York Times

THE WEEK IN REVIEW

Section 4

Sunday, August 11, 1974

The Power Passes

The Sad, Swift Transition From Nixon to Ford

"...I have felt it was my duty...to make every possible effort to complete the term of office to which you elected me. In the past few days...it has become evident to me that I no longer have a strong enough political base in the Congress to justify continuing that effort...With the disappearance of that base, I now believe that the constitutional purpose has been served...

"I shall resign the Presidency...By taking this action, I hope that I will have hastened the start of that process of healing which is so desperately needed...I regret deeply any injuries that may have been done in the course of the events that led to this decision..."

"...I am acutely aware that you have not elected me as your President by your ballots. So I ask you to confirm me as your President with your prayers...I believe that truth is the glue that holds governments together...That bond, though stained, is unbroken...In all my public and private acts as your President, I expect to follow my instincts of openness and candor...

"...our long national nightmare is over. Our Constitution works. Our great republic is a government of laws and not of men...As we bind up the internal wounds of Watergate...I ask again your prayers for Richard Nixon and for his family.

"May our former President who brought peace to millions, find it for himself..."

—Gerald R. Ford at his swearing-in

The New President: Reassurances

The Old President: Damaging Admission

The New President: A New Atmosphere

INDEX

MORE ON THE TRANSITION

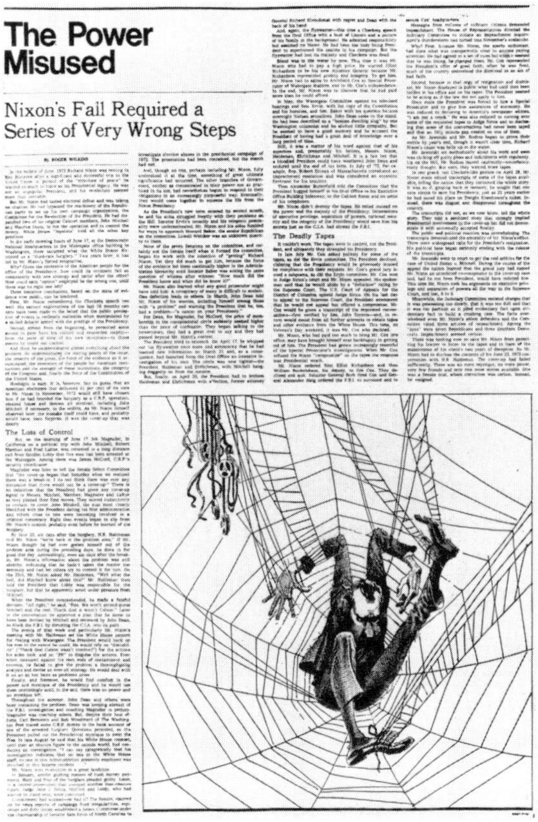

The Power Misused

Nixon's Fail Required a Series of Very Wrong Steps

By ROGER WILKINS

The Loss of Control

The Deadly Tapes

595

MELBA
ESCAPED FROM DEVIL'S ISLAND
MUTT & JEFF SAT & SUN
FRAN
BARRY

The Bronx: Hillside Homes

"...Clarence Stein at the peak of his power and imagination..."

One hundred feet west of the Boston Post Road near 222nd Street in the East Bronx, hidden behind the Melba Cinema and a strip of stores, lunchrooms, and bars, Hillside Homes continues—as over the past 40 years—to provide the physical locus for a unique New York neighborhood. The work of Clarence Stein at the peak of his power and imagination, Hillside Homes (*see picture*) revives half-forgotten memories of the 1930's in America. The economic system lay gasping, almost inert (Stein wrote that the bricklayers at Hillside in 1933 were so rusty from unemployment that they took months to limber up). People had lost confidence in their immediate environment, and lived only in their hope of the future. Hillside Homes' apartments originally rented for $11 per room per month, and it sometimes paid its sponsors the earnings they were entitled by law to make: 6 per cent per year on their actual invested capital above the federal mortgage. Its purpose was not merely to provide shelter and put people to work; Stein intended it as social environment, and planned it so that people would meet face-to-face, interact with each other, and perhaps recover their self-confidence in the experience of solving shared problems.

Hillside Homes cannot be observed from the outside; it can only be experienced on a walk through. Starting at 221st Street, at the highest grade, the visitor finds his way downhill, from courtyard to courtyard, playground to wading pool. The form of this neighborhood suggests the bed of a rocky brook in which water gathers to form pools and back eddies, and then moves along more quickly through archways into other pools downstream. The analogy is imperfect because water tends to scour the rocks it moves over, while people leave their marks behind, as in the murals on some of the playground walls, and in the community rooms.

Sometimes, alas, the people also leave their litter behind; the neighborhood sense of Hillside has not eliminated the cost of maintaining its public spaces, some of which seem designed only for the litter of a less affluent age. But 1,400 families live here at a time; some have flowed, in a sense, through Hillside, refreshed here, and have moved elsewhere into their own homes.

SPANISH & AMERICAN PRODUCTS
Casa America BAKERY
PHILIP GRODKO MEATS & POULTRY

Queens: Jackson Heights

"...With good luck the area can remain what it now seems to be—one of the city's rare stable interracial neighborhoods..."

596

595

Art Director Eric Seidman
Designer Eric Seidman
Artist John Cayea
Editor Al Marlens
Publisher The New York Times Week in Review

596

Art Directors Walter Bernard, Milton Glaser
Designer Walter Bernard
Artist Julian Allen
Writer Roger Starr
Publisher New York

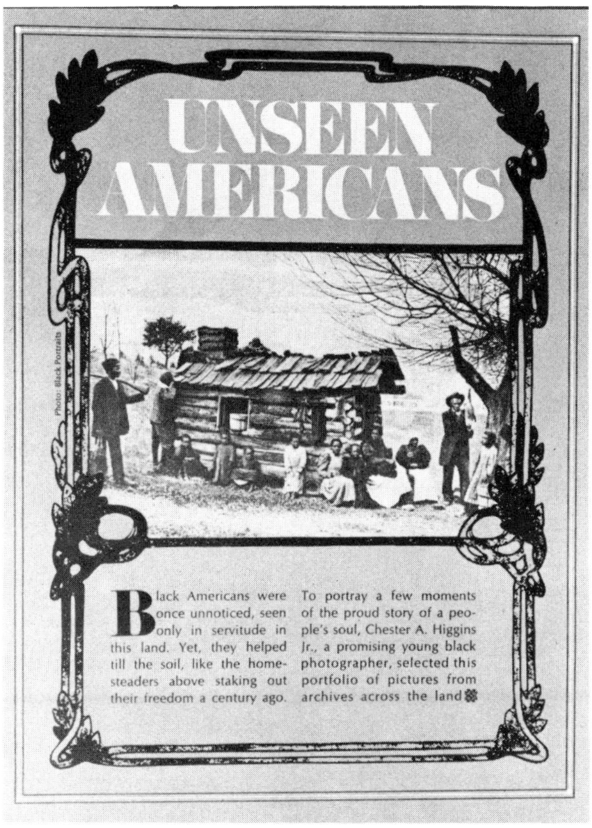
UNSEEN AMERICANS

Photo: Black Portraits

Black Americans were once unnoticed, seen only in servitude in this land. Yet, they helped till the soil, like the homesteaders above staking out their freedom a century ago. To portray a few moments of the proud story of a people's soul, Chester A. Higgins Jr., a promising young black photographer, selected this portfolio of pictures from archives across the land

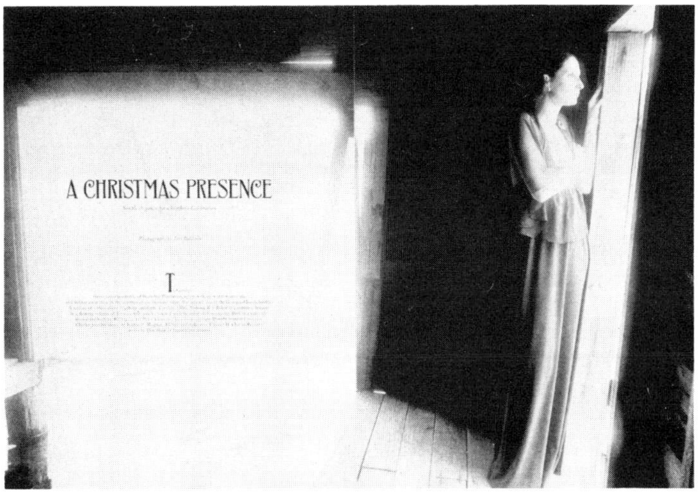
A CHRISTMAS PRESENCE

597

599

597
Art Director Raymond Waites
Designers Janice Warner
Raymond Hooper
Writer Ann Francis
Publisher A.D. Magazine

599
Art Director Nancy Kent
Designer Nancy Kent
Photographer Joel Baldwin
Editor Anne Kampmann
Writer Mary Louise Ransdell
Publisher Town & Country

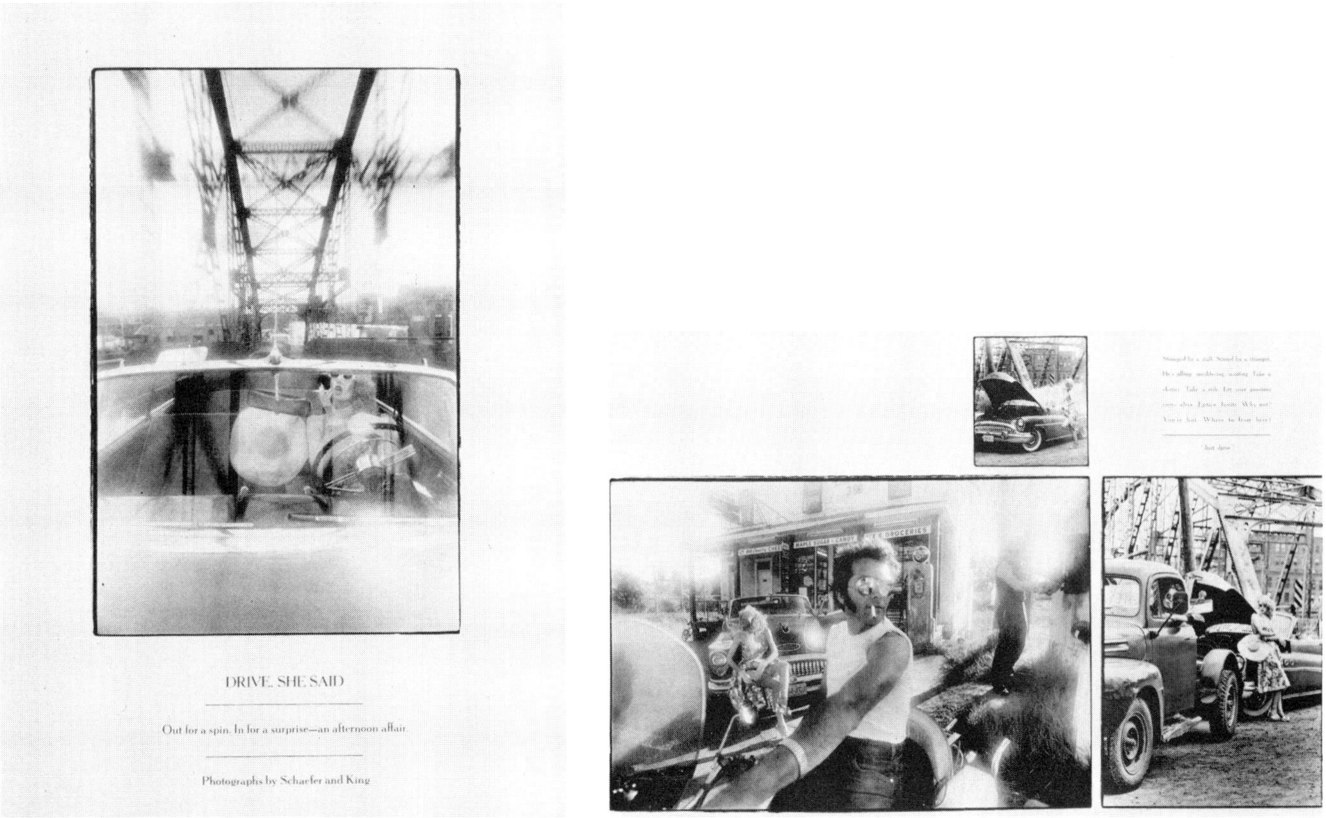
DRIVE, SHE SAID
Out for a spin. In for a surprise—an afternoon affair.
Photographs by Schaefer and King

600

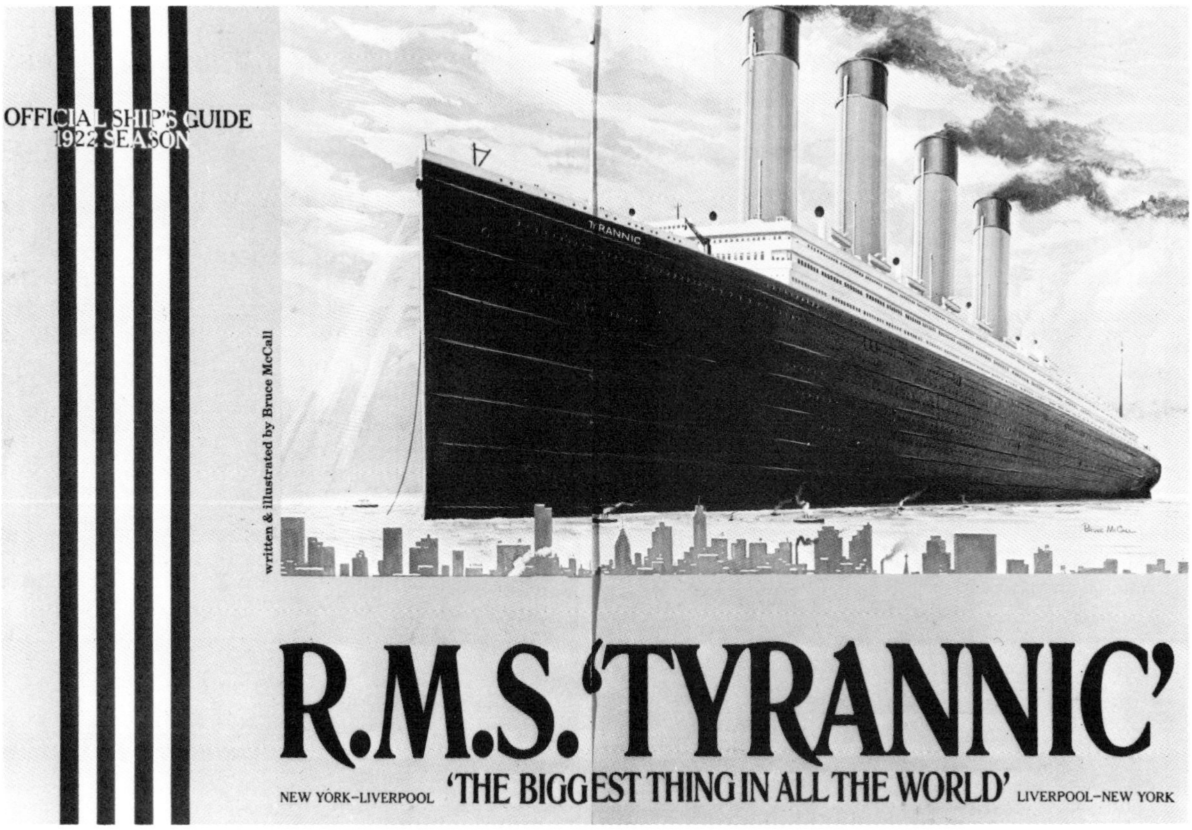
OFFICIAL SHIP'S GUIDE
1922 SEASON
written & illustrated by Bruce McCall
TYRANNIC
R.M.S. 'TYRANNIC'
NEW YORK–LIVERPOOL
'THE BIGGEST THING IN ALL THE WORLD'
LIVERPOOL–NEW YORK

601

600
Art Directors Art Kane
Carl Barile
Designers Claire Victor
George Moy
Photographer Schaefer and King
Publisher Viva

601
Art Director Michael Gross
Designers Bruce McCall
Michael Gross
Artist Bruce McCall
Writer Bruce McCall
Publisher National Lampoon

TOWN&COUNTRY
LOS ANGELES:
WORLDLY,
DIFFERENT
Against the city's graphic, adamantine backdrop of starkly bright highways and a whole slew of brand-new, brashly streamlined skyscrapers: the softest, driftiest, clingingest dresses by California's own masterful designers. Late-day fashions that are unsentimentally modern, playfully exciting, and possibly the most sophisticated in America.
Photographs by Silano

602

Stitch an Arty Dish
Have you a friend who's crazy about old-fashioned strawberry shortcake? Is there a shish kebab freak in your family? Or a man who'd rather eat spaghetti with meat sauce every day of his life? Almost everybody has some special food craving—and therein lies EPICURE's reason for saying, Why not immortalize that favorite food for a favorite person as a very personalized gift? Below and on the next three pages are four popular dishes translated into fabric "paintings" with a bit of scissors work and a sewing machine. All are suitable for framing for facing pillows or bibs of aprons—whatever fancy and preference dictate. And all are easy-dos, even by amateurs. Turn to page 72 for ways and means to stitch your own arty feast.
Spaghetti with Meat Sauce
Margaret Cusack

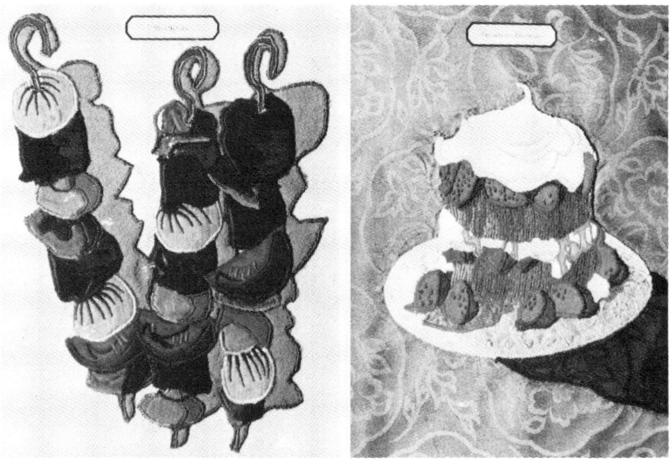

603

602
Art Director Nancy Kent
Designer Nancy Kent
Photographer Silano
Writer Mary Louise Ransdell
Publisher Town & Country

603
Art Director Fred Tobey
Designer Margaret Cusack
Artist Margaret Cusack
Publisher Epicure

SCOTT & ZELDA

THE BEAUTIFUL AND DAMNED

F. Scott Fitzgerald

ILLUSTRATIVE MATTER COPYRIGHT © 1974 BY FRANCES SCOTT FITZGERALD SMITH

AN AMERICAN HERITAGE BOOK SELECTION

Where Scott first saw Zelda, September, 1918

Scott as a first lieutenant and general's aide, 1918

... then they meet ...

... and fall in love ...

Zelda Sayre at nineteen—in the midst of her romance with Scott

Brilliant "Folly Ball" Given By Members of Les Mystery

With Scott in New York to start his career in April, 1919, Zelda toiled not—but she continued to spin, at least socially.

604

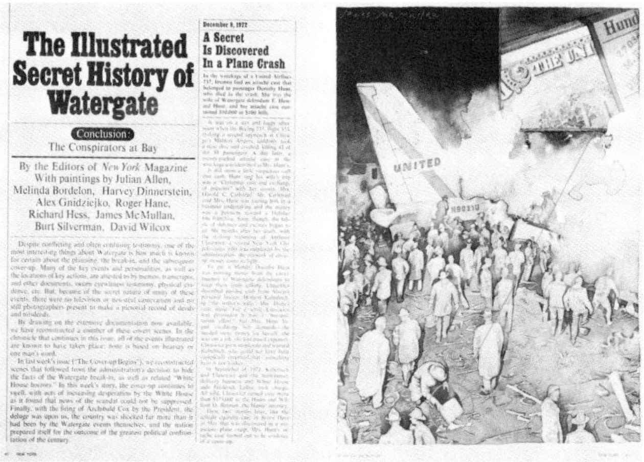

The Illustrated Secret History of Watergate

Conclusion: The Conspirators at Bay

By the Editors of *New York* Magazine With paintings by Julian Allen, Melinda Bordelon, Harvey Dinnerstein, Alex Gnidziejko, Roger Hane, Richard Hess, James McMullan, Burt Silverman, David Wilcox

December 8, 1972

A Secret Is Discovered In a Plane Crash

April 5, 1973

Ellsberg's Judge Gets an Offer

October 18, 1973

Cox Refuses Nixon Ultimatum

Christmas Week, 1972

Patrick Gray Burns Hunt's File

January 12, 1973

McCord Rejects Clemency Promise

March 21, 1973

Nixon Orders The Payment Of Hush Money

605

604
Art Director Emma Landau
Designer Emma Landau
Photographer Frances Scott Fitzgerald Smith Collection
Editor Ernest Halliday
Writer Ernest Halliday
Publisher American Heritage

605
Art Directors Milton Glaser, Walter Bernard
Designers Walter Bernard, Tom Bentkowski
Artists James McMullan, Julian Allen, Burt Silverman, Harvey Dinnerstein, Melinda Bordelon
Writer The Editors
Publisher New York

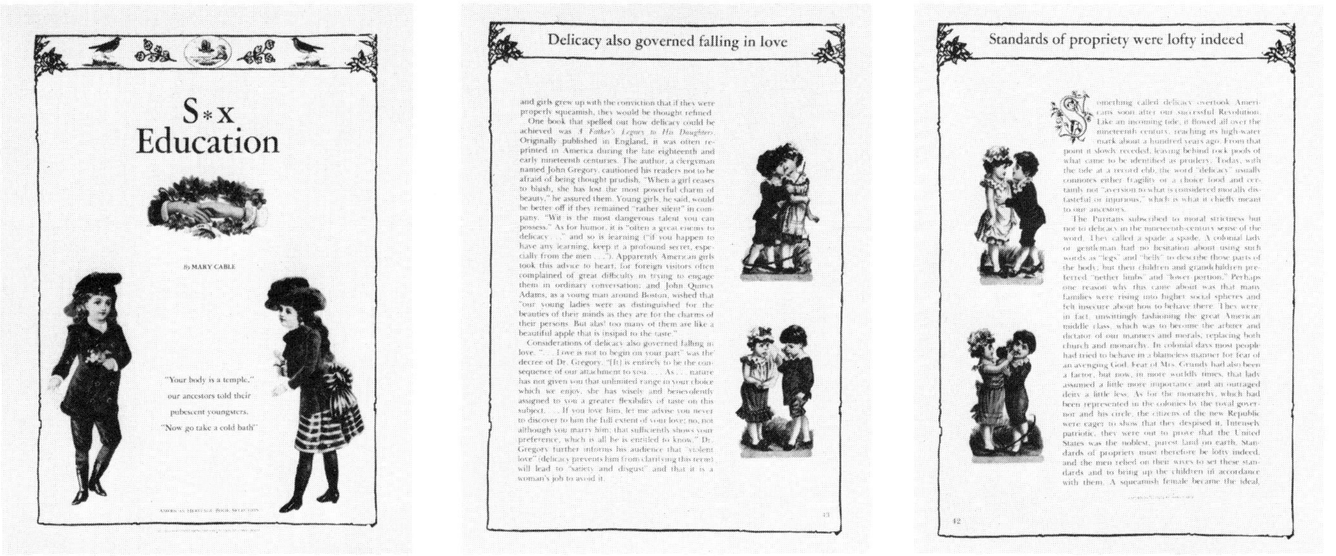
S*x Education
By MARY CABLE
"Your body is a temple," our ancestors told their pubescent youngsters. "Now go take a cold bath"
Delicacy also governed falling in love
Standards of propriety were lofty indeed

606

The Illustrated Secret History of Watergate
Part II: The Cover-up Begins
By the Editors of New York Magazine With paintings by Julian Allen, Melinda Bordelon, Harvey Dinnerstein, Alex Gnidziejko, Roger Hane, Richard Hess, James McMullan, Burt Silverman, David Wilcox
June 17, 1972
Liddy Tries To Involve the Attorney General
June 22, 1972
Martha Mitchell Is Manhandled But Unsilenced
Summer, 1972
"Deep Throat" Whispers The Secrets
September 15, 1972
Nixon Offers Dean Compliments In the Oval Office
phone
Summer, 1972
Cash Begins To Flow to The Defendants
"...Were the tapes to go to the Nixon Library with their expletives undeleted?..."

607

606
Art Director Emma Landau
Designer Emma Landau
Artist Carol Wald Collection
Editor Ernest Halliday
Writer Mary Cable
Publisher American Heritage

607
Art Directors Milton Glaser
Walter Bernard
Designers Walter Bernard
Tom Bentkowski
Artists David Wilcox
Julian Allen
Melinda Bordelon
Writers The Editors
Publisher New York

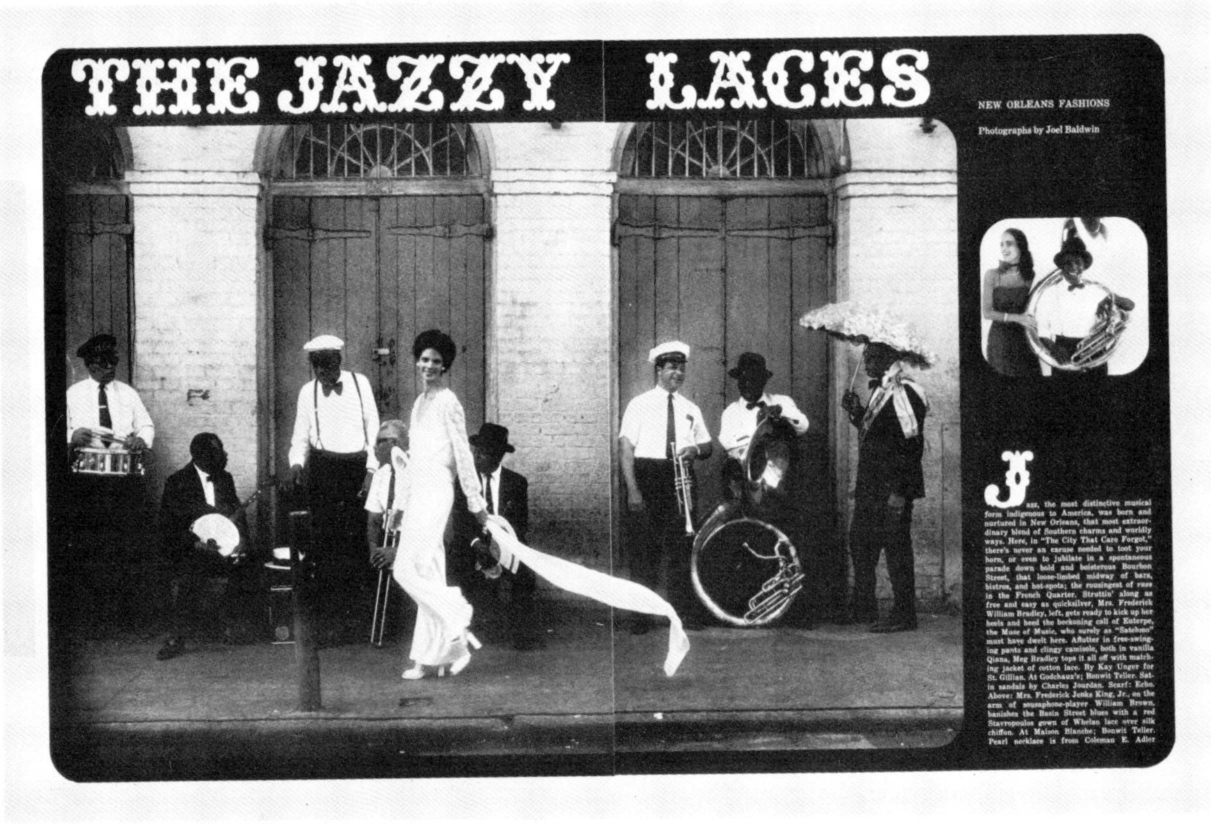

THE JAZZY LACES

NEW ORLEANS FASHIONS

Photographs by Joel Baldwin

Jazz, the most distinctive musical form indigenous to America, was born and nurtured in New Orleans, that most extraordinary blend of Southern charms and worldly ways. Here, in "The City That Care Forgot," there's never an excuse needed to toot your horn, or even to jubilate in a spontaneous parade down bold and boisterous Bourbon Street, that loose-limbed midway of bars, bistros, and hot-spots; the rousingest of rues in the French Quarter. Struttin' along as free and easy as quicksilver, Mrs. Frederick William Bradley, left, gets ready to kick up her heels and heed the beckoning call of Euterpe, the Muse of Music, who surely as "Satchmo" must have dwelt here. Aflutter in free-swinging pants and clingy camisole, both in vanilla Qiana, Meg Bradley tops it all off with matching jacket of cotton lace. By Kay Unger for St. Gillian. At Godchaux's; Bonwit Teller. Satin sandals by Charles Jourdan. Scarf: Echo. Above: Mrs. Frederick Jenks King, Jr., on the arm of sousaphone-player William Brown, banishes the Basin Street blues with a red Stavropoulos gown of Whelan lace over silk chiffon. At Maison Blanche; Bonwit Teller. Pearl necklace is from Coleman E. Adler

608

PETHOUSE
THE INTERNATIONAL MAGAZINE FOR MALES
JANUARY 1974 ONE DOLLAR
THE NAKED NAKED APE
VIVISECTION
TWO LEGS ARE
BETTER THAN NONE
SPAYED CATS
SADOMASCOTISM
THE LAST TABOO

609

608
Art Director Nancy Kent
Designer Linda B. Stillman
Photographer Joel Baldwin
Editor Anne Kampmann
Writer Richard Kagan
Publisher Town & Country

609
Art Director David Kaestle
Designer David Kaestle
Artist Dick Hess
Photographers David Kaestle
Schaefer and King
Vince Aiosa
Judy Hendra
Writer Tony Hendra
Publisher National Lampoon

IRVING PENN NEUTRAL GROUND PORTRAITURE

Worlds
in a Small Room

The power of Irving Penn's vision and the quality of his perception as a photographer have been working their peculiarly quiet but enduring magic on us for quite some time now in various modes: fashion photography, still life, scenes from far-away places, and especially in portraiture. Out of this over-all body of work, last presented in book form in *Moments Preserved* (1960) he has extracted a group of portraits widely varied in content but related in psychological approach. Any new book of Penn photographs would be an event, but *Worlds in a Small Room* (Grossman Publishers, 1974, $16.50) has special charm because it represents a labor of love, a personal project carried out over a period of more than 25 years: to record vanishing cultures and subcultures in terms of people in the neutral environment of a studio. In some cases the people came to the studio; other times Penn brought the studio to them, as he explains in his introduction to the book reproduced below. In either case, photographer and subject became involved amid a climate of mutual respect in a timeless environment that serves to intensify individual and cultural uniqueness. A selection of these extraordinary images, which are both anthropological documents of great value and an expression of the photographer's personal vision, are reproduced on the following gravure pages. *Arthur Goldsmith*

I share with many people the feeling that there is a sweetness and constancy to light that falls into a studio from the north sky that sets it beyond any other illumination. It is a light of such penetrating clarity that even a simple object lying by chance in such a light takes on an inner glow, almost a voluptuousness. This cold north light has a quality which painters have always admired, and which the early studio photographers made the fullest use of. It is this light that makes some of these studio portraits sing with an intensity not bettered by later photographers with more sophisticated means at

From WORLDS IN A SMALL ROOM by Irving Penn
Copyright © 1974 by Irving Penn
All rights reserved
Reprinted by permission of Grossman Publishers

114

MOUNTAIN CHILDREN, CUZCO, PERU
© 1960 by the Conde Nast Publications Inc.

610

MEMORIES

PHOTOGRAPHS BY MAUREEN LAMBRAY

Standing amid the shrouded furniture in the old Back Bay mansion once filled with gay children and deep laughter, she was bathed in a warm, milky light that evoked scenes of past joy, of Jack's first novel, of Alison, breaking the news of her engagement, and of that memorable afternoon when the three sisters had listened to Edward's abdication speech.

Her robe by Harriet Love Shop, N.Y.C. Hairstyles: Pascal

610
Art Director Shinichiro Tora
Designer Shinichiro Tora
Photographer Irving Penn
Writers Arthur Goldsmith
Irving Penn
Publisher Popular Photography

611
Art Director Ahmad Sadiq
Designers Frank DeVino
Hector Marrero
Photographer Maureen Lambray
Publisher Viva

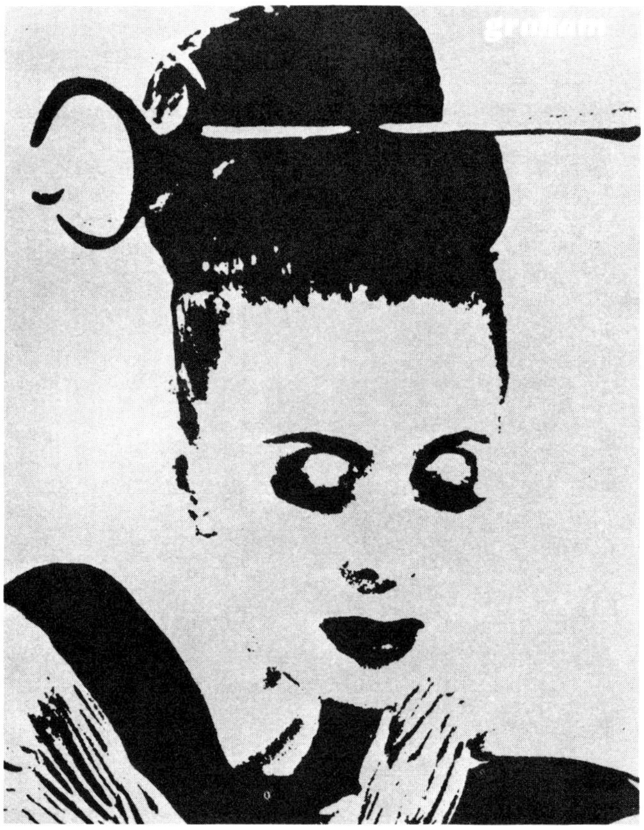
graham

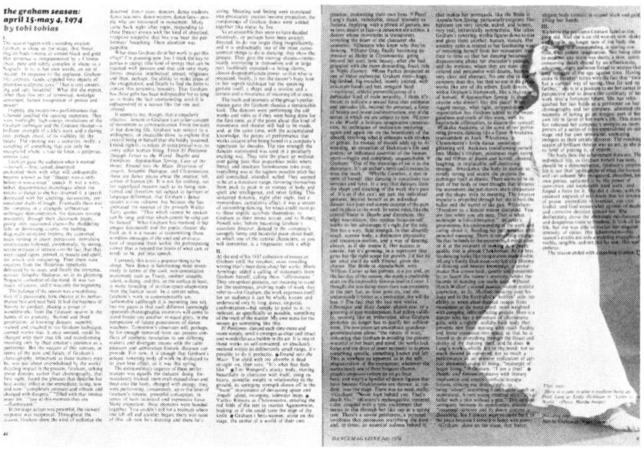
the graham season:
april 15-may 4, 1974
by tobi tobias

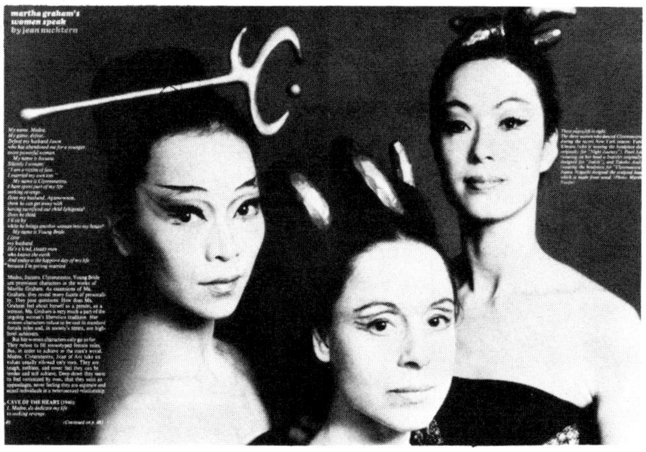
martha graham's
women speak
by jean nuchtern

612

612
Art Director Herbert Migdoll
Designers Herbert Migdoll
Augustus Ginnochio
Photographers Martha Swope
Frederika Davis
Editors William Como
Joel Shapiro
Richard Philip
Doris Hering
Writers Tobi Tobias
Jean Nuchtern
Publisher Dance Magazine

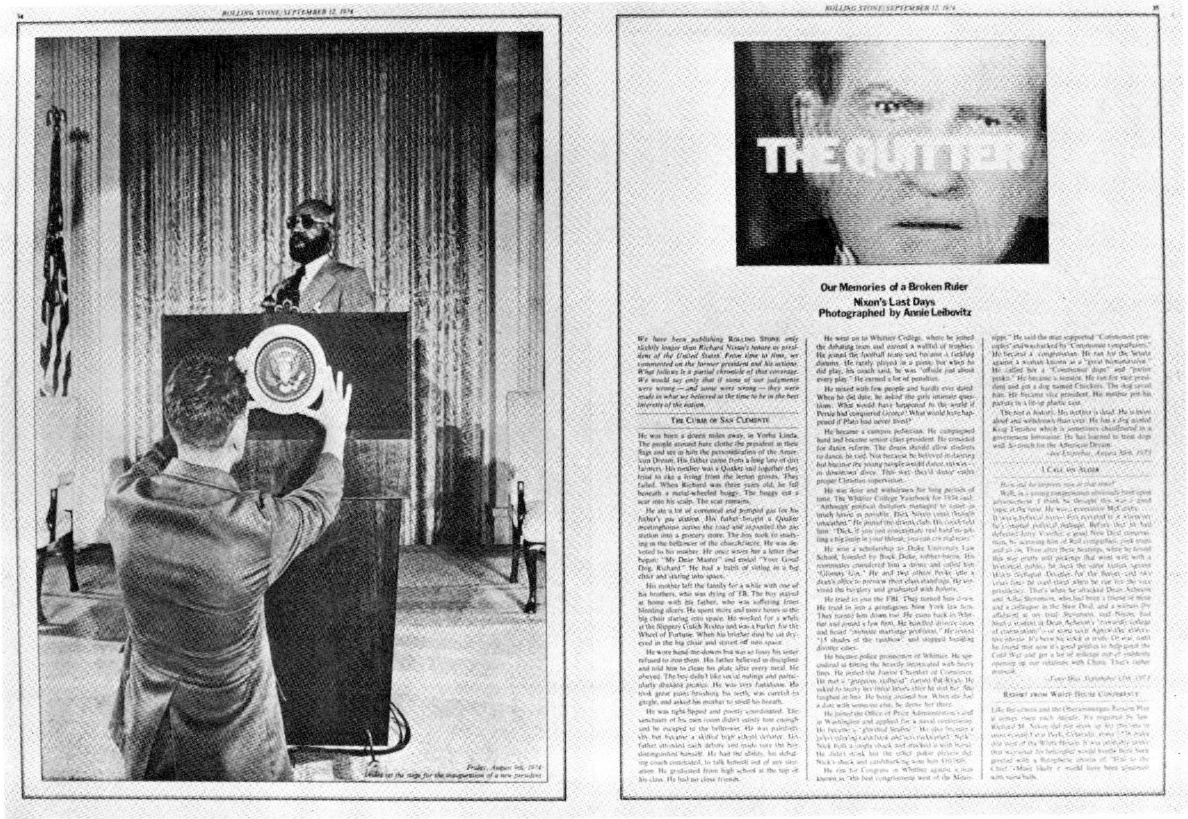

ROLLING STONE/SEPTEMBER 12, 1974

THE QUITTER

Our Memories of a Broken Ruler
Nixon's Last Days
Photographed by Annie Leibovitz

We have been publishing ROLLING STONE *only slightly longer than Richard Nixon's tenure as president of the United States. From time to time, we commented on the former president and his actions. What follows is a partial chronicle of that coverage. We would say only that if some of our judgments were wrong — and some were wrong — they were made in what we believed at the time to be in the best interests of the nation.*

THE CURSE OF SAN CLEMENTE

He was born a dozen miles away, in Yorba Linda. The people around here clothe the president in their flags and see in him the personification of the American Dream. His father came from a long line of dirt farmers. His mother was a Quaker and together they tried to eke a living from the lemon groves. They failed. When Richard was three years old, he fell beneath a metal-wheeled buggy. The buggy cut a scar into his scalp. The scar remains.

He ate a lot of cornmeal and pumped gas for his father's gas station. His father bought a Quaker meetinghouse across the road and expanded the gas station into a grocery store. The boy took to studying in the belltower of the church/store. He was devoted to his mother. He once wrote her a letter that began: "My Dear Master" and ended "Your Good Dog, Richard." He had a habit of sitting in a big chair and staring into space.

His mother left the family for a while with one of his brothers, who was dying of TB. The boy stayed at home with his father, who was suffering from bleeding ulcers. He spent more and more hours in the big chair staring into space. He worked for a while at the Slippery Gulch Rodeo and was a barker for the Wheel of Fortune. When his brother died he sat dry-eyed in the big chair and stared off into space.

He wore hand-me-downs but was so fussy his sister refused to iron them. His father believed in discipline and told him to clean his plate after every meal. He obeyed. The boy didn't like social outings and particularly dreaded picnics. He was very fastidious. He took great pains brushing his teeth, was careful to gargle, and asked his mother to smell his breath.

He was tight-lipped and poorly coordinated. The sanctuary of his own room didn't satisfy him enough and he escaped to the belltower. He was painfully shy but became a skilled high school debater. His father attended each debate and made sure the boy distinguished himself. He had the ability, his debating coach concluded, to talk himself out of any situation. He graduated from high school at the top of his class. He had no close friends.

He went on to Whittier College, where he joined the debating team and earned a wallful of trophies. He joined the football team and became a tackling dummy. He rarely played in a game, but when he did play, his coach said, he was "offside just about every play." He earned a lot of penalties.

He mixed with few people and hardly ever dated. When he did date, he asked the girls intimate questions. What would have happened to the world if Persia had conquered Greece? What would have happened if Plato had never lived?

He became a campus politician. He campaigned hard and became senior class president. He crusaded for dance reform. The deans should allow students to dance, he said. Not because he believed in dancing but because the young people would dance anyway—in downtown dives. This way they'd dance under proper Christian supervision.

He was dour and withdrawn for long periods of time. The Whittier College Yearbook for 1934 said: "Although political dictators managed to cause as much havoc as possible, Dick Nixon came through unscathed." He joined the drama club. His coach told him: "Dick, if you just concentrate real hard on getting a big lump in your throat, you can cry real tears."

He won a scholarship to Duke University Law School, founded by Buck Duke, robber-baron. His roommates considered him a drone and called him "Gloomy Gus." He and two others broke into a dean's office to preview their class standings. He survived the burglary and graduated with honors.

He tried to join the FBI. They turned him down. He tried to join a prestigious New York law firm. They turned him down too. He came back to Whittier and joined a law firm. He handled divorce cases and heard "intimate marriage problems." He turned "15 shades of the rainbow" and stopped handling divorce cases.

He became police prosecutor of Whittier. He specialized at hitting the heavily intoxicated with heavy fines. He joined the Junior Chamber of Commerce. He met a "gorgeous redhead" named Pat Ryan. He asked to marry her three hours after he met her. She laughed at him. He hung around her. When she had a date with someone else, he drove her there.

He joined the Office of Price Administration's staff in Washington and applied for a naval commission. He became a "glorified Seabee." He also became a poker-playing cardshark and was nicknamed "Nick." Nick built a single shack and stocked it with booze. He didn't drink but the other poker players did. Nick's shack and cardsharking won him $10,000.

He ran for Congress in Whittier against a man known as "the best congressman west of the Mississippi." He said the man supported "Communist principles" and was backed by "Communist sympathizers." He became a congressman. He ran for the Senate against a woman known as a "great humanitarian." He called her a "Communist dupe" and "parlor pinko." He became a senator. He ran for vice president and got a dog named Checkers. The dog saved him. He became vice president. His mother put his picture in a lit-up plastic case.

The rest is history. His mother is dead. He is more aloof and withdrawn than ever. He has a dog named King Timahoe which is sometimes chauffeured in a government limousine. He has learned to treat dogs well. So much for the American Dream.

—Joe Eszterhas, August 30th, 1973

I CALL ON ALGER

How did he impress you at that time?

Well, as a young congressman obviously bent upon advancement. I think he thought this was a good topic at the time. He was a premature McCarthy. ... It was a political issue—he's resorted to it whenever he's needed political mileage. Before that he had defeated Jerry Voorhis, a good New Deal congressman, by accusing him of Red sympathies, pink traits and so on. Then after these hearings, when he found this was pretty soft pickings that went well with a hysterical public, he used the same tactics against Helen Gahagan Douglas for the Senate and two years later he used them when he ran for the vice presidency. That's when he attacked Dean Acheson and Adlai Stevenson, who had been a friend of mine and a colleague in the New Deal, and a witness [by affidavit] at my trial. Stevenson, said Nixon, had been a student at Dean Acheson's "cowardly college of communism"—or some such Agnew-like alliterative phrase. It's been his stock in trade. Or was, until he found that now it's good politics to help quiet the Cold War and get a lot of mileage out of suddenly opening up our relations with China. That's rather ironical.

—Tony Hiss, September 13th, 1973

REPORT FROM WHITE HOUSE CONFERENCE

Like the census and the [illegible] it comes once each decade. It's required by law. Richard M. Nixon did not show up for this one in snow-bound Estes Park, Colorado, some 1,776 miles due west of the White House. It was probably better that way since his helicopter would hardly have been greeted with a [illegible] chorus of "Hail to the Chief." More likely it would have been plastered with snowballs.

Friday, August 9th, 1974
Aides set the stage for the inauguration of a new president

613

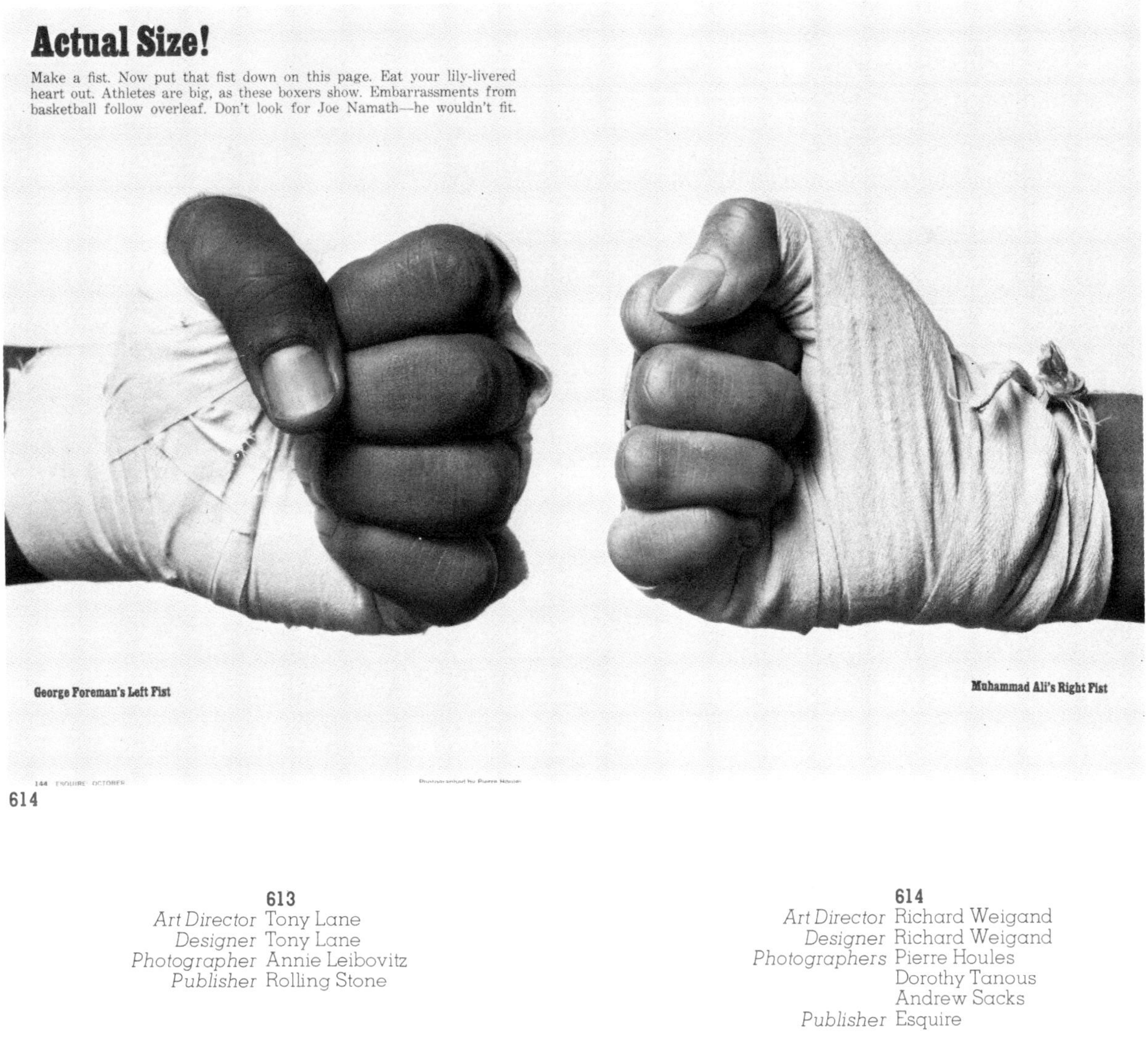

Actual Size!

Make a fist. Now put that fist down on this page. Eat your lily-livered heart out. Athletes are big, as these boxers show. Embarrassments from basketball follow overleaf. Don't look for Joe Namath—he wouldn't fit.

George Foreman's Left Fist

Muhammad Ali's Right Fist

144 ESQUIRE: OCTOBER

Photographed by Pierre Houles

614

613
Art Director Tony Lane
Designer Tony Lane
Photographer Annie Leibovitz
Publisher Rolling Stone

614
Art Director Richard Weigand
Designer Richard Weigand
Photographers Pierre Houles
Dorothy Tanous
Andrew Sacks
Publisher Esquire

CTW
SESAME STREET
MAGAZINE
Shapes Bingo
Ernie and Bert
Mailman Maze
And More!
615

HOLLINS
617

All New Material
$2.50
NATIONAL
LAMPOON
1964 High School Yearbook Parody
Plus: School Newspaper, Literary Magazine, Basketball Program, Report Card, Diploma, Detention Slips, Fake ID, Cootie Catcher, Cheater Slicks, Beaver Shots, Feel-Ups, Fake-Outs, Gross-Outs, Chug-a-Lugs, Wheat Jeans, Pressed Ham, Hang-a-Louie, Get Bent.
618

GOLD

615
Art Director Henry Wolf
Designer Gary Schenck
Publisher Sesame Street Magazine
Agency Henry Wolf Productions

617
Art Director Robert J. Rytter
Designer Robert J. Rytter
Photographers Various
Writers John Allen
Lorna Kirkwood
Tamasin Roop
Publisher Hollins College
Agency The North Charles Street Design Organization

618
Art Director David Kaestle
Designer David Kaestle
Artists Alan Rose
Marc Arcineaux
Mara McAffee
Photographers David Kaestle
Vince Aiosa
Robert Pakter
Writers Doug Kenny
P. J. O'Rourke
Publisher National Lampoon

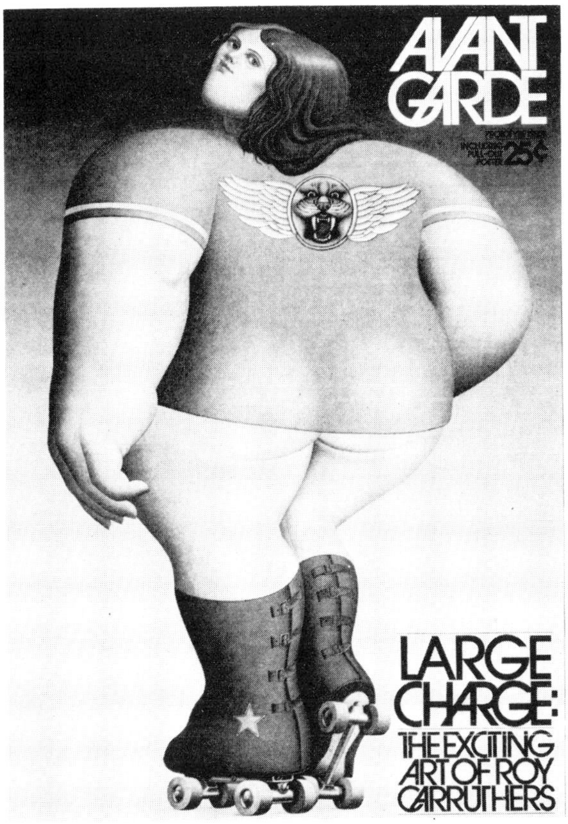
AVANT GARDE
LARGE CHARGE: THE EXCITING ART OF ROY CARRUTHERS

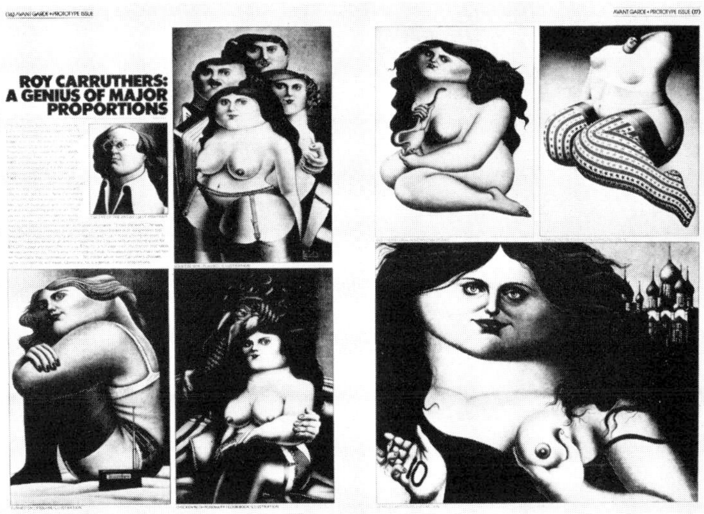
ROY CARRUTHERS: A GENIUS OF MAJOR PROPORTIONS

619

The New York Times Magazine
NOVEMBER 24, 1974 / SECTION 6
Thanksgiving, with a conscience
CONTENTS: PAGE 10
Thanksgiving Menu 1974
Chilled Artichoke
Sunflower Seeds Vinaigrette
Clear Borscht
Sesame Seed Wafers
Vegetarian Coulibiac
Sour Cream Sauce
Broccoli Purée
Corn Relish
Bean Sprout & Citrus Salad on Watercress
Pumpkin Flan
Fresh Apple Cider

620

The New York Times Magazine
FEBRUARY 24, 1974 SECTION 6
ПЕПСИ-КОЛА
The genie of East-West trade: Out of the bottle / CONTENTS PAGE 9

621

619
Art Director Herb Lubalin
Designer Hoi Ling Chu
Artist Roy Carruthers
Editor Ralph Ginzburg
Publisher Avant Garde
Agency Lubalin, Smith, Carnase

620
Art Director Henry Wolf
Designer Henry Wolf
Photographer Henry Wolf
Publisher The New York Times Magazine
Agency Henry Wolf Productions

621
Art Director Ruth Ansel
Designer Ruth Ansel
Photographer Allen Green
Editors Lewis Bergman
Jack Rosenthal
Publisher The New York Times Magazine

FIFTY CENTS
MAY 27, 1974
TIME
MID-EAST MASSACRES

622

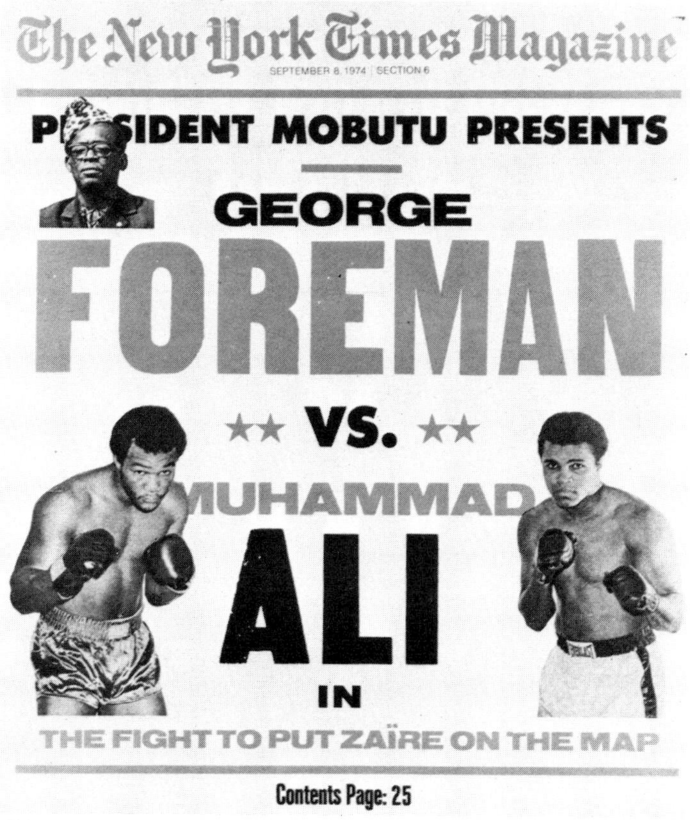
The New York Times Magazine
SEPTEMBER 8, 1974 | SECTION 6
PRESIDENT MOBUTU PRESENTS
GEORGE
FOREMAN
VS.
MUHAMMAD
ALI
IN
THE FIGHT TO PUT ZAÏRE ON THE MAP
Contents Page: 25

623

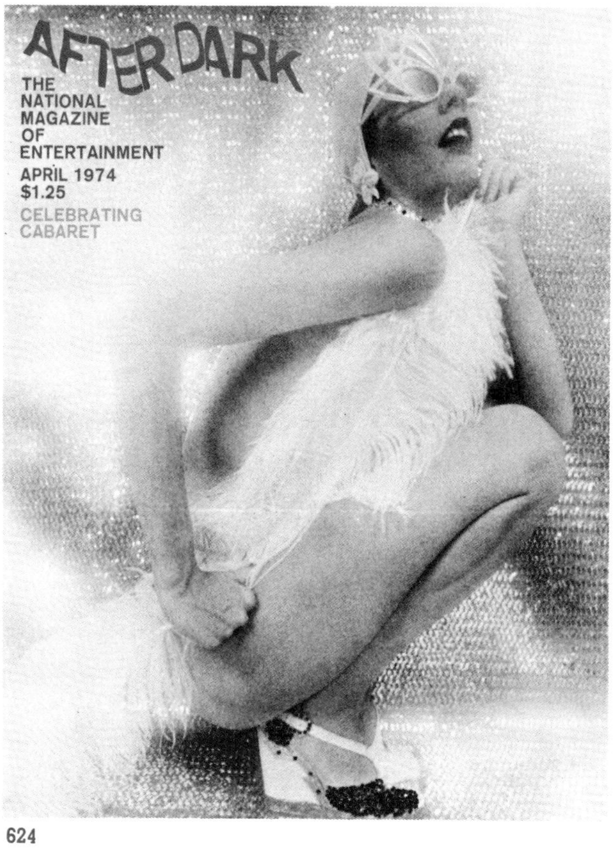
AFTER DARK
THE NATIONAL MAGAZINE OF ENTERTAINMENT
APRIL 1974
$1.25
CELEBRATING CABARET

624

622
Art Director David Merrill
Designer David Merrill
Artist David Merrill
Photographer U.P.I.
Editor Henry Anatole Grunwald
Publisher Time Magazine

623
Art Director Ruth Ansel
Designer Ruth Ansel
Artist Ruth Ansel
Editors Lewis Bergman
Jack Rosenthal
Publisher The New York Times Magazine

624
Art Director Herbert Migdoll
Designers Herbert Migdoll
Augustus Ginnochio
Photographer Rick Shaefer
Writer William Como
Publisher After Dark

HUDSON VALLEY
50¢
October
1974
THE HECTIC LIFE
OF A TOWN JUSTICE
FALL FOLIAGE TOUR
COMPLETE OCTOBER
CALENDAR OF EVENTS
EVERYBODY EATS OUR APPLES

625

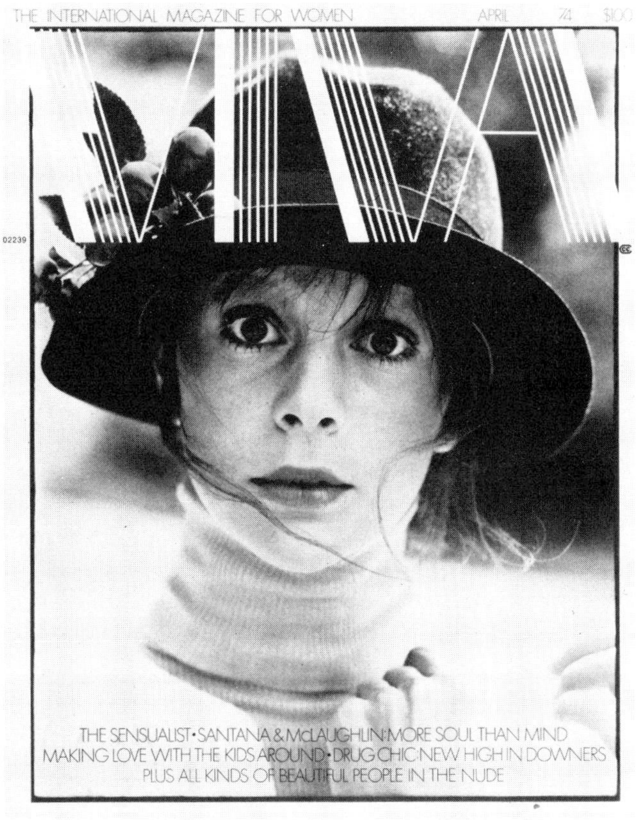
THE INTERNATIONAL MAGAZINE FOR WOMEN
APRIL
74
$1.00
VIVA
THE SENSUALIST • SANTANA & McLAUGHLIN: MORE SOUL THAN MIND
MAKING LOVE WITH THE KIDS AROUND • DRUG CHIC: NEW HIGH IN DOWNERS
PLUS ALL KINDS OF BEAUTIFUL PEOPLE IN THE NUDE

626

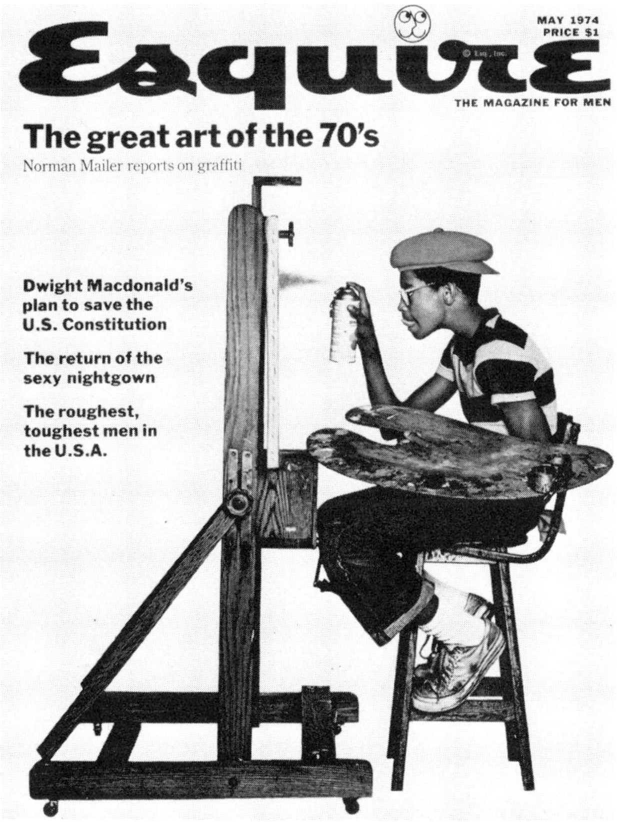
MAY 1974
PRICE $1
Esquire
THE MAGAZINE FOR MEN
The great art of the 70's
Norman Mailer reports on graffiti
Dwight Macdonald's plan to save the U.S. Constitution
The return of the sexy nightgown
The roughest, toughest men in the U.S.A.

627

625
Art Director Marilyn Hoffner
Designers Marilyn Hoffner
Al Greenberg
Photographer Ron Rozman
Publisher Hudson Valley Magazine

626
Art Director Ahmad Sadiq
Designers Frank DeVino
Hector Marrero
Photographer Stan Shaffer
Publisher Viva

627
Art Director Richard Weigand
Designer Jean Paul Goude
Photographer Jean Paul Goude
Publisher Esquire

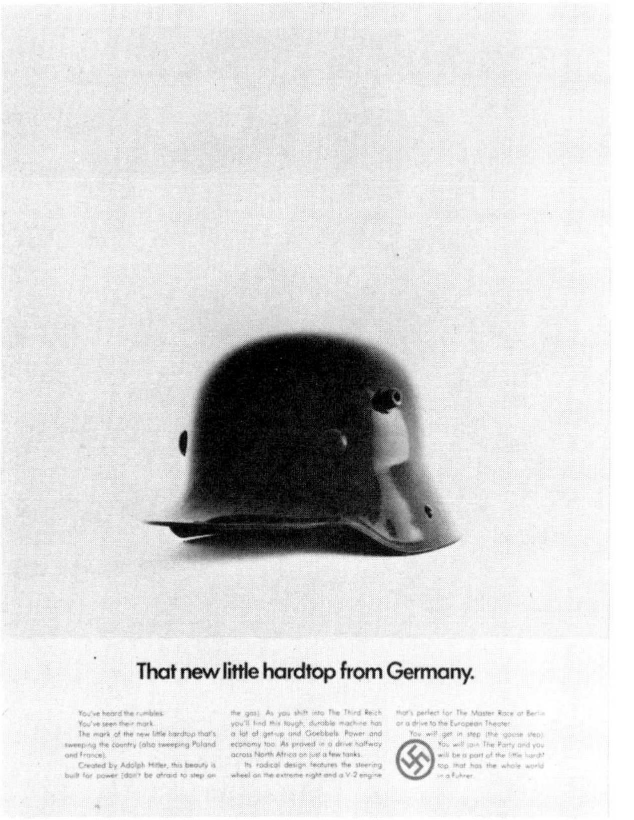
That new little hardtop from Germany.

628

Squeezed between rising insurance premiums and the escalating threat of malpractice litigation, many physicians work in a climate of increasing tension.

629

Bertsch & Cooper design advertisements, books, booklets and posters, originate type faces, and draw special ornament and decorative borders to be used along with type. Their studio is equipped to supply typography befitting their designs. 59 E. Van Buren St. Chicago
Harrison 7771
Leaves from
MAN dwells
GLORY impends
CLIMATE like tropics
REAL sailor
Swing TUNE
JIG played on jug
PRONG antelope
Amplify inspired REVUE
MYSTERY grows as days pass
RUGS colorful
MICE play
MAIZE
Cat is AWAY
ambrosia
NEW game devised
PINKISH
xylophonist
Quaint old CAPE
EARLY fashions viewed
Basket picnics under ELMS
The Wizard of Oz
LET'S NEVER FORGET HIM

630

628
Art Director Larry Sons
Designer John Green
Photographer Francisco/Booth
Writer Larry Sons
Publisher The Dallas/Ft. Worth Society of Visual Communications
Agency The Richards Group

629
Art Director Joe Giacalone
Designers Joe Giacalone
Jim Kolar
Sue Connors
Photographer Charles Shotwell
Writer Carl Burkard
Publisher Prism
American Medical Assoc.

630
Art Director Herb Lubalin
Designer Herb Lubalin
Artist Oz Cooper
Editor Herb Lubalin
Writer Jack Anson Finke
Publisher U & lc
International Typeface Corp
Agency Lubalin, Smith, Carnase

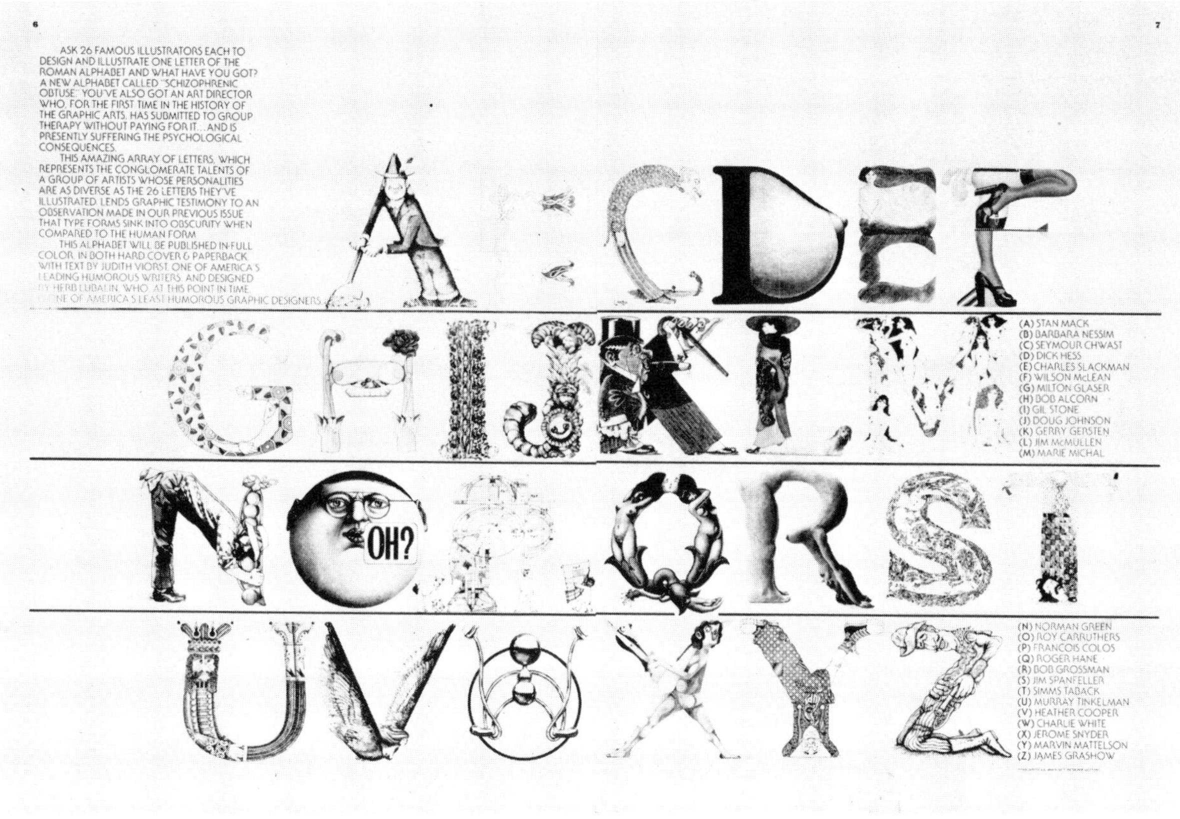
6
7
ASK 26 FAMOUS ILLUSTRATORS EACH TO DESIGN AND ILLUSTRATE ONE LETTER OF THE ROMAN ALPHABET AND WHAT HAVE YOU GOT? A NEW ALPHABET CALLED "SCHIZOPHRENIC OBTUSE" YOU'VE ALSO GOT AN ART DIRECTOR WHO, FOR THE FIRST TIME IN THE HISTORY OF THE GRAPHIC ARTS, HAS SUBMITTED TO GROUP THERAPY WITHOUT PAYING FOR IT... AND IS PRESENTLY SUFFERING THE PSYCHOLOGICAL CONSEQUENCES.
THIS AMAZING ARRAY OF LETTERS, WHICH REPRESENTS THE CONGLOMERATE TALENTS OF A GROUP OF ARTISTS WHOSE PERSONALITIES ARE AS DIVERSE AS THE 26 LETTERS THEY'VE ILLUSTRATED, LENDS GRAPHIC TESTIMONY TO AN OBSERVATION MADE IN OUR PREVIOUS ISSUE THAT TYPE FORMS SINK INTO OBSCURITY WHEN COMPARED TO THE HUMAN FORM.
THIS ALPHABET WILL BE PUBLISHED IN FULL COLOR, IN BOTH HARD COVER & PAPERBACK WITH TEXT BY JUDITH VIORST, ONE OF AMERICA'S LEADING HUMOROUS WRITERS, AND DESIGNED BY HERB LUBALIN, WHO, AT THIS POINT IN TIME, IS ONE OF AMERICA'S LEAST HUMOROUS GRAPHIC DESIGNERS.
OH?
(A) STAN MACK
(B) BARBARA NESSIM
(C) SEYMOUR CHWAST
(D) DICK HESS
(E) CHARLES SLACKMAN
(F) WILSON McLEAN
(G) MILTON GLASER
(H) BOB ALCORN
(I) GIL STONE
(J) DOUG JOHNSON
(K) GERRY GERSTEN
(L) JIM McMULLEN
(M) MARIE MICHAL
(N) NORMAN GREEN
(O) ROY CARRUTHERS
(P) FRANCOIS COLOS
(Q) ROGER HANE
(R) BOB GROSSMAN
(S) JIM SPANFELLER
(T) SIMMS TABACK
(U) MURRAY TINKELMAN
(V) HEATHER COOPER
(W) CHARLIE WHITE
(X) JEROME SNYDER
(Y) MARVIN MATTELSON
(Z) JAMES GRASHOW

631

20
21
Something for Everybody from U&lc.
TYPOMANIA
WHY IS THE KING OF HEARTS THE ONLY ONE THAT HASN'T A MOUSTACHE ?
HOW I GAVE HERB LUBALIN THE FINGER AND LIVED TO TELL THE STORY.
BY PETER KATZ
A writer owned an asterisk, And kept it in his den, Where he wrote tales (which had large sales) of frail and erring men; And always, when he reached the point Where carping censors lurk, He called upon the Asterisk To do his dirty work
I am the voice of today, the herald of tomorrow... I coin for you the enchanting tale, the philosopher's moralizing, and the poet's visions... I am the leaden army that conquers the world— I am type.
FREDERIC GOUDY
HEAD LINE! BODY COPY FOOT NOTE
Where did it come from?
A good thing about gossip is that it is within everybody's reach, and it is much more interesting than any other form of speech.
OGDEN NASH
GOSSIP
Fly-Speck: The prototype of punctuation.
AMBROSE BIERCE

632

631
Art Director Herb Lubalin
Designer Herb Lubalin
Artists Various
Editor Herb Lubalin
Writer Herb Lubalin
Publisher U & lc
International Typeface Corp.
Agency Lubalin, Smith, Carnase

632
Art Director Herb Lubalin
Designer Herb Lubalin
Artists Gerry Gersten
Peter Katz
Editor Herb Lubalin
Writers Herb Lubalin
Jack Anson Finke
Publisher U & lc
International Typeface Corp.
Agency Lubalin, Smith, Carnase

12

13

DEFINITIONS FROM THE DEVIL'S DICTIONARY BY AMBROSE BIERCE
ILLUSTRATED BY GERRY GERSTEN

A

Achievement, *n.* The death of endeavor and the birth of disgust.

Admiral, *n.* That part of a war-ship which does the talking while the figure-head does the thinking.

Affianced, *pp.* Fitted with an ankle-ring for the ball and chain.

Agitator, *n.* A statesman who shakes the fruit trees of his neighbors—to dislodge the worms.

Air, *n.* A nutritious substance supplied by a bountiful Providence for the fattening of the poor.

Alone, *adj.* In bad company.

Ambidextrous, *adj.* Able to pick with equal skill a right-hand pocket or a left.

Ass, *n.* A public singer with a good voice but no ear. In Virginia City, Nevada, he is called the Washoe Canary, in Dakota, the Senator, and everywhere the Donkey.

Auctioneer, *n.* The man who proclaims with a hammer that he has picked a pocket with his tongue.

B

Bait, *n.* A preparation that renders the hook more palatable. The best kind is beauty.

Beauty, *n.* The power by which a woman charms a lover and terrifies a husband.

Belladonna, *n.* In Italian a beautiful lady; in English a deadly poison. A striking example of the essential identity of the two tongues.

Birth, *n.* The first and direst of all disasters. As to the nature of it there appears to be no uniformity. Castor and Pollux were born from the egg. Pallas came out of a skull. Galatea was once a block of stone. Peresilis, who wrote in the tenth century, avers that he grew up out of the ground where a priest had spilled holy water. It is known that Arimaxus was derived from a hole in the earth, made by a stroke of lightning. Leucomedon was the son of a cavern in Mount Ætna, and I have myself seen a man come out of a wine cellar.

Brain, *n.* An apparatus with which we think that we think. That which distinguishes the man who is content to be something from the man who wishes to do something. A man of great wealth, or one who has been pitchforked into high station, has commonly such a headful of brain that his neighbors cannot keep their hats on. In our civilization, and under our republican form of government, brain is so highly honored that it is rewarded by exemption from the cares of office.

Bride, *n.* A woman with a fine prospect of happiness behind her.

C

Cabbage, *n.* A familiar kitchen-garden vegetable about as large and wise as a man's head.

Cannibal, *n.* A gastronome of the old school who preserves the simple tastes and adheres to the natural diet of the pre-pork period.

Christian, *n.* One who believes that the New Testament is a divinely inspired book admirably suited to the spiritual needs of his neighbor. One who follows the teachings of Christ in so far as they are not inconsistent with a life of sin.

Circus, *n.* A place where horses, ponies and elephants are permitted to see men, women and children acting the fool.

Commerce, *n.* A kind of transaction in which A plunders from B the goods of C, and for compensation B picks the pocket of D of money belonging to E.

Connoisseur, *n.* A specialist who knows everything about something and nothing about anything else.

D

Dance, *v.i.* To leap about to the sound of tittering music, preferably with arms about your neighbor's wife or daughter. There are many kinds of dances, but all those requiring the participation of the two sexes have two characteristics in common; they are conspicuously innocent, and warmly loved by the vicious.

Day, *n.* A period of twenty-four hours, mostly misspent. This period is divided into two parts, the day proper and the night, or day improper—the former devoted to sins of business, the latter consecrated to the other sort. These two kinds of social activity overlap.

Deliberation, *n.* The act of examining one's bread to determine which side it is buttered on.

Deluge, *n.* A notable first experiment in baptism which washed away the sins (and sinners) of the world.

Deputy, *n.* A male relative of an office-holder, or of his bondsman. The deputy is commonly a beautiful young man, with a red necktie and an intricate system of cobwebs extending from his nose to his desk. When accidentally struck by the janitor's broom, he gives off a cloud of dust.

Diplomacy, *n.* The patriotic art of lying for one's country.

Distance, *n.* The only thing that the rich are willing for the poor to call theirs' and keep.

Duel, *n.* A formal ceremony preliminary to the reconciliation of two enemies. Great skill is necessary to its satisfactory observance; if awkwardly performed the most unexpected and deplorable consequences sometimes ensue. A long time ago a man lost his life in a duel.

E

Emotion, *n.* A prostrating disease caused by a determination of the heart to the head. It is sometimes accompanied by a copious discharge of hydrated chloride of sodium from the eyes.

Erudition, *n.* Dust shaken out of a book into an empty skull.

Eulogy, *n.* Praise of a person who has either the advantages of wealth and power, or the consideration to be dead.

F

Famous, *adj.* Conspicuously miserable.

Female, *n.* One of the opposing, or unfair, sex.

Fiddle, *n.* An instrument to tickle human ears by friction of a horse's tail on the entrails of a cat.

Finance, *n.* The art or science of managing revenues and resources for the best advantage of the manager. The pronunciation of this word with the i long and the accent on the first syllable is one of America's most precious discoveries and possessions.

Funeral, *n.* A pageant whereby we attest our respect for the dead by enriching the undertaker, and strengthen our grief by an expenditure that deepens our groans and doubles our tears.

G

Grave, *n.* A place in which the dead are laid to await the coming of the medical student.

Gravitation, *n.* The tendency of all bodies to approach one another with a strength proportioned to the quantity of matter they contain—the quantity of matter they contain being ascertained by the strength of their tendency to approach one another. This is a lovely and edifying illustration of how science, having made A the proof of B, makes B the proof of A.

H

Hand, *n.* A singular instrument worn at the end of a human arm and commonly thrust into somebody's pocket.

Hash, *x.* There is no definition for this word—nobody knows what hash is.

Hatred, *n.* A sentiment appropriate to the occasion of another's superiority.

Hearse, *n.* Death's baby carriage.

Hers, *pron.* His.

Homicide, *n.* The slaying of one human being by another. There are four kinds of homicide: felonious, excusable, justifiable and praiseworthy, but it makes no great difference to the person slain whether he fell by one kind or another—the classification is for advantage of the lawyers.

Husband, *n.* One who, having dined, is charged with the care of the plate.

I

Imagination, *n.* A warehouse of facts, with poet and liar in joint ownership.

Incompatibility, *n.* In matrimony a similarity of tastes, particularly the taste for domination. Incompatibility may, however, consist of a meek-eyed matron living just around the corner. It has even been known to wear a moustache.

Interpreter, *n.* One who enables two persons of different languages to understand each other by repeating to each what it would have been to the interpreter's advantage for the other to have said.

Intimacy, *n.* A relation into which fools are providentially drawn for their mutual destruction.

Irreligion, *n.* The principal one of the great faiths of the world.

J

Jealous, *adj.* Unduly concerned about the preservation of that which can be lost only if not worth keeping.

Justice, *n.* A commodity which in a more or less adulterated condition the State sells to the citizen as a reward for his allegiance, taxes and personal service.

K

Kill, *v.t.* To create a vacancy without nominating a successor.

Kindness, *n.* A brief preface to ten volumes of exaction.

King, *n.* A male person commonly known in America as a "crowned head," although he never wears a crown and has usually no head to speak of.

Kleptomaniac, *n.* A rich thief.

L

Lap, *n.* One of the most important organs of the female system—an admirable provision of nature for the repose of infancy, but chiefly useful in rural festivities to support plates of cold chicken and heads of adult males.

Learning, *n.* The kind of ignorance distinguishing the studious.

Lecturer, *n.* One with his hand in your pocket, his tongue in your ear and his faith in your patience.

Liar, *n.* A lawyer with a roving commission.

Liberty, *n.* One of Imagination's most precious possessions.

Life, *n.* A spiritual pickle preserving the body from decay. We live in daily apprehension of its loss, yet when lost it is not missed. The question, "Is life worth living?" has been much discussed, particularly by those who think it is not, many of whom have written at great length in support of their view and by careful observance of the laws of health enjoyed for long terms of years the honors of successful controversy.

Limb, *n.* The branch of a tree or the leg of an American woman.

Logic, *n.* The art of thinking and reasoning in strict accordance with the limitations and incapacities of the human misunderstanding. The basic of logic is the syllogism, consisting of a major and a minor premise and a conclusion—thus:

Major Premise: Sixty men can do a piece of work sixty times as quickly as one man.

Minor Premise: One man can dig a post-hole in sixty seconds; therefore—

Conclusion: Sixty men can dig a post-hole in one second.

This may be called the syllogism arithmetical, in which, by combining logic and mathematics, we obtain a double certainty and are twice blessed.

Longevity, *n.* Uncommon extension of the fear of death.

Love, *n.* A temporary insanity curable by marriage or by removal of the patient from the influences under which he incurred the disorder. This disease, like caries and many other ailments, is prevalent only among civilized races living under artificial conditions; barbarous nations breathing pure air and eating simple food enjoy immunity from its ravages. It is sometimes fatal, but more frequently to the physician than to the patient.

M

Magnificent, *adj.* Having a grandeur or splendor superior to that to which the spectator is accustomed, as the ears of an ass, to a rabbit, or the glory of a glow-worm, to a maggot.

Maiden, *n.* A young person of the unfair sex addicted to clewless conduct and views that madden to crime. The genus has a wide geographical distribution, being found wherever sought and deplored wherever found. The maiden is not altogether unpleasing to the eye, nor (without her piano and her views) insupportable to the ear, though in respect to comeliness distinctly inferior to the rainbow, and, with regard to the part of her

633

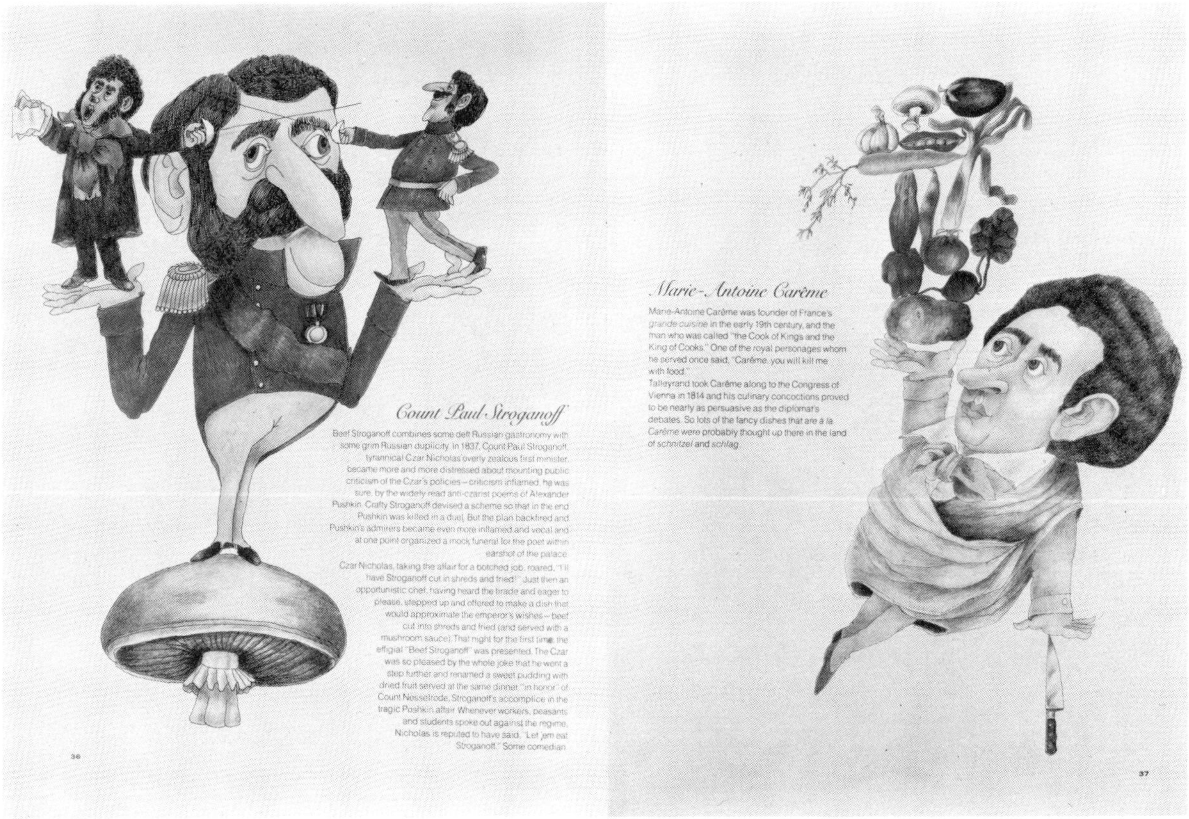

Count Paul Stroganoff

Beef Stroganoff combines some deft Russian gastronomy with some grim Russian duplicity. In 1837, Count Paul Stroganoff, tyrannical Czar Nicholas' overly zealous first minister, became more and more distressed about mounting public criticism of the Czar's policies—criticism inflamed, he was sure, by the widely read anti-czarist poems of Alexander Pushkin. Crafty Stroganoff devised a scheme so that in the end Pushkin was killed in a duel. But the plan backfired and Pushkin's admirers became even more inflamed and vocal and at one point organized a mock funeral for the poet within earshot of the palace.

Czar Nicholas, taking the affair for a botched job, roared, "I'll have Stroganoff cut in shreds and fried!" Just then an opportunistic chef, having heard the tirade and eager to please, stepped up and offered to make a dish that would approximate the emperor's wishes—beef cut into shreds and fried (and served with a mushroom sauce). That night for the first time, the effigial "Beef Stroganoff" was presented. The Czar was so pleased by the whole joke that he went a step further and renamed a sweet pudding with dried fruit served at the same dinner "in honor" of Count Nesselrode, Stroganoff's accomplice in the tragic Pushkin affair. Whenever workers, peasants and students spoke out against the regime, Nicholas is reputed to have said, "Let 'em eat Stroganoff." Some comedian.

36

Marie-Antoine Carême

Marie-Antoine Carême was founder of France's *grande cuisine* in the early 19th century, and the man who was called "the Cook of Kings and the King of Cooks." One of the royal personages whom he served once said, "Carême, you will kill me with food."

Talleyrand took Carême along to the Congress of Vienna in 1814 and his culinary concoctions proved to be nearly as persuasive as the diplomat's debates. So lots of the fancy dishes that are *à la Carême* were probably thought up there in the land of *schnitzel* and *schlag*.

37

634

633
Art Director Herb Lubalin
Designer Herb Lubalin
Artist Gerry Gersten
Editor Herb Lubalin
Writer Ambrose Bierce
Publisher U & lc
International Typeface Corp.
Agency Lubalin, Smith, Carnase

634
Art Director Robert Hallock
Artist Jerome Snyder
Publisher Lithopinion
Amalgamated Lithographers of America

U&lc.

Aa Bb Cc Dd Ee Ff Gg Hh Ii Jj Kk Ll Mm Nn Oo Pp Qq Rr Ss Tt Uu Vv Ww Xx Yy Zz 1234567890&ÆŒ$¢£%!?()[]

UPPER AND LOWER CASE, THE INTERNATIONAL JOURNAL OF TYPOGRAPHICS — PUBLISHED BY THE INTERNATIONAL TYPEFACE CORPORATION, VOLUME ONE, NUMBER THREE 1974

In This Issue:

The First Alphabet
For eons of time, historians and scholars have accepted the Bible of Johann Gutenberg as our first example of printing. The editors of U&lc set the matter straight by producing, and telling about, our actual first use of movable type.

Editorial
The editors restate the purpose and intention of U&lc.

The Mecklenburg Declaration
In 1819, an alleged "first" Declaration of Independence appeared in the newspapers, purportedly adopted in 1775. If genuine, it would have made Thomas Jefferson an out-and-out plagiarist. Jack Finke tells this astonishing, true, yet little known story of historical plagiarism.

The Wizard of Oz
Every art director and typographic designer owes a measure of his skills to the influence of this towering figure of American Typography.

XPO-I
As President of the Art Directors Club, Herb Lubalin created the concept of a First Communications Exposition. Here, he reveals XPO's raison d'etre, its successes, its problems, and its future outlook for bringing together the various disciplines relating to the graphic arts.

The Devil's Dictionary
Ambrose Bierce is known as one of America's great writers. He was also one of our delicious humorists. His "Devil's Dictionary" is a prominent instance of this, and some choice examples are reproduced here from A to Z.

My Best With Letters
Helmut Krone, Bradbury Thompson, Mo Lebowitz, and Ivan Chermayeff join the growing list of outstanding designers contributing their one "best" as a regular feature of U&lc.

Ms.
The first of a new series of articles devoted to the many talented women in communications, the kickoff being devoted to the superior work of Annegret Beier of the Paris office of Lubalin, Delpire et Cie, and one of Europe's finest graphic designers.

Something For Everybody
Featurettes, aphorisms, cartoons, and you name it. Another regular feature of U&lc.

Selling Ice Cubes To An Eskimo
Herb Lubalin in high old form, as he takes off on a pet subject—dimensions. With great good humor he traces the difficulties he encountered trying to sell a three-dimensional logo to some astute corporate executive graphic design buyer—accompanied by some elegant illustrations of the turndowns, still up for grabs to the nearest, and smartest, buyer.

Letters To The Editor
Unblushingly, we present random samples from the virtual flood of mail that continues to pour in from all parts of the globe.

What's New From ITC
A preview showing of the very newest in ITC typeface designs: **Lubalin Graph** and **American Typewriter**—now being offered through ITC subscribers.

XPO 1 THE FIRST COMMUNICATIONS EXPOSITION

le bestiaire jeu

NBCABC

THE FIRST ALPHABET

"WHO'S GUTENBERG?" ASKS ANCIENT MEDITERRANEAN GRAPHIC DESIGNER

The question in the subhead may not be as facetious as it sounds. For in 1908, with the archaeological discovery in Crete of the **Phaistos Disk**, all traditionally-accepted concepts of the "invention" of printing by Johann Gutenberg had to be pushed backward in time at least as far as the second millennium B.C. The actual name of that first "graphic designer" is, unfortunately, lost to us. In those days, there seemed to be no grab for credits: no by-lines have yet been found by scientists on the clay tablets of the Babylonians or the Egyptians or the Etruscans.

Aside from its discovery, a striking feature of this Cretan find—a clay disk with alphabetic or hieroglyphic figures imprinted in spirals on both sides—is that, for the first time, the different symbols were imposed individually on the wet clay. Another way of saying that the **Phaistos Disk** was printed using movable type some thousands of years before the name Gutenberg was even heard of.

The whole question of just when it was that the alphabet was invented is an intriguing one. Although generally attributed to the Phoenicians, this doesn't mean that man did not write before that time, but simply that he did not use an actual alphabet to enable him to spell out words using individual letters instead of pictures—as with the original Egyptian hieroglyphics and the Chinese ideographs, or with the cuneiform wedge writing of the Babylonians representing complete syllables. As a matter of record, spelling by syllables is still effectively used in modern Japanese and Korean scripts, but in general it is cumbersome because of the many additional number of symbols needed, and is not as effective as the true alphabet.

The initial Phoenician or North Semitic alphabet—from which all other true alphabets are descended—has been authentically traced back to Byblos, Lebanon (**biblia, bibliography, bibliophile,** et al) where it was in use more than 4000 years ago. And it is generally held that the earliest **phonetic** alphabet—in which written symbols stand for sounds rather than for ideas or objects—appears in inscriptions found in the vicinity of Mount Sinai, dating from approximately the fifteenth century B.C. And it was this early Semitic Alphabet, adopted by the Greeks, that later gave rise to the Roman, from which our present system of writing stems.

It is of especial interest that the Semitic names of the letters—**aleph, beth, gimel, daleth,** and so on—give a clear clue to the pictograph origin of the phonetic alphabet. **Aleph** is the Semitic word for **ox,** and the earliest form of our letter A is definitely a picture of the head of an ox; the same holds true for **beth,** Semitic for **house; gimel,** Semitic for **camel,** and all the way on to the end of the character list.

The Rosetta Stone. A tri-lingual three foot diorite slab, found by Napoleon in 1799 near Rosetta at Giza. Its singular inscription written in hieroglyphs, demotic Egyptian, and Greek enabled Champollion to decipher the mysterious language of the ancient Egyptians.

Babylonian Clay Tablet. An example of the cuneiform system of wedge-shaped writing representing complete symbols, introduced about the middle of the third millennium B.C. and readily adaptable to the Semitic dialects prevalent in Syria/Palestine.

U&lc.

Editorial:

THE MECKLENBURG DECLARATION: WAS THOMAS JEFFERSON A PLAGIARIST?

635

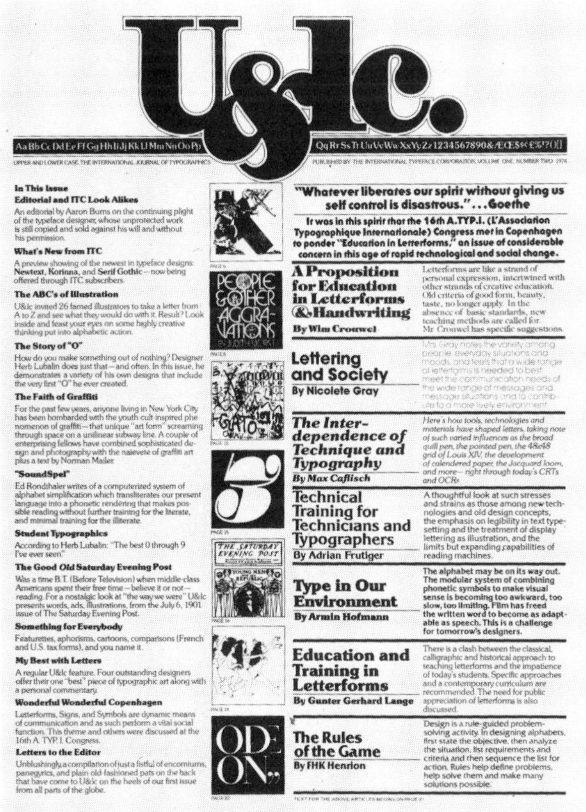
U&lc.

Aa Bb Cc Dd Ee Ff Gg Hh Ii Jj Kk Ll Mm Nn Oo Pp Qq Rr Ss Tt Uu Vv Ww Xx Yy Zz 1234567890&ÆŒ$¢£%!?()[]

UPPER AND LOWER CASE, THE INTERNATIONAL JOURNAL OF TYPOGRAPHICS — PUBLISHED BY THE INTERNATIONAL TYPEFACE CORPORATION, VOLUME ONE, NUMBER TWO 1974

In This Issue

Editorial and ITC Look Alikes
An editorial by Aaron Burns on the continuing plight of the typeface designer, whose unprotected work is still copied and sold against his will and without his permission.

What's New from ITC
A preview showing of the newest in typeface designs: **Newtext, Korinna,** and **Serif Gothic**—now being offered through ITC subscribers.

The ABC's of Illustration
U&lc invited 26 famed illustrators to take a letter from A to Z and see what they would do with it. Result? Look inside and feast your eyes on some highly creative thinking put into alphabetic action.

The Story of "O"
How do you make something out of nothing? Designer Herb Lubalin does just that—and often. In this issue, he demonstrates a variety of his own designs that include the very first "O" he ever created.

The Faith of Graffiti
For the past few years, anyone living in New York City has been bombarded with the youth cult inspired phenomenon of graffiti—that unique "art form" screaming through space on a unilinear subway line. A couple of enterprising fellows have combined sophisticated design and photography with the naievete of graffiti art plus a text by Norman Mailer.

"SoundSpel"
Ed Rondthaler writes of a computerized system of alphabet simplification which transliterates our present language into a phonetic rendering that makes possible reading without further training for the literate, and minimal training for the illiterate.

Student Typographics
According to Herb Lubalin: "The best 0 through 9 I've ever seen."

The Good *Old* Saturday Evening Post
Was a time B.T. (Before Television) when middle-class Americans spent their free time—believe it or not—reading. For a nostalgic look at "the way we were" U&lc presents words, ads, illustrations, from the July 6, 1901 issue of The Saturday Evening Post.

Something for Everybody
Featurettes, aphorisms, cartoons, comparisons (French and U.S. tax forms), and you name it.

My Best with Letters
A regular U&lc feature. Four outstanding designers offer their one "best" piece of typographic art along with a personal commentary.

Wonderful Wonderful Copenhagen
Letterforms, Signs, and Symbols are dynamic means of communication and as such perform a vital social function. This theme and others were discussed at the 16th A. TYP. I. Congress.

Letters to the Editor
Unblushingly, a compilation of just a fistful of encomiums, panegyrics, and plain old-fashioned pats on the back that have come to U&lc on the heels of our first issue from all parts of the globe.

PEOPLE & OTHER AGGRAVATIONS

THE SATURDAY EVENING POST

ODEON,,

"Whatever liberates our spirit without giving us self control is disastrous."...Goethe

It was in this spirit that the 16th A.TYP.I. (L'Association Typographique Internationale) Congress met in Copenhagen to ponder "Education in Letterforms," an issue of considerable concern in this age of rapid technological and social change.

A Proposition for Education in Letterforms & Handwriting
By Wim Crouwel
Letterforms are like a strand of personal expression, intertwined with other strands of creative education. Old criteria of good form, beauty, taste, no longer apply. In the absence of basic standards, new teaching methods are called for. Mr. Crouwel has specific suggestions.

Lettering and Society
By Nicolete Gray
Mrs. Gray notes the variety among people, everyday situations and moods, and feels that a wide range of letterforms is needed to best meet the communication needs of the wide range of messages and message situations and to contribute to a more lively environment.

The Interdependence of Technique and Typography
By Max Caflisch
Here's how tools, technologies and materials have shaped letters, taking note of such varied influences as the broad quill pen, the pointed pen, the 48x48 grid of Louis XIV, the development of calendered paper, the Jacquard loom, and more—right through today's CRTs and OCRs

Technical Training for Technicians and Typographers
By Adrian Frutiger
A thoughtful look at such stresses and strains as those among new technologies and old design concepts, the emphasis on legibility in text typesetting and the treatment of display lettering as illustration, and the limits but expanding capabilities of reading machines.

Type in Our Environment
By Armin Hofmann
The alphabet may be on its way out. The modular system of combining phonetic symbols to make visual sense is becoming too awkward, too slow, too limiting. Film has freed the written word to become as adaptable as speech. This is a challenge for tomorrow's designers.

Education and Training in Letterforms
By Gunter Gerhard Lange
There is a clash between the classical, calligraphic and historical approach to teaching letterforms and the impatience of today's students. Specific approaches and a contemporary curriculum are recommended. The need for public appreciation of letterforms is also discussed.

The Rules of the Game
By FHK Henrion
Design is a rule-guided problem-solving activity. In designing alphabets, first state the objective, then analyze the situation, list requirements and criteria and then sequence the list for action. Rules help define problems, help solve them and make many solutions possible.

TEXT FOR THE ABOVE ARTICLES BEGINS ON PAGE 21

Something for Everybody from U&lc.

LOGO PHAG

"AMPERSAND: THE SIGN & IS CALLED THE AMPERSAND, FROM THE PHRASE 'AND PER SE AND' OR '& BY ITSELF MEANS 'AND.' THE CHARACTER IS BELIEVED TO HAVE ORIGINATED AS AN ABBREVIATION OF THE LATIN ET MEANING 'AND.' PRONUNCIATION? AM-PER-SAND.

"CHAUVINISM"

"EGGHEAD"

"MEATHEAD"

"HOT DOG"

"AVANT-GARDE"

MARRIAGE

1973 Déclaration des revenus

PICA—AN ABNORMAL CRAVING FOR CERTAIN UNNATURAL FOODS, AS PICKLES AND ICE CREAM, SOMETIMES OCCURRING IN PREGNANCY, HYSTERIA, AND CHLOROSIS.

636

SILVER

635
Art Director Herb Lubalin
Designer Herb Lubalin
Artists Various
Editors Herb Lubalin
Aaron Burns
Jack Anson Finke
Ed Rondthaler
Publisher U & lc
International Typeface Corp.
Agency Lubalin, Smith, Carnase

636
Art Director Herb Lubalin
Designer Herb Lubalin
Artists Various
Editors Herb Lubalin
Aaron Burns
Jack Anson Finke
Ed Rondthaler
Publisher U & lc
International Typeface Corp.
Agency Lubalin, Smith, Carnase

CRIME IN THE SCHOOLS
by Jeremiah B. McKenna
The police last year arrested 219 school age children for murder, 353 for rape, 8056 for robbery and 252 for arson. Many of these children were back in class after only a month, effectively transforming the city's schools into sanctuaries for criminals who prey upon their fellow students.
New York Affairs
Volume I Number 3 1974
New York Affairs
Volume I Number 3 1974

637

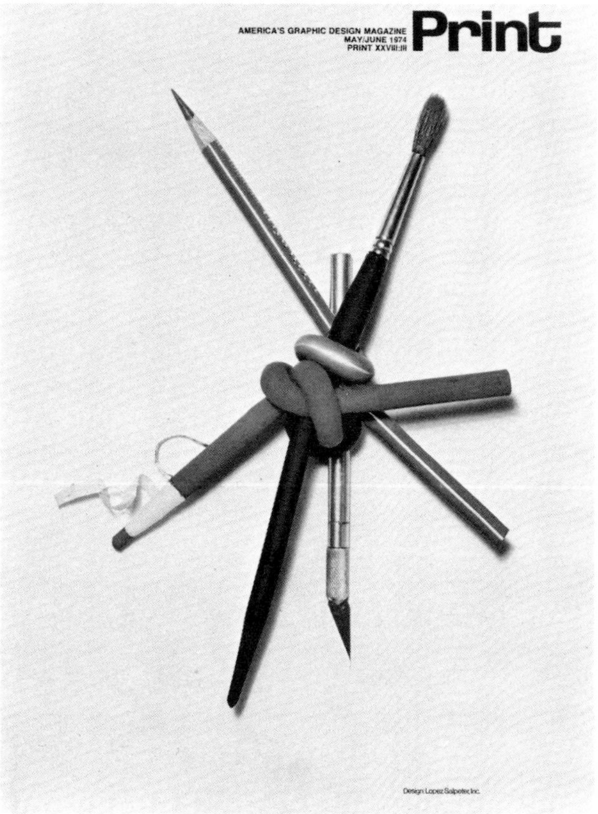
AMERICA'S GRAPHIC DESIGN MAGAZINE
MAY/JUNE 1974
PRINT XXVIII:III
Print

638

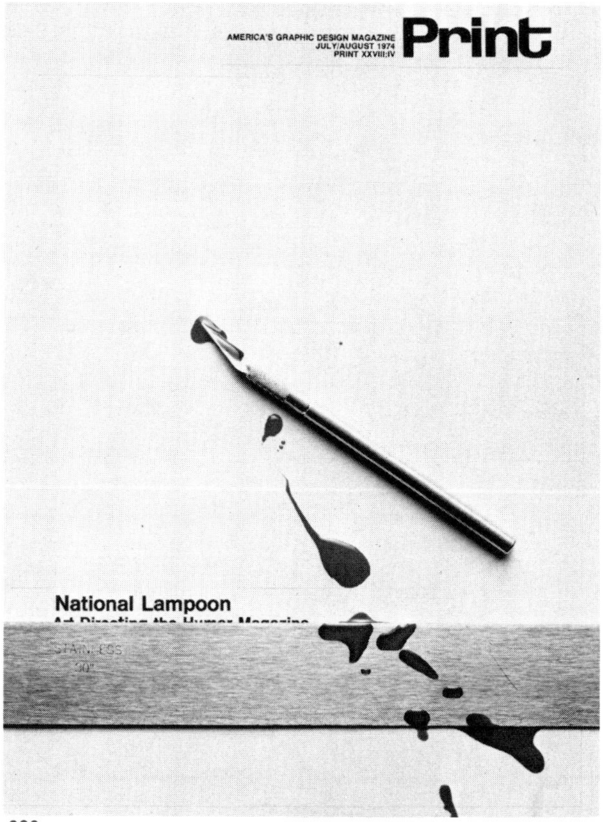
AMERICA'S GRAPHIC DESIGN MAGAZINE
JULY/AUGUST 1974
PRINT XXVIII:IV
Print
National Lampoon

639

SILVER

637
Art Director Samuel N. Antupit
Designer Samuel N. Antupit
Artist Alan Cober
Photographer Saalmon Bernstein
Publisher New York Affairs
Agency Antupit & Others

638
Art Director Bob Salpeter
Designer Bob Salpeter
Artist Madeline Silverman
Photographer Will Nardelli
Publisher Print Magazine
Agency Lopez Salpeter

639
Art Director Andy Kner
Designers David Kaestle
Michael Gross
Photographer Dick Frank
Writers Henry Beard
David Kaestle
Michael Gross
Doug Kenny
Publisher Print Magazine
Agency Pellegrini, Kaestle & Gross

PRACTICAL
FOR PHYSICIANS
PSYCHOLOGY
A HARCOURT BRACE JOVANOVICH PUBLICATION
SEPTEMBER/OCTOBER 1974
Ashley Montagu on medicine
Self-help recovery therapy
Teenagers and sex
Anorexia Nervosa: Diet out of control

641

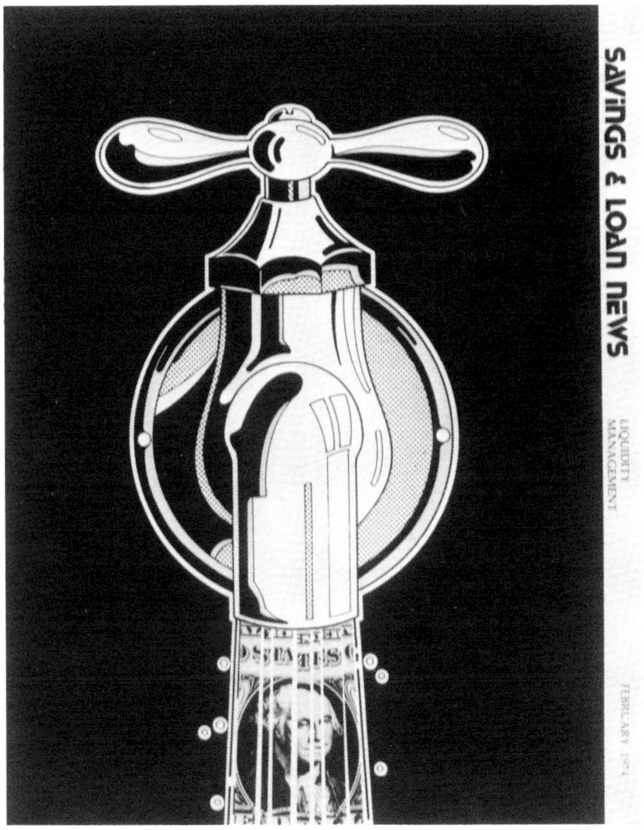
SAVINGS & LOAN NEWS
LIQUIDITY MANAGEMENT

642

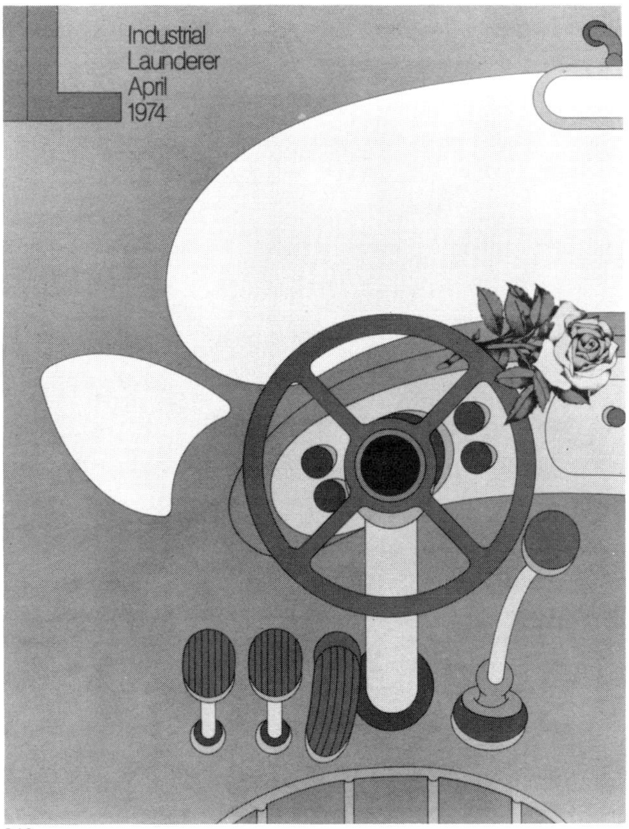
Industrial
Launderer
April
1974

643

641
Art Director Paul Nemesure
Designer Paul Nemesure
Photographer Laszlo Hege
Writer Hilde Bruch
Publisher Practical Psychology
Agency Harcourt Brace Jovanovich

642
Art Director Jim Lienhart
Designer Jim Lienhart
Artists Bill Biderbost
Art Factory
Writers Hoyt Mathews
James Kendall
Publisher Savings & Loan News
Agency Jim Leinhart
Murrie-White & Assoc.

643
Art Director Jack Lefkowitz
Designers Pam Lefkowitz
Jack Lefkowitz
Artists Pam Lefkowitz
Jack Lefkowitz
Editor James L. Trichon
Publisher Industrial Launderers
Institute of Industrial Launderers
Agency Jack Lefkowitz

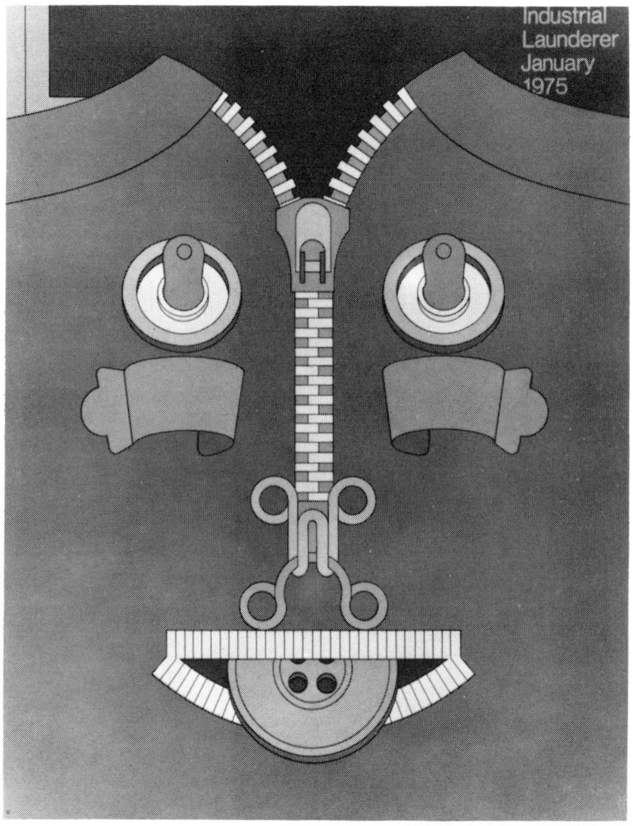
Industrial
Launderer
January
1975

644

A Photographic Treasury from the American Past
THE WAY LIFE WAS

646

644
Art Director Jack Lefkowitz
Designers Pam Lefkowitz
Jack Lefkowitz
Artists Pam Lefkowitz
Jack Lefkowitz
Editor James L. Trichon
Publisher Industrial Launderers
Institute of Industrial Launderers
Agency Jack Lefkowitz

646
Art Director Massimo Vignelli
Designers Massimo Vignelli
Gudrun Buettner
Writer Jeffrey Simpson
Publisher Praeger Books

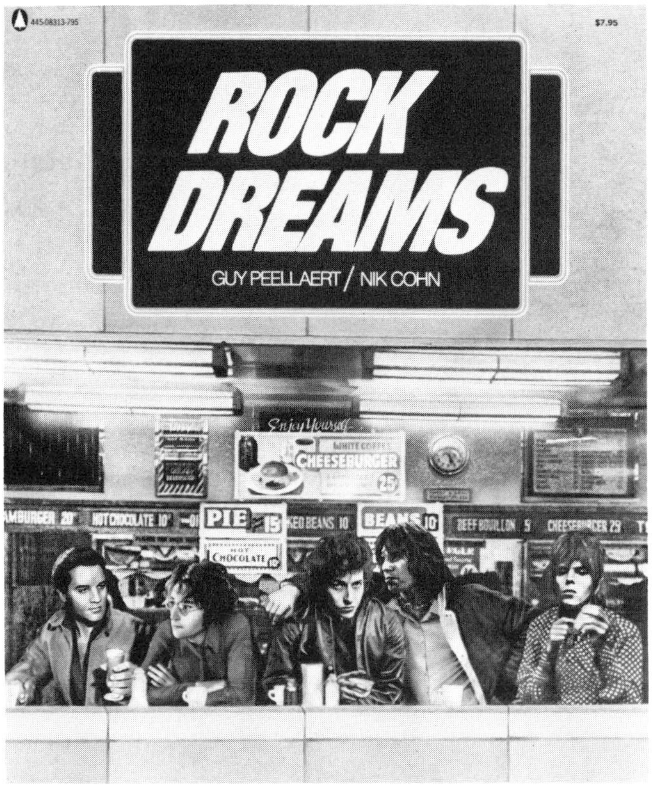
$7.95
ROCK DREAMS
GUY PEELLAERT / NIK COHN
CHEESEBURGER
PIE
BEANS
HOT CHOCOLATE

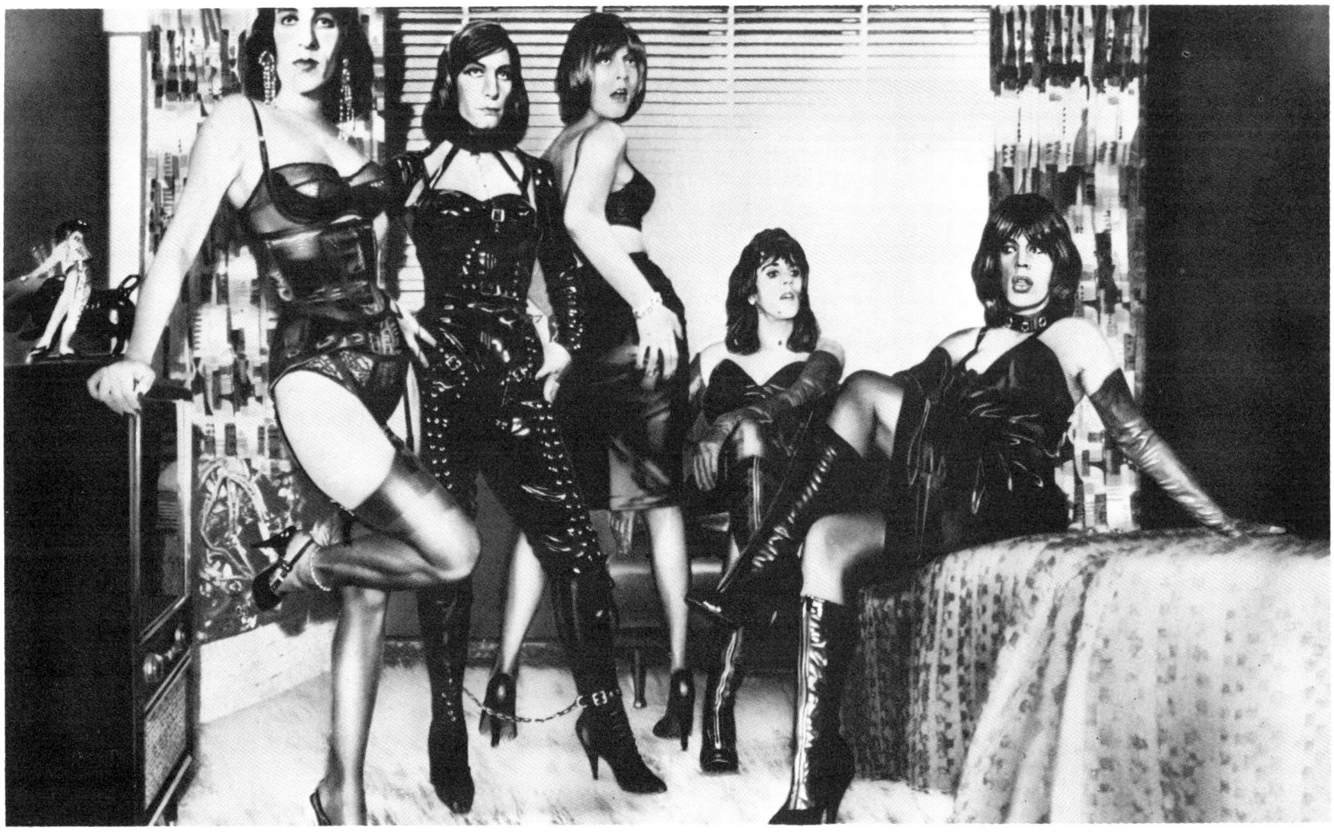

647

647
Art Director Edward Rofheart
Artist Guy Peellaert
Writer Nik Cohn
Publisher Popular Library

Atlas of Cerebral Angiography with Anatomic Correlation
Margaret M. Waddington, M.D.

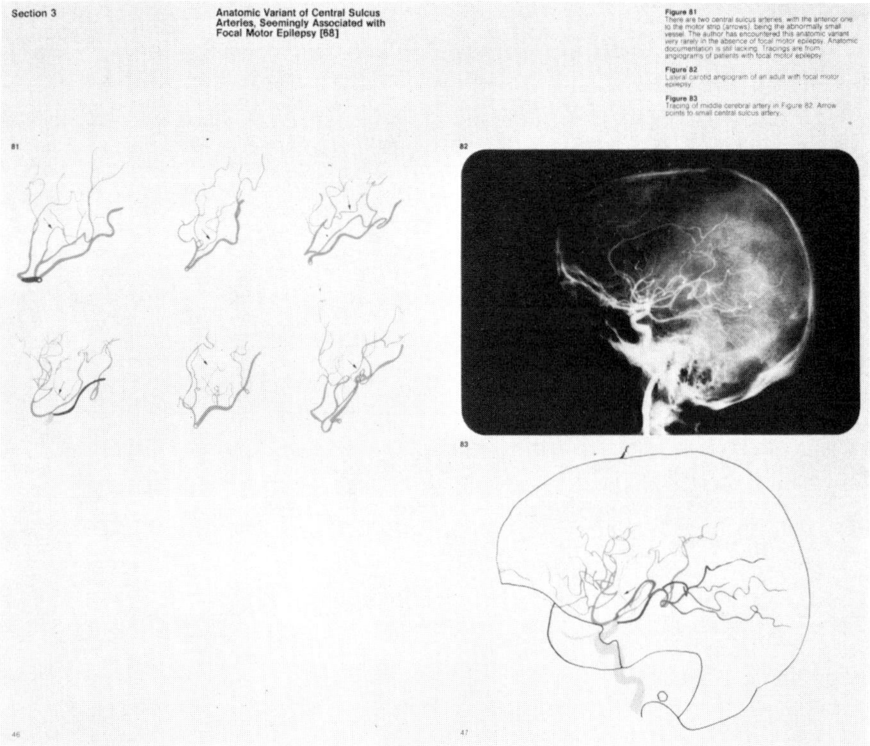
Section 3
Anatomic Variant of Central Sulcus Arteries, Seemingly Associated with Focal Motor Epilepsy [68]
Figure 81
There are two central sulcus arteries, with the anterior one to the motor strip (arrows) being the abnormally small vessel. The author has encountered this anatomic variant very rarely in the absence of focal motor epilepsy. Anatomic documentation is still lacking. Tracings are from angiograms of patients with focal motor epilepsy.
Figure 82
Lateral carotid angiogram of an adult with focal motor epilepsy.
Figure 83
Tracing of middle cerebral artery in Figure 82. Arrow points to small central sulcus artery.
81
82
83
46
47

648

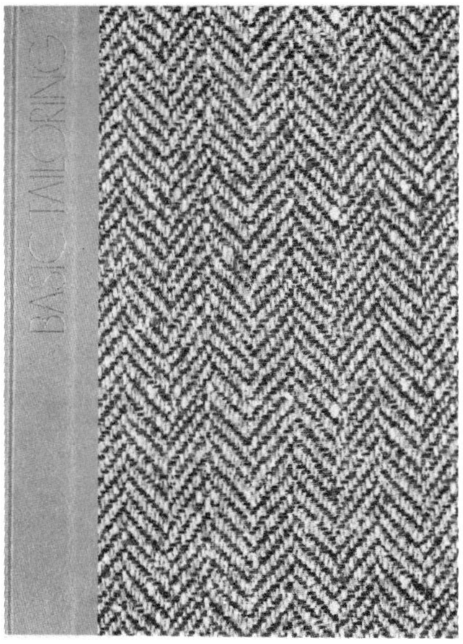
BASIC TAILORING

Classic clothes for tailoring
Fine tailoring rests on a base of certain classic fabrics—primarily the woolens and worsteds shown on these pages. Besides having a stylishly dignified look, these materials possess a rare degree of body and strength that enables them to hold a tailored shape.
The source of their strength and substance is the weave, which is dense and compact, and produces a relatively hard, smooth finish. In the case of the worsteds, the yarns have been tightly twisted for extra toughness. The navy serge at far left, the glen plaid below it, and the beige gabardine at bottom are all worsteds. The Saxony plaid and houndstooth check at far right—both hard woolens—have the same body and are almost as tough. Any of these fabrics would be perfect for a business suit. And the bolder plaid woolen (third from left) is right for a tailored jacket, or for a striking pair of party trousers.

649

648
Art Director Massimo Vignelli
Designer Massimo Vignelli
Writer Margaret M. Waddington, M.D.
Publisher Little, Brown & Co.

649
Art Director Sheldon Cotler
Designer Virginia Gianakos
Artist Harold Corhan
Writer Carlotta Kerwin
Publisher Time-Life Books

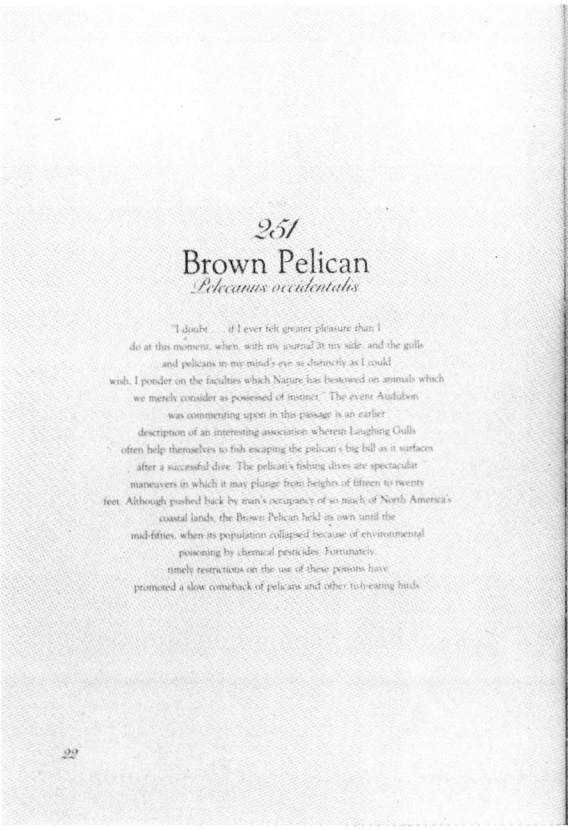

251
Brown Pelican
Pelecanus occidentalis

"I doubt . . . if I ever felt greater pleasure than I do at this moment, when, with my journal at my side, and the gulls and pelicans in my mind's eye as distinctly as I could wish, I ponder on the faculties which Nature has bestowed on animals which we merely consider as possessed of instinct." The event Audubon was commenting upon in this passage is an earlier description of an interesting association wherein Laughing Gulls often help themselves to fish escaping the pelican's big bill as it surfaces after a successful dive. The pelican's fishing dives are spectacular maneuvers in which it may plunge from heights of fifteen to twenty feet. Although pushed back by man's occupancy of so much of North America's coastal lands, the Brown Pelican held its own until the mid-fifties, when its population collapsed because of environmental poisoning by chemical pesticides. Fortunately, timely restrictions on the use of these poisons have promoted a slow comeback of pelicans and other fish-eating birds.

22

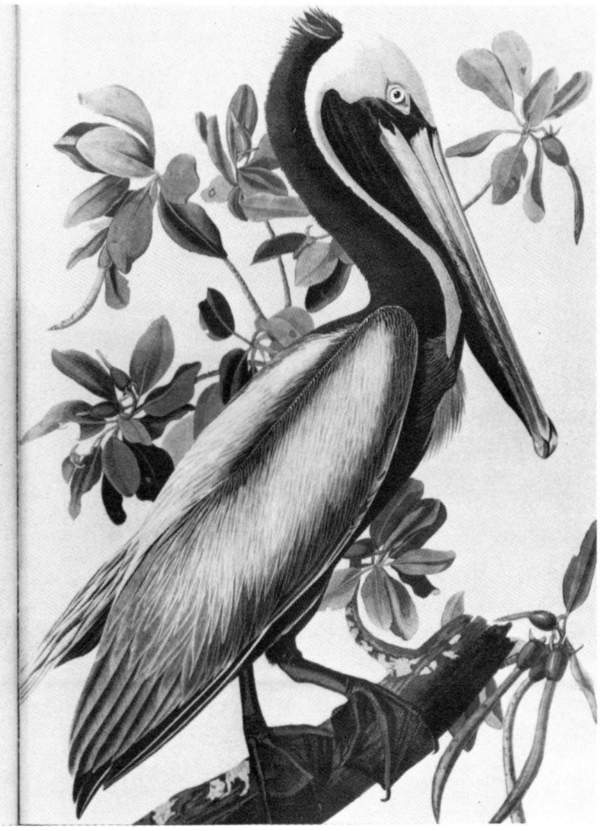

650

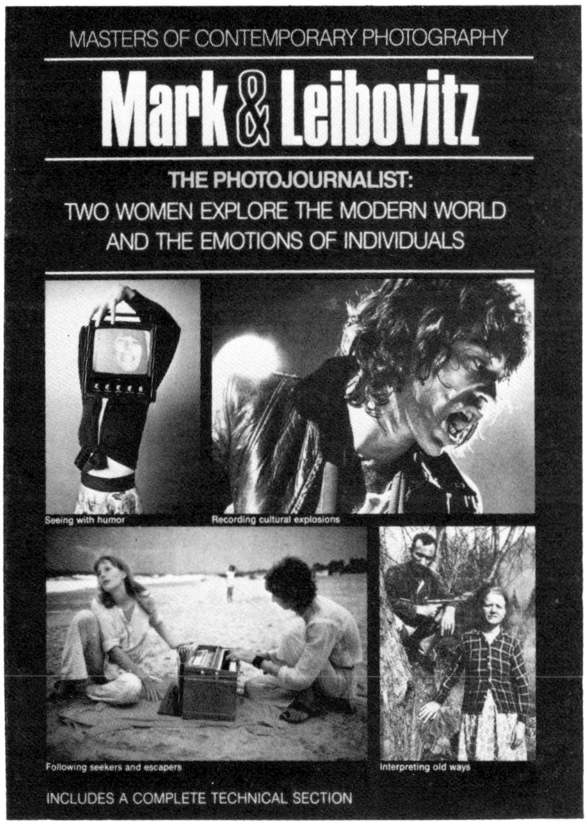
MASTERS OF CONTEMPORARY PHOTOGRAPHY
Mark & Leibovitz
THE PHOTOJOURNALIST:
TWO WOMEN EXPLORE THE MODERN WORLD
AND THE EMOTIONS OF INDIVIDUALS
Seeing with humor
Recording cultural explosions
Following seekers and escapers
Interpreting old ways
INCLUDES A COMPLETE TECHNICAL SECTION

652

GOLD

650
Art Director Albert Squillace
Designer Albert Squillace
Artist John James Audubon
Writer Roland Clement
Publishers Ridge Press
Grosset & Dunlap

652
Art Director Will Hopkins
Designer Will Hopkins
Photographers Mary Ellen Mark
Annie Liebovitz
Writers John Poppy
Adrianne Marcus
Publishers Alskog
T. Y. Crowell

MASTERS OF CONTEMPORARY PHOTOGRAPHY
Fusco & McBride
THE PHOTO ESSAY:
HOW TO SHARE ACTION AND IDEALS
THROUGH PICTURES
Finding new awareness of the world
Preserving history
Capturing the senses
Making symbols work
INCLUDES A COMPLETE TECHNICAL SECTION

653

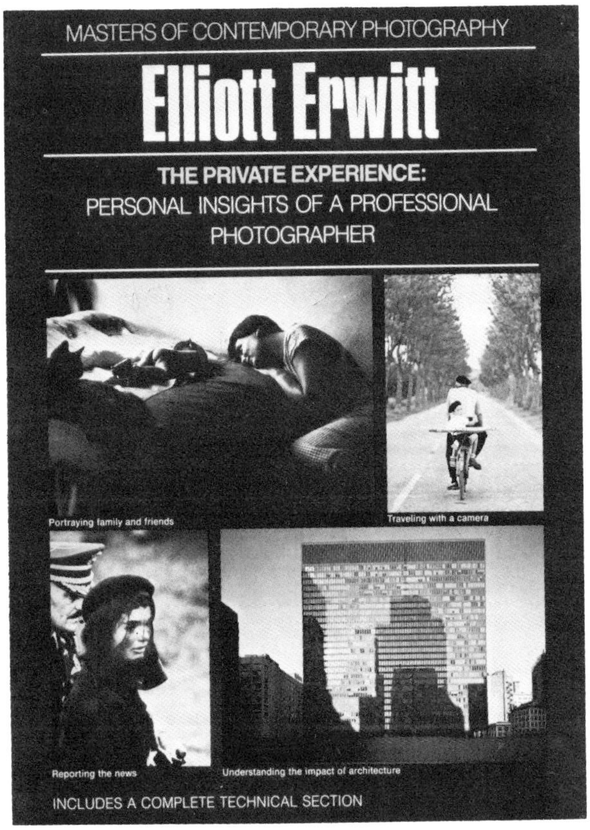
MASTERS OF CONTEMPORARY PHOTOGRAPHY
Elliott Erwitt
THE PRIVATE EXPERIENCE:
PERSONAL INSIGHTS OF A PROFESSIONAL
PHOTOGRAPHER
Portraying family and friends
Traveling with a camera
Reporting the news
Understanding the impact of architecture
INCLUDES A COMPLETE TECHNICAL SECTION

MASTERS OF CONTEMPORARY PHOTOGRAPHY
the Private Experience:
Elliott Erwitt

654

653
Art Director Will Hopkins
Designer Will Hopkins
Photographers Paul Fusco
Will McBride
Writers John Poppy
Tom Moran
Publishers Alskog
T. Y. Crowell

654
Art Director Will Hopkins
Designer Will Hopkins
Photographer Elliott Erwitt
Writers John Poppy
Sean Callahan
Publishers Alskog
T. Y. Crowell

MASTERS OF CONTEMPORARY PHOTOGRAPHY
Bert Stern
THE PHOTO ILLUSTRATION:
A RESTLESS MAN'S REWARDS FOR CREATING
IMAGES FROM IDEAS
Improving advertisements
Translating fashion and glamor into an "American Dream"
Exploring a new portraiture
INCLUDES A COMPLETE TECHNICAL SECTION

655

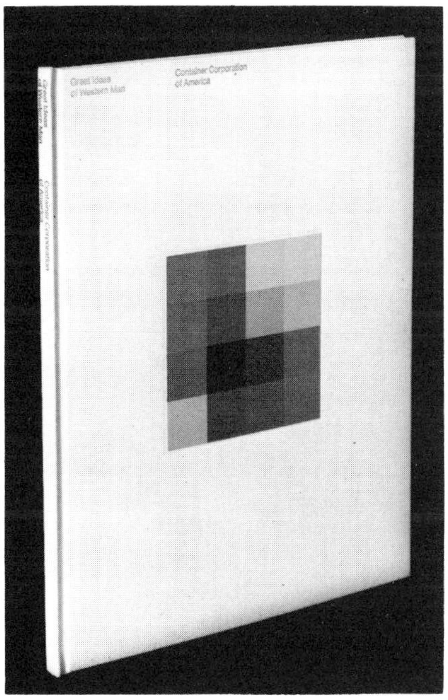

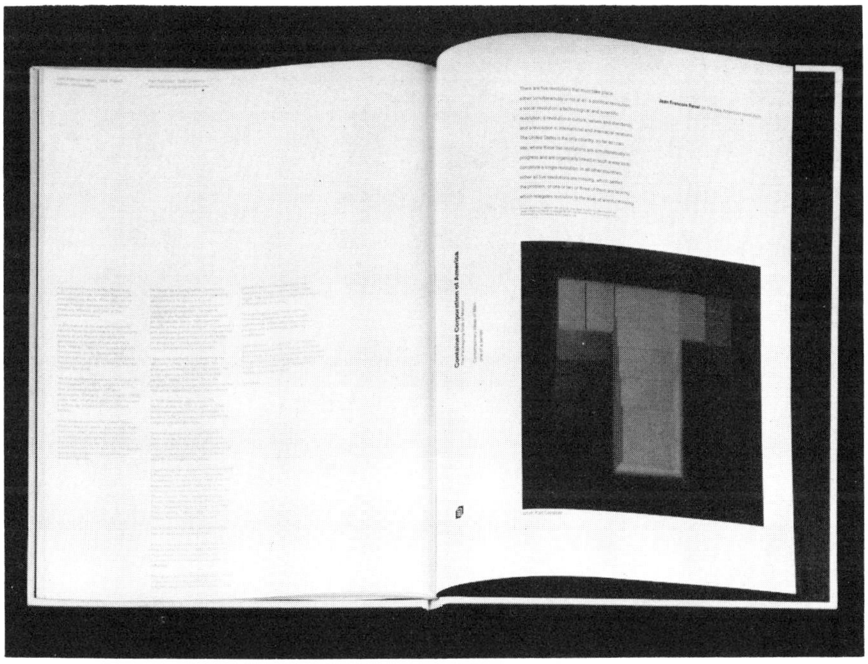

656

655
Art Director Will Hopkins
Designer Will Hopkins
Photographer Bert Stern
Writer John Poppy
Publishers Alskog
T. Y. Crowell

656
Art Director Bill Bonnell III
Designer Bill Bonnell III
Artist Bill Bonnell III
Editor Rhodes Patterson
Publisher Container Corporation of America
Agency Container Corporation Communications Dept.

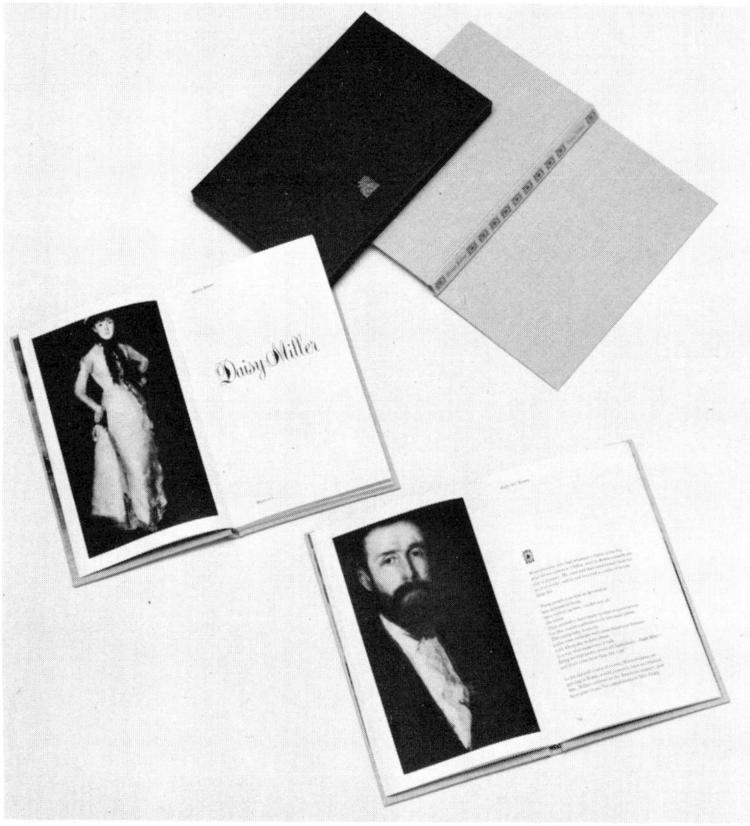
Daisy Miller

657

ON TIME
1975
APPOINTMENT CALENDAR
THE MUSEUM OF MODERN ART
NEW YORK

659

On the set with the great movies and stars of the last three decades
THE PLATINUM YEARS
by Bob Willoughby / Text by Richard Schickel

660

657
Art Director Bradbury Thompson
Designer Bradbury Thompson
Artists James NcNeill Whistler
John Singer Sargent
Writers Henry James
Jean A. Bradnick
Publisher Westvaco Corp.

659
Art Director Jon Lopez
Designer Jon Lopez
Photographers Various
Editor Mary Lee Bandy
Writer Marjorie Munsterberg
Publisher The Museum of Modern Art
Agency Jon Lopez Design

660
Art Director Albert Squillace
Designer Albert Squillace
Photographer Bob Willoughby
Writer Richard Schickel
Publishers Ridge Press
Random House

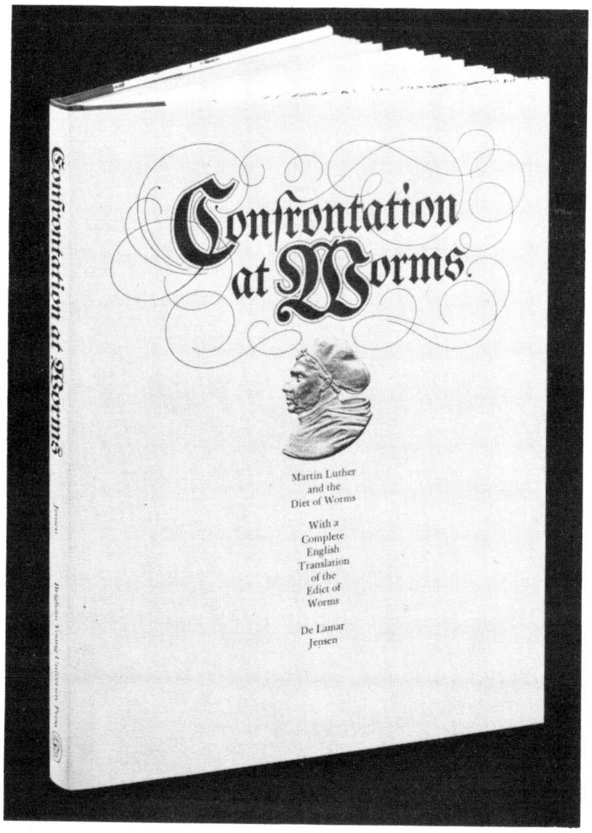
Confrontation at Worms
Confrontation at Worms
Martin Luther
and the
Diet of Worms
With a
Complete
English
Translation
of the
Edict of
Worms
De Lamar
Jensen

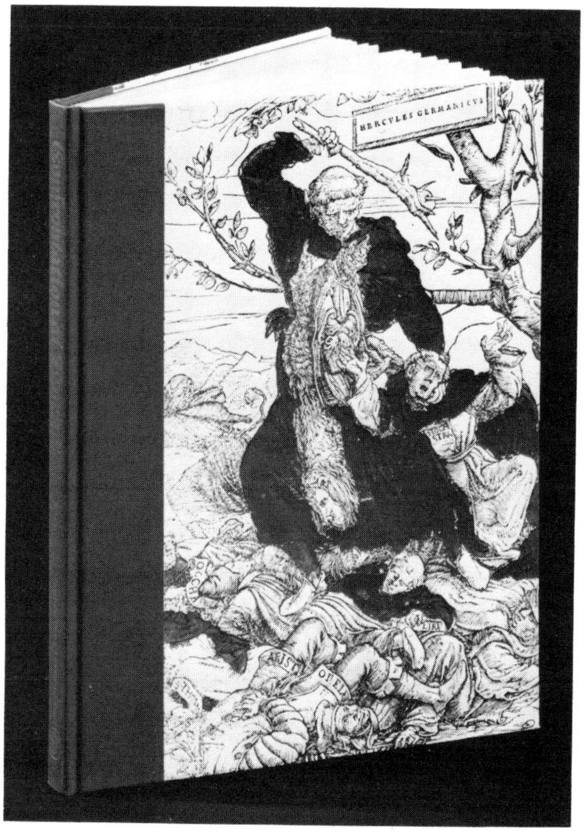
HERCVLES GERMANICVS

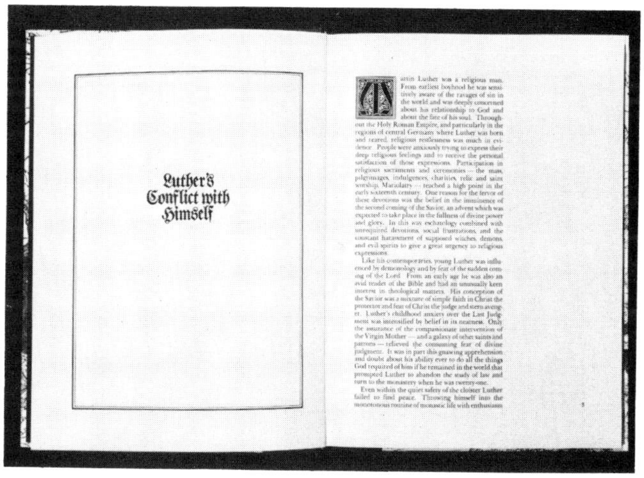
Luther's
Conflict with
Himself

661

661
Art Director McRay Magleby
Designer McRay Magleby
Artist David Canaan
Writers DeLamar Jensen
John Drayton
Publisher Brigham Young University Press
Agency Graphic Communications Dept.
Brigham Young University

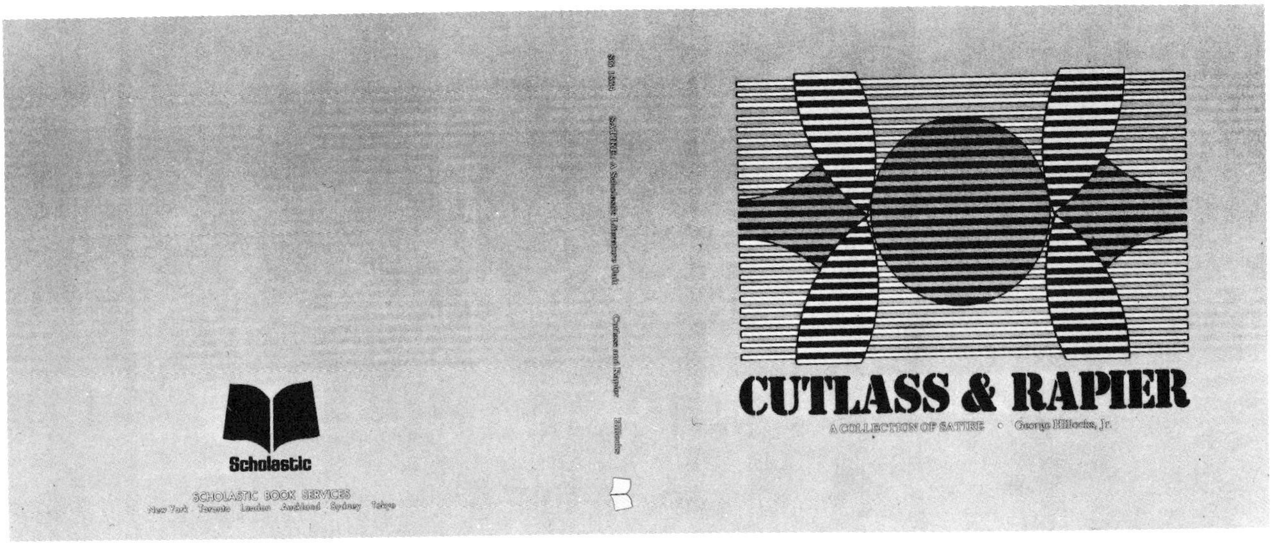

CUTLASS & RAPIER
A COLLECTION OF SATIRE • George Hillocks, Jr.
Scholastic
SCHOLASTIC BOOK SERVICES
New York Toronto London Auckland Sydney Tokyo

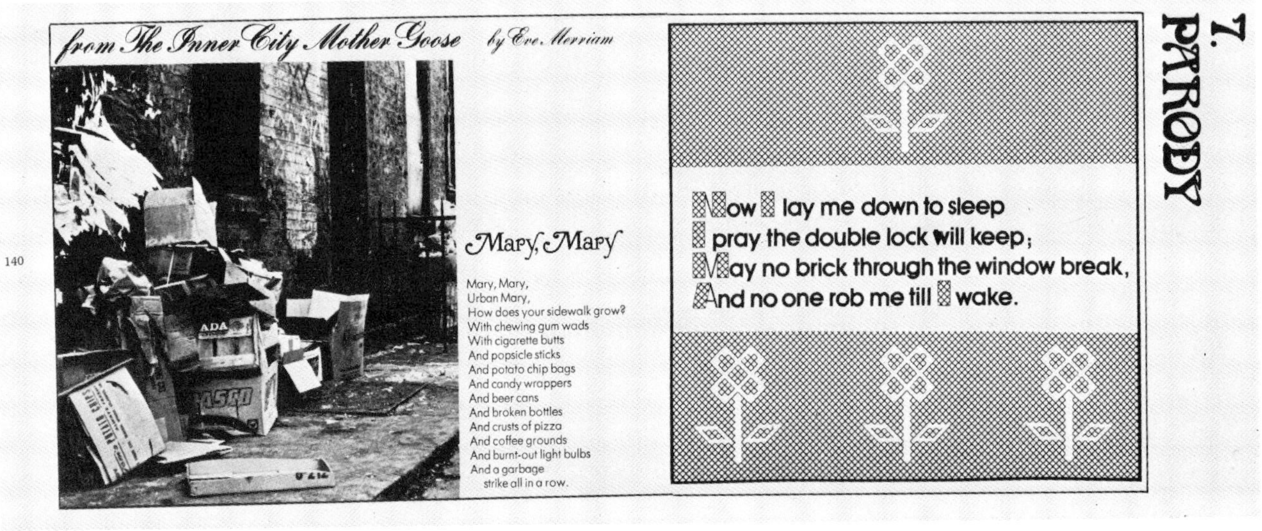

from The Inner City Mother Goose by Eve Merriam
140
Mary, Mary
Mary, Mary,
Urban Mary,
How does your sidewalk grow?
With chewing gum wads
With cigarette butts
And popsicle sticks
And potato chip bags
And candy wrappers
And beer cans
And broken bottles
And crusts of pizza
And coffee grounds
And burnt-out light bulbs
And a garbage
strike all in a row.
Now I lay me down to sleep
I pray the double lock will keep;
May no brick through the window break,
And no one rob me till I wake.
7. PARODY

52
5. THE PEOPLE IN CHARGE

From NO KNOWN SURVIVORS by David Levine

662

662
Art Director Bonnie Bishop
Designer Patricia H. Wosczyk
Artists Various
Photographers Burk Uzzle
Margaret Bourke-White
Various
Editor Judith Bauer Stamper
Publisher Scholastic Magazines

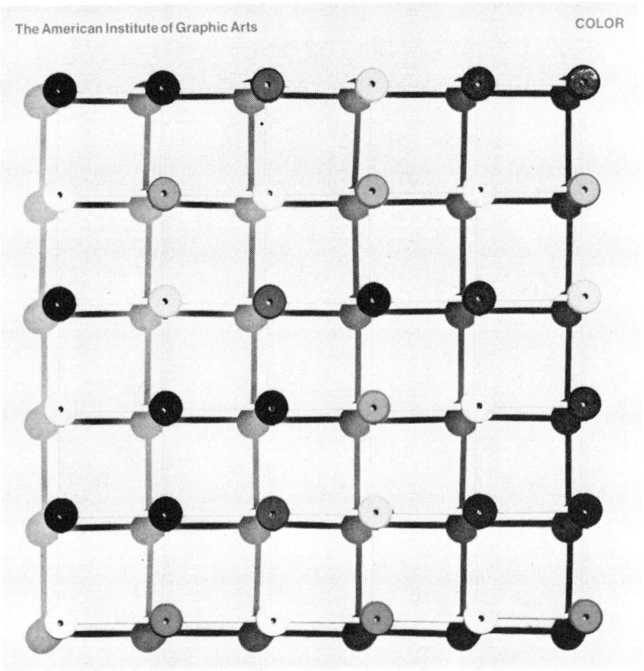
The American Institute of Graphic Arts
COLOR

663

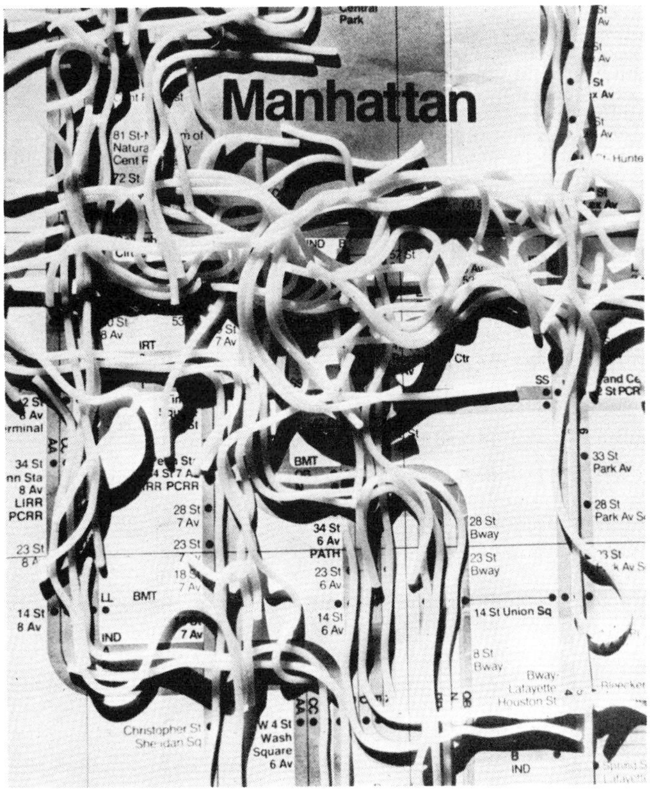
Manhattan
14 St Union Sq
Christopher St
Sheridan Sq
W 4 St
Wash
Square
6 Av

664

663
Art Director James Miho
Designer James Miho
Artist American Institute of Graphic Arts Members
Writer David Brown
Publisher Champion Papers

664
Art Director Cipe Pineles
Designers Karlong Shiv
Melissa Schreiber
AnnaMarie Beleznay
Barbara Freeman
Bruce Handler
Editorial Design Students
Artists Editorial Design Students
Photographers Editorial Design Students
Writers Editorial Design Students
Publisher Parsons School of Design

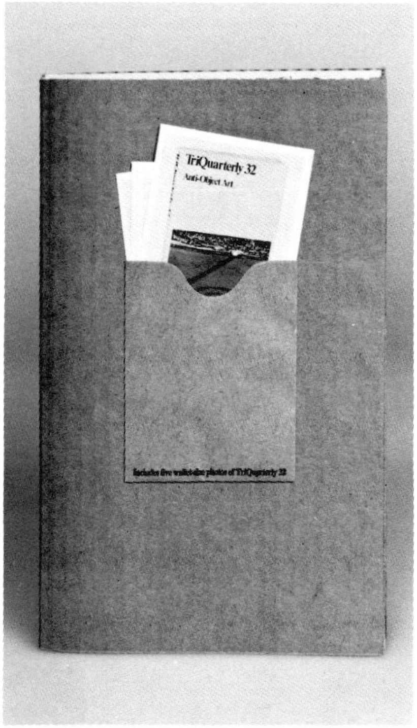
TriQuarterly 32
Anti-Object Art

Richard Long

Line in Ireland
1974

Sol LeWitt

The location of a rectangle

A RECTANGLE WHICH IS FORMED AND ENCLOSED BY FOUR LINES. THE FIRST OF WHICH IS DRAWN FROM A POINT HALFWAY BETWEEN A POINT HALFWAY BETWEEN THE CENTER OF THE PAGE (SQUARE OR WALL) AND THE UPPER LEFT CORNER AND THE MIDPOINT OF THE LEFT SIDE AND THE UPPER LEFT CORNER TO A POINT HALFWAY BETWEEN THE MIDPOINT OF THE TOP SIDE AND THE UPPER RIGHT CORNER, THE SECOND LINE FROM A POINT HALFWAY BETWEEN THE START OF THE FIRST LINE AND A POINT HALFWAY BETWEEN THE MIDPOINT OF THE TOP SIDE AND THE UPPER LEFT CORNER TO A POINT HALFWAY BETWEEN THE CENTER OF THE PAGE (SQUARE OR WALL) AND THE LOWER LEFT CORNER AND THE MIDPOINT OF THE BOTTOM SIDE. THE THIRD

665

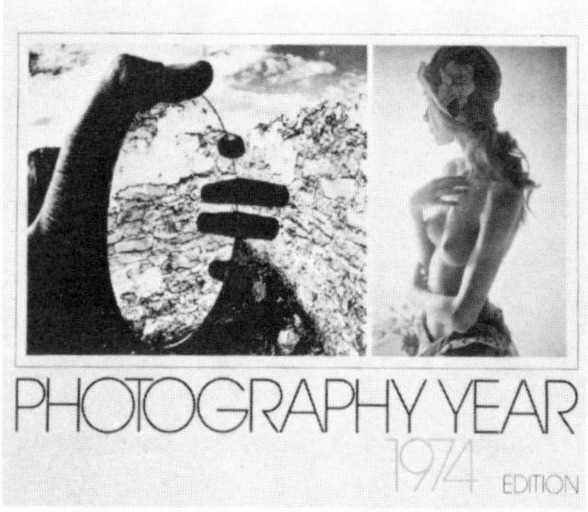
PHOTOGRAPHY YEAR
1974 EDITION

666

665
Art Director Lawrence Levy
Designer Lawrence Levy
Editors Elliott Anderson
John Perreault
Lawrence Levy
Publisher Northwestern University
TriQuarterly
Agency Lawrence Levy Design/Film

666
Art Director Sheldon Cotler
Designer Sheldon Cotler
Editor Sheldon Cotler
Publisher Time-Life Books

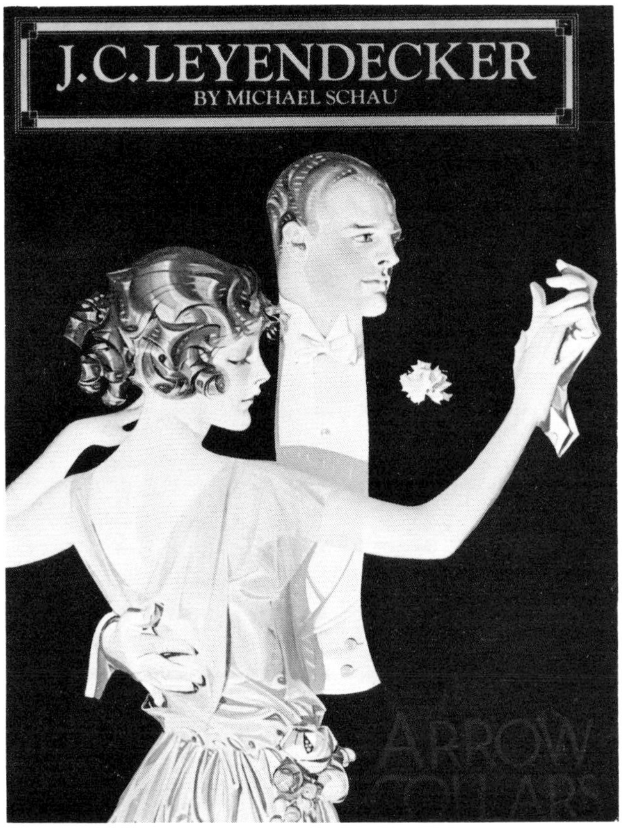
J.C.LEYENDECKER
BY MICHAEL SCHAU
ARROW
COLLARS

MAGAZINE COVERS

667

667
Art Directors Bob Fillie
Jim Craig
Designer Bob Fillie
Writers Michael Schau
Editor Sue Davis
Publisher Watson-Guptill Publications

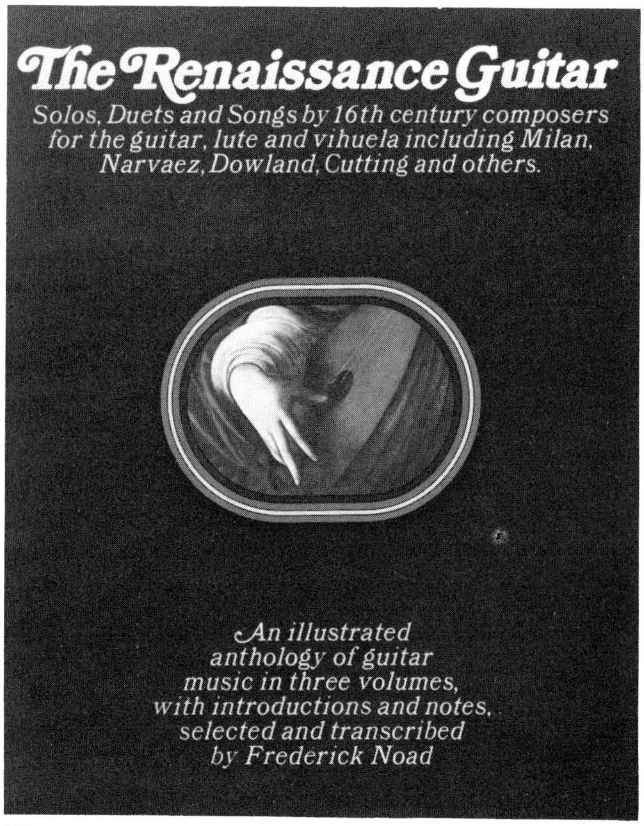
The Renaissance Guitar
Solos, Duets and Songs by 16th century composers for the guitar, lute and vihuela including Milan, Narvaez, Dowland, Cutting and others.
An illustrated anthology of guitar music in three volumes, with introductions and notes, selected and transcribed by Frederick Noad

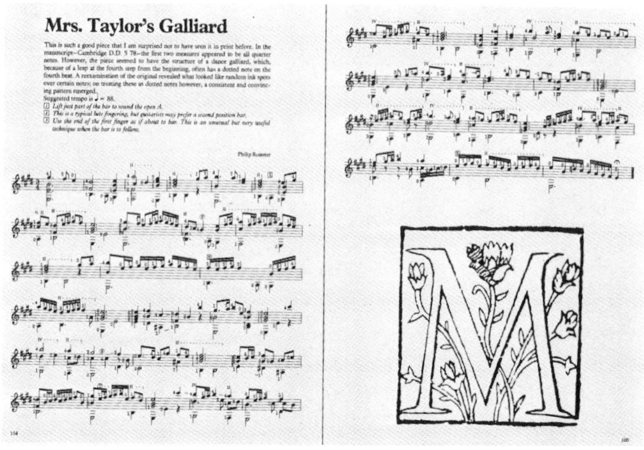
Mrs. Taylor's Galliard

668

Clawhammer Banjo
Traditional Appalachian banjo tunes transcribed in tablature and based on the playing of Wade Ward, Fred Cockerham, Henry Reed, Frank George and others. With tunings and all basic right and left hand techniques: drop-thumbing, the "Galax lick," pull-offs, slides and plucking. By Miles Krassen. Oak Publications/$4.95
instruction record included

Pretty Little Dog
CHAPTER 3

669

668
Art Director Iris Weinstein
Designer Iris Weinstein
Writer Frederick Noad
Publisher Ariel Music Publications

669
Art Director Iris Weinstein
Designers Jeanne Hammons
Ira Haskell
Photographers Herbert Wise
Jeanne Hammons
Writer Miles Krassen
Publisher Oak Publications

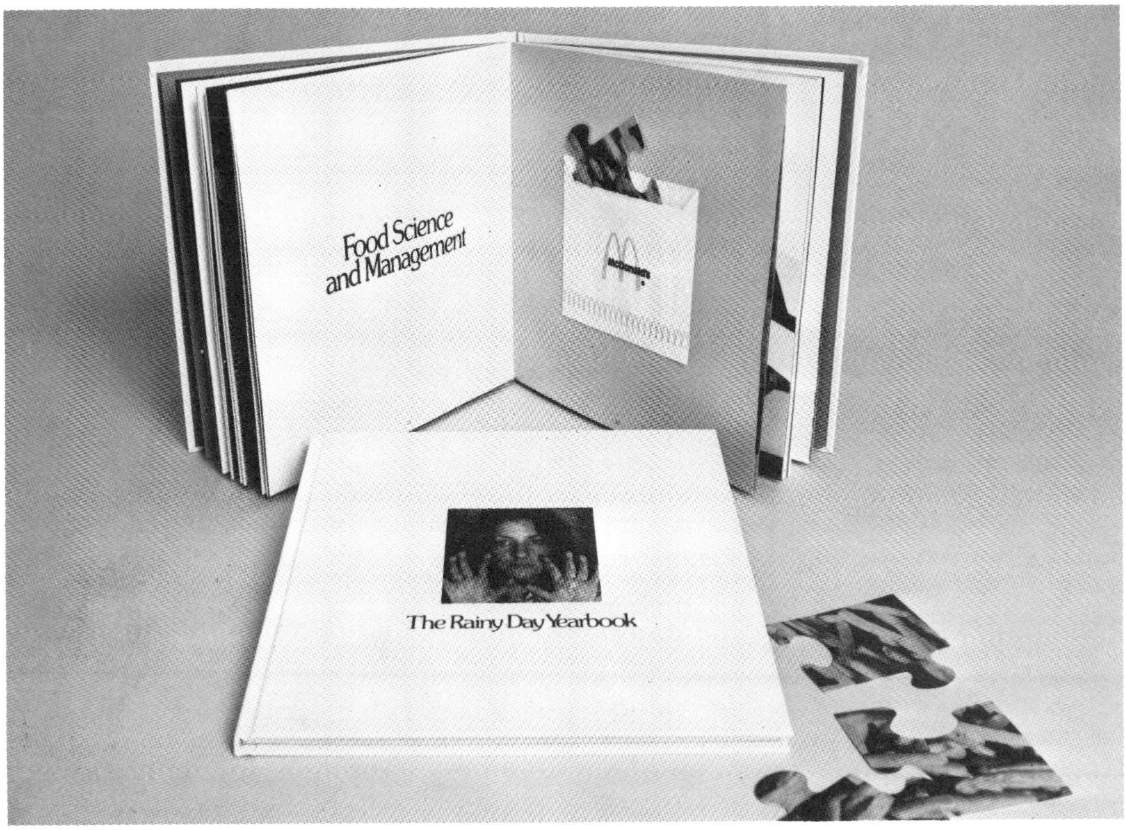
Food Science and Management
McDonald's
The Rainy Day Yearbook

670

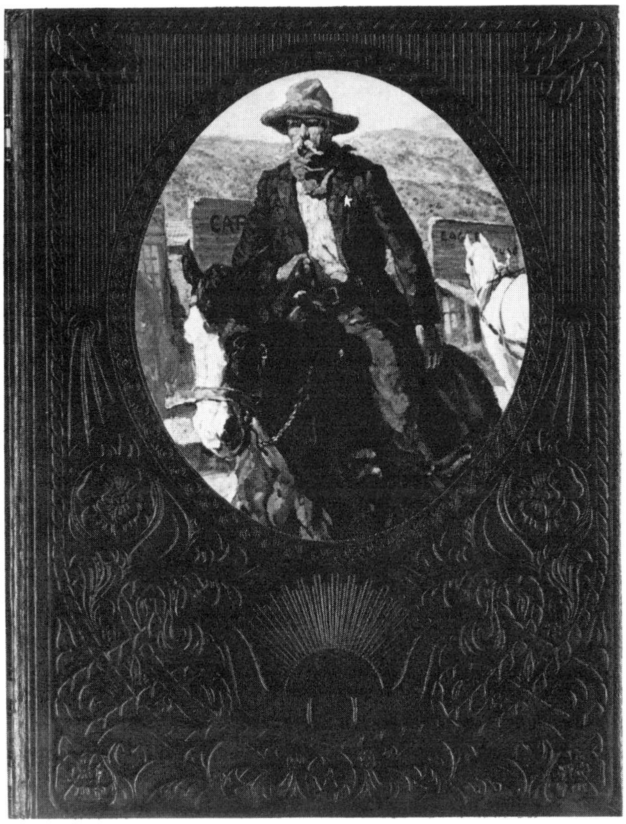

6 Frontier justice, vigilante style

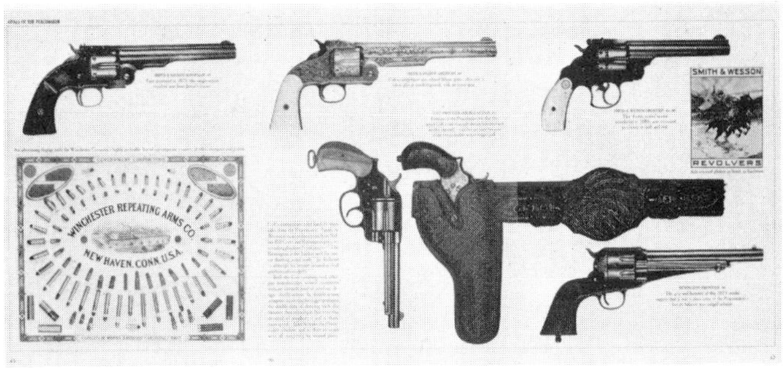
SMITH & WESSON
REVOLVERS
WINCHESTER REPEATING ARMS CO.
NEW HAVEN, CONN. U.S.A.

671

670
Art Directors Steve Kasloff
Dennis Machlica
Designers Steve Kasloff
Dennis Machlica
Artists Various
Photographer Dennis Machlica
Editor Steve Kasloff
Publisher Pratt Institute
Prattonia

671
Art Director Sheldon Cotler
Designer Herbert H. Quarmby
Writers Paul Trachtman
Editors, Time-Life Books
Publisher Time-Life Books

2
FABULOUS
FLIGHTS
IN FABRIC

672

A novel by MARK DINTENFASS
Figure 8

673

672
Art Director Sheldon Cotler
Designer Virginia Gianakos
Photographer Ryszard Horowitz
Writer Carlotta Kerwin
Publisher Time-Life Books

673
Art Director Frank Metz
Designer Wendell Minor
Artist Wendell Minor
Publisher Simon and Schuster
Agency Wendell Minor Design

EDWARD THE RAKE
By John Pearson

674

A BIT OF A SHUNT UP THE RIVER
DESMOND CORY
A CRIME CLUB SELECTION

675

674
Art Director Harris Lewine
Designer Stan Zagorski
Artist Stan Zagorski
Publisher Harcourt Brace Jovanovich

675
Art Director Rallou M. Hamshaw
Designer Lawrence Ratzkin
Artist Lawrence Ratzkin
Publisher Doubleday & Co.

Of Thee, Nevertheless,
I Sing
An Essay on American Political Values
by William Lee Miller

676

THE NOTHING BOOK
Wanna Make Something Of It?
For: poets, cooks, travelers, writers, diarists, students, comedians, brides, grandparents, decorators, kids, tourists, doodlers, secretaries, list-makers, forgetters, artists, sketchers, businesswomen, businessmen, leaf-pressers, gift-givers, minimalists, and all of us who've ever wanted to do a book.

677

Humphrey
BOGART
Nathaniel
BENCHLEY
BOGART
BENCHLEY
KARSH
OTTAWA
088862
Little, Brown

678

676
Art Director Harris Lewine
Designer Lawrence Ratzkin
Photographer Lawrence Ratzkin
Publisher Harcourt Brace Jovanovich

677
Art Director Alan Peckolick
Designer Alan Peckolick
Artist Lubalin, Smith, Carnase
Publisher Crown Publishers
Agency Lubalin, Smith, Carnase

678
Art Director Char Lappan
Designer Bernie LaCasse
Artist Bernie LaCasse
Photographer Karsh
Writer Roger Donald
Publisher Little, Brown & Co.

Falkenhorst
A Novel by MARK RASCOVICH
Falkenhorst
A Novel by MARK RASCOVICH
HOLT
RINEHART
WINSTON

679

679
Art Director Robert Reed
Designer Wendell Minor
Artist Wendell Minor
Writer Mark Rascovich
Publisher Holt, Rinehart and Winston

DESIGN

GRAPHIC DESIGN

Complete Sales Promotion Pieces	680–743
Sales Promotion Covers	744–749
Complete Annual Reports	750–784
Annual Report Covers	785–787
House Organs	788–793
Direct Mail	794–809
Box Design	810–822
Can Design	823
Bottle Designs	824
Album Covers	825–846
Calendars	848–853
Posters	854–909
Point of Sale Designs	910–914
Sales Presentations	915–923
Letterheads	924–940
Trademarks & Logotypes	941–972
Complete Corporate Identity Programs	973–984
Architectural Graphics	985–989

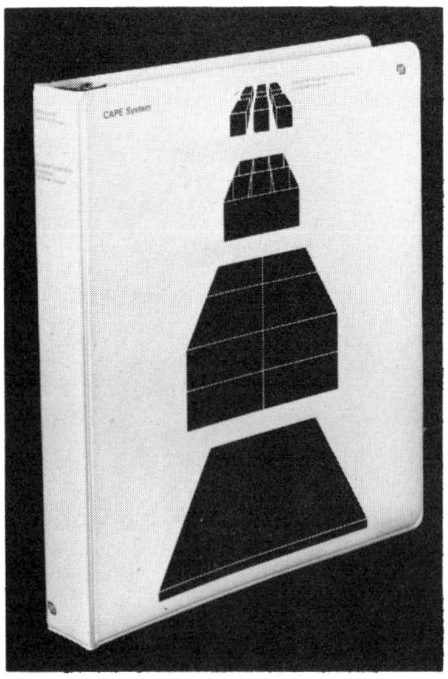

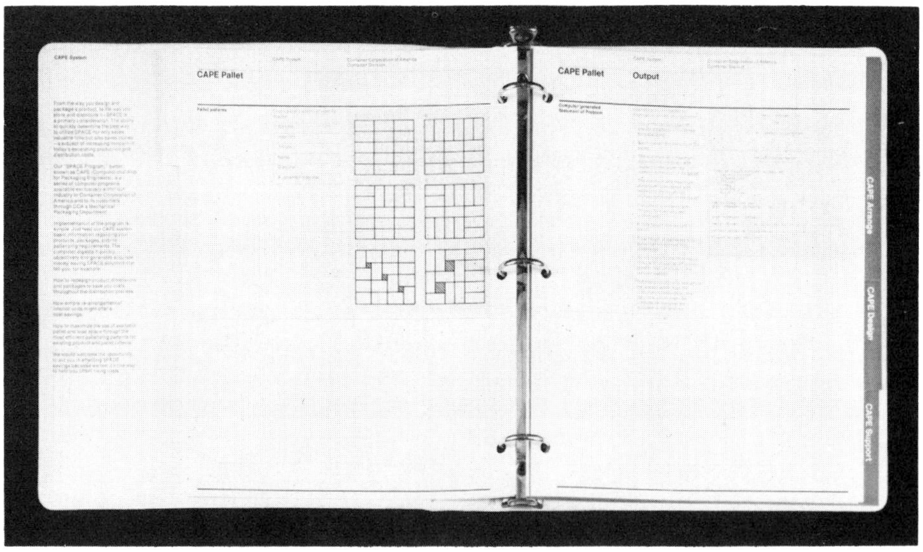
CAPE Pallet
CAPE Pallet
Output

680

CBS
TELEVISION
Network
Press
INFORMATION
GUIDE
1974-75
PROGRAMS
Information
Biographies

681

680
Art Director Bill Bonnell III
Designer William McDowell
Artist Mas Nakagawa
Agency Container Corporation Communications Dept.
Client Container Corporation of America

681
Art Director Lou Dorfsman
Designer Kiyoshi Kanai
Artist Ray Cruz
Agency CBS/Broadcast Group
Client CBS Television Network

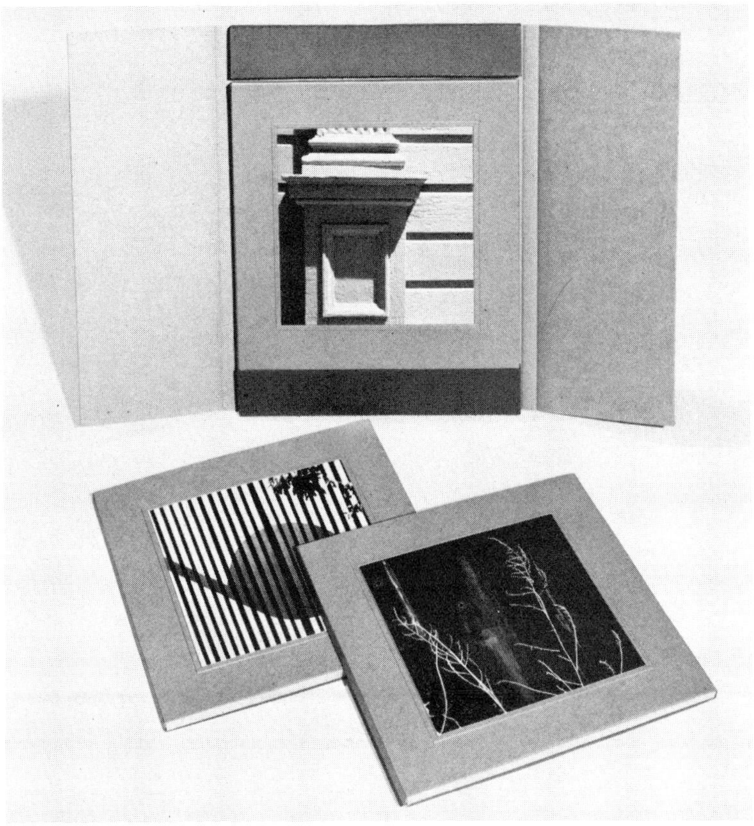

682

CELEBRATING FIFTY YEARS OF FASHION
OUR ANNIVERSARY ARRAY OF DESIGNER INSPIRATIONS
SAKS FIFTH AVENUE

684

682
Art Director Primo Angeli
Designer Primo Angeli
Artist Nancy Kennedy
Photographer Tom Abels
Writer Emil Korenic
Agency Primo Angeli Graphics
Client Sandy-Babcock, Architects

684
Art Director Max Jorden
Designer Max Jorden
Agency Saks Fifth Avenue
Client Saks Fifth Avenue

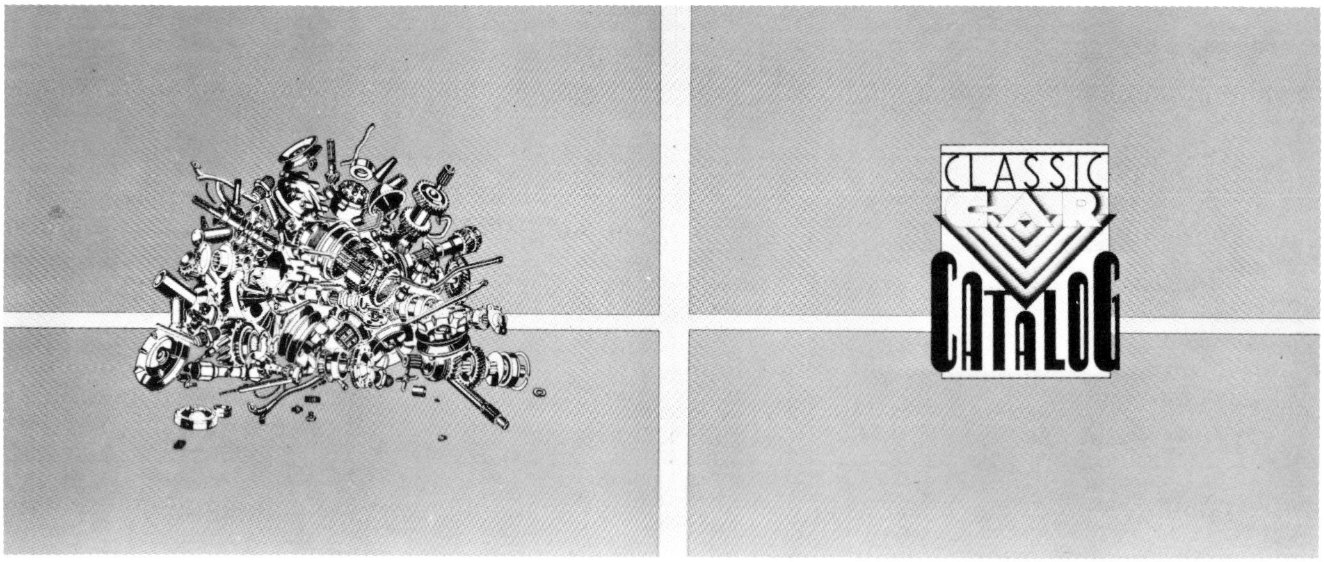
CLASSIC
CATALOG

1942 Chevrolet Limousine

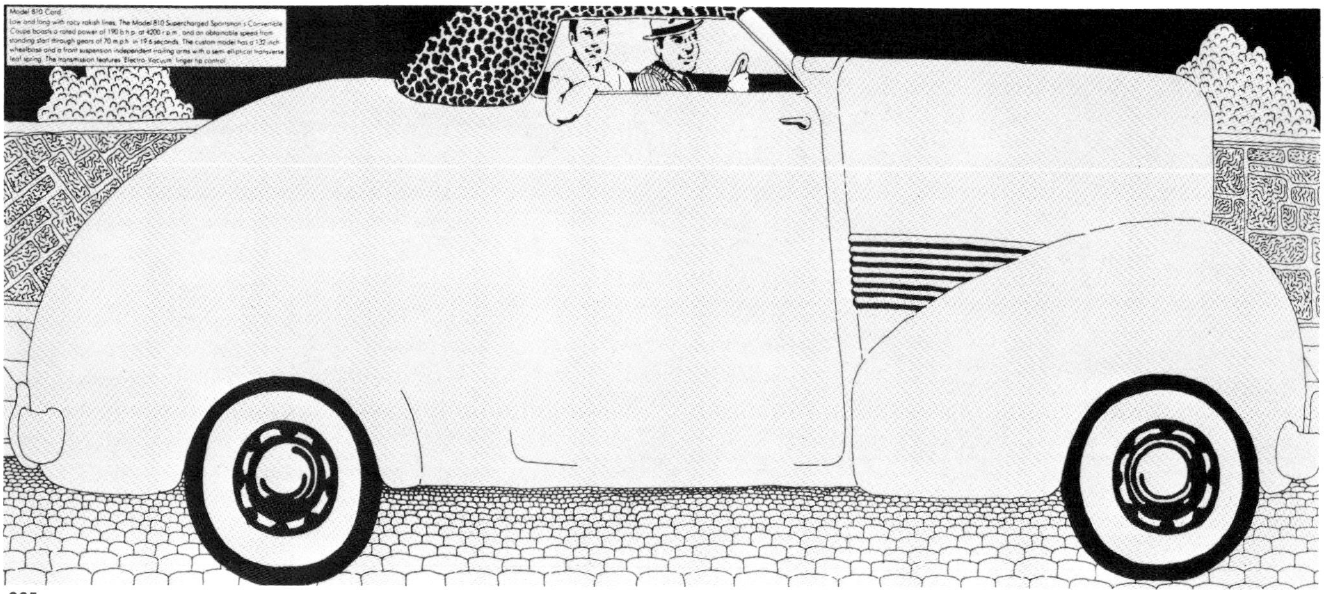
Model 810 Cord.
Low and long with racy rakish lines. The Model 810 Supercharged Sportsman's Convertible Coupe boasts a rated power of 190 b.h.p. at 4200 r.p.m., and an obtainable speed from standing start through gears of 70 m.p.h. in 19.6 seconds. The custom model has a 132 inch wheelbase and a front suspension independent trailing arms with a semi-elliptical transverse leaf spring. The transmission features 'Electro-Vacuum' finger tip control.

685

685
Art Director Seymour Chwast
Designer Seymour Chwast
Artists Seymour Chwast
Haruo Miyauchi
Christian Piper
Agency Push Pin Studios
Client Push Pin Studios

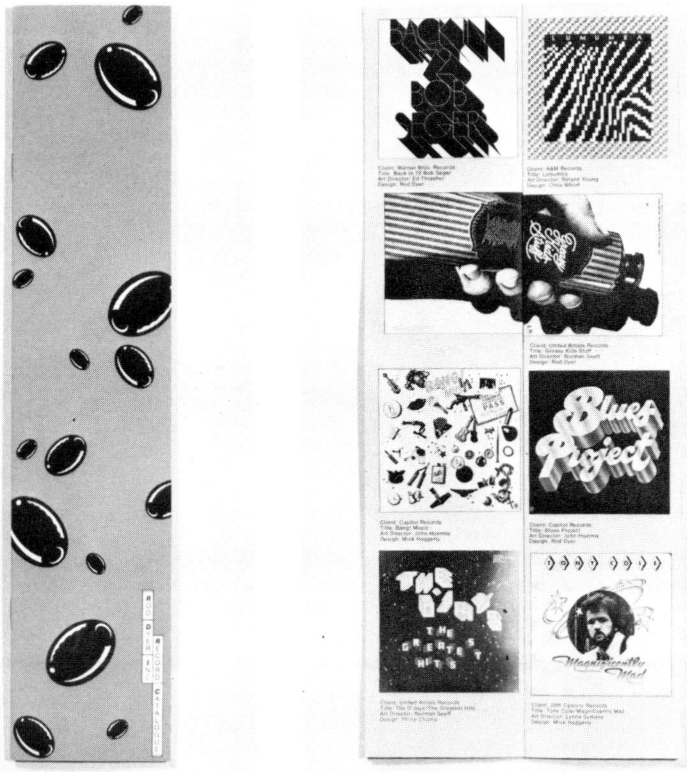
Blues Project

686

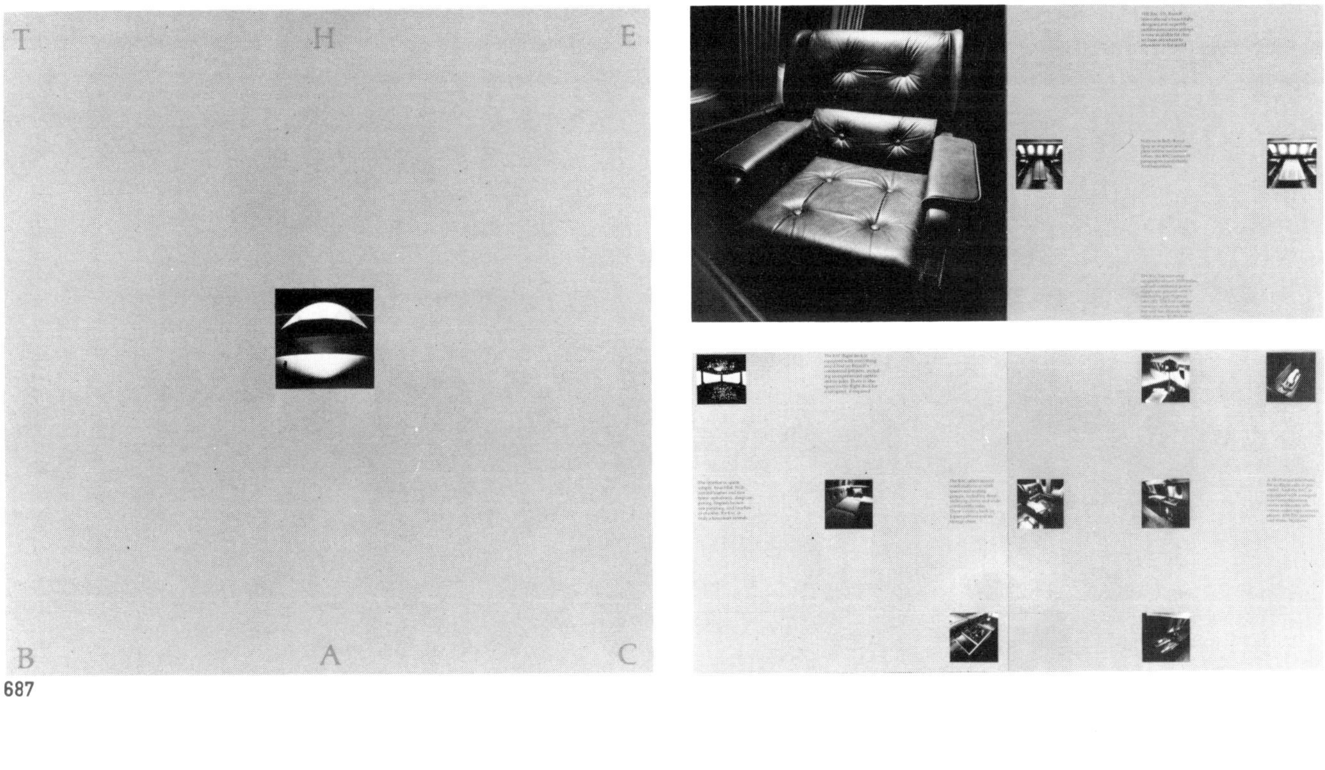
T H E
B A C

687

686
Art Director Rod Dyer
Designer Rod Dyer
Artist Mick Haggerty
Agency Rod Dyer, Inc.
Client Rod Dyer

687
Art Directors Woody Pirtle
Stan Richards
Designer Woody Pirtle
Artists Woody Pirtle
Chris Hill
Photographers Greg Booth
Francisco & Booth
Writer Cap Pannell
Agency The Richards Group
Client Braniff International

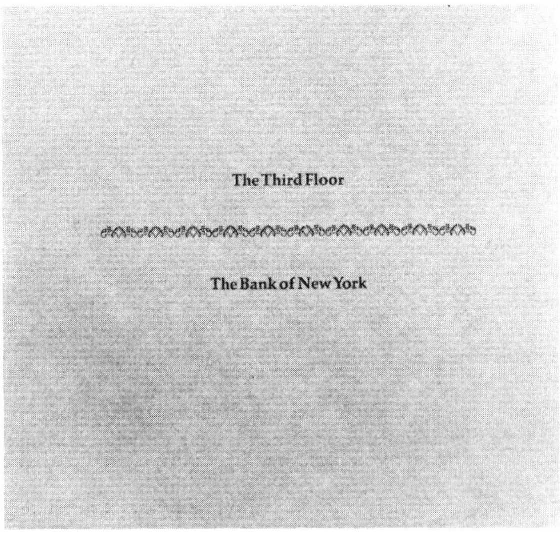
The Third Floor
The Bank of New York

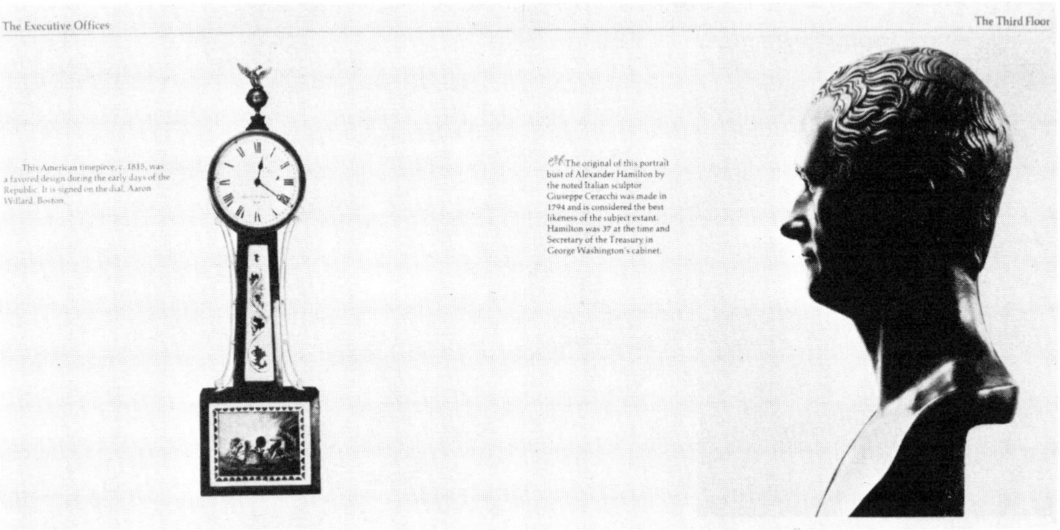
The Executive Offices
The Third Floor
This American timepiece, c. 1815, was a favored design during the early days of the Republic. It is signed on the dial, Aaron Willard, Boston.
The original of this portrait bust of Alexander Hamilton by the noted Italian sculptor Giuseppe Ceracchi was made in 1794 and is considered the best likeness of the subject extant. Hamilton was 37 at the time and Secretary of the Treasury in George Washington's cabinet.

688

688
Art Director Richard Perlman
Designer Richard Perlman
Photographers Herb Goro
Henry Humphrey
Writers Ken Bacon
James Beuchner
Agency Richard Perlman, Inc.
Client The Bank of New York

The Team
Stimulating ingredients.
A blend of ideas.
A satisfying combination.

THE IDEA
The challenge and mind meet.
They ignite.
Quickly! Before it's gone!

689

689
Art Director Harold Printup, Jr.
Designer Harold Printup, Jr.
Artist Donna Neal
Photographer Harold Printup, Jr.
Writers Donna Neal
Louise Rishoff
Agency Harold Printup Graphic Design Studio
Client Harold Printup Graphic Design Studio

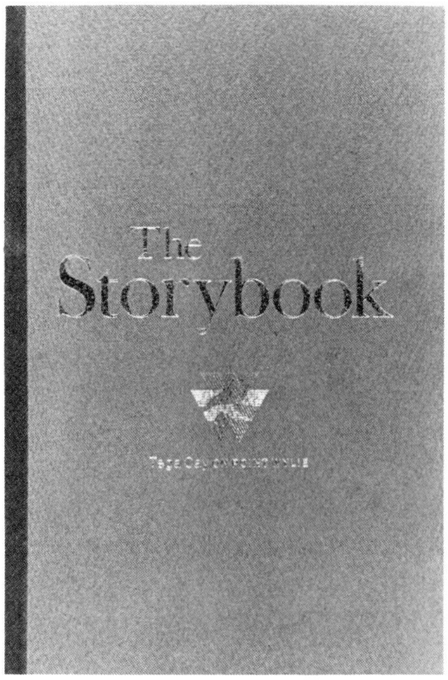

The
Storybook

Your new neighbors at Tega Cay are people who were searching for an honest answer to the question of how and where to live their lives. Possibly the very same questions that now pose themselves to you.

They are people whose basic wants and needs are in part similar to your own. Yet whose tastes and backgrounds vary so that Tega Cay has become a community of genuine spirit, thrust and human dimension.

Here, the family down the street is more than merely a name on the mailbox or a polite wave on the way to work.

For this is a caring community. A place where people reach out.

*"We've made more friends in one year at Tega Cay than we had in our entire lives."**

19

Listen at the dawn as a choir of robins welcomes in the new day. To the sounds of children as they run free to explore the out-of-doors. Secure and content.

Listen for the whonk of a racket and the whoosh of a club. A splash from the pool or a rrrrrr from the lake. A clippity clop.

Listen to yourself having fun at the clubhouse. Meeting old friends and making new ones. Here you can find solace for a love-six set or celebrate that hole-in-one.

Listen during a summer's eve when the cricket draws his bow and a hush falls over the land. Silence like this is music to the ears.

A symphony for all seasons.

*"Once I was on the patio about six in the morning. The sun was coming up, the fog was lifting out of the valley . . . it was the most fantastic sight I've ever seen."**

14 15

690

690
Art Director Grant Treaster, Jr.
Designer Grant Treaster, Jr.
Artist Janie Case
Writer Ron Levin
Agency Group Four, Inc.
Client Tega Cay

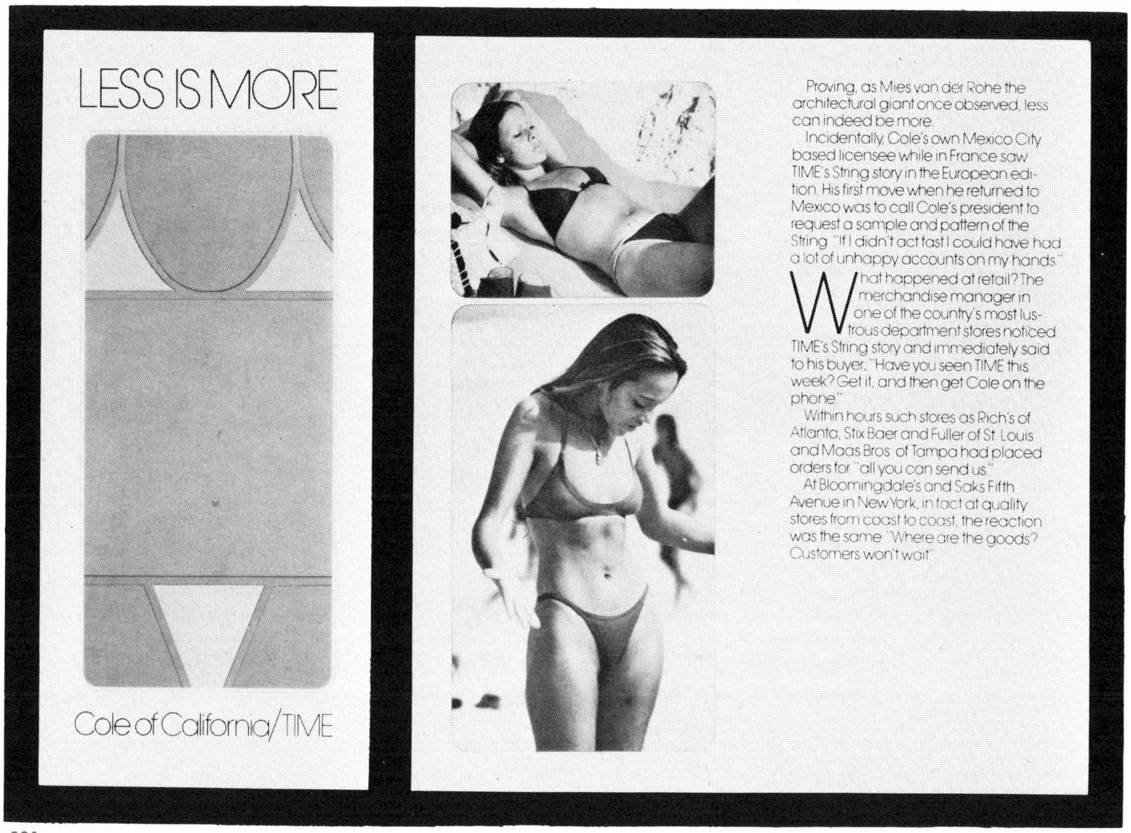
LESS IS MORE
Cole of California/TIME
Proving, as Mies van der Rohe the architectural giant once observed, less can indeed be more.
Incidentally, Cole's own Mexico City based licensee while in France saw TIME's String story in the European edition. His first move when he returned to Mexico was to call Cole's president to request a sample and pattern of the String. "If I didn't act fast I could have had a lot of unhappy accounts on my hands."
What happened at retail? The merchandise manager in one of the country's most lustrous department stores noticed TIME's String story and immediately said to his buyer, "Have you seen TIME this week? Get it, and then get Cole on the phone."
Within hours such stores as Rich's of Atlanta, Stix Baer and Fuller of St. Louis and Maas Bros. of Tampa had placed orders for "all you can send us."
At Bloomingdale's and Saks Fifth Avenue in New York, in fact at quality stores from coast to coast, the reaction was the same: "Where are the goods? Customers won't wait."

691

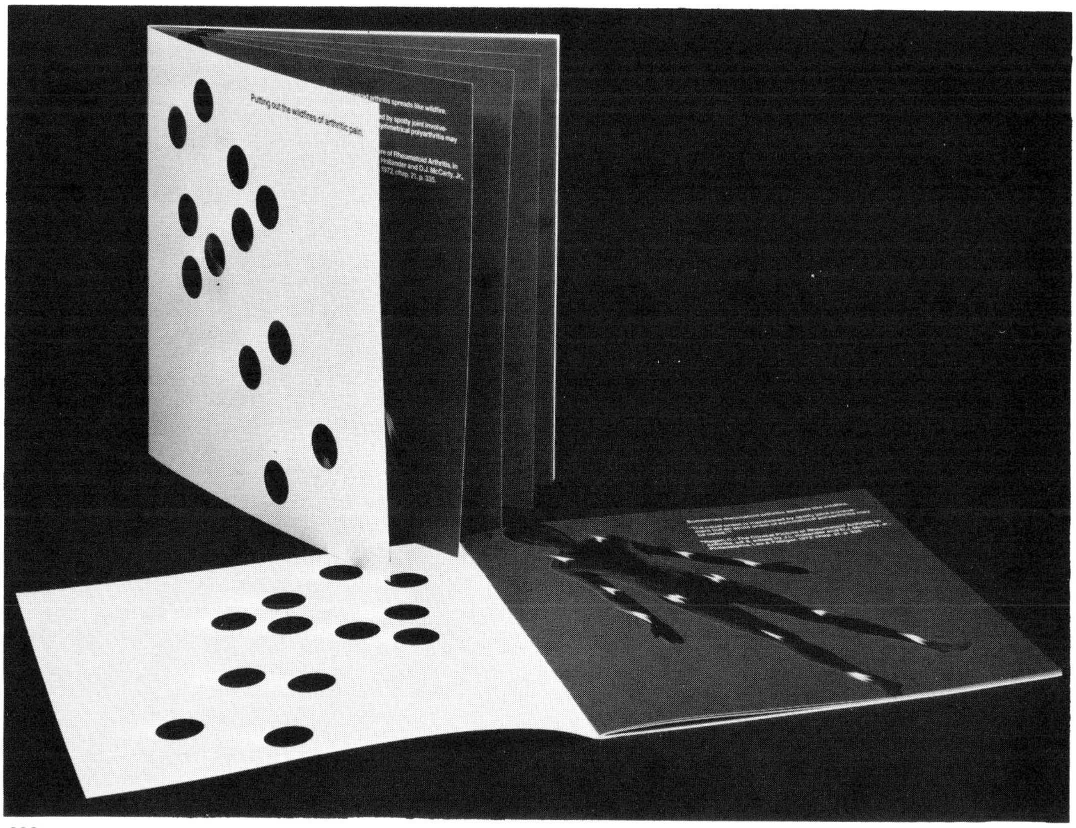
Putting out the wildfires of arthritic pain.

692

691
Art Director Walter Lefmann
Designer Susan Skoorka
Artist Susan Skoorka
Writer John Murphy
Agency Time, Inc.
Client Time Magazine

692
Art Director Bob Paganucci
Designer Bob Paganucci
Photographer Ed Gallucci
Writer Louis Ares
Agency Geigy Pharmaceuticals
Client Geigy Pharmaceuticals

Unsolicited testimonials (no kidding) from some of the food brokers who flipped out over the new Ocean Spray labels designed by Lois/Chajet Design Group, Inc.

...they look exceptionally nice and should result in greater business for all of us. They really show imagination and whoever designed them is to be congratulated.
...beautiful labels...
...We think they are outstanding, and very cleverly conceived. Your originality is to be complimented. ...a quality and freshness that is unmistakable. The display of all these labels on the retailer's shelves will be most impressive.
...the new labels are terrific!
Ocean Spray you have "done it again." We received the new labels—they are fantastic. Don't know who designed these labels but they did a beautiful job.
...most attractive! Even more important to us, they seem to tie all Ocean Spray drink items together.
...these are the finest looking labels that we have seen and certainly should have a tremendous impact on Mrs. Consumer.
...a definite improvement, and will improve sales at the retail level.
Gentlemen, we thank you.
Ocean Spray
Cranprune
Ocean Spray
Cran·Grape

693

ONE ELOQUENT IRISH JESUIT
MALACHI MARTIN ON PROTESTANTISM

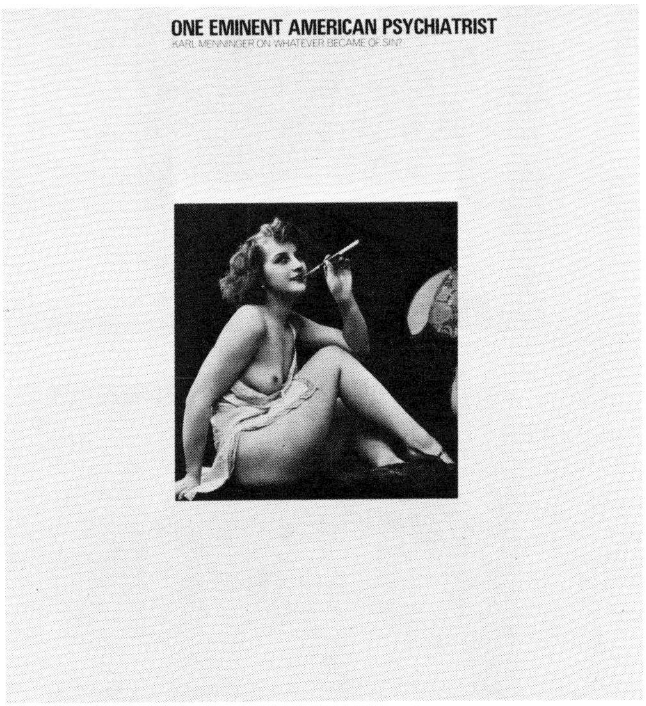
ONE EMINENT AMERICAN PSYCHIATRIST
KARL MENNINGER ON WHATEVER BECAME OF SIN?

IN ONE ISSUE:
APRIL'S INTELLECTUAL DIGEST
Poet, priest and psychiatrist, headliners and by-liners, laureates of Pulitzer and Nobel. Meet them, as our readers will, in INTELLECTUAL DIGEST. Every month it offers commentary and viewpoints from those worth hearing, culled from over 300 journals of significance, and many new books published around the world.
INTELLECTUAL DIGEST spans the globe—and the full range of man's curiosity, answering questions about not-so-average subjects asked by not-so-average minds. Minds quick to respond—one way or the other—to a Buckley or a Lorenz, to a Singer or a Menninger. Minds that want and need to be informed, illuminated, enriched, stretched.
That kind of intelligence and drive, as you'd suspect, sets these readers apart—and up, demographically. Pick any yardstick and you'll find our readers lead the leaders.* If someone is one of the 250,000 who buy INTELLECTUAL DIGEST, or one of the 1,000,000 people who read it, you already know he's inquisitive... and acquisitive.
JUSTICE
Intellectual Digest
ENRICH YOURSELF
(AND YOUR ADVERTISING)

694

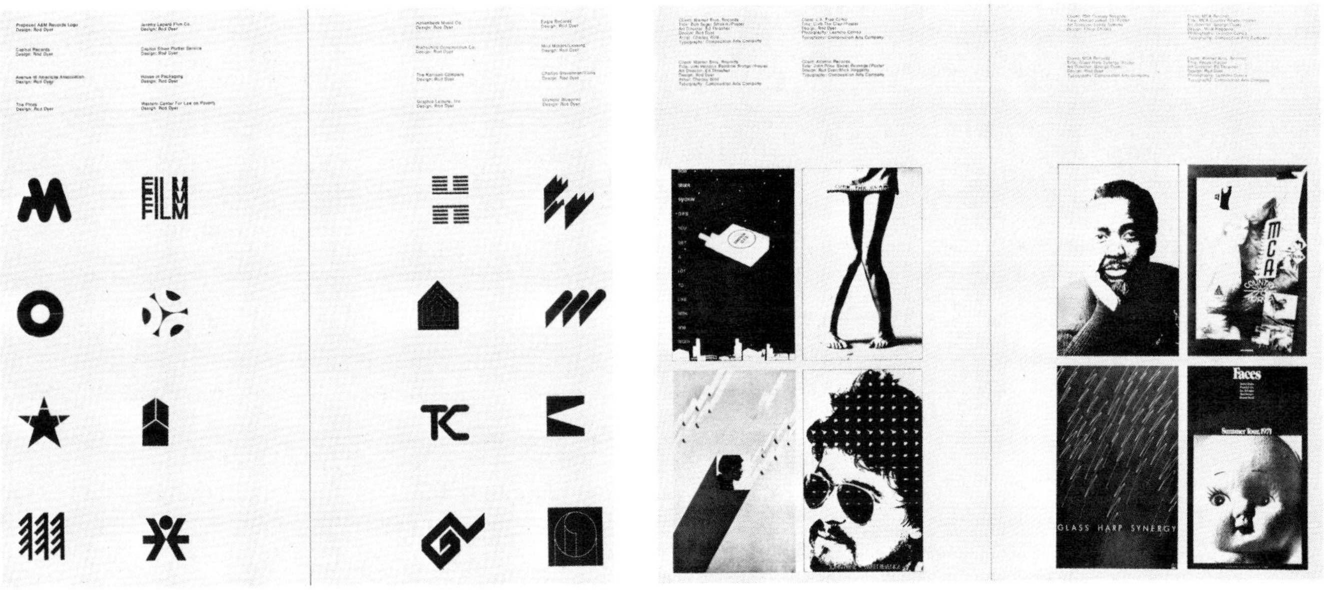

695

693
Art Director Kurt Weihs
Designers Kurt Weihs
Catherine Levine
Photographer Tasso Vendikos
Writer George Lois
Agency Lois/Chajet Design Group
Client Lois/Chajet Design Group

694
Art Director Herb Stern
Designer Asa Johnson
Artist Asa Johnson
Photographers Blair Pittman
Herb Stern
UPI
Culver
Writer Robin Jones
Agency Ziff-Davis Publishing
Client Intellectual Digest

695
Art Director Rod Dyer
Designer Rod Dyer
Artist Rod Dyer
Agency Rod Dyer, Inc.
Client Rod Dyer

FINAL
The Big Time
FILMS INC. NEWS
Follow the Party Line! Book Films Incorporated
Films Inc. Serves Student Film Chairpeople!
Take a great leap forward & offer 19 new showcase titles!
Power to The Viewer
Chairman's Choice
Chairman's Choice

696

Humphrey Browning MacDougall meets the grumph.

Last year Humphrey Browning MacDougall won fifteen major national creative awards. (And we swept the local awards scene with seven first place Hatch bowls and nine Art Directors' medals.)
EGO TRIPS FOR THE CREATIVES.

697

696
Art Director Peter Nevraumont
Designer John Van Hamersveld
Photographer Phil Fewsmith
Writer Peter Nevraumont
Agency The Art Factory
Client Films Inc.

697
Art Director Dick Gage
Writer Jamie Putian
Agency Humphrey Browning MacDougall
Client Humphrey Browning MacDougall

698
Art Director Irwin Goldberg
Designer Irwin Goldberg
Photographer Buddy Endress
Writers Irwin Goldberg
Bob Larimer
Agency Nadler & Larimer
Client Tulchin Productions

HANK AARON
RED AUERBACH
GEORGE BLANDA
TOMMY BOLT
JOHN BUCYK
ROY CAMPANELLA
WILT CHAMBERLAIN
JERRY COLEMAN
DAVE COWENS
KIKI CUTTER
ROMAN GABRIEL
JOE GARAGIOLA
PANCHO GONZALES
GAIL GOODRICH
SONNY GOSSICK
ROCKY GRAZIANO
BOB GRIESE
HAPPY HAIRSTON
HARLEM GLOBETROTTERS
FRANCO HARRIS
JOHN HAVLICEK
TOM HEINSOHN
PAMELA SUE HIGGINS
GIL HODGES
PAUL HORNUNG
FRANK HOWARD
PHIL JACKSON
ALEX KARRAS
BILLIE JEAN KING
TONY LIMA
SPARKY LYLE
MICKEY MANTLE
DAVE MARR
JIM McMILLAN
LENNY MOORE
FRANK NELSON
HEIZE OKAWA
BUD PALMER
JOHN PENNEL
GEORGE PLIMPTON
PHIL RIZZUTO
JACKIE ROBINSON
FRANK ROBINSON
RALPH SALVON
TOM SEAVER
ROGER STAUBACH
JIM THOMAS
KEN VENTURI
JERRY WEST
JO JO WHITE
DICK WILLIAMS
FRED WILLIAMSON

TULCHIN PRODUCTIONS LTD.
HAS FILMED AND VIDEOTAPED ALL THE
SPORTS CELEBRITIES ON THIS LOCKER.
WE'VE PRODUCED MORE SPORTS
COMMERCIALS THAN JUST ABOUT ANYONE
ELSE IN THE BUSINESS.
BEFORE YOU SHOOT YOUR NEXT
JOCK SPOT SEE OUR REEL. CALL:
HERIS STENZEL, TED BAYLIS, DICK DE MAIO.
(212) 532-3453

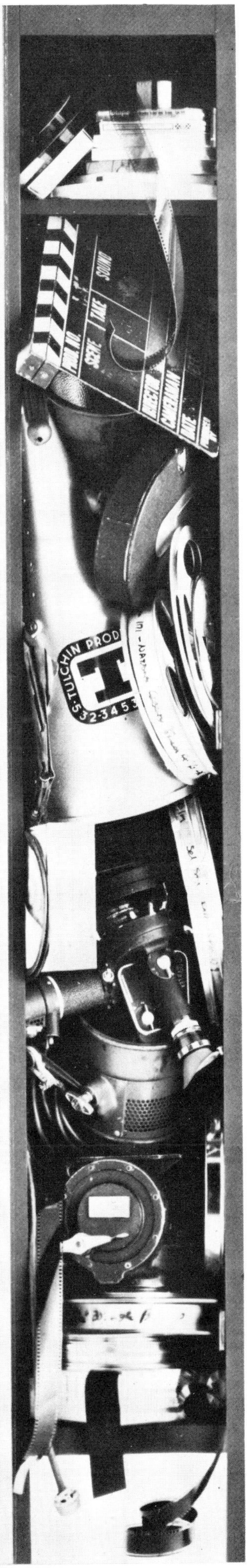

TULCHIN PRODUCTIONS LTD., 107 E.38TH ST., N.Y. 10016

The problem is not usually with the carrot, it's all in how you dangle it.
Thankyou BRAND
TEENIE
GOLDEN
FINGERLING
carrots
LENGTH CUT
"country kitchen good"
NET WT. 8¼ OZ.

699

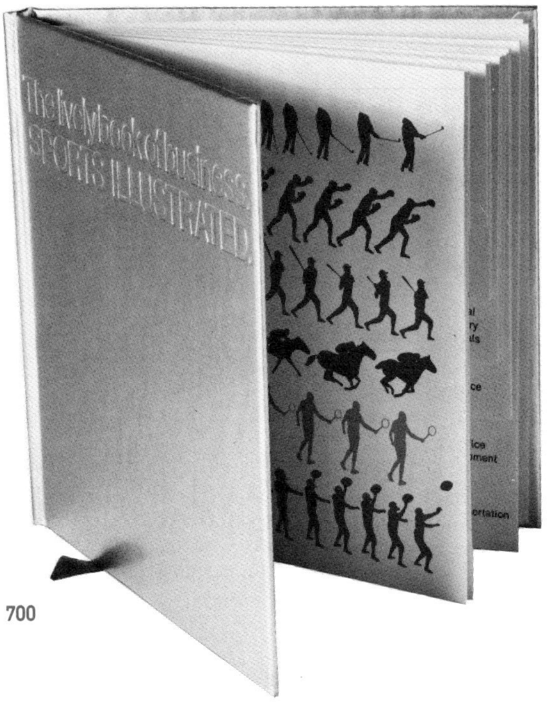
The lively book of business
SPORTS ILLUSTRATED

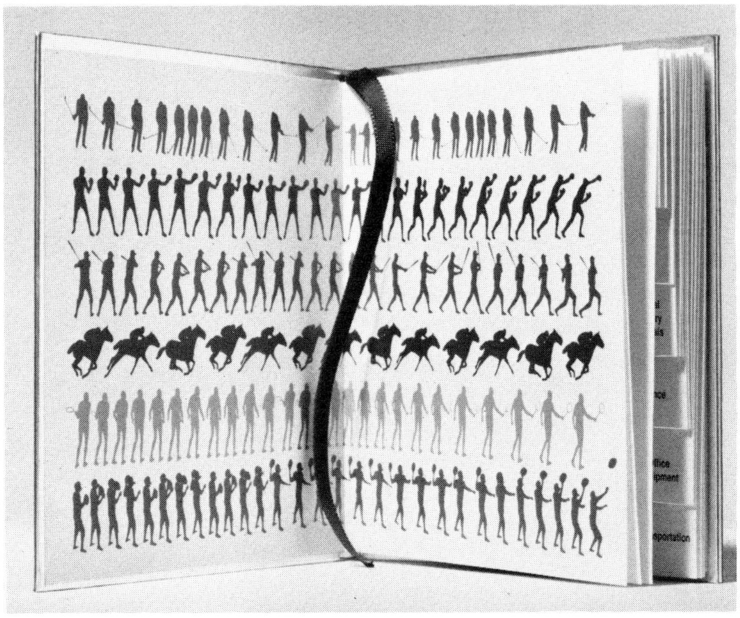

700

699
Art Director John McEown
Designer John McEown
Photographers Allan Starr
Markow Studio
Writer J. C. Whitted
Agency The Roberts Group
Client J. C. Whitted and Assoc.

700
Art Director S. B. Berliner
Designer S. B. Berliner
Artists James Miho
Champion Paper Co.
Writer Jack Counihan
Agency Time, Inc.
Client Sports Illustrated

ATLAS FOUNDRY
& MACHINE CO.
Seventy Five
Celebrating 75 years with Atlas Foundry & Machine Company

701

These are the wines of OZ. Wines to suit every taste, every meal, every occasion. In this select company, all are superb and all are unique. Each of them has been tasted and approved prior to selection by one of the world's most knowledgeable and respected wine authorities. Together they compose a cellar of unusual dimension and breadth. If you wish suggestions, the sommelier will be delighted to assist you. Joy and health are the gifts of wine, and they are priceless. As is the custom of fine European restaurants, OZ also proffers its own vin de maison. Personally selected by the owner, each has an individuality of its own and each is an excellent value.

THE WINE OF OZ

702

701
Art Director Ken Dankwardt
Designer Ken Dankwardt
Artist Ken Dankwardt
Photographer Tom Upper
Writers Kurt Jacobson
Mike Mayes
Agency Graves & Assoc.
Client Atlas Foundry & Machine Co.

702
Art Director Woody Pirtle
Designer Woody Pirtle
Artist Woody Pirtle
Writer Stan Richards
Agency The Richards Group
Client Oz Restaurant & Disco

THE ONE SHOW IS COMING APART

THE ONE SHOW
When The Art Directors Club and The Copy Club joined together, we had a very big baby: The One Show.
The Show fused The Copy Club's Gold Key Awards and The Art Directors Club Awards for Advertising, Editorial and Design into one huge award: a giant gold pencil.
Since that beginning three years ago, The One Show has grown enormously.
It's come to the point where in order to judge the show properly, exhibit the show intelligently, and present the show unboringly, the show must come to terms with itself.
So we've split The One Show into two shows which we'll still call The One Show.
The One Show International Advertising Awards.
The One Show International Editorial & Graphic Design Awards.
Each One Show will be judged separately by the leading practitioners in its field.
Each will have its own celebration. An event in which there's enough time to give the awards the dignity they deserve. To say nothing of a little entertainment on the side.
The two One Shows have separate instruction folders as you can see. If you're in Advertising, use the Advertising folder and throw away the one for Editorial and Design.
If you're in Editorial or Design fill out that folder and throw away the one for Advertising.
If you're in both, use both.
You'll have two judgings to be judged in, two celebrations to celebrate.
Lucky you.

703

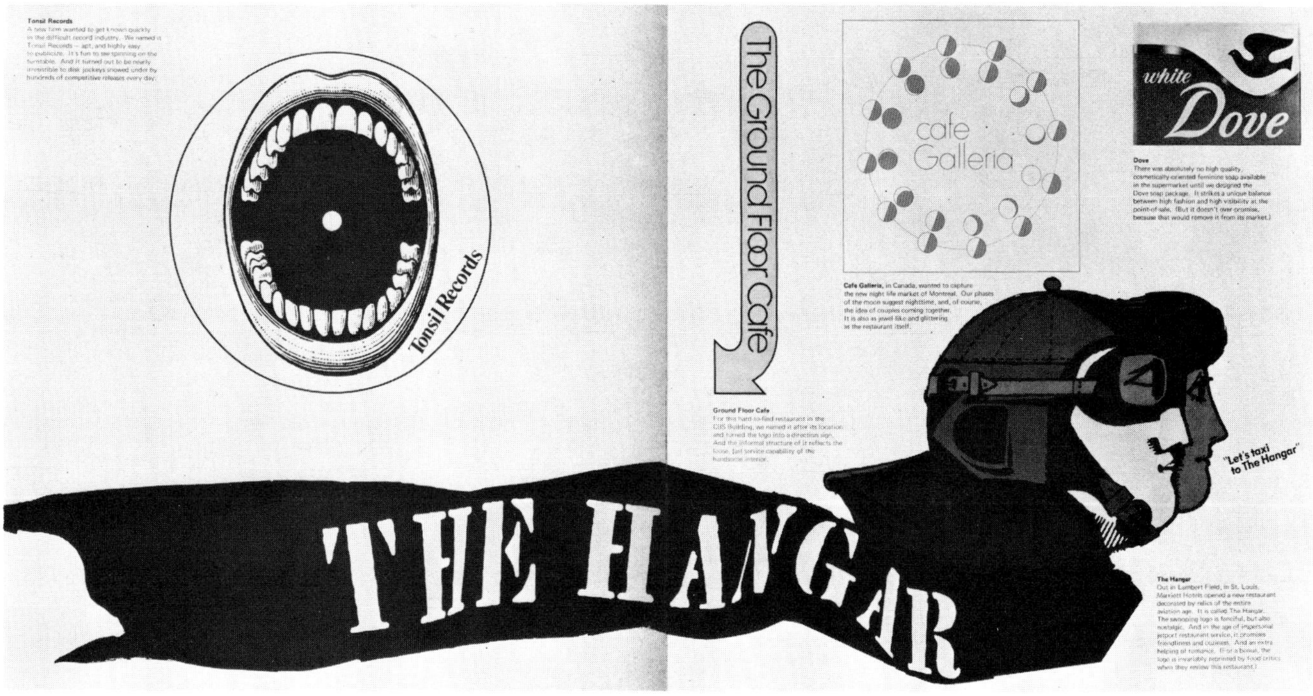
Tonsil Records
The Ground Floor Cafe
cafe Galleria
white Dove
"Let's taxi to The Hangar"
THE HANGAR

704

703
Art Director Bernie Zlotnick
Designer Bernie Zlotnick
Artists Tom Carnase
Chuck Cassidy
Writers Dave Altschiller
Faith Popcorn
Agency Barnett, Zlotnick Advertising
Client The Art Directors Club of New York

704
Art Directors Tom Courtos
George Lois
Kurt Weihs
Designer Tom Courtos
Writer Ron Holland
Agency Lois/Chajet Design Group
Client Lois/Chajet Design Group

A day on the farm with the Honda ATC 90 K2.
Many farmers and ranchers are discovering that the Honda ATC 90 K2 is an all-terrain, all-weather beast of burden. It rolls merrily along over rocks, sand, light snow and bumpy trails, through mud and shallow streams. It features a Honda spark arrestor/muffler to help protect the environment. A strong Honda warranty to protect you. During the week, it can help you with all sorts of work. On the weekend, it's a fun ride for the entire family. The Honda ATC 90 K2—it can make any day on the farm more rewarding.
Specifications on the Honda ATC 90 K2
HONDA
Good things happen on a Honda.

705

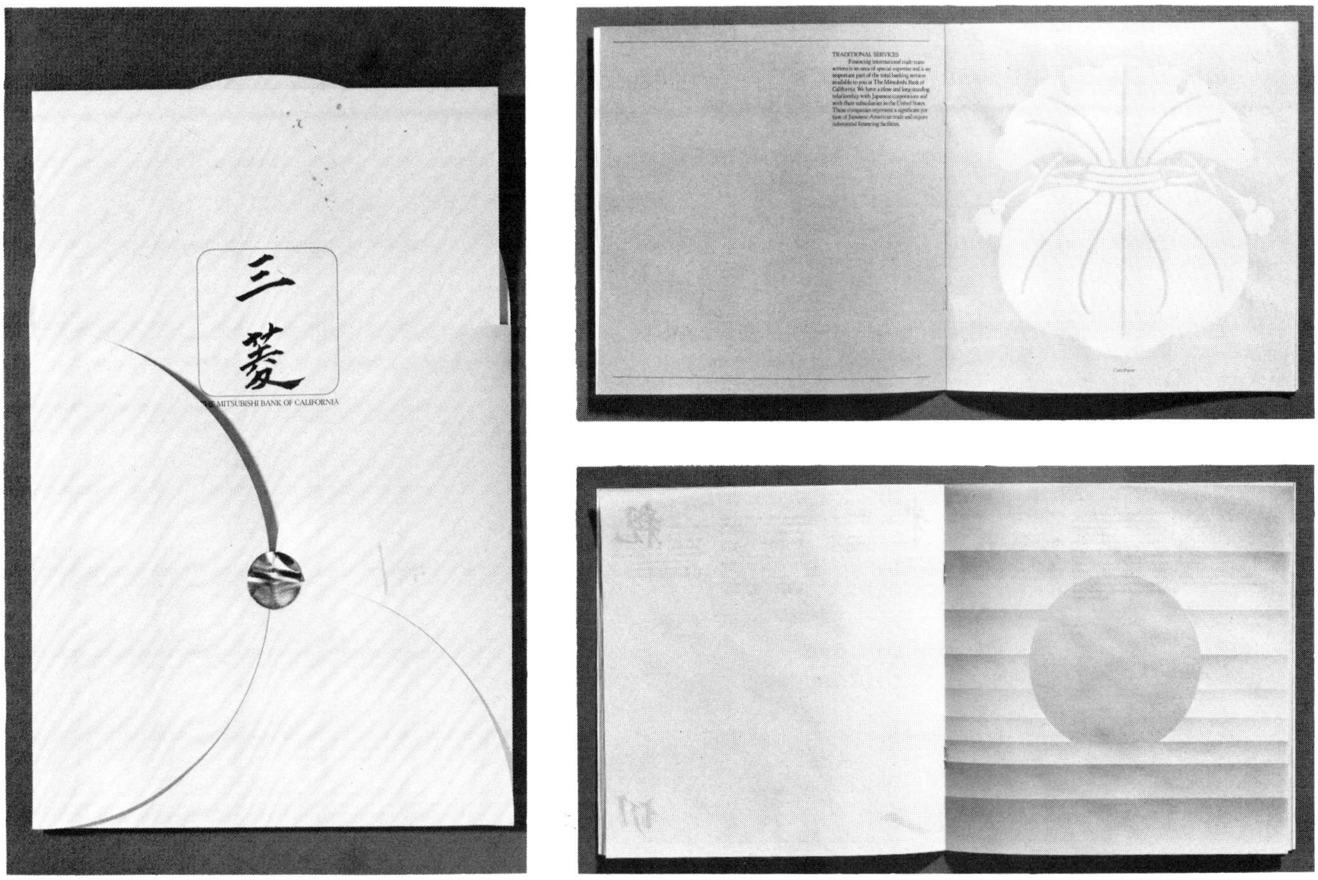
三菱
THE MITSUBISHI BANK OF CALIFORNIA
TRADITIONAL SERVICES

706

705
Art Director Leland Miyawaki
Designer Leland Miyawaki
Photographer Jim Miller
Writer Lee Livingston
Agency Grey Advertising
Los Angeles
Client American Honda Motor Co.

706
Art Director Gene Dispara
Designer Nicolas Sidjakov
Artist Nicolas Sidjakov
Agency Needham, Harper & Steers
Los Angeles
Client Mitsubishi Bank of California

THE
WEATHER
MACHINE

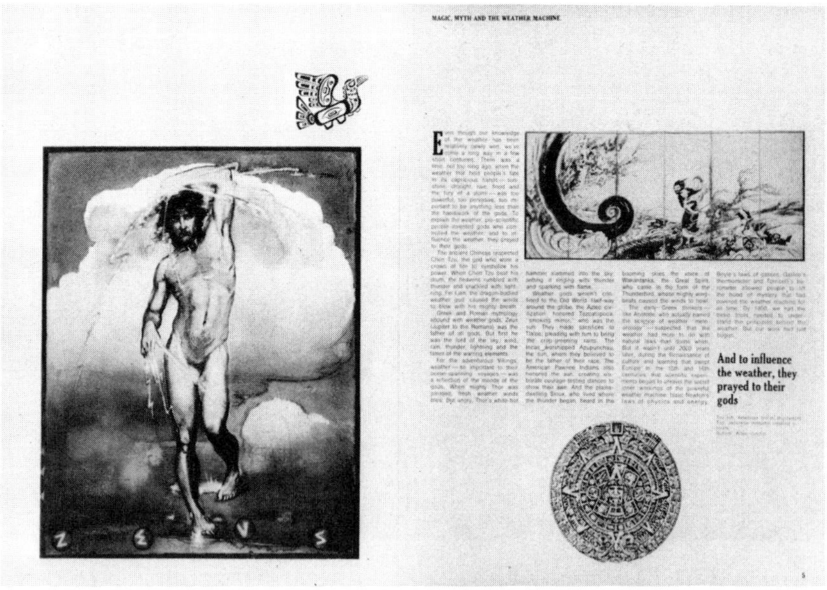
MAGIC, MYTH AND THE WEATHER MACHINE
Z E V S
And to influence the weather, they prayed to their gods

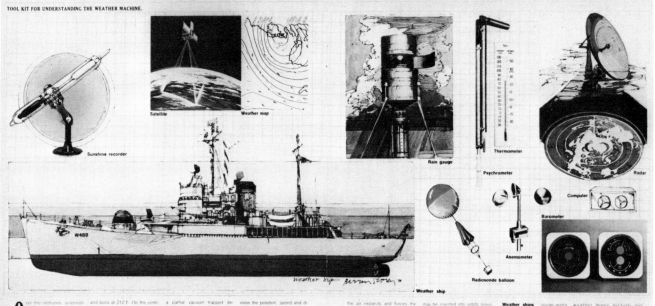

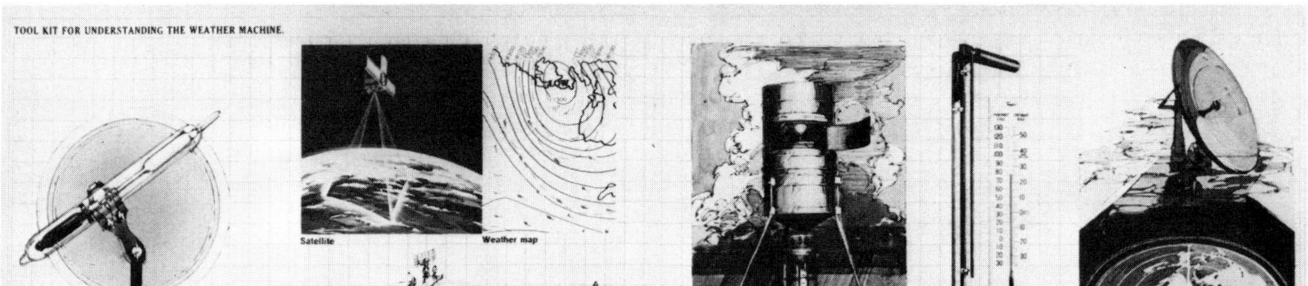
TOOL KIT FOR UNDERSTANDING THE WEATHER MACHINE.
Satellite
Weather map
Sunshine recorder
Rain gauge
Thermometer
Psychrometer
Radar
Computer
Barometer
Anemometer
Radiosonde balloon
W489
Weather ship
20
21

707

707
Art Director B. Martin Pedersen
Designer B. Martin Pedersen
Artists Daniel Maffia
Dick Hess
Barron Storey
Writer Dave Brown
Agency Pedersen Design
Client Champion Papers

SOIL
A PINCH OF MELBOURNE SOIL. ONE OF THE WORLD'S FINEST FOR GROWING TREES. FROM WEYERHAEUSER.
"The soil out of which such men as he are made is good to be born on, good to live on, good to die for and to be buried in."
James Russell Lowell
"Our soil belongs also to unborn generations."
Sam Rayburn
"Not every soil can bear all things."
Virgil

Q. Why the soil survey?
A. Since soils are a key to High Yield Forestry, we must know what kinds, where, how much and how good.
To survey anything across millions of acres is a big job, but to map soils beneath the surface is impossible by traditional dig-and-look methods.
A different approach was needed. The goal was to break down the immense acreage into units of uniform character.
The landform.
With the help of aerial photography, soil scientists learned to read the wrinkled face of the land, to recognize the forces that shaped the terrain and created each soil.
Once the association between a specific landform and soil was established, the soil scientist, by identifying landforms on aerial photos, was able to predict that soil, even in remote and unvisited areas.
This unique technique was tested first in the rugged and glaciated country of the Snoqualmie Falls Tree Farm. The survey then progressed through the foothills of the Washington Cascades, across to the rich soils of the coast and then on to Oregon.
Today, the forest soils of over 4 million acres in the Pacific Northwest have been surveyed by Weyerhaeuser. The goal by 1980: all Weyerhaeuser land, including the pine regions in Eastern Oregon, Arkansas, Alabama, Mississippi, Oklahoma and North Carolina.

708
Art Director Martin Banke
Designer Martin Banke
Artist Mike Casad
Photographers Martin Banke
Jan Osborne
Writer David Steel
Agency Cole & Weber
Client Weyerhaeuser Co.

Ralph Bu
Without the contributions of foundations, corporations, and individuals, only a part of the Indian achievement at BYU would have been possible. Their donations largely support the assistance projects off-campus and some of the students' learning experiences outside the classroom. Funds contributed always go to specific programs directly benefitting students or participants; and an accounting is always given of results achieved (see next page). The contributions are *not* dissipated in staff salaries, supplies costs, or other regular operating expenses to which the University budget is already committed. Moreover, the University devotes some of its own funds to every externally supported project. Thus, contributions are used entirely to educate more Native Americans, in a university program unique in its proven effectiveness.

709

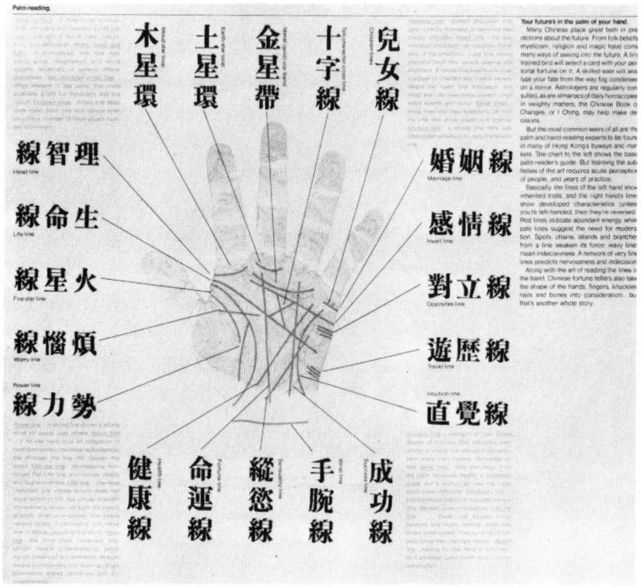
Palm reading.
木星環
土星環
金星帶
十字線
兒女線
線智理
Head line
線命生
Life line
線星火
Fire star line
線惱煩
Worry line
Power line
線力勢
婚姻線
Marriage line
感情線
Heart line
對立線
Opposites line
遊歷線
Travel line
Intuition line
直覺線
健康線
命運線
縱慾線
手腕線
成功線
Your future's in the palm of your hand.
Many Chinese place great faith in pre
dictions about the future. From folk beliefs
mysticism, religion and magic have come
many ways of seeing into the future. A tiny
trained bird will select a card with your per
sonal fortune on it. A skilled seer will ana
lyze your fate from the way fog condenses
on a mirror. Astrologers are regularly con
sulted, as are almanacs of daily horoscopes
In weighty matters, the Chinese Book o
Changes, or I Ching, may help make de
cisions.
But the most common seers of all are the
palm and hand reading experts to be found
in many of Hong Kong's byways and mar
kets. The chart to the left shows the basic
palm reader's guide. But learning the sub
tleties of the art requires acute perception
of people, and years of practice.
Basically the lines of the left hand show
inherited traits, and the right hand's lines
show developed characteristics (unless
you're left-handed, then they're reversed.
Red lines indicate abundant energy, while
pale lines suggest the need for modera
tion. Spots, chains, islands and branches
from a line weaken its force; wavy lines
mean indecisiveness. A network of very fine
lines predicts nervousness and indecision
Along with the art of reading the lines in
the hand, Chinese fortune tellers also take
the shape of the hands, fingers, knuckles
nails and bones into consideration... but
that's another whole story.

Champion Papers
Imagination XVIII
Hong Kong
冠軍紙
想像十
八香港

710

SILVER

709
Art Director James Cross
Designer James Cross
Photographer Marvin Silver
Writer C. Terry Warner
Agency James Cross Design Office
Client Brigham Young University

710
Art Director James Miho
Designer James Miho
Artists Norman Macdonanld
Barry Zaid
Ying Wei Tang
Marjorie Guarcello
Photographers Jerry Sarapochiello
Run Run Shaw
Museu Luis De Camoes
Writer David Brown
Agency Champion Papers
Client Champion Papers

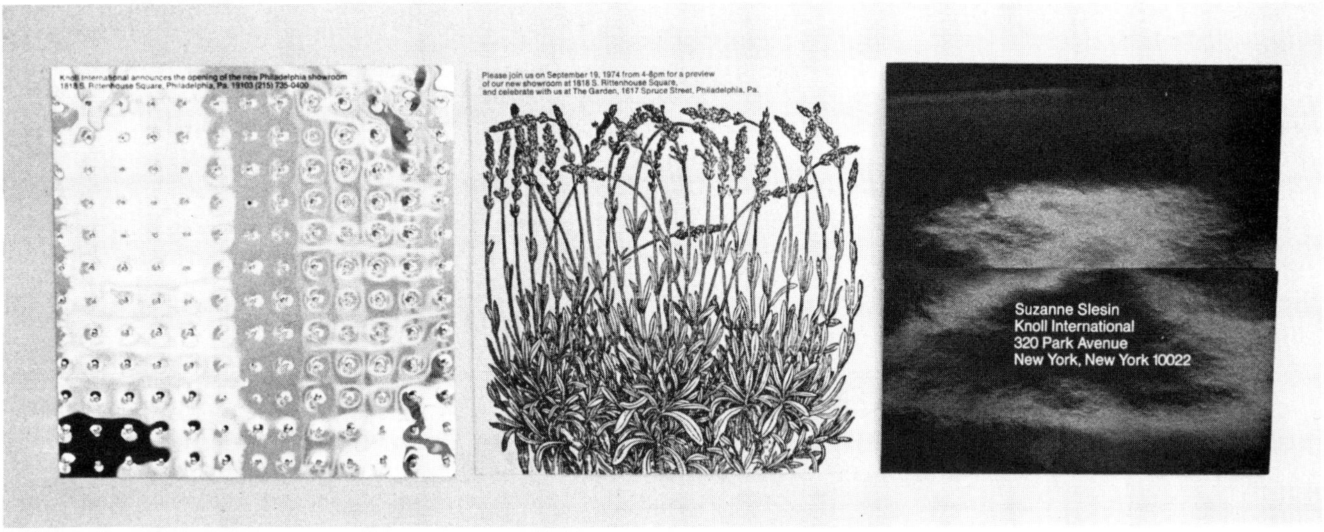

Knoll International announces the opening of the new Philadelphia showroom
1818 S. Rittenhouse Square, Philadelphia, Pa. 19103 (215) 735-0400
Please join us on September 19, 1974 from 4-8pm for a preview
of our new showroom at 1818 S. Rittenhouse Square,
and celebrate with us at The Garden, 1617 Spruce Street, Philadelphia, Pa.
Suzanne Slesin
Knoll International
320 Park Avenue
New York, New York 10022

711

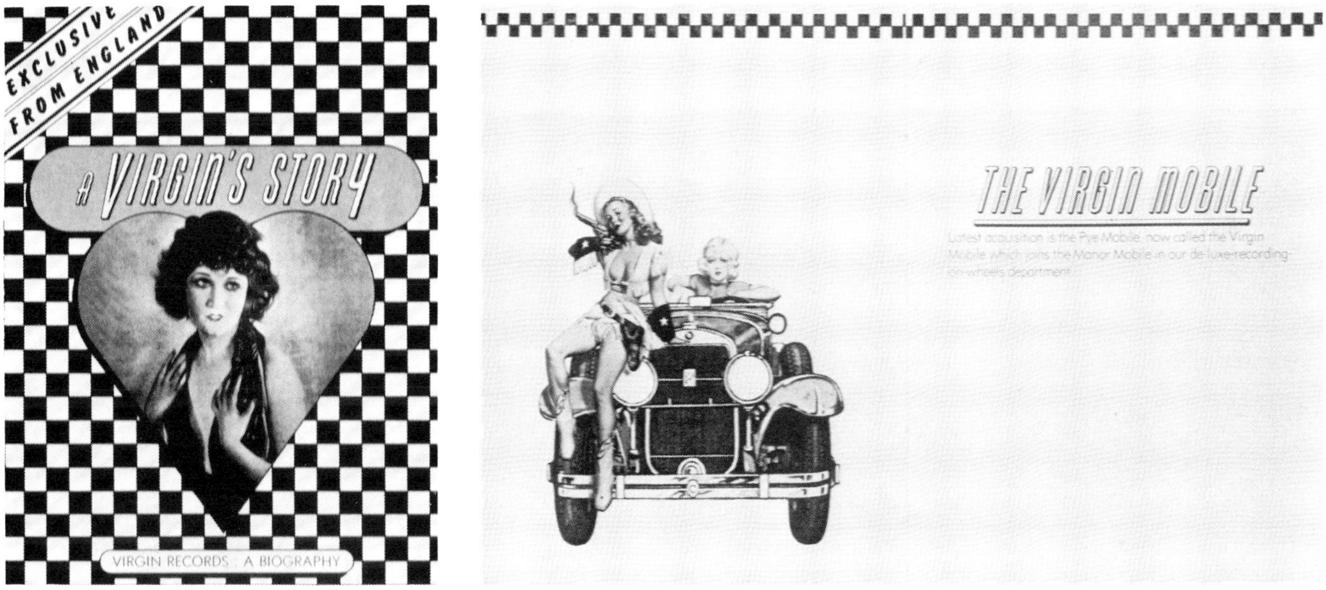

EXCLUSIVE
FROM ENGLAND
A VIRGIN'S STORY
VIRGIN RECORDS : A BIOGRAPHY
THE VIRGIN MOBILE
Latest acquisition is the Pye Mobile, now called the Virgin Mobile which joins the Manor Mobile in our de-luxe-recording-on-wheels department.

712

711
Art Director Marjorie Katz
Designer Marjorie Katz
Writer Suzanne Slesin
Agency Knoll International
Client Knoll International

712
Art Director Bob Defrin
Designer Paula Scher
Agency Atlantic Records
Client Virgin Records

Boscobel
Restoration

713

713

Art Director George Klauber
Designer George Klauber
Photographers Frank Moscati
Danny Wann
Charlotte Brooks
George Klauber
Writers Joseph T. Butler
Fred Stanyer
Agency George Klauber
Client Boscobel Restoration

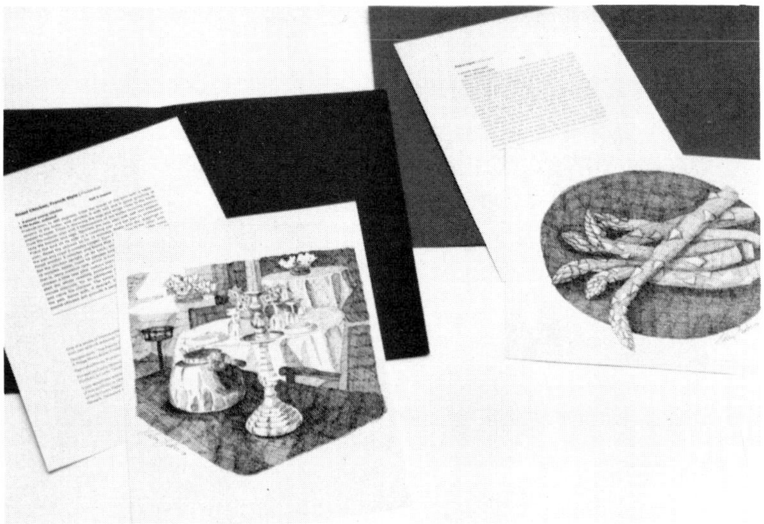

714

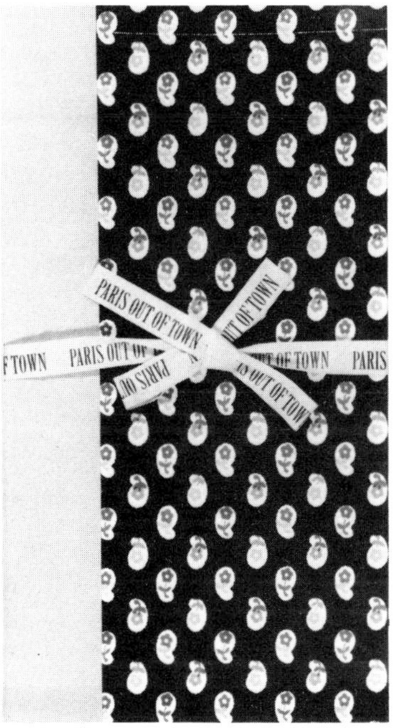
PARIS OUT OF TOWN

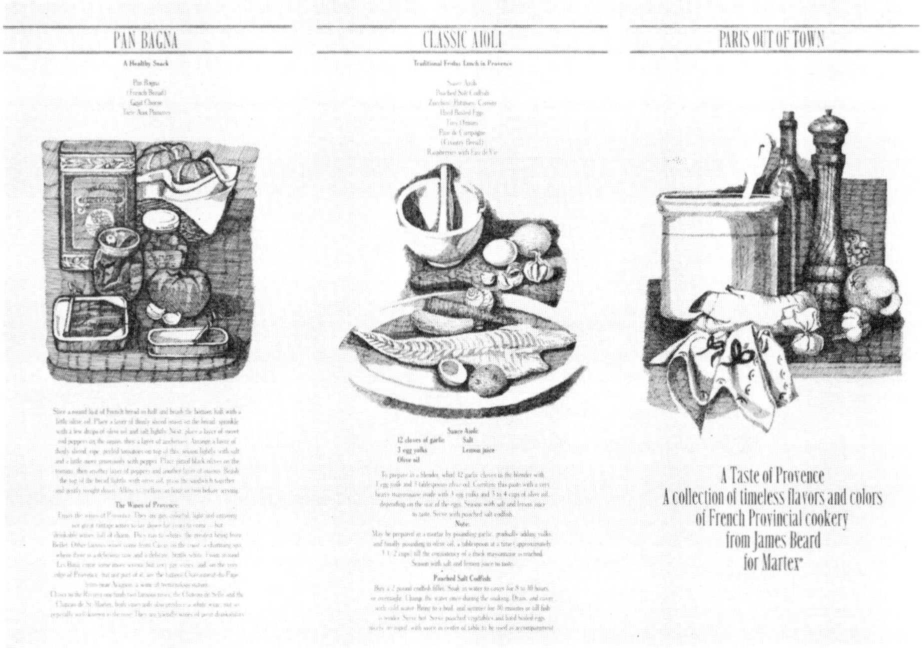
PAN BAGNA
A Healthy Snack
CLASSIC AIOLI
Traditional Friday Lunch in Provence
PARIS OUT OF TOWN
A Taste of Provence
A collection of timeless flavors and colors
of French Provincial cookery
from James Beard
for Martex

715

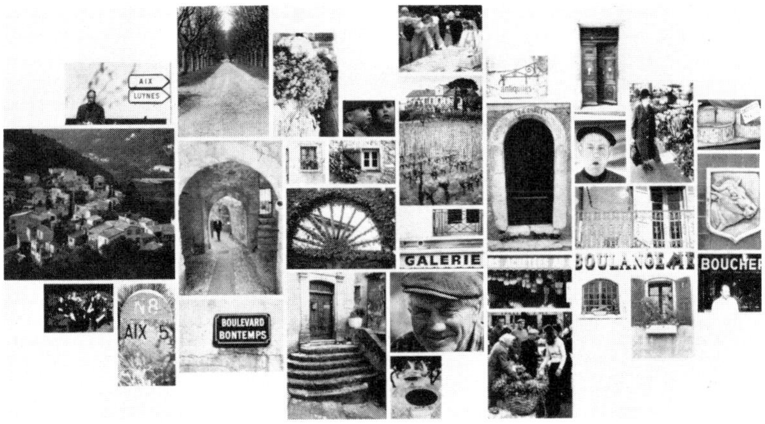
AIX
LUYNES
GALERIE
BOUCHER
BOULEVARD BONTEMPS

714
Art Director Irwin Rothman
Designer Helen Federico
Artist Helen Federico
Agency Pioneer-Moss Reproductions Corp.
Client Pioneer-Moss Reproductions Corp.

715
Art Director Don Ervin
Designer Ray Behar
Artist Helen Federico
Photographer Jerry Abramowitz
Agency Siegel & Gale
Client West Point Pepperell

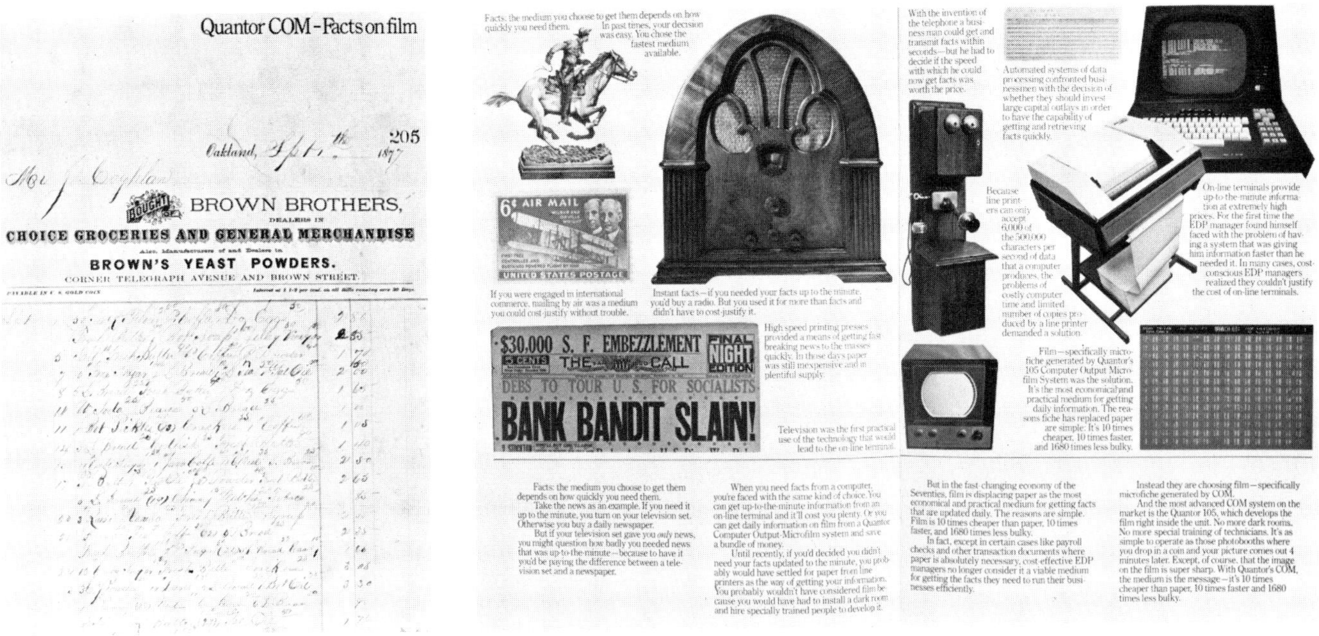
Quantor COM - Facts on film
BROWN BROTHERS,
DEALERS IN
CHOICE GROCERIES AND GENERAL MERCHANDISE
BROWN'S YEAST POWDERS.
CORNER TELEGRAPH AVENUE AND BROWN STREET.
Facts: the medium you choose to get them depends on how quickly you need them. In past times, your decision was easy. You chose the fastest medium available.
AIR MAIL
UNITED STATES POSTAGE
If you were engaged in international commerce, mailing by air was a medium you could cost-justify without trouble.
Instant facts—if you needed your facts up to the minute, you'd buy a radio. But you used it for more than facts and didn't have to cost-justify it.
$30,000 S. F. EMBEZZLEMENT
FINAL NIGHT EDITION
THE CALL
DEBS TO TOUR U. S. FOR SOCIALISTS
BANK BANDIT SLAIN!
High speed printing presses provided a means of getting fast breaking news to the masses quickly. In those days paper was still inexpensive and in plentiful supply.
Television was the first practical use of the technology that would lead to the on-line terminal.
With the invention of the telephone a business man could get and transmit facts within seconds—but he had to decide if the speed with which he could now get facts was worth the price.
Automated systems of data processing confronted businessmen with the decision of whether they should invest large capital outlays in order to have the capability of getting and retrieving facts quickly.
Because line printers can only accept 6,000 of the 500,000 characters per second of data that a computer produces, the problems of costly computer time and limited number of copies produced by a line printer demanded a solution.
On-line terminals provide up-to-the-minute information at extremely high prices. For the first time the EDP manager found himself faced with the problem of having a system that was giving him information faster than he needed it. In many cases, cost-conscious EDP managers realized they couldn't justify the cost of on-line terminals.
Film—specifically microfiche generated by Quantor's 105 Computer Output Microfilm System was the solution. It's the most economical and practical medium for getting daily information. The reasons fiche has replaced paper are simple: It's 10 times cheaper, 10 times faster, and 1680 times less bulky.
Facts: the medium you choose to get them depends on how quickly you need them.
Take the news as an example. If you need it up to the minute, you turn on your television set. Otherwise you buy a daily newspaper.
But if your television set gave you only news, you might question how badly you needed news that was up-to-the-minute—because to have it you'd be paying the difference between a television set and a newspaper.
When you need facts from a computer, you're faced with the same kind of choice. You can get up-to-the-minute information from an on-line terminal and it'll cost you plenty. Or you can get daily information on film from a Quantor Computer Output-Microfilm system and save a bundle of money.
Until recently, if you'd decided you didn't need your facts updated to the minute, you probably would have settled for paper from line printers as the way of getting your information. You probably wouldn't have considered film because you would have had to install a dark room and hire specially trained people to develop it.
But in the fast-changing economy of the Seventies, film is displacing paper as the most economical and practical medium for getting facts that are updated daily. The reasons are simple. Film is 10 times cheaper than paper, 10 times faster, and 1680 times less bulky.
In fact, except in certain cases like payroll checks and other transaction documents where paper is absolutely necessary, cost-effective EDP managers no longer consider it a viable medium for getting the facts they need to run their businesses efficiently.
Instead they are choosing film—specifically microfiche generated by COM.
And the most advanced COM system on the market is the Quantor 105, which develops the film right inside the unit. No more dark rooms. No more special training of technicians. It's as simple to operate as those photobooths where you drop in a coin and your picture comes out 4 minutes later. Except, of course, that the image on the film is super sharp. With Quantor's COM, the medium is the message—it's 10 times cheaper than paper, 10 times faster and 1680 times less bulky.

716

PepsiCo, Inc.
Products
& Services

717

716
Art Director Jerry Leonhardt
Designer Nicolas Sidjakov
Artists John Hyatt
Nicolas Sidjakov
Photographer Don Shapiro
Writer Tom Livingston
Agency Regis McKenna
Client Quantor Corp.

717
Art Director Stan Eisenman
Designer Eisenman and Enock
Photographer Arnold Beckerman
Writer Bill Brown
Agency Eisenman and Enock
Client PepsiCo

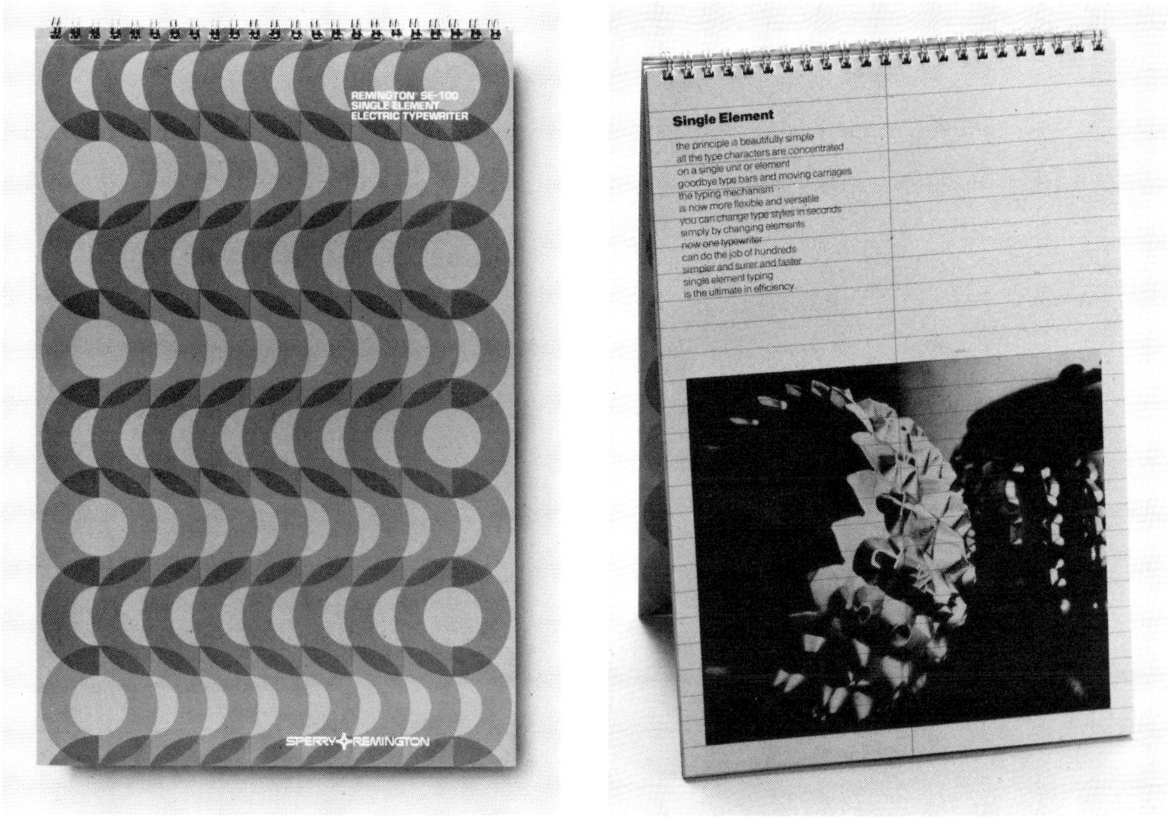
REMINGTON SE-100
SINGLE ELEMENT
ELECTRIC TYPEWRITER
SPERRY REMINGTON
Single Element
the principle is beautifully simple
all the type characters are concentrated
on a single unit or element
goodbye type bars and moving carriages
the typing mechanism
is now more flexible and versatile
you can change type styles in seconds
simply by changing elements
now one typewriter
can do the job of hundreds
simpler and surer and faster
single element typing
is the ultimate in efficiency

718

REED
"Reed's very tough and incredibly satisfying."
Student
Class of 1972
"...small, intimate classes, where emphasis may be placed on 'the idea'."

719

718
Art Director Ford, Byrne & Assoc.
Designer Ford, Byrne & Assoc.
Artist Ford, Byrne & Assoc.
Photographer Frank Leone
Writer Donald Falk
Agency Ford, Byrne & Assoc.
Client Sperry-Remington

719
Art Directors Robin Rickabaugh
Heidi Rickabaugh
Designer Robin Rickabaugh
Artists Robin Rickabaugh
Heidi Rickabaugh
Photographer Ron Finne
Editor Ann Granning-Bennet
Agency Robin Rickabaugh
Client Reed College

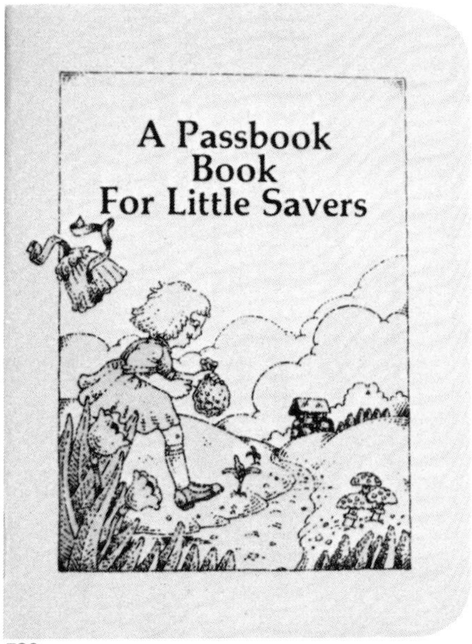
A Passbook
Book
For Little Savers

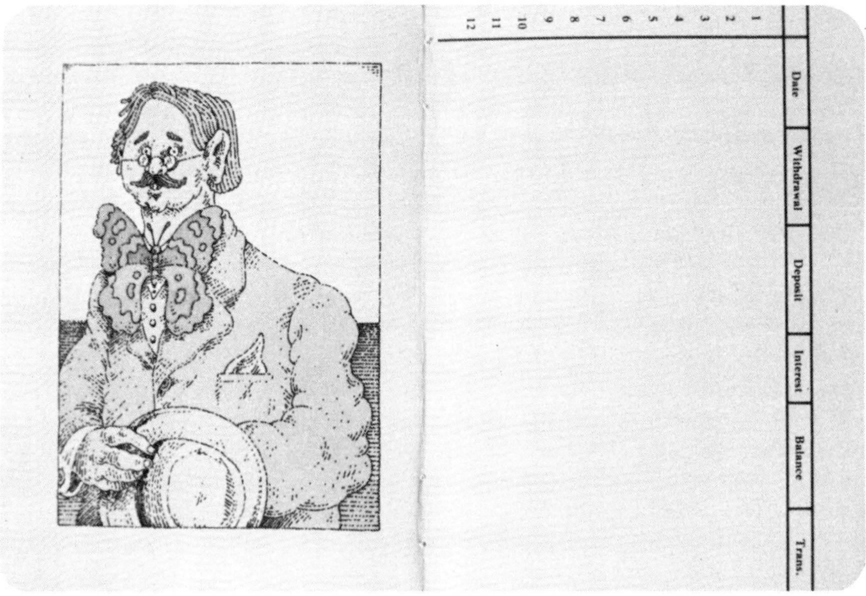
1
2
3
4
5
6
7
8
9
10
11
12
Date
Withdrawal
Deposit
Interest
Balance
Trans.

720

SCHAAK · ALLIED
RADIO CATALOGUE OF THE AIR
Inside is everything you need to know about audio, Timmy!
What's an audio, Uncle Allie?

HOW HI THE FI?

"I hate to be the one to tell you," a guy named Fred told our Uncle Allie, "but I've discovered something that will probably put Schaak and Allied Stores out of business."

Uncle Allie was interested, of course, and he accepted an invitation to visit Fred's home for a refreshment and the mysterious revelation.

Indeed, Fred's "discovery" was a fascinating device. An oil company had offered it to him through its credit card's "special merchandise" division. For a 30-day free home trial. And only $129.95 if he decided to keep it.

It was a radio, yes. AM, FM and FM Stereo. With a record player cleverly built into the top. And a slot for inserting 8-track cartridges into its front. Dials and switches galore. Plus two compact loudspeakers with sufficient cord to position them about 10 feet apart.

"Now I know your Schaak and Allied Stores charge as much as several hundred dollars for equipment that does all this," Fred told Uncle Allie. "I know this will shake you up. But best you learn about it from a friend. Listen!"

Switch on. Tone arm down.

"Listen! Just listen!" Fred repeated.

It was loud. As much volume for $129.95 as Uncle Allie had ever heard. When Fred finally switched it off, Uncle Allie could hear a dog down the street baying in agony.

"Why," the host asked compassionately, "would anybody buy expensive stuff from Schaak and Allied Stores when a low cost system like this is available?"

"Bring your record over to my house," Uncle Allie replied. "My Scotch is not as good as yours. But I'd like you to compare sounds."

Uncle Allie has what some would call a "conservative" system. He doesn't believe that good sound has to cost an arm and leg. And he's cheap! Allie poured a couple of Scotches. And put Fred's record on his turntable.

"Come on," Fred bellowed. "You switched records on me."

Uncle Allie denied it.

"But this record has violins. My record didn't have any violins on it."

Yes, it was the same record. And, aside from some record noise, it played back very much like the original music session must have sounded.

(The record noise, Allie explained, probably resulted from record damage caused by the relatively heavy-tracking cartridge in the tone arm of Fred's record player — damage that could have been avoided had lighter-tracking equipment been used.)

Yes, there were violins on Fred's record all the time. But his mail-order system would not separate the strings from the simple *essence* of what the music was intended to sound like.

That's what Fred bought for $129.95. Equipment that would reproduce the essence of the original recorded sounds.

Uncle Allie on the other hand, had spent a few extra hundred dollars for his system because he wanted to hear those sounds reproduced as realistically as possible. Strings, horns, woodwinds, percussion — each as separate and distinct as if the orchestra were performing in his living room.

Fred had been satisfied with this essence. Until he heard Allie's better system. Then he, too, wanted the better system.

You might be satisfied with your essence — even after you hear our better system. And, for you, Schaak and Allied Stores feature many excellent buys in lower-priced systems priced around $129.95. Sometimes even less. And we won't look down our noses at you when you come in to choose one.

But if your taste-level requires more of the full, rich reality of the original sound of the music, voice, etc., you're going to have to spend more money for the technology and hardware required to accurately reproduce all the sounds that are so carefully recorded onto a disc or tape recording or transmitted by a radio station.

How much more technology and hardware? Depends how high your taste-level runs and how much of that taste-level you feel you must satisfy. And the main job of the Schaak/Allied staff is to help you find the system that maximizes your listening enjoyment without minimizing your financial position.

What you don't see is what you get.

Fred's $129.95 30-day free home trial system (he returned it before the end of 30 days) was a "package" of functions that are included in more sophisticated equipment. In this case:

Speakers—to generate sound waves as "instructed" by electrical signals coming from the power amplifier.

Power amplifier—to transform relatively weak signals coming to it from the pre-amplifier into signals sufficiently strong to drive the speakers.

FRED
ONLY $129.95
THAT'S NOT MY STYLE!
CLINK!
RECEIVERS, AMPS, TUNERS · STEREO & QUAD

721

720
Art Director Elwood H. Smith
Designer Elwood H. Smith
Artist Elwood H. Smith
Writer Elwood H. Smith
Agency Elwood H. Smith Design/Illustration
Client Lakeshore Bank & Trust Co.

721
Art Director Meredythe Jones
Designers Bill Hogan, Paul Ginther, Meredythe Jones
Artists Pete Bastiansen, Dave Rubenstein
Photographers Don Thoen, Paul Hagen, Alan Forrest
Editor Paul Hagen
Writers Ron Dick, Steve Rossi, Bob Murray
Agency Serendipity
Client Schaak Electronics

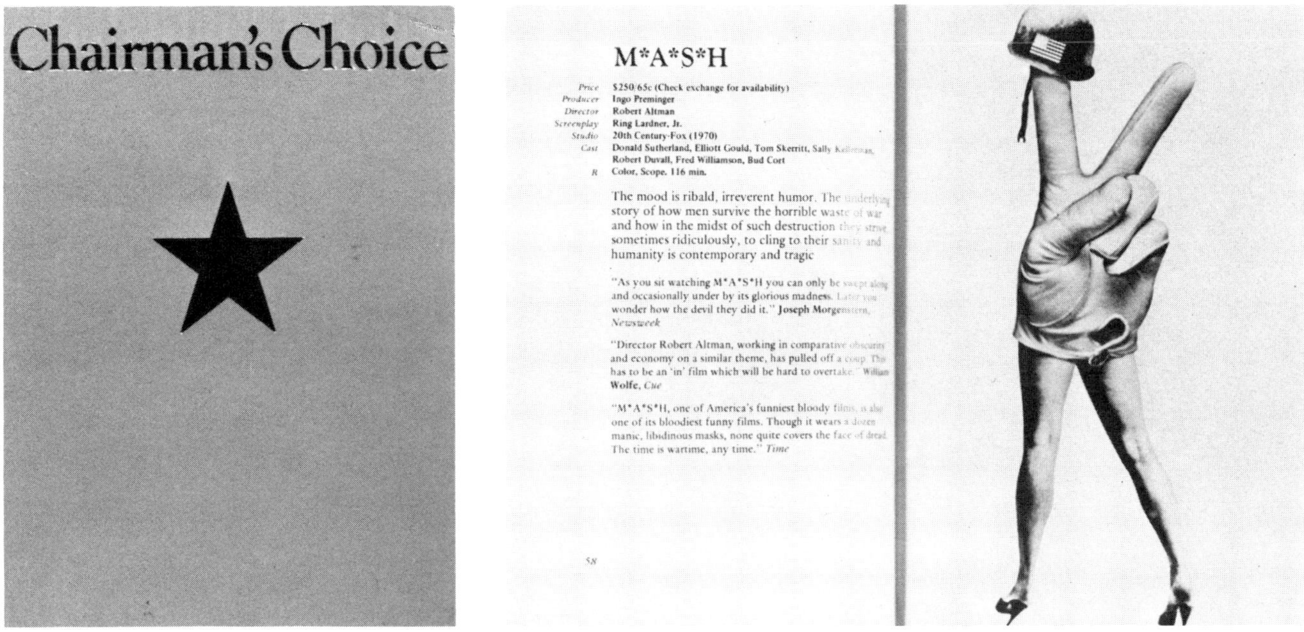
Chairman's Choice
M*A*S*H
Price $250/65c (Check exchange for availability)
Producer Ingo Preminger
Director Robert Altman
Screenplay Ring Lardner, Jr.
Studio 20th Century-Fox (1970)
Cast Donald Sutherland, Elliott Gould, Tom Skerritt, Sally Kellerman, Robert Duvall, Fred Williamson, Bud Cort
R Color, Scope. 116 min.
The mood is ribald, irreverent humor. The underlying story of how men survive the horrible waste of war and how in the midst of such destruction they strive, sometimes ridiculously, to cling to their sanity and humanity is contemporary and tragic
"As you sit watching M*A*S*H you can only be swept along and occasionally under by its glorious madness. Later you wonder how the devil they did it." Joseph Morgenstern, Newsweek
"Director Robert Altman, working in comparative obscurity and economy on a similar theme, has pulled off a coup. This has to be an 'in' film which will be hard to overtake." William Wolfe, Cue
"M*A*S*H, one of America's funniest bloody films, is also one of its bloodiest funny films. Though it wears a dozen manic, libidinous masks, none quite covers the face of dread. The time is wartime, any time." Time
58

722

Griffith Park

723

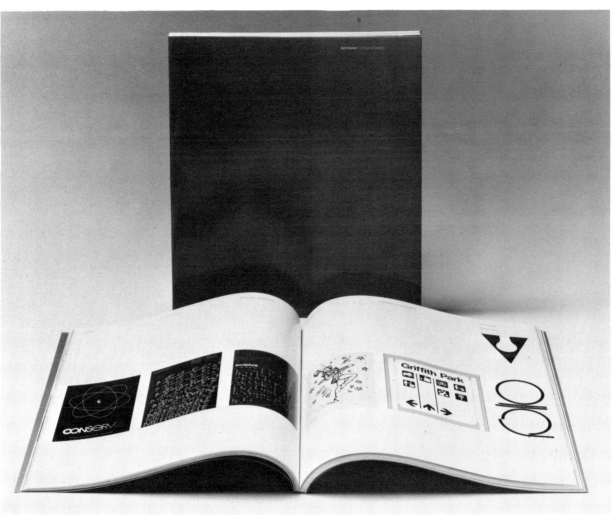

722
Art Director Peter Nevraumont
Designer John Van Hamersveld
Writer Peter Nevraumont
Agency The Art Factory
Client Films Inc.

723
Art Director Don Kubly
Designer Edwin Love
Photographer Edward Handler
Writer Rosalie M. Stapleton
Agency Art Center College of Design
Client Art Center College of Design

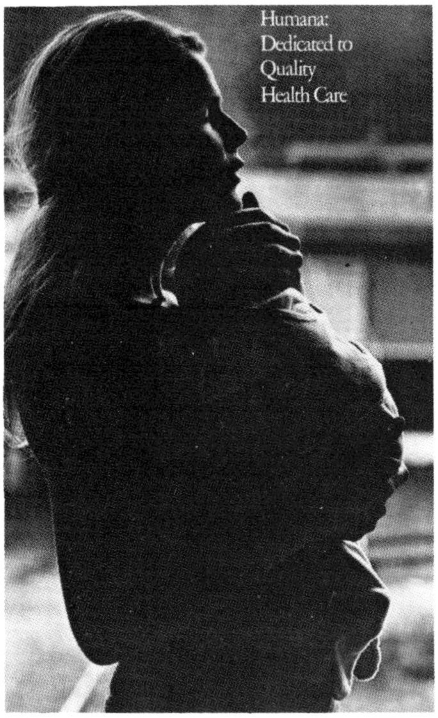
Humana:
Dedicated to
Quality
Health Care

hospital—so that health needs for the community can be handled in one place, whether they involve visits to the doctors' offices, referrals to the hospital on an outpatient basis for x-rays and tests, or hospitalization for treatment.

When existing hospitals come under the HUMANA management, extensive improvements and additions in service, where needed, are put into effect.

New coronary and intensive care units, facilities for outpatient services, and other renovations are characteristic of these hospitals after they have been evaluated in terms of local needs by HUMANA and representatives of the community.

Adequate emergency services—including the proper number of emergency rooms as well as facilities for emergency surgery—are top-priority attributes of HUMANA hospitals.

All needs, in fact, are weighed: operating rooms, recovery rooms, intensive care unit, coronary care unit, maternity section, psychiatric unit, outpatient surgery section, ambulatory care facilities, and other considerations.

The patient room in a typical new HUMANA hospital is equipped with piped-in oxygen and vacuum, a bed with electric controls, and a nurse-call system that lets patients talk with the personnel at the nursing station. Each room has its own complete bathroom facilities, telephone, and color television. Advanced electronic data systems are being tested by HUMANA and installed in many of its hospitals to improve speed and accuracy of response to physicians' orders.

Latest condition monitoring devices are used. In fact, purchase of sophisticated equipment—such as a laser coagulator, daylight process x-ray system, gamma camera, and a remote control radiology room utilizing the Telegem system—is an ongoing activity.

HUMANA and Professional Standards. Because hospitals offer such vital service, they are subject to various regulations, which may differ from community to community and from state to state. All of our hospitals are properly licensed at all appropriate levels of government. It is company policy that each hospital maintain its good standing and cooperate fully with public officials in qualitative improvement.

But on a corporate level as well as on the local Board of Trustees level, HUMANA adheres to the highest professional standards, above and beyond the mere minimum required by law.

To be certain that its facilities are a co-ordinated part of the community's total health care delivery system, HUMANA works within the comprehensive health planning process.

Every hospital that HUMANA builds is designed to meet the requirements of the Joint Commission on Accreditation of Hospitals.

Application for accreditation is made as soon as the hospital

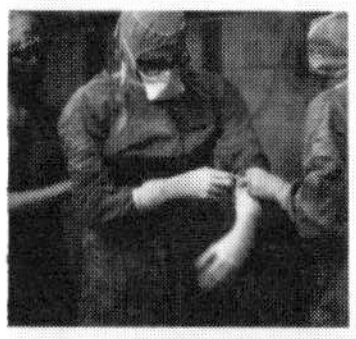

completes the waiting period stipulated by the Joint Commission and all such inspections to date have resulted in accreditation.

A number of hospitals the company acquired were not accredited. We have been bringing these hospitals up to accreditation standards through remodeling or replacement of the buildings.

Education and Training. HUMANA has established its own continuing education program for physicians on the medical staffs of its hospitals.

The company already conducts an extensive medical education program at St. Joseph Infirmary, a 500-bed facility. There are residents in internal medicine, general surgery, pediatrics, obstetrics/gynecology, radiology, and orthopedics. There are also straight, rotating, and mixed internships in this medical education program, which is affiliated with the University of Louisville.

HUMANA's concern with qualified nursing and paramedical personnel is reflected in the fact that many of the company's hospitals have affiliations with educational institutions in their communities for the training of nurses and technicians. The quality of the medical, nursing and paramedical staffs is described in the following section.

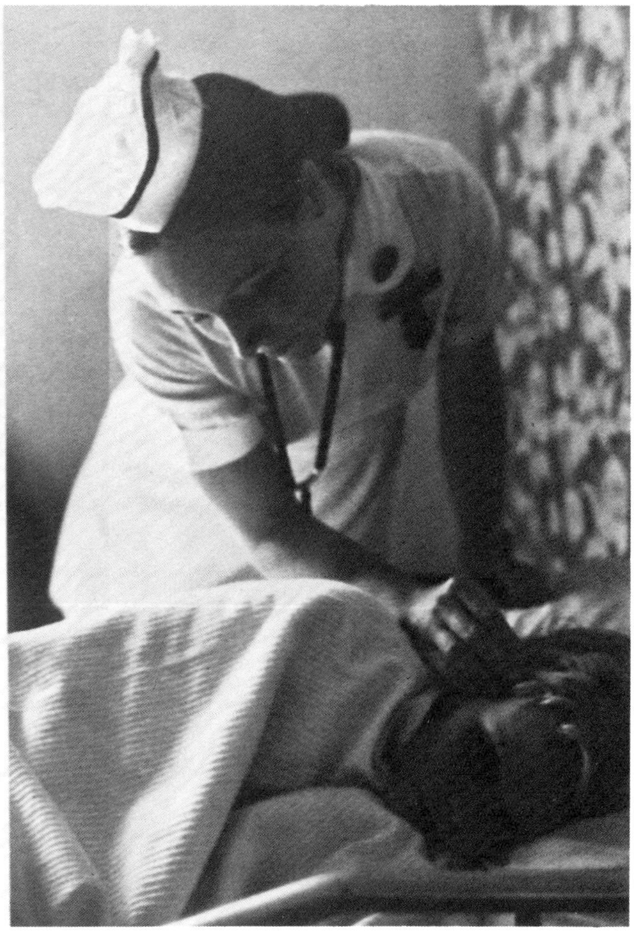

724

724
Art Director Frank Deleno
Designer Frank Deleno
Photographer Bruce Davidson
Writer Charles Webb
Agency Lippincott & Margulies
Client Humana

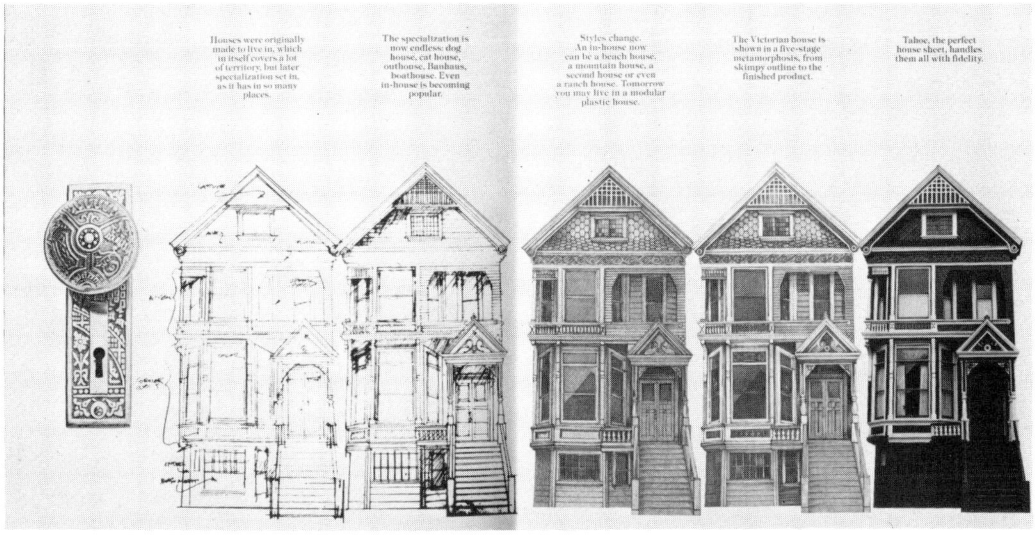
Houses were originally made to live in, which in itself covers a lot of territory, but later specialization set in, as it has in so many places.
The specialization is now endless: dog house, cat house, outhouse, Bauhaus, boathouse. Even in-house is becoming popular.
Styles change. An in-house now can be a beach house, a mountain house, a second house or even a ranch house. Tomorrow you may live in a modular plastic house.
The Victorian house is shown in a five-stage metamorphosis, from skimpy outline to the finished product.
Tahoe, the perfect house sheet, handles them all with fidelity.

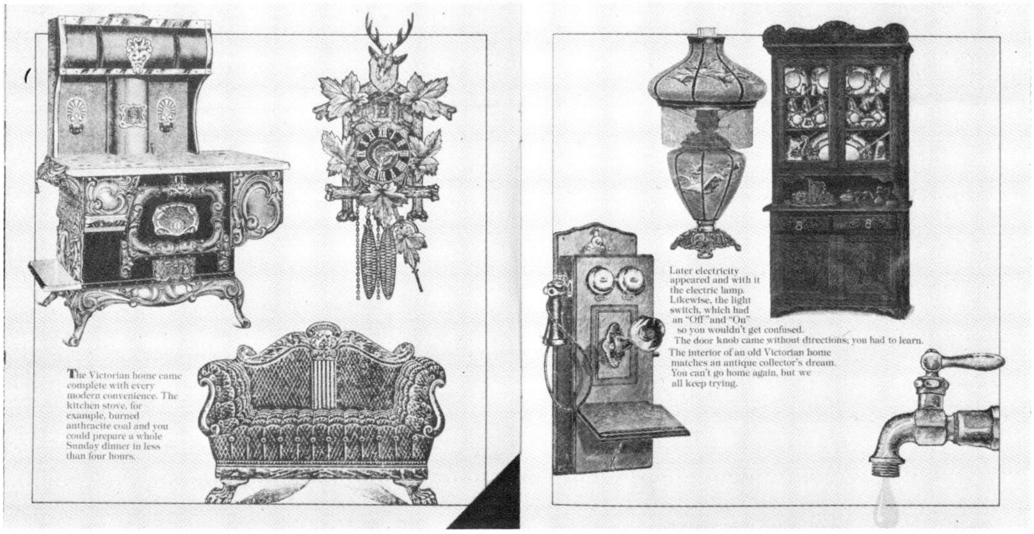
The Victorian home came complete with every modern convenience. The kitchen stove, for example, burned anthracite coal and you could prepare a whole Sunday dinner in less than four hours.
Later electricity appeared and with it the electric lamp. Likewise, the light switch, which had an "Off" and "On" so you wouldn't get confused.
The door knob came without directions; you had to learn.
The interior of an old Victorian home matches an antique collector's dream. You can't go home again, but we all keep trying.

725

725
Art Director Steve Jacobs
Designer Steve Jacobs
Artist Dennis Ziemienski
Photographers Bill Arbogast
Don Silverek
Writer Maxwell Arnold
Agency Steven Jacobs Design
Client Simpson Lee Paper Co.

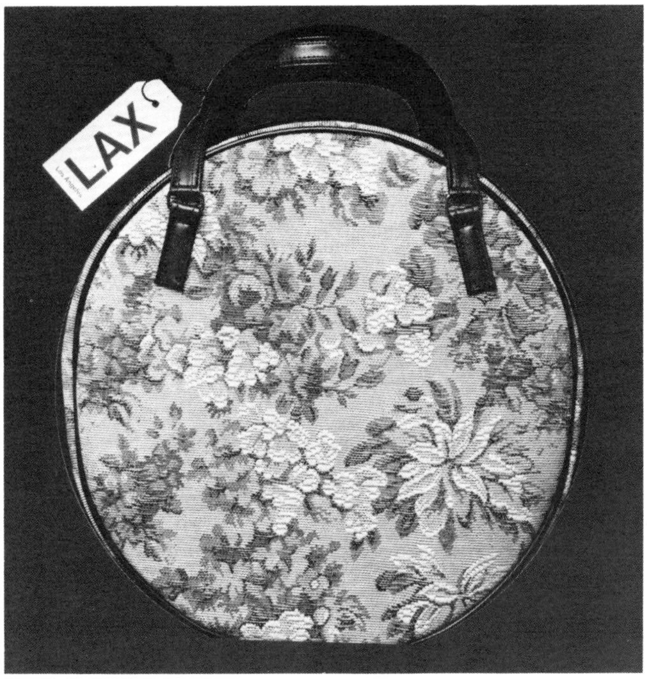
LAX

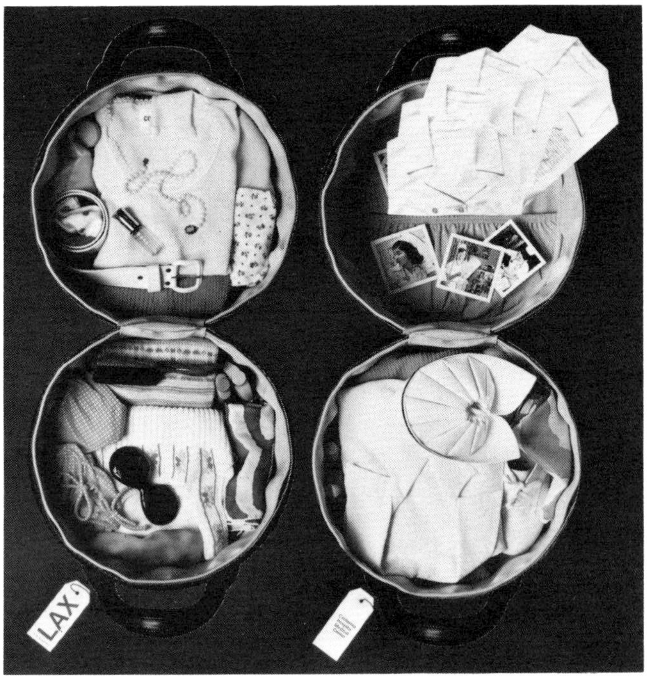
LAX

726

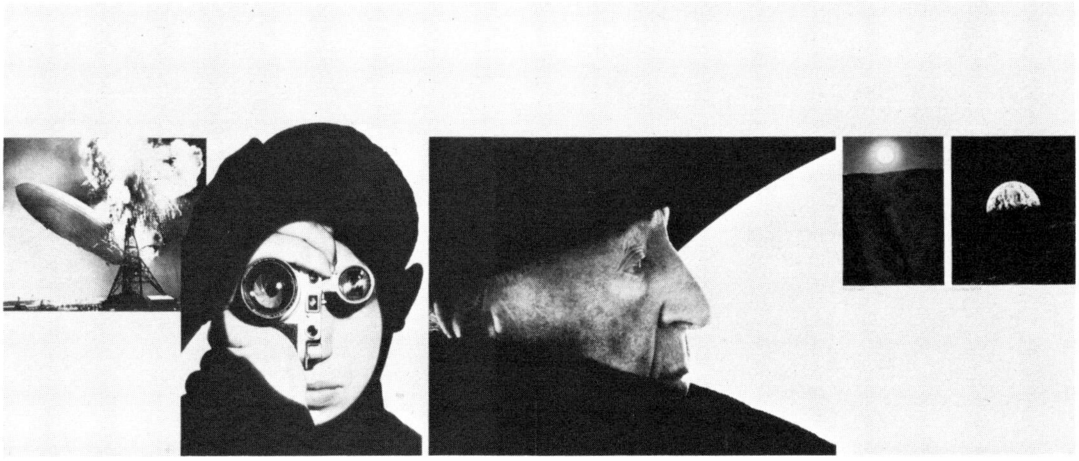

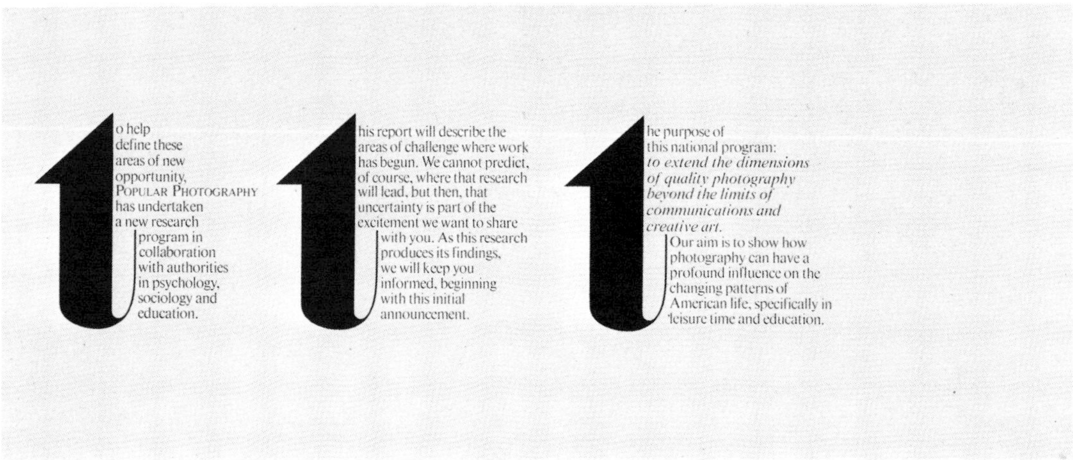
o help define these areas of new opportunity, POPULAR PHOTOGRAPHY has undertaken a new research program in collaboration with authorities in psychology, sociology and education.
his report will describe the areas of challenge where work has begun. We cannot predict, of course, where that research will lead, but then, that uncertainty is part of the excitement we want to share with you. As this research produces its findings, we will keep you informed, beginning with this initial announcement.
he purpose of this national program: *to extend the dimensions of quality photography beyond the limits of communications and creative art.*
Our aim is to show how photography can have a profound influence on the changing patterns of American life, specifically in leisure time and education.

727

726
Art Director John Anselmo
Designers John Anselmo, Thomas Bloch, Cathy Krollpfeiffer
Photographer Allen D. Walker
Writer Jean Hall
Agency John Anselmo Design Assoc.
Client Lutheran Hospital California

727
Art Director Herb Stern
Designer Herb Stern
Photographers Various
Writer Robin Jones
Agency Ziff-Davis Publishing
Client Popular Photography

728
Art Directors Dennis Mazzella, Kurt Weihs
Designers Dennis Mazzella, Kurt Weihs
Photographer Tom Weihs
Writer Wally Weis
Agency Lois Holland Callaway
Client Bricklin Vehicle Corp.

The Bricklin's gull-wing doors:
You'll think they're ahead of their time.
We think they're about time.
Of the Bricklin's many design innovations, its gull-wing doors are the most evident.
Besides adding to the appeal of the car, gull-wing doors are also quite practical.
As well as safer than ordinary doors.
Since they open almost vertically, you can get in and out of the car with ease even when you have less than 12" of clearance. Which also means you're less likely to bang your own doors or the other guy's car.
They're safer because they open up and out of the way of traffic, kids on bicycles, even pedestrians, who have been known to walk into opening car doors on occasion.
An optional electro-hydraulic system opens and closes the doors at the touch of a button. And when they close, they lock automatically, cutting down on the possibility of theft and the attendant accidents stolen vehicles are likely to get involved in.
All things considered, it's obvious that gull-wing doors weren't put on the Bricklin just for looks.

The Bricklin's safety features:
You'll think they're ahead of their time.
We think they're about time.
We think the Bricklin is the first mass-produced automobile worthy of the label, Safety Vehicle.
It has an energy absorbing bumper system capable of absorbing impacts in excess of existing government requirements.
The fuel tank is protected on five sides by steel members. Rather than simply strapped to the body and left almost fully exposed as on most cars.
A steel roll cage surrounds the passenger compartment, providing much greater, all around protection than any standard frame.
The instrument panel is fully padded and easily readable.
The weight distribution and aerodynamics of the car afford effortless and precise handling.
Radial tires are standard.
And, of course, the Bricklin comes standard with the full complement of mandatory safety equipment found on all other cars.

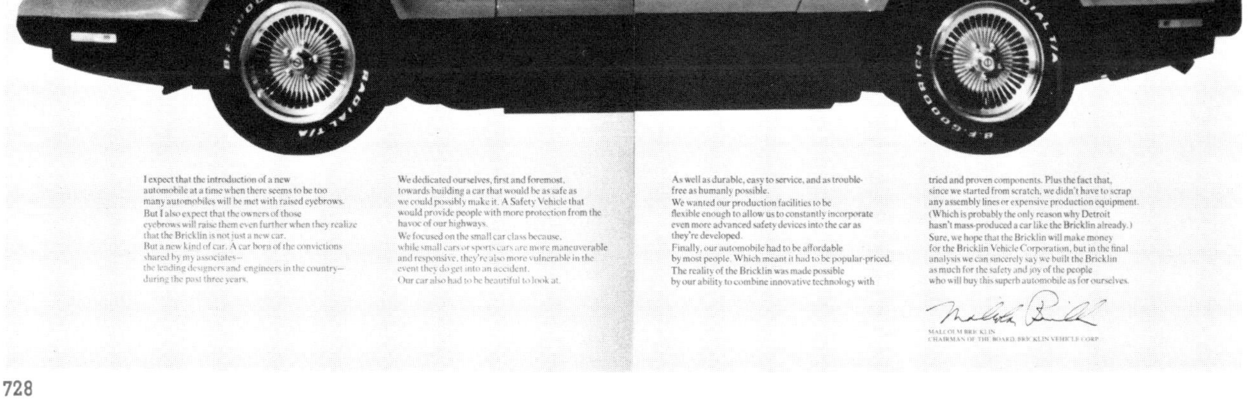
I expect that the introduction of a new automobile at a time when there seems to be too many automobiles will be met with raised eyebrows.
But I also expect that the owners of those eyebrows will raise them even further when they realize that the Bricklin is not just a new car.
But a new kind of car. A car born of the convictions shared by my associates— the leading designers and engineers in the country— during the past three years.
We dedicated ourselves, first and foremost, towards building a car that would be as safe as we could possibly make it. A Safety Vehicle that would provide people with more protection from the havoc of our highways.
We focused on the small car class because, while small cars or sports cars are more maneuverable and responsive, they're also more vulnerable in the event they do get into an accident.
Our car also had to be beautiful to look at.
As well as durable, easy to service, and as trouble-free as humanly possible.
We wanted our production facilities to be flexible enough to allow us to constantly incorporate even more advanced safety devices into the car as they're developed.
Finally, our automobile had to be affordable by most people. Which meant it had to be popular-priced.
The reality of the Bricklin was made possible by our ability to combine innovative technology with tried and proven components. Plus the fact that, since we started from scratch, we didn't have to scrap any assembly lines or expensive production equipment.
(Which is probably the only reason why Detroit hasn't mass-produced a car like the Bricklin already.)
Sure, we hope that the Bricklin will make money for the Bricklin Vehicle Corporation, but in the final analysis we can sincerely say we built the Bricklin as much for the safety and joy of the people who will buy this superb automobile as for ourselves.
MALCOLM BRICKLIN
CHAIRMAN OF THE BOARD, BRICKLIN VEHICLE CORP.

DMC
DMC

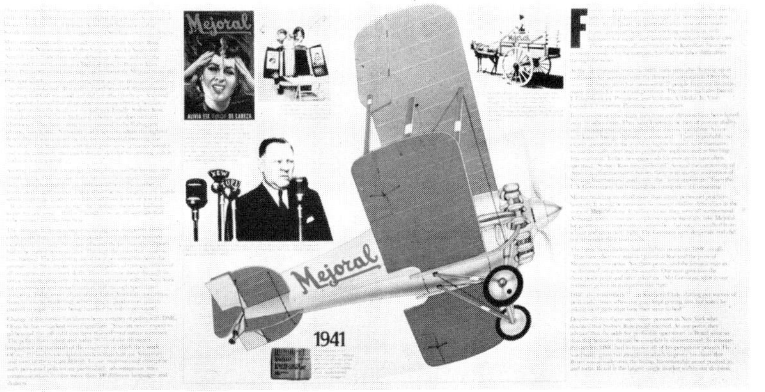
Mejoral
Mejoral
1941

729

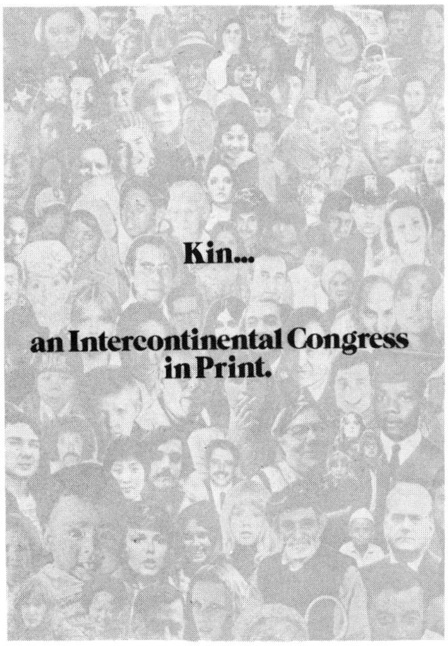
Kin...
an Intercontinental Congress in Print.

TAKE GOOD CARE OF SELF LONG JOURNEY AHEAD KEEP STRENGTH GOOD IDEAS LOVE IN HEART HATRED BURY IN DEEP EARTH SPREAD SELF LIKE GIANT TO FOUR WINDS
Lithograph
Robert Indiana
Poem
Walasse Ting

Let us impart all the blessings we possess, or ask for ourselves, to the whole family of mankind.
GEORGE WASHINGTON
The American Revolution Bicentennial celebrates the way men from many lands joined and became kin in the cause of liberty.

730

729
Art Directors Herbert R. Nubel
Kit Hinrichs
Designers Kit Hinrichs
Paul Hardy
Artists Various
Writers D. Kenneth Dill
J. Robert Chaffer
Agency Hinrichs Design Assoc.
Client Sterling International

730
Art Director Mort Rubenstein
Designer Mort Rubenstein
Artist Tony Palladino
Writer Sam Tankel
Agency International Cultural Exchange
Client International Cultural Exchange

The One Show
IN THE WINTER OF 1974 128 ART DIRECTORS, COPY WRITERS AND GRAPHIC DESIGNERS SPENT A TOTAL OF 5,200 HOURS JUDGING 10,000 PIECES OF DESIGN AND ADVERTISING. ONLY 1059 WERE CONSIDERED GOOD ENOUGH TO GET INTO THIS BOOK.
1974

731

Office Buildings

732

731
Art Director Alan Peckolick
Designer Alan Peckolick
Artists Tom Carnase
Lubalin, Smith, Carnase
Editors Jo Yanow
Jennifer Place
Charles Rosner
Agency Lubalin, Smith, Carnase
Client The Art Directors Club
of New York

732
Art Director James Cross
Designer Kenton Lotz
Photographers Various
Writer Kurt Meyer
Agency James Cross Design Office
Client Kurt Meyer and Assoc.

Villas de San Alma
Welcome to the Villas de San Alma... a unique contemporary lot-line cluster home community in Palo Alto. The Villas de San Alma was conceived by Dividend Industries, Inc. to appeal to people with extraordinary taste. The 26 homes are

Featuring
Homeowners Association
The Space.
$

733

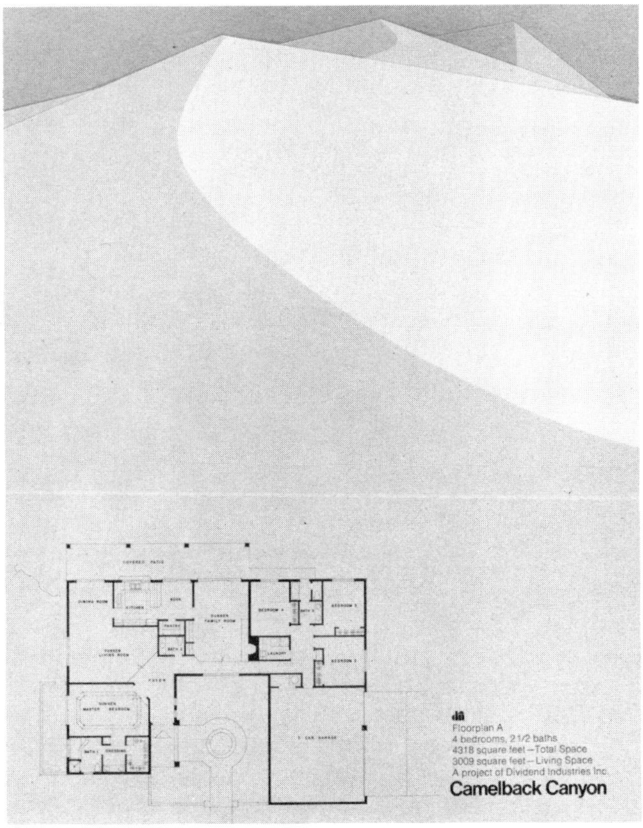
Floorplan A
4 bedrooms, 2 1/2 baths
4318 square feet—Total Space
3009 square feet—Living Space
A project of Dividend Industries Inc.
Camelback Canyon

733A

733
Art Director David Gauger
Designer David Gauger
Artists David Gauger
Paul Greenwell
Writer Larry Silva
Agency Gauger Sparks Silva
Client Dividend Industries

733a
Art Director Walter Sparks
Designer Walter Sparks
Artists Walter Sparks
Paul Greenwell
Writer Larry Silva
Agency Gauger Sparks Silva
Client Dividend Industries

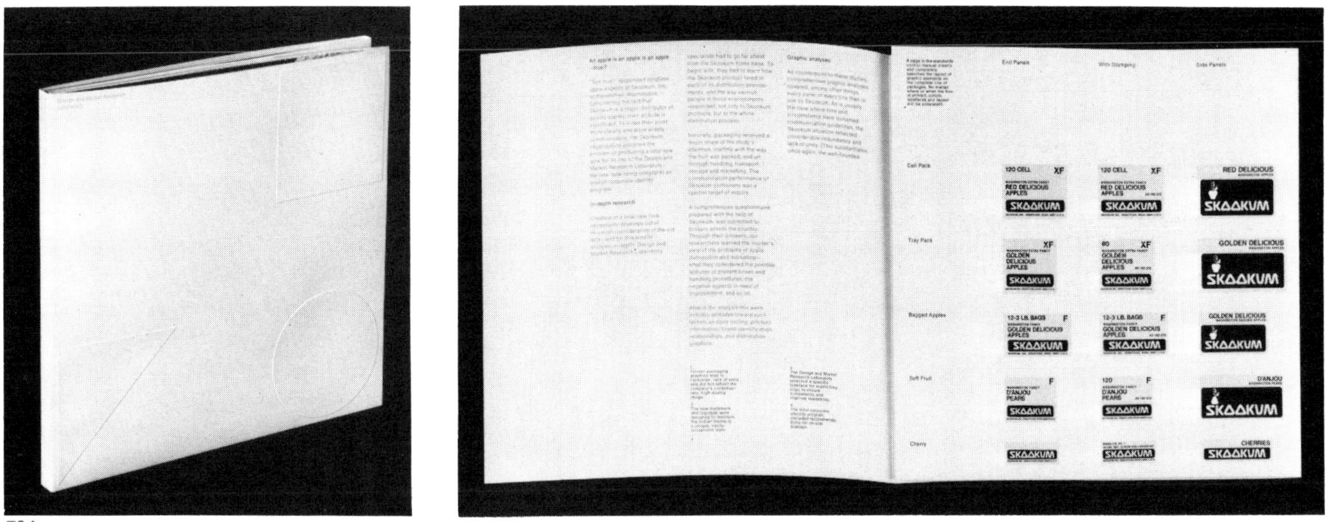

734

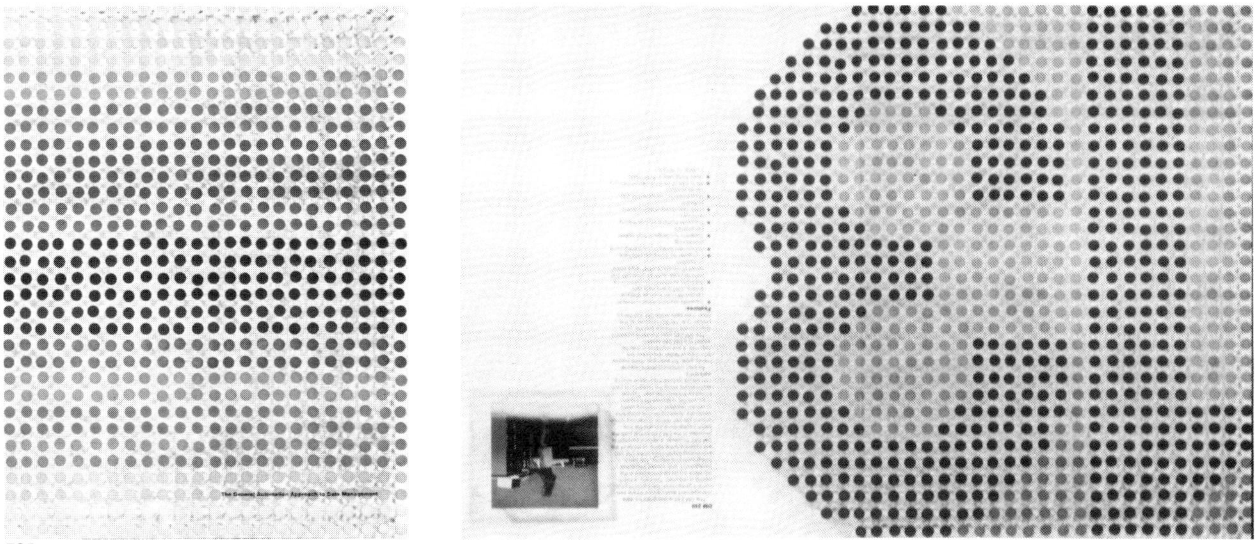

735

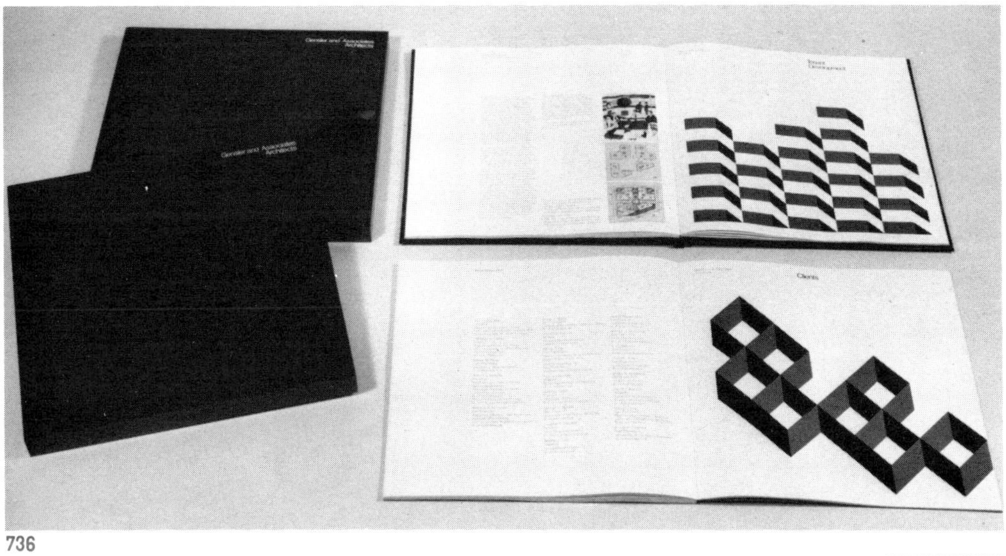

736

GOLD

734
Art Director Bill Bonnell III
Designer Bill Bonnell III
Photographers Stan Jorstad
Nick Costanza
Editor Rhodes Patterson
Agency Container Corporation
Communications Dept.
Client Container Corporation of America

735
Art Director John Anselmo
Designers John Anselmo
Thomas Bloch
Cathy Krollpfeiffer
Photographer Allen D. Walker
Writer Paul Eisner
Agency John Anselmo Design Assoc.
Client General Automation

736
Art Director Harry Murphy
Designer Harry Murphy
Artist Kate Keating
Writer Art Odel
Agency Harry Murphy & Friends
Client Gensler & Assoc.
Architects

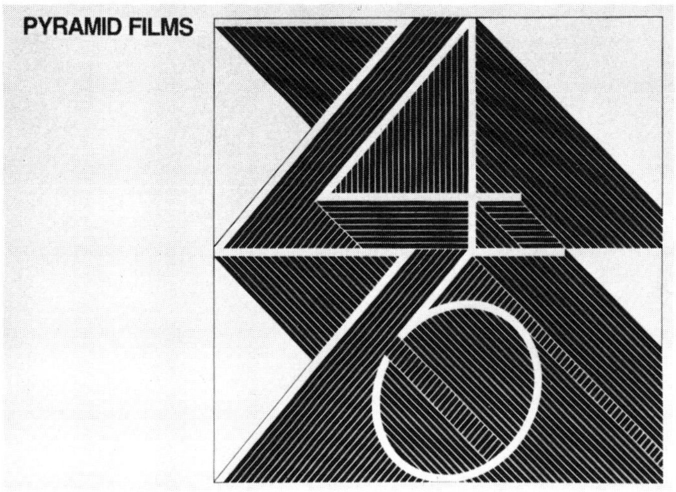
PYRAMID FILMS

PYRAMID

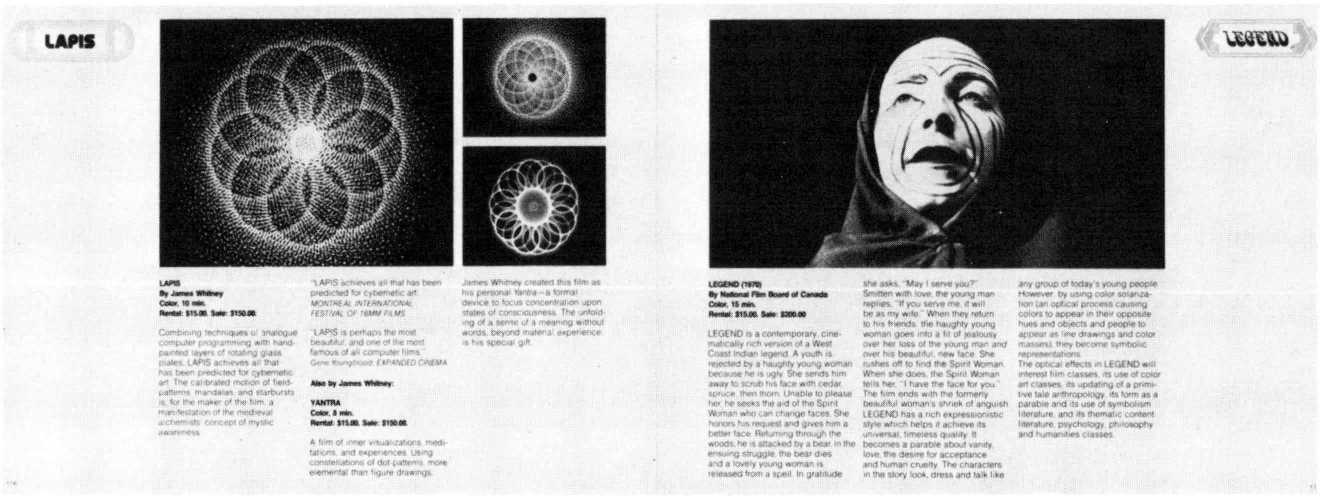
LAPIS
LEGEND
LAPIS
By James Whitney
Color, 10 min.
Rental: $15.00. Sale: $150.00.
Combining techniques of analogue computer programming with hand-painted layers of rotating glass plates, LAPIS achieves all that has been predicted for cybernetic art. The calibrated motion of field-patterns, mandalas, and starbursts is, for the maker of the film, a manifestation of the medieval alchemists' concept of mystic awareness.
"LAPIS achieves all that has been predicted for cybernetic art." MONTREAL INTERNATIONAL FESTIVAL OF 16MM FILMS
"LAPIS is perhaps the most beautiful, and one of the most famous of all computer films." Gene Youngblood, EXPANDED CINEMA
Also by James Whitney:
YANTRA
Color, 8 min.
Rental: $15.00. Sale: $150.00.
A film of inner visualizations, meditations, and experiences. Using constellations of dot-patterns, more elemental than figure drawings.
James Whitney created this film as his personal Yantra—a formal device to focus concentration upon states of consciousness. The unfolding of a sense of a meaning without words, beyond material experience, is his special gift.
LEGEND (1970)
By National Film Board of Canada
Color, 15 min.
Rental: $15.00. Sale: $200.00
LEGEND is a contemporary, cinematically rich version of a West Coast Indian legend. A youth is rejected by a haughty young woman because he is ugly. She sends him away to scrub his face with cedar, spruce, then thorn. Unable to please her, he seeks the aid of the Spirit Woman who can change faces. She honors his request and gives him a better face. Returning through the woods, he is attacked by a bear. In the ensuing struggle, the bear dies and a lovely young woman is released from a spell. In gratitude she asks, "May I serve you?" Smitten with love, the young man replies, "If you serve me, it will be as my wife." When they return to his friends, the haughty young woman goes into a fit of jealousy over her loss of the young man and over his beautiful, new face. She rushes off to find the Spirit Woman. When she does, the Spirit Woman tells her, "I have the face for you." The film ends with the formerly beautiful woman's shriek of anguish. LEGEND has a rich expressionistic style which helps it achieve its universal, timeless quality. It becomes a parable about vanity, love, the desire for acceptance and human cruelty. The characters in the story look, dress and talk like any group of today's young people. However, by using color solarization (an optical process causing colors to appear in their opposite hues and objects and people to appear as line drawings and color masses), they become symbolic representations.
The optical effects in LEGEND will interest film classes, its use of color art classes, its updating of a primitive tale anthropology, its form as a parable and its use of symbolism literature, and its thematic content literature, psychology, philosophy and humanities classes.

737

737
Art Directors Art Goodman
Nancy Von Lauderback
Designers Mamoru Shimokochi
Michael Mills
Saul Bass & Assoc.
Artists Mamoru Shimokochi
Saul Bass & Assoc.
Agency Saul Bass & Assoc.
Client Pyramid Films

ÆE

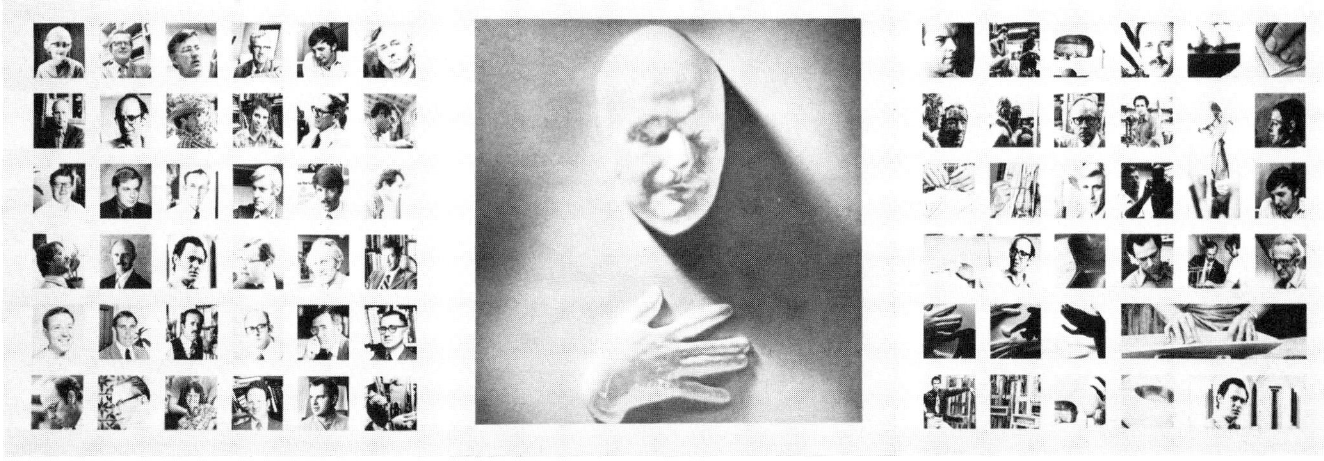

738

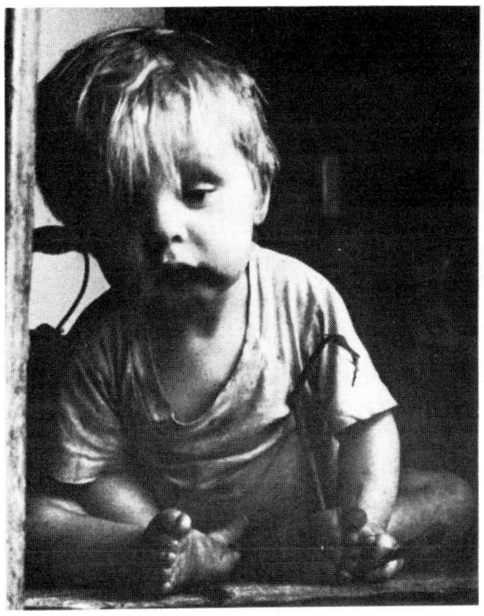

Wherever there is a human problem,
there will be a design engineer trying to find a solution.

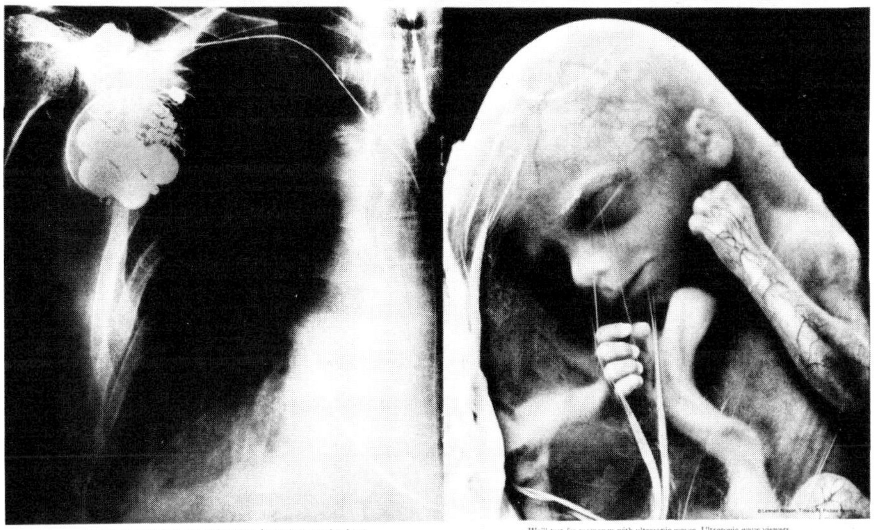

You may pace your heart with nuclear power. Longer-lasting nuclear heart pacemaker batteries are almost here. Design engineers will make them happen.
We'll test for pregnancy with ultrasonic waves. Ultrasonic wave viewers will be able to determine a pregnancy in the first month. With no danger from radiation. Design engineers will make them happen.

739

738
Art Director McRay Magleby
Designers Michael Kawasaki
Ron Eddington
Artist Michael Kawasaki
Photographers Rick Nye
George Brown
Writer Peter L. Myer
Agency Graphic Communications Dept.
Brigham Young University
Client Brigham Young University

739
Art Director Tom Gilday
Designer Tom Gilday
Photographer Jan Czyrba
Writer Mike Marino
Agency Griswold-Eshleman
Client Machine Design Magazine

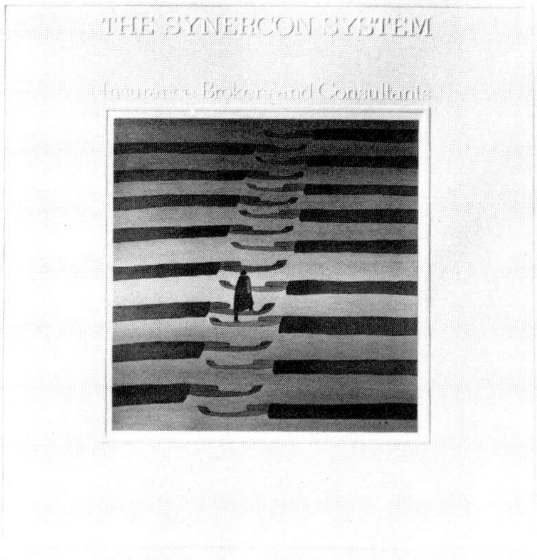
THE SYNERCON SYSTEM
Insurance Brokers and Consultants

Property rating was arbitrary and inadequate. There had to be something better.

The old way was based on factors that had little to do with the incidence or the extent of loss.

Like roof vents.

For years roof vents had been considered necessary for highly protected properties. Yet, recent studies indicate that, in most cases, the use of roof vents may tend to increase the severity of loss.

What was needed was a method of analyzing the causes and the costs of loss based on empirical data, not hypothesis.

Our research found a way. A way of projecting the frequency and severity of loss over a given period of time. And of measuring the probability that the loss will cost more, or less, than a fixed amount. And that makes it manageable.

Because of our work, risk management is no longer the guessing game it once was.

You don't trade dollar for dollar with an insurance company and come out ahead.

You look for ways to reduce risk. To maintain comprehensive coverage at a favorable rate.

We call it loss prevention engineering. It means fewer losses. Less extensive losses.

We've made it a science. Our engineers are seasoned professionals. Making inspections and recommendations that will lower claim frequency. Helping to contain the size of loss. Aiding in OSHA compliance. Appraising and establishing replacement costs. Advising on the location and design of new construction. And doing it all with a recognized expertise.

From hard hats to hard toe boots, from amusement parks to operating rooms, loss prevention engineering is working for our clients.

Claims should be settled quickly and fairly. From a position of strength.

When a claim occurs, we process it all the way. From insured to insurer and back. We advise clients, and our own underwriters, on the extent and limits of coverage. We adjust marine averages, particular and general. And we help direct settlement strategy.

Under the cash flow concept of risk financing, claims are a business expense and should be controlled as such. At Synercon, we monitor claim trends and make the necessary adjustments in loss prevention. We help each of our client's operating units

Our research has led risk management out of the chasm of conjecture.

run his business. But we've bonded enough successful contractors — many in *Engineering News Record's* top 400 — to have some pretty good ideas on what works and what doesn't. And we think sharing what we know makes better business.

Better business begins at home.

Over 200 firms a year go bankrupt because of employee dishonesty. And yet many businesses, well-insured in other areas, lack adequate crime protection. With us, fidelity coverage, plus the experience to design the most effective protection for varying risks, is all part of the plan.

With group marketing, more is less.

An association of homogeneous groups with fixed insurance expenses can pool premiums and claims, and pass the resulting profit back to the group members. As reduced premiums, dividends, or both. And the larger the group, the lower the cost.

We bring together homogeneous groups of individuals and businesses from across the country: trade associations, professional associations, national retail operations, credit unions. And we design and develop comprehensive coverage for each risk grouping. It might be specific liability coverage for associations of automobile dealers. Or a complete package for national food franchises. Whatever the need, we can meet it.

Our experience in writing homogeneous risks, and our network of affiliates, marketing the group-coverage concept, are bringing together more and more groups. So that their insurance can cost less.

Group coverage reduces cost. So we started grouping the groups.

740

740
Art Director Bill Barnes
Designer Dave Pfister
Artist Folon
Writer Cliff Probst
Agency Harmon & Crook Advertising
Client Synercon

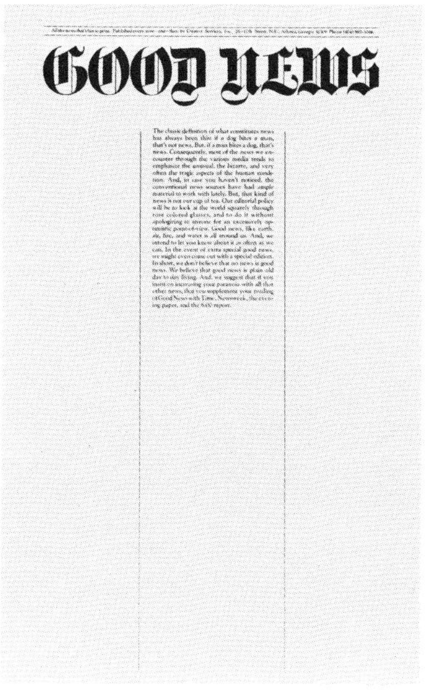
GOOD NEWS

AT LAST, GOOD NEWS FOR YOUR A.M. EAR
Dear Ann,
Dear Agony in Detroit,

WHAT DO YOU KNOW?
Better View for You!
• A Chicago bottling company has exploded the myth that non-returnable bottles are bad for business in the beverage industry.
ZODIAC NEWS SERVICE
You Call Em!
No Crash for Louis' Lunch
Creative Services
Good News for You!
• MORE BAD NEWS FOR RICHARD NIXON. The Orange County, California, tax collector has increased the valuation of Nixon's oceanfront estate at San Clemente.
a Sure Cure!
Four British researchers, writing in the Medical Journal THE LANCET, report that Vitamin C helps remove excess alcohol from the bloodstream.
ZODIAC NEWS SERVICE
Whats Up?
• A New York artist named Neke Carson paints portraits with his ass.
Village Voice (W. Taurins)
the interview
Seasonal Sport Seen Spiraling
THE UNICORN HUNTING SEASON IS OVER...
Catch 22
• A 20-year-old purse snatcher got more than he bargained for at a San Jose, California, shopping center.
Good Mews
Rita the Cat
Knows where it's at,
Creative Services
the carolina craftsmen's christmas classic
The Town Liar
New Energy Discovery Claimed by Baltimore Scientists!
The Dixie Star
Creative Services
Mayor uses Utility Co. to Lower Property Tax!
• Henry Orleau of Chineca, Ohio was re-elected to an unprecedented 5th term as mayor in a landslide victory.
Pennsylvania Penn
NO RELIEF IN SIGHT!
• Sources say Martha Mitchell claims that after three years she hasn't been able to find a plumber that could tell her what is wrong with her John.
TRUE FACT
PEELING FOR TOP BANANA!
Ah-Mazing
• According to an impeccable source, a spokesman for the National Restaurant Association announced Tuesday, at their 1974 convention, that the Association is well aware that a joint is no longer a place to get something to eat.
Going Down Laughing
ZODIAC NEWS SERVICE
Bag Man (bags) Federal Funds
ZODIAC NEWS SERVICE
Lively News
• Due to the newsprint shortage, no obituary section appears in this paper.

740A

740A
Art Director Thomas Wood
Designer Thomas Wood
Artists Various
Writers Dick Grant
Robert Solomon
Ray Garrett
Steve Parks
Agency Creative Services, Inc.
Client Creative Services, Inc.

PEOPLE
&JOBS
A Forecast of Population, Households, Labor Force and Jobs in the New York-New Jersey-Connecticut Metropolitan Region: 1975-1990
Published by
The Port Authority
of New York and New Jersey

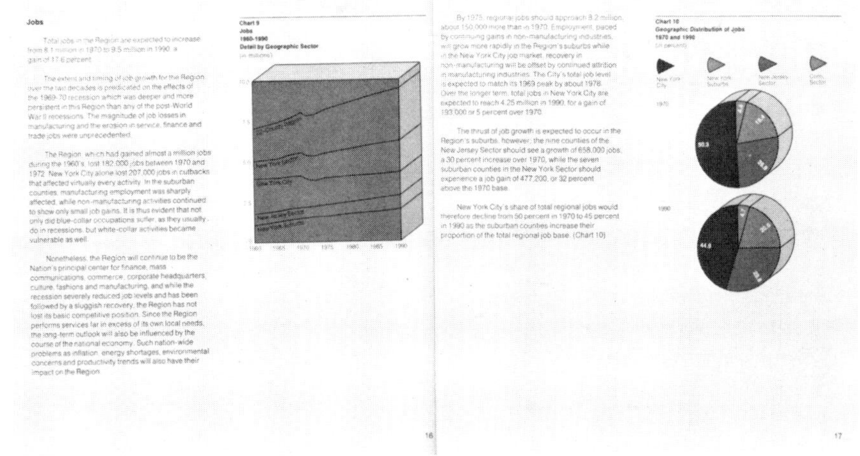
Jobs

Total jobs in the Region are expected to increase from 8.1 million in 1970 to 9.5 million in 1990, a gain of 17.6 percent.

The extent and timing of job growth for the Region over the two decades is predicated on the effects of the 1969-70 recession which was deeper and more persistent in this Region than any of the post-World War II recessions. The magnitude of job losses in manufacturing and the erosion in service, finance and trade jobs were unprecedented.

The Region, which had gained almost a million jobs during the 1960's, lost 182,000 jobs between 1970 and 1972. New York City alone lost 207,000 jobs in cutbacks that affected virtually every activity. In the suburban counties, manufacturing employment was sharply affected, while non-manufacturing activities continued to show only small job gains. It is thus evident that not only did blue-collar occupations suffer, as they usually do in recessions, but white-collar activities became vulnerable as well.

Nonetheless, the Region will continue to be the Nation's principal center for finance, mass communications, commerce, corporate headquarters, culture, fashions and manufacturing, and while the recession severely reduced job levels and has been followed by a sluggish recovery, the Region has not lost its basic competitive position. Since the Region performs services far in excess of its own local needs, the long-term outlook will also be influenced by the course of the national economy. Such nation-wide problems as inflation, energy shortages, environmental concerns and productivity trends will also have their impact on the Region.

Chart 9
Jobs
1960-1990
Detail by Geographic Sector

16

By 1975, regional jobs should approach 8.2 million, about 150,000 more than in 1970. Employment, paced by continuing gains in non-manufacturing industries, will grow more rapidly in the Region's suburbs while in the New York City job market, recovery in non-manufacturing will be offset by continued attrition in manufacturing industries. The City's total job level is expected to match its 1969 peak by about 1978. Over the longer term, total jobs in New York City are expected to reach 4.25 million in 1990, for a gain of 193,000 or 5 percent over 1970.

The thrust of job growth is expected to occur in the Region's suburbs, however; the nine counties of the New Jersey Sector should see a growth of 658,000 jobs, a 30 percent increase over 1970, while the seven suburban counties in the New York Sector should experience a job gain of 477,200, or 32 percent above the 1970 base.

New York City's share of total regional jobs would therefore decline from 50 percent in 1970 to 45 percent in 1990 as the suburban counties increase their proportion of the total regional job base. (Chart 10)

Chart 10
Geographic Distribution of Jobs
1970 and 1990

17

741

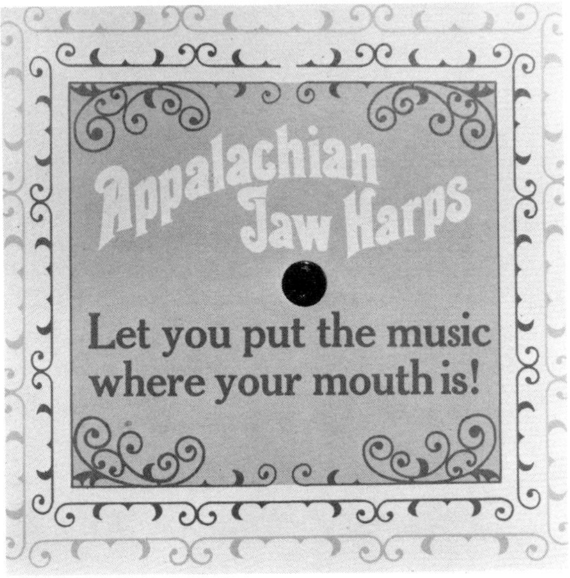
Appalachian
Jaw Harps
Let you put the music
where your mouth is!

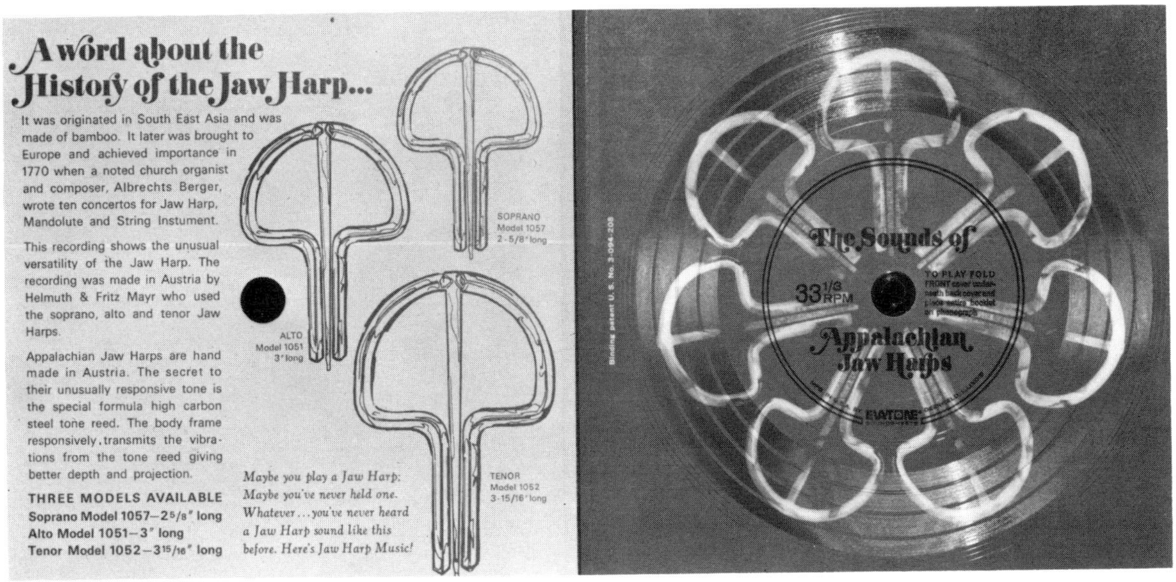
A word about the
History of the Jaw Harp...
It was originated in South East Asia and was made of bamboo. It later was brought to Europe and achieved importance in 1770 when a noted church organist and composer, Albrechts Berger, wrote ten concertos for Jaw Harp, Mandolute and String Instument.
This recording shows the unusual versatility of the Jaw Harp. The recording was made in Austria by Helmuth & Fritz Mayr who used the soprano, alto and tenor Jaw Harps.
Appalachian Jaw Harps are hand made in Austria. The secret to their unusually responsive tone is the special formula high carbon steel tone reed. The body frame responsively, transmits the vibrations from the tone reed giving better depth and projection.
THREE MODELS AVAILABLE
Soprano Model 1057—2 5/8" long
Alto Model 1051—3" long
Tenor Model 1052—3 15/16" long
SOPRANO
Model 1057
2-5/8" long
ALTO
Model 1051
3" long
TENOR
Model 1052
3-15/16" long
Maybe you play a Jaw Harp;
Maybe you've never held one.
Whatever... you've never heard
a Jaw Harp sound like this
before. Here's Jaw Harp Music!
The Sounds of
33 1/3 RPM
Appalachian
Jaw Harps

742

741
Designer Jim McWilliams
Writers Raymond Spungin
Rosemary Scanlon
Agency Port Authority
of New York and
New Jersey
Client Port Authority
of New York and
New Jersey

742
Art Director Ted Hyman
Designer James Gormley
Artist James Gormley
Photographer James Gormley
Writer Ted Hyman
Agency Brendel Typographic
Service
Client St. Louis Music
Supply Co.

Columbia
Pictures
Television
Features
for the '70's
VOL.
ONE

743

Good Morning America

744

If the building of the "Harvey Gamage" is worth the paper it's printed on...

745

743
Art Directors Marvin Korman
Cristos Gianakos
Stephen Ancona
Designer Cristos Gianakos
Artist John Sagan
Writers Marvin Korman
Paul Shrage
Agency Ancona/Gianakos Inc.
Client Columbia Pictures

744
Art Director Bo Costello
Artist Fred Otnes
Writer Bill Guisewite
Agency Willis/Case/Harwood
Client Mead Corp.

745
Art Directors Jim Witham
Ralph Moxcey
Artist Charles Hoar
Photographer Bill Bruin
Writer Nelson Lofstedt
Agency Humphrey Browning
MacDougall
Client S.D. Warren Co.

EDUCATED MAN
MAN
MAMMAL
BIRD
REPTILE
AMPHIBIAN
FISH
INVERTEBRATE
JELLY FISH
New School Bulletin / Fall 1974
Volume 32, Number 1, August 5, 1974

746

DALLAS
LITHO
CLUB

746A

Adam's Rib by Wamsutta

747

746
Art Director Howard Levine
Designer Edward Sorel
Artist Edward Sorel
Agency Edward Sorel Assoc.
Client The New School for Social Research

746A
Art Director Glenn Baxter
Designer Glenn Baxter
Photographer Kenn Lawrence
Agency Baxter/Seivert Assoc.
Client Dallas Litho Club

747
Art Director Michael Allen Ende
Designer Michael Allen Ende
Artists Neal Barr
David Vine
Photographers Neal Barr
David Vine
Writer Sharon Demarest
Agency Irving Miller, Inc.
Client Wamsutta Mills

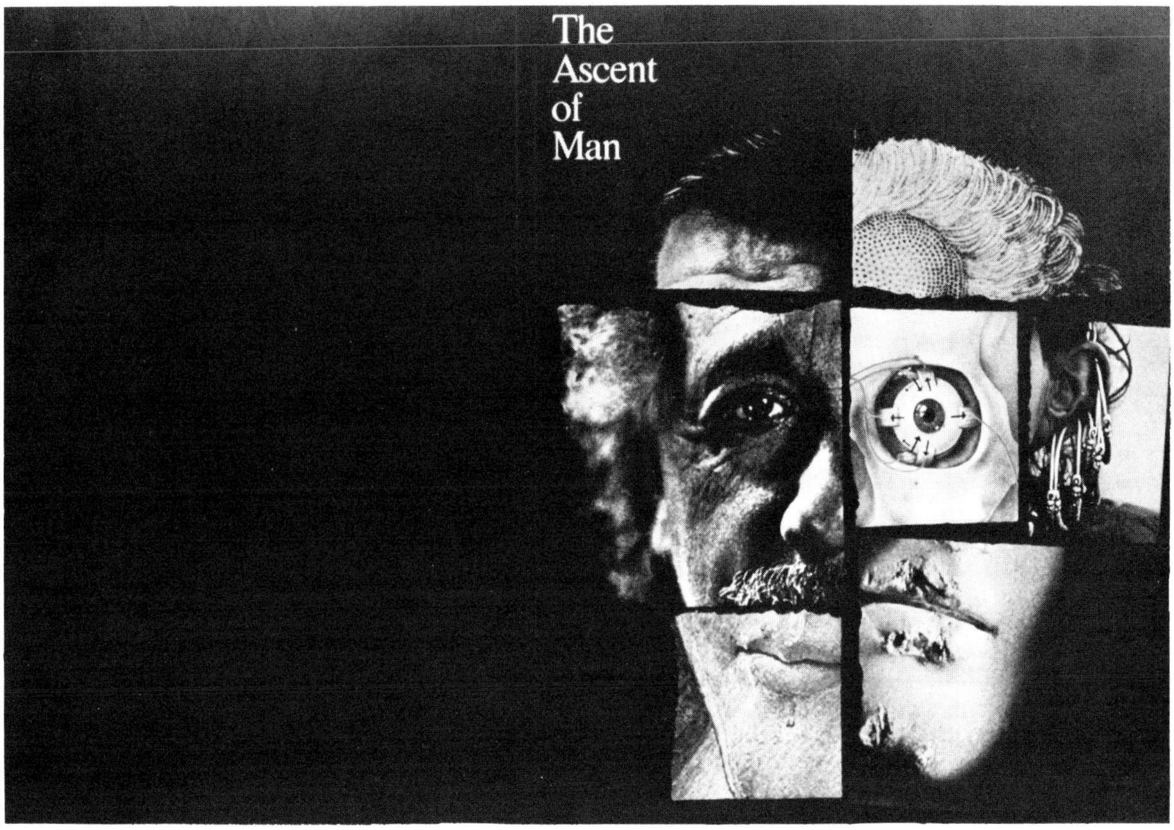
The
Ascent
of
Man

748

T H E
B A C

749

748
Art Director Ivan Chermayeff
Designer Ivan Chermayeff
Artist Ivan Chermayeff
Agency Chermayeff & Geismar Assoc.
Client Mobil Oil Corp.
for P.B.A.

749
Art Directors Woody Pirtle
Stan Richards
Designer Woody Pirtle
Artists Woody Pirtle
Chris Hill
Photographers Greg Booth
Francisco & Booth
Writer Cap Pannell
Agency The Richards Group
Client Braniff International

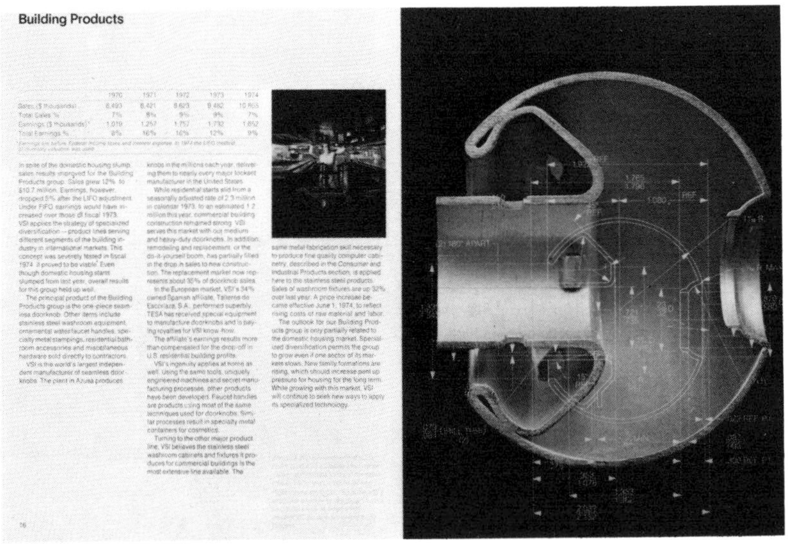
Building Products

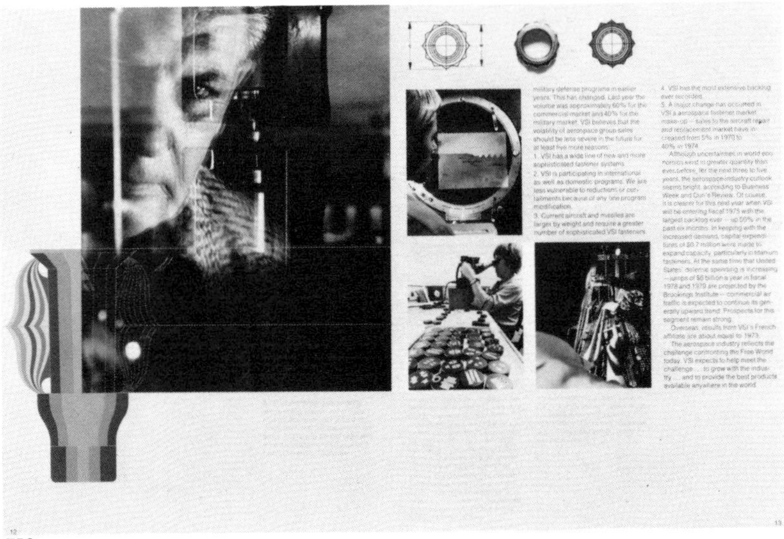

750

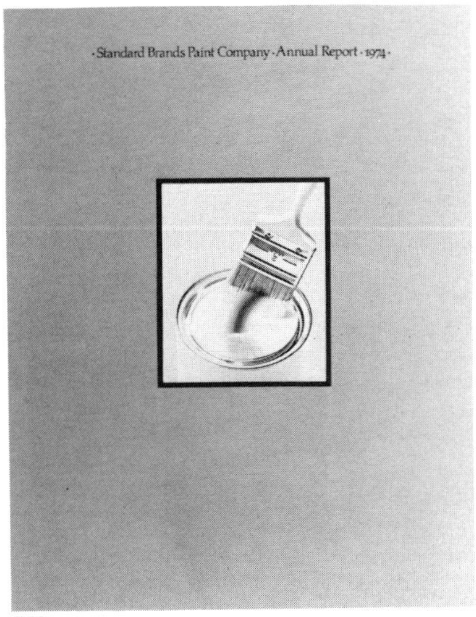
·Standard Brands Paint Company·Annual Report·1974·

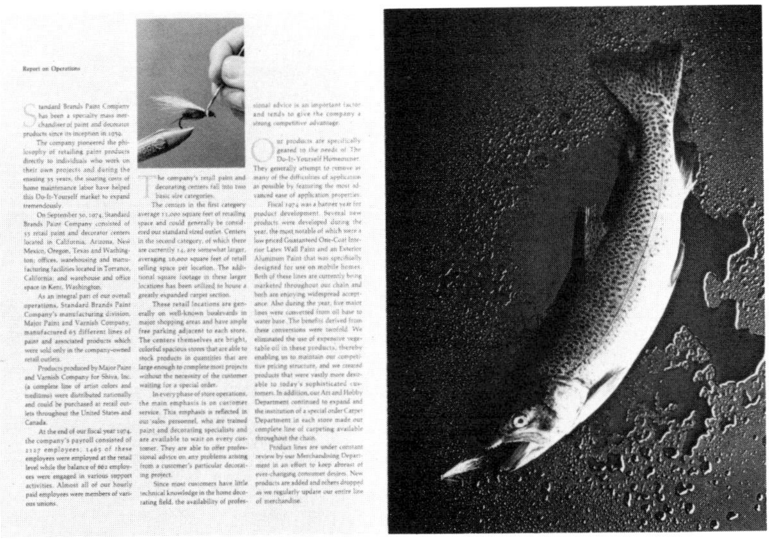
Report on Operations

751

750
Art Director Robert Miles Runyan
Designer Ron Jefferies
Artist Ron Jefferies
Photographer Ken Whitmore
Writer Ted Schmitt
Agency Robert Miles Runyan & Assoc.
Client VSI Corp.

751
Art Director Don Weller
Designers Don Weller
Chikako Matsubayashi
Artist Richard Huebner
Photographer Roger Marshutz
Writer Sheldon Weinstein
Agency The Weller Institute
Client Standard Brands Paint Co.

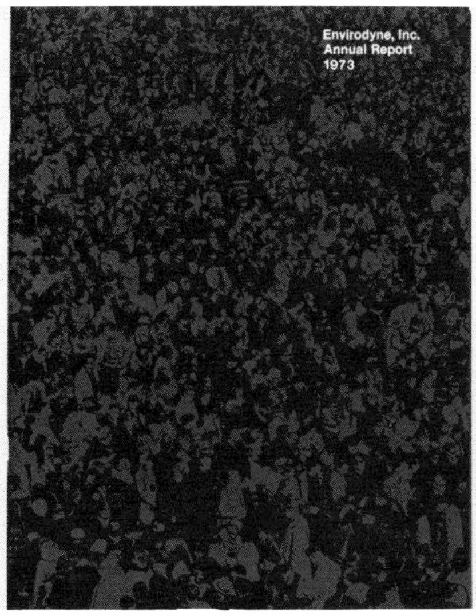
Envirodyne, Inc.
Annual Report
1973

Energy Systems and
Services Group

752

The telltale hair by Redken

752A

752
Art Director Tartak/Libera
Designer Tartak/Libera
Artist Joan D. Libera
Photographers Bob Waterman
Jerry Socher
Donald H. Tartak
Writers Dr. Ronald K. Linde
Dr. Gerald A. Marxman
Maxine Linde
Agency Tartak/Libera Design
Client Envirodyne, Inc.

752A
Art Directors James Van Noy
Armand Gauthier
Designer James Van Noy
Artists David Candioty
Bill Millikan
Photographers Don R. Tyson
C. George Lefeber
Writer Ronald M. DiSalvo
Agency Van Noy & Co.
Client Redken Laboratories

10

12 Corporate banking has been a primary strength of United California Bank since its inception in California. Time has blurred even faint memory of those pioneering days; horse-drawn carriages and leather-bound ledgers have long since been replaced by jumbo jets and electronic data processing.

Yet for all the dramatic transformations that continue to occur in the worlds of business and banking, the nature of the corporate banking partnership itself remains constant. Today, as yesterday, UCB corporate banking helps business and industry grow.

Over the years, the financial requirements of corporations have become increasingly complex and markedly different from the requirements of other bank customer groups. Unlike individuals and small retail establishments, for example, corporations must deal with challenges unique not only to their particular industries, but deriving also from the broader arena in which all businesses compete.

That is why UCB has established a Corporate Banking Group, concentrating solely on the needs of business and dedicated to meeting those needs in the most effective manner. UCB provides varied and sophisticated services for companies of all sizes and descriptions, keeping pace with change even as our customers diversify and adapt to the sometimes harsh realities of today's marketplace.

business is designed around one individual: the Corporate Banker. Above all, corporate bankers are skilled and experienced banking officers, with all of UCB's resources at their disposal. Their charter is the orchestration of those resources to best meet the needs of corporate customers. Their sole responsibility is to serve the business community.

The UCB Corporate Banker is a professional trained to meet the exacting requirements of today's business market. Free from administrative routine, they are decision-makers, not middlemen, with the ability to eliminate red tape and avoid delays. The UCB Corporate Banker devotes full and undivided attention to the customer and, as a result, is able to contribute fresh insights, advance new perspectives, and then follow through with recommendations and actions.

This means that the corporate customer need never take a back seat to other activities requiring the Corporate Banker's attention, nor suffer the inconvenience and frustration of dealing with committees. In short, the customers have at their disposal the full-time service of a single decision-maker, one who has responsibility for the entire corporate banking relationship. 13

Manufacturing and Distribution

UCB's concept of service to business is designed around the UCB Corporate Banker, whose most valuable asset is understanding and thorough knowledge of his customer. UCB has found that the acquisition and effective use of such knowledge is best served by assigning corporate bankers to specific businesses. Banking officers specializing in the operations of California-based manufacturers and distributors, for example, are assigned to UCB's State Division. The many corporate banking services UCB offers to manufacturers and distributors include providing alternative methods for acquiring new capital equipment, assisting in accomplishing diversification programs, and supplying loans to support accounts receivable, finance inventories, modernize facilities, develop new products and enter new and expanding markets.

A long time UCB customer, Western Digital Corporation of Newport Beach, California, is engaged in designing, developing and manufacturing micro-electronic circuits used in the electronics industry. Shown in large photo are Western Digital Corporation president Al Phillips, and UCB vice president Rod Dunagan.

Financial Review
United California Bank Building
Personal Banking

753

Lomas & Nettleton Mortgage Investors, 1974 Annual Report

Lomas & Nettleton Mortgage Investors, 1974 Annual Report

754

753
Art Director James Cross
Designer Emmett Morava
Photographer Marvin Silver
Writer Lloyd B. Dennis
Agency James Cross Design Office
Client United California Bank

754
Art Director Jack Summerford
Designer Jack Summerford
Photographers Greg Booth
Bettman Archives
UPI
Amon Carter Museum
Writer John Stone
Agencies Glenn, Bozell, &
Jacobs Public Relations
The Richards Group
Client Lomas & Nettleton
Mortgage Investors

12 Among the projects completed in 1973 was a marine loading facility for Petromer Trend in Irian Jaya, Indonesia. The marine terminal, pipelines, and process facility were engineered and built by Fluor Ocean Services in six months. Another Fluor company, South Pacific Oil, is a member of the Petromer Trend group.

The company also performed the preliminary design of the offshore tanker terminal for the Louisiana Offshore Oil Production installation, which will be one of the largest such projects in the world. Fluor Ocean Services also completed the marine terminal design and assisted in the construction planning for the Trans-Alaska crude oil pipeline program's Valdez terminal.

Representative of projects currently under way is the managing contractor assignment for a natural-gas liquids plant in the Java Sea. This will be the world's first such facility to be located offshore. In association with Fluor Engineers and Constructors' Houston Division, the company is responsible for all marine facilities, including four platform-mounted flow stations, 40 miles of submarine pipelines, a central process platform, and a marine loading terminal. Completion is set for 1975.

In May of 1973, this subsidiary sold much of its offshore construction equipment located in the Gulf of Mexico for approximately $15.6 million. Sale of this equipment has enabled Fluor Ocean Services to concentrate its efforts in more specialized engineering and construction projects within the offshore industry.

The increasingly rapid development of offshore areas and the growing importance of facilities such as marine terminals and offshore platforms indicate numerous opportunities for Fluor Ocean Services' capabilities worldwide.

DRILLING SERVICES

	1973	1972
Earnings Before Taxes	$ 8,396,000	$ 7,275,000
Revenues	32,227,000	27,145,000
Backlog	34,520,000	12,000,000

The highest utilization rate of drilling equipment since Fluor Drilling Services was formed highlighted that subsidiary's fiscal year. In 1973, utilization of offshore operating units reached 89.9 percent – one of the highest rates in the industry. This resulted from long-term contracts for the company's floating barges and renewed government lease sales, which kept the subsidiary's shallow-water equipment in the Gulf of Mexico busy.

Fluor Drilling Services' five barges are all at work in waters outside the United States. In the Far East, the WODECO IV is drilling off Taiwan, the WODECO VI offshore Kalimantan (Borneo), and the WODECO VII in the South China Sea. The WODECO III is on long-term assignment in the Persian Gulf, and the WODECO V is carrying out exploratory drilling for a group – in which Fluor is a participant – in the Aegean Sea off Greece.

In the Gulf of Mexico, the company has four rigs – Mr. Arthur, Mr. Gus, Mr. Mel, and Mr. Sam. Mr. Mel, the new jack-up rig commissioned at the beginning of the fiscal year, enjoyed 100-percent utilization throughout the year. It is capable of drilling at 350-foot water depths.

The company made commitments for two additional offshore drilling rigs during fiscal 1973. The first is the conversion of a former oil tanker into a self-propelled drilling vessel. It will be able to moor in water depths to 750 feet and drill to 25,000 feet. The new drillship, to be called the WODECO VIII, will provide quarters for 109 crewmen. It is scheduled for completion in mid-1974 at a cost of approximately $20 million.

Ray Pasternak is Fluor Utah's Project Director on Southern Peru Copper Corporation's new mining and processing complex being built in Cuajone, Peru. Major activity in this project is taking place at an elevation of more than 11,000 feet in the Andes Mountains, but all components of the project are spread over a 750-square-mile area from Ilo on Peru's coast to Lake Suches, which is 16,000 feet high. With Pasternak is Engineer Cesar Serpa.

755

Lomas & Nettleton Financial Corporation 1974 Annual Report to Stockholders
and Supplemental Report to Institutional Mortgage Investors

756

755
Art Director James Cross
Designer James Cross
Photographer Marvin Silver
Writers Paul Etter
Walter Russler
Agency James Cross Design Office
Client Fluor Corp.

756
Art Directors Stan Richards
Ron Sullivan
Designer Ron Sullivan
Artist Ron Sullivan
Photographers Greg Booth
Francisco & Booth
Writer John Stone
Agencies Glenn, Bozell, &
Jacobs Public Relations
The Richards Group
Client Lomas & Nettleton
Financial Corp.

Xerox Corporation 1973 Annual Report
XEROX

"Color copying is the kind of innovation we expect of Xerox managers," said Dr. Murray, investment consultant to institutions holding Xerox stock, "but no one really knows how much of a market awaits the Xerox 6500. Educational effort will be required to establish the dimension that color can add to information delivery processes."
The Xerox color copier uses magnetic brushes, above, to reproduce a spectrum of hues from cyan, magenta and yellow.
Lined up and awaiting final test, right, are new Xerox 3100 copiers. Thanks to the results of our research and second-generation xerographic technology, this compact, portable device is bringing convenience and improved copies to many new Xerox customers throughout the United States and in Europe.

757

USI
U.S. Industries, Inc. Annual Report 1973

Children's birthday parties are times for wearing funny hats and opening presents. It's also the time for putting on party clothes like Polly Flinders dresses from Baylis and boy's outfits from Sturdi-Wear/Mark.
All-weather outerwear from Excelled and Jerold for men and women, respectively, provide the right degree of warmth, comfort and good looks. And they are versatile enough to keep you well-dressed, whatever the hour.
Jeans are what's happening today. Jeans combine informality with comfort and durability. Today, young men wear Cheap Jeans and young women wear Hillbilly Jeans while watching a movie—or making one.

758

757
Art Director John D. Hough
Designer Thomas Geismar
Photographers George Haling
Bunt Glinn
Agency Chermayeff & Geismar Assoc.
Client Xerox Corp.

758
Art Director Alicia Landon
Designer Alicia Landon
Photographer Bill Farrell
Agency Corporate Annual Reports
Client U.S. Industries

Annual
Report
ARISTAR
1974

maxwell
home furnishings

759

759
Art Director Eugene J. Grossman
Designers Eugene J. Grossman
A. Zurcher
Photographer Paul Kopelow
Writers L. Burnett
T. Taulbee
Agency Anspach Grossman
Portugal
Client Aristar

H. J. Heinz Company Annual Report 1974

Public Service

Nigeria is a stately woman bearing a tray of food (a special treat, those baked beans, and don't spoil our enjoyment by talking to us about proteins)—bright-hued garments at a kith-and-kin Sunday lunch in Lagos. Heinz has markets in Nigeria ... also in Greece, Singapore, Luxembourg, Egypt, Bulgaria, Argentina, Vietnam, Finland, Spain, Guam, Malta, Malawi, Chile and Fiji.

HEINZ
BAKED

760

760
Art Director Peter Harrison
Designer Jay Tribich
Photographer Bruce Davidson
Writer Thomas McIntosh
Agency Harrison Assoc.
Client H. J. Heinz Co.

SCM Corporation Annual Report 1974

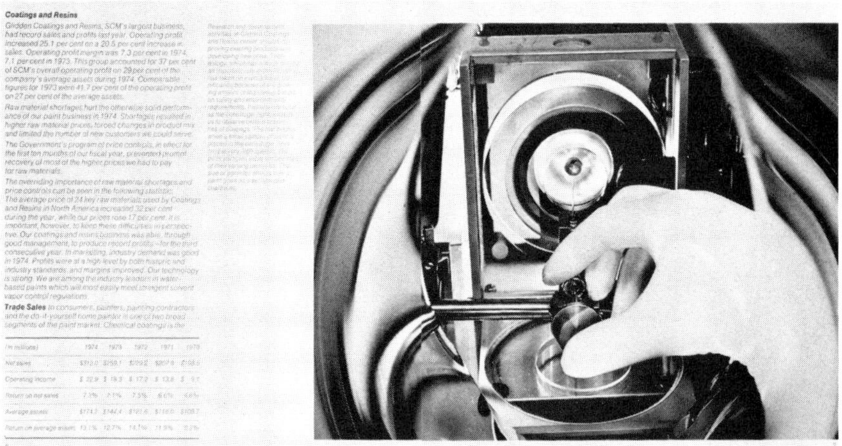
Coatings and Resins

761

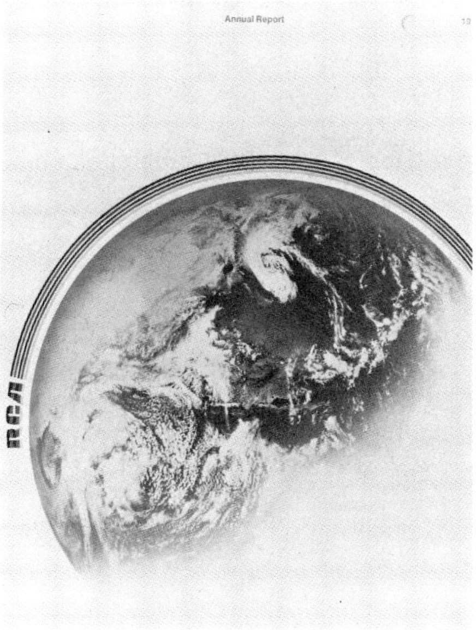
Annual Report
RCA

Other Products and Services
Reading

762

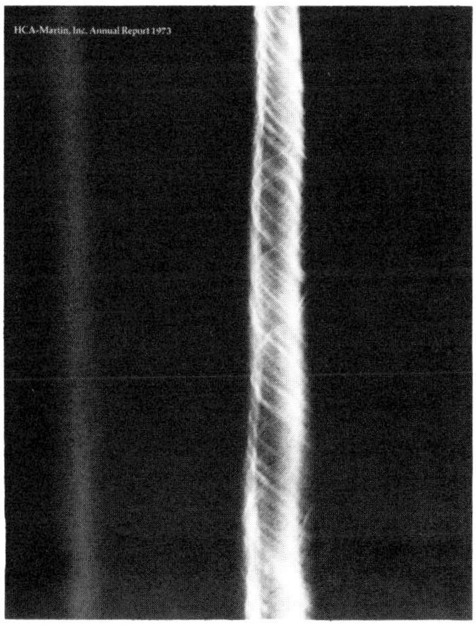
HCA-Martin, Inc. Annual Report 1973

763

761
Art Director Peter Harrison
Designer Peter Harrison
Photographer Wolf Von Dem Bussche
Writer SCM Corporate Communications Dept.
Agency Harrison Assoc.
Client SCM Corp.

762
Art Director Sheldon Seidler
Designers Sheldon Seidler
Chris Lawrence
Photographer Bruce Davidson
Agency Sheldon Seidler Inc.
Client RCA

763
Art Director Len Fury
Designer Len Fury
Photographer Gary Gladstone
Agency Corporate Annual Reports
Client Martin Processing

Herman Miller People Report to the Stockholders
Yes, Virginia, it does rain on picnics – even Herman Miller picnics!

People Working Together
We can talk about this all day, but it is only talk until you see how people actually do participate and work together to achieve our common goals.
Time management seminar – first of many training events coming – held in Education Center last month
Snider, Duthler, Snook head top performers after nine months
26
27

764

Cabot, Cabot & Forbes Land Trust
1974 Annual Report
$2.60
We paid a cash dividend of $2.60 per share for this fiscal year.

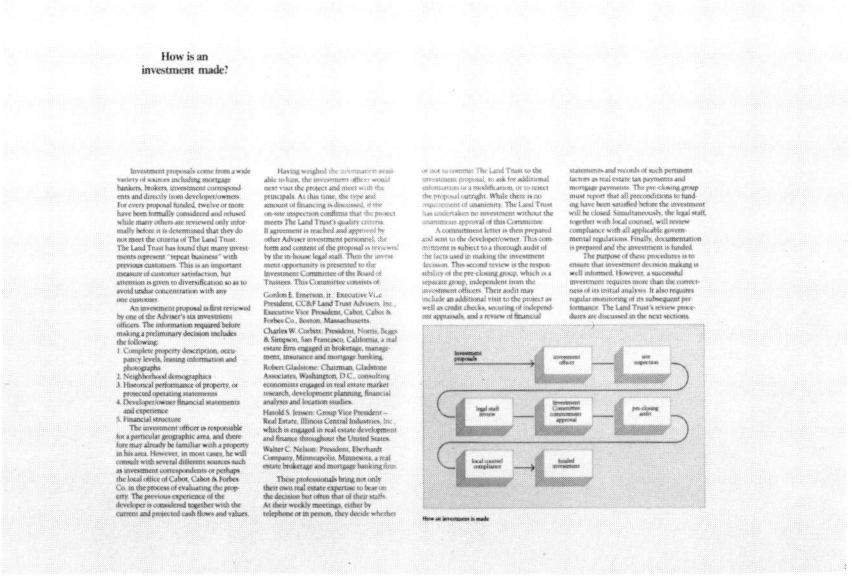
How is an investment made?
How an investment is made

765

764
Art Director John Massey
Designers John Massey
Janet Kasko
Photographer Herman Miller Staff
Writer Hugh DePree
Agency Center for Advanced Research in Design
Client Herman Miller

765
Art Directors Richard Stack
Stan Malcolm
Designer Roy Hughes
Artist Robert Cipriani
Photographer Steve Hansen
Writers Richard Stack
Charles Angle
Agency Cabot, Cabot & Forbes
Client Cabot, Cabot & Forbes Land Trust

Mobil

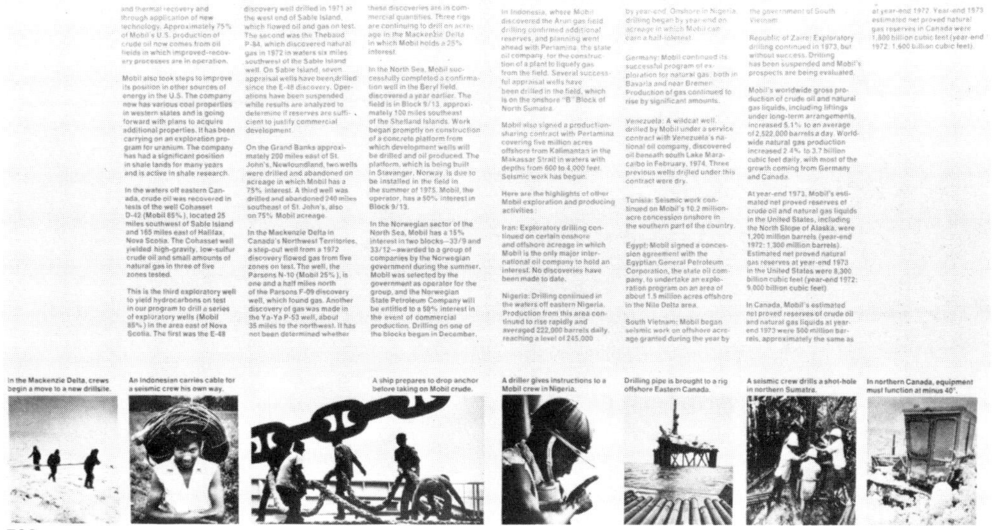

and thermal recovery and through application of new technology. Approximately 75% of Mobil's U.S. production of crude oil now comes from oil fields in which improved-recovery processes are in operation.

Mobil also took steps to improve its position in other sources of energy in the U.S. The company now has various coal properties in western states and is going forward with plans to acquire additional properties. It has been carrying on an exploration program for uranium. The company has had a significant position in shale lands for many years and is active in shale research.

In the waters off eastern Canada, crude oil was recovered in tests of the well Cohasset D-42 (Mobil 85%), located 25 miles southwest of Sable Island and 165 miles east of Halifax, Nova Scotia. The Cohasset well yielded high-gravity, low-sulfur crude oil and small amounts of natural gas in three of five zones tested.

This is the third exploratory well to yield hydrocarbons on test in our program to drill a series of exploratory wells (Mobil 85%) in the area east of Nova Scotia. The first was the E-48 discovery well drilled in 1971 at the west end of Sable Island, which flowed oil and gas on test. The second was the Thebaud P-84, which discovered natural gas in 1972 in waters six miles southwest of the Sable Island well. On Sable Island, seven appraisal wells have been drilled since the E-48 discovery. Operations have been suspended while results are analyzed to determine if reserves are sufficient to justify commercial development.

On the Grand Banks approximately 200 miles east of St. John's, Newfoundland, two wells were drilled and abandoned on acreage in which Mobil has a 75% interest. A third well was drilled and abandoned 240 miles southeast of St. John's, also on 75% Mobil acreage.

In the Mackenzie Delta in Canada's Northwest Territories, a step-out well from a 1972 discovery flowed gas from five zones on test. The well, the Parsons N-10 (Mobil 25%), is one and a half miles north of the Parsons F-09 discovery well, which found gas. Another discovery of gas was made in the Ya-Ya P-53 well, about 35 miles to the northwest. It has not been determined whether these discoveries are in commercial quantities. Three rigs are continuing to drill on acreage in the Mackenzie Delta in which Mobil holds a 25% interest.

In the North Sea, Mobil successfully completed a confirmation well in the Beryl field, discovered a year earlier. The field is in Block 9/13, approximately 100 miles southeast of the Shetland Islands. Work began promptly on construction of a concrete platform from which development wells will be drilled and oil produced. The platform, which is being built in Stavanger, Norway, is due to be installed in the field in the summer of 1975. Mobil, the operator, has a 50% interest in Block 9/13.

In the Norwegian sector of the North Sea, Mobil has a 15% interest in two blocks—33/9 and 33/12—awarded to a group of companies by the Norwegian government during the summer. Mobil was selected by the government as operator for the group, and the Norwegian State Petroleum Company will be entitled to a 50% interest in the event of commercial production. Drilling on one of the blocks began in December.

In Indonesia, where Mobil discovered the Arun gas field, drilling confirmed additional reserves, and planning went ahead with Pertamina, the state oil company, for the construction of a plant to liquefy gas from the field. Several successful appraisal wells have been drilled in the field, which is on the onshore "B" Block of North Sumatra.

Mobil also signed a production-sharing contract with Pertamina covering five million acres offshore from Kalimantan in the Makassar Strait in waters with depths from 600 to 4,000 feet. Seismic work has begun.

Here are the highlights of other Mobil exploration and producing activities:

Iran: Exploratory drilling continued on certain onshore and offshore acreage in which Mobil is the only major international oil company to hold an interest. No discoveries have been made to date.

Nigeria: Drilling continued in the waters off eastern Nigeria. Production from this area continued to rise rapidly and averaged 222,000 barrels daily, reaching a level of 245,000 by year-end. Onshore in Nigeria, drilling began by year-end on acreage in which Mobil can earn a half-interest.

Germany: Mobil continued its successful program of exploration for natural gas, both in Bavaria and near Bremen. Production of gas continued to rise by significant amounts.

Venezuela: A wildcat well, drilled by Mobil under a service contract with Venezuela's national oil company, discovered oil beneath south Lake Maracaibo in February, 1974. Three previous wells drilled under this contract were dry.

Tunisia: Seismic work continued on Mobil's 10.2 million-acre concession onshore in the southern part of the country.

Egypt: Mobil signed a concession agreement with the Egyptian General Petroleum Corporation, the state oil company, to undertake an exploration program on an area of about 1.5 million acres offshore in the Nile Delta area.

South Vietnam: Mobil began seismic work on offshore acreage granted during the year by the government of South Vietnam.

Republic of Zaire: Exploratory drilling continued in 1973, but without success. Drilling has been suspended and Mobil's prospects are being evaluated.

Mobil's worldwide gross production of crude oil and natural gas liquids, including liftings under long-term arrangements, increased 5.1% to an average of 2,522,000 barrels a day. Worldwide natural gas production increased 2.4% to 3.7 billion cubic feet daily, with most of the growth coming from Germany and Canada.

At year-end 1973, Mobil's estimated net proved reserves of crude oil and natural gas liquids in the United States, including the North Slope of Alaska, were 1,200 million barrels (year-end 1972: 1,300 million barrels). Estimated net proved natural gas reserves at year-end 1973 in the United States were 8,300 billion cubic feet (year-end 1972: 9,000 billion cubic feet).

In Canada, Mobil's estimated net proved reserves of crude oil and natural gas liquids at year-end 1973 were 500 million barrels, approximately the same as at year-end 1972. Year-end 1973 estimated net proved natural gas reserves in Canada were 1,800 billion cubic feet (year-end 1972: 1,600 billion cubic feet).

In the Mackenzie Delta, crews begin a move to a new drillsite.

An Indonesian carries cable for a seismic crew his own way.

A ship prepares to drop anchor before taking on Mobil crude.

A driller gives instructions to a Mobil crew in Nigeria.

Drilling pipe is brought to a rig offshore Eastern Canada.

A seismic crew drills a shot-hole in northern Sumatra.

In northern Canada, equipment must function at minus 40°.

766

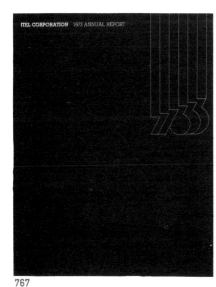
ITEL CORPORATION 1973 ANNUAL REPORT

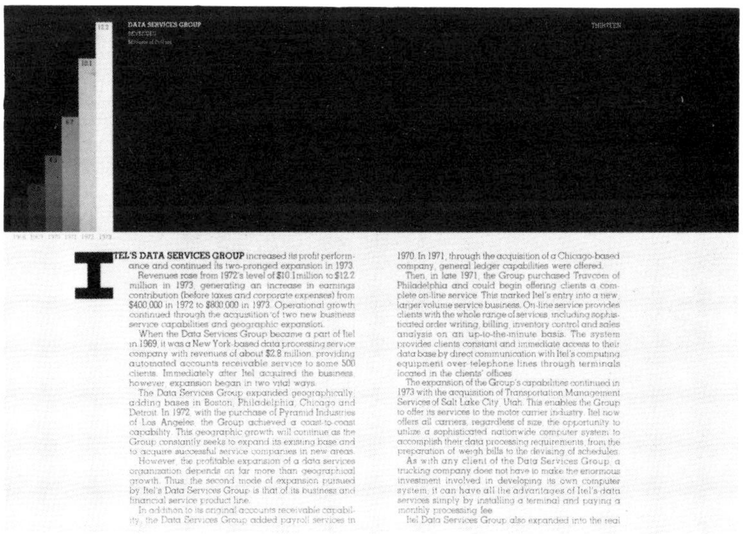
DATA SERVICES GROUP
THIRTEEN
12.2
10.1

ITEL'S DATA SERVICES GROUP increased its profit performance and continued its two-pronged expansion in 1973.

Revenues rose from 1972's level of $10.1 million to $12.2 million in 1973, generating an increase in earnings contribution (before taxes and corporate expenses) from $400,000 in 1972 to $800,000 in 1973. Operational growth continued through the acquisition of two new business service capabilities and geographic expansion.

When the Data Services Group became a part of Itel in 1969, it was a New York-based data processing service company with revenues of about $2.8 million, providing automated accounts receivable service to some 500 clients. Immediately after Itel acquired the business, however, expansion began in two vital ways.

The Data Services Group expanded geographically, adding bases in Boston, Philadelphia, Chicago and Detroit. In 1972, with the purchase of Pyramid Industries of Los Angeles, the Group achieved a coast-to-coast capability. This geographic growth will continue as the Group constantly seeks to expand its existing base and to acquire successful service companies in new areas.

However, the profitable expansion of a data services organization depends on far more than geographical growth. Thus, the second mode of expansion pursued by Itel's Data Services Group is that of its business and financial service product line.

In addition to its original accounts receivable capability, the Data Services Group added payroll services in 1970. In 1971, through the acquisition of a Chicago-based company, general ledger capabilities were offered.

Then, in late 1971, the Group purchased Travcom of Philadelphia and could begin offering clients a complete on-line service. This marked Itel's entry into a new, larger volume service business. On-line service provides clients with the whole range of services, including sophisticated order writing, billing, inventory control and sales analysis on an up-to-the-minute basis. The system provides clients constant and immediate access to their data base by direct communication with Itel's computing equipment over telephone lines through terminals located in the clients' offices.

The expansion of the Group's capabilities continued in 1973 with the acquisition of Transportation Management Services of Salt Lake City, Utah. This enables the Group to offer its services to the motor carrier industry. Itel now offers all carriers, regardless of size, the opportunity to utilize a sophisticated nationwide computer system to accomplish their data processing requirements, from the preparation of weigh bills to the devising of schedules.

As with any client of the Data Services Group, a trucking company does not have to make the enormous investment involved in developing its own computer system; it can have all the advantages of Itel's data services simply by installing a terminal and paying a monthly processing fee.

Itel Data Services Group also expanded into the real

767

766
Art Director Sheldon Seidler
Designer Sheldon Seidler
Photographers Various
Agency Sheldon Seidler Inc.
Client Mobil Oil Corp.

767
Art Director Thom LaPerle
Designer Thom LaPerle
Artist Thom LaPerle
Writer Kekst & Co. Staff
Agency LaPerle/Assoc.
Client Itel Corp.

Distillers Corporation-
Seagrams Limited
Annual Report 1974

rranean littoral and trade was based on local shortages. Fragments of amphorae remind us that the ancient Greeks traded their wine over great distances, probably even to Cornwall in search of tin, but the origins of the modern international wine trade lie in the late Middle Ages, and had their most important impetus when Eleanor of Aquitaine married Henry II of England in the twelfth century. In accordance with what the historian H. A. L. Fisher calls "the disastrous notions of that feudal age", a vast area of southwestern France was transferred to the crown of England. A trade of Bordeaux wine for English wool developed rapidly.

By the sixteenth century the wine trade flourished on all the trade routes of the West, not only from Bordeaux to England (by then Bordeaux was reunited with France but the wine trade ties remained as strong as ever), but from Bordeaux to all the North Sea and Baltic ports, from Cyprus and Crete to London and Amsterdam; from Italy across the Brenner; from the vineyards of Hungary to the luxurious Polish court, newly moved to Warsaw. As trade grew, so did the need to regulate it. The Vintners' Company in London, founded in the fourteenth century, had a prime responsibility to control the quality of wine sold in the city. In Warsaw tavern owners were compelled to display signs to indicate whether the wine they sold was finest Hungarian or coarse Moldavian. In Italy buyers demanded sworn guarantees of a wine's origin, and such a document sworn to by Barone Ricasoli in 1696 is still in the files at Brolio Castle. In France, growers' fraternities like the Jurade of St. Emilion were formed to exercise jealous control over the quality of wine sold with their town's name. All of these were forerunners of the national and international controls of our contemporary wine trade.

If the marriage of Eleanor of Aquitaine gave the first strong impetus to the wine trade, late seventeenth century commerce and politics gave it the shape it has today. Arnaud de Pontac, appointed first president of the *Parlement* of Guyenne in Bordeaux in 1653, came from a rich and influential family. The wine from his estate at Haut Brion near Bordeaux was at first sold in much the same way as other agricultural produce of the time. Then Pontac conceived the idea of using the prestige of his name and his estate to sell it. In 1663 Samuel Pepys wrote in his diary that at the Royal Oak Tavern in London he "drank a sort of French wine called Ho Bryan that had a good and most particular taste that I never met with". This is the first known reference to Chateau Haut Brion, and the first known reference to a wine of a particular, *named* chateau being offered for sale.

The Pontac family developed their innovative marketing idea with skill and soon were selling their wine at prices up to three times as high as any other wine in London. Their success encouraged others. Between 1703 and 1711 the London Gazette carried advertisements for four "chateaux" of Bordeaux. They were Haut Brion, Margaux, Latour and Lafite—which were to emerge, a hundred and fifty years later, as the four "first" growths of the 1855 classification (a classification based on market prices for the Bordeaux growths during the previous quarter-century). With the identification of wine, it became possible for the con-

10

Brolio is one of the great Chianti. Bersano Barolo ... comparable to the finest wines in the world; both are from Seagram companies. Below: Bronze bust of "A Young Bacchante" by Jean Baptiste Carpeaux, from the collection of the Wine Museum of San Francisco, a contribution to the community by Alfred Fromm, Chairman of Fromm & Sichel, a Seagram subsidiary.

Financial Report

Contents

30 Financial Review
35 Consolidated Statement of Income and Retained Earnings
36 Consolidated Balance Sheet
38 Consolidated Statement of Changes in Financial Position
39 Summary of Significant Accounting Policies
40 Notes to Consolidated Financial Statements
41 Auditors' Report
42 Fifteen-Year Financial Summary
44 Directory

29

768

768
Art Director Arnold Saks
Designers Arnold Saks
Tomas Nittner
Photographers Phil Marco
Arthur Schatz
Writer The Jonathan Rinehart Group
Agency Arnold Saks, Inc.
Client The Seagram Co.

"They say you get better care in a teaching hospital. But I don't want any of those youngsters taking care of me while they're still learning how."
"I don't want any of my money going for pie-in-the-sky research. I just want to pay for the care I'm getting."
"If you don't have the money, forget it. You can't get good medical care."
REPORT for the YEARS 1971–72 and 1972–73
"Hospitals are always crying the blues about money. I don't believe it. Between big donors and government money, they can get all they need and more."
"Why is there almost continual disagreement between Blue Cross and the hospitals? It's difficult to know who's wrong and who's right and meanwhile costs keep going up."
If you need medical care, you can get it — with or without money. Hospitals don't like to admit it, but it's true.
Last year the Hospital of the University of Pennsylvania gave away $2.5 million worth of care. Some of it went to people who arrived at the emergency room in critical condition — those whose health needs could not be disregarded, despite the fact that they lacked money. Some went to patients whose insurance lapsed before they were physically able to be discharged from the hospital. A large portion went to outpatients on welfare or medical assistance; their health coverage offers the hospital only a meager reimbursement which nowhere nearly approaches the actual cost of providing the care. This $2.5 million represents the loss that hospitals attempt to recoup from patients who pay — those covered by Blue Cross or other health insurance.
Throughout its facilities and services, the quality of care that the Hospital of the University of Pennsylvania offers is singular, of one caliber. The old image of open wards is a thing of the past at most hospitals, and certainly it is here. Most of the Hospital's 700 beds are semi-private; the two remaining multi-bed units are due for closing or renovation during the coming year.
So has outpatient care outgrown its old image. Specialization has reached the clinics, which now number more than 40 and cater to all types of medical need. Outpatient services include a hip clinic, a knee clinic, an acne clinic, a hypertension clinic, and many others which minister to highly specific conditions. This year the Hospital opened a walk-in clinic, which allows non-emergency patients to simply 'walk in' without an appointment and receive immediate attention for general medical problems.
Charges for the outpatient clinics have not been raised in three years. The standard charge per visit is scaled down according to a patient's ability to pay.
Hospitals cannot afford to give away care; but nor can they afford to neglect the needs of the critically ill. Health care is always available to those who really need it.

769

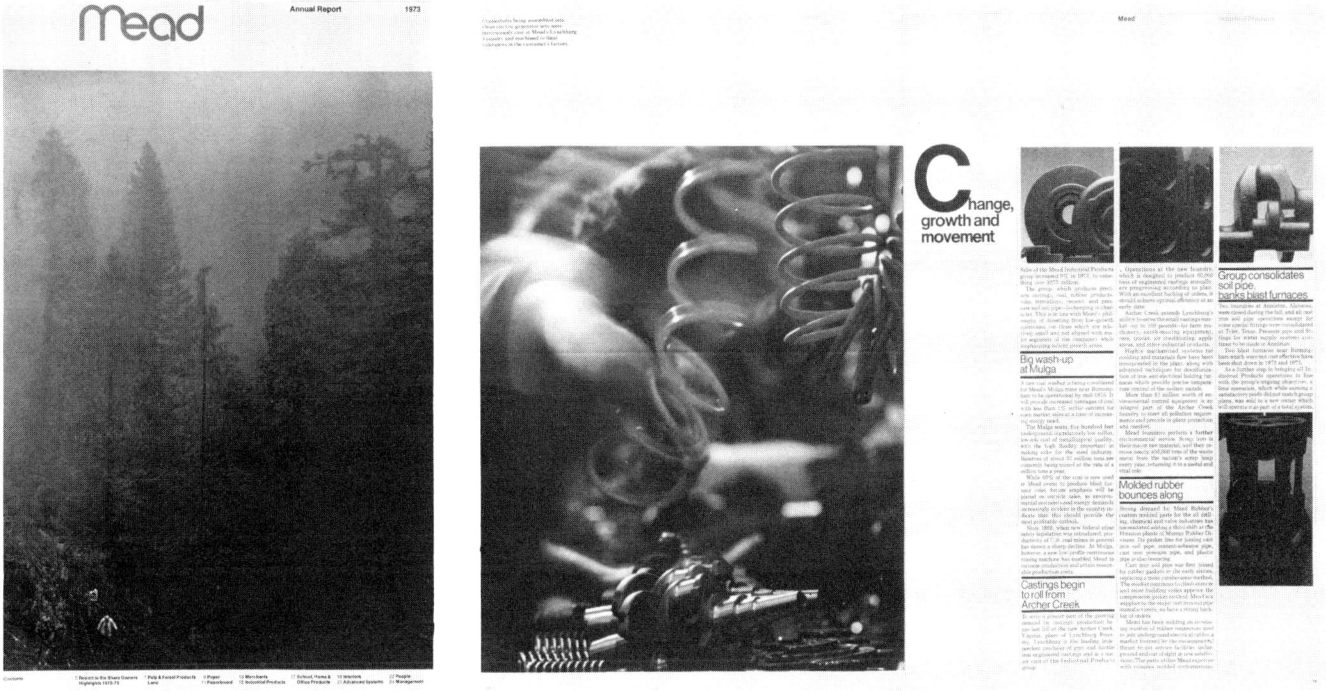

Mead
Annual Report
1973
Mead
Change, growth and movement
Big wash-up at Mulga
Molded rubber bounces along
Castings begin to roll from Archer Creek
Group consolidates soil pipe, banks blast furnaces

780

769
Art Director Robert J. Rytter
Designer Robert J. Rytter
Photographers George Krause
Various
Writers Marilyn Castaldi
Bernice A. Thieblot
Agency North Charles Street Design Organization
Client Hospital of the University of Pennsylvania

780
Art Director Sheldon Seidler
Designer Sheldon Seidler
Photographers Erich Hartmann
Burk Uzzle
Dawson Jones
Kent Schellenger
Mort Schreiber
John Paul Endress
Pete Turner
Writer Harry P. Carruth, Jr.
Agency Sheldon Seidler Inc.
Client Mead Corp.

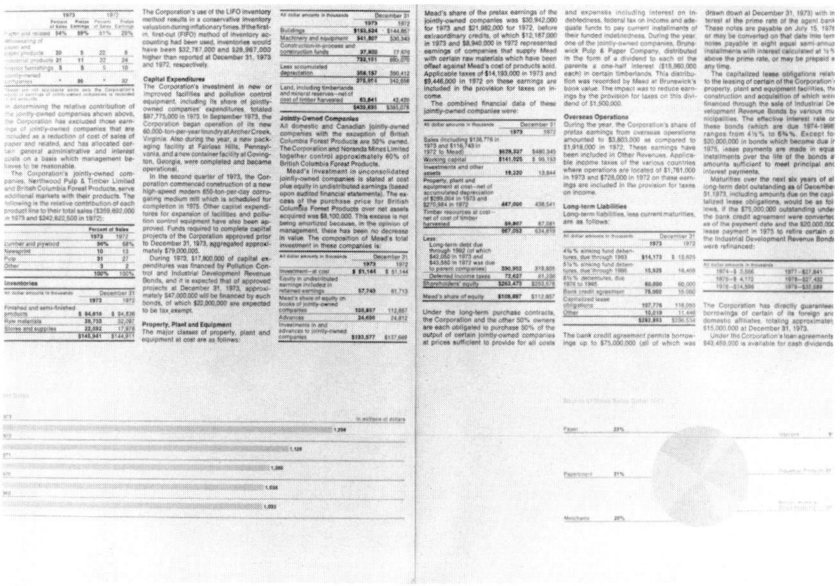

781

782

781
Art Director Sheldon Seidler
Designers Sheldon Seidler
Bill Mihalik
Agency Sheldon Seidler Inc.
Client Mead Corp.

782
Art Director James Cross
Designer James Cross
Photographer Marvin Silver
Writers Paul Etter
Walter Russler
Agency James Cross Design Office
Client Fluor Corp.

The SX-70 Experience

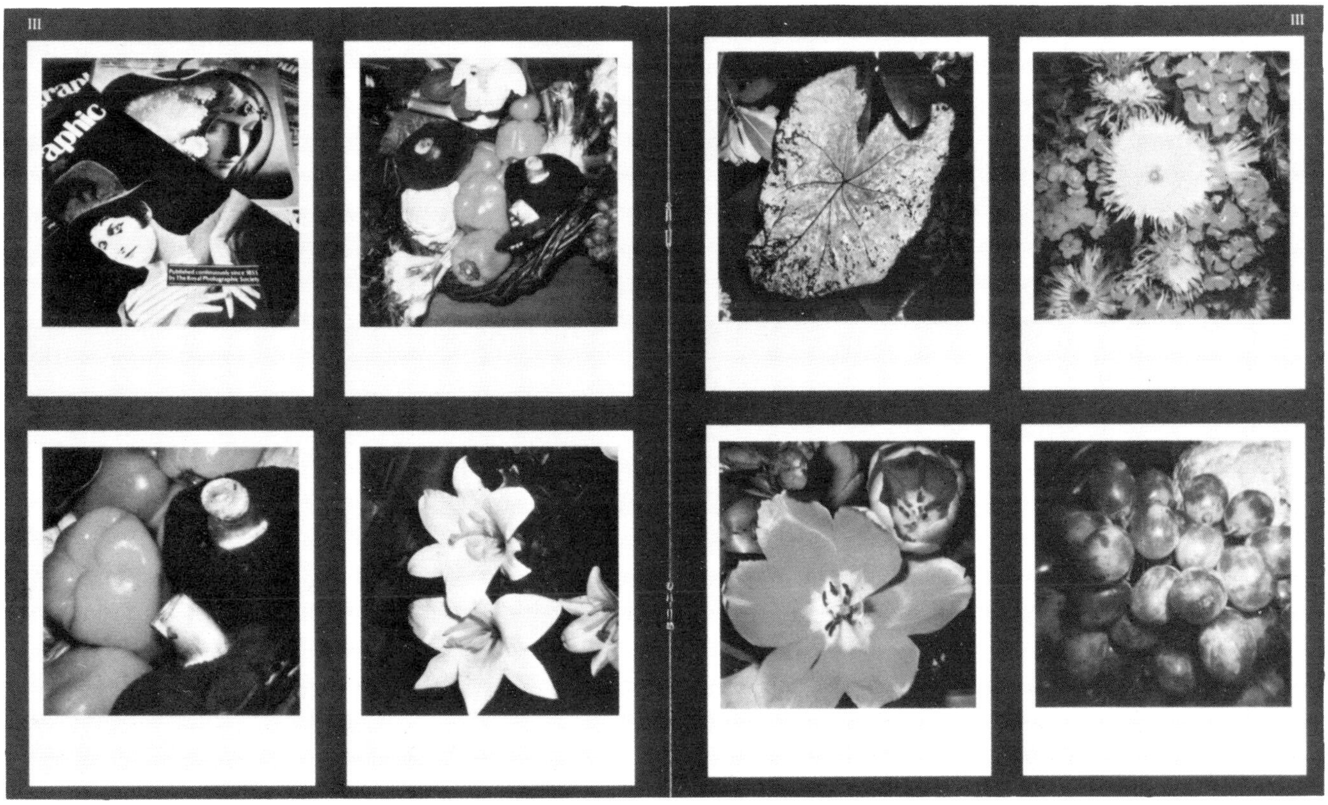

783

783
Art Director William Field
Designer Jean Benton
Photographer Edwin Land
Writer Edwin Land
Agency Polaroid Corp.
Client Polaroid Corp.

Torin
Finances. Torin's financial position is strong. Stockholders' equity now stands at $19.05 per share, an 8.5% increase during 1973.
We increased our dividend during the year by 25% – the maximum allowable under federal guidelines. We recognize this dividend is conservative, approximately 25% of earnings, when compared with other companies of similar size. We anticipate an improvement in payout generally comparable to our growth in earnings.
In 1973 our capital investment program totaled $934,000 compared with $1,300,000 plan and $712,000 expended in 1972. The major outlays were for increased capacity in Belgium, Indiana and Torrington divisions and land in Australia. The balance maintained our very high standard of machinery and equipment.
In 1974 we plan to spend approximately $1,750,000, a figure ballooned by the building of the Australian plant. We expect a like figure in 1975 when we anticipate a demand for increased capacity to meet our domestic growth.
Summary. 1973 was a fine year – 1974 has some unknowns but we have done a lot to cushion the possible downturns. We will implement a five year strategy to maximize results by gaining leadership positions in carefully chosen markets. The energy crisis will present opportunities as well as problems because industries using air moving equipment will be seeking improvements in efficiency. Torin's future lies in working with customers to improve their product. Torin's strength lies in the people who did such a beautiful job in 1973 and who will create the success of 1974.

784

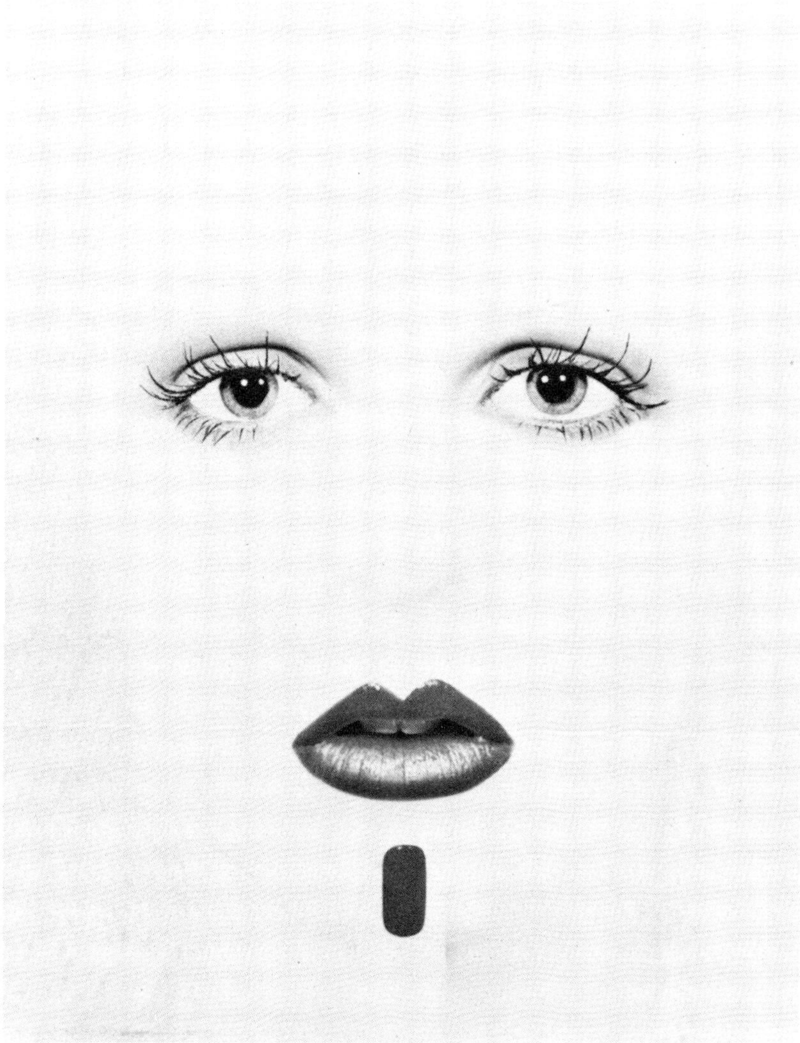

785

784
Art Director Ivan Chermayeff
Designers Ivan Chermayeff
Steven Haines
Photographer Ivan Chermayeff
Agency Chermayeff & Geismar Assoc.
Client Torin Corp.

785
Art Director Robert S. Nemser
Designer Robert S. Nemser
Artist Clyde McWilliams
Photographer John Zoiner
Writer Bass & Co.
Agency Nemser & Howard
Client Monica Simone Cosmetics

TEXSTAR
TEX-73
ANNUAL REPORT

786

Lomas & Nettleton Mortgage Investors, 1974 Annual Report
Lomas & Nettleton Mortgage Investors, 1974 Annual Report

787

786
Art Directors David Kaestle
Robert Pellegrini
Designers David Kaestle
Robert Pellegrini
Photographer Dick Frank
Writer William Schechter
Agency Pellegrini
Kaestle & Gross
Client Textar Corp.

787
Art Director Jack Summerford
Designer Jack Summerford
Photographers Greg Booth
Amon Carter Museum
Writer John Stone
Agencies Glenn, Bozell, & Jacobs
Public Relations
The Richards Group
Client Lomas & Nettleton
Mortgage Investors

Six patient perspectives of the Utah State Hospital
IMAGES

"In other hospitals, patients have no say-so at all. Here, the patients with the help of the staff, run much of what is done. Each patient's treatment is set up individually — no two of us have the same program. If there's something positive we do, we receive positive reinforcement; something negative — something the staff is trying to correct — negative reinforcement. ■ "I love helping in the unit. My need to help others is uncommonly strong, probably because of the length of time I've spent in institutions — 18 years. ■ "I'm a person who gets high — without alcohol or drugs — and I can't control it. Then I go into the depression part. I can show you seventeen stab wounds in my chest and umpteen-hundred suicidal attempts on my arms. I've drank Lysol and Drano, too — that's how depressed I've gotten. However, since I've been here I haven't cut myself even one time. I attribute this to a small attendant-to-patient ratio (one to six) and a lot of care and peer pressure. ■ "The message I take with me when I go out on panels is that Utah citizens are lucky to have this facility . . . that they ought to come forth, participate, and find out what mental illness is all about. It's time for people to take a look and ask themselves, 'What am I doing and what can I do?'"
Image 2: Karen
"When I first came here I was on the verge of divorcing my wife. I can see now that many of the problems I had with her were my fault — not hers. I had to go somewhere where I could get a little help. I had been in two rest homes . . . seemed like they couldn't help me. ■ "Some days little things will hurt me, but I don't let them stay with me. Inside an hour I'm back pitching again and building. I'm going to do things in the next ten years; I'm not washed up just because I'm seventy-three. ■ "The staff helps those poor people who can't help themselves, but when a man's able . . . well, they let him help himself, and he's better for it. ■ "This is a place to get well — mentally, physically, spiritually. If you fall down one day, the nurses and doctors get you on your feet the next. I can't help but say that this is one of the best hospitals in the United States — not just in Utah. ■ "I'm a better man today than I have ever been. These people have taken an interest in me . . . they've done everything possible to help me."
Image 3: Frank

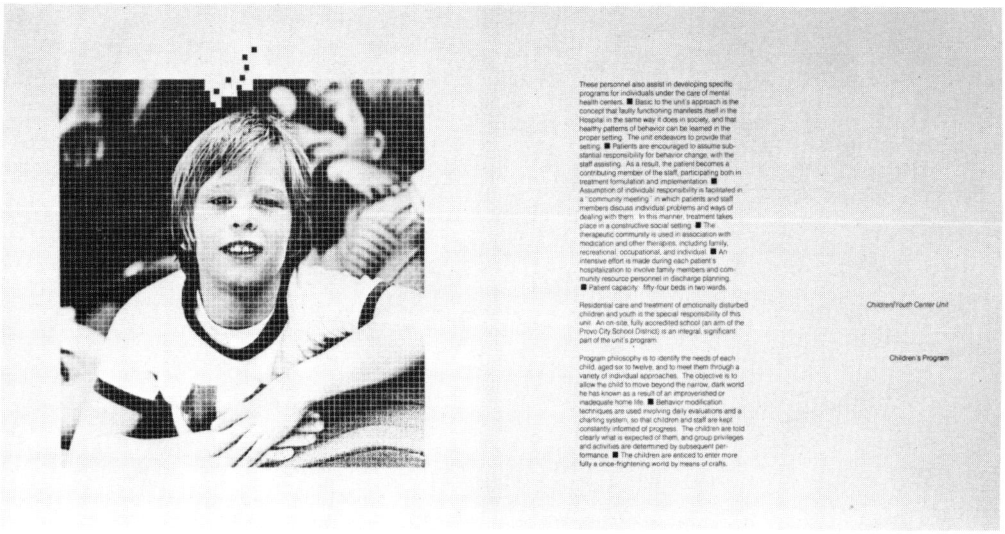
These personnel also assist in developing specific programs for individuals under the care of mental health centers. ■ Basic to the unit's approach is the concept that faulty functioning manifests itself in the Hospital in the same way it does in society, and that healthy patterns of behavior can be learned in the proper setting. The unit endeavors to provide that setting. ■ Patients are encouraged to assume substantial responsibility for behavior change, with the staff assisting. As a result, the patient becomes a contributing member of the staff, participating both in treatment formulation and implementation. ■ Assumption of individual responsibility is facilitated in a "community meeting" in which patients and staff members discuss individual problems and ways of dealing with them. In this manner, treatment takes place in a constructive social setting. ■ The therapeutic community is used in association with medication and other therapies, including family, recreational, occupational, and individual. ■ An intensive effort is made during each patient's hospitalization to involve family members and community resource personnel in discharge planning. ■ Patient capacity: fifty-four beds in two wards.
Residential care and treatment of emotionally disturbed children and youth is the special responsibility of this unit. An on-site, fully accredited school (an arm of the Provo City School District) is an integral, significant part of the unit's program.
Children/Youth Center Unit
Program philosophy is to identify the needs of each child, aged six to twelve, and to meet them through a variety of individual approaches. The objective is to allow the child to move beyond the narrow, dark world he has known as a result of an impoverished or inadequate home life. ■ Behavior modification techniques are used involving daily evaluations and a charting system, so that children and staff are kept constantly informed of progress. The children are told clearly what is expected of them, and group privileges and activities are determined by subsequent performance. ■ The children are enticed to enter more fully a once-frightening world by means of crafts.
Children's Program

788

788
Art Director McRay Magleby
Designer McRay Magleby
Artist McRay Magleby
Photographer Don. O. Thorpe
Writer Paul H. Schneiter
Agency Graphic Communications Dept.
Brigham Young University
Client Utah State Hospital

U&lc.
UPPER AND LOWER CASE, THE INTERNATIONAL JOURNAL OF TYPOGRAPHICS
PUBLISHED BY THE INTERNATIONAL TYPEFACE CORPORATION. VOLUME ONE, NUMBER THREE 1974
In This Issue:
The First Alphabet
Editorial
The Mecklenburg Declaration
The Wizard of Oz
XPO-1
The Devil's Dictionary
My Best With Letters
Ms.
Something For Everybody
Selling Ice Cubes To An Eskimo
Letters To The Editor
What's New From ITC
THE FIRST ALPHABET
"WHO'S GUTENBERG?" ASKS ANCIENT MEDITERRANEAN GRAPHIC DESIGNER
XPO-1 THE FIRST COMMUNICATIONS EXPOSITION
NBCABC

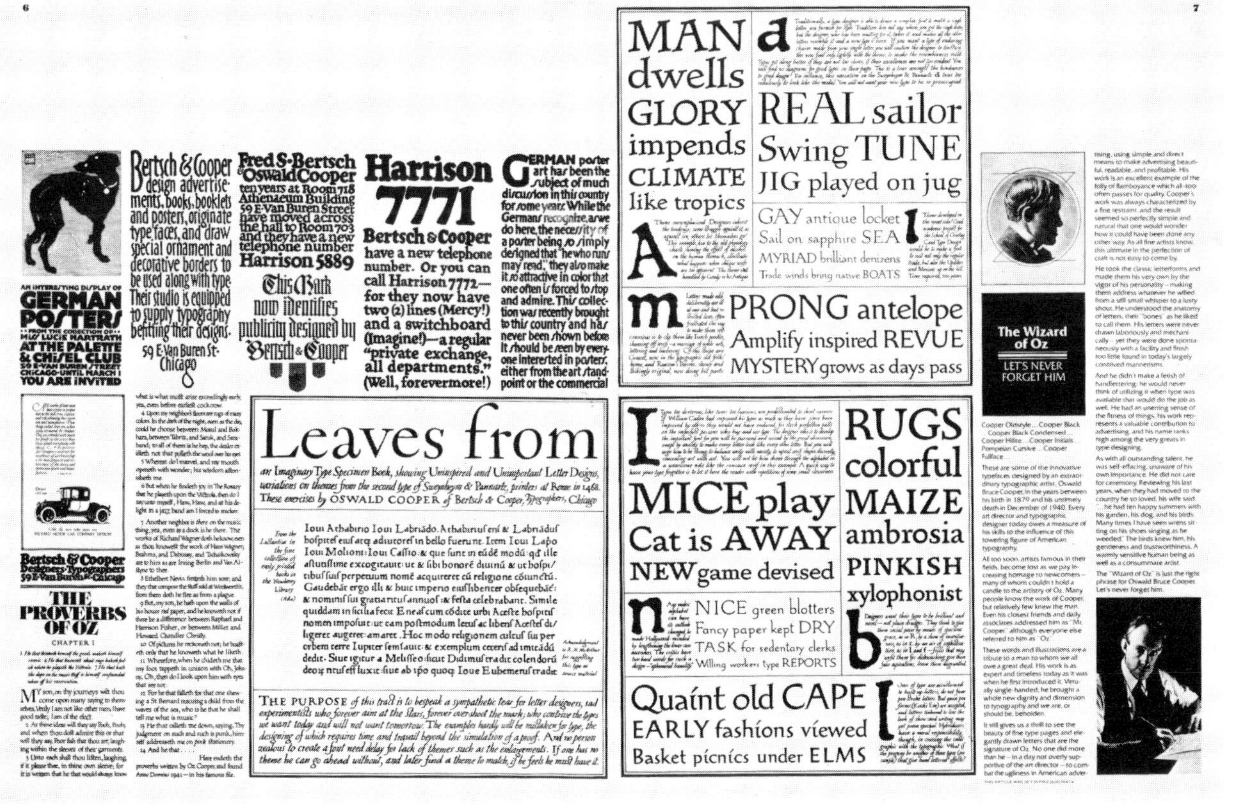
6
7
Bertsch & Cooper design advertisements, books, booklets and posters, originate type faces, and draw special ornament and decorative borders to be used along with type. Their studio is equipped to supply typography befitting their designs. 59 E. Van Buren St. Chicago
Fred S. Bertsch Oswald Cooper ten years at Room 718 Athenaeum Building 59 E. Van Buren Street have moved across the hall to Room 703 and they have a new telephone number Harrison 5889
Harrison 7771
Bertsch & Cooper have a new telephone number. Or you can call Harrison 7772—for they now have two (2) lines (Mercy!) and a switchboard (Imagine!)—a regular "private exchange, all departments." (Well, forevermore!)
AN INTERESTING DISPLAY OF GERMAN POSTERS AT THE PALETTE & CHISEL CLUB YOU ARE INVITED
Bertsch & Cooper Designers Typographers 59 E. Van Buren St. Chicago
THE PROVERBS OF OZ
CHAPTER I
MAN dwells GLORY impends CLIMATE like tropics
REAL sailor Swing TUNE JIG played on jug
GAY antique locket Sail on sapphire SEA MYRIAD brilliant denizens Trade winds bring native BOATS
PRONG antelope Amplify inspired REVUE MYSTERY grows as days pass
Leaves from an Imaginary Type Specimen Book, showing Uninspired and Unimportant Letter Designs, variations on themes from the second type of Sweynheym & Pannartz, printers at Rome in 1468. These exercises by OSWALD COOPER of Bertsch & Cooper, Typographers, Chicago
MICE play Cat is AWAY NEW game devised
RUGS colorful MAIZE ambrosia PINKISH xylophonist
NICE green blotters Fancy paper kept DRY TASK for sedentary clerks Willing workers type REPORTS
Quaint old CAPE EARLY fashions viewed Basket picnics under ELMS
The Wizard of Oz
LET'S NEVER FORGET HIM

789

789

Art Director Herb Lubalin
Designer Herb Lubalin
Artists Gerry Gersten
Peter Katz
Photographer Simone Cherpitel
Editors Herb Lubalin
Aaron Burns
Jack Anson Finke
Ed Rondthaler
Agency Lubalin, Smith, Carnase
Client U & lc
International Typeface Corp.

U&lc.
"Whatever liberates our spirit without giving us self control is disastrous."...Goethe
A Proposition for Education in Letterforms & Handwriting
Lettering and Society
The Interdependence of Technique and Typography
Technical Training for Technicians and Typographers
Type in Our Environment
Education and Training in Letterforms
The Rules of the Game
OD ON
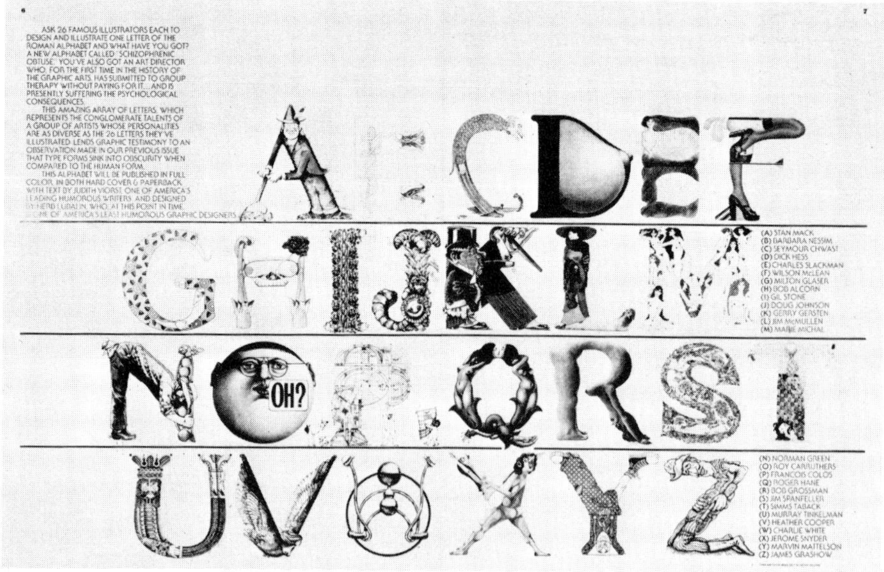
ASK 26 FAMOUS ILLUSTRATORS EACH TO DESIGN AND ILLUSTRATE ONE LETTER OF THE ROMAN ALPHABET AND WHAT HAVE YOU GOT? A NEW ALPHABET CALLED "SCHIZOPHRENIC OBTUSE."
OH?
(A) STAN MACK
(B) BARBARA NESSIM
(C) SEYMOUR CHWAST
(D) DICK HESS
(E) CHARLES SLACKMAN
(F) WILSON McLEAN
(G) MILTON GLASER
(H) BOB ALCORN
(I) GIL STONE
(J) DOUG JOHNSON
(K) GERRY GERSTEN
(L) JIM McMULLEN
(M) MARIE MICHAL
(N) NORMAN GREEN
(O) ROY CARRUTHERS
(P) FRANCOIS COLOS
(Q) ROGER HANE
(R) BOB GROSSMAN
(S) JIM SPANFELLER
(T) SIMMS TABACK
(U) MURRAY TINKELMAN
(V) HEATHER COOPER
(W) CHARLIE WHITE
(X) JEROME SNYDER
(Y) MARVIN MATTELSON
(Z) JAMES GRASHOW

790

Champion Papers The Printing Salesman's Herald Book 33

791

790
Art Director Herb Lubalin
Designer Herb Lubalin
Artists Various
Editors Herb Lubalin
Aaron Burns
Jack Anson Finke
Ed Rondthaler
Agency Lubalin, Smith, Carnase
Client U & lc
International Typeface Corp.

791
Art Director J. Malcolm Grear
Designer Malcolm Grear Designers
Photographers Susan Newkirk
Bert Beaver
Mark Silber
Sibyl Wilson
Aaron Siskind
Writers Michael Corey
Champion Papers Staff
Agency Malcolm Grear Designers
Client Champion Papers

792

FREE BROADCAST JOURNALISM:
TWO ASSESSMENTS, OVER THE COURSE
OF TWO DECADES, OF THE
GROWING CHALLENGE THAT CONFRONTS IT
BY WILLIAM S. PALEY
1954

793

792
Art Director Don Weller
Designer Don Weller
Photographer Chris Callis
Agency The Weller Institute
Client Art Directors Club of Los Angeles

793
Art Director Lou Dorfsman
Designer Ted Andresakes
Writer Arthur Tourtellot
Agency CBS/Broadcast Group
Client CBS

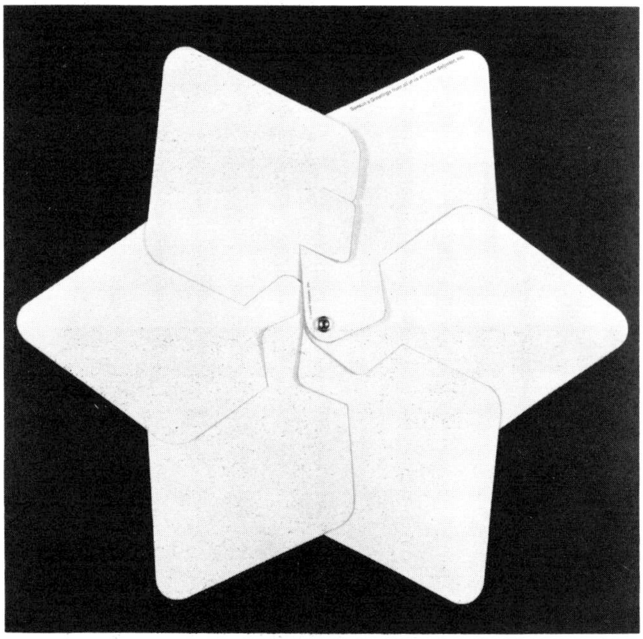

794

INTRODUCING
ON DESIGNERS SATURDAY
OCTOBER 18 AND 19
THE NEW, SINGULAR FAMILY
OF WARD BENNETT FABRICS
FRESH—ORIGINAL—ELEGANT
UPHOLSTERY CLOTHS CRAFTED WITH
THE SAME CARE YOU DEMAND
OF HIS FURNITURE
WARD BENNETT DESIGNS
FOR BRICKEL ASSOCIATES INC.
515 MADISON AVENUE
NEW YORK, NEW YORK 10022
(212) MU 8-2233

795

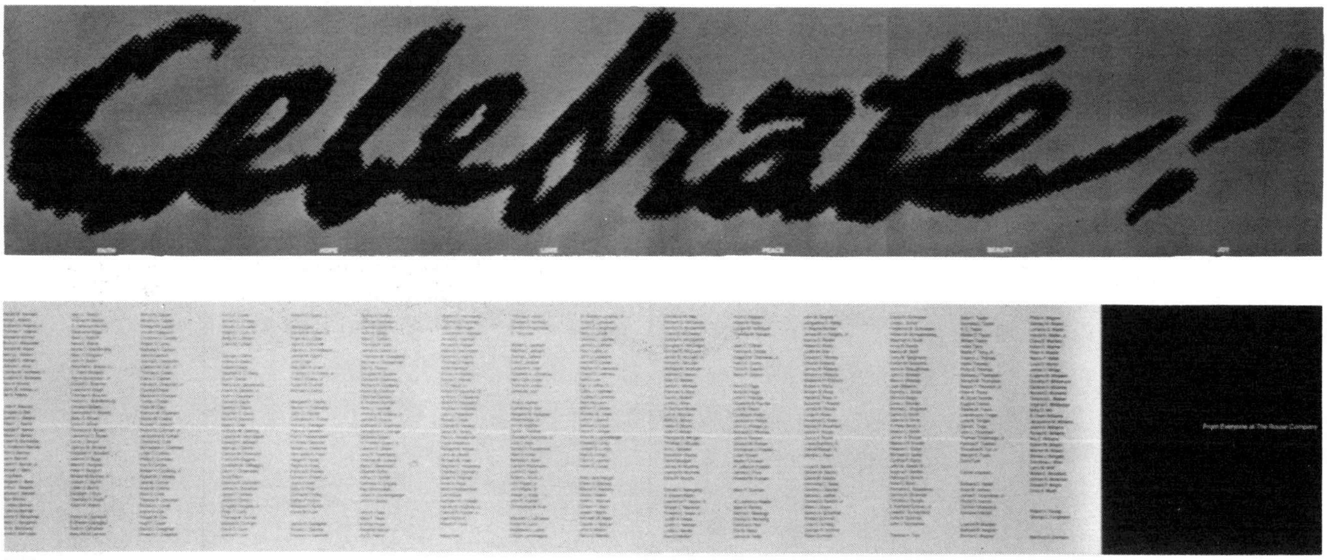
Celebrate!

796

794
Art Director Bob Salpeter
Designer Bob Salpeter
Artist Judy Reiser
Agency Lopez Salpeter
Client Lopez Salpeter

795
Art Director Peter Bradford
Designers Peter Bradford
Ward Bennett
Photographer Michael Pateman
Writers Peter Bradford
Ward Bennett
Agency Peter Bradford and Assoc.
Client Brickel Assoc.

796
Art Director Ed Gold
Designers Bob Holland
David Crowder
Artist Bob Holland
Writer Scott Ditch
Agency Barton-Gillet Co.
Client The Rouse Co.

797

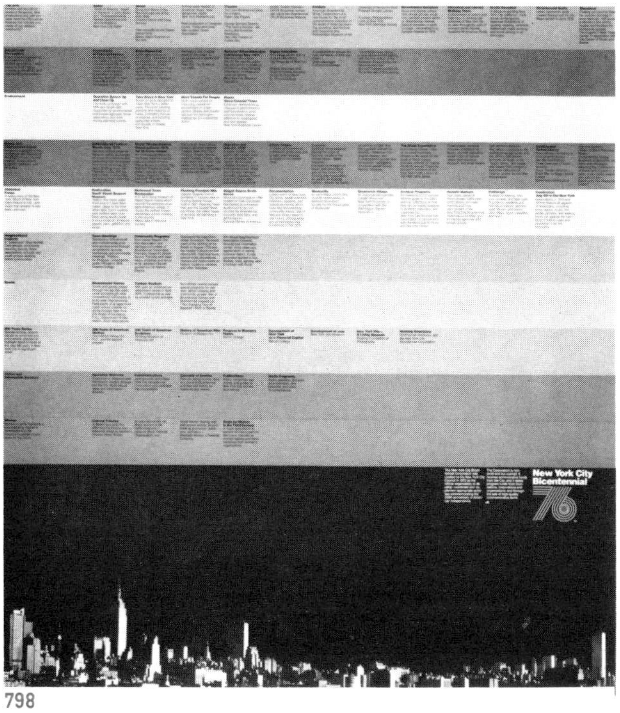
New York City
Bicentennial
76

798

76
New York City
Bicentennial

797
Designer Cosimo Scianna
Photographer Cosimo Scianna
Agency Cosimo's Studio
Client Cosimo's Studio

798
Art Director Eugene J. Grossman
Designer Eugene J. Grossman
Agency Anspach Grossman Portugal
Client New York City
Bicentennial Commission

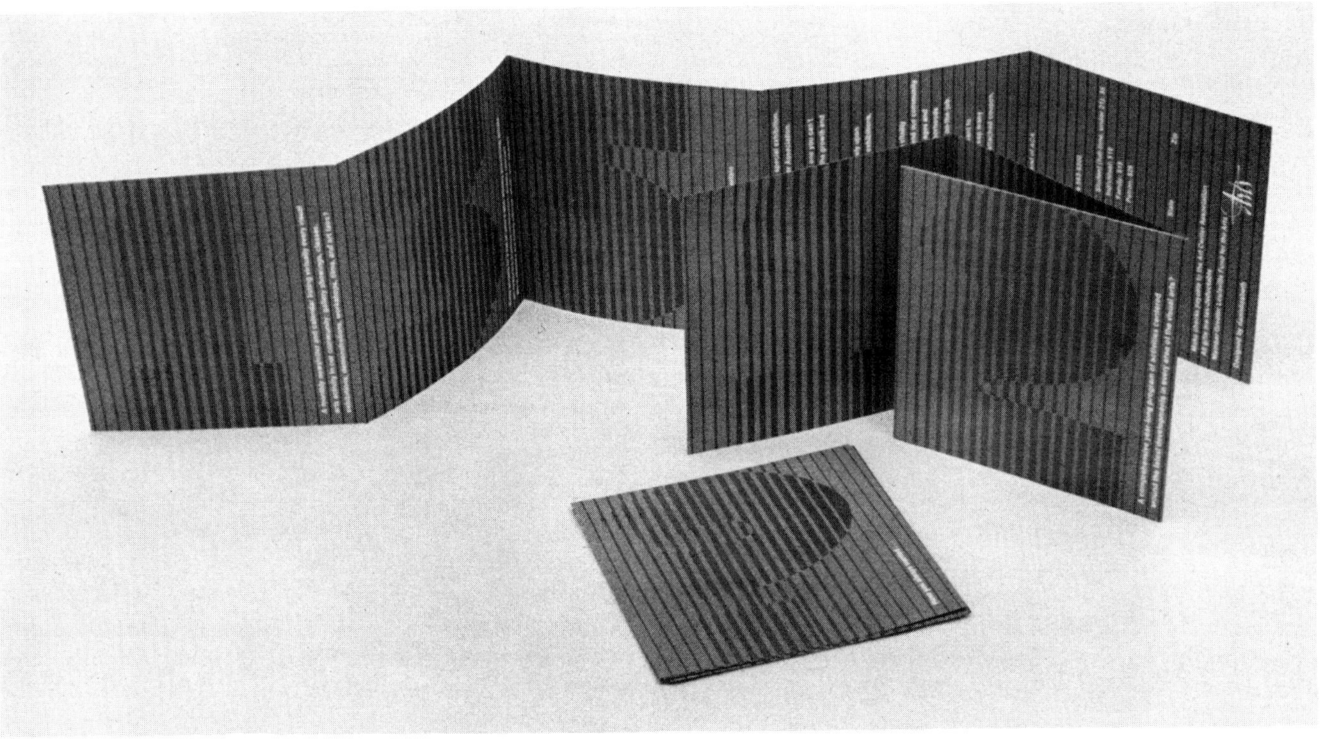

799

YEARUP.
Happy Nineteen Hundred Seventy-Five/Gauger Sparks Silva.

800

799
Art Directors Daniel Boyarski
Elizabeth Marschke
Designers Daniel Boyarski
Elizabeth Marschke
Writer Robert H. Roach
Agency Daniel Boyarski &
Elizabeth Marschke
Client The Art Center Assoc.

800
Art Director David Gauger
Designer David Gauger
Artist David Gauger
Writer David Gauger
Agency Gauger Sparks Silva
Client Gauger Sparks Silva

Tangents XV
Designs for the haunted house

801

LOVE
PEACE
GLEE

802

801
Art Director Rick Horton
Designer Rick Horton
Artist Gateway Studios
Photographer Boulevard Photographic
Writer Alan Van Dine
Agency Van Dine Horton McNamara
Client Koppers Co.

802
Art Directors Robin Rickabaugh
Heidi Rickabaugh
Designer Robin Rickabaugh
Artist Robin Rickabaugh
Writer Robin Rickabaugh
Agency Heidi & Robin Rickabaugh
Client Heidi & Robin Rickabaugh

address: zip code: area code: prefix: line number:
1314900172134842525

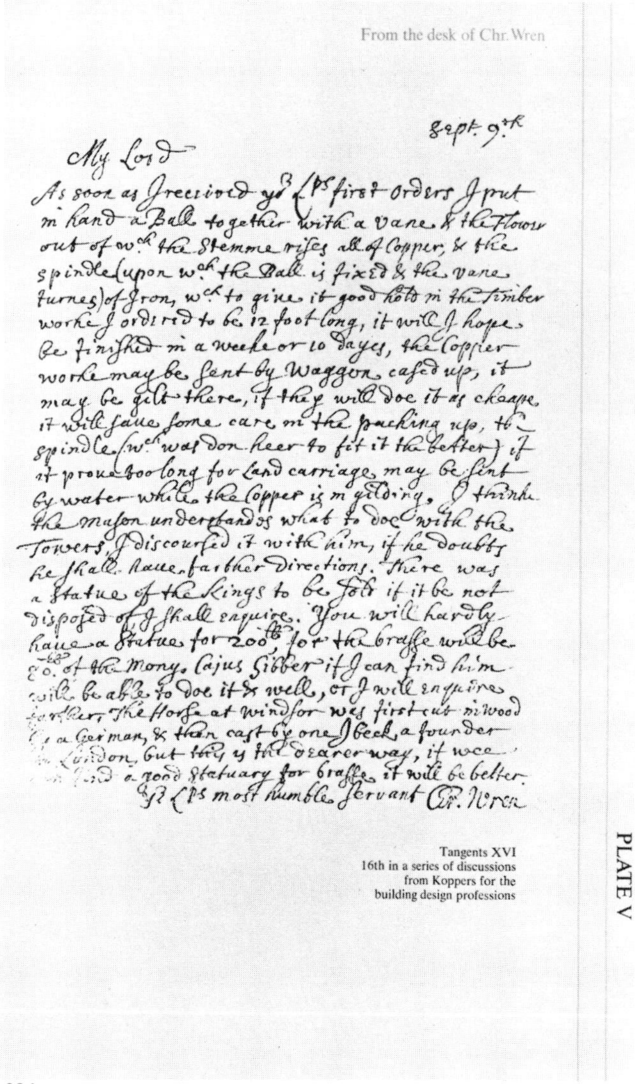
From the desk of Chr. Wren
Tangents XVI
16th in a series of discussions
from Koppers for the
building design professions
PLATE V

804

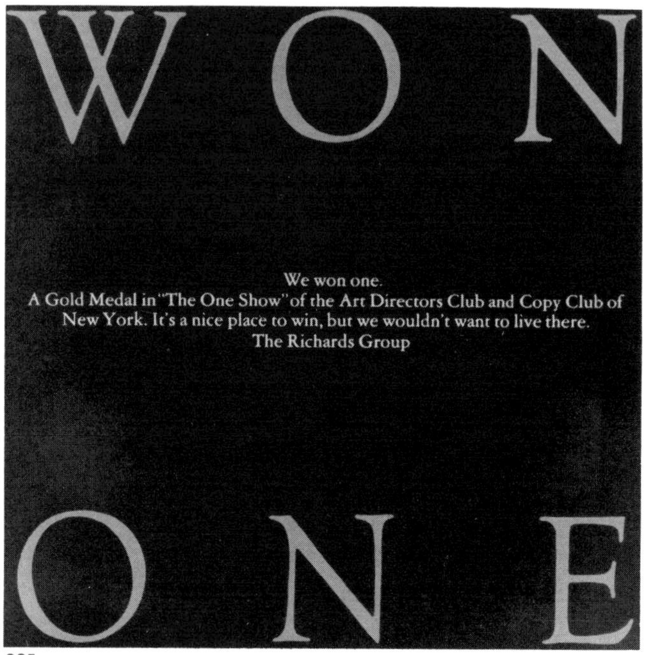
WON
We won one.
A Gold Medal in "The One Show" of the Art Directors Club and Copy Club of New York. It's a nice place to win, but we wouldn't want to live there.
The Richards Group
ONE

805

SILVER

803
Art Director James Cross
Designer James Cross
Agency James Cross Design Office
Client James Cross Design Office

804
Art Director Rick Horton
Designer Rick Horton
Artist Gateway Studios
Photographer Ed Zak
Writer Alan Van Dine
Agency Van Dine Horton McNamara
Client Koppers Co.

805
Art Director Woody Pirtle
Designer Woody Pirtle
Artist Woody Pirtle
Writer Larry Sons
Agency The Richards Group
Client The Richards Group

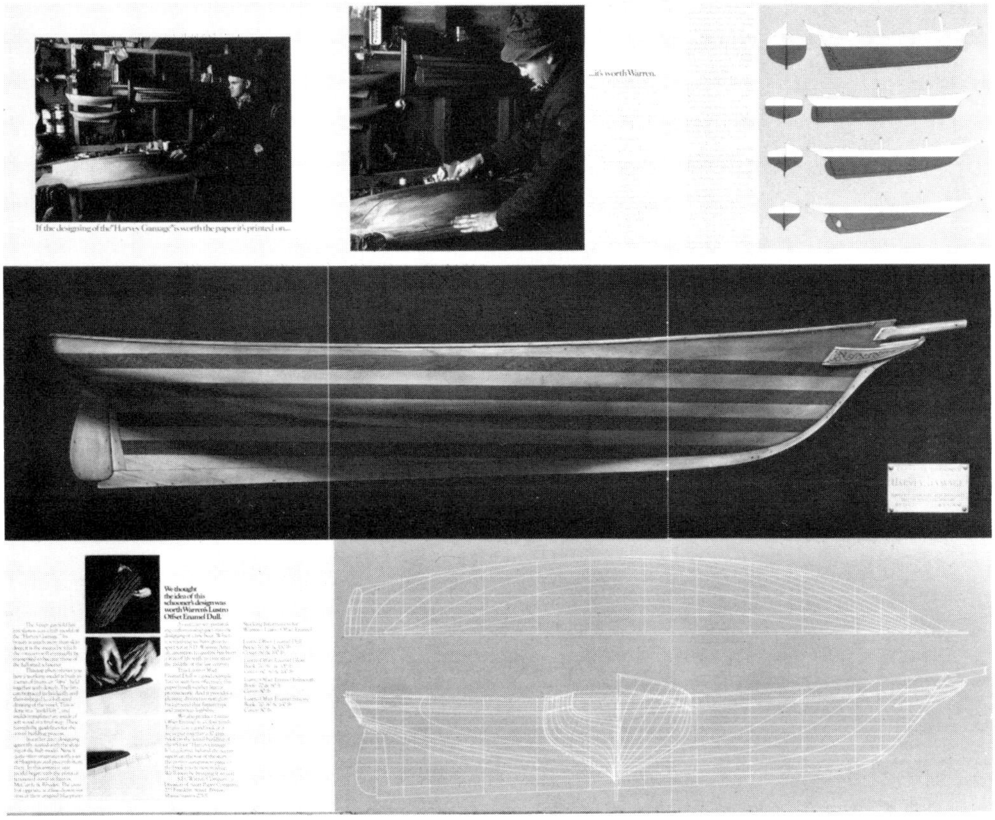
If the designing of the "Harvey Gamage" is worth the paper it's printed on...
...it's worth Warren.
We thought the idea of this schooner's design was worth Warren's Lustro Offset Enamel Dull.

806

Precision Instrument Corp.
464 Oak Street
Ridgefield, New Jersey
07657

The Biomedical Manufacturer's Self-diagnosis Kit
Take a close look at the medical research in your state
Could your productivity use a little boost?
Are you located in the heart of a market?
Is your state government hot or cold toward you?
Do your employees' lifestyles have them feeling depressed?
Could your distribution picture be a little brighter?
MICHIGAN

807

806
Art Directors Jim Witham
Ralph Moxcey
Artist Charles Hoar
Photographer Bill Bruin
Writer Nelson Lofstedt
Agency Humphrey Browning MacDougall
Client S. D. Warren Co.

807
Art Director Edd Mangino
Designer Edd Mangino
Artist George Gaadt
Writer John Altomare
Agency W. B. Doner & Co.
Client Michigan Office of Economic Expansion

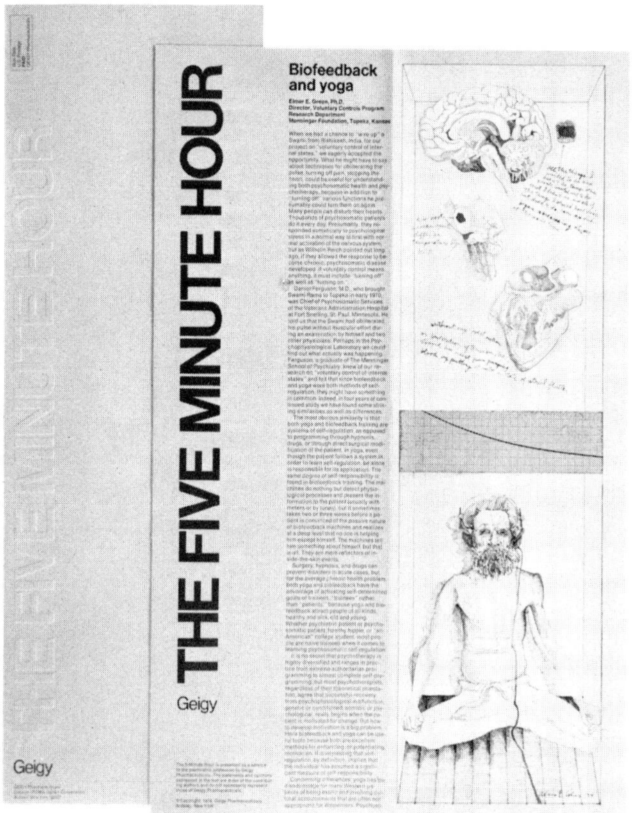
THE FIVE MINUTE HOUR
Geigy
Biofeedback and yoga
Geigy

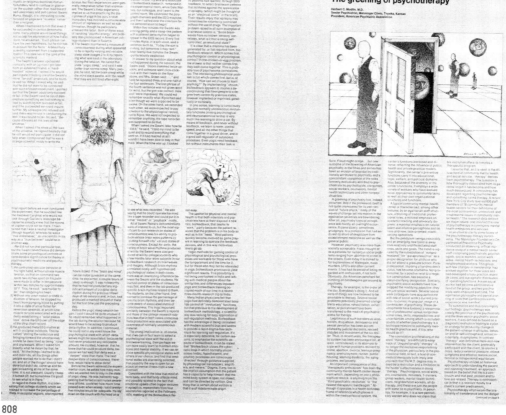

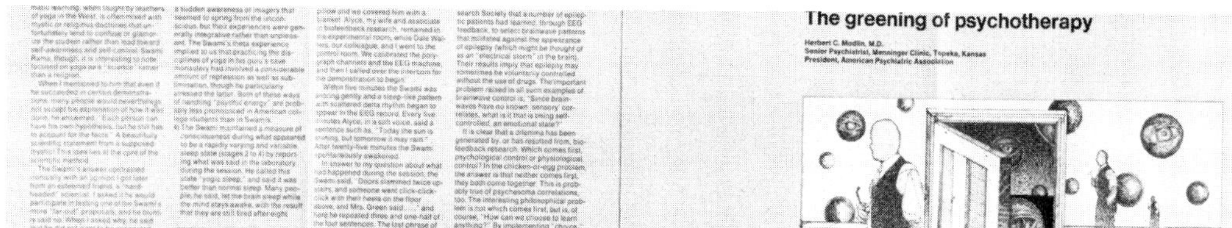
The greening of psychotherapy
Herbert C. Modlin, M.D.
Senior Psychiatrist, Menninger Clinic, Topeka, Kansas
President, American Psychiatric Association

808

808
Art Director Bob Paganucci
Designer Bob Paganucci
Artist Alan E. Cober
Writer Geigy Pharmaceuticals Staff
Agency Geigy Pharmaceuticals
Client Geigy Pharmaceuticals

Janice Fudyma
&
Craig Bernhardt
invite you to join them
while they marry
Saturday,
April 27, 1974
1 o'clock
Theological Seminary Chapel
W. James St. & College Ave.
Lancaster, Pa.

809

wordplay
UhHuh
Shine
AtLast
ForSure
Groovy
RedHot
SoGood
BabyTalk
NoWay
HotDog
Really
Cuckoo
AhYes
Crash
Abracadabra
Thanks!
OhWow
Ciao
Gotcha
Yassou
InShort
OhBoy
unReal
Bananas
RockOn
25 Different 5x5 NoteCards &
Envelopes, Mixed Colors $8.00
BirthdayBook
740 Madison Avenue
New York 10021
212-249-2408

810

LotsaHearts
LotsaFlowers
LotsaLove
LotsaLaughs
ps:
I love you
You
Zing
I Brought
You a Present
You Send Me
HeyYou
pitapat
Thinking of You
From A Friend
OhWow

811

SILVER

809
Art Directors Craig Bernhardt
Janice Fudyma
Artists Craig Bernhardt
Janice Fudyma
Writers Craig Bernhardt
Janice Fudyma
Agency Graphics-To-Go
Clients Craig Bernhardt
Janice Fudyma

810
Art Director Phelps K. Manning
Designer William R. Tobias
Writers Phelps K. Manning
William R. Tobias
Agency BirthdayBook
Client BirthdayBook

811
Art Director Phelps K. Manning
Designer William R. Tobias
Writers Phelps K. Manning
William R. Tobias
Agency BirthdayBook
Client BirthdayBook

MIYAKO
MIYAKO
20 CLASS A FILTER CIGARETTES

812

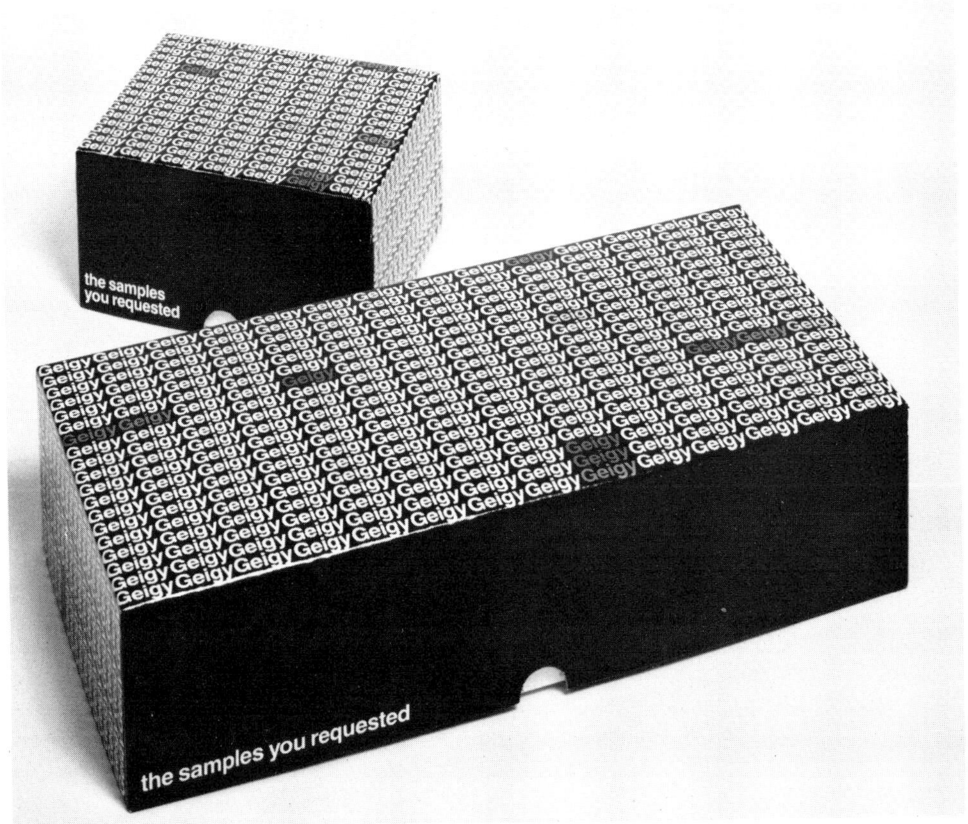
the samples
you requested
the samples you requested

813

812
Art Director James Black
Designers J. Downs
J. Davenport
Agency Moonink Inc.
Client Philip Morris

813
Art Director Bob Paganucci
Designer Bob Paganucci
Agency Geigy Pharmaceuticals
Client Geigy Pharmaceuticals

ABC
74/75
ABC
74/75

814

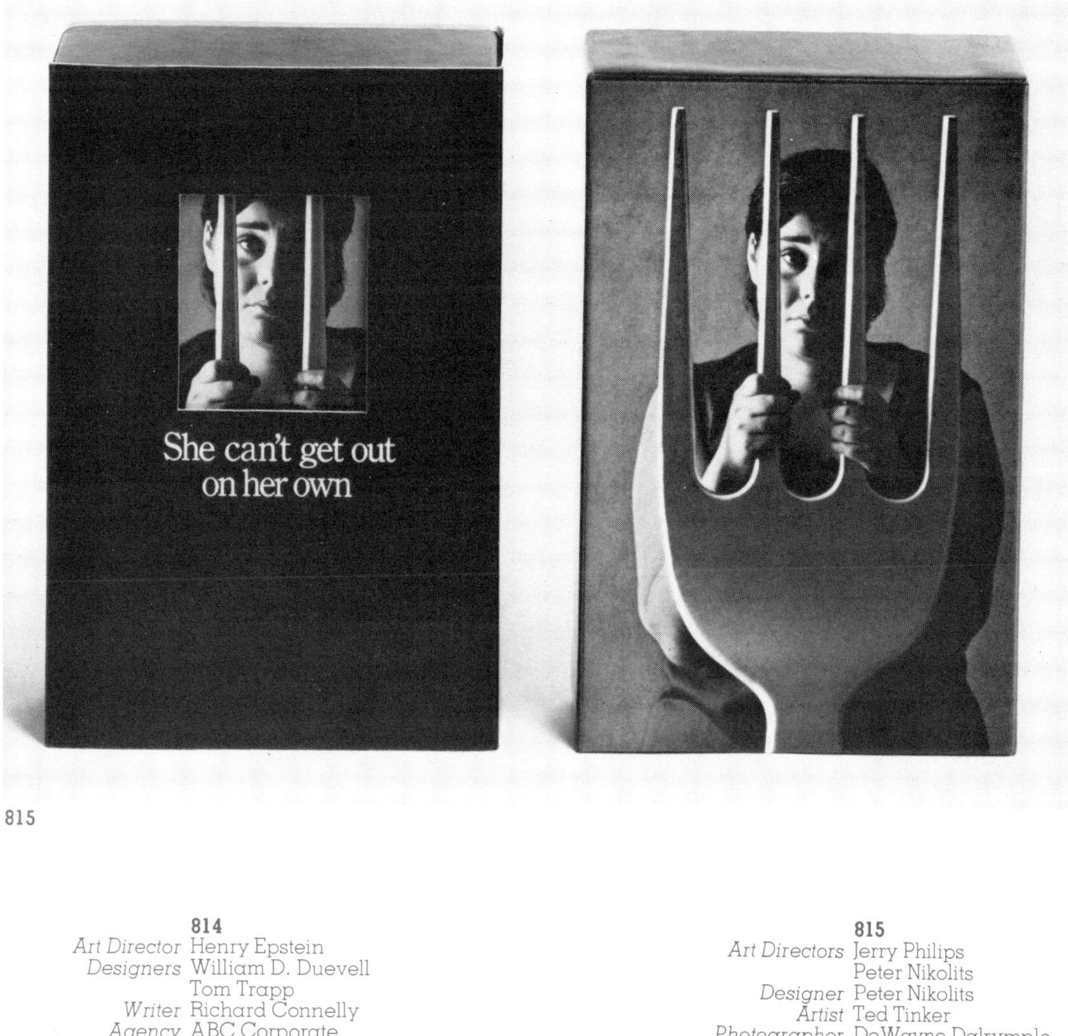
She can't get out
on her own

815

814
Art Director Henry Epstein
Designers William D. Duevell
Tom Trapp
Writer Richard Connelly
Agency ABC Corporate
Art Dept.
Client ABC Public Relations

815
Art Directors Jerry Philips
Peter Nikolits
Designer Peter Nikolits
Artist Ted Tinker
Photographer DeWayne Dalrymple
Agency Kallir, Philips, Ross
Client Beecham-Massengill
Pharmaceuticals

h2ok
PORTABLE DRINKING WATER PURIFIER
h2ok
PORTABLE DRINKING WATER PURIFIER

816

Westminster Sports
Official Table Tennis Set
Westminster Sports

817

816
Art Director Ed Bailey
Designers Ed Bailey
Jim Osborn
Artist John Boatright
Photographer Tom Kelley
Writers John Malmo
Glenda Collier
Agency John Malmo Advertising
Client Better Living Laboratories

817
Art Director Robert P. Gersin
Designers Paul Hanson
V. Lorenzo Porcelli
Photographer Melabee M. Miller
Agency Robert P. Gersin Assoc.
Client Westminster Sports

818

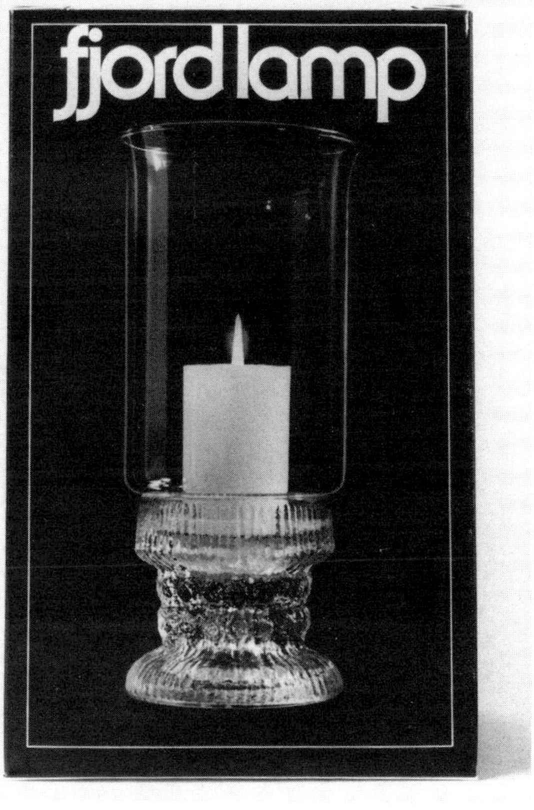
fjord lamp

819

818
Art Director Ken Macey
Designers Androus Noyes
Gary Porcano
Agency deMartin Marona
Cranstoun Downes
Client L'eggs Products

819
Art Director Len Moser
Designer Len Moser
Artist Marini, Climes & Guip
Photographer David VanDeveer
Agency George Hill Co.
Client l. e. smith glass co.

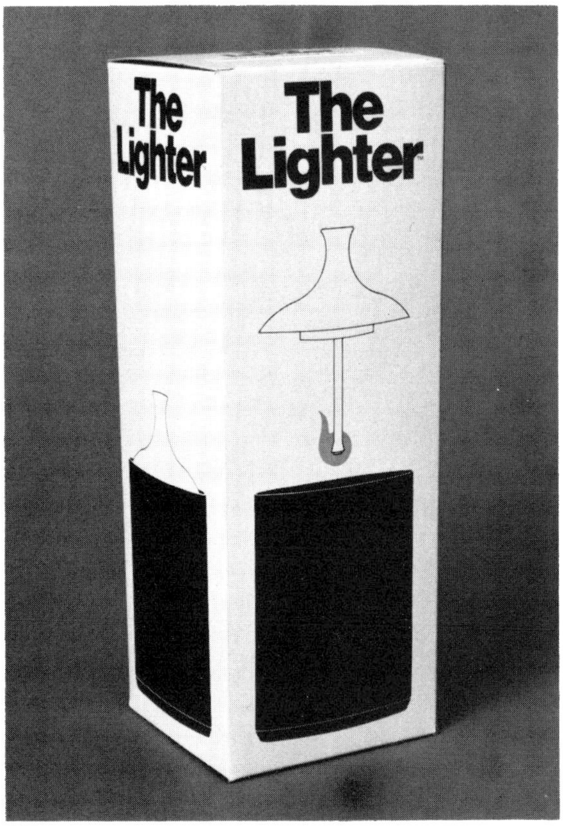
The Lighter
The Lighter

820

Textiles:
Samples
Knoll

821

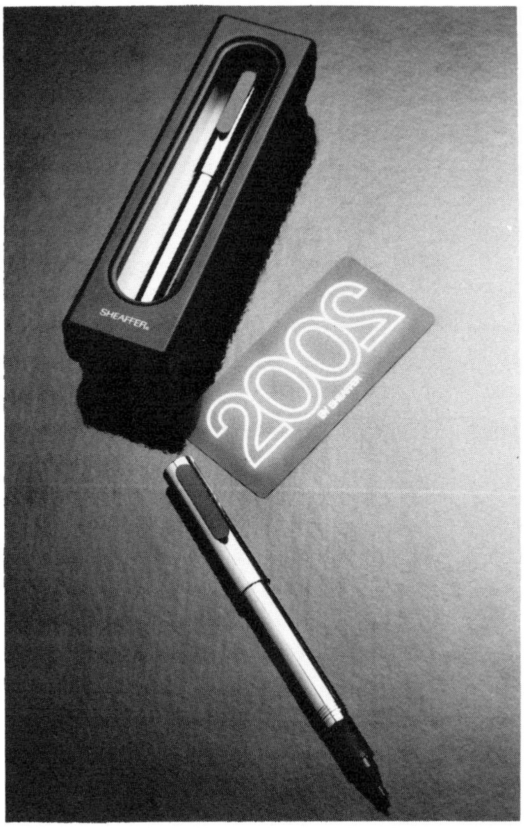
SHEAFFER

822

820
Art Director Fabian Melgar
Designer Fabian Melgar
Artist Fabian Melgar
Writer Fabian Melgar
Agency Fabian Melgar Advertising
Client Westminster Industries

821
Art Director Marjorie Katz
Designer Marjorie Katz
Agency Knoll International
Client Knoll Textiles

822
Art Director Robert W. Hain
Designers Fred Hadtke
Paul Gensior
Pete Connolly
Pete Dillon
Agency Robert Hain Assoc.
Client W. A. Sheaffer Pen Co.

TEA
50
BAGS
NET WT. 4 OZ.
114 GRAMS
Paul Revere

823

PASTENE
CHABLIS
Superior
California
ALCOHOL 12% BY VOLUME
PASTENE
CHIANTI
Superior
California
ALCOHOL 12% BY VOLUME
PASTENE
VIN ROSÉ
Superior
California
ALCOHOL 12% BY VOLUME

824

823
Art Director Edward Morrill
Designer Edward Morrill
Agency Werbin & Morrill
Client Salada Foods

824
Art Director Tom Courtos
Designer Tom Courtos
Artist Tom Courtos
Agency Lois/Chajet Design Group
Client Pastene Wine & Spirits Co.

Lighthouse
Good Day

825

REDWING DEAD OR ALIVE

826

ahmad jamal '73

827

825
Art Director Ted Pettus
Artist Margaret Cusack
Agency Kameny Assoc.
Client Polydor Records

826
Art Director Tony Lane
Designer Tony Lane
Photographer Tony Lane
Agency Fantasy Records
Client Fantasy Records

827
Art Director Rod Dyer
Designer Philip Chiang
Artist Philip Chiang
Photographer Norman Seeff
Agency Rod Dyer, Inc.
Client 20th Century Records

CHARLES IVES
THE 100TH ANNIVERSARY
1874–1974

828

GOLD

828

Art Directors John Berg
Henrietta Condak
Designer Henrietta Condak
Artist Richard Hess
Agency Columbia Records
Client Columbia Records

830

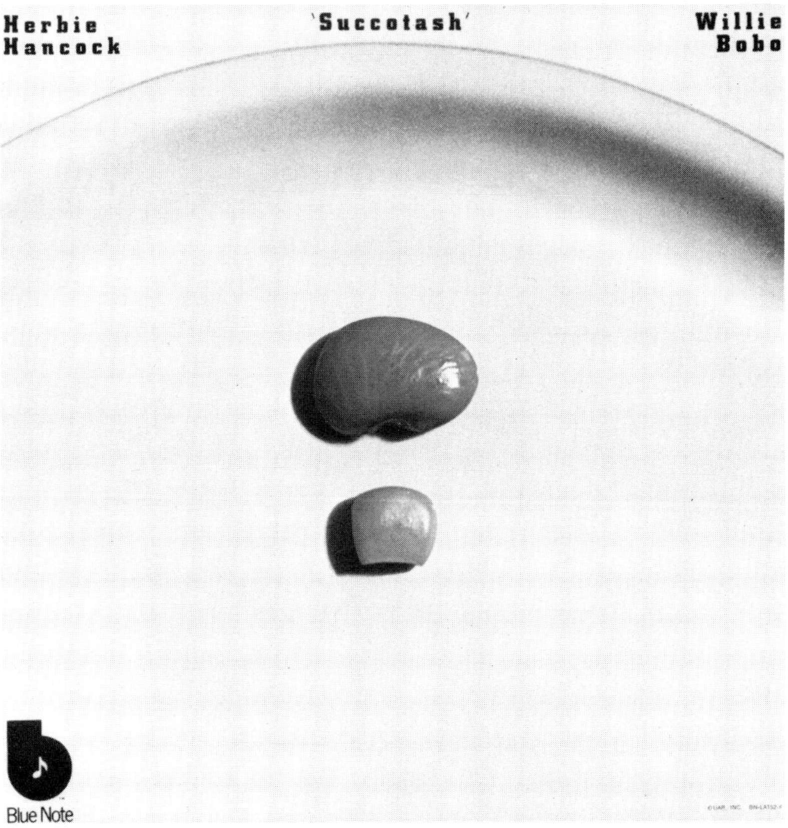

Herbie
Hancock
'Succotash'
Willie
Bobo
Blue Note

831

830
Art Director Ron Coro
Designer Milton Glaser
Artist Milton Glaser
Agency Epic Records Div.
CBS Records
Client Epic Records Div.
CBS Records

831
Art Director Mike Salisbury
Designer Mike Salisbury
Photographer Mike Salisbury
Agency United Artists Artists
Client Blue Note Records

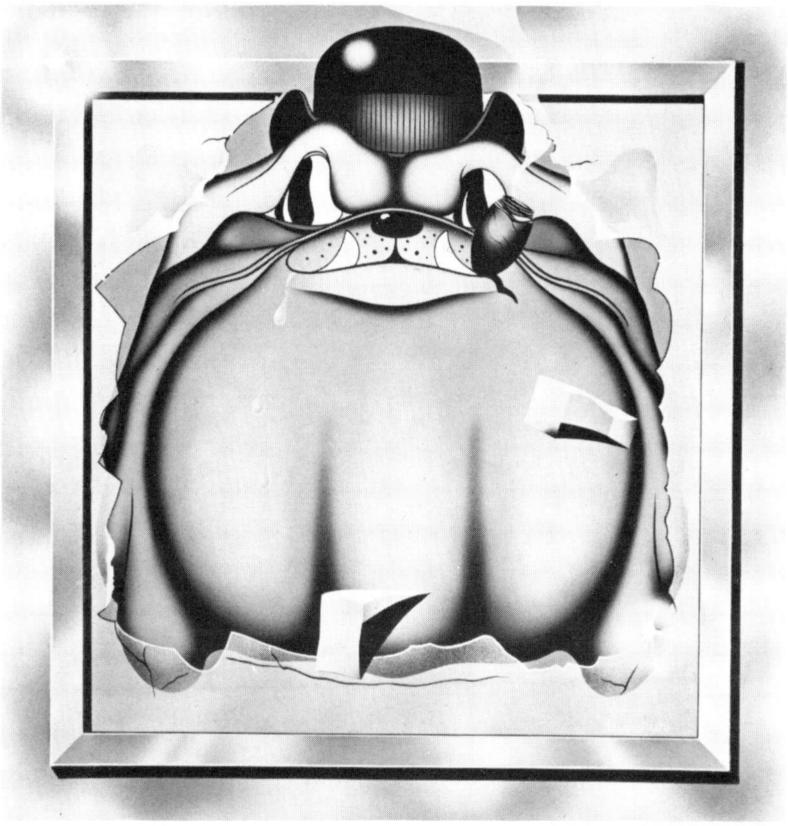

832

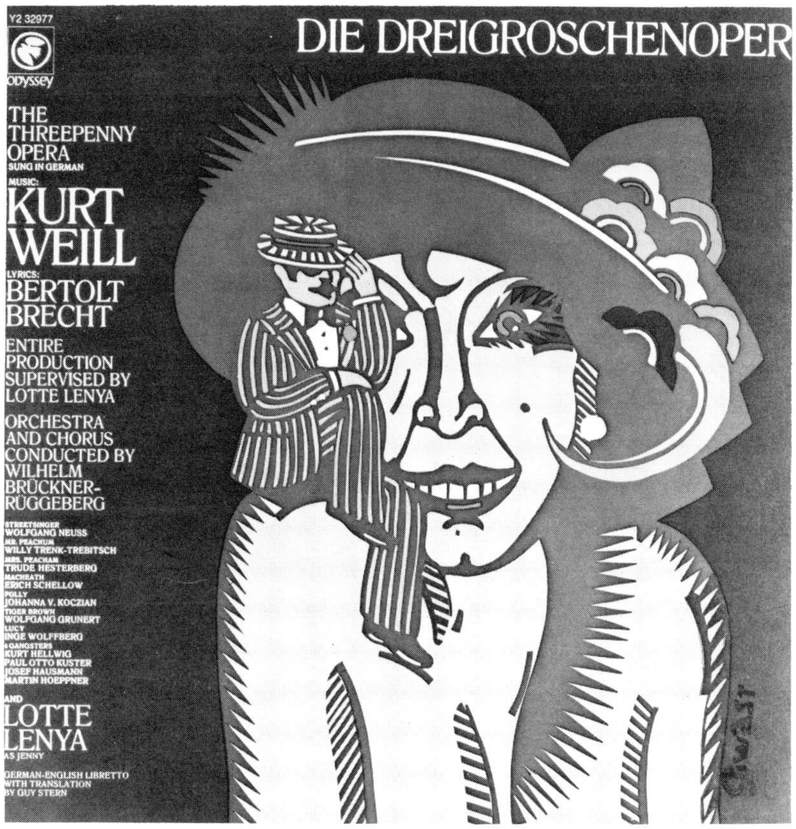
Y2 32977
odyssey
DIE DREIGROSCHENOPER
THE THREEPENNY OPERA
SUNG IN GERMAN
MUSIC:
KURT WEILL
LYRICS:
BERTOLT BRECHT
ENTIRE PRODUCTION SUPERVISED BY LOTTE LENYA
ORCHESTRA AND CHORUS CONDUCTED BY WILHELM BRÜCKNER-RÜGGEBERG
STREETSINGER WOLFGANG NEUSS
MR. PEACHUM WILLY TRENK-TREBITSCH
MRS. PEACHAM TRUDE HESTERBERG
MACHEATH ERICH SCHELLOW
POLLY JOHANNA V. KOCZIAN
TIGER BROWN WOLFGANG GRUNERT
LUCY INGE WOLFFBERG
4 GANGSTERS KURT HELLWIG PAUL OTTO KUSTER JOSEF HAUSMANN MARTIN HOEPPNER
AND
LOTTE LENYA
AS JENNY
GERMAN-ENGLISH LIBRETTO WITH TRANSLATION BY GUY STERN
Chwast

833

832
Art Director Milton Sincoff
Designer Milton Sincoff
Artist Tom Upshur
Agency Buddah Records
Client Buddah Records

833
Art Directors John Berg
Eloise Smith
Designer Seymour Chwast
Artist Seymour Chwast
Agency Push Pin Studios
Client Odyssey Records Div.
CBS Records

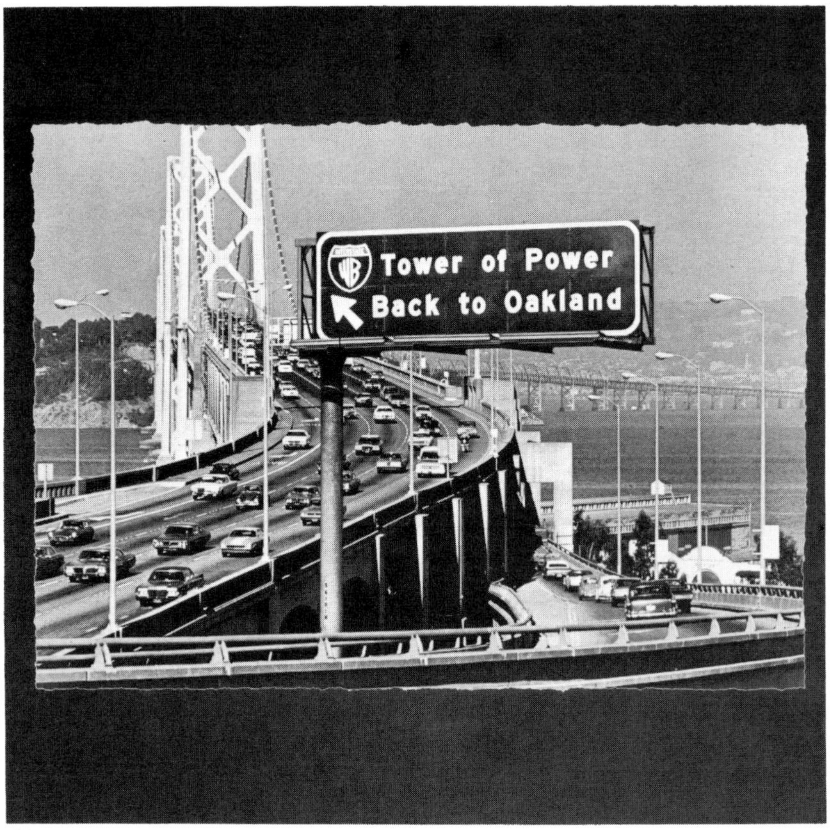
Tower of Power
Back to Oakland

835

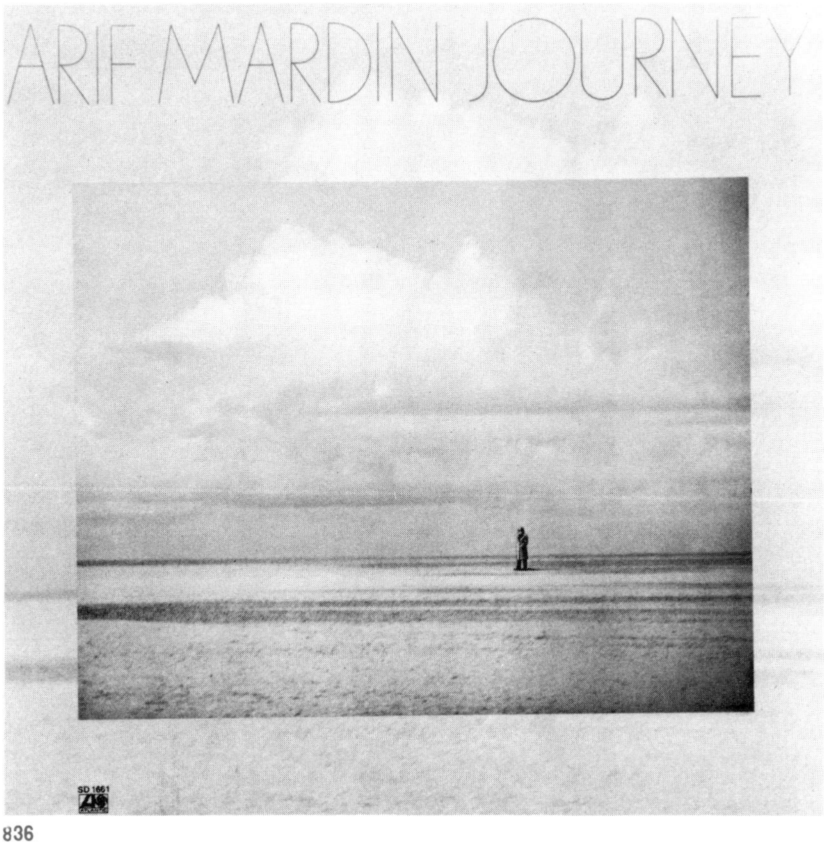
ARIF MARDIN JOURNEY

836

835
Art Directors Ed Thrasher
Bruce Steinberg
Designer Bruce Steinberg
Photographer Bruce Steinberg
Writers Stephen Kupka
Emilio Castillo
Agency Bruce Steinberg
Client Warner Bros. Records

836
Art Director Bob Defrin
Designer Basil Pao
Photographers Chris Callas
Martin Schreiber
Agency Atlantic Records
Client Atlantic Records

EDDIE HARRIS IS IT IN
Palombi '74

837

837
Art Director Bob Defrin
Designer Basil Pao
Artist Peter Palombi
Agency Atlantic Records
Client Atlantic Records

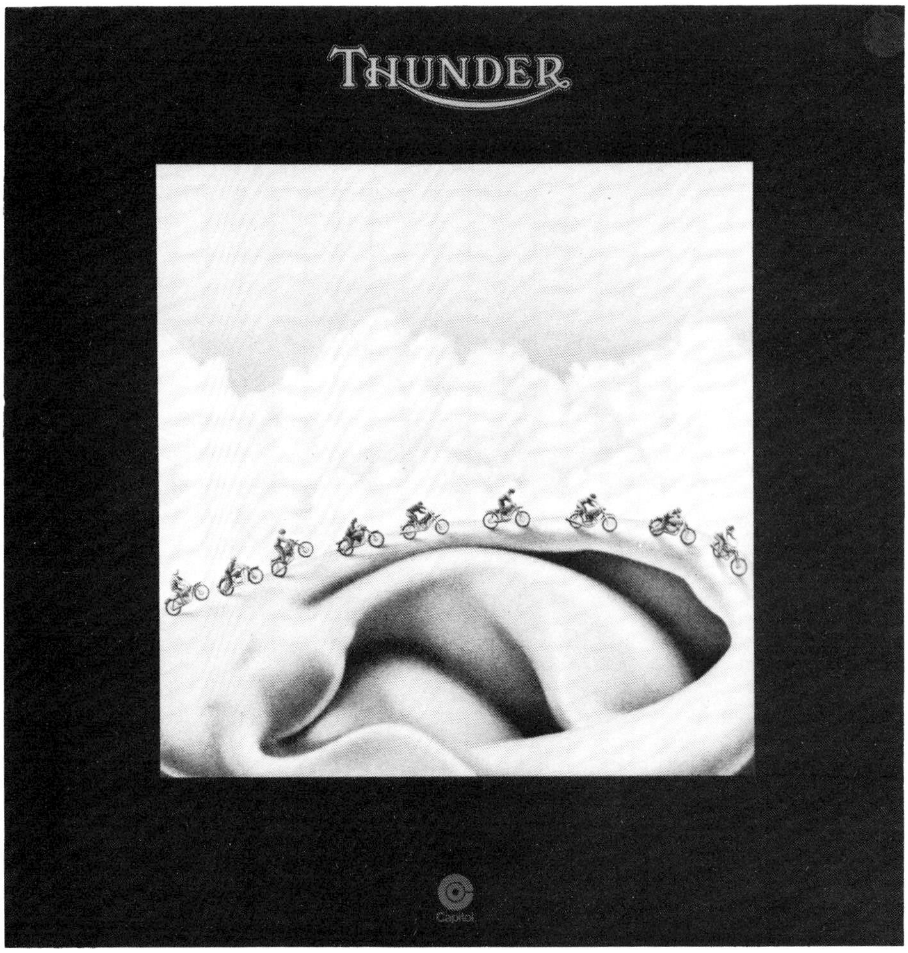
THUNDER
Capitol

838

Arthur, Hurley & Gottlieb

839

Chicago

840

SILVER

838
Art Director Woody Pirtle
Designer Woody Pirtle
Artists Bill Jenkins
Woody Pirtle
Agency The Richards Group
Client Capitol Records

839
Art Director Roland Young
Designer Mick Haggerty
Artist Mick Haggerty
Photographer George Jerman
Agency Art Attack
Client A&M Records

840
Art Director John Berg
Designers John Berg
Nick Fasciano
Artist Nick Fasciano
Agency Columbia Records
Client Columbia Records

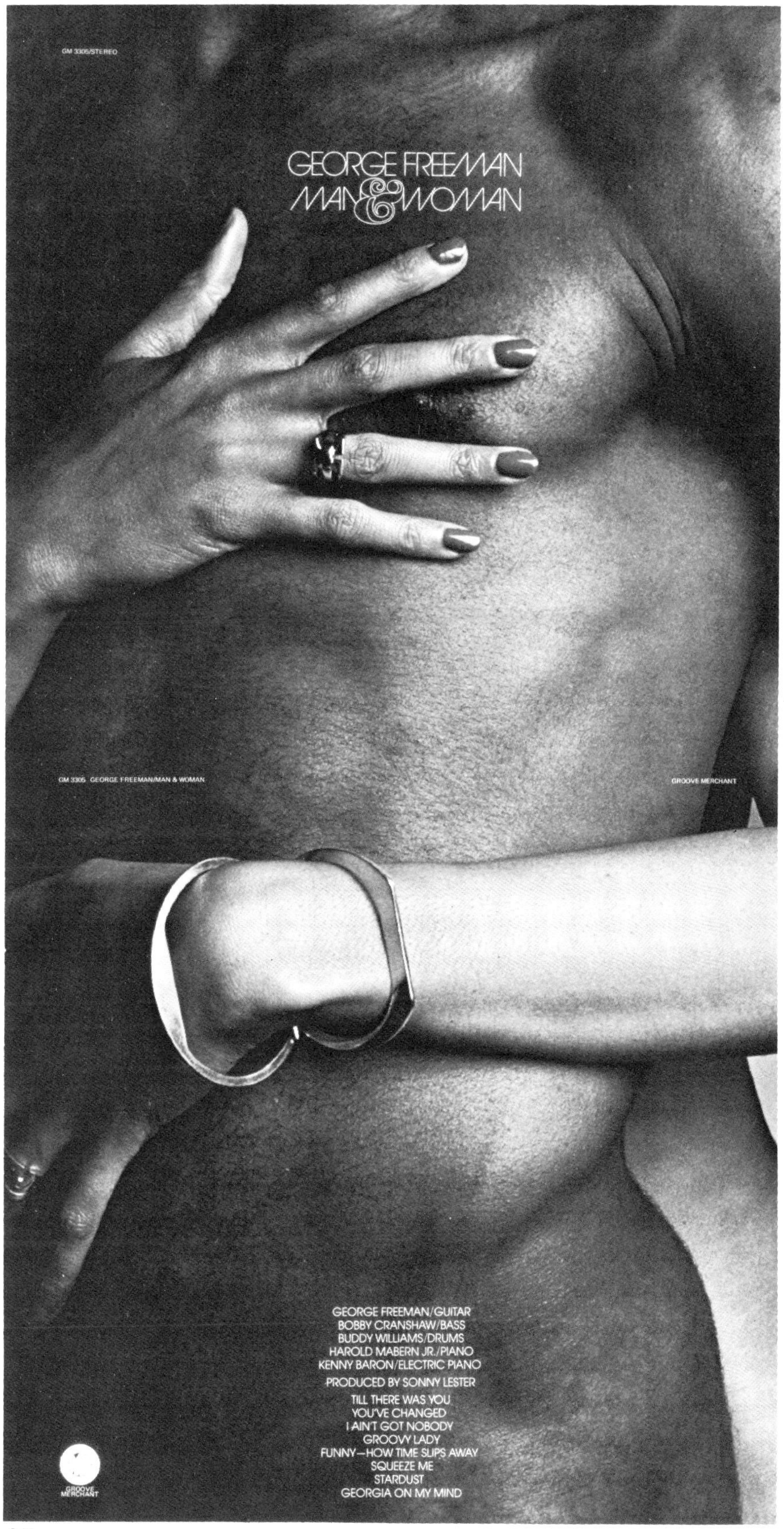
GM 3305/STEREO
GEORGE FREEMAN
MAN & WOMAN
GM 3305 GEORGE FREEMAN/MAN & WOMAN
GROOVE MERCHANT
GEORGE FREEMAN/GUITAR
BOBBY CRANSHAW/BASS
BUDDY WILLIAMS/DRUMS
HAROLD MABERN JR./PIANO
KENNY BARON/ELECTRIC PIANO
PRODUCED BY SONNY LESTER
TILL THERE WAS YOU
YOU'VE CHANGED
I AIN'T GOT NOBODY
GROOVY LADY
FUNNY—HOW TIME SLIPS AWAY
SQUEEZE ME
STARDUST
GEORGIA ON MY MIND
GROOVE MERCHANT

841

841
Art Directors David Lartaud
Frank Daniel
Designer David Lartaud
Photographer Manny Gonzales
Agency Pickwick International
Client Groove Merchant Records

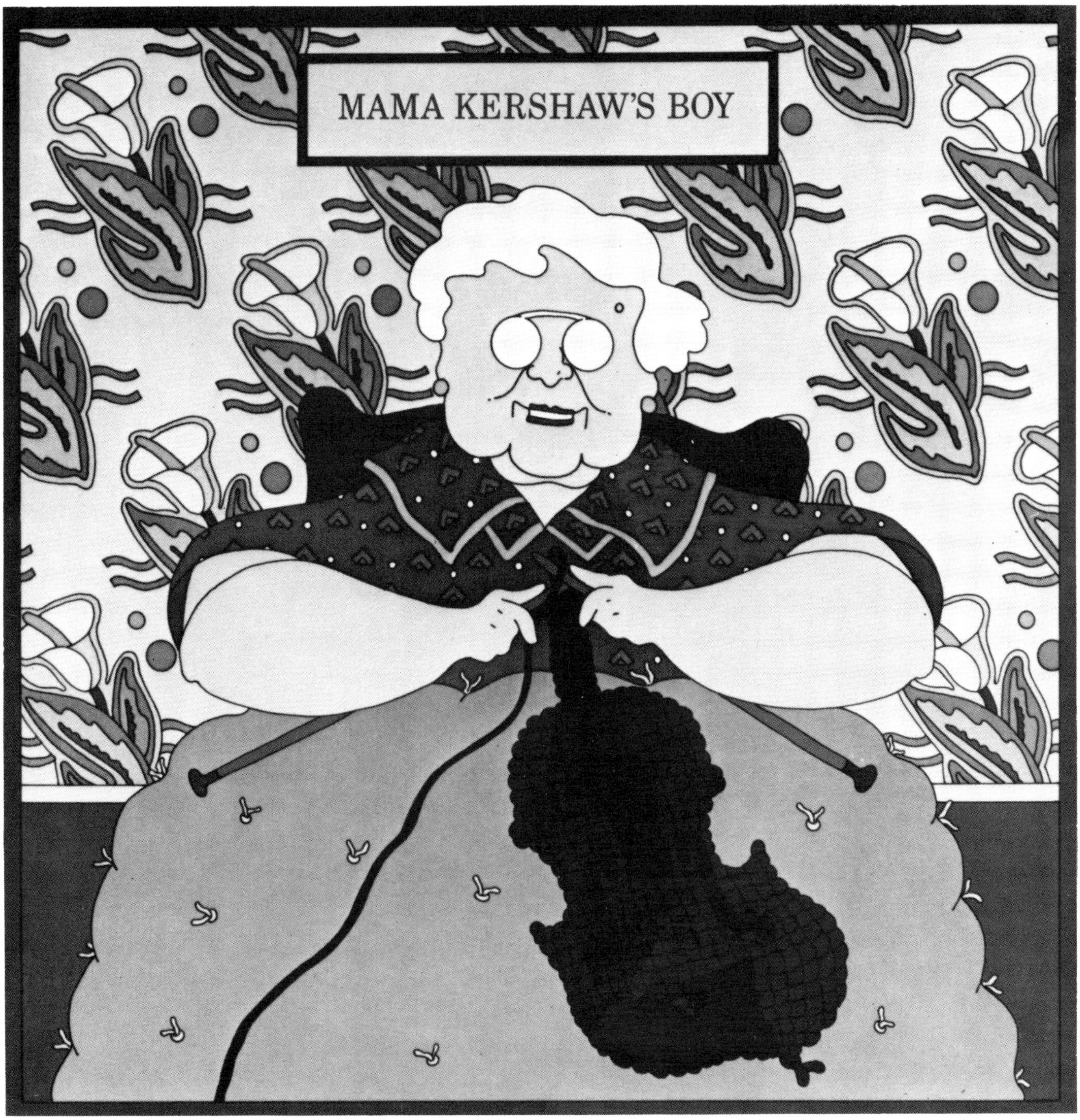
MAMA KERSHAW'S BOY

842

842
Art Director Ed Thrasher
Designers John Casado
Barbara Casado
Artists John Casado
Barbara Casado
Agency Warner Bros. Records
Client Warner Bros. Records

Lorraine Ellison

843

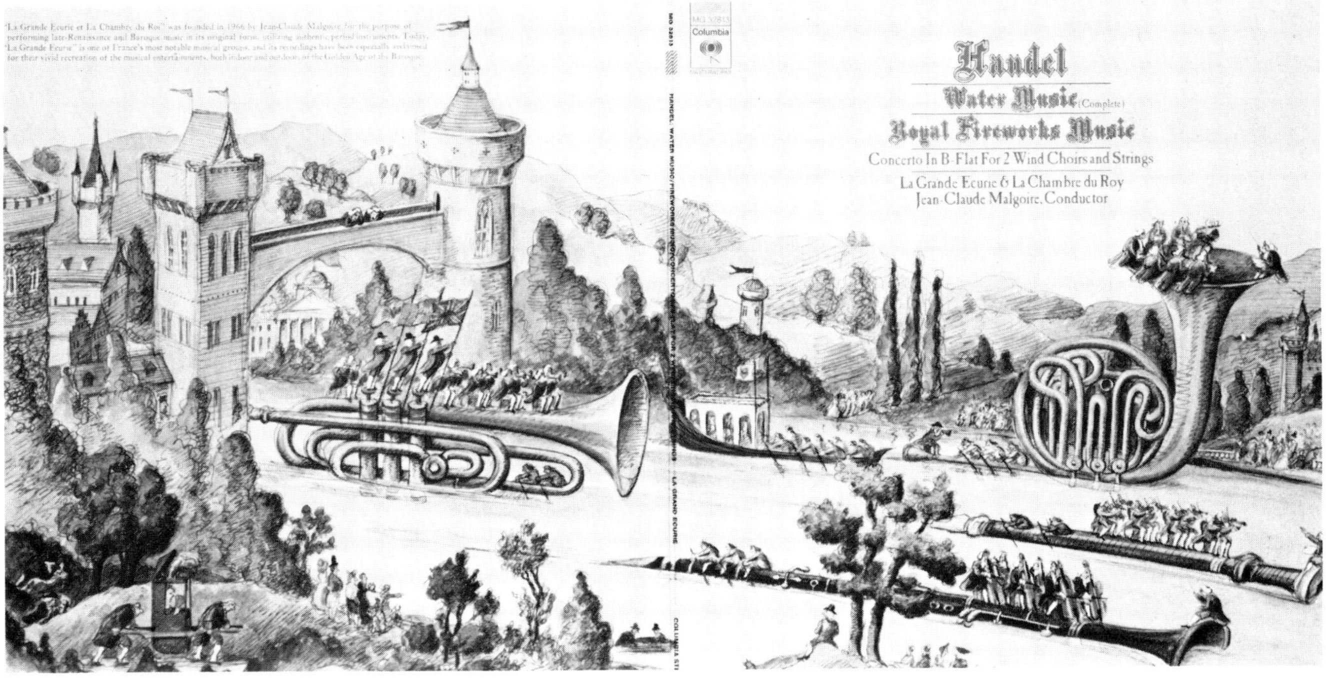
Columbia
Handel
Water Music (Complete)
Royal Fireworks Music
Concerto In B-Flat For 2 Wind Choirs and Strings
La Grande Ecurie & La Chambre du Roy
Jean-Claude Malgoire, Conductor

844

843
Art Director Ed Thrasher
Designer Gribbitt
Photographer Gary Gross
Agency Warner Bros. Records
Client Warner Bros. Records

844
Art Director John Berg
Designer John Berg
Artist Edward Sorel
Agency Columbia Records
Client Columbia Records

SOUNDS OF
SOLID COUNTRY
POUCH
U.S. MARINE CORPS PUBLIC SERVICE PROGRAMS

845

Chicago

846

Y 32884
Columbia
odyssey
VIVALDI
THE FOUR SEASONS
YOSHIO UNNO
violinist and conductor
The NHK String Ensemble

847

845
Art Director William J. Conlon
Designer William J. Conlon
Artist Mabey Trousdell
Writer Tim Sullivan
Agency J. Walter Thompson
Client U.S. Marine Corps

846
Art Director John Berg
Designers Nick Fasciano
John Berg
Artist Dallas Cap & Emblem Co.
Agency Columbia Records
Client Columbia Records

847
Art Director John Berg
Designer John Berg
Photographer Jay Maisel
Agency Columbia Records
Client Columbia Records

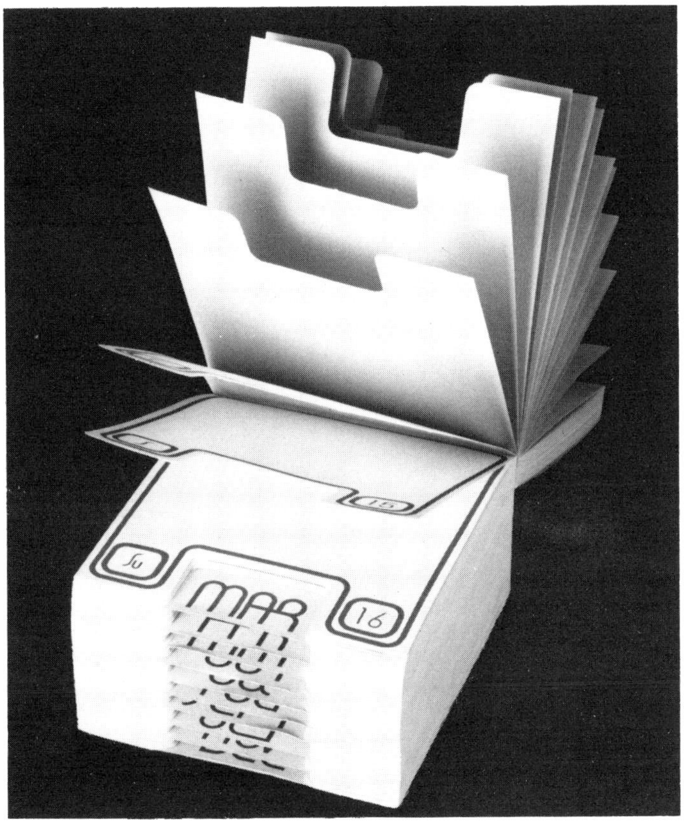

848

Push Pin Graphic

849

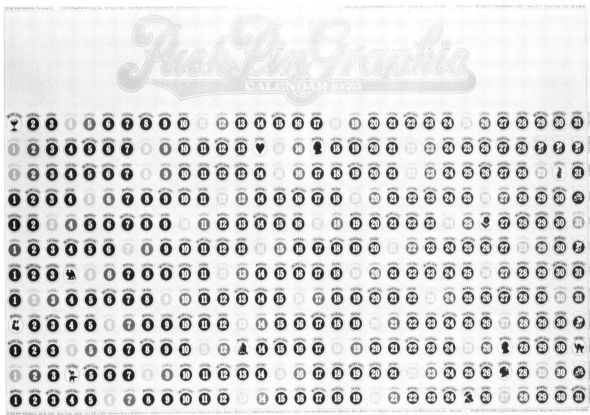

848
Art Director Lamont Thomas
Designer Lamont Thomas
Artist Lamont Thomas
Agency Cliff Covington Design
Client Cliff Covington Design

849
Art Director Seymour Chwast
Designer Seymour Chwast
Agency Push Pin Studios
Client Push Pin Studios

Hermann Hesse 1975 Calendar Illustrated by Milton Glaser

MAY

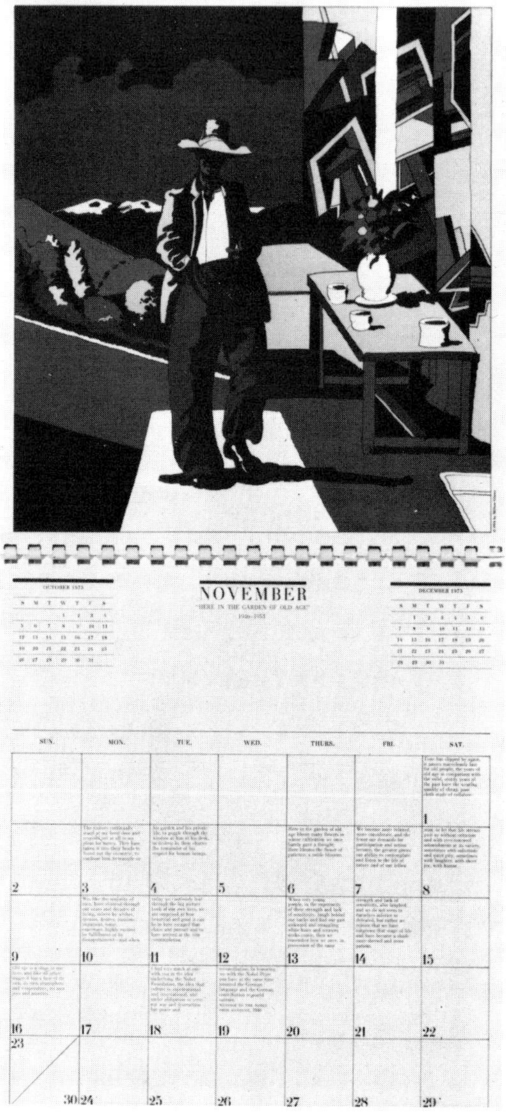
NOVEMBER

850

SILVER

850
Art Director Dorris Janowitz
Designer Milton Glaser
Artist Milton Glaser
Editor Linda Lee
Agency Farrar, Straus & Giroux
Client Farrar, Straus & Giroux

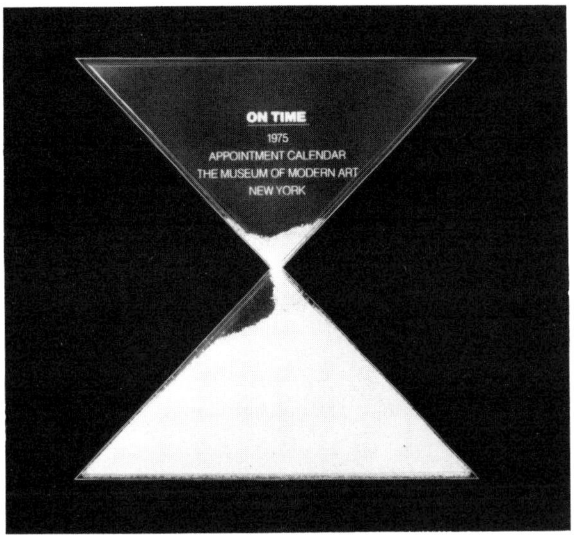
ON TIME
1975
APPOINTMENT CALENDAR
THE MUSEUM OF MODERN ART
NEW YORK

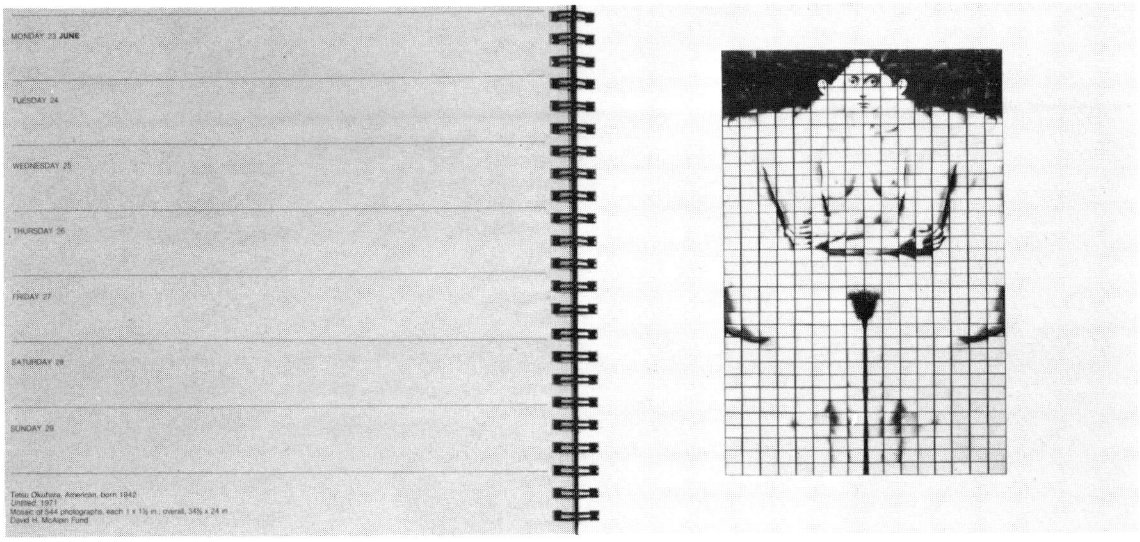
MONDAY 23 JUNE
TUESDAY 24
WEDNESDAY 25
THURSDAY 26
FRIDAY 27
SATURDAY 28
SUNDAY 29
Tetsu Okuhara, American, born 1942
Untitled. 1971
Mosaic of 544 photographs, each 1 x 1½ in.; overall, 34⅝ x 24 in.
David H. McAlpin Fund

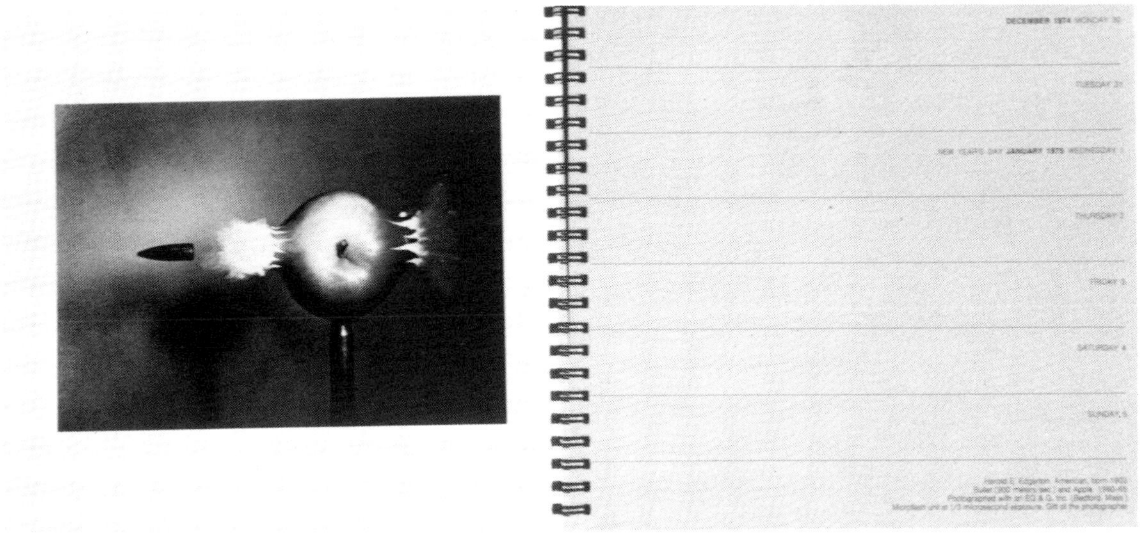
DECEMBER 1974 MONDAY 30
TUESDAY 31
NEW YEAR'S DAY JANUARY 1975 WEDNESDAY 1
THURSDAY 2
FRIDAY 3
SATURDAY 4
SUNDAY 5

851

851
Art Director Jon Lopez
Designer Jon Lopez
Photographers Various
Editor Mary Lee Bandy
Writer Marjorie Munsterberg
Agency Jon Lopez Design
Client Museum of Modern Art

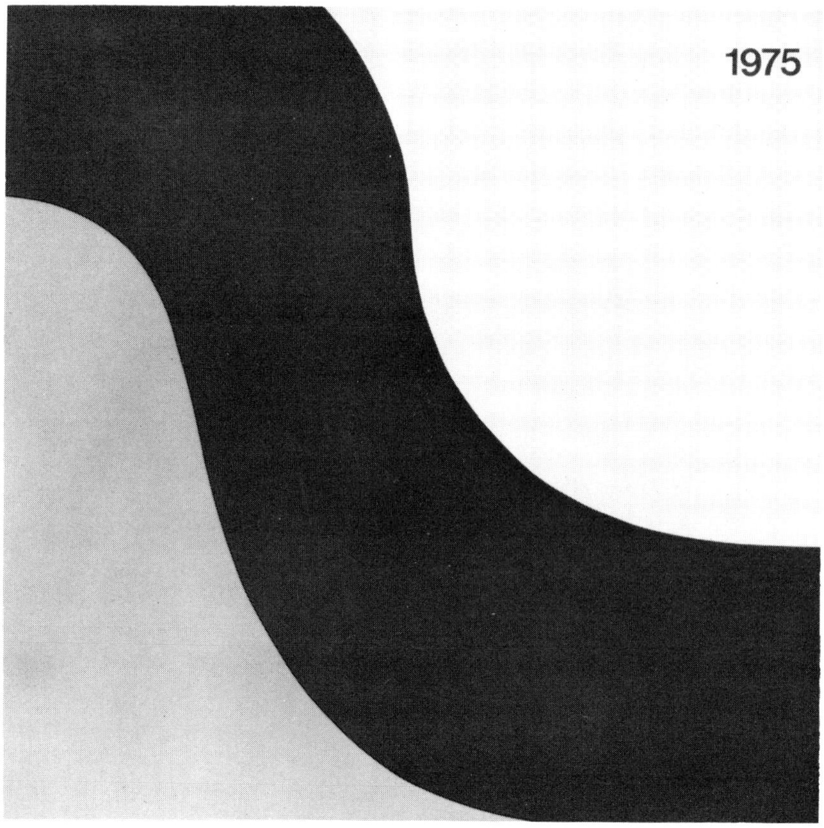
1975

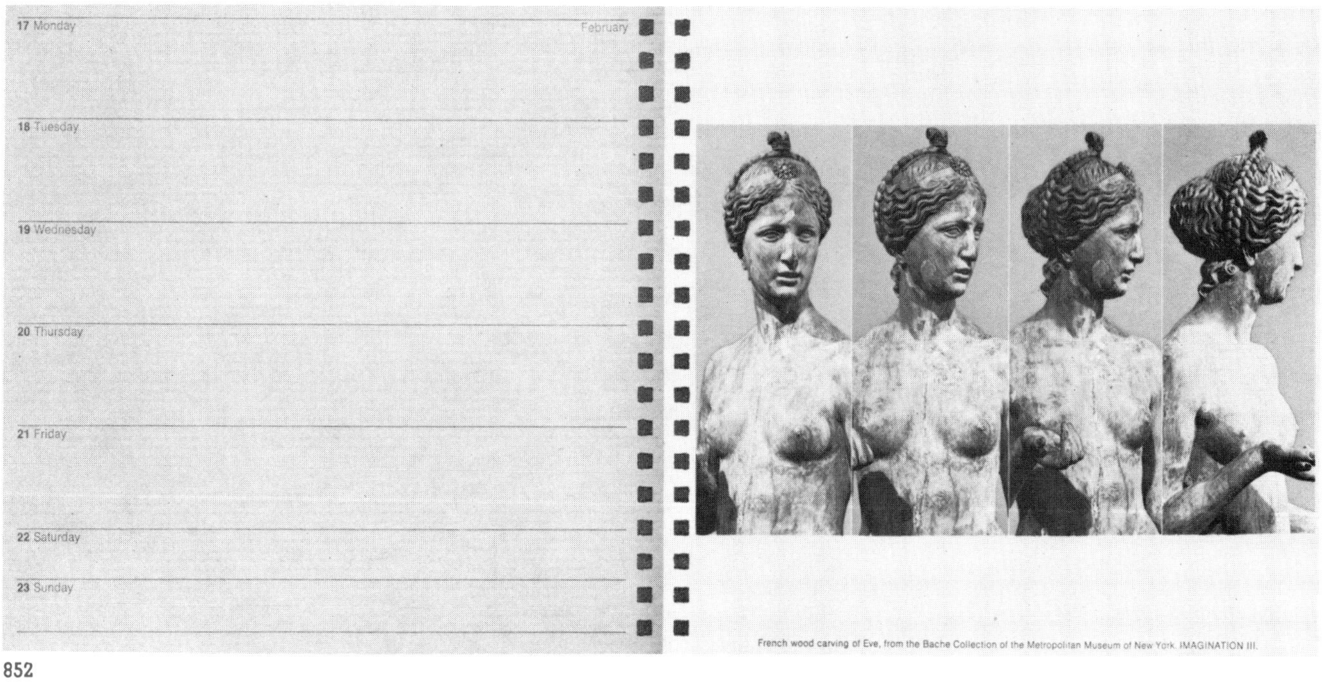
17 Monday
February
18 Tuesday
19 Wednesday
20 Thursday
21 Friday
22 Saturday
23 Sunday
French wood carving of Eve, from the Bache Collection of the Metropolitan Museum of New York. IMAGINATION III.

852

852
Art Director James Miho
Designer Tomoko Miho
Writer David Brown
Agency Champion Papers
Client Champion Papers

FASTLIVIN
OCTOBER 1975
PEPSI

COOLTALKIN
FEBRUARY 1975
PEPSI
PEPSI

GOODBUZZIN
MAY 1975
PEPSI

HIGHWALKIN
SEPTEMBER 1975
PEPSI

853

853
Art Director Judy Smith
Designers Seymour Chwast
Milton Glaser
Artists Seymour Chwast
Milton Glaser
Doug Gervasi
Haruo Miyauchi
Christian Piper
George Stavrinos
Agency Boase Massimi Pollitt
London
Client Pepsi-International

BROOKLYN
CHEL-SEA
THEATRE COUNTRY
Brooklyn;
home of the Best Play
and the Best Musical of 1974.
Last year, Brooklyn's Chelsea Theater Center
won the New York Drama Critics Awards
for Best Play (David Storey's The Contractor)
and Best Musical (Leonard Bernstein's Candide).
That's a little like winning the World Series
and the Super Bowl in the same season.
If you want to catch the action this year,
subscribe now for the coming season.
The Chelsea Theater Center
at the Brooklyn Academy of Music.
For information call: 783-5110

854

Give everybody Cutty!
SCOTS WHISKY
86 Proof

855

854
Art Director Doug Johnson
Designer Herb Bossardt
Artist Doug Johnson
Writers Doug Johnson
Michael David
Agency Performing Dogs
Client Chelsea Theater Center of Brooklyn

855
Art Director Steve Kambanis
Designer Steve Kambanis
Photographer Allen Vogel
Writer Ron Holland
Agency Lois Holland Callaway
Client Buckingham Corp.

Knoll Textiles: The Collection
December 11 1973-January 4, 1974
745 Fifth Avenue, New York

856

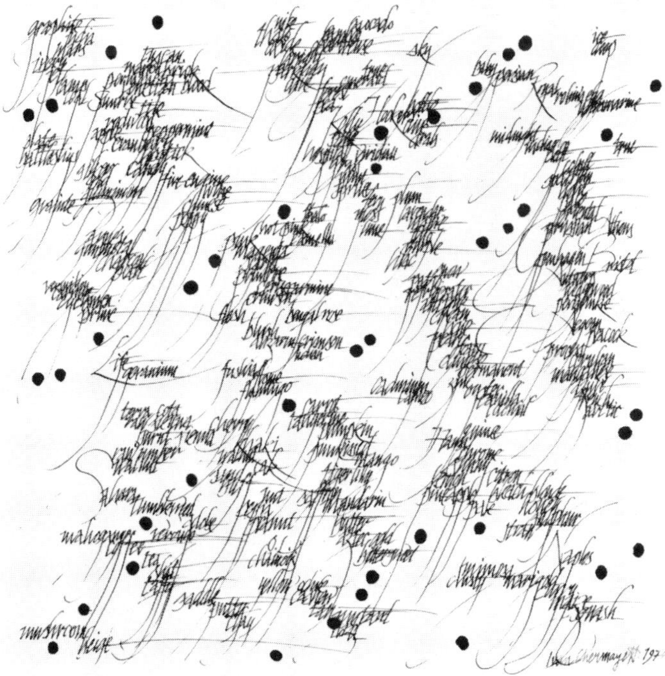

857

SILVER

856
Art Director Marjorie Katz
Designer Jim Garrison
Photographer Rudolf Beck
Agency Knoll International
Client Knoll Textiles

857
Art Director James Miho
Designer James Miho
Artist Ivan Chermayeff
Agency Chermayeff & Geismar Assoc.
Client American Institute of Graphic Arts

Dodgers
NY GIANTS
THE WAY IT WAS
Great sports events recaptured on TV Thursdays 8pm Channel 13
Mobil

858

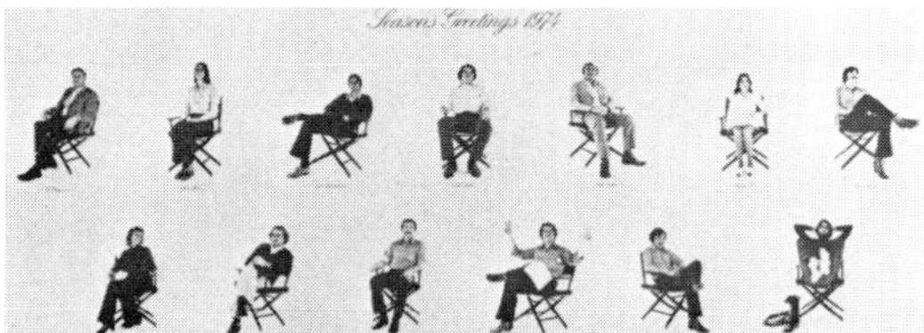
Seasons Greetings 1974

859

858
Art Director Irwin Glusker
Designer Irwin Glusker
Artist Richard Hess
Writer Gordon Bowman
Agency Irwin Glusker
Client Mobil Oil Corp.

859
Art Director Richard Burns
Designers Doug Akagi
John Clark
Photographer John Andersen
Writers Scott Buchanan
Peter Walker
Agency SWA Communications
Client SWA Communications

Having a talent isn't worth much unless you know what to do with it.
Degree and Non-Degree Programs. Day and Evening.
Film, Photography, Media Arts (Advertising, Fashion, Illustration, Design), Crafts (Ceramics, Jewelry)
Fine Arts (Painting, Sculpture, Printmaking), Video Tape, Dance, Humanities
School of Visual Arts
209 East 23rd Street, New York, New York 10010 · (212) 679-7350
Drawing by Marshall Arisman

860

GRAPHIC DESIGN

860
Art Directors Richard Wilde
Marshall Arisman
Designer Richard Wilde
Artist Marshall Arisman
Writer Dee Ito
Agency School of Visual Arts
Client School of Visual Arts

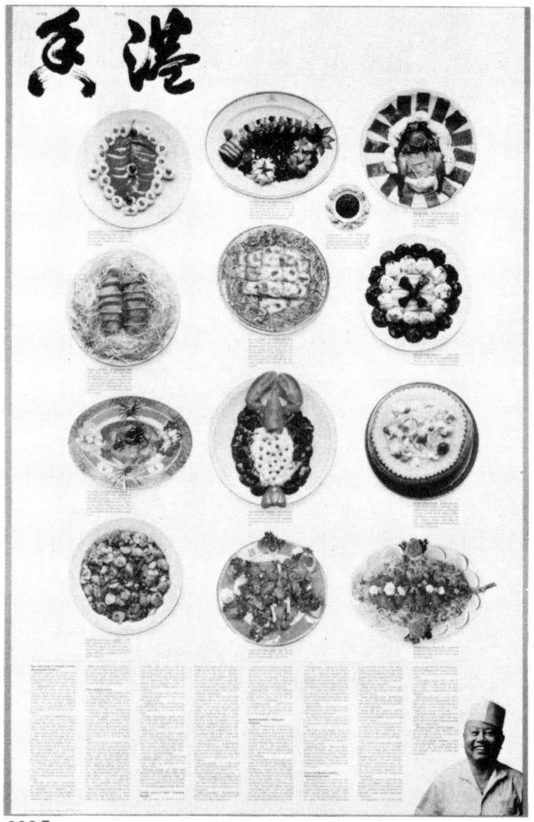

860A

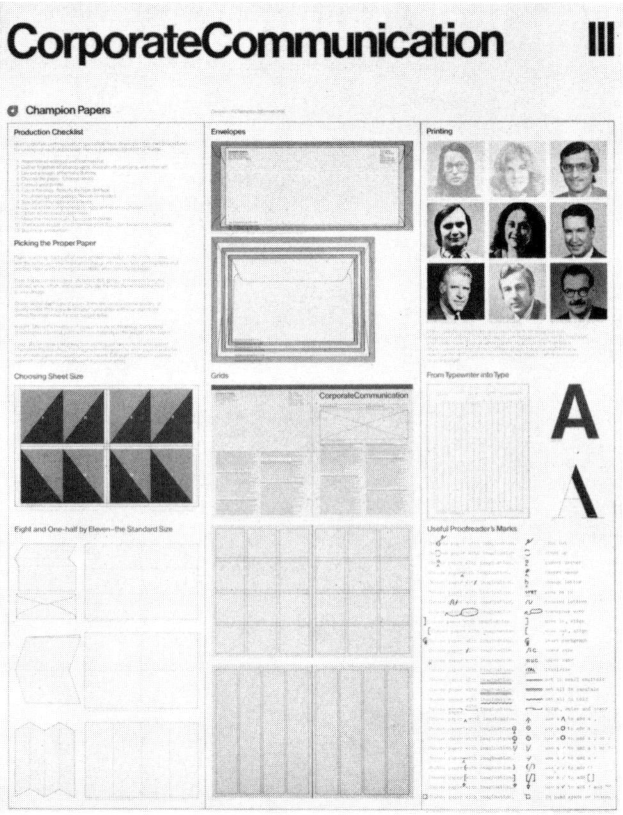
CorporateCommunication III
Champion Papers
Production Checklist
Picking the Proper Paper
Envelopes
Printing
Choosing Sheet Size
Grids
From Typewriter into Type
A
Eight and One-half by Eleven—the Standard Size
Useful Proofreader's Marks

861

There are certain truths which are true no matter how much the world may question or deny them. In the economic realm, for instance, you cannot legislate the poor into freedom by legislating the wealthy out of it. You cannot multiply wealth by dividing it. Governments cannot give to people what they do not first take away from people. And that which one man receives without working for, another man must work for without receiving it. And nothing can kill the initiative of a people quicker than for half to get the idea they need not work because the other half will feed them, and for the other half to get the idea it does no good to work since someone else receives the rewards.

862

860A
Art Director James Miho
Designer James Miho
Photographer Jerry Sarapeochiello
Writer David Brown
Agency Champion Papers
Client Champion Papers

861
Art Director James Miho
Designer Tomoko Miho
Artist Marjorie Guarcello
Writer David Brown
Agency Champion Papers
Client Champion Papers

862
Art Director Steve Jacobs
Designer Steve Jacobs
Writer Edgerton Minnesota Enterprise
Agency Steven Jacobs Design
Client Steven Jacobs Design

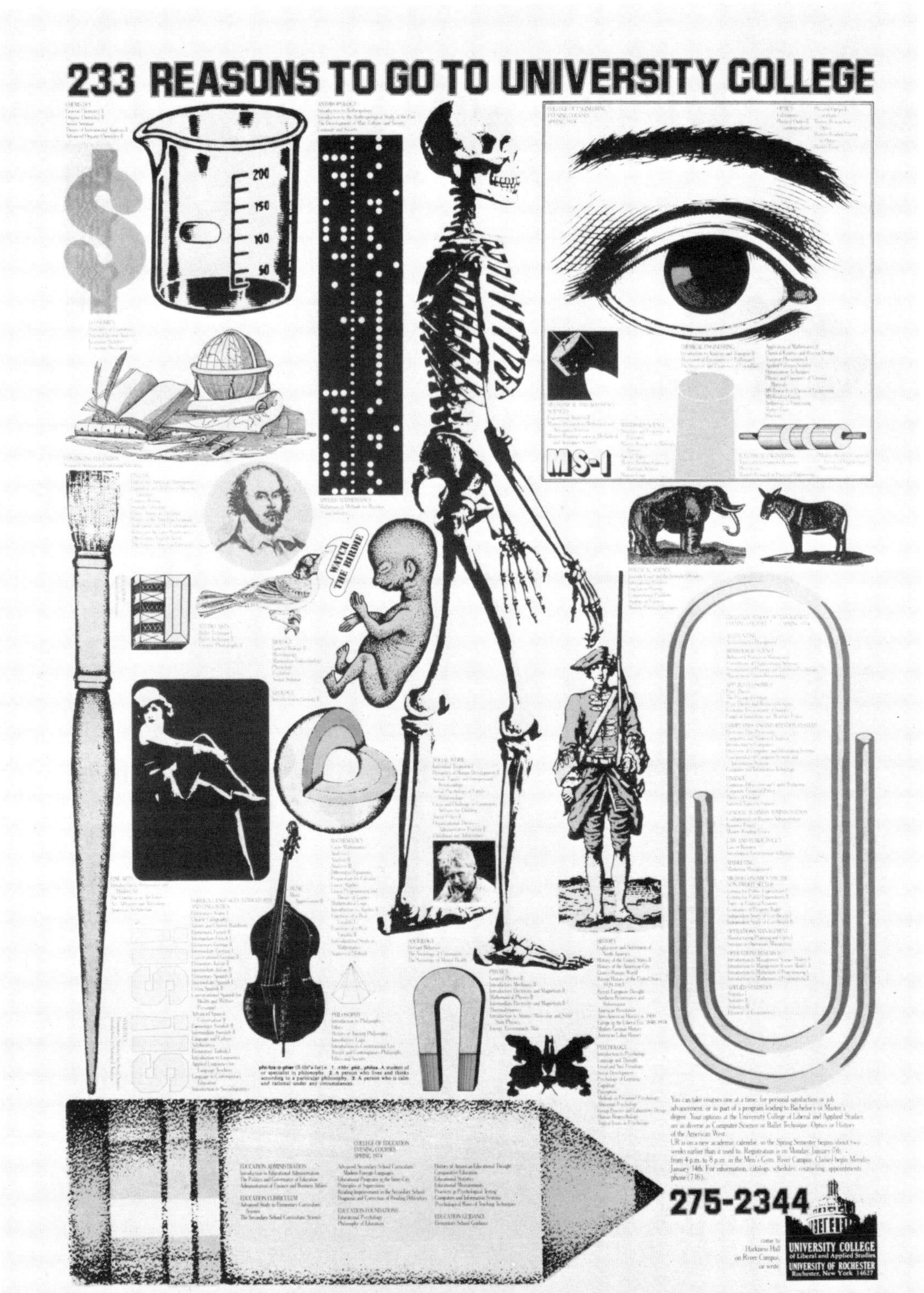
233 REASONS TO GO TO UNIVERSITY COLLEGE
WATCH THE BIRDIE
MS-1
275-2344
come to Harkness Hall on River Campus, or write:
UNIVERSITY COLLEGE
of Liberal and Applied Studies
UNIVERSITY OF ROCHESTER
Rochester, New York 14627

863

863
Art Director John Kuchera
Designer Mabey Trousdell
Artist Mabey Trousdell
Writer James S. Peck
Agency Hutchins/Darcy
Client University College
University of Rochester

The Return of
OOM
PAH
PAH
an exhibition of The American Brass Band
81st Street Entrance
January 7-February 3

864

CITY CENTER OF MUSIC AND DRAMA, INC. PRESENTS THE
ALVIN AILEY
CITY CENTER DANCE THEATER
THREE WEEKS
DECEMBER 3-22, 1974
CITY CENTER 55TH STREET THEATER
131 WEST 55TH STREET NEW YORK CITY

865

Best Wishes and A Happy New Year.

866

864
Art Director Stuart Silver
Designer Melanie Roher
Artist Melanie Roher
Agency Metropolitan Museum of Art
Client Metropolitan Museum of Art

865
Art Director Michael Hampton
Designer Michael Hampton
Artist Michael Hampton
Agency Michael Hampton
Client City Center Dance Theater

866
Art Director Ralph Parenio
Designer Ralph Parenio
Writer Susan Johnson
Agency Ralph Parenio Graphic Design
Client Ralph Parenio Graphic Design

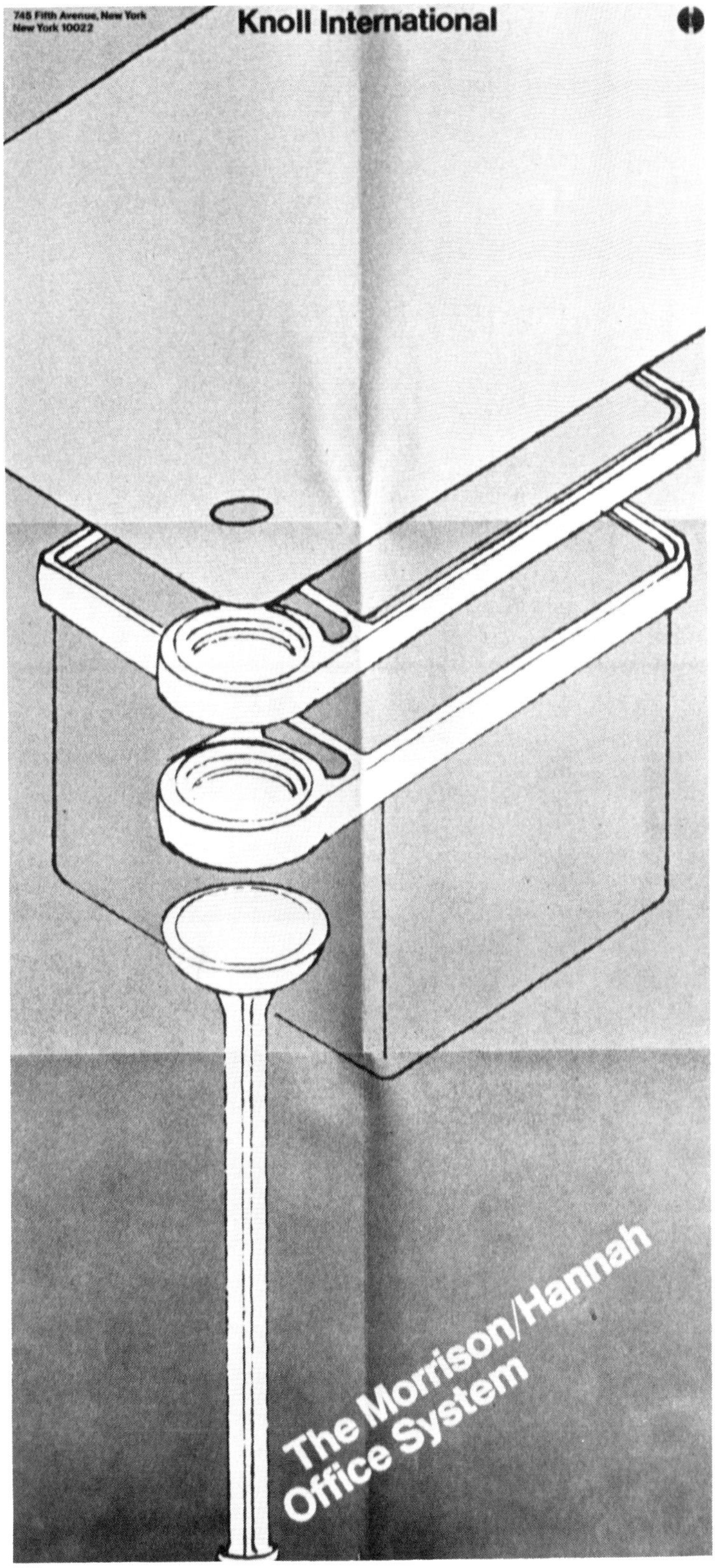
745 Fifth Avenue, New York
New York 10022
Knoll International
The Morrison/Hannah
Office System

867

867
Art Director Marjorie Katz
Designer Marjorie Katz
Artist Michael Donovan
Writer Suzanne Slesin
Agency Knoll International
Client Knoll International

Joy

868

American Society of Landscape Architecture Foundation
Publications
Outstanding publications and programmed teaching materials are available from the American Society of Landscape Architecture Foundation publications office. For a complete listing, prices and ordering information write to:
American Society of Landscape Architecture Foundation
Publications Department
1750 Old Meadow Road
McLean, Virginia 22101

869

868
Art Director Ralph Parenio
Designer Ralph Parenio
Photographer Maury Garber
Agency Ralph Parenio/Graphic Design
Client Ralph Parenio/Graphic Design

869
Art Director David J. Franek
Designer David J. Franek
Artist David J. Franek
Agency Ashton-Worthington
Client American Society of Landscape Architecture Foundation

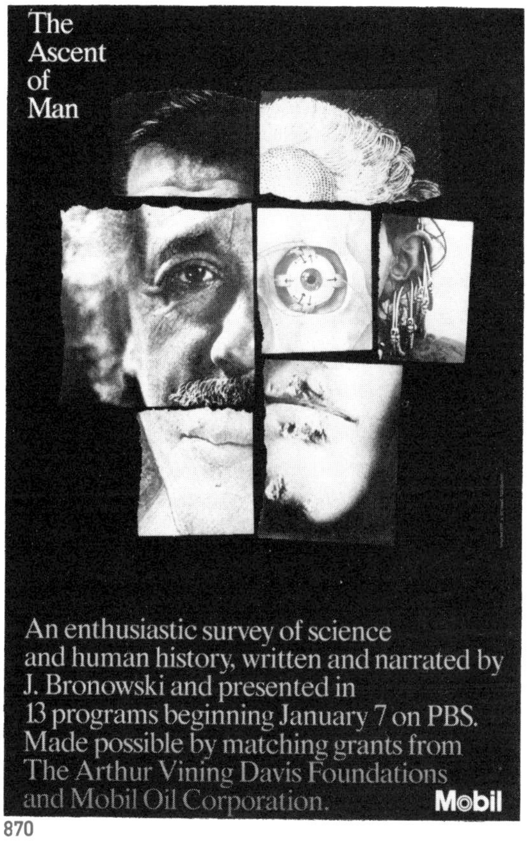
The Ascent of Man
An enthusiastic survey of science and human history, written and narrated by J. Bronowski and presented in 13 programs beginning January 7 on PBS. Made possible by matching grants from The Arthur Vining Davis Foundations and Mobil Oil Corporation.
Mobil

870

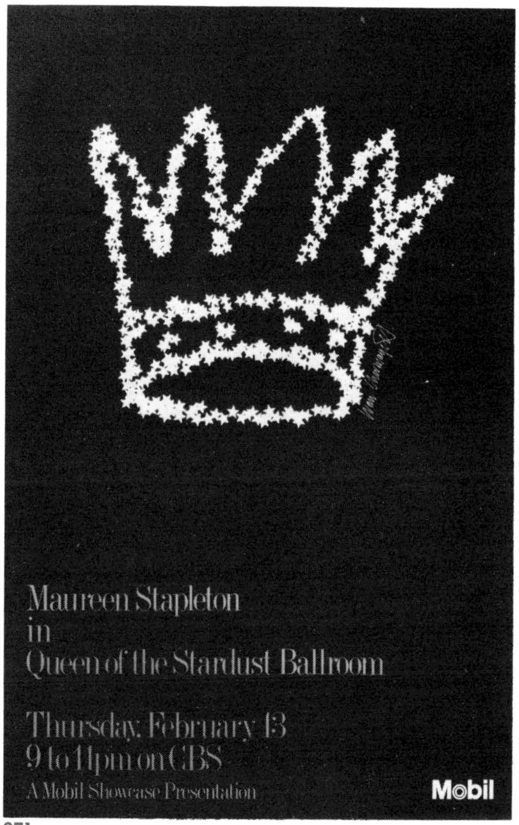
Maureen Stapleton
in
Queen of the Stardust Ballroom
Thursday, February 13
9 to 11pm on CBS
A Mobil Showcase Presentation
Mobil

871

Summergarden
The Museum of Modern Art
Sculpture Garden
is open free
Fridays, Saturdays, and Sundays
6 to 11 PM
May 31 to September 29
8 West 54th Street
Evenings in the Sculpture Garden are
made possible by a grant from Mobil Oil Corporation

872

870
Art Director Ivan Chermayeff
Designer Ivan Chermayeff
Artist Ivan Chermayeff
Agency Chermayeff & Geismar Assoc.
Client Mobil Oil Corp.

871
Art Director Ivan Chermayeff
Designer Ivan Chermayeff
Artist Ivan Chermayeff
Agency Chermayeff & Geismar Assoc.
Client Mobil Oil Corp.

872
Art Director Ivan Chermayeff
Designer Ivan Chermayeff
Agency Chermayeff & Geismar Assoc.
Client Museum of Modern Art

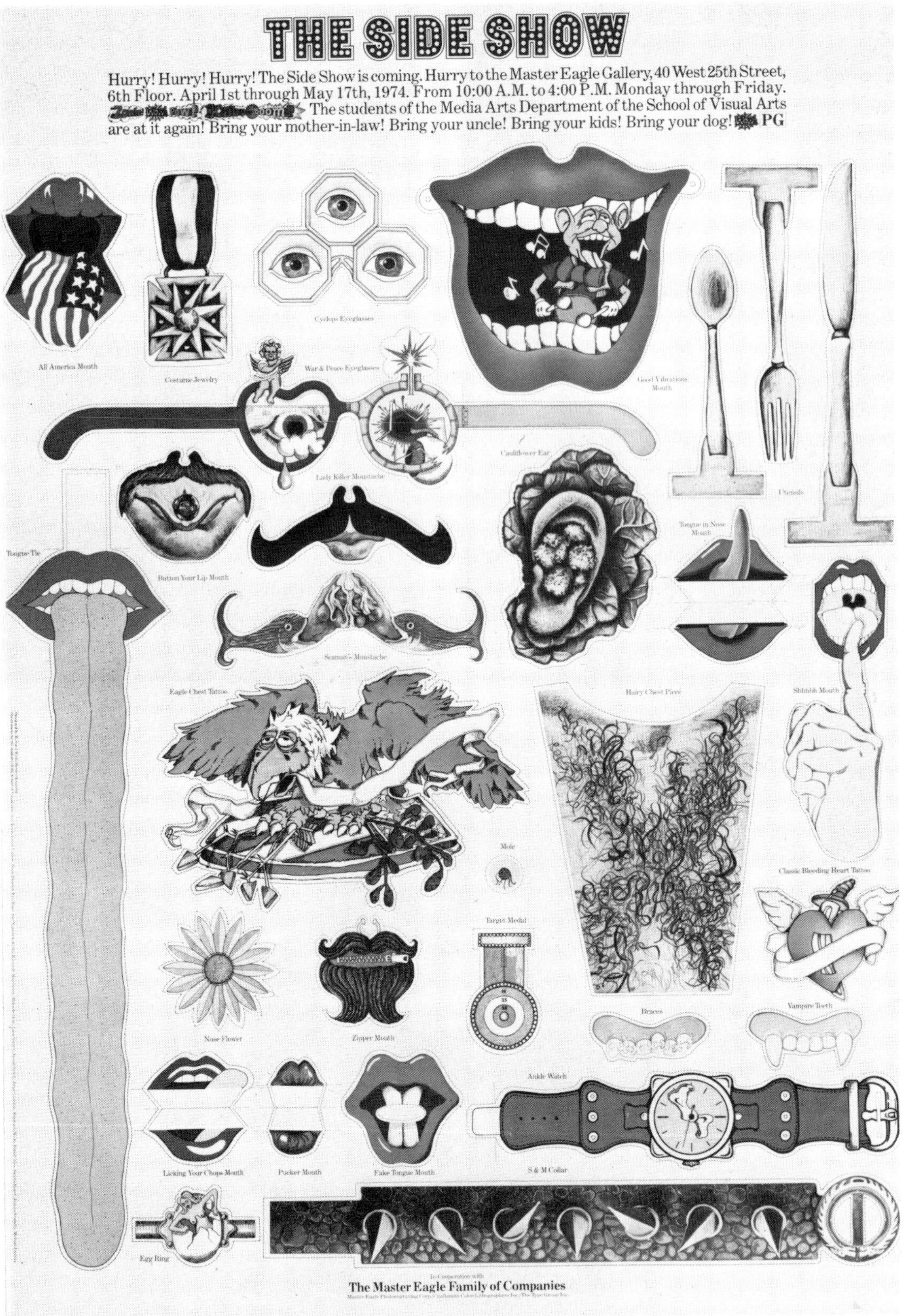
THE SIDE SHOW
Hurry! Hurry! Hurry! The Side Show is coming. Hurry to the Master Eagle Gallery, 40 West 25th Street, 6th Floor. April 1st through May 17th, 1974. From 10:00 A.M. to 4:00 P.M. Monday through Friday.
The students of the Media Arts Department of the School of Visual Arts are at it again! Bring your mother-in-law! Bring your uncle! Bring your kids! Bring your dog! PG
All America Mouth
Costume Jewelry
Cyclops Eyeglasses
War & Peace Eyeglasses
Good Vibrations Mouth
Cauliflower Ear
Lady Killer Moustache
Utensils
Tongue Tie
Button Your Lip Mouth
Tongue in Nose Mouth
Seaman's Moustache
Eagle Chest Tattoo
Hairy Chest Piece
Shhhhh Mouth
Mole
Classic Bleeding Heart Tattoo
Target Medal
Nose Flower
Zipper Mouth
Braces
Vampire Teeth
Ankle Watch
Licking Your Chops Mouth
Pucker Mouth
Fake Tongue Mouth
S & M Collar
Egg Ring
In Cooperation with
The Master Eagle Family of Companies

873

873
Art Directors Richard Wilde
Herb Bossardt
Designer Richard Wilde
Artists School of Visual Arts Students
Writers Dee Ito
Judi Wilde
Agency School of Visual Arts
Client School of Visual Arts

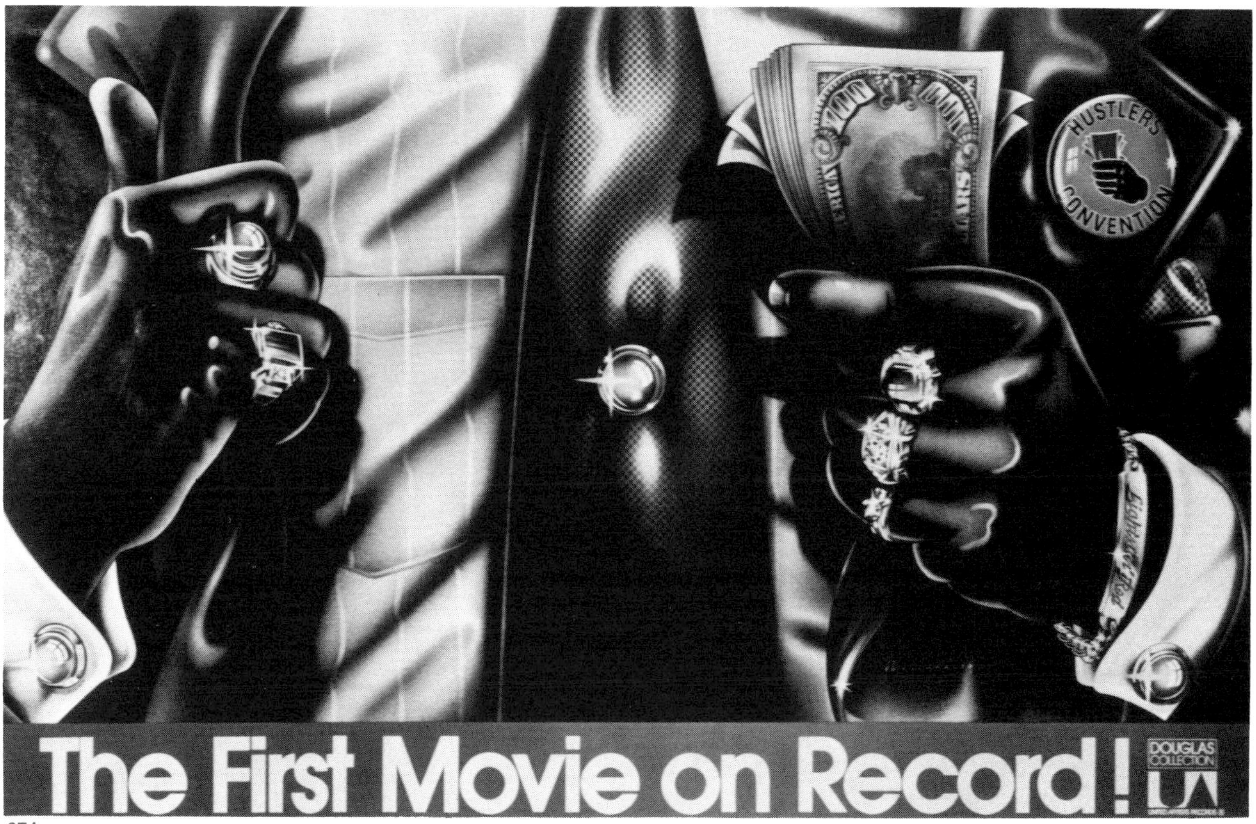
HUSTLER'S CONVENTION
The First Movie on Record!
DOUGLAS COLLECTION
UA
874

THE FRONTIER
874A

874
Art Director Craig Braun
Designer Mike Salisbury
Artist Dave Willardson
Writer Alan Douglas
Agency Craig Braun Inc.
Client United Artist Records

874A
Art Directors Jay Taylor
Bill Caldwell
Designer Don Komai
Artist Michael David Brown
Writer Jay Taylor
Agency United States Information Agency
Client United States Information Agency

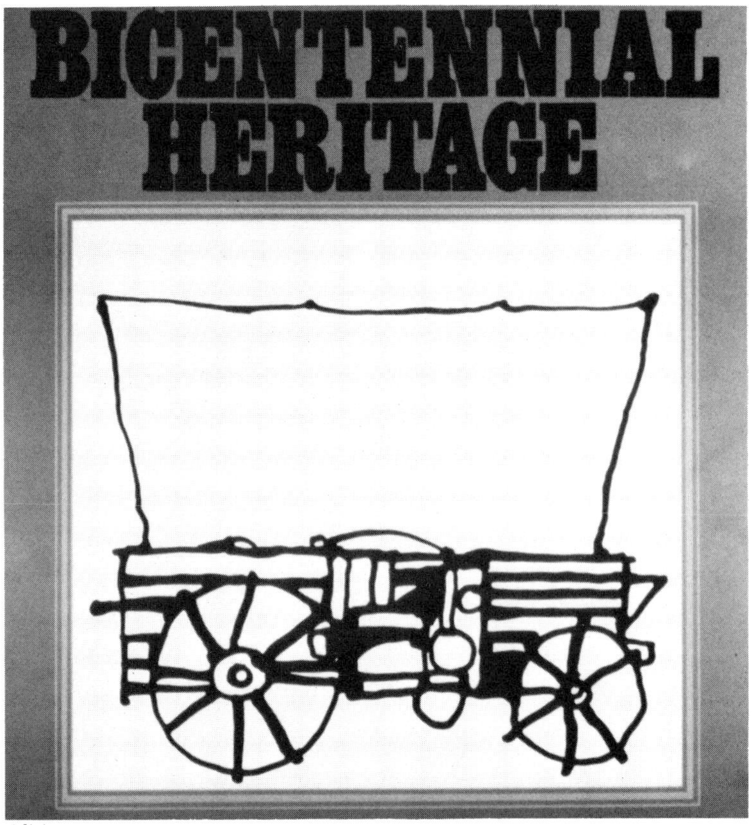
BICENTENNIAL
HERITAGE

875

THE
FRONTIER

876

875
Art Directors Jay Taylor
Bill Caldwell
Designer Don Komai
Artist Michael David Brown
Writer Jay Taylor
Agency United States
Information Agency
Client United States
Information Agency

876
Art Directors Jay Taylor
Bill Caldwell
Designer Don Komai
Artist Michael David Brown
Writer Jay Taylor
Agency United States
Information Agency
Client United States
Information Agency

The
A.E. Stickney
Memorial
Clam Bake
Arthur E. Stickney and a thousand of his closest friends
will launch two boats to George's Island on July 12th.
Unfortunately, only 275 of them will make it to the Clam Bake.
The first boat (departing at 3:30) has room for 200. The second
boat (departing at 3:30) has room for 75. That means unless
you're bringing a party of midgets you better make your
reservations soon. Call Kathy at the Ad Club (262-1100) and
tell her which boat you plan to board. $8 for members or $10 for
non-members paid in advance will assure you a spot on one
of them. The boats leave from Mass. Bay Lines on Rowe's Wharf.
At the other end there'll be lobsters, beer, the Ice House 5 + 2,
softball, contests, prizes in gay decorator colors, kites and frisbees.
Or you can just stand around and watch the neighborhood go.
But make your reservations early, or there'll be the same
275 droll people who show up every year.
Raindate: July 19

877

Saul Steinberg
constructions, drawings and lithographs
from the collection of
Chermayeff & Geismar Associates,
Institute of Contemporary Art,
955 Boylston Street, Boston,
May 11–June 20, 1974

878

878
Art Director Milt Wuilleumier
Designer Milt Wuilleumier
Photographer Mike Pierce
Writer Joan MacArthur
Agency Ingalls Assoc.
Client Advertising Club of Boston

879
Art Directors Ivan Chermayeff, Thomas Geismar
Designers Ivan Chermayeff, Thomas Geismar
Artist Saul Steinberg
Agency Chermayeff & Geismar Assoc.
Client Institution of Contemporary Art

aiga
AIGA
Computer Typesetting
and the New Technology
Shortages, Shortages, Shortages
Copyright and the Graphic Arts
Holiday Cheer
Save the Artist
Multimedia and the
Cookie Monster
The Economics of Long-Run
vs. Short-Run Manufacturing
Education: A Publisher's View
Fifty Books Show

880

The Architectural League of New York
AMERICAN DESIGN BETWEEN THE WARS 1920-1940
The Origins and Development of Rockefeller Center
Modernism: Styles and Movements
Modes of Modernity
Los Angeles in the Thirties 1931-1941

881

880
Art Director Judie Mills
Designers Mark Rubin
David Rubin
Artist Mark Rubin
Agency Mark Rubin Design
Client American Institute of Graphic Arts

881
Art Directors Massimo Vignelli
Cervin Robinson
Designer Massimo Vignelli
Photographer Cervin Robinson
Agency Vignelli Assoc.
Client Architectural League of New York

882

We the People join together to celebrate Philadelphia Bicentennial 1976

883

WE SELL MORE CARS THAN FORD, CHRYSLER,
CHEVROLET AND BUICK COMBINED.
MATCHBOX.

884

882
Art Director Bill Bonnell III
Designer Bill Bonnell III
Artist Bill Bonnell III
Writer Bill Bonnell III
Agency Container Corporation Communications Dept.
Clients Container Corporation of America
Frederic Ryder Gallery

883
Art Director Ford, Byrne & Assoc.
Designer Michael Chapman
Artist Michael Chapman
Agency Ford, Byrne & Assoc.
Client Print Club of Philadelphia

884
Art Director Allan Beaver
Designer Allan Beaver
Photographer Cailor/Resnick
Writer Larry Plapler
Agency Levine, Huntley, Schmidt
Client Lesney Products Corp.

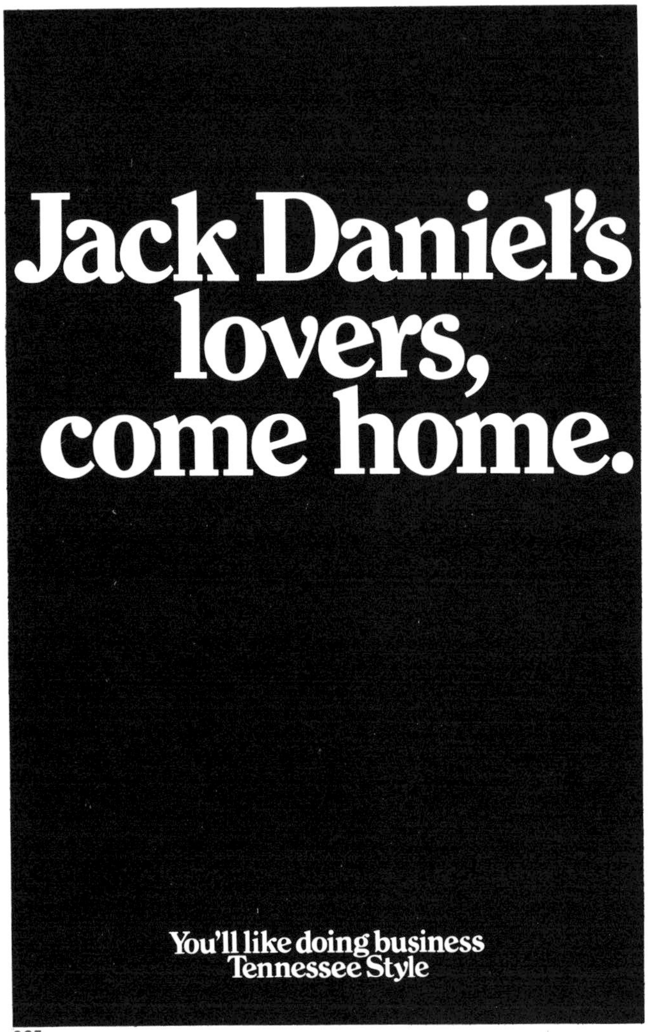
Jack Daniel's
lovers,
come home.
You'll like doing business
Tennessee Style

885

MAN OF THE YEAR
SMALL TALK
SLY & THE FAMILY STONE
SLY. "SMALL TALK." A NEW ALBUM. ON EPIC RECORDS AND TAPES

886

885
Art Director Bill Mostad
Designer Bill Mostad
Writer Vance Arbuckle
Agency Noble-Dury & Assoc.
Client Industrial Development Div.
State of Tennessee

886
Art Director Ted Bernstein
Designer Paula Scher
Artist Paula Scher
Writer Marty Pekar
Agency Columbia Records
Client Columbia Records

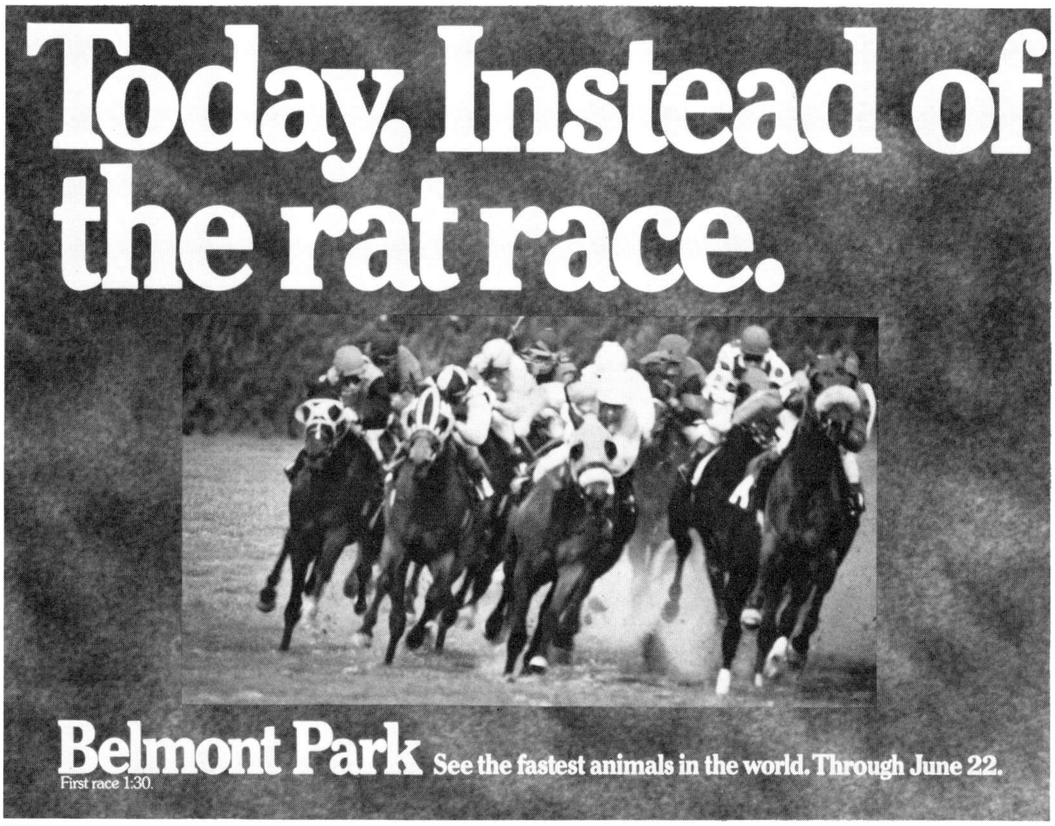
Today. Instead of the rat race.
Belmont Park See the fastest animals in the world. Through June 22.
First race 1:30.

887

We hate to see our name tossed around like this.

888

887
Art Director Harvey Gabor
Designer Harvey Gabor
Photographer Gus Boyd
Writer Rick Johnston
Agency McCann-Erickson
Client New York Racing Assoc.

888
Art Director Fred Caravetta
Designer Fred Caravetta
Photographer Bob Panuska
Writer Ray Allen
Agency Caravetta Allen Kinbrough
Client Burger King Corp.

The President's Men
Find out how they were found out –
in Playboy.
©1974, Playboy

889

Timme fake furs not only make you feel good when you buy them, but they're made with Creslan® acrylic fiber So they make you look good when you wear them. E. F. Timme & Son, Inc., 200 Madison Avenue, New York, N.Y. 10016
TIMME
Creslan
Fur-bearing animals everywhere request you look at Timme's family of fake furs.
SAVE THE TIGER
GRASHOW

890

889
Art Director Richard Manzo
Designer Richard Manzo
Artist Don Ivan Punchatz
Writer Irwin Kornblau
Agency Playboy Promotion Dept.
Client Playboy Magazine

890
Art Director Rob Lopes
Artist James Grashow
Writers Mike Lichtman
Larry Plapler
Agency Levine, Huntley, Schmidt
Client E. F. Timme & Son

Eat,
eat, eat.
Doesn't anybody drink anymore?
CHARLEY'S
EATING &
DRINKING
SALOON
LADIES INVITED/344 NEWBURY ST./267-8645 · CHESTNUT HILL MALL/244-1200

891

(212)
MU7-0700
FOR HOME DELIVERY
The New York Times

892

891
Art Director Tony Viola
Designer Dick Pantano
Artist Tony Viola
Writers Tony Winch
Seumas McGuire
Agency Hill, Holliday
Connors, Cosmopulos
Client Charley's Eating &
Drinking Saloon

892
Art Director Andrew Kner
Designer Andrew Kner
Photographer Vince Aiosa
Agency The New York Times
Client The New York Times

THE MUSIC MAN

893

TALON
SMART SHOPPERS READ THE SMALL PRINT.
A Talon zipper says a lot about the quality of the clothes it's in
Talon

895

"AMERICANA TEXTILE DESIGN COMPETITION"
$10,000 in prizes. Obtain entry forms from Art Dept... or write Riegel Textile Corporation, 260 Madison Ave., N.Y., N.Y. 10016

897

893
Art Director McRay Magleby
Designer McRay Magleby
Artists McRay Magleby
Karen Morales
Writer McRay Magleby
Agency Graphic Communications Dept.
Brigham Young University
Client Brigham Young University

895
Art Director Alan Chalfin
Designer Alan Chalfin
Artist Peter Lloyd
Writer Ken Baron
Agency DKG
Client Talon

897
Designers Jerry Leopold
Larry Wattman
Agency Poppe Tyson
Client Riegel Textile Corp.

MILLER & RHOADS
THE
BEST
of EVERYTHING

899

899
Art Director Rhea G. Cole
Designer Rhea G. Cole
Artist Rhea G. Cole
Agency Miller & Rhoads
Client Miller & Rhoads

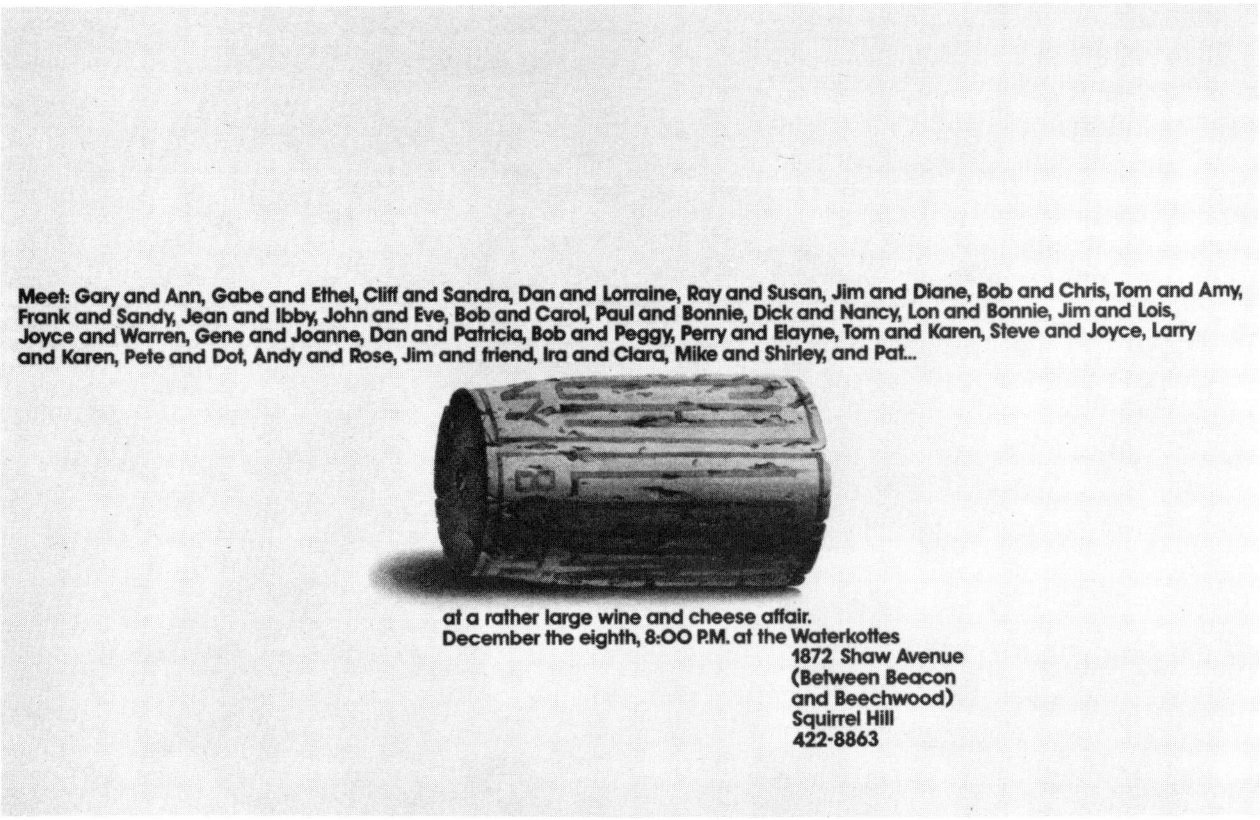
Meet: Gary and Ann, Gabe and Ethel, Cliff and Sandra, Dan and Lorraine, Ray and Susan, Jim and Diane, Bob and Chris, Tom and Amy, Frank and Sandy, Jean and Ibby, John and Eve, Bob and Carol, Paul and Bonnie, Dick and Nancy, Lon and Bonnie, Jim and Lois, Joyce and Warren, Gene and Joanne, Dan and Patricia, Bob and Peggy, Perry and Elayne, Tom and Karen, Steve and Joyce, Larry and Karen, Pete and Dot, Andy and Rose, Jim and friend, Ira and Clara, Mike and Shirley, and Pat...
at a rather large wine and cheese affair.
December the eighth, 8:00 P.M. at the Waterkottes
1872 Shaw Avenue
(Between Beacon
and Beechwood)
Squirrel Hill
422-8863

900

SENIOR NIGHT AT SIX FLAGS
MAY 2, 1975
SEE YOUR CLASS PRESIDENT OR ADVISOR FOR DETAILS.

901

900
Art Director Gabriel DiFiore
Designer Gabriel DiFiore
Artist Gabriel DiFiore
Writer Ray Werner
Agency DiFiore Assoc.
Client Mike Waterkotte

901
Art Director Bob Wages
Designer Bob Wages
Artist David Gaadt
Writer Sarah Ricks
Agency McDonald & Little
Client Six Flags Over Georgia

903

The New York Times
It goes to your head

904

903
Art Director Gabriel DiFiore
Designer Gabriel DiFiore
Artist Gabriel DiFiore
Writer Mike Waterkotte
Agency DiFiore Assoc.
Client Geyer Printing

904
Art Director Andrew Kner
Designer Andrew Kner
Artist Gary Solin
Writer Leonard Wright
Agency The New York Times
Client The New York Times

10th Chicago
International
Film Festival
November 8-21

905

The New York Times
MINIMUM-WAGE
BIPARTISAN PL
It goes to your head

906

905
Art Directors Saul Bass
Art Goodman
Designers Saul Bass
Art Goodman
Artist Saul Bass & Assoc.
Photographer Jerry White
Agency Saul Bass & Assoc.
Client Chicago International
Film Festival

906
Art Director Andrew Kner
Designer Andrew Kner
Artist Gary Solin
Writer Warren Abrams
Agency The New York Times
Client The New York Times

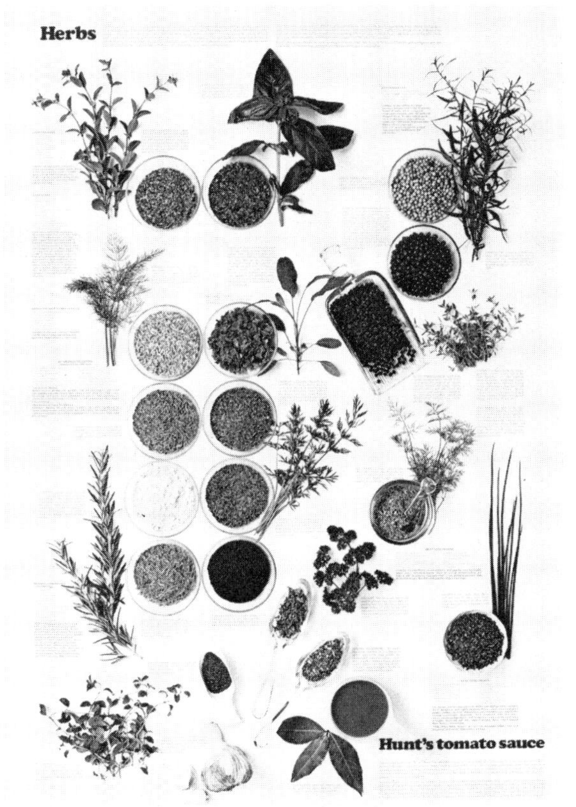
Herbs
Hunt's tomato sauce

Pasta
Hunt's tomato sauce

907

Hunt's

907
Art Director William McCaffery
Designer William McCaffery
Photographer Irwin Horowitz
Agency Norton Simon Communications
Client Hunt-Wesson Foods

908
Art Director William McCaffery
Designer William McCaffery
Photographer Irwin Horowitz
Writer Kelly Welles
Agency Norton Simon Communications
Client Hunt-Wesson Foods

909
Art Director William McCaffery
Designer Dana Cairns
Photographer Irwin Horowitz
Writer Kelly Welles
Agency Norton Simon Communications
Client Hunt-Wesson Foods

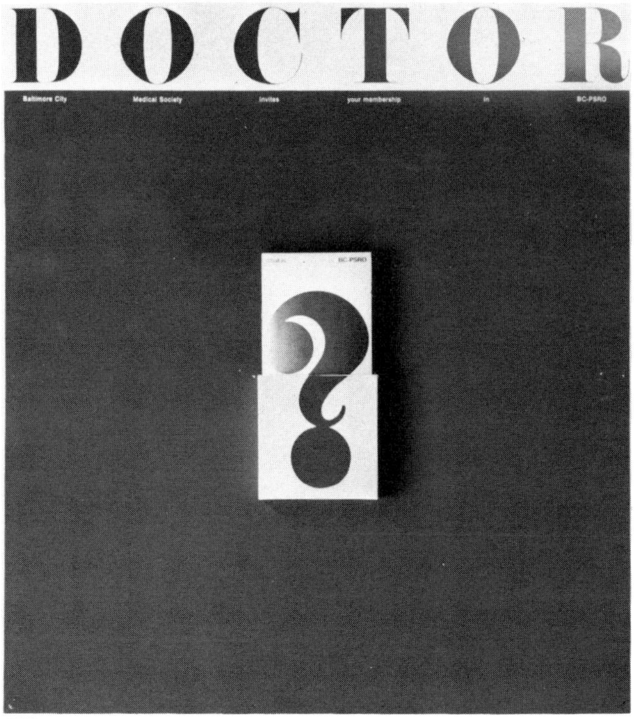
DOCTOR
Baltimore City
Medical Society
invites
your membership
in
BC-PSRO
BC-PSRO

910

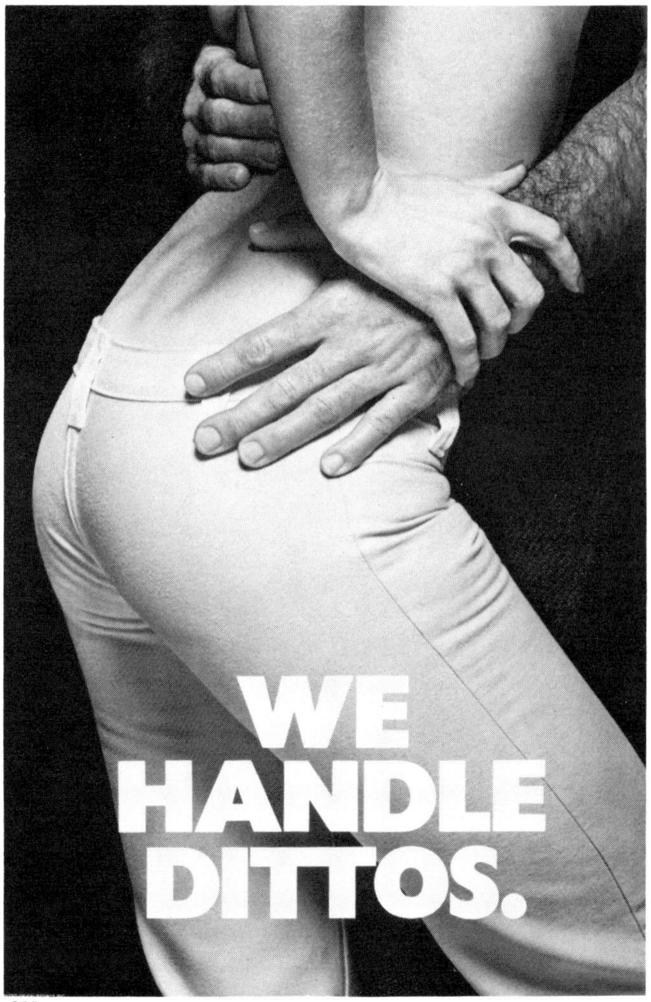
WE HANDLE DITTOS.

911

910
Art Director Robert O. Shelley
Designer Robert O. Shelley
Writer Bernice A. Thieblot
Agency North Charles Street Design Organization
Client Baltimore City Medical Society

911
Art Director Barry Carter
Designer James Van Noy
Artist Van Noy & Co. Staff
Photographer Albert Watson
Writers Barry Carter
Cliff Einstein
Agency Van Noy & Co.
Client Dailey & Assoc.

CELEBRATING
FIFTY YEARS
OF FASHION
SAKS FIFTH AVENUE

912

BOBBY
HUTCHERSON
Blue Note

MARLENA
SHAW
Blue Note

913

912
Art Director Max Jorden
Designer Max Jorden
Agency Saks Fifth Avenue
Client Saks Fifth Avenue

913
Art Director Lloyd Ziff
Designer Ria Lewerke
Photographers Doug Metzler
Albert Mackenzie Watson
Agency United Artists Artists
Client Blue Note Records

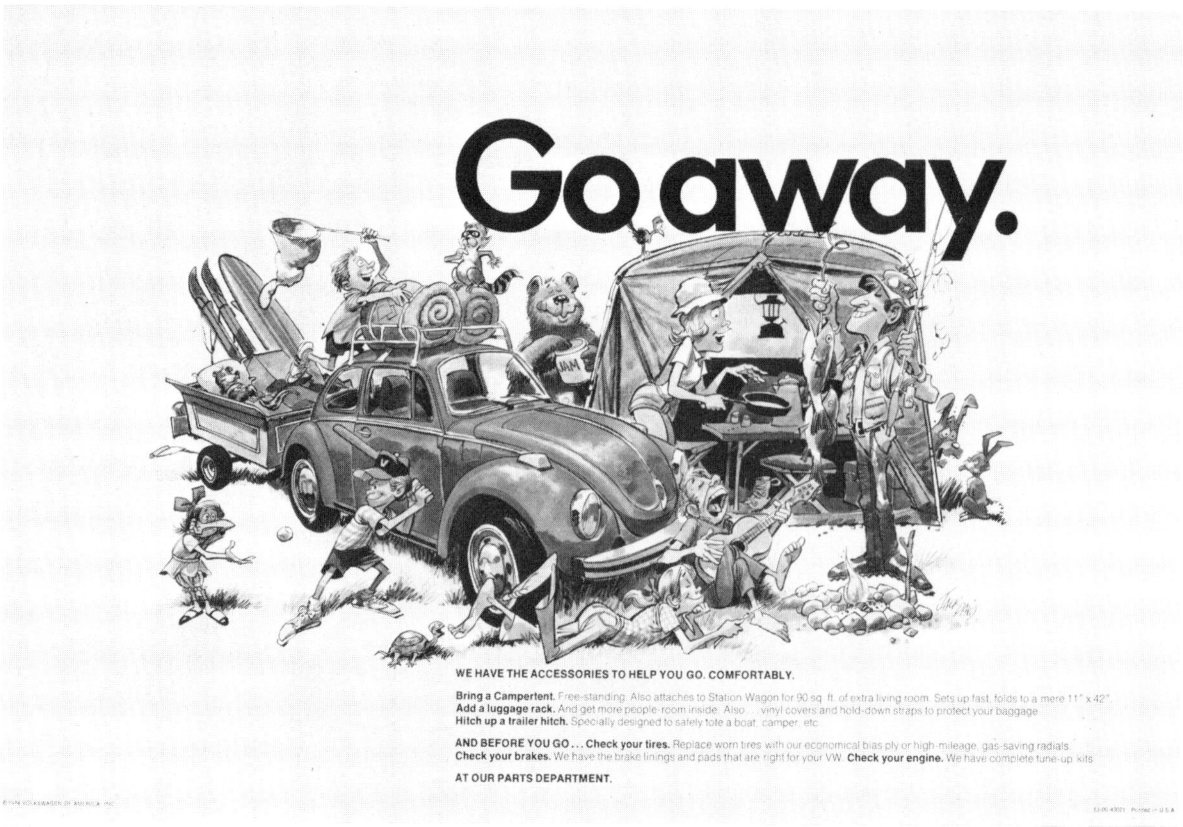
Go away.
WE HAVE THE ACCESSORIES TO HELP YOU GO. COMFORTABLY.
Bring a Campertent. Free-standing. Also attaches to Station Wagon for 90 sq. ft. of extra living room. Sets up fast, folds to a mere 11" x 42".
Add a luggage rack. And get more people-room inside. Also . . . vinyl covers and hold-down straps to protect your baggage.
Hitch up a trailer hitch. Specially designed to safely tote a boat, camper, etc.
AND BEFORE YOU GO . . . Check your tires. Replace worn tires with our economical bias ply or high-mileage, gas-saving radials.
Check your brakes. We have the brake linings and pads that are right for your VW. Check your engine. We have complete tune-up kits.
AT OUR PARTS DEPARTMENT.

914

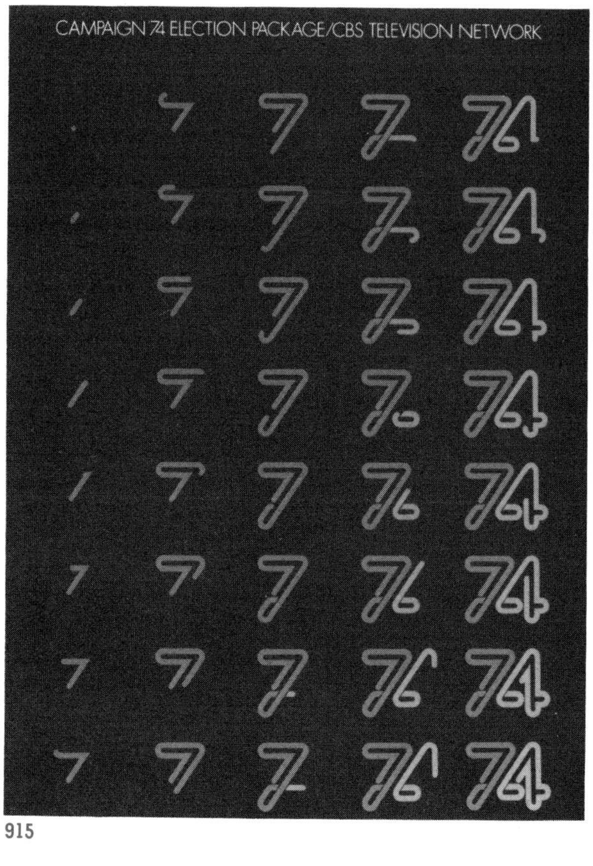
CAMPAIGN 74 ELECTION PACKAGE/CBS TELEVISION NETWORK

915

914
Art Director Peter Adler
Designer Fred Witzig
Artist Jack Davis
Writer Keith Connes
Agency Adler, Schwartz & Connes
Client Volkswagen of America Corp.

915
Art Director Lou Dorfsman
Designer Akihiko Seki
Artist Akihiko Seki
Agency CBS/Broadcast Group
Client CBS Television Network

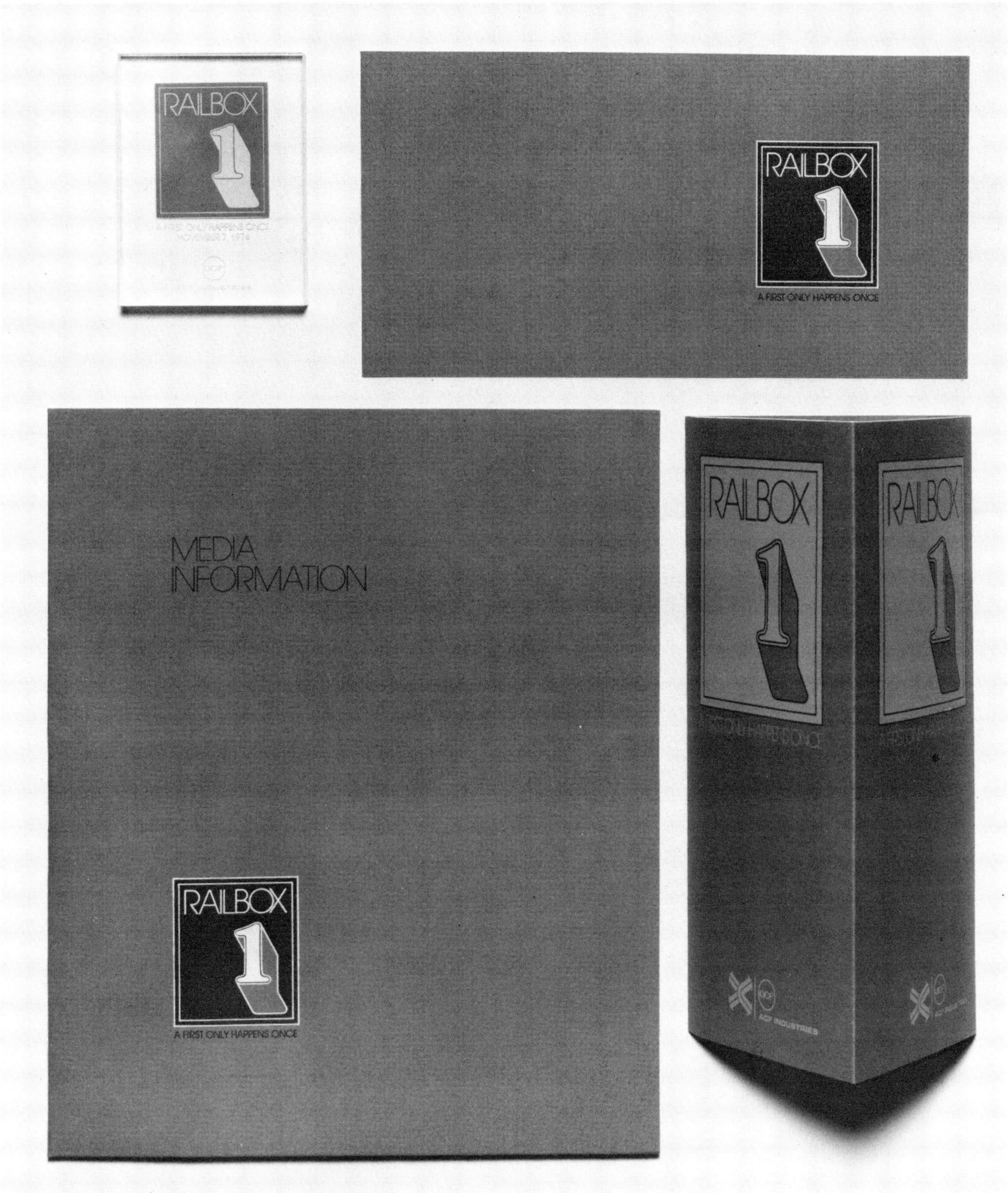
RAILBOX
1
A FIRST ONLY HAPPENS ONCE
NOVEMBER 7, 1974
RAILBOX
1
A FIRST ONLY HAPPENS ONCE
MEDIA
INFORMATION
RAILBOX
1
A FIRST ONLY HAPPENS ONCE
RAILBOX
1
RAILBOX
1
ACF INDUSTRIES

916

916
Art Director Frank Roth
Designer Becky Venegoni
Writer Mark Shyres
Agency Frank/James Productions
Client ACF Industries

Container Corporation
Container Corporation

917

Knoll

918

Knoll Textiles
Knoll

919

917
Art Director Bill Bonnell III
Designers Bill Bonnell III
Chris Ward
Artist Robert Padgett
Editor Rhodes Patterson
Agency Container Corporation
Communications Dept.
Client Container Corporation
of America

918
Art Director Marjorie Katz
Designer Marjorie Katz
Agency Knoll International
Client Knoll International

919
Art Director Marjorie Katz
Designer Marjorie Katz
Agency Knoll International
Client Knoll Textiles

CBS
MENU
FRENCH ONION SOUP
Toasted Croutons
ROAST SIRLOIN OF BEEF
Sauce Bordelaise
Asparagus Polonaise
Chocolate Sauce
COFFEE

from dear sir
to sincerely yours
in 3½ seconds...
REMINGTON® 140
ELECTROSTATIC
BOOK COPIER

921

920
Art Director Bruce Day
Designer Bruce Day
Agency Columbia Records
Client Columbia Records

921
Art Director Ford, Byrne & Assoc.
Designer Ford, Byrne & Assoc.
Artist Ford, Byrne & Assoc.
Writer Donald Falk
Agency Ford, Byrne & Assoc.
Client Sperry-Remington

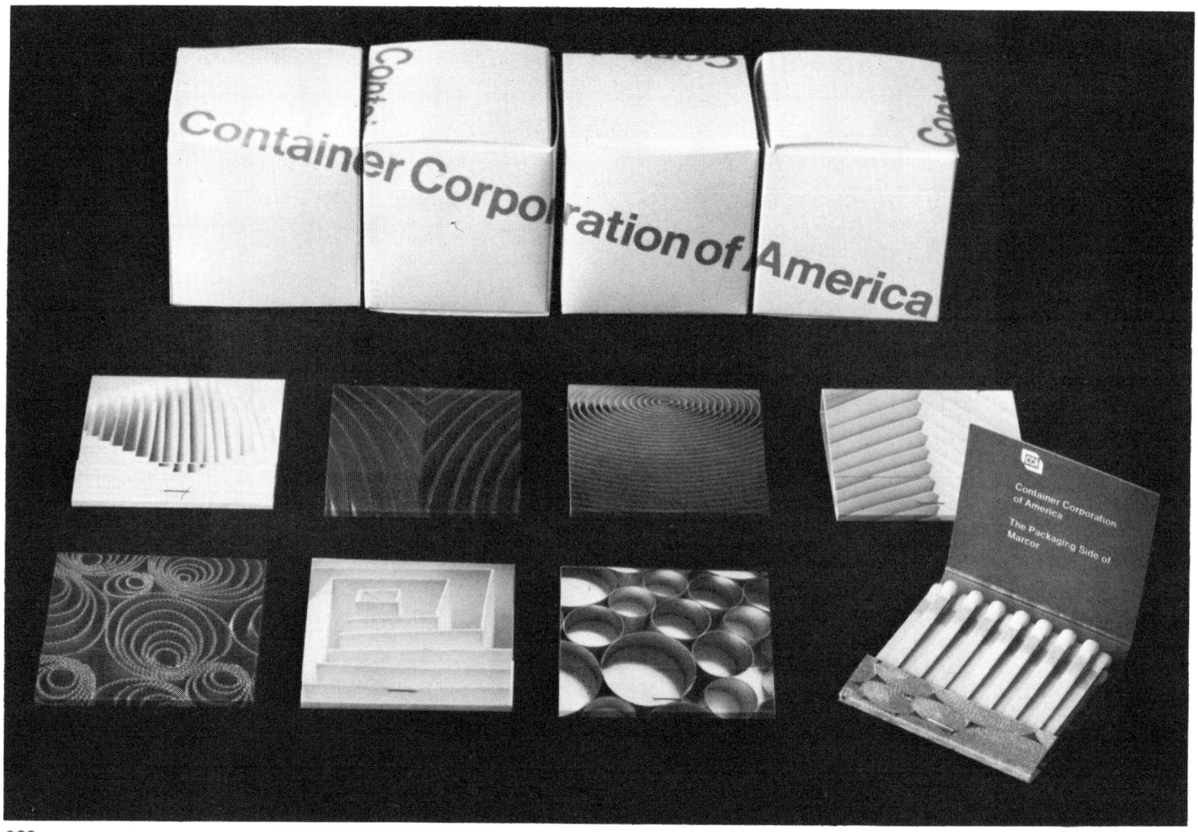
Container Corporation of America
Container Corporation of America
The Packaging Side of Marcor

922

Marketing & Design
No. Four
Published by the Marketing Design Alliance. 131 Riverside Drive, New York, N.Y. 10024. Tel. (212) 799-0095
Easy-to-use-Index for the busy reader.
Pick the subject that interests you most.
And see our solutions to problems in
sales, marketing, and communication.
PROMOTION MEDIA
Page 2
Packaging
Page 13
AudioVisual
Page 18
Corporate Identity
Page 20
Editorial
Page 27
& How We Can Help
Page 31

The Easy Way to Increase Sales:
That's the Easy Way to Increase Sales.
TRADE MAGAZINE
NEW Products
Ideas IN SALES

923

922
Art Director Bill Bonnell III
Designers Bill Bonnell III
Randy Hoffeld
Photographer Rudolf Janu
Writer Rhodes Patterson
Agency Container Corporation
Communications Dept.
Client Container Corporation
of America

923
Art Director Lawrence Miller
Designer Lawrence Miller
Artists Simms Taback
Reynold Ruffins
Writers Lawrence Miller
Vernon Mackie
Jim Johnston
Agency Marketing Design Alliance
Client Marketing Design Alliance

Michael A. McNeilly

924

924
Art Director Dennis S. Juett
Designer Dennis S. Juett
Artist Dennis S. Juett
Writer Michael A. McNeilly
Agency Dennis S. Juett & Assoc.
Client Michael A. McNeilly

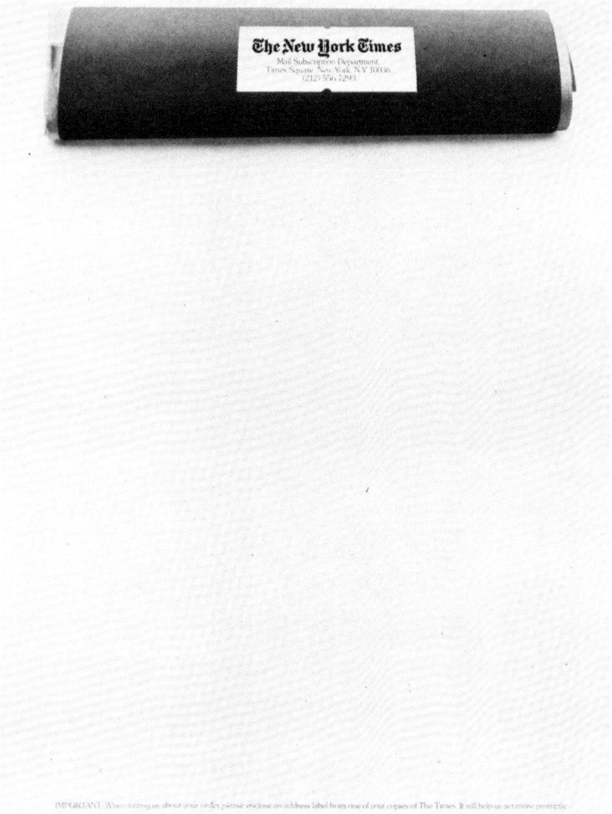
The New York Times

925

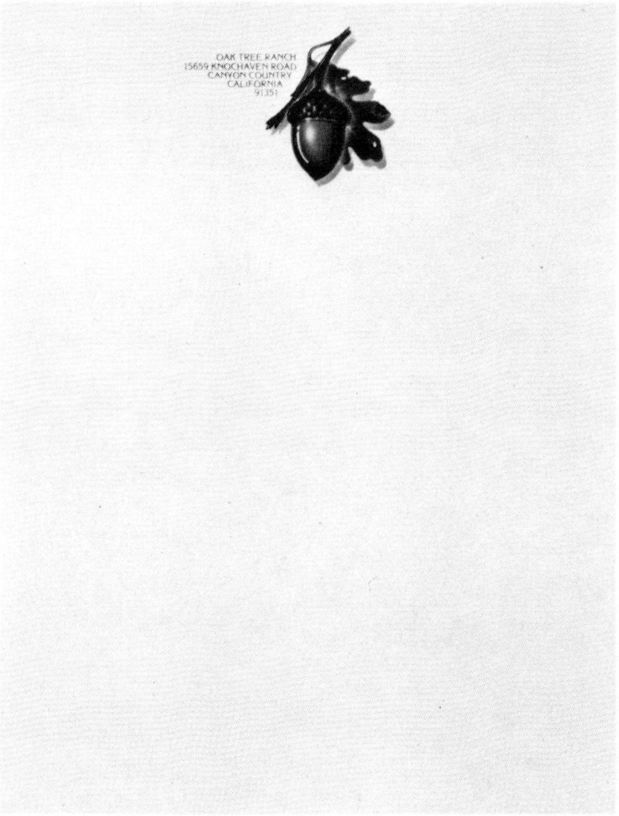
OAK TREE RANCH
15659 KNOCHAVEN ROAD
CANYON COUNTRY
CALIFORNIA
91351

926

COMPETITIVE NOTES
WABC-TV, Research and Sales Development, 1330 Avenue of the Americas, New York, 10019

927

925
Art Director Andrew Kner
Designer Peter Schaefer
Photographer Bill Aller
Agency The New York Times
Client The New York Times

926
Art Director Ed Thrasher
Designer Ed Thrasher
Artist Dave Willardson
Writer Ed Thrasher
Agency Ed Thrasher
Oaktree Ranch
Client Ed Thrasher
Oaktree Ranch

927
Art Director George McGinnis
Designer George McGinnis
Artist Taro Hiroshi Yamashita
Writer Mark Hanler
Agency Image Factory
Client WABC-TV
New York

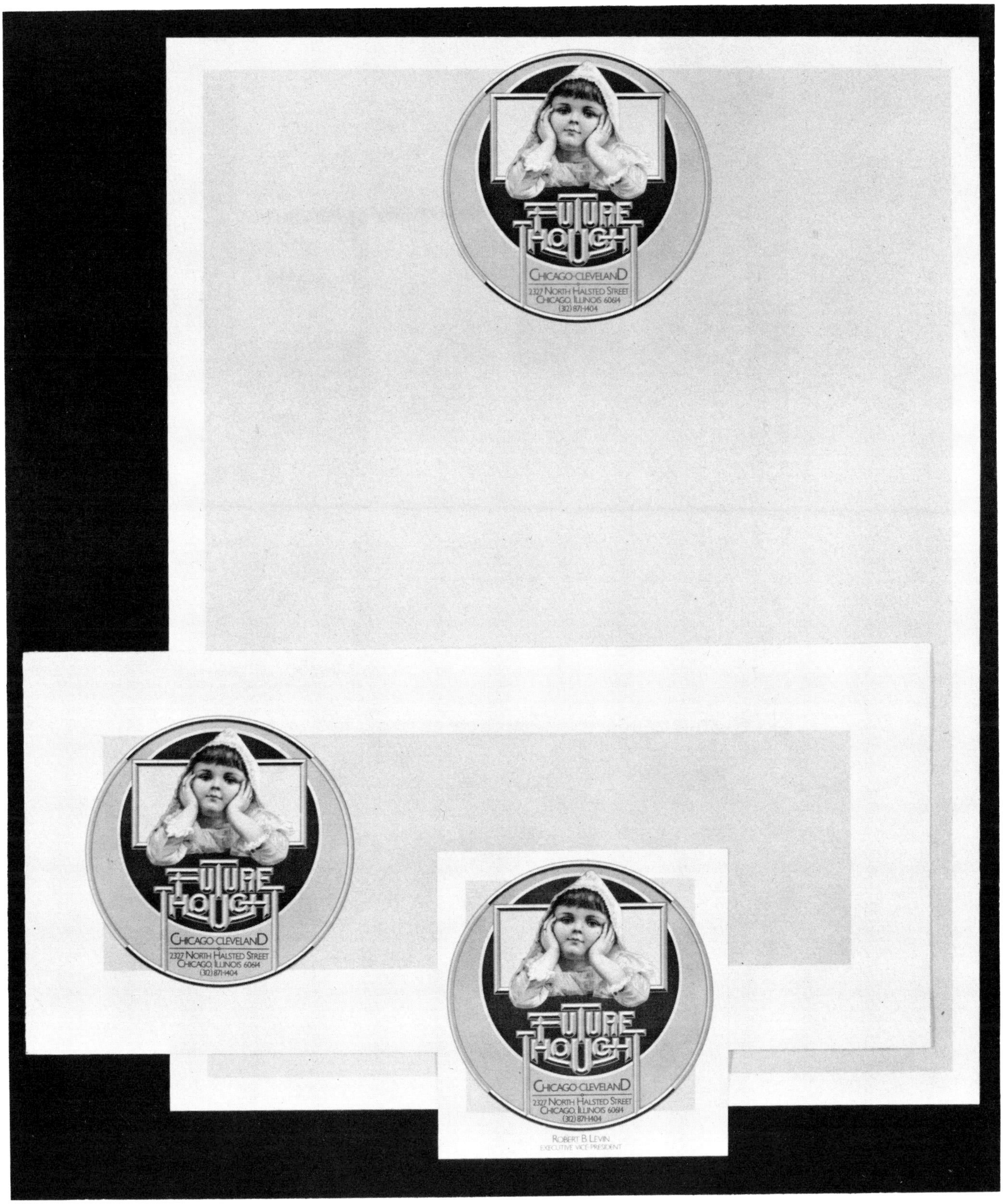
FUTURE THOUGHT
CHICAGO-CLEVELAND
2327 NORTH HALSTED STREET
CHICAGO, ILLINOIS 60614
(312) 871-1404
ROBERT B. LEVIN
EXECUTIVE VICE-PRESIDENT

928

SILVER

928
Art Director Peter Cotroulis
Designer Michael Doret
Artist Michael Doret
Agency Michael Doret, Inc.
Client Future Thought

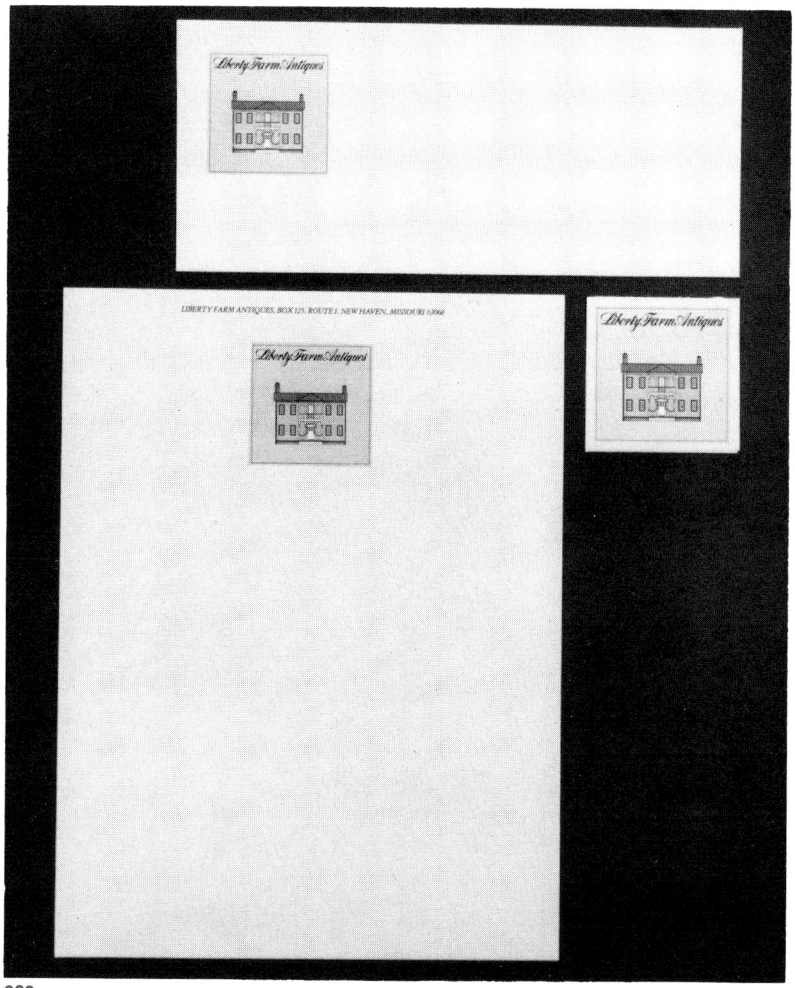
Liberty Farm Antiques
LIBERTY FARM ANTIQUES, BOX 125, ROUTE 1, NEW HAVEN, MISSOURI 63068
Liberty Farm Antiques
Liberty Farm Antiques

929

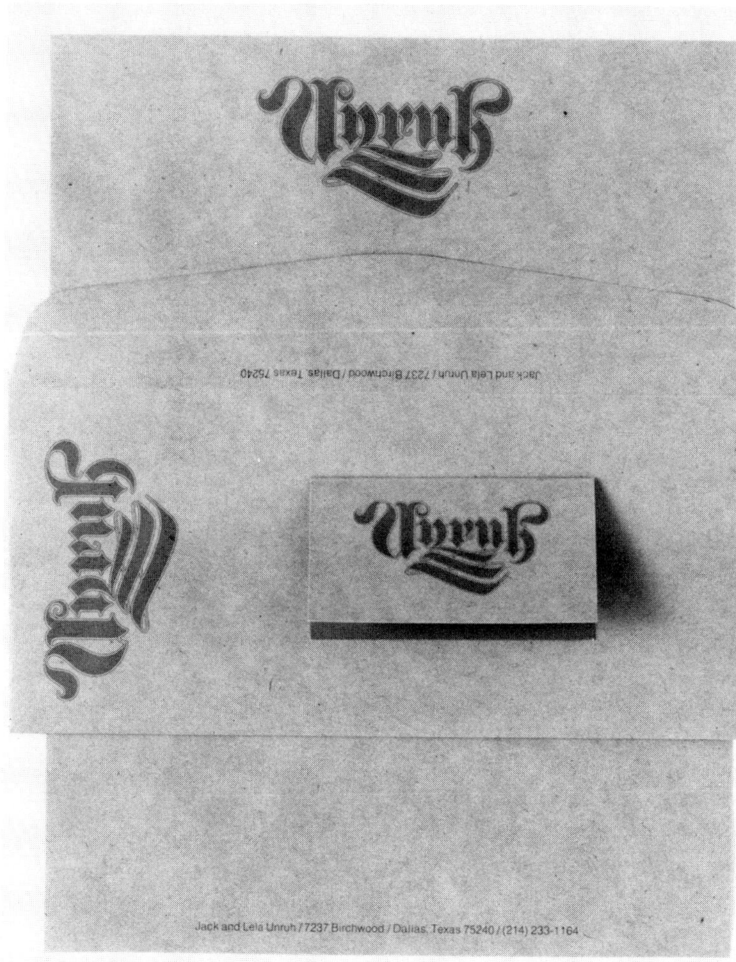
Unruh
Jack and Lela Unruh / 7237 Birchwood / Dallas, Texas 75240
Unruh
Unruh
Jack and Lela Unruh / 7237 Birchwood / Dallas, Texas 75240 / (214) 233-1164

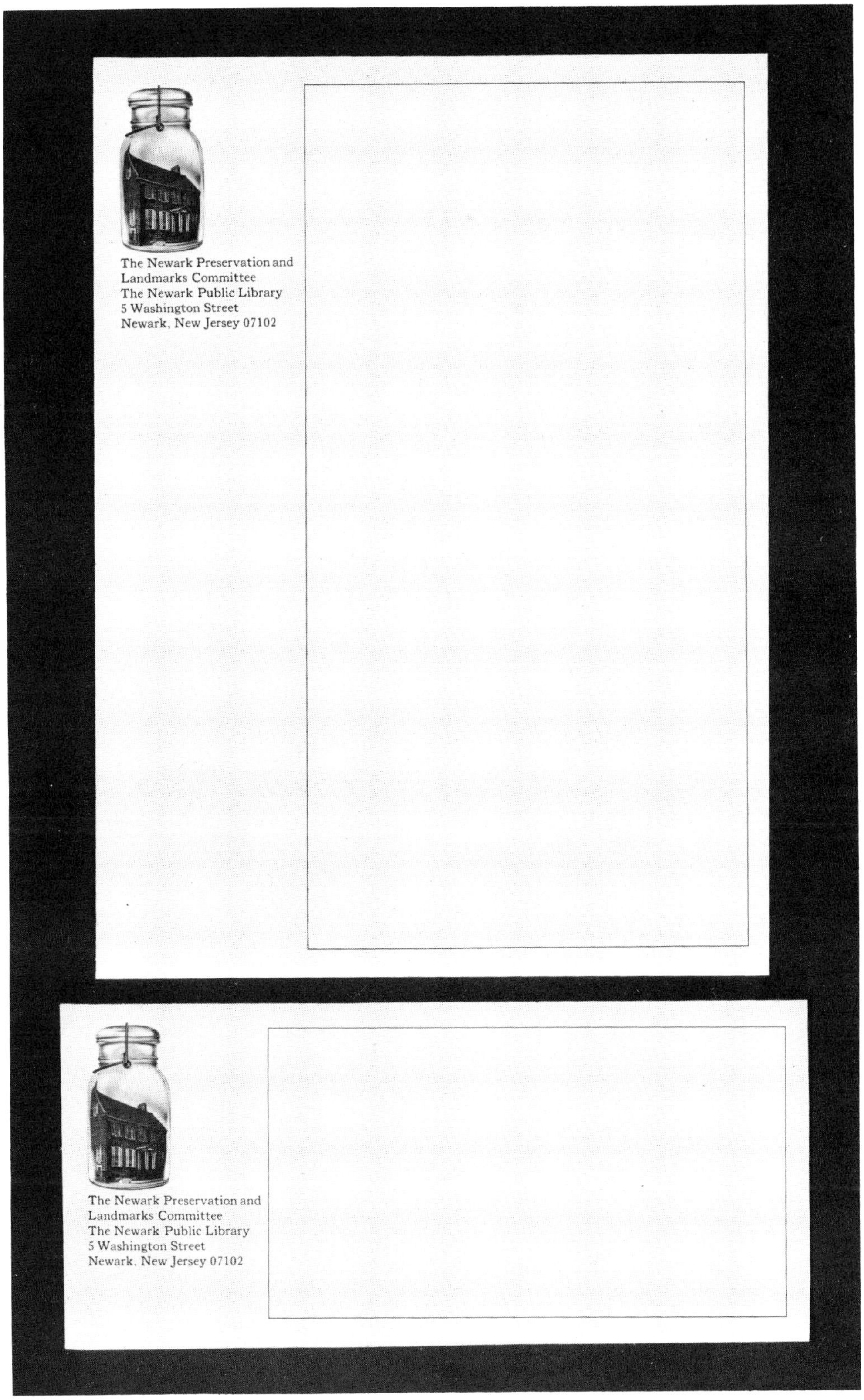
The Newark Preservation and
Landmarks Committee
The Newark Public Library
5 Washington Street
Newark, New Jersey 07102
The Newark Preservation and
Landmarks Committee
The Newark Public Library
5 Washington Street
Newark, New Jersey 07102

931

929
Art Director Frank Roth
Designer Michael Simpson
Artist Linda Recker
Writers Harry Hammer
Mark Shyres
Agency Frank/James Productions
Client Harry Hammer

930
Art Director Woody Pirtle
Designer Woody Pirtle
Artist Woody Pirtle
Agency The Richards Group
Client Jack Unruh

931
Art Directors Milt Simpson
Barbara Jo Leer
Designer Barbara Jo Leer
Artists Barbara Jo Leer
Compton Packenham
Photographer Ellsworth Schell
Editor Don Dust
Agency Johnson & Simpson
Graphic Designers
Clients The Newark Preservation
Landmarks Committee
Newark Public Library

OUT TO LUNCH
Produced by Children's Television Workshop
ABC December 10, 9:00 P.M. EST
A Mobil Showcase Theatre Presentation
From Frank Goodman Associates
251 West 57th Street, New York, N.Y. 10019
212-246-4180

932

DESIGNER'S SATURDAY
PO BOX 1103
FD ROOSEVELT BRANCH
NEW YORK, NEW YORK 10022
ATELIER INTERNATIONAL LTD
BRICKEL ASSOCIATES INC
CI DESIGNS
CUMBERLAND FURNITURE CORP
DIRECTIONAL CONTRACT FURNITURE
DUNBAR FURNITURE
EDWARD AXEL ROFFMAN
EPPINGER FURNITURE
FRITZ HANSEN INC
HARTER CORP
HARVEY PROBBER
HELIKON FURNITURE CO
HERMAN MILLER INC
ICF INC
INTREX INC
JENS RISOM DESIGN INC
JG FURNITURE CO
JOHN STUART INC
KNOLL INTERNATIONAL
LEHIGH—LEOPOLD
THE PACE COLLECTION INC
STENDIG INC
STOW/DAVIS FURNITURE CO
TURNER LTD

933

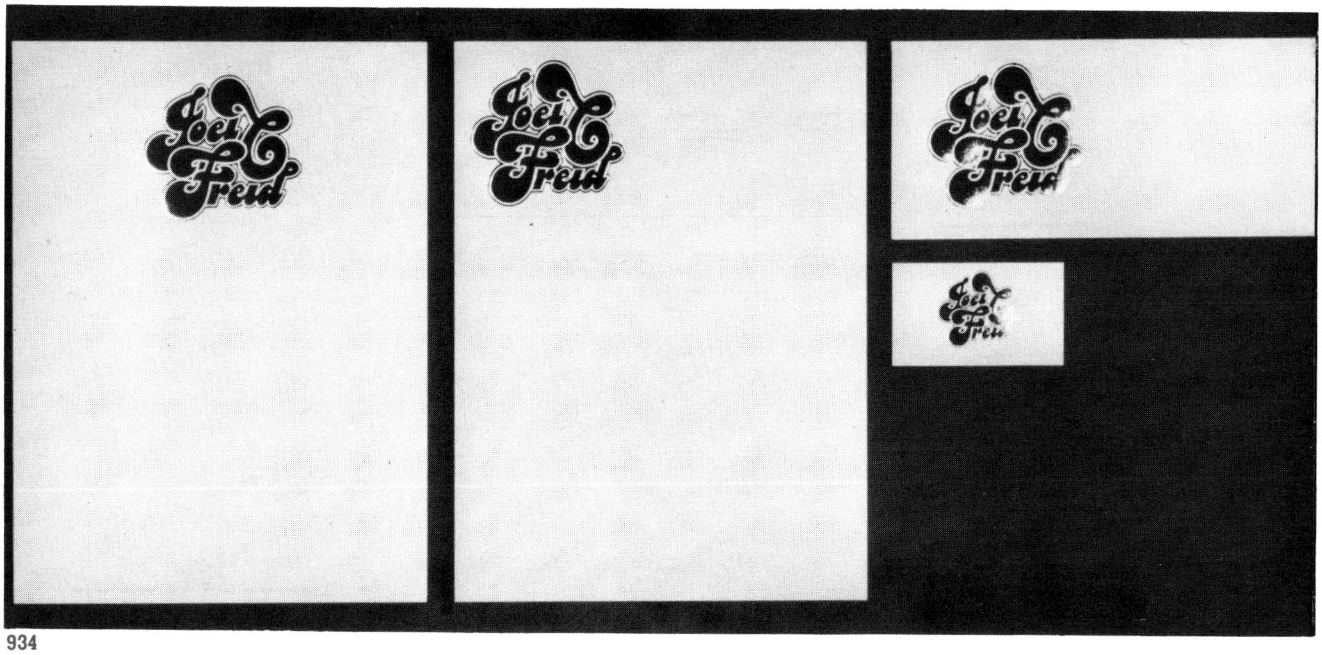

934

932
Art Director Ivan Chermayeff
Designer Ivan Chermayeff
Photographer Chermayeff & Geismar Assoc.
Agency Chermayeff & Geismar Assoc.
Client Mobil Oil Corp.

933
Art Director Marjorie Katz
Designer Marjorie Katz
Agency Marjorie Katz Graphic Design
Client New York Designer's Saturday Committee

934
Art Directors Ethel K. Freid
Joel C. Freid
Designer Ethel K. Freid
Artist Ethel K. Freid
Agency Joel C. Freid
Client Joel C. Freid

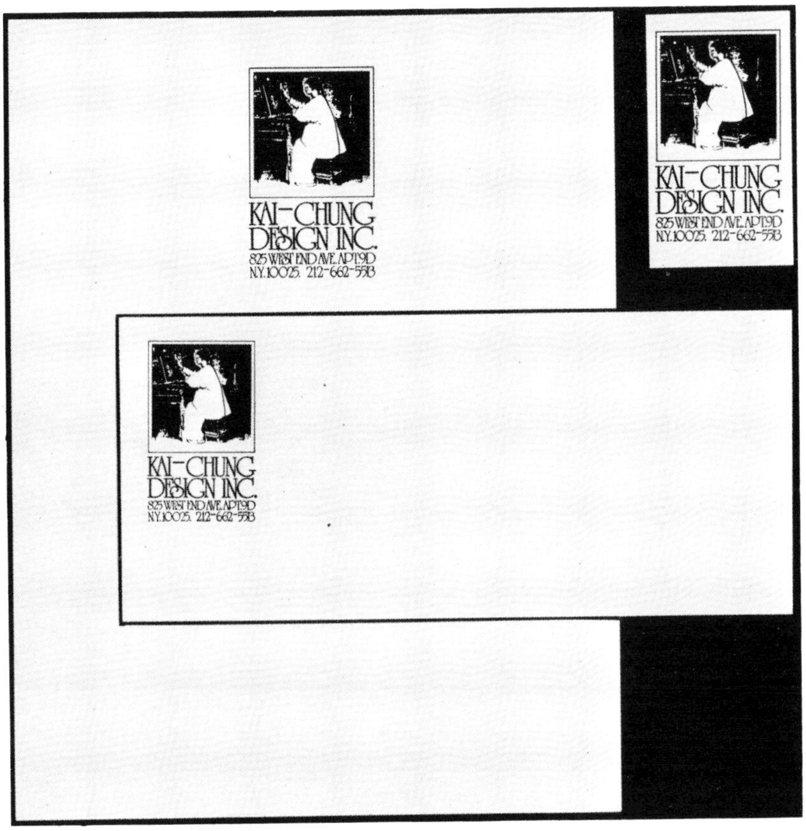
KAI-CHUNG
DESIGN INC.
825 WEST END AVE. APT 9D
N.Y. 10025. 212-662-5513
KAI-CHUNG
DESIGN INC.
825 WEST END AVE. APT 9D
N.Y. 10025. 212-662-5513
KAI-CHUNG
DESIGN INC.
825 WEST END AVE. APT 9D
N.Y. 10025. 212-662-5513

935

DILL
PRODUCTIONS
DILL PRODUCTIONS, P.O. BOX 402, FAIRFIELD, ALABAMA 35064 (205) 788-0064

936

935
Art Director Kai-Chung Lee
Designer Kai-Chung Lee
Artist Kai-Chung Lee
Agency Kai-Chung Design
Client Kai-Chung Design

936
Art Director Clyde Hogg
Designer Clyde Hogg
Artists Larry Bishop
Lisa Johnson
Agency Daniel, Riley &
Hogg Advertising
Client Dill Productions

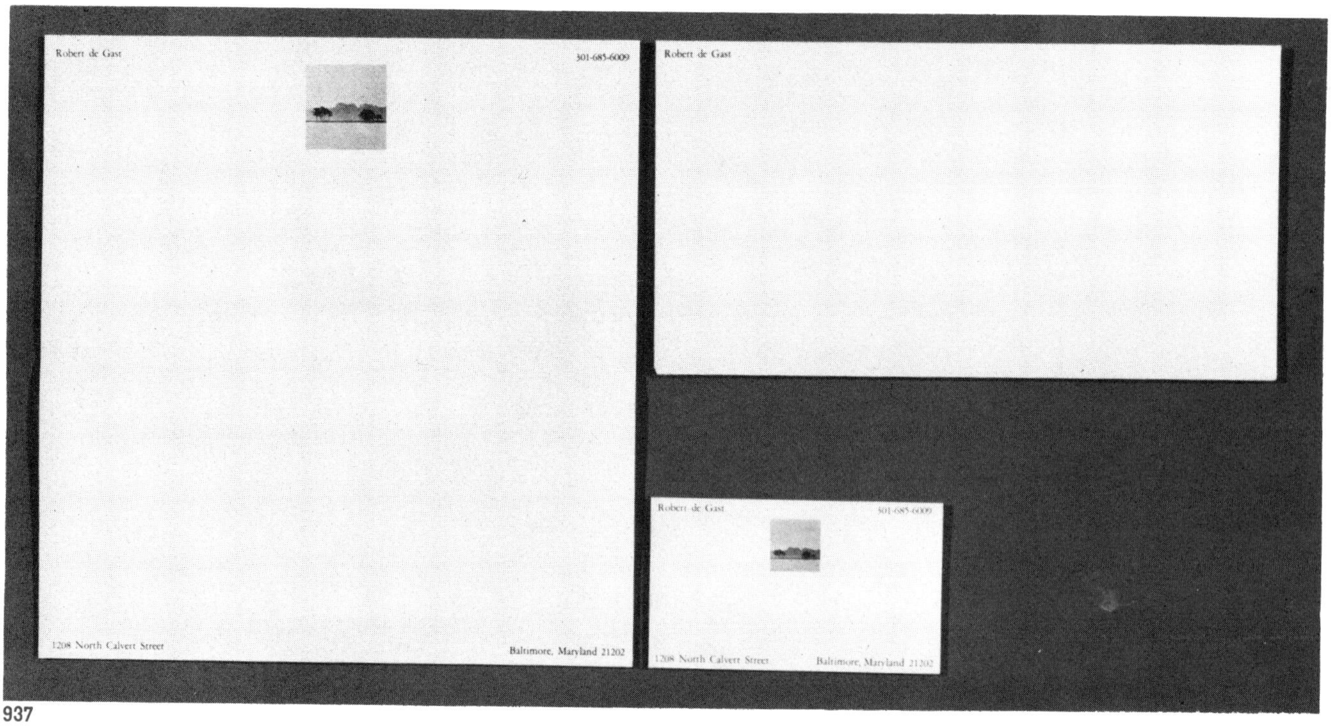
Robert de Gast
301-685-6009
1208 North Calvert Street
Baltimore, Maryland 21202
Robert de Gast
Robert de Gast
301-685-6009
1208 North Calvert Street
Baltimore, Maryland 21202

937

Sharon Grahnquist
Sharon Grahnquist

938

937
Art Director Robert J. Rytter
Designer Robert J. Rytter
Photographer Robert deGast
Agency The North Charles Street Design Operation
Client Robert deGast

938
Art Director Woody Pirtle
Designer Woody Pirtle
Artist Woody Pirtle
Agency The Richards Group
Client Sharon Grahnquist

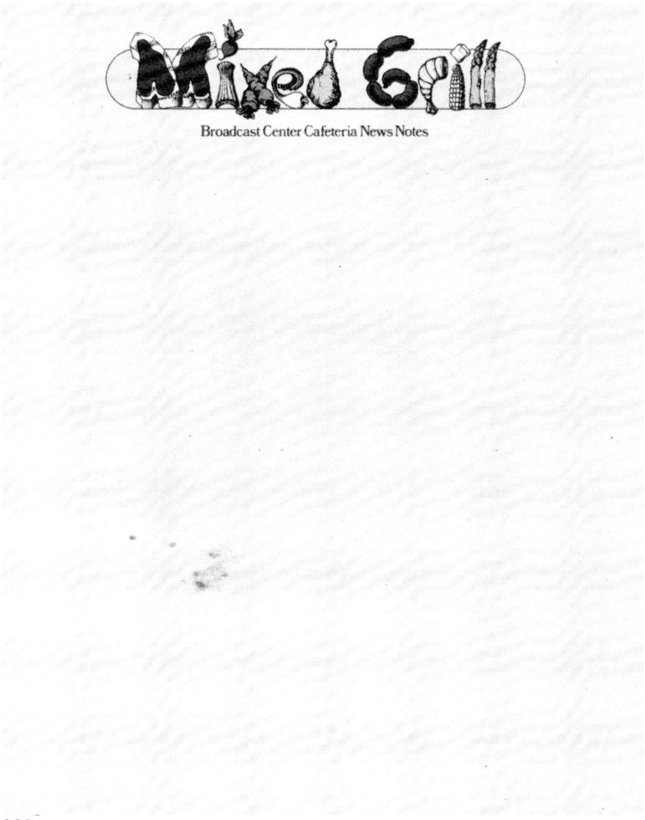
Mixed Grill
Broadcast Center Cafeteria News Notes

939

Fourth Annual Awards
for Communications
Excellence Sponsored
by Pittsburgh Advertising
Club and Pittsburgh
Radio and Television
Club.

940

ALEX MURAWSKI
REPRESENTED BY DANA EAKIN
(312)337-0332

941

939
Art Director Lou Dorfsman
Designer Jim Udell
Artist Isadore Seltzer
Agency CBS/Broadcast Group
Client CBS Television Network

940
Art Directors Joe McKenna
Gabriel DiFiore
Designer Gabriel DiFiore
Artists Tom Connors
DiFiore Assoc.
Agency DiFiore Assoc.
Client Fourth Annual
Ace Awards

941
Art Director Michael Doret
Designer Michael Doret
Artist Alex Murawski
Agency Michael Doret, Inc.
Client Alex Murawski

THE STATE OF WASHINGTON PRESENTS A DE MARTIN-MARONA CINEMA GROUP FILM

942

DANSK

943

942
Art Director Ed deMartin
Designer Ed deMartin
Agency deMartin Marona
Cranstoun Downes
Client State of Washington

943
Art Director Alan Peckolick
Designer Alan Peckolick
Artist Tom Carnase
Agency Lubalin, Smith, Carnase
Client Dansk International

SAKS FIFTH AVENUE
CELEBRATING OUR FIFTIETH CHRISTMAS

945

skeptic
THE FORUM FOR CONTEMPORARY HISTORY

946

945
Art Directors Max Jorden
Richard Martino
Agency Saks Fifth Avenue
Client Saks Fifth Avenue

946
Art Director Scott F. Reid
Designer Scott F. Reid
Artist Scott F. Reid
Agency Scott F. Reid & Assoc.
Client Forum for Contemporary History

947

948

949

947
Art Director Richard Nava
Designer Richard Nava
Artist Richard Nava
Agency Image Communications
Client Intercontinental Apparel

948
Art Director Richard Schneider
Designer Richard Schneider
Artist Richard Schneider
Agency Schneider Studio
Client Schneider Studio

949
Designers J. Downs
J. Davenport
Agency Moonink Inc.
Client Wittman Electric Service

951

950

952

950
Art Director Calvin Woo
Designer Calvin Woo
Artists Calvin Woo
Janis Sisty
Agency Humangraphic
Client Woo Chee Chong

951
Art Director Ken Parkhurst
Designer Ken Parkhurst
Artist Jean-Claude Muller
Agency Ken Parkhurst & Assoc.
Client Ladd, Kelsey & Woodard, A.I.A.

952
Art Director Jess Gruel
Designer Jess Gruel
Agency Larson/Bateman
Client Quadrant Development Co.

953

954

955

953
Art Directors Bob Kwait
Jim Clark
Designer Bob Kwait
Agency Griswold-Eshleman
Client B. F. Goodrich Engineered Systems

954
Art Director Alan Peckolick
Designer Alan Peckolick
Artist Tom Carnase
Agency Lubalin, Smith, Carnase
Client Helena Rubenstein

955
Art Director Ruut van den Hoed
Designer Ruut van den Hoed
Artist Ruut van den Hoed
Agency Design and Market Research Laboratory
Client Philadelphia 76

956

957

958

956
Art Director David Dobra
Designer Steve Rousso
Artist Steve Rousso
Agency The Workshop
Client American-Overseas Trading Corp.

957
Art Director Stan Baker
Designer Stan Baker
Artist Stan Baker
Agency CIBA-Geigy Corp.
Client CIBA-Geigy Corp.

958
Art Director Gerry Kano
Designer Gerry Kano
Artist Paul Bice, Jr.
Writers Monsignor William J. Barry
Bruce Russell
Agency Gerry Kano Design
Client Campaign for Human Development

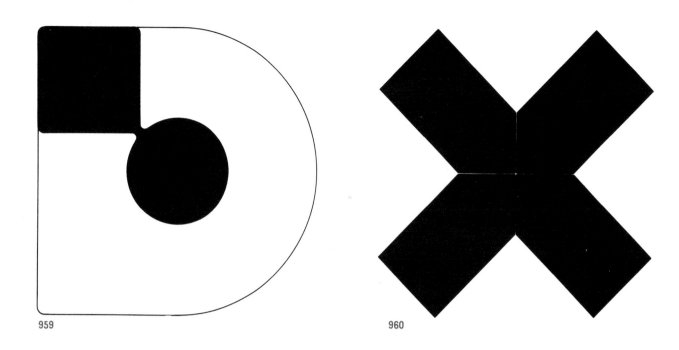

959

960

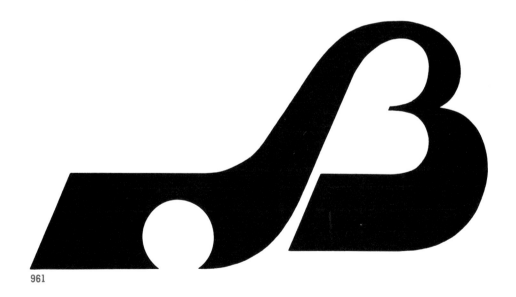

961

959
Art Director Jim Lienhart
Designer Jim Lienhart
Artist Jim Lienhart
Agency Jim Lienhart
Client Darby Lithography

960
Art Director John Dolby
Designer John Dolby
Artist John Dolby
Agency BBDM
Client St. Xavier College

961
Art Director Thomas L. Burden
Designers Jerry Dadds
Eucalpytus Tree Studio Staff
Artists Jerry Dadds
Eucalyptus Tree Studio
Agency Mathis, Burden & Charles
Client Baltimore Blades Ice Hockey

962

963

962
Art Director Robert A. Gale
Designer Robert A. Gale
Agency Siegel & Gale
Client Ram Ridge
Corporate Park
I.E.C. Development Ltd.

963
Art Director Joe Brooks
Artist Tom Carnase
Agency Lubalin, Smith, Carnase
Client Penthouse Magazine

FEELING GOOD

964

Summit University

965

964
Art Director Herb Lubalin
Designer Herb Lubalin
Artist Lubalin, Smith, Carnase
Agency Lubalin, Smith, Carnase
Client Public Broadcasting Service

965
Designer Marty Neumeier
Artist Marty Neumeier
Agency Marty Neumeier
Client Summit University

GrandCanyon
NATIONAL PARK LODGES

966

the Mouse trap
INC.

967

966
Art Director Primo Angeli
Designers Tandy Belew
Primo Angeli
Artist Tandy Belew
Agency Primo Angeli Graphics
Client Grand Canyon

967
Art Director John R. Chepelsky
Designer John R. Chepelsky
Artist John R. Chepelsky
Agency Brand-Edmonds Packett
Client The Mouse Trap

SUSAN COX
MICHAEL DORET
GRAPHIC & TYPOGRAPHIC DESIGN
CONTACT: SUSAN COX
TELEPHONE (312) 642-4349

968

969

968
Art Directors Michael Doret
Steve Stove
Designer Michael Doret
Artist Michael Doret
Agency Michael Doret, Inc.
Client Cox Leisure Time Industries

969
Art Director John Dolby
Designer John Dolby
Artist John Dolby
Agency Genesis
Client Recovery, Resource, Recycling

970

971

972

970
Art Director Clyde Hogg
Designer Clyde Hogg
Artist Larry Bishop
Agency Daniel, Riley & Hogg Advertising
Client WFL Birmingham Americans

971
Art Director Michael Kelly
Designer Michael Kelly
Artists Michael Kelly, John Kirckham
Photographer John Dolby
Agency BBDM
Client Franklin Picture Co.

972
Art Director Richard Erlanger
Designer Richard Erlanger
Artist Richard Erlanger
Agency Goodbye
Client Market Street

NIGHTTIME
CBS Television Network
SPECIALS
CBS Television Network
DAYTIME
SPORTS
CBS Television Network
NEWS
CBS News

973

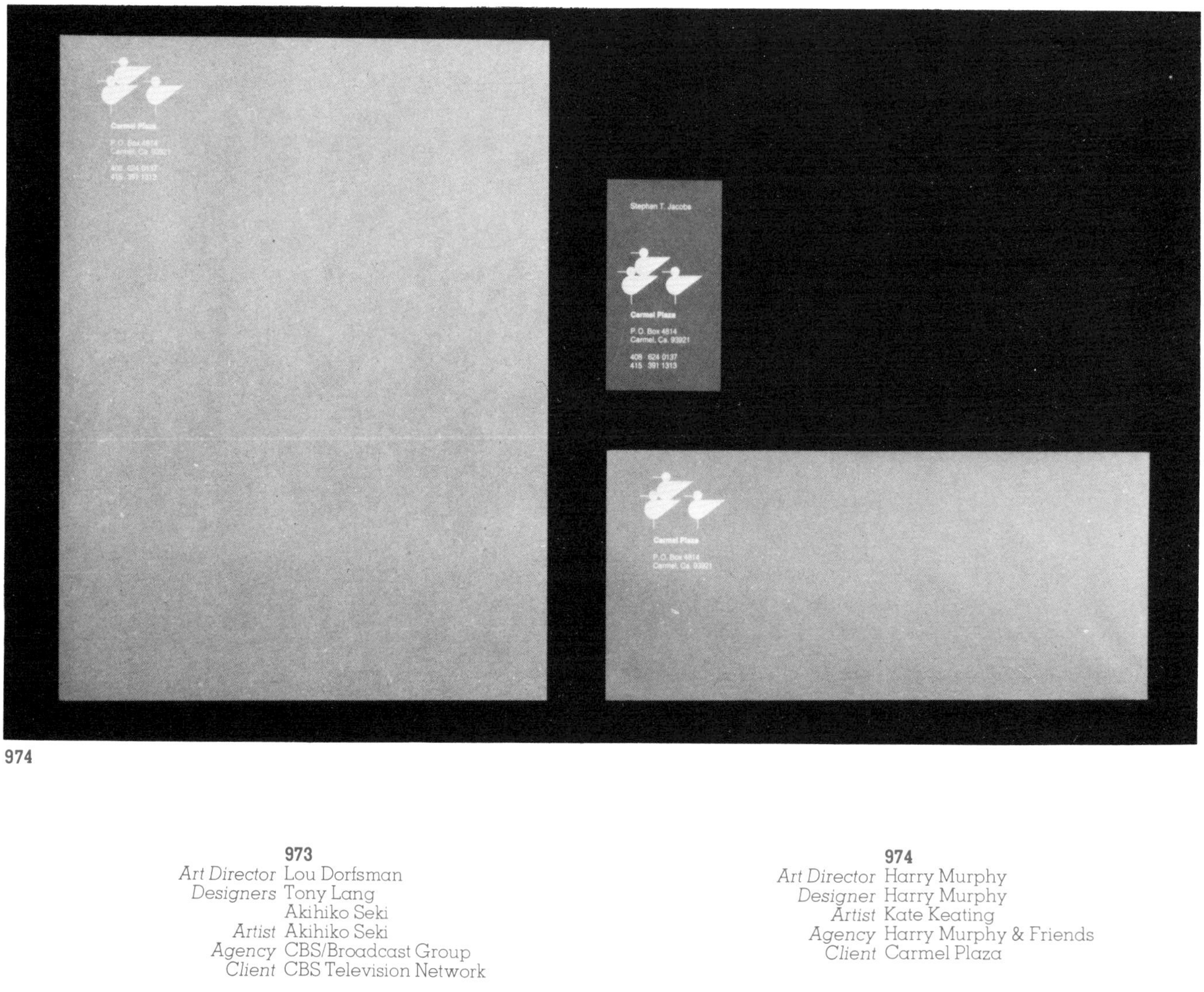
Stephan T. Jacobs
Carmel Plaza
P.O. Box 4814
Carmel, Ca. 93921
408 624 0137
415 391 1313

974

973
Art Director Lou Dorfsman
Designers Tony Lang
Akihiko Seki
Artist Akihiko Seki
Agency CBS/Broadcast Group
Client CBS Television Network

974
Art Director Harry Murphy
Designer Harry Murphy
Artist Kate Keating
Agency Harry Murphy & Friends
Client Carmel Plaza

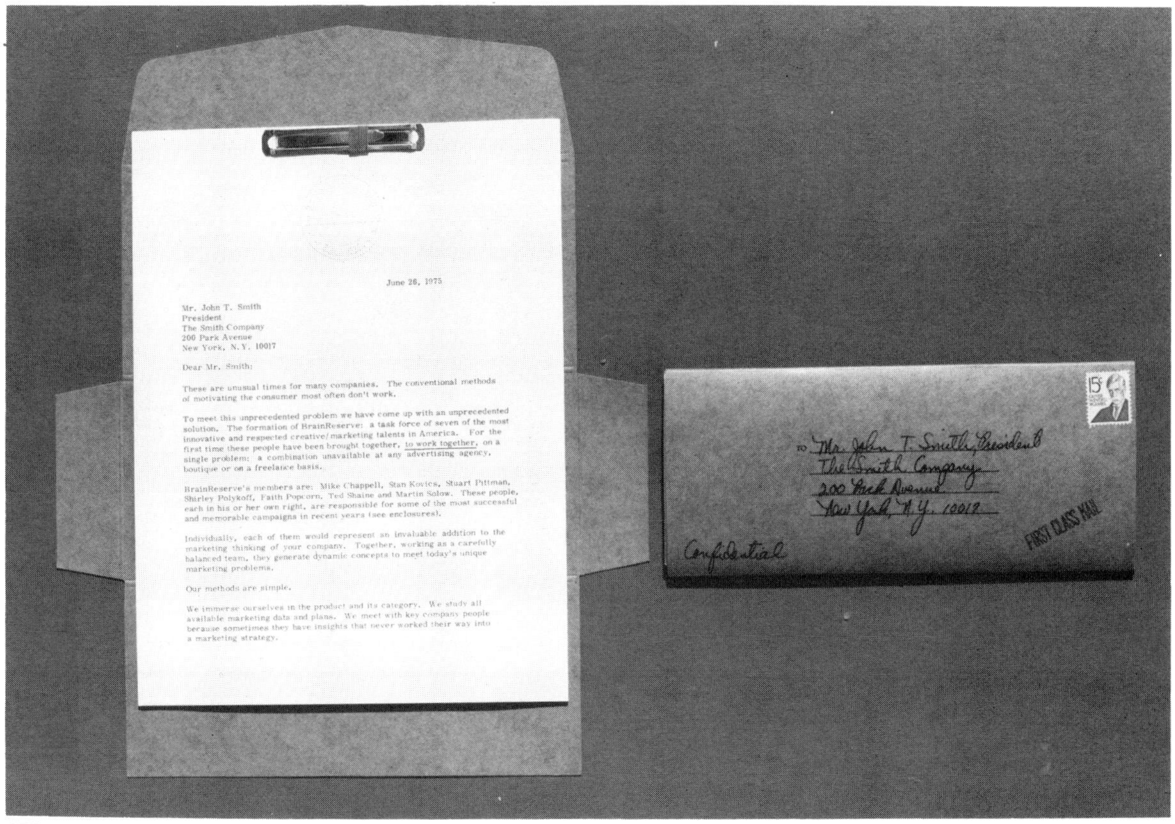
June 26, 1975
Mr. John T. Smith
President
The Smith Company
200 Park Avenue
New York, N.Y. 10017
Dear Mr. Smith:
These are unusual times for many companies. The conventional methods of motivating the consumer most often don't work.
To meet this unprecedented problem we have come up with an unprecedented solution. The formation of BrainReserve: a task force of seven of the most innovative and respected creative/marketing talents in America. For the first time these people have been brought together, to work together, on a single problem: a combination unavailable at any advertising agency, boutique or on a freelance basis.
BrainReserve's members are: Mike Chappell, Stan Kovics, Stuart Pittman, Shirley Polykoff, Faith Popcorn, Ted Shaine and Martin Solow. These people, each in his or her own right, are responsible for some of the most successful and memorable campaigns in recent years (see enclosures).
Individually, each of them would represent an invaluable addition to the marketing thinking of your company. Together, working as a carefully balanced team, they generate dynamic concepts to meet today's unique marketing problems.
Our methods are simple.
We immerse ourselves in the product and its category. We study all available marketing data and plans. We meet with key company people because sometimes they have insights that never worked their way into a marketing strategy.
15¢
Confidential
FIRST CLASS MAIL

975

976

975
Art Directors Stuart Pittman
Faith Popcorn
Designers Stuart Pittman
Faith Popcorn
Writers Faith Popcorn
Stuart Pittman
Agency BrainReserve
Client BrainReserve

976
Art Director Don Strandell
Designer Don Strandell
Artist Don Strandell
Agency Don Strandell Design
Client Bangtails Restaurant

DILL
PRODUCTIONS

977

PLANTINGS
UNLIMITED

978

977
Art Director Clyde Hogg
Designer Clyde Hogg
Artists Larry Bishop
Lisa Johnson
Agency Daniel, Riley & Hogg
Advertising
Client Dill Productions

978
Art Director Pete Traynor
Designer Pete Traynor
Artist Pete Traynor
Writer Douglass B. Forsyth
Agency Ashton-Worthington
Client Plantings Unlimited

abc
This Week
abc
Sunday
abc
Monday
abc
Tuesday
abc
Wednesday
abc
Thursday
abc
Friday
abc
Saturday
abc
Special!

979

U.S.
TEAM

980

979
Art Directors Robert Abel
Harry Marks
Designers Wayne Kimbell
Richard Taylor
Artists Richard Taylor
Wayne Kimbell
Photographers Richard Taylor
Richard Edlund
Client ABC-TV

980
Art Director Harry Murphy
Designer Harry Murphy
Artist Kate Keating
Agency Harry Murphy & Friends
Client U.S. Team Stores

THE FORCE
THE FORCE
"To play and enjoy"
THE FORCE
THE FORCE
THE FORCE
1975

981

The Art Directors Club, Inc.
Member of The Art Directors Club, Inc.
Membership Application

982

981
Art Director Ed Thrasher
Designer Ed Thrasher
Artist Peter Palombi
Writer Ed Thrasher
Agency Warner Bros. Records
Client Warner Bros. Records

982
Art Director Donald A. Adamec
Designer Donald A. Adamec
Artist Tom Carnase
Agency Adamec Assoc.
Client The Art Directors Club of New York

paul harris

983

UNITED

984

983
Art Directors Art Goodman
Vincent Carra
Saul Bass & Assoc. Staff
Designers Mamoru Shimokochi
Saul Bass & Assoc.
Artist Saul Bass & Assoc.
Agency Saul Bass & Assoc.
Client Paul Harris Stores

984
Art Directors Saul Bass
Art Goodman
Vincent Carra
Ron Lane
Designers Vincent Carra
Mamoru Shimokochi
Saul Bass & Assoc.
Artist Saul Bass & Assoc.
Agency Saul Bass & Assoc.
Client United Airlines

calm
MUFFLERS · SHOCKS
calm
calm
MUFFLERS · SHOCKS

985

shops Upper level
Walden Book Store
Eastern Airlines
Sandlers Shoes
Katzenjammer Haus
Pressman, Frohlich & Frost
Mayflower Coffee House
Pemberton Pub
Pressman, Frohlich & Frost

Exit
One Beacon Street
Parking
Center Plaza
PARKING

986

985
Designer F. Eugene Smith Assoc.
Agency F. Eugene Smith Assoc.
Client Standard Oil of Ohio

986
Art Director Robert A. Propper
Designer Robert A. Propper
Agency Propper/Elman
Client Center Plaza Assoc.

987

987
Art Director Harry Murphy
Designer Harry Murphy
Artists Victor Langer
Jim Anderson
Agency Harry Murphy & Friends
Client Security Pacific Bank

CineRentWest
Snazelle Films

CineRentWest
A Division of
Snazelle Films
San Francisco
(415) 864-4644

988

988
Art Director Harry Murphy
Designer Harry Murphy
Artists John Keane
Guy Joy
Jim Anderson
Agency Harry Murphy & Friends
Client Snazelle Films

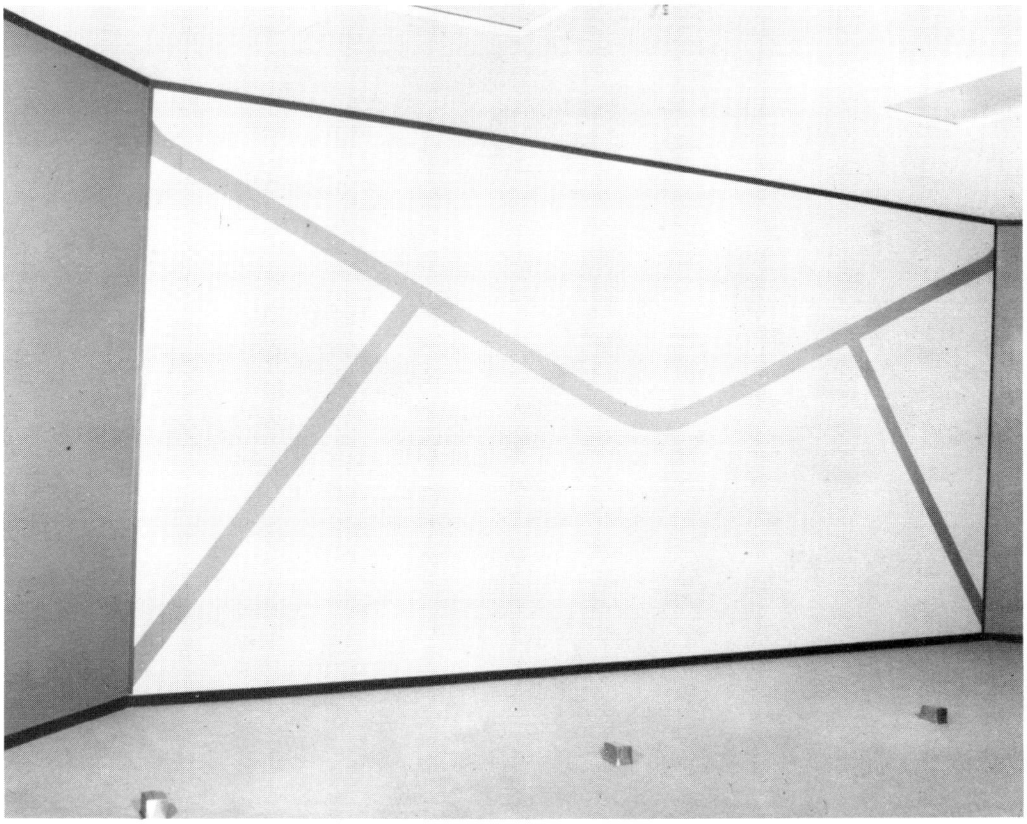

989

989
Art Director Harry Murphy
Designer Harry Murphy
Artists Victor Langer
Jim Anderson
Agency Harry Murphy & Friends
Client Security Pacific Bank

DESIGN

PHOTOGRAPHY & ART

Editorial Photography, b/w	990–996
Editorial Photography, color	997–1030
Sales Promotion Photography, b/w	1031–1032
Sales Promotion Photography, color	1033–1049
Book Photography, b/w	1050–1053
Cover Photography, b/w	1054
Cover Photography, color	1055–1060
Editorial Art, b/w	1062–1078
Editorial Art, color	1079–1113
Sales Promotion Art, b/w	1115–1117
Sales Promotion Art, color	1118–1125
Book Art, color	1126
Cover Art, color	1127–1133

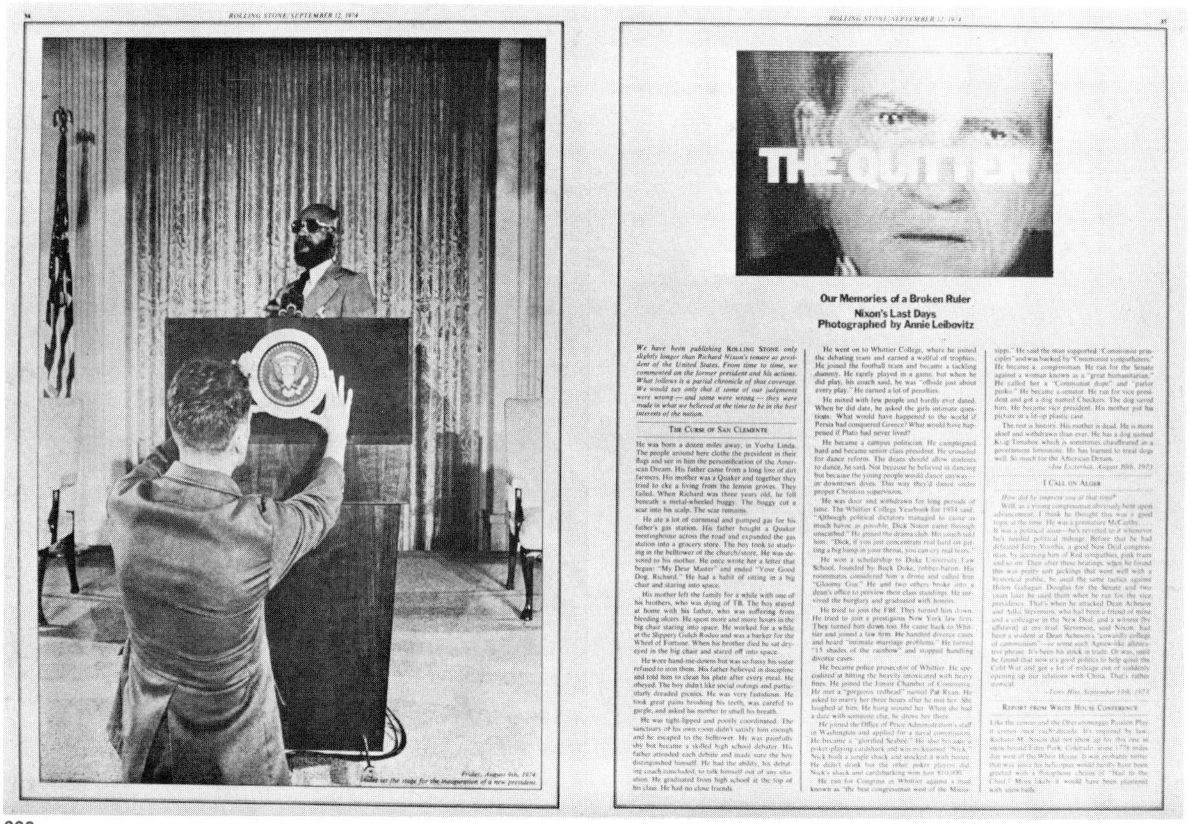
34 ROLLING STONE/SEPTEMBER 12, 1974

Friday, August 9th, 1974
[illegible] set the stage for the inauguration of a new president.

ROLLING STONE/SEPTEMBER 12, 1974 35

THE QUITTER

Our Memories of a Broken Ruler
Nixon's Last Days
Photographed by Annie Leibovitz

We have been publishing ROLLING STONE *only slightly longer than Richard Nixon's tenure as president of the United States. From time to time, we commented on the former president and his actions. What follows is a partial chronicle of that coverage. We would say only that if some of our judgments were wrong — and some were wrong — they were made in what we believed at the time to be in the best interests of the nation.*

THE CURSE OF SAN CLEMENTE

He was born a dozen miles away, in Yorba Linda. The people around here clothe the president in their flags and see in him the personification of the American Dream. His father came from a long line of dirt farmers. His mother was a Quaker and together they tried to eke a living from the lemon groves. They failed. When Richard was three years old, he fell beneath a metal-wheeled buggy. The buggy cut a scar into his scalp. The scar remains.

He ate a lot of cornmeal and pumped gas for his father's gas station. His father bought a Quaker meetinghouse across the road and expanded the gas station into a grocery store. The boy took to studying in the belltower of the church/store. He was devoted to his mother. He once wrote her a letter that began: "My Dear Master" and ended "Your Good Dog, Richard." He had a habit of sitting in a big chair and staring into space.

His mother left the family for a while with one of his brothers, who was dying of TB. The boy stayed at home with his father, who was suffering from bleeding ulcers. He spent more and more hours in the big chair staring into space. He worked for a while at the Slippery Gulch Rodeo and was a barker for the Wheel of Fortune. When his brother died he sat dry-eyed in the big chair and stared off into space.

He wore hand-me-downs but was so fussy his sister refused to iron them. His father believed in discipline and told him to clean his plate after every meal. He obeyed. The boy didn't like social outings and particularly dreaded picnics. He was very fastidious. He took great pains brushing his teeth, was careful to gargle, and asked his mother to smell his breath.

He was tight-lipped and poorly coordinated. The sanctuary of his own room didn't satisfy him enough and he escaped to the belltower. He was painfully shy but became a skilled high school debater. His father attended each debate and made sure the boy distinguished himself. He had the ability, his debating coach concluded, to talk himself out of any situation. He graduated from high school at the top of his class. He had no close friends.

He went on to Whittier College, where he joined the debating team and earned a wallful of trophies. He joined the football team and became a tackling dummy. He rarely played in a game, but when he did play, his coach said, he was "offside just about every play." He earned a lot of penalties.

He mixed with few people and hardly ever dated. When he did date, he asked the girls intimate questions: What would have happened to the world if Persia had conquered Greece? What would have happened if Plato had never lived?

He became a campus politician. He campaigned hard and became senior class president. He crusaded for dance reform. The deans should allow students to dance, he said. Not because he believed in dancing but because the young people would dance anyway—in downtown dives. This way they'd dance under proper Christian supervision.

He was dour and withdrawn for long periods of time. The Whittier College Yearbook for 1934 said: "Although political dictators managed to cause as much havoc as possible, Dick Nixon came through unscathed." He joined the drama club. His coach told him: "Dick, if you just concentrate real hard on getting a big lump in your throat, you can cry real tears."

He won a scholarship to Duke University Law School, founded by Buck Duke, robber-baron. His roommates considered him a drone and called him "Gloomy Gus." He and two others broke into a dean's office to preview their class standings. He survived the burglary and graduated with honors.

He tried to join the FBI. They turned him down. He tried to join a prestigious New York law firm. They turned him down too. He came back to Whittier and joined a law firm. He handled divorce cases and heard "intimate marriage problems." He turned "15 shades of the rainbow" and stopped handling divorce cases.

He became police prosecutor of Whittier. He specialized at hitting the heavily intoxicated with heavy fines. He joined the Junior Chamber of Commerce. He met a "gorgeous redhead" named Pat Ryan. He asked to marry her three hours after he met her. She laughed at him. He hung around her. When she had a date with someone else, he drove her there.

He joined the Office of Price Administration's staff in Washington and applied for a naval commission. He became a "glorified Seabee." He also became a poker-playing cardshark and was nicknamed "Nick." Nick built a jungle shack and stocked it with booze. He didn't drink but the other poker players did. Nick's shack and cardsharking won him $10,000.

He ran for Congress in Whittier against a man known as "the best congressman west of the Mississippi." He said the man supported "Communist principles" and was backed by "Communist sympathizers." He became a congressman. He ran for the Senate against a woman known as a "great humanitarian." He called her a "Communist dupe" and "parlor pinko." He became a senator. He ran for vice president and got a dog named Checkers. The dog saved him. He became vice president. His mother put his picture in a lit-up plastic case.

The rest is history. His mother is dead. He is more aloof and withdrawn than ever. He has a dog named King Timahoe which is sometimes chauffeured in a government limousine. He has learned to treat dogs well. So much for the American Dream.

—Joe Eszterhas, August 30th, 1973

I CALL ON ALGER

How did he impress you at that time?

Well, as a young congressman obviously bent upon advancement. I think he thought this was a good topic at the time. He was a premature McCarthy. . . . It was a political issue—he's reverted to it whenever he's needed political mileage. Before that he had defeated Jerry Voorhis, a good New Deal congressman, by accusing him of Red sympathies, pink traits and so on. Then after these hearings, when he found this was pretty soft pickings that went well with a hysterical public, he used the same tactics against Helen Gahagan Douglas for the Senate and two years later he used them when he ran for the vice presidency. That's when he attacked Dean Acheson and Adlai Stevenson, who had been a friend of mine and a colleague in the New Deal, and a witness [by affidavit] at my trial. Stevenson, said Nixon, had been a student at Dean Acheson's "cowardly college of communism"—or some such Agnew-like alliterative phrase. It's been his stock in trade. Or was, until he found that now it's good politics to help quiet the Cold War and get a lot of mileage out of suddenly opening up our relations with China. That's rather ironical.

—Tony Hiss, September 13th, 1973

REPORT FROM WHITE HOUSE CONFERENCE

Like the comet and the Oberammergau Passion Play it comes once each decade. It's required by law. Richard M. Nixon did not show up for this one in snow-bound Estes Park, Colorado, some 1778 miles due west of the White House. It was probably better that way since his helicopter would hardly have been greeted with a flutophone chorus of "Hail to the Chief." More likely it would have been plastered with snow balls.

990

991

990
Art Director Tony Lane
Designer Tony Lane
Photographer Annie Leibovitz
Publisher Rolling Stone

991
Art Director Ernest Scarfone
Designer Ernest Scarfone
Photographer Jean-Loup Sieff
Writer Julia Scully
Publisher Modern Photography

Detroit's Shattered Love Affair

BY BROCK YATES

It's already been rough…and there's more to come. But the break-up between Detroit and the Big Car is a fact and the industry is quite definitely on the make

• General Motors—flagship of that colossus of all businesses, automobile manufacturing—is still considered by stock market experts to be among the "Blue Chip" issues. Massive fortunes have been accumulated in portfolios thick with GM certificates and there is no question that shares in the world's largest corporation will remain a prestigious stock for the foreseeable future. Yet as The Corporation plunges into its traditional—if somewhat muted—hoopla of the 1975 car introductions, the hard fact is that within the past decade GM stock has declined over half its price. In the late summer of 1964, in the final moments before the industry slammed Titanic-fashion against the iceberg of safety and pollution legislation and mutiny broke out among its consumers, a share of General Motors common stock could be purchased for about $90. Today that same share costs roughly $45.

While this slump in value has been influenced in part by the complicated buying and selling tactics of the money managers who exert pressure on all stocks, the fact remains that market analysts describe GM and its associates who compose the Big Three (or Four if AMC is included) as "mature" industries. This means they are operating with a cyclical demand that can be plotted—even in the face of uncertainties like the Energy Crisis or international monetary fluctuations—with reasonable accuracy. By injecting such economic indicators as birth rates, scrappage rates, disposable income projections and car price indexes, men both within and without the industry can predict annual sales with surprising skill. (While the Energy Crisis will cause 1974 car sales to be about 18 per cent below 1973, it will remain—as several analysts had predicted, the *third* best selling year in history.)

But this predictability is not attractive to the men who buy and sell common stock because it implies a latent stagnation. "Quite simply, GM or Ford are producing no new technology," says one analyst. "Even if the rotary engine comes along … or steam … or electricity, it will probably not be enough to cause dramatic shifts in the market. And dramatic shifts brought about by new technology—the Xeroxes and IBMs—or life styles are what produce demand for stock. As long as the automobile industry provides a predictable demand from one year to the next and the short-term money market provides a better return on investment than GM dividends, the stock will probably continue its steady decline."

Is the American automobile industry over the hill? A tour through the environs of Detroit motordom implies nothing resembling decay, but conversely there is little indication of dynamism. A car builder's executive offices or research facility reminds you of a power plant or a new public library: sparsely furnished … and scrubbed and waxed to the verge of fetish. There are few people in sight and the place is permeated with an atmosphere of aseptic momentum that requires no human involvement other than routine fiddling with a few valves and buttons. The ambience is the same in such divergent buildings as the wood-paneled Lincoln-Mercury headquarters in Dearborn—which dates from the early days of the Ford empire—to the stolid splendor of the monster General Motors building on West Grand Boulevard in Detroit to the severe, Eero Saarinen-designed steel and glass boxes of the General Motors Styling and Technical Center in suburban Warren. Tidiness seems to be the primary mission. It appears that this industry is so old and so orderly that it knows no confusion or chaos, that it views the passage of time and events with the same placid aloofness as the Vatican or the Bank of England. If there is one simple emotion that can be attributed to this industry, it would be complacency.

It is the inner conviction of each employee that steadiness and continuity—the evolution rather than revolution which has produced a half-century of virtually uninterrupted prosperity—will overwhelm momentary fads and prickly external threats. And circumstances insure that this faith in the continuity will be self-sustaining and self-renewing because culture and commerce in Detroit are intertwined to a point where one cannot be separated from the other. Unlike a Seventh Avenue dress manufacturer whose relationship to ladies-ready-to-wear is highly abstract or the aerospace worker whose personal life has little involvement with his computers and rocket boosters, men and women in the automobile industry are participants in the fantasies upon which their empire is built. It is the living American Dream, complete with a split-level in the suburbs, a pool in the back yard and—most important—its driveway filled with a pair of opulent, shining automobiles. So the central theme of the industry and the cars it builds are a direct reflection of the middle-class life styles of Greater Detroit. "American cars are at their best in Detroit," says one expert. "The streets are wide and there is no premium on space in the suburbs, so parking lots can spread everywhere. The country is flat, so brakes and suspensions have never

OCTOBER 1974

992

Breach of promise

By Larry L. King

The bombshell that was the unpardonable Pardon should have registered as little more than a firecracker even on Watergate-stewed brains. Had we but consulted the record and available clues, we might have suspected—whether useful citizens or mere reporters—that it had been written in the stars. Richard Nixon probably knew it; likely he sensed in his craftier nooks that, should push come to shove, then Gerald R. Ford would prove as loyal as any old dog.

Ford's well-advertised Old Shep qualities, indeed, may account for why Nixon so cheerfully tapped him for Veep: it was nothing less than a form of disaster insurance. While the rest of us sailed for the obvious in explaining Ford's selection (he was of the Congress and loved by it, a body the slipping President needed quickly to shore up), Dick Nixon knew something everyone else forgot in the new numbness attending Spiro Agnew's fall and heightened Watergate suspicions: that Gerald Ford is one of the relatively few living Americans who not only admires Nixon but actually *likes* him.

Ideologically, the two are brothers: Ford voted for more than 90 percent of Nixon's legislative proposals, spoke out in defense of programs bogged in the congressional morass and otherwise carried faithful water. From their earliest days in the House of Representatives—Nixon came in '47, Ford followed in '49—they had appeared to be kindred spirits. One assumes that Jerry Ford had no notion, back then, of those dark secret furies agitating Dick Nixon's soul. They were young hail-fellow founding members of the Chowder and Marching Society, a group of double-conservative Republicans who regularly met to enjoy simple food and Middle America fellowship including sing-alongs during which Nixon punished the piano, Bob Michael of Illinois bellowed the desired key and Jerry Ford grinned. Even then Nixon was the star of the group, having bagged Alger Hiss, and the others deferred to him.

Though ever a loner and always uncertain of where he belonged, Dick Nixon took pains to return for Chowder and Marching Society functions even after moving on to the Senate and then to the vice-presidency; he donned the club apron and chef's hat, gamely offering that determined stiff grin. Feeling occasional golfing urges, he invited Jerry Ford's participation. In a minor way, Ford came close to being Nixon's early Bebe Rebozo. In 1965, by which time all sane people had given Dick Nixon up for politically dead, Ford told a journalist (though carefully placing it off the record so as not to offend others) that Nixon remained his presiden-

The public has been jilted again, this time by the unpardonable Pardon; but then, Jerry Ford's affair with Richard Nixon goes way, way back

tial choice. "He calls me and checks in with me, sometimes from pay phones at airports," Ford said. "Nelson Rockefeller and the others—well, they don't do that." When House Minority Leader Ford called on the apparently moribund Nixon to stump the country for party congressional hopefuls, he appreciated the quick response. "Dick's a team man," the old Michigan football star miscalculated. Ford places team men on a pedestal; like the late Speaker Sam Rayburn, he believes that the best way to get along is to go along. Certainly he went along with Dick Nixon almost from scratch.

Though President Nixon was contemptuous of the Congress, rarely taking it into his confidence or receiving its advice, he sometimes consulted Jerry Ford. Ford was one of precious few congressmen who received advance warning that Nixon intended to war on Cambodia; he offered his immediate approval and later passionately defended the new war in the House. As the Asian war bogged down under LBJ, Ford more than Nixon offered harsh criticism, not because President Johnson's war taxed the nation's resources and patience but because, in Ford's view, we were muffing a chance to win by failing to provide enough bombs, manpower and napalm.

Indeed, Ford always has been a loyal old Cold Warrior, one who consistently voted for the larger schemes of the Pentagon brass and who limited his examinations of weaponry systems to seeking what Eisenhower's secretary of Defense, Engine Charlie Wilson, called "the biggest bang for the buck." He went along with a successful dirty trick to provide covert CIA funding toward the defeat of a member of the Japanese Diet who had blocked a state visit by President Eisenhower; he voted for hush-hush funds to sponsor the disastrous U-2 spy flights over Russia; he fought Red China's admission to the United Nations, criticized John F. Kennedy for failing to succeed at the Bay of Pigs and otherwise believed with Dick Nixon and others who carried big sticks. (Two weeks ago, he asked Congress to increase appropriations for Vietnam to the level Nixon had originally requested.)

His willingness to do Dick Nixon's dirty work was perhaps most apparent in Ford's fruitless effort to bring impeachment proceedings against Supreme Court Justice William O. Douglas in retaliation for the U.S. Senate's refusal to confirm Judges Carswell and Haynsworth to the big court. Not even the youngest pageboy in the Republican cloakroom believes the idea originated with Ford: it was a brainchild of Nixon and Attorney General John Mitchell, one that disastrously backfired after they had Ford threaten to begin his impeachment attempt should the Senate fail to confirm. Once Justice Blackmun

993

992
Art Director Gene Butera
Designer Gene Butera
Photographer Doug Mesney
Writer Brock Yates
Publisher Car and Driver

993
Art Director Steve Phillips
Photographer Carl Fischer
Writer Larry L. King
Publisher New Times Magazine

Fashion

By Patricia Peterson

From the ground up

994

995

994
Art Director Ruth Ansel
Designer Ruth Ansel
Photographer Elliott Erwitt
Editor Mary Simons
Publisher The New York Times Magazine

995
Art Director Steve Heller
Designer Steve Heller
Photographer Jerry N. Uelsmann
Editor Charlotte Curtis
Publisher The New York Times Op-Ed Page

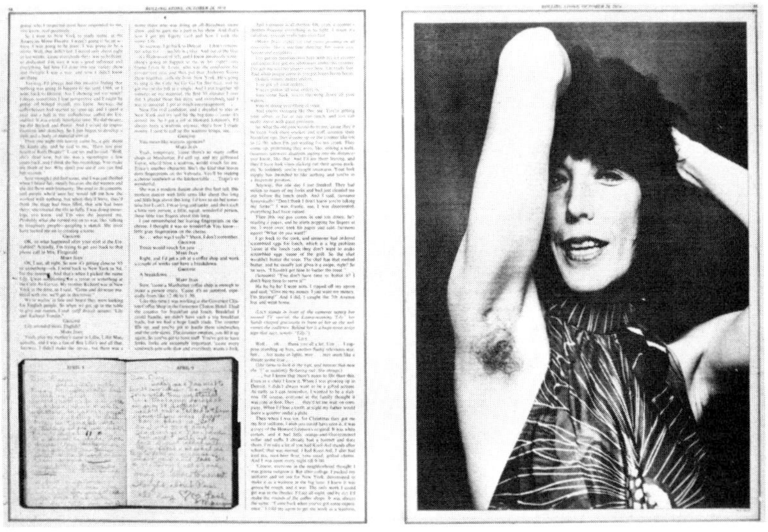

996

996
Art Director Tony Lane
Designer Tony Lane
Photographer Annie Leibovitz
Publisher Rolling Stone

997

997
Art Director David Moy
Designer Bette Lord
Photographer Bette Lord
Publisher The Washington Post

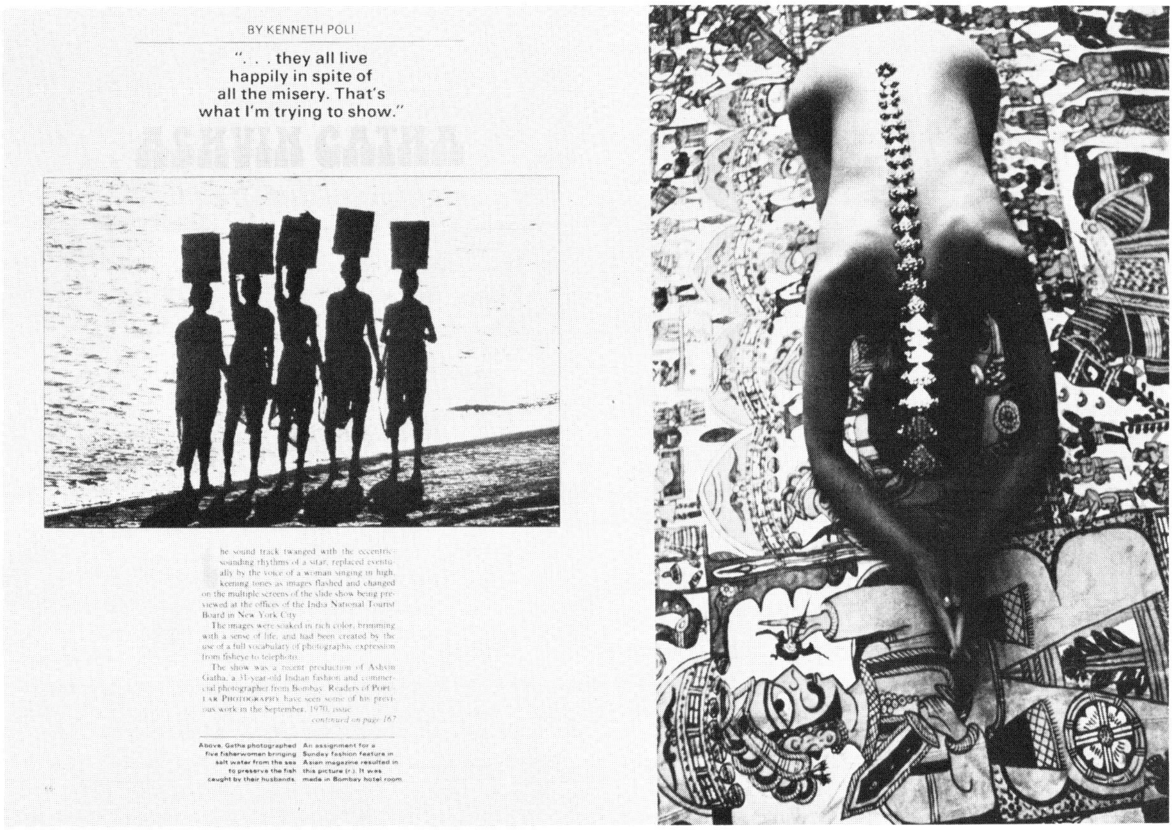

BY KENNETH POLI

"... they all live happily in spite of all the misery. That's what I'm trying to show."

ASHVIN GATHA

The sound track twanged with the eccentric-sounding rhythms of a sitar, replaced eventually by the voice of a woman singing in high, keening tones as images flashed and changed on the multiple screens of the slide show being previewed at the offices of the India National Tourist Board in New York City.

The images were soaked in rich color, brimming with a sense of life, and had been created by the use of a full vocabulary of photographic expression from fisheye to telephoto.

The show was a recent production of Ashvin Gatha, a 31-year-old Indian fashion and commercial photographer from Bombay. Readers of POPULAR PHOTOGRAPHY have seen some of his previous work in the September, 1970, issue.

continued on page 167

Above, Gatha photographed five fisherwoman bringing salt water from the sea to preserve the fish caught by their husbands.

An assignment for a Sunday fashion feature in Asian magazine resulted in this picture (r.). It was made in Bombay hotel room.

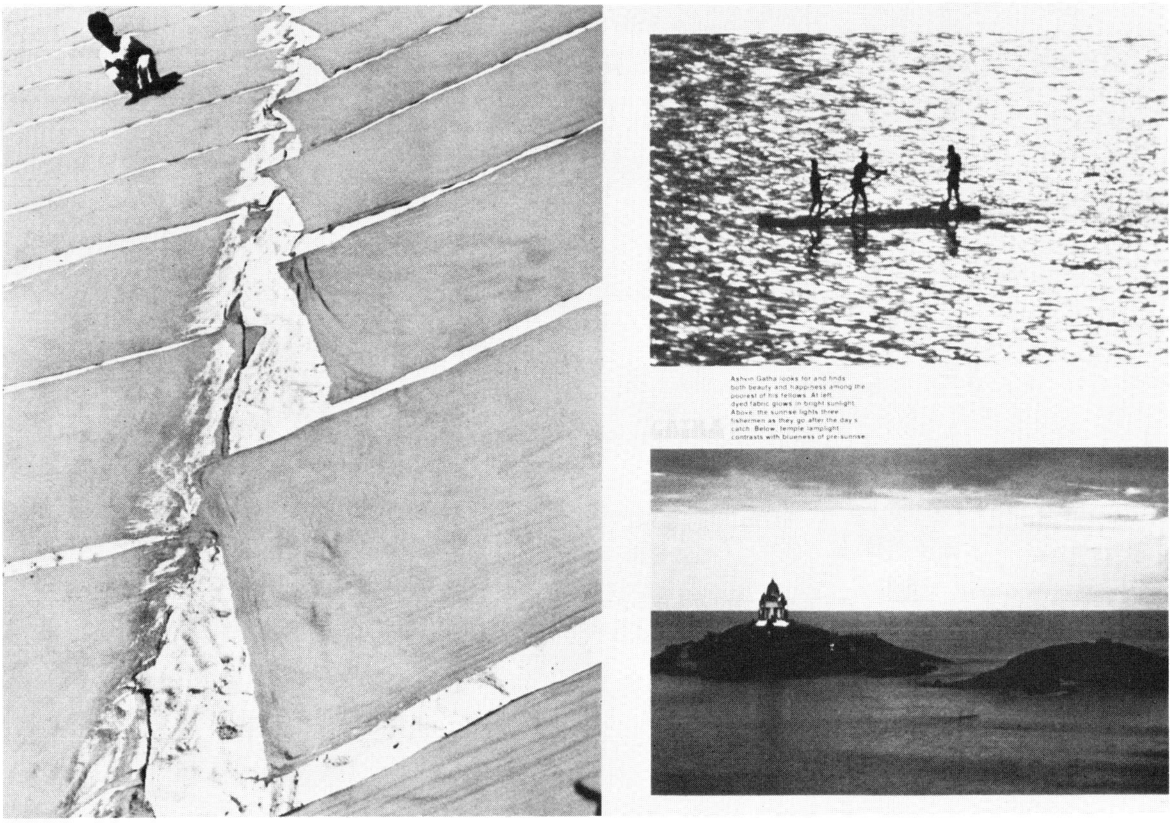

Ashvin Gatha looks for and finds both beauty and happiness among the poorest of his fellows. At left dyed fabric glows in bright sunlight. Above: the sunrise lights three fishermen as they go after the day's catch. Below, temple lamplight contrasts with blueness of pre-sunrise.

998

998

Art Director Shinichiro Tora
Designer Shinichiro Tora
Photographer Ashvin Gatha
Writer Kenneth Poli
Publisher Popular Photography

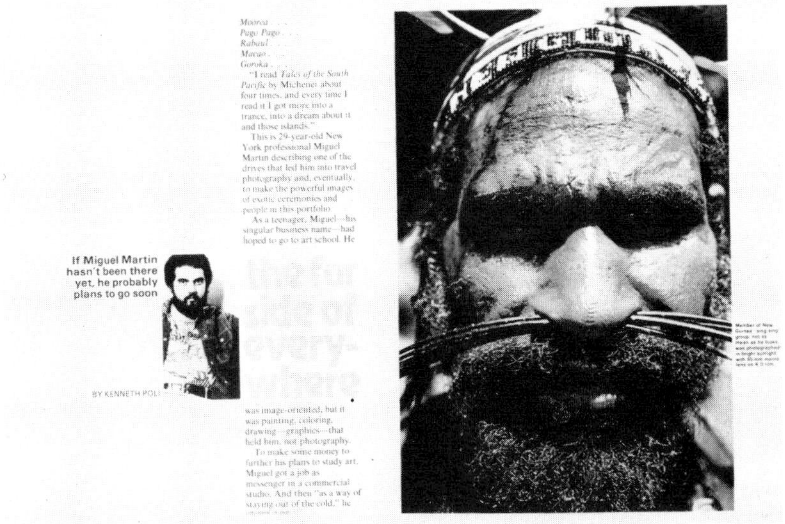
Moorea . . .
Pago Pago . . .
Rabaul . . .
Macao . . .
Goroka . . .
"I read Tales of the South Pacific by Michener about four times, and every time I read it I got more into a trance, into a dream about it and those islands."
This is 29-year-old New York professional Miguel Martin describing one of the drives that led him into travel photography and, eventually, to make the powerful images of exotic ceremonies and people in this portfolio.
As a teenager, Miguel—his singular business name—had hoped to go to art school. He
If Miguel Martin hasn't been there yet, he probably plans to go soon
the far side of every-where
BY KENNETH POLI
was image-oriented, but it was painting, coloring, drawing—graphics—that held him, not photography.
To make some money to further his plans to study art, Miguel got a job as messenger in a commercial studio. And then "as a way of staying out of the cold," he

the far side of every-where

the far side of every-where

999

999

Art Director Shinichiro Tora
Designer Shinichiro Tora
Photographer Miguel Martin
Writer Kenneth Poli
Publisher Popular Photography

Like a movie crew shooting a close-up of Hell, Bill Connelly and Joe Zimmer of Truck Co. 6 ride their firemen's boom near the explosive core of a chemical fire at the Columbia Southern Trucking terminal in Jersey City.

1001

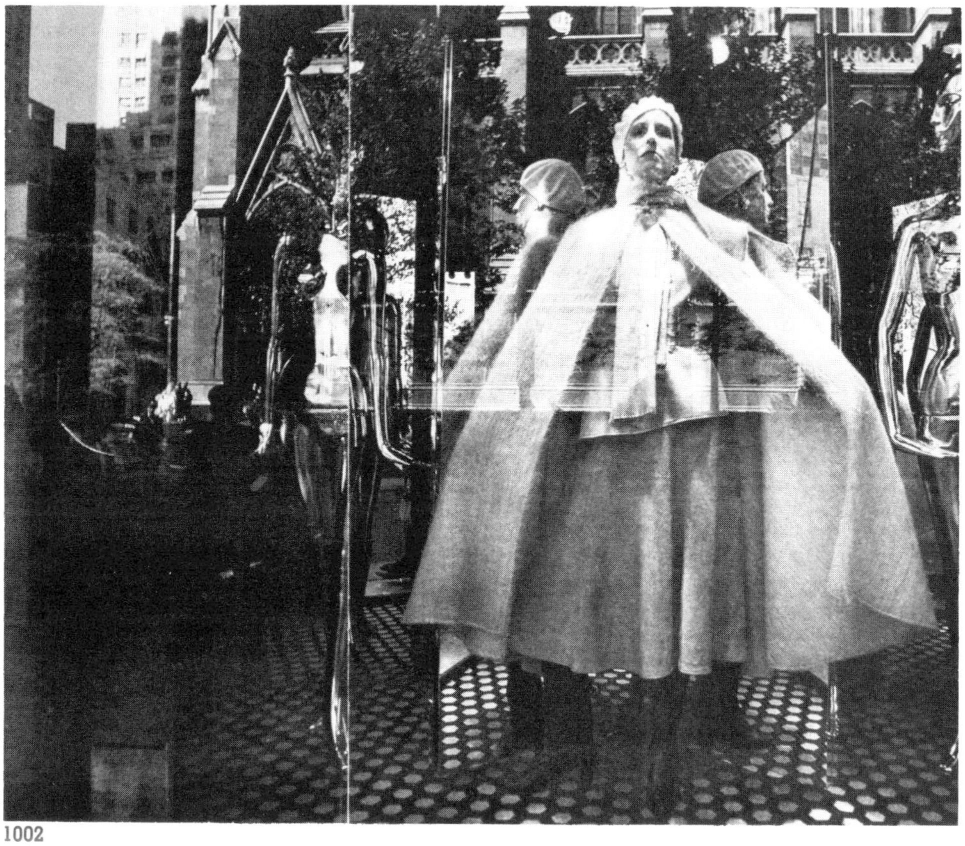

1002

PHOTOGRAPHY & ART

1001
Art Director Elton Robinson
Photographer Pete Turner
Publisher Life Special Reports
Time, Inc.

1002
Art Director Nancy Kent
Designer Nancy Kent
Photographer James H. Karales
Writer Mary Louise Ransdell
Publisher Town & Country

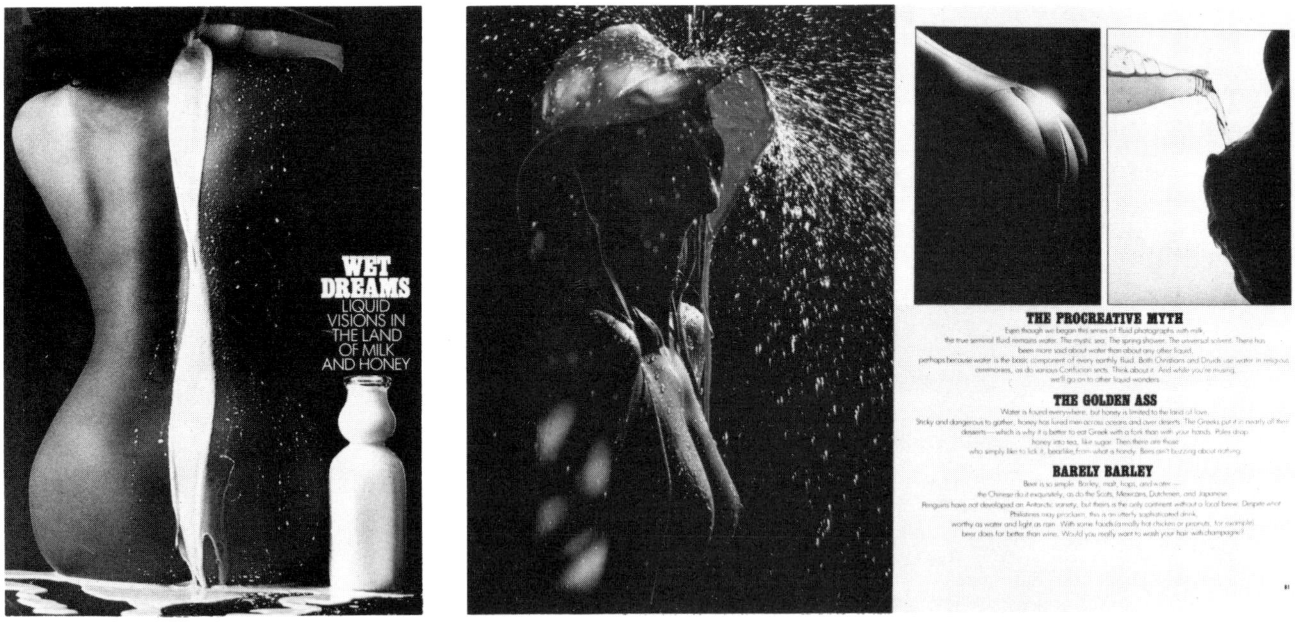

WET DREAMS

LIQUID VISIONS IN THE LAND OF MILK AND HONEY

THE PROCREATIVE MYTH

Even though we began this series of fluid photographs with milk, the true seminal fluid remains water. The mystic sea. The spring shower. The universal solvent. There has been more said about water than about any other liquid, perhaps because water is the basic component of every earthly fluid. Both Christians and Druids use water in religious ceremonies, as do various Confucian sects. Think about it. And while you're musing, we'll go on to other liquid wonders.

THE GOLDEN ASS

Water is found everywhere, but honey is limited to the land of love. Sticky and dangerous to gather, honey has lured men across oceans and over deserts. The Greeks put it in nearly all their desserts—which is why it is better to eat Greek with a fork than with your hands. Poles drop honey into tea, like sugar. Then there are those who simply like to lick it, bearlike, from what is handy. Bees ain't buzzing about nothing.

BARELY BARLEY

Beer is so simple. Barley, malt, hops, and water— the Chinese do it exquisitely, as do the Scots, Mexicans, Dutchmen, and Japanese. Penguins have not developed an Antarctic variety, but theirs is the only continent without a local brew. Despite what Philistines may proclaim, this is an utterly sophisticated drink, worthy as water and light as rain. With some foods (actually hot chicken or peanuts, for example) beer does far better than wine. Would you really want to wash your hair with champagne?

81

1003

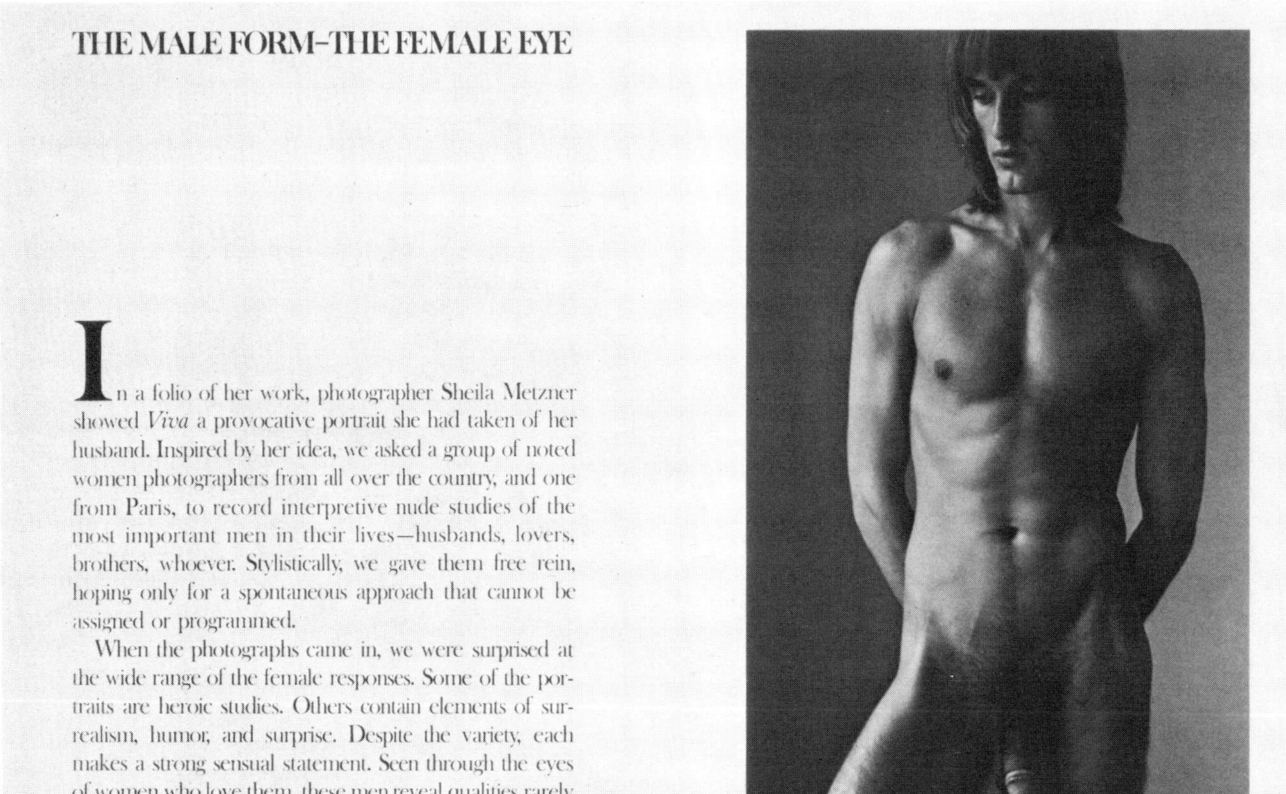

THE MALE FORM–THE FEMALE EYE

In a folio of her work, photographer Sheila Metzner showed *Viva* a provocative portrait she had taken of her husband. Inspired by her idea, we asked a group of noted women photographers from all over the country, and one from Paris, to record interpretive nude studies of the most important men in their lives—husbands, lovers, brothers, whoever. Stylistically, we gave them free rein, hoping only for a spontaneous approach that cannot be assigned or programmed.

When the photographs came in, we were surprised at the wide range of the female responses. Some of the portraits are heroic studies. Others contain elements of surrealism, humor, and surprise. Despite the variety, each makes a strong sensual statement. Seen through the eyes of women who love them, these men reveal qualities rarely captured on film.

TANA KALEYA

78 VIVA

1004

SILVER

1003
Art Director Don Menell
Designer Michael Brock
Photographer Larry Dale Gordon
Publisher Oui

1004
Art Director Ahmad Sadiq
Designers Frank DeVino
Hector Marrero
Photographers Lynn Davis
Tana Kaleya
Others
Publisher Viva

CLICK!

The Beautiful Bare Thigh Is Back

We love the naked flanks, the glossy skin, the elegance, the freedom. And all it takes is a frilly little waistling with provocatively dangling garters, a pair of sheer sheer stockings, and you. Black flounced with lace (right) dares to go solo over sandalfoot stockings that hug the thighs with stretchy lace tops. The set by Van Raalte, $8. Available at Bergdorf Goodman, New York; Foley's of Houston; Burdine's, Miami. Shoes: Golo.

Hip-hugger garter belt and matching bikini (above)... very French, very fresh. Both edged with eyelet stretch lace. The set, by John Kloss for Lily of France in Dacron stretch yarn, $6. Stockings: Round-the-clock. Shoes: Couture Collection at Chelsea Cobbler.

Photographs by Art Kane

62

1005

1006

1005
Art Director Roy Carruthers
Designer Carl Barile
Photographer Art Kane
Publisher Viva

1006
Art Director Ernest Scarfone
Designer Ernest Scarfone
Photographer Rodger Buchanan
Writer Agustus Wolfman
Publisher Nikon World

1007

WOMAN AS EROTIC FANTASY

PHOTOGRAPHS BY ART KANE

In Richard Lindner's work, the duality of his artistic nature is expressed in a compelling involvement with Woman as a symbol that has the force of an erotic obsession. Women dominate paintings that blend surrealism, caricature, theatricality, and fantasy in images of great formal power. He exposes the banality and compulsive quality of our environment with a unique style in which women are depicted as aggressive and unyielding, monstrous, even dangerous, yet he infuses them with a startling sexuality and an inherent humanity.

Born in 1901, Lindner grew up in Nuremberg. He fled to France in the Thirties and then, in 1941, to New York, where he became a successful fashion illustrator. Returning to painting in the Fifties, he gained public recognition during the ascendancy of pop art, a movement whose concern, like Lindner's, was with the poetic interpretation and intensification of experience through the use of distortion, spatial illusion, and the complex arrangement of our culture's symbols. Here, Art Kane gives photographic expression to Richard Lindner's painterly visions of women as seductresses whose exotic, heavy makeup is both disguise and revelation.

1008

1007
Art Director Ernest Scarfone
Designer Ernest Scarfone
Photographer Alan Kaplan
Publisher Nikon World

1008
Art Director Carl Barile
Designer Carl Barile
Photographer Art Kane
Publisher Viva

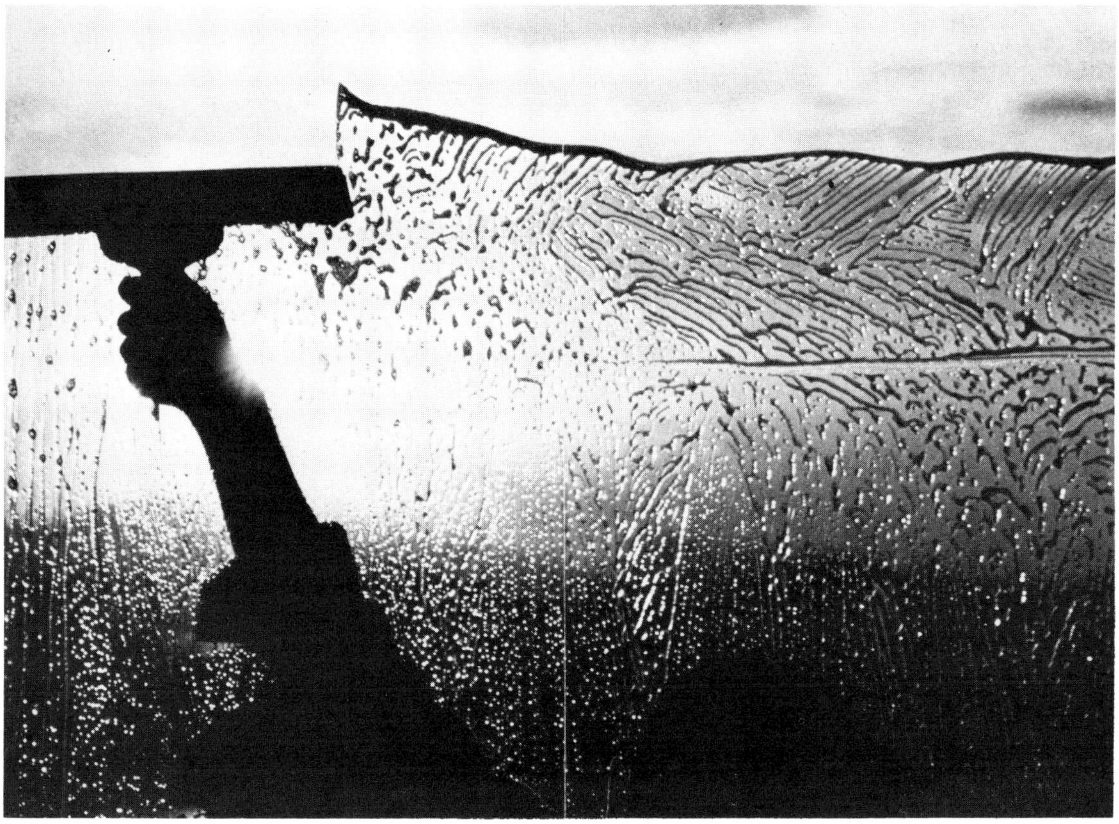

1009

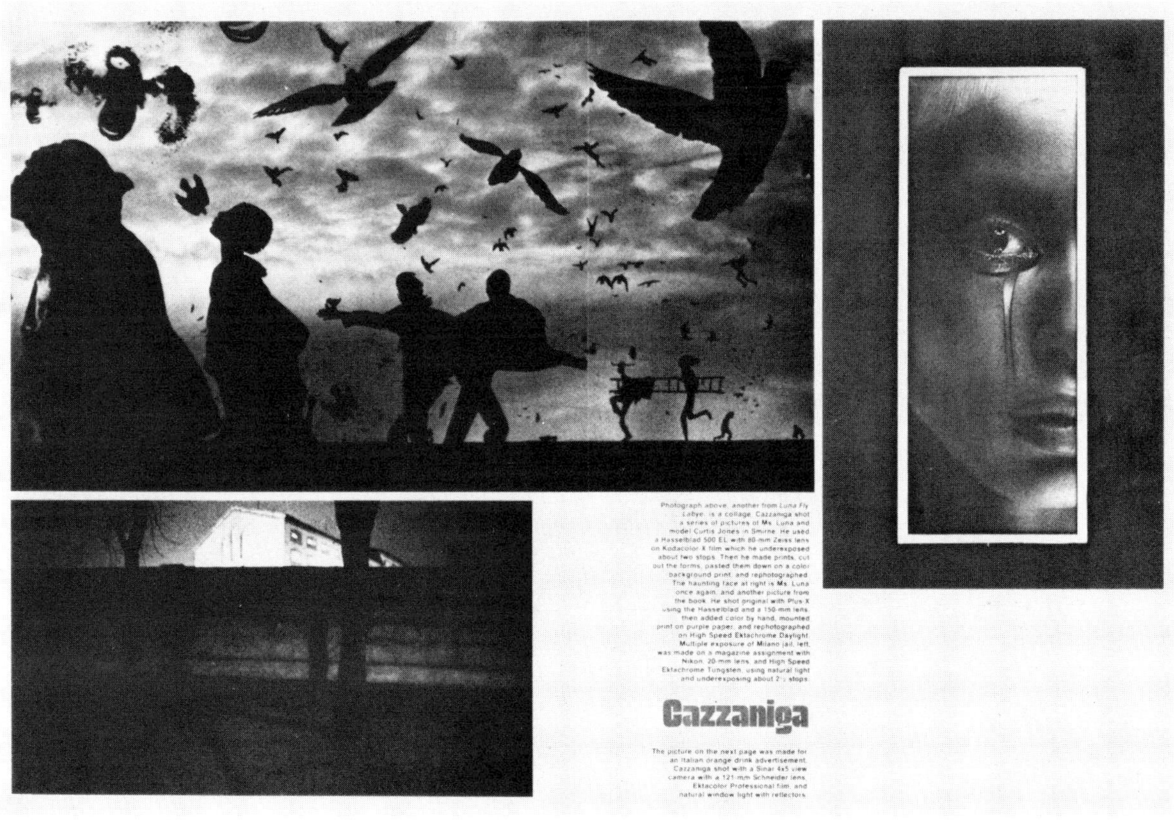

Photograph above, another from *Luna Fly Labye*, is a collage. Cazzaniga shot a series of pictures of Ms. Luna and model Curtis Jones in Smirne. He used a Hasselblad 500 EL with 80-mm Zeiss lens on Kodacolor X film which he underexposed about two stops. Then he made prints, cut out the forms, pasted them down on a color background print, and rephotographed. The haunting face at right is Ms. Luna once again, and another picture from the book. He shot original with Plus-X using the Hasselblad and a 150-mm lens, then added color by hand, mounted print on purple paper, and rephotographed on High Speed Ektachrome Daylight. Multiple exposure of Milano jail, left, was made on a magazine assignment with Nikon, 20-mm lens, and High Speed Ektachrome Tungsten, using natural light and underexposing about 2½ stops.

Cazzaniga

The picture on the next page was made for an Italian orange drink advertisement. Cazzaniga shot with a Sinar 4x5 view camera with a 121-mm Schneider lens, Ektacolor Professional film, and natural window light with reflectors.

1010

1009
Art Director Ernest Scarfone
Designer Ernest Scarfone
Photographer Jay Maisel
Writer Julia Scully
Publisher Modern Photography

1010
Art Director Shinichiro Tora
Designer Shinichiro Tora
Photographer Luigi Cazzaniga
Writer Richard Busch
Publisher Popular Photography

1011

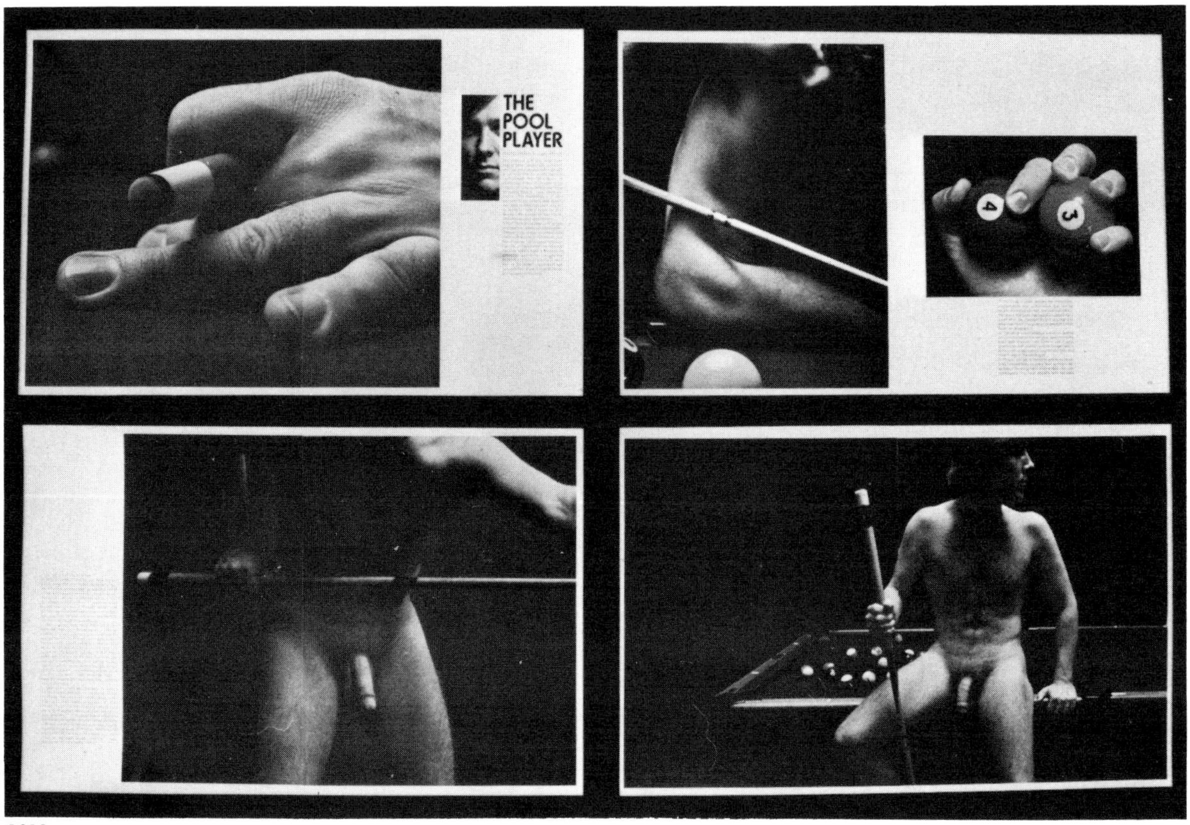
THE
POOL
PLAYER

1012

1011
Art Director Ernest Scarfone
Designer Ernest Scarfone
Photographer André Martin
Writer Julia Scully
Publisher Modern Photography

1012
Art Directors Art Kane
Ahmad Sadiq
Designer Frank DeVino
Photographer Carl Fischer
Publisher Viva

This Edwardian feast, which outdoes even that famous one prepared on television by Mrs. Bridges for King Edward VII, begins, at left, with raw oysters dolloped with mimosa sauce and red caviar dribbled with lemon juice and served with chilled Dom Perignon Champagne from Moet et Chandon. Two soups follow, a thickish sturgeon potage garnished with tiger lily buds (in tureen) and a thin wild mushroom bouillon with a passatelli garnish (in bowl), both taken with a cold Moselle, Bernkastler Doctor und Graben Spatlese, and a rusk or two. Above, the meal continues with a sauced turbot poached in Chablis surrounded by shrimp, mussels, quenelles of whiting, baby lobsters and fleurons of flaky pastry. The Chablis accompanies the dish. Next, upper right and on plate, a partridge pie. A claret, Chateau Margaux, is drunk with this course. The bottle was cropped from the picture but can be seen overleaf.

1013

In 1952 Lee Grant appeared headed for acting fame. She had scored a big hit in a small part as the freaked-out shoplifter in the Broadway play Detective Story. Then she did the movie version and won a Cannes Film Festival Award.
It was at that point that the anti-Red hysteria of the McCarthy period almost destroyed her. Because she had married a blacklisted writer named Arnold Manoff, she suddenly found herself unable to get work in Hollywood. For twelve lean years she took what she could get off-Broadway and with the few courageous producers who ignored the blacklist. In 1958 she faced the House Un-American Activities Committee, denied being a Communist, and then defiantly took the Fifth Amendment as they attempted to terrorize her into informing on friends and fellow workers.
Somehow she survived and fought her way back. Last October she coproduced, codirected, and performed in "The Shape of Things," a CBS special by and about women. She recently completed the film The Internecine Project, starring opposite James Coburn. Her track record includes the lead in the Broadway comedy hit The Prisoner of Second Avenue and the title role in Electra for Joseph Papp's New York Shakespeare Festival Theater. She also did Two for the Seesaw, and won an Obie award for her off-Broadway performance in Jean Genet's The Maids.
Probably her most incredible achievement was in the dreary but wildly successful TV series "Peyton Place," in which she triumphed over a script of outstanding mediocrity to win an Emmy.
Lee moved from New York to Malibu in 1966, but she is Manhattan born and bred and proud of it. She now lives with her second husband, producer-director Joe Feury in a red barnlike house overlooking the Pacific. They share it with their newly adopted daughter and assorted dogs and cats. Over the fireplace are huge blow-ups of Dinah, Lee's seventeen-year-old daughter who is away at a California college. Dinah looks like a cross between her mother and Liza Minnelli.
Lee greeted Viva interviewer Linda Kuehl at the appointed afternoon hour. She looked sleepy and harassed. She wore no eye makeup, as if to say, "See, I haven't done the Hollywood number on you." Her straw-colored hair was worn in the slightly disheveled state that seems to excite men. Her skin was translucently pale, unmarked by the California sun. She wore faded jeans, an old black sweater, a gray flannel blazer, and yellow-tinted Gloria Steinems. She sat in a faded blue-and-white floral armchair, nibbling saltines and sipping Tab.
In talking about herself, she vacillates from "I am a realist" to "I am a child." They may both mean the same thing. She plays to her audience even in an interview. She endears, cajoles, cons, and rationalizes, but she usually protects her inner core of privacy—except for sudden, spontaneous bursts of self-revelation. Her parting words were, "I don't think I've ever talked so much to anybody in my life, outside of my diary when I was twelve. I may have to have you shot as you board the plane!"
VIVA interview
LEE GRANT
Viva: Are you as "supermodern" and "superhip" as many people say you are?
Grant: I guess hip is the avant-garde of what's doing in relationships. At this time, hip might be like going to bed with other women, right? So, no, I'm not hip—I'm not going to bed with other women. Many of my younger friends of twenty-two and twenty-three are into it because there aren't any younger men available. And when they have an involvement with a man, they find the relationship is very rocky, very painful. They find the guys aren't there when they need them. They can rely more on their girl friends than on their men friends. So where it's permissible to have sex with a girl, they do.
Viva: Why do you personally reject bisexuality?
Grant: I don't know. This past year I was supposed to do a picture with Tuesday Weld about two women in love. We had a director and a producer and we were actually getting close to a deal. Then the Supreme Court passed the censorship thing and everybody backed away. But in the process of thinking about the part, I explored the possibility. Given the framework of the story, it certainly seemed possible. If I were in a situation where a man wasn't
47

1014

1013
Art Director Richard Weigand
Designer Richard Weigand
Photographer Henry Wolf
Writer Roy Andries de Groot
Publisher Esquire

1014
Art Director Ahmad Sadiq
Designers Frank DeVino
Hector Marrero
Photographer Jean Pagliuso
Publisher Viva

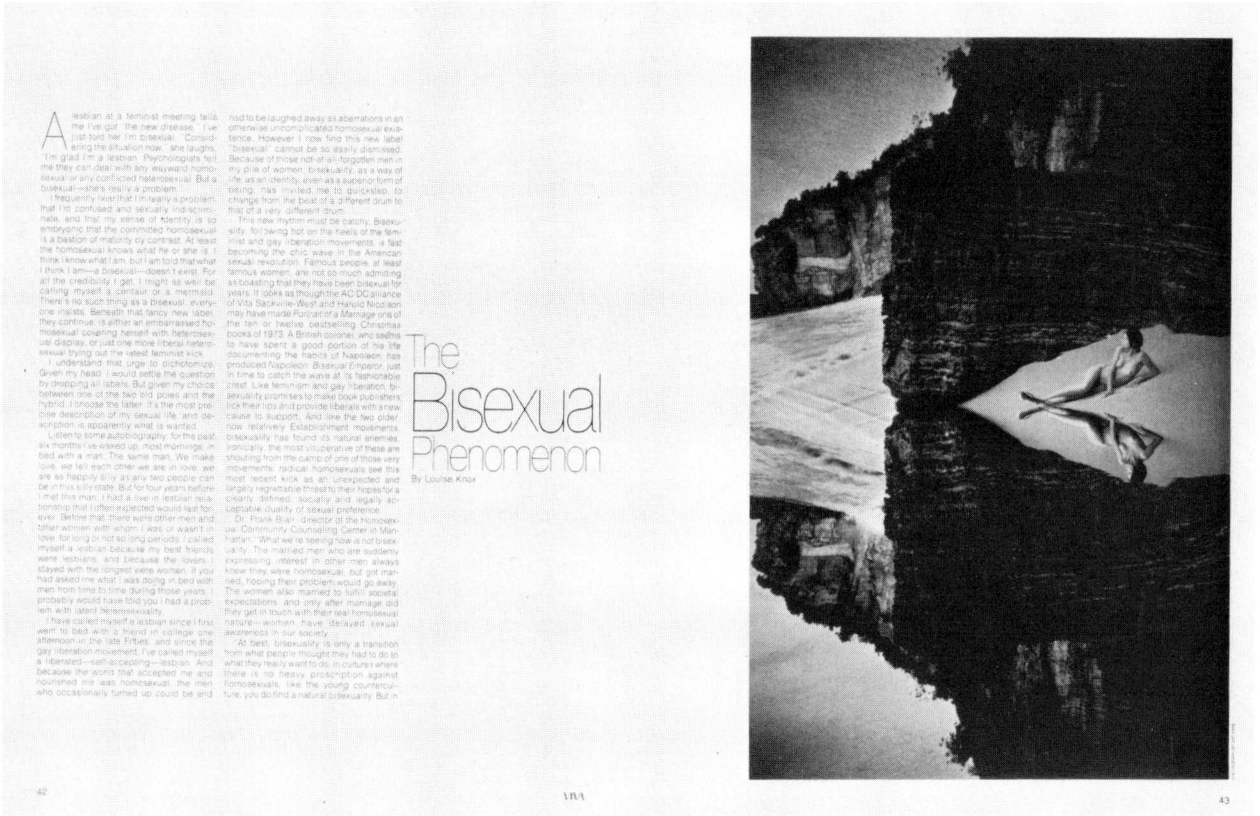
The Bisexual Phenomenon
By Louise Knox

1015

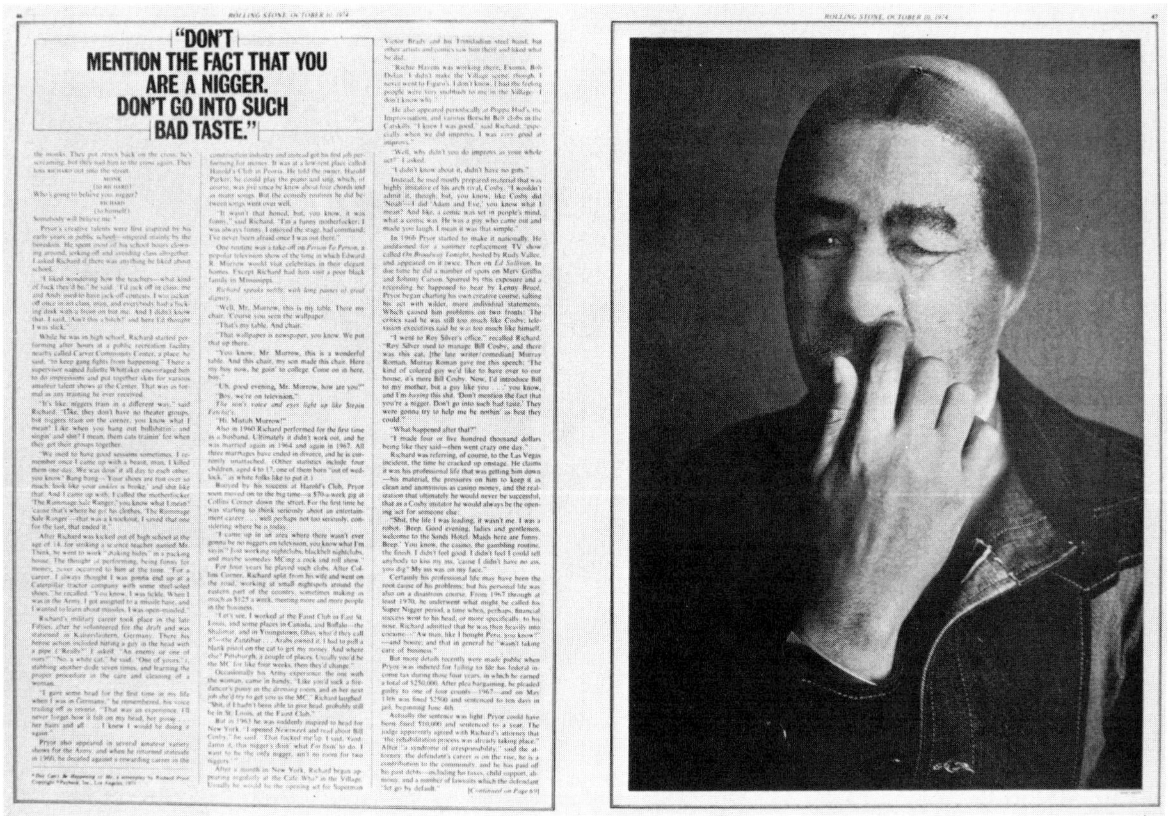
"DON'T MENTION THE FACT THAT YOU ARE A NIGGER. DON'T GO INTO SUCH BAD TASTE."

1016

1015
Art Director Ahmad Sadiq
Designers Hector Marrero
Frank DeVino
Photographer Art Kane
Publisher Viva

1016
Art Director Tony Lane
Designer Tony Lane
Photographer Annie Leibovitz
Publisher Rolling Stone

1017

1018

1017
Art Director Gene Butera
Designer Gene Butera
Photographer Gene Butera
Writer William Jeanes
Publisher Car and Driver

1018
Art Director Ernest Scarfone
Designer Ernest Scarfone
Photographer Rodger Buchanan
Writer Agustus Wolfman
Publisher Nikon World

MEMORIES
PHOTOGRAPHS BY MAUREEN LAMBRAY
Standing amid the shrouded furniture in the old Back Bay mansion once filled with gay children and deep laughter, she was bathed in a warm, milky light that evoked scenes of past joy, of Jack's first novel, of Alison, breaking the news of her engagement, and of that memorable afternoon when the three sisters had listened to Edward's abdication speech.
Her robe by Harriet Love Shop, N.Y.C. Hairstyles: Pascal

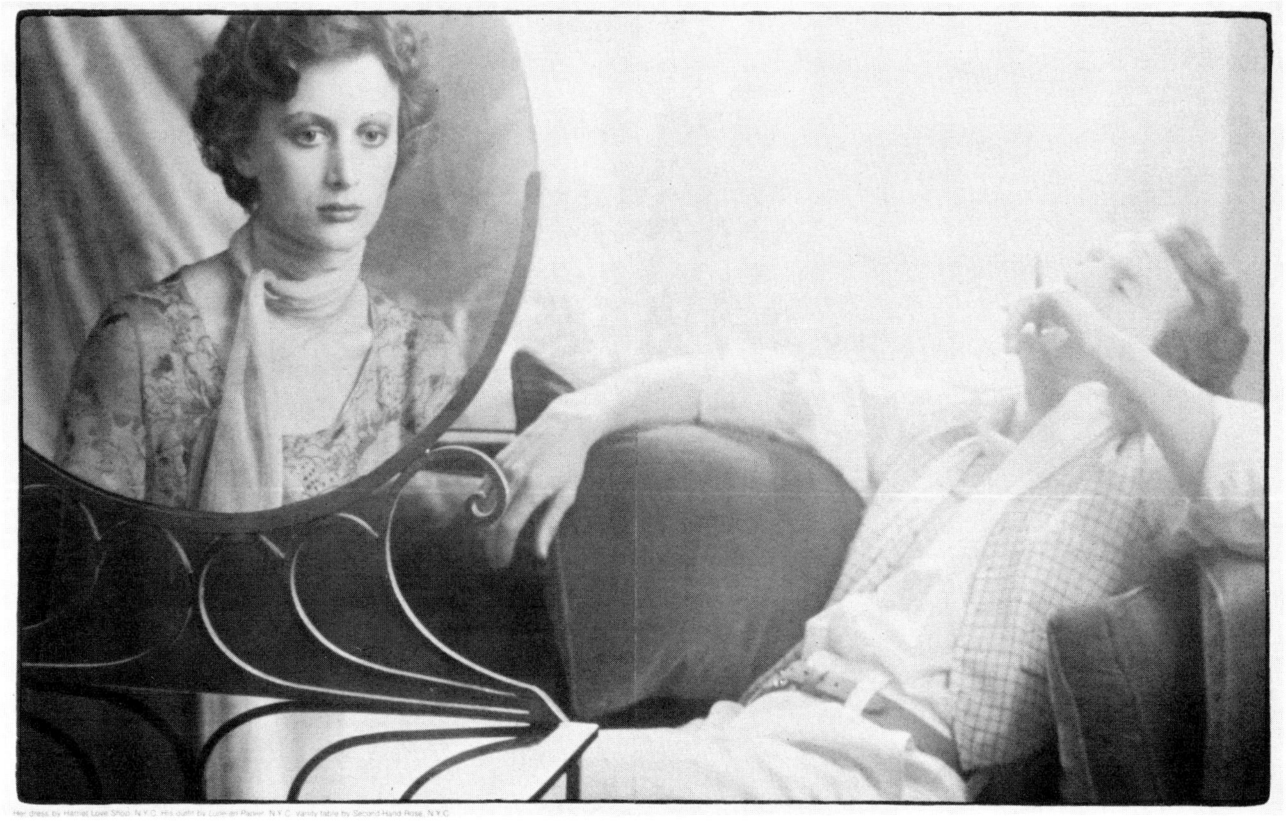

1020

1020
Art Director Ahmad Sadiq
Designers Frank DeVino
Hector Marrero
Photographer Maureen Lambray
Publisher Viva

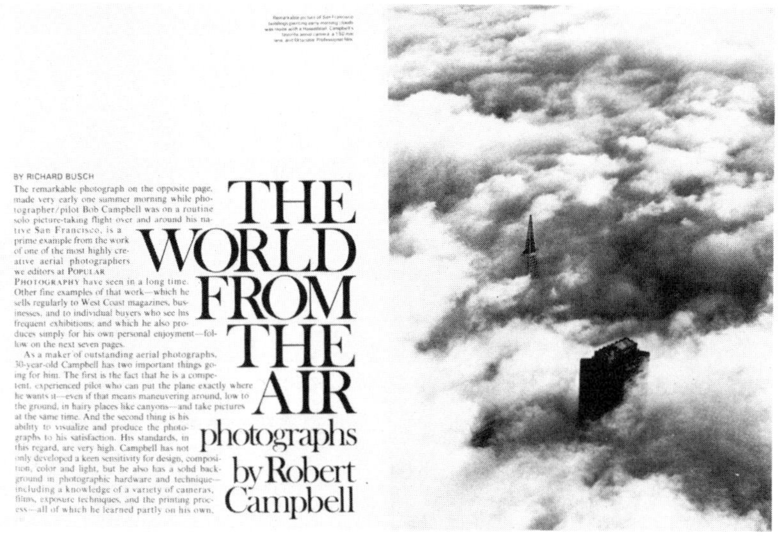

THE WORLD FROM THE AIR

photographs by Robert Campbell

BY RICHARD BUSCH

The remarkable photograph on the opposite page, made very early one summer morning while photographer/pilot Bob Campbell was on a routine solo picture-taking flight over and around his native San Francisco, is a prime example from the work of one of the most highly creative aerial photographers we editors at POPULAR PHOTOGRAPHY have seen in a long time. Other fine examples of that work—which he sells regularly to West Coast magazines, businesses, and to individual buyers who see his frequent exhibitions; and which he also produces simply for his own personal enjoyment—follow on the next seven pages.

As a maker of outstanding aerial photographs, 30-year-old Campbell has two important things going for him. The first is the fact that he is a competent, experienced pilot who can put the plane exactly where he wants it—even if that means maneuvering around, low to the ground, in hairy places like canyons—and take pictures at the same time. And the second thing is his ability to visualize and produce the photographs to his satisfaction. His standards, in this regard, are very high. Campbell has not only developed a keen sensitivity for design, composition, color and light, but he also has a solid background in photographic hardware and technique—including a knowledge of a variety of cameras, films, exposure techniques, and the printing process—all of which he learned partly on his own.

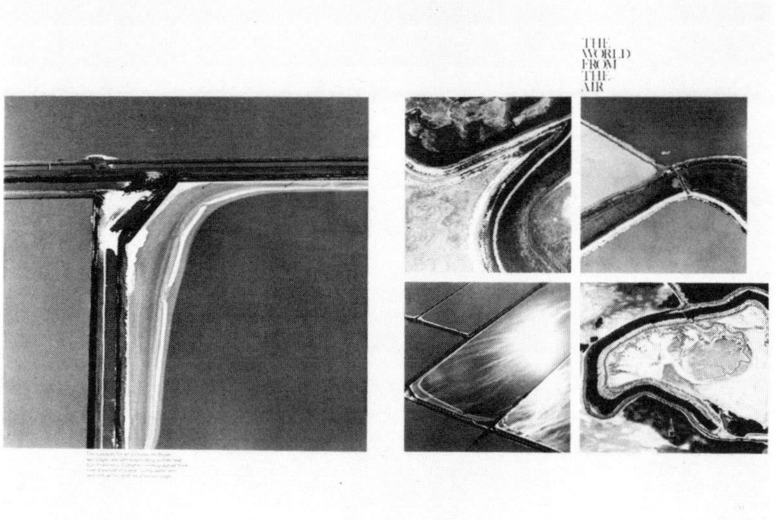
THE WORLD FROM THE AIR

THE WORLD FROM THE AIR

1022

1022
Art Director Shinichiro Tora
Designer Shinichiro Tora
Photographer Robert Campbell
Writer Richard Busch
Publisher Popular Photography

1023

THE KITCHEN
A STORY IN PICTURES BY ART KANE

1023
Art Director Ernest Scarfone
Designer Ernest Scarfone
Photographer André Martin
Writer Julia Scully
Publisher Modern Photography

1024
Art Director Carl Barile
Designers Art Kane
Carl Barile
Photographer Art Kane
Publisher Viva

VIVA FASHION

BARELY COVERED

Minimal Suits For Maximum Exposure

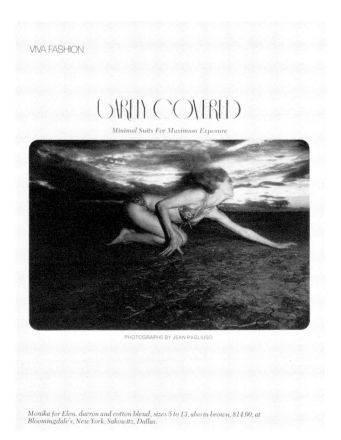

PHOTOGRAPHS BY JEAN PAGLIUSO

Monika for Elon, dacron and cotton blend, sizes 5 to 13, also in brown, $14.00, at Bloomingdale's, New York; Sakowitz, Dallas.

Gottex of Israel, Lycra and nylon, sizes 8 to 14, $26.00, at Saks Fifth Avenue, New York.

Jer-Sea of Sweden, silk polyester, sizes 6 to 14, $22.00, at Bonwit Teller, New York.

1025

1025

Art Director Ahmad Sadiq
Designers Art Kane
Frank DeVino
Hector Marrero
Photographer Jean Pagliuso
Publisher Viva

Images born of private dreams, then synthesized in the darkroom: it's the fantasy world of

KUYTAE HWANG

BY CHARLES REYNOLDS

For the first 100 years or so of its brief history, the art of photography was mostly dedicated to showing us aspects of the real world we live in—its scenic wonders, its momentous events and its everyday happenings, its people great and small. Frequently transformed by the sensibilities of the fine photographers who perceived and captured these things on film, they were called to our attention through the medium of the camera. Today through photography and the various media which transmit it, we have seen a great many things many times over. We have seen the Taj Mahal and the landscape of the moon. The horrors of war have been shown us so many times that the result is we have become numbed to their shock. Even the most far-out sexual subjects are rapidly becoming part of the visual commonplace with the relaxing of taboos within the world of communications.

All of this is having its reaction in the directions in which young photographers are moving. Rather than showing us the outside world in its infinite variety for the thousandth or millionth time, many have chosen to turn their vision inward and reveal to us a world of private dreams and fantasies both staged for the camera and synthesized in the darkroom. The work of Kuytae Hwang, a South Korean-born photographer who has lived in Los Angeles for the last eight years, is a fascinating example of this growing trend.

Starting out as a black-and-white photographer for a newspaper in Seoul, Hwang's photographic interests switched from straight photojournalism to created graphic pictures in high-contrast black-and-white to color. Finally he settled on the Type R printing process which made it possible for him to combine two or more color photographs in the darkroom to create his final, highly personal fantasy image.

Hwang feels that many things which are either ugly or commonplace to the eye can be made beautiful or compelling through the medium of photographic combination. "I want to explore dimensions that are not in the so-called world of reality before the camera but in the worlds I think of. I want to show in my pictures the concepts of hard-to-express fantasies and thoughts. These can be beautiful, mysterious, or frightening, depending on how you look at them. For example, sometimes when I am driving and I see many cars passing me, I feel fearful. I associate a car with a scary monster, even though it is operated by and for man. I have never actually seen a car driven by a sinister-looking giant owl, but this was the frightening image I wanted to express. By combining two photographs in the darkroom, I was able to express my feelings about the automobile. A car is a very convenient means of life in America, but it is also a monster. I'm operating that monster every day."

Hwang will often use filters when photographing the images which are later to be combined in the darkroom to get a specific effect. He also frequently combines pictures taken in 120 format with those taken in 35-mm in order to get a final composite image. His standard working equipment is a Nikon F with 50-mm lenses. Which lens and camera he uses for each part of the image depends upon his preconceived idea of how that segment should appear in the final composite print. For example, in the car and owl picture, the owl was photographed with the Hasselblad and a 250-mm lens, while the extreme wide-angle shot of the car was made with the Nikon F and 20-mm lens.

In some of Hwang's photographs he strives not to create a surrealistic fantasy effect but merely a poetic image that would be difficult for him to achieve in any other way but composite printing. Of his picture of the moon reflected in a pool of water he comments, "Once upon a time, there was a famous poet called Yee Ta Bek in China. There is a famous story about him that when he saw a beautiful moon reflected on a crystal lake, being very charmed with it, he jumped into the lake to catch the moon and never came out. It is almost impossible to find such a romantic subject around my life in the American city so full of smog, noise, and mechanism. I added a moon to the reflection of a building and falling leaves in a small pond. Is it a little poetic at all?"

Kuytae Hwang has recently had a one-man show in the Press Hall in Seoul, Korea (January 1973) followed by the Pentax Gallery in Tokyo (April 1973). He has also participated in various group shows both in the U.S. and abroad. He feels that he has been influenced by Edmund Teske, with whom he studied at U.C.L.A.; and by the work of Ernst Haas, which he likes very much while acknowledging that it is very different from his own. He is currently opening his own color lab (specializing in Type R color printing) in a suburb of Los Angeles.

Bizarre image of owl driving red automobile was made by combining telephoto shot of bird with wide-angle shot of car, on one Type R print.

1026

1027

1026
Art Director Shinichiro Tora
Designer Shinichiro Tora
Photographer Kuytae Hwang
Writer Charles Reynold
Publisher Popular Photography

1027
Art Director Ernest Scarfone
Designer Ernest Scarfone
Photographer Rodger Buchanan
Writer Agustus Wolfman
Publisher Nikon World

JAY MAISEL

UN SOLITAIRE A LA RECHERCHE DES BEAUTES URBAINES

Tout entretien avec Jay Maisel commence par le même acte de foi. « Il y a, dit-il, deux choses que j'aime par-dessus tout : l'amour et la photographie ». N'étant pas dans notre propos de développer le premier point, nous nous sommes surtout intéressés au second et à ces photos réalisées entre 1965 et 1973 à New York, en Californie et dans le Montana, sélectionnées par l'auteur lui-même. Jay Maisel vit à New York dans une vieille banque désaffectée, l'ex-« Germania Bank », située dans le Bowery, le quartier des clochards. C'est plusieurs centaines de milliers de dollars qu'il lui en a coûté pour rénover cet immeuble de quatre étages, tous décorés de marbre, de boiseries et de cuivres. Comme Maisel n'a ni « book » ni agent, il expose ses photos d'une façon permanente sur tous les murs, pour ses clients éventuels. Dans les anciens coffres du sous-sol, il a entreposé matériel, négatifs et archives. Le reste lui sert d'habitation. Ce sont d'immenses pièces où s'entassent des milliers d'objets. « Je collectionne tout. Je suis un mélange d'amateur d'art et de chiffonnier. » C'est à l'âge de vingt-trois ans, en 1953, que Jay Maisel est venu à la photographie. Un temps, il s'était essayé à la peinture, mais s'était ravisé. Le pas décisif, il l'a franchi un jour de cette année-là, quand, étudiant à l'université de Yale, son professeur Buckminster Fuller lui a prêté un appareil. Pendant un an, il est donc photographe le jour et boulanger la nuit, pour payer ses études. Tous les mardis, il se rend à New York pour montrer ses clichés. Son premier client sera le magazine « Dance », puis un groupe pharma- (suite page 93)

1028

1028
Art Director Regis Pagnez
Designer Eric Colmet-Daage
Photographer Jay Maisel
Editor Jean Jacques Naudet
Publisher Daniel Filipacchi
Paris

1029

1030

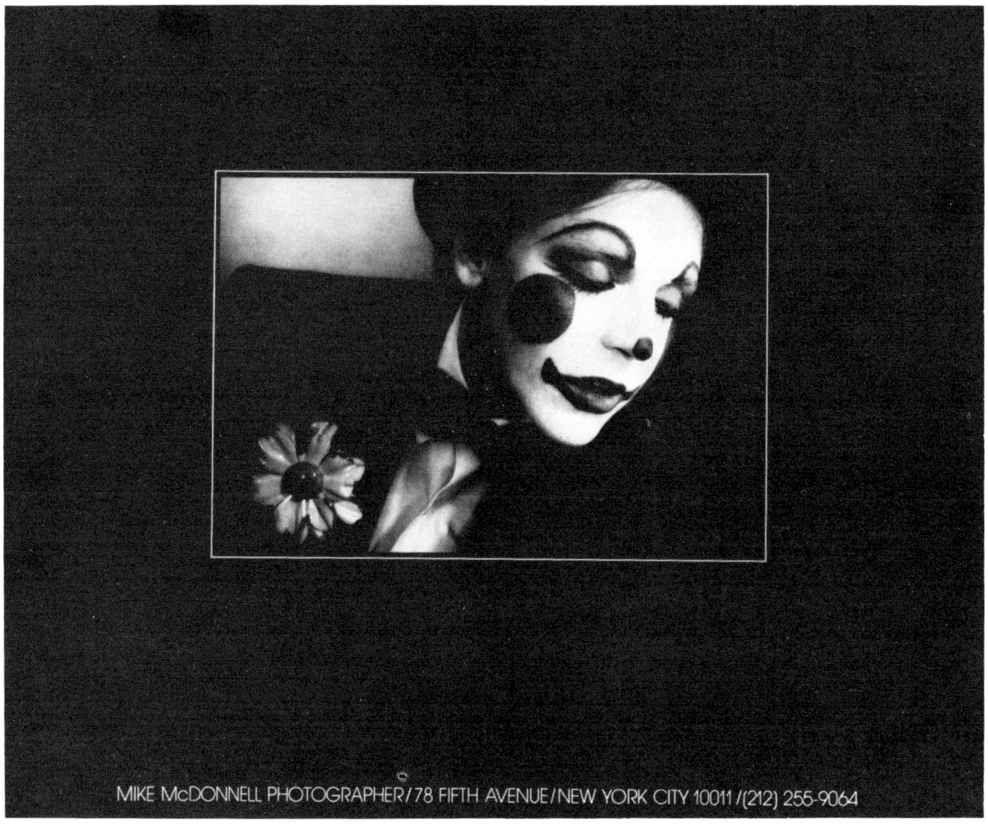
MIKE McDONNELL PHOTOGRAPHER/78 FIFTH AVENUE/NEW YORK CITY 10011/(212) 255-9064

1031

1029
Art Director Ernest Scarfone
Designer Ernest Scarfone
Photographer André Martin
Writer Julia Scully
Publisher Modern Photography

1030
Art Director Ernest Scarfone
Designer Ernest Scarfone
Photographer Alan Kaplan
Writer Agustus Wolfman
Publisher Nikon World

1031
Designer Phil Slager
Photographer Mike McDonnell
Client Mike McDonnell Photographer

Your old love, the Divisumma printing calculator, has been replaced by the new Logos 50/60.
Have an office romance with Olivetti.
That love affair between American business and Olivetti calculators goes on and on—spurred by a new generation of electronic printing calculators called the Logos 50/60. What makes the Logos lovable is: A buffered keyboard that operates so fast you can race 12 steps ahead of the printer. 0 and 00 and 000 keys for fast entry.
A print-out with large letters automatically separated by thousands for easy reading.
A cartridge ribbon and externally mounted paper tape for easy, clean reloading.
A fantastic capacity— the Logos 55, 58 and 59 have 16 digits and the 68 (shown) has 23! And the new Logos calculators are made by Oljvetti. So you know they're beautifully designed, reliable, backed by alert, dependable service.
What's not to love?
olivetti
OLIVETTI CORPORATION OF AMERICA, 500 PARK AVE., NEW YORK CITY 10022

Start an office romance with Olivetti.

Your slightest wish commands our Mastermind Word Processing System.
Have an office romance with Olivetti.
It's easy to fall in love with the Mastermind (otherwise known as the Olivetti S-14 word processing system). You never have to type anything over again because of mistakes or revisions. With the Mastermind you type the original only once. Changes are fed into it in seconds. Then—zing—out come perfect copies.Automatically.
At three words a second! The Mastermind has practically an unlimited capacity.
Because its memory bank uses Olivetti's cartridges with a 150 page storage capacity!
Also, unlike other systems, with the Mastermind you don't have to learn a new typing method.
It uses the standard keyboard of the famous Olivetti Editor (the typewriter with a brain!).
The Mastermind can be seen at 80 Olivetti district offices or by contacting any of our 700 exclusive agents. (They also carry our complete line of office typewriters.)
Make a date with Olivetti.
olivetti
OLIVETTI CORPORATION OF AMERICA, 500 PARK AVE., NEW YORK CITY 10022

You'll become infatuated with our P-603 accounting system, we promise.
Have an office romance with Olivetti.
Thousands of businessmen wonder how they ever did without it. Because this system, using the Olivetti P-603 microcomputer, does the day-to-day bookkeeping, invoicing, payroll, sales analyses, etc.—at one of the lowest costs in the business. It's a modular system that you can expand as your business expands. (Programs can be created right on the machine, using magnetic program cards.) So it handles everything you need handled today and in the future. And it's backed up by terrific Olivetti service—with trained personnel in 80 district offices and through hundreds of exclusive Olivetti agents. Look us up in the Yellow Pages under "Accounting Systems" and make a date today. (We've installed over 100,000 accounting machines all over the world.)
olivetti
OLIVETTI CORPORATION OF AMERICA, 500 PARK AVE., NEW YORK CITY 10022

1032

1032
Art Director Kurt Weihs
Designer Kurt Weihs
Photographer Carl Fischer
Writer Rudy Fiala
Agency Lois Holland Callaway
Client Olivetti Corp. of America

1033

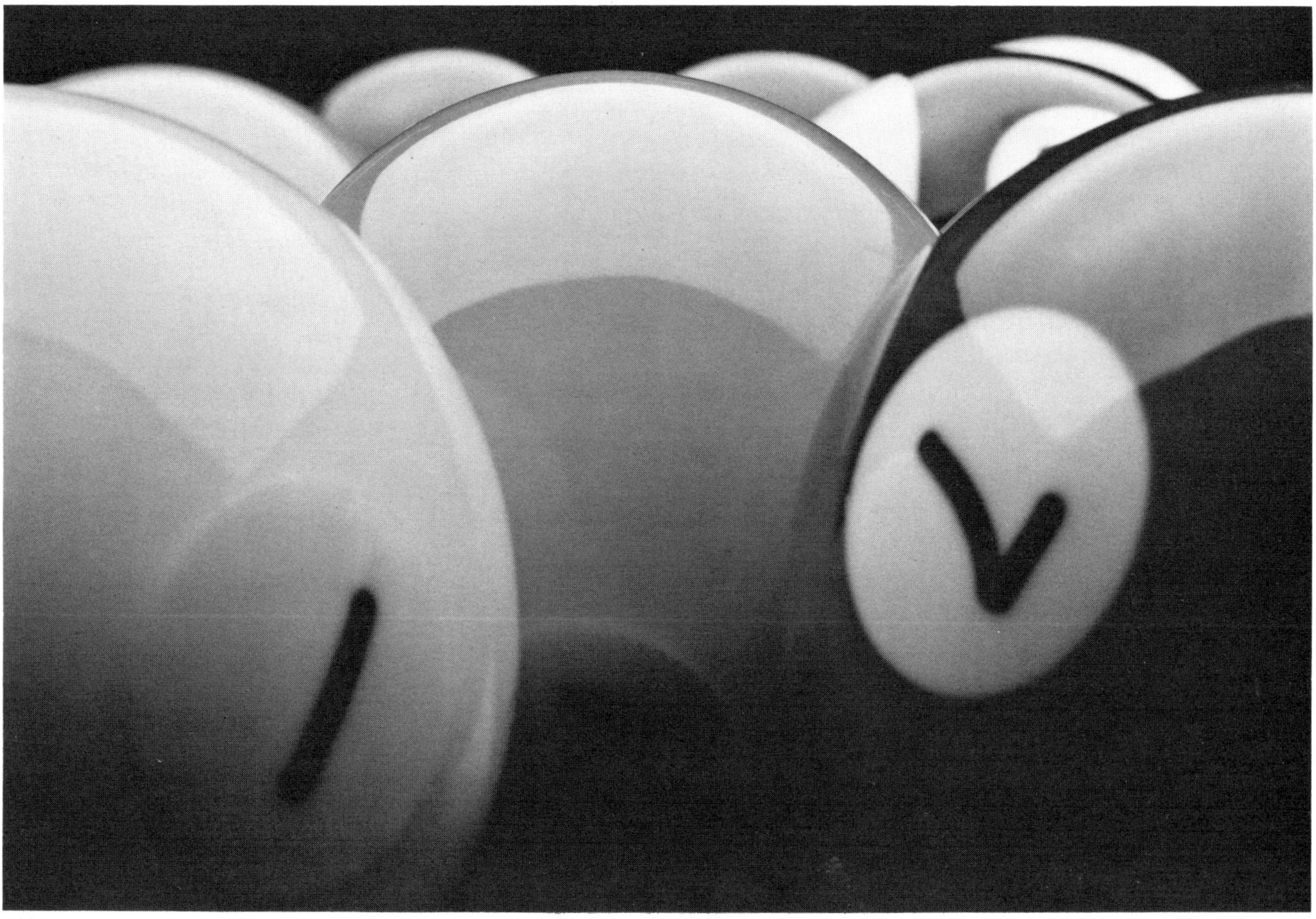

1034

SILVER

1033
Art Directors Boyd Jacobsen
Lee Ruggles
Designer Boyd Jacobsen
Photographer Craig Simpson
Writer John vanderZee
Agency McCann-Erickson
San Francisco
Client Wells Fargo Bank

1034
Art Director Lowell Williams
Photographer Ron Scott
Agency Environmark
Client The Woodlands

1035

1035
Art Director Fred C. Kidder
Photographer Keith Axelson
Writer Lyle Hoffman
Agency Kidder Axelson & Assoc.
Client Northwest Paper Div.
Potlatch Corp.

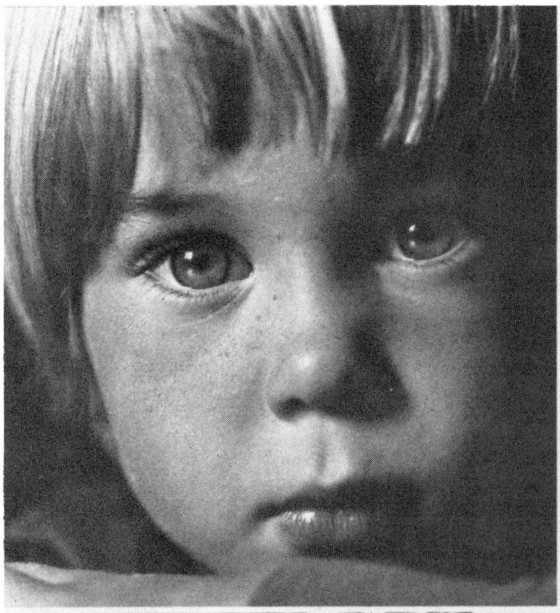

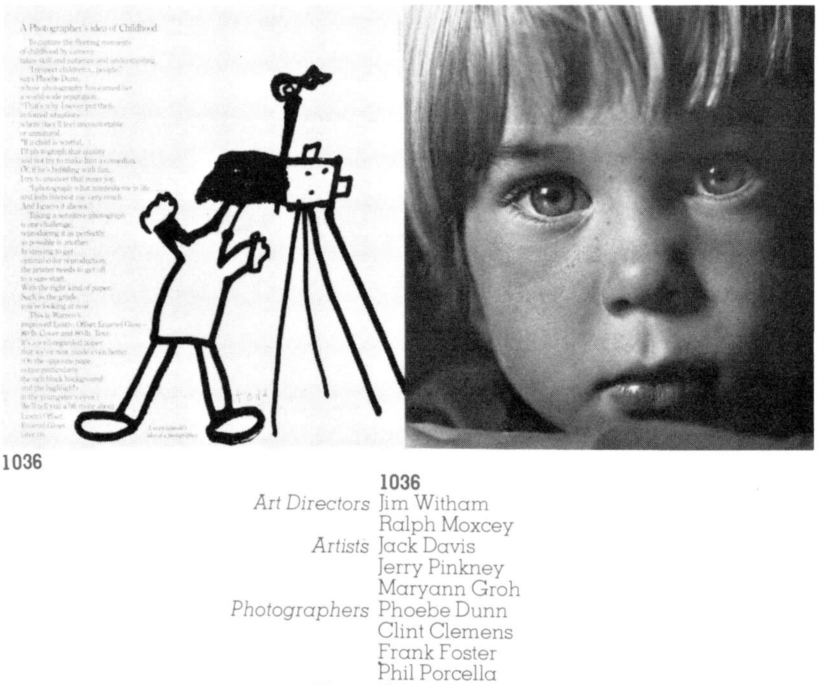
A Photographer's idea of Childhood

1036

1036

Art Directors Jim Witham
Ralph Moxcey
Artists Jack Davis
Jerry Pinkney
Maryann Groh
Photographers Phoebe Dunn
Clint Clemens
Frank Foster
Phil Porcella
Writer Nelson Lofstedt
Agency Humphrey Browning MacDougall
Client S. D. Warren Co.

If technical ideas are worth the paper they're printed on...

...they're worth Warren.

1037

1037
Art Directors Jim Witham
Ralph Moxcey
Artist Gary Fugiwara
Photographer Karl Faller
Writer Nelson Lofstedt
Agency Humphrey Browning MacDougall
Client S. D. Warren Co.

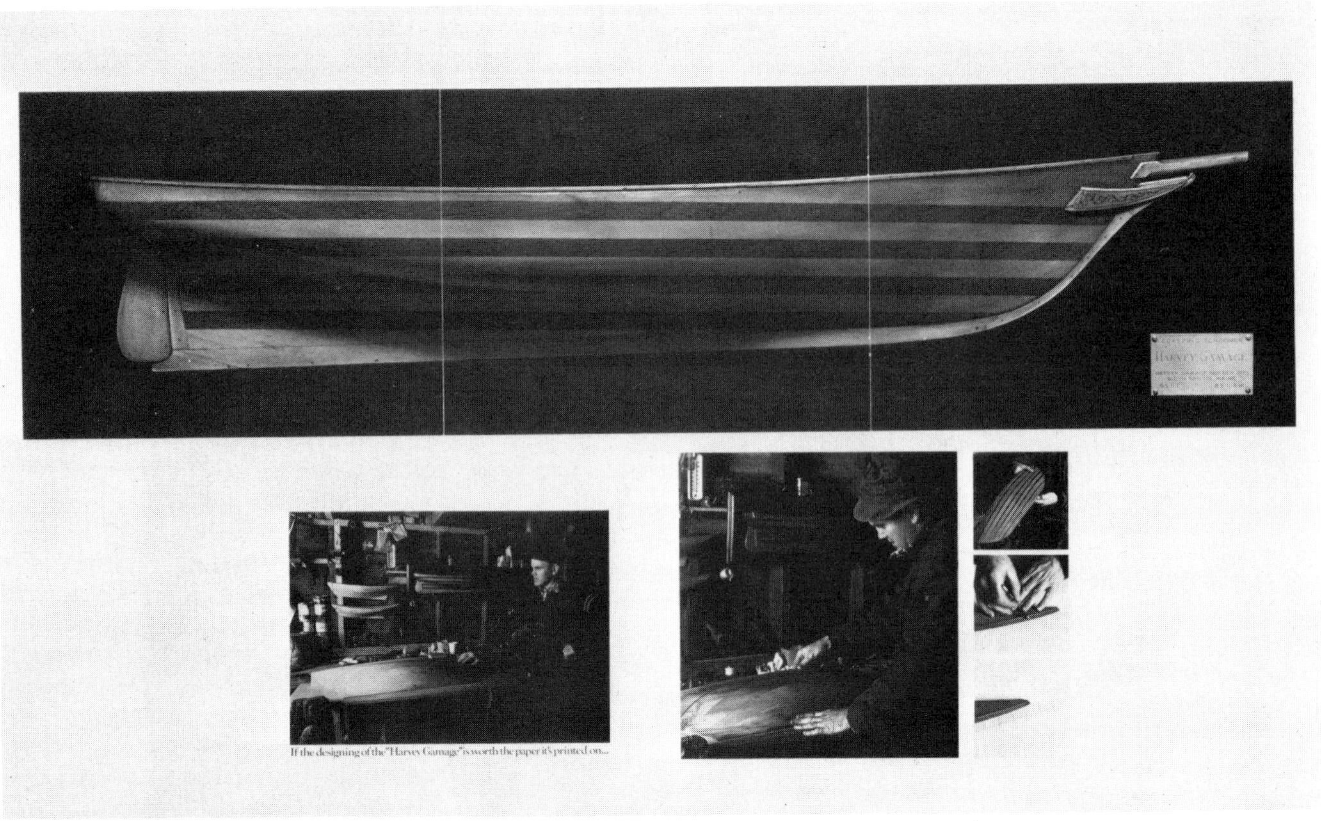
If the designing of the "Harvey Gamage" is worth the paper it's printed on...

1038

THE WEATHER MACHINE

LIVING WITH THE WEATHER MACHINE
Weather has changed the course of human history
22

1039

1038
Art Directors Jim Witham
Ralph Moxcey
Artist Charles Hoar
Photographer Bill Bruin
Writer Nelson Lofstedt
Agency Humphrey Browning MacDougall
Client S. D. Warren Co.

1039
Art Director B. Martin Pedersen
Designer B. Martin Pedersen
Photographer Pete Turner
Writer Dave Brown
Agency Pedersen Design
Client Champion Papers

1040

Light up your fingers
with Gold Lance Class Rings.
RINGS!
GOLD LANCE

1041

1040
Art Director Lester A. Barnett
Photographer Steve Steigman
Agency Klemtner Advertising
Client Pfizer Laboratories

1041
Art Director Jay Loucks
Designer Jay Loucks
Photographer Ron Scott
Writer Bruce Davis
Agency Bruce, Henry & Davis
Client Gold Lance Rings

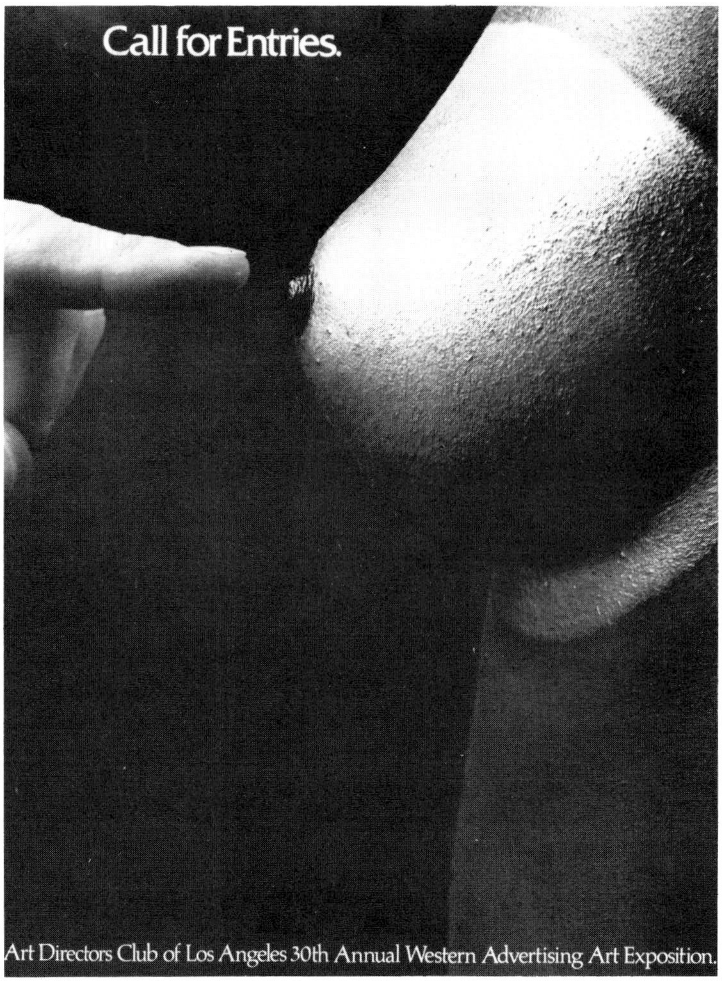
Call for Entries.
Art Directors Club of Los Angeles 30th Annual Western Advertising Art Exposition.
1042

...it's worth Warren.
1043

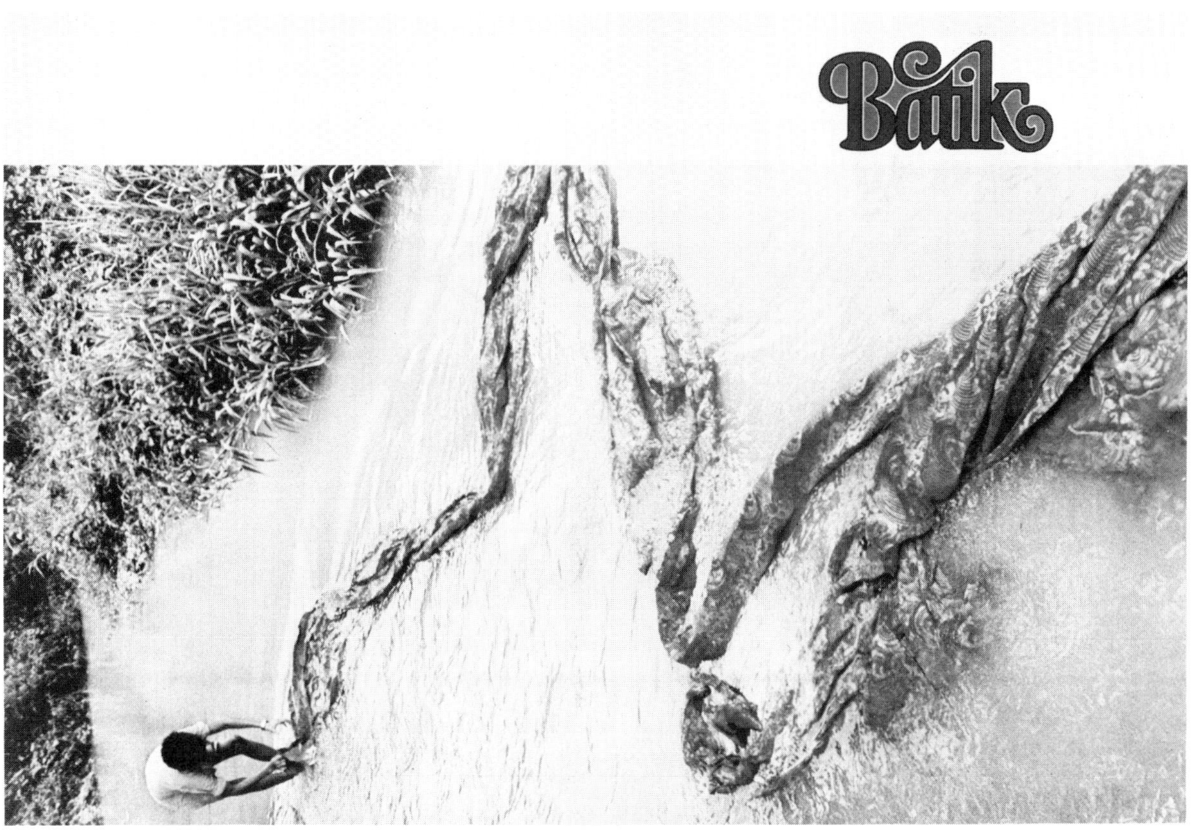
Batik

Batik

1045

1042
Art Director Archie Boston
Designer Archie Boston
Photographer Roger Marshutz
Writer Archie Boston
Agency Botsford Ketchum Los Angeles
Client Art Directors Club of Los Angeles

1043
Art Directors Jim Witham, Ralph Moxcey
Artist Charles Hoar
Photographer Bill Bruin
Writer Nelson Lofstedt
Agency Humphrey Browning MacDougall
Client S. D. Warren Co.

1045
Art Director John J. Conley
Designer John J. Conley
Photographers Ray Cranbourne, Black Star
Editor Sharon Comey
Agency Exxon Chemical Co.
Client Chemsphere Exxon Chemical Co.

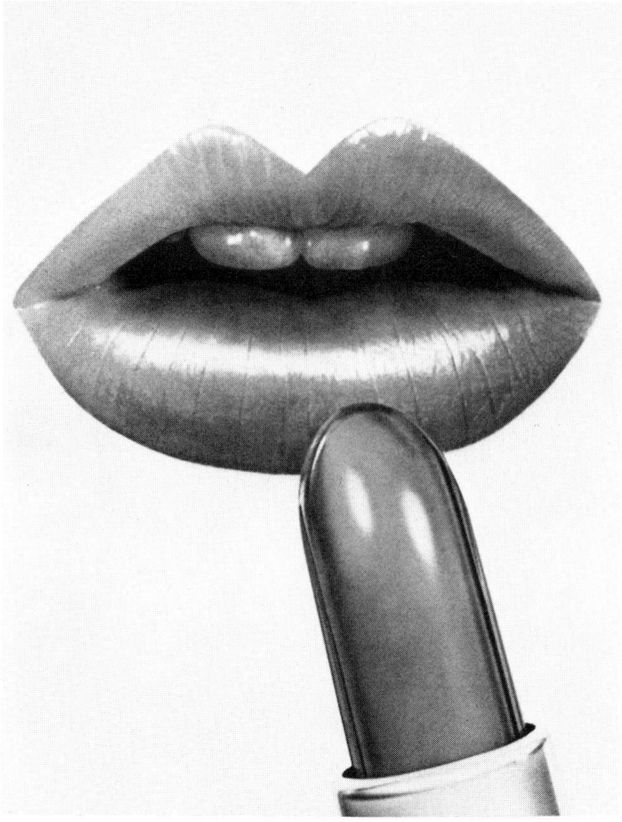

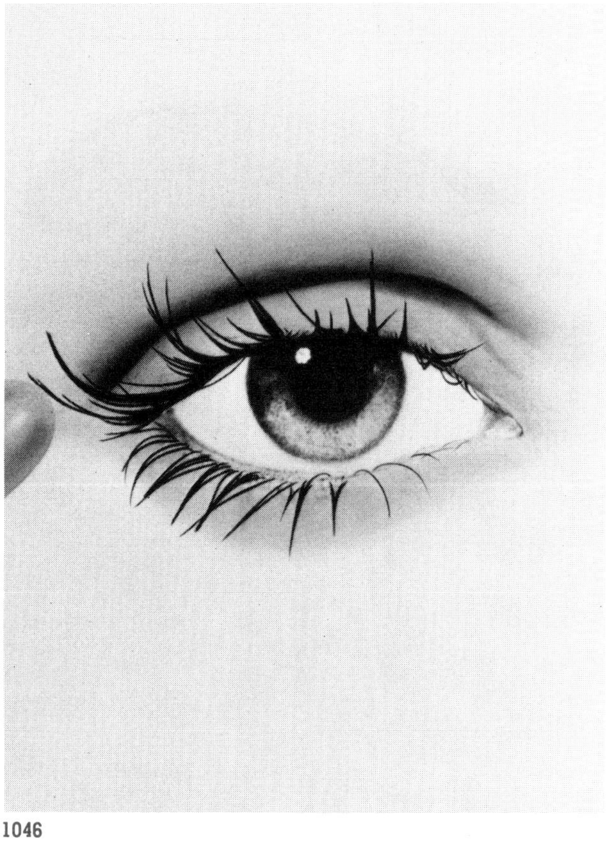

1046

1046
Art Director Robert S. Nemser
Designer Robert S. Nemser
Artist Clyde McWilliams
Photographer John Zoiner
Writer Bass & Co.
Agency Nemser & Howard
Client Monica Simone Cosmetics

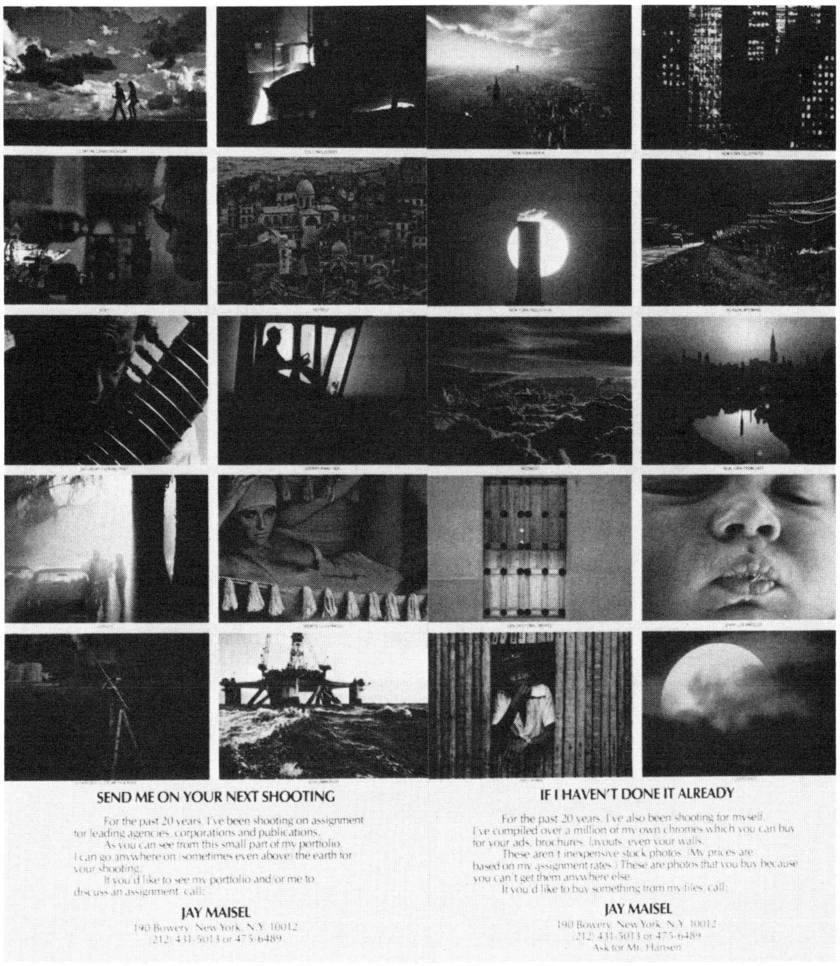
SEND ME ON YOUR NEXT SHOOTING
For the past 20 years, I've been shooting on assignment for leading agencies, corporations and publications.
As you can see from this small part of my portfolio, I can go anywhere on (sometimes even above) the earth for your shooting.
If you'd like to see my portfolio and/or me to discuss an assignment, call:
JAY MAISEL
190 Bowery, New York, N.Y. 10012
(212) 431-5013 or 475-6489
IF I HAVEN'T DONE IT ALREADY
For the past 20 years, I've also been shooting for myself. I've compiled over a million of my own chromes which you can buy for your ads, brochures, layouts, even your walls.
These aren't inexpensive stock photos. (My prices are based on my assignment rates.) These are photos that you buy because you can't get them anywhere else.
If you'd like to buy something from my files, call:
JAY MAISEL
190 Bowery, New York, N.Y. 10012
(212) 431-5013 or 475-6489
Ask for Mr. Hansen

1047

·Standard Brands Paint Company·Annual Report·1974·
Report on Operations

1048

1047
Art Director Marty Goldstein
Designer Marty Goldstein
Photographer Jay Maisel
Writer Stu Waldman
Agency Jay Maisel
Client Jay Maisel

1048
Art Director Don Weller
Designers Don Weller
Chikako Matsubayashi
Artist Richard Huebner
Photographer Roger Marshutz
Writer Sheldon Weinstein
Agency The Weller Institute
Client Standard Brands Paint Co.

SEE JAMAICA FROM TOP
TO BOTTOM.
airJamaica
WE MAKE YOU FEEL GOOD ALL OVER.

1049

1050

SILVER

1049
Art Director Peter Welsch
Designer Peter Welsch
Photographer Robert Phillips
Writer Gene Tashoff
Agency Ketchum, MacLeod & Grove
Client Air Jamaica

1050
Art Director Don Weller
Designer Don Weller
Photographer Chris Callis
Agency The Weller Institute
Client Art Directors Club of Los Angeles

Hot Shots
• Photographs by Norman Seeff •

1051

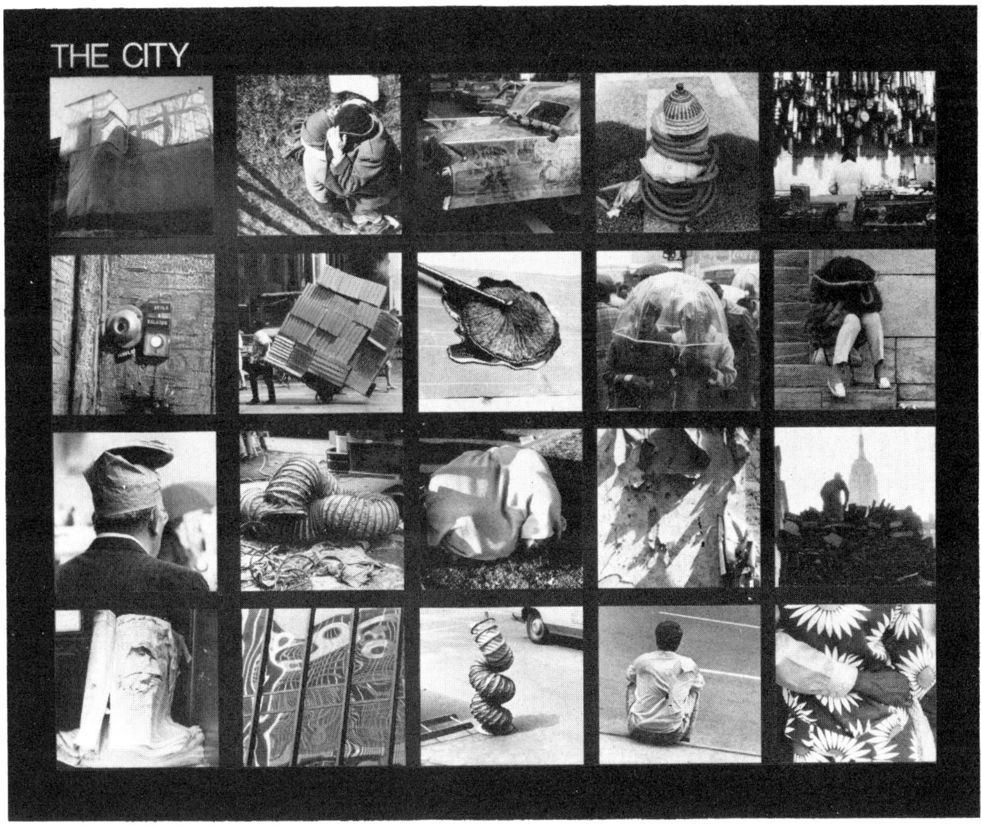
THE CITY

1052

GOLD

1051
Art Director Herbert Wise
Designer Norman Seeff
Photographer Norman Seeff
Publisher Flash Books

1052
Art Director Ned Harris
Designer Ned Harris
Artist Ned Harris
Agency Wallack & Harris
Client Van Nostrand-Reinhold

ADLA

Hovering Haze over Hose

West Peak, Hose Valley

Hose Lake & Recreation

1053

1053
Art Director Don Weller
Designer Don Weller
Photographer Francis T. Ho
Writer Francis T. Ho
Agency The Weller Institute
Client Art Directors Club of Los Angeles

1054

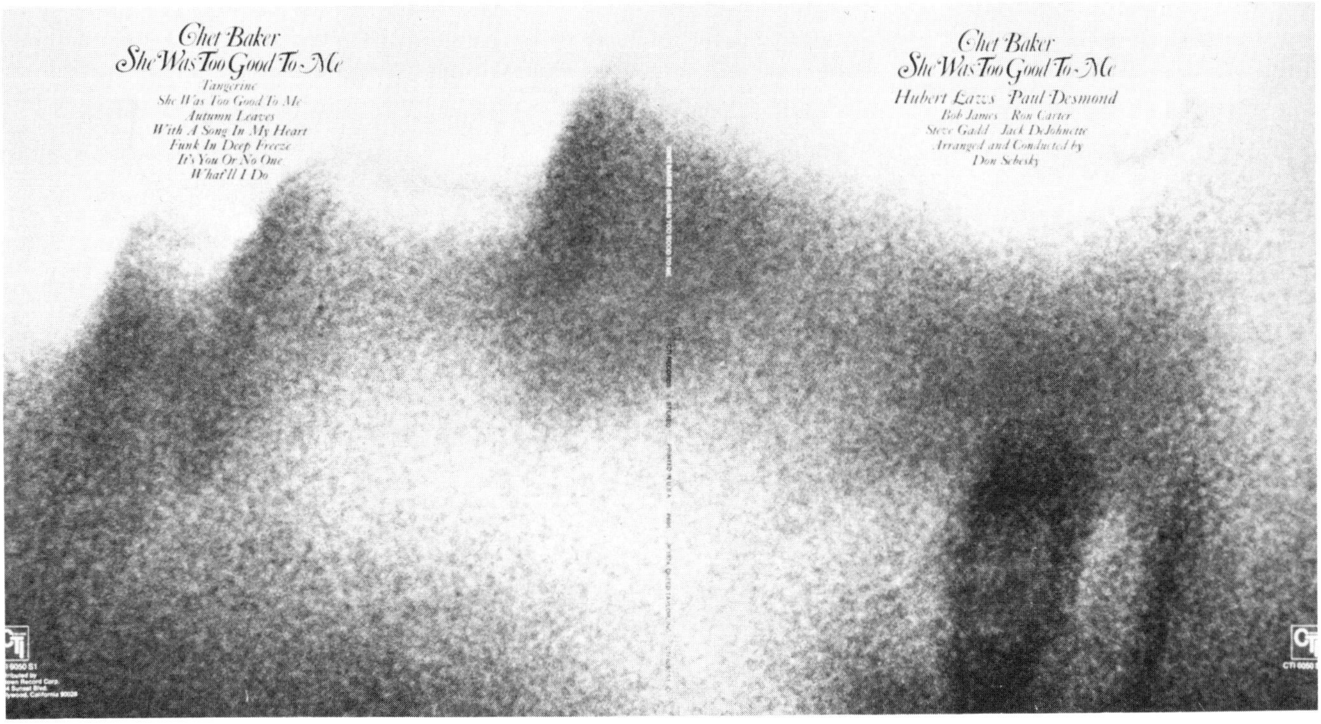
Chet Baker
She Was Too Good To Me
Tangerine
She Was Too Good To Me
Autumn Leaves
With A Song In My Heart
Funk In Deep Freeze
It's You Or No One
What'll I Do
Chet Baker
She Was Too Good To Me
Hubert Laws Paul Desmond
Bob James Ron Carter
Steve Gadd Jack DeJohnette
Arranged and Conducted by
Don Sebesky

1055

SILVER

1054
Art Director Ruth Ansel
Designer Ruth Ansel
Photographer Bob Adelman
Publisher The New York Times Magazine

1055
Art Director Bob Ciano
Photographer Pete Turner
Client CTI Records

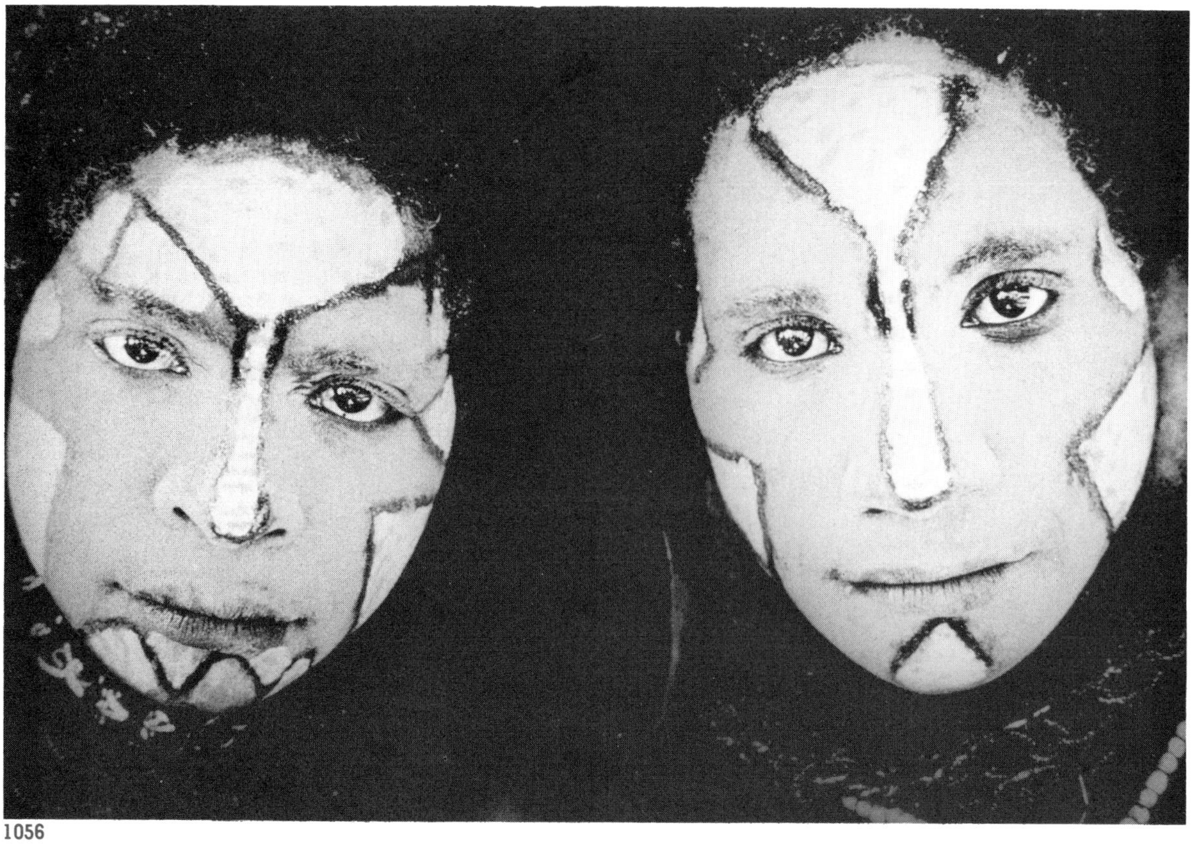

1056

FOLIO
THE SUNSHINE
EXPERIENCE 1974

1057

1056
Art Director Bob Ciano
Photographer Pete Turner
Client CTI Records

1057
Art Director Henry Wolf
Designer Henry Wolf
Photographer Henry Wolf
Agency Henry Wolf Productions
Client Saks Fifth Avenue

Texasgulf
Road Atlas

1058

Where Texans Go To Meet Their Subconscious
How Poor Emergency Medical Care Can Kill You
The Premature Retirement of Price Daniel, Jr.
TexasMonthly
Texas Exposed!
See page 81

1059

1058
Art Director Joan Cassidy
Photographer Larry Mayea
Client Texasgulf

1059
Art Director Sybil Broyles
Photographer Ron Scott
Editor Bill Broyles
Publisher Texas Monthly Magazine

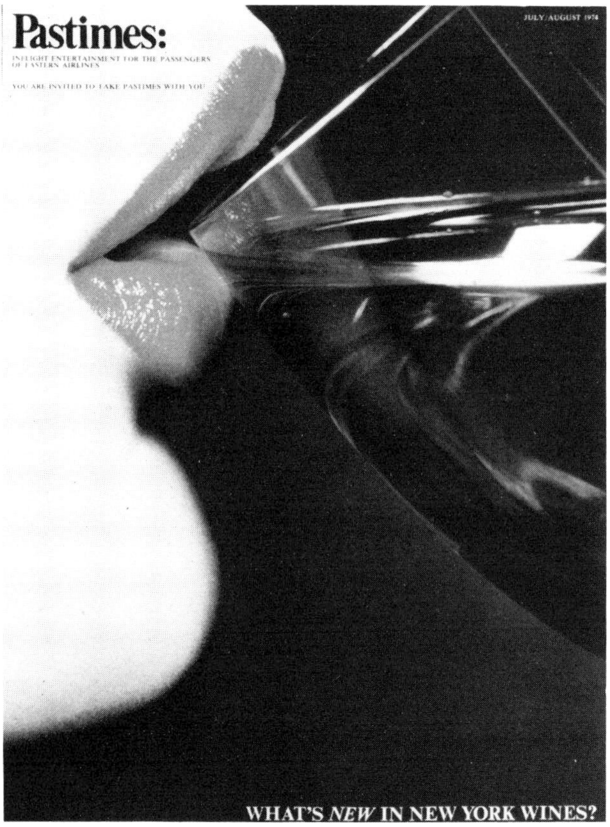
Pastimes:
INFLIGHT ENTERTAINMENT FOR THE PASSENGERS OF EASTERN AIRLINES
YOU ARE INVITED TO TAKE PASTIMES WITH YOU
JULY/AUGUST 1974
WHAT'S *NEW* IN NEW YORK WINES?

1060

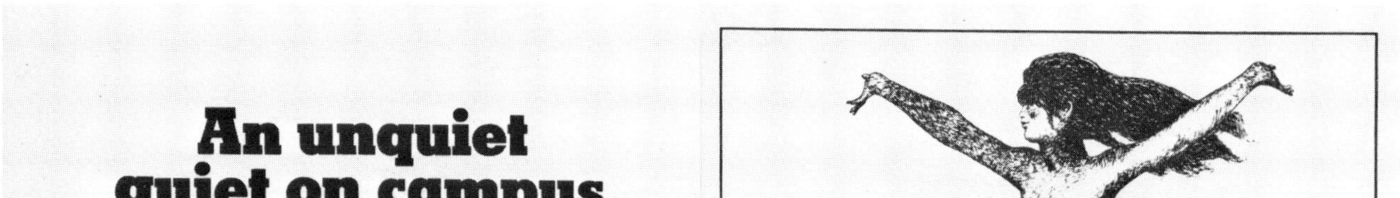

An unquiet quiet on campus

Causing a widely traveled and well-endowed observer to conclude that there has been an end to barbarism but also to freedom, and that excellence is yielding to impotence

By Ronald Berman

At the end of the sixties the academic world gratefully welcomed the cessation of violence. It assumed that campus problems were finite and political; with their disappearance, we would be back to normal. The academy hoped for tranquillity and, attaining it, confused it with order. Few realized at the beginning of the seventies that an entirely new set of problems had arisen and that their solution depended on values and traditions that were dealt a staggering blow in the sixties. The traditional university was imperfect but equitable. The same cannot be said of today's.

The seventies began with a shortage of money caused by a shortage of public confidence. There have been other external problems: fluctuations in the student population; inflation; changes in Federal and state education policies; the sudden constriction of employment. But internal problems are even more severe. We have been left with a politicized environment in which disinterested argument is at a loss. The curriculum is more or less in shreds after its attempts to reflect, with ever increasing speed for most of a decade, the relevancies of the moment. Students are without grades and requirements, while professors are without traditional responsibilities; in both cases there is great anxiety about loss of structure and equity. A new generation of academics has appeared, but, having for some years now argued the superior claims of politics, they find themselves unhappily detained by subjects merely parochial. Innovation, a concept rightly honored when most necessary, has become sterile and mechanical. In the race to attract foundation funds—and because it implies a certain style—innovation has become more of an end than a means. Finally, students are evidently bored by the kind of debate long familiar on campus and are deserting the liberal arts for the vocations in enormous numbers. Because of these issues, the campus is naturally agitated. Because of the difficulty of their solution, it is in a state of anxiety, not to say depression.

The report of the Carnegie Commission states that the universities are undergoing a trauma of self-doubt. Kenneth Clark has written in The American Scholar that they have shown an abject failure of nerve. A great variety of such statements on the crisis of confidence in education are now appearing. None of them refer simply to the issues I have just described. They apply to the conditions those issues have both created and encountered. I would put the matter this way: The essential loss of the past decade was not material but moral. The attention of the public was focused on violence, barbarism and physical destruction; what escaped notice was the end of discourse, objectivity and freedom. Without these, academe is powerless to face the issues and is, in fact, in a state of twittering inertia.

A brief historical review may be useful. There have been two revolutionary changes on campus, one material and the other political. From 1958 to 1968 the American university boomed along with the rest of the economy. There were many benefits as intellectual life became part of the knowledge industry: decent wages and research facilities; *carrière ouverte aux talents*; the end of cultural isolation. But on the whole the experience resembled nothing so much as the effect of the capitalist ethic on medievalism, at least as described by Marx and Engels. If the old campus was paternalistic, the new one was frigidly aloof—there were verifiable stories of students at Berkeley whose only direct contact with their professors was a single annual conversation. Burkeian affection for people, places and institutions disappeared; it was replaced by a freedom easily confused with neglect. The campus atmosphere changed in a way reminiscent of the opening of "Hard Times," in which the prisons looked like hospitals and the schools looked like prisons.

The role of the administration expanded even beyond those horizons foreseen by Jacques Barzun in his "Teacher in America." A large state university in the sixties would have literally thousands of clerks, advisers, maintenance men, technicians, staff assistants, deans, deanlets and deanlings. As the decade advanced, they were joined by psychological counselors, racial and sexual advisers, "affirmative-action" personnel and directors of various remedial or research projects. In short, education became typically an enterprise of the state, supported by tax moneys and similar to other state bureaucracies. While it was certainly a good thing to have undergraduate education demythologized, it was an error to turn it into an assembly line.

The script for the sixties was perhaps implied by the work of Emile Durkheim, the first modern sociologist and our great theorist of social decay. Students with few connections to their teachers, inhabiting campuses unintelligible without a road map, sitting in classes by the hundreds or thousands, became the natural consistituency for unrest. It was only natural for them to turn to exaggerated "community," or "humanity," or "commitment," because these had recently been in such short supply. And it was only natural that they should be led into fearful excess, if we are to be guided by that body of work which, from Arendt to Palmer to Talmon, describes the passage from revolutionary expectancy to disillusion.

With the uproar over ownership of the Bancroft Strip, the sidewalk in Berkeley reserved for student causes, intellectual life—the knowledge industry itself—became historically transformed. The earthly issues and tactics of protest engendered problems by 1970 that virtually no one in 1964 had predicted. The first issues were free speech and Vietnam; the first tactics were occupation of physical space, varieties of rudeness, ingenious harassment. But the tactics escalated to armed confrontation (Cornell), mob violence (Berkeley), arson (Stanford), blackmail (San Francisco State) and murder (Wisconsin). We became accustomed to the destruction of records and property and the disruption of education. There were fatalities on campus by bomb and self-immolation—not to mention self-destruction by narcotics.

The tactics changed because the issues changed. Although the Vietnamese war was unmistakably the central issue, it was also *(Continued on Page 17)*

Ronald Berman is chairman of the National Endowment for the Humanities in Washington, D.C.

1062

1060
Art Director B. Martin Pedersen
Designer B. Martin Pedersen
Photographer Pat Field
Writer Tom Humber
Publisher Pastimes
Agency Pedersen Design

1062
Art Director Ruth Ansel
Artist Brad Holland
Editors Lewis Bergman
Jack Rosenthal
Publisher The New York Times Magazine

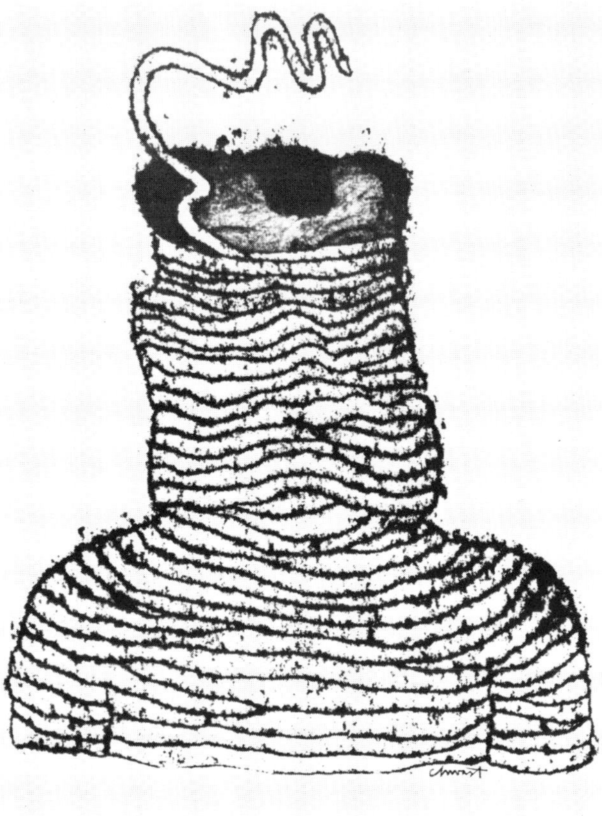

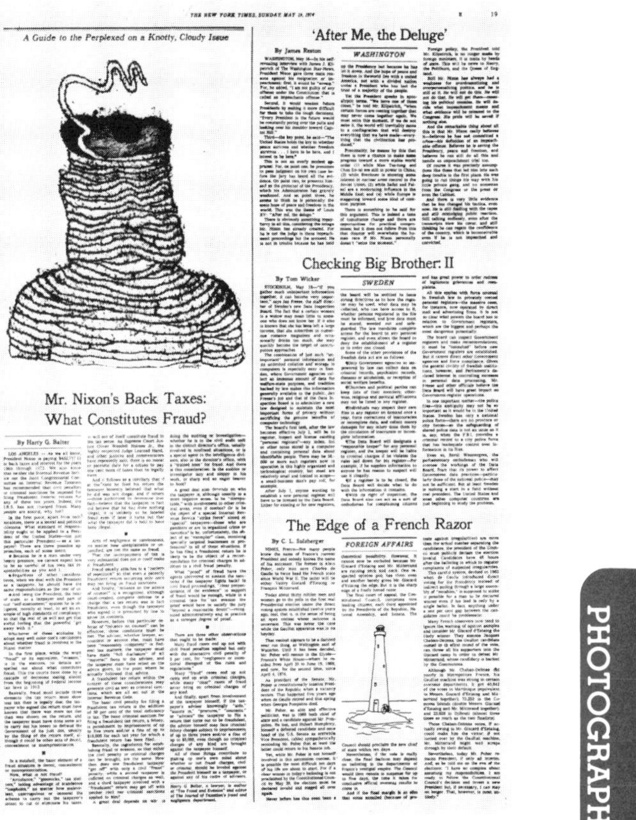

A Guide to the Perplexed on a Knotty, Cloudy Issue

'After Me, the Deluge'

Checking Big Brother: II

Mr. Nixon's Back Taxes: What Constitutes Fraud?

The Edge of a French Razor

1063

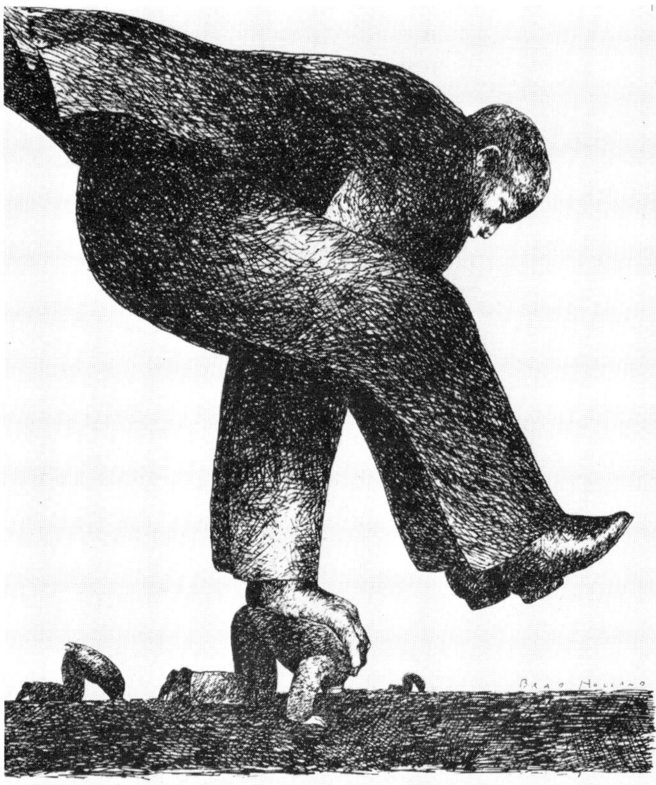

The New York Times Magazine | April 14, 1974

The painful DeFunis case raises the specters of racism and anti-Semitism

Discriminating to end discrimination

By Nina Totenberg

The two men walking across the University of Washington campus in Seattle looked like any two professors just chatting away. But they weren't. They were lawyers. Suddenly, the older gray-haired man turned to his companion and said, "You know, Jim, if the Regents don't let that kid into law school, I'm going to sue the university. It'll be a big case, and I'll take it all the way to the Supreme Court if I have to. And I'll win." The younger man smiled to himself, amused at his friend's saber-rattling.

Three years later, in February, the same two men, Joe Diamond and Jim Wilson, sat on the teams at opposing tables for counsel. The place was the United States Supreme Court, and the case that had been just a seedling in 1971 had blossomed into one of the potential landmark cases of the decade. At issue is the whole concept of affirmative-action programs—programs that give preference to minority groups in such areas as school admissions and employment in order to compensate for past discrimination.

The case involves Marco DeFunis Jr., a white, Phi Beta Kappa college graduate who was denied admission to the University of Washington Law School in 1971. DeFunis's college grades and Law School Aptitude Test scores were higher than those of 36 minority students—blacks, Chicanos, Indians—who were accepted by the law school. DeFunis claims he was the victim of reverse racial discrimination. He asserts that racial discrimination of any kind is a violation of his constitutional right to equal protection of the law. The university claims that "benign" discrimination—discrimination to aid historically disadvantaged minorities—is within the law. It asserts that without an affirmative-action program to aid minorities, the law school would be "lily white," and that it is the duty of the law school both to provide a diversified student body and to help correct the appalling shortage of minority lawyers in the nation.

However the Supreme Court decides the issue—and even if the Court does not decide it definitively—the case of *DeFunis v. Odegaard* (the defendant recently retired as president of the university) has brought the Court and the nation to a painful point in history. No longer are the choices easy ones. No longer is it a simple choice of a crumbling old schoolhouse for blacks and a sparkling new school for whites; no longer is it a simple matter of a person's dark skin excluding him from a vote, or a drink at the soda fountain, or a job. The heart of American ideology is equality of opportunity and success based on individual merit. From its inception, this nation fought to undo the notion of aristocracy, at least in principle. At the same time the nation was discriminating officially and viciously against blacks and other brown-skinned groups, denying them a decent education, a decent wage, decent housing and, most of all, equal opportunity.

In 1954, the Supreme Court in its historic *Brown v. Board of Education* case pushed the country firmly down the path of racial equality. Since then, the Court, at every chance, has torn down remaining barriers to equal opportunity. But now the Court, like much of the nation, finds itself caught between two of its most cherished ideals. It must decide which is more important: to continue to do everything possible to correct the effects of centuries of racial discrimination, or to remain faithful to the American ideal of a strict merit system.

The question is so painful that it has split the traditional liberal alliance of labor, Jewish and civil-rights groups. Suddenly most of the Jewish and labor organizations are joined with big business in opposing civil-rights groups, while the Government itself is split from agency to agency. Indeed, the question is so painful that it has, on occasion, brought to the surface usually repressed feelings of racism and anti-Semitism.

DeFunis himself is a Jew, though he does not argue that the university discriminated against him because of that. The reason for all the emotionalism over the case is the accumulated resentment of every white man who believes that a black or a woman was given preference over him in getting a job or a promotion. Business has always disliked affirmative action because it means constant pressure to do this or that, from the Government or some other outside group. But now business has been joined for the first time by hard-core labor, predominantly white and male, which fears that affirmative action would take its jobs away. Jews have deserted the old civil-rights coalition because they see the DeFunis case as a matter of quotas, and quotas are anathema to Jews because they were used for so many centuries to keep Jews out of universities.

Marco DeFunis's journey to the Supreme Court began in 1971 when he was rejected by the University of Washington Law School for the second time. A resident of Seattle, he had received his college degree from the university and done a year of graduate work there, while working part-time for the Seattle Park Department. He had been accepted at four other law schools and had just about decided to go to the University of Oregon in Eugene, where tuition would be the same as at U.W. But there was a problem: DeFunis had lined up an office job in a Seattle law firm and neither he nor his wife, a dental assistant, could make nearly as much money in Eugene. They figured that his going to law school in Oregon would cost them about $1,500 a year in lost salaries; DeFunis's father, a furniture salesman, could give them only limited financial help.

Enter Craig Sternberg, a one-time college fraternity brother of DeFunis's who was already a practicing attorney in Seattle. Sternberg offered to help, and spoke to the senior law partner in his firm about DeFunis. The partner, Josef Diamond, was intrigued—partly because the situtation offended his sense of rightness, and partly because he had a couple of well-to-do clients who had children not as qualified as DeFunis who were having trouble getting into law school. Diamond took over the DeFunis case. After numerous unsuccessful meetings with the law-school dean, the admissions committee chairman and the board of regents, he brought a lawsuit. Following a trial in a local court, the judge issued an order compelling the university to admit DeFunis to the 1971 freshman class. The university complied and then appealed to the Washington State Supreme Court, which reversed the ruling of the trial judge.

By this time, DeFunis was well into law school; he thought the university would probably let him stay, and wasn't enthusiastic about appealing. After all, being called the "house bigot" wasn't much fun; there were at least a couple of incidents, his lawyer says, when DeFunis walked into the library and encountered a group of black students who pointed him out as a bigot and promptly got up and left. But despite his uncomfortable position, DeFunis agreed to press his case when Diamond noted that the university was then legally free to throw him out. An appeal was brought to the Supreme Court and Justice William O. Douglas issued an order that has kept him in school until the present.

Now 25 years old, he is expected to graduate in May. His legal education, however, will be far more expensive than he ever *(Continued on Page 36)*

Nina Totenberg is Washington editor of New Times magazine. She previously covered the Supreme Court for The National Observer.

9

1064

1063
Art Director George Delmerico
Designer George Delmerico
Artist Seymour Chwast
Editor Charlotte Curtis
Publisher The New York Times Op-Ed Page

1064
Art Director Ruth Ansel
Artist Brad Holland
Editors Lewis Bergman, Jack Rosenthal
Publisher The New York Times Magazine

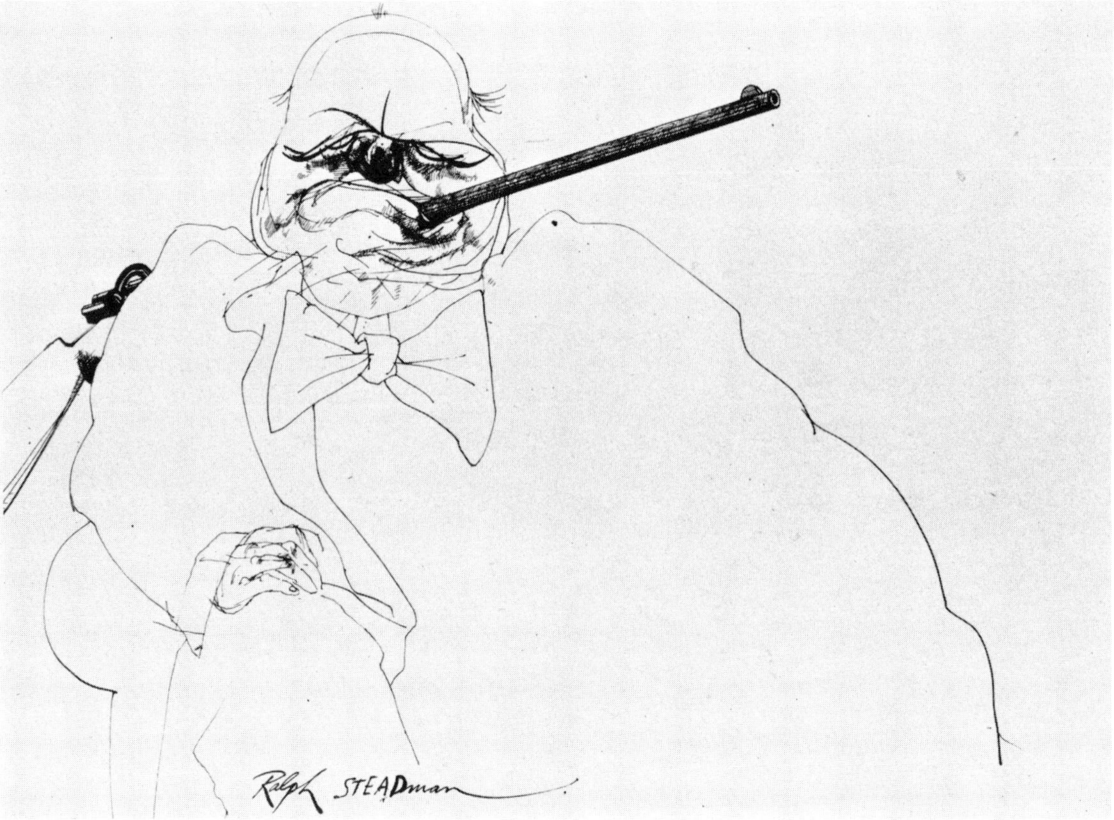
Ralph STEADman

1065

The New York Times Magazine | August 18, 1974

Last days in the bunker

By William Safire

WASHINGTON. "We've known that something terrible was going to happen since last Thursday," Julie Nixon Eisenhower told a friend a few hours before her father's resignation, exactly one week after the President had revealed incriminating evidence to his closest aides.

On Incrimination Day—Aug. 1—the White House bunker began its final weeks of siege. The first aides to hear the crushing tapes reported bleakly, "It's not 'more of the same,'" and others immediately said, "Throw in the towel." Although some of his attorneys had accepted the need for resignation since the Supreme Court decision, the President, strongly supported by his family, resisted.

"Do you think the staff can be kept in line?" Julie had asked a hard-line aide, as lawyer James St. Clair led the charge for resignation. The aide said he thought so, if the President was prepared to say, most uncharacteristically, that he was profoundly sorry for holding back evidence; he gave Julie, who passed them on to her father, some not-altogether-cheery lines from Dryden: "I will lay me down for to bleed awhile/Then I'll rise and fight with you again."

That was what Mr. Nixon tried to do in the death throes of his Presidency. "It doesn't matter to him about his health," Julie explained; "his life is ruined." As the one who loves him most fiercely and probably understands him best, his younger daughter was primarily concerned with the death of his spirit.

He gave it a final go, with the statement over his last weekend admitting "variance" with the facts, and waited to see if the reaction would make it impossible to win the Senate trial. He had not thought the June, 1972, tapes were that significant, he told aides, adding that if those tapes ended the fight now, they would have ended it whenever they had been released. As the last storm broke, aide Richard Moore put forward a suggestion that he step aside under the provisions of the 25th Amendment, appointing Mr. Ford as acting President for a time, but chief of staff Alexander Haig, who was worried about national security in a time of paralysis, said that route was not Nixon's way, that the President would make a clean decision one way or the other.

The mood in the White House on Wednesday, Aug. 7, was a distillate of moods of other eras when the Executive Mansion became a bunker—in the time of Teapot Dome, or the Depression, or after the Tet offensive in Vietnam—and crowds began to gather around the iron fence, photographers training telephoto lenses on the men scurrying around inside. In his E.O.B. office, after his cottage-cheese-and-fruit lunch, the President stopped asking for lists of reasons why it would be wrong to resign and began to outline a speech on resignation. Ray Price, who had worked with him on his Miami acceptance address exactly six years before, started a draft.

At 5:45 on Decision Day, the President went across West Executive Avenue to the White House, told a policeman to get Ollie Atkins, the photographer, for a picture in the Rose Garden, and appeared there in a few moments with daughter Tricia. He told Atkins he wanted a formal shot with his arm around her. Then the President and his older daughter went upstairs to the third-floor "California Room," where Mrs. Nixon, Rose Mary Woods, Ed Cox, and David and Julie Eisenhower were waiting. They ate dinner on trays and Mr. Nixon broke the news to his family that they would be "packing up and going home to California."

"You know him, with his sense of history," said Julie later. "He wanted Ollie there to get a picture." When the photographer arrived at 7 P.M., he entered a room that contained four tearful women and three glum men, but his appearance broke the spell: A cheer went up for Ollie, tension-relieving laughter, and the President proceeded to do his thing of setting up an awkward, strung-out picture, with everybody in it. Ollie cried a little himself, and took what he describes as "the President's idea of what a picture should be," with the family locking arms together. "I used a flash, because the available light would have made it even more pathetic, with the tears." David Eisenhower asked him to take it again, because "I'm a blinker."

The moment the group broke up, Julie broke down, and the President moved to comfort her and Ollie began to take the unposed photographs that best punctuate the end of a political career. That night, the President spent hours with Secretary Kissinger, and the following morning—as it became known he would be going on television to resign—he met with the man he had chosen to succeed himself.

On Resignation Day, Julie was still choking back bitter tears at "hypocrisy," but the atmosphere inside the bunker and around the nation perceptibly softened. The President, who remembered how he had to hail a cab to the airport when he left Washington in defeat 13 years before, made sure that this time he left in some dignity. At his emotional farewell to his Cabinet and staff, he showed he had learned what had gone wrong with himself and his Administration, passing along the hardest-earned advice of any President: "Those who hate you don't win—unless you hate them, and then you destroy yourself."

The manner of Mr. Nixon's departure gave his supporters a lift, not the "lift of a driving dream" he had promised long ago, but a respite from a constantly sinking sensation that was the Watergate nightmare. Those who served him in his first term, as well as those who staggered through the slings and arrows of his aborted second term, were refreshed by the arrival of reality.

For a long time, it had been a useful sense of unreality that had kept men in the White House at their posts, along with a measure of hope and the President's ability to inspire confidence. What had it been like those last months inside the bunker? It may be instructive to examine how the people on the inside reacted to the bursts of fresh defections, the shellings of criticism, the impacts of court decisions, the rumbling sounds of the erosion of foundations, leading up to the Big Bomb—the revelation by the President that he had been holding back evidence—and the final days of Richard Nixon's Presidency.

"Last days in the bunker" may be a cruel headline for this article, recalling as it does the last days of Hitler and his henchmen in the rubble of Berlin. But the metaphor, though not the comparison of characters, has some validity: In the final days, the Nixon White House had become the center of inaction, the walled capital city of the state of siege, a combination shelter, sanctuary, last barricade and law library. And in their time of adversity, those who kept the faith sometimes turned to gallows humor to keep their spirits up. Before the fall, the White House staff had adopted a new tradition: Whenever a meeting on whatever subject broke up, the last man out of the room turned off the lights and shouted back into the darkness, for the record: "But it would be wrong!"

Others lapsed into gloom. Consider the mood of the man who had what was widely conceded to be the hardest job in the White House. He is Mort Allin, 32, a chubby, once good-humored former schoolteacher who prepared the President's daily news summary. When a tape gap was discovered or another jury came in with another conviction, other staffers could forget to watch the news that night or hurriedly turn to another page of their newspaper, but Mort Allin had to watch it all, read it all, and put in pithy summary the worst of the record.

In the old days, Mort could balance a blast with a bouquet, send a cheery cartoon along with the Herblockages. But during the siege, as in Chinese water torture, he was doomed to the day-after-day production of the dreariest daily publication in America, and he hated every moment of it.

Leonard Garment, a serious man who retained his sense of humor, was the author of the bunker's bonniest mot: "Stonewalling doth not misprision make." A few weeks ago, a couple of cleaning men from the General Services Administration came by to ask if they could wash his furniture. "I'm clean," the lawyer said automatically, but then said O.K. To his surprise, the men began working up a sudsy lather and applying it with gusto around the room. As multicolored bubbles floated near his desk, the President's counselor observed, "You suppose anybody believes that this is the way life goes on at the White House? These G.S.A. gentlemen represent stability and continuity—and just look at the way they go after that dirt."

Garment side-stepped some foam and walked to the window of his office, which used to be Charles Colson's office, to which Garment had moved after a few months in the office that used to belong to John Dean: "Nothing wrong with my morale. And who ever heard of jumping from a first-story window?"

In patrolling the darkened halls of the Old Executive Office Building next door (many of the lights were turned off *(Continued on Page 40)*

William Safire, a columnist for The Times, was formerly a Presidential speech-writer in the Nixon Administration.

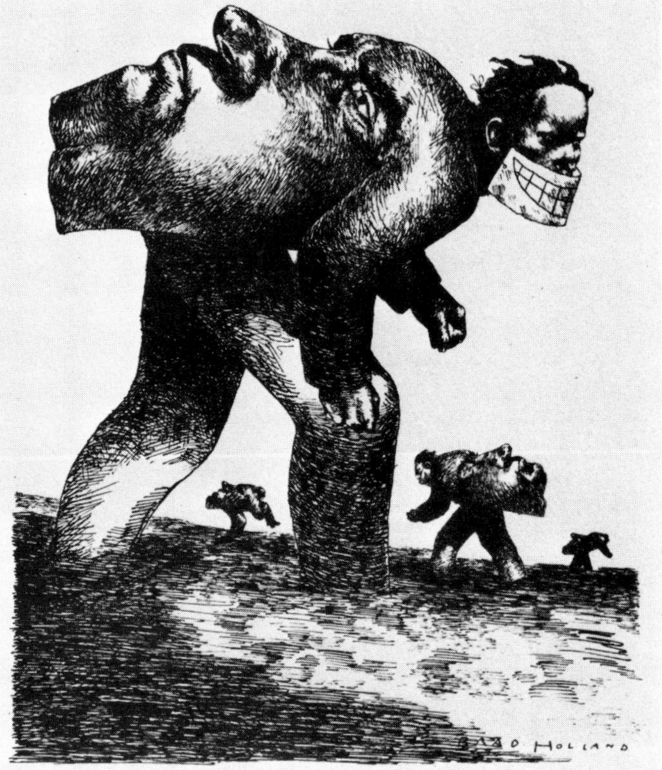

1066

1065
Art Director Tony Lane
Designer Tony Lane
Artist Ralph Steadman
Publisher Rolling Stone

1066
Art Director Ruth Ansel
Artist Brad Holland
Editors Lewis Bergman
Jack Rosenthal
Publisher New York Times Magazine

1067

THE NEW YORK TIMES, SATURDAY, MAY 11, 1974

The Politics Of Divorce

By C. L. Sulzberger

FOREIGN AFFAIRS

'The issue is really whether the Church in Italy should have even vestigial temporal power.'

The Press as Cloak and Suitor

By Roger Morris

Mother Up Against The Wall

By Russell Baker

OBSERVER

1068

1067
Art Director George Delmerico
Designer George Delmerico
Artist Michael Mathias Prechtl
Editor Charlotte Curtis
Publisher The New York Times Op-Ed Page

1068
Art Director Ruth Ansel
Designer Seymour Chwast
Artist Seymour Chwast
Editors Lewis Bergman
Jack Rosenthal
Publisher The New York Times Magazine

The New York Times

Section 4

THE WEEK IN REVIEW

The Bad Alternatives

Mr. Nixon Opts For the Inquiry On Impeachment . . .

An Exception Gone Awry

Dealing With The Terrorists

"Any government of Israel will do everything in its power to cut off the hands that want to harm a child, an adult, a settlement, a town or a village."

. . . Mrs. Meir Breaks Her Own Rule, and Fails

INDEX

1069

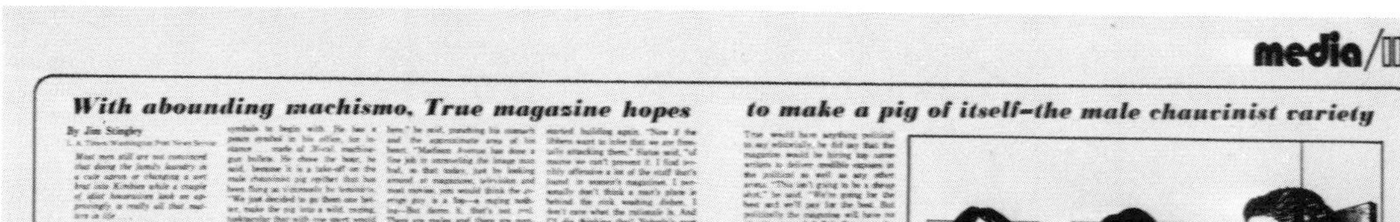

media/II

With abounding machismo, True magazine hopes to make a pig of itself—the male chauvinist variety

By Jim Stingley

IN SHORT

Transmedia

Women's vote

Harrison E. Salisbury: On TV.

Gov. Wilson: Ads attached.

1070

1069
Art Director Eric Siedman
Artist Brad Holland
Publisher The New York Times Week in Review

1070
Art Director Morris Neuwirth
Designer Gary Viskupic
Writer Jim Stingley
Publisher Newsday

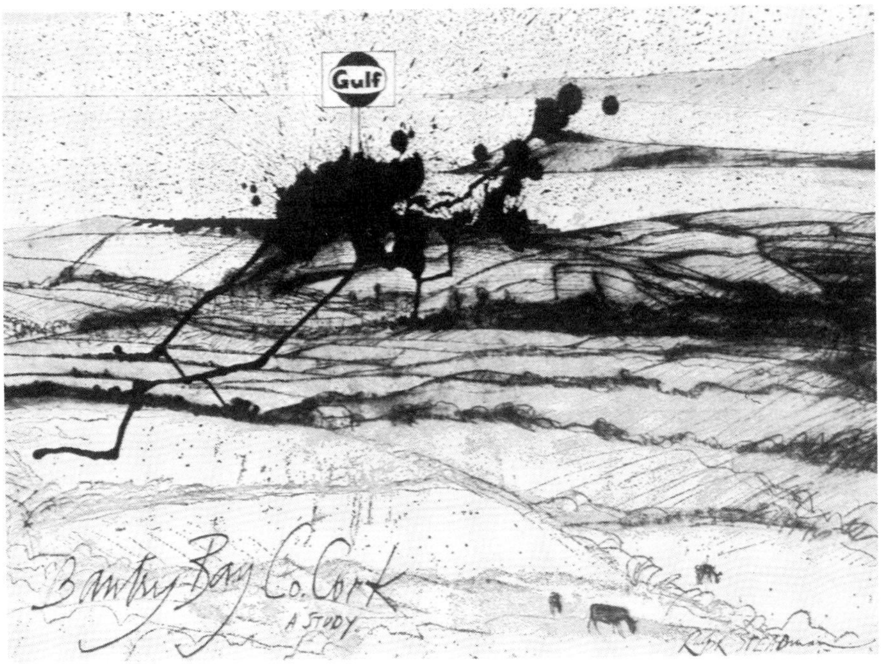
Gulf
Bantry Bay Co. Cork
A STUDY

Law and Vengeance

The House Guests of Bantry Bay

It's All About to Come Tumbling Down

1071

How many brave but irrelevant books must women writers write to prove they can write like men?

Who's afraid of Erica Jong?

By Norma Rosen

An invention: Let us suppose a woman who wants to enter the new territory of feminist thinking through books. She is 30-ish, a homemaker and mother of small children. Let's call her Fredericka, because it is a derivative of a man's name; and let's say that before now she received her image of herself from men. In college, male teachers teaching ideas held by men about "man"; in novels, male authors writing about men as heroes and women as consorts—that sort of thing.

Suppose Fredericka went to the library and asked a friendly librarian to help her sample books on "feminist themes," or maybe the library has thoughtfully arranged shelves of such books. What might Fredericka find?

Impossible to mention them all—all the novelists and poets and heroines and genres and modes and views; all the new young writers and rediscovered older writers and revivals of long-dead ones—that crowd those shelves. So much, it appears, has been pent up for so long. "Who are we?" women—the newly self-conscious group—ask themselves. Fredericka looks through the images provided by writers to find some clues.

Let's suppose that Fredericka is lucky enough to find on the shelves this first visit some of the novels (they go out fast) of sexual revolution and breakthrough. Here are the new heroines who hurl themselves into life and sex with so much intelligence, so much experience, so much experiment that it's as if they had in mind Virginia Woolf's lament and warning: Shakespeare's sister never went anywhere or was allowed to do anything, and so even with Shakespeare's talent, could not have been Shakespeare.

After only a few years of consciousness-raising—which may turn out to be the quickest, cheapest and friendliest form of self-help attitude-reforming in the annals of psychological therapy—not to mention deep-self-scrutiny (physical as well as mental), reading in their own history and other labors, women writers have leaped over the barbed-wire fences to a new sexual honesty and self-exposure.

Not so long ago, any writer worth her salt struggled to write herself free of the epithet "woman writer." "Damned scribbling women," Hawthorne fumed. Woman writers, sob sisters, the three-named ladies. (I had heard nothing but sneers for the three-named ladies, so I junked my family name—it's gone forever.) Out of the loins of the woman's movement, the term woman writer is born again. Separatist? Regressive? Separatism to end separatism, war to end war. Paradox enough. There is only one literature, that is human literature, and all who can, participate and contribute. Need we repeat—nothing human is alien to me? Yes.

Yet there's no doubt that in the last few years there has been an outpouring of writing by women about women. It is as if the woman's movement gave a kind of support that led to an exuberant letting go, out of imagination or memory. Some of it very good writing, some of it art, some of it confessional and documentary—interesting because the confessed and documented matters haven't been written about before.

So be it. Making a separate category of women writers is a kind of holding pattern then, till themes and responses and methods worked by women are also given safe conduct in the world.

Clearly the atmosphere around women who write is slowly but surely improving. They are freer to create out of a larger range of styles and attitudes than before. And reviews, apart from an occasional dreadful "affirmative action" review, in which a woman is set to review a woman with the obvious purpose of redressing a general wrong instead of addressing a particular book, have gotten a bit more fair-minded toward women.

Still, every writer will have her own list of reviewing grievances from before the enlightenment. Here are mine:

Book I: Reviewer praises it for charm, for playfulness, for being "an idyll . . . about unsuccessful people working for an unsuccessful company . . . [in] go-getting America . . ." But it wasn't "corrosive enough. (1) Who said I wanted to be corrosive at all? (2) The desire for corrosiveness is an aspect of the received idea that books must be "active," that is, "masculine," that is: "Don't just stand there depicting something and making us see how it works—give it a kick!"

Book II: Review opens with an Anthony Burgess quote: *He* prefers books with "a strong male thrust, an almost pedantic allusiveness and a brutal intellectual content." Reviewer tries to grope his way out of his own trap: "But surely the appetite for honest emotional goods is not exclusively feminine?"

Book III (this time, alas! a woman reviewer): ". . . One cannot read this novel without stumbling over queries about the female condition. (If only this topic might stay in the garage for a while! It just isn't one of our primary national problems.)"

And now back to the shelves.

Had Fredericka been under the impression that masturbation was exclusively a male, not female, subject in fiction? There is "Marcella," by Marilyn Coffey, a novel whose content is almost exclusively female adolescent sexuality and masturbation.

Were women supposed to be passive and submissive? There is a new woman who is swashbuckling and adventuring, picaresque; who hunts adventure and men. Fredericka takes out Erica Jong's "Fear of Flying" and finds that the heroine adores males with all the fervor Humbert lavished on Lolita, and rivals his passion with hers for male bodies, male smells, male ejaculations.

Were women supposed to be masochists? The new heroine seeks pleasure and is the first to walk out when it wanes, as Alix Kates Shulman's heroine does in "Memoirs of an Ex-Prom Queen."

Were they supposed to be "ladylike," modest in speech and manner? Then what used to be called "locker-room talk" would be welcomed into the house, and women would speak it as easily as men.

Fredericka staggers home with her load of books and finds herself admiring. How brave these women are! They defy the father, the husband; they defy the analyst himself! They are all, these heroines, wound into analysis and analysts (Lois Gould's novel is called "Final Analysis")—married to them, having affairs with them, telling their stories to them, *seeing through them* ("You see, you must now learn to agzept yourzelf as a vooman . . .").

Without masochism, who would be analyzed? Who would pay to be flogged? Those heroines, having cut themselves off from one unsatisfactory safety, the unsatisfactory husband, want to hold themselves back from running to the next safety, the next unsatisfactory husband; to refuse also the trap of unsatisfactory liaison with analyst. Unless it is analyst as lover, in which case analyst is stripped down to full pomposity. In "Fear of Flying," the analyst-lover leads the heroine in a week-long romp through the woods without timetable in order to teach her how to give herself to existential life, then leaves abruptly for his next appointment.

They hack away, these women, at the ground under their own feet, sacrificing the old ways of safety, forcing themselves to face the void. Mapless and chartless, at the close of their books they are deep into their own hair—they have cut it and it will never (Continued on Page 18)

Norma Rosen is the author of "Green," "Joy to Levine!" and "Touching Evil," and is currently working on a new novel.

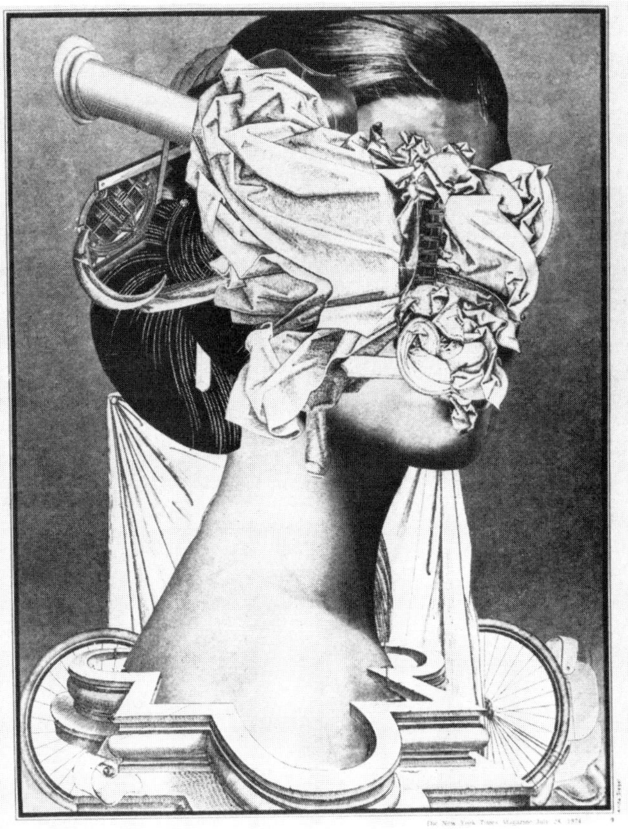

1072

1071
Art Director Steve Heller
Designer Steve Heller
Artist Ralph Steadman
Editor Charlotte Curtis
Publisher The New York Times Op-Ed Page

1072
Art Director Ruth Ansel
Designer Ruth Ansel
Artist Anita Siegel
Editors Lewis Bergman
Jack Rosenthal
Publisher The New York Times Magazine

1073

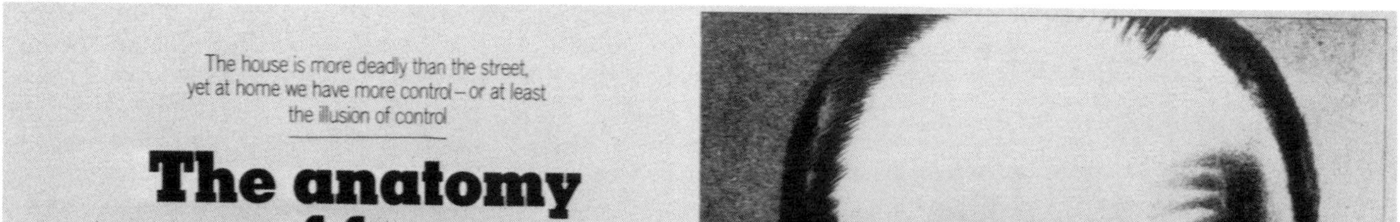
The house is more deadly than the street, yet at home we have more control—or at least the illusion of control

The anatomy of fear

By Maggie Scarf

Dangers we face (based on estimates for 1972 by the National Safety Council and the F.B.I.)

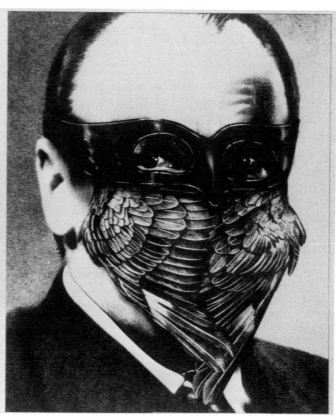

1074

GOLD

1073
Art Directors Milton Glaser
Walter Bernard
Designers Milton Glaser
Walter Bernard
Artist David Levine
Publisher New York

1074
Art Director Ruth Ansel
Designer Ruth Ansel
Artist Christian Piper
Editor Lewis Bergman
Jack Rosenthal
Publisher The New York Times Magazine

1075

Nontravelers are not "take-charge persons," says one psychologist who has studied them for an airline. They tend to be neurotically "territory-bounded" and beset by "generalized anxieties" and "powerlessness."

1076

1075
Art Director Joe Brooks
Designer Honey Kandel
Artist Edward Sorel
Publisher Penthouse

1076
Art Director Robert Melson
Designer Robert Melson
Artist R. O. Blechman
Publisher The New York Times Travel and Resorts

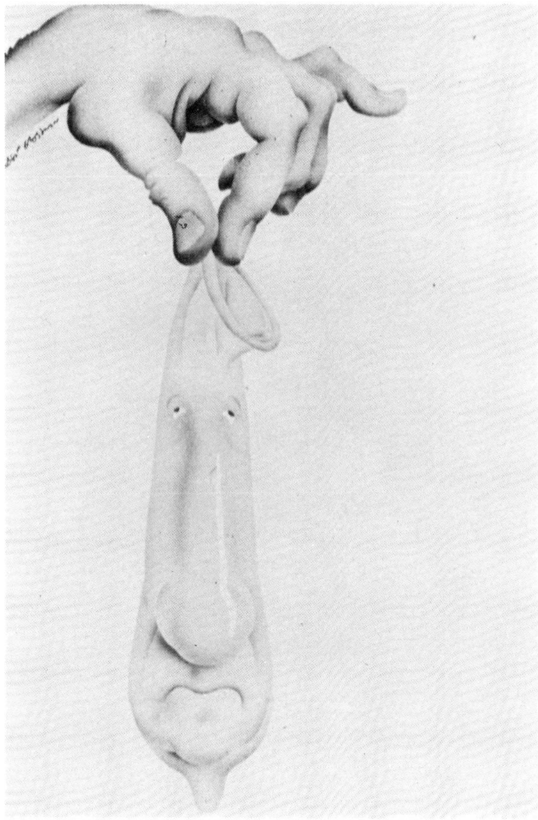

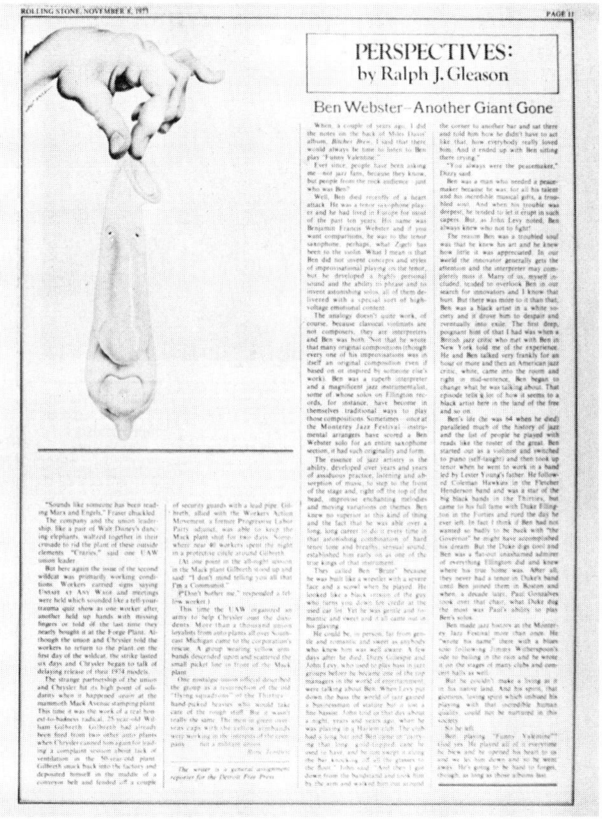

ROLLING STONE, NOVEMBER 6, 1975 PAGE 11

PERSPECTIVES:
by Ralph J. Gleason

Ben Webster—Another Giant Gone

1077

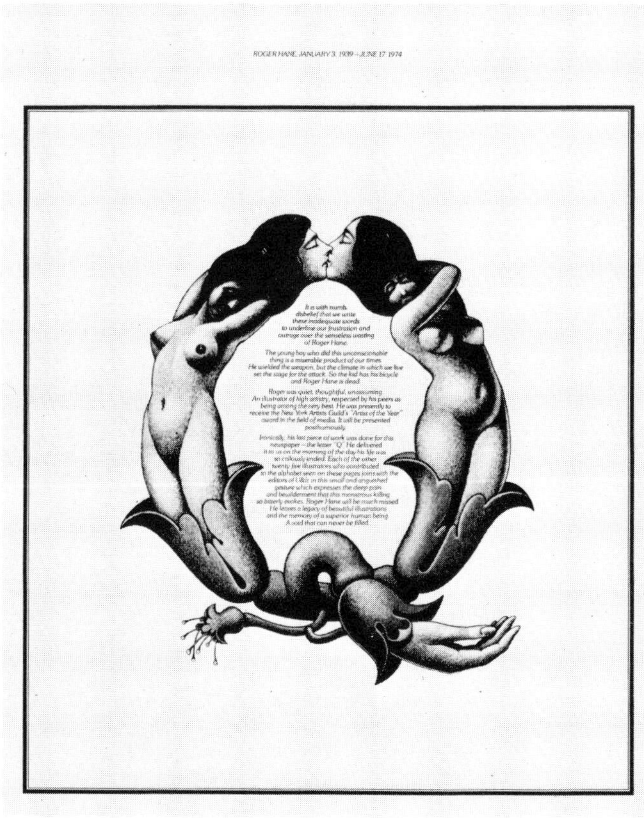

ROGER HANE, JANUARY 3, 1939—JUNE 17, 1974
It is with numb disbelief that we write these inadequate words to underline our frustration and outrage over the senseless wasting of Roger Hane.
The young boy who did this unconscionable thing is a miserable product of our times. He wielded the weapon, but the climate in which we live set the stage for the attack. So the kid has his bicycle and Roger Hane is dead.
Roger was quiet, thoughtful, unassuming. An illustrator of high artistry, respected by his peers as being among the very best. He was presently to receive the New York Artists Guild's "Artist of the Year" award in the field of media. It will be presented posthumously.
Ironically, his last piece of work was done for this newspaper—the letter "Q". He delivered it to us on the morning of the day his life was so callously ended. Each of the other twenty five illustrators who contributed to the alphabet seen on these pages joins with the editors of U&lc in this small and anguished gesture which expresses the deep pain and bewilderment that this monstrous killing so bitterly evokes. Roger Hane will be much missed. He leaves a legacy of beautiful illustrations and the memory of a superior human being. A void that can never be filled.

1078

1077
Art Director Mike Salisbury
Designers Mike Salisbury
Lloyd Ziff
Artist Robert Grossman
Publisher Rolling Stone

1078
Art Director Herb Lubalin
Designer Herb Lubalin
Artist Roger Hane
Editor Herb Lubalin
Writer Jack Anson Finke
Publisher U & lc
International Typeface Corp.

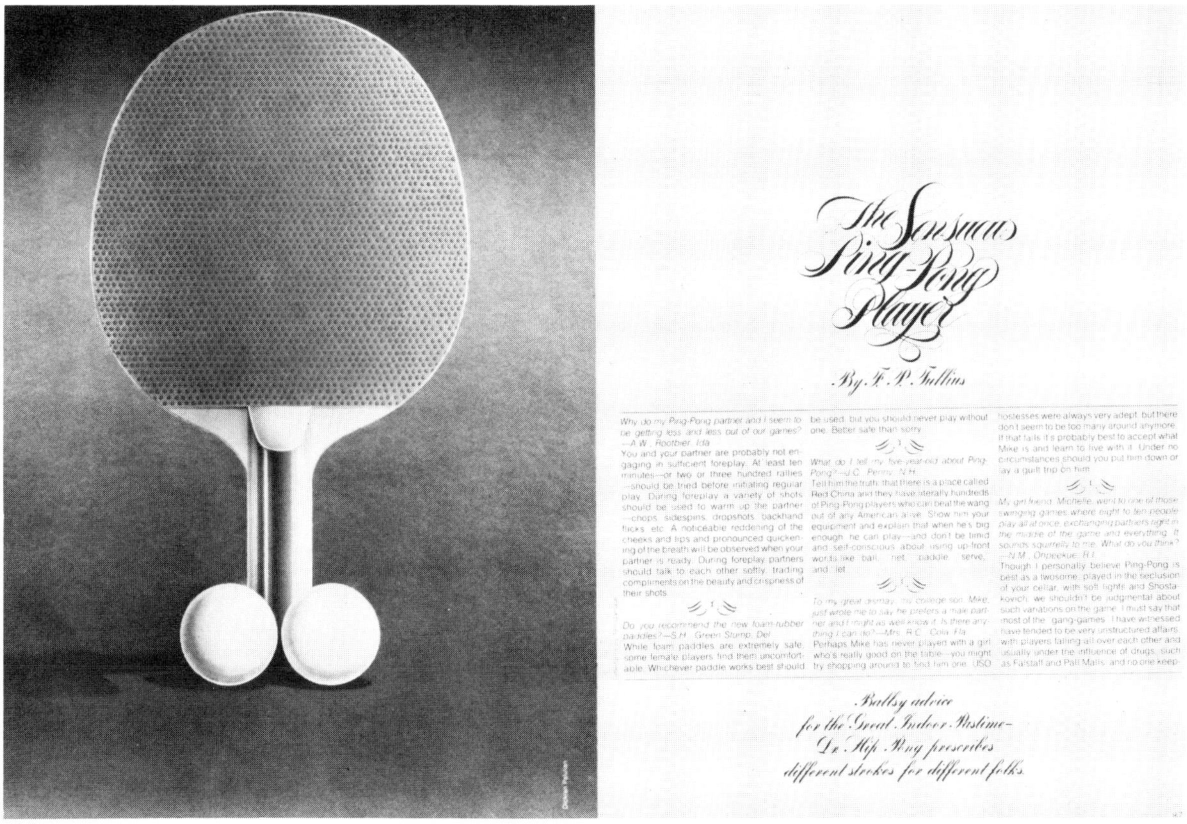

The Sensuous Ping-Pong Player

By F. P. Tullius

Why do my Ping-Pong partner and I seem to be getting less and less out of our games? —A.W., Rootbier, Ida.

You and your partner are probably not engaging in sufficient foreplay. At least ten minutes—or two or three hundred rallies—should be tried before initiating regular play. During foreplay a variety of shots should be used to warm up the partner—chops, sidespins, dropshots, backhand flicks, etc. A noticeable reddening of the cheeks and lips and pronounced quickening of the breath will be observed when your partner is ready. During foreplay partners should talk to each other softly, trading compliments on the beauty and crispness of their shots.

Do you recommend the new foam-rubber paddles?—S.H., Green Stump, Del.

While foam paddles are extremely safe, some female players find them uncomfortable. Whichever paddle works best should be used, but you should never play without one. Better safe than sorry.

What do I tell my five-year-old about Ping-Pong?—J.C., Penny, N.H.

Tell him the truth: that there is a place called Red China and they have literally hundreds of Ping-Pong players who can beat the wang out of any American alive. Show him your equipment and explain that when he's big enough, he can play—and don't be timid and self-conscious about using up-front words like "ball," "net," "paddle," "serve," and "let."

To my great dismay, my college son, Mike, just wrote me to say he prefers a male partner and I might as well know it. Is there anything I can do?—Mrs. R.C., Cola, Fla.

Perhaps Mike has never played with a girl who's really good on the table—you might try shopping around to find him one. USO hostesses were always very adept, but there don't seem to be too many around anymore. If that fails it's probably best to accept what Mike is and learn to live with it. Under no circumstances should you put him down or lay a guilt trip on him.

My girl friend, Michelle, went to one of those swinging games where eight to ten people play all at once, exchanging partners right in the middle of the game and everything. It sounds squirrelly to me. What do you think? —N.M., Onpeekue, R.I.

Though I personally believe Ping-Pong is best as a twosome, played in the seclusion of your cellar, with soft lights and Shostakovich, we shouldn't be judgmental about such variations on the game. I must say that most of the "gang-games" I have witnessed have tended to be very unstructured affairs, with players falling all over each other and usually under the influence of drugs, such as Falstaff and Pall Malls, and no one keep-

Ballsy advice for the Great Indoor Pastime—Dr. Hip Pong prescribes different strokes for different folks.

1079

Colonel Matt Winn; Aristides, the first Derby winner (with jockey Oliver Lewis up); and the start of the 1914 Derby—in which the field was sent off with the crack of a whip—figure in artist Wilson McClean's nostalgic portrayal of America's greatest sport classic. During the Derby's first quarter century many of the winning jockeys were black.

AMERICA'S GREATEST RACE

The Kentucky Derby

BY PETER CHEW

Someone once asked Irvin S. Cobb, the homespun philosopher of Paducah, to tell what made the Kentucky Derby so special. Said Cobb:

"If I could do that, I'd have a larynx of spun silver and the tongue of an anointed angel. But if you can imagine a track that's like a bracelet of molten gold encircling a greensward that's like a patch of emerald velvet. . . . All the pretty girls in the state turning the grandstand into a brocaded terrace of beauty and color such as the hanging gardens of Babylon never equaled. . . . All the assembled sports of the nation going crazy at once down in the paddock. . . . And just yonder in the yellow dust, the gallant kings and noble queens of the kingdom . . . each a vision of courage and heart and speed. . . . But what's the use? Until you go to Kentucky and with your own eyes behold the Derby, you ain't never been nowheres and you ain't never seen nothin'!"

Well, the Kentucky Derby hasn't been like that for some time. But Cobb was right. The Derby is America's greatest horse race. It ranks with the World Series, the Indianapolis 500, the Davis Cup and the Super Bowl. And this year, on the afternoon of May 4, when millions of Americans switch on their TV sets they will be witnessing the one-hundredth running of the mile and a quarter race for three-year-olds that has become known as "the most exciting two minutes in sports."

There are older stakes in America, the Preakness and the Belmont for instance, and $100,000 races without number, but the Derby is the oldest *continuously run* classic. And no matter what horsemen say about the race's deficiencies as an intelligent test of the nation's best three-year-olds, most agree that they all want to win this one.

Stardust, riches and a measure of immortality attend the owners, breeders, trainers, jockeys and grooms connected with a Derby winner. The instant the winning colt flashes under the wire (only one filly has ever won), he's usually worth at least $1 million for stud purposes. Some horses have been syndicated for four and five times that amount. Secretariat was syndicated before the race in early 1973 for $6,080,000; the syndicators figured the colt had the best chance to win the Derby. Secretariat won, and the members, who each paid $190,000 for the privilege of breeding one mare a year to Secretariat, were relieved. When Secretariat went on to take the Preakness and Belmont in awesome style, the value of the shares rose even higher.

Horsemen agree there is no more difficult race to get ready for than the

continued on page 55

1080

1079
Art Director Joe Brooks
Designer Joe Brooks
Artist Dickran Palulian
Publisher Penthouse

1080
Art Director Norman S. Hotz
Designer Gail Tauber
Artist Wilson McLean
Publisher Travel & Leisure

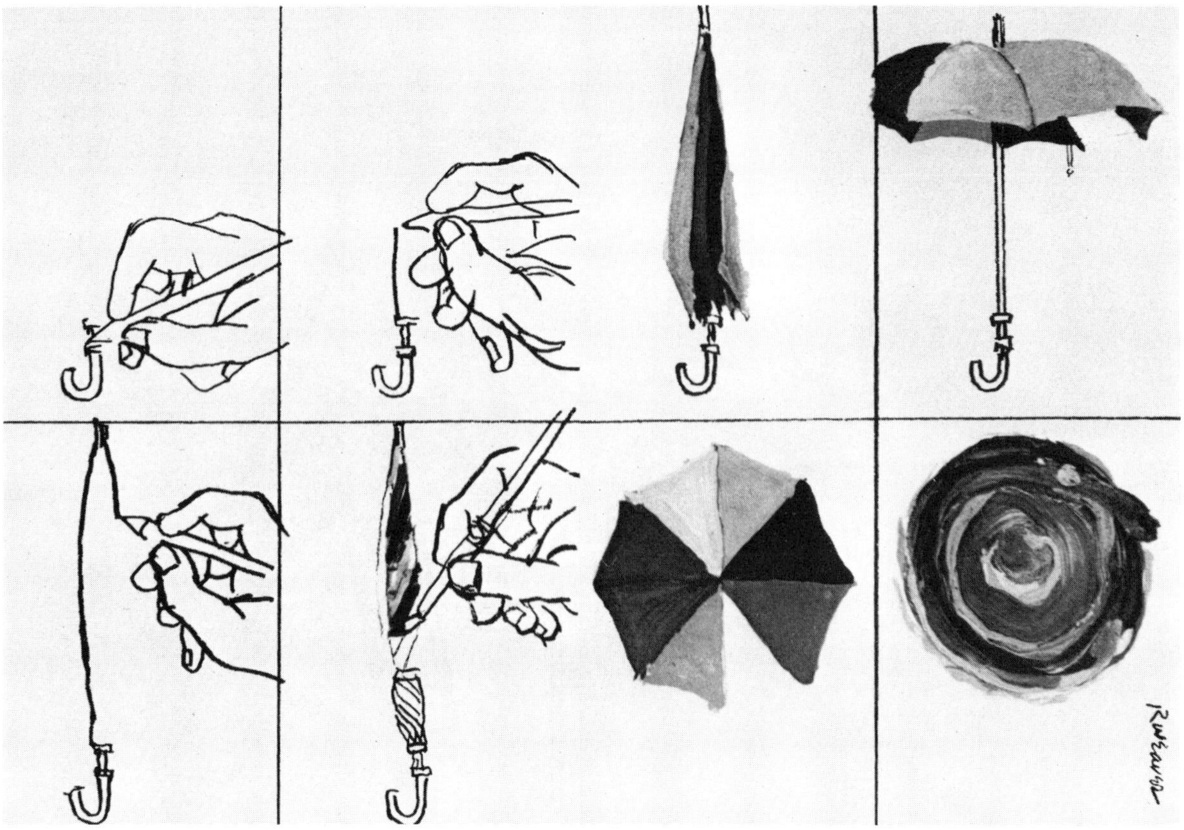

1081

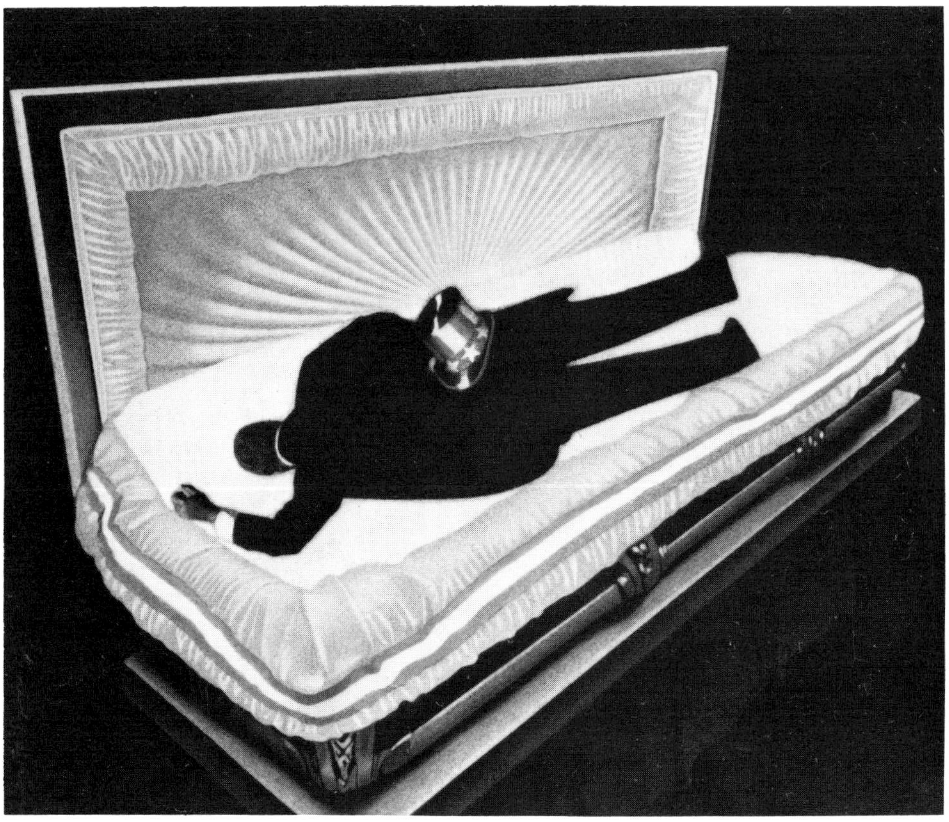

1082

1081
Art Director Henry Wolf
Designer Gary Schenck
Artist Robert Weaver
Publisher Sesame Street Magazine
Agency Henry Wolf Productions

1082
Art Director Joe Brooks
Designer Joe Brooks
Artist Alex Gnidziejko
Publisher Penthouse

Who's Coming to Lunch? Answer on back cover.
¿Quienes vienen a almorzar? Respuesta en la contraportada.

1083

CONOCO74
NUMBER 2
CELEBRATION!
First Oil: The Fabulous 101 pg. 3
Coal Mountains, Coal Men pg. 10
So You Work for an Oil Company? pg. 24

1086

1083
Art Director Henry Wolf
Designer Gary Schenck
Artist Dave Willardson
Publisher Sesame Street Magazine
Agency Henry Wolf Productions

1086
Art Director Milt Simpson
Designer Gretchen Ackerman
Artist Alan E. Cober
Editor Maury Bates
Agency Johnson & Simpson Graphic Designers
Client Conoco Continental Oil Co.

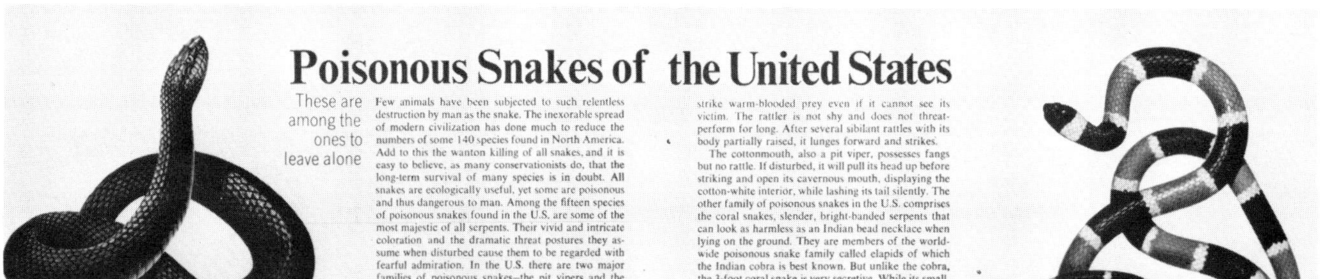

Poisonous Snakes of the United States

These are among the ones to leave alone

Few animals have been subjected to such relentless destruction by man as the snake. The inexorable spread of modern civilization has done much to reduce the numbers of some 140 species found in North America. Add to this the wanton killing of all snakes, and it is easy to believe, as many conservationists do, that the long-term survival of many species is in doubt. All snakes are ecologically useful, yet some are poisonous and thus dangerous to man. Among the fifteen species of poisonous snakes found in the U.S. are some of the most majestic of all serpents. Their vivid and intricate coloration and the dramatic threat postures they assume when disturbed cause them to be regarded with fearful admiration. In the U.S. there are two major families of poisonous snakes–the pit vipers and the elapids. Rattlesnakes belong to the pit viper family and are best known for their habit of rattling the horny segments of their tails—as a warning. They possess enormous movable fangs that rotate forward when the snake opens its mouth to bite but otherwise are folded back in the mouth. The 6 or 7-foot Western diamondback rattler, along with its even larger Eastern cousin, is the largest of our poisonous snakes. It has a stylish pattern over its heavy body and a characteristic triangular-shaped head. Its vertical eye slits and immovable eyelids are typical of many snakes, but in addition, it has unique sensory pits on either side of the head that help the snake to locate and strike warm-blooded prey even if it cannot see its victim. The rattler is not shy and does not threat-perform for long. After several sibilant rattles with its body partially raised, it lunges forward and strikes.

The cottonmouth, also a pit viper, possesses fangs but no rattle. If disturbed, it will pull its head up before striking and open its cavernous mouth, displaying the cotton-white interior, while lashing its tail silently. The other family of poisonous snakes in the U.S. comprises the coral snakes, slender, bright-banded serpents that can look as harmless as an Indian bead necklace when lying on the ground. They are members of the worldwide poisonous snake family called elapids of which the Indian cobra is best known. But unlike the cobra, the 3-foot coral snake is very secretive. While its small, immovable fangs may be simple and primitive, its venom, drop for drop, is much more potent and dangerous than that of the rattlers. But because it is such a shy snake, found largely in Florida and adjacent southern states, few people ever see it. The venom that poisonous snakes inject into a wound through their fangs is potent and even deadly, but the possibility of death from a bite is very slight. There is good antivenin for all snake poisons now, but prompt treatment is imperative. The best advice about snakes is that which was emblazoned on a Colonial flag: "Don't tread on me"–for their sake, as well as yours.

—PAT HUNT

Cottonmouth
Agkistrodon piscivorus piscivorus

Eastern Coral Snake
Micrurus fulvius

Western Diamondback Rattlesnake
Crotalus atrox

ILLUSTRATED BY JOHN WILSON

1087

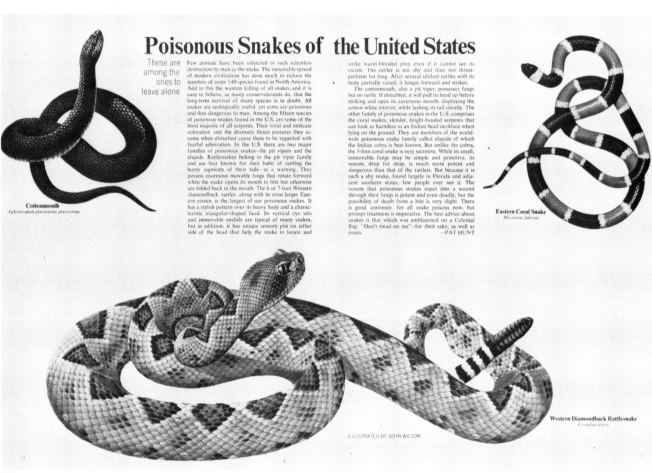

1087
Art Director Norman S. Hotz
Designer Gail Tauber
Artist John Wilson
Publisher Travel & Leisure

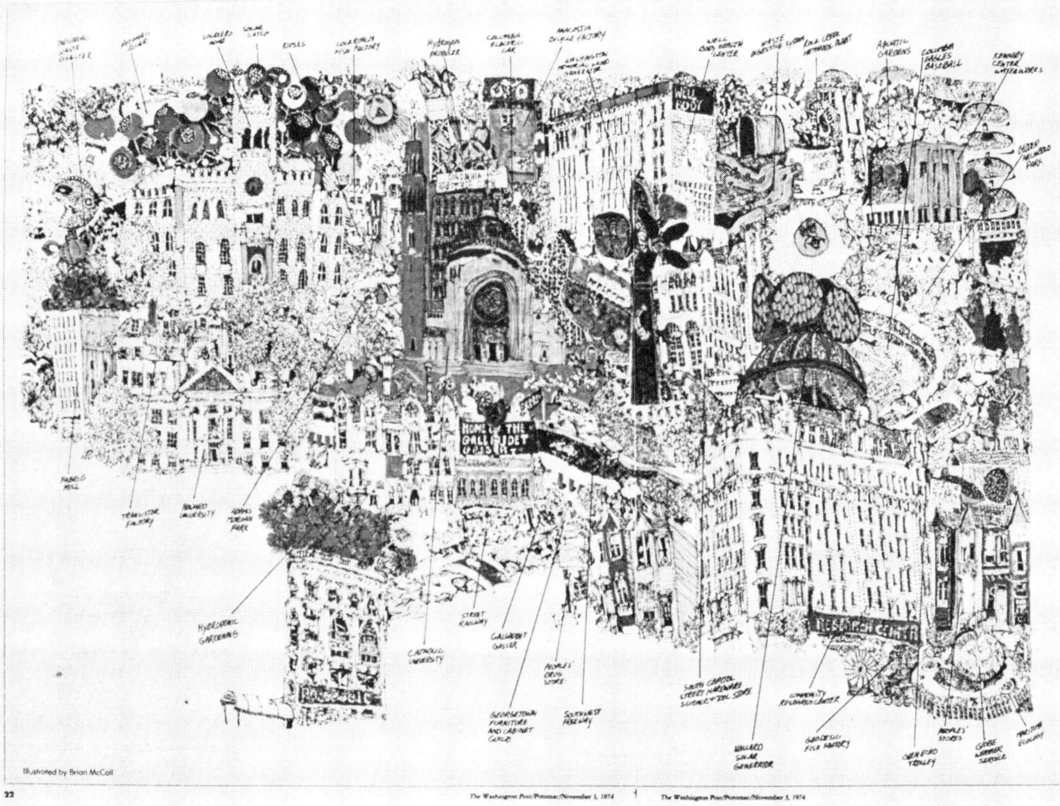

Illustrated by Brian McCall

Washington Utopia

An Election Eve Dream

By Karl Hess

Exactly ten years after the District's first home rule primary election, it will be 1984, the date famed for predictions of the ultimate rule of Big Brother.

In a Washington and an America following a path of centralized power over an expanded bureaucracy, the 1984 elections here could be merely a ritual support of a puppet city government — a little brother for the Big Brother ruler.

But the signs are not all pointing that way. Indeed, heady new whiffs of freedom seem to be sensed everywhere. By 1984, Washington, free and bountiful, could be a dream, not a nightmare, come true. If so, a chronicler of the time might reflect on the decade in this way:

It came as no particular surprise to anyone that the first of the great changes came in the Adams-Morgan section, that mixed 60-block bag of artists, craftsmen, businessmen, anti-businessmen, bureaucrats, cooperators, radicals, conservatives, welfare families, workers of all kinds, loafers, hucksters, hypsters, and hipsters.

Shortly after the first mayoral election as a matter of fact, during a neighborhood street fair, the fairgoers by obvious conspiratorial arrangement simply tore up the entire street, blocked it at both ends, and began preparing the ground for planting. In the spring the first flowers appeared. By the end of the summer the entire neighborhood was not only using the street as a park but was supplying a significant part of its nutrition from the gardens which checkerboarded the street. Automobiles, in the meantime, parked very handily in angle-in lines at each end of the street.

The city, of course, had virtual fits about the citizen action in converting the street to a park. But, in the jockeying for power and politicking that marked the transition to home rule there were more situations in which the citizens could, literally, stand off the government while experimenting with their new-found freedom. And, in cases like the spontaneous park, the effects were so practical and popular that the forces of status quo looked silly anyway.

Continued on page 26

Karl Hess is a fellow with the Institute of Policy Studies. A writer and a welder, he is also project coordinator for Community Technology, Inc.

1088

Portrait of Jen

Remembrances From the Children's Cancer Ward

By Robert A. Becker

"The committee feels that since its inception of little more than two years ago, the National Cancer Program has made substantial progress. . . . The difficulty of the cancer problem is illustrated by the fact that in spite of the progress that has been made, one of every four of our citizens will develop cancer in their lifetime. According to the present trends, 665,000 new cases and nearly 350,000 deaths from cancer are expected in 1974."

Sen. Edward M. Kennedy
March 20, 1974

A nurse on the floor ushered us to a room and handed me a small, open-backed gown for Jen to wear.

"Leave my clothes on," the child insisted. "I want my shirt on. Don't take my shoes off." Jen was terrified. It was our seventh visit to Children's Hospital in three weeks, visits which invariably began in the outpatient clinic on the first floor with a technician pricking her finger for a blood sample, followed by a doctor's probings and palpations. The more recent trips, like this one, often turned into a two- or three-day stay in the hospital, much to Jen's growing dismay.

Ten months earlier, when Jennifer was 20 months old, her mother and I noticed a lump on her side after lifting her from the tub one Sunday night. She had been lethargic for a couple of weeks before that but the pediatrician said she was probably anemic and prescribed iron pills. After the swelling appeared though, we took her to Alexandria Hospital where they operated and discovered neuroblastoma, the most common form of solid-tumor cancer that strikes infants and toddlers.

In the months that followed, we had taken her to a private oncologist for chemotherapy every other week, and to the radiologist every day for the first two months. We were lucky. The combination of drugs and radiation had worked and produced what the doctors said was "complete remission," which simply meant there was no trace of the disease. It was not to be confused with a "cure."

Still, we had begun to allow ourselves the luxury of believing she just might be cured anyway, when suddenly, the lethargy, the failing appetite, the constant crying from the discomfort—and the tumor—all reappeared. A relapse.

Realizing there was little else he could do, the oncologist, a rather large man with an air of determined detachment, arranged for Jen's admission to the fouth floor of Children's Hospital—the children's cancer ward.

"Unproven remedies for the treatment of cancer are as old as the disease itself. Unfortunately, many patients with curable cancer also leave the care of competent physicians to be treated with a worthless, unproven remedy until a cure by accepted methods of treatment becomes impossible."

Unproven Methods of Cancer Treatment
The American Cancer Society, Inc.

But before Jen's first appointment at Children's, this bitter, abrupt change started me on the last stretch of a psychic marathon, a race known to countless families of the cancer-stricken—The Miracle Chase. I am talking now of hope and fear. Sunrise, sunset, the dread remains, the hope remains.

The senses are seized and the stomach alternately tightens, then churns. I had experienced this first at the Alexandria Hospital when we thought Jen would survive only a few weeks at most. Despite the fear, because of the fear, you keep functioning. In recent weeks, I had furiously researched and read all I could on neuroblastoma and where and how it was treated.

I placed phone calls all around the country to leading hospitals and clinics.

Was there any new treatment, any drug that looked hopeful? There were calls to Sloan Kettering, to Roswell Park, M.D. Anderson Hospital and Tumor Clinic in Houston, Texas, even to Dr. Andrew C. Ivy whose curative claims for Krebiozen in the late 1950s led to his indictment in 1964 (and subsequent acquittal) on 49 counts for violations of the Food, Drug and Cosmetic Act. But Dr. Ivy, now in his 70s, seemed more interested in attacking his persecutors of ten years ago and the consequent restricted use of his drugs than he was in their effects on neuroblastoma. Desperate for help, I found none. Most likely, there was none then to be found. There still isn't—for a variety of reasons.

Continued on page 37

Robert A. Becker is a free lance writer and member of the Candlelighters, Washington area group of parents of cancer-afflicted children.

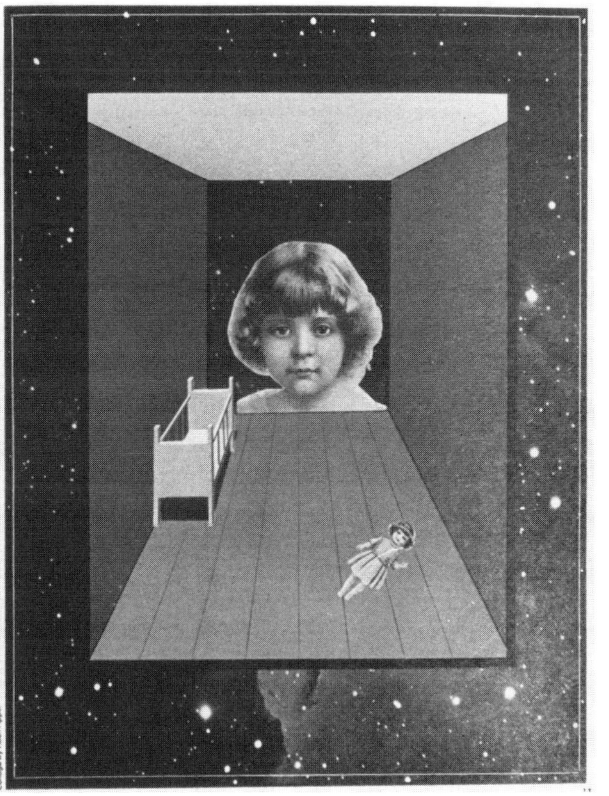

Collage by Allen Appel

1089

PHOTOGRAPHY & ART

1088
Art Director David Moy
Designer Brian McCall
Artist Brian McCall
Publisher The Washington Post
Potomac Magazine

1089
Art Director David Moy
Designer Allen Appel
Artist Allen Appel
Publisher The Washington Post
Potomac Magazine

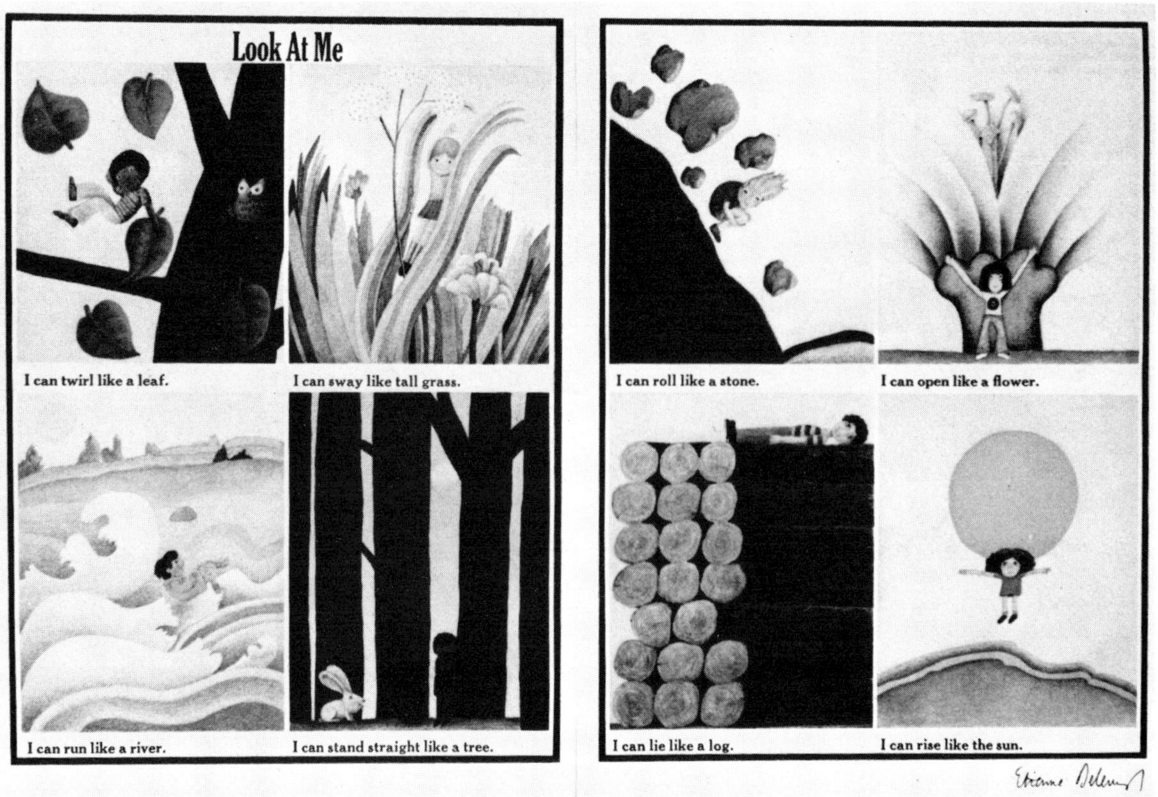
Look At Me
I can twirl like a leaf.
I can sway like tall grass.
I can run like a river.
I can stand straight like a tree.
I can roll like a stone.
I can open like a flower.
I can lie like a log.
I can rise like the sun.

1090

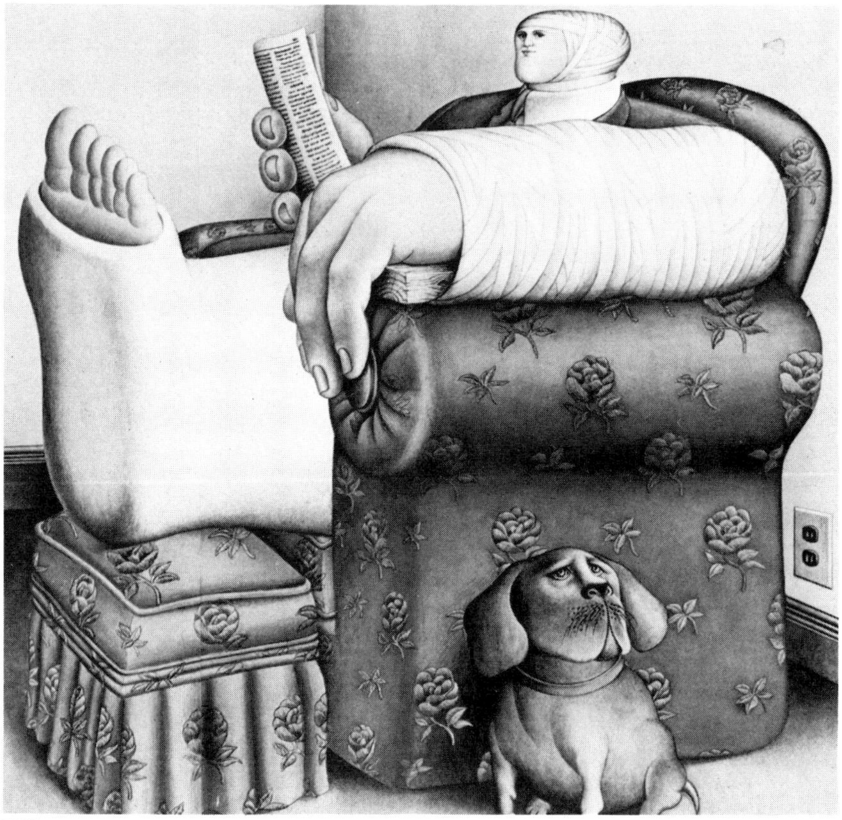

1091

1090
Art Director Henry Wolf
Designer Gary Schenck
Artist Etienne Delessert
Writer Jocelyn Gunnar
Publisher Sesame Street Magazine
Agency Henry Wolf Productions

1091
Art Director Joe Brooks
Designer Joe Brooks
Artist Roy Carruthers
Publisher Penthouse

The Washington Post
Potomac
Sunday, September 22, 1974
The Illusion of Post-Watergate Morality
Men's Fall Fashions
The Rise of Michigan Chic

1092

Find All the Words That Start with "CH."
See page 32 for answers.

1093

1092
Art Director David Moy
Designer John Heinly
Artist John Heinly
Publisher The Washington Post Potomac Magazine

1093
Art Director Mary Schenck
Artist Seymour Chwast
Publisher Sesame Street Magazine

They Loved Not Wisely But Too Well

Illustrated by Edward Sorel

"...Their only offense was that they loved too well—and then went ahead and told the American public about it..."

The tragedy of Richard Nixon is not that he has a soul too mean, a nature too petty, but that he has a personality too magnetic, an aura too blinding. Not only did his closest aides succumb to his charm, but even some who met him only briefly, outside the Oval Office, fell victim to his fatal gifts. These are the poor unfortunates who planned no burglary, tapped no phone, never even took a free malted milk. Their only offense was that they loved too well—and then went ahead and told the public about it. Their only crimes were of verbal excess, which is not even a misdemeanor.

"Nixon has sex appeal—he's slim and suntanned and . . . well, he's just sexy, that's all. And I call that charming."
—*Barbara Walters*
(*How to Talk With Practically Anybody About Practically Anything*, 1970)

"I have asked You for a moral and spiritual restoration in the land and give thanks that in Thy sovereignty Thou hast permitted Richard Nixon to lead us at this momentous hour of our history."
—*Billy Graham*
(*The New York Times Magazine*, June 8, 1969)

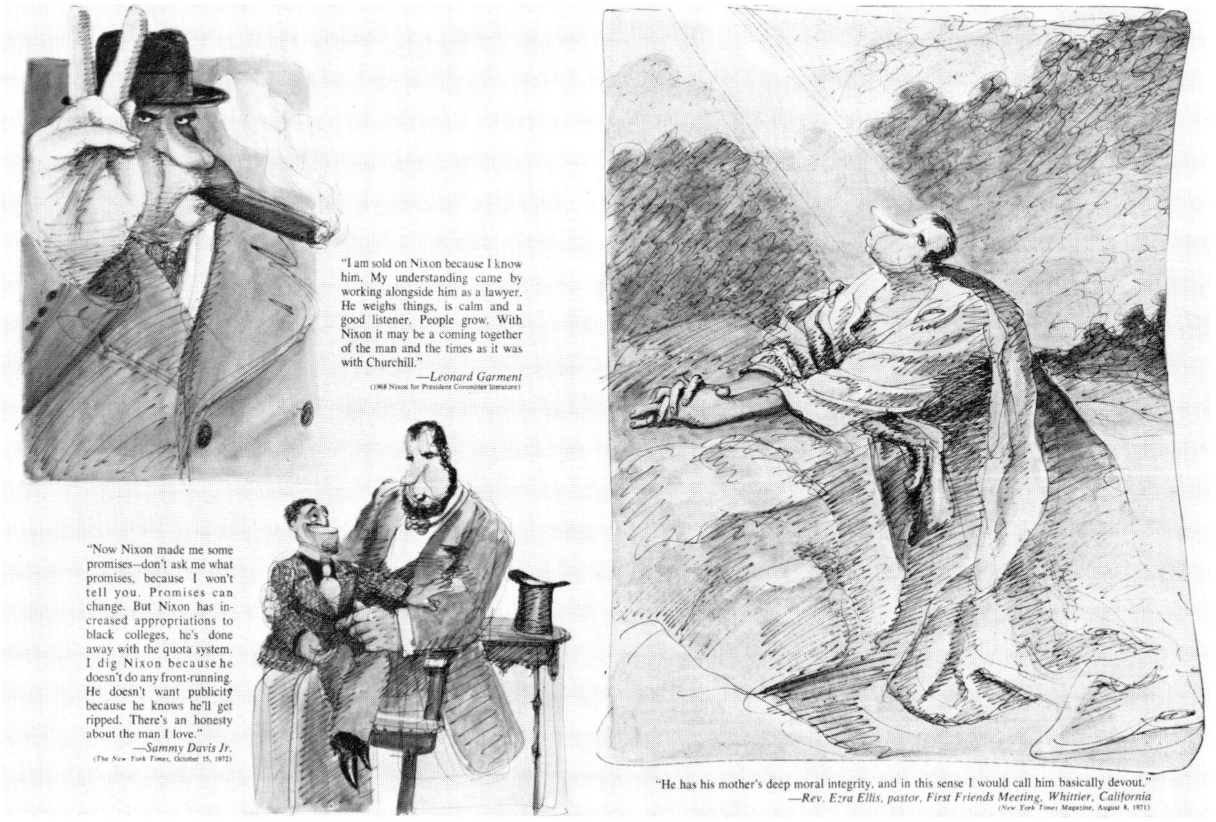

"I am sold on Nixon because I know him. My understanding came by working alongside him as a lawyer. He weighs things, is calm and a good listener. People grow. With Nixon it may be a coming together of the man and the times as it was with Churchill."
—*Leonard Garment*
(1968 Nixon for President Committee literature)

"Now Nixon made me some promises—don't ask me what promises, because I won't tell you. Promises can change. But Nixon has increased appropriations to black colleges, he's done away with the quota system. I dig Nixon because he doesn't do any front-running. He doesn't want publicity because he knows he'll get ripped. There's an honesty about the man I love."
—*Sammy Davis Jr.*
(*The New York Times*, October 15, 1972)

"He has his mother's deep moral integrity, and in this sense I would call him basically devout."
—*Rev. Ezra Ellis, pastor, First Friends Meeting, Whittier, California*
(*New York Times Magazine*, August 8, 1971)

1094

1094
Art Director Walter Bernard
Designer Edward Sorel
Artist Edward Sorel
Publisher New York

NEW TIMES
TOP OF THE NEWS

LBJ through Watergate-colored glasses

By Larry L. King

When they first began to back him into the fatal corner—*why'd you take that tax write-off for your papers, Mr. President? how many people have you bugged?*—Richard Nixon said in effect, well, that Lyndon Johnson had told him to do the former and, for that matter, LBJ had perhaps bugged more people than Scull and Bones. Yes, he leaned heavily on LBJ in his early defenses, knowing that at the end of his troubled reign Lyndon Johnson had left the presidency under the darkest cloud since Herbert Hoover. No doubt it appeared, to Richard Nixon, to be a convenient and profitable comparison; possibly he thanked his Quaker god.

But was it, now? Were the sins equal? No. Not, at least, by certain measurements of the runaway House Judiciary Committee, which, having voted three articles of impeachment against the President, failed, however, to stampede the proposition that Nixon's secret bombing of Cambodia constituted an impeachable offense. We might argue all night whether the committee *should* have: a private war, an undeclared war, a war covered up and denied even as it was being waged would appear on the surface, at least, closely akin to a major no-no. But they didn't indict RMN for it, anymore than they indicted LBJ for his own international deceptions—Gulf of Tonkin, Dominican Republic, all those false promises of light at the end of the endless Vietnam tunnel, all the secret escalations, all the falsespeak and phony kill-ratios and "pacified" vast areas or other official flimflams.

Probably that made Richard Nixon feel pretty good. Maybe he said to himself in whatever hideaway office he then occupied—or, perhaps, during solitary nocturnal misplayings of the White House piano—*well, we won that one, Lyndon, we are brothers under the skin, heh-heh.* Were they? And, if so, how much commonality did they share?

LBJ's faults are legendary: warts grew on him in grand profusion. There was much of the hog-caller in the man,

In the raised consciousness of impeachment, a fellow Texan examines the record of Richard Nixon's predecessor

something of the playground bully, a dash of the gambler who dealt off the bottom. His only brother recalls LBJ skinning him in a bicycle trade when they were kids and habitually cheating at dominoes. LBJ tom-catted around a bit outside his marriage, especially in his younger years, and occasionally took on excessive liquors. One night in the mid-1950s, after a Texas State Society function at the National Press Club, I saw a zonked LBJ—then Senate Majority Leader—in a small bar with Texas Congressmen Homer Thornberry and Jack Brooks. "I'm a powerful sumbitch, boys," he told them over drinks. "Do you realize what a powerful sumbitch I am?" He said it not once but a half dozen times, face flushed, arms waving, obviously a man full of himself, and in love with his future.

I sense that LBJ's financial affairs constituted his softest underbelly. He came from a state where, traditionally, public figures take no poverty vows: an amazing number of Texans in high places grow rich beyond their visible opportunities or brains. For years a Texas Establishment ran things. Conservative bankers, oil men, businessmen of all stripes—these were the powers in each congressional unit, and they operated their own grand duchies. Party ties were weak; during most of LBJ's career Texas was a one-party state with no single figure all-powerful; party discipline was nonexistent. Consequently, each office-seeker made a separate peace with the powers in his domain. The successful candidate cuddled up to the money boys—they held the power—and, once in office, thought little of using their positions or their friends to enrich themselves. Yes, persuasive arithmetic and regional custom are on the side of LBJ's having found that power bred money unless one beat it off with a stick.

The Johnson fortune is said to have been seeded by a $21,000 cash inheritance bequeathed to Lady Bird. In 1942, when her husband had been in Congress five years, Mrs. Johnson became the purchaser-of-record of radio station KTBC in Austin for $17,500; her net worth, including land inherited in Alabama, was listed as $64,000. By 1948, the year he was elected to the U.S. Senate, LBJ privately boasted of having made his first million. In 1964 Barry Goldwater's campaign oratory variously pegged the Johnson

Contributing Editor King, Visiting Ferris Professor of Journalism at Princeton, is at work on a biography of Lyndon Johnson.

64 NEW TIMES

1095

Struggle in the Far West

Isaac Blake was the kind who could take on the Standard giant in a no-holds-barred California price war—and laugh at the prospect.

THE CONTINENTAL OIL CO.

Perhaps it was San Francisco in the 1870s, a bustling city of 200,000 and the oil center of California. Perhaps it was the excitement of the harbor with barrels of kerosine piled high at the docks and the price of kerosine soaring back East and the rumors of new oil strikes down near the sleepy village of Los Angeles.

But when Isaac Blake stopped at San Francisco in 1874, the visit changed his life. Though he returned to the Rocky Mountain area where he founded the Continental Oil and Transportation Company in Ogden, Utah, in 1875, and shortly afterward the Continental Oil Company of Colorado, in Denver, California seemed to lure him back.

Once the Rocky Mountain companies were flourishing, Blake headed back to San Francisco for what were to be some of the most exciting, rewarding years of his life.

In 1877, Blake formed the Continental Oil and Transportation Company of California, with a plant in San Francisco where kerosine and other oils brought overland from the East could be stored in bulk and then measured into barrels or tins and sold. The company flourished, and within months Blake was building other plants.

Blake's rapid success in California was due as much to his imagination as an oil pioneer as his skill as an entrepreneur. One innovation was the introduction on the West Coast of a railroad tank car consisting of two large oil storage tanks at each end and a storage compartment for dry freight in the center. Continental also became noted for its special steel barrels encased in wooden staves and its five-gallon cans attached to a rocker. The rocker let the purchaser pour kerosine from the can without lifting it.

Within a year, Blake was not only selling products all along the coast but was evolving plans for marketing oils, lubricants, and waxes outside the United States. Although the extension of marketing into Mexico, Canada, and Pacific markets by ships was limited, it could be said that Continental was an international marketer as far back as 1878, when shipments were being sent to agents in the Hawaiian islands, Japan, and the Samoan islands.

By 1880, Continental had four offices in California, located in San Francisco, Los Angeles, Sacramento, and San Jose. Blake used them rather as centers from which to radiate an increasingly larger selling organization. By the end of 1880, he was advertising products available through outlets in Oakland, Stockton, Marysville, and San Diego.

Blake was always a man with an eye for new markets. In the fall of 1882, he purchased oil leases in California with the idea of ultimately developing and marketing fuel oil, although most oil marketers concentrated on selling lubricants and kerosine. But Californians had long been dissatisfied with coal, and Blake's idea was to substitute fuel oil and to work closely with gas companies, which already offered a very attractive market.

On October 26, 1882, Blake founded the Mission Transfer Company, incorporating it and staffing it with four Continental Oil and Transportation employees. The beginning of 1883 saw Isaac Blake pursuing an ambitious plan to lay a pipeline for Mission Transfer all the way from the Pico Oil Field to Ventura where he was going to build a steamer to carry the oil to San Francisco. This would be California's first pipeline. The plan necessitated laying pipeline across the property of A. C. Dietz. Mr. Dietz readily agreed at first, but later had a change of heart and ordered Blake's men off his property. It is characteristic of Blake that he took the case to court even though the ensuing litigation brought his operations almost completely to a halt. Persevering, he won the case in June 1884.

Continental, both on the West Coast and in the Rockies, was dependent upon a system of bulk stations. The typical bulk station consisted of two or three large wooden storage tanks of 500-barrel capacity, a storage warehouse, half a dozen tank wagons with teams of horses, a stable, and a small office.

In the early years, product was hauled in large barrels to customers. One nagging problem was that each barrel had to be delivered and then picked up and replaced. It was difficult for a customer to order a particular number of gallons, since he had to accept the whole barrel. Isaac Blake solved the problem by employing tank-wagon delivery. The wagons cut down on the awkwardness of having to wrestle heavy, bulky barrels off a cart. They also permitted the driver to pour out the exact gallonage ordered by the customer.

During the early 1870s, much of the oil products sold in California came from Jersey Standard refineries in the East, and arrived in clipper sailing ships from around Cape Horn. But by 1879 overland rail rates were dropping, and John D. Rockefeller and his companies decided it was time to start marketing products directly in California. In 1879, the Standard Oil Company (Ohio) opened an office in San Francisco.

For Isaac Blake, a blunt, outspoken man with a strong competitive streak, this was the kind of challenge he welcomed. Blake loved to bedevil competitors, taking personal delight in detailed research to pinpoint weak spots in the operations of other companies, particularly Standard Oil. When he found out, for instance, that Standard was weak in marketing lubrication

This article is excerpted, in part, from the forthcoming history of Continental Oil. The book will be published in 1975 as part of the observance of the company's one hundredth anniversary.

28 29

1096

1095
Art Director Steve Phillips
Designer Steve Phillips
Artist Bill Nelson
Editor John Larsen
Publisher New Times Magazine

1096
Art Director Milt Simpson
Designer Barbara Jo Leer
Artist Stan Hunter
Editor Maury Bates
Publisher Conoco
Continental Oil Co.
Agency Johnson & Simpson
Graphic Designers

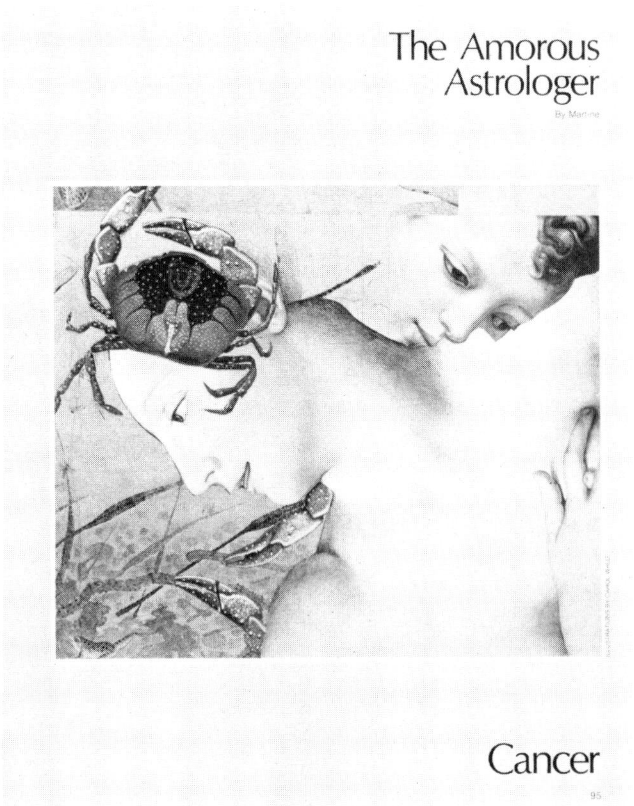

The Amorous
Astrologer
By Martine
Cancer
95

1097

LOVERS

By ROBERT CHATAIN

Spring transfigures even midtown. Concrete sidewalks split and send up thin curling stems, grass overgrows the caked dust lining curbside gutters, and lichens bloom on the wheel rims of parked cars. In freshly excavated foundations, windborne seeds germinate. Orange steel girders carry soft white vines toward the sun. Sterile demolition sites sprout weeds as readily as fallow fields, the broken glass and pulverized brick erupting with shoots and buds and broad-leaved plants flaunting pretty yellow flowers and concealing spines.

▷ In spring it was, then, that Eleanor Naso applied for her first, her very first job. She had come to midtown, I read, with only enough money to finance one week's search for employment. Of all the notes made by Chambers during his preliminary interview with her, this was the note which caught my attention.

▷ "One week?" I asked. "Really? How could you be sure you would find a job in just one week? You have no experience of any kind, your typing isn't good, you don't take stenography, and you admit to having no career ambitions in midtown. Why should anyone hire you?"

▷ Eleanor Naso, eighteen years old and coltish, brushed brown medium-length hair out of her eyes with a flip of her wrist. "I have a good imagination," she boasted.

▷ This, in fact, was corroborated by another of Chambers's notes: "Imaginative . . . romanticizes office atmosphere, environment, milieu . . . thinks midtown glamorous . . . art department?"

▷ "Besides," Eleanor Naso said, "someone *has* to hire me."

Ah, spring!

▷ Barely had Eleanor Naso begun work when the marriageable males of the office assumed their most colorful plumage and sang their loudest territorial songs from prominent perches in their various departments. Bernard, the gentle giant of the mail-room staff, wore khaki shirts with obsolete military insignia; he also showed Eleanor how to operate the office copy machine. Stuart, in accounting, bought a wide-ribbed corduroy jacket and offered to do Eleanor's income tax returns. Otto, the junior manager of the research department, put on his best starched laboratory coat and toured Eleanor through the tiers of test tubes and the tenement cages of mice and rats and guinea pigs. Young successful salesmen like Chuck Oates and Jack Flamm donned their flashiest suits, knotted their most luminous ties, and took turns spending their commissions on lunch dates with Eleanor at midtown's fancier restaurants. In the art department itself, where Eleanor's desk was installed, both Henry the photographer and Lyons the draftsman bent their energies toward making a favorable impression. Henry contented himself with a new nylon windbreaker and an exhibition of the inner workings of a miniature camera. Lyons, more aggressive, dressed in wild unruly prints and presented Eleanor with a hand-drawn street map of midtown lettered in a rakish slanting Gothic script.

▷ Which of these marriageable males did Eleanor Naso favor with her fondest smiles?

▷ "None of them, damn it," said my displeased secretary. "She's making a play for John, and Joanie is furious."

▷ "Are you sure?" I asked.

▷ "Of course I'm sure. Forget that Doris told me—Doris thinks people have orgasms when they shake hands. Forget that Angelo told me—Angelo thinks women short of menopause need bodyguards. You know who finally told me? Waxworks. When the smoke gets thick enough to bother him, there's got to be a fire."

John and Joanie were a pair. More than a pair, they were inseparable. Then Eleanor Naso applied for her very first job. . . .

46 VIVA 47

1098

SILVER

1097
Art Director Ahmad Sadiq
Designers Frank DeVino
Hector Marrero
Artist Carol Wald
Publisher Viva

1098
Art Director Ahmad Sadiq
Designers Frank Devino
Hector Marrero
Artist Christian Piper
Publisher Viva

THESE ARE NEW TIMES

The Trashing of America

The beverage and container companies of the U.S. have perpetrated a great hoax– the notion that recycling will save America from being buried in its own litter

By Roger Neville Williams

"You can't buy a can that we can't recycle," announce the can manufacturers in full-page newspaper ads. "At $200 a ton, some solid waste is too valuable to be wasted–Aluminum: Pass It On," says Alcoa. "And the Cans Keep Marching In," proclaims Reynolds Aluminum across two pages in *Newsweek*, claiming success for their recycling centers. Just about every aluminum can you buy these days, and you are buying more than ever before, will remind you in small earnest lettering to "Please Recycle," and that the "All-Aluminum Can" you are holding and intending to throw away is made of "Recyclable Aluminum."

The environmentalists call this ecopornography, a slick $10-million advertising campaign by the steel, glass, aluminum and container industries, along with the national soft-drink bottlers and brewers, to convince Americans that recycling, or, as industry likes to call it, "resource recovery," is the way to reduce litter, save energy and solve the environmental problems created by throwaway bottles and cans. They want to "keep America beautiful" by recycling the 60 billion bottles and cans that Americans throw away each year.

Alcoa's latest contribution to the burgeoning ecopornography is a colorful magazine advertisement telling you that "your next can of beer may have been a Coors can that was a Falstaff can that was a Carling can." Chances are, however, it wasn't. Fewer than 15 percent of all aluminum cans produced each year are recycled. According to the Aluminum Association, only one in seven aluminum beverage and beer cans came back for recycling last year, while some 10 billion ended up as litter or trash.

The statistics on nonreturnable bottles and steel cans are even worse–over 100 billion went into the garbage last year, 60 billion of them one-way beverage containers. And what happens to them then? Not even 1 percent of municipal wastes in the United States is recycled. Very little glass gets recycled, since there are only 100 glass-container redemption centers in the entire country. And despite what the can makers say in their ads, there is no great drive to recycle steel cans. Most steel beverage containers have aluminum flip-top lids, rendering them *unrecyclable* by any method because the aluminum contaminates the steel. A small percentage of the annual steel-can production is used as scrap in copper smelting, but none is made into steel again because of the tin lining. As for aluminum, in 1973, 1.6 billion cans were returned to Kaiser, Alcoa and Reynolds for recycling. But these companies, along with the container manufacturers, increased production of aluminum beverage cans during the same year *by 3.4 billion*–from 8.2 billion in 1972 to 11.6 billion in 1973. Thus, even with recycling, the number of aluminum beverage cans ending up as litter or garbage is increasing by 20 percent a year. America has been trashed good.

Like a city caught downwind of its own municipal burning, Americans in the late '60s were jerked into environmental consciousness and there was serious concern about the midden heap of throwaway

Free-lance journalist Williams last reported for NEW TIMES on Army deserter Eddie McNally (Exile on Main Street, May 3, 1974)

NEW TIMES

1099

1100

1099
Art Director Steve Phillips
Designer Steve Phillips
Artist Nicholas Gaetano
Editor John Larsen
Publisher New Times Magazine

1100
Art Director Art Kane
Artists Miriam Wosk
Carl Barile
Publisher Viva

Plain, fancy, sour or sweet, a stack is still

America's Favorite Breakfast

BY RICHARD BISSELL

Scientists tell us that pancakes, or griddle cakes, are the oldest way of eating cooked grain known to man. These same scientists recently told us that a glorious, awe-inspiring comet would flash across the sky causing mankind more thrills than the Sells-Floto circus. The comet never came up to snuff, which proves that the scientists don't know any more than you or I do about comets, pancakes or anything else. What a relief!

Evidently the first pancakes were made of pounded grain mixed with water and spread on a hot rock to cook. Benedict Arnold's soldiers used this same method on their starvation junket through the Maine woods to Quebec in 1775. But such primitive creations would be laughed back into the kitchen or onto the rock by the gourmet pancake fans of today. (Everything is "gourmet" now, including the "Business Men's Gourmet $1.35 Pot Roast Lunch with 2 Veg.")

Pancake people take their passion for the flat goodies very seriously indeed. The health food freaks are the most demanding, of course, as they will eat only hot cakes made of hazelnut flour cooked in prune oil. But at all levels standards are high and debates almost as tedious as those surrounding chili con carne.

In February, 1928, confronted by a stack of, to him, inadequate buckwheat cakes, my grandfather Lester Bissell threw them out of the window of his tenth-story suite at the Blackstone Hotel in Chicago, Illinois.

"Kate Straub would not feed buckwheats like that to a Milwaukee railroad section gang," was his explanation. Kate Straub was the cook back home in Dubuque, who made very sour buckwheat cakes. Which is the way they are supposed to be.

James McNeill Whistler startled the bon ton of London by serving American buckwheat cakes at his hoity-toity literary breakfasts. Enormous buckwheat orgies soon became the rage in Mayfair and were in some measure responsible for the worldwide buckwheat panic of 1883.

The Pennsylvania Dutch often stop guzzling *schnitz-un-gnepp* long enough to produce steaming towers of buckwheats containing cornmeal and potato water.

Out in the lumber camps of Wisconsin and Minnesota griddle cakes were called a "string of flats." A lumberjack would eat anything, even birch bark, if it was sprinkled with whiskey, but even without this incentive he would consume flats by the bale. Paul Bunyan's cook, Hot Biscuit Slim, assisted by Cream Puff Fatty, made pancakes as big around as poker tables.

In the last few years a new form of eatery has burst forth across our fruited plains, dubbed Pancake House. One philanthropic chain of this type has over 400 branch buffets where you can go right on in and stuff yourself into a doughy coma on Oregon Boysenberry Pancakes, Iowa Corn Pancakes, Maine Blueberry Pancakes, Georgia Pecan Pancakes, Banana-Nut Pancakes, French and German and Swedish pancakes and even (watch the bump) Chocolate Chip Pancakes.

The emporium I frequent says their ambrosial concoctions have been created by "Peter Masoobian, graduate of the famed Cordon Bleu in Paris, France." They also offer low-calorie maple syrup and adorable waitresses in miniskirts. This is but one of hundreds of pancake palaces throughout the land.

"Flapjacks" came into the American language as far back as the Revolution. A 1796 cookbook calls them "slapjacks." They have long been associated with olden times, the virtuous simple life and the world of the fearless woodsman.

"This story has naught to do," says Dan Beard, "with the effete luxury of degenerates, but is written for all those wholesome beings who love to sleep on sweet-smelling balsam, hear the music of the sizzling bacon and watch the gymnastics of the acrobatic flapjack."

Little did he know the way of the world.

At one end of the gourmet scale we observe two boy scouts burning some ready-mix stove lids over a camp fire. Far away in a Large City sit a duet of Beautiful Degenerates in a sybaritic ambience toying with *crêpes au citron* surrounded by white grapes. They're all eatin' pancakes.

Then we come to the salubrious sourdough.

I ate my first sourdough pancakes, fittingly enough, in Whitehorse, Yukon Territory. Life has been a Beautiful Event ever since. Sourdoughs are different. They have consistency. They don't melt in your mouth, they are chewy. No degenerates need apply.

Here's how to make sourdough pancakes without all that fiddling around with "starter" and crocks. This "receipt" comes from Dawson on the Yukon.

In the evening put 2 cups of warm water (110°) in a large bowl. Sprinkle on a package of dry yeast and stir up. Dump in 2 cups of flour and beat sturdily. Put a plate

Playwright and novelist Richard Bissell is at work on a humorous book about the American Revolution.

ILLUSTRATED BY DAVID WILCOX

1101

Across Australia by Train
From Sydney to Perth, the Indian-Pacific train spans the continent in three days
BY JOHN KENNETH GALBRAITH

1102

1101
Art Director Norman S. Hotz
Designer Gail Tauber
Artist David Wilcox
Publisher Travel & Leisure

1102
Art Director Norman S. Hotz
Designer Gail Tauber
Artist Paul Davis
Publisher Travel & Leisure

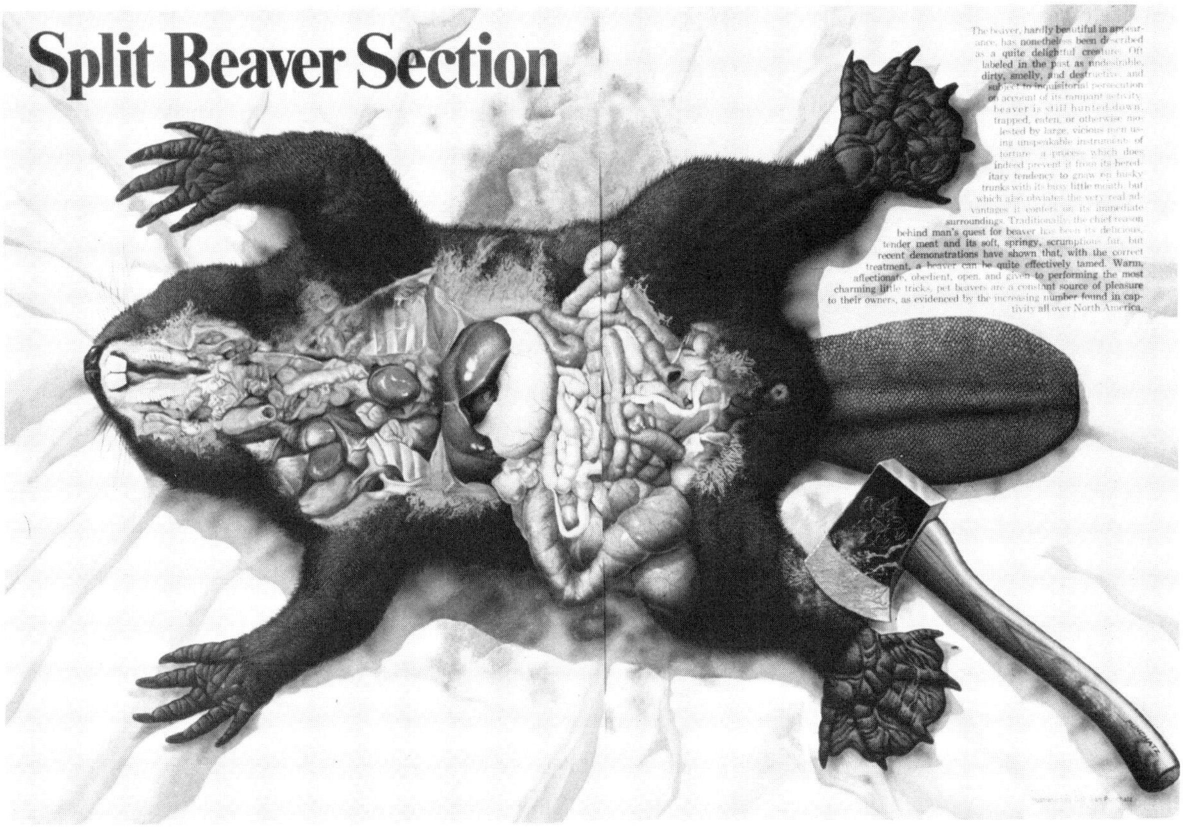

Split Beaver Section

The beaver, hardly beautiful in appearance, has nonetheless been described as a quite delightful creature. Oft labeled in the past as undesirable, dirty, smelly, and destructive, and subject to inquisitorial persecution on account of its rampant activity, beaver is still hunted down, trapped, eaten, or otherwise molested by large, vicious men using unspeakable instruments of torture, a process which does indeed prevent it from its hereditary tendency to gnaw on husky trunks with its busy little mouth, but which also obviates the very real advantages it confers on its immediate surroundings. Traditionally, the chief reason behind man's quest for beaver has been its delicious, tender meat and its soft, springy, scrumptious fur, but recent demonstrations have shown that, with the correct treatment, a beaver can be quite effectively tamed. Warm, affectionate, obedient, open, and given to performing the most charming little tricks, pet beavers are a constant source of pleasure to their owners, as evidenced by the increasing number found in captivity all over North America.

1103

Digging Up Wall Street

Reconstruction of the securities industry is changing the way people buy stocks, and could outmode the New York Stock Exchange.

by Jeffrey G. Madrick

For the investor with an independent flair, the road to the securities market is well marked. With solid credit and only a vague notion that he wants to buy a certain stock—say, General Electric—he can walk into a brokerage office, mention his mission to a receptionist and be assigned to an "account executive"; receive an opinion, often detailed, on the quality and potential of GE stock; consult about his financial needs; be apprised of alternative investments such as bonds, real estate investment trusts and mutual funds; place an order to buy, perhaps borrowing up to 50% of the purchase price on margin; and pay a fixed commission when he gets the bill.

In only a few years, this sequence will be dim history. An investor who wants to buy 100 shares of GE may still go to a broker's office, but the person he'll see will very likely be a clerk, who will check the price and availability of the shares on a nationwide quotations system and place the order. The customer will make out a check (or use his credit card), walk away with a receipt and pay a substantially lower commission charge than he would have paid in the past. If he wants any kind of analysis of his individual financial needs, the order clerk will send him to another office, or even to another firm, smaller but more attentive, catering to those who require personal attention. There he will be able to purchase information on stocks, bonds and mutual funds as well as an analysis of his personal portfolio. The price of such services may be quite high and may or may not include the cost of the securities transaction.

Such changes are not a dream, but the logical outcome of a far-reaching restructuring of the securities industry that is already under way. Even the 182-year-old New York Stock Exchange, now the major securities marketplace, may wither away once the system is reorganized to take over some of the basic NYSE functions. NYSE "specialists," often credited with keeping the market liquid and preventing wild swings in the price of stocks, may become obsolete. The effects of the restructuring will eventually filter down to every investor.

Street-level outlets

The future investor will have many alternative ways to invest, often at low commissions. His corporation may provide a payroll deduction plan whereby it deducts a designated amount of money each month and invests it in a mutual fund or one of several stocks. Many banks and brokerage firms already provide similar services, with the bank deducting the regular investment from a customer's checking account. The individual may be able to tie his life insurance to investments in stocks by buying variable life insurance. He can now buy an annuity that is tied to the stock market, and in the future most insurance salesmen will probably sell stocks or shares in mutual funds as well. Some forecasters even suggest that securities may some day be sold through retail stores and small, street-level outlets, made efficient by a high-speed computerized ordering network.

It is good old American competition, to which all brokers pay homage,

continued

Money FEBRUARY 1978 37

1104

1103
Art Director Michael Gross
Designer David Kaestle
Artist Don Ivan Punchatz
Writer Tony Hendra
Publisher National Lampoon

1104
Art Director Peter Rauch
Designer Robert Dougherty
Artist Edward Sorel
Writer Jeffrey Madrick
Publisher Money

Stop
Para
Go
Sigue
S. CHWAST
1105

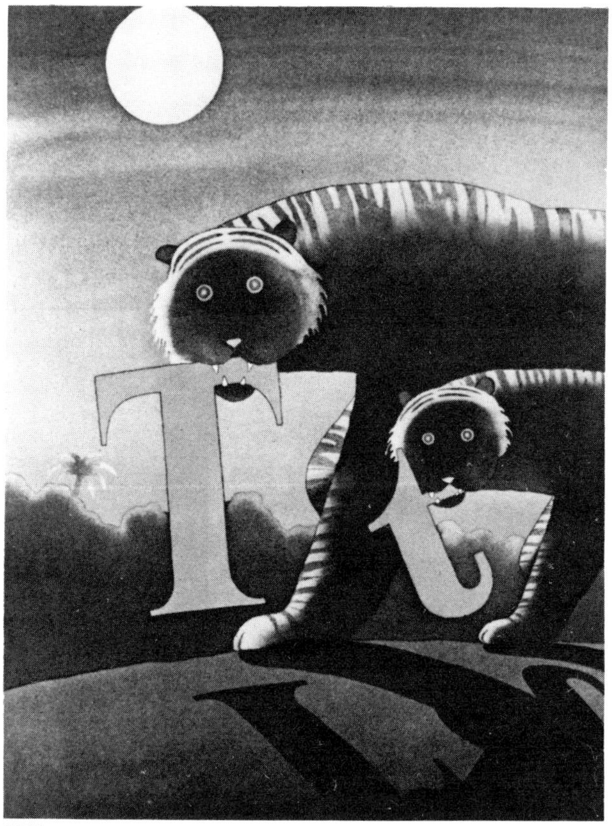
1106

1105
Art Director Henry Wolf
Designer Gary Schenck
Artist Seymour Chwast
Publisher Sesame Street Magazine
Agency Henry Wolf Productions

1106
Art Director Henry Wolf
Designer Gary Schenck
Artist Guy Billout
Publisher Sesame Street Magazine
Agency Henry Wolf Productions

Ralph STEADMAN

1108

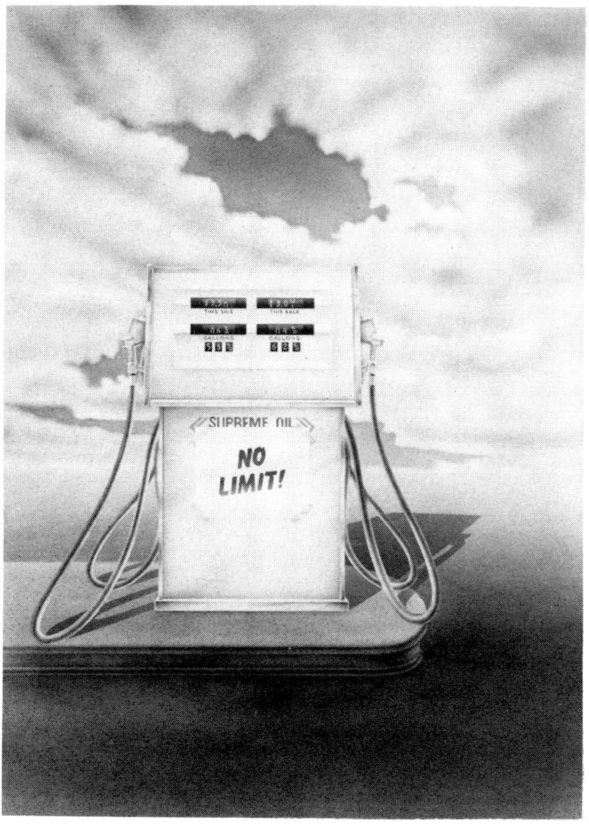
SUPREME OIL
NO LIMIT!

1108
Art Director Tony Lane
Designer Tony Lane
Artist Ralph Steadman
Publisher Rolling Stone

1110
Art Director Joe Brooks
Artist Dickran Palulian
Publisher Penthouse

Count Paul Stroganoff

Beef Stroganoff combines some deft Russian gastronomy with some grim Russian duplicity. In 1837, Count Paul Stroganoff, tyrannical Czar Nicholas' overly zealous first minister, became more and more distressed about mounting public criticism of the Czar's policies—criticism inflamed, he was sure, by the widely read anti-czarist poems of Alexander Pushkin. Crafty Stroganoff devised a scheme so that in the end Pushkin was killed in a duel. But the plan backfired and Pushkin's admirers became even more inflamed and vocal and at one point organized a mock funeral for the poet within earshot of the palace.

Czar Nicholas, taking the affair for a botched job, roared, "I'll have Stroganoff cut in shreds and fried!" Just then an opportunistic chef, having heard the tirade and eager to please, stepped up and offered to make a dish that would approximate the emperor's wishes—beef cut into shreds and fried (and served with a mushroom sauce). That night for the first time, the effigial "Beef Stroganoff" was presented. The Czar was so pleased by the whole joke that he went a step further and renamed a sweet pudding with dri..d fruit served at the same dinner "in honor" of Count Nesselrode, Stroganoff's accomplice in the tragic Pushkin affair. Whenever workers, peasants and students spoke out against the regime, Nicholas is reputed to have said, "Let 'em eat Stroganoff." Some comedian.

36

Marie-Antoine Carême

Marie-Antoine Carême was founder of France's *grande cuisine* in the early 19th century, and the man who was called "the Cook of Kings and the King of Cooks." One of the royal personages whom he served once said, "Carême, you will kill me with food."

Talleyrand took Carême along to the Congress of Vienna in 1814 and his culinary concoctions proved to be nearly as persuasive as the diplomat's debates. So lots of the fancy dishes that are *à la Carême* were probably thought up there in the land of *schnitzel* and *schlag*.

37

Prince Philippe de Condé

One of the grandnephews of Louis XIII, Prince Charles Philippe de Condé, had a sweet tooth when he was a child and thus spent a lot of time in the royal kitchens, pestering the cooks for sweets and frequently spoiling his dinner. The Master Chef, the illustrious Vincent de la Chapelle, could not refuse the youthful royal demands, but did hit upon the idea of coating certain meats, vegetables and fruits—that usually remained untouched by the Prince—with a sweet glaze made of sugar, egg whites and chopped nuts. His young friend could thus be tricked into eating more nutritious foods. It turned out that de Condé was not the only one fond of these creations and it wasn't long before glazed hams, fruits and pastries found their way onto the table of King Louis himself.

The King loved them and ordained that such candied delicacies should bear the name of the young Prince and his illustrious family.

Have some *condé*, little girl?

40

Antoine-Auguste Parmentier

The potato, today highly regarded by poor peasants as well as by privileged Parisians, had a difficult time gaining respectability as food in France. It always has been well-loved in most Northern European countries ever since its introduction from South America in the 16th century by Spanish traders and Sir Francis Drake (to whom the Germans even erected a statue for the job!). But the French thought it was unhealthful, so not until much later did the *pomme de terre* (apple of the earth) gain respectability in the culinary headquarters of Europe.

In 1771, French Army pharmacist Captain Antoine Parmentier was on duty in an occupied suburb of Hamburg during one of the many wars between France and Germany. One night his German cook served him a hearty, tasteful and varied dinner in the flickering candlelight of his tent. Parmentier smacked his lips first at the soup, then at the main course and finally at the dessert. *"Fantastique,"* he congratulated his cook. "What are these things?" Each and every course, it turned out, had been made from the noble *"Erde Apfel"* (earth apple).

After his discharge, back in France, Parmentier got a government grant, grew a whole field of potatoes and wrote a detailed scientific treatise on the tuber. His work sparked an enthusiasm only the French reserve for food, and for a while the King even adorned his buttonhole with a potato blossom Parmentier had given him. The regent was so impressed that he wanted to change the name of the vegetable to *parmentier*, but the modest pharmacist turned down the honor. Nonetheless *"parmentier"* is a method of cooking any number of dishes, all using the good old earth apple.

41

1111

1111

Art Director Robert Hallock
Designer Robert Hallock
Artist Jerome Snyder
Writers Sol Chaneles
Jim Harrison
Publisher Lithopinion
Amalgamated
Lithographers
of America

THEATER

THE DAY OF THE DAUPHIN

"...Joel Grey is committing himself to a full year of Broadway just when everybody else says the Broadway theater is dead..."

Joel Grey, suntanned and neat in blue jeans, white turtleneck, and white rough-cotton jacket, sits in Peacock Alley and sips his Campari and soda. It is August, and he's in New York for a few days, sleeping at the Waldorf in a room next to Frank Sinatra's, and spending the rest of his time in a dark theater watching unsaintly young actresses audition for the part of Saint Joan. He'll be back again later to begin rehearsals for the new musical, *Goodtime Charley*, but he's here now because he is the man who sells the tickets, and no one gets cast opposite him without his approval. "Joel Grey is a star," says a co-worker, "and his audiences consider him *their* star."

The last time he appeared on Broadway was in 1969, in *George M!*, when he played the man who owned Broadway. Before that, there was *Cabaret*, of course, for which he won a Tony, and then there was the movie version of *Cabaret*, for which he won an Oscar. A year ago, there was another movie called *Man on a Swing*, and always there is his very successful nightclub act. So why, when everybody's calling the Broadway theater dead, is Joel Grey committing himself to a year of it?

"Because when I was here last winter," he says, "I saw *A Moon for the Misbegotten* and *Candide*, and realized that the theater is still a tremendous part of my life. I've always said it didn't matter what the medium was—films, Broadway, off-Broadway, whatever—the part was the dictating circumstance. And this is one of the most demanding, interesting roles I've ever been offered."

In *Goodtime Charley*, it is the title role, the role of the Dauphin, who under the tutelage of Joan of Arc becomes Charles VII of France. Grey describes the show as "a love story. It's about what can happen to somebody if somebody else says, 'You're nice, and you're worthwhile.' Charley was dumb, the pawn of the court. They tried to destroy him. One day this young woman walks in and says, 'You're not dumb, you're not stupid, you're the king and you're beautiful.' And for a second he believes her and becomes an extraordinary man . . . a caring man, a feeling man. And whatever love she gave him is his forever."

Joel Grey, born Joel Katz 42 years ago in Cleveland, has wanted to be an actor forever. He made his professional debut when he was ten, as Pud in *On Borrowed Time* at the Cleveland Playhouse. He had a death scene, heard the audience weep, and was hooked. So, apparently, was a critic who wrote, "I can only say that the boy is phenomenal. He is as completely at home on the stage, without being in the slightest degree precocious, as any child I have ever seen."

During the week, Joel went to school, and on weekends, he appeared in revues with his father, comedian Mickey Katz. He changed his name to Joel Kaye. He danced, did impersonations of Johnny Ray, Frankie Laine, and Jerry Lewis, and he sang. Eddie Cantor caught him singing "Rumania, Rumania," and took over his career.

He put Joel on television, then directed him to the nightclub circuit. At nineteen, Joel was a headliner at the Copa and at the London Palladium. He had a nose job, changed his name to Joel Grey, and was miserable.

So he went back to acting, everywhere he could find it: at the Neighborhood Playhouse, in *December Bride*, in *The Littlest Revue*. On Broadway, he took over for Warren Berlinger in *Come Blow Your Horn* and for Tommy Steele in *Half a Sixpence*. He toured in *Stop the World, I Want to Get Off*. He did summer stock and worked for Guy Lombardo at Jones Beach. And then came *Cabaret*—and his dazzling portrayal of the Machiavellian emcee—which is where most of us came in.

In November, the Greys will leave their house at Malibu, sell their Fiat, pack their bags, their three cats, and their dog, and drive east in their white four-door Toyota station wagon to the apartment they've always kept on Central Park West. Joel's wife, Jo, comes from Brownsville in Brooklyn, and she's feeling pretty good about coming back to New York. His children—Jimmy, who is nine, and Jennifer, who is fourteen and has just had the braces taken off her teeth—are feeling even better about it.

Joel says that what he'll miss most about California is driving along the ocean and seeing sunsets. But he hates the idea of commuting on weekends, so the New York apartment will have to be a country home as well. "If I had my way," says the man who usually does, "we'd cover all the furniture with white canvas and fill the place with plants, trees, and art." (Recent acquisitions include a Richard Tuttle canvas called *Rag*, some Oldenburg prints, and two Rauschenberg paper sculptures.)

All the Greys have bikes, which they'll ride in the park, and Frisbees, which they'll toss. Joel and Jimmy fly kites together, play tennis, and take archery lessons. They'll go to the ballet ("I don't know where else you can see so many dance companies," says Joel), and to museums ("I could spend days in the Egyptian Room or the Chinese Room at the Met").

When they go marketing, they'll take the car over to Ninth Avenue. (In Majorca, where they spent part of the summer, Joel did all the marketing because he's the only one in the family who speaks Spanish. The butchers there, he reports, are all women.) And when they go out to dinner, they'll go to Gloucester House (where Joel orders lemon sole or lobster), the Dardanelles, Pearl's, the Russian Tea Room, and Nippon where he likes to sit at the Sushi bar. These are the restaurants that allow Joel Grey to weigh 119 pounds.

All of this will begin happening in November. Until then, he'll be doing his act—with trunk, top hat, and tap shoes—in London, Israel, San Francisco, and Las Vegas, where he plays and stays at the Riviera. And does he gamble? "I do my token slot-machine number," he says, "which means I'm willing to lose $10 a day.

"But," Joel Grey adds, "I don't lose." —Ellen Stock

Joel Grey, by James McMullan: *This November, Joel Grey (and his cats, dog, wife, and kids) returns to Broadway and Central Park West.*

1112

TWILIGHT of the GRIDIRON

Where Have All the Old Boys Gone?

by Robert Sherrill

All great institutions ultimately die. Oxydol's Ma Perkins, gone. Lucky Strike's Hit Parade, gone. George White's Scandals, gone. The Academy Awards are obviously dying. And now can it be true, as some say, that the Gridiron Club of Washington, D.C. is facing a perilous future? One does not, of course, actually mention death in the presence of so much richly contribed gusto and patrician buffoonery.

Continued

Robert Sherrill is Washington correspondent for The Nation

1113

1112
Art Director Walter Bernard
Artist James McMullan
Publisher New York

1113
Art Director David Moy
Designer John Heinly
Artist John Heinly
Publisher The Washington Post Potomac Magazine

1115

SILVER

1115
Art Director Harry Sehring
Designer Harry Sehring
Artist Brad Holland
Photographer George Krause
Writer John N. Rosen, M.D.
Maurice Peizer
Agency William Douglas McAdams
Client Roche Laboratories

1116
Art Director Dolores Gudzin
Designer Dolores Gudzin
Artist Wilson McLean
Agency N.B.C. Advertising Dept.
Client National Broadcasting Co.

1117
Art Director Richard Wilde
Designer Richard Wilde
Artist Robert Weaver
Writer Dee Ito
Agency School of Visual Arts
Client School of Visual Arts

Frankenstein
THE TRUE STORY

JAMES MASON • DAVID McCALLUM • AGNES MOOREHEAD • MARGARET LEIGHTON
MICHAEL SARRAZIN • MICHAEL WILDING • SIR JOHN GIELGUD • JANE SEYMOUR
SIR RALPH RICHARDSON • LEONARD WHITING • NICOLA PAGETT • CLARISSA KAYE
PART 1 TONIGHT 00:00PM NBC CHANNEL 00

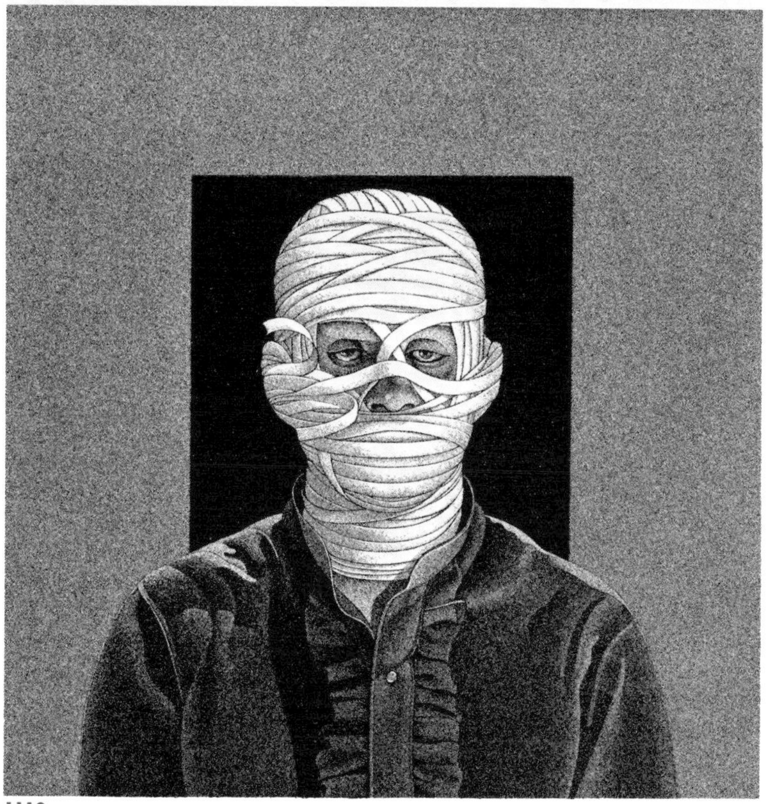

1116

Seeing is not believing

School of Visual Arts

1117

A Fourth of July Memento from
TIME
The Weekly Newsmagazine
The Stamp Act of 1765.
Nothing so outraged Colonial America as the Stamp Act of 1765. Imposed by King George III, the tax stamps were intended to help defray the expenses of defending, protecting and securing the British colonies and plantations in America.
Actually not stamps at all, most were embossments—much like a notary public seal. The Act required that a duty of from one half-penny to ten pounds be imposed not only on legal documents, but on every pamphlet, newspaper, marriage certificate or commercial paper—even playing cards.
The reaction of the colonists was swift. Sparked by the eloquence of 29 year-old Patrick Henry, Virginia led the colonies, all of whom eventually passed resolutions defining their rights. Protest meetings were held and the phrase "no taxation without representation" was widespread.
Major rioting greeted the arrival of ships bearing the first consignments of stamped papers. Many consignments were burned by the mob and every appointed distributor or "Stamp Master" was forced to resign his commission. The stamped sheets from England, quite literally, provided the tinder that ignited the colonies and foreshadowed the American revolution.
Never enforced, the Stamp Act was repealed exactly one-year after its passage.
Here to commemorate that early outcry for independence are faithful reproductions of four different America tax stamps. They come to you as a reminder from TIME, The Weekly Newsmagazine that this Independence Day our nation—well-informed and free—has much of which to be mindful; much for which to be grateful.
TIME July 4 1974
Anno Quinto Georgii III Regis

1118

1119

1118
Art Director Walter Lefmann
Designer Walter Lefmann
Artist Hal Fiedler
Writer Alan Martin
Agency Hal Fiedler
Client Time Magazine

1119
Art Directors Jim Witham
Ralph Moxcey
Artists Jack Davis
Jerry Pinkney
Maryann Groh
Photographers Phoebe Dunn
Clint Clemens
Frank Foster
Phil Porcella
Writer Nelson Lofstedt
Agency Humphrey Browning
MacDougall
Client S. D. Warren Co.

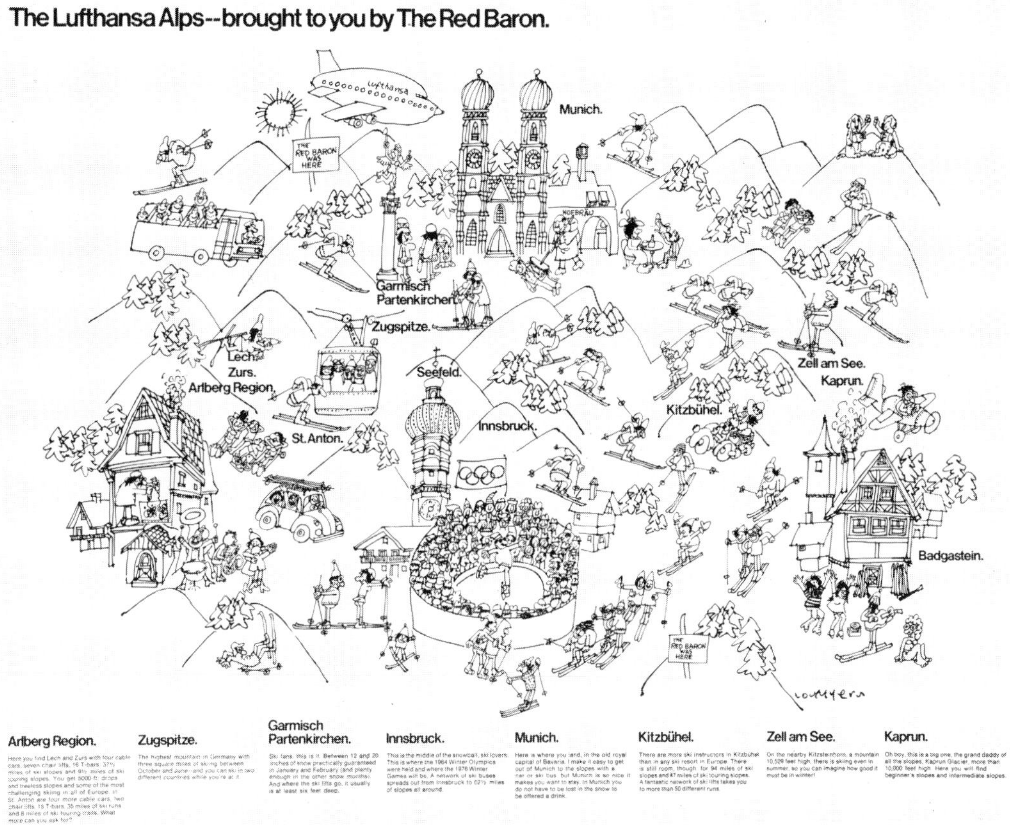
The Lufthansa Alps--brought to you by The Red Baron.
Munich.
THE RED BARON WAS HERE
Garmisch Partenkirchen.
Zugspitze.
Lech.
Zurs.
Arlberg Region.
Seefeld.
Innsbruck.
St. Anton.
Kitzbühel.
Zell am See.
Kaprun.
Badgastein.
Arlberg Region.
Here you find Lech and Zurs with four cable cars, seven chair lifts, 16 T-bars, 37½ miles of ski slopes and 9½ miles of ski touring slopes. You get 5000 ft. drops and treeless slopes and some of the most challenging skiing in all of Europe. In St. Anton are four more cable cars, two chair lifts, 15 T-bars, 35 miles of ski runs and 8 miles of ski touring trails. What more can you ask for?
Zugspitze.
The highest mountain in Germany with three square miles of skiing between October and June—and you can ski in two different countries while you're at it.
Garmisch Partenkirchen.
Ski fans, this is it. Between 12 and 20 inches of snow practically guaranteed in January and February (and plenty enough in the other snow months). And where the ski lifts go, it usually is at least six feet deep.
Innsbruck.
This is the middle of the snowball, ski lovers. This is where the 1964 Winter Olympics were held and where the 1976 Winter Games will be. A network of ski buses spreads out from Innsbruck to 62½ miles of slopes all around.
Munich.
Here is where you land, in the old royal capital of Bavaria. I make it easy to get out of Munich to the slopes with a car or ski bus, but Munich is so nice it makes you want to stay. In Munich you do not have to be lost in the snow to be offered a drink.
Kitzbühel.
There are more ski instructors in Kitzbühel than in any ski resort in Europe. There is still room, though, for 94 miles of ski slopes and 47 miles of ski touring slopes. A fantastic network of ski lifts takes you to more than 50 different runs.
Zell am See.
On the nearby Kitzsteinhorn, a mountain 10,529 feet high, there is skiing even in summer, so you can imagine how good it must be in winter!
Kaprun.
Oh boy, this is a big one, the grand daddy of all the slopes, Kaprun Glacier, more than 10,000 feet high. Here you will find beginner's slopes and intermediate slopes.

1120

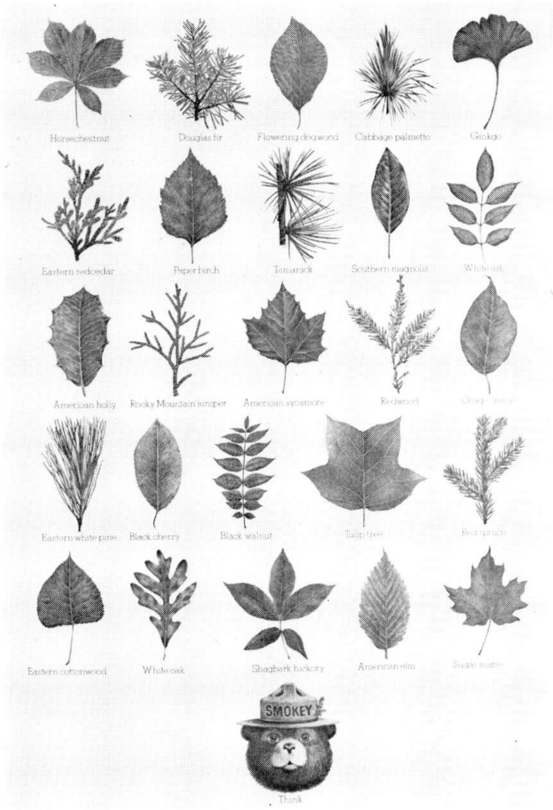
Horsechestnut
Douglas fir
Flowering dogwood
Cabbage palmetto
Ginkgo
Eastern redcedar
Paper birch
Tamarack
Southern magnolia
White ash
American holly
Rocky Mountain juniper
American sycamore
Redwood
Eastern white pine
Black cherry
Black walnut
Tulip tree
Eastern cottonwood
White oak
Shagbark hickory
American elm
Sugar maple
SMOKEY
Think.

1121

1120
Art Director Richard January
Designer Richard January
Artist Lou Myers
Writer Harry Reingold
Agency Reingold & Ricaud Advertising
Client Lufthansa German Airlines

1121
Art Directors Ann King
Judith Hersley
Designer Ann King
Artist Jerome Snyder
Writer Judith Hersley
Agency Foote, Cone & Belding Los Angeles
Client United States Department of Agriculture Forest Service

1122

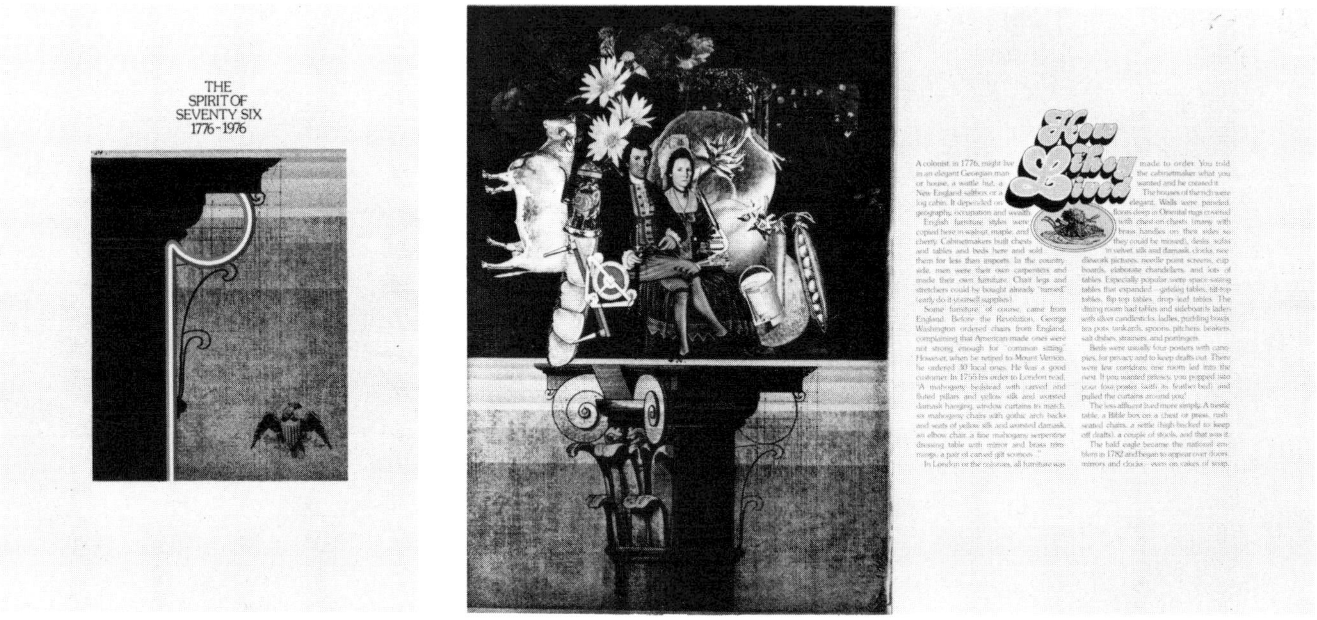
THE
SPIRIT OF
SEVENTY SIX
1776-1976
How They Lived

1123

1122
Art Director Rollin Binzer
Designer Charles E. White III
Artist Charles E. White III
Agency Fluid Drive
Client Rolling Stones

1123
Art Director Tom Clemente
Designer Lynne Moran
Artists Fred Otnes
Alex Tiani
Photographer Larry Karrasch
Writers Ray Stone
Hank Simons
Judy Ocko
Publisher Newspaper Advertising
Bureau

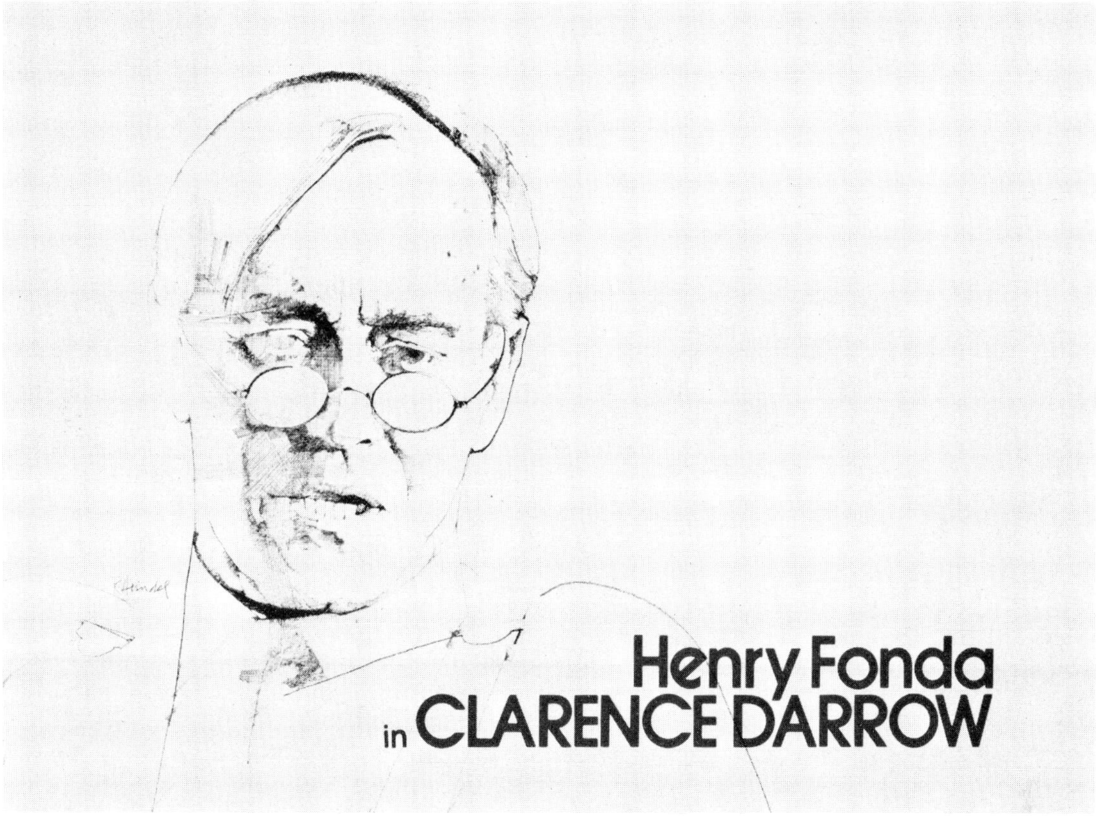
Henry Fonda
in CLARENCE DARROW

1124

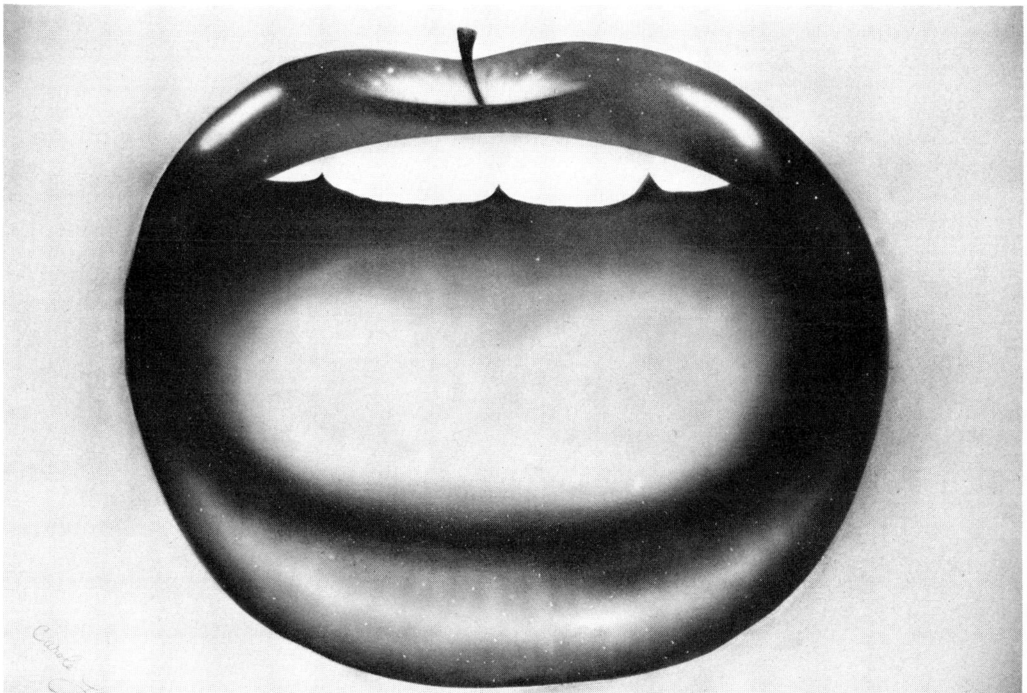
CAROLE JEAN, ILLUSTRATOR · 45 ORIOLE DRIVE · ROSLYN, NEW YORK 11576 516-484-4144
REPRESENTED BY: HEATHER SCHOEN · 684-5583

1124A

1124
Art Director Dolores Gudzin
Designer Dolores Gudzin
Artist Robert Heindel
Agency N.B.C. Advertising Dept.
Client National Broadcasting Co.

1124A
Art Director Carole Jean
Designer Carole Jean
Artist Carole Jean
Writer Carole Jean
Agency Carole Jean
Client Carole Jean

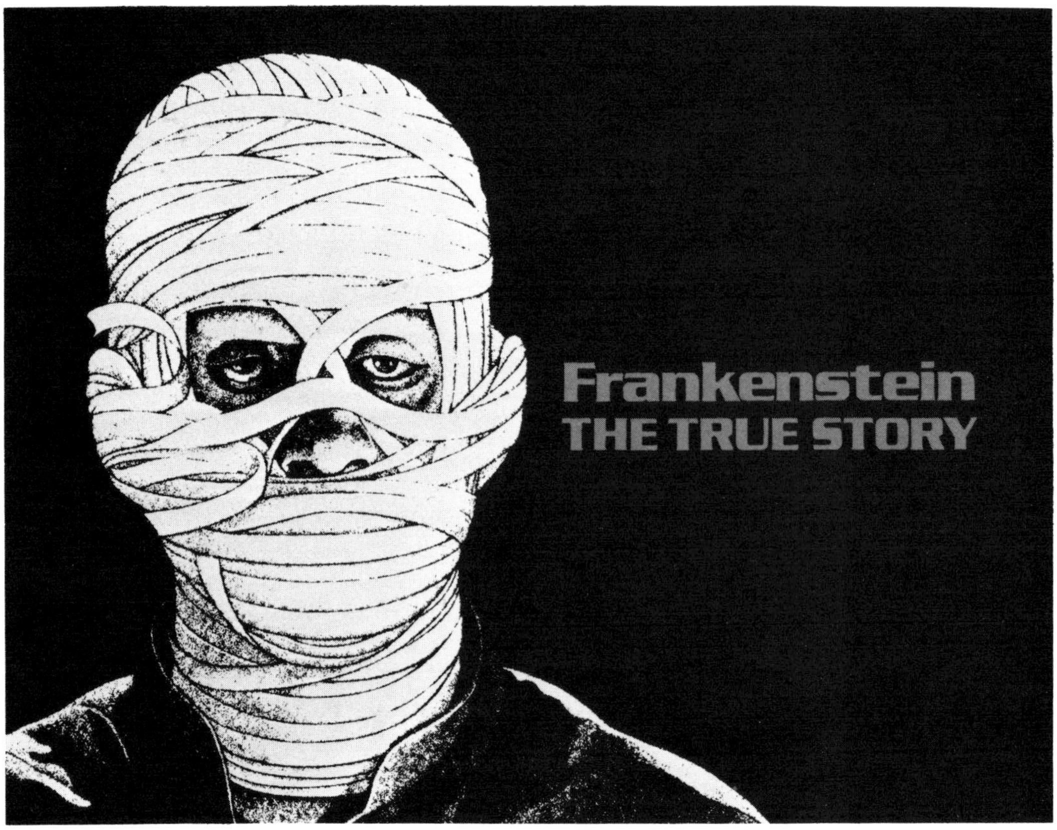
Frankenstein
THE TRUE STORY

1125

ELSEWHERE

1126

GOLD

1125
Art Director Dolores Gudzin
Designer Dolores Gudzin
Artist Wilson McLean
Agency N.B.C. Advertising Dept.
Client National Broadcasting Co.

1126
Art Director Uli Boege
Designer Uli Boege
Artist Uli Boege
Photographer Jean-Marie Guyaux
Writer Franz Kafka
translated by Uli Boege
Publisher Links Books

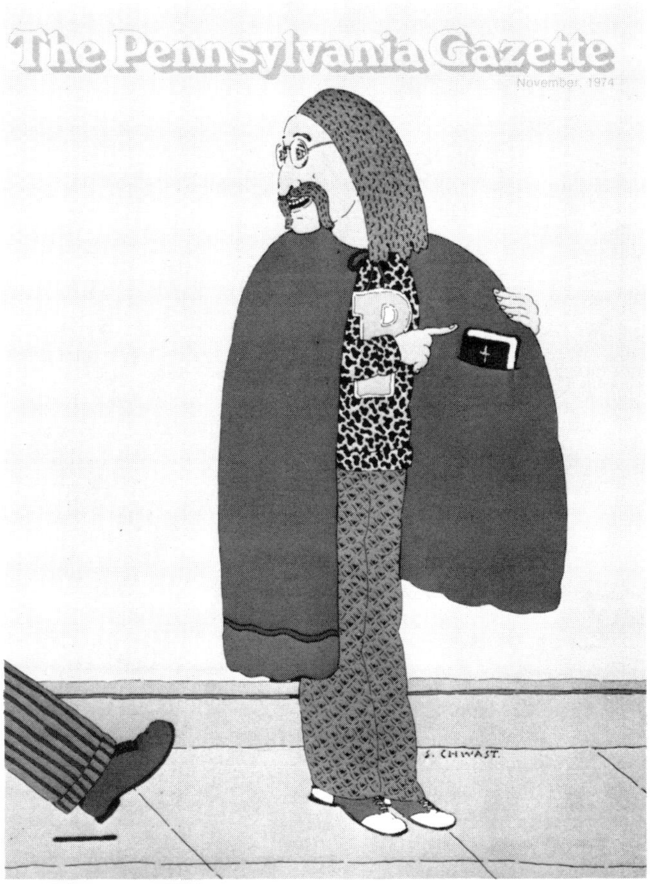
The Pennsylvania Gazette
November, 1974
S. CHWAST

1127

The New York Times Magazine
This
WILL SEE
US STILL
CHURNING
SATANIC
MILL

1128

1127
Art Director Tony Lyle
Designer Seymour Chwast
Artist Seymour Chwast
Publisher The Pennsylvania Gazette

1128
Art Director Ruth Ansel
Designer Ruth Ansel
Artist Ralph Steadman
Editors Lewis Bergman
Jack Rosenthal
Publisher The New York Times Magazine

AMERICA'S GRAPHIC DESIGN MAGAZINE
SEPTEMBER/OCTOBER 1974
PRINT XXVIII:V
Print

1129

The New York Times Magazine
NOVEMBER 3, 1974
SECTION 6
The
PENN CENTRAL
The Penn Central Cliffhanger
CONTENTS PAGE
10

1130

1129
Art Director Andrew Kner
Designer Istvan Orosz
Artist Istvan Orosz
Editor Martin Fox
Publisher Print

1130
Art Director Ruth Ansel
Designer Michael Doret
Artist Michael Doret
Editors Lewis Bergman
Jack Rosenthal
Publisher The New York Times Magazine

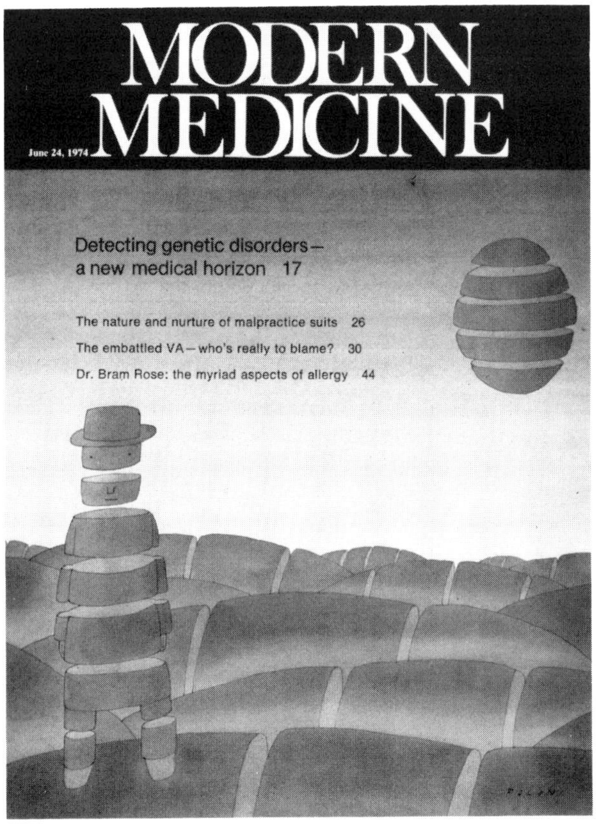
MODERN MEDICINE
June 24, 1974
Detecting genetic disorders—
a new medical horizon 17
The nature and nurture of malpractice suits 26
The embattled VA—who's really to blame? 30
Dr. Bram Rose: the myriad aspects of allergy 44

1131

The New York Times Magazine
AUGUST 25, 1974 | SECTION 6 | PART 1
CHW
AST

1132

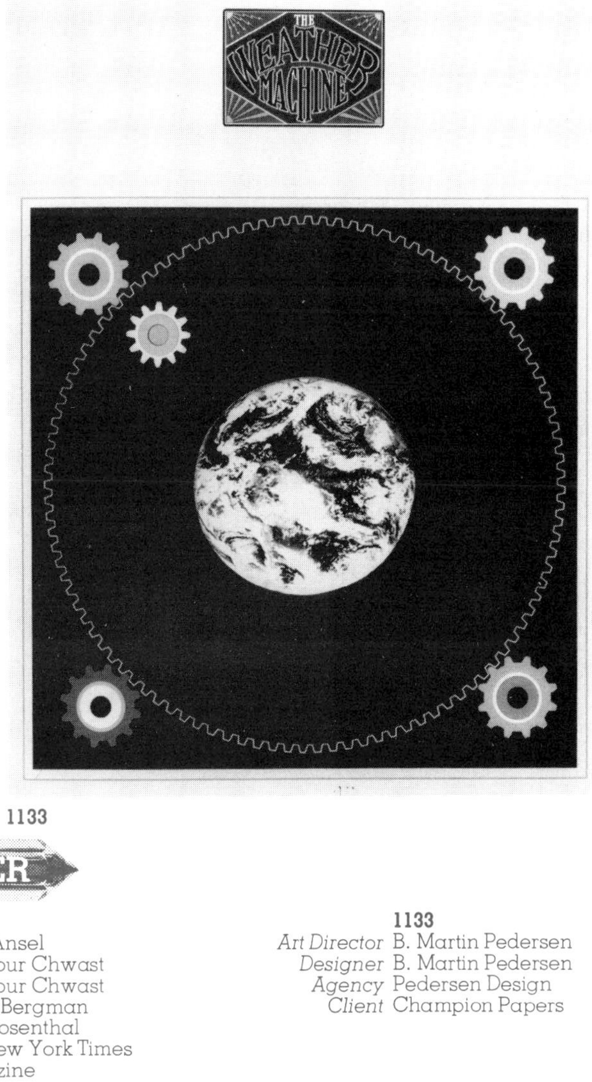
THE
WEATHER
MACHINE

1133

SILVER

1131
Art Director Phillip Dykstra
Designer Phillip Dykstra
Artist Jean Michel Folon
Publisher Modern Medicine

1132
Art Director Ruth Ansel
Designer Seymour Chwast
Artist Seymour Chwast
Editors Lewis Bergman
Jack Rosenthal
Publisher The New York Times
Magazine

1133
Art Director B. Martin Pedersen
Designer B. Martin Pedersen
Agency Pedersen Design
Client Champion Papers

INTERNATIONAL EDITORIAL DESIGN

International Consumer Magazine Design	1134–1144
International Trade Magazine Design	1145–1148
International Books	1153–1156
International Sales Promotion	1150–1152
International Direct Mail	1157–1158
International Packaging	1159–1161
International Calendars & Posters	1162–1169
International Letterheads, Trademarks & Logotypes	1172–1178
International Art	1179–1181
International Photography	1182

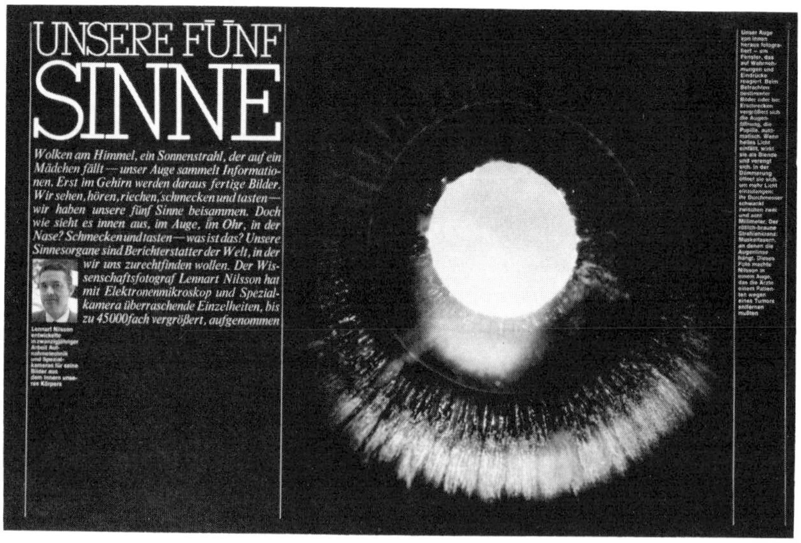
UNSERE FÜNF SINNE
Wolken am Himmel, ein Sonnenstrahl, der auf ein Mädchen fällt — unser Auge sammelt Informationen. Erst im Gehirn werden daraus fertige Bilder. Wir sehen, hören, riechen, schmecken und tasten — wir haben unsere fünf Sinne beisammen. Doch wie sieht es innen aus, im Auge, im Ohr, in der Nase? Schmecken und tasten — was ist das? Unsere Sinnesorgane sind Berichterstatter der Welt, in der wir uns zurechtfinden wollen. Der Wissenschaftsfotograf Lennart Nilsson hat mit Elektronenmikroskop und Spezialkamera überraschende Einzelheiten, bis zu 45000fach vergrößert, aufgenommen

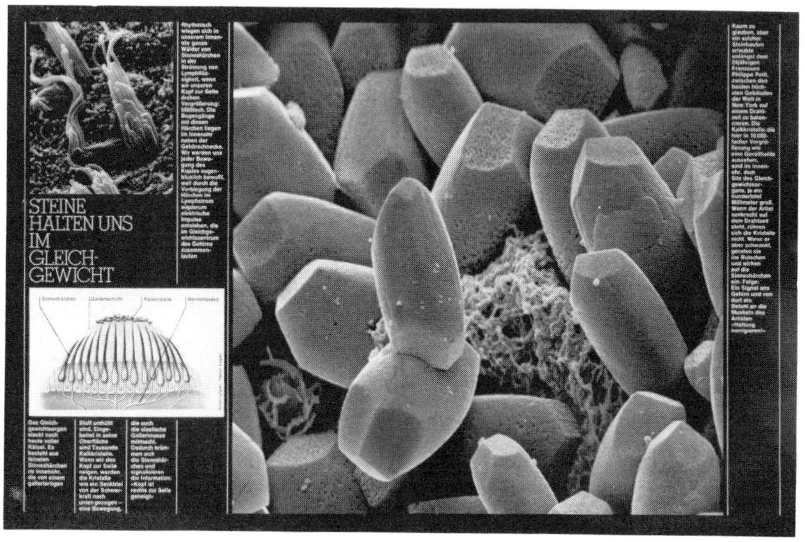
STEINE HALTEN UNS IM GLEICHGEWICHT

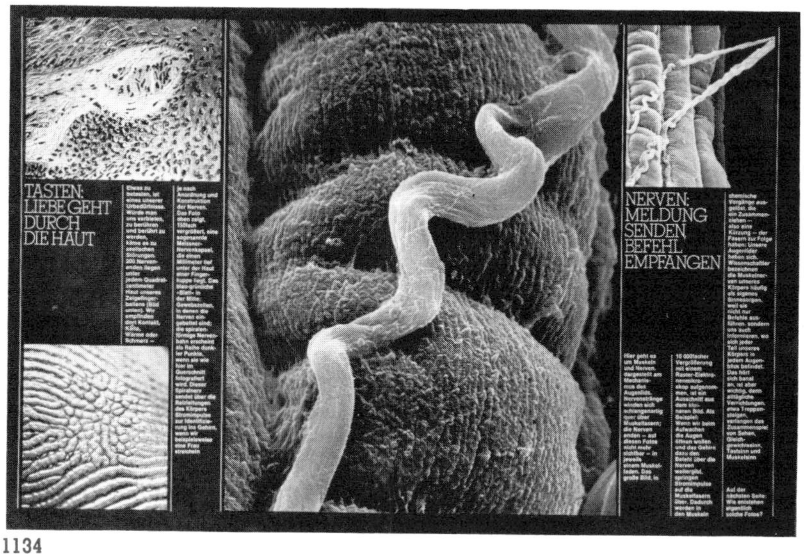
TASTEN: LIEBE GEHT DURCH DIE HAUT
NERVEN: MELDUNG SENDEN BEFEHL EMPFANGEN

1134

1134
Art Directors Rolf Gillhausen
Franz Kliebhan
Designer Karl-Heinz John
Photographer Lennart Nielsson
Writer Friedrich Abel
Publisher Stern Redaktion
West Germany

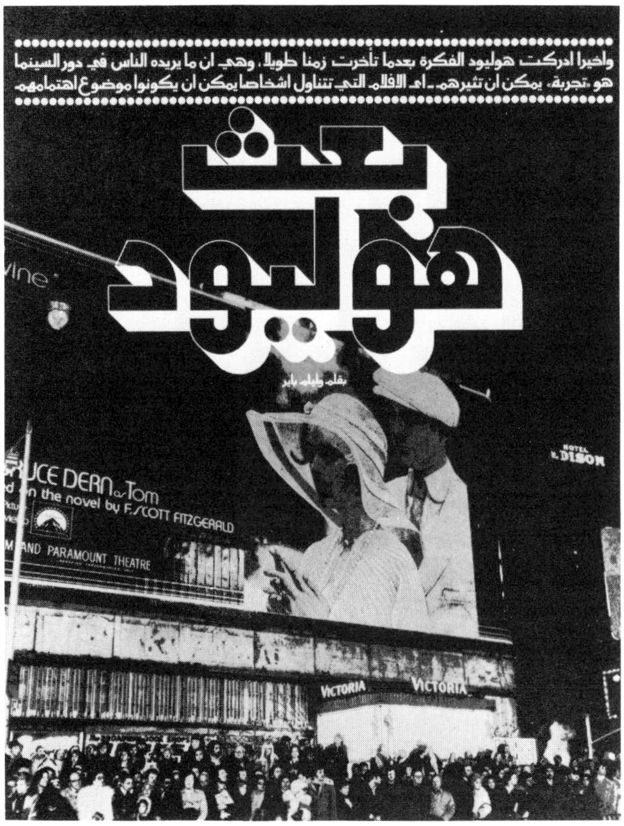
واخيرا ادركت هوليود الفكرة بعدما تأخرت زمنا طويلا، وهي ان ما يريده الناس في دور السينما
هو «تجربة» يمكن ان تثيرهم ـ اي الافلام التي تتناول اشخاصا يمكن ان يكونوا موضوع اهتمامهم.
بعث هوليود
F. SCOTT FITZGERALD
PARAMOUNT THEATRE
VICTORIA

المجال
عالم الفيلم المتغير
084044
ADMIT ONE
$2.75

جيل جديد من المخرجين
PANAVISION
R-300

1135

1135
Art Director Robert Banks
Designers Robert Banks
Sam Burlockoff
Artists Gerry Gersten
Jacob Knight
Editors James Baker
Ellen Toomey
Publisher United States Information Agency
Al-Majal Magazine

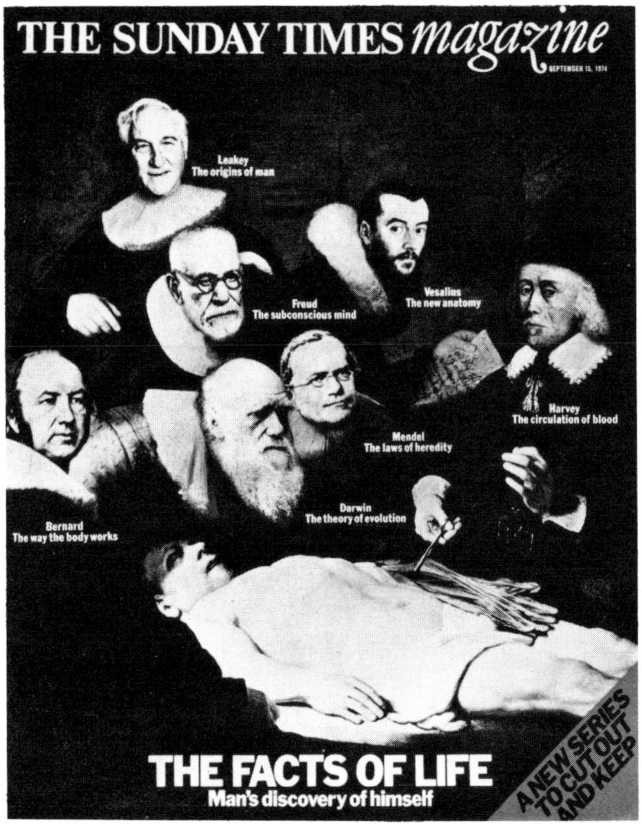
THE SUNDAY TIMES magazine
SEPTEMBER 15, 1974
Leakey
The origins of man
Freud
The subconscious mind
Vesalius
The new anatomy
Harvey
The circulation of blood
Mendel
The laws of heredity
Darwin
The theory of evolution
Bernard
The way the body works
THE FACTS OF LIFE
Man's discovery of himself
A NEW SERIES TO CUT OUT AND KEEP

THE
HUMAN
BODY
WHEREVER YOU ARE–
IT'S ALWAYS SPRINGTIME IN A
HUMAN
Singing in the rain Our illustration is a symbolic impression of the complicated physical and chemical mechanisms whereby the body maintains the equilibrium of the inner Man – keeping his cool when the going gets hot, consoled by inner warmth when icy winds blow – the phenomenon of the self-adjusting 'internal environment' observed scientifically by Claude Bernard (facing page), the distinguished 19th-century French researcher who is one of the founders of modern physiology
FACTS OF LIFE 57

Binet **1905**

Assessing human intelligence

Born in 1857, Alfred Binet was a pioneer of psychological testing whose early research was at the Salpêtriere hospital in Paris where he worked with Féré, a pupil of Jean-Martin Charcot (q.v.) studying hysteria and hypnotism.

In spite of prodigious quantities of very able work, Binet never became a professor. His main vehicle for the dissemination of idea was *L'Année Psychologique* which he founded with Henri Beaunis in 1894. Binet himself contributed many of the original articles in this annual – essays that were attempts at the objective new style of psychology and played a crucial role in disseminating this new work internationally.

Binet frequently worked in collaboration with others and his most famous combination was with T. Simon with whom in 1905 he produced the first intelligence scale – a series of 30 tests, the forerunner of intelligence tests as we know them. Binet had at his own suggestion been commissioned by the Ministry of Education to look into the education of the 'mentally abnormal' and his intelligence scale was designed to discriminate what we would now call the below average from the subnormal children. Binet's innovation was that he chose everyday activities: "Show me your nose" for a three-year-old, "Copy a square" for a five-year-old, "Tell me the days of the week" for a nine-year-old. Previously, psychologists had tried to reduce the assessment of intelligence to the measurement of physiological responses like reaction times.

A further innovation was the concept of mental age so that a child who passed all the tests up to and including those of an average six-year-old, but no more, would have a mental age of six years, though the chronological age might be greater or less. And the German, W. Stern, was later to refine Binet's work with the formula that compared mental age to chronological age (MA/CA x 100), thus producing "the intelligence quotient" – the now ubiquitous I.Q. (see right).

Suggest as many uses as you can for a hat and/or a banana

This is an example of the open-ended sort of 'creativity test' for which there is no single answer. Unlike a 'convergent' I.Q. test question which requests a single answer (London is to England as Paris is to . . . .) it invites 'divergence' of thought – and though it might seem pointless and exasperating to have to think beyond the everyday uses of a hat and/or a banana, it is no more or less pointless than filling in the blanks on an I.Q. test form. The range of different uses you can think up, moreover, does provide some external basis for comparing your imagination to that of others – though imagination, of course, is only one factor in creativity

What would happen if animals became more intelligent than men?

This is a 'consequences' type of creativity test which may seem fanciful at first sight but which, in fact, needs only a slight twist to test a subject's potential as an economic, political or social planner: what would happen if the world's backward countries found wealth to buy out the richest?

Think of a caption for this picture

Find a link word for each picture sequence

Attack Burn Blood

Door Traffic Bread

Comic Air Tease

Answers (or rather, Possible Responses)

I.Q. and creativity

If your I.Q. is below 70 you are mentally retarded. If your I.Q. is 100 you are of average intelligence, and above 140 you qualify as a genius – or more precisely as a genius at taking I.Q. (Intelligence Quotient) tests. Alfred Binet (opposite) showed how intelligence tests can provide a basis for assessing certain mental aptitudes, but they do not tell us all there is to know about a man's abilities, and this page shows some other ways of testing human potential.

Name the next number in this series: 2, 4, 6, 8. There can only be one answer (10), which is very neat and satisfying, just as there is no doubt about the missing word in "TOP is to BOTTOM as UP is to . . . ." But an artist working in certain perspectives might possibly answer "SIDEWAYS", and though he would fail his I.Q. test he might well create an original and thoroughly valid picture.

I.Q. tests, in other words, favour people who like to find just one correct answer to one question, encouraging people to 'converge' on one simple answer rather than viewing all the possibilities. But life is not like that, for many practical problems are ambiguous, accessible to no single solution, and noting this in 1946 the American psychologist Joy Guilford worked out tests (like these, left) to test open-ended or 'divergent' thinking.

For a time these were known as 'creativity tests', but to be truly creative you must do more than dream up, say, 50 different uses for a blanket. Liam Hudson examined a group of bright children that had, in real life, done things like designing a computer to race cars round a track, and many of them dismissed 'creativity tests' as silly – one little boy saying crossly he could only think of one use for a blanket and that was on a bed. While Getzels and Jackson, associates of Guilford, showed that though some people with high I.Q. scores do perform poorly in creativity tests, low I.Q. scorers are rarely 'creative'.

The two abilities, in fact, should tend to complement rather than contradict each other, for the really creative person needs not only the *divergent* ability to dream up and play around with all sorts of outlandish and even disturbing ideas – but also the *convergent* ruthlessness to pursue, test and track down the truly creative and practical solution.

86 FACTS OF LIFE

FACTS OF LIFE 87

1136

1136

Art Director Arnold Schwartzman
Designer Arnold Schwartzman
Artists Charles Raymond
Jean Lagarrigue
Seymour Chwast
Various
Photographers Donald Silverstein
Lester Bookbinder
Various
Writer Peter Ryan
Publisher The Sunday Times
Magazine
London

DAS
WESEN MIT DEM
SECHSTEN
SINN

WER SIE
VERSTEHEN
WILL, MUSS
SCHARFE
AUGEN
HABEN
KONNEN
KATZEN MIT DEN
AUGEN HOREN?

DIE LIEBE
DER KATZE
IST NUR
MIT GEDULD ZU
GEWINNEN

1137

1137

Art Directors Rolf Gillhausen
Franz Kliebhan
Designer Franz Braun
Artist Jochen Widmann
Writer Ortwin Fink
Publisher Stern Redaktion
West Germany

NOS VIEILLARDS EN FOYERS CLANDESTINS: DES MORTS VIVANTS?

DES FOYERS CLANDESTINS IL Y EN A QUELQUE 400 CONNUS, A MONTRÉAL SEULEMENT, OÙ LES TENANCIERS SONT AUSSI MISÉREUX QUE LES VIEILLARDS QU'ILS HÉBERGENT

par Jean-Pierre Nicaise

Ils sont près de 500 000 au Québec, 250 000 dans la seule ville de Montréal à avoir plus de 65 ans. Dans la phraséologie actuelle, nous disons que ce sont les gens du troisième âge. Dans la rue, on les appelle toujours "les vieillards". Sur ces 250 000 personnes de plus de 65 ans résidant à Montréal, 70 p.c. n'ont pour vivre que les prestations du gouvernement, soit au maximum $179.16 par mois au titre de la pension de vieillesse, récemment haussée (à la condition que d'éventuels autres revenus ne dépassent pas $24 par an). Mais avant même de citer quelques chiffres, il me semble que nous oublions trop souvent que ce sont ces hommes et ces femmes qui ont fait le Québec d'aujourd'hui; que nous oublions encore plus facilement que la grande majorité des personnes âgées ont gagné toute leur vie de bas salaires, ont vécu la crise économique et l'insécurité qu'elle a provoquée, ont eu peu ou pas de loisirs et sont loin d'être parvenues à une aisance financière qui leur permettrait de minimiser l'importance vitale que prend l'argent. Importance vitale, en effet, parce qu'on a formulé une relation entre l'argent, la liberté et l'autonomie. Aussi, lorsque les personnes âgées réclament plus d'argent, c'est le strict respect de leurs droits qu'elles réclament. Nombreux sont ceux qui estiment qu'une vie de travail donnée à la société vaut bien que celle-ci leur assure maintenant les moyens de vivre convenablement. Certes. Mais avant de rejeter ce qui suit sur les seules épaules du gouvernement, rappelons que les 433 545 personnes qui, au Québec, n'ont pour vivre que leur pension ont également mis au monde de nombreux enfants. Où sont-ils? Sur le bien-être social? Où sont les 21 héritiers de cet homme que j'ai rencontré vivant misérablement dans une chambre dans l'est de la rue Sainte-Catherine, avec 6 autres vieillards?

Les enfants disparus dans leur propre vie, on en vient ainsi à parler des pensions de vieillesse qui constituent trop souvent le seul revenu des personnes âgées. En effet, les fonds de retraite privés et le régime de rentes existent depuis trop peu d'années pour assurer à eux seuls un revenu convenable. Les $179 par mois de la pension suffisent-ils? Le service d'éducation permanente de l'université de Montréal a chiffré le budget-type minimum d'une personne âgée: $194 par mois, en 1972, avant la flambée des prix. Je vous laisse juge de ce minimum: $55 pour le loyer, $7 pour le téléphone, $22 en chauffage et électricité, $80 en nourriture, $5 pour les médicaments, $15 en vêtements, $10 en transport et 0 en loisirs. Il manque encore $15 pour arriver au minimum d'il y a deux ans. Alors, comment font-ils? Ils se placent, ou plus exactement ils essayent, où ils peuvent et de préférence dans les foyers subventionnés par le gouvernement. Toutefois, dans ces endroits, les places sont rares. Aussi, avant d'examiner la situation des plus favorisés, nous sommes-nous occupés du troupeau des laissés-pour-compte: les anémiques du porte-monnaie, les angoissés de solitude — ce cancer du monde moderne —, les malades rejetés par des hôpitaux débordés. Ensemble, ils forment une légion à la recherche d'un gîte, d'un terrier. Oh! ils le trouvent! On ne meurt plus sous les ormes disparus. Notre métropole qui masque ses lézardes sous d'humanistes murales aux couleurs bariolées et qui sait si bien nous donner à regarder jouer, a encore, hors des projecteurs, quelques taudis et quelques mercanti pour loger et s'occuper de ses vieux. Ce sont ces demeures — clandestines — et ces propriétaires — discrets — que nous avons visités pendant plus d'un mois. C'est donc à un portrait en filigrane de ce reportage que nous vous convions: à une image de ce qui nous attend (qui sait?) après-demain, et en tout cas, à la quotidienne réalité de l'âge d'or!

Toutefois, ne vous attendez pas à de spectaculaires révélations. Le troisième âge n'est pas couvert de guenilles trouées montrant un ventre creux. Tout juste ai-je pu rencontrer, de-ci, de-là, quelques réfrigérateurs vides, une poignée (une dizaine) de vieillards ficelés sur leurs lits — lesquels vieillards, du reste, avaient disparu une semaine plus tard, emmenés par un médecin anonyme vers une destination qui m'est encore inconnue —, pas mal de calards, coquerelles et autres bestioles, ainsi que des tenancières-ménagères comme je pensais qu'il n'en existait qu'en rêve et avec lesquelles il a bien fallu ruser. Rien pour du sensationnel à la une, pas de vieillards brûlant, point d'anecdotes dramatiques. Et c'est tant mieux!

Deux bonnes raisons à cela. Tout d'abord, les cas les plus désespérés, les plus sordides (Repentigny par exemple), se trouvent situés hors de Montréal: à Laval, sur la rive sud, ainsi que dans la proche campagne où les contrôles sont plus difficiles, moins organisés. Ensuite, parce que dans la ville de Montréal même, depuis un an, les services de santé, que dirige une femme remarquable, le Dr Antonine Paquin, se livrent à un véritable travail de sape envers les maisons clandestines (ainsi appelées parce qu'elles existent sans permis). Près de 3 000 lits ont déjà été découverts, recensés et régulièrement visités malgré un personnel trop peu nombreux mais efficace et doté de pouvoirs étendus, supérieurs à ceux des policiers. Ce harcèlement continuel qui fait gémir les logeurs a porté ses fruits. Vivant dans l'inquiétude des visites municipales, les tenanciers font attention sur l'essentiel: hygiène des locaux, nourriture.

Mais alors, que reproche-t-on à ces foyers clandestins? Le Dr Paquin nous le rappelle: insalubrité des locaux, entassement des patients, garde de malades sans compétence médicale, non respect des règlements d'incendie. Voilà ce qu'on trouve le plus souvent dans les quelque 400 foyers clandestins connus de Montréal. Hélas! sur le terrain, si je puis dire, l'énoncé s'avère exact. La trentaine de foyers que j'ai visités sont situés dans des maisons aux murs de bois, avec des installations électriques absolument insensées, souvent en étages (ne pensons pas à une évacuation d'urgence). Les lits, pratiquement les uns à côté des autres, occupent toute la place disponible dans les chambres. Une salle de bains pour 10 à 15 personnes est une bonne moyenne. Quant aux nombreux malades alités que j'ai rencontrés, qu'ils se cramponnent! Pas un, mais alors pas un des responsables de ces foyers n'a l'ombre d'une connaissance médicale élémentaire. Manque de chance de ma part! Pas un, non plus, n'a complété une 6e année. Mais j'ai cru comprendre que, sans doute reconnaissants, les malades finissent par mourir en silence, et le plus souvent pendant la nuit.

Suite page 4

1138

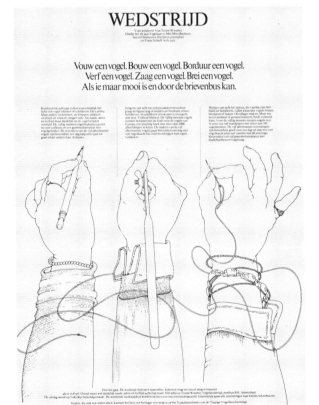

WEDSTRIJD
Voor kinderen. Van Trouw/Kwartet. Omdat het dit jaar Vogeljaar is. Met Mies Bouhuys, Sietzo Dikhuizen (freelance journalist) en Frans Schaeff in de jury.
Vouw een vogel. Bouw een vogel. Borduur een vogel. Verf een vogel. Zaag een vogel. Brei een vogel. Als ie maar mooi is en door de brievenbus kan.

Dit jaar is het Vogeljaar. Dat is hard nodig, want steeds meer vogels en vogelsoorten worden bedreigd. O.m. door verontreiniging van water, lucht en bodem, wegen- en woningbouw, hoogspanningsleidingen, recreatiedrukte en moderne landbouwmethoden.

1139

1138
Art Director Gilles Daigneault
Designers Gilles Daigneault
Robert Arsenault
Photographer Denis Plain
Publisher Perspectives
Montreal

1139
Art Director Herman Gerritzen
Artist Mariet Numan
Writer Paul Mertz
Publisher Trouw/Kwartet B. V.
Agency Prad B. V.
Amsterdam

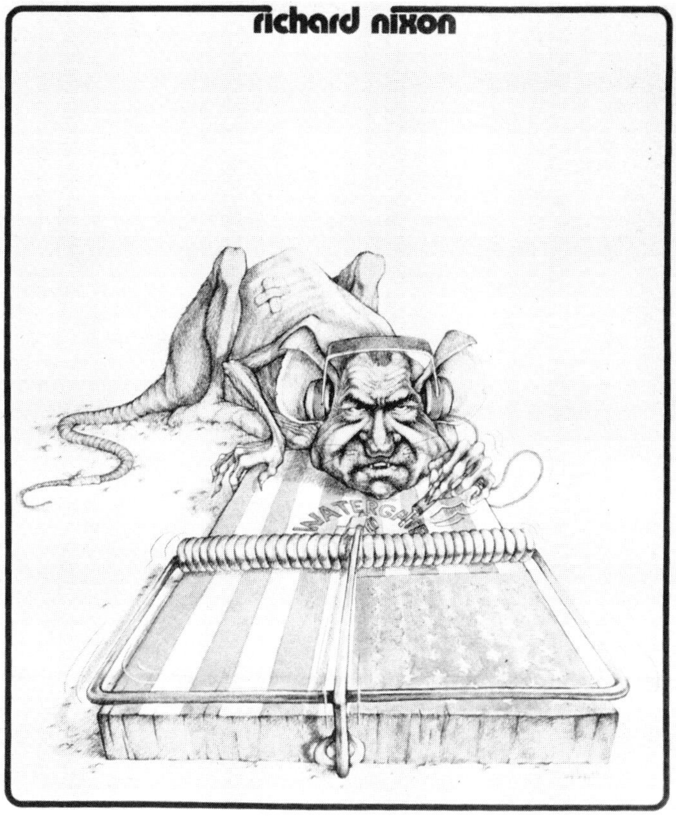
richard nixon
WATERGATE

1140

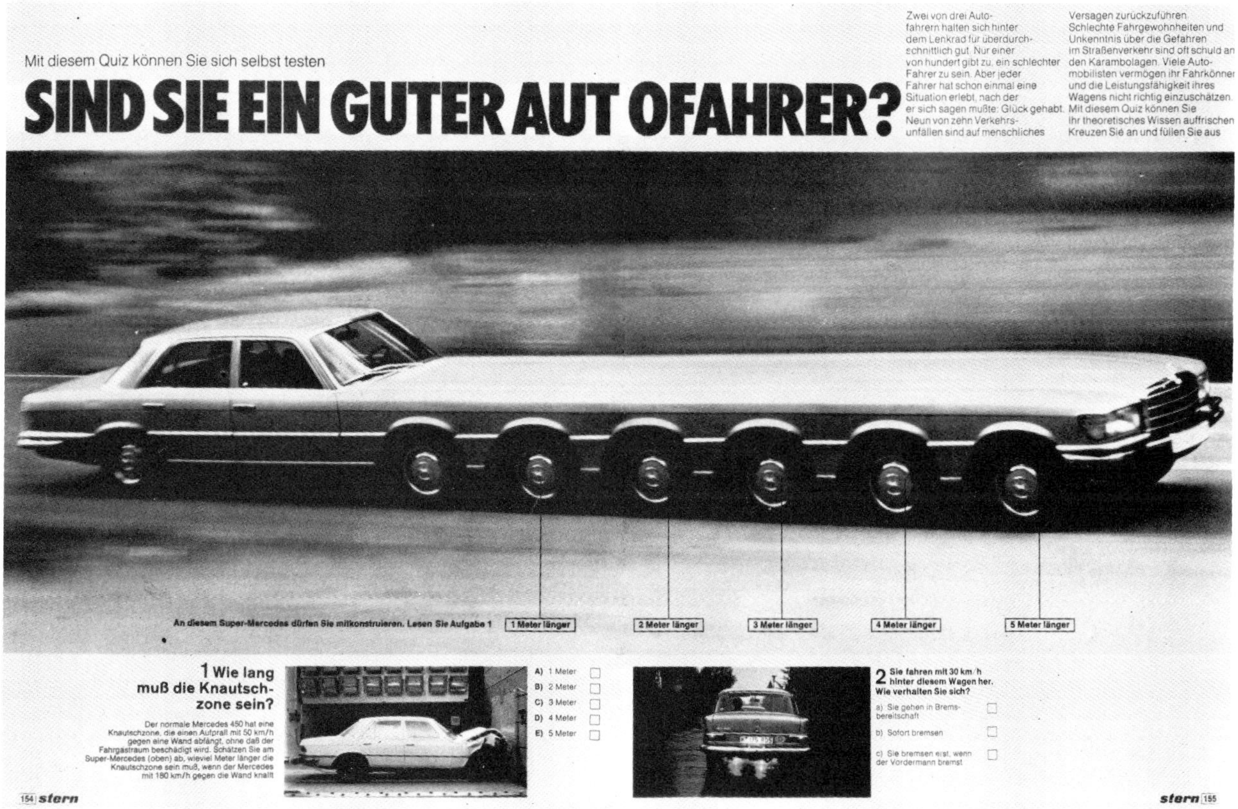

Mit diesem Quiz können Sie sich selbst testen

SIND SIE EIN GUTER AUT OFAHRER?

Zwei von drei Autofahrern halten sich hinter dem Lenkrad für überdurchschnittlich gut. Nur einer von hundert gibt zu, ein schlechter Fahrer zu sein. Aber jeder Fahrer hat schon einmal eine Situation erlebt, nach der er sich sagen mußte: Glück gehabt. Neun von zehn Verkehrsunfällen sind auf menschliches Versagen zurückzuführen. Schlechte Fahrgewohnheiten und Unkenntnis über die Gefahren im Straßenverkehr sind oft schuld an den Karambolagen. Viele Automobilisten vermögen ihr Fahrkönnen und die Leistungsfähigkeit ihres Wagens nicht richtig einzuschätzen. Mit diesem Quiz können Sie Ihr theoretisches Wissen auffrischen. Kreuzen Sie an und füllen Sie aus

An diesem Super-Mercedes dürfen Sie mitkonstruieren. Lesen Sie Aufgabe 1

1 Meter länger
2 Meter länger
3 Meter länger
4 Meter länger
5 Meter länger

1 Wie lang muß die Knautschzone sein?

Der normale Mercedes 450 hat eine Knautschzone, die einen Aufprall mit 50 km/h gegen eine Wand abfängt, ohne daß der Fahrgastraum beschädigt wird. Schätzen Sie am Super-Mercedes (oben) ab, wieviel Meter länger die Knautschzone sein muß, wenn der Mercedes mit 180 km/h gegen die Wand knallt

A) 1 Meter ☐
B) 2 Meter ☐
C) 3 Meter ☐
D) 4 Meter ☐
E) 5 Meter ☐

2 Sie fahren mit 30 km/h hinter diesem Wagen her. Wie verhalten Sie sich?

a) Sie gehen in Bremsbereitschaft ☐
b) Sofort bremsen ☐
c) Sie bremsen erst, wenn der Vordermann bremst ☐

154 stern

stern 155

1143

1140
Art Director Gilles Daigneault
Designer Gilles Daigneault
Artist Serge Chapleau
Publisher Perspectives
Montreal

1143
Art Director Wolfgang Behnken
Designer Norbert Kleiner
Artists Wolfgang Behnken
Hanno Engler
Writer Rudolf Rossberg
Publisher Stern Redaktion
West Germany

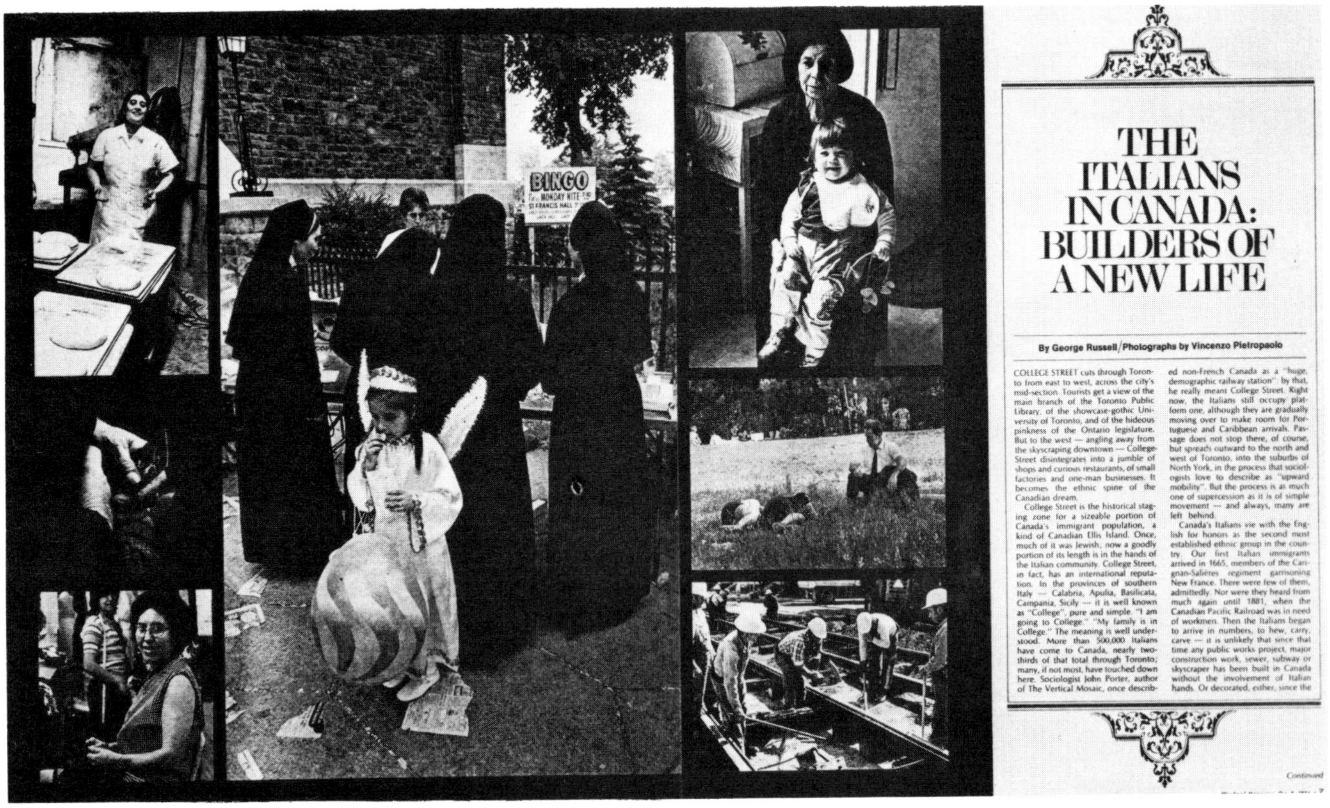
BINGO
MONDAY NITE
ST FRANCIS HALL

THE ITALIANS IN CANADA: BUILDERS OF A NEW LIFE

By George Russell/Photographs by Vincenzo Pietropaolo

COLLEGE STREET cuts through Toronto from east to west, across the city's mid-section. Tourists get a view of the main branch of the Toronto Public Library, of the showcase-gothic University of Toronto, and of the hideous pinkness of the Ontario legislature. But to the west — angling away from the skyscraping downtown — College Street disintegrates into a jumble of shops and curious restaurants, of small factories and one-man businesses. It becomes the ethnic spine of the Canadian dream.

College Street is the historical staging zone for a sizeable portion of Canada's immigrant population, a kind of Canadian Ellis Island. Once, much of it was Jewish; now a goodly portion of its length is in the hands of the Italian community. College Street, in fact, has an international reputation. In the provinces of southern Italy — Calabria, Apulia, Basilicata, Campania, Sicily — it is well known as "College", pure and simple. "I am going to College." "My family is in College." The meaning is well understood. More than 500,000 Italians have come to Canada, nearly two-thirds of that total through Toronto; many, if not most, have touched down here. Sociologist John Porter, author of The Vertical Mosaic, once described non-French Canada as a "huge, demographic railway station": by that, he really meant College Street. Right now, the Italians still occupy platform one, although they are gradually moving over to make room for Portuguese and Caribbean arrivals. Passage does not stop there, of course, but spreads outward to the north and west of Toronto, into the suburbs of North York, in the process that sociologists love to describe as "upward mobility". But the process is as much one of supercession as it is of simple movement — and always, many are left behind.

Canada's Italians vie with the English for honors as the second most established ethnic group in the country. Our first Italian immigrants arrived in 1665, members of the Carignan-Salières regiment garrisoning New France. There were few of them, admittedly. Nor were they heard from much again until 1881, when the Canadian Pacific Railroad was in need of workmen. Then the Italians began to arrive in numbers, to hew, carry, carve — it is unlikely that since that time any public works project, major construction work, sewer, subway or skyscraper has been built in Canada without the involvement of Italian hands. Or decorated, either, since the

Continued

1144

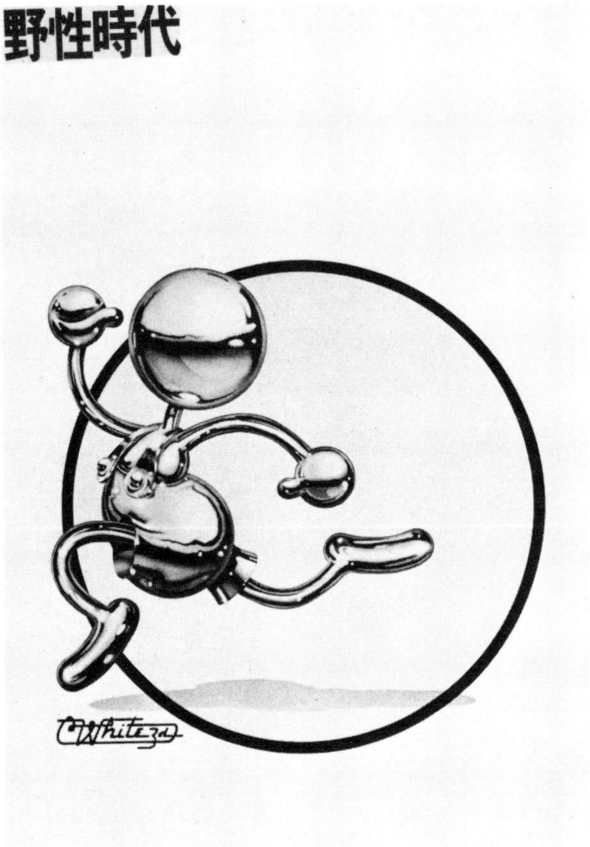
野性時代

1145

1144
Art Director Max Newton
Designer John McGuffie
Photographer Vincenzo Pietropaxolq
Publisher The Montreal Standard Weekend Magazine Montreal

1145
Art Director Eiko Ishioka
Designer Charles E. White III
Artist Charles E. White III
Agency Fluid Drive
Publisher Yasei Jidai Tokyo

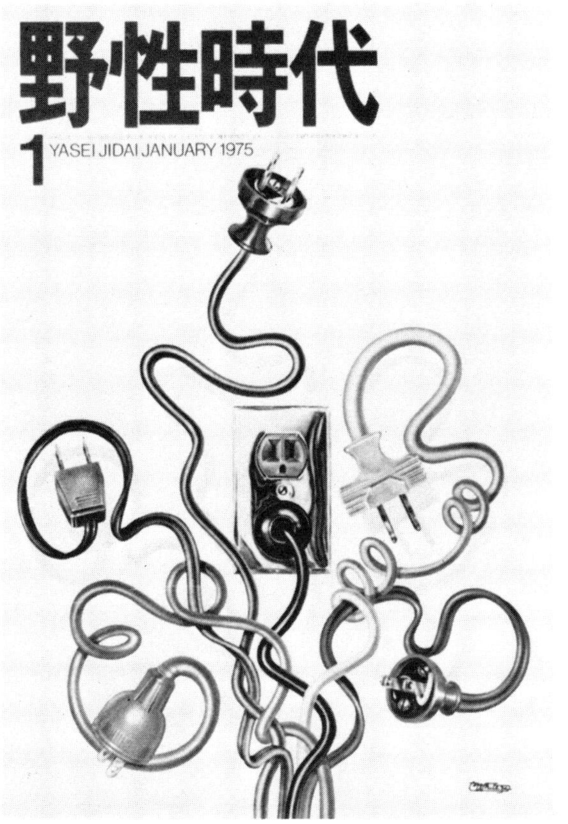
野性時代
1 YASEI JIDAI JANUARY 1975

1146

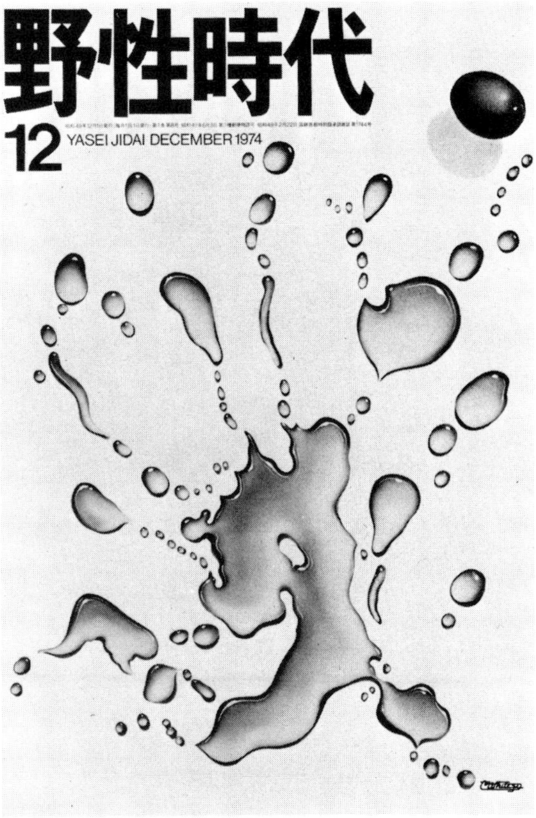
野性時代
12 YASEI JIDAI DECEMBER 1974

1147

野性時代
11 YASEI JIDAI NOVEMBE

1148

1146
Art Director Eiko Ishioka
Designer Charles E. White III
Artist Charles E. White III
Agency Fluid Drive
Publisher Yasei Jidai

1147
Art Director Eiko Ishioka
Designer Charles E. White III
Artist Charles E. White III
Agency Fluid Drive
Publisher Yasei Jidai

1148
Art Director Eiko Ishioka
Designer Charles E. White III
Artist Charles E. White III
Agency Fluid Drive
Publisher Yasei Jidai

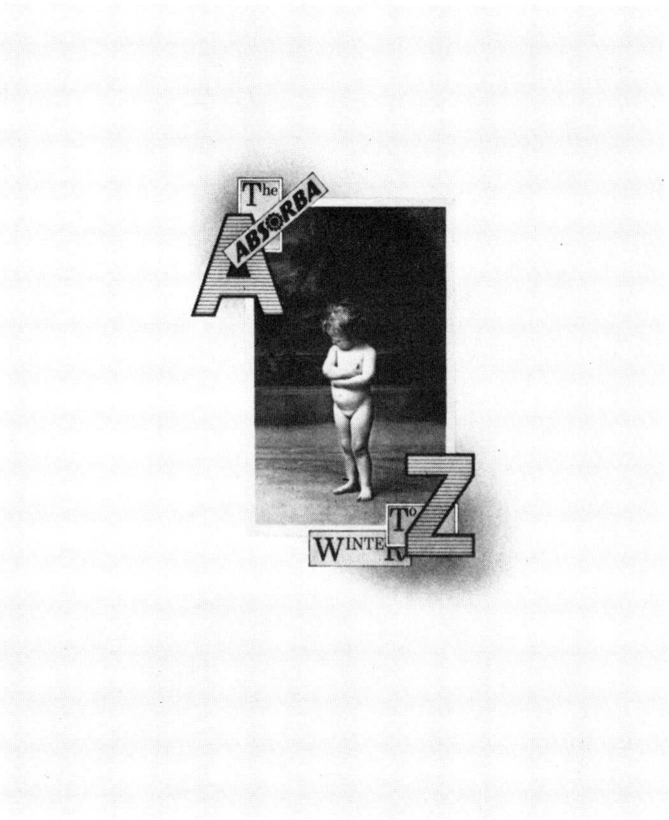
The
ABSORBA
A
Z
WINTE
To

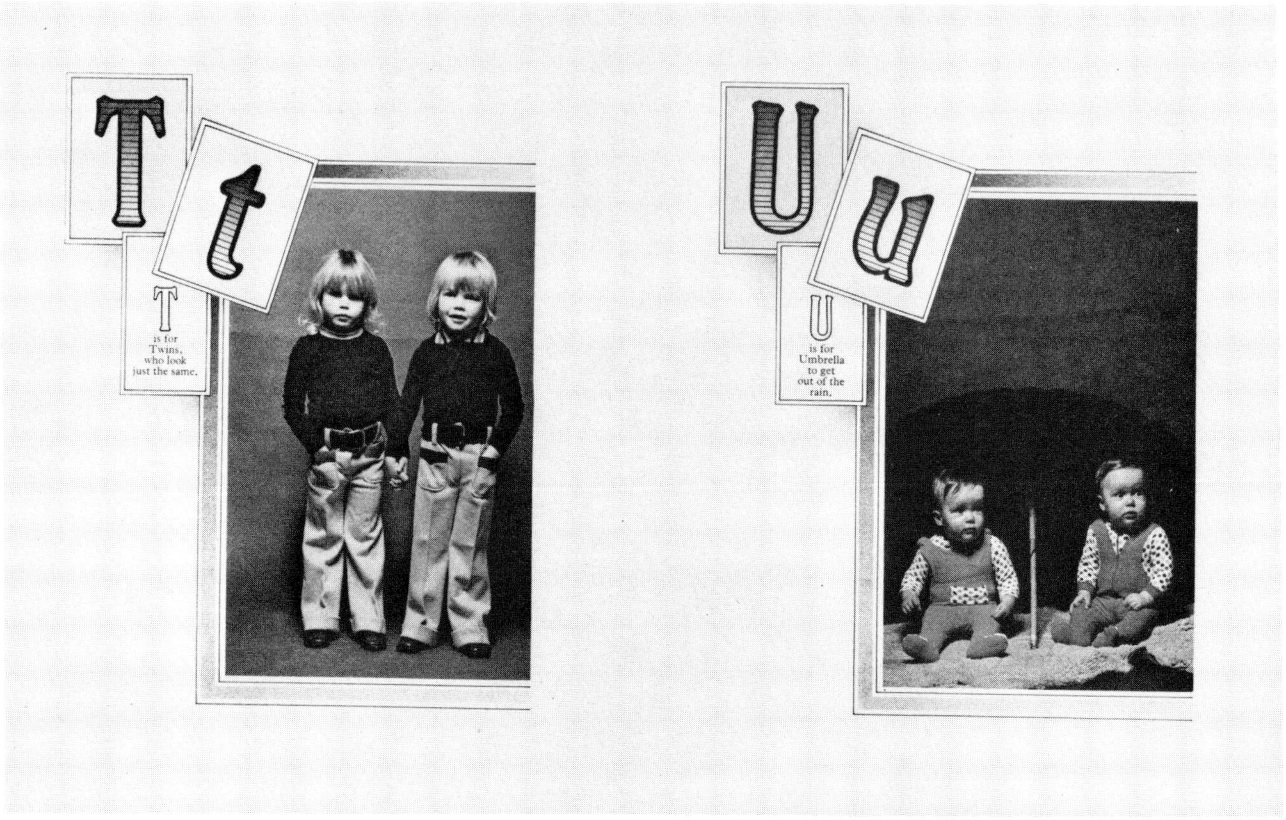
T
t
T
is for
Twins,
who look
just the same.
U
u
U
is for
Umbrella
to get
out of the
rain.

GOLD

1150
Art Director David Pocknell
Designer David Pocknell
Photographer Harri Peccinotti
Agency David Pocknell
Client Absorba Ltd.

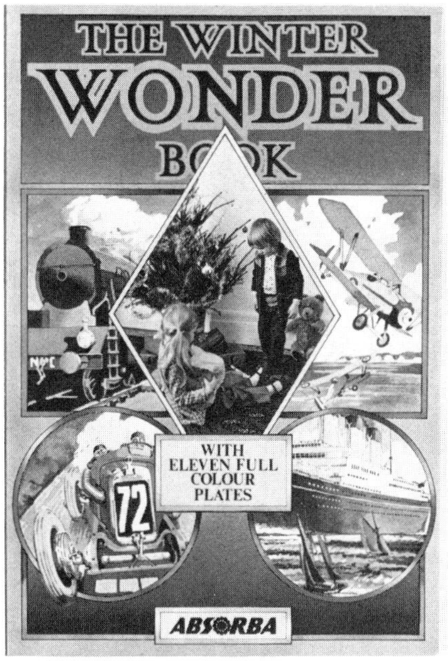
THE WINTER
WONDER
BOOK
WITH ELEVEN FULL COLOUR PLATES
72
ABSORBA

FOR YOU TO COLOUR!
Oliver
Aurocks 48806 Denim suit
Tamasin
Zamba 78805 Denim suit
Edouard 73050 Polo
Sean
Corlin 43716 Trouser
Slughi 43209 Shirt
Use felt pens and make this the most colourful page in the book.
8

9

5
Culotte **70120**
Chemise Américaine **70113**
6
Chemise Américaine **70114**
7
Chemise Américaine **70115**
5
6
7
FOR
BABY

1151
Art Director David Pocknell
Designer David Pocknell
Artist David Pocknell
Photographer Tony Evans
Writer David Pocknell
Agency David Pocknell Agency
London
Client Absorba Ltd.

Vacation Retreat
Business Retreat

1152

242 ST-B'WAY
SOUTH FERRY
BROADWAY LOCAL
Watching my name go by
Documented by Mervyn Kurlansky & Jon Naar. Text by Norman Mailer

1153

1152
Art Director Robert Burns
Designers Robert Burns
John Speakman
Artists Heather Cooper
Dawn Tennant
Photographer Tim Saunders
Writer Don Hewson
Agency Burns & Cooper Ltd.
Toronto
Client Canadian Government
Office of Tourism

1153
Art Director Mervyn Kurlansky
Designer Mervyn Kurlansky
Artists Citizens of
New York City
Photographer Jon Naar
Writer Norman Mailer
Publisher Mathews Miller
Dunbar Ltd.
Agency Pentagram Design
Partnership
London

bruemmer
THE ARCTIC

Top: Lousewort blooms on an island in the Bering Sea.
Carmine cap of a mushroom among dwarf willow leaves. Delicate grasses sway in the wind near the tundra's southern edge.
Male catkins of dwarf willows. Frail blossoms of the hardy broad-leaved willow herb.
Middle: Dwarf willow leaves in early fall. Purple saxifrage, the first flowers to bloom in the arctic spring.
Cinquefoil on an island off Alaska's west coast. Monkshood and goldenrod on a far
northern meadow. Cottongrass loves the moisture of an arctic marsh.
Tiny hairs protect the stems of the arctic poppy. The vivid red of bearberry leaves on the fall tundra.
Bottom: Kamchatka lily on Marmot Island, off Alaska's west coast. Arctic chamomile, the daisy of the north.

1155

1155
Designer Gilles Daigneault
Photographer Fred Bruemmer
Writer Fred Bruemmer
Publisher Optimum Publishing Co. Ltd.
Montreal

INT'L EDITORIAL ART & DESIGN

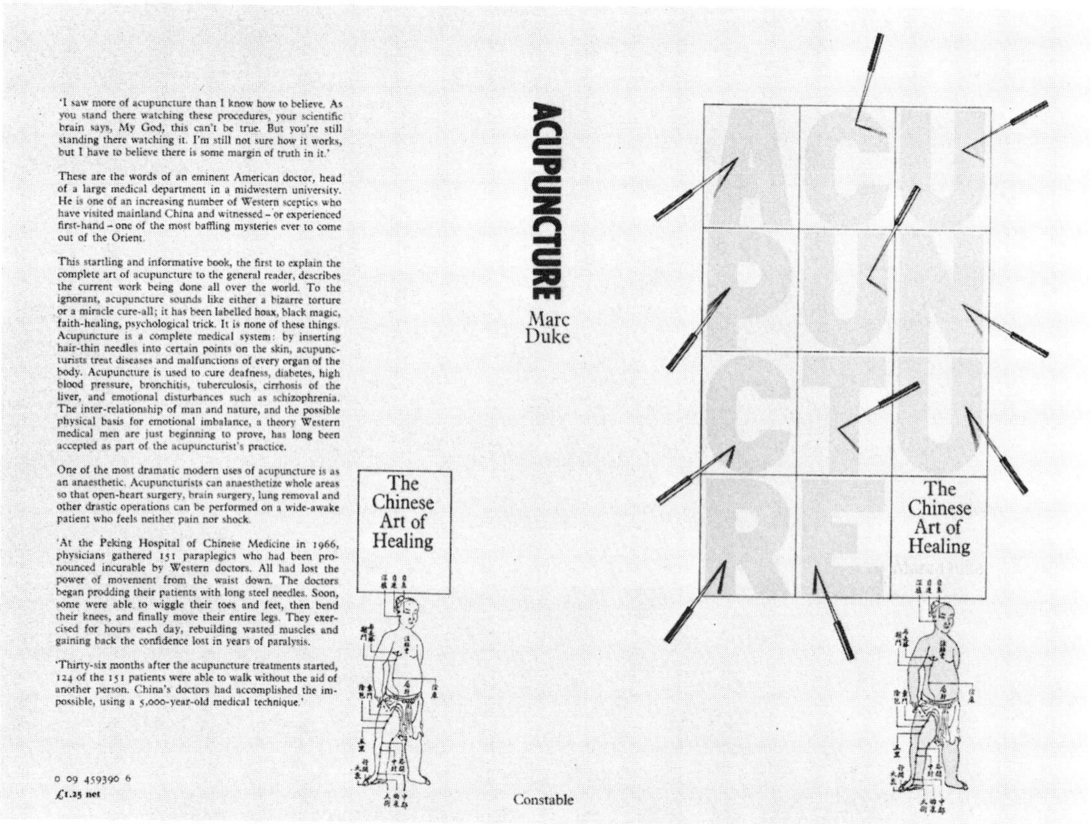
'I saw more of acupuncture than I know how to believe. As you stand there watching these procedures, your scientific brain says, My God, this can't be true. But you're still standing there watching it. I'm still not sure how it works, but I have to believe there is some margin of truth in it.'
These are the words of an eminent American doctor, head of a large medical department in a midwestern university. He is one of an increasing number of Western sceptics who have visited mainland China and witnessed – or experienced first-hand – one of the most baffling mysteries ever to come out of the Orient.
This startling and informative book, the first to explain the complete art of acupuncture to the general reader, describes the current work being done all over the world. To the ignorant, acupuncture sounds like either a bizarre torture or a miracle cure-all; it has been labelled hoax, black magic, faith-healing, psychological trick. It is none of these things. Acupuncture is a complete medical system: by inserting hair-thin needles into certain points on the skin, acupuncturists treat diseases and malfunctions of every organ of the body. Acupuncture is used to cure deafness, diabetes, high blood pressure, bronchitis, tuberculosis, cirrhosis of the liver, and emotional disturbances such as schizophrenia. The inter-relationship of man and nature, and the possible physical basis for emotional imbalance, a theory Western medical men are just beginning to prove, has long been accepted as part of the acupuncturist's practice.
One of the most dramatic modern uses of acupuncture is as an anaesthetic. Acupuncturists can anaesthetize whole areas so that open-heart surgery, brain surgery, lung removal and other drastic operations can be performed on a wide-awake patient who feels neither pain nor shock.
'At the Peking Hospital of Chinese Medicine in 1966, physicians gathered 151 paraplegics who had been pronounced incurable by Western doctors. All had lost the power of movement from the waist down. The doctors began prodding their patients with long steel needles. Soon, some were able to wiggle their toes and feet, then bend their knees, and finally move their entire legs. They exercised for hours each day, rebuilding wasted muscles and gaining back the confidence lost in years of paralysis.
'Thirty-six months after the acupuncture treatments started, 124 of the 151 patients were able to walk without the aid of another person. China's doctors had accomplished the impossible, using a 5,000-year-old medical technique.'
0 09 459390 6
£1.25 net
The Chinese Art of Healing
ACUPUNCTURE
Marc Duke
Constable
ACU
PUN
CTU
RE
The Chinese Art of Healing

1156

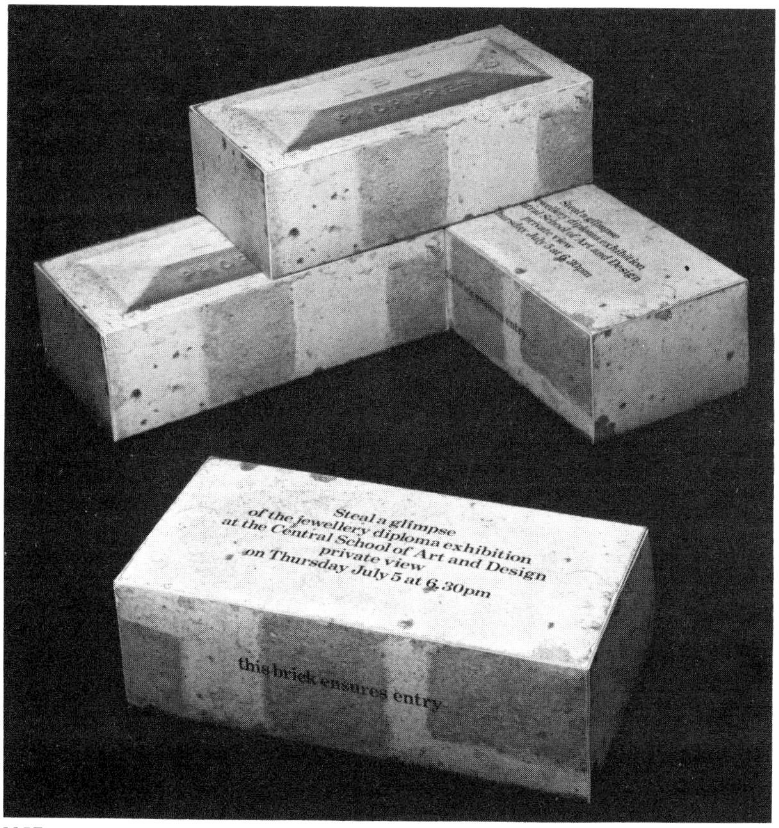
Steal a glimpse
of the jewellery diploma exhibition
at the Central School of Art and Design
private view
on Thursday July 5 at 6.30pm
this brick ensures entry

1157

1156
Art Director David Pocknell
Designer David Pocknell
Artist David Pocknell
Agency David Pocknell Agency
London
Client Constable and Co.

1157
Art Director Carole Ingham
Designer Carole Ingham
Agency Carole Ingham
London
Client Central School of Art Jewellery

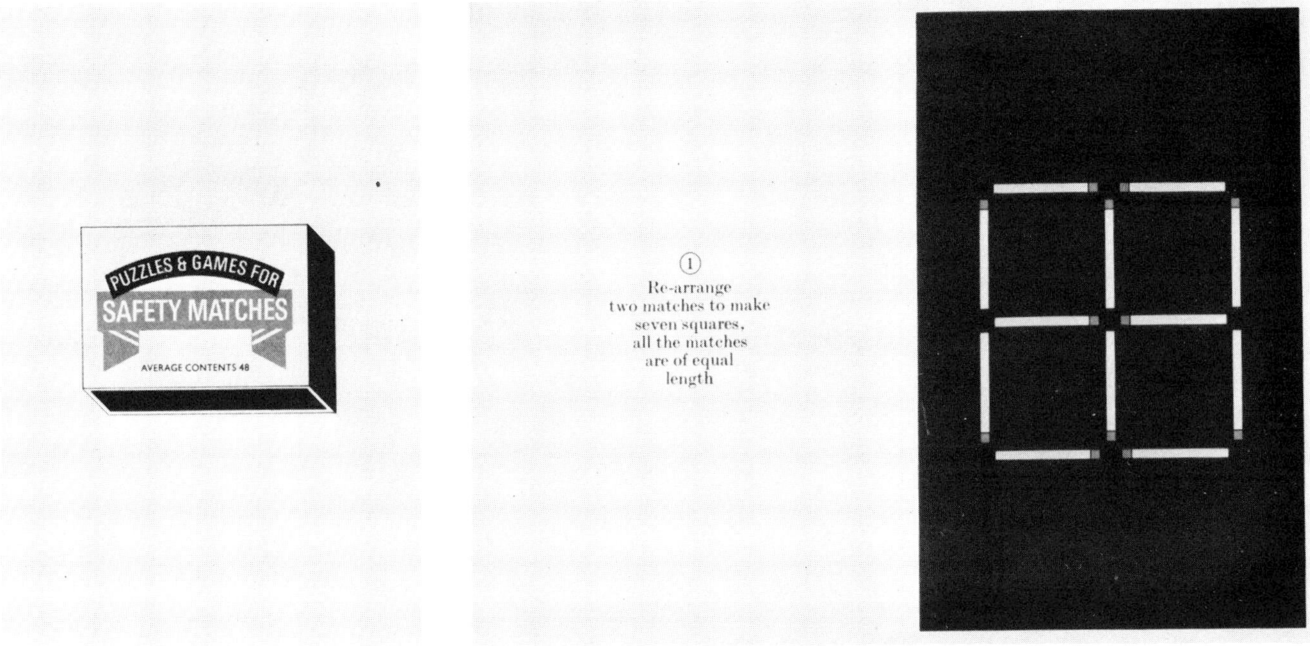
PUZZLES & GAMES FOR
SAFETY MATCHES
AVERAGE CONTENTS 48
1
Re-arrange
two matches to make
seven squares,
all the matches
are of equal
length

1158

福寿園

1159

1158
Art Director John McConnell
Designer John McConnell
Agency Pentagram Design Partnership London
Client Pentagram Design Partnership

1159
Art Director Tokihiko Kimata
Designers Takeo Yao
Takuzo Mizuno
Artist Kanyo Funazu
Agency Yao Design Co. Tokyo
Client Fukujuen Co. Ltd.

LOOK
Look
LOOK AT CHROMOLUX
ZANDERS

1160

CINZANO
CINZANO

1161

SILVER

1160
Art Directors Olaf Leu Design
Designers Olaf Leu
Fritz Hofrichter
Writer Prof. Berndt
Agency Zanders Feinpapiere GmbH
West Germany
Client Zanders Feinpapiere GmbH

1161
Art Director Rosette Holzer
Designer Stag
Photographer David Thorpe
Writer Pierre Berville
Agency Tragos Bonnange
Wiesendanger Ajroldi
Paris
Client Cinzano

APRIL APRIL AVRIL ABRIL
ZANDERS FEINPAPIERE GMBH BERGISCH GLADBACH UND DÜREN

FEBRUAR FEBRUARY FÉVRIER FEBRERO
ZANDERS FEINPAPIERE GMBH BERGISCH GLADBACH UND DÜREN

1162

MAYO
JUNIO

MARZO
ABRIL

1163

1162
Art Directors Olaf Leu Design
Zanders Werbeabteilung
Designers Olaf Leu Design
Fritz Hofrichter
Photographer Oskar Rainer
Publisher Zanders Feinpapiere GmbH
West Germany
Client Zanders Feinpapiere GmbH

1163
Art Director Tomás Vellvé
Designer Tomás Vellvé
Photographers Jaime Blassi
Jorge Blassi
Publisher Industrias Gráficas Casamajó
Barcelona
Client Industrias Gráficas Casamajó

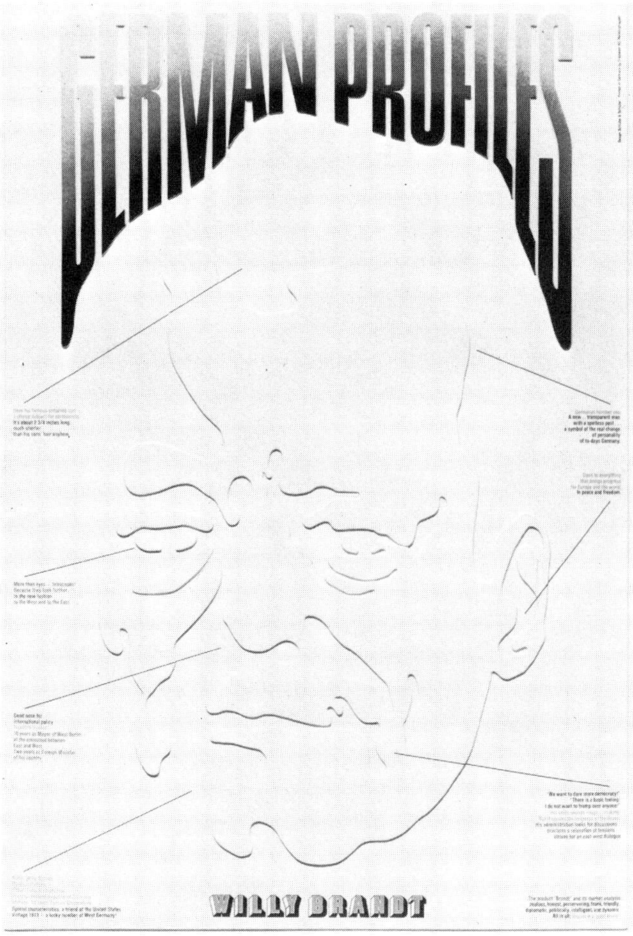
GERMAN PROFILES
WILLY BRANDT

1164

T.UNGERER

1165

GOLD

1164
Art Directors Doris Schlüter
Harald Schlüter
Designers Doris Schlüter
Harald Schlüter
Artists Doris Schlüter
Harald Schlüter
Writer Jürgen Mehl
Agency Schlüter, Schlüter
Mehl Ideealismus GmbH
West Germany
Client Inter Nationes

1165
Art Director Robert Pütz
Artist Tomi Ungerer
Writer Alfred Limbach
Agency Werbeagentur Robert Pütz
West Germany
Client Robert Pütz

I'm Jackie. Fly me.
A Photograph by Christa Peters
Represented by Mark Ramon
Tel: 01-834 1588
Telex: "Raymark" West Cham London 268312

1166

Wir bauen einen Regenbogen auch für Sie.
Werbeagentur Robert Pütz 5 Köln, Kleingedankstraße 11, Telefon 31 70 41, Telex 08 88 10 10

1167

INT'L EDITORIAL ART & DESIGN

SILVER

1166
Art Director Christa Peters
Designer David Sharp
Photographer Christa Peters
Publisher Christa Peters
London
Client Christa Peters

1167
Art Director Robert Pütz
Artist Uwe Brandi
Writer Alfred Limbach
Agency Werbeagentur Robert Pütz
West Germany
Client Robert Pütz

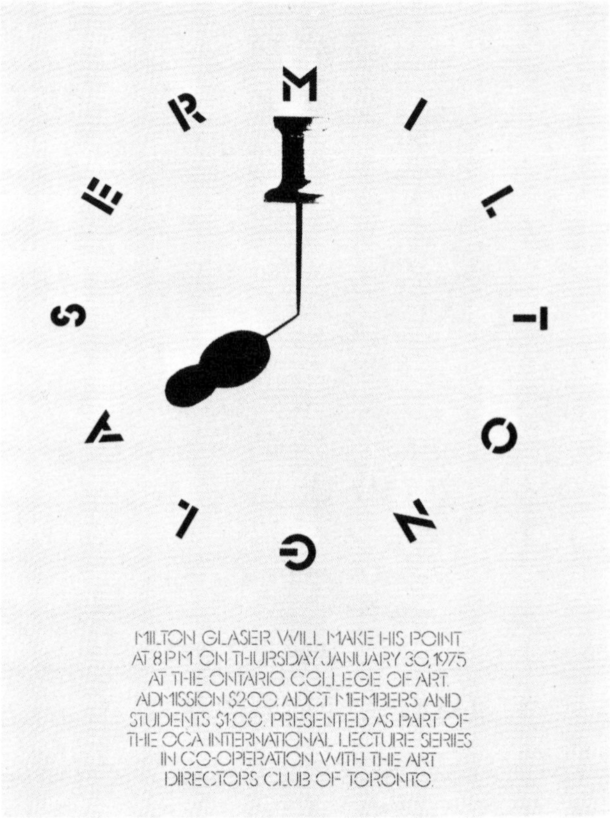
MILTON GLASER
MILTON GLASER WILL MAKE HIS POINT AT 8 P.M. ON THURSDAY JANUARY 30, 1975 AT THE ONTARIO COLLEGE OF ART. ADMISSION $2.00. ADCT MEMBERS AND STUDENTS $1.00. PRESENTED AS PART OF THE OCA INTERNATIONAL LECTURE SERIES IN CO-OPERATION WITH THE ART DIRECTORS CLUB OF TORONTO.

1169

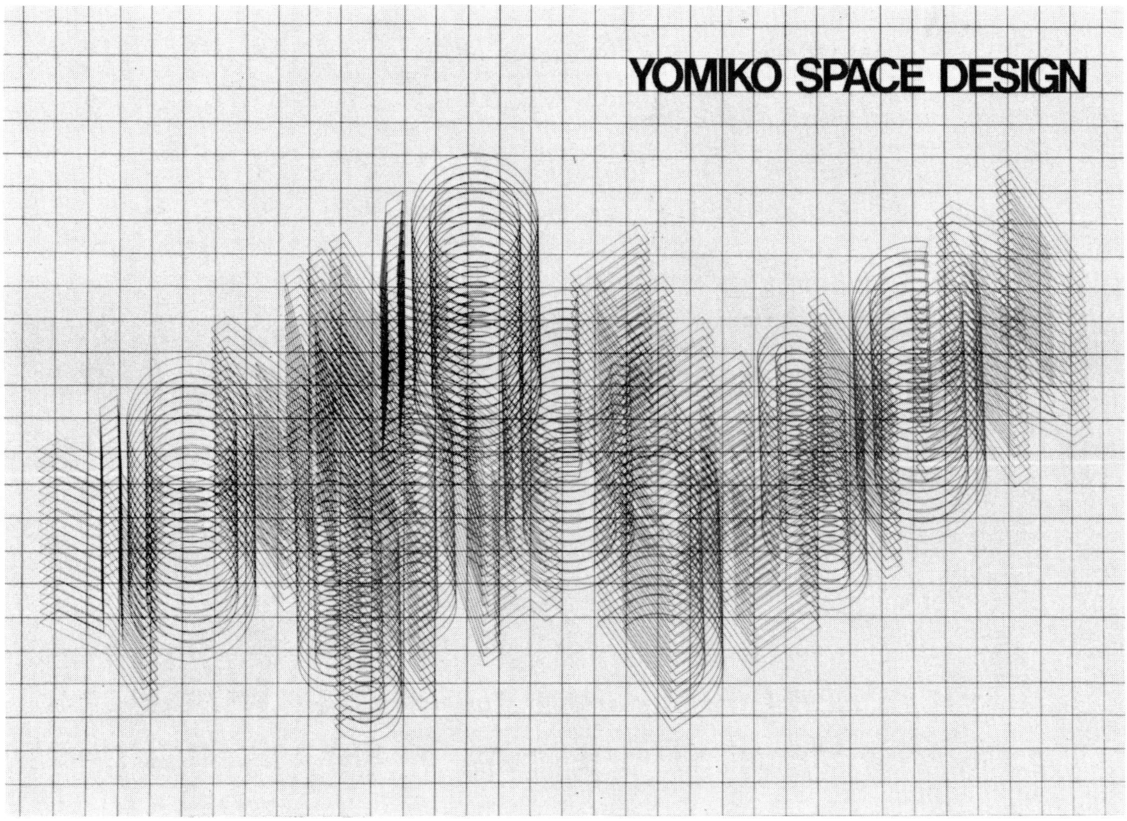
YOMIKO SPACE DESIGN

1170

1169
Art Director Robert Burns
Designer Robert Burns
Artists Heather Cooper
Paul Walker
Photographer Tim Saunders
Writer Robert Burns
Agency Burns & Cooper, Ltd.
Toronto
Client Ontario College of Art

1170
Art Director Takenobu Igarashi
Designer Takenobu Igarashi
Artist Takenobu Igarashi
Agency Yomiko Advertising
Tokyo
Client Yomiko Space Design

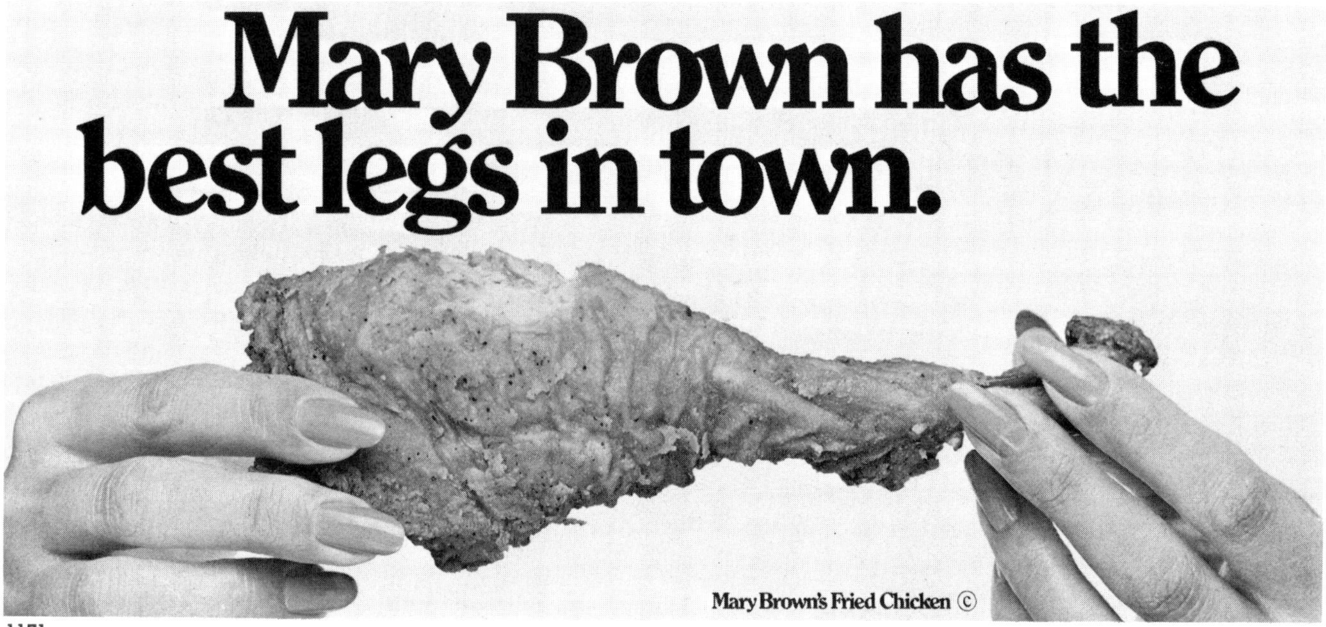
Mary Brown has the best legs in town.
Mary Brown's Fried Chicken ©

1171

BUNDESREPUBLIK DEUTSCHLAND
BUNDESPOST
DEUTSCHE
40
25 JAHRE
BUNDESREPUBLIK
DEUTSCHLAND
1949—1974

1172

1171
Art Director Raymond Lee
Designer Raymond Lee
Artist Dean Raynor
Photographer Rudi Von Tiederman
Writer Raymond Lee
Agency Raymond Lee & Assoc. Ltd.
Toronto
Client Mary Brown Canada Ltd.

1172
Art Director Helmut Langer
Designer Helmut Langer
Agency Langer Visualization
West Germany
Client Deutsche Bundespost

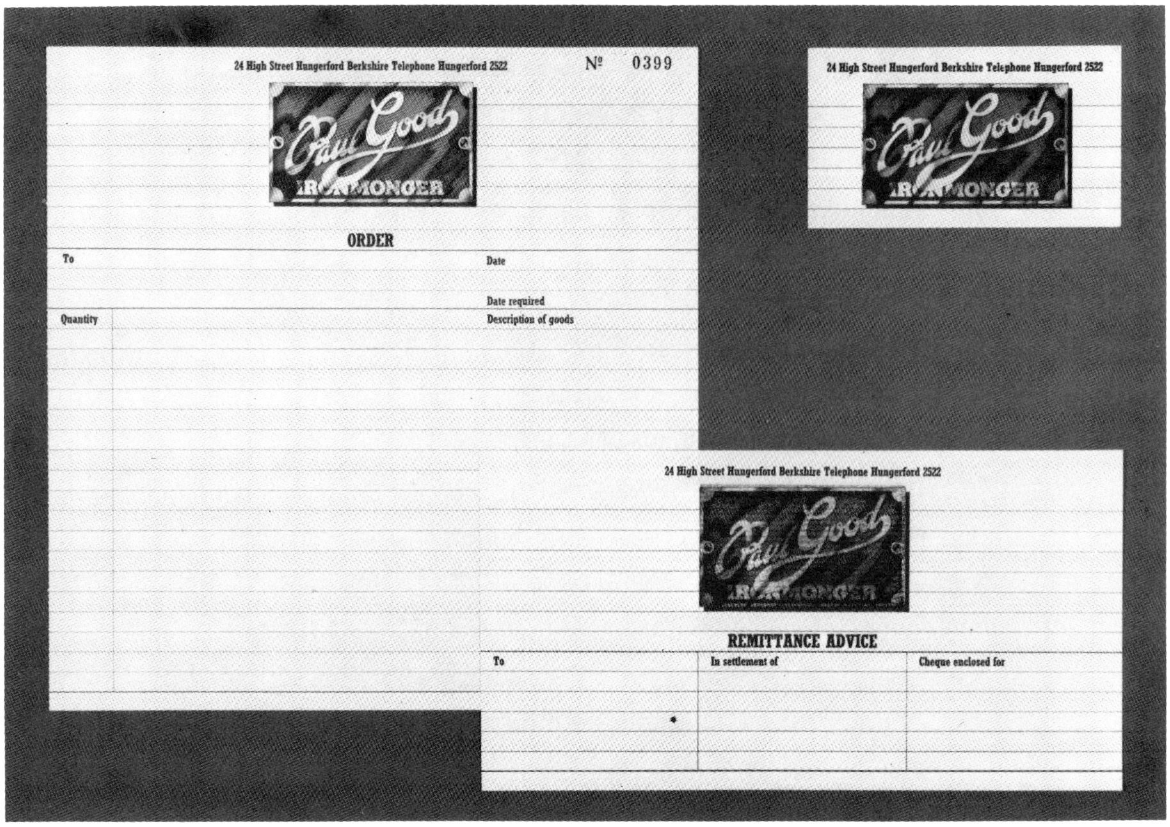
24 High Street Hungerford Berkshire Telephone Hungerford 2522
№ 0399
Paul Good
IRONMONGER
ORDER
To
Date
Date required
Quantity
Description of goods
24 High Street Hungerford Berkshire Telephone Hungerford 2522
Paul Good
IRONMONGER
24 High Street Hungerford Berkshire Telephone Hungerford 2522
Paul Good
IRONMONGER
REMITTANCE ADVICE
To
In settlement of
Cheque enclosed for

1173

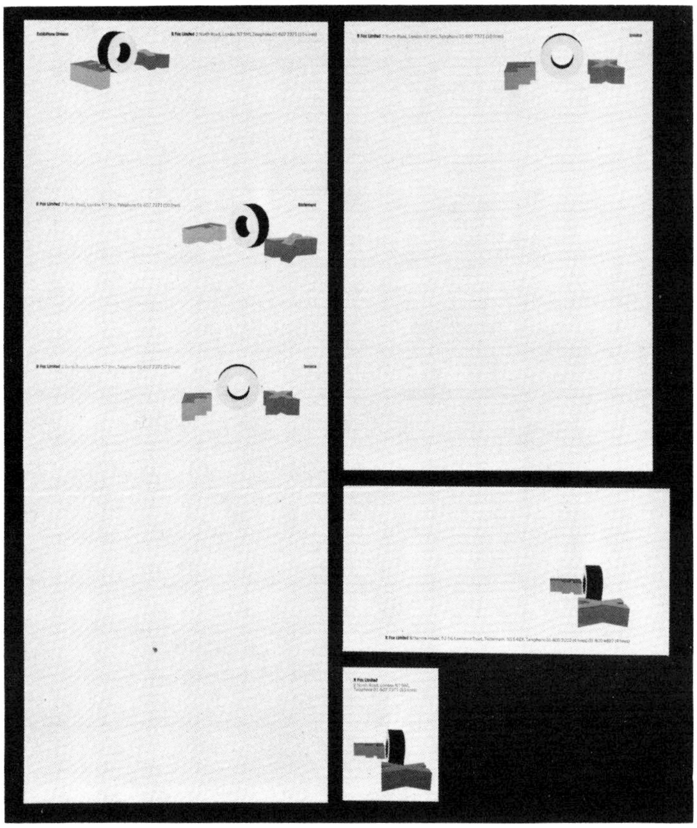

1174

GOLD

1173
Art Director David Pocknell
Designer David Pocknell
Artist David Pocknell
Agency David Pocknell Agency
London
Client Paul Good
Ironmonger

1174
Art Directors Marcello Minale
Brian Tattersfield
Designers Marcello Minale
Brian Tattersfield
Alex Maranzano
Agency Minale, Tattersfield
Provinciali Ltd.
London
Client Fox Ltd.

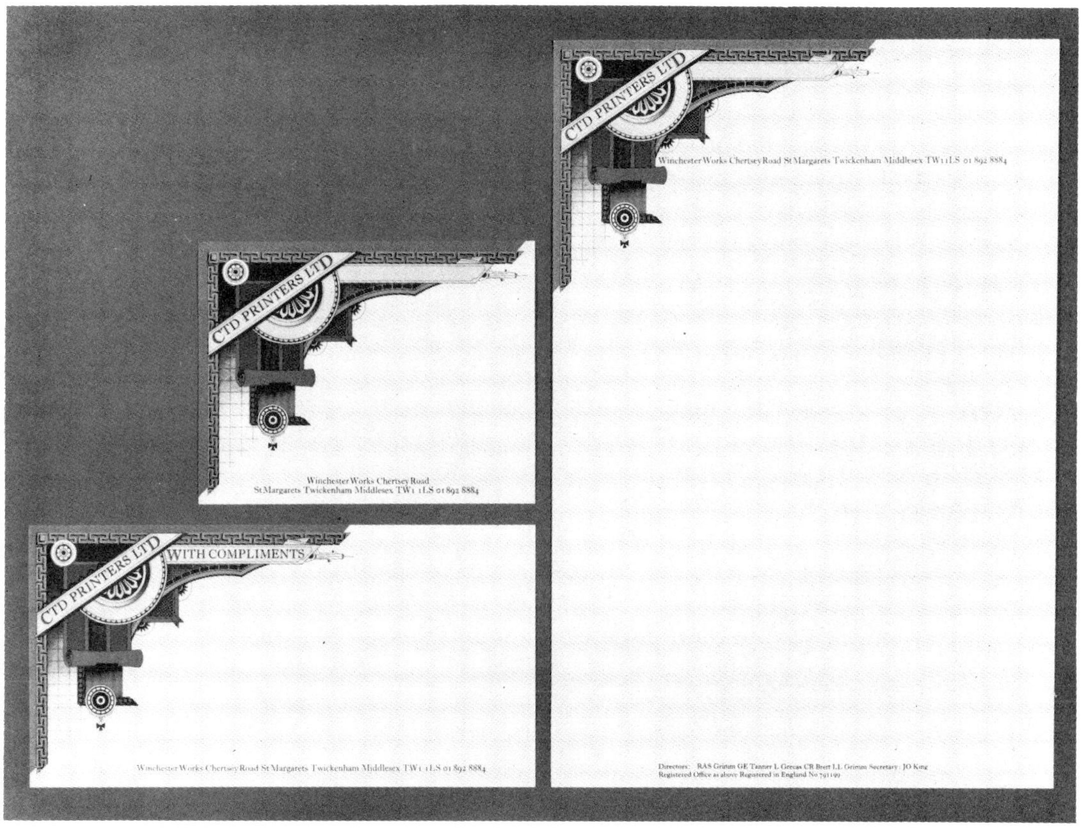
CTD PRINTERS LTD
Winchester Works Chertsey Road St Margarets Twickenham Middlesex TW1 1LS 01 892 8884
CTD PRINTERS LTD
Winchester Works Chertsey Road
St Margarets Twickenham Middlesex TW1 1LS 01 892 8884
CTD PRINTERS LTD
WITH COMPLIMENTS
Winchester Works Chertsey Road St Margarets Twickenham Middlesex TW1 1LS 01 892 8884

1175

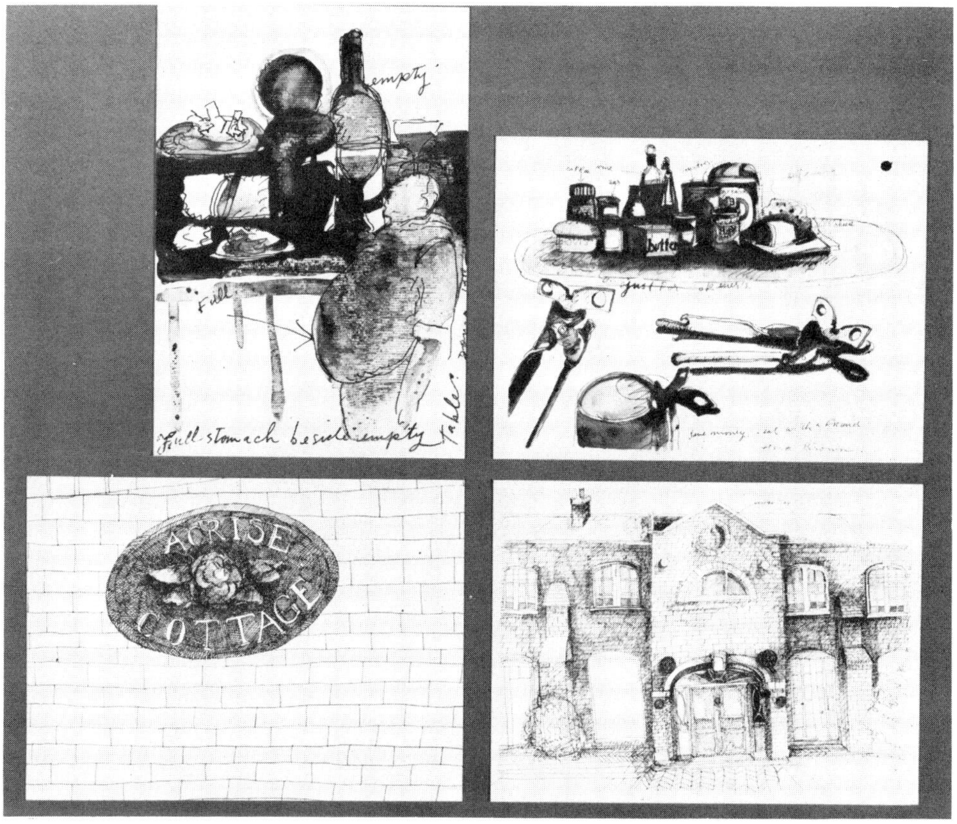
empty
Full
Full stomach beside empty table
ACRISE COTTAGE

1176

1175
Art Director David Pocknell
Designer David Pocknell
Artist David Pocknell
Agency David Pocknell Agency
London
Client CTD Printers Ltd.

1176
Art Director Alan Fletcher
Designer Alan Fletcher
Artist Donna Brown
Agency Pentagram Design
Partnership
London
Client Kenneth Grange

POP CROSS

1177

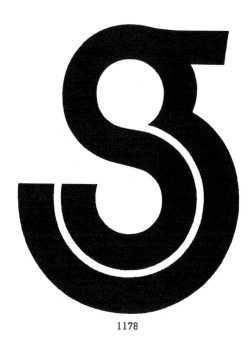

1178

1177
Art Director Annegret Beier
Designer Annegret Beier
Agency Lubalin, Delpire et Cie
Paris
Client Lubalin, Delpire et Cie

1178
Art Director Alan Peckolick
Designer Alan Peckolick
Artist Lubalin, Smith, Carnase
Agency Lubalin, Smith, Carnase
Client Societie General

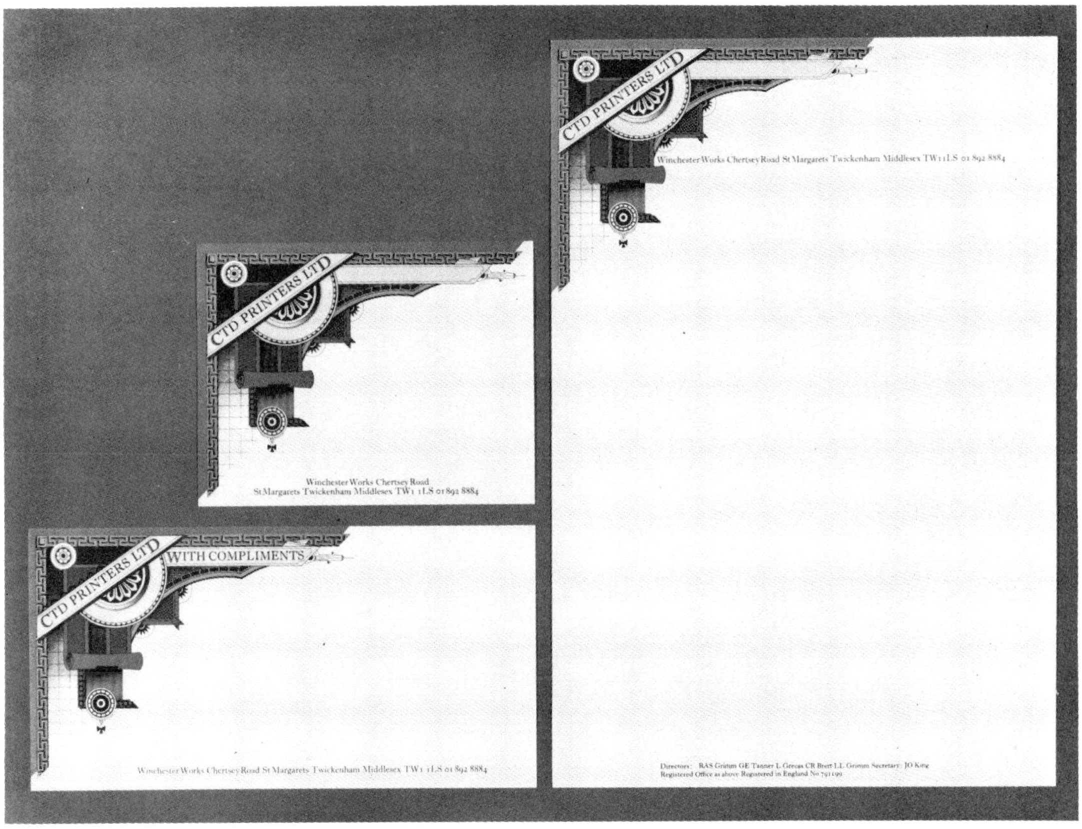
CTD PRINTERS LTD
Winchester Works Chertsey Road St Margarets Twickenham Middlesex TW1 1LS 01 892 8884
CTD PRINTERS LTD
Winchester Works Chertsey Road
St Margarets Twickenham Middlesex TW1 1LS 01 892 8884
CTD PRINTERS LTD
WITH COMPLIMENTS
Winchester Works Chertsey Road St Margarets Twickenham Middlesex TW1 1LS 01 892 8884

1175

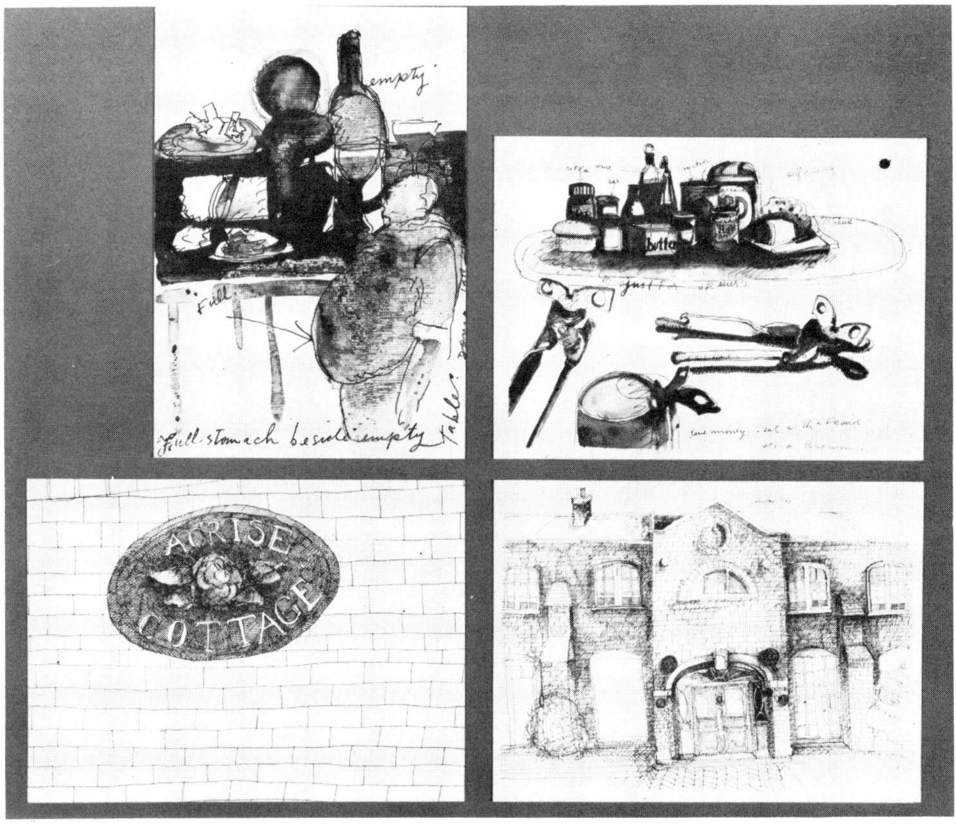
empty
Full
Full stomach beside empty table
ACRISE COTTAGE

1176

1175
Art Director David Pocknell
Designer David Pocknell
Artist David Pocknell
Agency David Pocknell Agency
London
Client CTD Printers Ltd.

1176
Art Director Alan Fletcher
Designer Alan Fletcher
Artist Donna Brown
Agency Pentagram Design
Partnership
London
Client Kenneth Grange

1177

1178

1177
Art Director Annegret Beier
Designer Annegret Beier
Agency Lubalin, Delpire et Cie
Paris
Client Lubalin, Delpire et Cie

1178
Art Director Alan Peckolick
Designer Alan Peckolick
Artist Lubalin, Smith, Carnase
Agency Lubalin, Smith, Carnase
Client Societie General

1179

1179
Designer Heather Cooper
Designer Heather Cooper
Artist Heather Cooper
Writer Heather Cooper
Agency Burns & Cooper Ltd.
Toronto
Client Burns & Cooper Ltd.

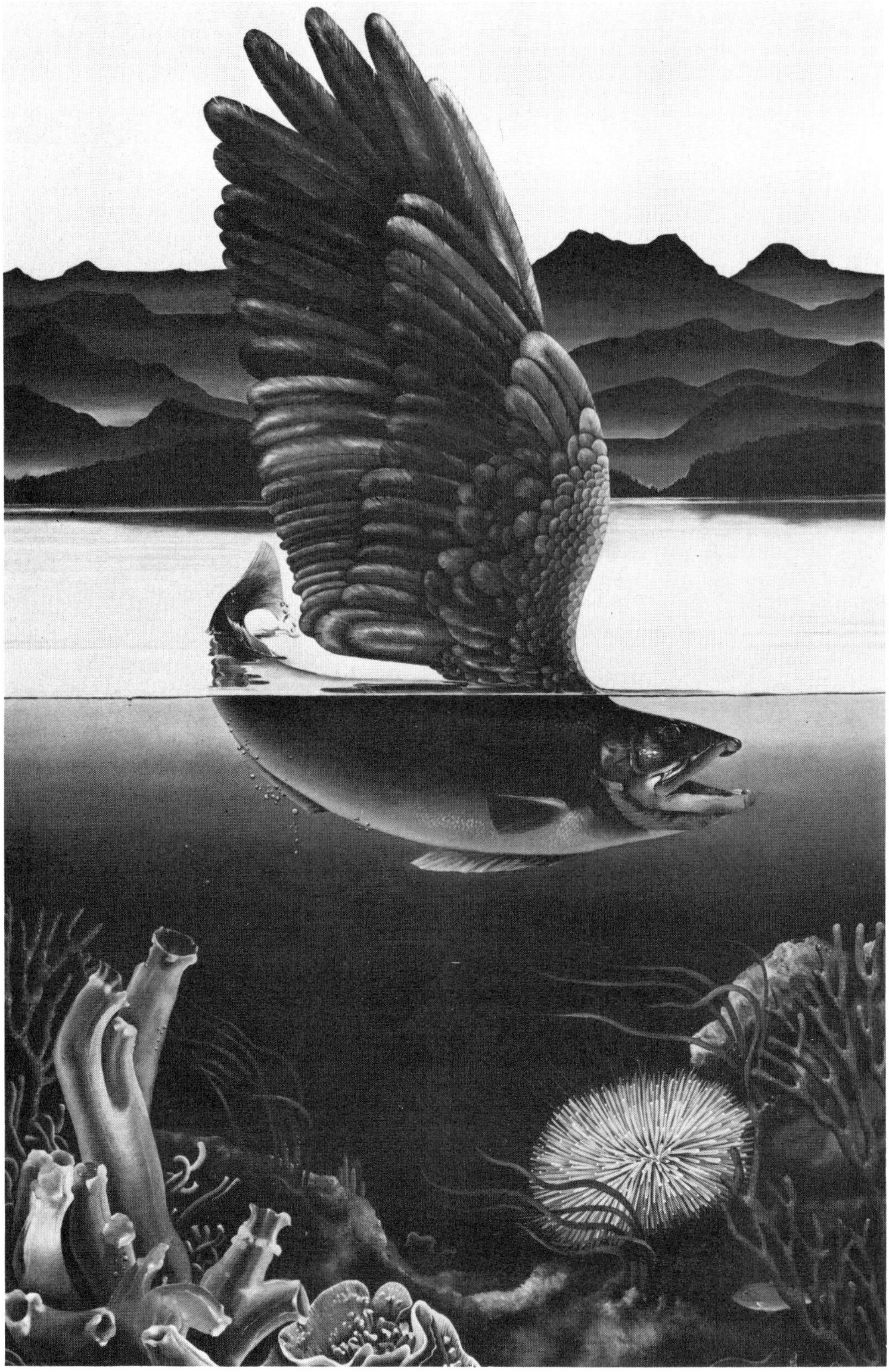

1180

1180
Art Director Robert Burns
Designers Robert Burns
John Speakman
Artist Heather Cooper
Photographer Tim Saunders
Writer Jim Hynes
Agency Burns & Cooper Ltd.
Toronto
Client Abitibi Provincial
Paper Co.

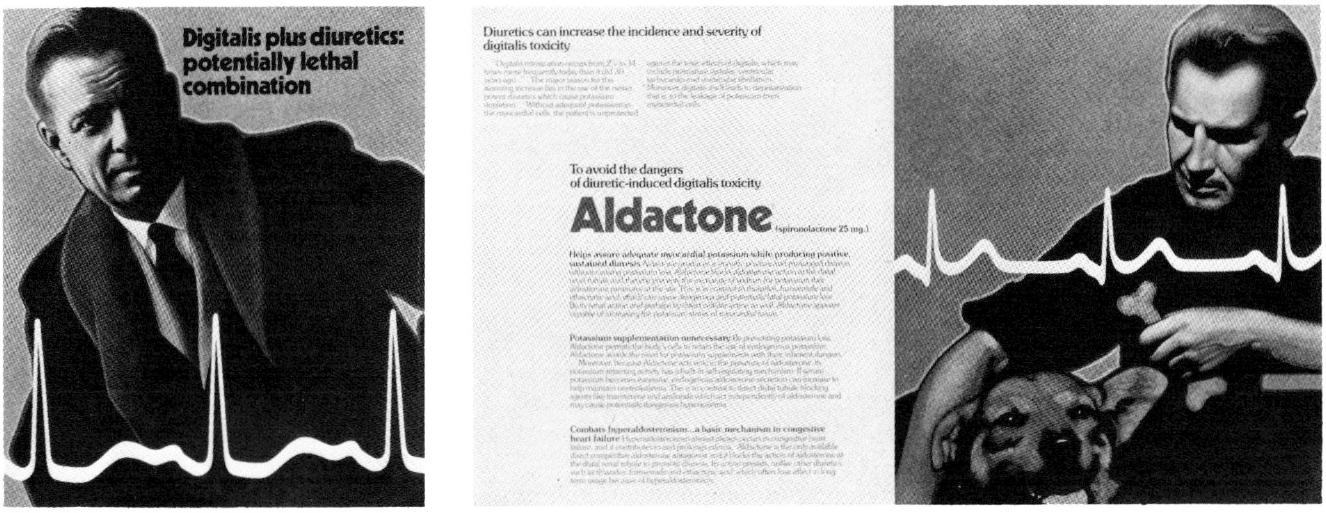
Digitalis plus diuretics: potentially lethal combination
Diuretics can increase the incidence and severity of digitalis toxicity
To avoid the dangers of diuretic-induced digitalis toxicity
Aldactone
(spironolactone 25 mg.)
Helps assure adequate myocardial potassium while producing positive, sustained diuresis
Potassium supplementation unnecessary
Combats hyperaldosteronism...a basic mechanism in congestive heart failure

1181

Heather Cooper

1182

1181
Art Director Leslie Sisman
Designer Leslie Sisman
Artist Alex Gnidzicjko
Writer Harry Smith
Client G. D. Searle International Co.

1182
Art Director Joe Brooks
Designer Heather Cooper
Artist Heather Cooper
Editor Jim Goode
Agency Burns & Cooper Ltd. Toronto
Client Penthouse

THE HALL OF FAME

M. F. Agha	1972
Lester Beall	
Alexey Brodovitch	
A. M. Cassandre	
René Clarke	
Robert Gage	
William Golden	
Paul Rand	
Charles Coiner	1973
Paul Smith	
Jack Tinker	
Will Burtin	1974
Leo Lionni	
Gordon Aymar	1975
Herbert Bayer	
Cipe Pineles	
Heyworth Campbell	
Alexander Liberman	
L. Moholy-Nagy	

Gordon C. Aymar

In between his graduation from Yale in 1914 and his service as a Signal Officer in the Navy in World War I, Gordon Aymar worked as art editor for two of the most exciting and influential magazines in American publishing history—*Vanity Fair* and *Harper's Weekly*.

At *Vanity Fair*, under editor-in-chief Frank Crowninshield, a remarkable staff came together. Some of the other editors were Robert Benchley, Dorothy Parker, and Robert Sherwood. The magazine was responsible, through its superb color plates, for the debut in print of such artists as Picasso, Matisse, Gauguin, Rouault, Epstein, Covarrubias, and Rockwell Kent. Noted photographers like Steichen, Bruehl, Horst, and Beaton appeared regularly.

And *Harper's Weekly*, the political and literary journal which was a force in American life from the Civil War period until its untimely demise in 1917, remains famous for the appearance on its pages of many of Thomas Nast's best-known cartoons. These two publications, then, were the extraordinary starting points of Aymar's long and distinguished career, as an art editor, an art director, and a widely-exhibited portrait painter.

After the war years, he went into advertising, becoming first an art director at J. Walter Thompson Company and later Vice President and Art Director of Compton Advertising, Inc. The accounts he worked on, either directly or as supervisor, were not only prodigious in number (involving almost 200 products and services) but in their great variety, ranging — in consumer pleasures, for example — from Peter Paul's candies to Harry Winston's diamonds. In addition, he designed or re-designed packages and trademarks in the most competitive marketing areas: foods, drugs, toiletries, tobacco, and liquor.

Aymar then became an independent art consultant for 13 years, and finally arrived at the point where he could spend all his time painting portraits. He has exhibited in museums and galleries throughout the country, from Bridgeport, Connecticut to Phoenix, Arizona to Seattle, Washington, as well as in the Montreal Art Museum and the Royal Society of Painters in Water Colour in London.

His work is in the collections of the Brooklyn Public Library, Pratt Institute, Yale University Art Gallery, Young & Rubicam, Inc., Ogilvy & Mather Inc. and many others. Aymar's series of photographs of St. Patrick's Cathedral are in the permanent study collection of MOMA. And he is also known for many books on advertising illustration, and on his other great love, sailing.

Aymar was charter president of the National Society of Art Directors, and president of the New York Art Directors Club in 1933–'34. He received the Art Director of the Year award in 1951.

We are gratified to have this new opportunity to recognize Gordon Aymar's outstanding contribution as an art director, and to pay homage to his continuing productive and creative life.

Herbert Bayer

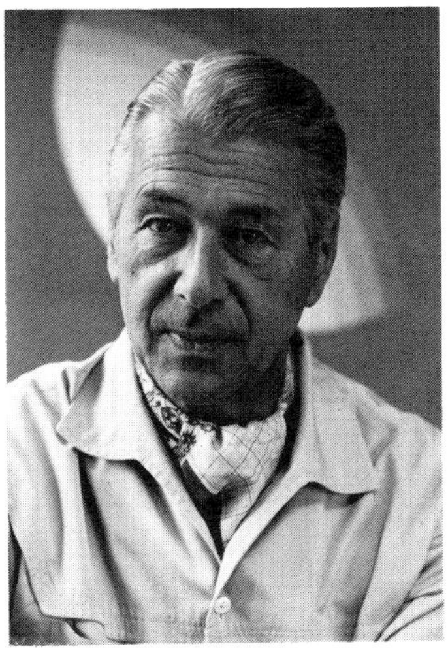

If Herbert Bayer had produced nothing after the age of 28, his accomplishments to that point alone would make him one of the great pioneers in visual communication.

Bayer is exactly as old as the century. He was born in Austria in 1900 and became a student at the Bauhaus in Weimar when he was 21. His main interests were typography and advertising, but as there was then no workshop in these subjects at the Bauhaus, he studied mural painting under Kandinsky.

Meanwhile, he and a few other students, encouraged by Moholy-Nagy, began experimenting with typography on their own. And from this period, when Bayer was 23, there is such distinctive work as the first Bauhaus book, other Bauhaus graphics, and the multi-digit (inflation) money he designed for the Thuringian government. There is his famous trademark for the Kraus Stained Glass Workshop, an elegantly balanced linear square divided into two squares and two rectangles.

Walter Gropius, observing this output, placed Bayer in charge of a Bauhaus workshop in typography in 1925. He taught for three years, then left for Berlin to work as a designer on his own.

The accomplishments of the early years also included his 1924 design for a remarkable structure, a street-car station and newspaper stand, in which strong horizontal and vertical planes cut through the station, forming open-sided spaces with red, yellow, blue, black, and white-painted walls. True to Bauhaus philosophy, Bayer constructed the station from prefabricated units to enable mass production.

In 1925, reacting to a general prevalence of bad type faces, Bayer designed Universal, a Grotesk type (which, after 50 years, today is a fashionable face). And also worthy of mention here are his extraordinary poster for the Kandinsky exhibit of 1926, and the work on Bauhaus publications of 1926 and '28.

When Bayer was 38, he came to the United States and began a new career of great distinction in advertising. In succession, he become consultant art director for J. Walter Thompson; and art director of Dorland International. He then formed what would be a long, fruitful association with the Container Corporation of America, which produced some of the most innovative and widely-applauded print advertising of the last several decades.

In recent years, Herbert Bayer has done much distinguished work as an architect, an interior designer, and a painter. Noteworthy is the book on Bayer, "The Way Beyond Art, The Work of Herbert Bayer," by Alexander Dorner. He has also authored and edited several volumes, including "Bauhaus 1919–1928," co-editor with Walter and Ise Gropius; "Herbert Bayer Book of Drawings;" "World Geo-Graphic Atlas;" A new book soon to be published on the artist is by Ida Rodriguez Prampolini.

He lives currently in Aspen, Colorado; Container Corporation Chairman Walter Paepcke had invited him to become design consultant of the Aspen development back in 1946.

We honor Herbert Bayer for the entire body of his work, grateful as we can be that the fireworks of the early years turned out to be only the curtain-raiser.

Heyworth Campbell

Heyworth Campbell once redesigned a newspaper. The result was so handsome and so original that Robert Benchley was impelled to "review" it in *The New Yorker*. The newspaper was *The Morning Telegraph*, and its new Campbell format, said Benchley, was "as beautiful as anything we have ever seen in a newspaper — we may just frame a copy and keep it to look at . . ."

That was Heyworth Campbell. Fresh from 17 years with Conde Nast, using in the *Telegraph* the prodigious talent that had been creating such distinctive styles for the pages of *Vogue*, *Vanity Fair*, and *House and Garden*.

Campbell, who was born in Philadelphia and attended art school there, came to New York in 1906. By 1910 he was art director for Nast, becoming widely recognized as a pioneer in magazine design, typography, and layout.

In 1927, Campbell entered advertising, joining the then Barton, Durstine & Osborne agency. As general account executive and art consultant on all accounts, he had much to do with campaigns for Atwater Kent, General Motors, General Electric, Arrow Collars, Bond Bread, R.H. Macy, and Abraham & Straus. His unusual around-the-corner name plate for A&S was used for decades as their advertising shingle.

Then he went on his own, with the Heyworth Campbell Studio, an art directing, design, and typographic service functioning on a one-at-a-time basis for a variety of accounts including *Good Housekeeping* promotion, Lederle Laboratories, Lucien LeLong, Butterick, and Dodge Publishing Co.

How did he go about redesigning a publication? "Oh, I don't know exactly," he said in an interview for *PM*, the production managers' journal. "I make an analysis of the publication, find out who it goes to, look over typical issues . . . Then analyze the editorial content, find out what they are trying to say . . . Then try to do it the way it should have been done in the first place."

And about print advertising, he remarked, "You start with the thought. Then come the words . . . You've got to look at your stuff with an editorial eye, from an impartial angle. It is or it isn't. If it isn't, chuck it — or get out of the business."

Heyworth Campbell was a founding member of the Art Directors Club, and its third president, serving in 1922 and 1923. He remained a member of the advisory board throughout his life.

Campbell's outlook never aged. He continued to learn and to grow until he died in 1953. And so we salute him with feelings akin to those expressed by Dr. M.F. Agha on Campbell's death: "We have all lost a friend and the world has lost one of the great workers in the field of art, to which he contributed so much." His memory will never die in our hearts.

Alexander Liberman

The *Washington Post* art critic Paul Richard, reviewing an Alexander Liberman retrospective a few years ago, made an essential point about this extraordinary man. "History lists few artists of the caliber of Liberman who have held, much less insulated their painting from, intellectually demanding full-time jobs." Putting it another way, history lists few art directors of the distinction of Alexander Liberman who have also achieved parallel distinction in the fine arts.

Liberman is editorial director of all Condé Nast publications in the United States and Europe. But this job — and painting — by no means exhaust his range. In 1971, an exhibit of his large metal sculptures marked the opening of the Hammarskjold sculpture garden in New York. Some years earlier, as a one-man photographer-writer team, he produced "The Artist in His Studio," a handsome, lively book on School of Paris artists. He is also the author of "Greece, Gods, and Art."

Liberman was born in Kiev, Russia, in 1912. His family moved to England during the revolutionary period, and he went to an English public school. "If you can survive that, you can conquer anything," says Liberman.

He studied at the École des Beaux Arts in Paris in the early 1930's. At 18 he became art editor of the French magazine *Vu*, working there from 1932 to 1936. With the Louvre, he made one of the first color films on painting, "La Femme Française." And in 1937 he won a Gold Medal at the Paris International Exhibition—prophetically, for his presentation on magazine design. Four years later Liberman came to New York and joined *Vogue*. He became Art Director in 1943, and was named to his present post in 1962.

Liberman's paintings and sculpture have been exhibited widely, and acquired by such museums as MOMA, the Tate, and the Chicago Art Institute, to name three of many.

He sees all of his work — as art director, painter, sculptor, photographer, editor — as a unified endeavor. "I don't believe in the 'masterpiece' idea," he said in an interview with Grace Glueck in *The New York Times*. "In an artist's involvement, all works are similar in value. What counts is the body of the work itself . . . I wish artists could all live into their eighties. It's toward the end, when one really knows one is going to die, that one is free to dare."

Liberman the artist/art director paused at that moment in the interview, and Liberman the editor took over. "If all that sounds pretentious," he said, "kill it." *The Times* didn't think so.

In saluting Alexander Liberman, we are also saluting the work he will do in his eighties, when he feels free to dare. It will be interesting to see the "daring" work of a man who was exploring hard-edge and minimalism long before more conventional artists turned to these modes, and whose concepts of magazine design have made such an enormous difference in the look of publications everywhere.

Laszo Moholy-Nagy

In a sense, the Bauhaus movement, in which L. Moholy-Nagy was so strong a moving spirit, sought to "co-opt" our industrial/technological environment before it could co-opt us.

A Utopian vision, and some would say a failed one. But for all of that, the achievements of this almost legendary center, in education and in design and function, continue to have immense influence throughout the world.

The Bauhaus under Walter Gropius gathered together in one place — Klee, Kandinsky, Feininger, Albers, Breuer, Bayer, Schlemmer — and Moholy-Nagy.

Of all these great names, Moholy was perhaps the most protean talent, the most versatile. As Hilton Kramer wrote in *The New York Times* a few years ago, Moholy "is an artist who still somehow resists the normal categories of criticism almost a quarter of a century after his death. One reason, of course, is his extraordinary versatility. Moholy was a painter, sculptor, designer, photographer, film-maker, teacher, and theoretician. He achieved distinction in all of these fields, and showed an unmistakable genius in several."

Laszlo Moholy-Nagy was born in Hungary in 1895. He started painting while recuperating from wounds suffered in World War I. He earned a degree in law, joined a poetry circle, and became a full-time artist in 1918. Gropius invited him to join the Bauhaus staff in 1923. He would remain until 1928, heading the metal workshop, developing techniques of painting with light, and editing Bauhaus publications. Moholy then went to Berlin, where he designed stage sets for the state opera and did experimental film work until the ominous political climate forced him to leave.

After two years in London, where he began his series of colored constructs in translucent materials which he called Space Modulators, he came to the United States in 1937. He brought the Bauhaus with him.

Moholy founded a school, The New Bauhaus, in Chicago. It failed, but he then opened the Institute of Design, which became recognized as one of the finest in the world in design, architecture, photography, and sculpture. The death of Moholy-Nagy only seven years after he began the Institute was a severe loss. He died at 51, of leukemia. But the same year that Moholy's Institute started, Gropius was appointed chairman of the Harvard School of Architecture. The following year, Mies van der Rohe (who had succeeded Gropius as head of the Dessau Bauhaus) moved to Chicago to establish the department of Architecture at the Illinois Institute of Technology. Josef Albers joined the staff of Black Mountain College in North Carolina.

And so Moholy and the Bauhaus would continue to put out new roots and reach new flowerings. As important as anything the man and the movement achieved was this cross-pollination among artists, spanning continents and oceans.

Gyorgy Kepes put it this way (in the Thirtieth Anniversary Issue of *Print*): "There were currents and cross-currents; artists absorbed other artists; each of them gave and took and altogether they formed one single creative community."

Cipe Pineles

During the worst depression this country has ever known, a 20-year-old artist named Cipe Pineles walked around New York tring to sell her paintings of sandwiches and Coca-Cola bottles. Several decades later, of course, magazines, like *McCall's* would indeed buy Cipe Pineles' still lifes of sandwiches, as would *Ladies Home Journal* her herbs, and *House Beautiful* her cheese cake.

In the intervening years, Miss Pineles became one of the most highly acclaimed magazine art directors and graphic designers in the country, design consultant for New York's Lincoln Center, and director of publication design at Parsons School of Design.

She was born in Vienna, attended high school in Brooklyn, and went to Pratt Institute where she won a Louis Comfort Tiffany Foundation Scholarship. After graduation, and what she calls an "adventurous" year in the still-life-painting business, she became assistant in 1932 to F.M. Agha, then art director of Condé Nast publications. She stayed at Condé Nast long enough to become a 10-year-test-case of The Art Directors Club's admission policy toward women, and did in fact becomes its first woman member.

In 1947, she moved to *Seventeen* as art director, introducing there the commissioning of leading painters to do fiction illustration (on the theory that young readers would have few barriers in accepting fine art). And so, the pages were graced by the work of Ben Shahn, Leonard Baskin, Raphael Soyer, Kuniyoshi, Doris Lee, Robert Osborn, Jan Balet, Joe Kaufman, Evalyne Ness, Lucille Corcos, Andy Warhol, Ed Reinhardt, Richard Lindner, and Jerome Snyder.

In 1950, Miss Pineles was named art director of Street & Smith's *Charm*, where she and Editor Helen Valentine redirected the publication to a then new consumer audience — women who work. She moved to another Street & Smith publication, *Mademoiselle*, leaving in 1961 to work as an independent designer and illustrator.

Cipe Pineles became design consultant to Lincoln Center in 1967, with the entire graphics program of the Center, from stationery to annual reports, under her supervision. Her communication assignments there also included the corporate symbol design and the monthly *Journal and Calendar of Events*.

In 1970 she joined the faculty of the Parsons School of Design, becoming as well director of publication design. The "Parsons Bread Book," produced as a class project, was republished by Harper & Row in 1974, and the original student version, "Bread," was included in the 1974 American Institute of Graphic Arts' prestigious "50 Books Of The Year" show.

She was married to William Golden for 20 years. Several years after his death in 1959 she married Will Burtin. Will Burtin died in 1972. Both of these distinguished members of our profession were posthumously elected to the Art Directors Club Hall of Fame, and Cipe Pineles holds the unique honor of being the third in her own family to be named to the Hall.

It is appropriate that C.P. breaks new ground. The first woman member of The ADC gives us the privilege of welcoming her as the first woman elected to our Hall of Fame.

THE ADC, INC.

Time Capsule
The One Show
Club Activities
Committee Reports
ADC Members
Index

Time Capsule

This is the 54th time materials such as the work in this volume have been exhibited. Each show since it all began in 1920 has set for us a reflection of our points of view and of how we lived then.

The editors decided to use this space to give a small sampling of ADC award winners from out of our rich graphic arts past. Our time capsule soupçon dips into each generation for a quick look at some of the images we used then in advertising, ad illustration, and editorial design . . . On the page opposite, Bernie Zlotnick, 1975 Show chairman, puts the 54th year into perspective.

CORAL GABLES
Miami Riviera
40 Miles of Water Front

1927

ivory

1935

1935

1945

TOASTIES

Tonight at 10:30 on channel 2
SEE IT NOW,
Report on South Africa
Sponsored by ALCOA,

1955

1975 Bernie Zlotnick
One Show Chairman

What is (as is said) "the state of our very special art form"? What can be found in a bad-economy year? Will we find new ideas or the same old-hat themes?

We found, and hope you concur, a surprisingly healthy total communications product. When we began we were not so sure.

We all knew what budget cutbacks had been made at all our places of work. Many people had been saying that creativity in advertising and design in the 70s had taken a downhill turn from which there was no road back. We had been hearing the prophets of doom citing the near-end of our business as we know it and for the work of art directors, designers, and copywriters. Everyone continues to look backwards with nostalgia to the creative revolution of the last decade where, it is true, our careers were made with a visibility and force entirely unknown to us working stiffs—when our industry came "of age."

Yet, the 1975 One Show seems to prove communications can not only survive but thrive, that big ideas can be created on smaller budgets. In spite of the doom-and-gloom-sayers, in a challenge to the sinking economy, it was a better year than others of the 70s. We had been looking for some bright new lights on the creative scene and we found some. While there were fewer run-away stand-out gold and silver medal winners in the overall view of the judges, they picked some fine winners and multitudinous good works in many groups. In sum, the Show is a going endeavor. And so is our work.

But the One Show 1975 represents an entity which is changing as it is growing, and some background can guide us at this point.

The Art Directors Club has been giving out awards to art directors for Advertising, Editorial, and Design for over 50 years. The Copy Club has been giving out awards to Copywriters for over 10 years. Three years ago they got together and created The One Show. The Advertising portion of The Show is jointly sponsored by the two major creative organizations as it is a natural evolution of the team relationship inherent in doing ads. The Editorial and Graphic Design portion is solely sponsored by the ADC.

Some important innovations were introduced into the 1975 Show. First, it was 'split' into two-Shows-in-one to give equal emphasis to the two major disciplines. Groups of jurors judged special areas — spending an average of 15 hours over several weeks. For the first time, International work was put into a separate category and a special jury invited to view that work. (Americans must see how much advertising and design of great worth is being done outside their country.) Following tradition, the juries were made up of the finest people our field has to offer, presidents of ad agencies, leading art directors, creative directors, artists, photographers, designers, editors. The jurors selected the finalists from the over 11,000 entries as well as the gold and silver medals.

The philosophies of the two co-chairmen of the different sections and their juries were similar but different in several ways. They ended up with a total show of over 1,100 works. About half is Advertising, half Editorial and Design. Work is not only New York-based but represents shops from around the country (and the world) and reveals a dissemination of creativity which soon will be global. Yet, Advertising judges selected many more medals. Twenty-seven golds and 32 silvers were awarded in Advertising, whereas 10 golds and 20 silvers were given in Editorial and Design.

The One Show is community-industry effort, a huge undertaking involving the time and talents of perhaps 300 individuals and firms. The Show seeks out new firms and artists to compete in an effort continually to discover, document, and communicate the best work done. It is a record of our progress as artists and craftsmen for study by professionals and students.

As the visuals, language, and themes we use in this work reflect our very life style, The One Show provides yet a bonus: we get a cultural set of images of 1975, a sociological and psychological panorama of our times. It is one of the best honest reflections we have of how we are, what we wear, how we think, what movies we like, how we bring up our children, where we work, and everything else which encompasses us.

Should the archeologist of 2075 unearth these works — TV commercials, posters, packages, photographs, books—he will see life as it was a century ago. And we think he will see some very fine 'art.'

Faith Popcorn
Co-Chairman, Advertising

Seymour Chwast
Co-Chairman, Editorial & Graphic Design

The Judging

As the pictures reveal, judging was intense during the many sessions held at the ADC for print categories—and at ad agencies and other facilities for broadcast.

PRINT ADVERTISING
JURORS:
Arnie Arlow
Allan Beaver
Alvin Chereskin
Dave Deutsch
Neil Drossman
Gene Federico
Peter Hirsch
Harry Jacobs
Kay Kavanagh
Stan Kovics
Larry Plapler
Marty Puris
Marty Solow
Bill Taubin
Bob Wilvers
CHAIRMEN:
Ed Butler
Irwin Goldberg

ADVERTISING & EDITORIAL, PHOTOGRAPHY & ART
JURORS:
Tom Carnase
Roy Carruthers
Alan E. Cober
Marie Cosindas
Helen Federico
Bob Freson
Gerry Gersten
Harold Krieger
Eugenia Louis
Jay Maisel
Jean Mallet
Barbara Nessim
Ernie Scarfone
Jerry Snyder
Kurt Weihs
Charles White III
CHAIRMEN:
Donald Adamec
Donald Duffy

RADIO COMMERCIALS
JURORS:
June Cerf
Jackie End
Steve Fenton
Steve Frey
Jack Jones
Toni Nathan
Geraldine Newman
Bretelle Selig
CHAIRMEN:
Kyle Dennis
Steve Lance

TV COMMERCIALS & FILMS

JURORS:
Barry Biederman
Jackie Brandwynne
Dick Calderhead
Jim Callaway
Neil Drossman
Pablo Ferro
Carol Ann Fine
Steve Frankfurt
Barney Melsky
Marv Mitchneck
Joan Murray
Bernie Owett
Bob Petrocelli
Charlie Piccirillo
Shirley Polykoff
Irwin Rothman
Sam Scali
Len Sirowitz
Elmer Skahan
Stanley Tannenbaum
Janet Wolfe
Lois Wyse
Bill Wurtzel
Ken Yagoda
Tony Zamora

CHAIRMEN:
Anita Daniels
Phil Becker
Mel Freedman
Hazel Goldgell
Adam Hanft
Flora Hanft

INTERNATIONAL ADVERTISING & EDITORIAL

JURORS:
Peter Brattinga
Robert Burns
Nicolai Canetti
Raymond Gfeller
Jean Paul Goude
Pierre Grimblat
David Hillman
Norberto Leon
George Nakano
David Pocknell
Klaus Schmidt
Jan Soderstrom
Paul Stephens

CHAIRMAN:
Ronné Bonder

EDITORIAL

JURORS:
Cipe Pineles
Bill Cadge
John Mack Carter
Verdun Cook
Michael Gross
Alvin Grossman
Will Hopkins
Herb Lubalin
Myles Ludwig
David Schneiderman

CHAIRMAN:
Roger Ferriter

GRAPHIC DESIGN

JURORS:
Ted Andresakes
John Berg
Ed Benguiat
Ivan Chermayeff
Dave Epstein
Helmut Krone
Jim Miho
Marty Moskof
Tony Palladino
Mort Rubenstein
Leslie Segal
Bradbury Thompson
George Tscherny

CHAIRMAN:
Alan Peckolick

Advertising Awards Night

The disciplines of Advertising and Design each had a night on the town for their aspects of The One Show. The celebration of the Gold and Silver Advertising honors took place during a dinner-and-show at New York's Waldorf-Astoria.

Industry spokespeople, winners of previous shows, talents who are the voices and faces of commercials participated in the event. Jerry Della Femina, Sam Scali, and Carl Ally did the print and television honors. Peter Max awarded advertising art. William 'B' Williams presented radio. Walter Wood, New York City's own Director for TV and Films, was a special presenter for public service. And, there were others. David Altschiller, Copy Club president, and Lou Dorfsman, out-going ADC president, spoke on the strengths of the creative competition and of the advertising business in general.

Surprise moments of hilarity were in store for the audience of 700 in viewing a specially-created film which had comedian Don Rickles poking good natured fun at the advertising professionals.

The audience stayed and danced until midnight.

Producer/Director: Wayne Lachman
Writer: Bernie Zlotnick
Composer/Conductor: Michael Gibson, Archangel Music
Audio-Visual Presentation: Jack Morton Productions
Film: Murray Bruce, Ed Kleban, Ampersand Productions
Slides/Graphics: Hans Weiss, Glen Samuels, Hans Assoc.
Film Editors: DJM Films, Ani-Live Films
Animation Designer: Wayne Lachman
Art Directors: Gerry Severson, Vince Marripodi
Animation Production: Colin Giles, Cel-Art Productions
Sound: The Mix Place
Radio Editor: Jennifer Gallagher

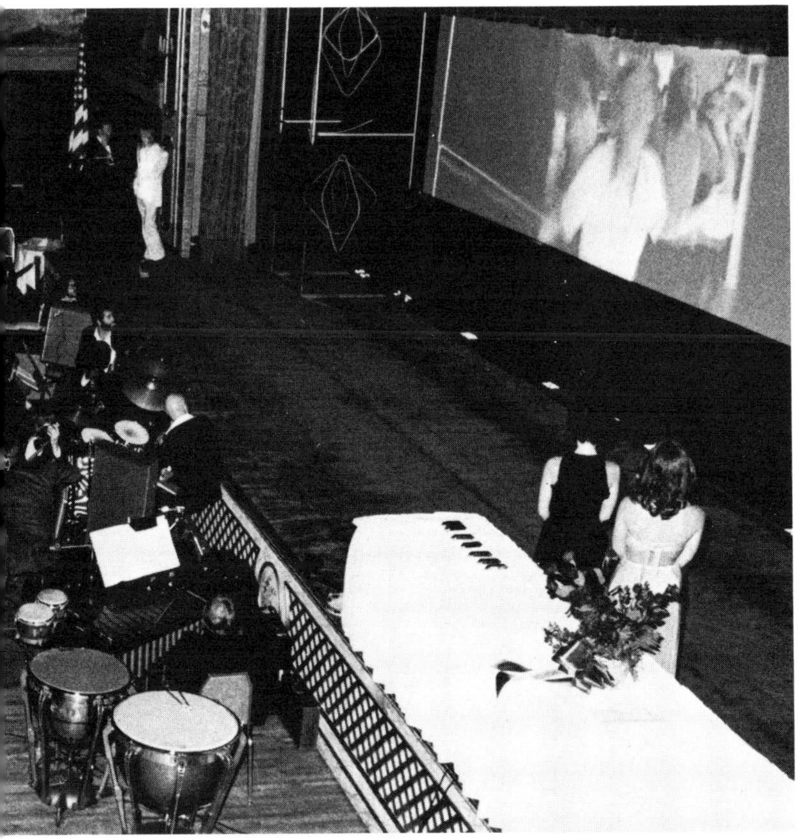

THE ONE SHOW

Editorial Awards Night

The Editorial and Graphic Awards at The Little Hippodrome, a New York discotheque, was an intimate and informal presentation. Art directors, photographers, and artists in all the specialties and print media were honored in The One Show's first such event. It was a time for socializing with old friends and peers, and more people came than anticipated.

Lou Dorfsman and Bernie Zlotnick led off the show and then turned the podium over to Jerome Snyder who was a masterful Master of Ceremonies for the program. Gold and Silver awards were presented in all the categories where the judges had awarded high scores and nominees for medals also were shown. The night provided another first—designers along with art directors received medals.

Again, some stayed to dance until midnight.

Audio Visual: Harry Joseph
Music: Anne Phillips, Bob Drake
Tickets: Glenda Spencer, Barbara Egan, Jackie Weir
Typographers/Printers: Tri Arts, Advertising Mailing Service

ONE SHOW:
Helpers: Teri Kerner, Paula Freedman, Students High School of Art and Design, Sara Behr, Ann Paley, Candy Greathouse, Chuck Cassidy, Norman Colp, Fred Marshall, Dozie Donalson, Ronné Bonder staff, Herbert M Rosenthal, Push Pin staff
One Show/ADC Directors and Staff: Jody Uttal, Jo Yanow, Jennifer Gallagher, Ruth Reis, Margarate McCarthy
Suppliers, Services, Facilities: Collier Photo Engraving, Pioneer-Moss, J. Walter Thompson, CBS, Carl Ally, Young & Rubicam, Smith, Greenland, Ross & Pento
Photographers: Harold Zipkowitz, Tom Yahashi
Mailing: Advertisers Mailing Service
Mechanicals: Chuck Cassidy
TV: Robert Smith

THE ONE SHOW

Exhibition

The One Show was seen by hundreds of New Yorkers and the industry during July in Union Carbide Building's second floor gallery facing Park Avenue.

David November took on the prodigious job of designing 'the world's largest show' of its kind. His display extended from one end of the spacious hall to the other (a city block). Bold mounted art work could be viewed from vantage points on the side streets. Banners in the huge windows heralded the Show for passersby. All manner of media—ads, posters, magazine designs—hung on panels with plenty of aisle room for browsing. There was a 'reading area' for books, a radio booth, a slide show of graphics. Designer November created a TV viewing space near one of the entrances: any noontime found people lined up to view their favorite commercials (for the hardy, there were three hours' worth without program interruptions!).

Leaving no area without the art director's touch, the lobbies downstairs carried this tease: "These are the silver award winners . . . go upstairs to see the gold!"

It was a media feast of sorts. Once again, the public nature of the exhibition enhances understanding about our work and is an education and entertainment for the uninitiated. For the rest of us, it was a once-a-year opportunity to review, analyze, criticize, and refresh ourselves on the judges' selections.

These are silver award winners.

Ads
Magazine Advertising

Show

Exhibition Designer: David November
Lobby Display Designer: Frank Skorski
Art Directors and Associates: Amelia Battaglio, Donald Lawson, Christopher Saxe, Aki Seki, Daphne Shuttleworth, Bill Snyder, Sally Miller Tomlinson, Grace Uhlig, Ana Lemos, Kathy Palladino, Wendy Byrne, Jonette Jacobson
One Show Staff Coordinators: Jody Utall, Wendy Addis, Fern Ramos, Jo Yanow
Post Production Facilities: Leslie Nathan, National Video Center
Video Equipment: Sony Corp.
Video Credits: Photography Dept., C.B.S. TV
Film Editors: Jack Anson Finke, Robert Smith
Radio Editor: Neil Dorfsman, Judrac
Photo Enlargements: Frankie Dee, Apco-Apedo
Printer: Hink House
Typographer: Latent Lettering
Assembly Facilities: Pioneer-Moss
Union Carbide Exhibits: Frank Scott, John Galvin

VOLVO
Come upstairs and see the gold.

The

The
Design

Luncheon Activities

This year's Wednesday lunch programs enjoyed growing interest from an ever greater variety of members, and a 50 percent increase in attendance.

With our own, and so many other art directors' love for films in mind, we introduced a film program, with selected rare and special shorts, classic TV commercials, and talks about the many film-related areas from movie advertising to computer animation.

There was a series of panel discussions on current subjects of concern in our work, such as political advertising and ethics in buying and selling art services.

And we had great fun with New York superlatives: the most beautiful model, superfood, the smoothest wine, the hairiest hair, and the dirtiest magazine.

FILM:
Seven young New York animators, Frank Mouris with his Oscar-winning 'Frank Film,' Richard Avedon, Charles Eames, Saul Bass, R.O. Blechman, the Club's TV commercials from "The Best of a Decade," 1960-1970.

DISCUSSIONS:
Harry Belafonte, Arthur Schlesinger, Fred Papert and Herb Lubalin on "Political Advertising", Ed Benguiat, George Abrams, John Schaedler on "The Letterer, today." Dick Hess, Joe Cahil, Shelly Coppel, Eunice Greenblatt on "Ethics."

FUN:
Jerome Snyder, Jean Paul Picot, Bert Greene, Al Goldstein, Paul McGregor, and Roy Carruthers.

Our thanks go to the speakers and moviemakers who helped us to create and maintain this active forum at the Club.

Constance Von Collande
Herbert M Rosenthal

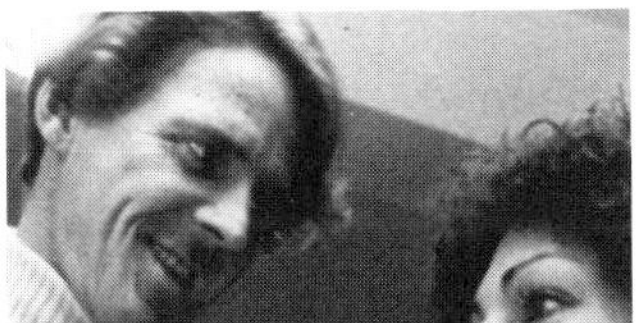

In-House Exhibits

This year the ADC Gallery worked as a *gallery*. In a very small space we have managed to present a wide range of things. The best way to illustrate this is to catalogue what was presented.

The "season" opened with a show of the Best Posters of 1974. This was done in conjunction with *Print* magazine which conducted the judging and published the results to coordinate with the opening of the show.

This was followed by an exhibit of Public Service Advertising by the students at the School of Visual Arts. All the work in the show, plus all installation of the show was handled by students from SVA.

The third show of the year proved to be the highlight. "Calligraphy and Lettering" opened to a turn-away crowd and succeeded in arousing interest for the duration of its run. In addition to people visiting the gallery, the show received publicity and coverage from *Print*, *Idea*, and *U&lc*. This publicity resulted in over 40 requests from schools and museums to have the show for themselves.

The final show of the year was the paintings of three ADC members, Ladislav Sutner, Adolph Treidler, and Ambrose Kennedy. This show brought together nostalgia and craft, and enlightened new members as to the superb work that has been done over the past fifty years.

By any gauge, the ADC Gallery had become established.

Committee
Len Fury, Harvey Gabor, Bob Ciano, Kit Hinrichs, Carveth Kramer, Bill Moore

Charley's

3
CADGE
3

Photos: Tom Yahashi

On The Road, Around The World

Brazil

W. Germany

Brazil

THE ONE SHOW 1974

Switzerland

The One Show

W. Germany

The ADC's Annual Shows have been seen by people of all cultures and persuasions for over a decade through tours arranged by the U.S.I.A. (United States Information Agency). We're told they have been 'good will' ambassadors for U.S. art-and-commerce—from Surinam to Seoul.

The last two One Shows went also to the Houston Museum of Contemporary Arts, Texas; Contemporary Arts Museum, São Paulo, Brazil; and Musée Des Arts Décoratifs, Lausanne, Switzerland. Best-of-Show commercials usually get separate viewings in these cities—by ad agencies, groups, and schools. The reel accompanied Lou Dorfsman as Mainichi Broadcasting's guest to Japan and member Shinichiro Tora organized exhibits of portions of the last Annual to three Japanese cities. Member Olaf Leu, with Klaus Schmidt of the United States, produced an extensive European tour to Munich, Duesseldorf, Frankfurt, Hamburg, and Amsterdam. Nearer to home base, faculty and students saw an exhibit arranged by Dorothy Hayes at New York City Community College.

Committee Reports 1974-75

ADVISORY BOARD

The Advisory Board is made up of past presidents of the Club. Their ideas don't necessarily coincide but their experience generally does. It was the need to utilize this experience which prompted the formation of this group many years ago. The Club gains the excitement and fresh ideas of new administrations which can be tempered with the battle-scarred experience of past presidents.

With the adoption of a new constitution a few years ago the Advisory Board became more visible and accessible. As a non-voting member of the Executive Board I participated in most of its meetings. There were times when the special experience of another member of the Advisory Board was required. And still other times I brought a particular subject to the entire Advisory Board for their guidance.

It is to the credit of this year's administration that our advice was actively sought and considered. The Club's activities have grown considerably in the last few years. Along with this growth comes an increase in problems. Every bit of experience and knowledge was sought in seeking the proper solutions.

The Advisory Board was conceived to utilize the experience of the Club's past presidents. In this past year it was called upon often . . . and it responded enthusiastically!

Bill Brockmeier
Chairman

MEMBERSHIP

Why should I join the Club? What do I get? What does the ADC do for its members and how can it be more of a 'members-first' organization?

These are questions which have arisen periodically but with greater insistency as our industry gets more sophisticated.

The Membership Committee tackled the basic consideration. Finding the answer was a reaffirmation for many of us. First of all, through the hard work of the president, Board, and our committee, we report that we added a group of new members from all the endeavors and they represent in total a formidable body of talent. (They are art directors from record companies, magazines and periodicals, film houses, and agencies; they are photographers and teachers, too.)

With applications coming in at a steady pace and fewer losses in membership due to attrition and "dropping out" we're in good shape. But late payment on dues is still problematic.

We have adopted a strong concern that the member comes first. A super get-acquainted lunch was held at the Club for new members as our guests, with president, Board, sponsors, proposers, and 130 members showed for the largest freebie ever.

Every member received an A.D. cube with a new corporate package consisting of letters from the president and all committees, information sheets on activites, a new certificate and card.

Last year we lowered our initiation fee to $50.00 for regular memberships and this year raised our membership dues to meet the cost of living to $130.00. We have opened our doors to new Corporate, Institutional/Educational, and Professional memberships and are happy to have aboard: New York Community College, Parsons School of Design, Mead Paper, Typographic Innovations, Union Camp, and Watson-Guptill Publications.

This all could not have been possible without the volunteering work and precious time of the people on the committee who wrote letters, made telephone calls, and did 100 other things. They instill the "I care attitude" which as become once again an important pillar of the Club: Donald Duffy, Nancy Greenberg, Dick MacFarlane, Mort Rubenstein, Ray Robertson, Meg Crane, Bob Greenwell, Bob Petrocelli, Pasquale Del Vecchio, Ray Podeszwa, Shinichiro Tora.

I hope that the future committees will have as much fun and involvement and goals to reach as we have had.

Donald Adamec
Chairman

EDUCATION

This year saw the tentative beginning of our Adoption Program. This could be one of the most meaningful and far-reaching projects ever initiated for students. Its ultimate success will depend on the willingness of more members to become involved, and the schools to live up to their first enthusiastic responses.

Entree into the professional milieu of a member is a unique experience for these chosen students, enriching and broadening the context of their study programs. They start to understand the realities of the business, pick up confidence, awareness, and the nuances that are just not available outside this experiment.

Our Evening Encounters this year under the imaginative direction of Anny Queyroy were even more widely attended.

Students need our input and encouragement, perhaps even more today than in previous years. Many members who see a lot of student portfolios have expressed strong feelings about their levels of preparedness. I would suggest that they now have an avenue to make their opinions count before the fact, rather than after.

Thanks again to committee members Alan Peckolick, David Pachman, John Okladek, Bob Farber, et al, for their ideas and efforts.

Stan Bloom
Chairman

At Christmas, the ADC ran a party for children of members with donations to go to UNICEF. *Photo: Jerome Gallagher*

SCHOLARSHIP

The Art Directors Club has earmarked $1,000 to go to two free-tuition art schools this year—Cooper Union and New York City Community College. Monies may go for the purchase of art materials which is very costly for students in these inflation times, or for dispersement at the discretion of the school. Board liaisons are Walter Kaprelian and Bob Bach.

HALL OF FAME

The Hall of Fame activity had George Krikorian at its helm. The membership again elected a distinguished Nominating Committee to analyze the traditions and high points in the development of graphic arts and select its outstanding members for special homage.

These individuals from the ADC were named to the Committee: Herb Lubalin, Eileen Hedy Schultz, George Lois, Jack Jamison, Arthur Hawkins, Bert Littman, Roy Tillotson, William Taubin, Aaron Burns, Gene Federico, George Giusti. Henry Wolf, 1974 Chairman, Lou Dorfsman, William Brockmeier, Paul Rand, and Robert Gage rounded out the group.

The Famers (whose stories lead off this section) were honored in a special event highlighting the fall-winter season.

LOU DORFSMAN 1974-1975

Between the covers of this weighty volume are 1,100 examples of the best in this business.

A parting message from a departing ex-president doesn't stand a chance surrounded by this rich lode of talent. So it is with a deep sense of security that I luxuriate in the following 'stream of consciousness' knowing full well that the 'noted' and 'read' scores should set an all time low.

On the whole the presidency of this Club added up to a year of frustration, hard work, wonder, joy and, mostly, a sense of renewal for me. Working with a first rate Executive Committee, members of the Advisory Board and the Club's full time administration in such close proximity turned into a privilege. (Much thanks to them for their perseverance, loyalty, and wisdom.)

The office of president provided, among many things, an opportunity for expanding one's point of view in areas I'm not in contact with otherwise — i.e. the social, political, and economic spheres of a non-profit organization. (Non-profit seems to be an inexact term.) Nothing seems to work in this society if it doesn't generate the financing to feed the machine. Under no condition does the landlord ever say "forget it!." Con Edison will turn off your power but never its pressure for payment of bills. The staff salaries are upon you with great regularity, pencils, paperclips, phones, petty cash, stamps!

And so it gets difficult to keep one's eye on those marvelous buzz words we dig so much: creativity, aesthetics, taste, style, concepts, etc. when the bills are piling up. My tenure provided a fair lesson in the economics of 'small business' in the world of reality. It turns out once again that you cannot do 'good' if you are not doing 'well.'

A pleasant money incident. When our financial plight was put before the Club membership with a request for a dues increase, members were sympathetic and realistic and voted overwhelmingly in favor of the increase.

I found special gratification in talking to and being talked back to by the members via those monthly president's Letters. The letters were an experiment in a determined effort to be totally candid with the membership on all aspects of the Club's activities. A policy of 'no information to be withheld' was instituted. The response proved the validity of an open system. I'm certain that it will continue.

A subject that will not easily be forgotten. The sickening incident of the bombing of the Glenda Spencer home in Queens. My pleas to the Club to help financially (for the restoration of the Spencer home) resulted in a generous outpouring of donations by members. Much thanks again. (The Spencers not only suffered the emotional and psychological effects of the dastardly act — but the humiliation of picking up the tab for the damage as well!)

A much happier event. Another first for the NYADC, an event that should add at least a glorious footnote (if not a chapter to the history of this Club). A woman has been elected president and not because she's a woman. Eileen Hedy Schultz will make a great president. She's a competent, hard working, knowledgeable person who is a terrific administrator and executive. She'll be backed up by an experienced Executive Board and I'll continue as liaison representing the Advisory Board. (This is a new system that should help to make for a smooth transition.)

In sum, my opportunity to participate in the workings of the Club and its activities at such close quarters brought into sharp focus what I'd suspected all along. This is an organization generally composed of creative, thoughtful, forward-looking men and women. A unique amalgam of talents, perhaps more unusual than any organization I can think of. And in its way more influential than most. We address millions of people through our work (in 30-second bursts on television) — many more millions in newspapers and magazines and we do it every day, many times a day, seven days a week — year after year. That's a lot of exposure and influence (and let's not forget that it carries with it a burden of great responsibility).

The wonderment that resides between the covers of this volume is an impressive testimonial to the talents, imagination, inventiveness, energy, and craft of the people in this business. 1,100 pieces representing the best of continuing rising standards in advertising copy and design, it's the biggest show ever. In this case big is beautiful.

EILEEN HEDY SCHULTZ 1975-1976

Jefferson wrote that "we must unite in common efforts for our common good" and that, in essence, is what we must do to maintain a healthy Club.

The Art Directors Club of New York is an organization dedicated to the furtherance of improving Industry standards and the extending of our aid in the education of young people entering our field. And not to be forgotten is the opportunity to meet, influence, and be influenced by the successful, experienced professionals in this field. It assures a continuous flow and exchange of ideas which is a healthy atmosphere for each and every member.

Our Industry is only as strong as we the communicators make it. And now, more than ever before, there's so much that we can do to make it stronger — not in our microcosm world of New York — but internationally. A network of communication among *all* communicators; a mutual admiration for the pioneers and leaders in our field which we recognize as world-wide; and a continuance of this exchange of talent and ideas that will insure a united and unbreakable bond within our profession long after we're gone. These are goals which we must work hard to achieve.

None of us is too sophisticated or too self-important that we can't learn from one another. None of us is too big to help those who are on their way up who would welcome a word of advice, an imparting of knowledge. No one is too small to offer wisdom of his own. We learn from each other and that's what gives us strength and unity.

I've never understood why there is dissension among us within our profession, or among factions within these areas. Disagreement is healthy. Dissension is destructive. Creativity is not limited to any one area. After all, we are all communicators.

In whatever area we're in, we should strive to be unified as never before: working together for the betterment of our profession and enjoying whenever possible the comaraderie of our fellow communicators — working together to insure the ideals of our profession and avoiding such factors as stagnation and the adherence to pre-conceived notions.

There's no way we can go forward except together, and no way anyone can win except by serving the urgent needs of our profession. In the months ahead, we look forward to continued growth, dedicated work in meaningful projects, better positioning of Art Directors on the decision-making level, and a unified membership to help achieve these goals.

1974-75 Board of Directors

President	Lou Dorfsman
1st Vice President	Herb Lubalin
2nd Vice President	Eileen Hedy Schultz
Treasurer	Marilyn Hoffner
Vice Treasurer	Gene Milbauer
Secretary	David Deutsch
Executive Committee	Gennaro Andreozzi
Executive Committee	Bob Bach
Executive Committee	Bruno Brugnatelli
Executive Committee	Walter Kaprelian
Executive Committee	George Lois
Executive Committee	Henry Wolf

1975-76 Board of Directors

President	Eileen Hedy Schultz
1st Vice President	Dave Davidian
2nd Vice President	Bill Taubin
Treasurer	Bob Greenwell
Vice Treasurer	Gene Milbauer
Secretary	George Krikorian
Executive Committee	Bob Bach
Executive Committee	Bruno Brugnatelli
Executive Committee	Tony Cappiello
Executive Committee	Walter Kaprelian
Executive Committee	Herb Lubalin
Executive Committee	Dick Ross

ADC MEMBERS

A

Aronson, Herman
Adamec, Donald
Adams, Gaylord
Adams, George C.
Addiss, Patricia
Adler, Jane
Adler, Peter
Adorney, Charles S.
Agha, M. F.
Aldoretta, Warren P.
Allen, Lorraine
Allner, Walter H.
Ammirati, Carlo
Andreozzi, Gennaro R
Andresakes, Ted
Ansel, Ruth
Anthony, Al
Anthony, Robert
Arlow, Arnold
Asano, Tadashi
Aymar, Gordon C.

B

Bach, Robert O.
Baer, Priscilla
Bailey, Li
Baker, Frank
Barbini, Edward
Barile, Carl
Barr, Carla
Barron, Don
Bartel, Clyde W.
Barton, Gladys
Basile, Matthew
Bastian, Rufus A.
Beaver, Allan
Beckerman, Jay
Bee, Noah
Belliveau, Peter
Bennett, Edward J.
Benson, Laurence Key
Berenter, William
Berg, John
Berkowitz, Seymour
Berliner, Saul
Bernstein, Ted
Berry, Park
Biondi, Aldo
Birbrower, Stewart
Blank, Peter
Blattner, Robert H.
Blend, Robert
Block, David S.
Blod, Francis
Blomquist, Arthur T.
Bloom Stan
Bode, Robert W.
Bonder, Ronné
Boothroyd, John Milne
Boroff, Sanford
Bossert, William T.
Bostrum, Thor F.
Boudreau, James
Bourges, Jean
Bowman, Harold A.
Boyd, Douglas
Braguin, Simeon
Brandt, Joan
Bratteson, Alfred
Brattinga, Pieter
Brauer, Fred J.
Braverman, Al
Brockmeier, William P.
Brody, Marc
Brody, Ruth
Brooke, John
Brugnatelli, Bruno E.
Brussel-Smith, Bernard
Brzoza, Walter C.
Bua, Charles
Buckley, William H.
Bunzak, William
Burns, Aaron
Burns, Herman F.
Burtin, Cipe Pineles

C

Cadge, William
Campanelli, Rocco E.
Campbell, Stuart
Canetti, Nicolai
Cappiello, Tony
Carlu, Jean
Carnase, Thomas
Cerullo, C. Edward
Cherry, John V.
Chiesa, Alfred F.
Chin, Kay
Church, Stanley
Chwast, Paula Scher
Chwast, Seymour
Ciano, Robert
Civale, Frank, Sr.
Clark, Herbert
Clarke, George P.
Clemente, Thomas F.
Cline, Mahlon A.
Clive, Robert
Closi, Victor
Coiner, Charles T.
Collins, Benjamin
Confalonieri, Giulio
Conley, John
Cook, John
Cook, Verdun P.
Costa, Ernest
Cotler, Sheldon
Cottingham, Edward M.
Counihan, Thomas J.
Craddock, Thomas J.
Craig, James Edward
Crane, Meg
Cranner, Brian
Crozier, John Robert
Cummings, Richard
Cummins, Jerry
Cupani, Joseph
Cutler, Charles

D

Dadmun, Royal
Dane, Norman R.
DaRold, Thierry L. H.
David, Stephanie
Davidian, David
Davis, Herman A.
Davis, Philip
deCesare, John
Dederick, Jay G., Jr.
Defrin, Bob
Del Sorbo, Joseph R.
Del Vecchio, Pat
Demner, Marius
Demoney, Jerry C.
Deppe, Florian R.
Deutsch, David S.
Diehl, Edward P.
Dignam, John F.
Dixon, Kenwood
Dolobowsky, Robert
Donald, Peter
Donatiello, Michael
Dorfsman, Louis
Dorian, Marc
Doyle, J. Wesley
Dubin, Morton
Duffy, Donald H.
Duffy, William R.
Dusek, Rudolph
Dymond, Joanna

E

Eckstein, Bernard
Edgar, Peter
Eidel, Zeneth
Eisenman, Stanley
Elton, Wallace
Emery, Rod A.
Engler, Elliot
Enock, David
Epstein, David
Epstein, Henry
Epstein, Lee
Erikson, Rolf
Ermoyan, Suren
Essman, Robert N.

F

Farber, Bob
Farrell, Abe
Federico, Gene
Feitler, Bea
Fenga, Michael
Fenton, Timothy
Fernandez, George R.
Fertik, Samuel A.
Finegold, Rupert J.
Finn, William
Fiorenza, Blanche
Firpo, Gonzalo
Fischer, Carl
Fitzgerald, John E.
Flack, Richard
Flock, Donald
Flynn, J. Walter
Foster, Robert
Fraioli, Jon M.
Francis, Robert D.
Frankel, Ted
Frankfurt, Stephen O.
Franznick, Philip E.
Freedman, Mel
Freyer, Fred
Friedman, Martin
Frost, Oren S.
Fujii, Satoru
Fujita, S. Neil
Fury, Leonard W.

G

Gabor, Harvey
Gage, Robert
Garlanda, Gene
Gatti, David
Gauss, Joseph T.
Gavasci, Alberto P.
Geoghegan, Walter B.
Georgi, Carl H.
Gering, Joseph
Germakian, Michael
Giammalvo, Nick
Gibbs, Edward
Gillis, Richard B.
Giusti, George
Glaser, Milton
Glessmann, Louis R.
Gluckman, Eric
Goff, Seymour R.
Gold, William
Goldberg, Irwin
Goldgell, Hazel
Goldman, Edward
Goldowsky, Eli
Golub, William
Grace, Roy
Graham, John

ADC MEMBERS

Green, Arnie
Greenberg, Albert
Greenberg, Nancy
Greene, Bert
Greenwell, Robert
Greller, Fred
Griffin, John J.
Griner, Norman
Grotz, Walter
Gruppo, Nelson
Guild, Lurelle, V.A.
Guild, S. Rollins

H

Hack, Robert H.
Haiman, Kurt
Halpern, George
Halvorsen, Everett
Handelman, Michael
Hanson, Thurland
Harris, Kenneth D.
Hartelius, Paul V., Jr.
Hautau, Janet
Havemeyer, Mitch
Hawkins, Arthur
Hayes, Dorothy
Heff, Saul
Heiffel, Eugene
Helleu, Jacques
Hemmick, Bud
Herman, Harvey
Heyman, Wesley F.
Hipwell, Grant I.
Hirsch, Peter M.
Hoashi, Jitsuo
Hodes, Ronald
Hoffman, Wallace R.
Hoffner, Marilyn
Holeywell, Arnold C.
Holtane, George
Hopkins, William P.
Horn, Steve
Hovanec, Joe
Howard, Hoyt
Howard, Mark
Hurd, Jud
Hungerford, Robert
Hurlburt, Allen F.
Hyatt, Morton

I

Iger, Martin
Irwin, William A.

J

Jaccoma, Edward G.
Jacobs, Harry M.
Jaggi, Mortiz S.
Jamison, John
Johnson, D. Carzell
Jones, Bob
Joslyn, Roger
Jossel, Leonard
Julia, Christian

K

Kambanis, Aristedes S.
Kambourian, Ron
Kanai, Kiyoshi
Kaprielian, Walter
Karsakov, Leonard
Katzen, Rachel
Kaufmann, M. R.
Keegan, Marcia
Keil, Tom S.
Kelley, Kenneth Roy
Kent, Nancy V.
Kenzer, Myron W.
Kittel, Frederick H.
Kleckner, Valerie
Klein, Gerald
Kner, Andrew
Knoepfler, Henry O.
Komai, Ray
Koos, John
Kosarin, Norman
Krauss, Oscar
Krikorian, George
Kurnit, Shep

L

LaGrone, Roy E.
Laird, James E.
Lamarque, Abril
Lambray, Maureen
Lampert, Harry
Larkin, John J.
LaMicela, Sebastian N.
LaRotonda, Anthony
Lavey, Kenneth H.
Lazzarotti, Sal
Leeds, Don
Leon, Norberto
Leonard, Jack
Leslie, Dr. Robert
Leu, Olaf
Levine, David T.
Levine, Irving
Levine, Richard
Levinson, Julian P.
Levy, Dean David
Leydenfrost, Robert
Liberman, Alexander
Light, Eugene
Lipton, Shelli
LiPuma, Sal
Littmann, Bert W.
Lockwood, Richard
Lois, George
Longo, Vincent R.
Longyear, William L.
Lotito, Rocco
Louise, John
Lowry, Alfred
Lubalin, Herbert
Ludekens, Fred
Luden, Richard B.
Luria, Richard
Lurin, Larry
Lyon, Robert W., Jr.

M

MacDonald, John
MacFarlane, Richard
MacInnes, David H.
Macri, Frank
Madia, Anthony
Madris, Ira B.
Magdoff, Samuel
Magnani, Louis A.
Malone, Martin J.
Mancino, Anthony
Manzo, Richard
Marinelli, Jack
Marshall, Al F.
Martin, Raymond M.
Martinott, Robert T.
Massey, John
Matyas, Theodore S.
Maximov, George
Mayhew, Marce
Mazzella, Dennis
McCaffery, William A.
McCallum, Robert
McCauley, Rita
McCoy, Kevin G.
McFadden, Keith
McGinnis, George
McOstrich, Priscilla
Medler, James V.
Menell, Don
Merlicek, Franz
Mesnick, Eve
Messina, Joseph
Messina, Vincent N.
Metzdorf, Lyle
Milbauer, Eugene
Miller, Larry
Minko, William
Mohtares, Alexander
Moore, William
Morang, Kenneth E.
Morgan, Burton A.
Morgan, Wendy Jo
Moriber, Jeffrey M.
Morrison, William R.
Morton, Thomas Throck
Moss, Tobias
Moy, George
Murray, John R., Jr.
Mutter, Ralph

N

Nappi, Nick
Newman, Charles A.
Nichols, Mary Ann
Nissen, Joseph
Nissenbaum, Judith
Noda, Ko
November, David
Nussbaum, Edward

O

O'Dell, Robert
Odette, Jack
O'Hehir, Joseph
Okladek, John
Olden, Georg
Olivo, Gary
Orr, Garrett P.
Osborn, Irene Charles
Otter, Robert David
Ottino, Larry
Owett, Bernard S.

P

Paccione, Onofrio
Pachman, David
Palladino, Tony
Parker, Paul E., Jr.
Paslavsky, Ivan
Pastorini, Frank
Peckolick, Alan
Peltola, John J.
Pento, Paul
Perel, Jules
Peter, John
Petrocelli, Robert H.
Peyton, Phillip
Pfeffer, Elmer
Phelps, Stewart J.
Philiba, Allan
Philips, Gerald M.
Philpotts, Randy
Pioppo, Ernest
Piotrowsky, Eugene
Pittmann, Stuart
Platt, Melvin
Pliskin, Robert

ADC MEMBERS

Podeszwa, Raymond
Pompiean, Thomas
Ponzian, Joel
Popcorn, Faith
Portuesi, Louis
Posnick, Paul
Post, Anthony
Pride, Benjamin
Propper, Robert
Prusmack, A. John
Pulise, Santo

Q

Queyroy, Anny

R

Rada, George A.
Radtke, Gary
Rafalaf, Jeffrey S.
Raffel, Samuel
Rand, Paul
Read, C. Richard
Redler, Harry
Reed, Robert C.
Reed, Samuel
Reed, Sheldon
Reeves, Patrick A.
Reinke, Fred
Reinke, Herbert O.
Reisinger, Dan
Ricotta, Edwin C.
Ritter, Arthur
Rizzo, Dominic G.
Robbins, Morris
Roberts, Kenneth
Robertson, Raymond
Robinson, Clark L.
Rocker, Harry
Rockwell, Harlow
Rofheart, Edward
Romagna, Leonard A.
Rondell, Lester
Rosenblum, Morris L.
Rosenthal, Herbert
Rosner, Charles
Ross, Andrew
Ross, Dick
Ross, James Francis
Roston, Arnold
Rothman, Irwin
Rubenfeld, Lester
Rubenstein, Mort
Rubin, Randee
Russell, Henry N.
Russo, John
Rustom, Mel
Ruther, Donald
Ruzicka, Thomas

S

Sadiq, Ahmad
St. Louis, Leonard A.
Saks, Robert
Salpeter, Robert
Santandrea, James, Jr.
Sauer, Hans
Scali, Sam
Scarfone, Ernest G.
Scheck, Henry
Schenk, Roland
Schiller, Lawrence
Schleider, Irene
Schneider, Richard M.
Schneider, William H.
Schreiber, Martin
Schultz, Eileen Hedy
Segal, Leslie
Seide, Allan
Seide, Ray
Seidler, Sheldon
Sellers, John L.
Shakery, Neil
Shear, Alexander
Sheldon, William
Shipenberg, Myron
Shomer, Harvey
Shutak, Sandra
Siano, Jerry J.
Silverberg, Sanford
Silverstein, Louis
Simkin, Blanche
Simpson, Milton
Sirowitz, Leonard
Skolnik, Jack
Smith, Paul
Smith, Robert Sherrick
Smokler, Jerold
Snyder, Jerome
Sohmer, Steve
Solomon, Martin
Sosnow, Harold
Spelman III, Hoyt
Spiegel, Ben
Staperfeldt, Karsten
Stauf, Alexander
Stech, David H.
Stehling, Wendy
Steinbrenner, Karl H.
Stenzel, Alfred B.
Stern, Charles
Stevens, Martin
Stone, Bernard
Stone, Loren B.
Storch, Otto
Strosahl, William
Sturtevant, Ira
Suares, Jean-Claude
Sutnar, Ladislav
Sweret, Michael
Sykes, Philip

T

Tanaka, Soji
Tanassy, Tricia
Tarallo, Joseph
Tashian, Melcon
Taubin, William
Tesoro, Ciro
Thomas, Lamont
Thomas, Richard
Thompson, Bradbury
Thorner, Lynne
Tillotson, Roy W.
Tinker, John Hepburn
Todaro, John
Toledo, Harold
Tollin, Helaine Sharon
Tompkins, Gilbert
Tora, Shinichiro
Tortoriello, Don
Toth, Peter
Trasoff, Victor
Travisano, Ronald
Treidler, Adolph
Trumbauer, J. Robert
Tsao, Alex

U

Urbain, John A.
Urrutia, Frank

V

Velez, Miguel
Venti, Tony
Vitale, Frank A.
Von Collande, Constance

W

Wagener, Walter A.
Waivada, Ernest
Wall, Robert
Wallace, Joseph O.
Wallace, Robert G.
Wallis, Harold
Wassyng, Sy
Watt, James C.
Watts, Ron
Weber, Jessica Margot
Weihs, Kurt
Weinstein, Stephen
Weissberg, Robert
Weithas, Art
Wells, Sidney A.
Welti, Theo
Wheaton, Ned
Wheeler, Dennis
White, Peter A.
Wickham, Ronald V.
Wilbur, Gordon M.
Wilde, Richard
Wilkison, David E.
Wilvers, Robert
Winkler, Horst
Winnick, Karen B.
Witalis, Rupert
Wolf, Henry
Wollman, Michael
Wurtzel, William K.

Y

Yablonka, Hy
Yamamoto, Hidehito
Yonkovig, Zen
Yuranyi, Steve

Z

Zahor, Bruce
Zalon, Alfred
Zeidman, Robert
Zlotnick, Bernard

Corporate Members

Mead Paper
New York Community College
Parsons School of Design
Typographic Innovations
Union Camp
Watson-Guptill Publications

INDEX

Art Directors

Abel, Robert, 979
Adamec, Donald A., 982
Adler, Peter, 914
Alban, Ray, 404
Alderisio, Bill, 284
Amaral, Ken, 374
Ammirati, Ralph, 160
Ancona, Stephen, 743
Andelin, Gerald, 384
Anderson, Ron, 44, 252
Andreozzi, Gennaro, 80, 81, 113, 151
Angeli, Primo, 682, 966
Ansel, Ruth, 555, 565, 566, 579, 583, 621, 623,'994, 1054, 1062, 1064, 1066, 1068, 1072, 1074, 1128, 1130, 1132
Anselmo, John, 726, 735
Antupit, Samuel N., 637
Arisman, Marshall, 860A
Arlow, Arnie, 6, 42, 122
Armistead, John, 418
Aromando, Charley, 59, 133

Bailey, Ed, 816
Baker, Stan, 957
Balchunas, Tom, 148
Banke, Martin, 708
Banks, Robert, 1135
Barile, Carl, 591, 600, 1008, 1024
Barnes, Bill, 740
Barnett, Lester A., 1040
Baron, Harvey, 4, 8, 45
Basile, Matt, 387
Bass, Saul, 905, 983, 984
Baxter, Glenn, 746A
Beaver, Allan, 74, 120, 171, 195, 884
Behnken, Wolfgang, 1143
Beier, Annegret, 1177
Belliveau, Peter, 274
Bensusan, Al, 406
Berbrower, Stew, 455
Berg, John, 828, 833, 840, 844, 846, 847
Berliner, S. B., 700
Bernard, Walter, 596, 605, 607, 1073, 1094, 1107, 1112
Bernhardt, Craig, 809
Bernstein, Ted, 886
Berris, Ken, 13
Bianchi, Ed, 446
Binzer, Rollin, 1122
Bishop, Bonnie, 662
Black, James, 812
Block, Stan, 381, 496
Bloom, Merl, 464
Blum, Chris, 486, 487
Boege, Uli, 1126
Bonnell, Bill, III, 656, 680, 734, 882, 917, 922
Bossardt, Herb, 873
Boston, Archie, 1042
Boyarski, Daniel, 799
Bradford, Peter, 795
Braun, Craig, 874
Brooks, Joe, 963, 1075, 1079, 1082, 1091, 1110, 1182
Brown, Ray, 277
Brown, Richard, 197, 238, 239, 272
Broyles, Sybil, 1059
Burden, Thomas L., 961
Burns, Richard, 859
Burns, Robert, 1152, 1169, 1180
Burton, Jim, 104
Butera, Gene, 992, 1017
Byrne, Bob, 544, 547

Cadge, William, 554, 575, 576, 578, 585, 586, 592
Caggiano, John, 128, 430
Calderhead, Dick, 86, 159, 187
Caldwell, Bill, 874A, 875, 876
Campbell, Cathie, 131
Campanelli, Rocco, E., 102, 287
Capawana, Rod, 489
Cappadona, Joe, 211
Caravetta, Fred, 888
Carlisle, Gary, 27, 36
Carra, Vincent, 983, 984
Carruthers, Roy, 590, 1005
Carter, Barry, 911
Carvell, Lou, 77, 82
Cassidy, Joan, 1058
Cato, Bob, 175A
Cavanah, Earl, 46, 52
Cenatiempo, John, 163
Chalfin, Alan, 895
Chepelsky, John R., 967
Chermayeff, Ivan, 748, 784, 870, 871, 872, 879
Christy, Art, 293
Chwast, Seymour, 685, 849
Ciano, Bob, 1055, 1056
Ciccarone, Joe, 135
Clemente, Tom, 1123
Clark, Jim, 953
Clugston, Audrey, 440
Cohen, Harvey, 142
Cohen, Jeff, 60, 67, 103, 126
Cole, Rhea, G., 899
Collamer, Jerry, 236, 365, 425
Colletti, Louis, 28, 180, 408, 449A
Condak, Henrietta, 828
Conley, John J., 1045
Conlon, William J., 845
Cook, Verdun, 554, 578
Cooper, Heather, 1179
Cooperstein, Sam, 149
Corley, June, 246, 247, 248, 262
Coro, Ron, 830
Costello, Bo, 744
Cotler, Sheldon, 649, 666, 671, 672
Cotroulis, Peter, 928
Courtos, Tom, 704, 824
Craig, Jim, 667
Crethar, Lindsay, 518
Crolick, Sue, 34
Cross, James, 709, 732, 753, 755, 782, 803
Czernysz, Bob, 25, 26, 35, 170, 193
D'Amico, Dennis, 155, 288
Dankwardt, Ken, 701
Daigneault, Gilles, 1138, 1140, 1155
Daniel, Frank, 841
Danza, John, 41, 376A
Day, Bruce, 920
DeCew, Garth, 237
Defrin, Bob, 712, 836, 837
Deleno, Frank, 724
Della Monta, Rolland, 506A, 553
Delmerico, George, 1063, 1067
deMartin, Ed, 942
Deutsch, David, 102, 287
De Vito, Ron, 480
Di Benedetto, Ed, 267
DiFiore, Gabriel, 900, 903, 940
DiJoseph, Lou, 461
Di Paolo, Lew, 280
Dispara, Gene, 706
Dobra, David, 956
Dolby, John, 960, 969
Doret, Michael, 941, 968
Dorfsman, Lou, 23, 162, 494, 498, 498A, 504, 681, 793, 915, 939, 973
Dornfest, Stan, 505
Dubarle, Robert, 509, 521
Dyer, Rod, 686, 695, 827
Dykstra, Phillip, 1131

Eding, John, 186, 204
Eisenman, Stan, 717
Ende, Michael Allen, 747
Engel, Bob, 57, 112, 136, 454
Epstein, Henry, 814
Epstein, Lee, 184, 202, 264
Erlanger, Richard, 972
Ervin, Don, 715
Esposito, Jerry, 210

INDEX

Essman, Robert N., 556, 557, 558, 559, 560, 561
Euringer, George, 78

Federico, Gene, 914
Fiarman, Nate, 69, 221
Field, William, 783
Figliola, Vincent, 50
Fillhardt, Charles, 66
Fillie, Bob, 667
Flanagan, Ed, 232
Fletcher, Alan, 1176
Ford, Byrne & Assoc., 718, 883, 921
Franek, David J., 869
Frankfurt, Steve, 419
Freid, Ethel K., 934
Freid, Joel C., 934
Friedlander, Alan, 90
Friant, Norm, 234
Fromowitz, Mike, 516, 517
Fudyma, Janice, 809
Fury, Len, 763

Gabor, Harvey, 242, 373, 423, 887
Gage, Dick, 374, 697
Gage, Robert, 7, 383, 441, 443, 450, 471
Gagliano, Merrick, 257, 259
Gale, Robert A., 962
Gardner, Lee, 279
Gargano, Amil, 511
Gauger, David, 733, 800
Gauthier, Armand, 752A
Geismar, Thomas, 879
Gennarelli, Charles, 448A
Gersin, Robert P., 817
Gerritzen, Herman, 1139
Giacalone, Joe, 629
Gianakos, Cristos, 743
Gilday, Tom, 176, 250, 739
Gillhausen, Rolf, 1134, 1137
Gisonde, Nick, 72, 85, 132, 157
Glaser, Milton, 596, 605, 607, 1073, 1107
Glusker, Irwin, 858
Gold, Ed, 796
Gold, Jonis, 448
Goldberg, Irwin, 96, 115, 698
Goldman, Marvin, 79
Goldstein, Marty, 1047
Goodman, Alan, 58, 130
Goodman, Art, 737, 905, 983, 984
Grace, Roy, 68, 75, 137, 377
Graff, Steve, 64
Grear, J. Malcolm, 791
Gregorace, Joe, 97, 116, 142
Grey, Norman, 499
Groff, Ray, 205
Gross, Michael, 601, 1103
Grossman, Alvin, 593
Grossman, Eugene, 759, 798
Gruel, Jess, 952
Gudzin, Dolores, 294, 1116, 1124, 1125

Hackenberg, Norman & Assoc., 54, 198
Hain, Robert W., 822
Hallock, Robert, 634, 1111
Hampton, Michael, 685
Hamshaw, Rallou M., 675
Handloser, Jim, 478
Harris, Art, 271
Harris, Bill, 145
Harris, Ned, 1052
Harrison, Peter, 760, 761
Harrod, Brian, 522, 532, 533, 534, 549
Hass, Derrick, 546, 548
Hechtman, Hank, 292
Heller, Steve, 995, 1071
Hersley, Judith, 1121
Hill, Jeffery, 39, 156
Hinrichs, Kit, 729
Hoffner, Marilyn, 625
Hogg, Clyde, 936, 970, 977
Holland, Preuit, 22
Holzer, Rosette, 550, 1161
Hopkins, Will, 652, 653, 654, 655
Horton, Rick, 801, 804
Hotz, Norman S., 1080, 1087, 1101, 1102
Hough, John D., 757
Howard, Cary, 14
Howard, Mark, 492
Hyman, Ted, 742

Igarashi, Takenobu, 1170
Ingham, Carole, 1157
Ishioka, Eiko, 1145, 1146, 1147, 1148
Ishiura, Tadashi, 519

Jacobs, Steve, 725, 862
Jacobsen, Boyd, 1033
Janowitz, Dorris, 850
January, Richard, 1120
Jean, Carole, 1124A
Johnson, Doug, 854
Jones, Meredythe, 721
Jones, Paul, 62
Jones, Stan, 230
Jorden, Max, 684, 912, 945
Juett, Dennis S., 924

Kaestle, David, 609, 618, 786
Kambanis, Steve, 855
Kamp, Bill, 166, 172, 207, 216, 222, 367
Kane, Art, 590, 591, 600, 1012, 1100
Kano, Gerry, 958
Kasloff, Steve, 670
Katz, Marilyn, 289
Katz, Marjorie, 711, 821, 856, 867, 918, 919, 933
Kay, Allen, 65, 71, 92, 126, 243, 265, 361, 362
Kelly, Michael, 971
Kent, Nancy, 570, 599, 602, 608, 1002
Kidder, Fred C., 1035
Kimata, Tokihiko, 1159
Kimura, Ken, 368
King, Ann, 1121
Kingman, Peter, 218, 220, 225
Kirk, Frank, 417
Kittel, Fred, 150
Klauber, George, 713
Klein, Burt, 188
Kline, Alan, 182
Kner, Andy, 639, 892, 904, 906, 925, 1129
Koga, Hiroaki, 519
Korman, Marvin, 743
Krumwiede, Tom, 416, 429
Kubly, Don, 723
Kuchera, John, 863
Kupchick, Alan, 254, 255, 258, 261, 474
Kuperman, Bob, 53, 158
Kurlansky, Mervyn, 1153
Kuwata, Ben, 173, 181
Kwait, Bob, 174, 175, 176, 177, 178, 179, 201, 224, 953

Lacey, Jim, 486A
LaGattuta, Steve, 256
Landau, Emma, 604, 606
Landon, Alicia, 758
Langer, Andrew, 370, 458, 459, 460, 465
Lane, Tony, 564, 572, 581, 613, 826, 990, 996, 1016, 1065, 1108
Lane, Ron, 984
Langer, Helmut, 1172
LaPerle, Thom, 767
Lappan, Char, 678
Lartaud, David, 841
Lawlor, Mike, 99, 121, 145, 469
Lee, Kai-Chung, 935
Lee, Raymond, 1171
Leer, Barbara Jo, 931

INDEX

Lefkowitz, Jack, 643, 644
Lefmann, Walter, 691, 1118
Leichner, Mitch, 228
Leone, Anthony V., 299
Leonhardt, Jerry, 716
Leu, Olaf, 1160, 1162
Levine, Howard, 746
Levy, Lawrence, 665
Lew-Dave-Marv, 95, 111, 278, 283
Lewine, Harris, 674, 676
Lienhart, Jim, 642, 959
Light, Ann-Marie, 477
Lipsitt, Martin, 154
Littman, Wally, 140, 141
Lois, George, 704
Lopes, Rob, 1, 38, 100, 168, 364, 890
Lopez, Jon, 659, 851
Loucks, Jay, 1041
Lubalin, Herb, 619, 630, 631, 632, 633, 635, 636, 789, 790, 964, 1078
Lyle, Tony, 1127

McCaffery, William, 907, 908, 909
McCarron, Len, 457
McCarthy, Tom, 231
McConnell, John, 1158
Macey, Ken, 818
McEown, John, 699
McGinnis, George, 492, 927
Machlica, Dennis, 670
McKenna, Joe, 940
McWilliams, Jim, 741
Magleby, McRay, 661, 738, 788, 893
Mafia Staff, 510, 552
Malcolm, Stan, 765
Malone, Marty, 16
Mangino, Edd, 807
Manning, Phelps K., 810, 811
Manzo, Richard, 167, 889
Marchant, Bob, 512
Marino, Dom, 48
Mariucci, Jack, 217, 219, 226, 388
Marks, Harry, 979
Marschke, Elizabeth, 799
Martino, Richard, 40, 127, 945
Massey, John, 764
Matsumoto, Bob, 438, 439
Mazzella, Dennis, 728
Melgar, Fabian, 820
Melson, Robert, 1076
Menell, Don, 1003
Merrill, David, 622
Metz, Frank, 673
Metzdorf, Lyle, 215
Migdoll, Herbert, 612, 624
Miho, James, 663, 710, 852, 857, 860A, 861
Miksinski, Thaddeus A., Jr., 563, 569
Miller, Lawrence, 923
Miller, Randy, 273
Mills, Judie, 880
Minale, Marcello, 1174
Minch, Marty, 276, 281
Minnar, Horace, 51
Mitchneck, Marvin, 488
Miyawaki, Leland, 234, 705
Mohtares, Alexander, 146
Moore, David, 584
Monte, Janet, 101
Moore, Mary, 246, 247, 248, 262
Morgan, Joseph, 588
Morkel, A., 529
Morrill, Edward, 823
Moser, Len, 819
Mostad, Bill, 885
Moxcey, Ralph, 63, 375, 745, 806, 1036, 1037, 1038, 1043, 1119
Moy, David, 997, 1088, 1089, 1092, 1113
Murnak, Richard, 278A
Murphy, Bill, 235
Murphy, Harry, 736, 974, 980, 987, 988, 989
Nava, Richard, 947
Nemesure, Paul, 641
Nemser, Robert S., 785, 1046
Neumeier, Marty, 965
Neuwirth, Morris, 1070
Nevraumont, Peter, 696, 722
Newton, Max, 1144
Nickerson, Nick, 213
Nicolo, Frank, 380
Nikolits, Peter, 815
Nissen, Joseph, 117, 118, 153
Nubel, Herbert R., 729
Nussbaum, Ed, 483

Ohman, Steve,
Oliveto, Tony, 268, 271, 286
O'Neill, Brian, 253

Paganucci, Bob, 692, 808, 813
Pagnez, Regis, 1028
Parenio, Ralph, 866, 868
Paris, Peter, 119A
Parkhurst, Ken, 951
Paul, Arthur, 589
Peckolick, Alan, 677, 731, 943, 954, 1178
Pedersen, B. Martin, 707, 1039, 1060, 1133
Pellegrini, Robert, 786
Perlman, Richard, 688
Perretti, Jim, 157
Perry, Frank, 293
Peters, Christa, 1166
Petrocelli, Bob, 482
Pettus, Ted, 825
Pfeitter, Wally, 421
Philips, Jerry, 815
Phillips, Steve, 993, 1095, 1099
Piccirillo, Charles, 17, 29, 31, 61, 134, 391, 395, 397, 399, 901
Piccolo, Jack, 442
Pineles, Cipe, 664
Pirtle, Woody, 687, 702, 749, 805, 838, 930, 938
Pittman, Stuart, 70, 89, 90, 105, 143, 975
Platt, Mel, 87, 123, 124, 125, 144, 152
Pocknell, David, 1150, 1151, 1156, 1173, 1175
Popcorn, Faith, 70, 89, 90, 105, 143, 975
Pouzol, Philippe, 535
Powell, Ivan, 296
Printup, Harold, Jr., 689
Propper, Robert A., 986
Pütz, Robert, 1165, 1167

Rauch, Peter, 298, 1104
Reavley, Martin, 507, 550
Reed, Robert, 679
Reid, Scott F., 946
Reitzfeld, Robert, 15, 30, 32, 46, 55, 84, 98, 109, 114, 147, 392, 398, 431, 444, 445
Rice, Nancy, 44
Richards, Stan, 464, 687, 749, 756
Rickabaugh, Heidi, 719, 802
Rickabaugh, Robin, 719, 802
Robinson, Cervin, 881
Robinson, Elton, 1001
Rofheart, Edward, 647
Rogers, Frank, 185
Rogers, Peter, 138
Romano, Dave, 20
Rosenwasser, Stu, 475, 483
Rosoff, Gil, 490
Ross, Mark, 369, 427
Roth, Frank, 292, 916
Rothman, Irwin, 714
Rosenthal, Dan, 10
Rotundi, Ed, 164, 169, 392A, 396A, 401A, 425
Rubenstein, Mort, 730
Ruggles, Lee, 1033
Runyan, Robert Miles, 750
Rustom, Mel, 106

ADC, INC.

Rytter, Robert J., 617, 769, 937

Sadiq, Ahmad, 611, 626, 1004, 1014, 1015, 1020, 1025, 1097, 1098
Sailor, Chet, 94
Saks, Arnold, 768
Salisbury, Mike, 568, 571, 573, 577, 580, 831, 1077
Salpeter, Bob, 638, 794
Sausville, Ken, 195
Scalfone, Jim, 433
Scali, Sam, 161, 165, 244, 389, 394, 396, 400, 410, 412, 414, 415, 432
Scarfone, Ernest, 991, 1006, 1007, 1009, 1011, 1018, 1023, 1027, 1029, 1030
Scheihagen, Vin, 196, 366
Schenck, Mary, 1093
Schindelman, Joe, 200
Schlesinger, Bob, 428
Schlüter, Doris, 1164
Schlüter, Harald, 1164
Schneider, Richard, 948
Schofield, Stan, 199
Schubeck, Barbara, 263
Schwartz, Dan, 409
Schwartzman, Arnold, 1136
Schwenk, Reinhold, 49
Scianna, Cosimo, 797
Scordato, Nick, 21, 240
Sehring, Harry, 1115
Seidler, Sheldon, 762, 766, 780, 781
Siedman, Eric, 595, 1069
Severson, Gerry, 37
Shaine, Ted, 378, 424
Shankel, Georgia, 473
Shelley, Robert, O., 910
Sherman, Ivan, 107, 143
Siebke, Frank, 422
Sillen, David, 58
Silver, Al, 403, 413
Silver, Stuart, 864
Silverman, Hal, 269
Simpson, Milt, 931, 1086, 1096
Sincoff, Milton, 832
Singer, Paul, 209, 212, 223
Sisman, Leslie, 1181
Slagter, Phil, 1031
Slater, Don, 83, 453, 466
Smith, Bill, 420, 436, 437
Smith, Eloise, 833
Smith, Elwood H., 720
F. Eugene Smith Assoc. 985
Smith, Judy, 853
Smith, Tom, 214
Snope, Dan, 506
Sons, Larry, 628
Sparks, Walter, 733A
Squillace, Albert, 650, 660
Stack, Richard, 765
Starr, Bob, 266
Stern, Herb, 47, 694, 727
Stove, Steve, 968
Strandell, Don, 976
Sullivan, Ron, 756
Summerford, Jack, 754, 787
Swan, Jim, 451, 456, 468, 470
Sweney, Bill,

Tanen, Norman, 108, 372
Tartak/Libera, 752
Tattersfield, Brian, 1174
Taylor, Jay, 874A, 875, 876
Tesch, Mike, 76, 129, 376
Thomas, Dick, 203, 251
Thomas, Lamont, 848
Thompson, Bradbury, 657
Thrasher, Ed, 835, 842, 843, 926, 981
Tischler, Lois, 196
Title, Howard, 3, 9, 11, 43, 88
Tobey, Fred, 603
Tora, Shinichiro, 610, 998, 999, 1010, 1022, 1026
Torchia, Jerry, 229, 233
Torreano, Alan, 56, 418
Travisano, Ron, 183
Traynor, Pete, 978
Treaster, Grant, Jr., 690
Trembath, Gordon, 514, 515, 518, 520
Triolo, John, 411
Troncone, Reggie, 434
Tuck, Roy, 270, 275

Ulick, Michael, 467
Urban, Rick, 285

van den Hoed, Ruut, 955
Van Dusen, Ross, 447, 452
Van Noy, James, 752A
Varon, Hy, 18
Vellvé, Tomás, 1163
Vetere, Barry, 208
Vero, Frank, 371
Vignelli, Massimo, 646, 648, 881
Viola, Tony, 227, 241, 891
Von Lauderback, Nancy, 737

Wages, Bob, 901
Waites, Raymond, 597
Webber, Harry, 481
Weigand, Richard, 562, 574, 614, 627, 1013
Weihs, Kurt, 693, 704, 728, 1032
Weinschenker, Greg, 2, 5, 45
Weinstein, Bill, 245
Weinstein, Iris, 668, 669
Weiss, Dan, 435
Weisselberg, Stu, 24
Weller, Don, 751, 792, 1048, 1050, 1053
Welsch, Peter, 1049
Whitley, Jerry, 139
Wilde, Richard, 860A, 873, 1117
Williams, Lowell, 1034
Winslow, Michael, 93
Wise, Herbert, 1051
Witham, Jim, 745, 806, 1036, 1037, 1038, 1043, 1119
Withers, Mike, 154, 426
Wolf, Dick, 142
Wolf, Henry, 615, 620, 1057, 1081, 1083, 1090, 1105, 1106
Wolf, Jay, 379
Wolsky, Alan, 12
Woo, Calvin, 950
Wood, Thomas, 740A
Wu, Kong, 464
Wuilleumier, Milt, 260, 878

Yamashita, Mas, 393, 402
Young, Roland, 839
Yurcich, Tom, 297
Yustein, Mark, 19, 73, 110, 157, 189, 190, 191, 206

Zamora, Tony, 140, 141
Ziff, Lloyd, 913
Zlotnick, Bernie, 703

Designers

Ackerman, Gretchen, 1086
Adamec, Donald A., 982
Amber, Ted, 480
Ammirati, Ralph, 160
Akagi, Doug, 859
Alderisio, Bill, 284
Anderson, Ron, 44, 252
Andreozzi, Gennaro, 80, 81, 113, 151
Andresakes, Ted, 23, 162, 793
Angeli, Primo, 682, 966
Ansel, Ruth, 555, 565, 566, 579, 583, 621, 623, 994, 1054, 1072, 1074, 1128
Anselmo, John, 726, 735
Antupit, Samuel N., 637
Appel, Allen, 1089

INDEX

Aromando, Charley, 59, 133
Arsenault, Robert, 1138
Aso, Yasunobu, 519

Bailey, Ed, 816
Baker, Stan, 957
Banke, Martin, 708
Banks, Robert, 1135
Barile, Carl, 590, 1005, 1008
Baron, Harvey, 4, 8, 45
Bass, Saul, 737, 905, 983, 984
Baxter, Glenn, 746A
Beaver, Allan, 74, 171, 195, 884
Behar, Ray, 715
Beier, Annegret, 1177
Belew, Tandy, 966
Beleznay, AnnaMarie, 664
Bennett, Ward, 795
Bentkowski, Tom, 605, 607
Benton, Jean, 783
Berg, John, 840, 844, 846, 847
Berliner, S. B., 700
Bernard, Walter, 596, 605, 607, 1073, 1107
Bernhardt, Craig, 809
Berris, Ken, 13
Blechman, R. O., 489
Bloch, Thomas, 726, 735
Block, Stan, 381, 496
Boege, Uli, 1126
Bonnell, Bill, III, 565, 734, 882, 917, 922
Bossardt, Herb, 854
Boston, Archie, 1042
Boyarski, Daniel, 799
Bradford, Peter, 795
Braun, Franz, 1137
Brock, Michael, 1003
Brooks, Joe, 1079, 1082, 1091
Brown, Richard, 197, 238, 239, 272
Buettner, Gudrun, 646
Burlockoff, Sam, 1135
Burns, Robert, 1152, 1169, 1180
Butera, Gene, 992, 1017
Byrne, Bob, 544, 547

Caggiano, John, 128, 430
Cairns, Dana, 909
Campanelli, Rocco E., 102, 287
Campbell, Cathie, 131
Caravetta, Fred, 888
Carra, Vincent, 984
Casado, Barbara, 842
Casado, John, 842
Chalfin, Alan, 895
Chapman, Michael, 883
Chepelsky, John R., 967
Chermayeff, Ivan, 748, 784, 870, 871, 872, 879, 932
Chiang, Philip, 827
Chouinard, Roger, 486, 487
Christy, Art, 293
Chwast, Seymour, 475, 685, 833, 849, 853, 1068, 1127, 1132
Chu, Hoi Ling, 619
Ciccarone, Joe, 135
Clarke, James, 6, 42, 122
Clark, John, 859
Cole, Rhea G., 899
Collamer, Jerry, 236
Colletti, Louis, 180
Colmet-Daage, Eric, 1028
Condak, Henrietta, 828
Conley, John J., 1045
Conlon, William J., 845
Connolly, Pete, 822
Connors, Sue, 629
Cook, Verdun, 554
Cooper, Heather, 1179, 1182
Cotler, Sheldon, 666
Coughter, Peter J., Jr., 479
Courtos, Tom, 704, 824
Crolick, Sue, 34
Cross, James, 709, 755, 782, 803
Crowder, David, 796
Cusack, Margaret, 603

Dadds, Jerry, 961
Daigneault, Gilles, 1138, 1140, 1155
Dankwardt, Ken, 701
Davenport, J., 812, 949
Davis, Sy, 480
Day, Bruce, 920
deMartin, Ed, 942
Deleno, Frank, 724
Delmerico, George, 1063, 1067
Deutsch, David, 102, 287
DeVino, Frank, 611, 626, 1004, 1014, 1015, 1020, 1025, 1097, 1098
Didia, Hy, 12
DiFiore, Gabriel, 900, 903, 940
Dillon, Pete, 822
Di Paolo, Lew, 280
Dolby, John, 960, 969
Doret, Michael, 928, 941, 968, 1130
Dorfsman, Lou, 23, 162, 494, 498, 498A, 504
Dougherty, Robert, 1104
Dornfest, Stan, 505
Downs, J., 812, 949
Duevell, William D., 814
Dworkin, Joan, 1107
Dyer, Rod, 686, 695
Dykstra, Phillip, 1131

Eckstein, Arthur, 495
Eding, John, 186, 204
Eddington, Ron, 738
Eisenman and Enock, 717
Ende, Michael Allen, 747
Epstein, Lee, 184, 202, 264
Erlanger, Richard, 972
Essman, Robert N., 556, 557, 558, 559, 560, 561

Fasciano, Nick, 840, 846
Federico, Gene, 194
Federico, Helen, 714
Ferrara, Neil, 274
Fillhardt, Charles, 66
Fillie, Bob, 667
Flanagan, Ed, 232
Fletcher, Alan, 1176
Ford, Byrne & Assoc., 718, 921
Franek, David J., 869
Frankfurt, Steve, 414
Freeman, Barbara, 664
Freid, Ethel K., 934
Friant, Norm, 234
Fromowitz, Mike, 516, 517
Fudyma, Janice, 809
Fury, Len, 763

Gabor, Harvey, 242, 887
Gardner, Lee, 279
Gargano, Amil, 511
Gale, Robert A., 962
Garrison, Jim, 856
Gauger, David, 733, 800
Geiger, Michael, 278A
Geismar, Thomas, 757, 879
Gensior, Paul, 822
Gerstein, Mordy, 488
Giacalone, Joe, 629
Gianakos, Cristos, 743
Gianakos, Virginia, 649, 672
Gilday, Tom, 739
Ginnochio, Augustus, 612, 624
Ginther, Paul, 721
Gisonde, Nick, 72, 85, 132, 157
Glaser, Milton, 830, 850, 853, 1073
Glusker, Irwin, 858
Goldberg, Irwin, 96, 115, 698
Goldman, Marvin, 79
Goldstein, Marty, 1047
Goodman, Alan, 58, 130
Goodman, Art, 905
Gormley, James, 742
Graff, Steve, 64

INDEX

Grear, Malcolm, 791
Green, John, 628
Greenberg, Al, 625
Gribbitt, 843
Gross, Michael, 601, 639
Grossman, Alvin, 593
Grossman, Eugene, 759, 798
Gruel, Jess, 952
Gudzin, Dolores, 294, 1116, 1124, 1125

Hadtke, Fred, 822
Haggerty, Mick, 839
Haines, Steven, 784
Hammons, Jeanne, 669
Handler, Bruce, 664
Hanson, Paul, 817
Hallock, Robert, 1111
Hampton, Michael, 865
Hardy, Paul, 729
Harris, Bill, 145
Harris, Ned, 1052
Harrison, Peter, 761
Harrod, Brian, 522, 549
Haskell, Ira, 669
Hass, Derrick, 546, 548
Hechtman, Hank, 292
Heinly, John, 1092, 1113
Heller, Steve, 995, 1071
Hinrichs, Kit, 729
Hoffeld, Randy, 922
Hoffner, Marilyn, 625
Hofrichter, Fritz, 1160, 1162
Hogg, Clyde, 936, 970, 977
Hogan, Bill, 721
Holland, Bob, 796
Holland, Preuit, 22
Hooper, Raymond, 597
Hopkins, Will, 652, 653, 654, 655
Horton, Rick, 801, 804
Howard, Cary, 14
Hughes, Roy, 765

Igarashi, Takenobu, 1170
Ingham, Carole, 1157
Ishiura, Todashi, 519

Jacobs, Steve, 725, 862
Jacobsen, Boyd, 1033
January, Richard, 1120
Jean, Carole, 1124A
Jefferies, Ron, 750
John, Karl-Heinz, 1134
Johnson, Asa, 694
Jones, M., 721
Jones, Paul, 62
Jorden, Max, 40, 127, 684, 912
Juett, Dennis S., 924

Kaestle, David, 609, 618, 639, 786, 1103
Kambanis, Steve, 855
Kamp, Bill, 166, 172, 207, 216, 222
Kanai, Kiyoshi, 681
Kandel, Honey, 1075
Kane, Art, 1024
Kano, Gerry, 958
Kasko, Janet, 764
Kasloff, Steve, 670
Katz, Marilyn, 289
Katz, Marjorie, 711, 821, 867, 918, 919, 933
Kawasaki, Michael, 738
Keaton, James, 588
Kehe, John, 175A
Kelly, Michael, 971
Kent, Nancy, 570, 599, 602, 1002
Kimbell, Wayne, 979
King, Ann, 1121
Kingman, Peter, 225
Kirk, Frank, 417
Kittel, Fred, 150
Klauber, George, 713
Kline, Alan, 182
Klein, Burt, 188
Kleiner, Norbert, 1143
Kner, Andrew, 892, 904, 906
Kolar, Jim, 629
Komai, Don, 874A, 875, 876
Krollpfeiffer, Cathy, 726, 735
Kupchick, Alan, 254, 255, 258, 261
Kuperman, Bob, 53

Kurlansky, Mervyn, 1153
Kuwata, Ben, 173, 181

LaCasse, Bernie, 678
LaGattuta, Steve, 256
Landau, Emma, 604, 606
Landon, Alicia, 758
Lane, Tony, 564, 572, 581, 613, 826, 990, 996, 1016, 1065, 1108
Lang, Tony, 973
Langer, Helmut, 1172
LaPerle, Thom, 767
Lartaud, David, 841
Lawlor, Mike, 99, 121, 145
Lawrence, Chris, 762
Lee, Kai-Chung, 935
Lee, Raymond, 1171
Leer, Barbara Jo, 931, 1096
Leichner, Mitch, 228
Lefkowitz, Jack, 643, 644
Lefkowitz, Pam, 643, 644
Lefmann, Walter, 1118
Leone, Anthony V., 299
Leopold, Jerry, 897
Leu, Olaf, 1160, 1162
Levy, Lawrence, 665
Lew-Dave-Marv, 95, 111, 278, 283
Lewerke, Ria, 913
Lienhart, Jim, 642, 959
Lipsitt, Martin, 154
Littman, Wally, 140, 141
Lopes, Rob, 38, 168
Lopez, Jon, 659, 851
Lord, Bette, 997
Lotz, Kenton, 732
Loucks, Jay, 1041
Love, Edwin, 723
Lubalin, Herb, 630, 631, 632, 633, 635, 636, 789, 790, 964, 1078

McCabe, Edward A., 50
McCaffery, William, 907, 908
McCall, Bruce, 601
McCall, Brian, 1088
McConnell, John, 1158
McDowell, William, 680
McEown, John, 699
McGinnis, George, 492, 927
McGuffie, John, 1144
Machlica, Dennis, 670
Magleby, McRay, 661, 788, 893
Malone, Marty, 16
Mangino, Edd, 807
Manzo, Richard, 167, 889
Maranzano, Alex, 1174
Marchant, Bob, 512
Marino, Dom, 48
Mariucci, Jack, 217, 219, 226, 388
Marrero, Hector, 611, 626, 1004, 1014, 1015, 1020, 1025, 1097, 1098
Marschke, Elizabeth, 799
Massey, John, 764
Mazzella, Dennis, 728
Melgar, Fabian, 820
Merrill, David, 622
Melson, Robert, 1076
Metzdorf, Lyle, 215
Migdoll, Herbert, 612, 624
Mihalik, Bill, 781
Miho, James, 663, 857, 860A, 710
Miho, Tomoko, 852, 861
Miksinski, Thaddeus A., Jr., 569, 863
Miller, Lawrence, 923
Miller, Randy, 273
Mills, Michael, 737
Minale, Marcello, 1174
Minch, Marty, 276, 281
Minnar, Horace, 51
Minor, Wendell, 673, 679
Miyawaki, Leland, 234, 705
Mizuno, Takuzo, 1159
Mohtares, Alexander, 146
Moran, Lynne, 1123
Morava, Emmett, 753

Morgan, Joseph, 584
Morrill, Edward, 823
Moser, Len, 819
Mostad, Bill, 885
Moxcey, Ralph, 63
Moy, George, 600
Murphy, Bill, 235
Murphy, Harry, 736
Murphy, Harry, 736, 974, 980, 987, 988, 989
Nava, Richard, 947
Nemesure, Paul, 641
Nemser, Robert S., 785, 1046
Neumeier, Marty, 237
Nikolits, Peter, 815
Nittner, Tomas, 768
Noyes, Androus, 818
Nyquist, Ray, 208

O'Neill, Brian, 253
Orosz, Istvan, 1129
Osborn, Jim, 816

Paganucci, Bob, 692, 808, 813
Pantano, Dick, 227, 241, 891
Pao, Basil, 836, 837
Paris, Peter, 119A
Parenio, Ralph, 866, 868
Parkhurst, Ken, 951
Peckolick, Alan, 677, 731, 943, 954, 1178
Pedersen, B. Martin, 707, 1039, 1060, 1133
Pellegrini, Robert, 786
Perlman, Richard, 688
Perry, Frank, 293
Pfister, Dave, 740
Phillips, Steve, 1095, 1099
Pittman, Stuart, 975
Pirtle, Woody, 687, 702, 749, 805, 838, 930, 938
Platt, Mel, 123, 124, 125, 144, 152
Pocknell, David, 1150, 1151, 1156, 1173, 1175
Popcorn, Faith, 975
Porcano, Gary, 818
Porcelli, V. Lorenzo, 817
Powell, Ivan, 296
Printup, Harold, Jr., 689
Propper, Robert A., 986

Quarmby, Herbert H., 671

Ratzkin, Lawrence, 675, 676
Rauch, Peter, 298
Reid, Scott F., 946
Revsin, Ethan, 368
Rice, Nancy, 44
Rickabaugh, Robin, 719, 802
Roher, Melanie, 864
Rogers, Frank, 185
Rosenthal, Dan, 10
Rotundi, Ed, 164, 169
Rousso, Steve, 956
Rubin, David, 880
Rubin, Mark, 880
Rubenstein, Mort, 730
Rytter, Robert J., 617, 769, 937

Sailor, Chet, 94
Saks, Arnold, 768
Salisbury, Mike, 568, 580, 831, 1077
Salpeter, Bob, 638, 794
Salisbury, Mike, 874
Sausville, Ken, 195
Scarfone, Ernest, 991, 1006, 1007, 1009, 1011, 1018, 1023, 1027, 1029, 1030
Schaefer, Peter, 925
Schenck, Gary, 615, 1081, 1083, 1090, 1105, 1106
Scher, Paula, 712, 886
Schoenfield, Berni, 556, 557, 558, 559
Schlüter, Doris, 1164
Schlüter, Harald, 1164
Schneider, Richard, 948
Schreiber, Melissa, 664
Schubeck, Barbara, 86, 159, 187
Schwartzman, Arnold, 1136
Schwenk, Reinhold, 49
Scordato, Nick, 21, 240
Seeff, Norman, 1051
Sehring, Harry, 1115
Seidler, Sheldon, 762, 766, 780, 781
Seidman, Eric, 595
Seki, Akihiko, 915, 973
Sharp, David, 1166
Shelley, Robert O., 910
Shimokochi, Mamoru, 737, 983, 984
Shiv, Karlong, 664
Sidjakov, Nicolas, 706, 716
Silverman, Hal, 269
Silvermintz, Hal, 371
Simpson, Michael, 929
Sincoff, Milton, 832
Singer, Paul, 209, 212, 223
Sisman, Leslie, 1181
Skoorka, Susan, 691
Slater, Don, 83
Smith, Elwood H., 720
Smith, Tom, 214
Snope, Dan, 506
Sobel, Ed, 575, 576, 578, 585, 586, 592
Solazzo, Mike, 231
Sorel, Edward, 746, 1094
Sparks, Walter, 733A
Speakman, John, 1152, 1180
Squillace, Albert, 650, 660
Staebler, Tom, 582, 589
Stag, 1161
Steckiv, Irena, 251
Steinberg, Bruce, 835
Stern, Herb, 47, 727
Stillman, Linda B., 608
Strandell, Don, 976
Sullivan, Ron, 756
Summerford, Jack, 754, 787
Sweney, Bill, 249

Tanen, Norman, 108
Tartak/Libera, 752
Tattersfield, Brian, 1174
Tauber, Gail, 1080, 1087, 1101, 1102
Taylor, Richard, 979
Thomas, Dick, 203
Thomas, Lamont, 848
Thompson, Bradbury, 657
Thrasher, Ed, 926, 981
Title, Howard, 3, 9, 11, 43, 88
Tobias, William R., 810, 811
Torchia, Jerry, 229, 233
Tora, Shinichiro, 610, 998, 999, 1010, 1022, 1026
Trapp, Tom, 814
Travisano, Ron, 183
Traynor, Pete, 978
Treaster, Grant, Jr., 690
Trembath, Gordon, 514, 515, 518, 520
Tribich, Jay, 760
Trousdell, Mabey, 863
Tuck, Roy, 270, 275

Udell, Jim, 939

Varon, Hy, 18
Vignelli, Massimo, 646, 648, 881
Vellvé, Tomás, 1163
Van Noy, James, 752A
Van Hamersveld, John, 696, 722
Venegoni, Becky, 916
Van Hamersvela, John, 696, 722
Viskupic, Gary, 1070
Victor, Claire, 591, 600
Van Noy, James 911

Wadler, Scott, 52
Wages, Bob, 901
Ward, Chris, 917
Warner, Janice, 597
Wattman, Larry, 897
Weigand, Richard, 562, 574, 614, 1013
Weihs, Kurt, 693, 728, 1032
Weinschenker, Greg, 2, 5, 45

INDEX

Weinstein, Bill, 245
Weinstein, Iris, 668
Weiss, Dan, 435
Weisselberg, Stu, 24
Welsch, Peter, 1049
Weller, Don, 751, 792, 1048, 1050, 1053
Wilde, Richard, 860A, 873, 1117
Winslow, Michael, 93
Witzig, Fred, 914
White, Charles E., III, 1122, 1145, 1146, 1147, 1148
Wolf, Henry, 620, 1057
Woo, Calvin, 950
Wood, Thomas, 740A
Wosczyk, Patricia H., 662
Wosk, Miriam, 1100
Wuilleumier, Milt, 260, 878

Yao, Takeo, 1159
Yustein, Mark, 19, 73, 110, 189, 190, 191
Yurcich, Tom, 297

Zagorski, Stan, 674
Zamora, Tony, 140, 141
Ziff, Lloyd, 568, 571, 573, 577, 580, 1077
Zimmerman, Arthur, 115
Zlotnick, Bernie, 703
Zurcher, A., 759

Writers, Editors

Abel, Friedrich, 1134
Abrams, Warren, 906
Aczel, Peter, 86, 187
Gonzalez-Adame, Helio, 271, 286
Adams, Jean, 575
Agniel, Lucien, 563, 569
Alfano, Tony, 416, 429
Allen, John, 617
Allen, Ray, 888
Alston, Elizabeth, 585, 592
Altomare, John, 807
Altschiller, David, 68, 75, 78, 137, 376A, 377, 378, 703
Anderson, Elliott, 665
Angle, Charles, 765
Annarino, John, 393, 402
Anton, Frank, 195
Arbuckle, Vance, 885
Ardisson, Thierry, 521
Ares, Louis, 692
Arnold, Maxwell, 725
Arnott, Ann, 554
Atkinson, Tom, 278A
Attea, Tom, 461
August, Steve, 197

Bacon, Ken, 688
Baker, James, 1135
Balkan, David, 438
Bandy, Mary Lee, 659, 851
Baron, Ken, 895
Baron, Ray, 196
Barry, Monsignor William J., 958
Basile, Gretta, 387
Bass & Co., 785, 1046
Bates, Maury, 1086, 1096
Beard, Henry, 639
Becker, Mike, 455
Bell, Ted, 62
Bennet, Ann Granning, 719
Bennet, Jerry, 40, 127
Bennett, Ward, 795
Berger, Ron, 69, 211, 218, 220, 221, 225
Berger, Sandy, 154
Bergman, Lewis, 566, 579, 621, 623, 1062, 1064, 1066, 1068, 1072, 1074, 1128, 1130, 1132
Berkhard, Peter, 323, 352
Berndt, Prof., 1160
Berne, Jennifer, 6, 42, 87, 123, 124, 125, 144, 152, 356
Bernhardt, Craig, 809
Bernstein, Dick, 488
Berris, Ken, 313
Berville, Pierre, 507, 550, 1161
Beuchner, James, 688
Bierce, Ambrose, 633
Bishopric, Robert, 181
Bittmann, Jon, 253
Blache, Joan, 481
Blackmar, Dana, III, 39, 156
Blake, Stuart, 546
Blitzer, Patty Volk, 314
Bonnell, Bill, III, 882
Bookman, Mike, 240, 379
Borders, Bill, 339
Boston, Archie, 1042
Bowman, Gordon, 858
Bradford, Peter, 795
Bradnick, Jean A., 657
Brécard, France, 510, 552
Breen & Porter, 188
Brown, Bill, 280, 717
Brown, David, 663, 707, 710, 852, 860A, 861, 1039
Brown, Lawrence, 245
Broyles, Bill, 1059
Bruemmer, Fred, 1155
Bruce, Gregory, 310
Bruch, Hilde, 641
Brun, Isabelle, 509
Buchanan, Scott, 859
Bucholtz, Sandra, 34
Burkard, Carl, 629
Burnett, L., 759
Burns, Aaron, 635, 636, 789, 790
Burns, Robert, 1169
Busch, Richard, 1010, 1022
Bushell, Gordon, 140, 141
Butler, David, 230, 311, 318
Butler, Ed, 76, 129, 378, 424
Butler, Joseph T., 713
Buttke, Liz, 435

Cadman, Larry, 15, 46
Calet, Neil, 154
Calderhead, Dick, 159, 263
Caffrey, Edward, 403, 413
Callahan, Sean, 654
Canestro, Tony, 495
Caroline, Peter, 374
Carothers, Gibson, 462
Carr, Robert, 167
Carruth, Harry P., Jr., 780
Carter, Barry, 911
Castaldi, Marilyn, 769
Castillo, Emilio, 835
Castleman, George, 119A
Certner, Andy, 228
Cetta, Mike, 51
Cetta, Pat, 51
Chaffer, J. Robert, 729
Chandler, Ken, 504
Chaneles, Sol, 1111
Chaplin, Gordon, 574
Charof, Ken, 21, 478
Christy, Art, 293
Clairon, Michel, 506A, 553
Clement, Roland, 650
Cohen, Chuck, 3. 9, 11, 43, 88
Cohen, Deanna, 64
Cohen, Martin, 279, 293
Cohn, Nik, 647
Collier, Glenda, 816
Collins, Glenn, 555
Colodny, Lester, 71, 126
Comey, Sharon, 1045
Como, William, 612, 624
Connelly, Richard, 814
Connes, Keith, 914
Connolly, Mara, 456
Cooper, Heather, 1179
Copacino, Jim, 232
Corey, Michael, 791
Cornish, Peter, 148
Cotler, Sheldon, 666
Coughter, Peter J., Jr., 479
Counihan, Jack, 700
Coveny, Terry, 337
Cox, Michael, 56, 418

INDEX

Curtis, Charlotte, 995, 1063, 1067, 1071
Cutler, Laurel, 372

Dale, Lindsey, 512
David, Michael, 854
Davis, Bruce, 1041
Davis, Sue, 667
de Groot, Roy Andries, 1013
Demarest, Sharon, 747
Dennis, Lloyd B., 753
DePascal, Rich, 446
DePree, Hugh, 764
Dick, Ron, 721
Dickison, Don, 210
DiGiacomo, Frank, 381
Dill, D. Kenneth, 729
Dillon, Brian, 371
Dillon, Jack, 383
DiSalvo, Ronald M., 752A
Ditch, Scott, 796
Dixon, Hal, 355
Donald, Roger, 678
Dorfsman, Lou, 162, 498, 504
Douglas, Alan, 874
Drayton, John, 661
Drazen, Michael, 114, 321, 336, 408, 444, 449
Drier, William, 20
Drossman, Neil, 13, 73, 85, 110, 157, 158, 164, 169, 183
Du Charme, Lou, 419
Durfee, Jim, 41, 139, 424, 511
Dust, Don, 931
Dymond, Russ, 249, 335

Edgerton Minnesota Edterprise, 862
Einstein, Arthur, 131, 194
Einstein, Cliff, 911
Eisner, Paul, 735
Emmerling, John, 37
Etter, Paul, 755, 782
Evans, Peter, 135

Fabian, Joyce, 58, 130
Faems, Mike, 250
Falk, Donald, 718, 921
Feinberg, Robert, 140, 141
Ferrelli, Richard Gaetano, 434
Feuerman, Roger, 22, 185
Fiala, Rudy, 1032
Fine, Carole Anne, 2, 4, 5, 8, 45
Fink, Lloyd, 92, 103, 243
Fink, Ortwin, 1137
Fink, Roy, 265
Finke, Jack Anson, 630, 632, 635, 636, 789, 790, 1078
Fitzgerald, Judith Brolin, 417
Flamma, Ed, 360
Flaum, Harley, 324
Flynn, Peggy, 106
Ford, Barbara, 233
Forsyth, Douglass B., 978
Fox, Martin, 1129
Francis, Ann, 597
Fraser, Alan, 205, 362
Fraser, Susan, 130
Frey, Jeff, 407, 467
Fried, Herb, 480
Friedman, Hal, 482
Fromowitz, Mike, 516, 517
Frye, Harriet, 93
Fudyma, Janice, 809
Futterman, Enid, 254, 255, 258, 261, 309, 340, 358, 360A, 474

Gaffney, Michael, 229
Gans, Barbara, 356
Garland, Wayne, 512
Garrett, Ray, 740A
Gauger, David, 800
Geigy Pharmaceuticals Staff, 808
Giles, William, 39, 156
Gill, Mike, 516, 517
Ginzburg, Ralph, 619
Golden, Joy, 106
Goldsmith, A., 345
Goldsmith, Arthur, 610
Goode, Jim, 1182
Gorman, Jeff, 326, 327
Goward, Jon, 319, 320, 322, 330, 331
Gowl, Charles, 18
Grace, Marcia Bell, 217, 219, 226, 388
Grace, Roy, 443, 471
Grant, Dick, 740A
Greenburg, Dan, 582
Greenspon, Barry, 426
Grey, Norman, 345
Gross, Michael, 639
Grunwald, Henry Anatole, 622
Guisewite, Bill, 744
Gunnar, Jocelyn, 1090
Guskind, Elin, 338

Hackenberg, Norman & Assoc., 54, 198
Hadley, Don, 306, 307, 308, 384
Hagen, Paul, 721
Hall, Jean, 726
Halliday, Ernest, 604, 606
Hammer, Harry, 929
Hanft, Adam, 83, 105, 143, 453, 466, 496
Hanft, Ed, 117, 118, 153
Hanler, Mark, 927
Harris, Maureen, 590
Harrison, Jim, 1111
Hartzell, James W., 328, 440
Hass, Derrick, 548
Henderson, Ken, 260
Hendra, Tony, 609, 1103
Herbert, Jim, 256
Hering, Doris, 612
Hersley, Judith, 1121
Hewson, Don, 1152
Hildt, Robert, 380
Ho, Francis T., 1053
Hobbs, Whit, 203
Hoffman, Lyle, 1035
Holland, Ron, 704, 855
Honig, Marvin, 128, 430
Humber, Tom, 1060
Hunt, Lionel, 514, 515, 518, 520, 542
Hunter, Blake, 305
Hutchinson, Garrie, 520
Hyman, Ted, 742
Hynes, Jim, 1180

Irvine, Bill, 275
Issacson, Andrew, 163
Ito, Dee, 860A, 873, 1117

Jackson, Dick, 23
Jackson, John, 277
Jacobson, Kurt, 701
Jacobson, Marv, 97, 104, 116, 142
James, Henry, 657
Jean, Carole, 1124A
Jeanes, William, 1017
Jensen, DeLamar, 661
Johnson, Doug, 854
Johnson, Susan, 866
Johnson, Rick, 238, 239, 242, 272, 373, 887
Johnson, Rupert, 149
Johnston, Jim, 101, 333, 359, 923
Jones, Robin, 47, 694, 727
Just, Gemma, 284

Kaestle, David, 639
Kafka, Franz, 1126
Kagan, Richard, 608
Kampmann, Anne, 570, 599, 608
Kantor, Norman, 292
Karp, Marshall, 370, 458, 459, 465
Kasdan, Lawrence, 348
Kasloff, Steve, 670
Kassof, Ritch, 257, 259
Kavanagh, Kay, 19, 189, 190, 206, 315, 316, 343, 349
Kay, Allen, 60, 67
Kazmer, Allan, 522, 532, 533, 534, 549
Keane, Jack, 488
Kehe, John, 175A
Kelley, Brendan, 369
Kelly, Patrick, 376
Kendall, James, 642
Kenny, Doug, 618, 639
Kekst & Co. Staff, 767
Kerwin, Carlotta, 649, 672

INDEX

Kessler, Syd, 541
Kikuchi, Kazuo, 519
Kilzer, Robert G., 102, 287
King, Larry L., 993
Kirkwood, Lorna, 617
Klausner, Steve, 334
Klein, Burt, 14, 16
Klein, Murray L., 89, 107, 143
Koelker, Mike, 486, 487
Korenic, Emil, 682
Kornberger, Charlie, 142
Korey, Lois, 65, 126, 361, 362
Korman, Marvin, 743
Kornblau, Irwin, 889
Krassen, Miles, 669
Kupchick, Alan, 309
Kupka, Stephen, 835
Kwait, Bob, 953

LaMell, Joan, 483
LaMond, Joline, 477
Land, Edwin, 783
Lane, Bill, 150
Lane, Chet, 406
Larimer, Bob, 96, 115, 698
Larsen, John, 1095, 1099
Lee, Linda, 850
Lee, Raymond, 1171
Leonard, Mike, 411
Levin, Bob, 586
Levin, Ron, 690
Levinsohn, Roger, 60
Levinson, Larry, 145, 448A
Levy, Lawrence, 665
Lew-Dave-Marv, 95, 111, 278
Lichtman, Mike, 100, 364
Limbach, Alfred, 1165, 1167
Linde, Maxine, 752
Linde, Dr. Ronald K., 752
Linder, Dorothy, 268, 271, 473
Little, Tom, 448
Livingston, Lee, 705
Livingston, Tom, 716
Lofstedt, Nelson, 745, 806, 1036, 1037, 1038, 1043, 1119
Long, Forrest, 27, 36
Lord, Dick, 251
Lubalin, Herb, 630, 631J 632J 635, 636, 789, 790, 1078

McArthur, Joan, 235, 878
McCabe, Edward A., 15, 46, 84, 147, 161, 165, 244, 319, 320, 322, 330, 331, 389, 394, 396, 400, 410, 412, 414, 415, 432
McCall, Bruce, 601
McCarthy, Ruth L., 59, 133
McCarthy, Tom, 231
McElligott, Tom, 44, 252
McEwan, Morag, 285
McGuire, Seumas, 227, 241, 891
McIntosh, Thomas, 760
Mackie, Vernon, 923
McLoughlin, Bob, 457
McNamee, Thomas, 363
McNeilly, Michael A., 924
Madrick, Jeffrey, 1104
Mailer, Norman, 1153
Magleby, McRay, 893
Mallin, Bob, 344
Malmo, John, 816
Mangano, Mike, 17, 29, 31, 61, 99, 134, 145, 312, 391, 395, 397, 399, 901
Manning, Phelps K., 810, 811
Marcus, Adrianne, 652
Margulies, Paul, 80, 81, 113, 151
Margulies, Warren, 325
Marino, Mike, 174, 175, 176, 177, 178, 179, 201, 224, 739
Marlens, Al, 595
Martin, Alan, 1118
Marwick, Maureen, 593
Marxman, Dr. Gerald A., 752
Maskaleris, Dee, 489
Matheo, Bob, 266
Mathews, Hoyt, 642
Mayes, Mike, 701
Mehl, Jürgen, 1164
Melgar, Fabian, 820
Mertz, Paul, 1139
Messing, Paul, 324
Messner, Tom, 41
Metzdorf, Lyle, 215
Meyer, Kurt, 732
Meylan, Dick, 213
Michlin, Spencer, 350, 351, 464
Miesmer, Charlie, 497
Miles, Lee, 576
Miller, George, 324
Miller, Lawrence, 923
Miller, Randy, 273
Miller, Scott, 63, 375
Mills, Katina, 246, 247, 248, 262
Mitchell, George, 94
Mohtaries, Alexander, 146
Moran, Tom, 653
Mower, Eric, 325
Mullen, Ken, 544, 547
Munsterberg, Marjorie, 659, 851
Murdock, Richard, 310
Murray, Jill, 486A
Murphy, John, 691
Murray, Bob, 721
Musser, Dodds, 186, 204
Myer, Peter L., 738
Myers, Ray, 200
Myers, Roger, 289

Naiman, Art, 27, 36
Nash, Veronica, 246, 247, 248, 262
Nathan, Thomas J., 30, 32, 46, 55, 84, 98, 109, 147, 392, 398, 431, 445
Naudet, Jean Jacques, 1028
Navarro, J. R., 234
Neal, Donna, 689
Needleman, Robin, 433
Neufeld, Bert, 423
Nevraumont, Peter, 696, 722
Newsom, Hal, 463, 472, 506
Noad, Frederick, 668
Noble, John, 329
Norica, Michael, 142
Nuchtern, Jean, 612

Ocko, Judy, 1123
Odel, Art, 736
Oelbaum, Carol, 79
Ofenstein, Sharon, 584
Olmsted, Richard, 25, 26, 35, 170, 193
O'Neill, Brian, 253
O'Neill, Joe, 392A, 396A, 401A, 425A
O'Rielly, Curvin, 451, 470
O'Rourke, P. J., 618
Ostrof, Bernard, 182, 299

Pannell, Cap, 687, 749
Parker, Lore, 121
Parks, Steve, 740A
Parsons Editorial Design Students, 664
Pasnick, Nadine, 355
Patterson, Rhodes, 656, 734, 917, 922
Peck, James S., 863
Peizer, Maurice, 505, 1115
Pekar, Marty, 886
Penchina, Steve, 199
Penn, Irving, 610
Peppis, Phil, 468
Perreault, John, 665
Petit, Marie, 506A, 553
Pettus, Ted, 77, 82
Pfiffner, Jerry, 267
Philip, Richard, 612
Pierson, Stevie, 24, 341
Pittman, Stuart, 70, 90, 143, 975
Place, Jennifer, 731
Plapler, Larry, 1, 74, 100, 120, 171, 195, 207, 222, 884

Pocknell, David, 1150, 1151
Poli, Kenneth, 998, 999
Popcorn, Faith, 70, 90, 143, 703, 975
Poppy, John, 652, 653, 654, 655
Probst, Cliff, 740
Prouk, G., 529
Puris, Martin, 160
Putian, Jamie, 697

Quennessen, Marie, 535
Quirk, Bill, 12

Raboy, Dick, 53
Radish, Buddy, 421
Ransdell, Mary Louise, 570, 599, 602, 1002
Rascovich, Mark, 679
Reiner, Carl, 173
Reingold, Harry, 1120
Remley, Street, 542
Revsin, Ethan, 368
Reynold, Charles, 1026
Richards, Stan, 702
Richman, Mel, 422
Rickabaugh, Rebin, 719, 802
Ricks, Sarah, 901
The Jonathan Rinehart Group, 768
Rishoff, Louise, 689
Roach, Robert H., 799
Robinson, Phyllis, 7, 441, 450, 471
Romann, Gad, 434
Rondthaler, Ed, 636, 637, 789, 790
Roop, Tamasin, 617
Rosen, John N., M.D., 1115
Rosenfeld, Ronald M., 213
Rosenthal, Dan, 10
Rosenthal, Jack, 566, 579, 621, 623, 1062, 1064, 1066, 1068, 1072, 1074, 1128, 1130, 1132
Rosner, Charles, 731
Rosoff, Gil, 490
Rossberg, Rudolf, 1143
Rossi, Steve, 721
Rothschild, Diane, 442
Ruffin, Fran, 578
Russo, John, 157, 166, 172, 207, 216, 222
Russo, Nat, 122
Russell, Bruce, 958
Russell, Susan, 357
Russler, Walter, 755, 782
Russo, John, 313, 367
Ryan, Peter, 1136

Sammes, Jacques, 162
Saxon, Robert, 49
Scanlon, Rosemary, 741
Schau, Michael, 667
Schechter, William, 786
Schickel, Richard, 660
Schiera, Richard, 354
Schmidt, Denis, 469
Schmitt, Ted, 750
Schneiter, Paul H., 788
Schulman, Stan, 374
Schwartz, Harold, 366
SCM Corporate Communications Dept., 761
Scully, Julia, 991, 1009, 1011, 1023, 1029
Shapiro, Joel, 612
Shenfield, Mark, 72, 132
Shrage, Paul, 743
Shyres, Mark, 916, 929
Silva, Larry, 733, 733A
Silver, Gail, 419
Silverman, Hal, 184, 202, 264
Silverman, Jack, 108
Simons, Hank, 1123
Simons, Mary, 565, 583, 994
Simpson, Jeffrey, 646
Simpson, John, 360A
Slesin, Suzanne, 711, 867
Smith, Elwood H., 720
Smith, Harry, 1181
Smith, Nancy, 505
Smith, Steve, 404
Smith, Tom, 214
Snyder, Carl Philip, 589
Solomon, Robert, 740A
Sons, Larry, 628, 805
Sorel, Edward, 1107
Spector, Larry, 1, 38, 168, 180
Spungin, Raymond, 741
SRA Copy Group, 257, 259
Stabin, Howard, 404
Stack, Richard, 765
Stamper, Judith Bauer, 662
Stanyer, Fred, 713
Stapleton, Rosalie M., 723
Starr, Roger, 596
Steel, David, 708
Stein, Mel, 345, 499
Stingley, Jim, 1070
Stevens, Jay, 210
Stone, John, 754, 756, 787
Stone, Ray, 1123
Sundland, Bob, 447, 452
Sullivan, Tim, 845

Taketa, Terry, 439
Tantillo, Joe, 209, 212, 223
Tankel, Sam, 730
Tarlow, Dick, 155, 288
Tashoff, Gene, 1049
Taylor, Bill, 427
Taylor, Jay, 874A, 875, 876
Taulbee, T., 759
Theodore, Alan, 274
Thieblot, Bernice A., 769, 910
Thiem, Ray, 420, 436
Thomas, Tom, 57, 112, 136, 454
Thrasher, Ed, 926, 981
Till, Diane, 48
Tobias, Tobi, 612
Tobias, William R., 810, 811
Toomey, Ellen, 1135
Tourtellot, Arthur, 793
Trachtman, Paul, 671
Trahey, Jane, 138
Trichon, James L., 643, 644
Turner, Tom, 63
VanderZee, John, 1033
Van Dine, Alan, 801, 804
Veder, Bob, 475, 483

Waddington, Margaret M., M.D., 648
Wagner, Valerie, 236, 353, 365, 425
Waldman, Stu, 1047
Walker, Peter, 859
Waterkotte, Mike, 903
Warner, C. Terry, 709
Weinstein, Sheldon, 751, 1048
Weis, Wally, 728
Welles, Kelly, 908, 909
Wells, Hugh, 437
Werner, Ray, 900
Whitted, J. C., 699
Wiesendanger, Uli, 509
Wilde, Judi, 873
Winch, Tony, 227, 241, 891
Wolff, Jeff, 428
Wolfman, Agustus, 1006, 1018, 1027, 1030
Wolsky, Alan, 12
Woodward, Walt
Wright, Bob, 418
Wright, Curtis, 66
Wright, Leonard, 904

Yanow, Jo, 731
Yates, Brock, 992
Yurcich, Tom, 297
Yustein, Mark, 315, 316, 341, 349

Zechman, Jan, 208

Directors

Arlow, Arnie, 356
Adams, Don, 421

Barker, Howard, 461
Barre, Rosemary, 317
Beck, E., 529

INDEX

Becker, Harold, 417
Berne, Jennifer, 356
Best, Steve, 532
Bianchi, Ed, 451, 468, 470
Blechman, R. O., 486A
Borders, Bill, 339
Brooks, Alan, 499
Brooks, Bob, 530, 531
Brown, Barry, 396, 400, 411, 414
Budin, Elbert, 364, 478, 483

Caggiano, John, 430
Capawana, Rod, 489
Chouinard, Roger, 486, 487
Covington, Hil, 420, 476
Crowther, Duane, 487

Dale, Jim, 348
DeSort, Jack, 393
De Vito, Ralph, 480
DeVoto, Joe, 404
de Vries, Dave, 426
Dorfsman, Lou, 494, 498A
Dymond, Russ, 335

Eckstein, Arthur, 495
Elliot, Steve, 371

Field, Larry, 355, 463
Flaum, Harley, 324
Fraker, William, 448A

Gage, Robert, 383, 441, 443, 450, 471
Gerstein, Mordy, 488
Giraldi, Bob, 369, 379, 430, 482, 496
Goldblatt, Stephen, 534
Goldman, Marty, 387
Gomes, George, 409
Greenberg, Harvey, 354
Griner, Norman, 428, 474, 475
Gyrs, Bob, 447

Haboush, Victor, 368
Hadley, Don, 307

Hamburg, Harry, 402
Hanwright, Joe, 375
Harris, Denny, 425
Heimann, Richard, 464
Herman, Frank, 389, 394, 410, 412, 415, 432
Herriott, Paul, 533
Hoffman, David, 497
Horn, Steve, 370, 376, 388, 408, 449, 455, 458, 459, 460, 465, 469, 481, 483
Howard, Mark, 492

Israelson, Peter, 373

Kane, Art, 454
Kasdan, Lawrence, 348

Levin, Lear, 435, 457
Levine, Arnold, 363
Levine, Rick, 456, 461, 504
Loew, Dick, 377, 498
Lovinger, Jeff, 376A, 381, 453, 466

McGarr, Gene, 462
McGinnis, George, 492
Magri, Massimo, 378, 424
Mangano, Mike, 391, 397, 399
Margulies, Warren, 325
Marshall, Sandra, 306, 307
Maze, Jud, 422
Miller, Dick, 427
Mitchel, Bob, 490
Mower, Eric, 325
Myers, Sid, 416, 429

Nagata, David, 505

Olds, Mike, 463

Piccirillo, Charles, 391, 395, 397, 399
Pytka, Joe, 374

Remley, Street, 542
Reitzfeld, Robert, 392, 431

Rossetti, Dominic, 428
Rotondi, Ed, 396A

Sandbank, Henry, 398, 431, 445
Sedelmaier, Joe, 365, 368, 448
Snider, Dick, 384, 472
Sokolsky, Mel, 464
Stone, Dick, 419

Tardio, Neil, 433
Toback, Norman, 426
Taylor, Medford, 479
Thomas, Pascal, 535
Tortoriello, Don, 380
Trenner, Mickey, 361

Ulick, Michael, 423, 467

Vergess, Laurent, 362
Vine, David, 372

Watts, Ron, 360
Weissinger, Ralph, 392A, 396A, 401, 425A
Williams, Larry, 418

Zander, Jack, 466

Producers

Anabel, Thomas, 375
Andelin, Gerald, 384
Anderson, Tom, 457

Bacal, Nancy, 387, 446
Barre, Rosemary, 312, 317, 329, 391
Barrow, Barbara, 483
Becton, Sue, 467
Bernstein, Dick, 488
Bloom, Merl, Assoc., 337
Borders, Bill, 339
Boyriven, Patrick, 413
Bragg, George, 464

Calhoun, Susan, 388
Campbell, Nancy, 469
Carroll, Suzanne, 448
Chesloff, Paul, 417
Cigarini, John, 530, 531
Coleman, Fletcher, 433
Cole & Weber, 463, 472
Collins, Janet, 327
Conti, Paul, 314, 346
Coughter, Peter J., Jr., 479
Cowan, Barbara, 442
Coyne, Jim, 323, 352

Davis, David E., Jr., 440
DeBarros, Jim, 395, 397, 399
DeBona, Glenn, 403
Del Nunzio, Paula, 484
DePlautt, Suzanne, 313
De Vito, Ralph, 480
de Vries, Dave, 426
Dick Orkin Creative Services, 332
Disalvo, Frank, 430
Dorfsman, Lou, 494, 498, 498A
Durham, Magi, 496
Dymond, Russ, 335

Engle, Robert, 454

Fagin, Cliff, 383, 441, 443, 450, 471
Fahnestock, William, 532, 534
Fenton, Tom, 453, 466, 477
Field, Larry, 355
Flynn, Diane, 423

Goldberg, Richard, 504
Golden, Kathi, 344
Gomes-Loew, 377
Gorman, Jeff, 326
Gramaglia, John, 423, 467
Gray, Dennis, 357
Greenberg, Harvey, 354
Grey, Norman, 345, 499
Grumish, Jim, 393, 402
Guskind, Elin, 338

Hadley, Don, 306
Hall, Percy, 481

Harmon, Miles, 495
Hartog, Pam Den, 305, 447, 452
Hays, Karen, 533
Heyl, Virginia, 440
Hill, John, 350, 351
Hoeck, Kimberly, 411
Hudson, Molly A., 328

Infantino, Vinnie, 421, 428, 475, 483

Jensen, L., 529
Jeremias, Diane, 370, 458, 459, 460, 465

Kane, Mel, 311, 318, 438
Kasdan, Lawrence, 348
Keane, Jack, 488
Kearns, Maureen, 376A, 377
Kessler, Syd, 541
Kirchmeier, Susan, 372
Kreeger, Jerry, 374
Kuperman, Lewis, 316, 343, 349, 392A, 401A, 425A

Lacey, Jim, 485A
Landi, Phylis, 455
Lassman, Ira, 416, 429
Lee, Raymond, 541
Levy, Mark, 487

McGinnis, George, 492
McGrath, Tom, 409
Mangel, Bert, 371
Marshall, Sandra, 306, 307, 308
Matthies, Gil, 310
Mayo, Geoff, 461
Messina, Phil, 373
Mevorach, Linda, 456
Michels, Joanne, 426
Michlin, Spencer, 350
Miller, George, 324
Mitchneck, Marvin, 488
The Mix Place, 322
Mower, Eric, 325
Murray, Jill, 486A

Nathan, Thomas J., 392
National Recording, 315
Nicolo, Frank, 380
Novick, Steve, 309, 340, 358, 474

Paradise, Michael, 420, 436, 437
Perez, Manny, 473
Powers, Dennis, 451, 470
Puopolo, Lou, 410, 419

Rangell, Syd, 361, 362
Reitzfeld, Robert, 392
Remley, Street, 542
Revsin, Ethan, 368
Rosoff, Gil, 496
Ross, Mark, 427
Rubin, Manning, 421
Ruesing, Joanne, 406

Samama, Vera, 376A
Schenkel, Bob, 378, 424
Schulman, Paul, 448A
Scibetta, Joe, 379, 478
Scott, John, 481
Selig, Bertille, 419, 422
Sinclair, Sandy, 367
Smith, Billy Ray, 366
Springer, Reed, 439
Stein, Mel, 345, 499
Stevens, Judith, 427
Stewart, Brian, 462
Suarez, Phil, 369, 482
Swan, Jim, 468

Troncone, Reggie, 434

Ullett, Nick, 334

Warnick, Buck, 333
Wiland, Harry, 497
Wineapple, Patty, 360A
Wolf, Michael, 505
Worcester, Phil, 430
Wypich, Harry, 353, 365, 425

Yagoda, Ken, 359

Cameramen Cinematographers

Best, Steve, 532

Caparros, Ernie, 391, 395
Cotts, Gerald, 461
Cronewith, Jordan, 447

Davis, George, 488
Dubbleman, Richard, 383, 443, 450, 471

Evans, Tony, 1151

Goldblatt, Stephen, 534

Hoffman, David, 497
Howard, Mark, 492

Kalogeratos, Jerry E., 495
Kellgran, Ray, 533
Knoop, John, 480

McGinnis, George, 492
Mounier, Colin, 535

Nagata, David, 505

Peterman, Fred, 452

Roeg, Nicolas, 434
Rosson, Ed, 469

Stone, Dick, 419

Taylor, Medford, 479
Thorpe, David, 507
Townsand, Julian, 363

Music

Anacrusis Music, 314

Band, J. Geils, 338
Berg, Richard, 360A
Briggs, David, 310
Brooks, Joe, 317

Cohen, Michael, 358
Dawes Productions, Tom, 360

Golson, Bennie, 311
Grant & Murtaugh, 329

Handel, George F., 325
HEA Assoc., 333, 337, 359
Hill, John, 350

Labunski Productions, 328, 346
Lavsky's Music House, 325
Lucas/McFaul Productions, 357

Mathews, Dave, 344
Mega Music Corp., 310, 356
Michlin, Spencer, 350, 351
National Recording, 316, 321, 335, 336, 343, 349
Simpson, John, 360A

Production Companies

Ampersand Productions, 364, 379, 439, 478, 483, 496
A&R Recording Studio, 333, 359
Arthur Eckstein & Assoc., 495
Aura Recording, 309, 340
Avon Productions, 392A, 396A, 401A, 425A

Bell Sound, 306, 307, 308, 348
R. O. Blechman, Inc., 486A, 489
Braverman Productions, 440
Brillig Productions, 396, 400, 411, 414, 440
Brooks, Alan, 494

INDEX

Brooks Fulford Cramer Ltd., 530, 531

Cabell Eanes Advertising, 479
Coast Recorders, San Francisco, 353
Cole & Weber, 355
Crescendo Productions, 309, 358

Tom Dawes Productions, 360
DeSort/Sam, 393
Director's Circle, 494, 498A
Directors Studio, 383, 391, 395, 397, 399, 441, 442, 443, 450
D.S.I., 430
Duck Soup Productions, 486, 487
Duffix Productions, 367

Edstan Studio, 494, 498A
Entertainment Concepts, 421
EUE/Screen Gems, 361, 373, 380, 387, 413, 490
EUE Video, 371

Filmfair, 447
Flickers, 403, 422

James Garrett and Partners, 434
Generation Sound, 358
Giraldi Productions, 430, 482
Gomes/Loew, 409, 498
Grant & Murtaugh, 344
Grapevine Productions, 372
Griner Cuesta, 428, 475

Haboush Co., 368
Hamster Productions, 362
Denny Harris Inc., 425
Harvest Films, 452
HEA Productions, 337
Herriott, Paul, 533

Covington, Hil, 420, 436, 437
Horn/Griner Productions, 376, 388, 455, 469, 474, 481
Steve Horn, Inc., 370, 408, 444, 449, 458, 460, 465, 483

Image Factory, 492
Independent Artists, 448A

Kaleidoscope Films, 401, 467
Phil Kimmelman & Assoc., 488

Labunski Productions, 328
N. Lee Lacy, 384, 417, 463, 472
Stan Lang Productions, 473
Dick Levine Productions, 451, 470
Lear Levin Productions, 435, 457
Rick Levine Productions, 456, 461, 504
Lovinger, Tardio, Melsky, 381, 433, 453, 466

McGraw-Hill Pacific Productions, 402
Master Sound, 345
Mega Music, 356
Michlin & Hill, 350, 351, 464
Milan Films, 468
The Mix Place, 319, 320, 330, 331
Mobius Productions Ltd., 532
Mary Tyler Moore Productions, 477
Myers & Eisenstat, 416, 429

David Nagata Productions, 505

Dick Orkin Creative Services, 332

Pepper Studios, 542
Perpetual Motion, 371
Petersen Co., 426, 494, 498A
Phoenix Films Corp., 462
Politecne Cinematografica, 378, 424
Lou Puopolo, Inc., 418, 419

Quadrophonic Productions, 310

Rabko Television Productions Ltd., 529
Ramsey Enterprises, 404
Radio & Records, 326
Radio Band of America, 323, 324, 352
Rossetti Films, 428

Henry Sandbank Films, 398, 431
Scali, McCabe, Sloves, 392
SDC, 314
Sedelmaier Films, 365, 366, 448
Spectrum Studios, 339
Studio One, 327
Sunlight Pictures, 464

Talieson Productions, 480
Telema, 535
Televideo Productions, 389, 394, 410, 412, 415, 432
J. Walter Thompson, 334
Toback & Assoc., 426

Uncle Film Co., 423

Varied Directions, 497

Wakeford/Orloff, 375, 446, 464
WAMO, 541
Waterbarrel, 438
Wylde and Assoc., 374, 406, 427, 454

Zander's Animation Parlour, 466

Artists Photographers

Abels, Tom, 682
Abromowitz, Jerry, 154, 714
A/D Associates, 397
Adelman, Bob, 1054
Aiosa, Vince, 609, 618, 892
Alexander, David, 175A
Allen, Julian, 596, 605, 607
Aller, Bill, 925
American Institute of Graphic Arts Members, 663
Ammirati, Ralph, 160
Andersen, John, 859
Anderson, Jim, 988
Ansel, Ruth, 623
Antonio, 583
Aoki, Kazuo, 519
Appel, Allen, 1089
Arbogast, Bill, 725
Arcineaux, Marc, 618
Arisman, Marshall, 860A
Arton, Inc., 3, 9, 11, 43, 88
Art Factory, 642
Audubon, John James, 650, 660
Avedon, Richard, 50
Axelson, Keith, 1035
Azuma, Don, 167

Baker, Stan, 957
Baldwin, Joel, 570, 599, 608

INDEX

Bama, James, 256
Banke, Martin, 708
Barille, Carl, 1100
Barley, Bill, 233
Barr, Neal, 747
Barrious, Pedro, 40, 127
Bass, Saul, & Assoc., 905, 983, 984
Bastiansen, Pete, 721
Batlin, Lee, 125, 144
Battaglia, Lee, 584
Beale, John, 514, 515
Beaver, Allan, 120
Beaver, Bert, 791
Beck, Arthur, 78
Beck, Rudolf, 856
Beck, Stan, 162
Beckerman, Arnold, 73, 110, 157, 717
Behnken, Wolfgang, 1143
Belew, Tandy, 966
Bell, Bert, 549
Bender, Bob, 174, 175, 177, 178, 179, 201, 224
Bernhardt, Craig, 809
Bernstein, Saalmon, 637
Bettman Archives, 754, 787
Bice, Paul, Jr., 958
Biderbost, Bill, 642
Billout, Guy, 1106
Binzen, Bill, 565
Bishop, Edward, 260
Bishop, Larry, 936, 970, 977
Blackman, Barry, 569
Blanch, Bob, 44
Blassi, Jaime, 1163
Blassi, Jorge, 1163
Blechman, R. O., 298, 486A, 489, 1076
Blinkoff, Richard, 40, 127
Boatright, John, 816
Bocca, Del, 509
Boege, Uli, 1126
Bonnell, Bill, III, 656, 882
Bookbinder, Lester, 547, 1136
Booth, Greg, 754, 756, 787
Bordelon, Melinda, 605, 607
Bourdin, Guy, 510, 552
Bourke-White, Margaret, 662
Boulevard Photographic, 801
Bourne, Bob, 514, 515, 520
Boyd, Gus, 238, 239, 242, 887
Brandi, Uwe, 1167
Brooks, Charlotte, 713
Brown, Donna, 1176
Brown, George, 738
Brown, Michael David, 874A, 875, 876
Brown, Win, 506
Bruemmer, Fred, 1155
Bruin, Bill, 745, 806, 1038, 1043
Buchanan, Rodger, 1006, 1018, 1027
Budin, Elbert, 168
Butera, Gene, 1017

Cailor-Resnick, 21, 72, 74, 120, 132, 163, 171, 195, 884
Callas, Chris, 836, 1050
Calogero, Gene, 18
Campbell, Robert, 1022
Canaan, David, 661
Candioty, David, 752A
Carnase, Tom, 703, 731, 943, 954, 963, 982
Carr, Doug, 670
Carruthers, Roy, 299, 619, 1091
Casad, Mike, 708
Casado, Barbara, 842
Casado, John, 842
Case, Janie, 690
Cassidy, Chuck, 703
Cayea, John, 595
Cazzaniga, Luigi, 1010
Chadwick, Tabor, 94
Chapleau, Serge, 1140
Chapman, Michael, 883
Charles, Osborn, 140, 141
Chepelsky, John R., 967
Chermayeff, Ivan, 748, 784, 857, 870, 871
Cherpitel, Simone, 635, 789
Chiana, Philip,. 827
Chouinard, Roger, 486
Chwast, Seymour, 685, 833, 853, 1063, 1068, 1093, 1105, 1127, 1132, 1136
Cipriani, Robert, 765
Clemens, Clint, 1036, 1119
Cober, Alan E., 637, 808, 1086
Cochran, George, 13
Cohen, Jerry, 133
Cohen, Leonard, 182
Cohn, Irwin, 59, 133
Cole, Rhea G., 899
Collier, John, 3, 9, 11, 43, 88
Collins, Jim, 229
Conboy, John, 232
Connors, Tom, 940
Connors, William, 106
Cook, Verdun, 578, 585
Cooley, Gary, 466
Cooper, Heather, 1152, 1169, 1179, 1180, 1182
Cooper, Oz, 630
Cooperstein, Sam, 149
Corey, Chris, 36
Corhan, Harold, 649
Cosimo, 48, 217, 219, 226, 228, 797
Costanza, Nick, 734
Courtos, Tom, 824
Cowan, Frank, 17
Cranbourne, Ray, 1045
Crowther, Duane, 487
Cruz, Ray, 681
Curilla & Assoc., 214
Cusack, Margaret, 603, 825
Czyrba, Jan, 176, 250, 739

Dadds, Jerry, 961
Dale, Robert, 3, 43
Dallas Cap & Emblem Co., 846
Dalrymple, DeWayne, 815
D'Amico, Dennis, 155
Dankwardt, Ken, 701
Davidson, Bruce, 724, 760, 762
Davis, Frederika, 612
Davis, Hal, 114, 122
Davis, Jack, 914, 1036, 1119
Davis, Lynn, 1004
Davis, Paul, 1102
Davis, Vince, 486
deGast, Robert, 937
Delessert, Etienne, 1090
De Milt, Ron, 27, 36
Deschamps, Bob, 203
DiFiore, Gabriel, 900, 903
Dinnerstein, Harvey, 605
Dolby, John, 960, 969, 971
Dolce, Steve, 130
Dolgins, Alan, 161, 165
Donovan, Michael, 867
Doret, Michael, 928, 968, 1130
Dorfsman, Lou, 494, 498A
Doss, David, 246, 247, 248, 262
Doyle Dane Bernbach Studio, 546
Drackert, Thomas D., 34
Dube, Barbara, 260
Dublin, Rick, 44
Duffy, Brian, 512
Dunkley, Richard, 512
Dunn, Phoebe, 1036, 1119
Duskin, Ken, 64
Dyer, Rod, 695

Edwards, Gregory, 252
Ehrlich, George, 65, 126
Elgort, Arthur, 40, 127
Endress, Buddy, 698
Endress, John Paul, 131, 780
Engler, Hanno, 1143
Erlanger, Richard, 972

INDEX

Erwitt, Elliott, 654, 994
Eucalyptus Tree Studio, 961
Evans, Peter, 135

Faller, Karl, 1037
Farrell, Bill, 758
Fasciano, Nick, 23, 840
Fauchon, Daniel, 521
Federico, Helen, 714, 715
Fewsmith, Phil, 696, 722
Fiedler, Hal, 1118
Field, Pat, 1060
Fillhardt, Charles, 66
Finne, Ron, 719
Fisher, Carl, 3, 9, 11, 43, 85, 88, 92, 103, 117, 118, 131, 153, 157, 243, 265, 266, 267, 268, 271, 286, 993, 1012, 1032
Folon, Jean Michel, 740, 1131
Forer, Dan, 20
Forrest, Alan, 721
Foster, Frank, 231, 1036, 1119
Four by Five Inc., 116, 142
Francekevich, Al, 274
Francisco & Booth, 628, 687, 749, 756
Franek, David J., 869
Frank, Dick, 95, 278, 283, 639, 786
Freson, Robert, 108
Freid, Ethel K., 934
Fudyma, Janice, 809
Fugiwara, Gary, 1037
Funazu, Kanyo, 1159
Furuta, Carl, 157, 173, 230
Fusco, Paul, 653

Gaadt, David, 901
Gaadt, George, 807
Gaetano, Nicholas, 1099
Gallardo, Gervasio, 90, 143
Gallucci, Ed, 692
Garber, Maury, 868
Gateway Studios, 801, 804
Gatha, Ashvin, 998
Gauger, David, 733, 733A, 800
Gelberg, Bob, 16
Gersten, Gerry, 632, 633, 635, 789, 1135
Gerstein, Mordy, 488
Gervasi, Doug, 853
Getsug, Don, 44
Gladstone, Gary, 763
Glaser, Milton, 830, 850, 853
Glinn, Bunt, 757
Gnidziejko, Alex, 1082, 1181
Goodman, Alan, 58, 130
Gold, Charles, 58, 96, 130, 189, 190, 206
Gold, Mike, 586
Gonzales, Manny, 841
Gordon, Larry Dale, 1003
Gormley, James, 742
Goro, Herb, 688
Goude, Jean Paul, 562
Gould, Chester, 371
Grashow, James, 100, 890
Green, Allen, 621
Green, Norman, 87, 124, 125, 144
Groh, Maryann, 1036, 1119
Gross, Gary, 843
Grossman, Robert, 1077
Guarcello, Marjorie, 710, 861
Guyaux, Jean-Marie, 1126

Hagen, Paul, 721
Haggerty, Mick, 686, 839
Haling, George, 757
Hallström, Bjorn, Dr., 202
Hamilton, David, 284
Hammons, Jeanne, 669
Hampton, Michael, 865
Handler, Edward, 723
Hane, Roger, 1078
Hansen, Steve, 765
Harris, Michael, 6, 42
Harris, Ned, 1052
Hartmann, Erich, 780
Hausman, George, 780
Hege, Laszlo, 641
Heindel, Robert, 294, 1124
Heinly, John, 1092, 1113
Hendra, Judy, 609
Hering, Al, 670
Herrero, Lowell, 236
Hess, Dick, 609, 707, 828, 858
Hess, Milo, 670
Hiett, Steve, 590
Hill, Chris, 687, 749
Hinrichs, Kit, 729
Ho, Francis T., 1053
Hoar, Charles, 745, 806, 1038, 1043
Holland, Bob, 796
Holland, Brad, 1062, 1064, 1066, 1069
Holland, Ralph, 93
Horn, Steve, 80, 81, 84, 101, 113, 151
Horowitz, Irwin, 593, 907, 908, 909
Horowitz, Ryszard, 672
Houles, Pierre, 614
Howard, Jim, 40, 127
Howard, Mark, 492
Huebner, Richard, 751, 1048
Huffaker, Sandy, 200
Humphrey, Henry, 688
Hunter, Stan, 1096
Hwang, Kuytae, 1026
Hyatt, John, 716

Igarashi, Takenobu, 1170
Ingham, Carole, 1157

Janson, Henri, 186, 204
Janu, Rudolf, 922
Jean, Carole, 1124A
Jefferies, Ron, 750
Jenkins, Bill, 838
Jerman, George, 839
Johnson, Asa, 694
Johnson, Doug, 854
Johnson, Lisa, 936
Jones, Dawson, 780
Jorstad, Stan, 734
Joy, Guy, 988
Juett, Dennis S., 924

Kaestle, David, 609, 618
Kaleya, Tana, 1004
Kane, Art, 112, 591, 1005, 1008, 1015, 1024
Kaplan, Alan, 1007, 1030
Karales, James H., 1002
Karrasch, Larry, 1123
Kasloff, Steve, 670
Katz, Peter, 632, 635, 789
Kawasaki, Michael, 738
Kazu, 208
Keane, John, 988
Keating, Kate, 736, 974, 980
Kehe, John, 175A
Kelley, Tom, 816
Kelly, Michael, 971
Kennedy, Nancy, 682
Kew, Tony, 522
Kimbell, Wayne, 979
King, Bill, 138
Kirckham, John, 971
Klauber, George, 713
Knight, Jacob, 1135
Kopelow, Paul, 759
Krause, George, 769, 1115
Krieger, Harold, 576
Kuzmanoff, Leon, 160, 181, 279
Kwong, Sam, 234

LaCasse, Bernie, 678
LaGarrigue, Jean, 1136
Lambray, Maureen, 40, 127, 611, 1020
Langley, Dave, 126, 131
LaMonica, Chuck, 79, 145
Land, Edwin, 783
Lane, Tony, 826
Langer, Victor, 987, 989

INDEX

Langley, David, 31, 61, 71, 76, 129, 134, 158, 901
LaPerle, Thom, 767
Lawrence, Kenn, 746A
Lee, Bud, 574
Lee, Kai-Chung, 935
Leer, Barbara Jo, 931
Lefeber, C. George, 752A
Lefkowitz, Jack, 643, 644
Lefkowitz, Pam, 643, 644
Legname, Rudy, 99, 145, 209, 212, 223
Leibovitz, Annie, 571, 580, 613, 652, 990, 996, 1016
Leone, Frank, 718, 921
Le-Tan, Pierre, 556, 557, 558, 559, 560, 561
Levine, David, 577, 1073
Levins, Mike, 47
Libera, Joan D., 752
Lichtman, Michael, 28, 890
Lienhart, Jim, 959
Littlejohn, William, 384
Lloyd, Peter, 895
Lombardo, Ken, 13
Lord, Bette, 997
Lucka, Klaus, 12, 130
Ludwick, Gary, 185
Lyons, Marv, 269

McAffee, Mara, 618
McBride, Will, 653
McCall, Brian, 1088
McCall, Bruce, 601
McCarthy, Tom, 150
McCullin, Donald, 253
McDonnell, Mike, 1031
McGinnis, George, 162, 492
Machlica, Dennis, 670
McLean, Wilson, 1080, 1116, 1125
McMullan, James, 605, 1112
MacWeeney, Alen, 76, 104, 129
McWilliams, Clyde, 785, 1046
Madonald, Norman, 710
Maffia, Daniel, 707
Magleby, McRay, 788
Manoff, Richard K., 37
Maisel, Jay, 277, 847, 1009, 1028, 1047
Manzo, Richard, 889
Marco, Phil, 93, 97, 142, 768
Marini, Climes & Guip, 819
Mark, Mary Ellen, 652
Markow Studio, 699
Marshutz, Roger, 751, 1042, 1048
Martin, Andre, 1011, 1023, 1029
Martin, Miguel, 999
Mayea, Larry, 1058
Mazzurco, Phil, 244
Melgar, Fabian, 820
Menken, Howard, 126
Merrill, David, 622
Mesney, Doug, 992
Metzler, Doug, 913
Meyerowitz, Rick, 586
Michals, Duane, 555
Miho, James, 700
Miller, Jim, 705
Miller, Melabee M., 817
Miller, Randy, 273
Millikan, Bill, 752A
Minor, Wendell, 673, 679
Mitchel, Bob, 496
Miyauchi, Harvo, 685, 853
Monroe, Robert, 276, 281
Morales, Karen, 893
Morgan, Joseph, 584
Mori, Ken, 575
Morris, Brian, 518
Moscati, Frank, 713
Muller, Jean-Claude, 951
Murawski, Alex, 941
Myers, Lou, 68, 75, 137, 1120
Naar, Jon, 1153
Nadel, Marc, 159, 263
Nakagawa, Mas, 680
Nardelli, Will, 638
Nava, Richard, 947
Neal, Donna, 689
Nelson, Bill, 1095
Neumeier, Marty, 237, 965
Newkirk, Susan, 791
Nielsson, Lennart, 1134
Nishimura, Norman, 554, 578
Noble, Richard, 130, 170, 180, 193
Nones, Leonard, 585
Numan, Mariet, 1139
Nye, Rick, 738

Obremski, George, 275
O'Neill, Michael, 70, 89, 105, 123, 143, 152, 155, 288
Orosz, Istvan, 1129
Osborne, Jan, 708
Otnes, Fred, 744, 1123

Packenham, Compton, 931
Padgett, Robert, 917
Pagliuso, Jean, 1014, 1025
Pakter, Robert, 618
Palladino, Tony, 730
Palombi, Peter, 837, 981
Palulian, Dickran, 1079, 1110
Panuska, Bob, 189, 888
Papadopolous, Peter, 4, 5, 45, 76, 129, 211
Parsons Editorial Design Students, 644
Pateman, Mick, 137, 795
Patti, Joe, 247, 262
Paul, Arthur, 589
Peccinotti, Harri, 1150
Peellaert, Guy, 647
Penn, Irving, 610
Peters, Christa, 1166
Peterson, Gosta, 285
Petrucelli, Tony, 62, 121, 136, 137
Phillips, Robert, 588, 1049
Pierce, Mike, 878
Pietropaxola, Vincenzo, 1144
Pinkney, Jerry, 1036, 1119
Piper, Christian, 568, 685, 853, 1074, 1098
Pirtle, Woody, 196, 687, 702, 749, 805, 838, 930, 938
Pittman, Blair, 694
Plain, Denis, 1138
Pocknell, David, 1151, 1156, 1173, 1175
Porcella, Phil, 1036, 1119
Powell, Ivan, 296
Pozar, Pompeo, 582
Prechtl, Michael Mathias, 1067
Preston, Neal, 581
Proctor, Gillean, 516, 517
Punchatz, Don Ivan, 86, 187, 293, 889, 1103
Push Pin Studios, 9, 43, 849

Quidor, Philippe, 506A

Raab, Mike, 257
R & V Studio, 186, 204
Rainer, Oskar, 1162
Ratzkin, Lawrence, 675, 676
Raymond, Charles, 1136
Raynor, Dean, 1171
Recker, Linda, 929
Reid, Scott F., 946
Reilly, Chris, 506
Reiser, Judy, 794
Rickabaugh, Heidi, 719
Rickabaugh, Robin, 719, 802
Rinaldo, Ginny, 10·
Rindner, Jack, 578
The Roberts Group, 699
Robinson, Cervin, 881
Roher, Melanie, 864
Rose, Alan, 618

INDEX

Rougier, Michael, 47
Rousso, Steve, 956
Rozman, Ron, 625
Rubin, Mark, 880
Rubenstein, Dave, 721
Run Run Shaw, 710
Ruffins, Reynold, 923

Sachs, Cal, 206
Sacks, Andrew, 614
Sagan, John, 743
Samardge, Nick, 8, 45
Sandbank, Henry, 30, 32, 46, 49, 55, 98, 107, 109, 143, 147, 148, 184, 202
Sarapochiello, Jerry, 710, 860A
Sargent, John Singer, 657
Saunders, Tim, 1152, 1169
Schaffer and King, 609
Schatz, Arthur, 768
Schell, Ellsworth, 931
Schellenger, Kent, 780
Scher, Paula, 886
Schlüter, Doris, 1164
Schlüter, Harald, 1164
Schneider, Richard, 948
Schockner, Jan, 10
Schreiber, Martin, 836
Schreiber, Mort, 780
Scott, Ron, 1034, 1041, 1059
Seeff, Norman, 827, 1051
Seki, Akihiko, 915, 973
Seltzer, Isadore, 939
Seton, Tom, 115
Severson, Kent, 34
Shapiro, Don, 716
Shaefer, Rick, 624
Shaffer, Stan, 926
Shenfield, Mark, 132
Shimokochi, Mamoru, 737
Shotwell, Charles, 629
Sidjakov, Nicolas, 706, 716
Siebel, Barbara, 670
Sieff, Jean-Loup, 991
Siegel, Anita, 1072
Silano, 602
Silber, Mark, 791
Sillen, Larry, 29
Silver, Marvin, 709, 753, 755, 782
Silverek, Don, 725
Silverman, Burt, 605
Silverman, Madeline, 638
Silverstein, Donald, 1136
Simpson, Craig, 1033
Simpson, Nicki, 564
Siskind, Aaron, 791
Sisty, Janis, 950
Skoorka, Susan
Smith, Elwood H., 720
Smith, Gordon E., 592
Smiton, David, 105, 143
Snyder, Jerome, 634, 1111, 1121
Snyder, Joel, 198
Socher, Jerry, 752
Sokolosky, Melvin, 202, 264
Solin, Gary, 904, 906
Sommer, Mel, 486, 487
Somoroff, Ben, 102, 287
Sorel, Edward, 292, 746, 844, 1075, 1094, 1104, 1107
Spindell, David, 23
Stag, 550
Starr, Allan, 699
Stavrinos, George, 853
Steadman, Ralph, 579, 1065, 1071, 1108, 1128
Steigman, Stephen, 60, 67, 238, 272, 1040
Steinberg, Bruce, 835
Steinberg, Saul, 879
Stern, Bert, 57, 136, 655
Stern, Herb, 694
Stettner, Bill, 7
Stone, Bob, 79
Strand, Paul, 566
Storey, Barron, 707
Strandell, Don, 976
Sullivan, Ron, 756
Swope, Martha, 612

Taback, Simms, 923
Tanen, Norman, 108
Tang, Ying Wei, 710
Tanous, Dorothy, 614
Tartak, Donald H., 752
Taylor, Richard, 979
Tennant, Dawn, 1152
Thoen, Don, 44, 721
Thomas, Lamont, 848
Thorpe, David, 550, 1161
Thorpe, Don O., 788
Tiani, Alex, 1123
Tiadecki, Bill, 139
Tilley, Arthur, 249
Tinker, Ted, 815
Tirpack, Dave, 670
Tomlinson, Rich, 198
Toto, Joe, 136, 142, 157, 254, 255, 258, 261
Touchet, Leo, 563
Traynor, Pete, 978
Trousdell, Mabey, 845, 863
Turbeville, Deborah, 40, 127
Turnau, Jeff, 14
Turner, Pete, 77, 82, 83, 572, 780, 1001, 1039, 1055, 1056
Tyson, Don R., 752A
Tyson, Poppe, 897

Uelsmann, Jerry N., 995
Unangst, Andrew, 166
Ungerer, Tomi, 1165
Upper, Tom, 701
Upshur, Tom, 832
Uzzle, Burk, 662, 780

van den Hoed, Ruut, 955
VanDeveer, David, 819
Van Noy & Co. Staff, 911
Vendikos, Tasso, 693
Vicari, Jim, 146
Vine, David, 164, 169, 747
Viola, Tony, 227, 241, 891
Vogel, Allen, 19, 119A, 855
von dem Bussche, Wolf, 761
Von Tiederman, Rudi, 1171

Wald, Carol, 1097
Walker, Allen D., 726, 735
Walker, Paul, 1169
Wallach, Jack, 280
Walters, Tom, 22
Wann, Danny, 713
Warner Bros. Pictures, 573
Warren, Steve, 520
Waterkotte, Mike, 900
Waterman, Bob, 752
Watson, Albert, 911, 913
Weaver, Robert, 1081, 1117
Webb, Charles, 724
Weihs, Tom, 728
Whistler, James McNeill, 657
Whistlin Dixie, 1, 38, 172, 207, 216, 222
White, Charles E., III, 1122, 1145, 1146, 1147, 1148
White, Jerry, 905
Whitesides, Kim, 24
Whitmore, Ken, 750
Widmann, Jochen, 1137
Wilcox, David, 189, 206, 607, 1101
Willardson, Dave, 289, 874, 926, 1083
Willoughby, Bob, 660
Wilson, John, 1087
Wilson, Sibyl, 791
Winslow, Michael, 93
Wise, Herbert, 669
Wolf, Henry, 270, 620, 1013, 1057
Woo, Calvin, 950
Wosk, Miriam, 1100

Yamashita, Hiroshi, 927
Yurcich, Tom, 297

Zagorski, Stan, 674
Zaid, Barry, 710

Ziemienski, Dennis, 725
Zoiner, John, 785, 1046

Agencies

Aalders & Marchant, 512
ABC Corporate Art Dept., 814
Abel, Robert, 979
Adamec Associates, 982
Adler, Schwartz & Connes, 914
Alskog, 652, 653, 654, 655
Ammirati Puris AvRutick, 160
Ancona/Gianakos Inc., 743
Angeli Graphics, Primo, 682
Anselmo Design Assoc., John, 726, 735
Anspach Grossman Portugal, 759, 798
Antupit & Others, 637
APCL&K, 360
Ariel Music Publications, 668
Arlow Advertising, 356
Art Attack, 839
Art Center College of Design, 723
Art Factory, The, 696, 722
Ashton-Worthington, 869, 978
Atlantic Records, 338, 712, 836, 837
N. W. Ayer Abh International, 267, 420, 436, 437

BBDM, 960, 971
BBDO, 344, 350, 351, 371, 457, 462, 464
Barnett, Zlotnick Advertising, 703
Baron, Costello & Fine, 4, 5, 8, 45
Barton-Gillet Co., 796
Bass & Assoc., Saul, 737, 905, 983, 984
Bates Advertising, Ted, 79
Baxter/Seivert Assoc., 746A
Benton & Bowles, 97, 104, 116, 142, 149, 405, 406, 413
Bergthold, Fillhardt, & Wright, 66
BirthdayBook, 810, 811
Blechman, R. O., 298
Bloom Agency, The, 354
Blue Green, Inc., 203
Boase Massimi Pollitt, 853
Botsford Ketchum, 306, 307, 308, 384, 486A, 1042
Boyarski, Daniel, 799
Bradford and Assoc., Peter, 795
Brain Reserve, 975
Brand-Edmonds Packett, 967
Braun Inc., Craig, 874
Brendel Typographic Service, 742
Brigham Young University, 661, 738, 788, 893
Bruce, Henry & Davis, 1041
Buddah Records, 832
Burnett Ltd., Leo, 544, 547
Burns & Cooper Ltd., 1152, 1169, 1179, 1180, 1182

Cabell Eanes Advertising, 479
Cabot, Cabot & Forbes, 765
Calderhead, Jackson, 86, 159, 187, 263
Campbell-Ewald Co., 328, 440
Campaign Palace, The, 518, 520, 542
Caravetta Allen Kinbrough, 888
Cargill, Wilson & Acree, 22, 185, 229, 233
Carl Ally, 41, 68, 69, 75, 76, 78, 129, 137, 139, 211, 218, 220, 221, 225, 376, 376A, 377, 378, 424, 511
Case & McGrath, 411
CBS/Broadcast Group, 23, 162, 494, 498, 498A, 504, 681, 793, 915, 939, 973
Center for Advanced Research in Design, 764
Chalek & Dreyer, 380
Chalk, Nissen, Hanft, 117, 118, 153
Champion Papers, 663, 710, 852, 860A, 861
Chermayeff & Geismar Assoc., 748, 757, 784, 857, 870, 871, 872, 879, 932
Chiat/Day, 305, 447, 452
Chicago, 436
Chirurg & Cairns, 119A, 146
CIBA-Geigy Corp., 957
Cliff Covington Design, 848
Cole & Weber, 339, 355, 472, 506, 708
Collett Dickenson, 530, 531
Columbia Records, 828, 840, 844, 846, 847, 886, 920
Container Corporation Communications Dept., 656, 680, 734, 882, 917, 922
Continental Oil Company, 1096
Corporate Annual Reports, 758, 763
Cox & Co. Advertising, 56, 418
Creative Services, Inc., 740A
Cross Design Office, James, 709, 753, 755, 782, 803
Crowell, T. Y., 652, 653, 654, 655

Dailey & Assoc., 911
Dancer-Fitzgerald-Sample, 39, 156
Daniel, Riley & Hogg Advertising, 936, 970, 977
D'Arcy MacManus & Masius, 490
David, Oksner & Mitchneck, 488
Della Femina, Travisano & Partners, 13, 19, 72, 73, 85, 110, 132, 157, 158, 164, 169, 183, 189, 190, 206, 313, 315, 316, 343, 349, 392A, 396A, 401A, 425A
deMartin Marona Cranstoun Downes, 818, 942
Design and Market Research Laboratory, 955
Deutsch Assoc., David, 102, 287
DFK Sales Promotions, 480
DKG, 154, 209, 212, 223, 426, 895
DiFiore Assoc., 900, 903, 940
Doherty, Mann & Olshan, 21, 240, 379, 478
Doner & Co., W. B., 256, 348, 807
Doran Stein Grey, 345, 494
Doremus Uptown, 278A, 489
Doret, Inc., Michael, 928, 941, 968
Doyle Dane Bernbach, 7, 17, 24, 29, 31, 48,

INDEX

49, 61, 62, 64, 99, 128, 134, 145, 184, 186, 202, 204, 217, 219, 226, 228, 230, 264, 266, 311, 312, 314, 317, 318, 329, 346, 383, 388, 391, 393, 395, 397, 399, 402, 430, 433, 438, 439, 441, 442, 443, 448A, 450, 469, 471, 529, 546, 548, 901
Dyer, Inc., Rod, 686, 695, 827

Eisenman and Enock, 717
Environmark, 1034
Epic Records, 830
Epstein, Raboy Advertising, 53
Esty, William, 140, 141
Evans Advertising, Peter, 135
Exxon Chemical Co., 1045

Fantasy Records, 826
Farrar, Straus & Giroux, 850
Fiedler, Hal, 1118
Filipacchi, Daniel, 1028
Firestone & Assoc., 435
Fluid Drive, 1122, 1145, 1146, 1147, 1148
Foote, Cone, Belding, 269, 486, 487, 1121
Ford, Byrne & Assoc., 718, 883, 921
Frankfurt Communications, 419
Frank/James Productions, 916, 929
Freid, Joel C., 934
Fuller & Smith & Ross, 279, 293

Garth De Cew Group, 237
Gauger Sparks Silva, 733, 733A, 800
Gaynor & Ducas, 163
Geer, Du Bois, 277
Geigy Pharmaceuticals, 692, 808
Genesis, 969
Gersin Assoc., Robert P., 817
Gilbert, Felix & Sharf, 275
Glenn, Bozell, & Jacobs Public Relations, 754, 756, 787
Glusker, Irwin, 858
Goodbye, 972
Gotham Advertising, 363
Graphics-To-Go, 809
Graves & Assoc., 701
Grear Designers, Malcolm, 791
Greengage Assoc., 434
Grey Advertising, 234, 254, 255, 258, 261, 309, 340, 360A, 416, 421, 428, 429, 474, 475, 483, 705
Griswold-Eshelman, 174, 175, 177, 178, 179, 201, 214, 224, 250, 739, 953
Group Four, Inc., 690

Hackenberg, Norman & Assoc., 54, 198
Hain Assoc., Robert, 822
Hakuhodo Inc., 519
Hampton, Michael, 865
Harmon & Crook Advertising, 740
Harrison Assoc., 760, 761
Hayim & Company, 199
Hill Co., George, 819
Hill, Holliday, Connors Cosmopulos, 227, 241, 891
Hinrichs Design Assoc., 729
Humangraphic, 950
Hume, Smith, Mickelberry, 20
Humphrey Browning MacDougall, 63, 231, 246, 247, 248, 262, 374, 375, 697, 745, 806, 1036, 1037, 1038, 1043, 1119
Hutchins/Darcy, 863

Image Communications, 947
Image Factory, 927
Industrias Gráficas Casamajó, 1163
Ingalls Associates, 235, 260, 878
Intermarco Elvinger Neuilly, 535
International Cultural Exchange, 730

Jacobs Design, Steven, 725, 862
Jean, Carole, 1124A
Johnson & Simpson Graphic Designers, 931, 1086, 1096
Juett & Assoc., Dennis S., 924

Kai-Chung Design, 935
Kallir, Philips, Ross, 276, 281, 815
Kameny Assoc., 825
Kano Design, Gerry, 958
Karp, Marshall, 460
Katz Graphic Design, Marjorie, 933
Kenyon & Eckhardt, 409
Ketchum, MacLeod & Grove, 337, 1049
Kidder Axelson & Assoc., 1035
King & Partners, Lee, 292, 368
Klauber, George, 713
Klemtner Advertising, 1040
Knoll International, 711, 821, 856, 867, 918, 919
Knox Reeves Advertising, 44, 252
KSS&G, 95, 111, 278, 283

Langer Visualization, 1172
LaPerle/Assoc., 767
Larson/Bateman, 952
Lawler Ballard Little, 249, 335
Lawrence Levy Design/Film, 665
Leber Katz Partners, 58, 108, 130, 372
Lefkowitz, Jack, 643, 644
Levine, Huntley, Schmidt, 1, 38, 74, 100, 120, 166, 168, 171, 172, 180, 195, 207, 216, 222, 364, 367, 884, 890
Lewis & Gilman, 182, 299
Leinhart, Jim, 642, 959
Lippincott & Margulies, 724
Lois/Chajet Design Group, 693, 704, 824
Lois Holland Callaway, 728, 855, 1032
Lomas & Nettleton Mortgage Investors, 754, 787
Lopez Design, Jon, 659, 851
Lopez Salpeter, 638, 794
Lord, Geller, Federico, 131, 194, 251
Lubalin, Smith, Carnase, 630, 631, 632, 633, 636, 677, 731, 789, 790, 943, 954, 963, 964, 1177, 1178

McAdams, William Douglas, 274, 505, 1115
McDonald & Little, 448, 901
McCaffrey & McCall, 77, 82

McCann-Erickson, 236, 238, 239, 242, 352, 373, 425, 522, 532, 533, 534, 549, 887, 1033
McKenna, Regis, 716
McKinney & Silver, 93
Maimé Arnodin, Fayolle International, Assoc., 510, 522
Malmo Advertising, John, 816
Mathis, Burden & Charles, 961
Marketing Design Alliance, 923
Marschalk Co., The, 370, 458, 459, 460, 465
Marschke, Elizabeth, 799
Martin Landey, Arlow Advertising, 6, 42, 87, 122, 123, 124, 125, 144, 152, 356
Mastropaul Design, 296
Melgar Advertising, Fabian, 820
Metzdorf Advertising, 215
Meyer and Assoc., Kurt, 732
Minale, Tattersfield, Provinciali Ltd., 1174
Minnar Advertising, 51
Miller & Rhoads, 899
Miller, Inc., Irving, 747
Miller, Inc., Randy, 273
Moonink Inc., 812, 949
Murphy & Friends, Harry, 736, 974, 980, 987, 988, 989
Murrie-White & Assoc., 642

Nadler & Larimer, 96, 115, 698
National Broadcasting Co., 294, 1116, 1124, 1125
Needham, Harper & Steers, 60, 65, 71, 103, 126, 205, 243, 265, 361, 362, 706
Nemser & Howard, 785, 1046
New York Affairs, 637
Noble-Dury & Assoc., 94, 885
Norman, Craig & Kummel, 106
Northwestern University, 665
Norton Simon Communications, 907, 908, 909
North Charles Street Design Organization, The, 617, 769, 910, 937

Ogilvy & Mather, 369, 427
O'Neill Design, Brian, 253

Parenio, Ralph, Graphic Design, 866, 868
Parkhurst & Assoc., Ken, 951
Pastimes, 1060
Pearce & Partners Ltd., 530, 531
Pedersen Design, 707, 1039, 1060, 1133
Pellegrini, Kaestle & Gross, 639, 786
Pennsylvania Gazette, The, 1127
Pentagram Design Partnership, 1153, 1158, 1176
Performing Dogs, 854
Perlman, Inc., Richard, 688
Perspectives, 1138, 1140
Pickwick International, 841
Pioneer-Moss Reproductions Corp., 714
Playboy Promotion Department, 167
Polaroid Corp., 783
Port Authority of New York and New Jersey, 741
Primaute Advertising, 80, 81, 113, 151
Printup, Harold, Graphic Design Studio, 689
Pritchard Wood-Quadrant, 514, 515
Promption Plus, 232
Propper/Elman, 986
Push Pin Studios, 475, 685, 833, 849
Pütz, Robert, 1165, 1167

Raymond Lee & Assoc. Ltd., 541, 1171
Reid, Scott F., & Assoc., 946
Reingold & Ricaud Advertising, 1120
Richards Group, The, 628, 687, 702, 749, 756, 805, 838, 930, 938
Rickabaugh, Heidi & Robin, 719, 802
Rosenfeld, Sirowitz & Lawson, 83, 213, 381, 417, 466, 477, 496
Rotten End House, 456, 1150, 1151, 1173, 1175
Rubin Design, Mark, 880
Rumrill-Hoyt, 310
Runyan & Assoc., Robert Miles, 750

Sacks, Tarlow and Rosen, 155, 288
Saks Fifth Avenue, 40, 127, 684, 912, 945
Saks, Inc., Arnold, 768
Saunders Bell Hicks, 189
Sawdon & Bess, 324
Scali, McCabe, Sloves, 15, 28, 30, 46, 50, 52, 55, 84, 98, 109, 114, 147, 161, 165, 200, 244, 245, 319, 320, 321, 322, 330, 331, 336, 389, 394, 396, 398, 400, 404, 408, 410, 412, 414, 415, 431, 432, 444, 445, 449
Schack Advertising, Michael, 14, 16
Schlüter, Schlüter Mehl Ideealismus GmbH, 1164
Schneider Studio, 948
Sheldon Seidler Inc., 762, 766, 780, 781
Serendipity, 721
Shaller Rubin Assoc., 257, 259
Siegel & Gale, 715, 962
Silverman & Mower Advertising, 325
Smith, Elwood H., 720
Smith Assoc., F. Eugene, 985
Smith/Greenland Co., 70, 89, 90, 105, 107, 143
Spencer Michlin, 464
Strandell Design, Don, 976
Steinberg, Bruce, 835
Stern Redaktion, 1134, 1137, 1143
SWA Communications, 859
Synergie/K&E, 506A

Tartak/Libera Design, 752
Thompson, J. Walter, 150, 173, 181, 280, 284, 334, 516, 517, 845
Thrasher, Ed, 926
Tracy-Locke Advertising, 196, 366
Tragos Bonnange Wiesendanger Ajroldi, 507, 509, 521, 550, 1161
Trahey/Rogers, 138
Trouw/Kwartet B. V., 1139
TV Graphics, 297

United Artists Artists, 175A, 831, 913
United States Information Agency, 874A, 875, 876

Van Brunt & Co., 289
Van Dine Horton McNamara, 801, 804
Van Leeuwen Advertising, 210
Van Noy & Co., 752A
VanSant Dugdale, 357
Vignelli Assoc., 881
Visualscope, 492
Visual Arts, School of, 860A, 873, 1117

Wallack & Harris, 1052
Waring & LaRosa, 3, 9, 11, 43, 88
Warner Bros. Records, 842, 843, 981
Warren Muller Dolobowsky, 482
Warwick, Welsh & Miller, 18
Weitzman & Assoc., 10
Weller Institute, The, 751, 792, 1048, 1050, 1053
Wells, Rich, Greene, 401, 423, 467
Werbin & Morrill, 823
Whitted and Assoc., J. C., 699
Williams Advertising, Martin, 34
Willis/Case/Harwood, 744
Wilson Haight & Welch, 59, 133
Wolf Productions, Henry, 270, 615, 620, 1057, 1081, 1083, 1090, 1105, 1106
Wolsky & Friends, Alan, 12
Workshop, The, 956

Yao Design Co., 1159
Yomiko Advertising, 1170
Young & Rubicam International, 25, 26, 27, 35, 36, 57, 84, 112, 148, 170, 193, 268, 271, 285, 286, 323, 332, 333, 352, 387, 446, 451, 453, 454, 455, 456, 461, 468, 470, 473, 481

Zanders Feinpapiere GmbH, 1160, 1162
Zechman Lyke Vetere, 208, 326, 327

Publishers Publications

A.D. Magazine, 597
After Dark, 624
Al-Majal Magazine, 1135
Amalgamated Lithographers of America, 634, 1111
American Heritage, 604, 606
America Illustrated, 584
American Medical Assoc., 629
Avant Garde, 619

Car and Driver, 1017
Crown Publishers, 677

Dance Magazine, 612
Doubleday & Co., 675

Epicure, 603
Esquire, 574, 614, 1013

Flash Books, 1051

Harcourt Brace Jovanovich, 641, 674, 676
Hollins College, 617
Horizons USA, 588
Hudson Valley Magazine, 625

Intellectual Digest, 694
International Typeface Corp., 631, 636, 1078

Little, Brown & Co., 648, 678

McCall's, 593
Metropolitan Museum of Art, 864
Modern Photography, 991, 1009, 1011, 1023, 1029
Money, 1104
Montreal Standard, The, 1144
Museum of Modern Art, 659, 851

National Lampoon, 601, 609, 618, 1103
National Periodical Publications, 371
New Times Magazine, 993, 1095
New York, 596, 605, 607, 1073, 1094, 1107, 1112
New York Times, The, 555, 565, 566, 579, 583, 595, 620, 621, 623, 892, 904, 906, 925, 994, 995, 1054, 1062, 1063, 1064, 1066, 1067, 1068, 1069, 1071, 1072, 1074, 1076, 1128, 1130, 1132
Nikon World, 1006, 1007, 1018, 1027, 1030

Oak Publications, 669
Oui, 1003

Penthouse, 1075, 1079, 1082, 1091, 1110
Peters, Christa, 1166
Playboy Magazine, 582, 589, 889
Popular Library, 647
Popular Photography, 610, 727, 998, 999, 1010, 1022, 1026
Praeger Books, 646
Pratt Institute, 670
Print Magazine, 638, 1129

Redbook, 554, 575, 576, 578, 585, 586, 592
Ridge Press, 650, 660
Rolling Stone, 564, 568, 572, 573, 577, 580, 581, 613, 990, 996, 1016, 1065, 1077, 1108

Scholastic Magazines, 662
Sesame Street Magazine, 615, 1081, 1083, 1090, 1093, 1105, 1106
Simon and Schuster, 673

Texas Monthly Magazine, 1059
Topic Magazine, 563
Town & Country, 1002
Time, Inc., 666, 671, 691, 1001
Time-Life Books, 649
Travel & Leisure, 1087, 1101

Viva, 590, 591, 600, 611, 626, 1004, 1005, 1008, 1012, 1014, 1015, 1020, 1024, 1025, 1097, 1098, 1100

Washington Post, The, 997, 1088, 1089, 1092, 1113
Watson-Guptill Publications, 667

Ziff-Davis Publishing, 47, 694, 727

Clients

ABC-TV, 492, 814, 979
Abitibi Provincial Paper Co., 1180
Absorba Ltd., 1150, 1151

INDEX

ACF Industries, 916
Advertising Club of Boston, 878
Air Jamaica, 1049
Alitalia Airlines, 209, 212, 223
Allied Products Div., 488
Allison-Erwin Co., 22
A&M Records, 839
American Airlines, 24, 230, 279, 346
American Can Co., 396, 400, 414
American Express, 427
American Express Travelers Checks, 369
American Honda Motor Co., 234, 705
American Institute of Graphic Arts, 857, 880
American-Overseas Trading Corp., 956
American Re-Insurance Co., 278A
American Society of Landscape Architecture Foundation, 869
American Tourister, 217, 219, 226, 388
Anti Defamation League, 475
Atlantic Records, 338, 836, 837
Atlantis Sound, 10
Atlas Foundry & Machine Co., 701
Architectural League of New York, 881
Aristar, 759
Armour Food Co., 198
The Art Center Assoc., 799
Art Center College of Design, 723
The Art Directors Club of Los Angeles, 792, 1042, 1050, 1053
The Art Directors Club of New York, 703, 731, 982
Aurora Products Corp., 421
Austin, Nichols & Co., 96, 115

Baltimore, City of, 357
Bangtails Restaurant, 976
Baltimore Blades Ice Hockey, 961
Baltimore City Medical Society, 910
The Bank of New York, 688
Barney's Clothes, 28, 336, 408, 449
Bass, 119A
Bauer & Black, 63
Beaird-Poulan, 366
Beecham-Massengill Pharmaceuticals, 815
Beech-Nut Baby Food, 123, 152
Benson & Hedges Ltd., 530, 531
Bernhardt, Craig, 809
Better Homes & Gardens, 21
Better Living Laboratories, 816
BirthdayBook, 810, 811
Blue Note Records, 831, 913
Boehringer-Ingelheim Ltd., 280
Boeing Airplane Co., 463, 506
Boscobel Restoration, 713
Bowmar Instrument Corp., 381
BrainReserve, 975
Braniff International, 687, 749
Brickel Assoc., 795
Bricklin Vehicle Corp., 728
Brigham Young University, 661, 709, 738, 788, 893
Bristol-Myers Co., 323, 352
Buckingham Corp., 855
Buddah Records, 832
Burger King Corp., 888
Burlington, 469
Burns & Cooper Ltd., 1179
Business Week, 556, 557, 558, 559, 560, 561

Cabot, Cabot & Forbes Land Trust, 765
Cadbury Ltd., 547
Cadbury, Schweppes, Powell, 529
Calderhead, Jackson, 159, 263
Campaign for Human Development, 958
Campana Corp., 59, 133
Canadian Government Office of Tourism, 1152
Capitol Records, 838
Car and Driver, 992
Carmel Plaza, 974
Carrols Restaurants, 325
Carte Blanche, 19
CBS Television Network, 23, 162, 494, 498A, 504, 681, 793, 915, 939, 973
Celanese, 433
Center Plaza Associates, 986
Central School of Art Jewellery, 1157
Champion Papers, 707, 710, 791, 852, 860A, 861, 1039, 1133
Charley's Eating & Drinking Saloon, 227, 241, 891
Cheap Jeans, 356
Chelsea Theater Center of Brooklyn, 854
Chicago International Film Festival, 905
Chivas Regal, 99, 145
Christa Peters, 1166
Christian Children's Fund, 479
Christie, 522
Church World Service, 478
Ciba-Geigy Corp., 274
Cinzano, 507, 550, 1161
City Center Dance Theater, 865
Clarks Shoes Ltd., 514, 515
The Cleveland Darter Club, 297
Cliff Covington Design, 848
CLIO, 495
Club Mediterranee, 1, 38, 172, 207, 216, 222, 367, 506A
Columbia Pictures, 743
Columbia Records, 828, 840, 844, 846, 847, 886, 920
Consolidated Cigar Corp., 488
Constable and Co., 1156
Container Corporation of America, 656, 680, 734, 882, 917, 922
Continental Hair Products, 72, 132
Continental Oil Co., 1086
Converse Rubber Corp. 375
Cos Capone Philips House, 533
Cox Leisure Time Industries, 968
Creative Services, Inc., 740A
Cross Design Office, James, 732, 803
CTD Printers Ltd., 1175
CTI Records, 1055, 1056

Daily News, The, 164, 169, 183, 392A, 396A, 401A, 425A
Dallas/Ft. Worth Society of Visual

INDEX

Communications, The, 628
Dallas Litho Club, 746A
Dansk International, 943
Darby Lithography, 959
Darling-Fischer Mortuaries, 66
deGast, Robert, 937
Del Monte, 236, 353, 365, 425
Detroit News, The, 348
Deutsche Bundespost, 1172
Dill Productions, 936, 977
Dividend Industries, 733, 733A, 800
Dr. Pepper, 446, 451, 456, 461, 470
Dollar Savings Bank, 426
Doner & Co., W. B., 256
Dos Pesos Restaurants, 237
Dubbleman, Richard, 441
Dyer, Rod, 686, 695

Eagle Shirtmakers, 117, 118, 153
Eastern Airlines, 468
Eastman Kodak Co., 150, 173, 334
Einstein Moomjy, 4, 5, 8, 45
Emery Air Freight, 313
Envirodyne, Inc., 752
Epic Records, 363, 830
Esquire, 562
Ex Bier, 435
Excello Shirts, 166, 168, 364
Exxon Chemical Co., 1045

Fantasy Records, 826
Farberware, 70
Farrar, Straus & Giroux, 850
Fedders Corp., 409
Fiat-Roosevelt Motors, 68, 69, 75, 137, 211, 221, 377, 378, 424
Fidelity National, 345
Films Inc., 696, 722
First National City Corp., 240, 379
Fluor Corp., 755, 782
Fortune Magazine, 170, 193
Fortunoff, 6, 42
Forum for Contemporary History, 946
Four Roses Distillers, 140, 141
Fourth Annual Ace Awards, 940
Fox Ltd., 1174
Franklin Picture Co., 971
The Franklin Society Federal Savings & Loan Assoc.
Freid, Joel C., 934
French Government Tourist Office, 362
Fudyma, Janice, 809
Fukujuen Co. Ltd., 1159
Fulton National Bank, 335
Future Thought, 928

Garrard, 86, 187
GE Corporate, 457
Geigy Pharmaceuticals, 692, 808, 813
General Automation, 735
General Foods, 27, 36, 148, 455
General Motors, 328, 440
General Telephone, 311, 318
General Telephone & Electronics, 448A
General Wine & Spirits, 232
Gensler & Assoc., 736
Geyer Printing, 903
Gillette, 371
Gingiss International, 208, 326, 327
Gold Lance Rings, 1041
Good, Paul, 1173
Goodrich, B. F., 953
Grahnquist, Sharon, 938
Grand Canyon, 966
Grange, Kenneth, 1176
Great Lakes Mink Assoc., 138
Groove Merchant Records, 841
Grumman Corp., 293
GTE, 62, 228, 266
Guerlain, 80, 81, 113, 151
Guinness Canada, 516, 517

Hall Clothes, Robert, 406
Hammer, Harry, 929
Hammond Organ, 442
Hanes-Millis Sales Corp., 185
Harris Manufacturing Co., B. W., 120
Harris Stores, Paul, 983
Heinz Co., H. J., 760
Holland Cheese Exporters Assoc., 534, 549
Hohner, M., 310
Humana, 724
Hunt-Wesson Foods, 907, 908, 909
Hyatt Regency of Chicago, 54

IBM, 139, 277
Illinois Bell, 420, 436, 437
Industrias Gráficas Casamajó, 1163
Industry Week, 174, 175, 176, 177, 178, 179, 201, 224, 739
Inter Nationes, 1164
International Cultural Exchange, 730
International Fund for Animal Welfare, 532
International Typeface Corp., 632, 633, 789, 790
Institute of Industrial Launderers, 643, 644
Institution of Contemporary Art, 879
Intercontinental Apparel, 947
Itel Corp., 767

Jack-in-the-Box, 393, 402
Jacobs Design, Steven, 862
Japan Air Lines, 337
Jean, Carole, 1124A
Jockey International, 180
Joffrey Ballet, 309, 340
Johnson & Johnson, 285

Kadokawa Shoten Co. Ltd., 1122, 1145, 1146, 1147, 1148
Kai-Chung Design, 935
Kalso, 87, 124, 125, 144
King & Partners, Lee, 292
Kinney Shoe Corp., 324
Knoll, 711, 821, 856, 867, 918, 919
Kobrand Corp., 78
Komatsu, Ltd., 519
Konica Camera Co., 111, 283
Koppers Co., 801, 804
Korman Muffler, 214

Ladd, Kelsey & Woodard, A.I.A., 951
Lakeshore Bank & Trust Co., 720
Lancaster, 510, 552
Learning Disabilities, 260
Legal Aid Society, 473
L'eggs Products, 818
Lenox, 146
Lesney Products Corp., 74, 171, 195, 884
Levi Strauss, 486, 487
Liggett & Myers, 106

Links Books, 1126
Lois/Chajet Design Group, 693
Lomas & Nettleton Financial Corp., 756
London Central Office of Information, 546
London Times, The, 544, 1136
Lopez Salpeter, 794
Lufthansa German Airlines, 1120
Lutheran Church in American, 253
Lutheran Hospital California, 726

McNeil Laboratories, 276, 281
McNeilly, Michael A., 924
Max Factor, 917
The Mennen Co., 411
Marcal Paper Mills, 380
Marketing Design Alliance, 923
Market Street, 972
Martin Processing, 763
Mary Brown Canada Ltd., 1171
Massachusetts Society for the Prevention of Cruelty to Animals, 246, 247, 248, 262
Massachusetts State Lottery Commission, 231
Mathews Miller Dunbar Ltd., 1153
Mead Corp., 744, 780, 781
Media Networks, 160
Metropolitan Life Insurance Co., 57, 112, 136, 454
Metropolitan Museum of Art, 864
Metzdorf Advertising, 215
Michigan Office of Economic Expansion, 807
Midas Mufflers, 467
Miller, Herman, 764
Miller & Rhoads, 899
Milton Bradley Co., 332
Minneapolis Police Department, 252
Minor Design, Wendell, 673
Mitsubishi Bank of California, 706
Mobil Oil Corp., 368, 497, 766, 858
Mobil Oil Corp. for P.B.A., 748, 870, 871, 932
Modern Medicine, 1131
Mohawk Trail Concerts, 298
The Mouse Trap, 967
Museum of Modern Art, 872
Mutual of New York, 370, 458, 459, 460, 465

National Alliance of Businessmen, 268, 483
National Assoc. of Insurance Agents, 489
National Broadcasting Co., 294, 1124
National Emergency Civil Liberties Committee, 263
National Enquirer, 37
National Federation of Settlements, 257, 259
Nationwide Financial Services, 213
National Hemophilia Foundation, 482
National Highway Traffic Safety Administration, 360A
National Kidney Foundation, 480
National Retinitis Pigmentosa Foundation, 477
Neiman Marcus, 58, 130
Netherlands National Tourist Office, 108
New England Fish Co., 289
New School for Social Research, The, 746
New Times Communication Corp., 53
New Times Magazine, 1099
New York City Bicentennial Commission, 798
New York Designer's Saturday Committee, 933
New York Racing Association, 238, 239, 242, 272, 373, 887
New York State Board of Adoption, 254, 255, 258, 261, 354, 474
New York Times, The, 892, 925
New Yorker, The, 194
Newark Preservation Landmarks Committee Newark Public Library, The, 931
Newsday, 1070
Newspaper Advertising Bureau, 1123
Newsweek Magazine, 267
Nikon Camera, 270, 275
Noresco Ltd., 541
Norwich Pharmacal Co., 403, 413

Odyssey Records Div. CBS Records, 833
Ogden Recreation, 235
Olivetti Corp. of America, 1032
Oneida Silversmiths, 102, 287
Ontario College of Art, 1169
Optimum Publishing Co. Ltd., 1155
Oz Restaurant & Disco, 702
Pacific International, 339
Pacific Northwest Bell Telephone Co., 305
Pan American World Airways, 41, 218, 220, 221, 225, 376A
Parenio Graphic Design, Ralph, 866, 868
Parker Brothers, 374
Pastene Wine & Spirits Co., 824
Pentagram Design Partnership, 1158
Penthouse Magazine, 963, 1182
People Magazine, 26, 35
PepsiCo, 350, 351, 464, 717
Pepsi-International, 853
Perdue Farms, 161, 165, 200, 244, 319, 320, 322, 330, 331, 389, 394, 410, 412, 415, 432
Pfizer Laboratories, 1040
Philadelphia 76, 955
Philip Morris, 812
Pioneer-Moss Reproductions Corp., 714
Plantings Unlimited, 978
Playboy Magazine, 167
Polaroid Corp., 7, 184, 202, 264, 383, 441, 443, 450, 471, 783
Polydor Records, 825
Port Authority of New York and New Jersey, 741
Porta Bella, 14
The Potato Board, 486A
Potlatch Corp., 1035
Prad B. V., 1139
Primo Angeli Graphics, 966
Print Club of Philadelphia, 883
Print Magazine, 639

INDEX

Printup Graphic Design Studio, Harold, 689
Procter & Gamble, 97, 104, 116, 142
Public Broadcasting Service, 964
Push Pin Studios, 685, 849
Pütz, Robert, 1165, 1167
Pyramid Films, 737

Quadrant Development Co., 952
Quant Cosmetics, Mary, 512
Quantor Corp., 716

Rainier National Bank, 472
Ralston Purina, 73, 158, 423
Ram Ridge Corporate Park I.E.C. Development Ltd., 962
RCA, 762
R.E.C., 521
Recovery, Resource, Recycling, 969
Red Cross, Metropolitan Atlanta Chapter, 249
Redken Laboratories, 752A
Reed College, 719
Revlon, 50
Reynolds Tobacco Co., R. J., 39, 156
Rickabaugh, Heidi & Robin, 802
Riegel Textile Corp., 897
Roche Laboratories, 505, 1115
Roerig, 299
Rolling Stone, 203, 1122
Rolls Royce, 77, 82
The Rouse Co., 796
Rubenstein, Helena, 954
Ryder Truck Rental, 422
Saab-Scania of America, 56, 418
St. Francis Hotel, 355
St. Louis Music Supply Co., 742
St. Xavier College, 960
Saks Fifth Avenue, 40, 127, 684, 912, 945, 1057
Salada Foods, 823
Salt City Playhouse Performing Arts Center, 296
Sandy-Babcock Architects, 682
Scannon, Ltd., 122
Schaak Electronics, 721
Schieffelin & Co., 85, 110, 157, 189, 190, 206, 315, 316, 343, 349
Schneider Studio, 948
Schofield, Stan, 199
SCM Corp., 761
Scotti Muffler Centers, 404
Seacraft, 135
Seagram Co., The, 768
G. D. Searle & Co., 284, 1181
Security Pacific Bank, 987, 989
Seven Color Television, 520
Sheaffer Pen Co., W. A., 822
Shore's Discount Drugs, 16
Simmons Co., 101, 333, 387
Simone Cosmetics, Monica, 785, 1046
Simpson Lee Paper Co., 725
Six Flags Over Georgia, 901
Smith Glass Co., L. E., 819
Smithsonian Magazine, 18
Snazelle Films, 988
Societie General, 1178
Soligor, 95, 278
Somerset Importers, 89, 90, 105, 107, 143
Sony Corporation of America, 48, 49, 83, 128, 430, 453, 466
Sopalin, 535
South Carolina Electric & Gas, 229, 233
Southern Airways, 448
Southern California Gas Co., 438, 439
Southwest Airlines, 354
Sparks Steak House, 51
Sperry-Remington, 718, 921
Sports Illustrated, 700
Standard Brands Paint Co., 751, 1048
Standard Oil of Ohio, 985
State of South Carolina Division of Tourism, 93
Steinway & Sons, 131
Sterling International, 729
Storer Broadcasting Co., 163
Summit University, 965
Surdyk's Liquor Store, 44
Suzuki Motors, 269
Swissair, 3, 9, 11, 43, 88
Synercon, 740

Talon, 895
Tega Cay, 690
State of Tennessee, Industrial Development Div., 94
Terraillon, 509
Texasgulf, 1058
Textar Corp., 786
Ed Thrasher Oaktree Ranch, 926
3M Company, 344, 462
Time-Life Books, 672
Time-Life Video, 245
Time Magazine, 25, 622, 691, 1118
Timme & Son, E. F., 100, 890
Tonka Corp., 376
Topic Magazine, 569
Torin Corp., 784
Town & Country, 570, 599, 602, 608
Travel & Leisure, 1080, 1102
Travelers Insurance Cos., The, 76, 129
Trifari, Krussman and Fishel, 156, 288
Tulchin Productions, 698
20th Century Records, 827

Union Carbide Corp., 205, 271, 286
Union Underwear Co., 416, 429
United Airlines, 984
United Artists Records, 175A, 874
United California Bank, 753
United Jewish Appeal, 251
United Negro College Fund, 481
United States Air Force, 490
United States Department of Agriculture Forest Service, 1121
United States Department of Transportation, 360
United States Information Agency, 874A, 875, 876
USLIFE Savings & Loan Assoc., 447, 452
United States Shoe Corp., 372
United States Virgin Islands, 434
University College University of Rochester, 863
Unruh, Jack, 930

Urban League of Cleveland, 250
U.S. Industries, 758
U.S. Marine Corps, 845
U.S. Team Stores, 980

Van Heusen Co., 428
Van Leeuwen Productions, 210
Van Nostrand-Reinhold, 1052
Van Noy & Co., 911
Vick Chemical Co., 149
Virgin Records, 712
Visual Arts, School of, 860A, 873, 1117
Volare Shoe Co., 189
Volkswagen of America Corp., 17, 29, 31, 61, 64, 134, 312, 314, 317, 329, 391, 395, 397, 399, 901, 914
Volvo of America Corp., 15, 30, 32, 46, 52, 55, 84, 98, 109, 114, 147, 321, 392, 431, 444, 445
VSI Corp., 750

WABC-TV, 496, 927
WAGA TV-5 Atlanta, 499
Wamsutta Mills, 747
Warner Bros. Records, 835, 842, 843, 981
Warner Publishing, 419
Warren Co., S. D., 745, 806, 1036, 1037, 1038, 1043, 1119
State of Washington, 942
WCBS Newsradio 88, 498
WCCO Television, 34
Wells Fargo Bank San Francisco, 1033
West End Brewing Co., 13
West Point Pepperell, 154, 715
Westminster Industries, 820
Westminster Sports, 817
Westvaco Corp., 657
Weyerhaeuser Co., 708
WFL Birmingham Americans, 970
Wilson & Co., 196
Women's Recognition, 548
Wittman Electric Service, 949
Woo Chee Chong, 950
Woodlands, The, 1034
World Jai-Alai, 20
Wrangler, 518, 542
Wyeth Laboratories, 182

Xerox Corp., 60, 65, 67, 71, 93, 103, 126, 243, 265, 361, 757

Yamaha International Corp., 306, 307, 308, 384
Yardley of London, 79
Yomiko Space Design, 1170
Young & Rubicam International, 359

Zanders Feinpapiere GmbH, 1162

THE ONE SHOW

ADVERTISING

"Set the Futura and hold the mayo."

Great advertising ideas come any time, any place. For example, an art director may be struck with genius somewhere between the cold cuts and coffee. We know, because we have the napkin, layout, mayonnaise and all, in our files to prove it.

We're the Advertising Typographers Association of America. And if that art director isn't using one of our shops, he could be mighty disappointed with the quality and accuracy of the job he gets back the next day.

But to an ATA shop, that's all in a night's work. Because knowing our customers is a major part of our business.

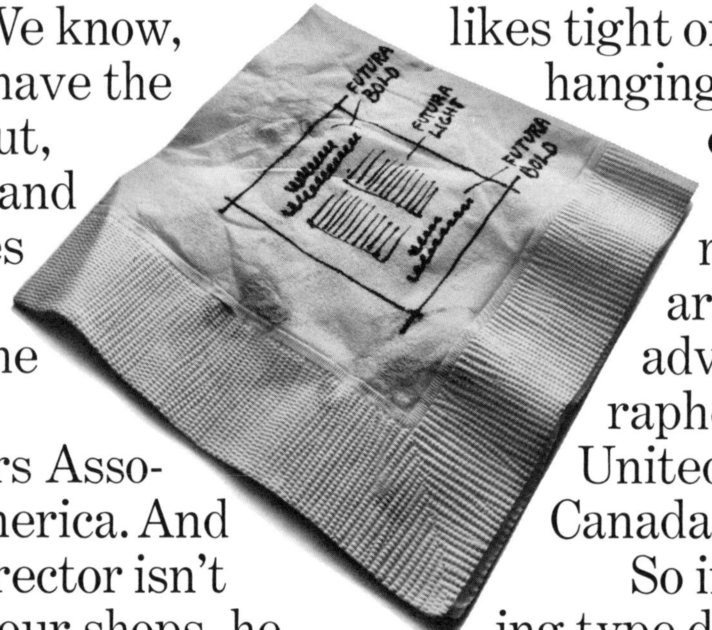
FUTURA BOLD
FUTURA LIGHT
FUTURA BOLD

Knowing that an art director at a certain agency likes tight or loose rags, hanging punctuation, or whatever is why our member shops are the foremost advertising typographers in the United States and Canada.

So if you're specing type down to the last character when you could be working on an idea for your next ad, call in an ATA shop. They'll help turn your ideas into the great ads you hoped they'd be.

The quality shops of ATA. We know your type.

Advertising Typographers Association of America, 461 Eighth Avenue, New York, N.Y. 10001, Walter A. Dew, Jr., Executive Secretary

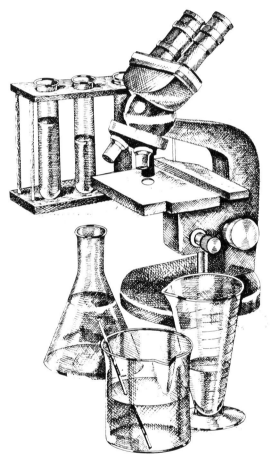

OCTOBER 1975
$1.25
American Artist
ICD

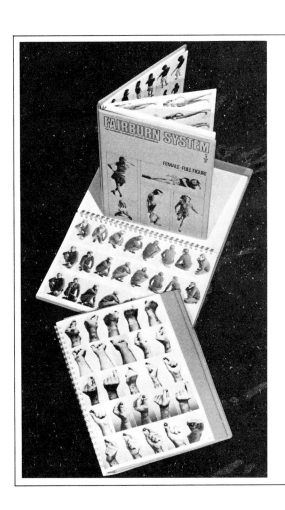

6 M.GRUMBACHER N.Y. RUBENS SERIES 187
000 M.GRUMBACHER N.Y. SERIES 187
M.GRUMBACHER N.Y. SERIES 187
G

Fit for a King!

The New 187 Series Rubens Extra-Selected Pure Red Sables from Grumbacher. Something very special, outshining the competition's best effort. Each jewel of a brush is hand-crafted from exotic, extra selected pure red Kolinsky sable, cupped to a generous, full-bodied shape and endowed with a resilient needle-sharp, split-proof point. Handles are designed for beauty and service in the richness and patina of natural gold. In 15 glittering sizes, from 000 through 12.

And the crowning touch—Grumbacher quality control. If the brushes don't pass you'll never see them. The ones that you will see (and buy) are truly fit for a King. You!

Grumbacher

M. GRUMBACHER, INC.,
460 West 34th Street, New York, N.Y. 10001
in Canada, M. GRUMBACHER OF CANADA, LTD.,
723 King Street West, Toronto, Ontario M5V 1N2

2022C080

PRODUCTS

ARTCADI™

Tools Shown Not Included

DRAWING DESK TOOL HOLDER Pat. Pend.

Designed for COMMERCIAL ARTISTS, ARCHITECTS, ENGINEERS & DRAFTSMEN And HOBBIESTS

- Designed to hold the hand tools that you use the most.
- Comes in three parts. Attaches to desk in seconds.

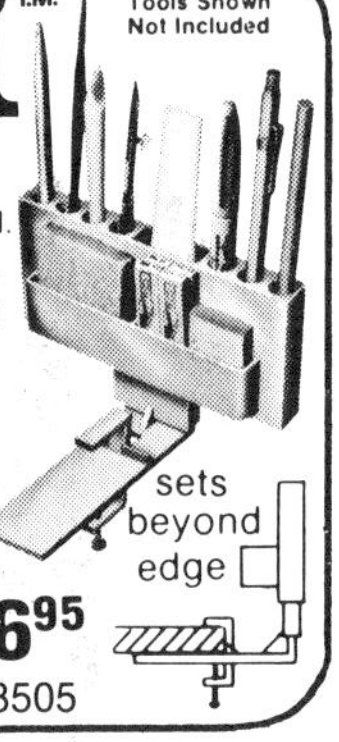
sets beyond edge

$6.95

Artcadi™ products
Lincoln, Nebraska 68505

---

the 'ARTISAN' **Artist's Projector**

our customers say:
'I am so pleased with the results... and it saves me time too'
'It's a pleasure to use'

Request free literature from
RIGYT-DAMAR
BOX 7587 TULSA, OKLA. 74105

PAINTING WORKSHOPS **U.S.A.**

Art Kraft
ART KRAFT

CANADA, HAWAII EUROPE, MEXICO EXCELLENT INSTRUCTORS
Special Group arrangements also available

For details write:
ARTKRAFT DIVISION | 2715 S. Memorial Dr., Tulsa, OK 74129
918 627-9797

SCHOOLS OF ART AND DESIGN

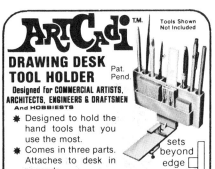

NEW JERSEY

du CRET SCHOOL OF THE ARTS
NEW JERSEY STATE APPROVED
559 Route 22, N. Plainfield, N.J. 07060
Tel.: (201) 757-7171-2

OHIO

the Columbus College of Art & Design
distinguished professional training geared to employment
47 north washington ave.
columbus, ohio 43215
(614)224-9101
request catalog ccda
est. 1879

fine arts
sculpture
ceramics
painting
printmaking
art therapy
commercial art
industrial design
interior design
magazine illustration
advertising design
retail advertising
photography
cartooning
fashion
tuition scholarships
financial aids
non-profit org.
b.f.a. degree

PENNSYLVANIA

CAREER IN ART *
hussian
SCHOOL OF ART
• WRITE OR PHONE FOR FREE CATALOGUE
1300 ARCH STREET SW, PHILA., PA. 19107 • 563-5727

Improve your art direction

IVY

Ivy School of Professional Art
UNIVERSITY AVENUE / PITTSBURGH,
PENNSYLVANIA 15214 / (412)323-8800

SERVICES

ALTON LITHO PRINTERS
Brochures — Promotional — Ad Books
QUALITY OFFSET
362 W. GARVEY AVE.
MONTEREY PARK, CA. 213/288-8211

---

photographic
Laboratory Service

35mm DUPLICATE SLIDES
16mm • 35mm super8mm
FILMSTRIPS

bēbĕll®
INCORPORATED
416 West 45 St. New York 10036
PHONE: (212) 245-8900
CABLE: LABSBEBELL, NEW YORK
WRITE, WIRE, PHONE FOR PRICE LIST

Graphics and Commercial Art Books for Professionals from Watson-Guptill...

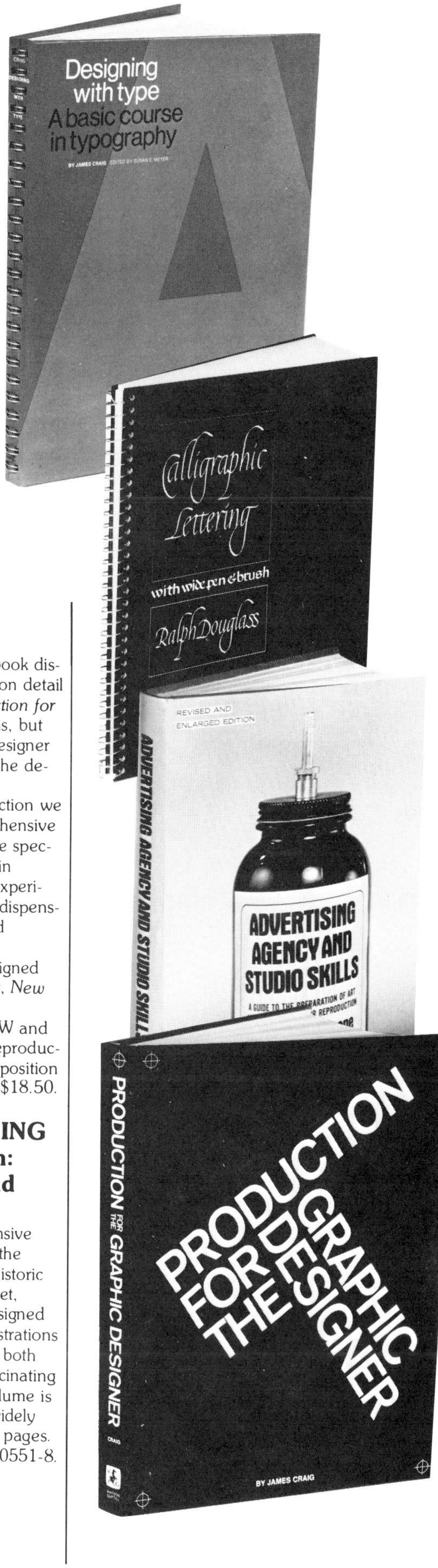
Designing with type
A basic course in typography
Calligraphic Lettering
with wide pen & brush
Ralph Douglass
REVISED AND ENLARGED EDITION
ADVERTISING AGENCY AND STUDIO SKILLS
PRODUCTION FOR THE GRAPHIC DESIGNER
BY JAMES CRAIG

ADVERTISING AGENCY AND STUDIO SKILLS
A Guide to the Preparation of Art and Mechanicals for Reproduction

By Tom Cardamone. An authoritative guide to the complicated procedures required by most art and production departments. The clear, concise text, aided by over 265 illustrations, examines such basic technical procedures as paste-ups, mechanicals, printing processes, specifications, *plus* hundreds of other invaluable tricks of the trade. An essential practical reference for students, teachers, commercial artists, and designers. 160 pages. 6 x 9. 256 illus. Index. 8230-0150-4. $7.95.

DESIGNING WITH TYPE
A Basic Course in Typography

By James Craig. Edited by Susan E. Meyer. A complete introduction to the fundamentals of typography that provides the student with all the basics needed for a career in graphic design. The author thoroughly examines five type faces—Garamond, Baskerville, Bodoni, Century Expanded, Helvetica; provides over 40 design projects; deals with the individual letter as a design element and as a means of communication; presents terminology; and discusses the various ways type is set. The student learns the units of measurement, wordspacing, letter spacing, and leading; how to comp type; how to arrange type on a page; and how to prepare copy for type. Also includes a chapter on display types with a gallery of over 100 specimens for additional or future use, as well as a list and discussion of the materials required. The final chapter offers design projects successfully used by the author in his years of teaching. 176 pages. 9 x 12. Over 180 typographic illus. Semi-Concealed Wire Binding. Bibl. Glossary. Index. 8230-1320-0. $11.95.

PRODUCTION FOR THE GRAPHIC DESIGNER

By James Craig. This authoritative book distills the enormous amount of production detail available into a single volume. *Production for the Graphic Designer* not only explains, but graphically illustrates *everything* the designer needs to know to produce the results he desires.

"It is easily the best book on production we have ever seen, and the most comprehensive and understandable with respect to the spectacular and revolutionary innovations in typesetting. This is a book that even experienced professionals will want . . . an indispensable working tool for professionals and teachers."—*American Artist.*

"Excellent, well conceived, well designed . . . extremely useful."—Milton Glaser, *New York Magazine.*

208 pages. 8½ x 11. Over 400 B&W and multicolor illus. 16 pages of full-color reproductions. Table of comparative photocomposition systems. Glossary. Bibl. 8230-4415-7. $18.50.

CALLIGRAPHIC LETTERING
With Wide Pen and Brush: Third Edition, Revised and Enlarged

By Ralph Douglass. This comprehensive handbook on calligraphic lettering for the commercial artist and student covers historic and modern styles, the Roman alphabet, scripts, brush lettering, and various designed letters and types. Step-by-step demonstrations promote easy understanding and help both novice and professional master the fascinating craft of calligraphy. This handsome volume is entirely hand lettered, and has been widely adopted for courses in calligraphy. 112 pages. 7⅞ x 10¼. Index. Spiral bound. 8230-0551-8. $7.95.

Watson-Guptill Publications, 2160 Patterson Street, Cincinnati, Ohio 45214

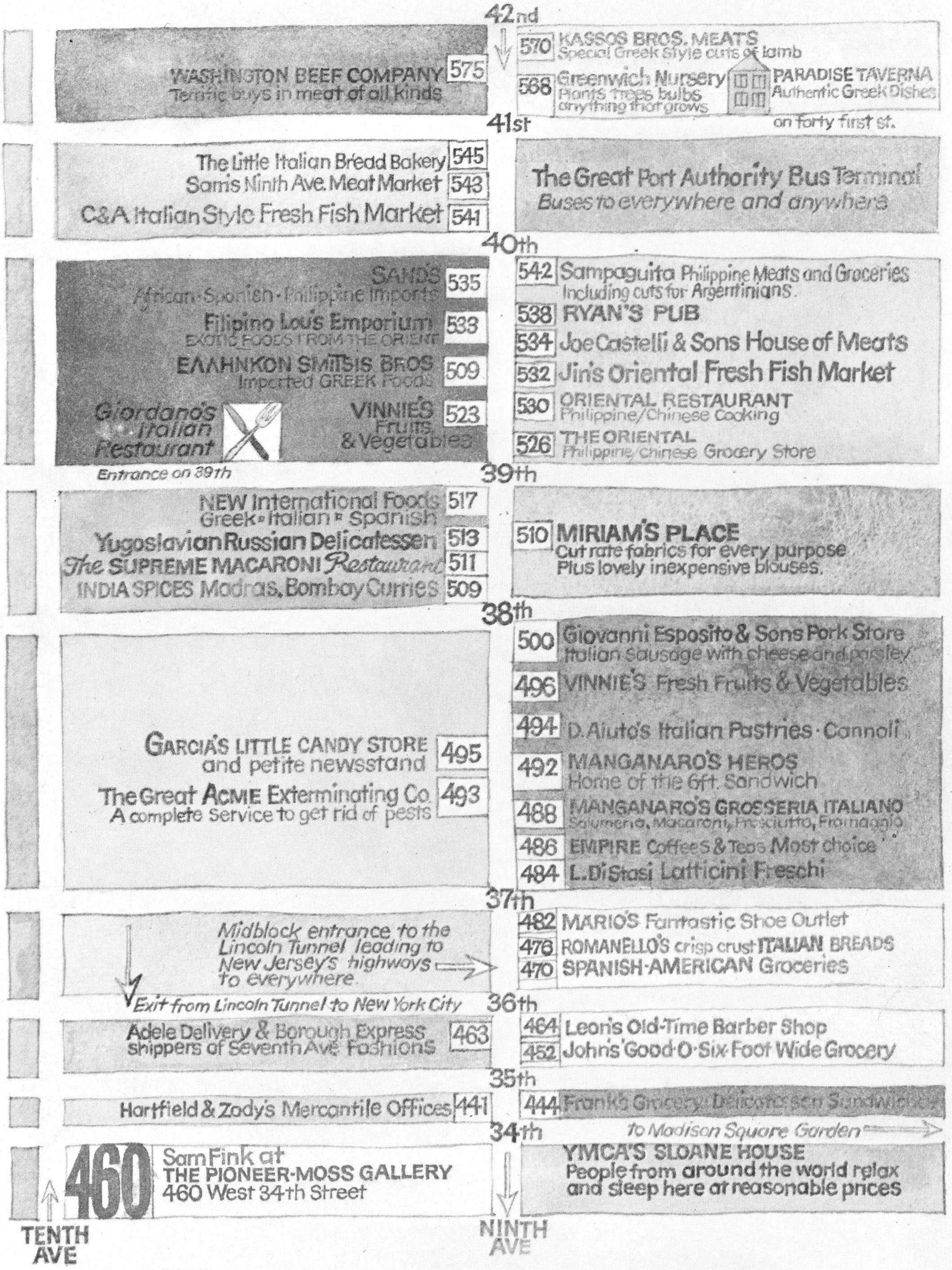

42nd
WASHINGTON BEEF COMPANY 575
Terrific buys in meat of all kinds
570 KASSOS BROS. MEATS
Special Greek Style cuts of lamb
568 Greenwich Nursery
Plants trees bulbs anything that grows
PARADISE TAVERNA
Authentic Greek Dishes
on forty first st.
41st
The Little Italian Bread Bakery 545
Sam's Ninth Ave. Meat Market 543
C&A Italian Style Fresh Fish Market 541
The Great Port Authority Bus Terminal
Buses to everywhere and anywhere
40th
SANDS 535
African · Spanish · Philippine Imports
Filipino Lou's Emporium 533
EXOTIC FOODS FROM THE ORIENT
ΕΛΛΗΝΚΟΝ SMITSIS BROS 509
Imported GREEK Foods
Giordano's Italian Restaurant
VINNIE'S Fruits & Vegetables 523
Entrance on 39th
542 Sampaguita Philippine Meats and Groceries
Including cuts for Argentinians.
538 RYAN'S PUB
534 Joe Castelli & Sons House of Meats
532 Jin's Oriental Fresh Fish Market
530 ORIENTAL RESTAURANT
Philippine/Chinese Cooking
526 THE ORIENTAL
Philippine/Chinese Grocery Store
39th
NEW International Foods 517
Greek · Italian · Spanish
Yugoslavian Russian Delicatessen 513
The SUPREME MACARONI Restaurant 511
INDIA SPICES Madras, Bombay Curries 509
510 MIRIAM'S PLACE
Cut rate fabrics for every purpose
Plus lovely inexpensive blouses.
38th
GARCIA'S LITTLE CANDY STORE 495
and petite newsstand
The Great ACME Exterminating Co. 493
A complete Service to get rid of pests
500 Giovanni Esposito & Sons Pork Store
Italian sausage with cheese and parsley
496 VINNIE'S Fresh Fruits & Vegetables
494 D. Aiuto's Italian Pastries · Cannoli
492 MANGANARO'S HEROS
Home of the 6ft. Sandwich
488 MANGANARO'S GROSSERIA ITALIANO
Salumeria, Macaroni, Prosciutto, Formaggio
486 EMPIRE Coffees & Teas Most choice
484 L. DiStasi Latticini Freschi
37th
Midblock entrance to the Lincoln Tunnel leading to New Jersey's highways to everywhere.
Exit from Lincoln Tunnel to New York City
482 MARIO'S Fantastic Shoe Outlet
476 ROMANELLO'S crisp crust ITALIAN BREADS
470 SPANISH-AMERICAN Groceries
36th
Adele Delivery & Borough Express shippers of Seventh Ave. Fashions 463
464 Leon's Old-Time Barber Shop
452 John's Good-O-Six-Foot Wide Grocery
35th
Hartfield & Zody's Mercantile Offices 441
444 Frank's Grocery · Delicatessen Sandwiches
34th
To Madison Square Garden
460
Sam Fink at
THE PIONEER-MOSS GALLERY
460 West 34th Street
YMCA'S SLOANE HOUSE
People from around the world relax and sleep here at reasonable prices
TENTH AVE
NINTH AVE

THE UNUSUAL AREA

With a small license on street widths and lengths

In an area in New York City where the Orient meets the West, where the Caribbean meets the Aegean, where exotic wares from around the world are at your fingertips there's an unusual art gallery that exhibits unusual work

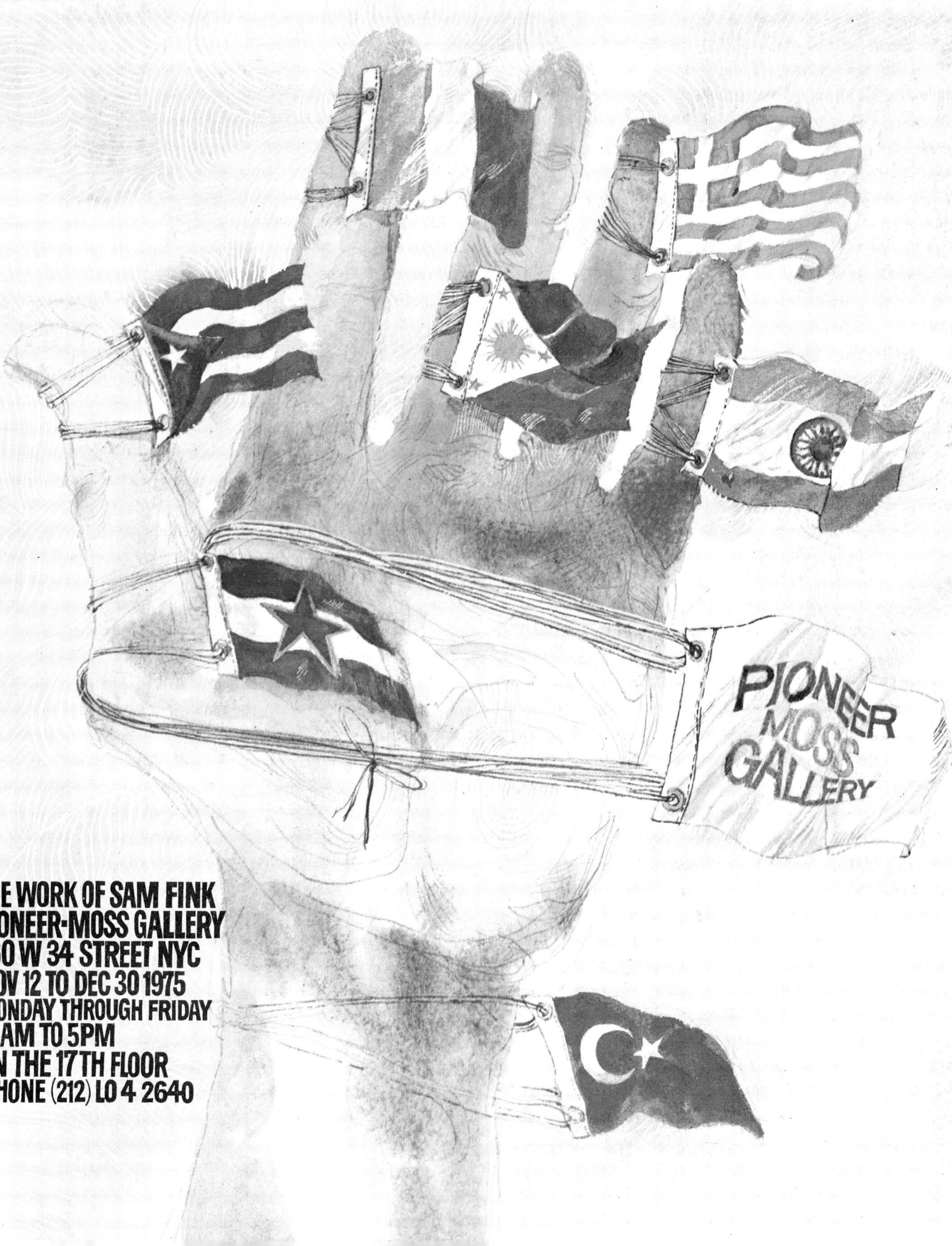
PIONEER
MOSS
GALLERY

THE WORK OF SAM FINK
PIONEER-MOSS GALLERY
460 W 34 STREET NYC
NOV 12 TO DEC 30 1975
MONDAY THROUGH FRIDAY
10 AM TO 5PM
ON THE 17 TH FLOOR
PHONE (212) LO 4 2640

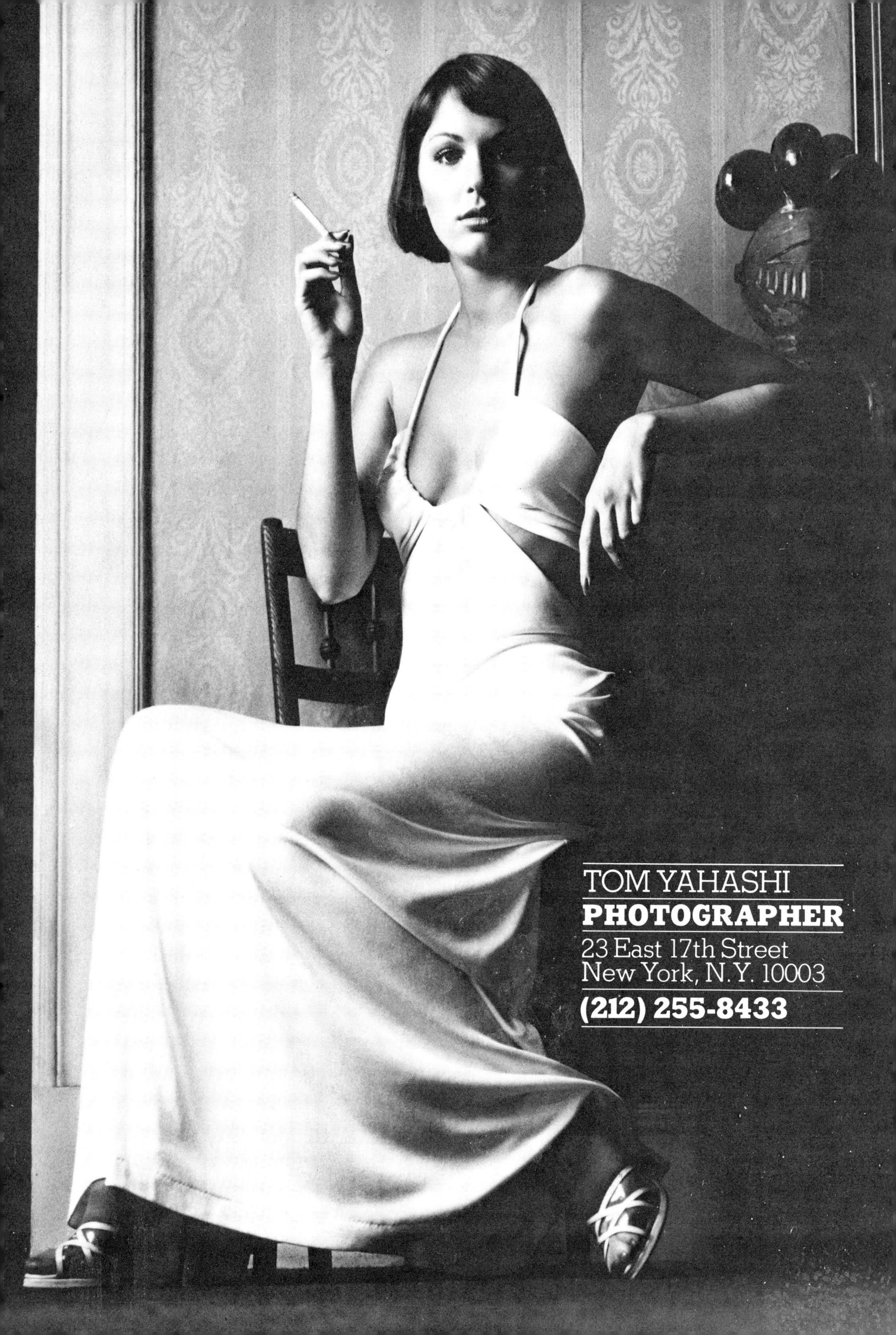
TOM YAHASHI
PHOTOGRAPHER
23 East 17th Street
New York, N.Y. 10003
(212) 255-8433

The Art Directors Club
Expresses

Heartfelt Thanks

To Hundreds of Individuals and Companies Who Support Its Programs During The Year.

Special Thanks in 1975 To:

Advertisers Mailing Service, Inc.
Artemis Offset
M.J. Baumwell Typography
Blueprint & Photoprint Masters
CBS, Inc.
Collier Photo Engraving Co., Inc.
the ComposingRoom inc
Crafton Graphic Co., Inc.
Daniel O. Reich, Inc.
Empire Typographers Inc.
Jack Anson Finke
Fischer-Partelow Inc.
Foodim Photo Prints Inc.
Fox River Paper Co.
G. J. Haerer Co.
Haber Typographers Inc.
Hinkhouse Inc.
Judrac Recording
Lees Art Store
Lindenmeyr Paper Corp.
Lubalin, Smith, Carnase
The Master Eagle Family of Companies
The Mix Place
MGA Graphics
Murray Hill Photo Print
National Video Center
Photo Lettering Inc.
Pioneer Moss Reproductions
The Print Shop
Quad Typographers
Sony Corporation
Steelograph Co.
Bill Stetner
Tatara Color Labs
The Type Group
The Typros
Tri-Arts Press Inc.
TypoGraphics Communications, Inc.
TypoGraphic Innovations, Inc.
Hans Weiss Associates
Tom Yahashi, Photography